GENERAL
HENRI GUISAN

GENERAL
HENRI GUISAN

COMMANDER-IN-CHIEF
OF THE SWISS ARMY
IN WORLD WAR II

BY
WILLI GAUTSCHI

Translated by
Karl Vonlanthen

FRONT STREET PRESS
Rockville Centre, NY

Published by
FRONT STREET PRESS

Library of Congress Cataloging-in-Publication Data

Gautschi, Willi, 1920-
    [General Henri Guisan. English]
    General Henri Guisan : Commander-in-Chief of the Swiss Army in World War
II / by Willi Gautschi ; translated by Karl Vonlanthen.
        p. cm.
    ISBN 0-9725572-0-2
    1. Guisan, Henri, 1874-1960. 2. World War, 1939-1945-Switzerland.
    3. Switzerland. Armee. I. Title

DQ207.G8G3713 2003
355'.0092-dc21
[B]

                                                        2003040892

CONTENTS

Foreword

By Admiral Thomas H. Moorer, U.S. Navy (Ret.)
Former Chairman of the U.S. Joint Chiefs of Staff

As a veteran of three wars, I have come to appreciate that the study of history is often the study of wars. This is not to say that much may not be learned from the study of phenomena far removed from the battlefield. But our world has been defined by the great conflicts and their outcomes. A study of the biographies of Generals Grant and Lee, for example, tells us much about our nation.

Switzerland's survival in World War II as a sovereign constitutional democracy was in large part a consequence of the nation's permanent military preparedness and its collective political will, true to 4th-century Roman historian Vegetius' "Si vis pacem, para bellum" ("If you want peace, prepare for war"). But one individual indisputably played a decisive role in Switzerland's World War II history: General Henri Guisan.

For the first time, acclaimed Swiss historian Willi Gautschi's landmark biography of Guisan is available in English. Anyone who has visited Switzerland knows that in virtually every Swiss city and town there is a landmark—a street or square—bearing Guisan's name. During the war, he came to symbolize not only extraordinary personal integrity but also the unified, strong national resistance to Nazism of all Swiss, be they of French, German, or Italian tongue. Though Switzerland is a country traditionally disinclined to be infatuated with heroic or charismatic figures—with the exception of William Tell—Guisan is indisputably the greatest popular hero of Switzerland of the 20th century.

Guisan is the great figure of the war years, having served as commander-in-chief of Switzerland's armed forces during the war, elected to this position by the Swiss Parliament in 1939. He inspired the military and civilian leaders and the population at large to embrace the strategy of resistance he devised. And with the benefit of scholarly hindsight he has come to embody and symbolize Switzerland's will to endure.

British Prime Minister Churchill at the end of World War II acknowledged that iron will when he said: "Of all the neutrals, Switzerland has the greatest right to distinction. She has been the sole international force linking the hideously sundered nations and ourselves. She has been a democratic state standing for freedom, in self-defense among her mountains, and in thought always on our side."

Gautschi's biography—six years in the making—is painstakingly researched. He draws on many sources and describes in exquisite detail how the Réduit (national redoubt) strategy developed by Guisan and his staff reinforced (by its military soundness) the will of Swiss political leaders and the public to hold firm in the face of encirclement and profound threat.

The lessons of military history are many. One is that peace is the product of a strength that deters attack in the first instance or overwhelms or confounds those who miscalculate. Switzerland's comprehensive and determined military preparedness in World War II raised the price of potential Nazi invasion.

This definitive study of General Guisan and the war years in Switzerland is an immensely valuable contribution to the military history of World War II. We are fortunate it is now available for the English-speaking public.

Acknowledgments

This book on the life and career of General Guisan turned out to be more voluminous than originally planned. In the course of its creation, which necessitated research lasting as long as World War II—that is, more than 6 years—the reference material raised additional questions that I felt had to be incorporated into the study.

I would like to express my special thanks to the following persons and organizations who promoted my efforts in many ways: The Swiss National Fund, which supported my work through a research grant; the Federal authorities, who granted me access to files that remained sealed beyond the official waiting period; several former colleagues and close friends of the General, as well as former participants in the Officers' Conspiracy and at the Rütli Meadow, who offered me authenticated information on their impressions and their parts in the events. I would like specifically to name retired Brigadier Max Häni, retired Colonels Denis van Berchem, Gerhart Schürch, Edmund Wehrli, and Otto Kellerhals, as well as retired Majors Jules Sandoz and Armand von Ernst, who entrusted me with valuable information during interviews and some of whom left with me materials and private correspondence for my perusal. Dr. Jürg Wille provided me with documents from the unpublished works of his father in Mariafeld.

I would like to thank the Director of the Federal Archives, Dr. Oscar Gauye, for his support during my research there, and his staff, especially Hans Kohler, Eduard Tschabold, and André Wälti, for their obliging assistance in finding source documents. In addition, I would like to acknowledge with gratitude the reliable services of the Archives of Contemporary History at the Swiss Federal Technical Institute in Zürich, whose director, Dr. Klaus Urner, provided me with useful information and, by organizing seminars with former magistrates, officers, and diplomats, made substantial contributions to this history of Switzerland during World War II.

Repeated conversations with the doyen of Swiss historiography, Professor Edgar Bonjour, with Professor Hans Rudolf Kurz, a historian who is a specialist on Guisan, and with Dr. Hans Senn, retired Corps Commander and former

Chief of the General Staff, resulted in a stimulating exchange of views on this complex subject. Dr. Hermann Böschenstein, whose vast knowledge of personal connections among the main figures of this book proved to be invaluable, read the manuscript and provided me with a lot of information and useful advice. The publisher of the original German version, Dr. Peter Keckeis, took an active part in bringing the project to fruition by providing advice and selecting the photographs for the book. Once again, my most heartfelt thanks go to my wife, Alice Gautschi-Weier, who devoted herself to this work and actively participated in its creation by typing the manuscript, correcting proofs, and assisting with the index.

During the past few years there have been public controversies surrounding attempts to discredit contemporary historical research. It would, of course, be impossible to verify all sources that were quoted by other authors, or else all historiography would come to a sudden standstill. However, I assume full responsibility for rendering correctly the sources I used myself. Professor Dr. Georg Müller of the University of Zürich volunteered to look over some critical chapters in terms of forensics, for which I am also much obliged.

Thanks to the efforts of Ambassador Faith Whittlesey and Georg Gyssler, who are encouraging the translation of classic Swiss history titles into English, this book is now available for English-speaking researchers and others interested in the difficult survival strategy of Switzerland during World War II.

I am grateful to Karl Vonlanthen for his careful translation and to Marco Ghiringhelli, John Gardner, and Don Hilty for their editing efforts. I also wish to thank Maurice Decoppet, President of the General Henri Guisan Foundation, for providing the photography for the dustcover of a painting of General Guisan by Herman Barrenscheen.

Permission to publish this work in English has been generously granted by its originators, Verlag Neue Zürcher Zeitung of Zürich, Switzerland. Gratefully acknowledged is partial funding by Presence Switzerland (PRS), The Ernst Göhner Foundation of Zug, Switzerland, and The Sophie and Karl Binding Foundation of Basel, Switzerland. I also thank the Swiss American Historical Society for their support in making this English translation available to the public.

—Willi Gautschi
Baden, in the spring of 2003

Introduction

Throughout Swiss history, no public figure has been as popular and widely admired, both while in office and afterward, as Henri Guisan, Commander-in-Chief of Switzerland's armed forces during World War II. Guisan's celebrity status surpasses even that of the glamorous General Henri Dufour, commander of the armed forces during the Civil War of 1848, who, for decades after the event, was regarded by portions of the population in the defeated cantons as the commander of the enemy. Transcending political, religious, and ideological boundaries, General Guisan—whose status rose to mythic proportions after his death—emerged as the outstanding unifying force among the Swiss—as the undisputed symbol of the spirit of resistance and unity—who was credited with Switzerland's being spared the horrors of war.

Even during his lifetime, Guisan was turned into a national father figure. His radiance was so encompassing that any reservations about him died down soon after they were voiced, and in the popular mind he was shielded from all criticism. His aura reached a magnitude that Switzerland had never before known, and has not known since. For instance, a farmer's wife from Canton Valais, in all seriousness, addressed the General in a letter as "Your Majesty."[1] Pierre Béguin, a staunch Guisan supporter, remarked that from an early period the commander-in-chief was credited with success for favorable outcomes with which he had nothing to do. If anyone had dared criticize Guisan, the people who revered and respected him would have ostracized that person. "Even if he had been responsible for the most serious errors, he would not have been held fully accountable for them. He could simply do whatever he wanted," wrote Béguin.[2] Many saw the General, who during a critical time seemed to embody the perfect union between the people and the army in matters of defense policy, as "their own better self."[3] They idealized Guisan, making him into a popular hero whose bright image must remain untarnished. It is hardly an exaggeration to say that reverence for Guisan took on a cult-like aspect.

Henri Guisan's life story, however, is far from spectacular. This physician's son had roots deeply anchored in his native region, to which a touch of nobility was added upon his becoming owner of the "Verte Rive" mansion outside Lausanne, on the shore of Lake Geneva. After encountering some initial difficulties, Guisan had a surprisingly conventional military career, rising, with some luck, to the top. Despite a typical military career, General Guisan presents, at one and the same time, a captivating and disarming phenomenon. How could a man whose education, talents, and performance were considered commonplace achieve such idolization in a small, democratic nation?

At the beginning of the war, Henri Guisan was not the undisputed choice for General, as one could gather from the present perspective and the adulation Guisan received after the war. Instead, both the political left and also a number of high-ranking army officers had reservations about Guisan's selection to be commander-in-chief. Once he was elected, the majority considered him to be the right man at the right time. Nevertheless, he had to overcome some mistrust, as well as fight insubordination and defeat a rebellious faction within the armed forces. Behind the scenes, out of public view because of wartime censorship, the commander-in-chief's authority came under attack, with disputes and infighting among senior leaders frequently occurring.

Many books have been written about General Guisan (cf. bibliography). In Switzerland no other contemporary figure, and certainly no other citizen of Canton Vaud, has received such wide attention in print. The most widely read biographies were intended to pay tribute and have thus contributed to idealizing the General. The one biography written in English, *Spying for Peace* (London 1961) by Jon Kimche, a dual British and Swiss national, is no exception, portraying Guisan as the country's only true hero. Kimche's well-meant book presents many facts correctly, but it contains a number of exaggerations that will be examined in the course of this study.

Professor Edgar Bonjour's report on Switzerland's neutrality during World War II,[4] written at the request of the Swiss government, paints an appropriate and not at all outdated picture of the commander-in-chief. However, new material has become available since its publication, making possible a more complete and specific account than Bonjour's report. Bonjour, as well as C. Ludwig in his report on Switzerland's refugee policy,[5] provided ample evidence that the army command's position sometimes diverged from, and in a few cases even clashed with, national political guidelines.

Publications on Guisan's life and Switzerland's history during World War II by renowned military historian H.R. Kurz are well known.[6] Bonjour, Kurz, and H. Böschenstein[7] did not hesitate to point out certain questionable activities of the General, but public opinion mostly shrugged its shoulders at a number of facts that could have somewhat discredited him.

In recent years, a number of special technical studies were published that shed new light on particular questions regarding Guisan's performance as commander-in-chief. Special mention should be made of studies written by historians V. Hofer, G. Kreis, D. Bourgeois, and O. Gauye,[8] which will be referred to later in this book. In 1984, a technical study by Federal Archives Director O. Gauye focused on the General's speech at the Rütli Meadow in 1940.[9] The report created a great uproar, as it revealed some new and controversial elements in Guisan's famous address to the Swiss officers' corps. In connection with his report, Gauye asked whether it was advisable to maintain the myth about Guisan's speech or whether, instead, new evidence should be shared openly with the public. In the interest of more precise historiography, Gauye rightly opted for publishing his findings unvarnished. There is no reason not to consider in a straightforward way delicate subjects such as the General's political views. To me, it seems to be a question of style and linguistic preference, rather than principle, whether the results of such studies should be viewed as scratches or retouches, or simply as additional details to the traditional image of Guisan. For my part, I prefer using the term "retouches," as I will argue in discussing specific incidents.

Primarily four published firsthand sources document General Guisan's activities as commander of Switzerland's armed forces from 1939 to 1945: (1) the General's own report to the Federal Parliament, supplemented by two volumes of reports by the three heads of the main army units and other direct subordinates;[10] (2) the reply to Guisan's report by the Federal Council in the form of a counter-report;[11] (3) the diaries of B. Barbey;[12] and (4) the General's conversations with R. Gafner,[13] which Guisan considered to be memoirs supplementing his official report. These four publications are the starting point of this book; I have turned to them again and again in all aspects of my work.

Barbey's diaries, published after 1945 with the General's encouragement, are highly informative. Barbey notes that Guisan gave him a free hand and "did not request one single change to be made to the text." Hence, the General agreed that some disturbing facts of which the general public had previously been unaware should be revealed through the chief of his personal staff. Both Barbey's diary and his tract, "Von Hauptquartier zu Hauptquartier" ("Back and Forth between Headquarters"), in which he reports on his role as liaison officer between the Swiss and French armies, contain various bits of information about the activities of the Swiss army staff and the General's closest collaborators that help to clarify certain matters. Comparison with files in the Federal Archives has established that Barbey's comments are, with few exceptions, perfectly reliable. Barbey wrote down his experiences and impressions "every evening," beginning in September 1939; he rightly called the volume "a bare diary, by definition, a principal type of contribution to historiography."[14]

Unfortunately, from a researcher's point of view, Barbey did not publish the full text of his diaries but made a selection, discarding parts "which did not deserve to go to print."[15] In spite of this selectivity, Barbey's sensational publication was viewed as a major indiscretion, especially in certain military circles. His revelations had a negative effect on his career, and he did not advance past the rank of lieutenant-colonel, despite his outstanding intellectual qualities and his qualifications as one of the General's closest collaborators (Guisan was no longer able to push for his protégé, either); and he also failed to be nominated as ambassador to France, despite his being highly qualified for the job and eager to obtain the post.[16]

Primary sources from World War II are available in abundance. Both the official files of the Federal authorities and the armed forces and materials from private sources are significant for historical research. The documents of the personal staff of the General alone amount to tens of thousands of files measuring 21 meters in the Federal Archives. Guisan's personal correspondence is another 10 meters long.[17] The numerous notes, drafts, and minutes are especially informative, as some of them contain handwritten remarks by the General or by his personal staff, permitting us to discover how the commander-in-chief made decisions. The files of the army staff and of the Federal Council, which have also been consulted, are at least as voluminous.

The fact that so much material is available to researchers is the result of a fortunate coincidence. After finishing his report to Parliament, Guisan left his own papers and the files of his personal staff in boxes at the barracks in Lausanne. Through a notary, he ordered the material to remain under his own control, and five years after his death "to be destroyed in the presence of Lt. Col. Barbey or Captain Marguth, or otherwise in the presence of a magistrate or officer authorized to serve as a witness."[18] Up to that time, only Barbey and Marguth were authorized to make use of the confidential documents.

Five years after Guisan's death, a controversy erupted over the legality of the planned destruction of the documents. Colonel Henry Guisan, the General's son, insisted on his father's will being executed, but the head of the military department, Federal Councilor Paul Chaudet, intervened in order to determine whether the papers should be preserved in the interest of history. The Federal government, spearheaded by Federal Councilor H.P. Tschudi, the head of the Department of the Interior, undertook to deal with the problem and try to find a way to save at least the military files, if not the General's personal files. A report from experts requested by Barbey and Marguth concluded that the documents had an official character and that the General had overstepped his authority by ordering them to be destroyed; therefore, his instruction was null and void from a legal viewpoint: "The General had no more right than any other magistrate or public official to decide for himself if some of his archives were private, or personal, and if he could dispose of them at his own will."[19] The notary and the trustees were relieved of their mandates, and the files were transferred to the Federal Archives.

The General never kept a diary, nor did he write memoirs. Moreover, he did not have much private correspondence, as he was not very keen on letter-writing. Hence, there is very little biographical data available directly from him. He rarely wrote to his wife, and when he did the letters were short. Henry Jr. told the author that Mrs. Guisan destroyed these letters before she died. Recently, though, Guisan's cashbook and a few notes were found in the basement of his house, "Verte Rive."[20] In this cashbook, which he kept from 1897, at the time he took over a farm in Chesalles-sur-Oron at the age of 23, to 1955, five years before his death, he painstakingly entered, on a daily basis except during the war, every income and expense item, listing his assets and liabilities at the end of each year.[21] Liliane Perrin was the first to write about this "Livre de comptes" in 1986; in addition, she recorded a wealth of details about the General's early life and his relatives that she had obtained from Guisan family members. Her book will be quoted in several places in this work, especially to resolve some issues about Guisan's private life and his family in connection with his career.

In order to obtain additional information on General Guisan's character and personality, I took into account the testimonies of his former associates.[22] Even though I am aware of the problematic nature of oral sources, I felt that the mood and the atmosphere surrounding special circumstances should be adequately represented in this book through the memories of Guisan's contemporaries. From conversations with members of the General's personal staff as well as with participants at the Officers' Conspiracy and at the Rütli, I derived interesting insights on several aspects of the subject matter.

This study does not intend to undermine the well-deserved memorial that the Swiss have erected to the General, nor to belittle the high esteem in which he is held. As indicated in the full title of this volume, its main objective is to use historical sources to clarify the problems that the army leadership was faced with during the period 1939 to 1945. Because of the complexities of World War II, the role of the army, with Guisan at its command, cannot be viewed in isolation. Inasmuch as the activities of the armed forces and those underlying politics are closely intertwined, the activities of the commander-in-chief have become a substantial part of the history of Switzerland's domestic and foreign policy.

J.R. von Salis writes that Switzerland's history during World War II was in fact "more trite than it appears from today's perspective: What were our aims? First, keep the war away from Switzerland; second, defend the country should it be attacked."[23] Before events are transformed into legend through a glorifying myth that seizes upon the extraordinary personality of General Guisan, historiography has the task of uncovering and perceiving the bare facts. The main undertaking consists in recognizing and recording each and every aspect of Guisan's role as commander-in-chief, which was significant. In addition, some light needs to be shed on several vague gray areas. While the author is fully aware that there is hardly any absolute historical truth, one can come very close to it by trying to be as objective as possible. The author is also aware of the fact that trying to establish substantive facts can sometimes detract from patriotic feelings. However, the General's accomplishments were significant enough to bear all the facts. He does not need to be lifted to a monumental level; any attempt to do so would constitute an insult to his memory. Even if this study keeps to the facts, it leaves the picture of an extraordinary performance by a man radiating immense inner power.

This volume focuses mainly on Switzerland's history during World War II. In order for it to be also a biography of Henri Guisan, the first chapters deal with the General's origin and early career, and the final chapters describe his late life.

As for me, the author of this study, I am a historian who was a young soldier at the time of the war. During the tense summer of 1940 I performed my initial obligatory military service and then remained on for some time to be promoted to officers' rank. During most of the period of mobilization I served as a warrant officer and later commanded an infantry company. I had the honor of personally meeting General Guisan on two occasions: the first while serving in the army in 1942 and the second as a civilian in 1951 in Zürich. During both encounters General Guisan left a deep impression on me.

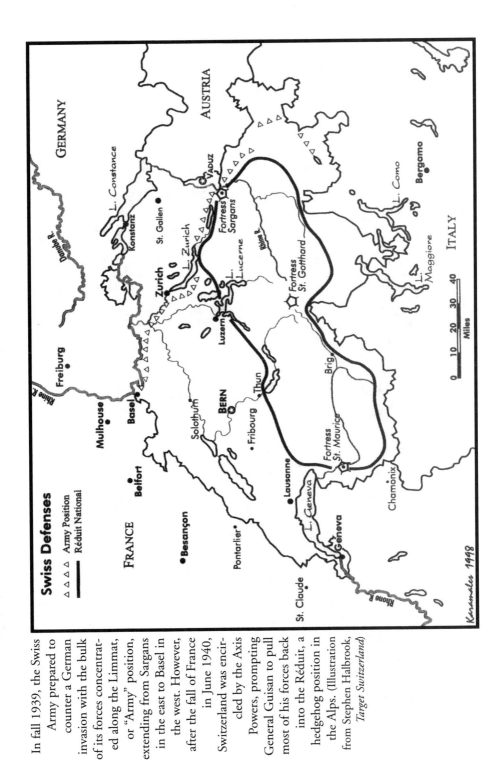

Swiss Defenses

△ △ △ △ Army Position
——— Réduit National

Karamales 1998

In fall 1939, the Swiss Army prepared to counter a German invasion with the bulk of its forces concentrated along the Limmat, or "Army" position, extending from Sargans in the east to Basel in the west. However, after the fall of France in June 1940, Switzerland was encircled by the Axis Powers, prompting General Guisan to pull most of his forces back into the Réduit, a hedgehog position in the Alps. (Illustration from Stephen Halbrook, *Target Switzerland*)

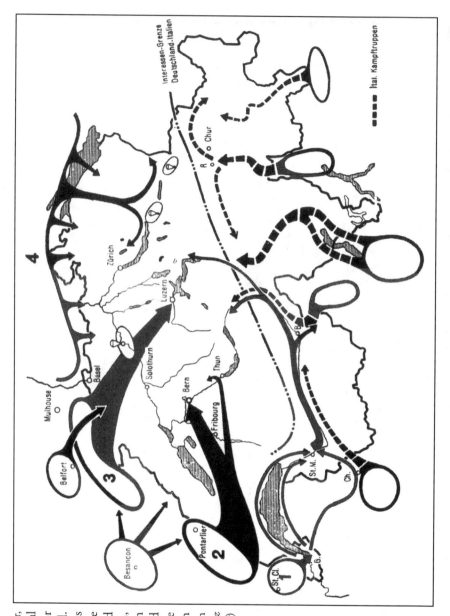

In the course of the war, Germany drafted several tentative plans for invading Switzerland. After completing its campaign in France, the German Army developed Operation Tannenbaum, at a time when Switzerland had drastically reduced the number of troops on duty. (Illustration from Werner Rings, *Die Schweiz im Krieg*)

I

Family History, Education, and Career (1874–1939)

Early Years

THE RECORDED GENEALOGY OF HENRI GUISAN, commander-in-chief of the Swiss Army during World War II, dates back to 1472, to the first mention in a document of someone named Guisan. The Guisan family came from the town of Avenches in Canton Vaud, in the southwestern, French-speaking part of Switzerland. At the beginning of the 16th century they belonged to the upper middle class of affluent farmers and bourgeois; they had the means to purchase land and rule over territory as well as hold posts as governors and judges.[1]

Guisan's direct ancestors were bourgeois, traceable back eight generations. There were no hereditary nobles among them, nor were they lower class. Both on his father's and mother's side, Guisan's ancestors embarked on military careers, or worked as physicians, lawyers, priests, and teachers, with others becoming merchants and artisans. The General once referred to his ancestors as having been "almost exclusively farmers,"[2] which is an overstatement. Most of them were upper-middle-class patricians living in the countryside.

Henri Guisan was born on October 21, 1874, in Mézières, as the eldest son of Charles-Ernest Guisan, a country doctor.[3] His grandfather had been a physician as well, while his great-grandfather had earned his living as a carpenter. His mother, Louise-Jeanne Bérangier, whose ancestors were Huguenots from the French Dauphinée, was the daughter of a businessman and grew up in Vevey, about 15 miles east of Lausanne.

Liliane Perrin, who researched Guisan's family history, discovered that the village priest had originally recorded Henri's birthdate as September 21, an error that was discovered some 16 years later, apparently in connection with young Guisan's confirmation. After some meticulous research, the cantonal government officially changed his birthdate to October 21.[4]

As an infant, Henri was in such poor health that he almost died a few months after birth. His mother, who at the time was at a spa trying to recover from tuberculosis, wrote to her husband in the spring of 1875 that she wanted to be notified by telegram in the event that her son's health worsened, so she could return home to "personally put him into his deathbed."[5]

Henri's mother died when he was 10 months old. Subsequently, one of Henri's aunts, Constante Guisan, oversaw the household, including the baby Henri.[6] Three years later, Charles-Ernest Guisan married his 26-year-old cousin, Blanche-Lina Guisan. The couple had five children together, three girls and two boys. Therefore, Henri grew up without his mother and with five half brothers and sisters. The General's son remarked that his father must "often have felt lonely" in this family situation.[7] When asked about his youth, the General himself told a student calling in on a radio show, "Even today I often reminisce about my early years and my dear parents."[8] In one of his conversations with Raymond Gafner, Guisan said about his childhood: "I have fond memories of my parents' home in Mézières, and of course I also remember my school years, during which I had many friends from the village and its surroundings who were mostly farmers' children. After school hours we enjoyed climbing trees, and during the fall we kept watch over the cattle. I also tremendously enjoyed accompanying my father on his sick calls and learning how to drive a carriage. My father had three horses, so I got to take him to the train station in the carriage, and in later years I went along with him on horseback."[9]

Henri Guisan's character was shaped during these early years of his life when he developed a close link with his native soil and a deep affection for the countryside and its people, especially the farming community. He also became fond of horses. The exact details of his youth are not very well documented; however, there are indications suggesting that Henri went through a "painful childhood that left distinctive marks" on him.[10]

At the age of 10, Henri was admitted to the Junior High School in Lausanne, where he lived at the "Mignot" boarding house. Cadet training was mandatory for his age group at the time. In the Lausanne Cadet Corps, the future General rose to the rank of non-commissioned officer.

Every weekend Henri went home to Mézières, walking 10 miles uphill on Saturday morning together with two friends, and back to Lausanne on Sunday evening, a trip that took three to four hours one way. "We had no other choice than to walk," Guisan said later, "because my parents would not spend any money on train or bus tickets, except when the weather was very bad."[11]

Judging from his grade sheets during high school, Henri Guisan was not a brilliant student. On his entrance exam to the junior high school, he scored 145 out of 220 points, finishing 31st among 37 passing candidates. Seven years later, during his senior year, he scored 201 out of 300 points, finishing 13th out of 15 passing students.[12] Apparently due to some difficulties in school, the 17-year-old took a break in 1891, spending several weeks with a minister's family, the Pichlers, in Kornwertheim, Württemberg, Germany, to prepare for his final high school exams. Even while serving as general, Guisan remained in contact with the Pichler family and wrote to them after the war that during his time as the supreme commander he "often reminisced with gratefulness about those days during my adolescence."[13]

At his father's request, Henri studied Latin and Greek in high school. "Latin was very useful to me later on, but Greek far less so," he said in retrospect.[14] Henri did not take advantage of the opportunity to study English, which was an elective subject at his school. In 1893, at the age of 19, Henri Guisan passed the final exams at the Lausanne High School, allowing him to enter a university.[15]

2

University Studies and Vocational Training

IT WAS NOT EASY FOR GUISAN TO CHOOSE his primary course of study at the University of Lausanne. His father would have liked him to study medicine to continue the family tradition, but he was, in his own words, "not in the mood for it." He first considered theology, another of his father's favorite subjects. "I told him I would try, and I did," he remembered. "However, I felt even less comfortable learning Hebrew than I did learning Greek, so I put theology aside and plunged into what I hoped would henceforth be my main occupation: science, especially chemistry."[1] One of Guisan's professors was a future Federal Councilor, Ernst Chuard, who lectured on agricultural chemistry and directed him toward his ultimate professional career as a farmer.[2] Guisan also made a short-lived attempt at studying law, and considered becoming a teacher.[3]

During the semesters when he was trying to find the most suitable university subject, Guisan joined the "Zofingia" fraternity in Lausanne, whose motto, "Home, Country, Friendship, Science," probably appealed to him. He was in contact with students from all the faculties and enjoyed the social life of the fraternity, which inspired him. "Problems of national interest were hardly ever on our minds," he recalled. "Instead, we rehearsed plays and prepared for other social gatherings. As far as I remember, we did not deal with important political or economic questions."[4] The only time Guisan performed as an actor in the annual fraternity play, he played the role of a woman.[5] One year he and two friends rode 100 miles on their bicycles to participate in the fraternity's annual national convention. On their way back, the three cyclists took a detour across the Brünig mountain pass.

One professor who influenced Guisan during his time at the university was the historian Edmond Rossier. Every other week, Rossier invited his students to his home for a seminar where they discussed historical topics.[6] It was most likely during these debates that Guisan gained knowledge of the essentials of European and Swiss history and came to realize the implications of freedom and democracy as major factors in building the Swiss Confederation. Moreover, the seminar discussions must have made clear to him that the duty to take up arms to defend these values and the country's independence was a basic political conviction throughout Switzerland's history.[7]

According to his records, Guisan also spent one semester at the University of Fribourg, along the language border between French- and German-speaking Switzerland. During that time, he worked on a farm on the outskirts of the town. The farm's owner, an aristocrat named de Diesbach, had promised his friend Dr. Guisan that he would teach his son "to do practical work."[8] During his stay at the farm, which was followed by another at the von Wattenwyls' estate in Oberdiessbach, Canton Bern, Henri Guisan made up his mind to study agriculture.

To follow his new career path, Guisan first attended the agricultural school in Ecully near Lyons, France, then one in Hohenheim in Württemberg, Germany, where his first application had been rejected because of lack of space. Among his papers, no diploma or certificate has been found from a school of agriculture. (His son confirmed that there was no such document.[9]) It seems that Guisan never called himself an "agronomist" or "certified farmer"; in his military record booklet, he was recorded, in 1893, simply as a "farmer."

During his stays in Canton Bern and in Württemberg, Guisan improved his Swiss German and High German language skills, and became familiar with German working methods and their different style of life. He learned to speak fluent German, and his intonation of the Bernese dialect of Swiss German was nearly perfect. Some authors claim that he also spoke perfect Italian and was able to express himself in Romansh.[10] However, when he was asked if he spoke all four of Switzerland's official languages, Guisan stated in 1949: "French, German, Swiss German—as much as you want. I understand some Italian but I don't speak it well at all. Whenever I have to address an Italian-speaking audience, I have to have my script corrected by a native speaker first. And I barely learned a few words of Romansh. . . . That's it, in a nutshell."[11]

Guisan not only spoke fluent German but also wrote it very well. Böschenstein mentions that in the 1920s the head of the military department, Federal Councilor Scheurer, had to mediate a dispute between Guisan and his French-speaking divisional commander, Bornard, because Guisan had submitted a report in German instead of French, his superior's native language.[12] Guisan's remarkable German language skills facilitated his contact with Swiss Germans. In fact, after retiring as commander-in-chief, he stated that speaking Swiss German had been "very useful" in his career.[13]

Due to his fondness for horses, Guisan initially intended to join the cavalry. However, at his father's request, and in order to be able to attend the agricultural school in Hohenheim, which happened to coincide with the cavalry training course, he asked to be transferred to a different mounted arm of the service. Hence, he was admitted to the field artillery, in which he accomplished his initial training course as a soldier in 1894. It is interesting to note that the authorization for Guisan's transfer was signed by General Johannes Herzog, who was then chief instructor in the cavalry, and two generals-to-be: Ulrich Wille, who led Switzerland's armed forces during World War I and was chief instructor in the artillery in 1894, and Guisan himself.[14] Thus the signatures of three of the four generals in Swiss history are present on the teenager's document of transfer.

At the end of the initial army training course, which lasted 57 days, Guisan was proposed as a candidate for officer training. He completed his officer training that same year and was promoted to lieutenant on December 15, 1894, at the age of 20.[15]

Guisan as a Farmer, Estate Owner, and Militia Officer

ONCE GUISAN HAD FINISHED HIS TRAINING as a farmer, he and his father agreed that he should purchase the "Bellevue" farm in Chesalles-sur-Oron. The money for Guisan's purchasing the farm at the age of 23 must have come from the inheritance he had received from his late mother, because his father was not very well off as a country doctor, and had to provide for the five children he had with his second wife.

According to his own account, Guisan moved to Chesalles-sur-Oron in the spring of 1897, though the civil authorities recorded "August 5, 1897"[1] as the official arrival date of "Guisan Henri, farmer."[2] At the end of the 19th century, this village on the border of Cantons Vaud and Fribourg consisted of 28 houses nestled in a hamlet with a few surrounding farmhouses. The total population of the community was 175. At the time of the purchase, the "Bellevue" property included about 35 acres of land and woods,[3] to which Guisan added another nine acres, making it a medium-sized farm. Guisan took over the furniture from his predecessor at a price of 197 Swiss francs.[4] He became owner of 30 head of cattle and six horses. The purchase price of the farm, including livestock and equipment, came to 98,000 francs.[5]

Guisan had planned ahead for his move to his first privately owned dwelling, purchasing, in March 1897, a barrel of Spanish white wine: "127 liters of Spanish wine at 0.35 francs per liter = 44.45 francs." The following spring, he spent 49.90 francs on 217 liters of "Roggen" wine, at a price of 0.23 francs a liter.[6]

In the fall of 1897, Henri Guisan married Mary Doelker, the daughter of a well-to-do merchant from Pully, whom he had been dating since high school and who was one year his junior.[7] In connection with the wedding, which took place on October 29, 1897, Guisan recorded expenses of 550 francs. His father-in-law recorded expenses of 150 francs, plus a dowry worth 11,500 francs.[8] In the wedding contract, dated October 20, 1897, the couple agreed on a separation of property. In addition, the contract stipulated that the surviving spouse was to have the right to the combined assets in case of the other's demise.[9] The couple remained married for 63 years, until death parted them; throughout all those years, they appeared to enjoy a harmonious relationship.[10]

Guisan tended his farm "practically by myself," as he said, although he had some helpers.[11] He detailed all his revenues in his cashbook. From April to December 1897, he earned a total of 2,897 francs, half of which came from milk sales.[12] Apparently Guisan was quite successful as a farmer, even though he was far from affluent. During those years, Guisan gained firsthand experience of the hardship of farming and became used to counting every penny.

When Guisan was summoned to an arms inspection in 1897, he recorded expenses of 70 centimes for a drink and 50 centimes for a cigar, plus two francs for getting a new gold braid sewn onto his officer's hat.[13] Judging from the entries in his cashbook, Guisan did not attend church very frequently, nor did he take time off from his job for hobbies or vacations. His only distraction was the military service, which many farmers and handymen at the time half-jokingly called "vacation time at the Confederation's expense." Guisan did not have much time for cultural and other events; the only expenses listed in his cashbook were three tickets to the "Zofingia" fraternity's annual play. Guisan subscribed to the "Nouvelliste" paper, while his wife had a subscription to the *Cri de Paris*, a fashion magazine.

Guisan held several honorary public offices in Chesalles-sur-Oron. As early as December 1897, the year he moved to the village, he was elected secretary of the village assembly ("Assemblée du Conseil général"). In this function, he had to take down the minutes of the assemblies, which were held two to three times a year.[14] The following year Guisan was named secretary of the poor-relief fund committee[15] and became a jury member on the cantonal court for a four-year term.[16] On November 17, 1901, he was elected to the village council, receiving 14 of 23 votes.[17] Guisan also joined the local fire brigade, which consisted of 27 men. He joined as a simple fireman since the positions of captain and lieutenant were already taken.[18]

When Guisan's father-in-law died in 1903, the Guisans left their farm in Chesalles-sur-Oron to move to the "Verte Rive" mansion in Pully outside Lausanne, located alongside Lake Geneva. Christ-Charles Doelker, a former baker, had built the house between 1867 and 1874 on a 2.7-acre property. Doelker's grandfather had immigrated to Switzerland from Württemberg as a cartwright in the early 1800s, and became a successful real estate agent and wheat wholesaler.[19] The property included a barn and stables for three to four horses, two to three cattle, and chickens that were tended by a stable lad and a shepherd.

Guisan kept his property in Chesalles-sur-Oron for several years after moving to Pully, first leaving the principal stable lad in charge of the farm, then leasing it to him. In 1906, he finally sold "Bellevue" to his tenant.[20] By this time, Guisan was no longer a simple farmer, but a landed gentleman. In 1910, he had the mansion in Pully partly redone and built an addition with a terrace, the ceiling of which was supported by columns.[21]

In Pully, Guisan also ran for public office. In late 1906 he was a candidate for the post of substitute on the town council, Pully's legislative branch, which consisted of 60 members, but he placed only fifth out of eight candidates.[22] Nevertheless, only one year later he entered the town council as the replacement for a citizen named Jules Collioud.[23] At the end of 1908, he was elected to the council's seven-member business administration committee ("Commission de Gestion"). Guisan was reelected to the town council in 1909, ranking 36th, and again in 1913, ranking 26th.[24]

Guisan was not a very active member of the council. He consistently missed most of the approximately 10 annual meetings, sometimes even without giving a reason. According to the council's records, he took part in four meetings in 1908 and three in 1910; in 1909, he missed all the meetings. In 1911, 13 meetings were held, of which Guisan missed six while giving a reason and another three without explanation. During World War I, he took part in one meeting each in 1915 and 1916 and missed all the meetings in 1917.[25] Guisan did not stand for reelection in 1917 but ran again in 1921, when he was elected by a narrow margin in the second round of voting.[26] He remained in office until 1929; that is, three years beyond his appointment as divisional commander. Overall, Henri Guisan served 18 years on the town council of Pully, from 1908 to 1917 and from 1922 to 1929.[27]

One should not underestimate the importance of the "Verte Rive" mansion in the progression of Guisan's career. The beautiful estate and the lifestyle of its owner were clear expressions of his financial independence. Even though Guisan did not brag about his lifestyle, he used the mansion to keep horses, ride, and invite guests to dinner at the table overlooking the lake and the French Alps. Meals served by his charming wife, outside on the terrace when weather permitted, with a good bottle of wine at hand, provided a pleasant atmosphere that made comrades in arms as well as superior officers, politicians, and journalists feel at ease. It is likely that Henri Guisan would not have had such an exceptional military career had he not been owner of the "Verte Rive" domain. As Liliane Perrin wrote, the estate "allowed him in part to become what he was."[28]

At "Verte Rive," Guisan began to focus on his military career with determination. After being promoted to captain, he first commanded the 4th Field Battery but had difficulties with his superiors. André Marcel vouches that, "unbelievable as this so far unknown fact may sound, the future General was declared unfit for service in one unit before being promoted to battalion commander."[29] Henry Guisan, the General's son, explained to me that his father was disdained primarily by the commander of the 1st Division at the time, Colonel Bornand, who resented the fact that Guisan refused to join the Radical Party of Vaud, of which Bornand was president. One statement said that Captain Guisan was not capable of commanding troops, nor could he be trained to do so.[30] Consequently, Guisan asked to be transferred to the 2nd Division, which mainly consisted of men from Canton Neuchâtel and Bern. His request was granted.

In 1908, Guisan began serving on the general staff of the armed forces. In addition, he began volunteering as a special instructor at the Bière training facility, located less than twenty miles from his home. From 1911 to 1913, after being promoted to major on the general staff, he taught artillery strategy to two training units. In courses given to the general staff, Guisan lectured on various topics.[31] He particularly liked this type of service as a trainer, admitting, "a special instructor has the privilege of being able to say, 'I am sorry that due to the harvest season or for some other reason, I cannot teach this particular course.'"[32]

Guisan recounted that at the request of Chief of the General Staff von Sprecher he was transferred from the artillery to the infantry in 1913. Guisan assumed command of the 24th Battalion, which consisted primarily of men from the Jura region. During the first part of World War I, he served with this unit for 119 days in the border area of the Ajoie valley and around the Hauenstein mountain.[33]

In 1916, Guisan served as a lieutenant colonel on the personal staff of von Sprecher, whose office was located in the Federal Building in Bern. During that time, he was in regular contact with General Ulrich Wille, whose command post was located in the Bellevue-Palace Hotel next door. Guisan explained, "I very often, albeit not quite every day, went to see the chief of the general staff with a document folder in my hand, had him read the documents and add his written comments, and then went to see General Wille to have the papers signed." General Wille always "made a very friendly impression" on Guisan. He was "extensive and very precise in handling everything, just like Colonel von Sprecher, who never left the slightest detail unfinished." Guisan later stated that the experience of dealing with two completely different commanders such as Wille and von Sprecher had been "very useful" to him as commander-in-chief during the Second World War.[34]

Lt. Colonel Guisan, one of von Sprecher's closest collaborators in the operational section, must have been well-informed of the secret negotiations that Switzerland's army command held with the French army in the spring of 1916 to discuss possible cooperation between the Swiss and French in case of a German attack.[35] It is very likely that Guisan was inspired by this World War I experience when he initiated his own secret cooperation talks with France in 1939–1940.[36]

In 1917, Guisan became chief of staff of the 2nd Division. In this function, and then as troop commander, he served under three commanders before taking command of the mixed German- and French-speaking division on his own in 1926.[37]

In August 1916, Guisan was chosen to accompany Lt. Colonel de Goumoëns, head of the operational section, on a visit to the front lines in eastern France. He wrote that "We were ordered to inspect, together with the military attachés stationed in Paris, the French front lines in the Argonnes, around Eparges and Verdun. There we saw how they were fighting under a defensive system which consisted of nothing but interconnected trenches, a kind of fortress in the field."[38] De Goumoëns and Guisan submitted a detailed 23-page report on the seven-day visit; drawings and addenda in Guisan's handwriting indicate that he was its main author.[39]

The two lieutenant colonels were impressed by the large number of motorized vehicles General Nivelle's French 1st Army had at its disposal: 12,000 trucks and just as many cars. Each truck could carry 28 to 32 men, including their arms and equipment. "This service is of the utmost importance," they wrote.[40]

On the negative side, Guisan remarked, "Both at the front and further back, the troops' uniforms are dirty, and so are their shoes, with the exception of some infantrymen and cavalrymen who are clean." During positional warfare, rifles seemed to have no great role to play. According to statements by front officers, the troops in the trenches used "artillery, hand-grenades, and knives" to fight. The two Swiss officers also noticed the number of automatic weapons in the infantry: Every regiment had three companies that operated eight machine guns each, and the British had plans to double that number. In addition, some machine guns had 18 barrels, allowing 18 shots to be fired simultaneously with one gun. The sector of front that had to be defended by a 150-man company was up to 800 meters wide.[41]

The Swiss visitors also inspected the French air force. Each French army corps included a group of six to ten aircraft, which were used mainly for reconnaissance or observing artillery fire. Moreover, the French had bombers and fighter aircraft that could fly at night as well as during the day. At a time when

the United States had not yet entered the war, the French air force was reinforced by a group of volunteer pilots from the United States who were commanded by French officers.[42]

The report concluded with criticisms on a number of points where the
Swiss believed they could do better, but above all it expressed admiration for the
French army, which in spite of setbacks had recovered its former fighting spirit at a time of utmost danger. On all parts of the front, the visitors received the
impression that the troops were "calmly fulfilling their duty," convinced, "without bragging at all," that the Germans would not win the war. Guisan recognized on the battlefield of Verdun that the determination to fight was a crucial
factor in winning a war, and that the Swiss "were far from matching the French,
who had come close to being defeated two years earlier, in that respect." In
summary, Guisan wrote, "In a war, in the first place you need soldiers and the
commanders who guide them. In Switzerland you often hear about the 'strategic understanding' of non-commissioned officers, but the strategy used by good
soldiers is perfectly sufficient!"[43]

The following year, in July 1917, Guisan had another opportunity to visit
front-line battlefields, in the sectors of the 7th and 8th French Armies in Lorraine
and the Vosges Mountains. However, this time he was the only Swiss officer present, "enjoying the privilege of accompanying Commander d'Harcourt in his car.
I could see a lot of details that I had missed in 1916, gaining useful information
on fortifications, trenches, and aligning troops in the woods."[44]

Guisan wrote a 25-page report on this mission,[45] in which he included
information on his first experience observing tanks. He noted that the initial
enthusiasm about their usefulness had somewhat abated, as the French had
"failed pitifully," 32 out of 100 tanks being immediately destroyed by the
Germans and others getting stuck in mud during the attack. Guisan viewed the
British tanks as better than the French ones, and he remarked that the crew
members were all volunteers "because life in the tanks is hell, and the death is
horrible."[46] In addition, he noticed that the air force had been reinforced, the
army now having five groups with 15 aircraft each, which were now deployed
on the army level, no longer on a corps level. The aircraft were flying at an average speed of 200 kilometers per hour and were able to climb to an altitude of
3,000 meters within ten minutes.[47]

Regarding the troops' morale, Guisan remarked that here and there some
mutinies had occurred, but overall the troops were in good spirits. He confirmed that General Pétain had to intervene personally to keep some colonial
units from deserting and to get them back into their positions. Also, France was
waiting for the support of the United States, which it expected to arrive on the
battlefields within eight months.[48]

During an inspection of the 7th French Army's trench system, Guisan was surprised to see that the front lines of the defending companies were much wider than the Swiss had assumed. In the Vosges Mountains, a company's front was one and a quarter miles wide, along the Marne River even two and a half miles wide. Both fronts had artillery support and were well equipped with heavy weapons, machine guns, and trench mortars.[49]

Guisan also noted that the French were using Alaskan huskies, able to pull loads of up to 1,750 pounds over long distances, to bring supplies to the troops in the wintertime regardless of weather conditions. Also, after successfully using carrier pigeons during the battle of Verdun, the French increased their number; the 8th Army, for example, had 1,700 carrier pigeons trained to fly by day and night.[50]

Guisan concluded optimistically that the French troops were convinced that they would succeed, even though the end of the war was not yet in sight.[51]

Toward the end of the First World War, Guisan was appointed commander of the 9th Infantry Regiment while holding on to his post as chief of staff of the 2nd Division; having multiple assignments simultaneously was possible at the time.[52] Most of Guisan's regiment consisted of men from the Jura region. It last served during the war in January 1918, and was called back in the spring of 1919 to help maintain order in Zürich,[53] one of the main hot spots of the civil unrest that swept across the country in November 1918 and the following months. Troops remained in Zürich until the summer of 1919 in case new riots flared.[54]

Guisan wrote a 15-page report on his regiment's four-week stay in Zürich.[55] One battalion had to guard sensitive areas in the city, while the two other battalions remained outside Zürich to perform regular training courses.[56] "We avoided having too many drills and boring exercises," Guisan wrote. Moreover, he cancelled long marches after several men complained of sore feet, replacing them with fitness classes and sports competitions.[57] Guisan also tried a new approach to lodging, finding host families for every soldier instead of quartering them in barracks. He considered this experiment very successful: "The benefits outweighed the disadvantages. My men were better rested, and the impact on their morale was just as important." In addition, Guisan was very pleased with the way his men were received by the families: "Many farmers left their houses open to the soldiers while they were out cultivating their fields. I did not receive one single complaint, which proves that there was perfect harmony between the farmers and the soldiers, who were grateful for what was done for them as well as for the confidence that was put in them."[58]

During the time the 9th Regiment stayed in Zürich, no major incidents occurred. May Day went by without any disturbances, pointing to a "substantial easing of the political tension in the country." Consequently, the Cantonal Executive Council of Zürich proposed that the Federal authorities "gradually reduce the number of troops occupying the city," as it believed that the labor movement was "not interested in revolutionary acts of violence if social reforms" were "introduced at a steady pace."[59] On May 26, railroad workers went on strike for four hours to add weight to their demand for lowering the number of working hours per week to 48. Less than two weeks later, another demonstration was dispersed without bloodshed. Guisan wrote about these events: "The labor protest of May 26 and the Communist demonstration of June 7 reinforced the troops in their conviction that their presence was necessary in Zürich."[60]

Divisional commander Biberstein commended Guisan and his troops for their "beautiful uniforms and their exemplary discipline that created a feeling of trust among the population. Everyone has great respect for them."[61] On June 10, the 9th Infantry Regiment was replaced by new troops; on June 13, it demobilized. That day and the following day, riots took place in Zürich, killing two people and injuring 25 others.[62]

Guisan later stated about the four weeks he spent in Zürich with his troops maintaining order, "I must say I was thrilled by the troops' morale. The battalions were well manned; my regiment had close to 3,000 men. They received the maximum pay for this type of service. Apart from a few incidents, everything went in a very orderly fashion. We had to take firm action on two occasions in order to disperse striking workers, which we did without any difficulty because my men proceeded with determination, as they were very upset with the strike leaders who were mostly foreigners. Being on duty to maintain order is no fun, but I had told my men beforehand that they would have to deal above all with foreign strike leaders trying to create turmoil in our country. Our good men from the Jura understood what I told them. The situation turned around, and the careless strike leaders had to give in to the loyal army."[63]

That statement, which Guisan made well after the Second World War, exemplifies his bias about the social unrest that swept across Switzerland in November 1918. His assumption that the strike leaders were mainly foreigners has since been disproven by historians.[64] As with many bourgeois, Guisan was traumatized by the serious crisis that shook the foundations of the Federal state in 1918. Above all, for decades afterward, he must have eyed Robert Grimm, the president of the union movement based in Olten (the so-called Olten Committee), which advocated massive strikes to obtain political results, as a leading exponent of socialist ideas who had to be defeated by all means. In a different context, Guisan explained that his experience while serving in Zürich in 1919 reinforced his conviction that it was necessary to create a climate of social stability during the time of World War II mobilization in order to prevent revolutionary movements from gaining momentum.[65]

At the end of 1921, Guisan was promoted to the rank of colonel and became commander of the 5th Infantry Brigade, which he headed during the large-scale training maneuvers in 1924. In addition, he continued teaching courses for the general staff and officers on a voluntary basis.[66] At the same time, at the request of the chief of the general staff, Guisan studied operational questions concerning a potential attack from the west,[67] analyzing the pros and cons of different formations that could be considered for defending the country. He wrote a study on his reflections in 1921–1922, followed by a memorandum in 1925[68] and a final report in 1926, citing figures for means of transportation and supplies, which were to serve as the basis for an operational plan for mobilizing troops on the western front. Guisan came to the conclusion that having an ally would increase the chances of resisting the enemy and of holding on to large areas of the country.[69]

Guisan's financial situation during his first years at "Verte Rive" was never critical, but he did encounter some difficulties. In 1916, as a lieutenant colonel, he earned a modest 4,630 Swiss francs in wages and fees. Guisan continued writing every expenditure and item of revenue in his cashbook. He earned several thousand Swiss francs a year in interest on his assets and occasionally made profits in the stock market. In 1916, after his father's death, he used his inheritance, which came from the sale of the doctor's office in Mézières, to have a bathroom and a fireplace installed at "Verte Rive." As an indication of Guisan's financial situation, he and his wife regularly rented out rooms at their mansion between 1909 and 1920, mostly to foreigners. In 1909, a Mr. Feiling paid 180 francs rent per month, in 1910 a Frédéric Smith paid 220 francs monthly, and in 1911 the total rent revenue amounted to about 2,600 francs. After 1912, Guisan no longer recorded rent revenues in his cashbook, noting that "rent was received by Mary," his wife.[70]

The Guisans' two children, Henry and Myriam, were born while they still lived in Chesalles.[71] Henry said that his father was firm with them. He did not beat them, nor did he shout, but he did not like to be contradicted; his verdict was always final. Henry remarked that his father was very fond of his family, but must not have been perfectly content spending too much time with them, as he was away 10 out of the 12 months of the year.[72]

Daughter Myriam found her father wonderful and caring "whenever he was home!" She had a very close relationship with her mother, visiting her in Pully every other week, even after she got married and moved to Bern.[73]

Myriam had fond memories of Christmas as a time of happiness for the family, even though the children did not receive their presents until New Year's Day.[74] Guisan was generous on these occasions, as seen in his cashbook entries in December 1928, when expenditure for Christmas gifts totaled 1,443 francs. His wife received a fur coat (300 francs), a shirt (55 francs), and chocolate (10 francs); his daughter got a fur coat (200 francs), a handbag (25 francs), and sweets (10 francs); and his son received a copy of the painting "Sentry at Les Rangiers," books, and chocolate (213 francs). Relatives and the employees also received presents.[75]

Considering these gifts and other financial information from the 1920s, Perrin exaggerates by calling those years as "rather tough" ("*plutôt dures*") for the Guisan family.[76] It is true, though, that Guisan could not have lived comfortably with his family exclusively on his pay as a colonel.

Some authors claim that Guisan did not know how to drive and never owned a car.[77] Guisan's cashbook, however, shows that he owned several cars from 1928 on. For example, in the spring of 1928, he purchased a "Falcon-Knight," including accessories, for 11,873 francs.[78] He passed his driving test for light vehicles on April 23, 1928.[79]

4

Guisan as Divisional Commander and Corps Commander

DESPITE FREQUENTLY VOLUNTEERING FOR SPECIAL TASKS, Guisan was seen merely as "the prototype of a militia officer"[1] by the instructional corps of the professional armed forces. In fact, Guisan was the only general in the history of the Swiss Confederation whose career all the way to the top level was through the militia. Even though he spent most of his time between 1908 and 1926 in the military, totaling about 3,560 days of service, he did not become a regular officer until he was 52 years old, when he was named a divisional commander.

On December 31, 1926, Colonel Guisan succeeded the newly appointed Corps Commander Sarasin from Geneva as commander of the 2nd Division. Guisan thanked the head of the Federal Department of Military Affairs, Federal Councilor Scheurer, for his upcoming promotion, writing, "I take on this great responsibility with joy, hoping that I will prove worthy of the trust which is put in me and that my performance will be to your entire satisfaction."[2] He must have been very excited about his promotion, as he signed the letter using his new title, "Col. Div.," one month before he actually assumed it.

When Guisan took over command of the 1st Division from retiring Divisional Commander Grosselin in March 1931, the troops, composed of French-speaking men from Cantons Vaud and Geneva, received him warmheartedly. However, Guisan only commanded the 1st Division for barely over a year, as he was promoted to corps commander on July 1, 1932, taking over command of the 2nd Corps from Colonel Scheibli, who had died.

German-speaking Switzerland welcomed Guisan's nomination as corps commander as much as did the French-speaking part of the country. *Der Bund,* a Bern newspaper, praised the 57-year-old, who spoke and wrote both French and German, for his military competence and his great charm, adding, "Those who know Colonel-Corps Commander Guisan are convinced that this outstanding soldier and congenial troop leader will have no trouble gaining the respect of the troops of the 2nd Army Corps."[3] The *Neue Zürcher Zeitung* agreed, saying that Guisan was well known beyond French-speaking Switzerland and made an "extremely fresh and stimulating" impression.[4]

Guisan later explained that he owed his promotion to commander of the 2nd Corps to the head of the Department of Military Affairs, Federal Councilor Rudolf Minger, who had succeeded K. Scheurer in 1930 and had "taken a liking" to him. "He wanted me to take over the command of a German-speaking army corps. . . . It was a big advantage for me to have commanded a bilingual brigade, followed by a bilingual division. Hence, I had absolutely no problems with the Swiss Germans when I joined the 2nd Corps. Moreover, I had the advantage of getting to know the two linguistic groups of our armed forces."[5]

Only 15 months later, in the fall of 1933, Guisan was offered command of the mixed German- and French-speaking 1st Army Corps to replace Colonel-Corps Commander Sarasin, who had died unexpectedly. This change allowed Guisan to acquaint himself with two-thirds of Switzerland's armed forces.[6]

With his promotion to corps commander, Guisan automatically became a member of the National Defense Committee (NDC), which was the Federal government's supreme advisory group in army-related matters and which met once a month under the chairmanship of the head of the Federal Department of Military Affairs. On July 28, 1932, when Guisan took part in his first NDC meeting, the committee consisted of Federal Councilor Minger, Chief of the General Staff Roost, the two other corps commanders, Sarasin (1st Corps) and Biberstein (3rd Corps), and Divisional Commander Ulrich Wille Jr., the chief instructor of the infantry.

Guisan hardly missed any meetings of the NDC and contributed regularly to the debates, usually through short interventions. Upon becoming the oldest serving member of the committee, he was often the first to speak, though without acting as the committee's spokesman, a role that Wille tended to assume once he had been promoted to corps commander. Guisan did not hesitate to express his own opinion, even when it diverged from that of the other members. A look at the minutes of NDC meetings shows that Guisan intervened mostly as an expert in questions relating to purchases and use of artillery, which was the arm of the service to which he originally belonged. When the NDC discussed abolishing the balloon troops, Guisan initially had doubts as to whether this was advisable because "long-range artillery [depended on data from] stationary observation points," adding that the Austrians had abolished balloons but then reintroduced them.[7] Guisan agreed to do away with the balloon troops only on the condition "that the artillery can be provided with a sufficient number of observation aircraft," and asked if it were not possible "to speed up the reinforcement of the air force."[8]

Guisan generally joined the rest of the National Defense Committee in requesting that the army be better armed and equipped. For instance, he advocated canceling all refresher courses for one year, so the expected savings of 18 to 20 million Swiss francs could be used to purchase heavy infantry weapons. He argued that "replacing our materiel" was "the most pressing matter. . . . The soldiers must have confidence in our weaponry, but currently they don't."[9]

In 1933, Jules Borel, commander of the 1st Division, made a formal request to do away with the rhythmic step in marching. The NDC debated the issue on several occasions, during which Guisan explained that the Swiss French were opposed to the rhythmic step, saying that they even objected to the phrase itself, "pas cadencé." Guisan continued: "The question of the rhythmic step is not new in French-speaking Switzerland. When I became commander of the 1st Division, I noticed that it had not been practiced for many years. The rhythmic step is unpopular."[10] After it had been decided that the mandatory pre-military training for male adolescents should no longer be performed with arms, Guisan told the NDC that this change had "left a bad impression on everyone," adding, "many believe that this is a concession to the Socialists and anti-military individuals." In 1934 he requested that armed pre-military training be reintroduced on a mandatory basis for all males between the ages of 16 and 20.[11]

It is interesting to note that during the 1930s the NDC discussed the usefulness of operational plans in the presence of Colonel-Corps Commander Guisan. In the spring of 1936, Chief of the General Staff Roost remarked, "We cannot prepare any deployment plans as this is the responsibility of the General. We can prepare positions ahead of time in order to block the enemy and to gain time for deploying troops. In case of mobilization, it is up to the corps commander where the troops should be positioned."[12] The corps commanders, including Guisan, did not contest this view. He agreed with the idea that army positions should be concentrated around the border fortifications, which were then being built. In the spring of 1935, Guisan commented during an NDC meeting, "In the first place, the fortifications boost border protection, allowing troops to fire from there on bridges and invasion routes. However, they have to be solid enough to be turned into army strongholds afterward."[13]

During the discussions in 1938 on whether to extend the duration of initial training courses, Guisan initially had reservations. However, after the September crisis prompted by Germany over Czechoslovakia, which was temporarily resolved by the Munich Pact, he stated that the courses did not last long enough and that he "would prefer a solution between four and eight months. Another option would be to have four months of initial training, followed by three months of service at the border. However, if the training courses are extended substantially, the question arises how that will affect officers living in the country. There is a risk that some segments of the population will not be represented among the officer corps anymore."[14]

In the summer of 1934, Corps Commander Guisan had the opportunity to attend, together with Divisional Commander de Diesbach, the large-scale maneuvers of the Italian army in the Apennines,[15] during which he met the King of Italy and Fascist dictator Benito Mussolini. Guisan later commented that his conversation with the "Duce" had been "very interesting; he had a very friendly attitude toward me, that is, toward Switzerland. I don't know whether this attitude lasted throughout the war; it is said that he tried to spare our country. I have not heard anything official about that."[16]

There is a 32-page report on this visit to Italy, including the encounter with Mussolini. Judging from the style and the handwritten additions by Guisan, the report was written primarily by de Diesbach, even though Guisan signed it.[17] In this report, the two Swiss officers expressed their deep admiration for the dictator, whose "miraculous qualities" helped to transform Italy, remarking, "He is the master, il Duce. This man is a genius who has the merit of having been able to discipline all forces of the nation." Guisan added in his handwriting, "He is two persons in one: the tough leader who is brutally frank; and he is charming when you see him smile and listen to him talk. He is respected, almost feared, with the prestige of a demigod, a man who rose from the people."[18] When Mussolini made his first appearance during the maneuvers, the officers of the troops that were engaged in training activities—generals and lieutenants alike—were visibly moved, and some were so reverent that they were about to lose their self-control. The spectators enthusiastically welcomed the dictator by shouting, "Duce! Duce!"; older people were weeping and crossed themselves.[19]

Mussolini was seen as trying to come across as a man of the people, dressing in a blue cap and a grey jacket. He also wore riding boots and pants, but no spurs or gloves, and he carried no cane. He had an unusually warm and open conversation with the two Swiss officers. When they talked about Lausanne, Guisan's hometown, Mussolini recalled his visit to that city and said he hoped that the old houses there, which bore witness to the past, would not all be torn down. He added jokingly, "Actually I should not say that, because I myself worked with a trowel in your country!"

The conversation soon turned to more serious matters, as Mussolini evoked the failed disarmament conference in Geneva. He explained to the Swiss visitors, "Switzerland's current political and military situation is of the utmost importance. Your country owes its position entirely to its determination to defend itself and safeguard its independence. As long as it maintains this attitude, it has nothing to fear from the neighboring powers." At this place in the report, Guisan added, "We have to be strong. Only those who are strong have friends. Hostilities will flare up before war is declared, because taking the enemy by surprise is the first rule of warfare! (So we should not rely on any treaty.) The second rule is that the winner will know how to justify why it entered the war."[20]

The day after the meeting, when the two Swiss officers arrived with some other visitors on the hill from which Mussolini watched the maneuvers, the Duce approached Guisan, showing him a newspaper and exclaiming joyfully, "Here is a picture of the two of us!" The following day, the same thing happened again. Mussolini presented Guisan a magazine, saying, "Here is another one."[21]

In view of these personal encounters, it is understandable that Guisan and de Diesbach considered Mussolini "a very simple and unbelievably attractive man." At the end of the report, much of which contained military data and analysis, the two officers once again discussed that "brilliant man," stating that the spiritual well-being of a country essentially depends on the attitude of the person who is at its helm.[22] From this statement, it appears that the two authors of the report had a tendency to believe that authoritarian leadership played an important role, and should in some instances even prevail over democratic institutions. Guisan concluded the report with the following handwritten remarks: "Feeling of trust, but above all [we] have to develop individual techn[ical] instruct[ion] of men in combat situations and of low-ranking officers." Guisan's favorable view of Mussolini, which lasted well into the Second World War, was undoubtedly influenced by the positive impression he had gained during his visit to Italy in 1934. It would be wrong, however, to assume that these warm feelings for the Duce, which were widespread in the 1930s, meant that Guisan leant in favor of Fascist ideologies; instead it appears that, along with many in the middle class, he welcomed the Fascist movement as a bulwark against the Bolshevik threat.

There is no record of Guisan's opinions about Hitler and National Socialism at that time, even when Hitler first came to power in 1933. However, one has the impression that Guisan had a more favorable view of Mussolini than of Hitler. There is no indication either that Guisan belonged to the group of people who clearly recognized the criminal nature of Hitler and his Third Reich at an early stage. In 1937, when the National Defense Committee discussed whether to accept Germany's invitation to attend the maneuvers of its 6th Army Corps—the so-called "Day of the Wehrmacht"—at the Nazi Party convention in Munich, Guisan did not express an opinion. According to the minutes of the meeting, however, Corps Commander Wille stated that Switzerland should attend the maneuvers but not the party convention, upon which Federal Councilor Minger decided to take up the matter with the Department of Foreign Affairs.[23]

There are conflicting opinions regarding Guisan's ability to assert himself as a military leader during his time as a corps commander. Foreign observers attending the maneuvers of the 2nd Division that were held in the fall of 1936 under Guisan's command were not very impressed with the troops' performance. The Austrian military attaché, for example, reported that the troops lacked strict leadership and were not encouraged to give their best. He had the impression that "the army had stagnated at a pre-World War I level" and would "be unable to put up resistance against an enemy with modern arms."[24] On the other hand, the Austrian observer conceded that the troops might have been spared more strenuous efforts because the military was in the process of getting a public loan approved. He also observed that training time was too short to allow the troops to perform according to the standards and requirements of a modern army.[25]

In the late summer of 1937, French Marshal Pétain attended the maneuvers of Switzerland's 1st Army Corps directed by Corps Commander Guisan, during which Guisan met the legendary victor of Verdun. The program for the day of September 5, 1937, included a gala reception with a dinner in Pétain's honor and a 45-minute personal meeting between Pétain and Guisan. Georg Kreis suggests that during this time the two men had a confidential exchange of opinions that became the foundation for the later talks about cooperation between the French and Swiss armies.[26]

The chief of Guisan's personal staff during the greater part of the war, Bernard Barbey, who was the Paris editor of the *Revue Hebdomadaire* at the time, had first established contact with Pétain in April 1936, after which he made a report to the Federal authorities in Bern. On that occasion, Pétain had expressed France's concern about Switzerland's lack of readiness to defend itself in the event of an attack. After setting up the Maginot Line between the Belgian and Swiss borders, the French counted on a strong Swiss military defense on their right flank. Pétain seems to have gained a favorable impression in that respect during his visit to the 1937 maneuvers; the French ambassador in Bern said in his report to Paris that the Marshal was very satisfied with the visit. Pétain was treated with reverence and was seated next to the Swiss Federal President on a special podium during the parade that concluded the maneuvers.

On September 10, Pétain invited Federal Councilor Minger, Guisan, and other high-ranking officers, including Corps Commander Wille, to a dinner at the French embassy in Bern.[27]

During that same year, Guisan was invited to France to attend maneuvers of the French armed forces in Normandy. Guisan later recounted that Marshal Pétain had personally invited him there during his visit to Switzerland. In France, he said, he "obtained valuable information, primarily about reservists whose regiments had been called up to participate in the maneuvers as a test. I gained the impression that these reservists were not as well trained as our territorial reserve troops. So our refresher courses during normal times are after all an excellent means of keeping our soldiers in shape."[28] Hence, Guisan was reassured through his impressions during these maneuvers that the training methods of Switzerland's militia army were effective.

Guisan was accompanied on his visit to France by Lieutenant Colonel Rudolf von Erlach, head of the operational section of the general staff. But attending the maneuvers was apparently not the only purpose of Guisan's visit. Kreis discovered that Guisan's visit had actually been arranged as early as August 1937, several weeks before Pétain visited Switzerland.[29] Even though the official mission report does not mention anything about meetings with the French army command, Guisan, unbeknownst to von Erlach, who was considered to be pro-German, must have held confidential talks with French General Gamelin about possible future military cooperation between the Swiss and French. Kreis came to this conclusion after analyzing, among other documents, the personal post–World War II correspondence between the two generals. In the summer of 1946, Guisan recalled in a letter to his French colleague that the 1937 maneuvers in Normandy allowed him to enjoy Gamelin's "generous hospitality and I was able to exchange views in friendship and confidence." The former French generalissimo used similar words in one of his letters to his Swiss counterpart, speaking of the "trustful relationship" he had with Guisan "in view of the common interests of our two nations."[30]

Guisan admired Pétain above all as a World War I hero, and continued to do so even after Pétain had created the authoritarian Vichy regime following France's armistice in 1940. To many Swiss French, including Guisan, Pétain was foremost, "the savior of France's last substance" by adapting to the hard reality of the defeat.[31] In the spring of 1941, Guisan wrote a letter to Pétain on the occasion of the latter's 86th birthday, saying that he still vividly and fondly remembered their meeting in 1937. He added that Pétain's moral and mental vigor was "comforting and enlightening" to all those who had been following his "efforts, from afar and nearby, for a quarter of a century, since the great days of Verdun."[32] In early 1944, when he thanked the Marshal for sending him his work, "La France Nouvelle," Guisan once again wrote to Pétain with admiration, albeit in a more subdued manner, saying that Pétain "had designed" France's renaissance, "the prospect of which has kept you going in a long and tough battle."[33]

Guisan also had personal confidential contact with a number of other French officers, including some generals who were about his age who were administrators or instructors at the Ecole Supérieure de Guerre in Paris. They included Generals Gaston Duffour, Raoul Voruz, and Victor Henri Schweissguth, as well as officers such as de Lannurien, Bordeaux, and Clément-Grandcour. Some of them visited Guisan at "Verte Rive" before the war, as indicated in Guisan's correspondence.[34] His visitors included, in the summer of 1938, General Alphonse Georges and his wife, who owned a chalet in Morzine in the French Alps across Lake Geneva. After 1945, Guisan renewed most of his contacts that had been interrupted by the war.

Since Guisan had no ambition of becoming a writer, there is very little material in print specifically authored by him. His best-known lecture, "The Soul of Our Army and the Social Role of an Officer," which he gave in 1934 in front of various military and non-military audiences in both French- and German-speaking Switzerland, was published in the *Neue Schweizer Rundschau* and printed as a brochure.[35] In this lecture, Guisan portrayed Switzerland's military tradition as an expression of the country's strong desire for freedom. He considered officers as links between the people and the armed forces, with a social obligation to serve as educators. He then went on to attack individuals friendly to Moscow, as well as "certain intellectuals and notorious pacifists with socialist ideas because of their ridiculous behavior and because they do not distance themselves" from Bolshevist ideas.[36]

In the spring of 1937, the *Schweizerische Hochschulzeitung*, a publication with official information pertaining to all public Swiss universities, focused on the topic of national defense. In this paper, Corps Commander Guisan wrote an article on "The Duties of University Graduates," stating that in an era of expected total war the hinterland would also be drawn into the conflict, allowing the equation, "Army = Nation."[37] He called on university students to believe in the future of Switzerland and to serve the country selflessly by becoming officers, because "the army needs brains that think and issue orders."[38]

On December 9, 1938, when he was already being viewed by many as Switzerland's future commander-in-chief, Guisan spoke in French on the topic of "Our People and Its Armed Forces" at the Swiss Federal Technical Institute in Zürich as part of a lecture series entitled "Switzerland in Europe." Even though he mainly repeated what he had said in his lectures four years earlier, the speech received wide attention, probably due to the international political situation at the time and Guisan's high rank. Guisan summarized his speech with the motto, "In order to be able to look ahead you have to be able to look back." As he may have been aware that he was on 'socialist' territory in Zürich, the corps commander omitted some of the anti-socialist statements he had made in 1934, speaking only of "hidden attacks" against the army and "its infiltration with the Soviet spirit." Above all, though, he invoked the old fighting spirit of the Swiss Confederation and encouraged his audience to be morally strong, nurturing a spirit of resistance in order to forge a moral unity between the people and the armed forces. This, he stated, was because "the soul of the people is also the soul of the army."[39]

5

Politics in the 1930s

THE POLITICAL MOVEMENTS THAT EMERGED in the 1920s and 1930s created serious tensions in Switzerland lasting well into the time of the Second World War; and though avowedly unconcerned with politics, Henri Guisan's attitude and reactions toward these movements had a profound impact upon his career. In spite of his apparently elitist lifestyle as an estate owner, Guisan generally enjoyed the reputation of a man of the people, with many republican and a few authoritarian qualities. He was very outgoing and joined a number of patriotic and military clubs, whose meetings he frequently attended. He even donated prizes for sports events.[1]

Throughout Guisan's career, his beliefs were identified with those of the traditional western Swiss farming and bourgeois communities. He demonstrated both conservative and liberal traits while also showing considerable understanding for the worries of society's disadvantaged. His conservative side manifested itself in his attachment to traditions and his rejection of new political ideas, especially those that emanated from the left. However, he also proved himself to be open and tolerant toward people with different opinions and religious beliefs. Moreover, he considered himself "an outright federalist," who favored maximum autonomy for the cantons in order to "prevent centralist tendencies from taking the upper hand."[2]

Above all, Guisan insisted that he was "apolitical." He stayed away from party politics, as he did not want to appear to be an officer who owed his military career to partisanship. In fact, he considered party politics to be detrimental to true patriotism.[3] According to his son, Guisan was never a member of any political party.[4] Nevertheless, even if Guisan was nonpartisan, one must recognize the fact that he did not focus exclusively on military matters but had a tendency to become involved in public dialogue. As commander-in-chief of the armed forces, Guisan gained a powerful platform for his views on the Federal political level.

Guisan was a member of the "Association Patriotique Vaudoise" (APV), an umbrella organization for officers' societies, rifle clubs, and other military groups, as well as for patriotic organizations in Canton Vaud. For a few years, while still a divisional commander, Guisan was vice-president of the APV, which joined the Swiss National Patriotic Federation (Schweizerischer Vaterländischer Verband, or SVV) in 1932.[5] The SVV was founded in early 1919 as the national umbrella organization for cantonal vigilance groups in reaction to the social unrest of November 1918. Its first president was Eugen Bircher, a medical doctor from Aarau and a captain on the army's general staff,[6] who was later promoted to corps commander during Guisan's tenure as commander-in-chief.

Guisan's activity as a member of the APV brought him into close contact with a group of French-speaking officers who were very critical of the Federal Parliament. For instance, Colonel de Diesbach from Fribourg, a leading member of that group and a personal friend of Guisan, stated at an SVV committee meeting in 1926 that the National Council was "a continuous threat to the country with its current mentality." Undoubtedly, de Diesbach referred to the programs of the numerous Social Democrats and other center-left representatives in the lower house of Parliament.[7] De Diesbach's idea of national renaissance was based on the concept of a corporate-run state resembling the one that existed in Italy—that is, traditional democracy should be forsaken in favor of a new state order based on professional employers' and employees' associations.

During the 1920s and 30s, Guisan shared some of de Diesbach's views regarding the Parliament. It can hardly be denied that Guisan was sympathetic toward corporatist ideas. Katharina Bretscher has indicated in a *Neue Zürcher Zeitung* article that Guisan's convictions came close to those expressed by Gonzague de Reynold in a 1929 essay entitled "Democracy and Switzerland: Essay on a Philosophy of Our History." Bretscher wrote: "When they promoted corporatism, many conservatives did not have foreign ideologies in mind but were filled with nostalgia about the good old days of the Swiss Confederation. De Reynold, for example, came to the conclusion that the patrician state order of the ancien régime was more democratic than the current egalitarian democracy."[8]

In his native canton, many viewed Guisan as an officer "rattling the saber" because of his constant appeals to the Federal authorities to improve the quality of armaments and training in order to improve the nation's defensive strength. Like others who advocated a strong Swiss Army after World War I, Guisan's actions were meant to counter a widespread antiwar mood, articulated in the saying, "Never again war!" Along these lines, Guisan opined in a 1934 lecture: "All those who hate the army do so because it is the embodiment of resistance, the bulwark that broke the Bolshevist wave in 1918."[9]

In the spring of 1934, Corps Commander Guisan addressed a confidential letter to the Federal Military Department, in which he expressed his concern about the political situation in Geneva. He explained that the local "Patriotic Association," a vigilance group, had indicated that the Geneva police were unreliable and would not be able to maintain order if riots broke out because they were under the control of a leftist cantonal government. Guisan wrote: "The arsenal is vulnerable to raids. In the past, the vigilance group had assisted the police on several occasions to protect it. Under the current government this is no longer possible."[10] He explained that Geneva's constitution had outlawed interventions by vigilance groups and he advised the Federal authorities to take all necessary precautions to protect the arsenal and to be ready to intervene promptly in Geneva. Moreover, he recommended preventing potential infiltration by "suspicious elements" from neighboring France. The Patriotic Association said it was willing to cooperate with the Military Intelligence Service because the Geneva cantonal government could not be trusted. Guisan offered his services as an intermediary between the Patriotic Association and the Federal Military Department, saying that he had already instructed the vigilance group to provide his liaison officer with relevant information.[11]

After the National Socialist Party took power in Germany in 1933, fascist groups began to gain influence in Switzerland under the so-called "Front" movement.[12] These Front organizations strove for an authoritarian Swiss state at the expense of the country's liberal democracy, and it had many sympathizers among the armed forces and civilians alike. However, they constituted only a small minority throughout the country. Ernst Nobs, a future Federal Councilor, described the atmosphere as follows: "During the Front movement, tens of thousands of harmless citizens filled the meeting rooms of the Front organizations. They were deeply impressed by the new language and appearance; their own fanatic behavior, kicking their feet and going wild, carried them away. People from all classes of society got involved; capitalists, the middle class, intellectuals, workers, and farmers; they were all convinced that their own personal wishes would be realized once the movement took control of the country. However, the leaders of the movement were bragging, spoke with impertinence, and were extremely arrogant and conceited."[13]

Not only those blinded by group fervor, but also some intelligent, moderate individuals began questioning Switzerland's democracy. As stated by Alice Meyer in 1965, "The 'proponents of renewal,' through their nationalist and promilitary behavior, gained considerable support among people who had initially eyed them with skepticism." Many middle-class citizens who feared Bolshevism were attracted by the distinctly anti-Marxist propaganda of the Front movement, and some believed that a durable new political force was on the rise.

During the first few years of this "renewal movement" in the early 1930s, Guisan may not have been unimpressed by the Front organizations, which emphasized patriotism and willingness to defend the country. Along with others, Guisan tended to believe that the Front movement could promote reflection on the Confederation's values and contribute to strengthening the military. As late as February 1939, Guisan was one of the National Defense Committee members who supported the promotion of a National Front member, Major Egli, who had received unfavorable reviews from the Social Democratic Executive Council of Basel. Egli's promotion was granted.[14]

It appears that at the time Guisan did not see a high risk of the army being infiltrated by officers who were members of Front organizations. During a discussion of the Front movement in the NDC in 1938, he told the committee members that in his army corps the group had "no importance."[15] Guisan's statement indicates that he either had a *laissez-faire* attitude toward the Front movement or was in large part ignorant of their activities. Later on, a number of legal investigations concluded that the Front had made serious attempts to gain influence in the armed forces.[16] Neither Guisan nor any other member on the National Defense Committee was aware of the fact that in 1936–1937 the national leader of the Front movement, Rolf Henne, had met on several occasions with a political strategist, Hermann Stegemann, to discuss useful methods for increasing the movement's impact in Switzerland.[17]

After Germany's attack on Scandinavia during the first year of World War II, in a confidential letter to the Head of the Military Department, General Guisan pointed out some imminent risks for Switzerland on the domestic front, including German immigrants, Swiss left and right extremists, and Jews. Guisan mentioned several reports, according to which "Jewish immigrants who have been granted asylum have turned into a rather important source of danger. Based on the experiences of Scandinavia, England, and Holland, this category of foreigners should not be disregarded. In today's situation, Switzerland can no longer afford to be compassionate and lenient; instead, it has to take a tough stand."[18] In this one instance, Guisan seems to have succumbed to German propaganda.

It would be unfair, however, to conclude from such remarks that Guisan was in principle anti-Semitic. On a personal level at least, he was not prejudiced against Jews, for some of his key staff during his time as supreme commander of the army were said to be of Jewish origin. In addition, Captain Henry Vogel, who played a key role on Guisan's personal staff as aide-de-camp between 1942 and the end of the war, had a Jewish wife. Jules Sandoz, who was Guisan's first adjutant for many years, told the author that he was unaware of any indication that would justify calling General Guisan anti-Semitic.[19]

The opinion of large parts of the population was determined for a long time by the traumatic experience of the social unrest of 1918, and above all by the fear of the destabilizing effect of Communism. Without realizing where the real danger came from, many believed that socially motivated agitation by left-wing parties and movements was the root cause of a gradual loss of identification with the Swiss Federal state. Guisan expressed a similar idea when he remarked that the spirit of the past required the Swiss "to be Swiss, above all, wherever we are," adding, "We must counter revolutionary mysticism and those who strive to drown our country in an anonymous Communist world organization with the myth of everlasting Switzerland."[20] Guisan was mainly concerned about potential Communist infiltration in the army. In 1934, he worried about a political meeting in Geneva during which Communist and socialist workers received the recommendation not to boycott military service but to learn how to manipulate arms in order to use them "against Swiss fascism and to seize power, once and for all."[21]

In 1936, the French General Lannurien reported to Paris that Federal Councilor Minger had voiced his concern, during a visit to view military maneuvers, about Switzerland being infested with Bolshevism and right-wing extremism from France. Corps Commander Guisan was reported to share Minger's apprehension, saying that Switzerland was more concerned about danger coming from France than from Germany. "We are afraid of you because of a possible infestation with Communism,"[22] he was quoted as telling his French host.

There was also considerable uneasiness about the Social Democratic Party in Switzerland, which was subject to constant criticism from the conservative right wing and center because of its 1917 party program, in which it denied the need for a Swiss Army and advocated a dictatorship by the proletarian masses. Social Democrats continued to be viewed with suspicion even after 1931, when there were increasing signs that they might review their party program.[23] After 1933, when the threat of totalitarianism had reached Swiss borders both to the south and the north, the Social Democrats began to acknowledge publicly that Switzerland needed the armed forces. When Robert Grimm, the leader of the movement spearheading the social unrest of 1918, expressed his personal support for the army at a convention of the Bernese Social Democratic party in 1933,[24] it was considered sensational news; but four years later no one was surprised when the national Social Democratic Party declared that it officially backed the army.[25] Nevertheless, conservatives continued to have doubts about the real intentions of the Social Democrats. It was said, for instance, that the Social Democrats were opportunists and had simply "glued a big Swiss cross onto their red Marxist flag."[26] Pro-army politicians who had been denounced as enemies of the working class for two decades by leftist politicians had trouble accepting them in their midst. Many were confused about Social Democrats who turned into militant army advocates and who were suddenly more serious about national defense than members of the Front.

A look at the minutes of Social Democratic Party committee meetings indicates that the party leaders took their support for the army seriously. For example, National Councilor Robert Grimm explained in the spring of 1939 that there was no question of advocating pacifist ideas and "collective security," since that would provide Hitler and Mussolini with a pretext to seize power in Switzerland. In the current situation, Grimm added, "If the Federal Council intended to perform political maneuvers with one of the totalitarian states, the people would immediately get rid of it."[27]

Guisan was among those who were skeptical for quite some time about the Social Democrats' new commitment to the armed forces, even if he may not have openly displayed his doubts. His mistrust was expressed in a confidential letter to Federal Councilor Minger in May 1940, months after becoming commander-in-chief, in which he stated, "At the present time it remains to be seen whether those Socialists [sic] who behave as if they were the ones who invented Swiss democracy will turn, directly or indirectly, into enemies of the State."[28]

Guisan's reservations about the Social Democrats and unionists were well known, especially in western Switzerland. Hence, many Social Democrats were in turn reluctant to give Guisan their support. In fact, in the spring of 1939 the Vaud cantonal Social Democratic Party considered launching a campaign against the corps commander in order to prevent him from being elected general in the future. They viewed Guisan as an "extremely cunning reactionary" and a "proclaimed enemy." However, the secretary of the cantonal party, Pierre Graber, recommended to his colleagues not to take any action, as Guisan "had been very clever at creating a large following among the armed forces and the people."[29] Moreover, Graber and national party leaders who discussed the matter in May 1939 were aware that any action taken against Guisan could be interpreted by political opponents as an indication that the Social Democrats were still anti-army and anti-patriotic. In addition, they realized that the only other potential candidate for the post of general was Ulrich Wille Jr., the son of World War I General Wille, whose reputation was somewhat blemished because he had paid several visits to National Socialist leaders in the Third Reich. Hence, the Social Democrats' decision not to undertake any move against Guisan was not a vote of confidence, but a reflection of their national political interests and the lack of qualified alternative candidates.

Following an increase in tensions on the international level in 1938, despite the Munich Pact, and after Germany occupied Czechoslovakia in early 1939,

Switzerland called up all emergency units of the border troops for the first time. However, in April 1939 the National Defense Committee believed the situation had become more stable. At one of its meetings, Guisan stated that the international financial and business community did not appear "to believe in an imminent war." Moreover, he considered as reassuring the fact that Germany had "authorized the delivery of big guns and gas masks from former Czechoslovakia to France and declared that it was willing to continue supplying France with materiel." In addition, Guisan explained that the United States was in the process of selling "large quantities of raw materials to Germany."[30]

At the following NDC meeting, in May 1939, Guisan, along with Federal Councilor Minger and Chief of the General Staff Labhart, continued to be optimistic about developments on the international stage, saying, "For us, the situation is much less alarming than it was four weeks ago."[31] However, Guisan indicated that the French "might soon get tired of Italy agitating them and could be forced to take action." Surprise attacks "should be expected in the air rather than at bridges," Guisan speculated, and he favored increasing the number of Swiss border troops by five to eight companies.[32]

On August 22, 1939, the day when the Nazi-Soviet non-aggression pact was made public, the NDC held its last meeting before the outbreak of general war. Federal Councilor Minger considered the situation "critical" and said it was "almost certain" that a war would break out. Nevertheless, for the time being he saw no reason for Switzerland to take special precautions on the military level. However, in case of an open conflict between Germany and Poland, Switzerland would immediately mobilize its troops. Guisan, who spoke next, as the oldest serving corps commander on the committee, explained that his views were generally identical to Minger's. He speculated that Germany and Russia would "agree to split Poland." On the other hand, he informed the committee that "high-ranking French officers" did not believe "a war would break out in September" because France "would not be able to count on substantial assistance from English territorial troops."[33]

Corps Commander Wille, who was viewed as an expert on the situation in Germany, stated that he did not believe a war was imminent, arguing that "the German armed forces do not have officers available yet. Hitler is interested in boosting his prestige by proceeding in a diplomatic manner. For now there is no danger for us; it would be better to refrain from taking any military precautions." Chief of the General Staff Labhart also recommended waiting and watching further developments before mobilizing any troops. Minger summarized the meeting by saying that there was overall agreement that Switzerland should wait and see what happened, but if the need arose the only option would be to mobilize all troops.[34]

Two participants, Wille and Labhart, took their own notes at that NDC meeting, which are interesting to analyze, as they indicate the clashing views on the committee about Germany's intentions. Wille was critical of the NDC chairman's and the committee majority's viewpoint, writing, "Federal Councilor Minger expresses his personal opinion, claims that for Hitler it is a matter of prestige to land another success (???). Federal Councilor believes that Hitler has probably already made up his mind to attack Poland, and possibly also Romania. Currently the situation is in Hitler's favor, but in case of a long-lasting war he won't prevail more than one year. Hitler and Mussolini are facing financial disasters, a revolution, or a war because of their armament efforts. A war can only be prevented by another agreement like the one in Munich, but Minger does not think it will come about."[35]

Wille recorded Guisan's opinion as follows: "Colonel-Corps Commander Guisan says quite a few things about his French friends, who consider the current situation as very serious, hopeless." Corps Commander Prisi, on the other hand, was convinced that, as Wille wrote, "Germany's and Italy's decisions are no longer based on rational thinking. Their goal is to destroy the British empire (!); for that purpose they are entering into an alliance with Japan." Wille expressed his critical opinion about the NDC members' statements with question marks or exclamation marks after some clauses. He summarized Labhart's viewpoint as "less pessimistic" with regard to a possible war because Germany could not risk a war on two fronts. Nevertheless, "Poland may have to give in because France is unlikely to open war against Germany but could do so against Italy."

Wille summarized his own view as follows: "Germany will not risk a war against England-France. It is not ready for war, neither on a military nor on an economic level." He wrote that Hitler was only interested in Danzig and would be satisfied to build "a corridor inside the corridor." Moreover, he wrote, "England and France are facing a difficult decision because an attack on the German western front will cost them a lot of time and bloodshed. They will have to assist Poland, but maybe just with a cannonade like at Valmy." At any rate, Wille considered Switzerland to lie "outside the main areas of tension" and it therefore was "not at risk."

According to Wille's notes, Colonel Masson, head of the army's Intelligence Service, attended the NDC meeting to inform its members of the number of troops mobilized by neighboring states. Germany had 2.2 million troops available, 1.5 million of whom were stationed on the eastern front and the remaining 700,000 in the Siegfried position facing west; France had called up 1.1 million troops, 500,000 of whom were deployed to the Maginot Line; Italy had more than one million troops available.[36]

In his personal notes, Chief of the General Staff Labhart recounted the conflicting views: "The Federal Councilor and Colonel-Corps Commanders Guisan, Miescher, and Prisi consider the situation to be dangerous and think a war is very likely. Colonel-Corps Commander Wille and I, on the other hand, are more optimistic, thinking that Poland, in view of Germany's increasing military pressure, may be willing to make concessions to Germany regarding Danzig, a corridor and possibly some other territories as well."[37] Since the National Defense Committee unanimously agreed that the border troops or the entire armed forces should be called up in case the situation became critical, on August 23 Labhart, on his own initiative, ordered the army corps, the heads of service at the Federal Military Department, and the cantonal military authorities to prepare their staff and troops for a possible wartime mobilization.[38]

The contents of these statements make clear that the members of Switzerland's top military advisory group had totally diverging views on the international situation on the threshold of the Second World War. As it turned out, Minger, Guisan, and the majority of the National Defense Committee came closest to predicting the reality.

6

The General Is Elected

DURING THE LAST WEEK OF AUGUST 1939, when millions of mobilized troops faced each other in Europe ready to fight, top Swiss military and government officials continued to believe that war could be averted. Hans Frölicher, Switzerland's ambassador to Germany, and Colonel von Werdt, the Swiss military attaché in Berlin, went on vacation just as the German-Soviet non-aggression pact was made public on August 22, because they were convinced that "the political situation had stabilized."[1] The chargé d'affaires during Frölicher's absence in Berlin, Franz Kappeler, considered the non-aggression pact "a guarantee for peace." In part based on evaluations from the embassy in Berlin, Swiss Foreign Minister Motta, on August 27, predicted that there would be no war.[2]

On August 25, 1939, Chief of the General Staff Jakob Labhart continued to be optimistic about the political situation. He wrote in his diary: "I believe that a solution to the Polish issue may or most likely will be reached through negotiations. Germany is unlikely to risk a European war, which would be triggered by an attack on Poland. In such a conflict Germany's and Italy's prospects of a victory are slim. Our country faces no immediate danger."[3] The following day he told Rudolf Minger that the situation had "not changed."[4] Nevertheless, he ordered the entire general staff to be on standby on Saturday, August 26, at 12:00 hours, and requested that Colonel P. Wacker, one of his most important staff members, cut short his vacation to report to him. Even Colonel Gustav Däniker, a specialist on military affairs, told his comrade Oskar Germann that he did not think an armed conflict was about to break out, because in his view England would not go to war over Danzig.[5]

However, Switzerland's ambassador to France, Walter Stucki, had a different view of the military situation. On Saturday, August 26, he reported from Paris that the French army had called up an additional 700,000 men, and he recommended that Switzerland call up its border troops. This message alarmed Labhart, who requested a special Federal Council meeting to be held the next morning. He said that he did not believe French troops would attempt to march through Switzerland, but the situation required taking the necessary measures to call up the border troops.[6]

On that Sunday morning, Minger held a briefing with the most important members of the general staff prior to the cabinet meeting to analyze the situation, and concluded that the border troops should not be mobilized for the time being.[7] Hence, the Federal Council did not decide until Monday, August 28, to call up the border troops, after it had received a new situation report from Colonel von Erlach, the chief of the operational section of the general staff. Von Erlach had received military intelligence reports about massive troop concentrations along Switzerland's western border, leading him to the conclusion that France was preparing to intervene on behalf of Poland via northern Italy and Austria, and would have to penetrate Swiss territory to do so. "The fact that French Supreme Commander Gamelin reassured our Military Attaché in Paris that France had no intention of marching through Switzerland should not prevent us from doing what is necessary in view of the existing military situation," von Erlach wrote in his report.[8]

The Federal Council met again at 4 p.m. on Monday and decided that the border troops should report to their duty stations the following morning, August 29. No other troops were placed on call, however. On that Monday evening, Federal President Etter addressed the nation in a radio announcement to explain the cabinet's decision and to urge the population to remain calm.[9]

Interestingly, during their discussions of the situation on August 27 and 28, the top officers on the general staff did not take into account a possible military threat from Germany, but feared an infringement of Switzerland's neutrality only from the French side. Moreover, it was the speculation about a possible French move that caused the Swiss to mobilize all troops at the end of the month. Chief of the Operational Section von Erlach asked a member of his staff, Lieutenant-Colonel Gonard, to outline the consequences of a possible invasion by the French troops massed along the Swiss border. Gonard came to the conclusion that "the six or seven divisions stationed along the border would be able to rush through the Jura Mountains in no time and occupy the access roads to the Jura" to keep them open for following troops. "These troops have all the necessary arms as well as motorized and armored means for combat," he added. "They do not have to use roads to advance and, given their number and composition, can proceed on a large front. Hence, our roadblocks are not very useful; they can easily be bypassed or removed. . . . In areas without fortifications, our border troops are largely outnumbered and less well armed than the French; therefore they will be able to hold out only for a few hours."[10]

The chief of the general staff and his head of the operational section had not been informed of the top-secret private talks that Corps Commander Guisan had held with the French high command. Consequently, they interpreted the massing of French troops along the Swiss border as a deployment in preparation for an offensive rather than what it actually was—preparation for French assistance to Switzerland in case of a German attack on France via Swiss territory. Guisan may have kept silent about this misinterpretation by the general staff because it helped to maintain the appearance of Switzerland's neutrality. Even two months later, Chief of the General Staff Labhart insisted, "The border troops and, a few days later, the entire armed forces, were called up mainly due to the French threat along our western border."[11]

Switzerland's Constitution stipulates: "Only in a national emergency shall Parliament elect a commander-in-chief who will have the rank of general, but only for the duration of the emergency. He is the only general in the Swiss Army."[12] The emergency clause in the Constitution signifies that Switzerland does not need to wait until a war breaks out to elect a commander-in-chief but is required to do so as soon as a large contingent of the army is called up to maintain the country's neutrality and sovereignty.[13] That was the case on August 29, 1939, when the Federal Council called up all border troops, about 50,000 men, plus the staff of the army units, the mobilization teams, the air surveillance units, and the minelayers.

The election of the general was scheduled for the following day, Wednesday, August 30, at 5:00 p.m. The Federal Council unanimously proposed as candidate Henri Guisan, the oldest serving corps commander.[14] Guisan was 64, close to the regular retirement age, but looked younger, and he had been in command of several army units for thirteen and a half years, seven of them as corps commander.

On the election day, the political parties met prior to the Parliament's meeting to deliberate on the candidate they would officially support. All decided to back Guisan. At 5:00 p.m., the Chairman of the National Council, Henri Valloton, opened the joint session of both chambers of Parliament. The public and diplomats filled the spectators' seats. On the floor, 229 out of 231 members of both houses were present, some wearing their military uniforms. National Councilor Hans Müller wrote, "The atmosphere reflected determination and solemnity."[15]

There was no debate. Guisan was elected on the first ballot with 204 votes, representing an unusually large majority of 90 percent. Colonel Jules Borel, commander of the 2nd Division, received 21 votes. Two votes went to other individuals, and two ballot papers were handed in blank.[16] Most of the votes for Borel came from French-speaking Social Democrats who had not forgotten about the political views held by Guisan in the 1920s and 1930s. The two Communist members most likely cast the two blank ballot papers.

Immediately following the election, Guisan was sworn in as commander-in-chief. He stood in front of the assembly to take the oath: "I vow to remain loyal to the Confederation, to protect and defend with my own life, to the best of my ability, together with the troops entrusted to me, Switzerland's sovereignty and neutrality, and to follow precisely the instructions the Federal Council is to give to me regarding the final goal to be accomplished through the armed forces' service." Everyone who listened to the live broadcast on the national radio heard Guisan say, at the end, "*je le jure*" ("I swear").[17]

The chairman of the National Council Valloton then addressed the newly elected general:

> We know that your ability, your extensive military experience, your determination, and your resolution make you a military leader who will be met with obedience, respect, and love. And we know that your friendliness and moderation will guarantee a good relationship between political and military authorities. General, please tell the armed forces that the Parliament, the nation, and the cantons have full confidence in them. Everyone, from the General all the way down to the youngest soldier, is prepared to give his life to safeguard Switzerland's independence, neutrality, and freedom. And please also tell the armed forces that they are not alone; all Swiss, men and women, old and young, alive and dead, will be standing guard with them at the border. General, we entrust to your care our country, which we love with all our hearts and which we shall under no circumstances surrender to any aggressor, wherever he may come from. God bless your mission, General! God bless our country and our army![18]

After the swearing-in ceremony, all seven Federal Councilors and the chairmen of the two chambers of Parliament congratulated Guisan. When Guisan and the political authorities appeared on the steps in front of the Parliament building, the crowd in the square welcomed him with enthusiasm and spontaneously began singing the National Anthem. Guisan later recalled these moments as "unforgettable" and said he was "deeply impressed" by the ceremony and the crowd outside that received him.[19]

Guisan was not surprised at his election. In fact, he had been anticipating it for several months. In a letter to Chief of the General Staff Labhart, for instance, Guisan wrote, "I had prepared myself, both mentally and morally, to take on this responsibility so I would be ready to exercise the Supreme

Command without having to deliberate what would be the most efficient way of doing the job. Hence, I was neither surprised nor caught off my guard."[20]

Following a ceremony in front of the Parliament building, the government invited the newly elected general to a dinner at its reception house in Kehrsatz outside Bern, from which Guisan returned to Lausanne to spend the night at his home.[21] The next morning, on August 31, he returned to Bern to issue his first orders and organize his office. In the afternoon Guisan drove to Fribourg to hand over to Colonel Petitpierre, his former chief of staff, the files of the 1st Army Corps.[22] The same day, at Guisan's recommendation, the Federal Council named Jakob Labhart, who had been Chief of the General Staff at the Federal Military Department, "Chief of the General Staff of the Armed Forces." Labhart explains in his diary that the General came to see him in his office at 10 a.m. to discuss "personnel matters, particularly the choice of the General's adjutant. Then we talked about the general situation and came to the conclusion that for the time being no further troops needed to be called up."[23]

In his first order to the armed forces issued on that same day, Guisan informed the troops of his assuming the supreme command, writing, "Officers, non-commissioned officers, and soldiers: The Federal Parliament has entrusted me with the Supreme Command of the Armed Forces. I am aware of this great responsibility, but I take it on with confidence and pride because I know the spirit with which the army is imbued. I know that during this critical period of time each one of you is ready and willing to fulfill your duty at the post assigned to you."[24] This was probably the shortest of the numerous orders that Guisan communicated to his troops during nearly six years of service.

On the same day, August 31, the government officially declared, through its embassies in 40 nations, that the Swiss Confederation was "determined to maintain its neutrality under all circumstances, toward all powers."[25]

The people's reaction to Guisan's election was very positive. In all four linguistic areas of the country a large majority were convinced that the right man had been chosen to lead the armed forces. When German-speaking border troops in eastern Switzerland heard the news on the radio, they applauded the election result, saying that they welcomed being commanded by that "officer from western Switzerland," even though they were "soldiers from the opposite side of the country."[26]

The press also generally expressed its satisfaction about the outcome of the election; moreover, they were impressed by the near-unanimous approval that Guisan had received, interpreting it as a sign of harmony and moral unity among the people at a time of uncertainty.[27] However, a few left-wing papers had reservations about Guisan because of his former ties with right-wing conservatives. In a commentary that was most likely written by National Councilor

Meierhans, the Zürich newspaper *Volksrecht* explained, "We had reasons to be suspicious [about the General's election] because of the candidate's past political activities. However, we put our doubts aside because we expect *General* Guisan to act differently than *Colonel* Guisan. When he was elected Supreme Commander, he must have realized that it is now his duty to be moderate in matters of party politics and absolutely impartial in order to earn the trust that will allow him to fulfill his difficult task. In addition, in western Switzerland lingering feelings of being left aside should subside now that one of them has been called to take on responsibility."[28]

A number of officers, especially in and around Zürich, were not as pleased as the general population with the prospect of being commanded by a man whose qualities as a military leader they questioned. Trained in a Prussian style reminiscent of the Swiss commander during World War I, General Wille, these officers were wondering whether Guisan had the analytical and quick mind, the strategic talent, and the energy needed to assert himself and to accomplish the complex tasks awaiting the commander-in-chief. Colonel-Corps Commander Ulrich Wille Jr., who had hoped to become general himself, wrote to his wife, "I have kept my calm about the outcome of the election by thinking that, seen objectively, the main powers will not go to war, and General Guisan will not have to deal with any situation that is critical for the Swiss Confederation. On a personal level I am pleased to note that Guisan's having been preferred over me has nothing to do with my own qualifications."[29] Wille tended to believe that Guisan's "lack of personality" as well as his "being nice and obedient" were the main reasons for his successful election, as the cabinet and the Parliament wanted to deal with an accommodating commander-in-chief.[30]

Colonel Gustav Däniker called Guisan's election "a typical example of bad defense policy," arguing that "the Federal Council that proposed the candidate had received a clear picture of the actual situation in the last few years, and many members of Parliament who elected the General had detailed information about personnel matters in the army, and yet they simply 'went along' with the rest, taking the line of least resistance. I believe," Däniker went on, "that the electorate's first concern should have been to put the most capable commander in charge of the armed forces; instead, they made many compromises."[31] Däniker did not say in his letter who he thought was "the most capable commander," but it was quite obvious that he could only have had in mind his direct superior, Colonel-Corps Commander Wille, the Chief Instructor of the Infantry.

The public in neighboring countries had to deal with their own pressing matters during that critical time and hardly took note of the election of Switzerland's commander-in-chief. Foreign diplomats, however, reported on the event to their governments. France's ambassador to Switzerland, Charles Alphand, was particularly pleased with Guisan's election. He told Paris that a general from western Switzerland would be better suited to resist possible German claims, stating, "In case they [the Swiss] had to appeal to the western powers for assistance, a general who is French-speaking and has a French cultural background would be more willing to cooperate with our army."[32] In a later report, France's military attaché, Colonel Chauvin, presented a surprising picture of General Guisan, remarking, "He is very easy to influence, which makes him susceptible to the various successive actions of his entourage and of the officials he encounters. He is aware of this, and that is undoubtedly the reason why he reacts, frequently and readily, by verbally demonstrating his authority. Intellectually he is not very profound, and he is not particularly cultivated. He makes no secret of his sympathies, which are largely in France's favor. . . . However, he has more serious concerns about Germany. In the beginning, he thought that he had nothing to fear from Italy." Chauvin further reported that Guisan's fellow citizens viewed the general as someone who was "rather ostentatious" and superficial, which was "probably due to his temper," and fond of living in solemn splendor, which he "most likely [did] in order to keep up his spirit."[33]

A report by a French military attaché in 1936 had been more flattering about Guisan, qualifying him with the words, "soul of a leader, trainer of men, perhaps a little too impulsive, needs someone with a clear mind who is level-headed and objective, always self-possessed to get his strategic concepts on target."[34] The German opinion of Guisan was concise, saying he was "clever, very prudent, displaying a correct attitude, even though his sympathies appear to be on the side of the Western powers."[35]

The Federal Council decided on September 1, only two days after Guisan's election, to call up the entire armed forces. For two days, Chief of the General Staff Labhart and his operational section had deliberated whether the mobilization of all troops was necessary. When the news of Germany's invasion of Poland was confirmed during the morning of September 1, the answer to their question became clear. General Guisan, who had been flown in from Lausanne earlier that morning, went to see Labhart in his office. Labhart wrote in his diary, which constitutes an excellent contemporary source document with its sober and matter-of-fact style, "10:00 until 10:15 a.m., the General comes to see me before the Federal Council meeting. I brief him on the situation and request to have general mobilization ordered and to put the public transport companies under wartime operation. . . . The General accept[s] my proposal and [takes] the maps to go to the Federal Council meeting."[36]

At 10:15 a.m., the Federal Council called the commander-in-chief into its meeting to be briefed on the international political situation and to explain the army's request for mobilization. At 10:55 a.m., the Cabinet unanimously decided to call up all troops. A public announcement was made at 11 a.m. saying that the troops had to present themselves at their respective assembly points on Saturday, September 2.[37]

The order for general mobilization triggered a number of pre-planned activities. On September 1, the arsenals were manned with army personnel who were to issue all pertinent material to the army corps the next day. The Federal railways were ordered to make transportation available for the troops and materiel. The general mobilization was announced on the radio, by telephone and telegraph, as well as in the printed press.[38]

Following the cabinet meeting, the General received the official terms of reference from the Federal Council for his task as commander-in-chief. Based on a draft by the army staff, the terms of reference included the following six points:

1. It is your responsibility to safeguard the country's independence and integrity with all suitable military means. In particular, it is up to you to propose to the Federal Council if and when additional army units or the entire armed forces are to be called up.

2. The neighboring and other interested powers have received a declaration stating that Switzerland will remain strictly neutral in case of a war. Therefore, as long as our borders and our independence are not threatened by a foreign power, you shall take all measures in view of preserving Switzerland's neutrality.

3. Only the Federal authorities have the right to declare war, conclude peace agreements, and enter alliances.

4. If hostilities erupt between a neighboring state and us that are not simply local incidents, all instructions regarding the preservation of neutrality become null and void. Instead, Switzerland assumes the position of a power at war with all rights attached to it. You shall then be given a free hand for carrying out military operations within and beyond the borders of our country. If small enemy troop formations intrude on our territory by mistake or for a limited time in isolated areas, you shall report without delay on the incident and on measures you have taken to immediately restore the state of law.

5. When Switzerland enters into a state of war, you are authorized to conclude conventions with the neighboring commands of a foreign army, as long as they involve a temporary and strictly military solution of incidents of local importance. However, only the Federal

Council is authorized to conclude military conventions, which involve the entire troops of both armed forces.

6. If necessary, the army shall be available at the domestic front to protect the political authorities in the execution of their rights and duties and to keep the legal system functioning without disruption.[39]

These terms of reference, to which the Federal Council made a few editorial changes without altering the content, had been drafted on August 30 by Colonel von Erlach at the request of Chief of the General Staff Labhart and were based on the instructions issued to General Wille in 1914.[40]

The first article, which defined the general's authority in matters of mobilizing troops, gave rise to a controversy between the army command and the political authorities. On September 2, General Guisan met with Labhart to discuss the official duties. They decided to have the terms of reference analyzed from a legal viewpoint by Colonel Logoz, Professor of Law at the University of Geneva and legal advisor to the army staff.[41] Logoz came to the conclusion that the German version diverged from the French version, as it contained some small linguistic variations that could lead to different interpretations.[42] In a letter dated September 4, Guisan informed the Federal Council of Logoz' findings and asked to have the matter clarified.[43] Since the cabinet did not answer, Guisan wrote another letter to the Federal Council on October 11, suggesting that the General be authorized to call up troops to the size of a regiment, while mobilizing the entire armed forces would remain the cabinet's responsibility.[44] The Federal Council replied to Guisan's proposal during its meeting of November 3, insisting that according to the law only the cabinet was authorized to call up troops. However, it was willing to grant Guisan the right to summon troops up to the size of companies, while he would have to "make a formal request to the Federal Council" for mobilizing larger army units.[45]

In a letter dated November 7, Guisan countered that the expression "formal request" could be interpreted in such a way that the Federal Council might be under no obligation to grant the general's request for calling up troops. The Head of the Military Department replied that the Federal Council had no intention of changing the existing law, which was not up to the executive branch of the government in any event.[46]

The wording of the terms of reference may have appeared as a small problem. However, during World War II, the question of who had the right to mobilize troops caused friction on several occasions between the Federal Council and General Guisan.

II

COMMANDER-IN-CHIEF OF THE ARMED FORCES DURING WORLD WAR II (1939–1945)

The First Army Positions, 1939–1940

WITH THE WARTIME MOBILIZATION of the entire Swiss armed forces on September 2, 1939, General Guisan now had about 430,000 combat troops and 200,000 auxiliary forces available to accomplish his task.[1] Most troops arrived at their assembly points on schedule, though a few incidents and misunderstandings occurred. In the 1st Army Corps, Guisan's own, 50 horses were missing from the 1st Division's Battalion 14, and 20 horses from Section 2 of the field artillery. There were a few complaints about a lack of officers. Also, a report stated, "200 horses that were supposed to be available in Moudon were sent to Interlaken, so the units are short of horses for the officers."[2]

In his postwar report, the chief of the general staff remarked that "many troops did not have sufficient arms" and those that were available were often "outdated," as "the relatively large armament credits approved before the war had not been turned into weapons yet. Above all, there was a lack of anti-tank and anti-aircraft weapons; some of the artillery weapons were made in the last century."[3]

When Divisional Commander Bandi, head of the Air Force and Anti-Aircraft Defense, informed General Guisan on August 31 that the Federal Council had just authorized selling 30 three-inch Oerlikon antiaircraft weapons to France, the commander-in-chief, through his chief of staff, intervened to request that these arms be made available to the Swiss Army instead. Federal Councilor Minger replied on the evening of September 1, the day before the weapons were to be shipped to France, that he had "presented the matter to the Federal President and to Federal Councilor Motta, but both gentlemen refused to review the earlier cabinet decision."[4] However, the following morning the Federal Council discussed the matter again, and on September 3 it decided unanimously not to export the Oerlikon weapons to France so Switzerland's own antiaircraft defense could use them.[5]

This example demonstrates how difficult it was for the army to get its armament program into place. It must be said that the inadequate arms supply at the outbreak of the war was the result of hesitation by those military and political circles, especially the Social Democrats, who had resisted allocating the necessary funds to the national defense budget. It was not until 1937 that they stepped up their efforts in favor of armament. Guisan commented on this fact in a diplomatic manner by stating, "Even if everything was not the way it had been requested by those who were responsible for the security of the country, the efforts in favor of our defense were met with remarkable respect abroad."[6]

The first operational directives issued by the commander-in-chief to his immediate subordinates at the time of mobilization were terse, stating, "Upon completing mobilization, the troops shall take in the previously prepared mobilization positions."[7] The general staff before the war had determined these positions, which were nothing but temporary quarters in strategic places.

On the morning of September 2, the first day of mobilization, Chief of the General Staff Labhart and Colonel Frick, Assistant Chief of Staff for the Front, went to see the General to submit for approval the draft of Operations Order No. 1, which had also been prepared before the outbreak of the war.[8] In this order, the General instructed the troops to advance from the mobilization positions into suitable standby positions, or so-called "neutrality" positions. It read: "The armed forces shall prepare themselves to protect the country from any infringement of its neutrality by land or by air and to defend it against any aggressor."[9] The three army corps were to be stationed in the western, northern, and northeastern parts of Switzerland, respectively, behind the border areas. The 3rd and 8th Divisions were to remain on standby in the Bernese Seeland and the Upper Aargau to be able to assist any corps that might need reinforcements. "The southern front was covered by the troops that had mobilized in Graubünden, the Gotthard area, Ticino, and Valais and that were partly under the direct supervision of the Army Command [i.e., the mountain and border brigades in those areas]."[10] Operations Order No. 1, a copy of which was submitted to Federal Councilor Minger at the General's request, went into effect on September 2.[11]

The armed forces, as stipulated under this first operational order, were to be positioned along a major part of the Swiss plateau. These positions were "in line with the idea of neutrality," according to which troops could not be deployed in an individual area "until hostilities broke out, or until an attack became a possibility because [an opponent] was making preparations that could lead to a military action against Switzerland."[12]

It is striking that the General, in his reports, did not make a clear distinction between the terms "mobilization positions" and "neutrality positions."[13] Even after the war, he used the two expressions interchangeably when he told Gafner, "The first positions taken in by the army were called mobilization positions, or rather, post-mobilization positions. That means we went into neutrality positions or stand-by positions."[14] Hans Frick, a future corps commander, later objected to this lack of distinction in a letter to the Head of the Military Department, writing, "We can only prepare a deployment of troops that is a 'coverage deployment' in all directions, the way it was presented to the General by his staff when he assumed the supreme command and which he approved without modifications. Contrary to the General's opinion, this positioning of the armed forces, which the General erroneously called 'mobilization positions'—which were something completely different, namely the positions where the troops were quartered once mobilization was completed until they received new orders—was a deployment, even if it was not directed against one single enemy."[15]

At first glance, Switzerland's basic strategic position in September 1939 appeared to be the same as during earlier European conflicts.[16] As during the Franco-Prussian War of 1870–1871 and at the beginning of World War I, Switzerland was once again facing the risk of an invasion by either or both of two neighboring powers which might attempt to outflank their opponent across neutral Swiss territory. However, the situation this time was somewhat different, insofar as Germany had attacked France in 1914, whereas in 1939 France declared war on Germany because it was allied with Poland to protect Danzig (in Polish, Gdansk), a city with which many French were unfamiliar. Therefore, the idea of "dying for Danzig" was unpopular with many French, who viewed the outbreak of war as unnecessary. These circumstances, as well as Germany's push toward the east, established a constellation of pressures quite different from those of 1914.

When the news broke on September 3 that France and Great Britain had decided to honor their alliance with Poland by declaring war on Germany, all Swiss Army staff and troops were put on maximum alert, as the consequences of the declaration of war were uncertain. During the five weeks of Germany's Polish campaign, the Swiss armed forces remained in their "neutrality" positions, while the state of alert was partly lifted. At the same time, General Guisan requested that the army's general staff draft plans to prepare positions that could be held in the case of a German attack. The commander-in-chief and some of his advisors had concluded, upon analyzing the overall situation, that the most likely threat came from Germany. As Guisan later explained, "The reasons for this [supposition] were obvious. It had become clear already at that point that Germany's goal was to conquer new territory, as it failed to explore all options for a peaceful resolution of the conflict with Poland but instead initiated its offensive during the final days of August. And once the German Wehrmacht had completed its first campaign with a victory within an unexpectedly short period of time, it was able to withdraw all available troops from the east to deploy them on the western front."[17]

Further, the general political situation in Europe was such that, "[Unlike] during the First World War, the only potential [opponent] was Germany, and perhaps Italy. The Western Allies could not afford to launch an offensive against Switzerland for political reasons, as that would have contradicted their war objectives."[18] Also, from a military point of view, it did not make much sense for the Allies to march through Switzerland while the majority of Germany's armies were engaged in combat in Poland and only a few units were stationed on the western front. A frontal attack into Germany was more promising than making a detour through Switzerland and having to fight the Swiss Army before reaching German territory. Guisan and his staff also discarded the possibility of a French offensive because "they did not think France was capable of taking such action."[19]

The planning of defensive positions against a possible German attack took quite some time. Hence, in his postwar report Guisan criticized the fact that he had no plans of operation available when he took over the command of the armed forces, which, he said, put Switzerland in a critical situation as it was not ready to defend itself.[20] However, the details given above put Guisan's criticism in perspective, because plans for the neutrality positions did exist and were perfectly adequate for the first phase of the war.[21]

When the army staff studied the question of where to station Swiss troops in order to counter a possible German offensive, they faced "a dilemma: should they opt for positions that were suitable for defending [the country] but that were located far within its borders, leaving vast areas open to the enemy (except for the border troops); or should the troops, for political and psychological reasons, be deployed close to the border, even if that meant that the prospects of successfully defending [Switzerland] were much slimmer?"[22] If popular sentiment were to be taken into account, the army had to be ready to defend the entire Swiss territory, as it had during earlier conflicts. However, the General decided, after consulting with his strategic advisor, Samuel Gonard, to give preference to a major troop deployment along the line "Lake Zürich–Limmat River–Bözberg Mountain–Hauenstein Mountain," well inside the Swiss border. Colonel Oskar Germann had suggested this defensive line to him in a draft plan of operations, the so-called 'Case North'.[23] Germann came to the conclusion that this line was most suitable from a strategic point of view, "particularly with regard to anti-tank defense and aircraft visibility."[24]

Germann's draft plan was submitted to Guisan on September 20, after being reviewed by von Erlach, Frick, and Labhart, who added some minor remarks to it. The commander-in-chief had Gonard look over the draft, and wrote as a comment, "yes." The General then noted on the draft, "completely correct."[25] Hence, it appears that Colonel Germann drafted not only the plan for the later 'Réduit' positions, but also the first defensive positions of September 1939.

In order to discuss the exact deployment areas for the troops under Case North, the General, without informing his chief of staff, sent Gonard on September 22 to meet individually with the commanders of the 3rd and 2nd Army Corps, Miescher and Prisi. Gonard briefed the General on these meetings the same day.[26]

The General's decision to prepare for Case North, which he seems to have made as early as September 21, caused the first frictions with Labhart. The chief of the general staff, who felt that he had been ignored, later reported to Rudolf Minger, "As early as during the night of September 21, the first orders were issued in preparation for Case North without involving the chief of the general staff's office. Consequently, I intervened with the General the next morning, explaining that I considered the time to be too early to start deploying troops for Case North, as the troop movements would not go unnoticed, thus jeopardizing our neutrality. Indeed, the General had all the necessary information at hand for deploying the troops; he and his [personal] staff used it behind my back to initiate the first troop deployments at that early stage."[27] Labhart had submitted Germann's draft plan of operations to the commander-in-chief "under the assumption that the proposal would be analyzed" with his involvement prior to taking any action on it. "However, that was not the case. This was a first indication of how much influence the General's personal staff actually had."[28] In his activity report, Gonard remarked regarding this matter that "it should be pointed out that especially during the preparations for Case North, the General's personal staff was instrumental in allowing the commander-in-chief of the armed forces to express his intentions directly to the subordinate commanders in the form of letters and instructions that were qualified as absolutely personal."[29]

The concept of establishing defensive positions along the Limmat River did not meet with unanimous approval. Its opponents would have liked to see the front line follow the Thur and Töss Rivers so as to include a considerably larger part of eastern Switzerland and the city of Zürich in the defensive strategy and to allow for deeper positions in the east. Yet the decision to forsake the Töss River in favor of the Limmat was taken because "if the enemy had been able to break through the lines at the lower Aare River, they could have turned, under favorable circumstances, the entire northern flank by attacking from behind."[30]

Guisan justified selecting the defensive front line by noting that "these army positions took into account the number of troops I had available and the terms of reference which the Federal Council had given to me, according to which I was to safeguard Switzerland's independence with all personnel and material means. . . . Based on observations I had made during operational courses and training maneuvers of the armed forces before the war, I decided to set the [northern] front along the line Sargans–Walenstadt–Linth Channel–Lake Zürich–Limmat River up to where it runs into the Aare River–Jura Mountain range from Aargau to Lake Neuchâtel–Mentue Creek–Lake Geneva. The southern front was determined by the line along the Alps which reinforced the border troops. Another defensive line on the southern front, covered by mobile troops, ran along the Rhone and Rhine rivers, including the fortresses of St-Maurice, St. Gotthard, and Sargans."[31]

By deciding to position the main armed forces in staggered formations far away from the Swiss border rather than at the border itself, Guisan discarded the doctrine on mobile warfare that had been officially adopted in 1927. He explained, "I was aware that abandoning eastern Switzerland and part of western Switzerland was a painful decision, but this solution imposed itself because we had to be strong in the rear positions. However, I had to ignore those who advocated further shortening the front to [a line] between Basel–Hauenstein–Napf–Gotthard, because giving up half of the country would have been irresponsible."[32] Hans Senn commented that the army command tried "to gain depth on the operational level mostly by positioning troops forward" because it realized that the Swiss infantry divisions would be unable to launch counterattacks against a mechanized enemy.[33]

Operations Order No. 2, dated October 4, explained to the troops the defense line under Case North. The line's "main focus [was] the area between Lake Zürich and the Hauenstein Mountain."[34] About the execution of the order, Gonard remarked, "From the autumn, the strongholds were ready and prepared to receive the troops. However, because of [Switzerland's] neutrality, not all troops were deployed there as originally planned but remained on standby."[35] Reserve troops, consisting of the reinforced 2nd Division, were originally positioned in the area between Lenzburg, Schöftland, and Gösgen. Order No. 2 defined the army units' combat areas as well as the boundaries between them. It also instructed the troops to build all kinds of obstacles between the line held by the border troops and the main defensive line and to prepare for destruction in certain areas to slow down the progress of an aggressor.

In addition, "The garrisons at the forts and pillboxes at the border and between the border and the defense line shall resist to the last shell, even if they have been bypassed and are totally isolated"[36]—a concept that would reappear frequently throughout the war. The border troops were told that they had to be ready to sacrifice their lives for their country. Corps Commander Lardelli had suggested bringing the southern border troops back into positions where the terrain was more suitable for defense, but Guisan wrote: "It is to be understood that the border troops shall maintain their positions without thinking about retreating and without hoping to be saved. They know their mission and are aware of the sacrifice that it entails."[37]

In line with the order to prepare the northern defensive front line, the troops began building fortifications, pillboxes for the infantry, and antitank barriers, an effort which took the entire winter of 1939–40. Guisan requested that this work be done "at a rapid pace" under the supervision of the chief engineer of the armed forces and the heads of the engineering troops in the different army units, adding, "Special attention shall be paid to the depth of the defensive installations and to the possibility of mutual fire coverage between its components." The barbed wire obstacles to be built in front of the field fortifications "shall be placed in a way that they can be taken under fire."[38] To prepare traps and demolition charges along the Limmat positions, half of the 32 reserve mine chambers inside the Simplon Tunnel were emptied because of the lack of other available explosives.[39] As Alfred Ernst wrote, "The heavy volume of construction work created considerable difficulties in the beginning, as we were not prepared for this important task. There were no drawings for the different types of structures; we did not use any carefully thought-out working methods, nor did we have prefabricated elements available. In addition, using troops to dig and do masonry work was not very efficient. It would have been better to use construction companies that would have done the job much faster."[40] W. Roesch discovered that it was not until May 1940 that uniform construction methods were applied in all areas.[41]

Prominent military historians such as A. Ernst and H. R. Kurz agree that the defensive front set up under Case North had a certain depth on the operational level thanks to the staggered defense zones, but lacked depth on the strategic level because of the linear positioning of the troops.[42] It is interesting to note that the Germans used the term "Guisan Line" for this initial defensive front stretching from the Limmat River along the Jura Mountains to Lake Geneva at least up to 1942, long after Switzerland's armed forces had retreated into the Réduit positions in the Alps.[43]

Some unit commanders complained that because two-thirds of the time was spent on construction work, they did not have enough time to engage the troops in training. The General responded by writing to the corps commanders in the early winter, "The first requirement was to fortify the ordered positions as fast as possible and without interruption. That is why combat exercises and other training activities had to be neglected. It was originally planned to make preparations for the previously scheduled maneuvers on the corps and divisional levels, but then I decided to cancel them in favor of training on the regiment level to give the middle and lower-ranking officers a chance to practice their skills." The General also urged the officers to "maintain and improve the troops' readiness and discipline by keeping a tight schedule and by being strict."[44]

Under Case North, the 3rd Army Corps commanded by Miescher was in charge of fortifying the Limmat position. Its left wing joined Prisi's 2nd Corps at the Aare River near Windisch. In case of an attack against one of these two corps, the 1st Corps, which was stationed in western Switzerland under Lardelli's command, was to send reinforcements.[45]

For quite some time, there was uncertainty about which fortification work had priority, about the combat strategy, and about the exact positioning of the front lines. At a meeting of the command of the 3rd Corps with the army's supreme command, Miescher explained, "On October 13, 1939, the General informed me that he disagreed with the 3rd Corps' interpretation of the positions. More specifically, he wanted us to move the front forward, all the way to the Limmat. Moreover, he did not fully agree with the order to position some troops ahead of the front line. There is consensus about their responsibilities, but there are difficulties when it comes to carrying out their missions because there are not enough material and explosives available to create the requested 'military desert' [sic!]." As the chief of staff of the 3rd Corps, Colonel Iselin, openly admitted, "It is not easy to comply with the General's order."[46]

A few days later, another meeting was held under the chairmanship of the commander-in-chief, in the presence of his Chief of Staff Labhart, to smooth out the differences. It was decided that the 3rd Corps should "present [new] studies and proposals for fortifying the defensive front at the Limmat," which was done on December 6. On December 15, the General replied that "for budgetary reasons he did not approve the fortification of the artillery positions. The General believes that the forts and pillboxes at the Limmat should be built first."[47] A major on the general staff remarked, "As late as in the winter of 1939–40 the General and the 6th Division disagreed on where to fight, at the river or further back."[48]

During the time of these discussions about warfare doctrine, combat strategies, and modifications to positions, discomforting news reached Switzerland that led to the "November Alert." As early as the end of September, after the conclusion of the Polish campaign, the first hints of an imminent German attack on the western front had caused some concern in the Swiss camp. General Guisan did not order but rather suggested that "Colonel Frick should organize a meeting with the German military attaché," apparently to investigate the Wehrmacht's intentions. However, when the news was verified, "no suspicious troop movements [had been] registered in the area between the Bodensee and Ulm that could lead to the conclusion that an attack on Switzerland was in the making." As it turned out, Chief of the General Staff Labhart wrote in his diary, "The news was once again exaggerated and had been disseminated by Capt. Hausamann."[49]

At the end of October, the signs of a looming crisis appeared to be more serious. Minister Stucki, the Swiss Ambassador to France, made a special trip to Bern to inform the Federal Council and the army command that the French were expecting an imminent German offensive. He recommended that Switzerland make the necessary arrangements to be able to enter "in contact with the French government in case of an attack." Labhart added in his diary, "[At] 18:00 hours we arrive at the General's; he informs us about his meeting with Minister Stucki, who said France was convinced that the Germans would attack, probably from two sides, which meant Switzerland would also be affected."[50] Even if Labhart and especially Assistant Chief of Staff Frick believed that the chances of such an offensive were slim at that moment, as a precaution the border troops were put on alert, and the troops on leave were called back. However, Guisan wrote that as "worrisome" as the November Alert was, "It did not incite us to deploy the troops according to Case North."[51]

In connection with calling the troops back from their leave during the November Alert, the General and his chief of staff had an interesting conversation, which Labhart recorded in his diary. "[On] October 26, at 8:30 hours, [the General] informed me over the telephone he had been told that the grape harvest in Vaud had not yet ended. Therefore he would personally tell Colonel-Corps Commander Lardelli [of the 1st Corps] to make some exceptions when calling back his troops. I pointed out that the harvest season was not finished in the Rhine valley, the Thurgau, and in Zürich's vineyards either, so the 3rd Army Corps should be granted the same exceptions. The General said he would personally take care of that."[52] May the commander-in-chief be excused for being most concerned about his friends, the winemakers of Vaud.

The state of alert transformed into a heightened phase of emergency after the failed assassination attempt on Hitler at the "Bürgerbräukeller" in Munich on November 8. German newspapers claimed that the traces of the would-be assassin led to Switzerland, and the Swiss feared that Germany would take reprisals against them. The Federal Council received alarming information and considered mobilizing the entire armed forces once again.[53] In this situation,

Colonel Hans Frick, Chief of the Operational Section, with the support of Labhart, suggested sending Professor Carl J. Burckhardt, who was on good terms with Hermann Göring, on a mission to Germany, under the pretext of a Red Cross assignment, in order to discover Germany's intentions toward Switzerland.[54] However, Professor Burckhardt was not available for a mission at the time, and the plan was dropped.[55]

The fears about a German move were not based on mere speculation: German sources indicate that the offensive against France was indeed originally scheduled to begin November 9 but was postponed a total of 14 times by Hitler, first until November 19, then until November 22, and finally until the spring of 1940.[56]

Swiss authorities made preparations to evacuate the civilian population in the event of hostilities on Swiss territory. One of the reception areas was located along Lake Geneva. The General's hometown, Pully, was expected to receive 1,200 evacuees, two or three of whom were to stay at the Guisan residence. Mrs. Guisan protested, saying that she would already receive her daughter with her two children from Bern in case of an evacuation. However, the mayor of Pully was not allowed to make any exceptions and replied in a polite letter, "We believe that you will be able to host two or three persons in addition to your daughter because everyone else will have to make room for others as well. However, I have taken note of your special situation; hence, our request will only become effective if a pressing need arises."[57]

The question of how to include the city of Zürich in the defense strategy received special attention during the early stages of the war. In a 46-page analysis, the command of the 3rd Army Corps made an "urgent request" to "defend the city. During the first construction phase, in the interest of the designated front line, the crossing points at the Limmat should be occupied and closed."[58] Upon Senator Klöti's and Zürich Executive Council Member Streuli's intervention, the General discussed with Corps Commander Miescher the usefulness of defending Zürich. They came to the conclusion that Zürich would not be declared an "open city"; instead, the current strategy would remain in effect, according to which tank traps and several bunkers were to be built.[59]

Four months later, during the height of Germany's Western campaign, Zürich's Executive Council and the two senators from Zürich wrote to the Federal Council to obtain additional information on the role that Switzerland's largest city would play in the event of an invasion. They pointed out that there was a contradiction between the determination to defend Zürich and the fact that "only very few measures [were] planned to protect the civilians," as current provisions would allow only 15,000 to 20,000 people to be evacuated, leaving more than 300,000 people behind in the city. By blowing up the bridges, all city installations would become useless, and "even the water supply for the neighborhoods on the right side of the river would be cut off." In view of these difficulties, the petitioners strongly urged the Federal government, in its "capacity as authority over the army command, to realize what it means, under modern combat methods, to commit a city with a population of 350,000 to destruction without protecting them at all. Either Zürich shall be turned into a fortress, in which case, in the interest of the troops and the civilian population, those evacuation measures shall be taken that have been applied everywhere else; or the Federal Council and the Army Command declare that taking evacuation measures is not possible, in which case they will not be able to take on the responsibility of defending the city of Zürich either. The city of Zürich is ready to make any sacrifice that may be necessary in the interest of defending our country. However, it urges the Federal Authorities to make a clear decision about its fate in case of a war and consequently to order the necessary measures."[60]

Germany's offensive in France was over before this serious matter could be considered twice and before Switzerland's military and political authorities could make a final decision. When the Réduit front was designed as a consequence of the new constellation around Switzerland, the strategic situation of Zürich changed. The example of Zürich shows how determined the General was to take on the enemy at the positions drafted under Case North, for he was willing to sacrifice Switzerland's most populated city as well as many other large and small towns located in the expected combat areas. The city of Basel, on the other hand, was on the front line and the army command's orders stated, "In case of an attack, Basel shall be defended house by house, street by street."[61]

The Linth Plain, located on the access route to Canton Glarus and the Pragel, Klausen, and Kisten mountain passes, played a particular role in the strategy along the front line. It had to be defended at all costs and was to be turned into marshland or to be flooded if the troops could no longer resist the enemy. On the Bodensee (Lake Constance) along the German border, which froze during the wintertime, the General had troops "cut out a five meter wide rift in the ice 200 to 300 meters from the shore, close enough to fire on [the enemy]." The blocks of ice cut out were "to be piled up along the rift to form a dam."[62]

Consistent with Switzerland's obligations as a neutral state, a plan of operations was formulated not only for Case North, but also for a less likely infringement of Switzerland's neutrality from the west through an Allied attack, even though the General initially failed to show much interest in it. The plan for Case West was initiated by the assistant chief of staff for the front, Colonel Hans Frick, who submitted a draft to the chief of the general staff in mid-

November 1939, which the latter forwarded to the General.[63] At that time, the General was not willing to take action on the proposed fortification of the defense line in the West, giving his chief of staff the "strictly confidential" information, "The Federal Government and I believe that at the present time the danger we encounter can only come from the north or the east, and perhaps later from the south. Therefore, any further discussion [of Case West] is superfluous." All operational, construction, and financial efforts were to be concentrated on the positions in the north. "In the west," the General said, "we shall do just what is necessary to avoid being accused of partiality."[64]

Labhart and other top-ranking officers on the general staff, including Colonel Frick, were concerned by the fact that Guisan's attention was almost exclusively directed to the north. Consequently, he decided to bring the matter before the General one more time.[65] He wrote a three-page letter to the General in the form of an exposé, in which he told his commander that he could "not deny" that the General's opinion caused "serious concerns" to him, as he believed he could "say that up to now Germany has, neither through its political position [sic!] toward us nor through positioning troops, provided any reason for us to be worried about an immediate threat." He agreed that it was advisable to remain cautious because the situation might change, but one should not totally rule out "an infringement of our neutrality from the West," as it was "dangerous to assume from the outset that one side present[ed] absolutely no risk."[66]

Labhart was meticulous, but in fact he was unduly concerned about the different military measures being undertaken to maintain this aspect of neutrality. He concluded his remarks to the General by writing, "I continue to believe that Switzerland has quite good chances of getting through this war without being drawn into the conflict. However, that requires making very prudent foreign policy decisions, which we must not jeopardize through military measures. Because the [anti-German] mood in the country strains our neutrality, it is all the more important that the political and military authorities remain strictly neutral."[67] These ideas were very close to those expressed by Marcel Pilet-Golaz, the Federal President in 1940, who was willing to make concessions to accommodate Germany's new hegemony in Europe and was heavily criticized for his views.

Guisan's initial reluctance to plan for a defense strategy on the western front also worried Colonel Logoz, the liaison officer between the government and the army command, who advised Federal President Pilet-Golaz at the end of January 1940 "to request that the army command accelerate the planning of Case West and begin drawing up a scenario in case we ask the Wehrmacht to intervene on our behalf."[68]

The commander-in-chief reassured his chief of staff at the end of 1939 that he would consider two defensive front lines in the west, one close to the French border between Lake Neuchâtel and Lake Geneva, following the Jorat Mountain and the Mentue and Paudèze river valleys, and one further inland from the Gempen Plateau towards Thun, adding that he personally preferred the one closer to the border. The General discarded a third front along the Sarine River, which military historian Alfred Ernst believes "would overall have been the most advantageous one,"[69] because he considered it "much too long."[70]

The General had the two options for the Western Front, which were subsequently called "Case West A" and "Case West B," analyzed in detail by the Operational Section in early 1940. However, the orders for a potential deployment of troops according to Case West A were not issued until March 9, and for Case West B only on April 22, 1940.[71] For Case West A, the deployment of reserve troops made up of two ad hoc divisions was planned. Border brigades 7 and 8 were to form "Division Sempach," and border brigades 5 and 6 were to form "Division Hallwil" under the command of Colonel K. Renold.[72]

Case West B foresaw a defensive front Basel–Hauenstein Mountain–Wigger River–Napf Mountain–Thun–St-Maurice, which was to be used if there was not enough time to deploy the troops according to Case West A. It meant that all of western Switzerland, including the capital Bern, would be forsaken. In case of an attack from the west, the Federal Council intended to move the seat of government to Lucerne; in the event of an attack from the north it planned to move to Lausanne.[73]

At the end of 1939, a total of 151,300 troops, just over one third of the entire armed forces, were on duty, most of whom were stationed near the planned northern front line to work on the fortifications.[74] The construction work for Case North was financed in part through credits that were to be used for fortifying the strongholds at the border. Labhart had informed a conference as early as September 29, one week before Operations Order No. 2 was issued, that the General had given instructions "to use the available credits mostly for fortifying the front lines and to stop using the funds for the border fortifications." Hence, fortifications like those at St-Ursanne on the Doubs River and along the Jura Mountains in Canton Neuchâtel, as well as the bridgehead over the Rhine at Schaffhausen were no longer reinforced, or the scheduled work was canceled altogether.[75] In addition, the Military Department reported, "The Federal Council authorized a credit of 40 million Swiss francs on October 30, 1939, mostly for fortifying the Limmat front line, and another credit of 90 million francs on March 26, 1940, based on a detailed request by the commander-in-chief. All of these 130 million francs were allocated to fortifying the planned front lines inside the country. . . . By January 1941, about 68 million francs had been spent."[76]

At the turn of the year 1939–40, some major reassignments occurred at the top level of the armed forces which even the General considered to be "of an unusual scope." Guisan named five new divisional commanders and one new corps commander.[77] The most sensational changes were the creation of a new army corps and the removal of the chief of the general staff from his office. The National Defense Committee had contemplated the creation of the 4th Army Corps as early as 1936. The chief of the general staff at that time, H. Roost, favored a new corps because it could provide "advantages in terms of the army's operational structure." Corps Commander Guisan agreed with this proposition, saying, "Four army corps would be better than three."[78] At the subsequent NDC meetings Guisan continued to advocate establishing a new army unit, calling it "extremely necessary"; however, he was in the minority, even if Federal Councilor Minger also tended to favor an additional corps.[79]

The General and his chief of staff agreed on the necessity for a new corps. As Labhart commented in the fall of 1939, "In my opinion, creating a fourth army corps has undisputable advantages in view of Case North and in view of troop deployments in general. . . . In my opinion, the organizational difficulties in connection with setting up the new structure will be relatively easy to surmount. However, I have some reservations about the availability of qualified officers for a new 4th Army Corps."[80] The available source documents do not indicate whether Labhart already suspected at that moment that he would be the one to set up and command the new corps.

The new army unit included the 7th Division, Mountain Brigade 12, Light Brigade 3, and Border Brigades 7 and 8, as well as the usual corps troops, heavy artillery, special weapons, and the garrison of the Sargans fortress. Under the new structure, which went into effect on a provisional basis on January 1, 1940, three army corps continued to hold the front lines to the north and northeast; the 4th Corps took control of the right wing, which included sectors previously held by the 3rd Corps. The task entrusted to Labhart was quite formidable, as he had to start from scratch recruiting personnel and organizing the new troops; moreover, he was in charge of expanding the Sargans fortress, which had been raised to the level of an army unit on January 4. Labhart chose Colonel Karl Kobelt, a hard-working former commander of an infantry regiment from eastern Switzerland, as his chief of staff.[81] The 1st and 3rd Army Corps received orders to supply the commander of the new corps immediately with all relevant instructions regarding Case North.[82] According to Operations Order No. 4, the 4th Corps had orders to "hold the positions to the right of the defensive front, between Sargans and Bendlikon (excluding Bendlikon). It shall cover the army's right wing in Graubünden." The 1st Corps, which had been deployed on the left wing, was ordered to remain on standby behind the front line in central Switzerland and to secure the Gotthard, St-Maurice, and the southern front.[83]

In the spring of 1940, before Germany began its western campaign, the General ordered the army staff to study a possible retreat of the armed forces to the Alps. Even if the Limmat front were to be held at all costs, Guisan requested that this question be examined, as a retreat might become necessary "after several weeks of battles" at the Limmat in order to prevent the enemy from breaking through the front line of decimated troops. This option was to be analyzed so that if a retreat contingency developed the staff would not to be taken by surprise. The study was to assume that "in all likelihood, if not most certainly," foreign troops would assist the Swiss Army to fight against a potential aggressor.[84] Hence, in early 1940 the General was cautious but optimistic, calculating that his armed forces, assisted by Allied troops, would be able to hold out at the prepared front lines "for several weeks."

Colonel Germann, who was also the author of this study,[85] proposed, "in view of the [expected] devastating fire of German tank and airborne troops," to withdraw the Swiss Army into positions located in the steep, tree-covered hills between Lake Zug and Lake Sempach, so that the troops could, "in the worst case, retreat to the mountains and gather new strength there to continue putting up resistance."[86] It is interesting to note that this study already used the concept of the Réduit, even if the word itself was not mentioned. When the General explained, in his postwar report, that his staff drafted the first plans for a front line in the Alps, as it was later stipulated under the Réduit strategy, in the spring of 1940, he undoubtedly referred to Germann's study.[87]

The draft for a possible retreat was simply a discussion of a strategic option; it did not indicate a predetermined intention. Alfred Ernst commented, "A retreat was planned only in case there was no prospect of further resisting the Germans on their march through the country and in case the French were willing to assist us by continuing to fight in our stead in the Plains. Before the summer of 1940, no serious consideration was given to a defensive war in the Alps to resist a German attack from several directions that aimed at incorporating Switzerland into the territory of the Axis powers."[88]

During the time of the "Phony War" of winter 1939–40—which was, for Switzerland, rather a "Phony Peace"—General Guisan skillfully managed to raise the level of preparedness among his troops by appealing to their sense of moral duty to their country. The commander-in-chief instilled trust, thus kindling the troops' spirit of resistance, sense of duty, and dedication. His personal appearances and the content of his orders encouraged the troops, promoted unity within the armed forces, and motivated them to fight should the need arise. Before the onset of winter, the General called on the army to be particularly vigilant in view of the unstable situation, explaining, in one of his orders, "Even though Europe has been at war for two months, our country has not been involved in the conflict so far. I have noticed that this fact has created some kind of peace psychosis among our armed forces that has also seized our people. This feeling of security is not at all justified. On the contrary, when soberly analyzing the situation one comes to the conclusion that unexpected events can instantly change our position. We are more at risk today than in September to be drawn into the war at any moment, against our will. It is therefore reckless to make the armed forces believe that a war is no longer possible. Such thinking would undermine the spirit of our troops and the material preparations."[89] Both the army and the people understood the General's sober, matter-of-fact language.

To acquaint himself with his unit commanders and troops during their first four months of active duty, from September to December 1939, the General visited the corps commanders on several occasions to hold talks and to conduct inspections. Moreover, he personally met with all twenty-two cantonal governments to introduce himself. Some cantons organized an official reception; others, such as Aargau, Solothurn, and the two Appenzells, simply received the General in their offices to establish first contact.[90] Guisan was particularly interested in getting acquainted with the Swiss in the eastern part of the country, which was not difficult for him because he spoke fluent German. He was met with approval everywhere. He later explained that these visits were "to a certain degree, a necessity." In addition, it was "a matter of courtesy for the General to introduce himself to the cantonal governments and to listen to their wishes regarding one or the other question. One had to make acquaintances!"[91] These many close contacts turned out to be very helpful during the long wartime duty to come. In his postwar report, the General commented, "In general, I remember as positive my relations with the members of the cantonal governments. With a few exceptions, the exchange of opinions, especially on the thorny question of leaves of absence, was very open and allowed both sides to reconcile interests that appeared to clash in the beginning."[92]

It is curious to note that during the time of the "Phony Peace," different high-ranking officers assessed the risks for Switzerland in strikingly different ways. Several unit commanders requested releasing the troops, arguing that the international military and political situation justified reducing the number of men on duty. Corps Commander Wille, for example, was optimistic and ruled out a German offensive in the West. He believed that the fact that everything was calm at the front lines abroad was a sign of a "balance of power in Europe, which is a prerequisite for a lasting peace between the major powers." "A German offensive," he added, "cannot bring about an immediate final victory, no matter where it is launched and how successful it may be in the first battles. A final victory will require many large battles. Time will work in favor of the Allies and the war will end with a German defeat. France and the English island cannot be conquered within a short period of time, even if the first [German] attacks are successful. The idea that England could be brought to capitulate through airborne attacks and a German landing does not stand up to closer scrutiny. If Germany launches an offensive against Belgium or Holland, the entire world will be alarmed once again as in 1914 and sooner or later America will intervene against Germany." In his optimistic analysis, Wille concluded that reason would command the Germans to stay put so as not to disturb the balance of power that was then in their favor. That way, "the other side of the Channel and the neutral countries, and above all the United States of America, will realize that Germany wanted nothing but to void the short-sighted Treaty of Versailles, which it did."[93]

Labhart made similar analyses in the spring of 1940, a few days before the German attacks on Norway and Denmark. As he wrote to the General, "Today the constellation is such that an attack by our neighbor to the north can be ruled out, at least as long as our neighbor to the south [Italy] maintains its neutrality and remains on good terms with our country. Everything indicates that in case Germany should take action, it would be directed against England in the first place; hence, Holland and Belgium will be far more at risk than Switzerland . . . . This analysis leads me to the definite conclusion that the troops that are on duty should be substantially reduced."[94] In early April 1940, Labhart recommended to the commander-in-chief that the major part of the armed forces be put on standby and only two to three divisions remain on duty.[95]

Wille and Labhart both underestimated Germany's aggressive ambitions. Guisan, on the other hand, recognized Hitler's demon-like determination and viewed the threatening situation objectively and, hence, correctly.

8

Replacing the Chief of the General Staff

IT DID NOT TAKE LONG FOR TENSIONS TO BUILD between the newly elected General and Corps Commander Labhart, who was seven years younger than Guisan and who had been named Chief of the General Staff by the Federal Council on Guisan's recommendation on August 31, 1939. The two leading figures in the army high command disagreed in their assessments of the international military and political situation as well as on the question of Case North. In addition, they did not get along because of their contrasting personalities.

Guisan had considered several other candidates before selecting Labhart for the position of chief of staff. Among those he contemplated were H. Frick, von Erlach, Gugger, Corbat, and (already at that time) J. Huber. He considered Labhart as rather disagreeable and had reservations about proposing him for the post. In his notebook Guisan wrote: "Politician, thinks about himself in the first place, does not study the subject matters, is not pro-active, passive, not honest. No instructions whatsoever to Frick."[1] However, Labhart had indisputable qualities on the organizational and operational levels, and as chief of the general staff section, a post he had held since 1936, had acquired profound knowledge of the internal structure of the military. These qualities apparently outweighed any reservations, so the General decided to recommend Labhart for the post.

Barbey, who introduced himself to Labhart at the beginning of the war in Spiez, where the general staff was headquartered, later wrote about Labhart's appearance: "He took my salute without saying a word. He is considered intelligent, a good organizer who focuses on the essentials, a dry person who does not have much contact. He has small, brown, sharp eyes, a pointed aquiline nose, a prominent chin, freckled skin, and a wide neck. When he enters the officers' mess hall at the hotel, about fifty officers of all ages and all ranks get up and slam their heels together. It all looks like some staff officer training course."[2]

Labhart had a tendency to be high-handed and obstinate, and had difficulty accepting the fact that someone else was above him. Robert Eibel, the chief secretary at the first "General's Office," told this author that it was "scandalous" how Labhart failed to inform the General of important orders during the first weeks of war-time service; the commander-in-chief found out about some of the orders "more or less by coincidence."[3] Guisan put Labhart in his place without delay. When he realized that his chief of staff had issued, on his own authority, operational and strategic orders to the commanders of the army units, he wrote to him, "In the future, any order issued by the Army Command that deals with operational or strategic questions pertaining to the front shall come exclusively from me. At the same time, I reserve the right to deal directly with my A[rmy] C[orps] commanders and the commanders of army units who are directly subordinated to me."[4] Guisan pointed out to Labhart that once the commander-in-chief had made a decision, all the general staff had to do was to act on the decision by preparing the relevant orders. He said he hoped that this clear distinction between their functions would be the basis for cooperation in an army command that would be free from frictions and conflicts in the future.

The differences between the General and his chief of staff did not go unnoticed among the army staff. At a briefing with the assistant chiefs of staff on September 22, Labhart openly criticized the commander-in-chief's decision to give priority to Case North, as well as the way he had issued orders in that connection.[5] Labhart had trouble accepting the definition of his role and did not seem to fully comply with the General's instructions. When the General informed him about his intention to transfer Light Brigade 2 to the 3rd Army Corps in order to reinforce the northern front, Labhart issued the respective order in his own name. The General immediately reacted by writing to Labhart, "This is, without the shadow of a doubt, a matter pertaining to the [supreme] command, on which the general staff could only make suggestions. No other interpretation is possible. I insist on this distinction and ask you to respect it in the future."[6] When Labhart tried to justify his action, the General replied to him in a seven-page letter, in which he once again emphasized the commander-in-chief's point of view and told Labhart that the times before the war when the general staff had extensive authority were over. "You, your Assistant Chiefs, and Heads of Section," Guisan wrote, "are not yet used to being subordinated to a command that makes requests and issues orders to you. The fact that I was

practically isolated until mid-September proves my point." Guisan reprimanded the chief of staff for his unwillingness to respect the General's views and
orders, and he insisted that the chief of the general staff's responsibilities had
"passed over entirely to the General" upon his election as commander-in-chief.[7]

In early October 1939, the General admonished Labhart again because he
had not been provided with adequate information on the progress of road construction at the Susten mountain pass. He emphasized that it was up to the
commander-in-chief to decide the pace of the work, explaining that he expected the road to be in condition for vehicles to cross the mountain in the fall of
1940. In a threatening tone he added, "This is not the first time I have had to
intervene in this matter, and I am telling you once again that I do not want to
be left in the dark about issues of such importance, nor do I want to be faced
with a *fait accompli*. If this happens again, I will draw the necessary conclusions."[8]

Labhart objected to the General's criticism and pointed out that he had discussed with him the continuation of the road construction at the Susten "on
several occasions," on September 5, 14, and 20. He added, "Since you had no
reservations and did not express a different opinion, it was safe for me to
assume that we both agreed. . . . To conclude, I would like to state that you have
been informed by me on the issue on several occasions; that I was authorized,
once you had approved of my viewpoint, to take action accordingly on the matter; and hence, that I did not face you with a *fait accompli*." This exchange of
letters created considerable friction, which Labhart expressed in the final sentence of his reply by writing, "I have to tell you that, in the interest of a fruitful collaboration between the General and the Chief of the General Staff, I very
much deplore the form of your letter, which was not even marked 'personal'
and was therefore opened by the office and was read by five gentlemen."[9]

Guisan felt obliged to formally demand that his authority, which he considered to be exclusive and absolute, be fully respected. By emphasizing that he
was determined to exercise his authority as commander-in-chief to the fullest,
he put Labhart in his place. His response to Labhart's suggestion to increase the
number of meetings between them was rather cold, as he replied that a more
frequent exchange of opinions was desirable and might be useful, but "I will
continue to make my decision only based on written studies or proposals which
you submit to me, in order for me to be able to analyze them in detail and make
my decisions in full knowledge of the facts. Hence, an exchange of views would
be advisable *before* you proceed to have the documents drafted on which I base
my decisions."[10]

It must be mentioned that the General's increasingly hostile tone in his
correspondence with his chief of staff was at least in part due to the striking cir-

cumstance that his letters and instructions were drafted, and in some cases also initiated, by Lieutenant-Colonel Gonard, who initialed them with "Go" or "-7-". Hence, the correspondence also reflected the long-lasting enmity between Labhart and his former associate Gonard, who had "left no good impression" on Labhart because he was ambitious and "a constant supporter of the politics of the Western Powers," as Labhart wrote in a letter to Federal Councilor Minger.[11]

During the late fall of 1939, the relationship between the General and his chief of staff appeared to stabilize on a level at which they kept their distance from each other. However, during that time tensions rose between the chief of the general staff and his deputy, Divisional Commander Huber, the assistant chief of staff for rearward affairs. Huber had already requested to be transferred before the war due to disagreements with Labhart.[12] In November 1939, Huber wrote a letter to the General asking him to be released from his post on the general staff to be assigned instead to the staff of the Federal Council, as he felt that he was "not the right man in the right place" and was "sick and tired of playing cat and mouse."[13] Huber's request came at a time when the General was studying the question of reassigning some staff members on the army command and it may have influenced his future deliberations.[14] In fact, Huber submitted his request at the right time, as it suited Guisan's plans for a reshuffling of the army staff.

On December 13, 1939, the General informed Labhart in writing that he had decided, upon analyzing the future makeup of the army staff, to replace him as chief of the general staff on a provisional basis with Divisional Commander Huber. However, he would give him the opportunity to command ad interim, as of January 1, 1940, the 4th Army Corps, which had yet to be established. At the same time, Labhart was asked to make suggestions as to the future composition of the new corps staff.[15]

There is no indication that talks were held prior to entrusting Labhart with the command of a corps. Labhart wrote in a note for the file that he had not been consulted about his new assignment or about the other changes at the top level of the army staff.[16] In a meeting with the General on December 15, he declared that he accepted his new task, confirming it in writing.[17] In addition to assuming the command of the 4th Army Corps, Labhart was told that he would formally continue to supervise the work of the general staff and would keep the official title of "Chief of the General Staff Section." As Ernst remarked, "These contradictory instructions created constant friction."[18]

The General's official order to establish a 4th Army Corps under the temporary command of the chief of the general staff was dated December 16, 1939.[19] Labhart was surprised to hear later that his reassignment had been a topic of conversation in Zürich several days before he had received the General's order.[20] When Heinz Häberlin, a former Federal Councilor who, like Labhart, was from Thurgau, heard the rumors, he wrote to Labhart, "I had a restless night. Last evening I heard that there was discord among the top officers of our armed forces. It was said that the General and his chief of staff communicated only in writing. Other high-ranking officers are said to display their discontent in public. Some of this dissatisfaction is said to be related to staff changes among the army command that are imminent or have already taken place. When I heard all this, it made me greatly concerned about our army. However, what I retained above all was the part about the army commanders not being able to talk with each other. *That must not happen!* Is any of this talk true, or is it mere gossip? I would ask the General the same question if he was the one who comes from Thurgau. . . ."[21] Labhart confirmed that there had been quarrels by replying, "Unfortunately some of the rumors that have reached your ears are true. I am the first one to regret that the situation has turned this way, but unfortunately forces were at work, which I could not stem, that sowed differences between the General and his subordinates, especially me."[22]

Guisan's personal notes clearly indicate why Labhart was removed from his post as chief of the general staff. The General scribbled, "Labh[art]: Sept[ember] 1, no operational instructions. No coordin[ation] at all. Impenetrable divisions. Only bo[rder] cov[erage] was in place. Current staff don't go because don't know how to obey, because have been their own masters until now. No contact between Chief of G. S. and me! Hardly ever comes to see me. Period of time Sept. 1–25, Chief of G. S. disqualified, they laughed about the General, saying he was good for visits with governments. It can't go on like that. . . ."[23]

During the first months of the war, the tensions between the General and his chief of staff did not reach the public ear or eye. Hence, the announcement, toward the end of 1939, of Labhart's replacement came as a surprise. Before an official communiqué was published, waves of rumors circulated in the streets and "the boldest allegations ran through the country like wildfire."[24] Labhart remarked in his diary that several newspapers had published his assignment as commander of the 4th Army Corps ahead of the official announcement in an "incorrect manner," adding, "Some newspapers were confiscated, and investigations have been opened against two journalists."[25] The official announcement that ended up being published by the press office of the army staff sounded as though Labhart had been promoted rather than demoted. It stated: "In the framework of the staff changes among the Armed Forces ordered by the General, as of January 1, ad interim Colonel-Corps Commander Labhart, Chief of the General Staff of the Armed Forces, will temporarily assume the command of a large unit, while maintaining his current position. During his absence, his current deputy, Colonel-Divisional Commander Huber, Assistant Chief of Staff for Rearward Affairs, will carry out the tasks of the Chief of the General Staff."[26]

It is striking how cautiously the commander-in-chief proceeded to remove Labhart from his post as chief of the general staff, the effect of which was to put him on the sidelines. There is no doubt that he wanted to allow Labhart to save his reputation, thereby avoiding any undesired commotion among the chief of staff's many supporters. In a meeting with Labhart, the General explained to him that Huber's role was "simply that of a deputy," adding that he had ordered the change in order to give Huber a chance to acquaint himself with the job, since Labhart "might get sick one day." Labhart replied that in that case his role as corps commander was not clear, because it remained to be determined whether he would stay on as commander or return to his job as chief of the general staff if a critical situation occurred. The General told Labhart that he had thought about this possibility and had come to the conclusion that Corps Commander Lardelli would take over the command of the 4th Army Corps, Divisional Commander Borel the command of the 1st Army Corps, Divisional Commander Flückiger the command of Borel's 2nd Division, and Huber the command of Flückiger's 7th Division. Labhart liked this proposal but mentioned that as a consequence he would have to inform himself, "once a week, on the state of affairs on the general staff."[27] The General was reluctant to grant that request, as he feared that Huber might feel limited in his actions; he insisted that Labhart first discuss the matter with Colonel-Divisional Commander Huber.

The General's official order to make Divisional Commander Jakob Huber ad interim Chief of the General Staff as of January 1, 1940, was dated December 18, 1939.[28] One week earlier, the Federal Council had noted and approved the General's intention to reassign Labhart and to temporarily make Huber his chief of staff. Three months later, Huber was informed in writing by the General that the Federal Council, at its meeting on March 26, had elected him Chief of the General Staff of the Armed Forces in replacement of Corps Commander Labhart.[29] On the same day, Labhart received a written notice from the General informing him that he had been relieved of his duties as chief of the general staff and had been confirmed as commander of the 4th Army Corps.[30]

Gonard drafted a detailed note, probably for Guisan's official meeting with Huber, outlining the commander-in-chief's terms of reference for his chief of staff. The first three of the six points stated:

1. We expect you, above all, to *stimulate, on an intellectual level,* the general staff which has had no guidance so far and has not received sufficient impetus.
2. You will receive top-notch staff as direct subordinates. Given their qualifications, I insist that they be consulted, that their point of view be taken into account whenever it is deemed justified, and that they be granted, although directly [sic], the necessary freedom of action. This is indispensable in order for them to feel that they have their own responsibilities.
3. When selecting people for different functions, the determining factor is their *ability,* not their age or rank. I insist very much that this principle be adhered to."[31]

These terms, which Huber undoubtedly accepted in view of the prospect of his new promotion, indicated that other changes were planned among the army staff. In fact, during the following weeks the Assistant Chief of Staff for the Front, Colonel H. Frick, and the Chief of the Operational Section, Colonel von Erlach, were also replaced. Moreover, Guisan ordered that all proposals pertaining to operational, strategic, fortification, or financial matters submitted by the commanders directly below him be addressed to the chief of the general staff for examination. Subsequently Huber was to inform the General "several times a week on the submitted proposals and on the major studies that [were] under way. . . . The Chief of the General Staff shall not only give his opinion and make suggestions on each proposal but also attach the necessary documents, such as draft orders or letters to be signed by the General, in order for the matter to be immediately liquidated."[32] The commander-in-chief added that it would be unacceptable to submit to him for decision issues of minor importance, especially in cases when subordinates stubbornly insisted on their point of view when there was nothing more to discuss.

Labhart handed over his duties as chief of the general staff to Huber before the Christmas holiday of 1939. He commented in his diary, "Afterwards I talk[ed] to him about a very personal matter, telling him several times that I [felt] hurt about the way he had proceeded. Colonel-Divisional Commander Huber is down and out. He is not happy at all about the future and only accepted [the new position] because he had received strict orders to do so."[33] Huber started crying during their conversation, which Labhart interpreted as an expression of depression and anger. Huber told Labhart that the other changes on the army staff had been "directly imposed" on him, without his being asked for an opinion. Labhart reminded his deputy that he remained chief of the general staff and therefore wished "to be consulted on a number of issues." In his diary he noted, most likely with satisfaction, "Colonel-Divisional Commander Huber is in favor of my coming here once a week to keep myself informed on current affairs."[34]

On December 30, Labhart held a final meeting with his staff to introduce his "deputy." In his final speech he said, among other things, "Gentlemen, as you know, the General has entrusted me with the interim command of the 4th Army Corps. In addition, he has ordered Colonel-Divisional Commander Huber to carry out the duties of the chief of the general staff during my absence. I will come back here from time to time to keep abreast of business."[35] Then Labhart went to see the General to report absent from duty; the General invited him to lunch, but Labhart "asked to be excused."[36]

Corps Commander Ulrich Wille was among those who were disappointed about the General's selection of his new chief of staff. He had counted on eventually succeeding Labhart in that position, as Guisan appeared to have given him reason to believe that he would take over the command of Main Unit I of the army staff. In late November 1939, the General had told Wille "confidentially that he [would] reassign Labhart as commander of the 4th Army Corps."[37] A few days later Wille wrote in his diary, "Gümligen—Meeting with the General re: replacement of Labhart, whose successor I am supposed to become."[38] Wille was skeptical about being able to work well with Guisan; nevertheless, he asked friends whether he should accept the post. Colonel Probst, the Chief Instructor of the Infantry, one of his subordinates, encouraged him to accept the offer, writing, "I believe that you should agree to it in spite of the serious reservations that you have. Even if you take on the major part of the responsibility, and even if you will undoubtedly encounter endless difficulties, one should not forget that something decisive can be done for the army and the country by taking that step. First of all, confidence in the [army] command will increase and be strengthened in the entire country and probably also abroad. Your name guarantees everything."[39] Probst's words may be considered to represent the view of a number of army instructors who were hoping that the army command would be restructured. Probst ended his letter saying that a new order "among the general staff and the adjutancy, in short, among the entire supreme command, [will] create a different atmosphere."

In early December 1939, the General was indeed seriously considering Wille as his future chief of staff, as indicated in two internal studies listing pros and cons of choosing Wille which were undertaken, without attribution, by two of Guisan's close associates. Kreis suggests that Gonard may have been the author of one of the studies,[40] which is likely because it contains several of his handwritten corrections. This first study states that a large number of officers from eastern Switzerland would strongly approve the choice, as Wille's intelligence and abilities would be better employed than in his current post. However, due to his character, difficulties would be expected, and French-speaking Switzerland, some corps commanders, and the Federal Council would be opposed to his nomination, even if Federal Councilor Minger would probably back it. The author of the study warned that "promoting to the second highest post of the army a man who has been intriguing throughout his life, a characteristic that everyone knows about, can trigger a reversal of opinion from which the entire armed forces would suffer."[41] The second study, possibly written by the General's adjutant, Major Mayer, came to a similar conclusion, stating that Wille's nomination could have negative effects on Guisan's prestige and position, as he would be held responsible for selecting Wille, an act which would have negative consequences on the army. In view of all circumstances, this study concluded, the only solution, "even if it is not very desirable, is to nominate Colonel Huber as Chief of the General Staff."[42]

Certainly, Guisan nominated Huber only after long deliberations. On December 11 Wille wrote in his diary, "Gümligen—Meeting with General, who drops me upon Minger's objection."[43] In the summer of 1940 Wille, who felt that he had been deceived, took up the matter once again in a personal letter to the General, reminding him that Guisan had promised, in early December 1939, to put him in Labhart's place as chief of the general staff, "even in case the Federal Council had reservations" about him. Wille accused the General of breaking his word, writing, "When we sat together in your office eight days later to discuss the same issue, you had changed your decision at the Federal Council's request."[44] Wille expressed his disappointment about not being considered for the post when he wrote, "I thank you for being nice to me, but perhaps that made me bear with too much patience the disregard for my 40 years of successful professional experience."[45]

The General waited five weeks before he responded to Wille's letter, denying ever making him a firm offer of the post of chief of the general staff. He stated that the way Wille remembered the situation did "not entirely correspond with the facts," adding, "you know that the nomination is up to the Federal Council. In our first meeting I simply told you about my intention to propose you for this post, depending on the circumstances. The Federal Council's reaction at the time made me give up this solution, of which I informed you in our second meeting."[46]

Wille apparently did not persist in pressing his point of view, since he did not reply to the General's answer. However, he wrote on Guisan's letter, "This account is correct with regard to the meeting that was held in Stadel on November 26, [1939]; but the General informed me in his office in Gümligen on December 4 that according to article 209 of the Military Regulations he would detail Colonel-Corps Commander Labhart as Chief of the General Staff; he could and would order me to the post in [Labhart's] place, even without the Federal Council's approval. I stand by what I wrote to the General on August 31, 1940, which is based on my diary entries of December 4 and 11, 1939."[47] It is strange that in connection with this controversy Wille did not approach Federal Councilor Minger to inquire about the facts, as he was on good terms with Minger, albeit not as close to him as was Guisan. It is possible that Wille was hoping to achieve his goal through other means, because during the year 1940 a pro-German group made a serious attempt at ousting Huber from his post as chief of the general staff in order to replace him with Wille (see Chapter 23 below).

The tensions surrounding the replacement of the chief of the general staff had repercussions until after the war, when special parliamentary committee hearings dealt with the General's report on wartime duty. Guisan evaded a pertinent question by explaining that he did not understand why some people thought he had replaced Labhart because he resented him. In the minutes of the hearing, the commander-in-chief's statement is summarized as follows: "He may not have valued Colonel-Corps Commander Labhart as his chief of staff, but he valued him as a corps commander."[48]

9

Cooperation with
Foreign Powers

AS A NEUTRAL STATE, SWITZERLAND WAS NOT ALLOWED to enter into any precautionary military agreements with foreign nations. However, in wartime,
cooperation with the opponent of an aggressor could be crucial. In his postwar
report, General Guisan wrote only a few lines on Switzerland's cooperation
with foreign powers, stating, "In the fall of 1939 . . . I ordered that two simultaneous studies be undertaken to facilitate cooperation with the Supreme
Command of the Allies or of the Wehrmacht in case hostilities broke out. These
studies contained general guidelines, which were established [by the army com-
mand] with legal advisors, on the extent to which our Army could, without giving up its independence, join forces with a foreign army in order to defend our
neutral country. Moreover, the studies determined the time frame and geographic limits that were to be applied if our Army participated in the war. They
also included an exposé by officers of the general staff on how such military
cooperation could be handled. These studies were an overview of Switzerland's
requirements, ideas, and requests."[1]

There is no doubt that in his report the General intentionally downplayed
the contacts and the quasi-agreements that existed with the French Supreme
Command regarding potential cooperation by merely calling them "studies."
The contacts regarding military cooperation had in fact reached such detailed
proportions with the Allies that they resulted, much to Guisan's embarrass-
ment, in thorny complications in both domestic and foreign policy. However,
the public found out about these complications only after the war.

Several authors agree that Guisan first established confidential contacts
with the French Army Command in the 1930s.[2] Kreis indicated that the term
"talks between the general staffs," which was frequently used in this context,
was not accurate. Even if the individual officers participating in the discussions

were members of the general staff, the talks were in no way official but private, based on personal connections.[3] From 1936 on, the head of Switzerland's intelligence service, Lieutenant-Colonel Dubois, and later Masson, secretly exchanged military information with the French Military Attaché in Bern, Lieutenant-Colonel de la Forest-Divonne, and with the Air Force Attaché, Commander Loriot, in a similar way as during World War I under the so-called "Colonel Affair."[4]

Guisan knew most French military leaders personally and was friends with some of them. As Barbey remarked, "Some were part of his generation and were his friends whom he had met during maneuvers or whom he had invited to his house at 'Verte Rive'."[5] One of them was General Victor H. Schweisguth, whose mother was Swiss and who owned a country estate at La Faraz in Vaud. He had accompanied Marshal Pétain during his 1937 review of Swiss maneuvers and was in charge of the French 8th Army Corps, stationed along the French-Swiss border, where he was in close contact with Guisan's 1st Army Corps.[6]

General Guisan later told an officer from western Switzerland, R.-H. Wüst, that in the fall of 1938 he had undertaken, as commander of the 1st Army Corps, and with the approval of Federal Councilor Minger, an unaccompanied mission in civilian clothes during which he visited the French 3rd Army Group in Alsace in order to acquaint himself with the southern part of the Maginot line and the French troops whose right wing ended at the Swiss border.[7] This several-day visit was the starting point for the cooperation talks during the winter of 1939–40. It is very likely that Guisan was inspired by the agreement called "Plan 'H'" that the Swiss and French general staffs had devised in 1917 during World War I in case Switzerland was drawn into the conflict.[8] The French apparently also drew on the experience and the files from the First World War, as the French liaison officer Garteiser showed Barbey "a copy of Plan 'H,' which General Weygand [had] established in 1917 together with Lieutenant-Colonel de Goumoëns of the 'Swiss Confederate' general staff," during one of Barbey's first contact visits to Paris in the fall of 1939.[9]

One month before war broke out, on July 31, on the instruction of Corps Commander Guisan, Colonel Petitpierre, chief of staff of the 1st Army Corps, met with Generals Gamelin and Georges at French Army headquarters in Paris to discuss, in the presence of Lieutenant-Colonel Garteiser, preliminaries for cooperation in case of war. The French supposedly suggested the meeting.[10] France, a major power, was as interested in knowing that its right flank was sufficiently secured as Switzerland was in knowing the details of possible assistance. Speaking on behalf of Guisan, Petitpierre explained the needs of the Swiss Army in the event of a German attack, while General Georges outlined the

French strategy should an intervention be necessary. The meeting at the French Army headquarters lasted more than an hour, from 11:25 a.m. to 12:35 p.m. The participants promised each other that the meeting and its topic would be kept strictly confidential. It was planned to have this first unofficial contact followed by another series of confidential talks in Lausanne between General Georges and Corps Commander Guisan in order to establish the details of cooperation.[11] However, because of the outbreak of the war, the Lausanne meeting did not take place.

Hans Senn discovered that the earliest instructions issued by Generals Georges and Garchéry "for the case of an invasion of Switzerland by our enemies," dated June 20 and July 19, 1939, are available to researchers at the "Service Historique de l'Armée de Terre Française (SHAT)" in Paris.[12] These instructions were in part drawn up before Petitpierre's visit to Paris and were later modified by General Gamelin. They considered possible cooperation—if the Swiss government made an express request for intervention—in the form of a forward defense strategy, according to which "French Army Group 3, consisting of the 6th and the 7th armies, [would] occupy and maintain as a pivotal position the Gempen Plateau, establish contact with the Swiss Army in the Jura and in the Aare valley, support it with heavy artillery, relieve its left wing on the defense line if possible, or at least take control of the area around Olten to block Germany's progress routes in the Jura mountains."[13]

The "key figure in the entire cooperation endeavor"[14] was Samuel Gonard, who was detailed as a training officer to the *Ecole supérieure de Guerre* in Paris from 1934 to 1936, where he was able to establish trusting relationships that facilitated cooperation between the two armed forces. Unfortunately not much is known about Gonard's actual part in the scheme. The documents contain very little direct evidence because Gonard chose not to put anything in writing. Even after the war, when he was corps commander, he refused to give any information on the issue, writing in 1963 that he had pledged secrecy to the General about a number of activities. As Guisan never relieved him of this obligation, he felt that he had made a lifetime commitment and was not willing to reveal anything, adding, "Because for me this is a matter of ethics and of my conscience."[15]

It would be wrong to assume that only French-speaking officers from western Switzerland were concerned with, or showed understanding of, the issue of cooperation with France. The leading staff officers prior to the war, Chief of the General Staff Labhart and his two Assistant Chiefs of Staff, Frick and von Erlach, who were all Swiss Germans, favored preparing for some type of cooperation on a theoretical operational level; however, for reasons of preserving neutrality they strictly opposed precautionary agreements with any side.

Another Swiss German officer, Oskar Germann, admitted that he had also "suggested preparing for the delicate and difficult task of cooperation as early as in September [1939] by asking Colonel Logoz, who was a special advisor to the General on legal and political issues, pertinent questions in Bern."[16]

During the first weeks of the war, when the Swiss Army was still in the "neutrality positions," Labhart wrote the General to propose considering a military convention with France. In his analysis, Labhart wrote, "[Because] we do not have sufficient troops to create operational and strategic reserve units, which prevents us from adding the necessary depth to our defense lines, the question should be studied from the outset whether we should not prepare a military convention [with France]. This convention would be submitted to the French Commander-in-Chief as soon as Germany began hostilities [against us] and would call for French troops to relieve the Swiss ones on a sector of the planned front line. In order to be able to carry out this substitution as fast as possible and in order to avoid mixing troops, the sector along the Jura should be proposed, whereby about three of our divisions would become available for other tasks and the front would be firmly established there. Support from the air force and the anti-aircraft defense would also be very useful."[17]

During October 1939, Labhart referred on several occasions in his diary to instructions that he had issued to prepare for cooperation with neighboring states; however, the contingencies tended to be drafted in a way that they were applicable to both the French and the German side. On October 4, he ordered Assistant Chief of Staff Frick "to immediately instruct Colonel Germann to come up with draft proposals for military conventions."[18] The following day he personally discussed the order with Germann, demanding that the matter be addressed without further delay with the legal advisors in charge, but that it be handled with "utmost confidentiality."[19] A little later, Chief of the General Staff Labhart informed Guisan about his instructions, writing, "Colonels Germann and Logoz shall establish the framework of the agreements. No other staff shall be involved with the project for the time being."[20]

During the last week of October, Logoz submitted to Labhart a draft proposal for a military convention, "plus an exposé on the military aspects of such a convention that was written by Colonel Germann."[21] Colonel Logoz was instructed to forward the two important documents to the General the same day. Unfortunately, Logoz' draft convention appears to be missing, as it could not be found at the Federal Archives; but Germann's detailed study on the military aspects of a convention with the Western Allies for Case North, dated October 24, has been preserved.[22] Labhart discussed the documents with Chief of Operations von Erlach and with the two authors, insisting that Case West, calling for a convention with Germany, be "dealt with at the same time."[23]

Federal Councilor Etter, standing in for Head of the Military Department Minger, who was on vacation at the time, was also informed about this part of the preparations for foreign cooperation. The General jotted on the front page of the study, "Informed Mr. Etter about the preliminary work for convention. When ready, will present to him. 31/10/1939."

In his analysis, Germann assumed that any infringement of Switzerland's neutrality and sovereignty by a belligerent party would make Switzerland the natural ally of the opposing party, leading "inevitably to military, political, and economic cooperation." However, he added, even if fast and frictionless cooperation was crucial and even if the Swiss and their potential ally "in large part shared a common fate," concluding a military convention in advance was out of the question because of Switzerland's neutrality. Nevertheless, preparations should be made to facilitate cooperation if the situation became critical. Therefore, "drafts of conventions, proposals, and supporting documents [should] be prepared that can be transmitted to the partner without delay whenever the need arises." Germann's analysis was very detailed and precise, containing all the principal information that Barbey took into account during his later contacts with Garteiser. General Guisan and Labhart reviewed the study and made annotations. Further, Gonard, the General's operational advisor, made substantial remarks, in some instances agreeing with and in other places questioning or rejecting Germann's ideas.[24]

According to Germann, the provisions to be made in view of potential assistance by France included the following points:[25]

1. A written draft of a military convention (the General remarked on this point, "we have to move ahead with this");
2. information on the structure of the Swiss Army and its strategy for Case North, including maps and copies of decisions and orders;
3. a proposal for the French to take over a sector of the western front (the General added, "probably Basel–Gempen?");
4. a request for support from the air force and the anti-aircraft defense (the General commented, "most urgently fighter planes. Without indicating our bases.");
5. a request for allocation of heavy artillery, indicating the number of required batteries (Guisan remarked, "count by groups or regiments, not by batteries");
6. information on preparations made, especially overview of the capacity of roads, railways, and train stations for transporting and receiving arriving troops.

In order to make the French troops' job easier, the Swiss would make available a sufficient number of relevant maps. Germann added, "As for the maps, one should study the possibility of having our 1:100,000 scale maps printed with woods colored in green, which is what French officers are used to" from their own maps, whose scale was 1:250,000. When Barbey took up this suggestion later to discuss it with the army staff, Chief of the General Staff Huber opposed printing the special maps because storing them would "take up a lot of space and thus become conspicuous." Hence, Huber decided to wait and bring up the issue with the national mapping agency only if tensions reached a high level.[26]

Germann believed that the French troops stationed west of Basel would be able to "occupy the sector near Liestal, including especially the strategically important Gempen Plateau, within a few hours, or at least as fast as it would take the Germans to cross the Rhine and to overcome the border troops' resistance." Since it was expected that a French army corps would take over the planned sector of the front in a timely manner, "it should suffice to position one of our battalions at the Gempen Plateau if Case North goes into effect in order to shield this important base against a surprise attack until the French troops arrive." Gonard challenged this assumption, writing in his comments that it was questionable that the French would agree to take over a sector of the Swiss front line only when it had already been attacked. This was an operation, Gonard wrote, which would not fit their strategic doctrine and which they would "not be keen on" carrying out, adding, "This would also lead to a certain scattering of their forces if they are preceded by a fierce opponent. They will have to be persuaded of this operation."[27] The task of convincing the French that it was possible to take over the assigned sector of the front only once hostilities had broken out was probably part of the mission that Barbey sought to accomplish in his talks with Garteiser.

The question of a joint supreme command in case of outside assistance was a separate problem. Ernst thinks that this "delicate question" must have been excluded during the talks, as Barbey did not mention it in his diary.[28] However, because Barbey discussed with Garteiser the provisions outlined by Germann in his study, and because the two liaison officers maintained a trusting relationship, there should be no reason to doubt that the question of the supreme command was also discussed.

Germann viewed an Allied Supreme Command as a prerequisite for joint military operations, writing, "We have to acknowledge from the beginning that there is a need for a unified supreme command. We also have to accept as a matter of fact that a representative of the large Allied Armed Forces will hold the supreme command, particularly since we have no reason to question their abilities. The only question is how much autonomy our own commanders will preserve." Even if "rationally speaking" there should in principle "be no disagreement" about the usefulness of a unified supreme command, it was possible that "opinions [might] diverge on details of its execution." Germann continued, "Should the supreme command be allowed to use the Swiss Army as it pleases? Reservations are due in this place that are based on the restrictions imposed on our own General by the military rules and regulations, according to which he has to adhere to the 'final goal' established by the Federal Council's instructions, which are in turn based on article 204 of the military rules and regulations. Even an Allied Supreme Command will be allowed to use the Swiss Army only for the tasks outlined by the political authorities who are in charge of our country. However, the Federal Council can and will of course adapt its instructions to new circumstances, making it possible to grant justified requests of the Allied Supreme Command."[29]

Germann's study states that any decisions on what the Swiss Army should do in addition to supporting an Allied deployment would have to be left up to the supreme military command, whose standards the Swiss could not really question. He admonished, "[personal] sensitivity is out of place in this respect," adding, "Orders of the supreme command regarding the tasks of our army as part of the entire operation are binding. The General ensures that they are executed with loyalty and strictness. Moreover, he can be put under the command of an Allied Army Group that carries out operations in Switzerland and includes major Allied forces in addition to our army."[30] The Swiss General should under all circumstances keep the immediate command and remain the sole authority in personnel matters of his army, but by subordinating his command to the Allied Supreme Command he would have to forego the freedom of making his own operational decisions. Germann explained: "What matters after all is the common interest in the final victory, the means for which shall be determined by the supreme command, by whose decisions we shall abide."[31]

Swiss and Allied units should not be mixed together, Germann suggested, so that Switzerland's own troops would continually remain under the command of a Swiss officer, "because only their own commanders know the troops' mentality and will be able get them to perform according to their best abilities." In addition, the study stated that colonial troops would not be welcome for missions in Switzerland.[32]

Even though Germann was aware that, because of Switzerland's neutrality, taking up negotiations or concluding a formal convention would be dangerous, he nevertheless asked whether "it would not be possible [to obtain] reliable information in a less binding manner," explaining, "[since] the Allies also have an interest in our making preparations for cooperation and, more particularly,

in our facilitating deployment of their troops for that purpose, it is not excluded that they will respond positively even to an unofficial proposition in that
matter."[33] In other words, Germann insinuated that it would be very useful to
reach an accord that was as precise and binding as possible without actually
signing a military convention.

Unknown to Germann at the time he submitted his study, top secret talks
between the French and Swiss had in fact been going on for some time on the
personal initiative of General Guisan. In addition to the contacts established by
Petitpierre, as described earlier, Barbey had gone on a mission to Paris at the
General's behest on September 24 to meet with Lieutenant-Colonel Garteiser,
whom he knew from his earlier professional activities there. Barbey later wrote
about this mission, "My task on that day mostly consisted of . . . establishing
contact with Garteiser and of recording what he would tell me. I felt very much
at the time and am even more aware of it now that this was merely the beginning of an experiment and that everything was up in the air. As much as I trusted Garteiser, I was careful not to get entangled, nor did I believe that I was lay-
ing the basis for working together on a real joint study before I knew in what
way the General wanted these initial talks to continue."[34]

The major purpose of the meeting, which took place at the "Deuxième
Bureau" of the French intelligence service, was to examine in what manner, if
at all, France could intervene on behalf of Switzerland, and also to establish a
code system with which they could call each other for a meeting "in Paris, Bern,
or somewhere halfway between the two places." After their meeting, on
September 28, the two liaison officers rode together on the Orient Express to
Switzerland. The following morning they arrived in Lausanne, where Garteiser
wished to meet with the General, to whom he appeared to have unconventional access.[35]

Garteiser had already been in Switzerland on August 30; on the evening of
the General's election he had the opportunity to meet with Guisan at "Verte
Rive,"[36] undoubtedly to convey to him the congratulations of his superior,
General Georges. However, it is unlikely that this was simply a courtesy visit. It
seems obvious that the occasion was used to verbally establish procedures in
preparation for Swiss-French military cooperation.

A few days after the first contacts between the two liaison officers, Garteiser
was still in Switzerland. Following another meeting with the General, he told
Barbey at the army headquarters in Spiez that Barbey's report on their meeting
in Paris had met with Guisan's approval.[37] Several days later the General personally and formally confirmed his order to Major Barbey to continue his confidential liaison activities, giving him confidential instructions in the presence of
Masson and Gonard and telling him at the end, "I trust you. Take the first

opportunity to travel, and as soon as you are back I expect you to brief me."[38] When he was about to depart the meeting, Barbey had the impression that he was suddenly ushered into an adjacent room. Later he realized that Chief of the General Staff Labhart had arrived for a surprise visit and was not supposed to see him there, as neither the general staff nor the Federal Council were to find out about the secret contacts with the French Army Command.

It is uncertain whether Minger, the Head of the Military Department, knew about the cooperation talks with France, and if he did, to what extent.[39] After Barbey returned from one liaison mission to France, the General indicated that in principle the time had come to inform the army staff. He added, however, "It would be very easy if I could speak as openly with Labhart as I can with Minger, but that is impossible."[40] Wüst wrote that Federal Councilor Minger was not only informed but had in fact encouraged Corps Commander Guisan as early as 1938 to enter into contact with the French Army.[41] However, it is improbable that Minger was informed about the extent to which the preparations for cooperation had advanced—at least the cabinet as a whole was not aware of anything, as indicated by the uproar that erupted later when the French cooperation files were discovered at La Charité.[42]

At the time when Germann submitted his study for Case North, Barbey was on his second mission to France on the General's orders. On Monday, October 23 and Tuesday, October 24, he discussed with Garteiser in Paris six points that were going to be "'the first step'—an expression used by Gamelin— of possible assistance by France to Switzerland at its request"; the question of how to organize the supreme command must have been one of the issues. The two officers, who had met in Paris before the war, shared professional interests as writers and were now dealing with each other in new roles under the unusual circumstances of the war. The two sides were very respectful of each other, as "[for] the first version of points one to six the conditional [was] used to indicate that these [were] suggestions, and efforts [were] made to use choice polite phrases."[43] After the talks in Paris, Garteiser took Barbey on a reconnaissance tour to the front at the Sundgau to identify suitable locations for the two armies to join forces. Close to the border, in the woods at Neuwiller, Barbey discovered that the French had placed four heavy pieces of 240mm artillery that were "only slightly anchored in the ground and camouflaged" and were aimed at the bridges of Basel.[44]

Following the reconnaissance, Barbey briefed Gonard, and then the General, on his mission, submitting "[Twenty] handwritten pages containing the six points drafted together with Garteiser, our observations in the field, and our common and individual suggestions. I [submitted] them to the General, who [received] me without anyone else present, paying me his full attention when welcoming me. I read my report to him, giving additional explanations. I [left] him the manuscript, which [was] the only existing copy; the General will keep it in his own or in Gonard's desk drawer. I will destroy the draft." The General declared that he agreed "with the proposed measures, making reservations concerning a few details."[45]

For the following meeting, Garteiser traveled to Switzerland to visit the front sector at the Gempen with Barbey. On November 18, the two officers examined possible locations on the Swiss side for the two armies to join. Garteiser opted for "contact to be made close to Basel," at the "Rock of Hegenheim."[46] One French division was to occupy the rock, while another division was to advance toward the Gempen Plateau via Lützel and the Birsig valley, backed by a colonial cavalry brigade that was to establish contact between the two larger units. In order to be able to occupy the Gempen Plateau as rapidly as possible, reconnaissance units were to be deployed ahead of these troops. The first priority was for French troops, consisting of an entire army corps supported by heavy artillery, to take over the organization of the defense in the sector around the Gempen, including the Ergolz valley. Upon returning from Gempen, Barbey briefed the commander-in-chief at the command post in Gümligen on that first idea for a French plan of operations, "showing the General on the two 'Special Jura Maps', at a scale of 1:50,000, the movements of the two large French units as outlined by Garteiser in the field during our reconnaissance mission to the Gempen."[47]

At the beginning of December, General Guisan, Barbey, and Gonard undertook a reconnaissance tour of the border area at Basel and the Gempen Plateau in order to analyze the projected French sector of the front. Barbey wrote: "The General jokingly pronounces 'Plateau' the way the people from Basel do and 'Gempen' the way 'Père' Besson [Commander of the 3rd French Army Group] does. We get out [of the car] to reconnoiter on foot the locations in the sector between Liestal–Gempen gallery–Münchenstein where Army Group 3 recommended some work to be done and to examine the artillery observation points suggested by Garteiser. Close to the Rhine, it seems to us that the Hardwald is quite sparsely covered, as there are no barriers all the way to the log house on the river bank across from the German village of Grenzach." At the harbor of Kleinbasel they noticed a number of barges that had been blocked there since the beginning of the war, putting the crews out of work. Barbey remarked, "Those boats would be an easy means to cross over. They must be prepared for destruction, and so must the Wiese bridge. Inside Basel, there are now a good number of barriers that are well positioned. But is that sufficient?" In the afternoon, the group approached the village of Neuwiller in Alsace from Allschwil, around where the Swiss front was to be linked to the southern end of the Maginot line for the time being. Then they climbed on top of the water tower at the Bruderholz in order to get an overview of the Rhine plain and the foothills of the Vosges Mountains. Barbey concluded his diary entry on that reconnaissance trip by explaining that its main purpose had been to give the General "a clear picture in the field of the measures that should facilitate carrying out the French intervention that has in principle been agreed on."[48]

It appears that the special orders to the 3rd French Army Group, which was designated to enter Switzerland under General Besson with nine divisions and brigades, were issued as Instruction No. 3 by the French Supreme Command as early as October 8.[49] However, at that time the Swiss were not informed about the details of French troop formations nor about their plan of action. Barbey wrote in his diary in December that he had remarked to Garteiser, "The makeup of the so-called French Intervention Army has not yet been precisely determined. We express the desire that this be done soon."[50]

The two liaison officers met again on several occasions during the winter of 1939–40, sometimes in the presence of Gonard, during which they also went on trips to the field. In early January 1940, they explored defense lines at the Venoge, Mentue, and Paudèze creeks; in March at the Wigger, along Lake Sempach, at the Limmat, and at the mouth of the Aare River; and in April in the Entlebuch valley and in the Napf area. They also frequently revisited the Gempen area, where "Garteiser [received] a firsthand impression of the steady progress of the work that was undertaken to prepare emplacements for guns, for which they had provided us with the drawings."[51]

Concerning the deployment of the air force, General Guisan believed that it had to be sacrificed if necessary, saying, "It has to be used audaciously from the outset because for now we don't have the means to distribute the aircraft on the ground and cover them."[52] Garteiser commented that there was a high risk that Switzerland's best planes—Messerschmitts purchased from Germany— could be shot down by Allied fighter planes in the heat of battle because they might be confused with Luftwaffe aircraft of the same type.

To improve defenses in the air, Guisan ordered additional confidential negotiations to be held to obtain assistance from the Allied air forces. Because the British air force units stationed on the continent were not placed under the French Supreme Command like their ground troops but remained under their own command, these confidential talks had to be held with the British. The General entrusted Divisional Commander Hans Bandi, commander of the Swiss Air Force, with this task. In early 1940 Bandi contacted the British Air Attaché in Bern, Commander F. W. F. West, in order to secure assistance by the Royal Air Force should the need arise. Most Swiss files containing documents relating to this cooperation were destroyed; however, the relevant British files are kept at the Public Record Office in London.[53] Peter A. Marti has written a conclusive article on the subject.[54]

Bandi reassured the British Attaché that "several aerodroms [sic] had been prepared also with the view that [they] could be utilized by the Allies." Bandi emphasized during his contacts that neither the Swiss general staff nor any staff member of the British embassy were to be informed about the subject of the talks, which had to remain "strictly within British walls."[55]

It appears that the British were not informed about the arrangements with France. Separate reconnaissance missions were made to identify possible aerodromes for French fighters. During the winter of 1939–40, Captain Sandoz, who was aide-de-camp and later first adjutant to the General, and who was vaguely informed about the cooperation talks with France, studied together with Barbey the conditions for aircraft movements at Witzwil on the plain east of Lake Neuchâtel. The terrain was considered to be suitable, and Barbey indicated that orders for setting up a temporary aerodrome would be issued.[56]

In February 1940, Gonard went to see the commander of Swiss Border Brigade 3, Colonel Du Pasquier in Neuchâtel, to inform him of the cooperation project. The university professor from Neuchâtel wrote about the meeting in his diary: "On our side, there are only four people who are informed: the General, Lt.-Col. Gonard, Major Barbey, and myself. Neither the general staff, nor the 2nd Army Corps must be informed at this time. We must be careful not to cause any friction so the Germans won't be able to claim that we are violating our neutrality."[57]

Du Pasquier was informed that he would be put in command of an ad hoc "Gempen" division, which would be responsible for defending that sector until the French arrived. Ten days later, the General personally confirmed to Du Pasquier his "possible mission to hold the Gempen Plateau in case of a German attack." Du Pasquier wrote: "[The General] tells me, 'I cannot allocate to you any means of transportation in advance because the general staff is unaware of the instructions that I have given you after establishing contact with the French Supreme Command. Therefore, you will have to manage with what you have!' I reply, 'So I will get the taxis of the Marne,' and he agrees. I tell him that I will do all I can."[58] Du Pasquier was very pleased about the exciting role with which he was entrusted should the storm break out, calling the mission "magnificent and interesting."[59]

During some of the succeeding meetings between Barbey and Garteiser, Du Pasquier was also present. He met the French liaison officer on March 26, 1940 at "Point Albert" on the border, writing about the meeting, "[Garteiser] gave Barbey an envelope containing studies and instructions by the [Main

Headquarters] of [Army Group 3], which I read in bed when I was back home; they are fascinating." Du Pasquier noticed that the French were very well informed about the situation of the Swiss and were willing to deploy 27 batteries of artillery to the Ergolz valley and the Gempen.[60] Three weeks later the three officers met once again, that time at Damvant.[61]

After going on reconnaissance tours, Garteiser sometimes went to see the General at the army headquarters in Gümligen. He was always dressed as a civilian, and nobody knew who he was except for the few officers who had been in contact with him. He was usually brought into Gonard's private quarters first, and even though he was a welcome visitor he was never invited to sit at the General's table.[62] During one of Garteiser's visits, Barbey wrote that the General was "in great shape, vigorous, beaming." The French officer expressed his admiration for Guisan, calling him a "great leader" and explaining after the meeting that it was regrettable that France did not have a similar commander-in-chief as a trump card.[63]

Toward the end of October 1939, Colonel Oskar Germann, the author of the draft for Case North, was ordered "to personally brief [the General] on the study for cooperation with the Western Allies at Gümligen Castle." Germann later wrote: "During the meeting, which lasted a little over half an hour, the General and I were all by ourselves; he asked me various questions and then said that he agreed. The reason for calling me into this meeting was probably the fact that he had already initiated, through Barbey, contact with French command posts."[64] Germann, who was opposed to direct preliminary talks with potential allies due to Switzerland's neutrality policy, was not let in on the confidential contacts. It was not until early November that Barbey received a copy of Germann's study, about which he wrote, "I am extremely pleased to see that this study, which uses exquisite military, legal, and . . . moral judgment, is based on principles that are very similar to those that Garteiser and I try to apply."[65]

Based on Germann's study, an army staff task force led by legal advisor Logoz was instructed to draft the provisions of a detailed military convention. Masson, Head of the Military Intelligence Section, informed Barbey on November 1 that he had been told to ask him to participate in that project "to have one common denominator for both tasks, and that is you." Barbey reflected, "Whatever happens, I will have to keep secret from the army staff the order that the General has given me. This is the condition *sine qua non* for it to succeed, at least for the time being. Masson agrees."[66]

From that moment on, Barbey played two roles at once. In the secluded, "comfortable, quiet Villa Reichen" in Langnau in the Emme Valley, where the army staff had its quarters since mid-October 1939, he participated in the official staff project; however, his thoughts remained primarily focused on the unofficial "Garteiser channel." Barbey wrote, "In the footsteps of Germann's study I elaborated the points that are connected like the studies that I was working on with Garteiser."[67]

Barbey had the delicate task of continually playing two tunes at once: on one hand, as the General's secret liaison officer, he was responsible for maintaining confidential contacts with the French Supreme Command; on the other hand, he had orders to cooperate with Germann and Logoz to make the preparations that the general staff deemed permissible for neutral Switzerland. Hence, he had the difficult and fascinating assignment to reconcile in an inconspicuous manner, with different methods, two projects that had similar goals. He accomplished this mission with an almost schizophrenic virtuosity. The arrangement to have a "common denominator" was artistic and simple at the same time; however, it could only work under the condition that those who were informed kept quiet and that utmost secrecy was maintained on both sides. Barbey said about his double role that the "amassing of more or less interrelated activities" forced him "to make breakneck moves like a quick-change artist."[68] He remained extremely discreet even when he dealt with high commanders. When he visited Divisional Commander Guillaume Favre at his sickbed in Merligen, he was asked whether the top military command had contemplated establishing contact with the Allies. He did not respond, pretending not to hear the question.[69]

General Guisan kept himself informed on a regular basis on the progress of the cooperation groundwork accomplished both by the army staff and by Barbey on his special mission. Even though the Swiss files were all destroyed, not everything about the accomplished work is speculation. The unwavering Germann gave a surprisingly precise account of his part, one that is more detailed than Barbey's. Because it is likely that thanks to Barbey's role as a coordinator, most of the results achieved by the army staff on the official project were brought into the confidential arrangements with the French, one can assume that Germann's propositions regarding France's fast, effective military intervention were actually agreed to in the form of commitments.

Germann stated: "I prepared the proposals for military cooperation including all necessary related documents. They dealt with the issue of the supreme command and the autonomy of our commanders within this framework; the urgent need for long-term resistance and offensive power by the air force and the anti-aircraft defense, tanks and heavy artillery; establishing the areas of operation including transportation facilities, authority as a police force, and requisitions in our country; information on available means, the structure of our army and its rearward formations. . . . The main considerations were the prospect of success and the attempt to avoid, as far as possible, mixing units and to clearly define the command. From these we derived propositions for the Allies to take over a sector of operations and to receive the required means of combat; for assigning the command, the rearward areas, and means of transportation. Moreover, we prepared meticulously precise technical material in order to allow the potential ally to intervene fast and effectively, such as maps with air force bases, indicating which ones were designated for use by its own air force, detailed maps of railroad and road networks available for deploying troops and sending supplies, artillery observation points in the sector assigned to the ally, reconnaissance of sectors for allied artillery that might be assigned to us. And of course the prepared material included maps with signed and unsigned copies of the combat order for our army. The proposals were concise, using terminology and map symbols that were familiar to the concerned officers; separate ones were drafted for the supreme command, for the air force, for the ground troops, for the commander of the army group designated for immediate cooperation, and often they were further classified within a command unit according to the level of urgency. The documents were to be submitted in advance to the respective command posts by carefully selected liaison officers if the need arose."[70]

The direct cooperation contacts with France were carefully hidden from Marcel Pilet-Golaz, who was Federal President in 1940 and became Switzerland's foreign minister after Federal Councilor Motta's death. Pilet-Golaz wished to gain insight on the preparations for cooperation when he began his tenure as president. His official request reached Guisan in a rather unusual way, Pilet-Golaz telling Colonel Logoz, who told Barbey, who in turn informed the General. The commander-in-chief granted the request.[71] Guisan mentioned the president's visit in his postwar report, writing that Pilet-Golaz listened to a briefing in Langnau, "which he approved."[72]

In Langnau, Logoz and Barbey (Huber being absent) received the president in the chief of the general staff's reception room. Logoz read the complete draft of the convention, and Barbey summarized "a part of the notes containing our suggestions and questions pertaining to military issues, without going into detail nor giving technical information."[73] The Federal President asked "two or three relevant questions" and had a few changes made to the text. At the same time, he insisted that "analogous studies be undertaken in parallel in view of cooperation with Germany."[74] Hence, Pilet-Golaz, who as foreign minister was the ultimate authority in matters of Switzerland's cooperation with foreign powers, did not obtain all the information about the preparations with France, being briefed only about the official work by the army staff but being left in the dark about the arrangements that had actually already been made with the French Supreme Command.

Given the twisted situation, errors were bound to occur. Consequently, rumors were not long in coming about Swiss cooperation with the Western Allies. High-ranking German officers believed even before the war that "Switzerland had concluded a military agreement with France directed against Germany."[75] In November 1939, a French detachment which appeared to belong to the forward troops of the proposed intervention unit requested to be admitted into the country at the border in the Leimen valley because they thought they had to protect the city of Basel against a German surprise attack. Labhart wrote about that incident in his diary: "Colonel Frick reports that according to information just received by the 2nd Army Corps a French column has arrived at the border, its commander explaining to our guards that he had to march into Switzerland to assist us. The telegram sent in by the 2nd Army Corps states that French officers explained that the deployment of French troops to the border was part of an exercise. However, the French, especially the reconnaissance officers, display a rather uninhibited behavior all along our border, which is not the best thing for our neutrality and which could give the opposite side ideas."[76] Another blunder occurred after the beginning of Germany's western campaign, when on the morning of May 15, 1940, at a time of utmost tension, a French reconnaissance unit asked to be let into the country near Lucelle, claiming that the Germans were attacking Basel and therefore they had instructions to advance to the Gempen Plateau.[77]

The Germans did indeed react. Germany's envoy to Switzerland, Otto Carl Köcher, raised the issue of rumors about arrangements between the Swiss and French armies when he met Pilet-Golaz to congratulate him on his assignment as foreign minister. After the meeting he reported to Berlin, "Pilet replied by insisting emphatically that he had asked to receive exact information on the measures taken until now [by the] army staff when he began his tenure as Federal President at the beginning of January. There were no arrangements whatsoever to which Germany could object. He did not deny that Swiss officers had personal contacts with French officers, but the same was true for Swiss German officers; most particularly, [he said that] the general staff of the Swiss sympathized with the German side. . . . Moreover, Pilet asserted that Swiss politics were not made by the military but by the civil authorities appointed to do so through the constitution."[78] Köcher concluded his report by indicating that the statements by the Federal President were "official reassurances in nature" that were deemed reliable.

During the first week of April 1940, the German Military Attaché took up the issue as well, telling Berlin, "Recently there have even been claims that General Guisan met with General Gamelin last month. The Ambassador and myself do not think that this information is credible. Hanesse [the air force attaché], however, who is not very interested in the Swiss to begin with, is convinced that it is true. . . . When you consider all the hearsay, it appears to be very possible that certain talks were held between Swiss and French military people. However, they can only have dealt with French assistance in case of a German attempt to march through Switzerland, which is still considered to be a possibility here."[79]

While attending a surgeons' convention in Berlin at the end of March 1940, Swiss Divisional Commander E. Bircher met with Colonel-General von Brauchitsch, Commander-in-Chief of the German Army, among others, and acting on General Guisan's orders, denied allegations of Switzerland having made any arrangements with France, saying, "There is nothing true about circulating rumors regarding cooperation."[80] As the rumors persisted, Germany's ambassador once again brought up the topic in a meeting with Pilet-Golaz. The answer he received now was even more reassuring than the first. The "Federal President underlined several times during the conversation that no military or political agreements at all had been made with France, as officially declared on the previous occasion."[81]

In spite of all denials, the contacts between Barbey and Garteiser continued as intensively as before. There are several indications that the talks held between France and Switzerland were more trusting, and the agreements regarding intervention were at least as far-reaching as those France made with Belgium and Holland, the two neutral countries attacked by Germany in May 1940 under the pretext that they cooperated with the Allies. Garteiser had complained to Barbey about Belgium's lack of cooperation as early as the fall of 1939, stating, "If the others up there on the left . . . you know who I mean, if the Belgians were as kind and did what we do with you, there would be one less thing to worry about."[82] General Georges also criticized the Belgians' unwillingness to communicate by telling Barbey in early 1940, "You cannot imagine the difficulties we had which prevented us from entering into contact with the Belgians until mid-January. Unfortunately, one cannot say that the situation has improved since then."[83]

Preparations by the army staff for possible cooperation with Germany, as had been suggested by Federal President Pilet-Golaz, had only second priority and were undertaken much later. Colonel Germann, who had to analyze Case West as well, wrote in his memoirs, "The study containing proposals for cooperation with the German Wehrmacht was concluded in March 1940."[84] That study, which is dated April 9, 1940, was almost as voluminous as the one on Case North and included a basic analysis of the circumstances that would have to be taken into account for cooperation with troops of the Third Reich if 'Case

West A' or 'Case West B' had to be applied.[85] In his introduction, Germann wrote in an almost apologetic tone, "In the event of an attack by the Western Allies we would naturally request assistance by Germany, just as we would consider the Western Allies to be our given allies in case of a German attack. Of course in both cases cooperation would only be possible under the condition that we obtain the necessary guarantees for our independence and territorial integrity as proposed in the draft of a military convention."[86]

Since for political reasons Switzerland could enter into contact with the National Socialists only after an attack had been launched or when "the Federal Council [considered] an attack to be imminent with certainty," preparations for cooperation had to be made without directly involving the potential partner, just as it had been stipulated by the army staff for Case North. Germann indicated that the principal problems would be the same as in the case of cooperation with the Western Allies. They included measures on the organizational level to facilitate German operations in Switzerland by such measures as information, reconnaissance, lodging, and the definition of its authority as a police force. There would also be a need for a unified supreme command while leaving the Swiss officers in charge of their own units; however, putting the Swiss Army under the command of a German Army Group should "be avoided as much as possible" but could not be excluded, especially if a large number of German troops would be engaged. Successfully defending the entire western front from Basel to the French-Italian border in the Alps, Germann calculated, would require 18 to 20 divisions, not including reserve troops. The Swiss Army had nine divisions at its disposal, which meant that it was nine to eleven divisions, or three to four army corps, short; in other words, at least one full German army would have had to come to Switzerland's assistance. The Germans would have been assigned the "northern half of the front, from Basel down to about the western edge of the Franches Montagnes–Lake Biel" as the sector to be defended by them. In addition, they would have been expected to support the Swiss Army with heavy artillery, aircraft, antiaircraft defense, and antitank defense.[87]

Germann noted that the operational questions would be more complex than in Case North because the General had left two possibilities, 'Case West A' and 'Case West B,' open for possible troop deployment. Therefore he thought it was useful to prepare "two completely separate files" to facilitate possible assistance from Germany, adding, "It will be up to the General to decide which of the two cases he wants to apply before Germany's cooperation is requested; hence, the decision will be made independently from the German Supreme Command's decisions. Documents relating our internal preparations should not be shown to them afterwards if they do not serve as a basis for their own decisions. Consequently, it is useful to also treat the two cases separately with regard to preparing orders."[88]

Even though Germann's study of Case West is quite detailed about several theoretical operational options, it appears to be somewhat less well researched than Case North, as though it had been done reluctantly. Moreover, it is striking that the text was not annotated either by the General or by Gonard—an indication that the army command did not pay much attention to the study and that no one made a critical analysis of it. The impression remains that a conscientious exercise was made for its own sake; no one was willing to identify with the study, and it was simply filed. Nevertheless, in early 1940 it was considered whether Major Berli should be asked to work out the details of issues relating to the general staff that were raised in the study.[89]

Berli was considered to be pro-German and was an expert on the Wehrmacht, as he had been detailed there before the war. Ernst wrote about Berli's task in connection with Case West, "In order to maintain a balance [of measures] our army command intended to establish contacts with the command of the German Armed Forces as well. However, it seems that these contacts did not progress very far."[90] The Swiss Army Command was very hesitant in this respect, as indicated in instructions that von Erlach, who had been promoted to chief of the Operational Section at the beginning of 1940, issued to Germann, stating, "The General has decided that Major Berli shall be informed only once he has made a decision on Case West. The proposals will be submitted to the General by mid-week, after discarding the idea of a front line along the Sarine river in favor of the one along the Mentue creek."[91] These words suggest that at the beginning of February 1940, Berli was not yet informed about a possible task in connection with Case West.

Berli's involvement remained within the framework of the official activities of the army staff; no confidential contacts were established that resembled those maintained by Barbey with French commanders. There are no indications, even in German documents, that such contacts existed, and Berli himself never made any statement on the subject. In his report on cooperation preliminaries, Barbey wrote about Berli's part: "In accordance with Colonel Germann, and in order to have a uniform structure for all files, Major Berli was authorized to consult the files that were prepared for France."[92] It should be clear that the files in question were only those prepared by the army staff as part of its normal work, not the ones dealing with Barbey's confidential contacts.

During the week before Easter 1940, Barbey once again went to France on the General's orders to have separate talks, in the presence of Garteiser, with Generalissimo Gamelin in Vincennes and with Generals Georges, Besson, and Daille at their respective command posts. Georges, who was commander of

France's northeastern front sector at that time, emphasized the "utmost importance" of the Gempen Plateau and expressed his satisfaction about the steady
progress of preparations there, adding, "On these hills the cooperation of our
two armies has to be sealed and worked out in every detail." Sending his best
regards to the Swiss commander-in-chief, he told Barbey, "And please tell
General Guisan to save some of the Lavaux wine for later that I had been
offered to drink before at 'Verte Rive'."[93]

The Gempen Plateau was also the main discussion topic with General
Besson. The commander of French Army Group 3 marked the positions on a
map where he wanted to have barriers and gun-emplacements built "in the
Gempen sector."[94] Later on, Garteiser gave Barbey technical data on 155mm
howitzers and an envelope containing the "measurements for the pill-boxes designated for the 75mm cannon."[95] General Guisan took note of the drawings
and had Gonard forward them confidentially to Prisi, the commander of the
2nd Army Corps. Under Prisi, at times "more than 1,000 men were busy building concrete structures" at the Gempen.[96] There is no doubt that Switzerland's
defensive measures in the area of the Gempen Plateau were carried out according to French plans.

It seems that Barbey's activities as a liaison officer with Garteiser did not
render Gonard's personal involvement in the cooperation talks unnecessary.
When Barbey briefed the General on his pre-Easter mission to Paris, Guisan
talked about "the usefulness of sending Gonard on a mission to France" but was
afraid of the "risks because such a trip would not go unnoticed."[97] As it turned
out, Gonard, the General's closest collaborator, was able to go on a mission after
all, as an opportunity presented itself for him to accompany a group of officers
invited to visit French Army Group 2 at the front in Lorraine.

The mission, which took place from April 17 to the 24th, was directed by
Colonel Montfort, a training officer, who was accompanied by three other
members of the general staff, Lieutenant-Colonel Gonard, Captain E. Widmer,
and Captain A. Schenk.[98] Gonard was to cross the border on the 17th by himself to join the rest of the team the following day in Paris.[99] The General commanded the participants not to say or write anything about their order to any
military or civilian individual or body.[100] No reports or notes were to be written. The head of the mission was instructed to brief the commander-in-chief
orally on April 30. A note for the file later specified that all files on the mission
to the western front had been destroyed on the General's orders.[101]

In spite of these instructions, there is a 30-page handwritten mission
report, of which five pages were written by Gonard on artillery-related matters,
and the rest which Montfort undoubtedly wrote on the General's orders after
briefing him. In the introduction, the report mentions that it was drafted in

accordance with verbal orders from the General,[102] implying that Guisan had instructed Montfort to leave out anything that had to do with the cooperation issue. The report contains detailed information on field fortifications, defense strategies, antitank and antiaircraft defense, command matters, and a lack of discipline, stating, "Frankly, the troops' uniforms, the internal service, and the care of their horses were bad"; however, it does not say one word about possible military cooperation. Nevertheless, talks are sure to have been held on that subject, at least by Gonard, because as Barbey noted on a meeting with Gonard after the mission returned home, "We compare the information that he was able to obtain during his trip to France with my own, and they are one hundred percent the same."[103] It is uncertain if Montfort was let in on the preparations for cooperation without participating in the talks held by Gonard. The fact that he was named head of the Swiss liaison team at the beginning of Germany's western campaign suggests that he was informed about the cooperation arrangements.

In regard to military cooperation with France, Germann had pointed out early on that there would be a need for liaison officers to be sent to the staff of the French intervention forces with the necessary documents in case of a German attack. A few days before Christmas 1939, Germann discussed the issue with Barbey, on which the latter noted, "[Germann] thinks that the moment has come to designate the liaison officers who would be detailed to the major units of the French Army on 'T' Day. He asked me to propose candidates, since they would mostly be Swiss French officers, and to prepare some sort of 'course' that should take place in February, before the expected large-scale offensive. Germann believes that the Wehrmacht will go on the offensive."[104] In early 1940 the staff assembled a tentative list of officers who would be ordered to enter into contact with Gamelin's general headquarters, the command of Besson's army group, and the army and air force staff immediately after the eruption of hostilities. General Guisan, who knew all the proposed officers personally, approved their selection.[105]

When the Swiss Military Intelligence Service reported a massing of German troops in the Black Forest at the beginning of the western offensive on May 10, 1940, an attack on Switzerland was considered imminent. Hence, Barbey was instructed by Chief of the General Staff Huber to call the proposed liaison officers for Case North for a briefing. The following eleven officers were concerned, most of whom were members of the general staff:

> Colonel Montfort, Army General Staff
> Colonel von Tscharner, office of the General's Adjutant
> Lieutenant Colonel von Muralt, 2nd Army Corps staff

Lieutenant Colonel Borel, 2nd Army Corps
Major Barbey, on the Army General Staff
Major Spahr, Railway Officer in the 1st Army Corps
Captain R. Frick, Army General Staff
Captain E. Primault, Air Force and Anti-Aircraft Defense staff
Captain Boissier, Training Officer on the General Staff
Colonel von Kalbermatten, commander of the base in Sion
Colonel Morand, office of the General's Adjutant.

They all met at the army headquarters in Langnau, where Barbey first told them that "they were to accomplish, in case of a war, a special, confidential mission on which they would at the present time not receive any further information, and that they should verbally and confidentially notify their commanders in person."[106]

The concerned commanders had to know that they would not have these officers available in case of war. Barbey wrote about this briefing in his diary: "Montfort, who is the highest-ranking officer and who would serve as head of mission if hostilities broke out, has asked me to hold a first briefing. My notes are ready: designation [of our officers] to the various levels of the French command, means of transportation, means of communication, amount of money available to each of them, etc., and not forgetting some information of psychological nature."[107] Afterward Barbey held individual or group briefings with the designated officers at the "Reichen Villa" in Langnau to inform them about the scope of the special confidential missions.

For ten days, May 15–25, the liaison officers were stationed in the border areas where they were to receive the French troops in case of an intervention. On the evening of May 14, expecting a German attack the following night, the General signed "individual mission orders for each liaison officer," which had been prepared by Barbey.[108] Barbey himself moved his quarters from Langnau to the Bristol Hotel in Bern, from where it was easier for him to maintain contact with the General in Gümligen and with the officers in the field. The cooperation files of the army staff, containing agreements, lists, and maps, which had been kept in a fireproof safe in Langnau until then, were put in a large suitcase—which Barbey called "the treasure chest"—and transported by car further west to the private home of an acquaintance near Neuenegg.

The binder containing the files of Guisan's confidential contacts with the French Supreme Command had been transferred from Gümligen to Montcherand, the private property of the Barbey family, the month before as a precautionary measure. The most important papers were kept in a sealed envelope, on which Barbey wrote, "In case that the undersigned passes away, please personally transmit this unopened envelope to General Guisan or Lieutenant-Colonel Gonard," and it was put in the family safe.[109]

Immediately after the beginning of the western campaign, on May 12, French liaison officer Garteiser traveled to Switzerland to meet with Petitpierre, Gonard, and Barbey in Fribourg. On the morning after the critical night of May 14–15, he again entered into contact with his Swiss counterparts. Garteiser, "who came and left like a whirlwind," reassured them that nothing would change regarding the plans of intervention, that in Army Group 3 not the slightest modifications were planned, and "in case of any change we would be notified." When the Swiss did not hear from the French officer for a few days, on May 17 Gonard was convinced that Army Group 3 had to have undergone "significant cuts" and that there was "no more Touchon Army that would be able to intervene on our behalf."[110]

On May 21, Barbey met Garteiser, who was bathed in sweat and who "carried an expression full of pain and worry on his face," at a secret location at the border in the Ajoie region. The French officer reported on the French defeat at the Meuse and its implications for the reserve troops that had been slated for deployment in Switzerland. Barbey remarked, "He was perfectly frank and did not try to embellish the picture," when he explained that the "terrible blow" in the north had made regrouping the army units necessary; hence, "Army Group 3 including the Touchon Army [has been] redeployed to the Aisne river. The 7th Army Corps [has been] withdrawn. Instead of this beautiful army corps we will only have a B-Series division which will form the 45th Army Corps together with a Polish division and a Colonial cavalry brigade." At least, he noted, its commander, General Daille, was a friend of Switzerland and was reliable.[111]

This information, according to which the French troops near the Swiss border were reduced and replaced by a corps with less fighting power, must have reached General Guisan on that same day, May 21. Consequently claims made by some that the French withdrew stealthily and abandoned the Swiss Army without informing it are incorrect. At another meeting, which took place three days later at the border, Garteiser explained to the Swiss liaison officer the structure of the 45th Army Corps, adding, "If you are attacked, the units will join your army at the indicated places with means that have been reduced to a minimum. As far as anyone can judge, they could not be reduced any further. . . . And then what? Either you will be able to resist, so everything will be ok; or else you will be forced to pull your troops back, but in what direction? Towards the Gotthard . . . or towards the Morvan?"[112]

When Barbey briefed the army command in Gümligen on this latest development, Gonard was quick to draw the operational conclusions, saying, "Our defense line will hold out for some time. Maybe it has already acted as a deterrent. The general situation has turned in such a way that we have to fathom not asking for, nor accepting, any French assistance; instead, we will have to base [our future strategy] on the Gotthard or on a National Réduit in a wide circle around it."[113] Hence, the key word "Réduit" [redoubt, or fortress], as outlined by Germann during the previous winter, was mentioned as early as a fortnight after the beginning of Germany's western offensive.

After General Weygand replaced Gamelin as the French Supreme Commander, Barbey received orders on June 5 to travel to Paris in order to attempt to meet with the new generalissimo. Guisan told Barbey, "This time I have fewer orders to give you than ever. You shall act according to the events and the atmosphere 'down there.' I do not personally know Weygand, but as soon as he is inclined to receive you, you will have to go see him, even more so if it is just a gesture. It is now or never that we can express our thankfulness to the French for the support that they offered us and prepared for us during better times. If we are attacked at the same time—the French in Alsace and we at our northern border—the two armies will have to join at our request as planned, even if they have only limited means available. However, if events take an unfavorable turn thereafter, you shall explain to them that we cannot determine in advance an established route for withdrawal. Do not say anything in that respect. Do your best. And do not forget that Weygand knows the case of Switzerland since accomplishing a mission to Bern in 1917."[114] This account shows how liberal General Guisan's orders were to Barbey, whose hands he shook "very warmly" when the liaison officer departed.

At Vincennes, where the French Supreme Command had its headquarters, Garteiser led Barbey into Weygand's office, which was sparsely furnished and resembled "a cell." The friendly but brief meeting resulted in Weygand's explanation, accompanied by hand movements expressing his regrets, that the way things had developed he could only promise deploying "at least one division."[115] At the same time, he offered a strategic piece of advice to be passed on to General Guisan, whom he said he would have liked to meet in person: "Multiply your anti-tank positions as we have been trying to do at a depth of 25 kilometers. But the terrain is much more favorable for you than it is for us. The bunkers that you have built will be the skeletons of those positions." When Barbey insisted that he wished the cooperation plans to remain secret, Weygand replied by saying, "I will do my best."[116]

During the days of Barbey's last visit to Paris, France's collapse had become practically a fact. The British Army had just evacuated the Continent from Dunkirk, the "Battle of France" was in full swing, and one week later German troops occupied the French capital. On June 8, Barbey returned to Bern and wrote a report on his mission, which he then brought to Gümligen. In his diary he noted, "This has without a doubt been my last report and my last trip to France for a long time, since I have received orders to assume the task of Chief of the Personal Staff as of Tuesday, June 11."[117]

Immediately after assuming his new position, Barbey had the opportunity to speak with General Guisan about the latest developments on the issue of cooperation, and to find out the General's view of the consequences that had to be drawn. In a memorandum on that meeting, drafted by Barbey, the General first mentioned the cooperation that had been planned, stating, "The issue of possibly requesting Allied cooperation in case of an attack on our territory has already resulted in a 'draft for a basic treaty' of legal nature and in notes of military nature, which contain a certain number of suggestions and requests for reinforcements in the event of cooperation. These notes were to be submitted, if the occasion should arise, to the Allied Command at the decision of the Federal Council."[118] These words indicate unambiguously that the Federal Council made the arrangements with France in the form of a tentative agreement that was subject to a request for intervention.

The memorandum continued by mentioning the two solutions that could be considered for putting up resistance: either requesting assistance from the Allies, if necessary, and cooperating with them by joining forces around Basel; or by fighting "to the utmost" with the Swiss Army's own means in the prepared positions. "Should a withdrawal have to be considered," the General suggested, "it could only be toward the center of the country. . . . In case we have to pull the troops back, the 'national réduit' at the St. Gotthard and in the Alps represents moral, historical, and traditional values."[119]

The General stated that in view of this situation, if cooperation with the Allies had to be renounced, only the second solution would be available, adding, "What matters most, though, is that the sense of the orders that I have issued shall not be modified by one bit; they instill into the Army its willingness to resist in its positions without thinking about retreating. I believe that carrying out these orders is currently our best guarantee. However, in case our resistance is broken in these positions, the choice between the two solutions mentioned above would be imposed on me by the development of the situation among the warring parties. Hence, I might have to approach the Federal Council with proposals in favor or against a request for cooperation with an Allied Army."[120] This passage makes clear that on June 13, the day before Paris fell, Guisan still considered French assistance to be possible despite all the setbacks they had suffered.

In the meantime, while defeat was looming over France, the Swiss cooperation files continued their odyssey. In Neuenegg, where they had been brought from Langnau, they no longer seemed to be safe considering the remarkable speed at which the Germans advanced. Chief of the General Staff Huber authorized their transfer to a place farther away from Bern and, hence, apparently less endangered. The choice fell on Wallenried Castle in the canton of Fribourg. Its owner, Albert de Castella, "a landed nobleman and cavalryman," who was acquainted with Barbey, helped find a suitable hiding place there: "a four-poster bed covered by a yellow curtain." In case of a red alert, the castle owner offered to sink the suitcase containing the files, the "treasure chest," in the pond.[121]

When France collapsed, the possibility of cooperation no longer existed. In his postwar report, General Guisan remarked, "When our country was facing a new situation toward the end of June 1940, after the German victory, Italy's entry into the war, and our being encircled by one single group of powers, I considered these files to be outdated and useless, so I ordered them destroyed."[122] There are conflicting accounts on the destruction of the files, which was not entirely successful. Barbey wrote a special report on it, saying that the files were destroyed on Huber's orders after the conclusion of the German-French armistice because there was no reason to keep them.[123] However, the files were in fact destroyed only three months later. On September 25, Captain on the General Staff Boissier reported to Chief of the General Staff Huber that the files of the "French-Swiss mission" had been destroyed as ordered.[124] Several dozen documents were listed one by one, among them the draft of the military convention. Huber noted about the issue, "[The files] should have been destroyed a long time ago. The whole matter was dealt with by the General's personal staff directly with the involved persons but apparently not with due care."[125]

The documents mentioned by Huber were undoubtedly the cooperation files prepared by the army staff. However, the additional files concerning the top secret special mission, which had been hidden at Montcherand, were destroyed as well. Barbey wrote, "When the army took up its positions in the Réduit, in July 1940, in order to adjust to the new situation, I returned the documents to the General, who decided to destroy them."[126] Consequently, the Swiss cooperation files as a whole were considered destroyed. However, there were some exceptions; a few documents were preserved because the original or a copy was unintentionally filed elsewhere. For instance, one of the documents listed as destroyed was Germann's study of Case North, the original of which was actually among the papers of the General's personal staff, as seen above.

In a confidential report in late summer 1940 on the preparations undertaken in connection with possible cooperation with France, Barbey only mentioned those carried out by the army staff on orders from Huber, without saying anything about his activities as the General's secret liaison officer and his arrangements with the French Army Command.[127] Hence, Barbey did not write anything that was not true, but what he said was less than half the truth. His statements served to cover up the facts.

In conclusion, one may say that internal preparations for cooperation with foreign powers in case of an infringement of Switzerland's independence are part of the legitimate tasks of a responsible army command in a neutral country. Taking precautions in order to guarantee military cooperation with an intervening army, which could be called for assistance if necessary, is a normal part of the army staff's activities. There is no real reason why tentative agreements should not be concluded with both parties at war in case of a conflict, without using secret diplomatic channels. Such open conventions could eliminate in advance misunderstandings regarding Switzerland's willingness to remain neutral and might at the same time serve as an additional deterrent.[128] Both sides would know clearly, by means of a pact, that as soon as Switzerland was drawn into the conflict it would no longer be neutral.

Guisan's risky cooperation contacts with the French Supreme Command, which began before the outbreak of the war, are understandable in view of the situation at the time. However, from a viewpoint of neutrality policy they are to some extent open to objection. Edgar Bonjour calls them "daring border cases" for a neutral state, which will always raise questions, even if they do not violate neutrality laws.[129] Corps Commander Labhart and later Federal Councilor Kobelt strictly rejected such contacts, considering them to be incompatible with Swiss neutrality. When Labhart was told by Colonel Logoz in November 1939, when he was still chief of the general staff, that General Guisan had said that "a telephone call from the border was all it would take" to alert General Gamelin and Georges, he immediately expressed "serious reservations about such a procedure because it would violate our neutrality and could hardly be kept secret." Both officers agreed that "the General's way of handling the issue [was] questionable and the consequences for our country [would be] alarming if the public found out about it."[130]

Labhart's successor, Huber, who was not fully informed about the confidential contacts with France, also had serious reservations about the cooperation plans, although he did not express them quite as sharply as Labhart.[131] In a confidential address to the army staff in 1942, the Head of the Military Department, Federal Councilor Kobelt, demanded that neutrality be adhered to in the strictest manner, adding that the Federal Government considered remaining neutral "an objective for the State, not just a means to an end."[132] When, after the war, he found out about the full scope of secret cooperation with the French Army, he called the General's arrangements "an act of anti-neutral behavior."[133]

Even if General Guisan's arrangements were made only as a precaution in case of a German attack, and under the condition that the Federal Council requested Allied assistance, the Germans could have used them as a pretext to take action against Switzerland under the claim that they constituted a serious infringement of Swiss neutrality. Guisan, who overstepped his authority, was undoubtedly aware of the risk he had taken, but apparently considered it to be the lesser evil. He accepted the responsibility for his actions, even though he may not have found it easy to bear. On all other occasions, the General had an indisputable understanding of neutrality and tried to adhere to it. In his instructions to the troops on how they were expected to apply neutrality he insisted that they not do anything while being on duty or off duty that could be interpreted as favoring a belligerent power, as anti-neutral in any way, or that would be incompatible with Switzerland's interests as a neutral state.[134]

Nevertheless, General Guisan did not consider neutrality an end in itself but as a foreign policy instrument to safeguard the country's independence. This view was formulated by State Law Professor Carl Hilty in the 19th century and coincided with that of von Sprecher, the Chief of the General Staff during World War I, who was Guisan's superior at that time. The creed "Switzerland does not exist because of neutrality but neutrality exists because of Switzerland" was advocated during the Second World War most particularly by the University of Basel.[135] Guisan viewed the Third Reich as a potential opponent quite early. Consequently, he took more serious precautions against invasion from the north than from the west. By doing so, the commander-in-chief may have had the right instinct but gave top military and political leaders grounds for criticism against him. When the Germans discovered the French copies of the military cooperation files at La-Charité-sur-Loire, they considered Switzerland's arrangements with France a serious violation of its neutrality.

10

The General's Personal Staff

EVEN THOUGH MOBILIZATION OF THE TROOPS was planned efficiently and carried out smoothly (except for the few minor incidents mentioned above), much less attention was paid to preparations for the army command; in fact, these preparations were quite insufficient. As Bracher explained, "Important steps had not been prepared at all," making the first workdays "not very satisfactory" for the staff that was called up on August 31, 1939.[1] Chief of the General Staff Labhart criticized his own work, writing, "The space is far too limited in the Federal Government Building to fit all staff members. Several gentlemen have to work in their lodgings, which makes it difficult to work efficiently. Wartime quarters will have to be prepared well in advance in the future, especially the telephone lines."[2]

The Staff Secretary, Lieutenant R. Eibel, who was designated the Commander-in-Chief's Head of Chancellory, was summoned to Bern by telephone on August 31 to immediately prepare the General's office. During the first four days, the General's office was set up at the Bellevue-Palace Hotel next to the Federal Government Building where "little or nothing had been prepared or organized; we did not even have typewriters available."[3] General Guisan also complained about this lack of organization, saying that he was completely without assistance and had to find his closest aides on his own. "In order to have somebody available right away," he recalled, "I called up my adjutant from the 1st Army Corps"; in addition, he used Scouts from Bern as guards and messengers at his temporary quarters, commending them later for their excellent work "as couriers and keeping pushy people out of my office."[4]

According to an ordinance dated January 4, 1938, on the organization of the army staff, a "General's office," consisting of five officers, including two adjutants, two aides, and a staff secretary, and additional auxiliary staff, was to be established whenever the armed forces were called to active duty. These five direct subordinates, who were joined by another staff secretary shortly afterward, were the General's closest collaborators during the first three weeks of wartime duty. The army staff had its quarters first in Bern and then transferred to Spiez on September 5, 1939.[5]

Implementing a "General's office" required that all command matters and decisions would be handled by the actual general staff in Main Section I, especially by its operational section.[6] However, General Guisan soon realized that he needed more staff, most particularly an experienced officer from the general staff who could advise him on operational and strategic issues. For this role, he chose Samuel Gonard, a graduate from the "Ecole supérieure de Guerre" in Paris who had just been promoted to lieutenant colonel and who had been working with Roger Masson in the Intelligence Service for some time. Gonard officially joined the General's office on September 20[7] as an officer dealing with matters pertaining to the general staff, but he had undoubtedly served as a confidential advisor prior to then.

Two weeks later, the commander-in-chief told his chief of staff in writing that he would expand his office because it was unorganized and understaffed. In addition, he changed its name to the "Personal Staff of the General" ("Etat-major particulier du Général") in order to reflect its function as a command unit. The leader of this personal staff, who was to organize and delegate the work for the General, was to be a high-ranking officer who could be assisted by additional general staff officers if necessary. Guisan told Labhart that he had selected Lieutenant-Colonel Gonard as the chief of his personal staff, who would henceforth have the same position and authority as the chief of staff of an army unit.[8] This decision was the basis for adding a new level of command structure to the Swiss Army, which Corps Commander Huber later criticized as "the root cause of the worst evil of the time of active duty" from 1939 to 1945.[9]

Chief of the General Staff Labhart, who had not been consulted on the matter, subsequently tried to cancel the formation of the personal staff, although he dutifully informed the commanders of the army units and the Military Department about the change.[10] In a seven-page letter to the General, Labhart expressed his opposition to setting up the new organ, explaining, "Please allow me to note that there is hardly any room for an additional body between the commander-in-chief and the chief of the general staff that studies the proposals submitted by the subordinate commanders or by the chief of the general staff. I would like to express my serious reservations, as interposing one or several officers between you and me could lead to a dangerous repetition of tasks and overlapping of responsibilities, which could have grave consequences."[11]

Handwritten annotations on Labhart's letter indicate that the General had the letter answered by his young collaborator Gonard, and that the latter was the main driving force behind the new body. Gonard remarked that, among other things, "Practical experience has shown the opposite [of Labhart's concerns] to be true," and later that, "This body is not supposed to be interposed between the General and the chief of the general staff but is placed next to the General." Gonard commented on Labhart's request to reconsider whether there was a need for a personal staff by writing, "This was well thought out and has turned out to be indispensable."[12]

Labhart did not succeed in convincing the General. In his response, which was also seven pages long, General Guisan explained that he considered the personal staff a working instrument that should analyze problems and write the drafts of his statements, decisions, and correspondence as commander-in-chief, thereby allowing him to focus on issues of more profound importance. He added that he considered it necessary to have on his side—"not between you and me"—officers "who are capable of not only understanding my intentions but also presenting them the way in which I want them to be presented."[13]

The General continued by explaining that his long experience as a commander of army units had allowed him to get "precise ideas" on how a commander-in-chief had to organize his work. He had no intention of disregarding either this valuable experience or the insight he had gained in 1916, when he was working for Chief of the General Staff von Sprecher. The idea that he might establish a position parallel to that of the chief of the general staff and in competition with him had "never crossed my mind." On the contrary, he said, "I would not like you to consider my collaborators as obstacles to harmoniously executing the command but as a vehicle that facilitates relations." Moreover, Guisan argued that a personal staff was common among several foreign armies and had passed the test of time there. At the end of the letter, the commander-in-chief told Labhart that he expected the chief of the general staff to come and see him in the future, not the other way around, and hoped that his explanation of the future organization of the supreme command was clear.[14]

A Swiss general is authorized to have a personal staff, as he has the right to establish the country's order of battle, and hence also to organize the army staff, as he wishes. Labhart did not intend to challenge this authority. However, by virtue of having a second staff unit, the direct contact between the commander-in-chief and the chief of the general staff was considerably reduced. Because, as of October, the headquarters of the army staff was located in Langnau in the Emme valley and the General's quarters were in Gümligen, 25 kilometers or at least 30 minutes away by car, most communication took place by way of written correspondence. Gümligen Castle was chosen as the General's command post at the suggestion of Adjutant-Major A. von Ernst. The decision in favor of this location was probably made because the General's aide, B. Barbey, was a nephew of the castle owner.[15] Labhart later wrote that separating the two quarters made "conditions for a responsible chief of the general staff unacceptable."[16]

The increase in tedious exchanges of letters and other written correspondence necessitated hiring additional personnel on both staffs. The General's personal staff included fifty men at one point; his closest collaborators included between five and twelve officers, while the auxiliary staff, such as office aides, kitchen personnel, and telephone and telegraph operators, consisted of an average of 30 to 35 men during the 2,180 days of war-time duty.[17] In addition, one infantry company was permanently on duty to watch the General's quarters; one platoon stood on guard, while the rest of the troops were engaged in training activities. At night they were reinforced by a pack of watchdogs. The members of the personal staff sometimes had to participate in practice alerts.

Compared with the rest of the army staff, the number of the General's personal staff was modest. The army staff increased more than sixfold within a year, from 408 at the outbreak of the war to 2,600 in the fall of 1940. The number of officers alone rose from 183 to 675.[18] Armin Meili, the director of the 1939 National Fair, who was called up in February 1940 to serve as an artillery colonel at the army headquarters in Langnau, wrote that he found "an idyllic administrative situation." He added, however, "I did not like the atmosphere among the army staff that included about 1,000 men. General Guisan lives far away in the charming small castle of Gümligen. It seems to me that he has very little contact with Langnau; instead, he has his own 'Personal Staff'."[19]

Apart from the reasons advanced by Guisan himself, other authors speculate about additional motivations the General may have had for recruiting a personal staff. Chapuisat thinks that because the Swiss entirely trusted the General, he was swamped with invitations and letters asking questions or giving advice; therefore hiring a special staff was the only way to handle all this correspondence.[20] This view is not very convincing, for the original General's office could certainly have handled the additional correspondence. Kreis advances a more credible argument, saying that Guisan created the special staff mostly to be able to prepare the secret cooperation plans with France without being disturbed.[21] This aspect may indeed have played a part in the General's thinking. However, the main reason must have been the lack of trust in, and tensions with, his chief of staff, Labhart. Bracher explained that setting up the personal staff "created a balance against the difficulties and clashes surrounding the Chief of the General Staff."[22] On the other hand, Federal Councilor Kobelt told a number of National Councilors that it was precisely by establishing a personal staff that the relationship between the General and Labhart became marred.[23]

The official job descriptions for the officers of the special staff were written by the chief of the personal staff and then signed by the General. The order, originally drafted by Gonard and slightly modified on several occasions, established, among other things, that another officer on the general staff would serve as the chief of staff's deputy and was to deal strictly with military issues. He was to open and distribute all incoming mail, a task which was to be handled by the chief of staff himself when his deputy was absent. He was to take care of all correspondence with the directly subordinate commanders and with civil bodies regarding operational, training, personnel, and equipment issues. The 1st adjutant, supported by a 2nd adjutant, was to handle the General's civil and private matters, such as invitations, sports issues, and cases of assistance. He was to decide who would be admitted to the General's quarters and was to be in charge of the commander-in-chief's security outside his quarters; moreover, he was to keep the command post's diary and manage the General's relief fund. The chief of staff was authorized to delegate to the 1st adjutant the execution of military tasks, while the 1st adjutant could pass on some correspondence to the head of chancellery or another qualified secretary. The 1st aide, assisted by a 2nd aide, was in charge of personnel matters below officer rank and had to handle issues pertaining to military law and cases of reprieve. The chief of staff himself was to handle personnel matters dealing with officers. In addition, the 1st aide was to be the strategic commander of the General's quarters and supervisor of the guards. The head of chancellery, a staff secretary who reported to the 1st aide, was responsible for all chancellery work and the accounts, as well as the encoding and the mail service.[24]

The most influential positions were undoubtedly held by the General's closest, and at the same time most loyal, collaborators, Gonard and Barbey, who succeeded each other as chief of the personal staff. The two staff officers were friends and had intellectual capabilities that Guisan lacked; hence, they complemented him perfectly. Gonard was able to conceptualize operational matters, while Barbey was intelligent and an exceptionally good writer. Their achievements behind the scene as advisors to the General were outstanding. It is difficult to say which of the two had more influence on the General's decisions.[25] Guisan trusted both, and both played a substantial role in the General's decision-making process. Boissier, Häni, and Wanner, captains on the general staff who were in regular contact with some members of the personal staff, tended to think that Gonard was the key figure and was able to win most recognition for himself apart from the General.[26]

Gonard recorded that on September 19 or 20 he was ordered to serve as a general staff officer in the General's office after working under Labhart. He wrote that for two weeks Labhart had not said one single word to him, "except during a short conversation when I reported absent from duty to begin my new job."[27] During that conversation, Labhart harshly criticized the General's decision to call up a general staff officer to serve in his office.

Once Gonard had assumed his new post as chief of the General's personal staff, he wrote the replies to studies regarding operational matters which the chief of the general staff submitted to the commander-in-chief, usually initialing them with "Go" on the letterhead.[28] Studies submitted by Labhart, the assistant chiefs of staff, and the corps commanders were annotated by Gonard, indicating that at the General's request he had reviewed them.

Gonard must have gained considerable influence with the General as early as the fall of 1939; as Guisan often said when problems occurred, "We will discuss that with Gonard."[29] Barbey considered "finding Gonard a stroke of luck at the right time," because his brainpower was an exceptional asset to the commander-in-chief. As Barbey described, "[Gonard] quickly devours his dinner and then spends his evening working. He loves to launch ideas; he is perfectly at ease designing and constructing them. He does not like pounding away at one idea for a long time."[30] Guisan acknowledged his collaborator's performance and versatility by writing about him to the Head of the Military Department, "I believe that this officer has common sense, shows initiative, is well organized, and conceptualizes, assimilates and works with ease and swiftness."[31] Even Federal Councilor Pilet-Golaz, who admitted that he did not like Gonard "very much," praised his qualities and told the General, "Gonard is your man!"[32] After replacing Germann as Chief of the Operational Section in June 1940, Gonard remained in close contact with the General's personal staff and went to see the General, to whose office he had free access anytime, almost every day.[33]

Major Barbey started his new job as Chief of the Personal Staff on June 11, 1940, at Gümligen Castle, after receiving a short introductory briefing by Gonard the day before. Barbey wrote in his diary, "[At] 14 hours I report to the General in the large living-room on the second floor, which is his office. Inside the wood-paneled walls his voice sounds warm and weighty; I remember it from the time he inspected my squadron when I did my initial army training. His eyes are very clear; he has a youthful smile in his tanned face, which has age spots scattered here and there. [The General said to me] 'Welcome . . . I know that I can trust you . . . we don't have much time, so let's get to work.'"[34] The first task, which the new chief of staff had to accomplish, was to draft an order of the day to the troops in case the armed forces had to prove themselves for the first time in combat.[35]

Barbey, who had a brilliant, elegant writing style and was a fascinating intellectual figure, became Guisan's closest collaborator along with Gonard. As chief of the personal staff, he was not merely an executor but the General's guiding intellectual force, and in several areas his indispensable assistant. He fulfilled his delicate task as the General's confidential secretary with devotion and discretion, and at the same time revered his "chief," as Guisan was called by his personal staff, with genuine affection. Barbey, a man of letters, a Parisian *belletrist*, had a kind of aggressive intelligence, which he expressed in a tight, logical manner.

Within a short period, Barbey became the distinguished yet undisputed autocrat among the General's personal staff. He soon became indispensable due to his analytical powers, profound knowledge, and organizational talents. When the General made public appearances, Barbey discreetly directed the events from behind the scenes. Working away from the limelight appears to have provided Barbey great satisfaction. When he thought that he could handle something on his own, he went ahead and made a decision. Whenever he believed that he could relieve the General of some of his workload by preparing decisions and solving problems, he did not hesitate to do so. He described his own task as an initiator and mediator by reminding himself, "Remember that the main responsibility of an officer serving on the general staff is to assemble the requirements which the chief needs to deliberate and make decisions. . . . The chief for his part has to slow down ambitious and impatient newcomers. I recall the words which Marshal Pétain pronounced to the officers on his staff in 1917: 'Seek to report to me above all the things that are reliable, not the things that are pleasant to hear!'"[36]

Gonard and Barbey often discussed operational matters strictly between themselves before presenting them to the General in the form of suggestions. For example, discussions between the two officers preceded the drafting of Operations Orders No. 11 and 12, which announced the army's retreat into the 'Réduit' positions. Gonard wrote five pages to Barbey on this subject, undoubtedly intending to use his successor as an accomplice to plead his case with the General. Gonard argued that the positions along the Limmat had to be abandoned while there was still time in order to concentrate all forces in the Alps. He wrote to Barbey: "We have to be able to hold the national *Réduit* at all cost. Personally, I do not think that we can do this with the few forces (that are provided for in [Order] No. 11!); I believe that we will be very swiftly defeated in two strikes." He said that he could understand that from an emotional point of view the positions along the Limmat should be maintained, but from an operational viewpoint it did not make sense because the army had to be strong where it intended to establish itself, which could only be in the *Réduit*. By planning to use more than half of the armed forces to support the weaker half of the army, Gonard claimed, a military success would be questionable from the start, adding, "to sum it up, I do not believe that the army will be able to resist for more than ten days with the adopted defense system."[37] Gonard and Barbey sometimes also held discussions prior to meetings that the commander-in-chief held with the Federal Council, the chief of the general staff, or the corps commanders. As a result of these discussions, Barbey supplied the General with relevant documents and notes which the General used to argue his case.

Barbey was clearly in charge whenever the General was absent. The General's direct subordinates, including the chief of the general staff, occasionally received orders that were not only drafted but also initiated by Barbey. Some army unit commanders did not fail to notice this fact. In a conversation with Barbey, Corps Commander Borel remarked, "*You* wrote to me . . . hence, if I want to write to the commander-in-chief, I inevitably have to address my letter to you. . . . You and Gonard are the ones who will write the reply."[38] When Borel raised the issue again on a later occasion, Barbey responded that he would propose to the General to have letters to the commander of the 1st Army Corps written by another officer on the personal staff. After the war, Borel complained to Federal Councilor Kobelt that the General tended to avoid resolving issues directly during a conversation and instead chose to do so in writing. Borel told Kobelt, "The General preferred to have some of his close collaborators write elegant and courteous letters, which he signed, of course."[39] Borel believed that many issues became complicated through this method and sometimes even turned into polemics.

The personal staff insisted at an early stage that correspondence had to be written in a correct manner. In a letter drafted by Gonard, the General explained that military documents submitted to him by the army staff in French were full of mistakes, making it impossible for him to sign and forward them. Consequently, he was forced to have some documents rewritten by his personal staff. Hence, he urged the subordinates concerned to have French texts or translations written by officers proficient in the language.[40] Barbey, who as a professional writer was demanding as well, continued these efforts at improving the style of military correspondence, saying that he wanted everyone to avoid using "the administrative style and formulae found in rules and regulations." Instead, the language should be lively. He asked the army staff to look for "an editor among public officials or elsewhere, a military person or a civilian who will not violate the language." The head of the chancellery admitted that he had been looking for someone for quite some time but that it was "very difficult, or actually almost impossible, to find someone suitable."[41] Not everyone appreciated Barbey's talents as a writer. Huber remarked, "the General and his working instrument took pleasure" in writing, of which "the Federal Council [got] a taste as well."[42]

Before important meetings, for example with the head of the Military Department, the chief of the general staff, or the corps commanders, Barbey not only put together the agenda for the General but also supplied him with ideas by jotting down the pros and cons in connection with specific items, raising questions, and offering arguments which the General could use during discussions. These "notes intended strictly for the commander-in-chief's personal perusal" were generally several pages long, unsigned, and often undated. As early as June 18, one week after assuming his new position, Barbey prepared documents for the General's briefing with a delegation of the Federal Council in which the military and political situation was discussed after the Pétain government had submitted a request for an armistice to Germany. There is evidence that Barbey, and occasionally Bracher, prepared notes for Guisan's meetings on at least nine occasions in 1941.[43]

In several instances, criticism voiced by the commander-in-chief about the manner in which direct subordinates handled their work was actually initiated by Barbey. For example, when Chief of the General Staff Huber was asked to submit a study on "Case West 1942" at the initiative of the General's personal staff, Guisan wrote to Huber, "I am hereby asking you to have studies undertaken for me to analyze which include the following elements: an outline of the strategy to be adopted, with possible variations, showing on maps the possible defense lines to be held by the army units; and a note on how the current mobilization system would have to be adjusted to fit the new strategy."[44] When Huber handed in his study one week later, Barbey was the first to look it over. In his written remarks for the General's attention, he complained that an analysis of the current situation, which should be the usual starting point for any work done by the general staff, was missing. Barbey remarked that without this analysis, all subsequent ideas were "vague and incomplete" hypotheses.[45] Based on that criticism, General Guisan called Huber to a meeting to discuss the study.[46]

After the war, Corps Commander Huber told the head of the Military Department about specific incidents which proved that "the working instrument was not as harmless as the General likes to think." For instance, he said that he "happened to receive misdirected letters" which showed that proposals for promotions were "pre-arranged and initiated" by Barbey and other officers. However, Huber continued, "I was not able to determine if the General fooled me or if the chief of his personal staff fooled him."[47]

The chief of the personal staff could make suggestions of any kind at any time to the General. There were two ways of proceeding: either he addressed an issue at an early stage during a conversation, whereupon the General promised to analyze it within a short period of time; or he submitted his own analysis in the form of written proposals for the General to sign and forward to the Federal Council, the chief of the general staff, or the corps commanders.[48]

Barbey had a kind of intuition that allowed him to be in tune with the General's way of thinking most of the time. He got to know the "chief" quite well during journeys they took together in the car. Barbey wrote, "I love these long car rides. The General talks about all kinds of things. We inspect the troops, and he gives me the opportunity to get to know his ideas and intentions. That makes my work all the easier. Hence, I know in advance his opinion or intentions on almost all the items on the agenda, which allows me to prepare his decisions on issues which are raised in his correspondence and to submit to him texts for signature of which some are final versions and some are drafts."[49] On their way back from a review of maneuvers performed by the 4th Army Corps in eastern Switzerland, Guisan once asked Barbey, "Did you write down all my comments? I intend to use the conclusions which I have drawn from these maneuvers. You shall put everything in writing, right away. . . ." On this occasion, Barbey remarked about the 69-year-old General that "Even after spending a long day outside, during which he continually has to adapt to new situations, he never appears to be tired and never has an urge to yawn. What a trump card he is in this game!"[50]

While Barbey was chief of the personal staff, subordinate officers sometimes had to inspect army units. In the spring of 1941, some officers, including Captains Bracher and Zimmermann and First Lieutenant Marguth, were sent to army units to check how far the work had progressed in their positions and to report back to the commander-in-chief.[51] Barbey wrote in a report that such inspections were necessary because the army units' own progress reports often contained "formal errors" or were "imprecise." In other cases, the work requested by the army staff took too long, making "inquiries" necessary.[52]

The members of the personal staff considered the General a driving force who inspired them to excel through his enthusiasm, optimism, open spirit, and magnanimity. As a leader, he refrained from using a strict and systematic style, showing instead his warm-heartedness, obliging nature, and spontaneity.[53] His good mood was contagious; and his mental liveliness and dynamism influenced his staff, making their jobs enjoyable. Jules Sandoz, who served as the General's 1st Adjutant for many years, explained that the only times that the atmosphere was unpleasant at the command post was on days when the General had to dismiss or reprimand a commander. Sandoz could see that the commander-in-chief was occasionally tired, but he was never disheartened.[54] The language was informal among the staff. Guisan was always polite and friendly and wished to be surrounded by well-mannered people. Eibel, the Head of Chancellery, remembered seeing the General indignant on only one occasion, when he found out that a letter had been answered without permission. "He banged his fist on the table and was swearing, but after that this unpleasant matter was done and over with."[55] Barbey mentioned several examples to illustrate the poise and optimism of his superior; in addition, the General was never intrusive but "extremely discreet by nature."[56]

Soon after the armed forces retreated to the *Réduit* positions, the question arose as to where the command posts should be relocated. The large army staff had actually moved in May 1940 from Langnau to Worb, where the means of communication were more adequate. The chief of the general staff suggested that the army staff should be transferred to a new location along the "periphery of the central area" as "soon as possible, but no later than next spring." Guisan agreed with this idea but wanted to keep his own command post somewhere near the Federal Council's office as long as the government stayed in Bern. Consequently, he proposed putting the army staff somewhere along Lake Thun before moving them to an actual wartime command post in the mountains.[57] Huber chose Interlaken, which the General accepted in December 1940.[58]

There was some concern about Interlaken being a suitable place for receiving the army staff, even though several hotels were able to accommodate them, as they had been empty for some time. The military intelligence service warned that "many individuals [live there] who do not have a steady income, who are embittered and susceptible to foreign ideologies." It said that the spa resort had "a disproportionately high number of extremists on both ends [of the political spectrum]." Moreover, the intelligence service explained that experience had shown that hotel personnel, "in many cases even the hotel owner himself," were easy targets for foreign intelligence service agents, "mostly because hotel personnel generally do not think that there is anything wrong with accepting money from foreigners, as they are used to receiving tips as part of their salary." Hence, there was a great risk that these people could render inadmissible services if they received payment. In addition, the intelligence service warned that in a vacation place like Interlaken, where the municipality was in charge of registering guests, "a reliable screening process for foreigners does not exist." In order to lower the risks of espionage, the intelligence service planned to tap telephones on a large scale.[59]

On April 1, 1941, "once the heating season was over," the General's personal staff moved from Gümligen Castle to Interlaken, where they had to be fully operational at 13:00 hours.[60] It took two hours to transport all their material in nine trucks to the new premises. Unloading and setting up the command post took another one and a half hours.[61] Barbey and Bracher, the two general staff officers on the General's personal staff, and von Ernst and Sandoz, the General's adjutants, who were all cavalrymen, rode their horses from Bern. The two local officers, Bracher and von Ernst, agreed on "an approximate route in the bushes along the Aare River."[62]

In Interlaken, the General and the officers on the personal staff moved into the "Cranz Villa," a spacious and comfortable residence located on the Gartenstrasse. Hotels and some private individuals, including "some ladies from Interlaken who generously contributed to furnishing the rooms," supplied the furniture.[63] Barbey noted about the new quarters, "trivial construction material of average quality; imitation marble that is already cracked on the staircase. They had plenty of bathrooms with top-notch equipment, which would thrill a spoiled woman. But we will continue living here like monks! There are just as many balconies, but they all face the backside of hotels, overlooking fir trees and sequoias, villas built in the Alpine style of the 1910s, and yards that are all overhung with laundry drying in the wind. Facing south is a lawn, a small orchard, and four ornamental aspen trees. . . . The General has set up his office in the southwestern corner of the building on the third floor; he is annoyed about the ugly lilac-colored carpet."[64]

In Interlaken, the General's personal staff and the army staff were reunited in the same town, but the two quarters were still fifteen minutes apart, allowing the personal staff to continue working according to their own agenda. The General explained that in Interlaken "the team spirit, the spirit of cheerfully working together without envy," could be cherished and strengthened.[65] The entire personal staff worked together in harmony, there were hardly any tensions, there was no animosity, and no small cliques formed.[66] During common meals, both French and German were spoken.[67] Marguth recounted that during meals they often talked about work. However, two other members of the personal staff stated that although they may have talked about current events that made the headlines on a particular day, military and political matters were taboo, and so were heated discussions, as mealtimes had to be "peaceful and quiet."[68] A visitor remarked about the General's command post after his first visit there, "The setting is very nice and the impression is generally one of elegance. Two waiters dressed in white jackets serve the meals."[69] After meals, they always played cards; the General usually teamed up with one of his adjutants, usually Captain Sandoz. Guisan was happy when he won a game; he did not like to lose, but he never got annoyed when he did.[70]

On the occasion of Guisan's 67th birthday, on October 21, 1941, the personal staff invited a number of army staff members to dinner because the General wished to "strengthen the bond of comradeship" between the staff members on that evening. It was the first time that the two bodies of staff sat that "close to each other." Since space was limited at the Villa, not all army staff members could be invited; some who were left out felt hurt and thought that they had fallen "out of favor" with the General.[71] The mood during the meal itself was rather low, and Huber was "silent." However, "the white wine from Pully cheered everyone up," so that during dessert they started singing songs. Barbey recounted: "At the end, we all stood in a big circle with our arms folded, holding each other's hands to sing the farewell song. Several men, including Huber, Tscharner, Masson . . . became carried away with the rhythmical dancing around the General." Barbey concluded his account of the birthday party by writing, "Without having too many illusions about bringing the two bodies closer together in the long term, I think that this was a nice evening and, above all, the fact that it could take place at all is a good sign."[72]

In Interlaken, the personal staff had a getaway place for weekends, a mobile wood cabin set up for the General on the shore of Lake Thun. Barbey explained, "The cabin has three rooms plus a porch. In the evening sun, one can smell the lovely scents of wood, grass, and water. . . . When the weather is good, we go to have dinner there; we get there on foot, on horseback, or by car. We start with a homemade aperitif consisting of grapefruit and Pernod. If the telephone did not constantly ring, we would be able to enjoy the quiet moments there between the stressful days."[73] After dinner, the General and his staff usually played a game of bowls on two improvised courts until night fell. Quite frequently Guisan spent his spare time in Bern, where he owned a small apartment, which his wife used mostly during the winter in order to be close to him and to their daughter.[74]

The personal staff set up a wartime command post west of Interlaken, at the foot of the Wagner Canyon near Unspunnen, in the event of a surprise attack or bombings. It consisted of two caverns, measuring 12 by 6.7 meters each, and a hallway. It could be closed with an armor-plated door and was furnished with basic equipment; it was heated and ventilated and had electric lights and six telephone lines. Mattresses were made available for the General and his staff to sleep on should the need arise. A five-day food supply was stocked there for 200 men.[75] The personal staff and the rest of the army staff would have continued to be located in separate places in the event of an emergency, as a different cave was prepared for the army staff outside Interlaken.

A special railway train was made available for the General to use on official visits and inspections. The General wrote about his travel activities in his postwar report: "For most of my journeys I used the car, which was the most convenient way of traveling, or the train in order to save on gasoline and tires, and sometimes also the plane. Moreover, I had a special train available which allowed me to go on trips for several days; I brought my files with me and was able to work and live in the railway car together with my Personal Staff."[76]

The instructions for furnishing two special command trains were issued in the fall of 1940. One of the trains had to be available at all times in Erstfeld, in eastern Switzerland, and the other in Spiez on Lake Thun. The General emphasized in his order, "I insist that the trains must be able to be moved elsewhere quickly and without the slightest incident whenever the need arises."[77] He asked about the possibility of stationing the trains on sidings or in tunnels.

Each train had six cars in addition to the locomotive. One belonged to the General and his closest associates as an office and for sleeping; one was a dining car, which could also be used as a conference room; a third was transformed into an office for the chancellery and included bunk beds for the chancellery staff. The others included a first-aid station, which contained straw bags for the guards, couriers, and telephone and radio operators to sleep on; a car designated for transporting luggage and cargo; and a final open car, which carried motor vehicles. One train provided space for a total of 60 people, including the railway personnel.[78] The food supply carried on the train was calculated to last three days. Acetylene lamps and candles supplemented the lighting and heating system, which was supplied by battery power and a gasoline generator. Communication with the outside world was maintained by radio and by telephone and telegraph during stops. The remodeling and furnishing cost several thousand francs and was carried out by the Federal Railways' garage within a short period of time. The Federal Railways and the Bern-Lötschberg-Simplon Railways supplied their cars free of charge, while the Dining Car and Sleeping Car Company charged 12.50 francs per day rent for their cars, which had to be paid by the army.[79]

From December 4 to 7, 1940, the General and his staff took a test ride on the command train to eastern Switzerland together with Federal Councilor Minger, Chief of the General Staff Huber, Military Railway Director Paschoud and other officers, bringing the total number of passengers to 52. They left Gümligen on the evening of December 4 and spent the night aboard the train on a siding in Walenstadt. On the following day, they inspected the Sargans fortress and spent the second night at the train station in Weesen. Then they inspected the front line held by the 7th Division and Light Brigade 3 and spent the next night in Birmensdorf in Canton Zürich. The following morning, Federal Councilor Minger and the General took the salute at a parade of the 6th Division in Zürich. On December 7, at 12:43 p.m., they arrived back in Gümligen. The test ride was considered "satisfactory," although the passengers had to sleep "in icy cold beds in the sleeping car" because the heating did not work well.[80]

Members of the personal staff were full of praise for the convenient command train during later occasions, as the journeys to the various parts of the country were comfortable and the staff were able to get their work done on the road and live an autonomous life.[81] The chief of the personal staff liked the mobile command post because it allowed him "to see a lot and to work effectively by having all the auxiliary personnel and files at hand." During the fifth year of the war, Barbey commended the railway personnel "on all levels, from the director all the way down to the station manager, for their friendliness and carefully considered instructions."[82] The army's counterespionage service received continuous confidential information on the train schedule in order to be able to organize security measures and put the train under discreet guard during its stopovers.[83]

The General's personal staff also had mobile command posts available on the road and on waterways. Motorboats and barges were organized to be able to move the command post around on Lake Lucerne, Lake Thun, and Lake Brienz.[84] In the spring of 1942, the mobile command post on the road consisted of two dozen vehicles; a command car and a special command tent were designed according to Marguth's instructions.[85] The mobile command post on the road was tested in early 1941 during a field exercise at Zwieselberg above Lake Thun. A C-35 observation aircraft followed the exercise and took photographs to see how well it was camouflaged. Several detachments guarded the bivouac with automatic guns. Barbey wrote that after having dinner at the edge of the woods, playing cards as usual, and drinking a "mediocre Cognac," the staff spent the night in the tent.[86]

All those who served on the General's personal staff had to make a special vow of secrecy, by which they felt bound until the end of their lives.[87] To a large degree the officers considered themselves as acolytes, the ordained servants of a General whom they revered as a father, even as they maintained their formal military discipline. The personal staff consisted of a group of extremely loyal captains and staff officers, on average 20 to 30 years younger than the General—a younger generation inspired by the desire to serve the country and its people by fully dedicating themselves to the "Chief." The French word "*patron*" conveys many facets of the relationship the staff had with their General; they respected him as the head of family and their employer, their sponsor and tutor, who was at the same time their venerable master. Barbey explained that working for the General enabled him to always keep his "imagination and belief" alive, adding, "We have the impression that we try to protect this advocate for the people almost in spite of himself."[88]

The General may, in a certain way, have viewed his personal staff as a substitute for his family. When he was among this team of devoted young men, he felt relaxed, efficient, and happy. There was a warm atmosphere among them, they felt purposeful and united, there were no half-hearted coalitions, and they were able to trust each other. Guisan needed this kind of support and loyalty,

and the importance of the personal staff for the General's strong emotional stability should not be underestimated. The "Chief" had personal contact with
each staff member. Marguth stated that the officers on the personal staff were
isolated from the outside world but they were "amply rewarded through the
General's presence and the trust."[89] As of March 17, 1944, the General had the
French name for this group of his closest associates changed from "Etat-major
particulier du Général" (Special Staff of the General) to "Etat-major *personnel*
du Général" (Personal Staff of the General);[90] the adjective "personal" had been
used in German from the start.

After the war, in an after-dinner speech at "Verte Rive," Gonard thanked
the General for taking the bold risk of choosing young, relatively inexperienced
officers to work with him and for putting his trust in them, adding, "You called
them to serve by giving them the benefit of the doubt and entrusted them with
high commands or important staff posts at an early stage in their careers."[91]

During the war, about thirty officers served in different functions on the
General's personal staff. It is striking that Guisan had a tendency to select officers from old aristocratic families, such as van Berchem, von Ernst, von Sinner,
von Haller, von Tscharner, and of course Barbey, most of whom belonged to the
cavalry or artillery. In addition, he had an inclination to pick general staff officers who were part of the militia rather than the professional instructional staff.
The General's closest collaborators came almost exclusively from French-speaking Switzerland and were Protestant.[92]

Officers who did not fit in with the personal staff for one reason or another were replaced in an inconspicuous manner by being sent on leave and simply not being called back to duty. This happened to Head of Chancellery Eibel
and 1st Adjutant Mayer, who had both helped to establish the personal staff but
became *personae non gratae* soon after Barbey succeeded Gonard as chief. They
remained on leave or were detailed to another unit for the rest of the war. Eibel
believed that he was dismissed because Social Democrat National Councilor H.
Oprecht had objected to his right-wing political activities.[93]

Adjutant A. Mayer was dropped after trying, in 1940, to publish a book
entitled *Autour d'un chef* ("Around a Commander"), in which he described the
commander-in-chief's actions from his own perspective. Barbey considered the
work to be of little literary value and too reverent of the General, making him
and other readers fear that it could backfire on him. He informed the General
in writing that the book was "really dangerous" for him at the present time
because the public might be inclined to believe that the flattering remarks
about Guisan were written with his consent, or even at his request. In Barbey's
view, "this plea 'pro domo' and 'pro persona,' published at the end of 1940, will
surprise and disconcert the readers; it might even cause a scandal. More partic-

ularly, it will provide the General's opponents with a formidable argument to pretend, in a most unfair manner, that he is overly concerned about his image and that he has spent some of his time to receive homages and gifts."[94] The book, of which 10,000 copies had already been printed and which was sure to become a best-seller at a time when the General's popularity was on the rise, was confiscated and destroyed.[95] Only a few pages of the book's proofs have been preserved.[96] After taking extended sick leave in 1941, Major Mayer was not called back to serve on the personal staff and was replaced by Major A. von Ernst, who had already been fulfilling the tasks of an adjutant at the time.

The personal staff was not only Guisan's main working instrument but at the same time his family while he was on duty, a sworn community, and his confidential power base. His chief of staff Barbey did not have "any illusions about the feelings that my position and activities triggered among many people," including top commanders and "many less important gentlemen," explaining that he had heard rumors which made him feel surrounded by "constant or wavering animosity."[97] The personal staff was indeed the center of the army's nervous system where all-important decisions were forged. Of course, Guisan always made the final decision and assumed full responsibility. It would be erroneous to claim that Guisan was kept on a leash by his close collaborators on the personal staff or that he let decision-making power pass from his hands. However, since the General used to consult with his advisors frequently, officers like Gonard and Barbey must have felt to some degree like his managers. It is understandable that these assistants were able to exercise considerable personal influence on the General, as they were constantly around him, interpreted his wishes, and by keeping track of his agenda decided in part who could see the commander-in-chief and for how long.

The members of the personal staff were also responsible for maintaining the General's image as an integrating figure and as the embodiment of the spirit of resistance in the country. They skillfully used the media during the period of wartime censorship to boost the commander-in-chief's status.[98] The General's public appearances during Swiss National Day, other holidays, and commemorative services were carefully staged to maximize favorable publicity. In addition, the General was the center of attention at military shows, parades, ceremonies for the promotion of officers, and soldiers' Christmas parties, which contributed to increasing his prestige and, consequently, enhancing the reputation of the armed forces. The personal staff was very inventive in creating and utilizing opportunities to promote the commander-in-chief's status and personality, thereby forming a deep psychological impact that, by Swiss standards, was quite unusual. These efforts were not unjustified in view of the situation, as many people needed a symbolic figure with whose spirit of resistance they could identify. Guisan's personality and communicative skills definitely helped to make him a national father figure, but there is no doubt that the officers on his personal staff who took on the role of public relations agents helped build this image with determination.

One means of promoting the General's image was through photographs. Any photograph that the media wanted to publish had to be approved by the personal staff. In some cases, the General himself made the final decision.[99] Many photographs were marked "publication strictly prohibited." In some instances, a bunch of flowers or a cigarette had to be cropped because they were considered, respectively, non-military or anti-athletic. As an example, the head of chancellory on the personal staff wrote underneath one picture, "Publication allowed only on condition that the flowers which the General holds in his hands are cropped."[100]

Guisan, as commander-in-chief, felt fully responsible for the armed forces. He did not only want to be called General but wished to be actively in charge of the army and to leave his personal mark on it through his personal staff. All correspondence was processed through his office, as he wished to be fully informed of everything that was going on (though he had a "certain aversion to writing"[101]). His favorite occupation was to deal directly with the troops rather than with paperwork. He was able to delegate tasks without losing track of the overall state of affairs. He was present at all times, even if he sometimes took his time to make a decision. By delegating tasks, the General was able to focus on comprehensive matters pertaining to the army command, especially the decisive psychological issue of increasing military strength by promoting national unity and the spirit of resistance.

In addition to his personal staff, the General relied on a number of other devoted young officers who served as informants and advisors, including Captains Hausamann, Ernst, Häni, and Meyer. They were allowed to see him at any time without having to go through official channels. Some of them had participated in the so-called "Officers' Conspiracy."[102] These enterprising and zealous officers provided the General with confidential information, and Guisan heeded their advice. In their reports, which they generally delivered verbally and only very rarely in writing, they did not hesitate to bring discomforting facts to his attention. Hausamann and Meyer's personal information was very revealing in that respect.[103]

In spite of the personal staff's attempt to keep a low profile in its duties, there was some whispering about the General's "court."[104] However, no substantial criticism was voiced during the war, even if some officers in Zürich liked to make fun of "the latest fad of the General's personal staff."[105] The harshest critic was Chief of the General Staff Huber, who remained adamant that the personal staff be dissolved, and his negative opinion temporarily marred relations between him and the General. Huber wrote to the commander-in-chief: "I suspect that the Personal Staff owes its creation to your mistrust in my predecessor. [The General made an annotation to this statement, writing, "No."] If the Chief of the General Staff enjoys the General's trust, interposing a Personal Staff is not only useless but actually hampers the entire management. I have on several occasions requested verbally that it be abolished; let me herewith do it once again in formally writing to you."[106]

The General replied that he was "surprised and distressed" by Huber's vehement attitude, adding that he had been under the impression that Huber trusted him as fully as he trusted Huber, and that their fruitful cooperation could not be blemished by any other parties. He claimed that the purpose of the personal staff was the same as that of the former "General's office," explaining, "by changing, in the course of wartime duty, the name of the General's office to 'Personal Staff of the General,' I had absolutely no intention of failing to recognize the other bodies of the army command; I simply wanted to replace an expression which was too administrative as a military term." Moreover, he said that Huber had never told him that he was dissatisfied with the existing situation, and that he did not have any knowledge of any abuse of power by officers of his staff, concluding, "I have therefore difficulty explaining to myself your sudden change of attitude toward the Personal Staff."[107] The correspondence is an indication of the underlying tension that existed between the commander-in-chief and the chief of the general staff. However, Huber was unsuccessful in bringing about a change of the status quo.

General Guisan later used similar arguments to defend his establishment of a personal staff. In his postwar report, he called that body indispensable, even though there was no provision for it in the military regulations. The chief of the general staff, on the other hand, continued to claim that it was dispensable.[108] In a conversation with Gafner, Guisan justified placing the army general staff and his personal staff in different locations by advancing "strategic and safety reasons," among others, because enemy bombings were possible.[109] In addition, he explained that his "personal working instrument" was essential for him to be able to keep in touch with the entire population, adding, "The General is very busy, so he has to have a general staff officer, who can be his Chief of Staff, available to study the files which are submitted to the General in order to present them to him in daily briefings for decision-making. That is all the more necessary because the General is solicited by everyone and will hardly find the time to examine all incoming files, let alone to study them in detail. Having them examined and summarized by a general staff officer facilitates his making decisions."[110]

It is obvious that these explanations did not address the main arguments put forward by the personal staff's opponents, because an "office" like the one that existed at the beginning of the war could have relieved the General of some of his duties just as well as a "personal staff," if it had been manned with qualified personnel. Virtually all directly concerned persons, except the General and the members of the personal staff themselves, had serious reservations about the special organ or strictly opposed it because they considered it harmful. The two chiefs of the general staff, Labhart and Huber, were joined by other subordinates of Guisan, such as corps commanders Borel, Constam, Frick, and later de Montmollin, Corbat, and others, who voiced their opposition to the personal staff. Corbat echoed Huber's criticism by writing, "This body is not only useless in times of war; in fact it is already detrimental in times of active duty."[111]

Constam argued that it was understandable that the General's office had been enlarged in view of the commander-in-chief's volume of work. However, he continued, "it was an error to call in a personal staff of the General to intervene between the General and the chief of the general staff and between the General and the corps commanders to participate in the operational and strategic preparations for a war. This error has to be avoided in the future, as [the personal staff] undoubtedly had an averse effect on the understanding and the trusting relationship that has to exist between the commander-in-chief and his closest assistant [the chief of the general staff] during a war."[112] Corps Commander Frick went even further when he wrote to the Head of the Military Department, "[The worst thing is] that if the supreme command is structured in such a way, it is bound to fail in case of a crisis."[113]

After the war, the personal staff was discussed at length because it had dealt with operational studies and had drafted relevant orders, and most of all because the role that it played behind the scenes had not always been clear. During World War I, the Swiss Army Command had been contained in one single structure, quartered at the Bellevue-Palace Hotel in Bern. One staff member remembered, "Every evening at 5 o'clock, Chief [of the General Staff von Sprecher] took his briefcase and went to see General [Wille]. The two top commanders never needed to communicate anything in writing. There was only one general staff . . .; there was no need for a second staff."[114] In connection with a revision of the 1938 ordinance on the organization of the army staff, Chief of the General Staff de Montmollin told a special parliamentary committee after World War II that he would maintain the General's office but would at the same time consider the possibility of assigning a captain or major from the general staff to the General if necessary, adding, "I think going beyond that would be very difficult."[115]

On balance, the impression prevails that the personal staff was hardly a useful body from a military point of view, even if it was established with good intentions in 1939 and made a significant contribution to the General's performance. It was a specific solution to a special leadership problem during the Second World War in view of the divergence of opinions existing in the upper ranks of the army command at the time; and it was tailor-made for the special temperament of the commander-in-chief.

Investigation of the Front Movement

AT A BRIEFING WITH HIS DIRECT SUBORDINATES at the end of April 1940, three weeks after Germany's invasion of Denmark and Norway, General Guisan discussed some of the officers' political opinions, explaining, "The army command has received a flood of letters which question the reliability of a large number of officers. At the present time, five simultaneous investigations are under way. The General is asking the army commanders to pay full attention to these cases."[1] Chief of the General Staff Huber stated that "defeatist propaganda [had been] carried out actively for a very long time and [was] very effective in Switzerland, undermining our country." He suggested dismissing untrustworthy personnel, saying, "Strict sanctions have to be enforced on undependable officers. Officers, non-commissioned officers, and soldiers on the staffs, most particularly the drivers, have to be closely supervised. People who are in debt are very suspicious, as they are the first to be allured by foreign propaganda. Unfortunately it is unpleasant to note that some officers are also defeatist and have doubts about our army's ability to put up any resistance."[2]

Huber's analysis was based on an investigation by Colonel O. Zumbrunn, head of the police section on the army staff, who had mentioned in an earlier report that "the poison of defeatism" was being administered "drop by drop in order for larger and more efficient doses to be applied at the right time."[3]

The General noted, probably as a result of the briefing of April 29:

Examine whether *personnel* on the staff are reliable (driver, secr[etary], aides, etc.) Officers with connections to foreign countries. German maids. Investigate *Nazi off[icers]* in the army corps. In 5 cases (Reber, Riggenbach, Mutterer, Spörri, Othmar Maag), file is being prep[ared] by Bracher. *Defeatism* among certain officers (Zurich) who criticize the measures taken and claim that we could not resist the Germans at all at the border, etc. *Col[onel] Däniker*, Major Berli, defeatist, saying that we could not defend ourselves against Germany. *Wille* opposes org[anization] of bo[rder] tr[oops] and [bo]rder forti[fications]. Meeting in Meilen to celebrate Germany's invasion of Denmark and Norway. — Champagne.[4]

These notes were undoubtedly a summary of information received by the army's counter-intelligence service, the source of which, however, cannot be verified.

On May 10, 1940, the day the decision was made to mobilize all troops for the second time, Guisan ordered an investigation against officers who held right-wing extremist ideas "to examine how long the concerned officers had been members of the National Front, what activities they had carried out there, and to what extent they were aware of the movement's spirit of violence and rebellion and its foreign connections." In addition, the question was to be examined "whether the suspects' ideology and political activities [were] compatible with the oath to the flag, according to which every officer has to swear loyalty to the Swiss Confederation, to sacrifice his life to defend the country and its constitution, and to do everything that is required to safeguard the honor and liberty of the country."[5]

According to the order, the chief of the general staff, the corps commanders, the commander of the air force and anti-aircraft defense, the chief instructors, and the heads of section of the army staff had to make sure that their direct superiors examined the suspects in accordance with official procedure. The suspects were to be told that they were under investigation based on information gathered by the police section of the territorial service on the army staff, and that it was in the interest of the country as well as in their own interest to tell the truth and nothing but the truth, because the accusations raised against the officers of the Front movement had created "great concern among the troops and the population." The sources of the confidential information received from civil police were not to be revealed. The investigation was to be completed speedily and its results were to be communicated to the chief of the general staff by June 5.

Chief of the General Staff Huber submitted the draft of the order, which was undoubtedly written by Colonel Zumbrunn, to General Guisan on May 6. On the following day, Colonel Zumbrunn submitted to the office of the army staff "the list with the names of the suspected officers, to the attention of the Chief of the General Staff."[6] Once the investigation was opened, the General informed the Head of the Military Department that he had "ordered all officers to be investigated whose patriotic attitude, based on existing files, could appear as unreliable. They included "approximately 150 officers in the entire armed forces." Their direct superiors had received "the top secret files on the suspects" in order to carry out their examination.[7]

There are conflicting indications about the exact number of officers who were subject to the investigation. In his postwar report, the General mentioned 124 suspects.[8] In a letter to the General, the chief of the general staff wrote about 122 suspects.[9] The individual army corps reported the following in their ranks:

1st Army Corps	11	
2nd Army Corps	40	
3rd Army Corps	29	
4th Army Corps	15	
Territorial reserve and others	31	
Total	126	(One of whom was said to be a Communist.)[10]

Current affairs commentator P. Schmid-Ammann had already demanded in the *Nation* newspaper before the war that officers who belonged to the Front movement be dismissed. "At the present time," he wrote, "each and every Swiss officer has to be aware that it is not enough anymore to pronounce patriotic phrases, and that this is not about knocking Switzerland into some authoritarian shape or overhauling it according to the German model. This is about defending democratic Switzerland with its current liberties and rights, or else it is not worth defending at all because Switzerland is only thinkable, and thus can only exist, as a democratic state."[11]

At the outbreak of the war, the Federal Council, based on the decree of August 30 for "measures to protect the country and to safeguard its neutrality," banned all propaganda in the army that could be a potential threat to the state.[12] When the draft of the ban was discussed, the Federal Council expressed "some reservations about banning right-wing extremist propaganda, as it [was] less dangerous" than Communist propaganda. Federal Prosecutor Franz Stämpfli disagreed, writing to the representative of the army command who was being consulted on the issue that "the various right-wing extremist groups should be prevented from infiltrating the army with their propaganda."[13]

When the investigation of the Front movement was completed, the General informed Federal Councilor Minger of the results in a confidential report, stating, "The list of officers who were known or suspected of having connections with extremist parties, 'Alliances' or 'Fronts,' was compiled by the military police based on information received from civil police authorities on the local, cantonal, and federal levels. Considering the speed with which the list was compiled and in view of the fact that inquiries would have had to be made in all of Switzerland, the army could not include its own observations in the files. As expected, the results of the investigation are reassuring. Based on the existing files and the requests formulated by the direct superiors and the army unit commanders, special sanctions had to be envisaged against only nine officers. The military courts will handle three cases. For the six other cases, I reserve the right to decide if and where the officers will serve in the future. I may suspend some of them from office. In an order dated June 24, 1940, I told the rest of the officers who had been under investigation that the case was closed and that I and their superiors had confidence in them."[14]

The General provided a more detailed account of the investigation in his postwar report, writing, "The list included 124 names: eleven staff officers, 14 captains, and 16 low-ranking officers were alleged members of the 'Front' Movement; twelve staff officers, 17 captains, and 54 low-ranking officers were alleged 'National Socialists' or 'Fascists.' As we had hoped, the investigation yielded satisfactory results. Based on requests made by the soldiers' direct superiors and unit commanders, only the cases of seven officers were further investigated. Three cases were referred to the military courts; special steps were taken in the four other cases, the officers being suspended from office." Guisan explained that most officers understood the purpose of the investigation, adding, "The minutes and reports written by the superiors of all ranks clearly indicated that officers of all ages, ranks, and arms had a very high sense of military honor. The concerned officers underwent the investigation as soldiers, and of their own accord provided the information that was requested from them on their political opinions. From that moment forward, they were allowed to speak out about any new investigation against them that lacked any evidence."[15]

The General wrote to the officers who came out of the investigation with a clean record that their cases could be considered closed, explaining that most had welcomed the investigation as it "cleared the air" and permitted "full confidence" to be placed in those who had been exonerated; moreover, "the military honor of these officers remains unblemished. If anyone feels that nevertheless his honor has been attacked, he is herewith rehabilitated."[16] The General reported that he summoned the seven officers who were suspended from duty to his office and "told them to their faces what I thought of them."[17]

The Front movement and its sympathizers harshly criticized the investigation and the way it was handled. Because the investigated and rehabilitated officers included such high-ranking staff officers as Colonels Gustav Däniker and Fritz Heitz, their supporters intervened on their behalf to protest the investigation, which they considered as humiliating censorship. Corps Commander Wille, who initially cloaked his criticism as an attack against Chief of the General Staff Huber, wrote to the General, "I feel sorry for the Chief of the General Staff if he believes that the army has to be purged of 'unreliable officers,' because if that is the case his faith in the army cannot be rock solid. By mistrusting Swiss officers, the army's confidence will suffer severe damages from the top down. Since hearing him say, at the briefing of the corps commanders in April, that he feared officers were betraying the country, and since hearing him announce the large-scale interventions by police today, I have been very worried and the fact that I bear part of the responsibility, even if it is only on the surface, makes me suffer."[18]

Bircher, the commander of the 5th Division, also attempted to defend the officers in his unit who belonged to the Front movement against the investigation initiated by the army command. In an official letter to the General, he wrote that "the snooping activities introduced in the armed forces [have brought about] unpleasant and questionable practices," adding, "I would like to state that *I* am solely responsible for my officers' spirit and their dutifully fulfilling their tasks; under no circumstances shall I tolerate the fact that an organization using Bolshevik methods is spying behind my back on officers who are my subordinates because they have been maliciously denounced." Bircher said that it was "high time" to "put a halt" to these snooping activities, "as the damage which they have caused is substantial and can hardly be fully assessed at this time." This divisional commander from Aargau, who compared the practices of the army and the counter-intelligence service to the methods of Soviet Communists, ended his letter by demanding that it was "just as important, if not more important, to take measures against the informants and to punish them severely."[19]

In a personal letter to the General, Colonel Däniker, who was virtually undisputed at the time and enjoyed widespread popularity, protested against the "dishonorable" investigation into officers' political opinions which, he argued, destroyed subordinates' confidence in the army command. Däniker went on: "Due to the most cowardly and perfidious denunciations, the most serious allegation has been raised against dutiful officers that they can possibly face—that is, their being disloyal to the flag. No one dared to say what the allegations were based upon or who the dubious informants were. Hence, these were cases of the worst and most despicable kind of snooping, which is a disgrace for an army and destroys the highest principles, which a soldier cherishes in every army. The questioning carried out by our superiors was an insult; the investigation would not have been necessary if it had not been based on mistrust on the part of some superior command."[20]

When the General failed to respond to his letter, Däniker wrote a formal five-page-long complaint in which he called the investigation and the way in which it was conducted inexplicable because it was based on "perfidious denunciation." He stated that as a colonel on the general staff he was displeased with the summary rehabilitation of all officers and refused to accept it.[21] However, the commander-in-chief refused to discuss the matter and demanded that Colonel Däniker accept the decision, adding, "I expect you to behave as a disciplined soldier."[22]

Lower-ranking officers who appreciated the efforts that the officers belonging to the Front movement made to fulfill their duties, expressed their outrage about the investigation as well. In a letter to his parents, Captain E. Wehrli, interim commander of the Zürich-based Fusilier Battalion 69, wrote after the critical days of May 1940: "Instead of moaning about unreliable officers—as far as I can see, the officers who formerly belonged to the Front movement are all very respectful and very reliable—it would be better to look for those who are responsible for the matters that were delayed. The Radical party and the other government parties are to blame for that. I think that a change in the cabinet would be good for us as well. However, we are no longer able to do that. . . . Yet once we return to our civilian life, we will have to face a tremendous job and will have to re-establish order in our country."[23] In this letter, Wehrli expressed an opinion shared by many younger people who were angry because they felt Switzerland to be militarily inferior, and who were determined to hold accountable those whom they thought were responsible for lack of preparedness.

During the investigation of the Front movement, the first clashes occurred between some German-friendly officers from eastern Switzerland and the commander-in-chief. During the summer of 1940, Wille, the Chief Instructor, once again complained to Guisan: "General, in May you ordered an investigation of the officers of the so-called Front movement to be carried out. The army command created a system of 'white registration cards for officers who were to be put under investigation.' Also, in another 'confidential' step, surveillance officers were introduced in our armed forces, a non-Swiss and undemocratic institution. For example, a general staff officer was ordered by the army police to watch his own chief of staff. Instruction officers were spied on without their chief instructor's knowledge. As Head of Main Section III and Chief Instructor, I can no longer talk to young soldiers and officers about loyalty and honor when such institutions exist and I have to be evasive when officers wonder about this new practice in our country and in our army."[24]

General Guisan defended the investigation he had ordered, saying that the procedure, which was designed to uncover facts, should not be called snooping and denouncing, even if some subordinate officers committed some "blunders." Moreover, he explained that in a circular dated June 24, 1940, after the investigation had been closed, he told the cleared officers that he had full confidence in them; hence, he considered the matter to be clarified.[25]

Wille made annotations to Guisan's letter, probably to prepare for a discussion with the General. Wille wrote, among other things, that "the key phrase about the 'unreliable officers who are sympathetic towards foreign countries' was pronounced by the chief of the general staff at the briefing with the corps commanders on April 29, 1940; it was directed exclusively against all those who were considered to be pro-German, not against those who openly admitted to being pro-French/pro-English." Wille added that the fact that the General ordered the investigation against his will because of political pressure did not relieve him of his "responsibility for the procedure," since he was the one who had signed the order.[26]

In a letter to Däniker, Wille claimed that he knew "the General had not ordered the 'investigation' on his own initiative or that of an office of the army command but due to pressure from the Federal Military Department, or some irresponsible politicians, above all members of the Federal Parliament."[27] During a subsequent meeting with Federal Councilor Kobelt, the new Head of the Military Department, Wille complained "several times and in a very passionate manner" about the surveillance and the investigation of officers belonging to the Front movement, calling it "a scandal which the public would deal with once free speech was re-established." He said that he was under surveillance as well, adding that the names of the informants were not revealed; on the contrary, the informants were granted protection."[28]

The General admitted that mistakes were made during the investigation. Studying the files, the impression prevails that in some cases attempts were made to settle old scores with private or political opponents by denouncing them. In some cases, officers were declared suspicious who turned out to be perfectly respectable. For example, Lieutenant-Colonel H. Streuli, Chief Engineer of Border Brigade 6, a member of Zürich's cantonal government and a Federal Councilor-to-be, was investigated by mistake.[29] The fact that the investigation of the Front movement was flawed is also exemplified by the case of First Lieutenant O. Reimann, a right-wing extremist who was sentenced to death for treason two years later and was executed. He was questioned but managed to talk his way out of the allegations and was rehabilitated.[30] Many other right-wing extremists also successfully slipped through loopholes in the investigation.

Parliamentary committees later criticized the investigation as being too lenient. Councilor of State E. Klöti, the mayor of Zürich, said that he was "absolutely dissatisfied" with the results, explaining, "I believe that it was rather strange that the superior officer was put in charge of telling the suspect that he had to question him. In 1942, as city mayor I found out about cases of officers belonging to the Front movement who were declared not guilty after a criminal investigation and consequently stayed on posts for which they were unfit because of their mentality, which could be considered as non-democratic."[31] National Councilor H. Oprecht voiced a similar criticism, saying, "The way the clean-up operation was carried out was not very fortunate insofar as the immediate superiors of suspected officers handled the investigation. An immediate superior is unable to ensure that such a delicate offense will be investigated in an objective manner."[32]

The investigation of the Front movement left an ambiguous impression. The files on which it was based did not seem very substantial. They had been compiled by the military police of the territorial service, Group Ic of the army staff, which acted in coordination with the Federal Prosecutor's office. At the beginning of the war, Chief of the General Staff Labhart had issued a directive stating, "In order for the army command to be able to support the federal prosecutor's activities and to intervene in command matters if necessary, a central military office has to be designated which collects all military reports and information."[33] The army command was not very satisfied with the work performed by the military police. Chief of the General Staff Huber wrote to its head, Colonel Zumbrunn, "The mistakes committed [during the investigation] have stunned and enraged the concerned officers and their commanders alike; moreover, because these incidents have occurred so frequently there are doubts about the reliability of the military police. You have put the army command in general and the commander-in-chief of the armed forces in particular in an uncomfortable position." Huber demanded: "In the future, the information provided by the police section must be accurate and has to be verified in order to be deemed reliable."[34]

The flaws of the investigation were obvious to the army staff, causing a controversy among them about the usefulness of the procedure. General Guisan explained to the Federal Council that "this procedure is unprecedented and must not be repeated."[35] The Military Attorney General later wrote about the investigation: "In the spring of 1940, the army command tried to initiate a general purge. However, it encountered enormous difficulties substantiating the allegations and was facing other obstacles, making the operation a flop."[36] It was undoubtedly because of the bothersome incidents connected with the investigation that Colonel Zumbrunn was replaced by Lt. Colonel Roger Lang from Geneva as head of the military police.

When he was corps commander after the war, Alfred Ernst still believed that the investigation of the Front movement had been unsatisfactory only because it was suspended prematurely due to Germany's victories in the West "in order not to irritate Germany."[37] However, this view is not tenable because from the beginning General Guisan had established June 5 as the deadline for submitting the investigation reports, a time when the battle in the West was far from decided. Nevertheless, it may not be unjustified to assume that superior officers questioned members of the Front movement rather delicately in view of the Wehrmacht's overwhelming victories taking place at the same time. Shortly after France's defeat, Wille wrote to Däniker of his conviction that "the operation suggested to the General [would] not be carried out anymore today."[38]

Not all opponents of the Front understood why members of the movement, who advocated the "New Europe" proclaimed by the Third Reich, were so speedily rehabilitated. To all appearances, there indeed seemed to be a connection between the end of the investigation and Germany's victories on the battlefields in France. As Captain on the General Staff Ernst, a participant in the Officers' Conspiracy, wrote to the chief justice of the 8th Division, "By taking the foreign political situation into account, the General fully rehabilitated the officers belonging to the Front movement. I do not claim that these officers were traitors. However, it appeared strange to us that the same officers who used to be considered suspicious were all of a sudden supposed to be reliable just because the situation in Europe had changed in Germany's favor."[39] Ernst explained that he had never been a sympathizer of the Front movement but admitted that he did "not *a priori* consider every member of the Front movement to be a traitor; there were good officers and patriots who originally joined the 'Front' because they believed that it instilled in them the soldier-like spirit that we hoped would then imbue the state. In the beginning it appeared to do just that. However, as time went by, it became obvious that the 'Front' was more and more directed toward Germany and took over German ideologies. Comrades whom I respect left the Movement at that time. It is not acceptable at all to call these people disloyal to their country."[40]

H. Hausamann, a staff member of Army Intelligence who was among the first officers to find out that traitors were hiding out in the Front movement, made similar distinctions between some of its members, saying, "There were some officers in the Front of whom one knew very well that they would never betray their country. They had joined the Front when a large number of people were attracted to the movement. . . . In addition to the officers who were members of the Fronts there were a number of 'sympathizers,' officers who did not become formal members of a 'Front' but had officer friends who did. These officers turned into a strong and influential force for the Fronts, as several of them held key positions or significant command posts in the army."[41]

The "purge" may have yielded very few immediate results, but it clearly separated the pro-German from the pro-Allied camps. Stalwart Front members who had not been investigated or had emerged unharmed from the investigation felt justified in their activities and at first gained the upper hand. However, they betrayed themselves by showing even more openly their support of Hitler's Germany after the Wehrmacht's victory in the West—and by doing so they increasingly isolated themselves. Hausamann wrote: "Some members of the Front became impertinent, starting to talk about 'claiming leadership' and similar things. These officers had General Guisan's photograph removed in the barracks to have it replaced by that of General Wille. [The counter-intelligence service] listened in on some disturbing telephone conversations between officers who were members or sympathizers of the Fronts and the German legation. Soldiers and even officers bluntly declared that they did not believe there would be any fighting [against Germany]."[42] Hausamann stated that after France's collapse the officers who unwaveringly believed in a western-style democracy had to go through a "time of real suffering," adding, "the sympathizers of the members of the Front movement began to rebel, and Federal Councilor Pilet-Golaz lent an open ear to them."[43] As is generally the case when someone or some cause is successful, numerous hangers-on began manifesting themselves.

During the first week of August 1940, the "Action for National Resistance" reported that the propaganda of the Front movement had significantly intensified and had become the "number one" threat to Switzerland. Even if it was too early to judge its effects, the "passivity on the national side [was] certainly not suitable to hold back those who [hesitated to join the Movement]."[44] The army command did not fail to notice this threatening development, which was looming in spite of the investigation of the Front movement and the Rütli report. General Guisan was told during a meeting of the Swiss Association of Non-Commissioned Officers in Lugano that in several towns propaganda efforts had been stepped up to "use [officers and NCOs] for the current political revival movements." In reaction to this news, the General wrote a "memorandum regarding the warning about political movements" which he handed out to the corps commanders and the chief of the general staff during an army conference on October 19, 1940. During a discussion of the memo, Corps Commander Prisi indicated that "undeniably, the 5th Division is a particularly fertile breeding-ground" for the Fronts, adding that even if the officers stayed away from politics while on duty they displayed "a benevolently indifferent attitude" toward the "National Movement of Switzerland," the new umbrella organization of the Fronts.[45]

General Guisan did not order any additional investigation after the "purge" of spring 1940, even though it was suggested to him. In his postwar report,

Guisan wrote, "[This investigation]—as painful as it was—was necessary in order to maintain the confidence in, the discipline within, and the reputation of the army. The investigation, whose scope was limited to the officers' corps, was an exceptional measure that could not be repeated. When the Head of the Military Department requested, in April 1944, that I should carry out a 'purge' in the armed forces, I was of the opinion that it was not advisable to grant this request, which was primarily formulated in reaction to a debate in the parliament about the case of a high-ranking officer who had been convicted of treason."[46]

The unusually extensive steps taken by cantonal police forces and the counter-intelligence service of the army to watch individuals who appeared to be unreliable were increasingly successful. For some time, denouncing became an activity that was considered an honorable patriotic duty. J. R. von Salis, who was an independent commentator on a weekly radio show during the war, wrote, "Nobody was protected from being suspected of advancing ideologies at that time—including myself."[47] Some soldiers were constantly on their guard in order not to be mistakenly suspected of wrongdoing. Captain on the General Staff E. Wehrli wrote to his mother at the end of June 1940: "I have to be careful what I write because we have a police force that dares to open the letters of officers who they believe are not model citizens."[48]

When Switzerland was struggling to survive, it indeed did not hesitate to use methods that did not always correspond to the ideals of a liberal state founded on the rule of law. During World War II, Swiss citizens and soldiers had to make significant concessions in regard to their cherished individual freedoms. But the description of one foreign historian, who described Switzerland's behavior as "Helvetian Fascism,"[49] is surely exaggerated. Similarly, the phrase "Helvetian totalitarianism" used by H.-U. Jost[50] should be mentioned in quotation marks only, as the investigatory activities were not based on aggressive ideology but employed only at that time as a defense mechanism. General Guisan may have believed that using these methods was ugly, but they did not seem unjustified as measures applied by a democracy in self-defense during an exceptional situation.

12

Alert During Germany's 1940 Western Campaign

SHORTLY AFTER THE BEGINNING OF OPERATION "Weserübung," Germany's invasion of Denmark and Norway, Federal Councilor Etter informed the Department of Military Affairs that he had received confidential information from "a well-informed source who is a friend of ours" that "in eight to ten days an offensive is very likely to be launched in the West across Holland and Belgium." He added that Germany and Italy had agreed not to attack Switzerland if "our press remained silent" and if "a panic [was avoided] among civilians and the military." Federal Councilor Minger, the head of the Military Department, forwarded the information to the General, who in turn forwarded it to the head of Swiss Military Intelligence, Masson.[1]

On April 18, the Federal Council and the General issued common instructions on "how reservists shall react in case of a surprise attack" by a foreign power. The commander-in-chief had initiated these joint instructions, which were submitted to the Cabinet for approval by Federal Councilor Minger[2] and signed by Federal President Pilet-Golaz and Vice Chancellor Leimgruber as representatives of the government. Referring to the experience in Scandinavia, where saboteurs, parachutists, and a "fifth column" had caused considerable confusion, the instructions clearly expressed a strong determination to put up resistance. They read, "All soldiers shall immediately be subject to martial laws and traditions when 'wartime mobilization in case of a surprise attack' is ordered. It is every officer's duty to gather all soldiers and to fight ruthlessly and vehemently against parachutists, air infantry, and saboteurs. When no officer or non-commissioned officer is present, every soldier shall act on his own initiative, using his entire strength. . . . Should information be dissipated through the radio, flyers, or other means that questions the Federal Council's and the army command's determination to put up resistance, it shall be considered an invention of enemy propaganda. Our country shall defend itself to the utmost, with all means, against any aggressor."[3]

These instructions were required to be glued into every soldier's record booklet and posted in every town for the public to read. Both people and press applauded the unambiguous language that was directed against any potential aggressor.[4]

At the same time, the General asked the Federal Council to give him the authority to independently proclaim a state of mobilization if communication with the Federal Government was interrupted in the event of a surprise attack.[5] The General also issued an order instructing all officers and non-commissioned officers to carry their pistols instead of their sabers when going on leave. Moreover, the armed forces were informed that a small amount of ammunition would be distributed shortly to all soldiers on call.[6] To ensure that the order to 'mobilize all troops in the event of a surprise attack' was transmitted, radio stations, telegraphs, and couriers were to be prepared and flyers printed to be thrown out of aircraft over the corps assembly points and the cantonal capitals.[7]

In his conversations with Gafner after the war, General Guisan explained that he did not think Switzerland's intelligence service had been informed in advance of Germany's attack on Denmark and Norway.[8] However, Barbey wrote in his diary that Captain Ernst, the head of the "German Desk" at the intelligence service, told him on the day of the invasion that "he had received reliable information about the aggression three weeks earlier [but] was unable to follow up on it because X considered it to be far-fetched."[9] Notes written by Major Daniel support the latter version, stating that because a German attack on Scandinavia was very improbable, a high-ranking officer of the intelligence service blocked an agency report from being transmitted to Intelligence Chief Masson.[10] The information, which of course turned out to be accurate, apparently came from the "Viking" line, which the intelligence service did not yet fully trust. As Masson later explained, "At the end of March, 1940, more than three weeks before the beginning of Germany's attack on Denmark and Norway, one of our trusted informants who maintained useful contacts with the supreme command of the Wehrmacht came to see us in Basel to inform us of the imminent operations in Scandinavia, which he said would definitely begin before the end of April. In April, our informant came back and told us about the imminent western campaign, which he said could begin any day after May 7. He explained to us that Holland and Belgium's neutrality would be infringed but that Switzerland was not endangered. He added that we should not be bluffed by troop movements in southern Germany, which would serve exclusively to tie French troops to the upper part of the Rhine River."[11]

To demonstrate Switzerland's determination to resist an aggressor at all costs, local civil defense units were established even before Germany's western push. At an army briefing on April 29, Chief of the General Staff Huber explained that volunteer defense units were being planned to reinforce the country's combat potential. Huber continued: "These local civil defense units should be organized in every town to fight against saboteurs and parachute troops."[12] They were to be placed under the command of officers or NCOs who were no longer serving or had been suspended. The General added that "the war material administration [had] a stock of 70,000 old guns with ammunition which [could] be made available to local defense units."[13] During the first week of May 1940, General Guisan officially requested that the Federal Council approve the formation of armed "surveillance and defense troops." Their tasks were "to prevent sabotage; immediately fight against every foreign intruder; maintain order and security in the town. . . . Creating these local defense units is extremely urgent; hence, I request that the Federal Council authorize me to proceed as soon as possible."[14]

The Federal Council acted without delay, granting the General's request three days later, on May 7, reserving, however, the right to determine the units' organizational statutes at a later date.[15] On the day after the second mobilization of the entire armed forces, the General issued the instructions for the local civil defense units, which were to report to the territorial service of the army.[16]

Following Germany's invasions of Holland, Belgium, and Luxembourg, through which the Wehrmacht launched its primary assault on France, on May 11, the Federal Council, at the General's request, called up the entire armed forces for the second time since the start of the war. The General had held separate briefings with Chief of Intelligence Masson, Chief of the General Staff Huber, and his Adjutant Dollfus at Gümligen on May 9 to examine the need for mobilizing the troops.[17] First news of the beginning of the German offensive in the west reached the General's personal staff at 3:00 a.m. on May 10. In view of this information, the General canceled an inspection of the Light Troops scheduled for that day and drove to the army staff's headquarters in Langnau instead, accompanied by his adjutant, von Ernst, and his aide, Marguth. The diary of the army staff stated: "At about 09:00 hours, General arrives to discuss the situation. The assistant chiefs of staff Ia to Ic have also been summoned. At about 10:30 hours, the General leaves for Bern to see the Federal Council with the signed request for re-mobilizing the armed forces in his hands."[18] Hence, the briefing with the General was attended not only by Chief of the General Staff Huber but also by officers von Erlach (Ia), Marty (Ib), and Dubois (Ic).

The General's meeting with the Federal Council lasted one hour, after

DER OBERBEFEHLSHABER DER ARMEE

9272   *CH*

GENÖSS·····ISS
ANDEPA·····NT   A.H.Q., 15. 5. 40.
16. MAI 1940
0 4 . 1 4

Armeebefehl
======================

Die neuesten Kriegsereignisse bestätigen, dass dort, wo selbst wenige
entschlossene Kämpfer genügt hätten, das feindliche Vorwärtskommen zu verun-
möglichen, deren Versagen dem Feind gestatteten, zunächst in die so entstan-
denen Lücken einzudringen, sie rasch zu erweitern und sodann vorwärts zu stos-
sen. Dieses Versagen Einzelner ist mit die Ursache des täglichen Vordringens
gewisser Truppen.

Ich erinnere an die hohe Pflicht des Soldaten, an Ort und Stelle er-
bittert Widerstand zu leisten. Verzögerungskampf führen nur zum vornherein
und durch besondern höheren Befehl bestimmte Truppen. Ueberalldort, wo
H a l t e n befohlen ist, macht es sich jeder Kämpfer, auch wenn er auf sich
allein angewiesen ist, zur Gewissenspflicht, auf der ihm zugewiesenen Stelle
zu kämpfen. Die Schützentrupps, ob überholt oder umringelt, kämpfen in ihrer
Stellung bis keine Munition mehr vorhanden ist. Dann kommt die blanke Waffe
an die Reihe..... Die Mitrailleure, die Kanoniere der Schweren Waffen, die
Artilleristen, ob im Bunker oder auf dem Feld, verlassen ihre Waffen nicht
und zerstören sie, bevor sich der Gegner ihrer bemächtigt. Dann kämpfen Be-
dienungsmannschaften weiter wie Schützentrupps. Solange ein Mann noch eine
Patrone hat oder sich seiner blanken Waffen noch zu bedienen vermag, ergibt
er sich nicht.

Damit weiss jeder, was ich von ihm erwarte und was sein einziger Ge-
danke sein bereit zu sein, das Leben einzusetzen, dort, wo ihn die Pflicht
hingerufen hat.

Der General:

Guisan

Ist allen Kampftruppen
sofort zur Kenntnis zu
bringen.

34

Original copy of General Guisan's order to the Armed Forces during the heightened
alert on May 15, 1940. (BAr)

which it was agreed that calling up the entire armed forces was absolutely necessary.[19] At 12:30 hours, an official announcement was made to call up the troops on the following day at 09:00 hours. After returning to his command post, the General went for a ride on his horse between 5 and 6 p.m.[20] Toward the evening of that same memorable day, Lieutenant-Colonel Gonard returned from his interim command post at Infantry Regiment 7 to once again assume the position of head of the Personal Staff. Colonel Perrenoud had filled in for him in his absence.[21]

On May 11, the day before Pentecost—a "particularly beautiful, sunny spring day"—the troops reported to their duty stations according to schedule; no incidents occurred. Several sources agreed that the troops were in even better spirits than in 1939.[22] The combat troops numbered 450,000 and the auxiliary troops another 250,000, bringing the total to 700,000 men, an increase of more than ten percent since 1939.[23]

The General issued an order of the day to the troops in which he wrote: "Our army is ready to fulfill its duty at all the borders. It will defend the liberty of our country with all its energy against any aggressor. If necessary, we will all sacrifice our lives for our children and for the future of our beautiful country. . . . The motto is simple: Let us stay calm, strong, united. That is how we will remain a free people." Once again he admonished the troops, "If any news is spread through the radio, flyers, or other media which questions the Federal Council's or the General's spirit of resistance, it shall be considered a lie disseminated by defeatist propaganda."[24] This order had been prepared the previous day. Barbey explained that he had to "review the text of the order for the first day of mobilization with the General toward the evening."[25] Before midnight, Barbey brought the French version to army headquarters in Langnau to have it translated into German. Between 23:25 hours and 00:10 hours, the order was transmitted by telegraph in French and German; at 04:30 hours, printed copies were distributed by special couriers.[26]

On the evening of May 11, the intelligence service believed it had serious evidence that a German invasion of Switzerland was imminent. As early as May 10, Germany had begun to mass troops near its borders with Switzerland.[27] Masson and the army staff expected an attack to be staged during the night of May 14–15. On the previous night, Barbey submitted for Huber's approval the cooperation plans that had been arranged with France regarding the deployment of liaison officers. When he got to the army headquarters at midnight, Huber, "who is usually not a night owl," was still at work, "displaying the same calmness as usual, despite the rumors that say that the critical moment has arrived, that [the attack] will happen during the night of May 14–15."[28] The following day, Barbey wrote, "Since this morning, the news and rumors have been accumulating, unanimously saying, 'It will happen tonight between 2 and 4 a.m.' I have packed my officer's bag."[29]

On three occasions during that night, Masson personally inquired of the command of the 2nd Army Corps, in whose border sector the Germans were expected to launch their invasion, whether there were signs of an imminent attack. The captain on the general staff who answered Masson's calls remembered "having to repeat three times that our border troops could see nothing suspicious; no extraordinary troop movements (artillery, engineer troops) [were] sighted" as far as 25 miles into the Black Forest.[30] Masson later recounted that the intelligence service was "a place of calm and quiet when the events of May 1940 shook up Western Europe."[31] Several of his contemporaries seriously questioned his view. Pilet-Golaz recalled that the fear was great and had seized some of the army staff as well, adding, "On Tuesday, 14 May, at the first hour of the day, I had a meeting with Colonel Masson, whom I found to be in a state of worrisome excitement. Alas, what's more, he was not the only one."[32]

Several reports stated that the panic was fanned through rumors that had been spread by members of the army staff. Max Iklé, a future director of the Swiss National Bank who was serving in Langnau as a first lieutenant at the time, wrote to this author: "During those days, there was tremendous nervousness; it emanated from the Assistant Chief of Staff for the Front, Colonel Gugger, and spread to the entire army staff and to the entire armed forces; it reached as far as the bunkers at the border."[33] Colonel Germann, who had gone to Langnau at the time to witness the atmosphere, confirmed that "the panic about an imminent attack on our country . . . also seized some officers on the army staff."[34] Captain René Hentsch confidentially reported to the General that several people had told him that civilians "were insistently asked" to run for shelter because Switzerland would be attacked by the Germans during the night of May 14–15 between 2 and 3 A.M. Hentsch continued his report by stating, "What is particularly grave about this matter is the fact that the panic was caused by officers on the army staff and apparently even by quite high-ranking officers. It also appears that the wives of several of these officers called up their friends left and right to advise them to flee. An officer on your personal staff is also said to be among those who alarmed the public."[35] Corps Commander Wille informed the General that "some civilians and troops [were] very concerned about how nervous some top leaders [were] among the army staff" and that it was "disturbing how some gentlemen of the army staff [were] nervous and alarmed colonels' families during the night of May 14–15, urging them to flee."[36] There is no evidence in the archives to support these statements. It seems that the General did not have the matter investigated. Moreover, Kreis researched this issue and concluded that there were no files in the Military Attorney General's office to support claims that officers deserted their troops.[37]

In the army staff's diary there was no indication of any agitation at the command post, where a state of alert was declared at 22:00 hours. However, the army headquarters received a number of telephone calls during the night of May 14–15 that suggested the country was on the verge of panic, especially people in the border areas of northern and eastern Switzerland. One entry read: "03:40 hours, cantonal cabinet member Dr. Römer from St. Gallen asks why no evacuation has been ordered for the civilians along the German border in Canton St. Gallen in view of the attack that is expected to occur in one hour." At 03:50 hours, territorial command post No. 6 called to say that it would like to "requisition private vehicles in order to evacuate the major banks, which had received information that an attack was imminent on Switzerland"; at 06:30 hours, "Dr. Läger, a civilian from the banking community, [asked] whether it was correct that the city of Basel was to be evacuated." Captain on the General Staff Adrian Prisi, the duty officer and diary writer, explained that he tried to calm some of the callers himself while referring others to Colonel W. Müller, the deputy chief of the intelligence service, adding, "Colonel Müller informs me of the general situation; he makes an appeal to remain calm. Evacuating the banks at the current time would create a complete panic. He says that he reassured cabinet member Römer. He believes that the panic has been caused by Prof. Meyer from Zürich who has been calling people all over Switzerland to spread stories of atrocities."[38] It is interesting to note that Professor Karl Meyer, chairman of the history department at the University of Zürich, was suspected of being a panic-monger during the critical days of May 1940. In fact, he contributed greatly to the resistance movement against Nazi Germany.[39]

The General's personal staff in Gümligen kept cool. R. Eibel, who was on duty at the General's headquarters during the night of May 14–15, reported that "the atmosphere [around Guisan] was calm and composed; there was no sign of agitation. On the evening of the day after Whitmonday [May 14, 1940], Masson was invited for dinner there. After being briefed by Masson on the situation, Guisan wanted to know if they should move into the war command post. Masson replied that his job was to provide the information needed to assess the situation and that the decision was up to the General. Gonard told the staff members, 'If something happens, it will be tonight toward dawn. What matters most is that you are rested. I order you to go to sleep.'" Eibel spent the night next to the telephone, writing farewell letters. The telephone rang only once, near dawn. The duty officer thought that this would be the call informing the General the attack had begun; instead, a quiet voice announced, "checking the line."[40]

The General indeed appears to have decided to move into the secret command post in a bomb-proof cavern at a quarry in Bolligen, which he had set up two days earlier.[41] The personal staff's diary mentioned, "[At] 22:05 hours, the General leaves his headquarters for the night. With him are Divisional Commander Huber, Captain Huber, and First Lieutenant Frey. First Lieutenant Marguth is in charge of the night guards at the headquarters." The next morning, the diary recorded, "[At] 07:50, the General returns to his headquarters, accompanied by First Lieutenant Frey. From 10:45 to 11:35, the General went for a horseback ride. From 12:55 to 13:10, he receives Major Barbey."[42] According to these entries, the commander-in-chief did not spend the night of the alert in his bed at Gümligen Castle.

Even though the night during which a German attack was expected went by without incident, the state of alert remained in force. On the morning of May 15, a situation report signed by Masson—undoubtedly compiled by A. Ernst, the head of the "German Desk"—stated that the area from the Black Forest and Hegau to Ulm still appeared to be densely occupied by German troops, including motorized heavy artillery, adding, "Details not verifiable; however, I am convinced that the numerous motorized couriers that have been observed there are not just driving around the area; troops must already be stationed off the main roads, unless they are advance command troops that are getting quarters ready." The report suggested that several powerful German divisions were present in that area, concluding, "It is possible that the Germans will carry out the attack through our country and reach their operational goal through the Jura Mountains with less than forty divisions if they manage to inflict a decisive defeat on the French Army in the north. It is possible that the attack, which I consider to be particularly promising in the Frick Valley, will be launched from the southern part of the Black Forest across the Rhine and get past our army's positions without using a lot of heavy artillery. An attack could be launched without our receiving any additional substantial information about movements of German troops and their going into position. It is impossible for us to know when the number of divisions needed for an attack will be available."[43] The report ended by suggesting that it was necessary to continue acting as if "the attack was possible at any moment." Colonel Claude Du Pasquier, commander of Border Brigade 3, who was to assume the command of the ad hoc "Gempen" division in the event of a German invasion, wrote in his diary that after the critical days around the weekend of Pentecost, Masson considered "the risk of a German attack at 80 percent. Charming!"[44]

Also on the morning of May 15, Chief of the General Staff Huber held a briefing during which he informed the staff that the orders for triggering Case North were ready, adding, "The state of alert of [May] 14 to 15 was ordered because a German attack was reportedly imminent and Italy was expected to enter the war at any moment. The risk still exists. The state of absolute readiness has to be maintained; no slackening is allowed."[45] He explained that the order for moving to the martial command post in Langnau had already been issued; making the quarters bombproof was a top priority. Assistant Chief of Staff for the Front Gugger specified that the current news was "rather reassuring" and that the state of alert had been lifted during the daytime for the border troops, the mountain brigades, and the Sargans fortress; it would go into effect again during the night.[46]

The memorable night of heightened alert, during which signs of nervousness and gloom surfaced, prompted the General to write an order to the troops to clarify once again what he expected each one of them to do. He wrote: "I recall the soldiers' great duty to put up bitter resistance in their positions. [The] strategy of delaying the enemy [shall be used] only in the beginning and by specific troops upon special higher order. Wherever the order has been issued to halt, every fighter shall dutifully fight at the spot assigned to him even if he is on his own. The troops of privates that have been bypassed or surrounded shall continue fighting in their positions until they have no ammunition left. Then they shall use their hand weapons. . . . As long as a man has one shell left or is able to use his hand weapon, he shall not surrender."[47] This order, which was published on May 15 in the press as well, provided new moral support, even to the panic-stricken civilians.

Another order of the day was prepared for the event of a German attack, which was to be read to the troops as soon as the fighting had started. Two drafts of this order were written in French, each with handwritten corrections by Guisan; hence, there is no doubt that the General was its author or was at least personally involved in its formulation. One of the drafts read:

> The storm which has engulfed Europe has now reached Switzerland as well. The moment of the great trial, of privation and sacrifices has come. During the coming days, the army's and the entire population's resistance will be tested. The army is determined to fiercely defend every inch of our territory. I know that the country will prove itself worthy of its past, of its six centuries of history, honor, and loyalty. I am confident that everyone will do his duty. The only thing that counts today is Switzerland. It must remain ours. Our motto is "hold out." As our ancestors did, we bow only to God. May God protect my country.[48]

The second draft stated: "At the border the blood of the confederates has started flowing, the blood of war and of freedom. We shall not be forced to the ground by an invasion."[49] If there were any further need to prove General Guisan's determination to fight, these drafts of an order of the day are compelling evidence.

As rumors circulated about an imminent German invasion during the week of Pentecost 1940, a panic spread among the population living in the border areas and in major cities. A constant stream of evacuees left the urban centers of Basel and Zürich in their vehicles to seek shelter in central and western Switzerland and the Grisons. In an internal general staff memo, Major Daniel wrote that it was no exaggeration to say that some people had lost their head, "[most] particularly the well-to-do class which should have set an example. Those of us who were driving on Switzerland's roads during that time will never forget the exodus of cars and people from eastern and northern Switzerland towards western Switzerland and the mountains."[50]

In his postwar report, General Guisan mentioned the "wave of panic" that rolled over the country in May 1940, adding, "There was an exodus of civilians who fled from apparently threatened areas and especially from the big cities to go to the areas of the country that were considered safe, to French-speaking Switzerland, the Alps, and Ticino. It was above all the people who owned a car who left."[51] The General later explained that he was criticized for using the word "panic" in his report but insisted that the term was justified, saying, "Reports received at the headquarters during the night of May 14–15 mentioned large-scale hurried evacuations by parts of the civilian population. We do not want to close our eyes to this chapter."[52]

Myriam, the General's daughter who lived in Bern with her family, also took part in the exodus. Perrin recounted: "During the first big alert of May 1940, when a German invasion was looming, [Myriam] escaped to her parents' home in Pully 'after hastily putting her two children into large laundry baskets in which she had packed some clothes.' If an invasion took place it would come from the north, so Pully seemed to be a safe haven."[53]

The mass exodus of people from the cities was the news of the day. Germany's envoy Köcher reported to Berlin, "Federal Councilor Celio made some bitter comments about the well-to-do people from Basel and Zurich fleeing head over heels. He said that the mass of the population received the impression that they were left behind unprotected. Some were even said to tell the runaways not to expect to be welcomed back with open arms, as they would not hesitate to make themselves comfortable in rich people's homes if they got desperate."[54]

Civil authorities and foreign diplomats in Bern also expected a German invasion during these days. In some residences for foreign legations, preparations were made for an emergency evacuation. Federal President Pilet-Golaz reported, "I saw with my own eyes that blackened pieces of documents were burned in a hurry and without discretion rose from the gardens that surrounded the [villas]. Diplomats called me up to say goodbye and to wish me luck."[55] Pilet-Golaz himself hardly slept two or three hours a night during those days. He spent the night of May 15–16 at the secret command post that had been prepared for the Federal Council and informed the army command where he could be reached. He and the General were convinced that Hitler was determined to attack Switzerland if the German troops failed to advance on the right, or northern, wing through the Low Countries. After May 15, Pilet-Golaz agreed with Guisan that strategic developments in the north made a German attack on Switzerland unnecessary, but he admitted that he had no "irrefutable" proof for his view.[56]

Ulrich von Hassel, a German diplomat who arrived in Switzerland on May 11 to visit his wife who was taking a cure in Arosa, noted that the military preparations in the country left the impression of "a real panic." "Switzerland," he described, "looks like a highly mobilized country that is at war—much more so than Germany! You virtually stumble across troops everywhere. There is talk of interning the Germans, and the good people of Zürich and Basel are bringing their wives and children to the mountains. The idea of paratroopers and the 'fifth column' is spreading fear and terror. At public buildings, bridges, etc. in Zürich you see barbed wire, barricades, etc."[57]

There may have been some signs of fear and despair here and there, but there was still determination to face the aggressor. P. Schmid-Ammann, who stood on guard at the border with a group of fusiliers from the territorial reserve troops, gave an account of the atmosphere there, writing, "I had ammunition for my light machine-gun, but I knew that in one or two hours the fighting would start and the ammunition would be sufficient to put up resistance for half an hour at the most, and then I would be done with. . . . We would have gone all out. Everyone from privates to the colonel was determined to resist. We could hardly believe that anything would happen to us. And we would not have been afraid if something had happened. We even said, 'may they come.'"[58]

Captain on the General Staff E. Wehrli wrote to his parents, "It is probable that we will not be attacked," even though he admitted that it was not impossible either.[59] He noticed "one thing above all. In our unit, there is absolutely no agitation; on the contrary, the atmosphere is excellent. Perhaps this is not the case everywhere, but it is in large parts of my battalion. The civilians are much more restless; it is a disgrace to see all those people fleeing to western Switzerland in their cars. It is a disgrace above all because our people say, 'You see, the big wheels who have the means bring their families into safety, while the proletarians remain at the front and their families stay at home in the neighborhoods adjacent to the Limmat front; they cannot afford to evacuate their families."[60]

During the critical hours of May 1940, the telephone network was on the brink of breaking down due to the "unusually high volume" of calls, forcing the telephone company to limit calls to three minutes. Telephone calls among the military were not limited at first; however, when the waiting time for calls between the troops and the army command reached forty to fifty minutes, they were restricted to twelve minutes, bringing down the waiting time to fifteen minutes. The restriction was lifted again, though, because there was concern that the commander-in-chief might have to limit the duration of his calls as well. The longest calls registered at the army command during mid-May 1940 were 25 and 35 minutes.[61]

In view of the apparent risk of a German attack during the week of Pentecost, Guisan faced the difficult question whether he should deploy his troops according to Case North. He decided to delay an all-out deployment as long as possible. The border troops took up their positions, but the positions along the Limmat front were not fully manned. In his postwar report, the General commented on this decision: "After mobilizing the entire armed forces on May 11, we could not take in all the positions that had been identified under the plan of operations for Case North because we had to take into account our country's neutrality. However, we deployed the troops as close as possible to these positions."[62] The General kept troops back not only to abide by Switzerland's neutrality but also for strategic reasons, explaining, "Indeed, the only problem that we kept facing was as follows: Was it advisable to continue exposing the western front as stipulated under Case North and to deploy the entire 1st Division to the Limmat, to the sector of the 'Dietikon Group'? Should the ad hoc 'Gempen' division be formed without delay and be deployed to its sector? . . . I was reluctant to tie down these reserve troops by deploying them to the front as long as there was a chance that I might need them later in another hot spot."[63]

In line with the General's decision, Chief of the General Staff Huber explained during a briefing on the evening of May 10 that "the main reason for mobilizing the troops are the closed borders. We do not know what is going on behind them. We are not scheduled to go into any particular positions for now; only a few movements will be carried out. Generally speaking the troops shall remain at their assembly points."[64]

Some undated handwritten notes by Guisan must have been written during those days of waiting and anxiety as a result of discussions with Huber. They read: "Don't be impressed by sensational news. Remain calm in case of combat around Basel. Don't get drawn into conflict."[65]

On May 14, the General issued special operations order No. 4, instructing the Geneva troops of the 1st Division to go into position the following night in the sector Bremgarten–Dietikon on the Limmat front.[66] This gradual movement of troops to the northwest at the expense of the western front was undoubtedly in line with the French cooperation talks, but it did not fully correspond to the plan of operations stipulated under Case North,[67] as some authors erroneously believe.[68]

Those critical days and nights following the second mobilization of the entire armed forces on May 11 were felt to be the most serious military threat to Switzerland during World War II. Initially historians agreed.[69] General Guisan wrote about the night of May 14–15, when the "panic-like agitation" peaked: "At that moment, without exactly knowing why, our country was in a period of utmost military danger. If the German offensive, which we suddenly noticed was concentrated at the Meuse River, at the level of Sedan, had not been successful, there would have been the risk of a second operation to be launched intending to bypass the right wing of the French defense line. This bypassing movement could have been carried out on Swiss territory. German forces appeared to be ready to intervene for that purpose."[70] Guisan added that even after the successful German breakthrough at the Meuse, their "mysterious troops [remained] concentrated in the Black Forest," keeping up the threat in that area.

Huber expressed a similar view, stating, "In the course of the battle of France a secondary 'Operation Switzerland' was looming. The [German] forces needed for such an operation were positioned at a short distance." He added that "the time around May 15 [was] particularly critical for Switzerland, when the German push was temporarily slowed down in front of the defensive wall at Sedan."[71]

General Guisan and Chief of the General Staff Huber remained convinced until the end of their lives that Switzerland was "never as close to getting entangled in the war" as during those days in May 1940. However, historiography has shown that the two top military leaders were wrong in this respect.[72]

Once it became more and more obvious that Germany's western offensive would end to France's disadvantage, and once the German troops started moving south, beginning to surround Switzerland, the Swiss forces gradually moved from their positions at the Limmat to the northwest and then to the southwest. Italy's entry into the war on June 10 as Germany's ally was all the more alarming. After Paris fell on June 14, the General's personal staff was sad and depressed, albeit neither discouraged nor desperate. It took them hours to recover from the shock of the news and to refocus on the idea of resistance.[73] The march of German troops into Paris was a sad event not only for those who had intellectual and cultural ties with France but also for those who cherished the idea of liberty. Barbey wrote in his diary: "Paris occupied! Don't have the heart to write more about it."[74] The following day the fortress of Verdun fell as well.

Denis de Rougemont, a writer who served in Bern as a lieutenant of the territorial reserve in the "Army and Home" section at the time, contributed a lead article to the daily *Gazette de Lausanne* on June 17 entitled, "At this hour when Paris . . ." In the article he explained that every idler was able to recognize the city's beauty, but the German conquerors would never be capable of recognizing its spiritual significance. Without mentioning Hitler's name, de Rougemont used the phrase, "the tragic powerlessness of this victorious conqueror." On the same day, the author was scolded by a member of the General's personal staff for insulting a foreign head of state, thereby jeopardizing the country's safety, adding, "That's grave, that's very grave." His superior in the military summoned him to his office to tell him that the German Ambassador had protested the article and that as a consequence he might be brought before a military court. Two days later, his colonel informed him that the General had personally sentenced him to 15 days of detention, which de Rougemont was allowed to serve at his home.[75] This incident shows that even Guisan and his entourage were initially bothered by the shock of the German victory and clearly believed that further danger was near.

Gonard explained that operational moves were made before "the German tanks arrived at the western foothills of the Jura mountains; we shifted our defense line to the west and kept extending it in that direction. . . . The depth at the Mentue river was increased with troops that had previously been stationed at the Limmat."[76] These troop movements had begun as early as the night of June 4–5 when the left wing of the defense line in the sector of the Gempen Plateau and the Upper Hauenstein Mountain was reinforced by troops from the 7th and 2nd Divisions once the French troops that were supposed to assist the Swiss were redeployed elsewhere. Moreover, the bridges across the Aare River between Thun and Biel were prepared for destruction and part of the army staff was moved from Langnau to Ittigen.[77] One week later, once the second phase of the battle of France was in full swing following Italy's declaration of war, the new situation prompted the commander-in-chief to reinforce further the defensive line in the west.

The General's deliberations, formulated by Barbey, indicate that based on information received on the French strategy, any assistance from France could henceforth only be symbolic and would serve to establish contact between the two armed forces. Any cooperation would take place on a much smaller scale than originally planned. It was likely that the French air force and antiaircraft defense would still be available, but in principle no French intervention troops would be deployed to Switzerland by road and railroad to seal the Swiss front line and to relieve some of its units. Guisan continued: "In case we don't ask for Allied assistance nor create a link with them right away, we will probably not get another chance to ask for assistance at a later date. Our strategy will have to focus on a withdrawal in a different direction, generally toward the center of the country, the foothills of the Alps and the St. Gotthard region."[78] At that moment, on June 13, in view of the looming French defeat, the Swiss Army command for the first time hinted at a strategic withdrawal into a *Réduit* in the Alps. It did not mention the possibility of retreating to French territory.[79]

A new strategic approach had already been considered a few weeks earlier, on May 25, when the commander-in-chief requested that the chief of the general staff examine alternatives to the defense strategies prepared for Case North and Case West. In a situation report undoubtedly written by Gonard, the General declared that the planned front line should be held as long as possible; nevertheless, the possibility of evacuating the troops should not be excluded in case incursions happened at the front that could not be re-sealed. In the event of a withdrawal, the following should be considered: "We must have a place to withdraw to. This place can be either positions held by fresh troops or a region where the difficult terrain would allow us to reorganize our resistance efficiently." The General explained that for the first option to be available an agreement would have to exist with the opponent of an aggressor which would allow the ally to occupy a rearward position on which the Swiss troops could fall back. The second option would come into play if no outside assistance was available and the Swiss would have to defend themselves solely with their own means. In this case, the foothills of the Alps and the Alps would be the natural choice of location for a withdrawal of the army, allowing Switzerland to fulfill its traditional historic task of guarding the Alpine mountain passes. Hence, Guisan concluded, "For Case N[orth] the first alternative means that the army would have to pull back toward the W[est]; the second alternative on the other hand means that we would have to withdraw toward the S[outh]."[80] In this explanation, the idea of the *Réduit* was also clearly on the General's mind even if he did not mention the word itself.

Chief of the General Staff Huber reported at a briefing on June 16 that the first troops of the German panzer group led by General Guderian had arrived at the Swiss border checkpoint near Porrentruy earlier that day.[81] The General later erroneously wrote that the German troops arrived at the border only on June 20.[82] After personally visiting the border checkpoint, Guderian immediately ordered his troops to turn around and continue their way northeast parallel to the Swiss border in order to join up with Dollmann's army that was advancing south along the Rhine, thereby encircling the 45th French Army Corps headed by General Daille that was pulling back from Burgundy.[83] Through this maneuver, the last French units that were supposed to assist Switzerland were doomed.

Very soon "large masses of refugees" began crowding Switzerland's borders. On June 16, close to 2,000 people arrived in Switzerland through the checkpoint at Boncourt.[84] On the evening of June 19, General Daille showed up at the checkpoint at Goumois, requesting that the troops of his 45th Army Corps—consisting of the French 67th Division, the Polish 2nd Division, and the 2nd Colonial Cavalry Brigade from Morocco—be admitted to Switzerland to avoid being caught and imprisoned by the Germans. They were disarmed and interned. Unlike in 1871, when Bourbaki's army was interned during the Franco-Prussian War, no written agreement was drafted to define the terms for Daille's troops to cross the border. In a briefing on June 20, Huber reported, "No convention has been signed with General Daille regarding crossing the border. The equipment and arms are being collected in the border area, and so are the vehicles and carts. The carts needed by the interned troops, especially for kitchens, will stay with them. The infantry troops are exhausted and will not be able to walk all the way to Biel. They will have to be transported there by rail and motorized vehicles."[85] Daille's corps that crossed the Swiss border during the night of June 19–20 included 29,700 Frenchmen and Moroccans, 12,000 Poles, and small detachments of Belgians and English. Overall they numbered 43,000 men, equipped with 7,800 horses and 1,600 motor vehicles.[86]

For some time it was not clear if an additional 150,000 men belonging to the French 8th Army, which was stationed in Sundgau, would also request to be interned in Switzerland.[87] However, Guderian's panzer troops stayed away from the Swiss border to keep Switzerland out of the line of fire, a consideration for which Federal President Pilet-Golaz thanked German Ambassador Köcher, who reported to Berlin, "[Mr. Pilet-Golaz confirmed that] it would have been easy for the Germans to instigate incidents at the border by ruthlessly chasing the French troops. However [he said], the German troops stopped several kilometers before the border and hence allowed the Swiss Army to fulfill its obligation as a neutral party by disarming the crossing [French] troops."[88]

General Guisan drove to the border to witness the crossing of the 45th French Corps. During the visit, he spoke not only with French General Daille and Polish General Prugar but also with interned troops to hear their stories.[89] It must have been during one of these conversations or shortly afterward that Captain Sandoz, the General's adjutant, witnessed members of a German patrol that had arrived at the Swiss border spit at the Swiss General.[90]

In the late afternoon of June 20, Jakob Huber also took a trip to the front to gain a firsthand impression of the situation. The officer who accompanied him, Captain Prisi, wrote: "At the southern entrance to the village of Lyss, we meet about ten French motorcycle riders who are unaccompanied. Chief stops them. They tell us that they have received orders to ride to Interlaken where they are supposed to meet their comrades who have been sent there by train. On our way to Biel we keep running into individual motorcycle riders, cars, and trucks heading toward Bern. They don't seem to have specific orders, heading toward the center of the country without supervision by our army. In Brügg, we run into colonial troops who leave a positive impression by standing to attention and saluting. Before reaching the Plateau of Reuchenette, we run into a column of bicycle riders about the size of a company riding toward Biel in a disciplined manner. It is striking that the bicycles, some of which are in bad shape, are not uniform. . . . Generally the impression prevails that almost all the officers are missing, which puts the columns of refugees into a state of disarray. Otherwise the troops do not look overly tired, and considering the fact that they are refugees they have generally kept their composure. We notice that most of them are shaved and salute, even if they do so in a nonchalant way."[91]

Following the internment of the French, some Swiss officers expressed doubts about the fighting spirit of the troops that had been earmarked to intervene on Switzerland's behalf in the event of a German attack. As Charles Daniel, an officer on the general staff, commented, "The operations of June 1940 demonstrated what the 45th Army Corps was really worth; its 67th Division completely lost its cohesion after a few days of combat of average intensity."[92] It was an irony of fate that the troops who were supposed to assist Switzerland in case of a German attack were those who sought shelter in Switzerland themselves and became internees. Instead of providing assistance, they put an additional burden on the Swiss Army, which had to allocate troops to watch the more than 40,000 interned men of Daille's corps.[93] Barbey, who was sent to Biel on the General's orders to assess the situation, was appalled at the chaos that reigned there. As a consequence, he suggested immediately replacing the commander of the town, as he was "incompetent and not up to the task."[94]

As preparations had been insufficient and the "Section for Prisoners and Internees" was unable to handle the large number of internment cases, the General established a special commissioner's office in charge of accomplishing the numerous organizational tasks in direct cooperation with the chief of the general staff and the Department of Foreign Affairs.[95] The General appointed Colonel Johannes von Muralt, the former assistant chief of staff for transports on the army staff, as "Federal Commissioner for Internment Matters."[96]

The internees were initially sent to the Bernese Oberland, the Napf region, and the Bernese lake district. The officers were allowed to take up quarters in hotels or, exceptionally, in private homes, while the other ranks were put up in barracks. The internees were occasionally asked to help out on farms and received a modest daily allowance.[97]

The pianist and former president of Poland, Paderewski, who was leading a secluded life on the shores of Lake Geneva, made a written request to Guisan to find the interned Polish men adequate jobs if possible, and asked him not to separate the officers from the other ranks. In his reply, Guisan promised to issue necessary instructions to grant the request.[98] The 45th French Corps managed to bring its cash box into Switzerland. It contained eight million French francs, which were exchanged into Swiss francs by the Swiss National Bank in accord with the army's general staff and used toward covering internment costs.[99]

The numerous civilian refugees who asked to be admitted to Switzerland posed a particular problem. On June 16, the General explained that it was impossible to admit the French civilians who were being hardpressed by advancing German troops; otherwise Switzerland would "be exposed to a variety of serious risks." He added, "The current situation among the warring parties beyond our borders is quite grave and confusing; hence, above all we must compromise neither our defense strategy nor possible changes that I may have to make to this strategy at any moment if the threat of an aggression materializes."[100] On the same day, Chief of the General Staff Huber explained at a briefing that the Federal Council had decided to admit, "in principle, children, mothers with children, old people, and handicapped persons. Admitting other people is out of the question."[101] The civilian refugees who were admitted were to be assembled around Porrentruy and to be evacuated by railway out of the dangerous border area. Three days later, on June 19, the commander-in-chief issued an additional order stating that members of labor groups were also to be considered civilians. Among civilians requesting to be admitted into the country, the only exceptions were to be made for those who were "under the threat of troops persecuting and firing at them."[102]

In the border area, people displayed their anti-German feelings while sympathizing with Daille's corps. Pilet-Golaz commented, "[Daille] was received as if he had been fighting heroically. . . . At the border, in the villages, and in the towns people were shouting, 'Down with the Krauts,' 'Down with the Macaronis.'"[103] In a meeting with the Federal President after visiting areas where the French troops were interned, Germany's Ambassador Köcher put forward "serious reservations about the way the internees were received and treated." The liaison officer between the government and the army command reported to the army staff about this meeting: "Germany's ambassador said that he had noticed the state of disarray in and around Biel, complaining most particularly about the fact that the officers were separated from the troops, that internees were sitting around restaurants without supervision, and that they were being celebrated virtually like heroes. The German minister did not hesitate to say that these incidents could have serious consequences."[104] The General refused to assume responsibility for civilians' behavior toward the internees, explaining, at an army briefing on June 22, "While the army behaves toward the interned soldiers according to the instructions, the same is not true of the population. The incidents that occurred at several places are indications that unfortunately the Federal Council failed to educate the people in time and to tell them how to behave toward internees."[105]

In view of the unpleasant circumstances, Guisan warned the Head of the Military Department, "Because of the development of the military, political, and diplomatic situation, our people *must stay calm.* I do not want to ring the alarm bell, but I believe that it is about time to let the people know that our neutrality obliges them to express their feelings with discretion and discipline. Whenever public manifestations that keep occurring *when civil refugees and military internees pass through town* express more than humanitarian and charitable feelings, they prove that our people do not understand that obligation and that necessity yet (for instance, incidents in Neuchâtel, Biel, etc.). It is therefore necessary to react while there is still time and *before this reaction is imposed on us* from the outside. The period of time from now until an armistice or even a peace agreement is signed will be crucial in this respect. We have received a sufficient number of warnings and lessons by now; even the slightest expression of our opinion, be it in writing or in speaking, is being monitored with utmost attention."[106]

Everyone in Switzerland was surprised by the complete collapse of France, one of Europe's major powers. Military experts had ruled out the possibility of a blitzkrieg against France. As Ernst observed, "We had not been able to predict this development. Nobody, not even officers of Army Intelligence, had reckoned with such a disastrous defeat of the Western Allies."[107] Due to the threatening situation, the chief of the general staff asked the commander-in-chief to urgently reinforce all crossing points in the Jura. Since no other troops were available, he recommended deploying infantry and artillery recruits there with 80 machine guns, 66 heavy guns, and 30 cannon.[108] Available infantry troops of Border Brigade 12 were regrouped under Colonel Montfort as the "Jorat" ad hoc formation in order to seal the area between Lake Neuchâtel and Lake Geneva.[109]

When the second stage of the Battle of France had begun after the British evacuation at Dunkirk, the Swiss Air Force became involved in combat with German aircraft that violated Switzerland's airspace. As General Guisan wrote about these incidents, "The police activities in the air on behalf of Switzerland's neutrality were an excellent exercise for our pilots. Especially in early June 1940, when the German offensive was in full swing in the west, our fighter pilots had the opportunity to compete with German pilots during battles. . . . The obvious fighting spirit with which our pilots accomplished their defensive tasks was an impressive demonstration of our willingness to put up resistance."[110] Once the entire armed forces had been called up for the second time, the six Messerschmitt-109E and four Morane-3800 emergency squadrons were in operation practically around the clock. The first confrontation took place on the afternoon of June 4. The front group reported that "[At] about 16:00 hours, a squadron of three German bombers was sighted on their way from Basel to Le Locle. A Me[sserschmitt] confronted these bombers and shot down two of them at Puoillerel and Boécourt. It appears that one Swiss was also injured during the battle and bailed out of the aircraft by parachute."[111]

The clashes between Swiss and German aircraft climaxed on June 8 in the area west of Porrentruy: "Eight to 12 Swiss fighters and at least 32 German fighter aircraft of type Me-110" were involved in a real dogfight.[112] The Swiss pilots excelled, showing their determination in the air; two were killed and another was seriously injured, but several German aircraft were hit, forced to turn around and head toward France. Another Messerschmitt was shot down over Triengen, Canton Lucerne. The courageous demonstration of the Swiss pilots' willingness to defend their country did not fail to impress the Germans. The Italian ambassador, Tamaro, who was generally not very well disposed toward Switzerland, was impressed as well, reporting to Rome, "It is said that the Swiss Air Force is actually already at war and that its immediate reaction proves that it is determined to demonstrate its neutrality. What is certain is that it would wage a bitter struggle against Germany and Italy. But would it do so against the French? At least until now no French aircraft has been intercepted, even though it is hardly possible that none has shown up on this side of the border. The Swiss are lying in wait; no sooner does a German aircraft fly across the border than the shooting spree begins."[113] On the Swiss side, however, some people were critical about the air force's interventions. W. Hörning, one of the fighter pilots, stated: "I still hear the voices of some wavering Confederates who condemned our actions as provocations, believing that the war was almost over and that it was dangerous to provoke the 'Führer of the thousand-year Reich' with such nonsense."[114]

Following the Swiss success in shooting down Luftwaffe fighter planes, which infuriated Hitler and Goering, the Germans tried to retaliate by infiltrating saboteurs into Switzerland. They were supposed to destroy military aircraft on Swiss airfields during the night of June 16–17. However, an observant railway employee reported the suspicious-looking agents and they were arrested before they could carry out their scheme.[115] These incidents sharply heightened tensions with Germany during the final stage of the Western campaign. Even though the acts of sabotage were prevented, it was not certain if they were a simple attempt at retaliation or comprised the beginning of an extensive operation against Switzerland. The situation appeared to be all the more uncertain as the uncovering of the sabotage scheme coincided with the first large bodies of German troops arriving at Switzerland's western border. Huber declared a state of alert for members of the general staff serving at the front on June 16 at 18:00 hours, explaining, "We have to be ready tonight, especially the territorial service. The troops in Bern have to be ready to protect the Federal Palace and to defend the city."[116]

The staff at the General's command post was on its guard against attempts of sabotage as well. On the evening of June 16, Barbey imposed a number of safety measures on the officers of the personal staff because there were fears of a coup against the headquarters.[117] Undoubtedly remembering the apparently threatening situation, the General later wrote, "We ran the risk of getting involved in the war, under the most confusing and unfavorable conditions, at the same time as the Battle of France was drawing to its close and the conquest of Western Europe was almost completed and was about to be replaced by the problems of the 'New Europe.'"[118]

On June 5 and again on June 19, Germany's Ambassador Köcher submitted protest notes to the Swiss government in Bern, asking for damages and apologies for shooting down German aircraft. Pilet-Golaz described the second note as "really not very reassuring."[119] Switzerland's Federal President tried to treat the matter in a dilatory manner by meeting Köcher and having Switzerland's Ambassador Frölicher call on Berlin to discuss the issue. At first Switzerland ignored Germany's demand "that the Swiss government pronounce a formal apology for these scandalous incidents and that it compensate Germany for the material and bodily damages suffered."[120] In the second note, the government of the Reich called the incidents a "flagrant hostile act" and threatened, practically in the form of an ultimatum, that "should such incidents happen again, [we shall] forego any written correspondence and defend German interests in a different way."[121] Federal President Pilet-Golaz was worried and received the General that same night at 11 p.m. to show him the German note.[122] After this second warning, and following additional diplomatic controversies and a dramatic meeting with General Guisan, the Federal Council finally agreed, a week after the armistice in France, to apologize in a roundabout manner.[123]

Meanwhile, on June 17, the French government under the elderly Marshal

Pétain, who had replaced Prime Minister Reynaud, had requested negotiations with Hitler. Four days later, an armistice was declared that went into effect on June 25, sealing France's capitulation.[124] With the ceasefire, Switzerland breathed a sigh of relief. General Guisan called his corps commanders to a briefing on June 22 to discuss demobilizing some of the troops once the armistice became effective. He jotted down the following notes: "Partial demobilization to be envisaged as soon as the armistice goes into effect.—Do not wait for pressure to be applied by Axis powers.—Only a potential opponent from now on.—Danger from the interior.—Unfriendly gesture to keep entire armed forces on duty, Italy has no troops at our S[outhern] front. General staff is studying possibility of demobilization.—Who will demobilize first?—Prop[osals] by army commanders."

In the unlikely event of a simultaneous attack from the north, west, and "maybe also from the east," the following solutions were considered: (1) holding the advanced positions; (2) going into a hedgehog position in the foothills of the Alps; or (3) withdrawing right away to the center of the country and conducting training activities.[125] Corps Commander Wille commented in connection with the briefing, "Prisi wants to keep the armed troops in the forward positions!!!!!!"[126]

The commander-in-chief recognized that, by moving troops west, the defense line "appeared to be sealed on the left wing of the front, but in fact this was questionable." He described how on June 25, the day of the French armistice, the Swiss Army held positions that left "the impression of a strip that did not have the same depth everywhere and that embraced our country at various distances from the border. In one place the positions were anchored around a fortified spot, elsewhere in the foothills of the Jura and the Alps; in the west, they followed watercourses and woods that had not yet been prepared for a defensive war. A positional map of that time draws a too favorable picture of the degree of security we had established for the event of an attack that could be launched simultaneously on all fronts. We had neither the necessary density nor strategic depth."[127]

As Germann explained, the collapse of the Western Allies' defense "was not only a deeply shocking event for us but it also prompted us to review our military preparations in a critical manner."[128] The most pressing question was how Switzerland would be able to mount any long-term resistance against an attack by the Wehrmacht if blitzkrieg tactics had managed to bring about the downfall of a former military power like France in as little as one and a half months. Others believed that the greater danger loomed on the political rather than the military level. In May 1940, Wehrli commented, not without good reason, that if Germany was victorious over France, Switzerland would be in need of a bold leader "who is cunning enough to control the country's fate."[129]

13

Orders to the Armed Forces in June 1940

THE INSTRUCTIONS AND ORDERS THAT GENERAL GUISAN ISSUED in early June 1940 in reaction to the threat of Germany's western offensive deserve close examination, as they had a tremendous effect on the morale of both the troops and the general public.

At the end of May, only a few weeks after launching its attacks on Holland, Belgium, and northern France, Germany's offensive bore its first results. The French army was retreating at a fast pace and British troops were forced to withdraw from the continent, staging an emergency sealift at Dunkirk.[1] Because of the Third Reich's rapid advances, the general public and the military in Switzerland began to display signs of despair. What could a militia army hope to accomplish against the German enemy if armies with modern equipment such as the British and the French, which were believed to be the best managed in the world, were forced to capitulate?

At this crucial moment of anguish for the Swiss population, on June 3, 1940, General Guisan issued two separate orders to the armed forces that helped boost morale among the disheartened and rekindle the spirit of resistance among those who despaired.

In the text of the first order, issued as an order of the day, Guisan began by referring to the fatal tragedies that other small countries had suffered, and then continued:

> Let us never forget that the Swiss are an armed people who are determined to preserve their independence. Every Swiss is horrified by the mere thought that his country could be occupied by a foreign power; his living conditions, without exception, whether he is a farmer, a

worker, or an intellectual, would change drastically. Every soldier knows why he has taken up arms, and day-by-day he should become more and more aware of the honorable task with which he has been entrusted—safeguarding our national heritage!

We have to defend ourselves, and we *can* do it. We are in a privileged position, as our country's topography is our first-rate ally. In other words, if the entire army works toward the same goal, no one will be able to walk over the country! It is not surprising that in our history there are many examples where we put up heroic, successful resistance against opponents outnumbering us tenfold. We are prepared to meet the challenges of new military strategies, as we have taken steps to counter them. The majorities of our positions are in mountainous or overgrown terrain, where aircraft cannot see us and where armored troops will have difficulties advancing.

However, we need to improve our moral readiness. Lack of respect for women, alcohol abuse, as well as any form of lack of self-control are unworthy of a Swiss soldier. Even more important than material and moral readiness, though, is *mental* preparedness. Our ancestors were well aware of that, as they knelt down before every battle to pay reverence to Almighty God. Thanks to God's protection, Switzerland is virtually the only small European nation that has been spared the horrors of an invasion. We should all keep God in our hearts; every soldier should join his wife, parents, and children in praying to Him. Moreover, every unit should be joyful, be ready to help each other, trust each other, and be willing to make sacrifices every day. At a time when the thunder of bombardments could awaken us at any hour, the feeling of being united is absolutely indispensable to the nation.

Let us counter defeatist propaganda with the spirit of the mountaineers of Uri, Schwyz, and Unterwalden on August 1, 1291. They had no outside assistance but put their trust in themselves and in God when they swore to free themselves from all foreign dominance. That is the only way our country will be really strong and our army will be ready. The motto is simple: Hold out![2]

The second text which General Guisan distributed to his unit commanders and the media that day was a general order in which he encouraged the troops to be ready to fight and gave detailed instructions how to successfully counter a possible attack. After pointing out Germany's new offensive methods during its victories in Belgium, Holland, and France, the commander-in-chief urged "Swiss soldiers of all ranks and arms" to keep in mind and follow at all times, "even during battles and in the hardship of war," the following principles:

> When you fight for your home country you are willing to risk your life without conditions. This has been true for centuries and does not change when new weaponry or new fighting methods are used. The enemy is successful not so much because of the material effects of its arms but much more so because its opponents who could continue to fight give up.
>
> No one shall be deterred by airborne attacks from accomplishing his task. You can and have to hold out to the last minute while performing your duty if dive bombers attack, the same way our soldiers tenaciously and courageously maintained their positions against the ceaseless artillery attacks during World War I. No matter what the danger, you shall continue fighting or keeping your territory under surveillance. Staff officers shall not interrupt their work either. If you have orders to run to the front, you shall not stop midway. Only the rearward area and resting troops shall observe air-raid warnings.
>
> No one shall leave his post if tanks come rushing on or roll over the flanks to attack from behind. If you are unable to stop them with your own weapons, you must trust the troops behind you to defeat them. Remember that even if a few tanks manage to break through the lines, you will prevent reinforcement troops from following through if you hold out in your positions. An enemy's isolated victory turns into a total victory only if you consider the battle to be lost and believe that you can no longer defend yourselves.
>
> No one shall leave his post if parachutists have landed behind him. Your task remains the same: If you are at the front, keep your position. Count on your leaders to deploy reserve troops or mobile units to defeat these enemies. Should you ever despair and feel that there is no way out, think of the 1,500 troops who died a hero's death in 1444 at St. Jakob near Basel to save our nation, and have attained immortal fame throughout Switzerland because of their courage.[3]

The General attached an instructional document entitled "Objective: Maintaining the Troops' Morale" to these two texts when he distributed them among the army unit commanders. The two texts were to be read to all troops without delay, the first text "in an adequate manner," and the second "in a way to leave a lasting impression." The General's instruction continued by saying, "Before presenting them, the unit commanders shall personally get to know the

Draft of handwritten letter by Corps Commander Ulrich Wille dated May 21, 1940, requesting that General Guisan allow him to go to battle with Infantry Regiment 25 in case of war. (ArMa) meaning and the spirit of the texts. It will be their responsibility henceforth to apply these principles in order to prepare the troops for combat." He urged the company commanders to go beyond reading the orders and explain to their troops the advantages of Switzerland being a free country and the need for it to remain independent. They should point out that with the existing fortresses and the favorable terrain as its most powerful ally, Switzerland could be successfully defended.[4]

The stirring appeals made by Guisan during the critical time of Germany's western offensive, and which were disseminated in all of Switzerland's press, considerably boosted morale among the troops and met a welcome response among the general population. Even abroad they did not go unnoticed. Ernst Nobs, a Social Democrat in Zürich's cantonal executive branch at the time, wrote, "The General's last orders have made an excellent and lasting impression on all Swiss! He told everyone that according to its tradition, Switzerland will follow Finland's example, not Norway's."[5]

In the days following the publication of these orders, Guisan received many letters of acknowledgment from all segments of the population. Some were exuberant in thanking him for his inspiring words. Numerous people congratulated him on his warnings regarding the lack of respect for women and alcohol abuse as well as on his appeal to pray and have faith in God. Individual believers, as well as Catholic and Protestant Church organizations, applauded his courage in publicly expressing his reverence for God. A devout family from the Bernese Oberland thanked the General for his "courage to profess [his] faith in God, on whose assistance and grace everything depends even nowadays. We pray for you every day so that you may have wisdom and the guidance of God to accomplish this great and responsible task."[6]

The two documents, which are often cited verbatim in Swiss history books as examples of Switzerland's determination to resist the German enemy, are typical of Guisan's ability to touch the spirit and soul of the army, as well as of the people as a whole. E. Bonjour, H. R. Kurz, and E. Chapuisat reprinted one or both texts.[7] More than once, Guisan himself later emphasized the significance of the two orders. In his own account of the six years of mobilization, he wrote that he found it important to "offer commanders what we liked to call 'ammunition,' that is, considerations on which to elaborate when speaking to their troops." Guisan then went on to reprint lengthy excerpts from the two orders.[8] On another occasion, he considered his order of the day of June 3 to be "the order that met with the most positive response in our country."[9]

The question remains who wrote the texts. It is known that unlike Generals Wille and Dufour, who composed their orders to the armed forces on their own,[10] General Guisan drew on skilled writers who edited most of his speeches, military orders, and other correspondence. Hence, it appears likely that some-one else had a hand in the two famous documents in question.

There is conclusive written evidence in the case of the order of the day of June 3—it was undoubtedly written by Edmond Grin, a theology professor at the University of Lausanne and a distant relative of General Guisan. Grin gave the eulogy at the General's funeral and mentioned on that occasion that the commander-in-chief had approached him in the spring of 1940 about writing an order of the day to elevate the "swaying hearts." Guisan told him the text should "have a clear religious, even a Christian overtone, as I am convinced that without the assistance of the Almighty we will not accomplish anything suffi-cient. We have to do all we can on the military level, but we must not forget that beyond the human effort there is God. He never abandons those who defend a cause that reflects His will."[11] Letters to his wife confirm that the order that Grin was asked to write was indeed that of June 3, 1940. Grin served tem-porarily as a private in the infantry as part of "Uncle Henri's" personal staff and told his wife about the draft he submitted to the General.[12] He sent her a copy of the draft, and though she praised him for its overall contents, she did not like the passage on the "thunder of bombardments." Grin replied, "It was Uncle Henri who insisted on using this phrase. I had difficulties weaving it into the text. But since he is the one who will sign off on it . . ."[13]

On the afternoon of May 31, Grin was called into the General's office. "Uncle Henri told me, 'I approve of the text. However, events have happened in Holland and Belgium (capitulation) that have left the country and the army in shock. You hear a lot of people say: Useless to defend ourselves if . . . However, that is nonsense! Our country is easy to defend, and our army is ready to do so. You should add one page elaborating on that idea.' I replied, 'I com-pletely agree with you, General.'" Grin went back to his room to revise the text according to the General's desire. "Until four in the morning I couldn't get one single thought on paper," he wrote to his wife. "But then, between four and five, everything became clear and I had my two pages together. Shortly after six o'clock, I submitted the document all typed up to Uncle Henri. He told me he would look at it the next day."[14] The revised text was distributed to the troops without further corrections on June 3, 1940. As this example shows, Guisan generally not only assumed responsibility for documents by affixing his signa-ture to them but actually took an active part in the editing process.

The draft of the second text of June 3 was most definitely written by the Chief Instructor, Corps Commander Ulrich Wille, as evidenced by documents found at the Federal Archives in Bern and at the Mariafeld Archives. Wille sub-mitted several pages of memoranda to the General on May 31 "including two drafts of orders and a personal memo. All three documents relate to the war against the German Army and the prevention of incursions. I have acted on your written orders of May 21, 1940, no. 9530, to come up with instructions how to respond to dive-bomber and tank attacks," he explained to Guisan.[15] Wille advised the General to prepare the army better on the "material and mental levels," which, he argued, would have to include the following three components: "Concentration of all available war material for a decisive battle; staggering of sizeable reserve troops and anti-tank weaponry along expected enemy incursion lines; and improving morale among leaders and troops to incite them to unfaltering resistance." Wille's elaborations express his determination to fight the enemy. He ended his memo to Guisan with a recommendation to "issue a general order to the armed forces similar to the one I have included in order to strengthen the staff's and the troops' morale."[16]

Guisan underlined phrases and made handwritten remarks in the margins of the drafts, indicating that he studied Wille's contributions carefully. He marked with a question mark in red ink the passage "uncertainty has befallen even our leaders." On June 2, he forwarded the seven-page document to Chief of the General Staff Huber for his review, remarking, "Personal and confidential [and] to be returned to me." Huber made some critical comments on the document, even though he agreed with it "in many respects."[17] Huber criticized Wille for becoming involved in operational matters and disliked his idea of pulling back the border troops. On the other hand, Huber indicated that he, too, had suggested "on several occasions that we have to concentrate most of our efforts on holding the chosen positions and should not sacrifice useful troops in a so-called delaying war."[18]

Wille's memorandum expresses the personal opinion of a high-ranking officer and appears to reflect, to a certain degree, the uneasiness some key staff members may have felt over the measures the General had taken up until that time.[19]

In addition to the memorandum and the draft of an order to the armed forces, Wille provided Guisan with detailed proposals on combat strategies. Guisan adopted them and passed them on as secret orders to all unit commanders. Wille's proposals suggested "immediately re-examining and re-regulating" all positions under the following principles:

1. The main focus has to shift to the potential attack points by tank units. The troops have to be more staggered there. If the Germans launch an invasion, they must be annihilated in a vigorous counterattack.
2. At these potential attack points, regimental and divisional reserve troops must be added to the battalion reserve troops in staggered formations in order to stop an attack in the long run. . . .

3. Tanks that manage to break through the front line must be stopped at all costs by the troops behind the lines. Attempts should be made to create blockades by shooting individual tanks in places where subsequent tanks cannot take another route. Where it is possible to approach tanks under cover, assault troops should take them on in close combat, especially at dawn.

Wille added that because of the lack of anti-tank weapons, the weapons of the artillery should also be used to fight tanks if necessary. The necessary restructuring of units should begin without delay and should be granted "utmost urgency."[20] Guisan accepted these proposals, making only minor editorial changes. For instance, the passages ordering the unit commanders to build up resistance had all been included in Wille's proposal.

In addition to the written instructions mentioned by Wille, it was undoubtedly during a meeting with the General on May 23 in Gümligen that he was encouraged to submit the memorandum and the drafts of the two orders. Wille was dissatisfied because he felt that he was merely idling in his position as Chief Instructor. Consequently, he considered returning to Infantry Regiment 25, which he had commanded in the 1920s, explaining in a draft of a letter to the General that "my argument for this request is the fact that for the last ten days, since the armed forces were mobilized for the second time, I have come to realize that I will sit around doing absolutely nothing if we get involved in the war. The only thing that I have been ordered to do during these ten days was to inform Swiss Federal officers, including Colonel Däniker of the general staff, of the doubts that are expressed in the commander-in-chief's police files about their loyalty to the country and about their oath to the flag."[21]

Wille did not send this letter; however, he undoubtedly brought up the subject at his meeting with the General the following day, as one of his handwritten notes in preparation for the meeting read: "2. To infantry regiment 25 (11 May–)."[22] During the meeting, Wille probably received orders from the General to put his thoughts in writing and to draft some orders to the troops, perhaps to prove that he was determined to fight. Wille may have been reluctant to carry out the order because he thought he had reasons to believe that the German Wehrmacht had no intention of attacking Switzerland. Nevertheless, he dutifully accomplished the task together with the staff of Main Section III.

Wille did not claim sole authorship of the proposals. In his memorandum to Guisan, he mentioned Colonel Hans Frick, a corps commander-to-be, and Colonel Gustav Däniker as co-authors. He explained, "My collaborators Colonel Frick and Colonel Däniker and I had great difficulties writing the draft. If instructions are too long they are not very compelling; if they are too short they sound like clichés or platitudes."[23] Certain style characteristics indicate that Frick, who is also believed to be the author of the military rules and regulations of 1933, made a major contribution to the draft.

There is clear evidence that the proposed order Wille submitted to the General on May 31 was identical to the order to the armed forces that Guisan issued on June 3. Not one single word was changed. The General indeed thanked Wille for submitting the proposals and sent him copies of the printed orders along with his letter of thanks.[24]

The fact that Wille authored the army orders of June 3 is nothing short of sensational, because he was a proclaimed opponent of General Guisan. As a matter of fact, because his authorship was kept a secret during the war, and even beyond 1945, the Chief Instructor became known mainly for his subsequent pro-German attitude and for publicly promoting appeasement and defeatism, culminating in a virtual conspiracy against General Guisan (see Chapters 21 and 25).

Historians may eventually produce a number of hypotheses to explain why Corps Commander Wille agreed to write what was to become one of General Guisan's most famous orders to the armed forces. He may have been a shrewd rival, staging a power struggle against the General behind the scenes. Whatever may have been his reasons for acting as he did, Wille's example illustrates the complexity of the question of resistance versus accommodation. Looking beneath the surface, the situation in that critical summer of 1940 cannot simply be reduced to shades of black and white.

The young Henri Guisan (right) with fellow Zofingia fraternity members at the University of Lausanne. (BAr)

Lieutenant Colonel Guisan (second from left) in discussion with an unidentified French officer during a 1916 fact-finding mission to the front at Verdun. (BAr)

Corps Commander Guisan is introduced to King Victor Emanuel III and Fascist leader Benito Mussolini, the Duce, during the 1934 Italian maneuvers. To Guisan's right stands Swiss Divisional Commander de Diesbach. (BAr)

Colonel Guisan speaking with French Marshal Henri Pétain during the 1937 maneuvers of Guisan's 1st Army Corps. (BAr)

The General's office staff in front of the "Olvido Villa" in Spiez, September 1939. From left to right, 1st Lieutenant Eberhardt, staff secretary; Captain Spinner, aide; Lt. Colonel von Sinner, 1st adjutant; General Guisan; Captain Baumgartner, 2nd adjutant; 1st Lieutenant Schild, 2nd adjutant; Lieutenant R. Eibel, staff secretary. (Photo courtesy of Dr. R. Eibel)

In front of Gümligen Castle in late 1939, from left to right, Corps Commander
Rudolf Miescher, General Henri Guisan, Corps Commander Fritz Prisi, and Corps
Commander Renzo Lardelli. (Photo by Hans Steiner, Bern)

At the beginning of 1940, Colonel-Corps Commander Jakob Labhart was pushed aside as Chief of the General Staff and was put in charge of the new 4th Army Corps. This photograph was taken at a time when Labhart (center) was still divisional commander. Pictured with him are Colonels Jordi (right) and Bandi (left). (BAr)

In June 1940, the 45th Corps of the French Army–which had once been earmarked to fight alongside the Swiss in the event of a German attack–was disarmed and interned in Switzerland. (BAr)

Officers of the General's "Personal Staff" in front of Gümligen Castle, from left to right, Captain Mario Marguth; unidentified person; Major Bernard Barbey; General Guisan; Lt. Colonel Samuel Gonard. (BAr)

General Guisan boarding his command train in Interlaken. (BAr)

Captain Alfred Ernst, left, Head of Bureau D, which analyzed information pertaining to Germany, and Captain Max Waibel, Head of Intelligence Procurement Bureau No. 1, called "Rigi." They are pictured standing in front of the barracks in Thun where they were serving sentences the General had pronounced against them for being the main initiators of the "Officers' Alliance." (Photo from Braunschweig's archives)

As long as he was Head of the Military Department, Federal Councilor Rudolf Minger (second from right) tried to mediate between Federal Councilor Pilet-Golaz (center, carrying white gloves) and General Guisan (far right), who were both natives of Canton Vaud. The General would have liked Claude Du Pasquier from Neuchâtel (second from left), who was informed about the secret cooperation talks with France, to become Minger's successor in the government. (BAr)

Fusilier Private First Class Edmond Grin, a theology professor at the University of Lausanne, performing a Sunday service in the field near Gümligen Castle in early 1940. (Photo from the archives of M. Eglin)

Chief of the General Staff Jakob Huber (right) consulting with General Guisan during winter maneuvers. Huber was promoted from Colonel-Divisional Commander to Colonel-Corps Commander at the end of 1940. (BAr)

The General inspecting a group of fusiliers. (BAr)

The General attending a convention of the Women's Auxiliary Service (FHD) in Zürich. Pictured to his left is G. Haemmerli-Schindler, President of Zürich's cantonal FHD section; in the background is Adjutant General Ruggero Dollfus. (Photo from the author's personal archives)

Abendausgabe
Preis 10 Pfennig

Berliner

Mittwoch, 3. Juli 1940

Lokal-Anzeiger

Organ für die Reichshauptstadt

Nummer 157 A   Bezugsbedingungen und Anzeigenpreise sind in der Morgenausgabe angegeben   59. Jahrgang

Die Geheimakten Gamelins

Sensationeller Dokumentenfund an der Loire

Wie die kleinen Völker Europas auf die Schlachtbank geführt werden sollten
Anschlag gegen Schwedens Erzgruben und Rumäniens und Rußlands Oelquellen
Rumänien, Türkei, Griechenland, Jugoslawien sollten für den Westen Krieg führen

Seite 7/8   Illustrierter Beobachter   1940 / Folge 39

Ein Güterzug weltgeschichtlicher Enthüllungen

On July 3, 1940, a Berlin newspaper, the *Lokal-Anzeiger*, reported the discovery of a train full of confidential files at La Charité-sur-Loire, France. The documents contained details of the secret plans for Swiss-French military cooperation. (Photo from the author's private archives)

After France's Defeat

As EARLY AS JUNE 23, THE DAY AFTER FRANCE SIGNED the armistice with Germany, and two days before it went into effect, Guisan issued new orders in view of the completely altered situation in Europe:

1. No new fortification projects shall be started along the existing defense line. Any unused portion of the credit shall not be used for new projects.
2. The projects under construction shall be completed if they fulfill the following criteria: a) they are very important permanent constructions; b) they are so far advanced that completing them is justified; c) the corps commanders and the commander of the 9th Division shall decide which projects fulfill these criteria.
3. Work on barriers and traps shall be halted, with the exception of infrastructure that is an integral part of a project's defensive concept. Work on the anti-tank barriers in the sectors of the 2nd and 3rd Army Corps shall be halted.
4. Starting on June 24, 1940, the barricades in the cities of Basel and Bern shall be removed.[1]

These instructions were the result of a briefing that the commander-in-chief held with his subordinate commanders in Bern to discuss regrouping the armed forces following the rapid collapse of France. The minutes of the briefing stated:

The General is convinced that the Germans will now apply primarily political and economic pressure and are unlikely to consider any military action [against Switzerland]. Switzerland will serve as a useful transit country for the Axis Powers; its Alpine railroad network should remain intact in order to be available for transit traffic, which is bound to increase. Nevertheless, we have to expect Germany to threaten invading Switzerland, particularly if we put up resistance against its economic and political threats. We must be prepared for the event of an attack.[2]

The army command initially hesitated implementing the strategic conclusions that it had to draw from the new situation. Above all, it was extremely reluctant to give up its existing positions. During a briefing with the 2nd Army Corps, Prisi explained that a hedgehog position at the Gotthard or positions in the foothills of the Alps were "generally not accepted"; instead, he asked that the border positions be reinforced and the army remain in its current positions to complete the fortification projects in progress. Divisional Commander Bircher, who usually disagreed with his superior Prisi, also expressed his preference for fighting in the existing positions, even though he said that an attack was unlikely because "the Germans do not have any intention of staging a war against us, [hence] withdrawing to a position at the Gotthard does not make any sense."[3]

In spite of these internal discussions, on June 25 the commander-in-chief issued an initial order aimed at regrouping the armed forces, which could be interpreted as the first stage toward realizing a new strategic concept. According to the order, "As of July 5, 1940, the army units shall be regrouped along the main axis of their sectors so as to be able to seal it in its full depth. Combat training shall continue."[4] Meanwhile, the army staff was struggling to prepare an operational analysis. The General wrote about this stage in his postwar report, saying, "To brace ourselves for external and internal dangers, it was most of all necessary to make a new assessment of the situation, and the army command had to make a series of logical decisions; in other words, it had to make an evaluation that also took into account concerns of a psychological nature."[5] As Ernst Schürch put it, after being surrounded by the Axis Powers, Switzerland was "like an egg in an armored fist."[6]

At lunchtime on June 25, the day when the armistice in France went into effect, three members of the Swiss Federal Council addressed the nation over the radio, in French (by Federal President Pilet-Golaz), German (by Councilor Etter), and Italian (by Councilor Celio). They promised that "some of the troops would immediately be demobilized" and others would follow later. They then spoke of "adapting to the new circumstances," explaining that "trodden paths should not be confused with traditions" and that one had to "look straight ahead. Important decisions [would] have to be made" to save the coun-

Geheime Kommandosache   114

Oberkommando des Heeres   H.Qu. OKH, den 16. August 1940

Gen St d H Op.Abt. (I)   Entwurf   3 Ausfertigungen

    Nr. 420/40 g Kdos.   3. Ausfertigung

                              An

                       Heeresgruppe C   2097/495

1.)   Die Heeresgruppe legt dem OKH Gen St d H Op.Abt. einen

      Operationsentwurf gegen die Schweiz vor.

2.)   Dem Operationsentwurf ist zu Grunde zu legen:

      a) Die Schweiz ist entschlossen,sich einem Einmarsch mit

          Einsatz aller Kräfte zu widersetzen.

      b) Italien beansprucht das Schweizer Gebiet südlich der

          Berner Alpen und Glarner Alpen als seinen Interessen-

          bereich.Es ist bereit,gleichzeitig mit dem Einmarsch

          deutscher Kräfte in die nördliche Schweiz in dieses

          Gebiet einzumarschieren.

          Gemeinsame Kommandoführung ist nicht vorgesehen.Jede

          Armee operiert selbständig.

      c) A.O.K. 12 führt die Operationen zur Besitznahme des

          schweizerischen Hoheitsgebietes nördlich der Berner

          Alpen und Glarner Alpen.

          12. Armee hat an einem von OKH zu bestimmenden X=Tag

          in breiter Front gleichzeitig die Schweizer Grenze zu

          überschreiten,dem deutschen Einmarsch entgegentretende

          eidgenössische Kräfte zu zerschlagen und möglichst

          schnell die Landeshauptstadt Bern mit umliegendem In-

          dustriebereich ,das Rüstungszentrum um Solothurn,Luzern

          und das Industriegebiet um Zürich ,anschließend das

          übrige deutsche Interessengebiet zu besetzen.

                              Die Operationen

Order from German Chief of the General Staff Franz Halder, dated August 16, 1940, instructing Army Group C to draft a plan of operations against Switzerland. (MArF)

try. These decisions would "have to be considered and made quickly, based on [the government's] own authority, without being able to consult on, discuss, and deliberate them." The speakers added that now was the time to forge a "national community through work and discipline," promising, "The Federal Council will find work for the Swiss at all costs." They continued by explaining that "the time [had] come for an internal renewal," and that every individual had to "give up his or her old self. . . . Events change at a rapid pace, so one has to adjust to this rhythm."[7]

The speech did not help to boost confidence among the Swiss. Bonjour did not hesitate to describe it as "a chaotic speech."[8] In the years since, Pilet-Golaz alone has usually been blamed for the controversial discourse. Yet this is somewhat unfair, even if he wrote most of it. The President spoke on behalf of a body of seven government representatives, even though the text was not submitted to the entire cabinet for approval before it was broadcast. Moreover, the other two cabinet members would have been unlikely to read the German and Italian versions had they not agreed with the content.[9] The speech was definitely made in the name of the entire government; the minutes of the subsequent cabinet meeting indicate that the Federal Council approved the speech after the fact and actually decided to rebroadcast it the same evening.[10]

The speech was not improvised. Pilet-Golaz had been working on it as early as June 23 when he wrote down some notes, which read, among other things, "Act instead of talking. Give instead of demanding . . . adapt to new circumstances . . . give oneself to the country. Serve . . ."[11] Some of these phrases were used in the speech. It appears that when writing it, Pilet-Golaz was influenced in part by letters from individuals recently returned from trips to Germany, telling him that they were concerned about Germany's drastic change of opinion about Switzerland.[12]

The address to the nation was a cautious expression of the desire to bring Switzerland into line with, and to persuade it to adjust to, the new balance of power. But reactions in the country were wildly various. In a confidential weekly report, Ernst von Schenck wrote that "the speech of the three Federal Councilors" had been the event of the week, dominating domestic politics and causing "extraordinarily divergent" reactions. He explained that it was "impossible to tell whether approving or disapproving voices are in the majority. The large majority of people who have reacted in a positive manner are part of the group that is more or less aware that their opinion will have consequences on the parliamentary 'system.'. . . They include, above all, the political groups that have been demanding a more powerful government for some time and believe that now their demand is more justified than ever. Among them are large parts of the conservatives, young liberals, members of the 'National Alliance of

Independents,' etc. However, it should be noted that one cannot generalize and some people from these groups have criticized the form or some phrases of the speech. Generally speaking, the younger generation has been more inclined to approve the speech than older generations." Moreover, von Schenck claimed that the army was "generally more inclined to heed the Federal Council's appeal than civilians," and negative comments were heard more often in Basel than elsewhere, as "in Basel people are perhaps traditionally more skeptical toward the Federal Council's points of view."[13]

There is no written evidence of how General Guisan reacted to the Federal Council's speech. Sandoz, the General's adjutant, assured this author that Guisan was not only disappointed but in fact furious about Pilet-Golaz' speech. He made no comments about it during lunch but did not hesitate to make his opinion known to his adjutant afterwards.[14] Hans Bracher, another member of Guisan's personal staff, recounted that the General was "saddened" by the fact that his friends on the Federal Council, especially Minger, failed to protest against the speech.[15] Writer Denis de Rougemont recorded in his diary that on the day after the speech an officer of the General's personal staff had told him, "For the first time in my life I was ashamed to be Swiss."[16] Based on these statements, there can be no doubt that von Schenck's comment that the army was "generally more inclined to heed the Federal Council's appeal" did not apply to the General and his entourage.

Other army commanders were also skeptical or reacted in a negative manner to the "speech of adjustment." Labhart wrote in his diary: "[The] Federal Council addresses the nation in a curious speech in which he [sic] points out the new situation and announces that the troops will be demobilized."[17] Prisi reported on his troops' reaction: "The Federal President's speech has been met with quite some disappointment. It is being viewed as a mental capitulation."[18] Some officers who were determined to put up resistance were "devastated" by the speech. Ernst remembered how he and his friends "were furious and threw our helmets on the ground because we felt cheated and betrayed."[19] Two decades later, Ernst had a somewhat more understanding view of the Federal Council's discourse when he wrote, "Rereading and analyzing the speech today, I have to admit that it does not sound quite as dramatic as we felt it to be at the time. There is no passage with an explicit demand to give up resistance. However, the speech must not only be analyzed according to its wording but also by taking into account what was read between the lines. More particularly, it must be seen in the context of the tense situation at the time. Its devastating effect was based more on what it concealed than what it stated."[20]

The controversial speech, which was felt to curry favor with the totalitarian spirit of fascism, did not say anything about Switzerland's traditional concepts of freedom and democracy, nor about independence and resistance. Fritz Wartenweiler, an educator who served in the "Home and Army" section as a captain, wrote a letter to the army command to express his concern about this lack, asking, "Why was there no mention of democracy, of freedom, of the Constitution? What will we have to expect when it comes to making decisions? Will they be conceived and made on the basis of Switzerland's idea of the State? Will 'adjusting to the pace of events' be in line with what we have until now considered to be the basis of the existence of the State and its people? What kind of renewal will there be?" Wartenweiler urged that the essence of Switzerland's reasons for existence should not be tampered with, especially at a time when totalitarian governments in powerful neighboring countries "are—temporarily—successful in the world." He demanded that the Federal Council clearly distance itself from the goals of the Front movement, unless it was willing to admit "that the road of renewal will be determined directly or indirectly by the spokespersons of the 'National Front' who are in touch with the powers that are—temporarily—victorious in Europe."[21]

Hausamann described how he and his friends did not believe their ears when they heard Pilet-Golaz' speech on the radio, adding that it triggered "an alarming flow of incoming news indicating that the troops were increasingly defeatist. As many as three sources said that troops tore the General's picture from the wall and trampled on it. They claimed that the fact that the General allowed such a speech to be aired was proof that he was hand-in-glove with the Federal Council. They also said that the troops might as well be sent home as they had been betrayed and sold."[22]

Opponents of the Federal Council's address, "from left to right, were concerned that [the government] was drafting a program that aimed to bring the country completely in line with the totalitarian powers, not only economically but also politically; [the] words that sounded like Pétain's" were considered to be inadequate.[23] Markus Feldmann, a future Federal Councilor, wrote the General that in his opinion Pilet-Golaz' speech was "on the verge of a cold coup d'etat."[24] The National Council's Proxy Committee met the day after the discourse was broadcast to protest against it. Only Roman Abt from Aargau congratulated the Federal Council on the speech, calling it "a masterpiece of its kind."[25] After the committee meeting, R. Grimm wrote to his fellow partisan, E. Nobs from the Social Democratic Party: "It is probably best not to say anything about Pilet's speech out of shame. He had to listen to some harsh comments yesterday in the committee meeting. Elsewhere people are all nervous, not knowing how to deal with the situation."[26] Adam considered that Pilet-Golaz' policy of appeasement put the Swiss government in an advantageous position on the foreign policy level by making the country look, through Germany's eyes, as if it had "come to its senses" and thereby become a potential partner for negotiations—an idea that may not be erroneous even if it is disturbing.[27]

During a conference of the Social Democratic Party, National Councilor H. Oprecht told the attendees that the Foreign Policy Committee had asked Federal President Pilet-Golaz very specifically "if Germany [had] really made any demands to Switzerland. Pilet replied very firmly that it had not and that all the hearsay about this matter was nothing but gossip."[28] W. Bringolf from Schaffhausen explained that he "no longer [had] confidence in the Federal Council" after Pilet made his speech.[29] Party president Oprecht declared, on behalf of the party leadership, "Federal President Pilet's speech is leading us astray. . . . The party and the unions have to take a clear stand against defeatism. It is above all the party's obligation to take action."[30] National Councilor Meierhans added that the central committee of the Association of Swiss Media had "almost unanimously condemned Pilet's speech."[31]

Others, even some of Guisan's close associates, initially expressed surprisingly positive opinions about the Federal Council's discourse. Claude Du Pasquier wrote in his diary that he was satisfied by the radio address, explaining, "This was a salutary warning announcing difficult times. The government will have to act with authority; there is no time for deliberating. The people should show real, profound solidarity—'give, don't demand.' This is the only way to salvation."[32] G. Duttweiler, the chairman of the National Alliance of Independents, was also reported to react positively to the speech, if only at first. Christian Gasser, a founding member of the Gotthard Alliance (see Chapter 18), wrote in his memoirs that he was in Duttweiler's company when he listened to the radio address at the Waage guild-house in Zürich, explaining, "Duttweiler's reaction showed how unstable many people's attitude was at the time. At first he was pleased, even thrilled, exclaiming, 'finally a new language!'"[33] Yet the following day he was one of the members of the National Council's Proxy Committee who vehemently criticized National Councilor Abt for praising Pilet's speech.[34]

Edmund Wehrli made an interesting comment typical of some younger Swiss, saying, "It is obvious that we will in large part have to adapt to the 'new world.' However, it would be totally wrong if the old guys tried to be trimmers. First of all, foreign countries do not trust them, and second, we do not trust them either. So much is alarmingly rotten in our State that there is only one solution: everyone who has been in the government until now has to be removed from office in order to be replaced by a new generation of leaders who will clean up the mess in the country first and who will not make foreign policy without having a spine. Our destiny may depend on how soon we are able to do the cleaning up of our own accord."[35]

The government's real position was unclear at first, providing proof of its insecurity. Two days after the Federal Council's speech, National Councilor Grimm wrote that he did "not have the impression that the leaders were determined to put up resistance and [would] coldly allow *Gleichschaltung* [streamlining, or synchronization] to take place instead."[36] Even one month later, National Councilor A. Oeri from Basel felt that it was necessary to remind the Federal Council of its duty, writing in a beseeching tone, "It would of course be useless to make foreign countries believe that Switzerland is determined to defend itself if this determination did not really exist or was bound to break down after a few days. That is not the way it is, though, dear sirs! A large majority of the Swiss and their army will defend themselves even if the political leadership should surrender and force the people to organize the defense against the Federal Council's will. I definitely hope that this will not happen. However, some civilians, officers, and soldiers are saying that it might become necessary to show patriotic disobedience."[37]

Pro-German individuals on the right of the political spectrum were particularly pleased both about Germany's victory over France and Pilet-Golaz' speech. Corps Commander Wille wrote to Däniker: "It almost seems that the French have come to their senses about their German neighbor before small-town Switzerland. The war against England and the final peace are likely to make it easier for us to come to our senses soon. Nevertheless, many people, such as Prof. Karl Meyer, who have taken the wrong path and are stuck there will not budge, so they will have to be removed from their positions in politics, in the military, the press, and academic circles."[38]

The members and supporters of the Front movement were understandably overjoyed at the Federal Council's statements, as they had reason to believe that their opinions were being supported. As a weekly report stated, "Many were pleased that the proclaimed policy would take the wind out of the sails of the Front movement and National Socialist propaganda. When a member of the Front movement commented that there would be nothing left for them to do, the statement was met with great satisfaction."[39] One leader of the Front, Major E. Leonhardt, who was in Berlin at the time, was encouraged by the events to call on the Swiss in mid-July 1940 to stage a National Socialist revolution. In a brochure, which was seized and consequently did not reach the public in large numbers, he wrote:

> People of Switzerland! We are calling on you at this crucial moment! Your future is in your hands. . . . You must decide between your current politicians, who are among those who have been defeated in the war, and the leaders of Swiss National Socialism, who are among

today's winners. . . . People of Switzerland! Make up your mind quickly! Make your decision before it is too late! Today's world is fast-paced. Time is running out! Switzerland will in the future only exist as a free National Socialist country, or it will not exist anymore at all![40]

Leonhardt bluntly demanded that Switzerland's current political and military leaders step down because they had failed, and instead make room for Swiss National Socialists. Guisan, who saw one of the brochures, marked this passage with a large exclamation mark in red ink, without making any further comment.[41]

Also on June 25, the commander-in-chief informed the Federal Council that the plan for discharging some of the troops and placing others on call was ready and could be implemented on July 3. At the same time, apparently in reaction to the controversial government declaration, he formally asked the Federal Council, in view of the fact that hostilities between the neighboring countries had ceased, "to confirm, or else specify, the mission with which the army has been entrusted as formulated in the terms of reference which the Federal Council addressed to the commander-in-chief of the armed forces on August 31, 1939, more specifically concerning point 2," that is, the mandate to safeguard the country's neutrality.[42]

The Head of the Military Department seemed surprised by the commander-in-chief's question and had his liaison officer Bracher find out what the General meant by his letter. Barbey informed Bracher that the letter had been "written at a time of uncertainty," when the signing of the armistice and its conditions were not yet known. In the meantime, though, the General had reached the conclusion that the terms of reference had in fact not changed, with the exception of point 5, concerning which one could remark that in all likelihood any cooperation with an ally was now out of the question unless the Axis Powers split apart. Given these facts, Barbey said that the General expected the Federal Council to simply confirm that in spite of the changes abroad it had no reason to modify the existing terms of reference. Bracher consequently submitted a draft of the cabinet's reply to the Head of the Military Department.[43]

Federal President Pilet-Golaz and Federal Chancellor Bovet signed this reply, which Bracher drafted in both German and French. It stated:

We consider that the suspension of hostilities between our neighbors does not necessitate these terms of reference to be modified for the time being. Since we have approved the project for demobilizing part of the armed forces which you submitted, and since you have in the meantime already issued the relevant orders, it does not seem advisable to us to elaborate further on this point. We will be interested to know what concepts you will submit to us for decision-making in order to take the measures that are necessary to safeguard the country's independence under the current situation, and we kindly ask you to inform us on this subject in due course.[44]

The government's reply was dated July 2 and reached the office of the General's personal staff two days later. Barbey wrote about this event in his diary: "I opened the Federal President's reply to the General tonight; terms of reference unchanged; the guidelines of August 31, 1939 remain in force both according to the letter and in spirit. Absolutely clear. The General has gone to bed. He is right. . . . I will show him the letter tomorrow; it does not change anything. Nothing could nor needed to change anyway, yet it was good, even necessary, to put this in writing."[45]

According to a note for the file at the Military Department, Bracher discussed the issue with Colonel Burgunder before drafting the government's reply to the General. Burgunder was recorded as saying that "for the time being the General's terms of reference did not need to be changed" but that it was "advisable that the General inform the Federal Council about his decisions regarding the future defense strategy."[46] The commander-in-chief replied to this request by informing the Federal Council, a few days later, about his decision to withdraw the troops to the Réduit positions.[47]

The General's first formal reaction to the armistice and to the Federal Council's radio address was an order of the day dated June 28, which was read to all troops. Above all he addressed the soldiers who were about to be discharged, thanking them for fulfilling their duty and asking them to remain vigilant and prepared. The General said:

> In a few days, some of you will return home. It is thanks to Almighty God's protection and the army that our country has been spared. You have been standing on guard for a long time. You have fulfilled your duty with discipline and dignity. In order to do that, you have had to make many sacrifices, for which the country is grateful to each one of you. . . . The army's mission is not accomplished. It will be the same tomorrow as it was yesterday and as it is today: to defend the honor and independence of our home country. In order to be able to continue fulfilling this mission, the army must continue training and remain in shape. Its mental strength and its resistance must be preserved. Only death relieves a Swiss soldier from his obligation to his homeland.[48]

Barbey explained that he wrote this order of the day "based on the General's notes," commenting, "He uses the word 'resistance.' What is it worth; hasn't it been used too often?"[49]

Guisan did not mention this order of the day in his postwar report. On the other hand, he gave a detailed account of his Order to the Armed Forces of July 2, which he later described as his first "parade" after France's collapse.[50] One has the impression that Guisan needed some time to overcome the shock of France's defeat and to regain his uncompromising spirit of resistance. In this order, at a time when the idea of the Réduit had, according to him, "not yet crystallized," the General made a public statement about his determination to resist any aggressor with all means. He used some of the ideas on which he later elaborated in his address to the unit commanders at the Rütli. The order read:

> I am warning the army about the risks that it could encounter both from the outside and the inside. The first risk consists of being carefree and trusting the current general situation. An armistice is not a peace agreement. Germany and Italy are still at war with England. The war can spill over to other countries unexpectedly, hit close to Switzerland and threaten our country. The second risk consists of a lack of trust in our own power of resistance. Certainly, the past battles have demon-strated how mighty the modern attack methods are, forcing much more powerful armies than ours to capitulate. However, this must not cause anyone to be defeatist nor to have doubts about our mission. We have a significant means available for our defense: our terrain! It boosts the number of our arms and increases their effectiveness. If it is used properly, it will turn into a fearsome ally. Our forests and mountains are full of ravines and canyons. The war has shown so far that they are unsurmountable barriers for tanks. Moreover, they provide efficient protection against air raids. It would be wrong to base our defense exclusively on these advantages. We must maintain our inner strength and unshakeable will. We shall fight even when we are not expected to win the battle. We shall fight for every inch of our soil and shall pre-serve the honor of the army and of our country.[51]

The order of July 2 unambiguously expressed the army's uncompromising willingness to defend the country and its determination to sell each soldier's life at a high price. However, somewhat in contradiction to this statement, the General simultaneously announced that part of the armed forces were to be demobilized. The first sentence of the order indicated that some troops would be discharged and put on call, "while the main body of the army remains on duty." This sentence was in fact misleading, as it was actually the "main body" that was demobilized on July 6; the orders for discharging them had already been prepared. After this, the contingent of serving troops dropped by two thirds, from 450,000 to about 150,000 men.[52]

Guisan later explained that the troops were discharged "to satisfy the needs of the agricultural community and industry."[53] This was certainly partly true, but before dismissing the troops an announcement was made that the staff and troops who were jobless or without an income would be kept on duty "unless they insist on being discharged."[54] This statement indicates that there were concerns about an increase in the unemployment rate. The soldiers who volunteered to continue serving were to be assigned to different corps or to be organized into new detachments. There is hardly any doubt that the large-scale demobilization was ordered much less for economic reasons than to indicate to the victorious German Reich that Switzerland was inclined to show understanding of the new situation.

Demobilizing the troops in the summer of 1940 considerably weakened Switzerland's defensive preparedness and could have been disastrous, as the country was unaware that it was in fact facing the most dangerous situation during the entire war. At the same time the Swiss were discharging most troops and regrouping their units, Germany's Army Unit C, battle-tested after gaining victory after victory, was stationed at Switzerland's western border. Its 29 infantry divisions, four motorized divisions, and four panzer divisions would have been sufficient to successfully carry out an "Operation Switzerland."[55] Guderian's panzer group alone, which was stationed in Burgundy, had 800 to 900 tanks, and the German 6th Mountain Division was also positioned close by.[56] As Roesch commented, "In this situation, the Swiss army was positioned along an arch between Sargans–Lake Zurich–Limmat–Jura–Lake Geneva that was about 360 kilometers long. West of Basel the sectors were not sufficiently prepared, or they were not prepared at all; the units were stretched out over these sectors, therefore lacking depth and reserve troops. The commander-in-chief of the Swiss Army had only the air force as a reserve."[57] The Germans did not fail to notice that the Swiss demobilized part of their army, estimating that in July they had "about 220,000 men" on duty and in August as few as 120,000 men.[58] At this period of time, the German Wehrmacht drafted operational studies for a campaign against Switzerland called "Operation Tannenbaum," which were discovered only after the war.[59]

During the panic of the week of Pentecost, Germany did not actually have any intention of attacking Switzerland. The Swiss and their army were deceived by a large-scale ploy, a hypothesis first formulated by Bourgeois and later proven true by Vetsch.[60] While in the spring of 1940 the military was fully prepared to counter a German attack, it did not suspect Germany would launch an offensive immediately after France's defeat, thus continuing defense measures were neglected. Alfred Ernst wrote, "The time between June 16 and the end of August 1940 was the only period during the entire war when Germany could have attacked Switzerland with superior forces without having to pull out troops elsewhere. During that time, our army was positioned along an improvised defensive arch that was much too long."[61] At that moment, Germany could have attacked the troops in the Limmat sector from behind by launching an invasion from the west, and could rapidly have rendered powerless the one-third of Switzerland's army that was on duty. Schaufelberger, a military historian, considered that a debacle would have been inevitable if the Germans had invaded at that time.[62]

Hans Senn recently discovered that Italy's general staff was also planning an operation against Switzerland, about which they held talks with Germany. The operation was initially supposed to be carried out on a small scale under plan "T" [Ticino] but was later extended to become plan "S" [Svizzera]. A memorandum dated July 7, 1940, stated that in the event of a German attack on Switzerland, all areas bordering the Alpine watershed were to be occupied by Italian troops so as to move the Italian-Swiss border further north. General Mario Vercellino was designated to lead the Italian troops during the operation. Mussolini would have preferred to have Switzerland as an amputated buffer state in the north. Other Italian plans talked about advancing via Malans and Maienfeld to the Linth Plain, or via the Gotthard to the basin of Schwyz, or via the Valais to the Bernese Oberland.[63] There is no doubt that Mussolini approved these plans as part of his irredentist concept.[64]

Guisan and the chief of the general staff praised Switzerland's intelligence service for the job it accomplished during the war, and Kurz echoed their opinion. However, H. R. Fuhrer was rather skeptical about its achievements, concluding that it was "by sheer luck" that its deficiencies in obtaining and evaluating information did not have "devastating" consequences.[65] The army's intelligence service had many merits, but in certain cases, which could have turned fatal, it did not function in a satisfactory manner.

W. Roesch's doctoral thesis gives an overview of the archive material and studies that exist regarding Germany's plans against Switzerland.[66] A study of "Operation Tannenbaum," dated September 6, 1940, concluded that at least 21 divisions, including five panzer divisions, three motorized divisions, and special troops would be required to take Switzerland within three to four days. An earlier study, "Case Green," dated June 25, 1940, calculated that nine divisions, including one panzer division and three motorized divisions, would be sufficient to lead a campaign that would not last more than two days.[67] Chief of the German General Staff, Colonel-General Franz Halder, personally analyzed the studies on October 17 and concluded that "eleven divisions, including six fast ones," should be "sufficient to accomplish the job."[68]

Neither Walter Brauchitsch, the commander-in-chief of the German Army, nor Hitler apparently had any direct influence on these studies, which can hardly be called plans of operation. Qualifying them as such would be an exaggeration; nevertheless, they were drafts and preliminary drawings that could have served as a basis for planning issues such as transport, supplies, deployments, and communication. The studies all took into account the Swiss Army's determination to fight and the preparations which it had made to defend the country. Moreover, they expressed a certain "reluctance to move into mountainous terrain."[69]

These factors were mentioned several times and without doubt helped to deter the Germans from attacking Switzerland, although they were unlikely to be the only reasons. Picker, who collected Hitler's dinner table conversations, claims that the "Führer" expressly forbade his army from invading Switzerland. When Guderian's panzer corps reached the Swiss border in June 1940, Hitler supposedly commented regarding the "problematic case of Switzerland . . . that the country was incomparably more valuable as a protectorate and as an international hub for diplomatic activities, intelligence activities, foreign currency transactions, and deliveries of goods that are in short supply, for example arms and armament supplies, than as a satellite state."[70] Even if Hitler's statement that there were no logical military reasons for conquering Switzerland was true, the country remained constantly at risk in view of Hitler's unpredictable, often irrational, decisions.

Corps Commander Prisi informed the General of another version of how confident the National Socialists were about defeating the Swiss, stating, "A secretary at the German Embassy in Bern allegedly said that Hitler would not have to sacrifice one single German soldier to conquer Switzerland. He said that as soon as the Germans had advanced far enough to the south, they would attack from the west on their way back to Germany rather than from the Rhine, thus surrounding the Swiss Army from the north and west and forcing it to capitulate."[71] When they were at the peak of success, the Germans hoped that the Swiss Confederation, or at least its German-speaking areas, would drop into the lap of the German empire without bloodshed.

Now that it had been completely surrounded by the Axis Powers, Switzerland began to experience increasing political and economic pressure, particularly from Germany. The country resembled an island that was thrown back on its own resources. In this difficult situation, the government, led by

Federal President Pilet-Golaz, proved willing to make considerable concessions, stretching to the limit an independent state's concept of dignity.

One concession made by the government was in connection with Germany's protests over the shooting down of German aircraft by the Swiss air force in June 1940. Frölicher, Switzerland's Ambassador to Germany, considered this moment to be the "most tense situation during the entire war."[72] Germany's Ambassador Köcher sent the Federal Council an ultimatum, demanding that it reply to the German protest note of June 19 by July 1 at 6:30 p.m.[73] The Federal Council invited Guisan into a meeting on July 1 at 3:15 p.m. in Federal President Pilet-Golaz' apartment. In the absence of Federal Councilor Obrecht, who was sick, the cabinet had already reached a unanimous decision to write an obliging note to the Germans, but wanted to hear the General's opinion before sending it off.[74] The Federal Council was willing to admit that the Swiss air force pilots had perhaps "flown over the border against strict orders and without their superiors' knowledge." In view of this possibility, the Federal Council said that it would not hesitate "to express its regrets about these incidents and . . . to apologize." In addition, Switzerland would make "provisions to compensate Germany for damages that were incurred, according to the German notes, by Swiss pilots outside Swiss territory" as soon as the necessary documents were presented.[75]

The fact that eight different drafts were written to formulate an adequate reply indicates that the Federal Council struggled to find the right words for an apology and that there were differences of opinion among the cabinet members, even though the minutes of the cabinet meeting did not mention this. The statement it eventually sent was an apology containing a number of qualifications. It indicated that the government was willing to make concessions by incriminating the Swiss pilots to a certain degree. Its decision was influenced in part by the fact that Germany denied visas to Isler and Magron, the two air force colonels whom the Federal President intended to send to Berlin to clear up misunderstandings with the competent German authorities.

The Federal President began the meeting with the General by asking whether Germany, by setting an ultimatum for making an apology, was looking for a pretext to attack Switzerland, or if the whole affair was just a matter of prestige. Pilet-Golaz considered that the second supposition was more likely, but explained that in any case the consequences would be painful. He added that refusing to meet the German demands could immediately trigger a war; that air bases and towns could be bombarded, the country could be occupied in part or in its entirety, acts of sabotage could be staged, or a city like Basel could be taken as a pledge. In this situation, the Federal President argued, when the country had to preserve its honor and its existence, any incident that could trigger a catastrophe had to be avoided until a peace agreement was signed. Nevertheless, the government wanted to hear the General's point of view.

Guisan's answer was firm. "You cannot ask me to agree," he said. "I would not be able to do that; first of all because this is a purely political matter; and above all, if I consented I would disavow my pilots, whose declarations are irrefutable, and through them my officers' corps and the armed forces as a whole. The facts are there." According to Guisan, there was no doubt whether the Swiss or the German pilots were right about respecting the Swiss national border, as he was convinced that "mine know the borderline far better." The commander-in-chief added that because the concessions proposed by the Federal Council would set "a dreadful precedent," he could not approve the cabinet's reply; however, he would not rebel against the Federal Council's decision. Pilet-Golaz replied, "I am not surprised by your answer. Had it been different, it would not have been a soldier's," whereupon Guisan conceded, "I recognize that one has to weigh the consequences of this reply, and if we refuse [to apologize], we will have to mobilize the entire armed forces." Pilet-Golaz added, "And a war will become inevitable. . . . You have given me the answer of a soldier. You give in to the Federal Council's decision without taking part in it nor agreeing with it. However, we count on you to intervene firmly, without any reservation, with the army if necessary." Guisan answered, "That is for sure. But don't ask me to do anything else against my officers, my pilots, and the army. I yield—and that's all."[76] The Federal Council's decision was clearly a concession to victorious Germany. As Bonjour put it, in view of the existing balance of power the Swiss were forced to "grin and bear it."[77]

On that same evening of July 1, Federal President Pilet-Golaz called Germany's Ambassador Köcher to a meeting at the Federal Palace to submit to him the government's verbal note. Following that meeting, Köcher was pleased to report to Berlin that Switzerland had "met the demands"; however, he said that the Federal President had explained to him, "It was very difficult for the Swiss government to accept Germany's version of the events because all official Swiss reports it had received contradicted that version. Nevertheless, the President said that he managed to convince the Federal Council that the unpleasant matter should be settled in a satisfactory manner as soon as possible in the interest of the future development of German-Swiss interests." Köcher wrote that Pilet-Golaz had made "an urgent appeal not to make public the course nor the results of these diplomatic talks, as that would severely harm the Federal Council's and his own authority, adding that it would not be in Germany's interest to see his authority as Federal President and Foreign Minister weakened."[78] After receiving this evasive apology, German Permanent

Secretary von Weizsäcker informed Switzerland's Ambassador Frölicher in Berlin that the dispute was settled.[79]

As another concession, at the suggestion of the Department of Foreign Affairs, the Federal Council decided to return 17 interned German airmen, whose aircraft had been shot down or who had had to perform emergency landings on Swiss territory during the war.[80] This gesture contradicted the law of neutrality, as Germany was still at war with Great Britain; and it was not the only favor that the Federal Council rendered the victorious German Reich. Captains Ernst, Hausamann, and Waibel, all leading figures in the "Officers' Alliance," noticed other signs of weakness in the Swiss government—for instance, the lawsuit against the German saboteurs (see Chapter 12) was delayed "on highest orders."[81] There were even rumors that the German Embassy had suggested exchanging the saboteurs.[82] However, these rumors could not be substantiated and according to Frölicher, the government of the Reich did "not have the shamelessness to officially plead the cause of these people."[83]

The Federal Council made largely one-sided concessions regarding print media. While Swiss newspapers were banned in Germany, Switzerland was inundated by German magazines and newspapers. Hausamann remarked that even the *Völkischer Beobachter*, the main paper of the Nazi Party, which had been banned for some time, "was suddenly available again at newsstands."[84] In addition, "at Germany's insistence," the Federal Council readmitted a leader of the Swiss section of the National Socialist Party and allowed other Nazi figures back into the country where they resumed their activities. Bonjour stated, "These officials actually performed the functions of regional representatives with the approval of the Swiss authorities."[85] Moreover, the Federal Council renounced making claims for damages suffered during Germany's bombardments of the towns of Kleinhüningen and Courrendlin, and instead compensated the victims with Federal funds. Also, under a new trade agreement concluded with Germany on August 9, following tough negotiations, Switzerland had to make substantial economic and financial concessions on the basis of clearing credits.[86]

France's rapid collapse had a very serious effect on Switzerland. After the debacle, it went through a period of weakness in both military and mental preparedness.[87] As General Guisan commented in his postwar report, "To be honest, we have to admit that during those five years and eight months we experienced a dramatic turn of events; that is, a situation neither the extent nor brutality of which we were able to imagine—being completely surrounded at the end of June 1940 after Germany's victory over the entire land forces in the west, with the exception of Great Britain's air and sea forces and mental strength, and America's latent power."[88] It may have been because of this shock that on July 4, 1940, the General made the following astonishing suggestion to the Federal Council:

> It seems natural and actually necessary to ask the German government, through diplomatic channels, to provide an explanation as to why some of its troops are stationed along our border. If the German government (and, if applicable, the Italian government) is able to give the Federal Council a reassuring explanation for the current or future presence of troops along and further behind our border, it will provide our government with a decisive element to evaluate the situation. . . . Whatever the German government's reply, it will give us an indication of the Reich's intentions toward us, an indication that will be as valuable for the political and economic sectors as it will be for the military.[89]

Odermatt considers that this suggestion may have been the General's first of several efforts to have a special diplomatic mission sent to Berlin to promote Switzerland's neutrality and to foster goodwill with the "Führer" by reinforcing cultural, artistic, and tourism ties with Germany.[90] These efforts continued until early 1941. It appears that the Swiss government did not take the General's proposal, which Minger forwarded to the Federal President, very seriously, as it did not respond to it in writing. Pilet-Golaz noted on the request, "To be returned to Military Department, as decided by the Federal Council. 7/12/1940," and Minger added on the same day, "Verbally informed the General about the Federal Council's comments."[91] By pointing out once again that German troops were still stationed at the border, Guisan reiterated his proposal, insisting, "I am providing you with this military information because I believe that it may also have substantial political implications. You may decide for yourselves if this situation would not justify reexamining the proposal I formulated in my letter of 7/4/1940 to undertake diplomatic steps in order to clarify the situation."[92] The Federal Council apparently did not consider the General's suggestion the second time either, as no mention was made of it in the minutes of the cabinet meetings around that time. The Secretary of the Military Department, Burgunder, wrote on the General's letter, "Matter said to be done and dealt with following yesterday's meeting between General/Head of Department. To be filed. 7/23/1940."[93] The final reply to the General's proposal was certainly negative, a fact that is remarkable insofar as it was communicated to him just three days before he addressed the army unit commanders at the Rütli.

Germany welcomed the subtle change of mood in Switzerland in favor of the Third Reich. In one of his reports in July 1940, Hans Hausamann wrote that the effect of Germany's victories on Switzerland's attitude actually "exceeded Germany's expectations." According to Hausamann, Germany believed that "Switzerland's sense of national identity [would] rapidly give way to a thinking along German, French, and Italian lines and the political and civil rights which had been uniting the Swiss [would] be relinquished." He added that Germany was convinced that "the Swiss authorities and parties actually make the largest contribution" toward dissolving the Swiss Confederation in this very effective manner "by resorting, at a time when the country reduces its military strength and adapts to the Axis Powers on the political and economic levels, to more and more semi-authoritarian measures which aim to secure food supplies and the people's economic existence, thereby preparing them perfectly for *Gleichschaltung*."[94]

15

The Officers' Conspiracy

IN REACTION TO THE DESPONDENCY THAT SEIZED Switzerland after the collapse of France, and following the Federal President's radio address of June 25, a group of young officers decided to create a group sworn to resist any aggressor under all circumstances. In his postwar report, the General wrote about the members of this so-called "Officers' Alliance":

> Some officers, most of whom were members of the general staff, came together because they shared concerns about the increasing defeatism in the army and among the population following France's defeat. Their intentions were actually commendable, as they feared that the government's and the population's determination to put up resistance could slacken in view of the effect of Germany's victories. They recruited other like-minded officers and tried to create an organization that sought to reiterate and strengthen the army's determination to put up total resistance against any enemy and support the army command in case it was subject to any pressure whatsoever. Even though these officers were prepared to act according to the orders issued to the armed forces that demanded they defend themselves 'under all circumstances,' a 'preliminary investigation' had to be ordered against them. Eight officers were disciplined, receiving sanctions ranging from 14 days of detention to a 'written reprimand' because they violated article 180 of the military's penal law on maintaining discipline. The rest of the 37 officers were not punished.[1]

Until now, no historical study has been made of the Officers' Alliance, an endeavor with many twists and turns, viewed as a heroic "conspiracy" by some, as a "Children's Crusade" by others, and as the "worst aberration ever" by others still. Officers who spearheaded the movement have written all the published, primary-source material and Bonjour's report was based mostly on their accounts.[2] In this chapter, these established facts will be summarized and supplemented with research based on documents made available for the first time to this author by the Military Attorney General's office.

Even the members of the group—which held its first meeting on July 21, 1940, in Lucerne—later disagreed about its nature. Some described it as a "conspiracy," others as an "alliance," and still others as a "movement." The key members clearly saw themselves as conspirators and did not hesitate to use the term "conspiracy," even after it was uncovered. One member went so far as to call it a "revolt of the general staff," or at least the prelude to a revolt.[3] In his account, Max Waibel, one of the group's proponents, used the term "Officers' Conspiracy" on several occasions and stated clearly, "We conspired." Even two decades later he declared that he "still stood by his view without reservations."[4] Gerhart Schürch, another member, agreed that the endeavor was a conspiracy in the sense that the group secretly prepared for the possibility of defying the authorities and staging a mutiny.[5] During the subsequent legal investigation of the group, Schürch explained, "We never had any intention to prepare a mutiny against a functioning army command; we prepared for the event that the army command was no longer the master of its own decisions."[6] In his notes describing the events, he frankly admitted, "When I signed the simple, binding document, I was fully aware that from a legal point of view this was a planned mutiny. I consciously accepted this fact."[7]

In a presentation he made to the founding convention in Lucerne, Alfred Ernst left little doubt that he felt the organization should have the character of a patriotic conspiracy. However, during the legal investigation, and in the title of his written account of the group's activities, he spoke of an "alliance."[8] Elsewhere he wrote that the group "intentionally paid little attention" to keeping its activities secret, explaining, "Our conspiracy methods were not very well developed. Due to our lack of experience, we made technical errors which soon resulted in our activities being uncovered."[9]

In contrast to the other members, Hans Hausamann strictly refused to call the endeavor a conspiracy, even though he described it as "a very serious matter." In an unpublished account, he reflected that the action, which many did not fully comprehend, was "in fact not a conspiracy [but a] movement."[10] Fritz Wanner believed that the undertaking was "something between a conspiracy and an alliance."[11]

From an organizational point of view, the endeavor appeared to be a union, intended to be an alliance, which had tendencies toward conspiracy; however, the members did not seem to be under any strict obligation to maintain secrecy. The action was a highly interesting case for the military courts as well, since they had to decide whether the group's contingency plans for mutiny or to violate army regulations should be treated as a matter of insubordination.

When Dr. W. Lützelschwab, a former prosecutor from Basel, proposed writing a history of the Officers' Alliance after the war, Ernst gave him all the files he had on the organization and wrote: "I am fully aware that we had the right basic attitude but made many errors back then. You must therefore absolutely not present us as heroes, which we were not. Most of all, politically speaking, we were appallingly naïve. Our careers were those of simple soldiers; we had a false sense of romanticism and totally misjudged the real political forces that existed among the Swiss." Ernst admitted that he was "a little ashamed" to reread the "romantic sentences [of that time], but they were written at a time when the situation was tense, and from a political viewpoint we were more or less childish—at least I was."[12]

Hausamann did not agree with Ernst's surprisingly candid account of the group's activities. When Ernst sent him a copy of his version of the events for comment before submitting it to Bonjour in 1963, he replied:

> If this account gets into Prof. Bonjour's (or someone else's) hands in its current version, we provide the ammunition that is needed to stab the 'conspirators' of 1940 in the back. . . . There is no need for us to declare, in retrospect, that we were a group of politically innocent people who were dilettantes even as conspirators. There is no need to do that because the material that I have submitted to Professor Bonjour proves that the opposite is true, that we were the ones who assessed the domestic and foreign political situation correctly. I have not sacrificed some of the best years of my life to be ridiculed after the fact for doing a good job. Moreover, the wording you use in some passages of your account does not correspond to the historical truth. Considering these facts, and in view of the fact that certain people would love to slap us in the face, it would be wrong to admit to anything that would make us a laughing-stock.[13]

Ernst, Hausamann, Waibel, and Schürch met on two occasions in February 1963 in Olten to discuss the position they should assume in view of future historiography. Ernst prepared a draft, which was subsequently corrected and shortened. In addition, Ernst, who had by then been promoted to divisional commander along with Waibel, took most of Hausamann's criticism into account. At the second meeting, on February 9, 1963, the modified version was approved.[14] Ernst asked his comrades to destroy the first draft, in which he had been too self-critical.[15]

1. Wir wollen unter allen Umständen bewaffneten Widerstand leisten, wenn vom Ausland Ansinnen an die Schweiz gestellt werden, die in irgend einer Weise ihre Unabhängigkeit oder ihre nationale Würde gefährden. Wer nach dem Erfolg des Widerstandes fragt, ist ein Verräter.

Der Verlust seiner staatlichen Unabhängigkeit ist das größte Unglück für ein Volk und wiegt unendlich schwerer als wirtschaftliche Not. Ein freies Volk ist fähig, sich aus wirtschaftlichem Niedergange wieder emporzuarbeiten. Ein Volk aber, das sich ohne Widerstand der Knechtschaft gefügt hat, verliert seine Daseinsberechtigung für immer.

2. Wir wollen eine starke, entschlußkräftige Regierung, die unabhängig von Parteien und Wirtschaftsgruppen sich ausschließlich vom Wohl des Landes leiten läßt.

3. Die neue Schweiz wird auf drei Grundgedanken beruhen:

    a) Soldatischer Kameradschaft und Disziplin;

    b) dem föderativen Prinzip als ewiger Grundlage der Eidgenossenschaft;

    c) der unbedingten Achtung vor der Einzelpersönlichkeit und der Familie.

Wir lehnen die Idee des totalen Staates eindeutig ab und verwerfen jegliche Einschränkung der Gewissensfreiheit durch den Staat.

4. Wir wollen nicht abrüsten, sondern schon jetzt, unter Anspannung aller Kräfte, am weitern Ausbau der Armee arbeiten.

Oath taken by members of the Officers' Alliance on July 21, 1940. (BAr)

All members of the movement agreed that Federal President Pilet-Golaz' radio address triggered the idea for the Officers' Alliance. August R. Lindt, the only member of the group who was not an officer, recalled that he had heard the broadcast on June 25 and had then called Captain Ernst, who was an old friend from his school days. They both viewed the speech with the same criticism and came to the "conclusion to make preparations, together with Captain Hans Hausamann, the head of Bureau 'Ha,' and Captain Max Waibel of the general staff," that would allow the army to fight even if the government capitulated and yielded to unacceptable demands from Nazi Germany.[16] In a private conversation, Lindt confirmed to this author that the concept of the Officers' Alliance was a spontaneous idea put forward by Ernst right after Pilet-Golaz' speech. He said that for a short time, they even considered staging a coup d'état. Captain W. Allgöwer, who served as an infantry instructor in Bern, was willing to occupy the Federal palace with his company of recruits; however, they quickly discarded that idea.[17] In his memoirs, Christian Gasser, a founding member of the Gotthard Alliance, also spoke of the idea of possibly launching a preventive action.[18] During the 1940 investigation Hausamann declared:

As a small group that met spontaneously in the second half of June 1940, we considered that the fighting spirit had to be rekindled everywhere at all costs. During several of these chance meetings, about five to seven officers were present. Because of my commitment to them I am not allowed to reveal their names. I was the one who pushed mostly for using all available means and every effort to fight against the spirit of resignation in the army and among the population. These occasional meetings gave rise to the idea of talking about these problems with a larger group of comrades.[19]

Ernst wrote about the spontaneous beginning of the officers' movement: "The idea to create an emergency organization to enforce armed resistance was developed by Colonel Waibel of the general staff, Captain Hausamann, A. R. Lindt, and myself. The other officers who participated in our action were recruited at a later stage and did not play a leading role."[20] For his part, Captain Waibel recounted: "In July, the two other captains and myself began organizing everything that was necessary to appeal to the army to fight in case the Federal Council or also the General should give in to political or military pressure by the Third Reich in order to 'peacefully' integrate our country into the new order of the National Socialist system."[21]

The group openly mistrusted the Federal Government. According to Hausamann, the officers who belonged to army intelligence and had access to inside information "no longer fully trusted all Federal Councilors."[22] Ernst wrote, "We knew that Federal Councilor Minger demanded to remain firm. However, we also knew that Federal Councilors Pilet-Golaz, Celio, and especially Wetter were ready to yield. Apparently the majority of the cabinet no longer believed that the war could turn around."[23] It is debatable whether the Federal Council, and in particular the Federal President, would have actually capitulated if the Third Reich had made any dishonorable demands in 1940; based on the information currently available, it is improbable.[24] Considering the Federal Council's sibylline radio address and other evidence of its apparent willingness to make concessions to victorious Germany, however, it is understandable that serious doubts were cast on the government's determination to put up resistance.

It is interesting to note that even the commander-in-chief's determination did not seem to be beyond a shadow of doubt. In his unpublished draft account of the Officers' Alliance, Ernst wrote:

> The General had close ties with the Federal Council; hence, it would have been understandable if he had not been able to revolt against the legitimate government to which he had vowed to be loyal. Our decision to create an organization that was to fight at all costs was made before the General's address to the unit commanders at the Rütli; at that time, he had not yet expressly declared that he would put up resistance under all circumstances. We were puzzled by the fact that he did not immediately react to the Federal President's radio address, so we thought it best to also prepare for the event that the General should give in to the capitulating Federal Council. If this had happened, we would have carried out our action without the General, even if the prospect of success would have been much slimmer.[25]

After being arrested, Ernst admitted to the investigating authorities: "I am convinced that the supreme command of the armed forces has every intention to put up resistance. However, I am not sure whether the political authorities will not put pressure on the army command to force it to give in." Consequently he and his friends vowed to engage in combat under all circumstances, even if they "were to disobey orders of the supreme command." In addition, Ernst conceded that he would "not refrain from committing illegal acts in order to accomplish the set goal."[26] Gerhart Schürch, one of the conspirators, explained to this author: "I would not go as far as saying that we mistrusted the General, but we certainly did not put very much trust in him at that time."[27]

The four leaders wrote to and spoke with other like-minded officers and personalities in order to boost their determination to fight. Hausamann told the editor of the *Berner Bund*:

> The people are just waiting to be called upon! And I guarantee you that they will be called upon. We are just waiting to see what position the parliament will assume. Should we give up just because a few big wheels are scared? . . . Now is the time to fight! Age is not important in this struggle because it is being fought on a mental level. Now comes the time of trial; now we shall see if everyone is really what others believed them to be; the victory will belong to the ones who are more enduring and determined.[28]

At the beginning of July, Ernst used his position as an intelligence officer to visit officers at various command posts to win them over to the group's cause.[29] He was most of all interested in recruiting a high-ranking staff officer who would be willing to lead the movement and to conduct an operation if necessary. At first, he believed that Colonel Gustav Däniker, the commander of the Walenstadt shooting practice facilities, would be suitable. He had met him in 1938 and was impressed by his "strong, fascinating personality" and his military capabilities. Ernst saw Däniker during a shooting practice in Graubunden and tried to find out his position. "In Arosa," he recalled, "we mostly talked about the question how our army could be made more powerful. We agreed on the technical military problems that we discussed. When I hinted at our plans to prevent our country from being subjugated [to Germany], Colonel Däniker did not respond. That is why I did not notice during that first visit that he completely disagreed with me on that point. I believed that he would join our cause; considering the high reputation he enjoyed among many officers, that seemed desirable to me."[30] Ernst held a second meeting with Däniker in Bern several days later, during which it became clear to him that their idea of Switzerland's policy toward Germany was fundamentally different. They said goodbye and never spoke with each other again. Ernst told the investigating authorities that Däniker's attitude was "one of the most bitter disappointments" for him and that he subsequently warned his comrades against keeping in touch with him.[31]

First Lieutenant Gerhart Schürch also played a role, albeit not a leading one, in the preliminary talks that led to the formation of the Officers' Alliance. He contacted Ernst, an old acquaintance, on his own initiative to inform him of his concern about the flagging determination to fight. He later wrote:

It had become clear to me what the country needed. If the General did not stand up and issue orders to resist, another personality who was well respected among the officers would have to do it. I wanted to ask Ernst what he thought about that idea and if he knew anyone who could take on that responsibility. I had already thought of Colonel Däniker, even though I disagreed with him (and with Ernst) on the question of the army command; however, I believed that Däniker might have the necessary stature and commanded general respect, at least from many officers. Captain Ernst summoned me to Worb; the meeting lasted 40 minutes. I will never forget how quickly it became clear that we perfectly agreed. Ernst explained to me that he would speak with Däniker and would then get back to me. A few days later, he told me over the telephone that he had come to the conclusion, after meeting with Däniker, that he was not the right man for us because he was convinced that Germany would carry away the final victory.[32]

The decision to go separate ways was mutual. As Däniker later explained to the General, "I pointed out to [Ernst] that his idea gave me cause for concern. I warned Captain Ernst and told him, 'Listen, if that is how you handle things, the army is doomed. This must not happen.' I refused to have anything to do with the whole matter."[33]

As a result of France's defeat, two conflicting factions emerged in Switzerland: on one side were unfaltering resistance fighters, while on the other were those willing to accommodate Germany because they were convinced of its absolute military might and consequently expected the Third Reich's final victory. After realizing to which side Däniker belonged, the conspirators started opposing him within their ranks.[34] Sorting out Däniker's position helped to clearly separate the two camps among the officers' corps. The leading figures of the two groups subsequently competed with each other to gain influence with the General.

Once Ernst realized that the well-respected Colonel Däniker was not a suitable leader for the resistance movement, he contacted Lieutenant-Colonel Wilhelm Werder, the chief of staff of the 5th Division. Werder later explained that Ernst had come to see him on three occasions to convince him to assume leadership of the movement. He also said that Ernst had assured him that Colonel Masson, the Chief of Intelligence, was "informed about the movement and approved of it, but because of his position he could not allow his name to be associated with it."[35] Even though Werder believed that "the army command approved" of the endeavor, he did not accept Ernst's offer right away; however, he did not decline it either, and seemed to try to gain time to make up his mind.

Before Werder made his final decision, Ernst and Waibel called for a meeting to be held in Lucerne on Sunday, July 21, 1940. The initiators had held preliminary talks with many of the invited officers; hence, they were already informed about the endeavor. In order to hide the purpose of the meeting from superior commanders, other officers were invited by telling them that a "briefing" was to be held for staff officers in the army units who were in charge of intelligence. Since the meeting was held on the premises of the army's Intelligence Bureau 1 at the "Schweizerhof," the participants' impression that this was an official military event was reinforced. One participant explained to this author that very few officers knew that they had been summoned to begin a conspiracy; most of them believed that the meeting was indeed intended to brief intelligence officers on the threatening military situation and to take the necessary precautions.[36]

The minutes of the examinations, which all participants had to undergo during the subsequent legal investigation, give a detailed account of the meeting in Lucerne, which lasted two to three hours.[37] The statements made by Captains Ernst, Waibel, Heberlein, Hunziker, and Uhlmann, as well as by First Lieutenants Schürch and Moser, were particularly precise and detailed. They all said that Captain Waibel, who made some opening remarks, chaired the meeting, the proceedings of which were "to be kept absolutely confidential and secret." Captains Ernst and Hausamann then made extensive presentations. Ernst, who spoke extemporaneously but held a manuscript in his hand, considered that it was urgent to strengthen the army's determination to resist an attack, and presented the plan for the creation of an organization designed "to put up armed resistance even if our superiors should order us to surrender." In every army unit, one officer should make sure that the troops fight under all circumstances. Ernst explained, "The subordinate commanders of the army units shall designate trustworthy men in the regiments, who shall in turn designate other trustworthy men in the battalions, et cetera, until every unit has officers in place who shall act on our orders." He exhorted the participants to choose the men very carefully. Only officers were to be considered who were "absolutely reliable and ready to fight" and whom their subordinates trusted; the commanders of the army units should "under no circumstances be let in" on the undertaking. It was not specified who would lead the organization. Captain Ernst only explained that a high-ranking staff officer was slated for the command, but that the officer in question was definitely not Colonel Däniker.

According to Ernst, the organization was to pursue three goals: (1) to propagate the determination to put up resistance until everyone was united; (2) to prevent capitulation under all circumstances; and (3) to prepare and carry out a reform in order to rebuild the army after the war. As Ernst elaborated:

> The first goal was most important. The second one was considered only in the event that the Federal Council or the army command capitulated. I imagined that we would warn the army units first and then put them on alert by issuing the code word 'Nidwalden' once it was irrefutable that the Federal Council would capitulate. The army units were to occupy the positions defined in the orders of the existing plan of operations. Then we would have informed the General and shown him the evidence of the imminent treason, expecting him to issue orders to fight. If he would not give orders, we would have issued the code word 'Nidwalden' anyway, thereby signaling the troops to fight.[38]

Ernst's passionate presentation did not fail to impress most participants at the meeting in Lucerne. However, some sober-minded officers had reservations. Captain Uhlmann recalled that Ernst seemed to be "very excited, [and] he spoke in a bombastic manner. At the end of his presentation, I remarked to one of my neighbors that I felt the situation was pictured in an overly pessimistic way. I know that Captain Ernst is very impulsive and tends to exaggerate."[39] Another participant commented that he considered the presentation "highly romantic."[40]

The notes that Ernst had prepared for his speech were confiscated by the investigators and kept on file. It is interesting to analyze the passages that he crossed out in the manuscript and apparently did not present in Lucerne. They indicate that he originally had farther-reaching goals in mind for the "Alliance" than those ultimately agreed to at the founding convention. He wrote, among other things, "We also have to be prepared for the worst-case scenario. If traitors pose a threat to our state's existence, we have to seize power and fight in order to prevent our country from being subjugated. We have gathered here to create an alliance that takes on this responsibility. Our Alliance should be organized according to military principles; one leader is in charge and issues orders, and we obey. Only a few of us will know the leader. We must not reveal his name so that no one will try to hinder him from doing his job."[41] Some other notes prepared by Ernst indicated that the state should henceforth be based on idealized soldierly qualities. At one point he jotted, "During these ten months of wartime duty we have come to know a new ideal; we have experienced the sense of comradeship, of voluntary subordination, and of individual responsibility. Even if we have not been fighting in the war, the spirit of the combatants at the front has imbued the units that are well managed. We want to preserve that spirit and use it to re-shape the lives of our people."[42]

Captain Hausamann spoke after Captain Ernst to make an assessment of the situation as seen by his intelligence network, Bureau 'Ha.' Uhlmann recounted that the second speaker "also pointed out how dangerous the situation appeared to be."[43] Hausamann later told Federal Councilor Kobelt that he attended the meeting in Lucerne without actually knowing what its goals were, explaining, "A few minutes before the beginning of the meeting, I was asked to give some information on the situation."[44] Hausamann told the meeting that the political authorities "covered up with economic arguments the fact that the country [was] being disarmed" and declared, "Those who ask if there are any prospects of successfully putting up resistance are traitors."[45] Hausamann told the investigating authorities that he said only a few sentences "extempore" at the meeting in Lucerne, making his assessment of the situation without notes. He claimed, "I do not remember what I said in detail. I said some general things."[46] However, among Hausamann's unpublished papers was a multi-page document entitled "Introductory remarks for the first meeting of the officers who decided to fight wherever they were stationed in the event of an attack, even if for some reason no such orders were given ('Officers' Conspiracy')." The first sentence read, "At the request of Captain Ernst of the general staff, the head of the [German] desk, I will make a short introductory assessment of the current international situation from my own perspective."[47] It is not inconceivable that Hausamann wrote down his presentation only after giving it. He wrote, among other things, "We are present here in our function as intelligence officers. Being what we are, all we can do is be vigilant in order to be prepared to fight at any given moment. . . . After the latest development on the international level everything once again depends on our remaining steadfast and resolute."[48] He spoke in measured tones and in a rather academic style, devoid of inflammatory phrases.

The main purpose of the meeting in Lucerne was the presentation and signing of a manifesto. Following a discussion among the participants, Hausamann read it to the officers and asked them to sign it. The manifesto contained the following four points:

1. We are determined to put up armed resistance under all circumstances against any foreign country that might have claims against Switzerland, which pose a threat to its independence or national honor. Those who ask if there are any prospects of successfully putting up resistance are traitors. Losing its independence is a people's greatest misfortune; it is infinitely more serious than suffering eco-

nomic hardship. Free people are capable of working their way up
from an economic downfall. However, a nation that is reduced to
servitude without putting up resistance permanently loses its right
of existence.

2. We want a government that is strong and capable of making its
   own decisions, which it bases exclusively on what is in the country's
   best interest. It must be independent of the interests of parties and
   economic groups.

3. The new Switzerland shall be based on three principles:
   a) military comradeship and discipline;
   b) the federalist principle, which is the eternal basis of the Swiss
      Confederation;
   c) an absolute respect for the individual and the family.
   We strictly refute the idea of a totalitarian state and reject any
   curtailment by the state of the freedom of conscience.

4. We do not want to disarm; instead, we want to begin strengthening the armed forces right away, using all our efforts.

Points two and three are clear evidence that the manifesto had not only
military but political aspects. Demanding a strong government and a "new
Switzerland" went beyond making an appeal to put up resistance at all costs;
consequently, one can conclude that provisions were made to take political
action if the Officers' Alliance had carried out its operation. Ernst was decidedly against a totalitarian state but considered that an authoritarian form of
democracy was desirable, making it necessary to grant far-reaching authority to
the government.[49]

Ernst drafted this declaration, which served as the basis for the oath that
the "conspirators" made in Lucerne. He "discussed and edited [it] several times"
with Captains Waibel and Burckhardt and presented it to Lt. Colonel Werder
before having it printed.[50] The manifesto was passed around during the meeting in Lucerne and "those who agreed with it signed it on the back."[51] Ernst
announced that the copy with the signatures would be "deposited in the safe of
the intelligence service."[52] The manifesto was signed "with the thought that an
attack was imminent. . . . [E]veryone was very serious about doing all he could
to prevent the country from capitulating in dishonor."[53] However, Captain
Allgöwer made a joke, asking his neighbor if ink would do or if everyone was
expected to sign with his own blood.[54]

A total of 18 participants signed the manifesto in Lucerne, while two officers declined. Major Rolf Zschokke from Aarau, who participated "as something like an observer" on orders of his Chief of Staff Werder, told his comrade

Burckhardt that he considered "Ernst to be somewhat of a dreamer" and did not sign.[55] Captain Edmund Wehrli from Zürich declared that he was in a moral conflict, stating, "I said that I agreed unconditionally with the cause which Ernst pleaded but explained that I did not like to be part of something of which I was not allowed to inform Colonel Däniker."[56] After the meeting, Wehrli wrote to Ernst to further explain his position: "You know what I think of Däniker. I do not want to follow a path that is different from his, as I fully trust him. Let me be more precise; you can count on me to act like the people of Unterwalden [more than six hundred years ago when they freed themselves from Hapsburg rule] and to do so within my scope of influence. However, I must ask you not to get me involved in an organization which you believe must be kept secret from Däniker (and probably from Wille and Frick as well), or else you will get me into a moral conflict from which I do not feel there is any way out."[57] He also told Ernst that by forming this movement he was about to split the officers' corps into two camps. He wrote, "Why are you driving a wedge of mistrust between our best officers when all of us who are young in age and spirit should stand united or at least discuss things openly nor have any secrets from each other, even if we do not agree on everything?"[58] Wehrli was asked to keep the meeting in Lucerne secret, but he informed Colonel Däniker about the activities and objectives of Ernst's group once the conspiracy had been uncovered.[59]

The officers who agreed to participate in the resistance group then discussed details on how to proceed. According to a snowball system, additional members were to be recruited among the staff of all corps. The intelligence office in Lucerne was to maintain contact with them through couriers. Within one week, as of July 29, the emergency organization was to be established on a large scale.[60] One of the participants remarked, "We left the meeting with instructions that were anything but clear."[61] One of the details that was discussed were the rules of communication; a secret code was to be established in order to be able to take action once the code word "Nidwalden" was pronounced. Captain Waibel drafted these rules and sent them to all participants in sealed envelopes that were marked "personal and confidential." Waibel was also designated as the one who would issue the code word. He explained, "If we had received information that the General refused to fight, we would have followed the order of April 18, 1940, according to which any such information was to be considered as enemy propaganda and we were to fight. Hence, we would have acted according to the order of April 18."[62]

Gerhart Schürch contributed to the group's preparations by securing the services of the Schwarzenburg radio station. The day after the meeting in Lucerne, he contacted the head of the shortwave radio service of the Swiss

Broadcasting Corporation, Paul Borsinger, with whom he was acquainted, and "was able to convince [him] of the need to act quickly in case our government displayed a defeatist attitude. . . . I informed Mr. Borsinger that the military resistance was organized and that it was crucial to get the radio station under the control of those who organized this resistance at the decisive moment."[63] Borsinger agreed right away "to go to Schwarzenburg immediately if an emergency occurred in order to carry out his orders." He planned to bring along an "absolutely reliable technician" from his staff to operate the radio station.

Schürch also mentally prepared the infantry company, which he commanded that summer on an interim basis, for an emergency. "The officers and non-commissioned officers were informed that they might have to act according to the order of April 18, 1940, very soon and ignore any information that the Federal Council or the army command had capitulated. They were to act exclusively on my orders under all circumstances. . . . We were waiting for the code word "Nidwalden" to be issued, and prepared for the case that we would have to act on our own responsibility if no further detailed instructions were to follow."[64]

Ernst, who called himself "No. 1," attempted to get Lt. Colonel Werder, the "Chief" of the movement, actively involved in the operation to consolidate its structure. During a meeting after the convention of Lucerne, he gained the impression that the chief of staff of the 5th Division agreed to take the lead. Ernst wanted to be able to look to Werder as the authoritative head of the Alliance. On August 1, he wrote to him, "Some gentlemen still seem to believe that we are an officers' club or some discussion group. It will be good for you to stress the fact that this is an organization in which orders are issued and followed and that you do not tolerate any shortcomings. We had better throw half-hearted and negligent gentlemen out of our organization. It is better to have a few absolutely reliable members than a lot of mere hangers-on."[65] In addition, Ernst submitted to his "Chief" a list of names of potential members in the divisions and light brigades. Werder approved the list and promised to personally find suitable officers in divisions 6 to 9.[66]

When the deadline for completing the organization's expansion turned out to be too soon, Lt. Colonel Werder ordered an extension of twelve days, during which its structure could be "put on a much more solid foundation." Hence, on July 29 the members received confidential instructions stating:

1. The domestic and foreign political situation of our country is still very serious. However, it appears that we will be granted a grace period before the crucial moment arrives. We have to make use of this extra time.

2. Consequently, your deadline for consolidating and expanding the organization in your area has been extended until 10 August, 08.00 hours. After this deadline, everything has to be prepared in a thorough and reliable manner so as to be able to deal with any situation. On 10 August, your final organizational charts for your army units will be picked up.[67]

This information was unsigned and said only, "on behalf of the Chief," which appears to be an indication that Werder's real relationship with the Officers' Alliance was up in the air. During the subsequent legal investigation, Werder slightly corrected Ernst's statement that he had unconditionally agreed to lead the organization. The minutes of the examination read: "Lieutenant-Colonel Werder claims that he made no definite commitment to Ernst regarding taking over the leadership [of the organization]; however, he declared that his actions allowed Ernst to conclude that he would eventually agree."[68] Up to the end, it was not clear how firmly Werder committed himself to the group. It cannot be excluded that bluffing took place and some intentional wrong assumptions were made. The ringleaders tried to promote the impression that high-ranking staff officers had made firm commitments to take on responsibility at a time when such commitments were merely wishful thinking. They hoped that everyone would follow along at the decisive moment if high-ranking officers approved of the organization.

Lieutenant-Colonel Werder told the investigating authorities that he had received the impression, during their meetings, that Ernst was "extremely tense and nervous" because of his concern about Switzerland's position, and "risked taking inappropriate and inadmissible steps." He claimed that his main reason for acceding to overtures from the movement was to keep it under control, explaining, "I felt responsible because I did not want to let the movement go astray, nor did I want them to make decisions that I would not approve. I realized that the gentlemen who were members of the movement were all honorable and had good intentions. I said to myself that a somewhat older officer had to make himself available for this good cause in order to prevent the young gentlemen from making wrong decisions and moves." Werder further explained that in order to prevent "the younger gentlemen from doing something without thinking it through," he gave Captain Ernst an answer "from which he could assume, with some certainty, that I would definitely be part [of the organization]. Hence, Captain Ernst could do nothing decisive without my knowing about it."[69]

Werder was also "concerned that the movement created by Captain Ernst [could have incited] certain officers to start a non-Swiss movement. . . . I thought that by joining it, I could help to prevent that from happening." Moreover, he ascertained that he would "never have opposed an order by the General or another superior" or encouraged others to do so, adding, "The only case where I would have put up resistance despite an 'order' would have been in the event that false information was disseminated after an invasion. In my opinion, this was the only case where, as the leader of the planned organization, I would have been under the obligation to make sure that everyone fights. In all other cases, where Switzerland was to make political or military concessions because it was put under pressure and was threatened by an invasion, I would under no circumstances have given any instructions."[70]

These statements by Werder, which undoubtedly reflected his true beliefs, indicate that the prospective leader of the officers' movement did not advocate the same unyielding attitude of total resistance as Ernst. It is possible that Werder, a well-versed legal professional, tried with his statements to avoid suffering severe legal sanctions; however, in view of the fact that the chief of staff of the 5th Division was a serious and discreet person, that seems rather unlikely. The impression prevails that Ernst and his fellow conspirators would have been fooled if an emergency had occurred.

On the other hand, it is not impossible that Ernst did not tell Werder everything about the conspirators' willingness to fight at all costs. During the investigation, Ernst stated that he informed Werder about the organization's objectives, "but not in a very concrete manner; [hence] most likely Lieutenant-Colonel Werder did not know exactly how determined I was in the event of an attack or an imminent invasion to go to combat even against clear orders by the army command."[71]

It is not unthinkable that certain things were intentionally left unclear in order to have a free hand to make far-reaching decisions at the appropriate moment. There is no doubt that Alfred Ernst was determined to fight at all costs. All statements indicate that he was imbued with the spirit of utmost resistance and was the unwavering, fearless driving force of the Officers' Conspiracy. However, from several statements he made during the legal investigation it becomes clear that he was not exclusively driven by military motivations but had a political agenda as well, even if it was not as important. During the excitement that followed his arrest, he declared:

I advocate a strong, determined government that orders what must be done without negotiating or making compromises. Consequently, I favor an authoritarian regime in the sense that I consider the parliament and the parties to be disastrous, at least in their current form. Nevertheless, I am a stout advocate of democracy in the sense that I would like the people to participate [in the decision-making process], first of all on a small scale on the town level, and then on the cantonal and federal levels. However, I do not think that they should participate by voting on issues which nobody understands anyway; instead, after being allowed to act on its own authority for some time, the government should be accountable to the people for the results which it has achieved.[72]

In this statement, Ernst expressed his aversion to the partisan state and the parliamentary system, a view that was similar to Guisan's in his earlier life.[73] However, Ernst went one major step further by declaring:

Those who want to be protected by the army should make sacrifices. In this respect, I am totally anti-capitalist. In fact, some capitalists are our worst enemies nowadays because money is their god and they will consequently strive to secure their possessions by appeasing Germany. I believe that a healthy new state will be built that is based on nationalist workers, farmers, and young intellectuals who do not think like materialists but like soldiers. I am allowed to be anti-capitalist because I personally have sizeable assets, so I will not be suspected of pleading my own case—on the contrary.[74]

Ernst later gave up his negative opinion about Switzerland's parliamentary democracy, and in 1963 he wrote:

The experience of the summer of 1940 quickly and completely opened my eyes. I realized that we had to rely on democratic forces in order to be able to successfully resist an attack from the outside. I have to point out this fact because otherwise the deposition I made on August 4, 1940 to the special prosecutor, Colonel Herzog, in which I explained the motivations for my actions, would not be understandable. I do not want to make excuses for the political mistakes that I made at the time. They were the consequence of my one-sided 'military' thinking, which is incomprehensible to me today, and my lack of political maturity. Many ideas that I advocated were common among the young generation in 1940.[75]

It is interesting to analyze whether there was a connection between the Officers' Conspiracy and the briefing General Guisan held at the Rütli Meadow. Strikingly, there is no written evidence that the General's upcoming briefing of the unit commanders was mentioned at the convention of July 21 in Lucerne, even though its date had been communicated to the commanders as early as July 18; hence, the officers of the general staff must have been informed about it. The witnesses whom this author was able to interview were surprised and said that they could not have known about the upcoming briefing at the Rütli when they were at the convention in Lucerne. However, the intelligence officers present—such as Captains Waibel, Ernst, and Hausamann—must have been informed days in advance about the confidential order summoning the unit commanders to the Rütli. It is possible that they did not mention it because it was strictly confidential. However, this author thinks it is more plausible that the upcoming briefing was not deemed important at first and that the ringleaders of the Officers' Alliance were skeptical because they could not know what the commander-in-chief would say in his first appearance after a prolonged period of silence. Schürch speculated that General Guisan may have been informed about the existence of the Officers' Alliance early on, thereby "considerably expediting" his decision to hold the briefing; however, this is very unlikely to be true.[76]

Even after the General's speech at the Rütli, in which he advocated unconditional resistance, the ringleaders did not consider their Alliance to be superfluous; instead, they decided to continue with their activities. Ernst told Lt. Colonel Werder, "The order issued by the General and the chief of the general staff makes many officers believe that our activities are in fact no longer necessary because they think that everything is all right now. However, this view is totally wrong and should be refuted in the first order that you issue. If we are not extremely vigilant and active there is a risk that the mood, which has somewhat improved, not least thanks to our very intensive propaganda, will shift again. This has to be prevented at all costs."[77]

Ernst considered himself to be in a dilemma, which he described as follows:

On one hand, the General's clear language and personal conviction, which had been less transparent before the briefing at the Rütli, reassured us. On the other hand, we thought that it was better to continue taking precautions. At that time, we had reason to be suspicious of declarations that were not followed by concrete actions; we considered that it was possible for the General to give in to pressure by the Federal Council. Moreover, we were convinced that the General would have been pleased to see that we had taken precautions in case he decided to rebel against an order by the Federal Council to capitulate. Based on these considerations, we decided to continue our activities.[78]

Ernst told the investigating authorities that the General's speech at the Rütli had "a very positive effect, but we are suspicious and no longer trust someone just because he says something nice."[79]

In agreement with Werder, Ernst called a second meeting to be held in Lucerne on August 4, at which only Ernst, Waibel, and the most trusted members from the army units would participate, and at which the command of the organization would be formally handed over to Lt. Colonel Werder.[80] On August 3, however, while he was working on the details for the meeting on the following day, Ernst was arrested in his office at Worb Castle as the first of the conspirators.[81] Colonel Herzog, Special Prosecutor and Senior Judge of the 8th Division, on the orders of General Guisan, who had consulted with the Military Attorney General before making his decision, made the arrest. At the same time, Herzog confiscated Ernst's files. On a notepad, Ernst had written, "Operation: explain that [it is] necessary more than ever before, in spite of Rütli."[82] The following morning, Captains Waibel and Hausamann were arrested in Lucerne.

The circumstances that led to the uncovering of the conspiracy were more complex than originally believed. Ernst was convinced that the General found out about the officers' secret activities because a courier erroneously transmitted a confidential message to the chief of staff of an army unit who did not know about the "Alliance." According to Ernst, "This chief of staff then informed his commander, and that is how Colonel-Corps Commander Labhart found out about it. He went to see the General to inform him; however, apparently he did not state everything correctly because, surprisingly, the General initially believed that we had instigated a pro-German conspiracy on behalf of the Front movement. Consequently, when I was arrested I had to point out to the special prosecutor that we intended to do exactly the opposite of what we were accused of. It was really a grotesque situation with a lot of unintended funny moments."[83]

The relevant files indicate that Ernst was correct about an initial misdirected message, but that the conspirators were in fact betrayed. Some officers from eastern Switzerland who had attended the meeting in Lucerne and signed the manifesto began having doubts whether their actions were honorable. Captain Heberlein said that he had "serious doubts if [the Alliance] pursued the right course." Hence, as early as the day after the convention in Lucerne, he informed his superior, Colonel Karl Kobelt, chief of staff of the 4th Army Corps, that he had participated in the meeting; however, at first he kept quiet about the signing of the manifesto and the formation of the special organization, explaining, "Once I looked at the meeting from a certain distance, I asked myself if it was really necessary and the right thing to create such an organization. . . . I was too embarrassed to admit to [Colonel Kobelt] that I had fallen under these people's spell."[84] Likewise, Captain Guido Hunziker from Aargau, who was not quite sure if the meeting in Lucerne was an official event held by the intelligence service, and was under the impression that "something was fishy about the whole matter," informed his superior, Major Schönenberger, the chief of staff of the Sargans Fortress.[85] Nevertheless, before going on leave he took precautions in the event that the code word "Nidwalden" was issued, and reported to Lucerne that he had "informed his deputy, Captain Holderegger of the general staff. During my absence, all messages shall be addressed to him."[86]

When Holderegger received the unsigned confidential message of July 29, he informed Major Schönenberger and Captains Hunziker and Heberlein. Schönenberger consequently called Hunziker and Heberlein to a meeting to get more information on the planned conclave in Lucerne. Heberlein later explained, "Major Schönenberger showed us in a very compelling manner that this was an organization within an organization, which was not permissible, and that the origin and the purpose of the signed declaration was not clear and had some political aspects. He pointed out that it could not be excluded that the whole endeavor carried with it additional hidden plans and intentions."[87] Schönenberger forbade Hunziker to attend the second conference, which was scheduled to take place on August 4, adding, "It was nonsense, both from a military and a moral point of view, for officers of the general staff who were informed about the Officers' Alliance to work against so-called unreliable commanders and chiefs of staff."[88] He informed the commander of the fortress, Brigadier Gubler, to discuss with him and Captain Holderegger what should be done about this matter, which "appeared to be more and more suspicious or was at least not correct from a military viewpoint." They considered "personally informing the General, or unofficially informing Colonel Masson first, or following the official procedure by informing the commander of the 4th Army Corps."[89]

Gubler decided to personally inform Corps Commander Labhart, who wrote about the meeting in his diary: "I arrive at the command post at 19.05 hours, where Colonel-Brigadier Gubler has been waiting for me for several hours. He informs me about a confidential document, which immediately leads me to launch an investigation that I conduct with the Chief of Staff [Kobelt] and Lieutenant-Colonel Schär. I ask the General for an urgent meeting on Saturday morning."[90] The following morning, Labhart traveled to Gümligen to inform the General of the status of his investigation. Labhart entered in his diary: "[Guisan] authorizes me to immediately contact the Senior Auditor at the Federal Palace; I arrive there at 9.30 hours."[91] The fate of the Officers'

Conspiracy was sealed. Senior Auditor Trüssel appointed a special prosecutor, had the conspirators arrested, and ordered a preliminary hearing of evidence to be conducted.

While waiting for the results of the preliminary hearing, Captains Waibel and Hausamann were kept under house arrest at the Schweizerhof Hotel in Lucerne, and Ernst remained in solitary confinement in his room in Worb. He wrote about this experience: "An ingenuous soldier from Valais stood on guard in front of my door with his loaded gun. We made friends quickly; he ate most of the copious meals that were prepared for me at the restaurant. In exchange, he let my wife visit me once in a while."[92]

Ernst spent 16 days, Waibel 15, and Hausamann 4 in their respective abodes awaiting the outcome of the preliminary hearings. Attempts were made to charge them with high treason, so they had to anticipate the possibility of spending several years in prison.[93] During this time of anxiousness, Ernst wrote to his wife:

> I don't know if I will ever be a soldier again or if they will take away my job. If they do, we'll have to start all over again. You will have to help me during the difficult period when I have to give up everything that was important to me. I am not afraid; things will work out. By the way, I am more and more convinced that our country is heading for a bitter end because the majority is careless, cowardly, and blind. If we could at least fight and die in combat, [our destiny] would be bearable; but I am more and more afraid that we will be appeased without fighting. You see, the only thing that worries me is the fact that I cannot be at my post at this time when I should be fighting more than ever against any kind of defeatism. But you know, they cannot kill our idea even if they lock us up. Who knows if locking us up won't actually advance our cause.[94]

Following his first interrogation, Ernst wrote to the investigating authorities that even after giving it some serious thought, he considered the activities for which he was arrested correct, adding, "Should I be mistaken, I am willing to bear the consequences of my conviction. I am certain that there can be cases when a soldier has no other choice but to disobey orders and break the law, for instance when there is concern that obeying an order would bring deep disgrace to the country. The only answer a soldier can give to an order like the one which Hácha and the Czech Supreme Commander issued at the time is disobedience."[95] Based on these considerations, Ernst said that he did not think he did anything illegal, adding, "In my opinion, the letter of the law is no longer very relevant when our country's liberty and independence are at stake." He referred to his former Professor of Constitutional and International Law at the University of Bern, Walther Burckhardt, "who always said that it did not make sense to follow and apply rules and regulations by the letter if they brought about the destruction of the state; they are in force only through the state."[96]

The officers who were arrested refused to reveal the names of their comrades and declared that they would bear "all the consequences" themselves. The investigators identified the head of the organization, Werder, only by comparing handwriting. However, the rest of the "conspirators" were identified through confiscated documents once the investigation had deepened. After undergoing his first interrogation, Hausamann asked the special prosecutor to add the following statement to the minutes: "I would give orders to fight no matter if I had orders to do so, or if I did not have any orders, or if I had orders not to fight."[97]

Those who were arrested soon became aware of the fact that Chief of the General Staff Huber sympathized with them. Moreover, they learned that "influential politicians from all parties were protecting" them and had intervened on their behalf with the General, who was also well disposed toward them.[98] The conspirators benefited from the fact that they had some trusting relationships with high-ranking officers and political leaders. Thus, Colonel W. Müller, Chief Security Officer of the Armed Forces, confidentially informed Captain Waibel about his upcoming arrest. Before he was arrested, Waibel managed to inform Lindt, who in turn warned other comrades, including "Chief" Werder, whom he went to see at the Aarauerhof Hotel in Aarau.[99] Corporal Lindt was not on the list of suspects at first, even though he was one of the founding members of the conspiracy, because the investigators were looking for a "Captain Lindt." Hausamann instructed Lindt to contact National Councilor Hans Oprecht of the Social Democratic Party, whom the latter did not know, to inform him about the arrests. Oprecht immediately informed Colonel Max Gafner, an influential member of the National Council and of Bern's cantonal cabinet, who in turn contacted General Guisan to make an appeal on behalf of those arrested. Ernst explained that he had reason to believe that Federal Councilor Minger, the Head of the Military Department, also intervened on their behalf. These interventions prevented "our enemies, most of all Federal Councilor Pilet, from enforcing very severe sanctions against us."[100]

When the preliminary hearing of evidence was concluded, General Guisan, at the request of the special prosecutor, ordered a preliminary military investigation based on article 110 of the army's penal law against the four main suspects: Ernst, Hausamann, Waibel, and Werder.[101] Senior Auditor Trüssel considered "the case to be anything but trivial" because the activities of the suspect-ed officers could have had "disastrous consequences for the army; their plan to go to combat in spite of different orders is not unquestionable." However, after concluding his investigation, Trüssel suggested to the General that the case should not be brought before the military courts; instead, some disciplinary action should be taken against the culprits.[102] Huber approved of this idea. As early as upon the conclusion of the hearing of evidence, he had written to the General:

> To me, discipline is not the same as blind obedience, but it is the obli-gation to do everything to the best of one's knowledge and belief that is in the interest of the received orders. The obligation to obey without condition no longer applies if a superior orders a subordinate to com-mit a crime or an offense (Rules and Regulations of the Army, clause 35; Penal Law of the Armed Forces, article 18) or asks him to do some-thing that is incompatible with a soldier's honor, for instance to break an oath which he has made. We made an oath to 'be loyal to the Swiss Confederation (not to the Federal Council nor to superiors), to sacri-fice our lives for defending our home country and its constitution, and to do everything that is necessary to safeguard the honor and liberty of our homeland.' The obligation to obey applies only as long as the received orders are in compliance with this oath. For example, if the commander of a fortress makes preparations to hand over the fortress to the enemy while it can still be defended, according to my interpre-tation of discipline, each and every subordinate who finds out about this intention does not only have the right but in fact the duty to shoot his commander or to put him out of action and to continue fighting on his own initiative. Overall, this principle applies to the entire armed forces. . . . The suspected officers made preparations only for the event that the Federal Council or the army command was to capitulate. In this situation, according to my opinion and interpretation, every sol-dier would not only have the right but the duty to disobey orders. It is regrettable that Captains Ernst and Waibel and their followers did not put more trust in the Federal Council and the army command; how-ever, considering their young age and fanaticism, this is to a certain extent understandable and excusable. . . . Captains Ernst and Waibel and their comrades should be commended for propagating the deter-mination to put up resistance. However, they should have done so openly; that way they would have been certain to have the support of the army command. A secret organization similar to the Freemasons

was totally unnecessary and could have undermined the trusting relationship within the armed forces. The activities of the suspected officers is not a crime nor an offense according to any article of the Penal
Law of the Armed Forces; however, they are in disagreement with the
military's code of conduct; hence, some disciplinary action will have to
be taken against the officers.[103]

The commander-in-chief followed the chief of the general staff's and the
senior auditor's recommendations to take disciplinary action against the leaders
of the officers' movement. In early October, he pronounced the following sentences[104]:

Capt. Ernst of the general staff	15 days of detention in seclusion
Capt. Waibel of the general staff	10 days of detention in seclusion
Capt. Hausamann	5 days of detention in seclusion
Lt. Col. Werder of the general staff	3 days of detention in seclusion
Capt. Wanner of the general staff	8 days of detention
Capt. Heberlein of the general staff	6 days of detention
Capt. Häni of the general staff	6 days of detention
1st Lt. Schürch	4 days of detention.

Major Gerber and Captains Uhlmann and Allgöwer of the general staff
were reprimanded in writing. The other members and sympathizers of the
movement were not punished. These sentences were even lighter than those the
chief of the general staff had proposed; Huber had requested 20 days of detention in seclusion for Ernst, 15 days for Waibel, and 10 days for Hausamann.[105]

On Thursday, September 29, General Guisan summoned the officers
whom he would punish to his command post in Gümligen to lecture them in
two groups. As Ernst recounted, "First he addressed the 'sympathizers' and then
the 'ringleaders.' He spoke to us in an open and benevolent manner. He
stressed the fact that our objective was correct but that we had chosen the
wrong means to accomplish it. Overall, he told us the same things that he later
wrote in his report to the Federal Council.[106] He told us that he would take disciplinary action against us by putting us in detention and that the case would
be closed thereafter. He explained that he still had full confidence in us. At the
end, he shook everybody's hand."[107] Max Häni, the officer who was put in
detention for six days, had the impression that the General's words resembled
"a coded eulogy rather than a lecture."[108] Captain Allgöwer was reportedly envi-
ous of his comrades because he was only reprimanded.[109]

In view of the fact that the officers made preparations for a conspiracy that aimed to collectively disobey orders, the sentences pronounced by the General were indeed mild. Hausamann actually wrote that he and his fellow conspirators accepted their punishments "as a matter of course; the officers concerned considered the fact that the General put them only in detention as evidence that he perfectly understood them. By pronouncing the sentences the way he did, he once again proved to be the General. If there was any need to bring the 'ringleaders' closer to the General, it was done through this act. This bond lasted through all phases of wartime duty."[110] The members of the Officers' Conspiracy, most particularly its leaders, became the General's strongest and most loyal supporters apart from the members of the personal staff.

Ernst, Waibel, and Hausamann had to serve their sentences during the month of October 1940 at the barracks in Thun. Waibel later wrote, "It was a quiet time during which we were able to take a break from the stressful work as intelligence officers and to discuss our upcoming tasks."[111] Ernst agreed that the days of detention were "pleasant in every respect. . . . We were allowed to work on private projects, take walks without supervision, and we generally enjoyed a high degree of freedom. Our guns were confiscated, but they were put in a wardrobe in our room that was easy to open so we could have taken them back if war had broken out."[112]

Ernst wrote to his superior, Colonel Masson, during the time of his detention:

> It is very well possible, or even probable, that you and I will perish in our combat against the Germans and their Swiss friends. However, if we remain faithful to our idea and believe in it up to the moment we die, it will rise again in a stronger and more genuine form. Real sacrifices have in the past always generated such tremendous energy that those who believed that everything was over ended up being mistaken. It is our responsibility to make sure that this sacrifice is made. We must be ready to die. However, we also have to do our utmost to get others to fight with us to the bitter end. [I admit that I am] no romantic who believes that death is beautiful and easy, nor do I know if I would be courageous in a gruesome battle or in a concentration camp. However, that is something no one can pretend to know. Hence, it will suffice in a first step to be ready to take the risk and trust that our faith will assist us during the most difficult moments. If we manage to show the courage to die for our idea—we may hope to do so if God is with us— we have gained everything. Our deaths will generate forces that the Germans will not be able to destroy. Perhaps they will destroy our entire country and occupy it for a long time, but one day our children

will manage to free themselves in our memory. In the end, their faith will be stronger than the brutal violence of the Germans and their Swiss friends.[113]

This statement demonstrates that Ernst did not regret his actions but was convinced that history would show he did the right thing. He also comforted comrades who were devastated by the punishment inflicted on them by the General and were concerned about their future careers. He wrote to Wanner:

Don't take this matter to heart. It is certainly a coincidence that you have to serve a longer sentence than others. No one will question your reliability and your qualities as a soldier. On the contrary, you will be viewed favorably because you joined our group. We will have to continue advocating our idea in a different, legal manner. It won't matter if we take risks by doing so. What matters most is our cause; our careers and personal comfort are secondary. I hope that we will end up reaching our objective in spite of all the difficulties we have encountered. The spirit that inspires above all our best and most valuable officers is a guarantee that we will be successful in the end. However, if we are wrong and it is too late, at least we want to die with honor. We want to stick together as comrades and continue fighting with appropriate means even if it would be easier to acquiesce.[114]

The General's postwar report mentioned that the Officers' Alliance had 37 members. These figures were subsequently also mentioned by some leaders of the movement in their accounts and became generally accepted as accurate. However, the existing files indicate that the actual number of participants at the meeting at the Schweizerhof in Lucerne was only 20, including 19 officers and Corporal Lindt. Eighteen of them stated under oath that they signed the declaration. It is safe to assume that other officers who were not present in Lucerne joined the Alliance later on, signing the declaration after the movement was founded.

The files from the Military Attorney General's office clearly indicate that a total of 32 individuals, including 31 officers and Corporal Lindt, were implicated in the investigation. At least half a dozen of them believed that they were not members of the conspiracy because they disliked Ernst's plan and did not wish to be associated with a special organization of conspirators even though they also advocated unconditional resistance. Hence, the Officers' Alliance had hardly two dozen members, not 37 as previously assumed. This number is close to the one Ernst originally mentioned. In 1945, he wrote in a letter to Cantonal government member Gafner from Bern, "About 20 officers, most of whom belonged to the general staff, were members of our organization. We had planned to considerably expand it when we were betrayed as a result of a coincidence."[115] It is impossible to determine the exact number of conspirators because Corporal Lindt burned the original list of members in the restroom of the Schweizerhof after the ringleaders had been arrested.[116] Lindt burned a second copy of the list in the presence of Captain Burckhardt at the chancellory of the 5th Division at the "Fleinergut" in Aarau.[117]

Strikingly, the Alliance had no members from French-speaking Switzerland. This fact was indeed pointed out at the meeting in Lucerne and it was consequently suggested "to also recruit [members from their midst], which was approved."[118] However, the conspiracy was uncovered before this could be done.

At first it appeared that the punished officers on the general staff would be transferred from the intelligence service to the troops. The Senior Auditor recommended, "I have serious reservations about keeping Captains Ernst, Waibel, and Hausamann in the intelligence service. In a report, the Chief of the General Staff of the Armed Forces considered that these officers should under no circumstances continue to be employed in the intelligence service, where their activities have turned out to be dangerous and disastrous."[119] The General annotated the document with the word "agreed," and had Captains Ernst, Waibel, and Hausamann suspended from office "until the case is closed; a decision on where they will serve thereafter will be made at a later date."[120] However, Masson convinced Chief of the General Staff Huber that the three experienced intelligence officers were indispensable because they had established confidential contacts with informants in foreign countries. Hence, once the sentences were pronounced, Huber wrote to the General, "The intelligence service is a very special link in the structure of the army command, having connections with numerous secret agents; personnel changes would therefore bring about great losses. It would be a disadvantage to increase the number of those who are informed. The past events have made the Chief of Intelligence aware that his subordinates will have to be supervised more closely in the future."[121] In another letter to the General, he reiterated his request not to replace any staff among the intelligence service for the time being. As long as "no specific cases [occurred] which [showed] that they [were] incapable" or failed to do their duty, Huber said that he would take "responsibility for them."[122]

Even if the Officers' Alliance failed in its immediate purpose, the ringleaders had a lasting influence in terms of the spirit of resistance. After Guisan's death Waibel stated, "In the summer of 1940, the General's position was not yet as clearly defined as it was later on. We were struggling with all available means to influence the commander-in-chief, just as our opponents did. For a long time, perhaps for too long, he was too cautious, thus risking being misunderstood by the people and the army. This crisis of confidence climaxed when General Guisan remained silent after Pilet-Golaz' speech. . . . This was particularly obvious for us as intelligence officers."[123]

One surprising result of the Officers' Conspiracy was the fact that the General actually went on to develop closer ties with its ringleaders. He authorized Captains Ernst, Hausamann, and Häni to contact him directly, without following official channels, at any time if they had new concerns about Switzerland's security.[124] Ernst stated, "The extent to which the chief of the general staff and the General personally trusted us, based on our activities, allowed us to counteract more efficiently than before the tendencies of the appeasers. The struggle continued for several years, but it lost more and more of its intensity as it became increasingly clear that Germany was headed for defeat."[125]

Captain Ernst later admitted that he felt less upset by his sentence than by the reason the General gave for imposing sanctions on him. He considered himself to be a resistance fighter and assumed that the General would fully approve of his activities. He did not think that he showed any lack of discipline, explaining, "The General was not quite clear regarding the question whether our actions were legal. On one hand he emphasized that it would not only have been our right but our duty as soldiers to fight if the determination to put up resistance had subsided due to pressure from abroad. On the other hand, though, he qualified our actions as a violation of the military's code of conduct. That is not very consistent; if we were authorized to act against a decision of the Federal Council or our superiors in the army, it is difficult to see why it was illegal to make preparations for that event."[126] Ernst gave an explanation for this contradiction:

> It seems to me that the General's ambiguous statement reflects the special problems that arise in connection with acting against orders. This is one of the contradictions of our existence that cannot be solved by logical reasoning. . . . The state cannot and must not allow any resistance to be made against it, or else it contradicts itself. However, the law is not the ultimate authority! There can be borderline cases where doing something illegal is mandatory in the interest of the law. In such cases, one cannot say, 'fiat justitia, pereat mundus!' ['May justice be rendered even if the world perishes because of it.'] Even in such exceptional cases, disobedience is not strictly legal, but it is justified from an ethical perspective.[127]

After serving their sentences, the hard-core conspirators Waibel, Ernst, Hausamann, and Lindt, together with two specialists on the political police, Willi Moser from Zürich and Emil Häberli from Basel, continued meeting at Waibel's office in Lucerne once a week as a working group to discuss possible activities and precautions.[128] There is no doubt that a significant lobby of resisters, of which there is no documentation or written account, was influenced by this panel, which had connections to politicians from all parties, most particularly the Social Democrats.

As another result of the Officers' Conspiracy, the national spirit of resistance was strengthened because the "Army and Home" Service of the armed forces was transformed from a simple organization that provided entertainment for serving soldiers to an efficient instrument that aimed to boost the army's and the population's mental readiness to defend the country. Ernst and his friends managed to get Colonel Oskar Frey—although he was not a member of the Officers' Alliance—and August R. Lindt nominated to the top positions of "Army and Home" when its new objectives were defined.[129] There was also an obvious connection between the Alliance and the civilian "Action for National Resistance," which was founded after the breakup of the Officers' Alliance, primarily on the initiative of Hausamann.[130]

As the internal military investigation of the Officers' Alliance was considered confidential, only a small number of people knew about it during the period of war. Neither the soldiers nor the public received specific information on the case that caused such concern to the army command at the time. However, the Federal President and high-ranking commanders were informed about the existence and the investigation of the Officers' Alliance. Unlike Guisan and Huber, who sympathized with the officers' cause, Federal President Pilet-Golaz and pro-German personalities criticized it harshly. Pilet-Golaz called the officers "ambitious newcomers [who are] more sectarian than critical" and expected them to be punished severely and suspended from the army.[131] In his correspondence with Federal Councilor Wetter, Corps Commander Wille considered that the existence of such "secret officers' alliances which, in an emergency, would replace the 'weak' Federal Council or possibly even the General, to take the responsibility for saving their home country into their own hands and appoint their own strong leader [were] far more dangerous than anything that has been revealed about the activities of some advocates of the [pro-German] revival movement."[132] Other critics remarked that Ernst and his friends tried to organize a "Children's Crusade."[133] During a parliamentary committee hearing, Eugen Bircher called the endeavor with its "supposed intentions . . . one of the most serious aberrations that has ever occurred."[134] Very recently, the *Staatsbürger* magazine called the undertaking the "ominous Officers' Alliance."[135] In addition, Karl Walde did not hide his skepticism about the manner in which the Officers' Alliance proceeded.[136]

Opinions about the purpose and usefulness of the Officers' Conspiracy diverge. It may have had good patriotic intentions but it also had a touch of the kind of romantic adventure common in a Scouts camp. It was bound to be uncovered, as its organization was amateurish and the ringleaders ignored some of the basic principles of secrecy. However, the idealistic conspirators were determined to follow de Gaulle's example by planning for a contingency when they would have to disobey orders. It is debatable whether, or to what extent, the endeavor could have been successful. Schürch accurately stated, "It was like a powder keg that was ready to receive the spark anytime; we knew that we were far from being alone."[137] In view of the tense political situation in Switzerland during the year 1940, there is no doubt that disobeying orders to capitulate would have triggered a lengthy civil war as in France.

The attempt to form a conspiracy to ensure that the army would fight—an ambition with some irony on the surface—may have surprised or even embarrassed General Guisan; but ultimately he must have been glad about it. Nevertheless, even if he agreed with the objectives of the Alliance, for disciplinary reasons he could not accept such unusual endeavors occurring in the armed forces. In his postwar report, he issued his final verdict on the matter, writing, "I would like to point out that these officers would not only have had the right to disobey orders but it would actually have been their duty as soldiers if the determination to put up resistance had dwindled due to pressure from abroad. They were wrong to keep their activities a secret; if they had done so in the open, I would not have had to intervene against them."[138]

The future showed that participation in the Officers' Conspiracy was not at all detrimental to the military careers of its members. Two participants at the meeting in Lucerne, Ernst and Uhlmann, actually rose to the rank of corps commander, the highest peacetime rank in the Swiss Army. Two others, Waibel and Burckhardt, were promoted to divisional commander, and Häni became a brigadier. More than a dozen others became colonels, and only a few, including Hausamann, did not advance past the rank of major. The only non-commissioned officer of the conspiracy, Corporal Lindt, became a foreign diplomat for Switzerland after the war. He was appointed Ambassador to the United States and later to the Soviet Union and to India before being nominated as the United Nations High Commissioner for Refugees. These careers may be an indication that the former "ambitious newcomers" were actually assertive, strong leaders who had a high degree of personal ambition.[139]

It appears to be an interesting coincidence that on the same day, July 21,

1940, when the Officers' Alliance was founded, the central committee of the Swiss Association of Non-Commissioned Officers met in Lucerne with the presidents of the cantonal clubs of non-commissioned officers. In a resolution that they transmitted to the General, the NCOs reiterated their determination not to be discouraged by events abroad and to defend Switzerland's liberty under all circumstances. In this resolution, they wrote, "The motto which our ancestors followed must apply today as well: 'Live as a free people, or die defending our freedom.' We are willing to also endure economic hardship for the sake of our independence. We prefer living in poverty than living as slaves."[140]

Briefing at the Rütli

ON JULY 25 OF THE FATEFUL YEAR 1940, General Guisan summoned his unit commanders to the Rütli Meadow for a meeting which has since entered every history book on Switzerland and has taken on legendary proportions. The event was meant to be a simple muster but in retrospect justifiably gained the status of a historic act as it had a tremendous impact on the entire country. The General wanted to communicate to the commanders the concept of his new defense strategy, the Réduit [Redoubt]. In his postwar report, he wrote, "The purpose of the briefing at the Rütli was to address the commanders of the army units to impress on them the spirit of the new solution that they had been chosen to implement."[1]

The commander-in-chief insisted on addressing the officers personally instead of giving them written instructions, explaining, "I wanted to speak to them in person, face to face, as a soldier speaks to soldiers. I could have done that in any meeting room or in any other manner, at historical battlefields like Morgarten or Sempach perhaps; however, it had to be done there, at the Rütli Meadow, the site of the birth of our independence, the place that had so many associations for everyone. I was convinced that there each one of them would understand me better than anywhere else."[2]

It is not easy to determine who first came up with the idea of holding a briefing at the Rütli, the meadow alongside Lake Lucerne where herdsmen termed "Companions of the Oath" had gathered, in 1291, to found the Swiss Confederation. Alfred Ernst stated that he had "repeatedly negotiated with the General's closest associates, above all with Major Barbey and Captain Bracher of the general staff, to try to get the General to make a public statement [in favor of unconditional resistance]." He believed that his and his friends' "intensive efforts contributed to bringing about the briefing at the Rütli."[3] Military historian Hans Rudolf Kurz agrees with this view.[4]

Some of the General's aides later indicated that Captain Bracher made the suggestion for the briefing. Barbey once told a student that Bracher was the first to mention the idea of a briefing at the Rütli, both to him and the General, and also made the most preparations for it.[5] Bracher's contemporary notes support this statement. He wrote that his suggestion was the result of several conversations with Captain Hausamann on the question of the most suitable means to counteract the increasing defeatism following France's capitulation. Bracher wrote in his diary, "As a result of these brainstorming sessions, I suggest to the General to muster the commanders somewhere in central Switzerland. This idea is approved; the briefing will be held at the Rütli."[6] Hence, the idea of holding a briefing with the unit commanders during this time of uncertainty was raised by a number of individuals, including Hausamann.

Barbey recounted an account of the moment on July 9 when the decision was made at Gümligen to hold the briefing, writing, "The General wants to address the commanders to explain to the executive body the meaning and the spirit of the measures that have been decided. Bracher, who was Secretary of the National Defense Committee before the war and is now liaison officer between the Head of the Military Department and the army staff, comes to see me. He has the same idea. . . . We walk back and forth on the terrace. Nature and history have provided us with the most suitable place, the 'sacred grounds' for this large assembly of the top commanders, which is the Rütli."[7] Von Ernst, the General's first adjutant, and his first aide Sandoz were sent on a reconnaissance mission to the Rütli. In Lucerne, they also inspected the steamer that was to carry the commanders across the lake to the meadow.[8]

Alfred Ernst wrote that he had "reservations about the way" in which the briefing would be carried out, "fearing a surprise attack by the Germans on the commanders of all levels who were to be gathered on one ship, and again at the Rütli Meadow, which is an easy target. I considered that it was irresponsible to risk having the entire command structure eradicated during that critical time. The officers of the general staff remained at their respective command posts; nevertheless, our resistance would have suffered a catastrophic blow in the event of hostilities if a large number of commanders had been eliminated. Therefore, I tried to convince the General that the risk was too great. I suggested that the General assemble the commanders one division at a time at secret places. My idea was rejected."[9]

The General wrote that he "did not hesitate to risk taking one single boat instead of spreading the risk."[10] However, both Lt. Colonel Marguth and Brigadier Bracher later said that the General initially believed the idea of a briefing at the Rütli to be too risky; hence, he had to be talked into doing it.[11] The fact that the commander-in-chief ended up assembling the commanders in one

Le Commandant en Chef
de l'Armée

FIDGENÖSSISCHES
MILITÄRDEPARTEMENT
✠ 16. AUG. 1940
CH. 23

Quartier Général de l'Armée,
le 18 juillet 1940.

No. 11706
1/ε/b

Aux Cdt. 1.- 4. C.A.
Au Cdt. 1. Div.
9. Div.
Trp. Av. et D.C.A.
Au Chef de l'E.M.G. de l'Armée.

1.   La situation présente m'invite à confirmer et à préciser à l'intention des officiers exerçant un commandement supérieur:

- le principe et le sens de notre défense nationale;
- les devoirs actuels du chef dans le cadre de l'Armée et du Pays.

2.   A cet effet, j'ai décidé de réunir les commandants des unités d'Armée et des corps de troupes des armes combattantes en un lieu central, où ils participeront à un rapport d'Armée.

3.   Le rapport d'Armée aura lieu le jeudi 25.7.40 sur la prairie du Rütli.

Y participeront:

a)   tous les commandants (sans leurs Etats-Majors), mobilisés et licenciés, des armes combattantes, de l'échelon bataillon et groupe et des échelons supérieurs, ainsi que les inspecteurs et commandants territoriaux et les commandants de villes;

b)   le Chef de l'Etat-Major Général de l'Armée.

4.   Le 25.7.40, durant l'absence de ces officiers, les Etats-Majors assureront la permanence du commandement.

5.   Le Chef et un photographe du Bureau de presse du Quartier Général de l'Armée assisteront au rapport. En dehors de ceux-ci, aucun journaliste, ni photographe, ne sera admis.

6.   Rendez-vous au débarcadère de Lucerne, à 1045. Retour à Lucerne à 1500, environ.

    Afin d'économiser l'essence, les participants utiliseront le chemin de fer pour se rendre à Lucerne (voir horaire annexé).

    Les officiers mobilisés voyageront avec bon de transport jusqu'à Lucerne et retour à leurs stationnements. Les officiers licenciés ne recevront pas de bon de transport; ils toucheront de leurs C.A. respectifs (suivant ordre de bataille administratif du 15.7.), du Cdt. des Trp.Av. et D.C.A. et du Groupe Id. de l'E.M.A., le remboursement du billet, les indemnités réglementaires et un jour de solde.

    L'usage des automobiles sera autorisé pour se rendre des stationnements à la gare la plus proche. A partir de Lucerne, le transport sera organisé par le Commandement de l'Armée. Un pique-nique sera préparé après le rapport.

7.   Tenue: casquette, pistolet, éventuellement manteau.

Le Général:

Annexe: extrait de l'horaire des CFF.

Copie: p.p.c. au Chef du Département militaire fédéral.

Order of July 18, 1940, to the officers participating in the briefing at the Rütli Meadow. (BAr) place may be an indication that he did not consider the military situation to be threatening, nor a German intervention to be imminent. Ernst commented, "I completely agree that the way in which the General decided to proceed was more impressive and effective than issuing orders to the commanders of the individual army units one at a time. However, even in retrospect my reservations concerning the risk of having our entire army command virtually paralyzed in one blow by the Germans did not seem to be entirely groundless. The fact that we were lucky does not prove that my reservations were unjustified."[12]

The General issued his order for the briefing at the Rütli on July 18, 1940, one week before the event. The three main points of the order, drafted by Barbey, read as follows:

> The current situation forces me to confirm and specify to the
> officers exercising a top command post:
> — the principle and the meaning of our national defense;
> — the current responsibilities of the commanders in the frame
> work of the armed forces and of the country.
> For this purpose, I have decided to assemble the commanders of
> the army units and of the combat troops at a central location in
> order to hold an army briefing.
> The army briefing shall take place on Thursday, July 25, 1940, at
> the Rütli Meadow.[13]

It is untrue that the participants were not told in advance where the briefing was going to be held, even though participants themselves have often said this.[14] The officers were to meet at 10:45 that morning at the dock in Lucerne. To save gasoline, they were to take the train instead of driving. The ship was due to arrive back in Lucerne at 3:00, allowing everyone to get back to his command post the same evening.

The General reported that "some basic precautions" had been taken for the boat trip; Colonel Jaquillard, Chief of Counterintelligence, received the relevant orders.[15] The ship, *Stadt Luzern*, was put under surveillance for several days and was searched on several occasions. Colonel Jaquillard ordered Corporal W. Lützelschwab, Counterintelligence Commissioner, to make sure that no act of sabotage could be carried out with explosives. The latter explained, "I carried out the order. I personally checked the ship together with an explosives expert on the evening before the trip, had two members of the army police watch it overnight, and checked it again in the middle of the night. The two police officers were sound asleep when I boarded the ship from a rowing boat." On the morning of the trip he once again searched the ship. However, he had serious doubts about the usefulness of his efforts, adding, "The instruments I had were so poor and the procedure was so amateurish that I made a sigh of relief once everything had gone well. I remember thinking to myself, 'We are all novices by carrying out such a briefing in public; however, the Nazis are as well, otherwise they would have seized the opportunity. That is a real consolation.'"[16]

It appears that not everyone kept the upcoming briefing a secret, as the boat ride on the *Stadt Luzern* was reportedly discussed at the Mostrose restaurant on the evening before it took place.[17] When the General arrived at the dock, a large crowd of the public had already gathered and they broke into applause. From landing stage three, the officers boarded the *Stadt Luzern*, the largest and most beautiful paddle steamer of the fleet on Lake Lucerne, which was generally used only on Sundays during the war. Barbey heard people whisper, "All eggs are in the same basket."[18] During the trip, two to three Morane fighter aircraft were flying in circles above the lake, and an armed motorboat equipped with a machine gun accompanied the ship.[19] Lieutenant Walter Dieterle, a communications officer, had arrived on board three hours before the departure to establish contact with the army staff[20] and the crew.[21] According to the regular schedule, the boat ride on the steamer from Lucerne to the Rütli lasts 87 minutes; unfortunately, no logbook entry has been preserved from that day.[22]

As head of transport, Major A. Perrig, the director of the steamer company, was personally responsible for the trip.[23] Bracher reported that the steamer left port on time, but Du Pasquier wrote that it took off late.[24] Otto Kellerhals noted in his diary: "Our ship is 20 minutes late, making the whole event unnecessarily hectic."[25] From the landing stage at the Rütli, the officers, including a communications officer who left his equipment behind on the ship, walked up to the meadow. The tenant of the Rütli house reported that it took about an hour from the time the steamer arrived to the moment when the briefing began. The General spent this time alone in the living room at the Rütli house concentrating on his upcoming speech. The tenants, the Ziegler-Zgraggen family, were asked to remain inside and shut all doors and windows during the briefing.[26]

All commanders of combat troops, down to battalions and sections, as well as territorial inspectors and commanders, were summoned to the briefing. Among the participants were quite a number of captains who were interim commanders and not promoted to major until the end of the year. With the exception of Chief of the General Staff Huber and the officers of the General's personal staff, no officers of the general staff were present, as they had to remain at their troops' command posts to ensure that the army remained ready to fight.[27]

At the Rütli Meadow, where four soldiers wearing steel helmets kept vigil around the flag of Battalion 87 from Uri, the participants stood in a semi-circle from which they could overlook the lake and the mountains of Schwyz. An outline had been handed out to the commanders instructing them how to line up. Barbey wrote, "The four corps commanders, Lardelli, Prisi, Miescher, and Labhart, as well as the commander of the Air Force and Anti-Aircraft Defense Bandi stand in the front. The divisional commanders and their subordinates stand behind them."[28] Miescher, the oldest serving corps commander, reported the officers present for the briefing. The General asked the participants to stand at ease and began his speech immediately. The speech lasted between 20 minutes and half an hour; however, there are conflicting accounts on the language he spoke. Two decades after the event, both Bracher and Marguth believed that Guisan had spoken in German.[29] Others recounted that he spoke in French but quoted in German from some letters that he pulled out of his pocket.[30] Otto Kellerhals, commander of an artillery unit, wrote in his diary on the evening of July 25: "Guisan speaks in French. He draws a pretty bleak picture."[31] Hence, it seems to be established that General Guisan spoke extemporaneously in French, without using a prepared text. He held some notes in his hand but used them only to quote a few sentences from letters, some of them in German.[32]

There is no verbatim record of the General's speech, but his candid, direct language impressed most listeners. Barbey summarized the speech in his diary, quoting Guisan:

> I have attached great importance to assembling you at this historic place, on this ground, which is a symbol of our independence, to inform you about the situation and to speak to you as a soldier addresses his peers. We have reached a turning point in our history. Switzerland's existence is at stake. Here the soldiers of 1940 will gain strength from the lessons and the spirit of the past in order to face the country's present and future with determination and hear the secret spell that emanates from this meadow. If we look straight ahead we shall master the ever-present difficulties which the Alliance of 1291 called the maliciousness of our times. . . .[33]

Barbey then stated that "resistance against any aggressor, wherever he may come from, and against the interior threat of defeatism, as well as trusting in the usefulness of resistance" were the main topics of the address. The General himself gave a similar account of his speech in his postwar report.[34]

Lt. Colonel Trachsel, commander of a regiment, wrote in the troops' diary upon his return from the briefing:

Above all, the General explained Switzerland's current political and military situation. Then he explained to us why the construction of fortifications at the border had been stopped and the bulk of the troops had been deployed to the foothills of the Alps. The reasons that he gave are absolutely plausible. Hopefully there will be enough time to bring all necessary troops and material behind the new lines. [There is] no question of discharging troops. A new task is awaiting us. All rumors about discharging troops must be stopped, and the people must be informed.[35]

Some officers were rather disappointed at the content of the commander-in-chief's speech, expecting something more substantial. Colonel Du Pasquier noted in his diary that the General had spoken "with great simplicity but the impression generally prevailed that what he told us was hardly worth the trip. He was actually very commonplace, and that is too bad. His spirit is clear and lively; he speaks as a chief but he lacks the culture that would allow him to put his words in a more impressive shape."[36] Otto Kellerhals had a good overall impression, but like many others did not consider the briefing to be particularly important at the time because it stated routine things.[37] Edmund Wehrli from Zürich voiced the most critical opinion: "When we were summoned to the briefing at the Rütli we were relieved. We expected the General to finally issue new orders and instructions regarding our combat strategy. However, for God's sake, he made nothing but a Sunday school sermon."[38] As late as 1985, he said that he regretted that the young commanders who were willing to fight failed to receive the precise instructions they had been craving for carrying out a war. "This inability to transmit orders to us faster was not likely to give us new confidence in the supreme command's capabilities," he maintained. "Many of us had trouble swallowing this interjection by the General."[39] Wehrli was convinced that top-ranking officers like Labhart and Constam were as disappointed as he was at the ordinary patriotic speech containing "commonplaces to strengthen the spirit of resistance."[40]

Ernst Uhlmann, a future corps commander, said, "Only few needed to hear the appeal. Constam agreed with this opinion."[41] Colonel Du Pasquier, who was usually a faithful supporter of Guisan, remarked to Sandoz, the General's first aide, while walking back to the boat after the briefing, that it was a shame that the General had not issued more precise directives for combat.[42] On the day of the briefing, Labhart laconically noted in his diary: "At 9.45 hours, I go to the army briefing at the Rütli together with the head of the artillery. Return at 16.00 hours."[43]

There is no record of the exact words the General used at the Rütli. Barbey told his comrade Sandoz afterward that he had prepared a manuscript for the speech and regretted that the General did not have the opportunity to make more use of it.[44] This 26-page manuscript was undoubtedly drafted by Barbey and was long treated with the utmost secrecy by the General's aides. In 1955, Captain Marguth wrote to another member of the General's former personal staff, expressing worry:

> Concerning the 'speech at the Rütli' I kindly ask you to urge the General not to make it available under any circumstances. Lt. Col. Barbey has asked me to prevent that from happening! Rightly so! For many years magistrates, journalists, historians, and officers have requested copies of this speech, and each time we have had to decline, also in the General's name. It contains things that could create a scandal, things that were not said. As long as the concerned individuals are alive, we have to be silent about it for human and political reasons. . . . This speech could be interpreted against the General and be detrimental to him and the army. Therefore, we have to mistrust everyone![45]

In 1962 Marguth, who initially acted as the General's trustee regarding unpublished material after the war, claimed that the draft of the speech at the Rütli had disappeared.[46]

As it turned out, Marguth's concerns were not unfounded. When Dr. Oscar Gauye, Director of the Swiss Federal Archives, published and annotated the entire text of the manuscript in 1984,[47] it was considered a sensational historical revelation and met with a great deal of negative emotion in some quarters. However, Gauye's work was based on meticulous scientific research. He gave compelling evidence that the domestic and foreign policy considerations expressed in the draft basically reflected the General's own convictions following France's collapse. It was not because the General disagreed with the ideas in the text that he did not follow it more closely during the speech, but because he did not have more time available to speak.[48]

The General undoubtedly quoted only very few passages verbatim from the manuscript, since he primarily spoke as if extempore. However, a few sentences and expressions recorded by participants and included in the official communiqué on the briefing at the Rütli are identical with the draft. Further, the General crossed out passages and made corrections to the manuscript, indicating that he had studied the draft in detail. He undoubtedly left out most of the text of the manuscript, since reading the entire 26 typewritten pages—15 pages of the actual speech and 11 pages of excerpts from letters—would have taken close to 90 minutes.

The participants who recalled the briefing all agreed that the General did not speak about matters of domestic and foreign policy, nor about revival ("*rénovation*") and a constitutional reform based on corporatism, nor about adjusting to the conditions of the new Europe. According to the draft, however, these issues were intended to be raised. The text stated, among other things:

What is happening in Europe will have repercussions on our country and on our political system and will perhaps bring about a change in our Constitution. We must evolve in order to adapt to the conditions of the new Europe. However, we must evolve on our own, without copying foreign countries. I am convinced that the old parties have lost their meaning. This is no longer about gaining seats in parliament; what counts is the ultimate interest of the country. To remain faithful to ourselves a national revival is needed. It can be based on our traditions. Switzerland wants to live its own life.[49]

At the Rütli, Guisan probably did not address censorship of the press either, yet the manuscript stated on this subject: "The German press is very aggressive toward us considering the attitude of our own media. However, our press has received enough warnings. I requested that the press be censored [by the army] but the Federal Council did not grant my request. I have therefore asked for the censorship to be supervised by the Federal Council because it is paradoxical that the army should be in charge of a censorship that is primarily of political character."[50]

Concerning the country's military and political situation after France's collapse, it is striking that in the manuscript the attitude of Fascist Italy toward Switzerland was viewed as "very benevolent." Hence, Switzerland's military leadership failed to recognize the real situation, as it is now known that the Italian Army's high command at that time was working on plans of operation against Switzerland just as Germany was.[51] The draft made no direct mention of the threat of right-wing extremism; however, it included a fierce attack against left-wing politicians, in particular against National Councilor and Member of the Bernese Cantonal Government Robert Grimm, who had put Fascists and National Socialists on the same level during a speech to the Bernese Social Democratic Party in February 1940, calling them "uncultivated, brutal, and gluttonous lansquenets and adventurers [who have] reverted to barbarism."[52] Guisan considered that in view of the foreign political situation, such attacks against the (supposedly) friendly neighboring state to the south were provocative and had to be suppressed.

The excerpts from letters attached to the draft included a German text entitled "The Red Enemies." It discussed the threat of Communism and stated that there were three distinct groups in Switzerland: those led by Humbert-Droz, by Nicole, and supporters of Trotsky, adding, "Today all these red enemies systematically attack the foundations of our state."[53] The participants at the Rütli whom this author was able to contact all agreed that the General did not speak about "Reds" nor about Grimm. However, on the day after the briefing he forwarded a letter to Federal Councilor Minger in which Colonel Perrier of the general staff, head of the Press and Radio Section, demanded that Grimm's "deplorable elaborations" should be publicly denounced because his writings would drive "our country straight into a disaster." Guisan annotated the letter, writing, "I agree with the opinion expressed above and fully support the officer's request."[54]

Minger made a wise political decision by refusing to grant Guisan's request; he forwarded the letter to the Federal President with the comment, "would be a concession to G[ermany]. Dealt with in a conversation with the General." If the army command had launched a public attack against Robert Grimm, the former head of the strike movement of 1918 who was still one of the most influential leaders of the labor movement during the war, it could have had nationwide repercussions. A rift with the Social Democrats, who had become resolute supporters of national defense, would have hampered domestic cohesion, and would undoubtedly have substantially weakened the political and military determination to put up resistance against any aggressor. It was a lucky coincidence that the General left this topic out of his speech.

The draft also included extensive explanations of the purpose of the new deployments of the armed forces, stating, "Your mission remains the same: hold out!" It declared that the armistice between Germany and France was not a peace agreement but merely signaled the conclusion of one stage of the war. Hence, the General had decided to move the bulk of the armed forces into positions in a "National Réduit" to defend the Alpine crossings around the Gotthard and to fulfill Switzerland's historic mission "at all costs." The combat strategy to be used in the Réduit positions included elements that had in essence already been formulated in the order to the armed forces of June 3: "React, form teams with specialists—volunteers and others—who shall try not only to stop the armored vehicles but to destroy them. If you do not have any field artillery or anti-tank guns available, make use of natural, reinforced, and artificial obstacles! Prepare alternative means of destruction! Set up anti-tank defense teams and imbue them with the spirit of coordination, courage, and audacity! Don't mind if you do not destroy the tanks! You shall destroy the infantry that follows on trucks. Maintain your freedom to decide, get ready, be prepared, command! Use every opportunity to protect the troops better. Your men must automatically dig individual holes."[55] These were specific pieces of tactical advice, which Captain Wehrli and other officers who were disappointed by the speech would have liked to hear. Apparently the General left out these passages because of the lack of time; at the end of the briefing, he informed the participants only that they would receive detailed written instructions for combat operations at a later date.[56]

The manuscript then took a stand against increasing despondency and defeatism, stating, in part in German, "The courage to hold out is no longer unwavering. This is partly the fault of the high-ranking officers. And of the windbags! And of the politicians! The most important battle that has to be carried out today is the fight against the opinion, 'it is useless.'"[57] He continued by explaining that the fighting spirit had begun to flag among certain high-ranking officers, some of whom went as far as declaring in public that they did not have much confidence in our capability to put up resistance. "Let me tell you loud and clear," the General went on, "so that every one of you may hear it today at the Rütli Meadow: such words are a crime. You do not have the right to say them to yourself, to your subordinates, to your country! These feelings and words are not worthy of a commander."

The General stated that it was wrong to suggest that Switzerland would not be able to defend itself and could hold out only a few days; if the army was determined to fight, it could put up effective resistance worthy of the country's honor and history. As the manuscript read, "Let me reiterate that even if our defense should become desperate, it would constitute a sacrifice that would later turn into success. If I repeat this once again here it is because I want it to be heard inside our country as well as beyond its borders." The General also warned, "I shall henceforth separate myself without hesitation from any officer, regardless of his rank, who lets himself go and pronounces defeatist words, thereby advancing intimidating foreign propaganda."[58] This warning was undoubtedly directed against Colonel Däniker and the group of officers supporting him.

It is uncertain which of these topics the General actually raised at the Rütli; nor is it possible to reconstruct the speech. Guisan himself declined to provide a copy of the address to those who asked him to do so. He wrote to an interested officer that there was "no complete text of the speech; I used only a few notes, the rest of the speech was made at my own discretion. Since my words were not to be published but were addressed exclusively to the present officers, no reporters were admitted. I have received several similar requests, especially after the end of wartime duty, from magistrates, historians, and journalists, and I have had to give them the same negative answer for the same reason, as reconstructing the speech based on the notes would not reflect the train of thought of that time."[59]

In spite of his reservations, Guisan later tried to reconstruct the speech anyway, recording on vinyl a combination of sentences from the order to the armed forces of July 25 and from the press release of July 29, 1940.[60]

The speech at the Rütli was short and concise. Once he finished speaking, the General saluted the battalion flag, and everyone else stood to attention. To some participants the simple conclusion appeared to be a renewal of the oath of independence of 1291. As one officer recounted, "Virtually everyone, even the toughest participants at the briefing, was moved to tears; we did not try to hide our tears, which turned into determination afterwards."[61] Barbey commented soberly, "The muster is finished. Dismissed. I approach the General. I do not know him well enough yet to recognize when he is moved, nor how he manifests his being moved. He marches back to the steamer at the head of the group together with Lardelli."[62]

During the ride back to Lucerne, the order to the armed forces dated July 25 was handed out, to be distributed to all units and read to the troops. This order summarized the main points of the General's briefing; it gave the reasons for his decision to deploy the troops to the Réduit positions and demanded that everyone remain determined to put up resistance. The key passages of the order read:

> I recently ordered our armed forces to be substantially rearranged. Many became aware of this at the moment when their unit was redeployed. They asked themselves why the completed fortifications were seemingly useless and why the army was still on duty at all. I know that you execute my orders even when the reasons for issuing them are not always apparent to you in the field. Nevertheless, I would like to inform you about the most important reasons. . . . The historical events that have happened recently have not in the least reduced our obligation to stand on guard. Currently there are more troops stationed beyond our borders than ever before, and they are excellent. What was unfathomable just a few weeks ago is a possibility today: we could be attacked simultaneously from all sides. The army must adapt to this new situation and shall adopt new positions which will allow it to defend itself effectively on every front. In this way it will fulfill its historic objective which has basically remained the same. . . . As long as millions of troops are stationed in Europe, and as long as substantial forces might launch an attack against us at any moment, the army shall remain on duty. No matter what happens, the fortifications that you have erected will remain useful; our sacrifices have not been in vain; our destiny is in our own hands. Do not listen to those who spread

defeatist news and cast doubts out of ignorance or maliciousness. Do not believe only in our right but also in our strength, with which we shall put up successful resistance if everyone has an iron will. Soldiers, on our upcoming National Day you shall keep in mind that the new positions I have assigned to you are those where under the new circumstances your arms and your courage will be best applied to our home country's advantage. Today I have gathered the top unit commanders at the Rütli, the cradle of our liberty, to give them this order to the armed forces, and I asked them to transmit it to you. Keep your confidence and your courage; your country is counting on you.[63]

This order showed the way not only to the troops but also to civilians. Kurz called it one of the "precious documents of Swiss history."[64] The original of the order was marked, "1/8/ae"; hence, its author was evidently Chief of the Personal Staff Barbey, who undoubtedly drafted it in part on the basis of some brief notes by the General. Guisan did not deny the importance of his close associate in connection with his appeals and orders, explaining to Gafner, "I took a few notes on small pieces of paper, which I then gave to the Chief of my Personal Staff; Lieutenant-Colonel Barbey, the well-known author who succeeded Colonel Gonard in this position in June 1940. [He] was virtually the ideal person for this task. Upon discussing the matter with him, I used to say to him, 'there you go; please draft the text!'"[65]

On the boat ride back to Lucerne, the participants at the briefing were offered cheese and ham sandwiches as well as beer and wine. Some officers from Zürich on the upper deck drank heavily and were boisterous, shouting, "Cheers, Henri."[66] Before arriving in Lucerne, the General joined individual groups of officers, exchanged a few words with them, and spoke with comrades from his early days in the military.[67] Alfred Schäfer thought he remembered that the General went from group to group and "shook everyone's hand, calling each one by his name."[68] The participants whom this author questioned all denied that this was true, relegating Schäfer's account to the realm of legend.[69]

A special train carried the participants from the Bernese Oberland and from western Switzerland back to Bern; the General was in a separate compartment with his personal staff. According to the official diary at the army headquarters, they arrived back in Gümligen "at 17.00 hours under cloudy skies."

There are conflicting accounts about the number of officers who participated at the briefing, ranging from 350 to 650. General Guisan himself spoke of 650 participants a week after the event, during a speech on August 1.[70] Attempts have been made to count the number of officers in photographs that were taken during the briefing. According to this method, the number was

485.[71] The number 650 could be correct, insofar as the *Stadt Luzern* had a capacity of 1,200 passengers. Photographs taken during the ride show that the ship was not full, as quite a number of seats were empty. Based on the Swiss Army's order of battle on May 1, 1940, considering that one or two percent of the officers may have been absent, and adding the officers of the General's personal staff, the number was 420.[72] This number is an estimate but might be close to the actual number of participants. The number 650 certainly seems too high.

It is understandable that with the passage of time many participants drew an idealized picture of that day at the Rütli Meadow. Even the weather was reported to be perfectly sunny; however army photographer Theo Frey, the only reporter admitted to the event, remembered that it was overcast during most shots that he took. It was warm but the light was diffuse, and it looked like rain.[73] This account is consistent with the records at the Swiss Meteorology Center, which recorded July 25, 1940, to be "mostly cloudy in the morning, with little sunshine, increasingly overcast in the afternoon, light rain starting from the northwest in the evening. Morning temperature 16 degrees Celsius, high of 24 degrees Celsius" in central Switzerland.[74]

Photographer Frey had received orders from Captain H. R. Schmid, head of the Press Bureau of the army staff, to be at the dock in Lucerne on July 25 to participate in a "top secret military event." He was on the *Stadt Luzern* to take a few shots of the boat trip as well as of the entire officers' corps. At the Rütli, the General wished him "good luck." To be able to capture the whole scene at the meadow, Frey had to climb a hill all the way to the edge of the woods, where blackthorn and blackberry bushes as well as army police hindered him from continuing on his way.[75] Hence, security at the Rütli was discreet but effective.

No other journalists were present at the briefing, except for two representatives of the Press Bureau of the army staff. Four days later, on July 29, an official press release informed the public about the event, stating that "the development of the situation caused" the General to hold a briefing with his unit commanders and to issue "orders to be watchful, [instructing them to] put up resolute resistance against any aggression from abroad as well as against any threat on the domestic front, such as weariness, defeatism, and lack of confidence in the usefulness of defending the country." The press release also summarized the main points of the General's speech and informed the public of the principal subjects of the order to the armed forces.[76]

It is striking to note that the media did not initially pay much attention to the briefing at the Rütli, as it appeared to be strictly a military affair. The articles on the event were surprisingly brief and were not accompanied by a single editorial. On July 30 and 31, however, some Swiss German and Swiss French newspapers published a "letter from the Rütli to a Swiss soldier," in which an officer gave an account of his personal impressions of the briefing and reiterated the army's determination to put up resolute resistance. It read, "Should God please to test us now, we are ready. Our task is to hold out!"[77] First Lieutenant Hugo Faesi, one of the representatives of the Press Bureau of the army staff who had attended the event, wrote the letter.[78] Three days later, the *Neue Zürcher Zeitung* published a "response by a Swiss soldier to the letter from the Rütli." In it, an anonymous author expressed the soldiers' thanks to and confidence in the army command, saying, "Swiss soldiers are so lucky to have leaders who anticipate and express their uncompromising determination to fight to the last drop of blood. We the soldiers follow them not because we have to but because we choose to. Our determination is as solid as the concrete that we use to build bunkers."[79]

Once it was publicized, the briefing at the Rütli received immediate attention from foreign diplomats in Bern, most particularly those from the Axis Powers. On July 30, German Ambassador Köcher telegraphed his Foreign Ministry that General Guisan had issued orders to be vigilant, referring to "malicious times." He commented, "There is absolutely no reason for this surprising move. I would like you to consider whether the Axis Powers should not jointly or individually intervene in writing to tell [the Swiss government] that we are puzzled by this new incitement of Swiss public opinion against Germany and Italy. If there is anything that could make the allied Axis Powers hesitate whether they want to maintain the same stance toward Switzerland, it is such untimely moves like the General's."[80] Hence, Germany accused the General, who was believed to be pro-British, of inciting the Swiss against it by appealing to his armed forces to remain determined to defend themselves.

The Swiss Military Attaché in Berlin, Colonel von Werdt, reported to Bern on August 6 that German authorities "most sharply" condemned the content of the press release because they viewed the statements about Switzerland's determination to defend itself as directed against Germany. "In my opinion there is a risk," von Werdt warned, "that they consider such remarks provocative. I consider that everything that is done to boost the determination to defend Switzerland will be viewed with the same suspicion in Germany; therefore, everything should be avoided that could be seen as provocative here."[81]

A diplomatic intervention against Switzerland was not long in the making. Reich Foreign Minister von Ribbentrop asked the Ambassador in Bern to address a note of protest to the Swiss Federal Council; the intervention was to be discussed with Italy first and to be submitted simultaneously by the two countries, albeit not jointly.[82] Germany's ambassador in Rome, Von Mackensen, submitted the text of the note, drafted by Köcher, to Italian Foreign Minister Ciano. Ciano noted in his diary, "Mackensen submits a draft of a joint protest note in Bern in reaction to an insulting speech by some general. We basically agree."[83] Mackensen sent a telegram to Berlin informing his authorities that Ciano reacted to the idea of a protest note "in a positive manner; in fact he was visibly pleased"—however, he wanted to consult with the Duce on the issue before signing off on the note.[84] The following day, Ciano informed von Mackensen that Mussolini "completely agreed" with the protest note proposed by Germany.[85] It seems ironic that General Guisan was accused of being a warmonger by the Italian dictator because of a speech in which (at least in the draft version) he sought to defend the supposedly Switzerland-friendly Italy against Grimm.

In his memoirs, Hans Frölicher, Switzerland's ambassador to Germany, strangely enough stated that Germany "made no official comment" about the briefing at the Rütli.[86] However, German Permanent Secretary von Weizsäcker wrote after a meeting with Frölicher on August 8 that he had told the Swiss ambassador he did not view General Guisan's speech with indifference, adding, "Without jumping to any conclusions, I told him that Guisan's remarks had left a bad impression on me as well and would probably have consequences."[87]

On the afternoon of August 13, the German ambassador, followed half an hour later by the Italian ambassador, presented their protest notes to the Swiss government in Bern. Federal Councilor Etter received them in the absence of Foreign Minister Pilet-Golaz, who was on vacation. The German note dated August 10 stated that the government of the Reich had taken note "with utmost surprise and displeasure at this event, which [it considered] to be nothing but a new incitement of Swiss public opinion against Germany and Italy"; it would hold the Swiss government "responsible for any further excesses that might be created through official statements by the commander of the Swiss Army."[88]

Etter wrote a detailed report on his meetings with the two ambassadors to the attention of the Department of Foreign Affairs, noting that he had tried to ease tensions and defend the General. He wrote:

> I remarked that I could not reply to the German government's declaration right away. Nevertheless, I remarked that Berlin had apparently made an interpretation of the General's statements different from what the General meant to say. I assured the Ambassador that the General had not had the slightest intention to agitate [the Swiss] against the Axis Powers. The Swiss did not interpret his order of the day in this way either. The General's remarks should not be interpreted in a negative but in a positive sense; he demanded that his soldiers fully accom-

plish their duty whatever may happen. I told him that I was entirely convinced that the General had absolutely no intention to agitate [his people] against the North or the South, explaining that he had merely the country's independence in mind, which precisely the General and the army were obliged to defend.[89]

Italian Ambassador Tamaro, who had been asked by his government to back up the German protest with a similar note, told Etter that "immediately after reading the order of the day in the press [he] sent the Italian Military Attaché to Colonel Masson to prompt him to urge the General to choose his words more discreetly and carefully in the future." Etter also defended the General before Tamaro, emphasizing that Switzerland's commander-in-chief had addressed "the army as a soldier" and that "his statements [should be seen] as those of a soldier; that the General, in his role as the top soldier of the country, had simply reminded the army of its duty to defend the country's independence against any attack. [I explained that] the army embodied the country's determination to defend itself, the national spirit, and the unity of the country. The real purpose of the soldier's statements was to stress in a positive manner this willingness to remain independent." Tamaro, who was otherwise not particularly well disposed toward Switzerland, seems to have agreed with this interpretation as he remarked, before leaving, "on a personal note, that his protest should not be taken too seriously." Federal Councilor Etter explained that it was difficult for him to remain composed while receiving the two protest notes; he admitted that he "had to make quite some efforts to remain calm and friendly, because I revolted as a human being and especially as an officer against the task entrusted to me to receive to the attention of the Federal Council a protest note from foreign powers against an order of the day by our General which I considered to be unjustified. What a difficult office this is."[90]

A delegation of the Federal Council subsequently discussed in what way the government should respond to the unpleasant protest notes by the Axis Powers. After consulting the General, Federal Councilor Etter, Minister Bonna, and Professor Logoz personally contributed to drafting a letter intended to calm Germany's and Italy's anger. It read:

The Federal Council trusts that the German and Italian governments are willing to maintain friendly relations with Switzerland. The German and Italian governments can count on Switzerland to show the same willingness on their behalf. . . . After consulting the General, the Swiss Federal Council wishes to clear up a misunderstanding which is apparently at the bottom of the declarations of August 13. The

General insisted right away that he had of course had absolutely no intention to make any statement against individual neighboring states, nor to incite the Swiss. The only purpose of his address to the Swiss Army was to instruct it that it had to stand on guard as long as there was no peace in Europe in order to fulfill its duty to defend the country's independence. Hence, the Commander-in-Chief had absolutely no intention to make allusions to German or Italian intentions that would be in contradiction with the present attitude of these neighboring states, which have respected Switzerland's independence and neutrality, a fact which the General himself pointed out.[91]

Ultimately the Federal Council did not send this written explanation but decided instead to give the two Axis ambassadors a verbal response based on the letter. Köcher reported to Berlin regarding the declaration, made by Federal President Pilet-Golaz, that "The Federal Councilor concluded by expressing his hope that the matter was closed through this declaration. He added, confidentially, 'I hope that from now on the General will not speak anymore.' He asked me to make sure that the public did not find out about our protest, as the Federal Council's position would not be strengthened if it became known."[92] At the same time, Köcher said that Baron von Bibra had received confidential information from Minister Feldscher that some important positions around the General were about to be reallocated, and "gentlemen [would] be put in these positions with whom Lieutenant-Colonel von Ilsemann will be able to speak more easily." Köcher considered this confidential information to be a concession on Switzerland's part. Meanwhile the Swiss legations in Berlin and Rome were informed by Bern that following the meetings held by the Federal President with Köcher and Tamaro, it was safe to assume that the matter, which was "very unpleasant for us," was closed.[93]

The briefing at the Rütli registered in Britain as well, albeit with some delay. In the fall of 1940, Switzerland's Ambassador Thurnherr reported from London that Britain "took note with interest and satisfaction of our General's courageous speech." The British press also mentioned it. Thurnherr explained that "politically the speech had a very positive effect, as it once again unambiguously confirmed our determination to safeguard our independence and liberty."[94]

From his reaction at the end of the meeting with Ambassador Köcher it is obvious that Federal President Pilet-Golaz disliked the General's speech at the Rütli. According to Wille, he had already expressed his "astonishment at some officers and other people still rattling their sabers and ignoring the real situation" when the press release of July 29 on the briefing was published.[95]

Wille, like his subordinates Däniker and Frick, had not been invited to the briefing at the Rütli because he did not command combat troops. The Chief Instructor remarked to Federal Councilor Etter that he did not want to criticize the General's speech but considered that it "unnecessarily emphasized successful resistance."[96]

According to a report submitted to the General in the fall of 1940 and subsequently forwarded to the Federal President, Däniker's reaction to the speech was particularly negative. The report stated:

Colonel Däniker was outraged by the General's speech at the Rütli. He considered that stressing the determination to put up resistance at a time when Switzerland had only one potential enemy left had to appear as a provocation. He said he knew that the speech was actually viewed as such in Germany, and Germany might want to test how determined Switzerland really was to put up resistance. Following the speech at the Rütli, Colonel Däniker wrote a letter to the General in which he told the Commander-in-Chief of the Armed Forces that he no longer had confidence in him. The General was said to reply to him that Däniker and his entourage might no longer have confidence in him but based on numerous letters he knew that the people did. Däniker qualified this reply as ridiculous; the General should have summoned him to his headquarters or had him arrested. [Däniker also said that] the General's position was becoming increasingly difficult because of his views on foreign politics. He said that he could imagine that the German Ambassador might soon demand that the General step down.[97]

General Guisan had probably received this report from "Bureau Ha." He annotated the passage about his foreign political views with the comment, "strictly neutral," and he put "?!" next to the sentence which said that he might soon be asked to step down. Däniker's letter to the General, which the report mentioned, could not be found among the colonel's correspondence or among the General's papers.

On August 1, in an order of the day, General Guisan reiterated the ideas he had expressed during the briefing at the Rütli, stating:

Based on the impression they have gained through eyewitness reports of the battles abroad, many ask themselves, 'Why put up resistance?' and they conclude, 'Whatever we do, we won't be able to defend ourselves.' To think like that is not worthy of a Swiss nor of a soldier.

Those who think like that shun their responsibilities. They ignore the natural strength of our country and the incomparable possibilities that the mountains and the wooded and varied terrain offer with their numerous obstacles and covers. May the strategy used in the battle of Morgarten be an everlasting example to you, soldiers, and to your commanders.

The General ordered his soldiers to think and act like Swiss, keeping in mind their responsibility toward the community, specifying: "To think like a Swiss means to honor one's neighbor as a human being, here and abroad. That is the reason why we put the law above power and humanity above profit and welfare. That is the reason why we enjoy linguistic, ethnic, and cultural diversity. That is the reason why we remain neutral in the struggle between major powers and try to understand them the way they are by remaining faithful to ourselves." He asked the soldiers to renew their oath to defend the flag and the state until they died, stating: "Swiss soldiers, you are not released from this oath. Let it be renewed on today's National Day and may it last forever, if God wills."[98]

The Swiss-French poet Denis de Rougemont contributed substantially to drafting the text of this order of the day, probably unbeknownst to the General. On July 10, while serving in Bern, de Rougemont noted in his diary that he got together with three officers of the general staff who had been asked to prepare a message by the General for the National Day. It is possible that one of the officers was Major Barbey, who was acquainted with de Rougemont. Since several hours of efforts did not result in a convincing draft, the poet took over the responsibility of writing it, explaining, "One cannot write as a group—they have entrusted me with writing the message on my own."[99] When the General's order of the day was published on August 1, the words looked familiar to de Rougemont, and he noticed that they were identical with the published part of the speech at the Rütli.[100] It is therefore possible that de Rougemont's contribution also had an influence on some passages of the draft of the General's speech at the Rütli, assuming the poet had submitted it before July 25.

The commander-in-chief also addressed the nation over the air at 6:30 a.m. on August 1, making statements that were similar to those in his order of the day. He referred to the briefing at the Rütli, declaring, "I personally believe that it is not only an obligation and a duty to defend ourselves but that we also have the means to do it. Defending ourselves not only means holding out but fighting with all our might and even destruction. If necessary, we must sell our lives at the highest possible price." He added that the entire population had to "think as Swiss do and act as Swiss do" according to the spirit of the Rütli.[101]

On the same day, Federal President Pilet-Golaz delivered an anything but defeatist radio address in which the government expressed patriotic greetings to the "armed forces, from the General to the simple soldiers," and declared that "liberty in harmony [was] the priority" and that the army's mission was "to be the guardian of the Alps—the fortress and at the same time the keystone of Europe."[102]

The General's briefing at the Rütli and speech on August 1 caused a noticeable shift in the public mood. Numerous speakers at local National Day celebrations referred to the words of resistance pronounced at the Rütli.[103] The weekly report by the Press and Radio Section on July 29 was mostly negative, stating, "The mood in the armed forces is still bad, and increasingly so. The soldiers are tired of being on duty, which has devastating consequences on the civilian population. Perhaps most of them think that a military threat no longer exists."[104] However, the report noted signs that the spirit of resistance was beginning to strengthen "among members of the army who have a positive attitude towards the state" and among civilians, explaining, "Soldiers, officers, and civilians alike talk about national disobedience and revolting against capitulation."[105]

The next report, published a week later, stated, "This week's highlights were the General's speech at the Rütli, or what became known of it directly or indirectly, and the General's speech on August 1. They had an extraordinary and profound effect on the elite and the people. Unconditionally advocating the national defense has created a new wave of confidence and has strengthened the determination to defend the country. Insecurity has given way to confidence. The future looks bright once again, or has at least become clear."[106] The report also mentioned, though, that some occasional criticism was still voiced, aimed in two directions:

> On one hand there are those who consider that Switzerland's defensive potential is weak even in the mountains; they do not have confidence in Swiss soldiers and their training, or they do not believe that it makes sense to stage a war in the mountains if the lowlands are abandoned to the enemy. On the other hand there are those—most of them belong to the Front movement or the industry or are defeatist—who continue denying that Switzerland can be defended at all. These people make negative or ironic comments about the General's speech in private conversations but not in public. However, these two tendencies clash sharply with the views of the large majority of the population.

A report by the 7th Division, which had been redeployed from eastern Switzerland to the Jura Mountains, stated that a "critical period [had] ended when the briefing at the Rütli defined a new objective."[107] However, it would be wrong to suppose that the mood changed dramatically everywhere. Several reports indicated that it was difficult to overcome despondency. As late as two weeks after the General's speech, a report by the 4th Army Corps mentioned "signs of fatigue and widespread defeatism."[108] As late as 19 days following the briefing, Hausamann informed the "Army and Home" service that he had received reports discussing a "really dramatic decline of the mood in the army and among the population." He said that estimates by "soldiers who [had] to be taken very seriously [indicated that] 75 percent of the troops no longer believe that they will be ordered to fight if necessary; 15 percent of the troops are indifferent; 10 percent are steadfast and reasonable but they are no longer able to assert themselves."[109] One month after the event at the Rütli, the army's adjutant general told Guisan that the reports from the various units and arms contained one common element: "The spirit of the troops has considerably deteriorated since part of the armed forces were demobilized on July 6, 1940."[110] This report did not mention anything about the mood having improved since July 25. During the same period the commander of a regiment from Valais reported to his superior: "The men begin to have doubts while they are on leave. The civilians consider the war to be over and the threat to be gone."[111]

Some people claimed that the briefing at the Rütli was in fact superfluous, though General Guisan always denied this view.[112] Shortly after the war, National Councilor Reichling, a key representative of the farming community who was a colonel in the army, denied that the troops or the population had ever heeded defeatist feelings or gone through a serious crisis; in 1946, he told a parliamentary committee, "It was not necessary for the General to boost anyone's confidence. The briefing at the Rütli was a nice affair but it was not needed as a booster shot in reaction to soldiers deviating from the path of duty."[113] Supporters of Wille and Däniker voiced similar opinions.

In spite of these critical comments, in this author's opinion there is no doubt that the briefing at the Rütli was the event that most helped to extract the army from a serious crisis, even if it took some time for the idea to sink in that putting up resistance made perfect sense. It is no exaggeration to say that at the Rütli some kind of miracle happened. The spirit of the Rütli emanated something magical. The General's briefing changed the basic attitude among the majority of the army and the population; despair and resignation gave way to the determination to brave any aggressor, no matter how powerful he was nor what happened, and if necessary, to sell oneself as dearly as possible. The briefing at the Rütli has rightfully gained the status of a historical turning point.

For the army of a democratic state it can be decisive that the people do not question the attitude of the command. The briefing at the Rütli made General Guisan a symbol of the unshakeable determination to resist. The General tackled and overcame a critical situation. One has the impression that the army, which had previously been subject to a number of mood swings, was finally imbued with the relentless fighting spirit that is generated by a soldier's confidence in his commander-in-chief. The instructions he issued at the Rütli indeed established General Guisan, whose leadership qualities had been questioned by his opponents, as commander-in-chief. The General's speech had not only military but political ramifications; his words lit a torch and gave direction to Switzerland's domestic and foreign policy during World War II. It established the General as the country's spiritual leader.

Nor has the spirit of the Rütli flagged. Forty years after the briefing, on July 25, 1980, a memorial service with 3,000 participants was held at the Rütli Meadow, during which Federal President Chevallaz recognized the occasion as a historic event. On the *Stadt Luzern*, the flagship of the fleet on Lake Lucerne, a relief by Franco Annoni was unveiled depicting the memorable boat ride to the Rütli.[114]

17

The Réduit Strategy

DEPLOYING THE ARMED FORCES TO THE RÉDUIT FRONT in the Alps was not a spontaneous decision; the briefing at the Rütli, at which the General informed unit commanders of the new strategy, was only the last step in a sequence of careful deliberations and plans. The actual idea of the Réduit strategy goes back to the nineteenth and even the eighteenth centuries. General Dufour had considered moving his army into positions in the heart of the country during the Civil War of 1848. Several historians have researched the origin of the concept.[1] General Guisan never claimed that the Réduit was his own idea, explaining that he was "the first to acknowledge that the basic idea came from people like Toepffer and Rambert."[2] In a speech after the war he pointed out, "There was certainly nothing ingenious about the idea of the Réduit. It was simply the most reasonable solution. Actually I tend to believe more and more that it was the only possible solution. Its implementation did not require tremendous intellectual efforts but above all some courage."[3]

Before the war, during an operational exercise in the spring of 1939, pulling the troops back into a central hedgehog position had already been planned in the event that superior German and Italian forces were to apply great pressure on the country; however, the strategy was not practiced during the maneuvers because of a lack of time.[4] According to this author's research into the files of the army staff, the expression "Réduit" was first used during the Second World War in November 1939 in connection with strategic deliberations. During the "Phony War" that followed the conclusion of Germany's campaign in Poland, the army staff discussed to what extent the existing fortifications should be reinforced. Colonel von Erlach, chief of the operational section, considered that "the Gotthard was still the central base for the army together with the fortresses of St-Maurice and Sargans." He added that if Switzerland had to fight on its own, without receiving any outside assistance, "the Gotthard would be of even greater importance, perhaps as a Réduit for the Swiss armed forces in the central Alps."[5]

During these discussions, Divisional Commander Huber, who was assistant chief of staff for rearward affairs at the time, was rather skeptical about a Réduit strategy's prospect of success. He recalled how such a proposal had been raised earlier by the commander of the 2nd Army Corps but had been refuted. "It was said," according to Huber, "that keeping a major army unit in the mountains under the current circumstances would hardly be feasible. It would require stocking a significant amount of additional provisions there, and special steps would have to be taken for the wartime economy. For these considerations the proposal was rejected. The Gotthard should not serve as a central position but as a barrier for traffic between the south and the north of the Alps."[6]

One month later, in mid-December 1939, Chief of the General Staff Labhart suggested that Guisan examine the possibility of shortening the existing defense line in case of simultaneous German and Italian attacks. He proposed pulling back the southern front, including the border troops, to positions at the Gotthard, and shortening the northeastern front to the area between Lake Zürich, the mountain passes of Glarus, and the Gotthard.[7] According to Labhart's proposal, the front at the Limmat would not have been abandoned, but the troops in the south would have been withdrawn to positions in the Alps. Franz Odermatt pointed out that General Guisan vehemently rejected that idea, which contained elements of the subsequent Réduit strategy, and it was not considered further for some time.[8] The commander-in-chief and his strategic advisor Gonard explained to the chief of the general staff, "We have to move all our troops forward in order to stall the enemy in the entire depth from the positions of the border troops to this front [at the Limmat]. The deeper the positions, the longer it will take the enemy to reach this front."[9]

After becoming chief of the general staff, Huber shared the General's and Gonard's views. The possibility of withdrawing to the foothills of the Alps was considered if the enemy took the front at the Limmat; however, during the winter of 1939–40, ideas resembling the Réduit strategy were only vaguely examined by some officers of the general staff, including Colonel Germann.[10] Huber probably first dealt with the possibility of a Réduit in central Switzerland in the second half of May 1940, as indicated by Germann in his memoirs.[11] On May 17, Germann concluded that if the front at the Limmat were to break down:

In my opinion, the bulk of the armed forces would have to be based in the foothills of the Alps, where they should defend the heart of the country like a fortress. Following the example of the people from Nidwalden who withstood the French invaders at the time, they should not give up, not even when there is nothing left to save but Switzerland's honor. There our army would actually perfectly fulfill its role as the custodian of the mountain passes across the Alps, a role that Italy has always acknowledged. In this perspective, the center of the country and the area around Lucerne have a special importance.[12]

A few days later, when the German panzer columns were standing at Dunkirk, the chief of the general staff forwarded Germann's report to the commander-in-chief without mentioning the possibility of withdrawing the troops to the Alps; instead, he emphasized the need "to defend the existing defense line with all our means. Consequently, we must use most of our resources to reinforce the existing front."[13] Huber initially had difficulty accepting the idea of redeploying the troops to positions in the center of the country. This author agrees with Odermatt that Huber, at that time, was determined to "fight unconditionally in the existing positions [and] perish with flying colors."[14]

In his response, which he gave only three days later, the General took a more nuanced stance than his chief of staff, as he did not exclude the possibility of withdrawing the troops to the Alps. He agreed that the existing defense line should be defended with all means as long as possible; nevertheless, considering the events in France he demanded that the possibility of pulling back the troops be examined. As he wrote, "Preparing to withdraw the army into the foothills of the Alps and the Alps has become the most likely solution that should be envisaged, no matter what the circumstances. This has become even more obvious these days due to the fact that a large number of [French] troops have apparently been withdrawn from our w[estern] border, probably in reaction to the ongoing battles in the north of France."[15] In view of the fact that by the end of May 1940 France was unlikely to be in a position to provide assistance to the Swiss Army, the General came to the conclusion that if the front at the Limmat were to collapse the only option would be to withdraw the armed forces into the foothills of the Alps and the Alps themselves. As he explained, "It goes without saying that if we are simultaneously attacked at the northern and the southern fronts, we will fight only to save our honor and all our troops will have to withdraw in a concentric way towards the Réduit at the Gotthard. In this case, the front will have to be concentrated at a central mountain range around the Gotthard. It is doubtful that we will be able to include Lucerne and the region of Schwyz and Brunnen in this defense strategy, as one has to admit that our means will be seriously curtailed."[16] It was at this point that the General for the first time embraced the idea of a Réduit. He agreed with Germann that seeking refuge in the Alps would allow Switzerland to fulfill its historic mission of guarding the routes across the Alps, even if it could do so only in a very limited area.

The study that Germann submitted on May 17, 1940 indeed included the original idea of the "Réduit National" of World War II.[17] From that moment on, the army staff and the General's personal staff began discussing the completely new idea of withdrawing the troops into a Réduit front, not as a last resort in the event of foreign military pressure but to prepare for combat there amid fortified positions in the Alps. Germann commented, "The novelty of my plan was that the bulk of the armed forces were to take positions in the Réduit, which are difficult to access and easy to defend against all sides, before an enemy launched an attack. There we would have been able to fight the decisive battle with all our energy. Meanwhile, the border troops and other advance troops were ordered to stall the intruding enemy, above all in order to allow the troops that were to be deployed to the Réduit to get ready for combat."[18]

Germann initially seems to have been the only advocate of this special strategy, but he soon received support from the army command. Even though the General and his chief of staff continued to believe for some time that the decisive battle would take place along the existing front in the plains, Germann was ordered to study in detail a possible withdrawal of the troops into the center of the country. During the last week of May, following the English-French debacle in northern France, Gonard told Barbey, "The general situation is such that we may have to forego requesting or accepting cooperation from the French; instead, we may have to back our defense on the Gotthard, or rather on a national Réduit covering a large area around the Gotthard. This is what Germann suggests in the plan that he started working on last winter."[19]

On June 13, the day before the Germans took Paris, Germann presented the tentative plan of his new defensive concept to the chief of the General's personal staff. Barbey wrote about this event, "Germann explains to me the last version of his draft of a national Réduit, which he calls 'Alpine Fortress' or 'Gotthard Fortress.' For the first time, this plan draws the ultimate consequences from a situation that may become reality from one day to the next, of being encircled and having to fight on all fronts at the same time. Germann defends the idea with powerful military and legal arguments. I present it to the General and notice how familiar it is to him."[20]

As the Germans were continuing their conquest of France and advancing toward Switzerland's western border in June 1940, another officer, Colonel H. Frick, also suggested examining the possibility of pulling back the armed forces into positions in the center of the country. Due to the fact that a considerable number of troops had been redeployed to the Jura and western Switzerland in order to reinforce the western front, the defense line in eastern Switzerland had been substantially weakened. When the 35th Regiment of the mountain infantry was also redeployed, Frick, who was commander of the ad-hoc "Linth Group," stationed on a 32-kilometer long sector of the front between Lake Zürich and the Walensee, was alarmed and wrote to his superior, Corps Commander Labhart, that his sector lacked depth, as did other sectors. He admonished that "the current positions have become useless and have to be replaced by others, as regrettable as it may be to abandon the expensive fortifications that have been built through hard work in the last several months."[21] Frick gave an extensive explanation of why this was necessary for reasons of strategy and neutrality, stating, "The army is the only thing that we can weigh against far-reaching German demands. We could declare that we are willing to discuss but that we would go to war if Germany made demands that infringe our honor and integrity, even though we would of course have no prospect of being successful."[22] He explained that the only thing that could contribute to successfully meeting exaggerated German demands was the determination to make "any thinkable sacrifice" to defend the country's liberty. Touching on the Réduit concept, he added:

> However, we can only take this approach if we concentrate the armed forces in positions that are suitable for their strength and where we can put up resistance without the enemy breaking through right away. Without going into detail, I fathom that these positions should be based around the Gotthard and extending [north] towards central Switzerland or [west] towards the Bernese Oberland. The entire armed forces including the border troops would have to be deployed to these hedgehog-like positions, while keeping sufficient mobile reserve troops available. It is obvious that preparations for this move would have to be ordered immediately; particularly, ammunition, provisions, and other indispensable material would have to be stocked there. [Consequently] I consider that it is absolutely necessary to explain to the commander-in-chief the situation of the Linth Group and of the 4th Army Corps as a whole and to request that the army be pulled back into a shortened front around a central area.[23]

Three days after Frick had made his appeal, when German troops had reached the Jura and were approaching Geneva, and Switzerland was about to be encircled by the Axis Powers, Corps Commander Labhart submitted a four-page situation report to the General. The report quoted extensively from Frick's analysis, as Labhart shared his subordinate's view. Labhart added, "There is no doubt that such a decision is very grave and will be difficult to make. However, during the difficult times that we are currently going through, wholehearted decisions are urgently needed if we want to survive with honor. I thought that it was absolutely necessary to briefly explain my view to you."[24] The commander-in-chief forwarded the proposal for examination and comment to the chief of the general staff the same day, as evidenced by his handwritten note on the document.

On June 22, 1940, the day when France asked Germany for an armistice, the General summoned his direct subordinates, the four corps commanders, the chief of the general staff, and Chief Instructor Wille, to a briefing in Bern. It is likely that Labhart's proposal prompted him to call the meeting, as Labhart himself speculated.[25]

The General had also received written situation reports from Gonard and Germann for the event. In his report, Gonard asked whether the army should not be pulled back into a central position in the mountains, which could include the Gotthard, the Bernese Oberland, and the area around the Napf mountain. He argued that on a less extended front in more favorable terrain the troops would be more concentrated, thereby increasing the prospect of putting up effective resistance.[26] However, he considered that withdrawing to a central position was a strategy that should only be applied when it appeared to be impossible to continue fighting at the existing front. After examining other options, Gonard concluded that in the event of an attack the existing front should be defended as long as possible. He suggested pulling uninvolved border troops and the Light Troops back behind the existing front line in order to reform them into powerful reserve troops, as "the army has absolutely no reserve troops left that would allow it to carry out even the slightest maneuvers."[27]

Germann reiterated his view that, considering the enemy's superiority in terms of tanks and aircraft, it would hardly be possible for the Swiss Army to withdraw to rearward positions once hostilities had broken out; hence, the existing front should be abandoned in favor of a Réduit while there was still time. He considered that the armed forces should remain in the existing positions only as long as the threat of an invasion was imminent, explaining, "If in the course of the war we should have any unexpected breathing space, it would be indispensable to forsake the existing strategy, as creating a Réduit is the only long-term solution."[28] Nevertheless, unlike Frick, Germann did not consider the existing front to be useless, as the well-constructed fortifications would help to stall the aggressor, thereby granting the troops more time to organize defenses at the new central front.

According to the minutes of the briefing on June 22, General Guisan opened the meeting by giving his own analysis of the situation, stating:

The purpose of today's briefing is to examine the general situation that is the result of the precipitate events of the last few weeks. The French armed forces have been defeated and are withdrawing southward while continuing to fight. The German Army is staying on their heels, attacking in several directions; it looks as if the two major attack routes follow the Rhone valley and further west in the general direction of Tours–Poitiers–Bordeaux. No major German units have come close to the Swiss border, as they continue south parallel to it. Individual small units have come in contact with our border posts before pulling back again. For the time being, there are no German troops in Upper Savoy; it does not look as if the Germans want to occupy the area south of Lake Geneva. However, German troops are in Bellegarde; hence, our communication lines with France are virtually interrupted.

In *Italy*, the situation has changed little. No activities have been observed. There are practically no Italian troops at the Swiss border. . . . Hardly any German troops are stationed east of Lake Constance, in Vorarlberg and the Allgäu, but there are troops north of the Rhine between Schaffhausen and Basel. A compact mass of German troops continues to be present in the Black Forest. There is a particularly large concentration of them in the Wiesen Valley.[29]

Speaking about the economic situation, the General remarked that Switzerland would have to brave rather difficult times and "widely ration all everyday necessities very shortly." Guisan said that he was personally convinced that the Germans would exercise primarily political and economic pressure on Switzerland and were unlikely to envisage any military action, explaining, "Switzerland is a valuable transit country for the Axis Powers; its railways across the Alps should remain intact in order to be available for their transit traffic, which is certain to increase. Nevertheless, we must be prepared for Germany to threaten us with an invasion at any given time, especially if we put up resistance against its threats." He concluded that in view of these facts, attacks from all sides could not be excluded. In order to defend the country, he considered that the army had three options:

1) *Hold out at the existing front line.* Advantage: we can rely on existing fortifications which will provide the necessary power to our defense. Drawback: the existing front is very long, tying down every single soldier of our troops. . . . When we established the current front line at the beginning of the war, we counted on having an ally who could take over a sector and defend it for us. Today no

such ally exists anymore, so we have to rely on our own forces to defend the entire front.

2) *Rely on part of the existing front line* by turning west and abandoning the positions that are not fortified. The advantage of this hedgehog position is that we can utilize the fortified sectors of the northern front from Sargans to the Hauenstein while abandoning the positions on the western front, which have hardly been fortified at all anyway; the troops that have been stationed there can be redeployed to the sector between Napf–Thun–St-Maurice. The drawback of this solution: a new western front has to be created that is not yet fortified at all. If we resort to this solution, we will have to start making preparations today to stock ammunition and food supplies along this new front.

3) *Pull the army back into a central area* that is defined to the north by the foothills of the Alps approximately on a line between Lake Zurich–Lake Lucerne–Napf–Thun. The advantage of this solution is that we will be very strong in the Alps; but [the disadvantage is that we] do not have a lot of resources and will use up the entire ammunition and food provisions very quickly. Moreover, this option requires that we surrender almost three-fourths of the country.[30]

The General explained that after weighing the pros and cons of the three options, he gave preference to the second one, which required:

a) orders be given to move ammunition and food provisions; and

b) some troops be redeployed from existing positions to a new sector. We do not intend to build fortifications in the new sector but to catch up on combat training, which has been missing in some places.

It is interesting to note that the General's initial idea of a Réduit did not include the construction of fortifications and other permanent structures; instead, the Réduit should serve as a training area in order to improve the troops' combat power.

The General also announced that the question of demobilizing some troops would be examined, stating, "At the time when the armistice goes into effect in France, we will not get around putting parts of the army off duty. It is better to prepare and carry out demobilization according to our own conditions before Germany makes any such demands."[31] However, he added that one would also have to take into account the employment situation, as an increase of the unemployment rate would have to be avoided. In addition, some troops would have to remain on duty "in order to counter possible attempts at a revolution."

By favoring an intermediate solution at the briefing, the commander-in-chief advocated a combination of the views that had been expressed by Frick, Germann, and Gonard. His explanations show that he did not embrace the idea of the Réduit from the start and had serious reservations about it.

During the subsequent discussion, it was striking that the General's suggestion was criticized on several accounts. Prisi opposed pulling back any troops, arguing that no matter where the front line was established, "in the front, in the middle, or back in a central area," the army would not be able to hold out for a long time. He added, "If the army has to sacrifice itself and perish, it is best to do so in the fortified positions that the troops are familiar with. Ultimately it is up to the political authorities, the Federal Council, if the army should establish a new front. The army's present mandate is to defend the country. If we pull it back into the Alps and surrender three-fourths of the country, the army no longer defends the country but just itself."[32] Prisi pointed out how difficult it would be to get fresh supplies in a central area, above all in case of a winter campaign. Moreover, the Germans could take in Switzerland's main economic and industrial base in the plains facing little resistance, without having to attack the Réduit. He only agreed with the idea to create central reserve troops in the heart of the country.

Chief of the General Staff Huber was skeptical as well. He advocated creating three divisions of reserve troops that should be on call in a central area, but he did not want to relinquish the existing front line at all. He pleaded that in view of the "certainty that we will perish anyway," the army should fight where it is strong, "which includes the existing front line that is by now well fortified." He added that in the mountains it would be difficult to get enough fresh supplies for the entire army. Moreover, the troops would not be sufficiently protected there, particularly above the tree line where they could easily be attacked by aircraft. Except for setting up the three divisions of reserve troops, Huber was against changing the existing defense strategy, as the army had to "protect the entire country and defend every inch of the native soil by using guerrilla tactics."[33]

Labhart referred to the proposal he had already submitted, and again advocated redeploying the troops to positions in the heart of the country quickly, saying that this would be "a full step, not just half a step."[34] Corps Commanders Wille and Miescher had similar views on the subject. Wille advocated a front that followed the line Lake Zurich–Einsiedeln–Lake Zug–Napf area–Simme

Valley–St-Maurice and was against scattering the troops across several front lines. He explained to Chief of the General Staff Huber that with the exception of the border troops, "all forces [should] be deployed to an area where we are strong." He argued that it was possible to stock an amount of ammunition and food in a central area that would allow the army to hold out substantially longer than in the weak existing positions, adding, "This redeployment will allow us to gain time and will require a lot of additional effort from the enemy. Germany's most important targets are still our Alpine railways. They do not want to occupy Switzerland's plains, which do not offer it anything that it does not already own. As long as we focus on energetically defending these targets and crucial mountain passes, we can more easily counter the threats of an armed power."[35] In this instance, Wille for the first time clearly expressed the dissuasive purpose of the Réduit strategy which Germann had hinted at and which later came to be accepted as the main reason for its usefulness.

In addition, Wille mentioned economic and political arguments to explain why the number of serving troops should be reduced, stating, "As you know, Germany demands that France immediately go back to work in order to be integrated into the war effort against England. In the same manner, Swiss industry could be awarded new orders because it is healthy and can begin production right away. All our industry has to do is to know how to secure these orders and consequently be integrated into the new economic policy of the Axis Powers."[36] These explanations demonstrate that Wille was a staunch supporter of the Réduit strategy but at the same time did not hesitate to speak in favor of indirectly supporting Germany's war against England.

At the end of the briefing, General Guisan concluded:

> Corps Commanders Wille, Miescher, and Labhart consider that following an armistice between Germany and France steps must be taken to pull the army back into a central area, where the troops should receive intensive combat training; in this central area, no fortifications should be constructed. Colonel-Corps Commander Prisi and Colonel-Divisional Commander Huber consider that the existing front should be maintained, while reducing the number of troops to create central reserve troops consisting of about three army units. They also acknowledge that there is a need to train the troops for combat. Colonel-Corps Commander Lardelli would like to wait for the Federal Council to make its decisions before taking any action; he tends to favor keeping the army at the existing front. Everyone who is present agrees that the border troops remain in their positions and that preparations be made to stock ammunition and food supplies closer to the center of the

country. With respect to dismissing troops, everyone agrees that following the armistice part of the armed forces should be demobilized, while taking into account the situation of the labor market; there are different opinions as to how many troops should be dismissed. Colonel-Divisional Commander Huber favors dismissing virtually the entire army if this can be justified in order to create a clear situation in case the troops have to be mobilized again. The other gentlemen are more in favor of gradually dismissing the troops and keeping some detachments in the existing positions to pack up. For the time being, the border troops should not be dismissed; they must stay on duty to reinforce the border police as well.[37]

There was agreement at the briefing that the existing front line was questionable and that the worsened general strategic situation would have consequences on the operational level. However, the army chiefs fundamentally disagreed on what those consequences would be. Corps Commander Prisi gave probably the most skeptical account of the mood that reigned among some of the corps commanders after the briefing. At a briefing with the divisional commanders of the 2nd Army Corps two days after the meeting with the General, on June 24, he explained that France had capitulated half a year too early to allow the Swiss Army to finish fortifying its existing front line. Because the army had no [outside] support left, he considered this to be the most unfavorable military and political situation in the history of the Swiss Confederation. He did not hide his opposition to pulling back troops to a central area, explaining that any kind of Réduit would "mean that we surrender all our precious cultural and industrial areas and relinquish all our essential means of transport, [which would have] a devastating effect on the army and the people. The hedgehog position at the Gotthard carries with it . . . every possible drawback. It will result in our army being encircled, starving to death, and capitulating. It is unacceptable."[38] Bircher, the commander of the division from Aargau who generally disagreed with Prisi, was also against the Réduit strategy.[39]

After the briefing of June 22, the commander-in-chief and the chief of the general staff agreed to have the future deployment strategy for the armed forces "analyzed independently" by Strüby, the assistant chief of staff for the front; Gonard, the head of the Operational Section; and Colonel Germann.[40] To establish a common starting point, two days later Chief of the General Staff Huber met with his subordinates Strüby and Gonard in the presence of Barbey, who wrote about this meeting:

The chief of the general staff unrolls a small map at a scale of

1:100,000 on which he drafted the new plan. The idea of the 'Réduit' which had been kept a secret until now is unveiled in the dusk of this summer day. An oval shape indicates where the front will run in the Alps. The army units are named at their respective positions: Mountain Brigade 12 and Sargans in the east; 7th, 8th, and 3rd Divisions in the north; 1st Division, Mountain Brigade 10 in the west and southwest; Mountain Brigade 11 and 9th Division in the south, covered by Border Brigade 9 in Ticino. The closed oval shape includes the three fortresses of Sargans, Gotthard, and Saint-Maurice. In the north, the 6th, 5th, 4th, and 2nd Divisions form a semicircle in the 'forward front.' This front is linked to the Réduit in the foothills of the Alps around Fribourg through a provisional division consisting of the three light brigades. We have agreed on this outline as a starting point for the studies. We discuss whether the fortified area around Saint-Maurice should be included in the Réduit—"Réduit" is really the word that imposes itself—or if it should be left to its own destiny, which would allow it to resist for two months. We decide to incorporate it in the Réduit.[41]

This vague concept, which left room for many options, had to be turned into a specific strategy. As early as the end of June, the General ordered no new fortifications at the existing front and completion only of certain others under construction.[42] These instructions indicate that by then the decision to pull back the defense line had already been made. On July 2, Huber presented Gonard's, Strüby's, and Germann's drafts to the General after examining them.

Germann submitted a study that was several pages long and included a "special report on the defense in the area of Schwyz (sector Pragel mountain pass–Lake Zug)." In this study, he repeated the most important arguments in favor of a central area in the Alps, stating, "In my opinion, the Réduit front aims to boost the power of resistance and thereby to demonstrate Switzerland's right to exist as an independent state and to allow the Federal authorities to make their own decisions on free Swiss territory, protected by the Réduit. Obviously this makes sense only if the willingness exists from the start to defend ourselves against demands that are incompatible with Switzerland's honor and independence."[43]

Germann advocated forming three strongholds within the Réduit: at the Gotthard, in the area between Unterwalden and Brünig, and in the Bernese Oberland. He did not think it was advisable to defend the canton of Glarus with special means, "as this would require too much effort"; but he favored including the area around Lucerne and the Valais in the defense concept.

Moreover, he recommended preparing the railways at the Gotthard, Lötschberg, and Simplon for destruction "to provide our diplomats with an asset that can prevent demands in the form of an ultimatum."[44] The General considered Germann's model, which advocated a very confined Réduit, as "the most consequential solution that draws the most extreme conclusions from the idea."[45]

Gonard's "Study for the Defense of a National Réduit" was 22 pages long.[46] In it, he proposed leaving the border troops in place and keeping the troops in the northeast in their existing positions. The rest, consisting of six divisions and two and a half mountain brigades, were to be redeployed to a central area that should be large enough to include as many routes across the Alps as possible, "which is why our country exists in the first place." Gonard concluded that the fortress of Sargans should remain outside the Réduit as a forward base, as it would be able to hold out on its own for an extended period of time.[47] Strangely, Guisan wrote in his postwar report that it was Gonard's idea to include all three fortified areas (Sargans, Gotthard, and Saint-Maurice) in the Réduit strategy, an opinion shared by Barbey but which was in fact erroneous, as evidenced by Gonard's original study.[48]

Strüby's shorter study, "Regrouping the Armed Forces," suggested staggering the army in three zones: the border troops, the covering troops, and the troops at the Réduit front.[49] He opposed abandoning the existing front, arguing that "it would be grave to completely give up the current defense line, which is very solid and fortified in some sectors. The troops have been busy for months building the fortifications and have constructed a number of solid bulwarks, pillboxes, and barriers. They are proud of their work and are convinced they will be able to resist any enemy for an extended period of time there." He added that if these positions were forsaken of the army's own accord, "the people's determination to put up resistance [would] be weakened and the army's resistance [would] be broken; [hence,] giving up the existing front line should not be considered." The General, who undoubtedly agreed with Strüby's arguments, annotated this passage in pencil, writing "psychological drawback."[50]

Strüby presented the option that Chief of the General Staff Huber preferred. His study incorporated the fortresses of Saint-Maurice and Sargans in the new defense line. Huber wrote to the General, "I agree with Strüby's proposal; it comes closest to the view which I expressed at the briefing of June 22, 1940." He argued that considering the threat that a German "fifth column" and parachutists posed it was necessary to "defend the territory of the entire country; [the troops have to] hold out in their respective positions to the last bullet."[51]

A further step toward deciding to withdraw the armed forces to the Réduit must have been taken on July 4, when the commander-in-chief and Barbey met with Huber, Strüby, Intelligence Chief Masson, and Gonard in Worb to examine the operational measures that would have to be taken immediately. Barbey's diary notes indicate how difficult it was for them to make essential decisions. He wrote:

> This is basically about setting up the army at definite positions in a national Réduit and at the same time about organizing this Réduit. The risk of such studies is that one tends to focus on the details. A few days ago, the Chief of the General Staff presented a first draft of a map which mentioned only the divisions and mountain brigades; the term 'army corps' was irrelevant. From there it takes only one step to go down to the levels below and to think in terms of combined regiments. . . . That is far from the level on which we are supposed to make our decisions. Logically speaking, one should say that this or that army corps is responsible for blocking this or that strategic direction. It would be even better to decide first what is the role of the front in the Alps (Réduit) and that of the forward front. At least we are getting to the objective, even though we do so from the wrong angle because our starting point is the terrain, kilometer by kilometer. We move from the tactical level to the strategic level, we start climbing from the bottom of the valley, as we are preoccupied by the requirements of the anti-tank defense, by the concept of bases that are fortified all around in a staggered, deep fashion. And all this is determined by one completely new experience, the campaign in France.[52]

Reading this passage, it seems that there was quite some uncertainty about the future strategy and that the discussion did not go in one direction. There was as yet no clear concept of the Réduit, and the group became entangled in details.

The following day, Barbey submitted to the General a comparative analysis of the three projects. He concluded, among other things, that Strüby's proposal, which Huber preferred, had the principal advantage that it could be achieved within a short period of time, while Gonard estimated that it would take three weeks to put his plan into effect, and Germann guessed that it would take at least three to four weeks for his project to be realized. Hence, Barbey said that the chief of the general staff had already issued orders on July 5 to prepare the first orders based on Strüby's plan.[53] Consequently, it appears that the decision in favor of pulling back the troops according to Strüby's proposal was made as early as July 4 or 5, three weeks before the briefing at the Rütli.

Nevertheless, the General called another briefing with the corps commanders for Saturday, July 6. The General planned to inform the Federal Council of the principle of a national Réduit under which two-thirds of the army would abandon three-fourths of the country's territory. At this meeting, it was to be discussed whether the Federal President should be told verbally or if the Head of the Military Department should be informed in writing.[54] In his notes on this briefing, the General wrote:

1. I gave everyone the opportunity to express himself and did not intervene.
2. The 3rd Army Corps [Miescher] spoke about the mentality of the troops, who no longer have confidence and are asking for something new! It is up to the commanders of the army corps to intervene where necessary, and the new elements are supplied through the reports of the Intelligence Service and through our instructions regarding the defense, including appendix. Up to commanders of the troops to keep troops busy! Sad that a Commander of an Army Corps noticed that the confidence lacks all the way to the Divisional Commander! Unity of doctrine lacks in this army corps.
3. Systematic opposition on the part of the three jealous ones.
4. Concept of defending exclusively the Alps is a mistake [because of] resources; what would the people say; not enough mountain troops. Population would also want to move to Réduit. Aviation would no longer be available. Population already protested against abandoning part of the territory beyond the current front line.[55]

From these notes, it appears that it was not easy for the General to defend his viewpoint. The "three jealous ones," a term which referred to Corps Commanders Wille, Labhart, and Miescher, did not oppose the idea of the Réduit per se, but keeping some troops at the existing front. Spearheaded by Wille, they criticized former decisions by the army command and opposed another "half measure," as they considered that the entire army except for the border troops should be withdrawn to a Réduit in the Alps. In a written declaration, which he read and asked to be added to the minutes, Wille explained, among other things, that although as Chief Instructor he was not involved in operational decisions of the army command, "as the oldest member of the National Defense Committee, which is currently out of function," he felt that he continued to bear some responsibility for preparing the national defense. He stated:

From the perspective of our future defensive potential, we must not spend another centime of the regular and special credits that have already been approved for the national defense on things that have to be considered outdated or at least questionable based on the current and the emerging military and political situation. . . . In my opinion, the orders that have been issued since the French-German armistice, according to which the fortifications under construction shall in general be completed, risk resulting in a waste of money, material, and manpower.[56]

Wille demanded that, most importantly, "a clear decision [had to be] made on the best combat strategy," adding that until such a decision was made all construction work should be halted "except on the projects that will definitely be useful." Furthermore, he criticized the decision to demobilize the troops so early; he would have "preferred to bring the troops into the [Réduit where] they could have deposited their material and then be sent home."

During the discussion of the advantages and drawbacks of the three proposals, Wille advocated defending the central area with the entire army, arguing that "the fortress of Sargans and the positions held by the border brigades should be the only positions maintained forward of the front line; so there should be no stalling battles in the area between the border troops and the new defense line of the army." Miescher supported Wille's view, explaining that a "new, extremely solid front" with numerous formations was necessary to "instill new confidence in the troops."[57]

Wille, who said that he wanted to "conduct a war, not defend the country," was countered by Prisi who, as at the first briefing two weeks earlier, opposed any Réduit strategy, arguing that the army could be encircled in the Alps and starved to the point that it would be forced to capitulate. The commander of the 2nd Army Corps explained, "Under the current circumstances it is useless to conduct a war if its only goal is to bring the army into safety in a refuge in the Alps. . . . It makes no sense to defend mountain tops and glaciers if the plains with their abundant economic resources and the majority of the population are surrendered to the enemy." Prisi was determined to fight and die in the existing positions; he expressed his determination with eloquence, stating, "By withdrawing to the Alps, the people's and the army's confidence would be shaken. A soldier is mentally more prepared to fight when the shelter of his home country is behind him than when he has to consider it as lost from the beginning. . . . The oath, which the army made refers to defending the country, its Constitution, its honor and liberty. Even nowadays it is worth perishing for an idea."[58]

Huber conceded that it would indeed be useless "to defend only rocks and glaciers"; however, he told Prisi that if an enemy managed to break through the existing front, which had become too weak given that no ally could assist the Swiss any longer, the country would perish anyway. He added, "That is why we plan to build up a rearward front with as few troops as possible, using the existing cornerstones of Sargans and Saint-Maurice. This is a compromise between the two options that are under discussion today, the one being a withdrawal of the entire army into the Alps, and the other for maintaining the existing front."[59] It is interesting to note that Huber continued to be rather skeptical about the new strategy, consistently avoiding the term 'Réduit' and speaking of "a rearward front" instead.

After four hours, the General concluded the meeting by summarizing its results as follows:

> Colonel-Corps Commanders Wille, Miescher, and Labhart consider that the entire army should be pulled back into the central area and only the border troops should remain outside of it. These gentlemen envisage an optimistic solution according to which the fortress of Sargans as well as the cities of Lucerne and Thun should be included within the front line of the central area. Colonel-Corps Commanders Prisi and Lardelli advocate maintaining the existing front line; only the Western front could perhaps be moved to the upper Birs river, the Taubenloch canyon, and the Sarine river. Today's interesting debate will allow the Commander-in-Chief to make a decision shortly.[60]

Labhart wrote in his diary about the meeting: "In the first place we discussed the positions of the army, which I consider to be completely untenable. The new proposal by the general staff would also result in splitting up the forces. My viewpoint is very clearly shared by Colonel-Corps Commanders Wille and Miescher. However, I fear that only half a step will be made."[61]

Corps Commander Prisi, who insisted on his viewpoint being accurately recorded, submitted a written declaration after the briefing that he asked to be added to the minutes. In it, he summarized his arguments but did not add any new points. Nevertheless, it demonstrates how important he considered the discussion about the new strategy. He implored the General to renounce withdrawing the army into a Réduit, as this would "not be 'a full step' but in fact the first step toward surrendering three-fourths of our territory and at the same time the beginning of an inglorious capitulation by the Swiss Army that would be necessary after a relatively short period of time." He emphasized once again that "our army, which has fewer troops and means, cannot be victorious against the battle-tried and triumphant armies of a superpower, [but it should at least] perish after courageously and heroically fighting the superior enemy in a hope-less battle, [thereby] saving our military honor [and] giving an example to our fellow human beings and to posterity."[62]

The General, who was undoubtedly impressed by his determination to fight, called Prisi into a meeting during which he tried to convince him of the usefulness of an intermediate solution. As Barbey noted in his diary, "This morning, the General received Prisi, the commander of the 2nd Army Corps; they had a long talk."[63] There is no record of the contents of the meeting; how-ever, *ex silentio* and from the subsequent instructions it can be concluded that the General managed to convince Prisi, whose allegiance he valued, of his point of view, or at least persuaded him to give up his opposition to the compromise. He may have made a concession to Prisi by letting the 2nd Army Corps stay in its existing positions in the Jura between Aargau and Basel.

After this meeting with Prisi, Guisan must have made his final decision about the future front line. Gonard wrote, probably referring to that day, July 9, 1940:

> Being the only witness, I still see how the General made the decision which has since entered the annals of our military history. He put both hands on a small map of Switzerland, his fingers resting on the forward front of that time. Then he briskly moved them to the foothills of the Alps, from Lake Geneva to Sargans, saying, 'This is where the army is now; that is where it shall move.' It was a decision that subsequently became the symbol of our absolute determination to resist, to be free and independent.[64]

Following the meeting with Prisi, the General called the chief of his per-sonal staff into his office and told him, "I want you to write to the chief of the general staff now. You have all the necessary information; you know what I want. Please get to work now. Then we shall write to the Federal Council to inform it of the measures that we shall take."[65] The following day, Guisan signed the directives and transmitted them as orders to Chief of the General Staff Huber.[66] The document, dated July 10, 1940, contained the General's decision to establish the Réduit. These directives were the basis for temporary Operations Order No. 11 of July 12, which covered the transition period, and for Operations Order No. 12 of July 17, in which the definite deployment into the Réduit positions was ordered.[67] According to a note he wrote to Barbey, Gonard had drafted both orders. The note read: "According to the General's orders, I am submitting to you this morning the draft of Operations Order No. 11, which I wrote yesterday evening based on the 'Directives' which had been submitted to me."[68] Gonard added that he deemed it necessary to issue two separate orders, as "one single order would be much too weighty; the final decision" would be included in Order No. 12.

On July 10, the General established the deadlines that had to be observed for regrouping the armed forces. Three days after the day on which the orders were issued, 'D-Day,' the internees were to be brought outside the Réduit ('D+3'). On 'D+4,' the army units were to begin their reconnaissance missions; on 'D+8,' the troops slated to be stationed along the forward front were to be deployed there; on 'D+15,' troops were to be deployed to the Réduit.[69]

Also on July 10, Huber met with the General in the morning and then called his four assistant chiefs of staff into a meeting to organize the regrouping of the army.[70] Later that day, he wrote a situation report on the General's behalf.[71] In the accompanying letter, Huber wrote, "If you agree with the draft, I will incorporate your changes and then make a sufficient number of copies to the attention of the Federal Council, including a French translation."[72] However, this seven-page situation report was not submitted to the government as such but served as the basis for a letter dated July 12 in which the Federal Council was informed about the establishment of the Réduit. Barbey had received orders to write the letter and explained:

> In this letter, some basic points will have to be highlighted: the concept of completely or partly forsaking the defense of large areas of the country in order to focus our main efforts on the Réduit; the emotional, mental, and material sacrifices that this solution entails; the deadlines for carrying out the changes, which the army staff estimates to take three or four weeks, up to the moment when the troops are established in their new positions and will be able to rely on elementary barriers and fortifications. The Federal Council must be informed about that. . . . And then there is another crucial issue: one has to make clear that one of the advantages of the Réduit is the fact that it will allow us to control and prepare for destruction the major routes across the Alps that link the two Axis Powers in the south and the north. As soon as we take control of these routes, the 'Réduit policy' can begin.[73]

The General made some slight changes to the draft and then signed it.

The memorandum dated July 12, entitled "Note concerning the new defense strategy," also remarked on the general situation following the armistice in France:

> Germany and Italy are not interested in bringing about new conflicts

as long as they have not broken England's resistance. On the other hand, though, it is incontestable that the direct passageways through our Alps are of importance, at least for Germany. As a consequence, Germany could be tempted to exercise economic, political, and even military pressure on Switzerland in order to gain free access to these passageways. Germany's demands could sooner or later become such that they are no longer compatible with our independence and our national honor. Switzerland can avoid the threat of a direct German attack only if the German Supreme Command becomes convinced, during its preparations, that a war against us would be long and costly and that it would kindle an unnecessary and dangerous conflict in the heart of Europe, thereby jeopardizing the execution of its plans. Consequently, henceforth our national defense has to have the purpose and the principle of showing to our neighbors that such a war would be a difficult and costly endeavor. If we are drawn into the conflict, we will have to sell ourselves as dearly as possible.[74]

It is not difficult to see that these arguments, which emphasized the dissuasive effect of the Réduit, had already been used by Germann in his first studies during spring 1940.[75]

In this memorandum, the General informed the Federal Council about the decision that he had made "in the framework of unchanged terms of reference" as a result of the altered military and political situation. He stated that "the country will be defended according to a new principle, that of staggering the troops in depth," explaining:

For this purpose, [I have] created three main resistance zones which shall be supplemented by a system of bases in the areas between these zones. The three resistance zones shall be as follows:
  − The border troops that shall maintain their current positions;
  − A forward front or safety front which takes advantage of the current front line between Lake Zurich and the Gempen Plateau and shall be extended in the west by a front following the general line of the Jura in Cantons Bern and Neuchâtel−Murten−Sarine river to the basin of Bulle;
  − A front in the center of the Alps (National Réduit) which shall be flanked by the fortresses of Sargans, St-Maurice, and the Gotthard.

As the General further described, "The mission of the border troops remains the same; the forward front or safety front shall block the invasion routes into the interior of the country. The troops in the Alps shall receive as many supplies as possible and hold out without thinking of withdrawal." He added that the defensive system between these three zones would consist of a dense network of objects prepared for destruction, and light detachments and territorial troops, assisted by local civil defense units, would have to stall the enemy. This combat strategy would make it necessary to regroup some of the internees; furthermore, it would be indispensable for the civilians to stay put. The General stated: "It is particularly important that the population does not flock towards the Réduit, where it would jeopardize the operations and would not have sufficient supplies available." He also suggested that in case of hostilities the seat of the government be transferred to Kandersteg and the army's command post to Altdorf. At the end of his letter, the General assured the Federal Council that the new concept could be in place by the beginning of August. In the meantime, all necessary steps would be taken to "ensure that the country is continually ready to be defended" during the time of the regrouping in spite of the difficulties of the operation.[76]

Several authors claim that in his letter of July 12 the General asked the government for its approval for redeploying the armed forces to the Réduit.[77] However, a careful analysis of the letter shows that this was not the case. Guisan simply informed the Federal Council about the new strategy, and he wrote, "I have made the following decision."[78] As commander-in-chief, he was under no obligation to ask the political authorities' permission on any military arrangement. In the Federal Council's reply to the General's postwar report, Guisan was criticized for not speaking with them before making such a far-reaching decision as deploying troops to the Réduit.[79] Guisan indeed failed to consult with the seven-member Federal Council, but he did ask Federal Councilor Minger, the Head of the Military Department, for his approval before making the decision on this special matter and communicating it to the government. As Guisan wrote, "I was able to reach a full agreement quickly during my meetings with the Head of the Military Department and, through him, with the Federal Council."[80]

In the files of the army staff, there is no indication of a written reply from the Federal Council to the General's letter. It was on the agenda of the Federal Council's meeting on July 16, but the minutes do not mention anything further. Federal President Pilet-Golaz personally informed Minger, who was unable to attend the meeting, about the issue when returning the letter to him. Pilet-Golaz wrote that he had informed the Federal Council about the General's letter and that he had made the following four points:

1) The distance between the seat of government and the General's command post should not be too great;

2) There should not be too many troops deployed to the so-called coverage positions;

3) It would be necessary to call up the troops, for example three divisions at a time, on a rotational basis;

4) It would be indispensable to prepare troops (light brigades and some regiments) to maintain law and order.

Pilet-Golaz considered the two last points to be most important. He told Minger that the Federal Council agreed with the General's measures after adding these four points. The Cabinet also emphasized the need to call up troops in a way "that is more useful to the national economy than has been the case until now. Mr. Wetter has been particularly keen on drawing the General's attention to this matter."[81]

Pilet-Golaz annotated the passage in the General's letter that stated Switzerland could no longer "automatically" rely on armed assistance from the enemy of a potential aggressor, writing, "That was never an issue, on the contrary." This remark confirms that the Federal President was completely in the dark about Guisan's cooperation agreements with France. In his report to Minger, Pilet-Golaz commented that the expression "automatically" was dangerous from a political perspective and not correct, stating, "We never envisaged that we would receive assistance automatically if we were attacked. On the contrary, we have at all times reserved the absolute right to call on foreign assistance or not. A document like this one could lead to completely wrong conclusions if it fell into the hands of propagandists one day."[82] One may wonder what went through Federal Councilor Minger's head when reading these remarks if he had been informed—as was entirely likely—about the cooperation talks with France.

The General was undoubtedly informed only verbally about the government's approval of the Réduit strategy. Minger probably communicated this information to him on July 16. Operations Order No. 12, which the General said was "the first document that was dictated by the idea of the Réduit,"[83] was dated July 17. At that time, though, the expression 'Réduit' was not yet associated with the idea of a decisive battle; the General explained that "through the influence of outside and inside circumstances [the idea of the Réduit] changed to that of the 'National Réduit,' a bulwark where the main resistance was concentrated and which included our three large fortified zones and, as an asset, the routes across the Alps—the Réduit that was to be defended by the bulk of our armed forces."[84]

According to Operations Order No. 12, the front of the central zone was to be established along the line Sargans–Linth Channel–Schindellegi–

Zugerberg–Rigi–Pilatus–Hohgant–Zulg (north of Thun)–Stockhorn–Kaiseregg–Dent de Lys–Chillon–St-Maurice–positions of mountain brigades 10 and 11–Gries mountain pass–Cristallina–Pizzo Campo Lungo–Scopi–Piz Guda–Tödi–Ringelspitz.[85] The 1st, 3rd, 7th, and 8th Divisions, which had been stationed in the plains and the Jura up until then, were to join the 9th Division and Mountain Brigades 10, 11, and 12 as well as the troops of the fortresses of Sargans, St-Maurice, and Gotthard at this new front and "hold out under all circumstances." This meant that a total of eight army units would be stationed in the Réduit, more than half of the armed forces excluding the border troops. This was more than Chief of the General Staff Huber had originally advocated. Four divisions, the 2nd, 4th, 5th, and 6th, as well as the three light brigades united into one light division, remained in the "forward front" which ran from the Limmat across the Gempen Plateau and the Jura at Neuchâtel to the Sarine.

It is interesting to note that under this concept, no reserve troops existed. In view of the fact that the Réduit ran across several regions connected by mountain passes, across which large troops could not switch positions in winter, the General had only the air force available as a mobile reserve. Having abandoned the concept of a strategic reserve, it would hardly have been possible to make operational modifications during a battle. The corps commanders would have had to fight on their own with their own reserves.[86] When the question of reinforcing the front at the northern banks of Lake Thun was raised in the late fall of 1940, Huber had to admit to Guisan, "The army has spent all its means and has no reserves left to occupy the ridge at Sigriswil."[87] In response to the view that reserve troops should be provided only at the level of the army units, the army corps did not have one-third of its troops available as reserves, as would have been desirable according to the general rule, but only one reinforced regiment.[88]

The reinforcement troops were not deployed to the Réduit all at once but little by little. Gonard explained: "The decision to deploy the bulk of the armed forces to the Alps had to be carried out in a way that we were capable of defending ourselves during the transition period, so as not to be caught by surprise in the middle of regrouping the army. Consequently, the transition from the old front to the Réduit was made step by step; the safety front that was strong in the beginning was later gradually dismantled in favor of the main front of the Réduit."[89] On August 18, one month after Operations Order No. 12 went into effect, the 6th Division was also redeployed from its positions at the Limmat to the Réduit. In his historical study, Roesch reconstructed in detail the changes made regarding the troop concentrations and front sectors during that time.[90]

The last, decisive stage was implemented in the spring of 1941, when Operations Order No. 13 ordered the troops that had remained at the forward front (the 2nd, 4th, and 5th Divisions) to pull back to the Réduit.[91] From that moment on, the entire field army, including all divisions and mountain brigades, amounting to twelve major units, plus the garrisons of the fortresses of Sargans, St-Maurice, and the Gotthard, were stationed in the Réduit. The zone between the border troops and this central front was manned only by the light troops and demolition detachments, which were to stall the enemy. Hence, more than ten months after the discussions with the corps commanders, the General, his chief of staff, and Operational Advisor Gonard ended up sharing the view that had originally been advocated by Wille, Labhart, and Miescher.[92]

Several commentators maintained that withdrawing to the Réduit front was not a heroic act but an emergency solution imposed by the military situation of early summer 1940, with consequent disadvantages for morale.[93] In fact, Huber himself called it an "extreme makeshift solution."[94] By deploying its troops to the Réduit, an undefeated army was, in effect, retreating to the mountains. Some officers considered the march into the interior of the country a "bloodless, silent defeat" and were overcome by "feelings of inferiority."[95] Colonel F. Wanner went so far as to call the withdrawal "a Swiss-style Dunkirk."[96]

In the central area, which had a population of 300,000, accommodations for the same number of soldiers had to be prepared. All kinds of supplies, food, and ammunition were stockpiled in this area for 600,000 people and 40,000 horses; the stocks were to last six to eight months in the event of a siege.[97] The Réduit was in fact comparable to one huge fortress. The commander-in-chief became personally involved in organizing the transport of supplies to the interior of the country, writing to his chief of staff, "During a recent trip to Zürich, I noticed that the army's iron supplies in Killwangen, which had begun to be stocked in the winter of 1939–40 for the construction of fortifications along the Limmat front, were still considerable. I would like to ask you to examine whether it would not be advisable to relocate this valuable material, at least temporarily, to a central place near the Réduit."[98]

Among the troops, there were emotional discussions about "abandoning" the country and their own families. Wilhelm Werder said, "The soldiers obeyed but they never really stopped worrying about those who remained up front."[99] To some degree, the redeployment had a positive effect on the troops' day-to-day morale, as the new environment of the Alps, with its lakes and glaciers, lifted their spirits; however, some men had initial difficulty getting used to their new mission because they interpreted it as too defensive. Barbey wrote about a reconnaissance the General undertook to the 1st Division, stationed in the foothills of the Alps in the canton of Fribourg: "When the unit commanders are asked about their plans and available materiel, very often you get confusing answers that are full of nonsense. There is no doubt that the materiel is insufficient, but there is also a lack of inventiveness and resolute thinking. No one, or almost no one, seems to know whether counterattacks will be launched, and how so."[100]

In a private conversation with the chief of his personal staff during the fall of 1940, the General was not very optimistic about the army's strength. Barbey recorded: "He considers that the border troops would be able to resist for two days on average, and so would the 'forward front.' Basically on the fourth or fifth day, the Réduit would be reached by tanks which precede the bulk of the motorized and non-motorized infantry by 24 hours. That is when the real battle would begin. We would have just enough time to begin fighting under acceptable conditions."[101] The General added that this was "a pessimistic calculation," but he expected the forward front to substantially affect the enemy's supply lines even if the enemy were able to break through the front in some sectors.

Aware that a defensive strategy carries the risk of applying a defensive mentality, the General issued orders to his troops to fight vigorously, emphasizing in the Réduit the spirit of aggressive resistance. He handed out "Instructions on Combat Tactics for the Defense" along with Operations Order No. 12 to the troops at the border, at the forward front, and in the central area.[102] These instructions, as well as additional directives dated August 13, 1940, which had been drafted at Gonard's request by Captain H. Frick, a training officer, were met with criticism from Chief Instructor Wille. Feeling ignored, Wille wrote a personal letter to the General, later followed by a lengthy complaint. In the latter he expressed serious reservations about the idea that henceforth the field artillery's primary mission was to fight against tanks, to compensate for an insufficient number of anti-tank weapons. Wille strictly opposed "handing out [to the training officers] the tactical rules contained [in the instructions] as a supreme doctrine by the commander-in-chief."[103]

Guisan's idea was to have his troops take advantage of the favorable terrain and use an aggressive, mobile defense even when the enemy was superior in materiel. He emphasized the "spirit of active resistance." At a briefing during maneuvers of the 1st and 3rd Divisions in the Réduit in the late fall of 1940 under the command of Corps Commander Miescher, the General explained, "In several instances I had the impression that the defense did not react vehemently nor fast enough. In each and every sector and position, a number of measures must be taken to fight tanks; more active and better trained anti-tank troops must be established; and everyone down to the rank-and-file must be indoctrinated with the determination to fight back."[104] However, it was initially difficult for the army to fulfill this demand, as in 1940 it did not have any anti-tank missiles, anti-tank mines, or flame-throwers available; moreover, the troops had not received sufficient training for close combat.

To improve aggressive combat tactics, Divisional Commander Constam of the 6th Division received orders in the winter of 1940–41 to draft new directives to temporarily replace outdated instructions from 1927. In January 1941, Constam submitted his draft, which included general ideas about combat tactics and guidelines for a mobile and active defense in the Réduit, to the commander-in-chief, who forwarded it to the chief of the general staff for examination.[105] Barbey noted that Constam's report instilled "confidence right away"[106] and he personally translated these "Instructions on Combat Tactics" into French. The General added them, in the form of an order, to Plan of Operations No. 13.[107]

The optimistic introduction to these instructions stated, among other things:

> A people that had to fight to become independent must not relinquish this independence without fighting. Those who are cowards and renounce their freedom will not find the strength to gain it back under more favorable circumstances. Those who are brave never think that a war is hopeless. Being brave is not only a matter of an individual's courage when he faces danger but to the same extent a matter of the expertise that he has gained through hard work, pain, and sacrifices, and that boosts his self-confidence. We must acquire this expertise by working constantly and consistently. We lack combat experience. Hence, we shall hold our own against a battle-tried opponent only if we draw the conclusions from the development [of the war abroad] that are relevant for us and then apply them through intensive training.[108]

With regards to combat tactics in the Réduit, the instructions explained that what mattered was "to do everything to defend the central area. . . . The Gotthard, Grimsel, and Lötschberg, which are the most important routes across the Alps, are the pawns that have been entrusted to us, the last refuges that we shall protect and never surrender. In our mountains, tenacious and well trained troops, even if they are outnumbered, are able to counter successfully an enemy who uses modern war materiel and combat methods." However, the instructions continued, it was crucial never to wait for an enemy attack "behind walls providing protection [but to launch] counterattacks with an aggressive spirit," supported by artillery. "Everyone must strive to fight the enemy at close range," which would make it "difficult, and in some instances impossible," for the enemy to use artillery and dive-bombers.[109]

To ensure that the Réduit would be effectively defended, the commander-in-chief demanded that the "battlefield be organized." For that purpose, on October 3 and 4, 1941, he summoned the unit commanders, their chiefs of staff and chief engineers, the chief instructors of the army and of the units, to attend demonstrations held by the 3rd and 6th Divisions in their sectors. The new Head of the Military Department, Federal Councilor Karl Kobelt, was invited as well.[110] During these demonstrations, Constam's arrangements were considered exemplary; the sector held by his 6th Division was said to be the best organized. Barbey noted:

> This is a precise, reliable, and convincing picture of the way we want the battlefield to be organized. In Unterägeri, after briefly outlining the purpose of this organization, the General asks Constam to speak. On a map, Constam explains the lineup of his division. We begin our visit at the banks of the Lorze river. . . . During an exercise involving two opposing groups, everyone sees how the sector has turned into a zone with an aggressive defense; the attacker is granted some freedom of movement so that counterattacks can be launched against him according to a number of plans. In the afternoon, we attend exercises involving sharpshooters and tanks which show aggressive battle tactics in the sector of Morgarten.[111]

Subsequently, individual divisions and groups of regiments carried out exercises and maneuvers in the different sectors of the central area. However, the troops were never all present in the Réduit simultaneously, and at times the total of serving troops dropped below 100,000 men. Guisan stated, "During the time of the war, the lowest number of troops, 70,000 men, were on duty in June 1942."[112]

To reinforce the defensive potential of the Réduit, Guisan, as early as the summer of 1940, issued instructions regarding the construction of fortifications. The first priority was given to anti-tank barriers in towns, followed by positions in open fields and concrete emplacements.[113] As Ernst remarked, "Once the troops had been deployed to the Réduit . . . the construction activities reached a level that our country had never experienced before in the domain of the military."[114] When Labhart initially opposed the construction of casemates for the artillery, arguing that the funds should be used to purchase tanks instead, the General replied, "I intend to make thrifty use of the funds that have been allocated for the construction of permanent structures and in particular of artillery casemates. These structures should allow us to resist for an extended period of time in case we are attacked during the current war. Moreover, they should not fall prey to rapid decay, thus becoming useless shortly after the end of mobilization" as had been the case with the earthwork fortifications during World War I, which were "virtually invisible" two decades later. The General stressed that the army should learn from this mistake, saying, "The structures we are building now must also be useful to those who will be called upon to defend Switzerland in 1960 or later."[115]

In the Réduit, most of the corps' and divisions' artillery was mounted on fortress-style gun carriages in caverns. To get the guns back on wheels, military technicians had to be called in; the procedure was scheduled to take three days.[116]

The cost to build the various structures in the Réduit was considerable. Originally the expenses were expected to amount to about 220 million Swiss francs. In early July 1940, 73 million of the 130 million francs that had been slated for the Limmat front were still available. These funds were reallocated for the fortifications in the Réduit and it was hoped that the amount would last until mid-1941. Meanwhile, requests for additional funds would be submitted.[117] Of the 73 million francs that were available right away, 29 million were allocated for reinforcing and expanding the fortress of Sargans, and 33 million were used for building the most urgent fortifications at the front of the central area.[118] During the following years, several additional credits had to be requested. Ultimately, the fortification of the Réduit between 1940 and 1945 cost around 900 million francs.[119] Gonard remarked that it was possible to provide the northern front of the Réduit from Sargans to St-Maurice "with an unbroken line of firing positions for the fortress artillery."[120]

In the event that the Swiss Army was encircled in the Réduit during a German attack, which was considered possible at any moment, Switzerland planned to ask England for military assistance. According to notes written by Chief of the General Staff Huber, it was planned to send a Swiss delegation from Belp or Thun to London by night in two DC-3 aircraft owned by Swissair to ask the British government for assistance. As a first step, the Swiss would request support by air; the British would be asked to bombard the attacking troops and their supply lines. In addition, the Swiss expected to receive support in the Réduit from 100 fighter aircraft and bombers (Spitfires and Hurricanes) as well as from paratroopers and transport troops. At a later stage, the Swiss would have liked to receive fuel, mines, explosives, food supplies, and medicine, which were to be air-dropped or flown to air bases within the Alps.[121]

From the moment it was planned to the time it was completed, the concept of the Réduit was not uncontested. Even if there was no public debate on the Réduit because of the censorship imposed on military issues, members of Parliament, the government, and the army itself continued to voice criticism against the idea. Chief of the General Staff Huber, who had for some time tried to keep the General from deploying the entire armed forces to the Réduit, wrote to him as late as the fall of 1940 saying, "Today some people in the military have a defeatist attitude precisely because of the front in the center of the country. These people have the impression that the majority of the country will be surrendered to the enemy without fighting and that the army will in fact only defend the least populated areas that have the least resources." Huber feared that increasing the number of troops in the central area would actually jeopardize the survival of the national fortress, at least as long as there were not enough food supplies and ammunition stocked there. He argued that by further augmenting the number of troops in the Réduit at the expense of the forward front, the power of resistance at the routes across the Jura and in the plains would be weakened, with "very serious consequences" because the enemy could

> rapidly advance to the front in the central area. . . . [I]t would have a highly unfavorable effect on the morale of the army and of the entire country if virtually the whole country were occupied during the first attack and the army was basically seeking refuge in the mountains. The possible consequences include a breakdown of the population, the establishment of a new government, and negotiations about the occupation. In that case, the enemy would not need to attack the Réduit front at all. He would occupy the country and starve the army in its positions in the Réduit.[122]

In the fall of 1941, when the General asked Borel, the new commander of the 1st Army Corps, whether he thought that he could hold his sector of the Réduit, the latter replied, "I think that we will be able to die with honor!" The General's entourage was "astonished" at this not very confident response.[123] One year later, Corps Commander Lardelli admitted to the commander-in-chief, "I do not like the idea of the Réduit front either. The Réduit is too small if it represents the home country that we defend; yet it is too large as a front that we must hold."[124]

It is striking to note that over the course of time some top commanders changed their minds about the Réduit. Corps Commander Labhart, who as we have seen was initially a staunch advocate of the Réduit, had doubts about its usefulness by 1942 and would have preferred to find a new solution. When it turned out that the Germans were facing unexpectedly dogged resistance during their Russian campaign, which they had launched in June 1941 with a string of impressive victories, Labhart wrote to Federal Councilor Kobelt, his former chief of staff, that in view of the constellation of power among the Axis in 1940, pulling back the armed forces to a Réduit front had been "an absolute necessity [considering] our weak forces." He remarked that since then, however, several things had completely changed, explaining, "Germany has enormous difficulties fending off the Russians. This is bound to continue the same way even if the Germans stage some more great victories and even if they should succeed in taking St. Petersburg and Moscow and advancing to the Caucasus. In the West, a second front is in the making, initially in the air, but it is just a matter of time until an attack is launched by land." Labhart considered that the Italians, on the other hand, were "taking part in the war only half-heartedly"; hence, Switzerland had "very little to fear anymore" from that side.[125]

Commenting on a critical analysis by Captain G. Züblin of the general staff, Major Bracher wrote in a report to the General in the fall of 1942 that in the summer of 1940 the Réduit had "indeed [been] an emergency solution [because] we had no other choice considering the circumstances as well as the amount of training and armament the army had at that time. [However] that is no reason to throw the baby out with the bathwater and condemn the Réduit just because the much-disputed General [sic!] carried out the idea instead of the gentlemen appointed by the grace of Mr. Wille and Mr. Däniker."[126] In certain cases one gains the impression that for opportunistic reasons some commanders tended toward particular views—even when dealing with issues that required objective thinking—simply to express their latent opposition to the commander-in-chief.

Unlike Labhart, Huber gradually became an advocate of the Réduit strategy. In the summer of 1942 he wrote to the General:

I continue to be convinced that at the present time [the Réduit] is the only way that allows our army and our government, and thus our State, to hold out for an extended period of time; [this strategy will] be more useful for the preservation of the State than an army which is crushed, dissolved, and deprived of a leader within a few weeks of fighting in the plains and a government which has fallen into the enemy's hands. The army command never intended to have the army wait in the Réduit until it is starved. If the enemy does not attack the Réduit, parts of the army shall make sorties from the Réduit and force the enemy to fight.[127]

Some members of the Federal Government were skeptical about the Réduit as well. Foreign Minister Pilet-Golaz later acknowledged that withdrawing the troops to the Réduit was correct from a military standpoint and very useful from a political angle, even though it was "cruel from the perspective of the country and of the population."[128] However, in 1943 he remarked to his liaison officer, Major Daniel, that he did not like the "rigidity" of the Réduit strategy because one could suddenly be faced with a situation for which the current defensive concept was not adequate.[129] Federal Councilor Stampfli, the Head of the Department of Economic Affairs, did not support the Réduit either; nor did he agree with several other decisions made by the commander-in-chief. In private, he did not hide his critical opinion, writing to Heinrich Walther, a National Councilor from Lucerne, that he considered the front in the Alps to "increase rather than diminish" the danger for Switzerland. He added: "Nevertheless, hundreds of millions of francs are sacrificed for this front, and nobody can speak out against it, or else he or she will be branded a defeatist."[130]

It is striking how patiently Guisan tolerated those who opposed the front in the heart of the country for military reasons. In 1942, he once again defended his decision during an exchange of letters with Labhart, writing:

According to my instructions of May 25, 1941 on combat tactics, I continue to stand by the principle that the central area must be defended with all means. In addition, surprise breakthroughs must be prevented, an objective which should be accomplished by a first continuous cordon which is based at natural or man-made anti-tank barriers. If the enemy invades the defense zone, he shall be destroyed and thrown back immediately beyond the first cordon by the actual defense, which is ready behind the first cordon in a terrain that has been prepared for the purpose. Carrying out these principles will be very difficult in some cases, yet I insist that this is the only possible way to defend us. Particularly if we are attacked by an enemy who is highly superior in the air, there is no way that a planned retreat can be carried out. On the contrary, each individual unit shall continue fighting in the area assigned to it even when it is encircled. This will make it possible to engage the enemy in combat and disorganize his attack in such a way that counterattacks can be launched to re-establish the situation [before the invasion]. I consider that it will be impossible to pull back part of the front against a well-organized enemy who attacks unimpeded if our artillery is not temporarily superior and if we do not have control over some air space, limited as it may be.[131]

The General reiterated his order not to conduct mobile warfare in the

Réduit in view of the army's inferiority in supplies; instead, the troops were to hold out and fight fiercely in their assigned positions.

From the summer of 1942 on, the army command also dealt with the question of what measures it should take in view of the Allies' expected second front in the West. Hence, at the end of June, the General issued orders to study a revised 'Case West' "as quickly as possible."[132] The studies resulted in the drafting of Plan of Operations No. 14 dated September 1, 1942, which was to go into effect only if necessary.[133] The plan stipulated that the bulk of the army would be deployed from the Réduit to Switzerland's western border. It was estimated that the move to the new front would take five days once the army was called up.[134] The problems connected with this plan were discussed at a number of conferences. During a meeting of the army staff, the General asked, "Which opponent would be most interested in the Réduit in the event of a battle in France between Germans and Anglo-Saxons?" He gave the answer himself, stating, "Above all the Germans, in order to maintain their communication lines with Italy, while the Anglo-Saxons will strive to destroy them."[135] Huber wrote a special memorandum entitled "The Plains, 1943" on the problems that were expected to occur during the changeover from the Réduit to the deployment of the troops in the lowlands.[136]

When Major König, a courier for the army command, returned to headquarters after delivering Operations Order No. 14 to the corps commanders, he reported that they were all favorable toward the new plans. As Barbey told the General, "To sum it up, everyone is pleased with the idea that the commander-in-chief has planned measures and issued orders that are intended to deal with the possibility of [Case] W[est]."[137] Only the chief of staff of the air force and antiaircraft defense had responded to the courier that the new operational plan was impossible to carry out and that he would submit a counterproposal. Barbey remarked on this matter that if officers were not able to execute Operations Order No. 14, the only solution was to ask them to resign so they could be replaced by more competent and more disciplined leaders.[138]

In June 1944, after the Allied landings in France, part of the Swiss Army left the Réduit to re-establish the western front; however, they did not proceed according to Operations Order No. 14 but according to orders which had by then been modified.[139] Plan of Operations No. 13, which defined the Réduit strategy, basically remained in effect until the end of the war and was formally canceled only in the summer of 1945. All relevant documents had to be returned to the operational section by the end of July 1945.[140] Nevertheless, the Réduit retained enduring importance as a fortification system. The General called it "a valuable legacy."[141] Even if, after the war, it was decided that a modernized Swiss army should not surrender the nation's industrial and agricultural areas to an enemy without putting up a fierce battle, the Réduit still maintained its significance as the country's last solid front.[142]

The command of the German Wehrmacht, based on intelligence information, regarded Switzerland's Réduit with respect. The Jura was viewed as a "mountain chain that acts as a defensive wall"; the Alps were considered "unsuitable" for operations except for the main access routes; and both areas were "difficult or impossible to use" in winter.[143] In 1942, an analysis of Switzerland made by Germany's army command stated that "the mountainous, scarcely populated center of Switzerland has been reinforced like a fortress and turned into a National Redoubt." It added that the access routes to that area had been effectively blocked. Germany's plans of operation against Switzerland took the formidable Réduit into account.[144]

In the fall of 1944, during a conversation with René Payot, an envoy of General Guisan, French General de Lattre de Tassigny praised the Réduit, calling it "Europe's largest fortress" and added, "The idea of your Réduit was ingenious. . . . I am convinced that you would have put up extremely dogged resistance in your mountains."[145] British Field Marshal Bernard Montgomery, who met Switzerland's commander-in-chief after the war, also said that he found the Réduit impressive, advising Guisan, "Perfect it; pierce even more holes into the rocks and fill them with additional automatic weapons!"[146]

All available documents prove that General Guisan was aware of the psychological drawbacks attached to the Réduit concept, and was reluctant to withdraw the army to the Alps. He finally did so only because of the constraints of the situation at the time. In his postwar report, he claimed that he and Huber had "made most basic strategic decisions without previously discussing them."[147] This statement, however, definitely did not apply to the decision about the Réduit. General Guisan sought advice from several sources, took his time, and hesitated as long as he dared. The commander-in-chief had the difficult task of choosing the most useful of several possible solutions, and to take the full responsibility for his choice. Guisan had the courage, in view of the circumstances, to bear the painful consequences and to assume the burden of a calculated risk. Kurz has rightfully stated, "The Réduit was not an invention but a decision."[148]

Pulling the troops back to a front in the center of the country was undoubtedly the army command's most important strategic decision during World War II.[149] The solution that Guisan chose in the midst of a delicate situation was strikingly simple and clear. Whatever one may think of the Réduit in retrospect, the concept served its purpose. Even though it was not very popular in the beginning, the Réduit became the quintessence of the nation's determination to resist. This shift in the way the Réduit was viewed was possible because the people trusted the commander-in-chief. For his part, Guisan succeeded in instilling among the army and public a feeling of confidence in the country's own strength. The symbolic character of the Rütli and the Gotthard played a role in this process that cannot be underestimated. From the German documents, it is indisputable that the Réduit strategy had the dissuasive effect for which the army command had hoped. Success proved the General to be right.

18

The National
Resistance Movement

ASIDE FROM HIS DUTIES AS COMMANDER-IN-CHIEF, General Guisan contributed both directly and indirectly to rekindling Switzerland's spirit of resistance, which had begun to strengthen once again as a result of his briefing at the Rütli and the announcement of the new national redoubt in the Alps. With direct participation, he was instrumental in the activities of the "Army and Home" section of the army staff and in the foundation of the public "Gotthard Alliance," while less overtly he was involved in the secretive "Action for National Resistance." These three organizations were rooted in different military and civilian sectors, yet they were closely intertwined by having common objectives and through the influence of a number of people active in at least two of the groups, although these links were not very obvious to outsiders.

Guisan contributed greatly to expanding the "Army and Home" section, which became a major link between the civilian population and the military during the war. It was probably the most effective instrument in strengthening the spirit of resistance throughout the country. It seems that Federal Councilor Etter, the Head of the Interior Department, originally initiated the idea for this service. In one of its first letters to the newly elected General, the Federal Council referred to Etter's idea to "immediately organize the creation of a body to handle the national propaganda" and asked the General to submit the name of an officer who could be put in charge of this task.[1] A few days later, the General submitted a list with three candidates: Major de Traz, Divisional Commander Favre, and Colonel Tenger of the general staff.[2]

The files of the General's office also include a report in which Samuel Haas, the director of the "Schweizer Mittelpresse," a conservative news agency, suggested establishing a body to deal with military propaganda and information. Haas wrote that because the war was expected to drag on for an extended period of time, it was "extremely important to create and maintain a reliable home front for the army and the national defense."[3]

On November 3, 1939, in an order regarding the "spirit of the troops," the General inaugurated the "Army and Home" section, which was to report to the adjutant general's office. The objective of the new service was to make sure that the troops remained in "an elevated state of mind . . . by contributing to keeping the troops in a good mood, by maintaining and advancing their patriotic spirit, by providing insight into the army's great responsibility, and by strengthening the bonds between the people and the army in a way that makes the army constantly feel close to the people."[4] Its activities were to include "radio broadcasts, films, plays, musical performances, lectures, and sports events." The "serious lectures, which require an extended attention span, were to be scheduled during work hours, the entertainment activities during off-hours." The order stated, "both are important, as there is a time for instruction and a time for fun."[5]

In early 1940, prior to Germany's western campaign, the Federal Council discussed the issue of state propaganda in a meeting attended by the General. During this discussion, the question was raised as to where patriotic propaganda ended for the people and where it started for the army. The minutes of the Cabinet meeting state, "The Federal President [Pilet-Golaz] explains that the propaganda intended for Switzerland or for foreign countries and the propaganda intended for the army should remain the government's responsibility. The Interior Department would be best suited to take over this task. The Head of the Department [Etter] agrees that it would be best to have his department handle propaganda. He said, however, that the department could not assume the role of a typical propaganda department. The General agrees with this organizational structure for propaganda matters but would like the Interior Department to stay in close contact with the army and its 'Army and Home' section."[6]

The army did not simply continue using the "Army and Home" service as a means to keep the troops in good spirits. As it turned out, during the Phony War and Germany's western campaign, the efforts undertaken by the Interior Department were not very effective. Guisan, aware that the national defense and the spirit of resistance required the support of the entire population, demanded that "Army and Home" extend its activities to reach civilians in the hinterland to inform them of the usefulness of, and the prospects for, military resistance. He asked that consequences be drawn from the lessons learned from the panic and rumor-mongering in Switzerland during Germany's French campaign. After the briefing at the Rütli, Guisan made himself the spokesperson of those who sought to reorganize "Army and Home" to make it an effective instrument to mentally prepare the entire population to defend Switzerland.

Captain Hans Hausamann played a leading role in this reorganization, together with other members of the Officers' Alliance. In a letter to the chief of the general staff, Hausamann had actually suggested setting up a similar military body, the "Swiss Research and Information Center," before the war.[7] In August 1940, Hausamann wrote to the head of the "Army and Home" section, "The troops lack information. It may be possible to keep everyone else out of the loop, but Swiss soldiers must be kept informed. Switzerland should do much more in this respect, because as civilians Swiss soldiers are used to receiving explanations about everything. It is good and necessary to keep things confidential, [but] one can go too far and do so in the wrong instances."[8]

At the same time, in a special report, Hausamann's Bureau "Ha" criticized Pilet-Golaz' National Day speech, stating, "Words like those expressed by the Federal President on August 1st, in which being able to work—for whom?— was called 'the highest thing next to life,' are incompatible with the need to maintain fighting spirit and the readiness to die at the highest possible level. They must be replaced quickly by a completely different spirit and a completely different way of appealing to the people and the army."[9]

In the late summer of 1940, the General formed a "special service for presentations within and outside the army," which was independent of "Army and Home." Its mission was to fight against defeatism.[10] Some younger officers of the intelligence service, including Hausamann and Captains Robert Frick and Max Waibel, were the first staff members of this so-called "General's Office for Public Outreach";[11] they were to explain war events and the purpose and the objectives of resistance, thereby counteracting any spirit of discouragement. As the General wrote about this matter in his postwar report:

> I, for my part, had ordered some officers, who were informed about all the problems of our national defense, to make presentations in order to explain to the population, as far as permitted under confidentiality regulations, the things that it was allowed to, and had to, know about the war events, the usefulness of our plans, and the means of our defense. The classes and presentations were an immediate success. Some of them were designated for the so-called 'informants'—that is, for people of all ages with various professional backgrounds who could in turn inform and influence the public, and some were directed toward the general public.[12]

This presentation team, which was soon overworked, had a limited impact. Hausamann consequently urged the General to expand the service, to integrate it into "Army and Home," and to nominate a new head for the section. He explained that "an officer who has become a colonel with honors is far from being a propagandist" and said that it was not surprising that the organization had not met its objectives. He advocated putting "a man at the helm of the 'Home and Army' section who is an officer from head to toe, who has a thorough political education, and who knows our people extremely well. He has to be a psychologist and be able to use the entire propaganda repertoire." Hausamann claimed that "Army and Home" was currently an office in which, "with a few exceptions, a group of dilettantes who are provided for by the army do a lot of mischief." In view of these shortcomings, he suggested "restructuring or expanding [this section] in order for it to fulfill the task that it is supposed to accomplish. This task consists of maintaining or creating, among the people and in the armed forces, the most favorable mental (and hence political) conditions for the army to do its job."[13]

A few weeks later, Hausamann struck the same chord again, writing in a special report:

> The things which 'Home and Army' gets away with are no longer tolerable. . . . In this connection, I would like to point out once again with utmost urgency that in times like the one that we have to go through now, when the army is waiting under arms, the activities of 'Army and Home' are particularly important. This section has to fight for the spirit of the army and the people; it has to maintain or create the most favorable mental conditions for the army to do its job wherever these conditions do not yet exist or where they have ceased to exist. Consequently, this section is an important instrument for the army command. The best man is barely good enough to head the 'Army and Home' section. It has become really urgent to identify this man and to put him in charge of 'Army and Home.'[14]

The General, who was aware that "it was not the army's overall responsibility to inform the public and to shape the mental attitude of the entire country," brought up the issue with Etter.[15] In February 1941, he wrote to him that everything should be done "to strengthen the country's mental attitude and nerves"; however, he said that the army could not "undertake this effort and tremendous task all by itself," as it did not have the necessary means to do so. He added, "This is the responsibility of the civilian authorities, and the army will be able to assist them in this endeavor."[16]

The General ultimately hoped to establish a national propaganda service under the direction of the army, which would, according to Barbey, "support the country's morale and inform the public both in Switzerland and abroad about the big problems that are of interest to our country."[17] The General had come to this conclusion, in part pressed by his entourage, following the experiences of the spring and summer of 1940. Through this new service, the efforts to strengthen morale in the hinterland were to receive a new dimension. However, because the Federal Council did not receive this idea with much enthusiasm, the General continued working with the means he had available through the army.

In spring 1941, the "Army and Home" section set up a sub-organization called the "Civilian Information Service," which organized presentations and classes to inform the population about issues pertaining to national defense. At the same time, Guisan put Colonel Oskar Frey from Schaffhausen in charge of the restructured "Army and Home" section. Barbey noted on this matter in his diary: "[The] General decides to entrust Oskar Frey, commander of Regiment 22, a circumspect, tireless, and eloquent man with an independent spirit, with the task of organizing 'Army and Home' and the 'Presentation Service.' A good solution."[18] This nomination, made after Germany's attacks on Yugoslavia and Greece brought morale among the Swiss to another low, had been influenced by two "conspirators" of the Officers' Alliance, Hausamann and Ernst, who had highly recommended the perfectly qualified Frey for this post. At the same time, they managed to have Corporal August R. Lindt put in charge of the "Civilian Information Service" to let him act "as a driving force there."[19]

In an order to the armed forces, which he opened by stating, "The longer our army is on duty and the longer the war lasts, the more individuals with a weak disposition begin to have doubts about our power to resist," the General announced that he had issued instructions to expand the activities of the "Army and Home" section.[20] This was the starting point of the Frey/Lindt era, during which a well-directed campaign was carried out among the population and in the army to promote the idea of resistance at all costs. The campaign did not rely on publicity or advertising; instead, civilians were directly informed in a blunt, matter-of-fact manner about details that the media were not allowed to divulge because of censorship. As it turned out, this was the most effective way to counter the foreign propaganda that aimed to spread fear among the Swiss through direct and indirect threats. A large number of fact sheets and pamphlets, frequently dealing with confidential subjects, were distributed to army units and key figures among the population. In addition, special "resistance letters" addressed military, economic, and political issues such as asylum regulations, foreign intelligence activities, treason, anti-democratic infiltration, and black marketeering. Beginning in 1941, a total of 34 resistance letters were published with a circulation of between 12,000 and 18,000 each.[21] "Army and Home" held more than 750 classes within and outside the army and gave about 6,500 presentations attended by a total of 833,000 individuals. A dense, nationwide information network, including more than 100,000 supporters and 7,000 correspondents, made it possible to influence the population and to sense the general mood at all times. The Adjutant General stated that "Army and Home" turned into "a real clearing organization."[22]

Not everyone was pleased with the extensive activities of the restructured section. In particular, individuals surrounding both Wille and Däniker tried to scheme, either openly or behind the scenes, against Frey's attempts to strengthen the Swiss polity. Däniker wrote to a fellow officer, Edgar Schumacher, that "amateurism and foolishness" were the order of the day in Switzerland, arguing, "It is nothing but a joke that of all people Oskar Frey is now head of the 'Army and Home' section and is therefore responsible for providing the army and the people with food for thought."[23] In a memorandum to the General, Corps Commander Wille criticized this new activity of the army, claiming, "The 'Army and Home' section is a well-meant but unsoldierly organization. One must no longer allow officers, government members, and party heads, who have been ordered to do so by this section, to publicly and semi-publicly stir up public opinion by using belligerent phrases and making warlike gestures. The superficial success [achieved by these activities] in our own country is proportionally much lower than the opposite effect [which is achieved] abroad. The present situation demands that we avoid rattling the sabre."[24] Corps Commander Labhart was skeptical as well, writing in his diary in the spring of 1941, "Colonel Oskar Frey shows up at the chief of staff's office, probably to make publicity for a presentation. I have given instructions that I do not wish this presentation, which is of a somewhat political nature, to be held."[25]

Even the Federal government voiced reservations about the army's public outreach activities. From the moment the Axis Powers protested Guisan's speech to the armed forces at the Rütli, the Federal Council mistrusted the General's public initiatives. This became very clear when Federal Councilor Etter advised the General not to make any proclamation on the first anniversary of the beginning of the Second World War, on September 1, 1940; instead, he should use the articles published by the Interior Department for the occasion. Etter wrote:

> I personally established the guidelines according to which the commemorative articles should be written. I consider that it is all right to commemorate this day in the press, and if the guidelines that I estab-

lished are respected, I believe this commemoration will have a positive effect. However, I do not think that it would be appropriate for the army to also mark the day, for example with an order of the day or any other special official event. It appears that these days certain foreign countries eye public statements by the army with special attention; in fact, I was made aware of that once again in a report by our diplomatic service today. [Hence, I consider] that we should be careful and restrain ourselves from publicizing events held by the army.[26]

In the summer of 1941, Federal Councilor Kobelt, the new Head of the Military Department, using budget cutbacks as a pretext, said that he would like to examine the possibility of closing down the "Army and Home" section. In a repeated exchange of letters and in debates with the Federal Council, and after consulting with the chief of the general staff and the adjutant general, Guisan successfully blocked this plan. The General's two subordinates agreed with him that the army should stop playing a role in influencing public morale only if the Federal Council would take over the lead instead, as suggested on several occasions, and do everything necessary to strengthen the spirit of resistance. The minutes of the internal consultation reported Adjutant General Dollfus stating: "Unlike the Federal Council, he considers Colonel Frey's resistance letters to be very important because they contribute to strengthening the morale. It is said that the Federal Council was prompted to make its request through a complaint by the German Legation (Bibra)."[27]

The General made it very clear that he would not approve closing down "Army and Home." In a meeting with Federal Councilor Etter at the end of 1941, Guisan once again emphasized the importance of this section, explaining that its activities were not only useful but necessary to maintain fighting spirit—"even that of the Notables"—at a high level as long as the Federal Council did not decide to establish its own "national propaganda service."[28] During another conference with a Cabinet delegation on January 26, 1942, the General reiterated his point of view, explaining that for obvious reasons the most vehement attacks against "Army and Home" came from the Front movement, young farmers, and the entourage of Colonel Däniker. He argued that there was a need for a Réduit not only for the military but also for the national spirit. The country's liberty and independence should be defended not only with weapons but also with a high morale so one would be willing to sacrifice oneself.[29]

The Federal Council's suspicion of "Army and Home" was also based on the fear that this service would allow the army to make its own policies, opposed to those of the government. In summer 1941, Federal Councilor Pilet-

Golaz wrote that a member of "Army and Home" had confidentially informed him that the way that section's activities were beginning to develop was dangerous because they had "anti-governmental tendencies." Some individuals in the section were said to be employed "to combat the government's policies and to spread ideologies."[30]

Some right-wing individuals tried to discredit the "Army and Home" section, whose spokesmen made attempts to get the workers to share the responsibility of defending the country, by accusing it of being subject to left-wing ideologies. As late as during the last year of the war, Lieutenant-Colonel Gilliard complained to the General that August Lindt had "a very leftist" attitude.[31]

Even Chief of the General Staff Huber feared that the army, which was supposed to stay out of politics, would be accused of becoming involved in political matters through the activities of "Army and Home." In a letter to Adjutant General Dollfus, Huber wrote:

> In his order no. 6011 of October 1, 1941 to the officers of the armed forces, the General, referring to its character and mission as an instrument of power of the State, said that the army was absolutely not allowed to play any part in molding political opinions, neither on the domestic nor on the foreign policy level. What applies to the army also applies to the army staff. During its official activities, an office of the army command must not work together with any political organization, be it publicly or secretly. I ask you to make sure that the 'Army and Home' section also adheres to these instructions.[32]

Huber intervened after finding out that "Army and Home" had established confidential contacts not only with military associations but also with a number of civilian organizations such as the Forum Helveticum and the National Sports Federation, as well as with political groups in order to involve them in its campaign to strengthen the spirit of resistance. He considered that this was a case of interference in politics.

What exactly was politics anyway, and how did Guisan define it? The General kept repeating verbally that the army, particularly its leaders, had to stay away from politics. Moreover, he issued the order to all officers referred to by Huber above, in which he said that the structure of the State precluded the army from playing "any part in molding political opinions." The General explained:

> What applies to the army as a whole also applies to every individual

soldier who is part of it. Because the military must maintain a uniform will, it is not acceptable to express nor to propagate political principles in the army which contradict the principles of the Constitution or the decisions made and measures taken by the branches of the constitutional government. It is the duty of every soldier to take heed of this rule, no matter what his rank and no matter where he presents himself in his function as a soldier.[33]

This order, which banned "any verbal or written political publicity," contradicted to a certain extent the objectives of "Army and Home," a section within the army that the General had established. However, this apparent contradiction shows that General Guisan considered "politics" merely as activities carried out by political parties, and more especially activities that were unconstitutional or subversive. Patriotic activities that promoted the spirit of resistance in order to assert the existence of the State were not "political" but an indispensable, natural, matter-of-course obligation.

In a personal memorandum for the file in early 1940, Guisan described his view:

> For some time now a large number of officers have been asked to join various political movements that are being created everywhere in the country. Some of these movements may move in a direction which threatens to more or less undermine the discipline and the mutual trust in the army. Hence, they are apt to worry public opinion. However, these worries bring about discord and disorder, thereby posing a threat to national security. An officer should be fully aware of his civic duties; but precisely because he is an officer he must abstain from any activities or propaganda that would allow politics to enter the army. As a civilian, he should always keep his duties as a soldier in mind. The principle that applies to commanders of all ranks and which determines all their actions is their loyalty to the oath that they made.[34]

The General's order preventing officers from being politically active was initiated by Captain Paul Meyer, alias Wolf Schwertenbach, and was targeted primarily at the activities of career officers surrounding Wille and Däniker. Captain Meyer, an intelligence officer who had received a special mission from the General to keep an eye on agitators against the army command in and around Zürich, wrote some personal notes, which are reliable and make it possible to discover the genesis of the order. According to these notes, on August 28, 1941, Meyer advised the General in a confidential meeting that something had to be done about Colonel Däniker, who was supported by some prominent officers, because it was "dangerous to let things run their course without intervening." Meyer reported that he told the General that his "kindness and forbearance [were] interpreted as weaknesses. . . . Däniker's case exists because of [the General's] forbearance regarding the political activities of some officers. By failing to intervene immediately, one would bring about a division among the officers' corps. One day they would have to choose between Däniker and Guisan. [The General] would have to prevent that from happening by immediately issuing an order to the armed forces to forbid the officers—even those who are off duty—from being politically active. . . . The army would have to be purged. It should be nothing but the General's powerful instrument." Meyer continued his account by writing that Guisan liked his suggestion. As he described, "[The] General thinks about it and then says that he agrees with this procedure. He asks me if I could draft an order to the armed forces which would have to be published in the newspapers. I tell him that every word would have to be thought over, but I would do it at the shores of Lake Constance where it was quiet."[35]

Meyer subsequently told his friend Dr. Wiesendanger, the commander of the Zürich police department, about his suggestion. The latter liked the idea of the order to the armed forces. He agreed that something had to be done in support of the commander-in-chief because the former staff of the 3rd Army Corps was upset with the General after he had dissolved their unit. A short time later, Meyer and Wiesendanger drafted the order to the armed forces at Wolfsberg Castle. Meyer wrote, "We start working before dinner. We both pull our drafts out of our pockets, and after going back and forth several times the order to the armed forces is on paper. The following morning, we go over the document once again, then my wife types it. Wiesendanger remarks, 'A powerful order.' I add, 'Maybe an appropriate order.' Then I dictate the cover letter."[36] In this "personal and confidential" cover letter to the commander-in-chief, Meyer once again emphasized the need for the "order to the armed forces, which should be published in the press, to ban as soon as possible any political activities by soldiers in order to keep the army pure."[37] The General waited one month before he issued the order, which was in fact a warning rather than a formal ban, to all officers.

The way in which this order to the armed forces originated had no direct link with the activities of "Army and Home," but it demonstrates that political propaganda was a delicate subject for the General and that he once again had young officers whom he trusted to advise him and to a degree even guide him. Even after the war, the General pointed out that he had never become involved in politics nor stood in opposition to the Federal Council. He once annotated

a letter written by a close associate by saying, "The army did not make any politics, nor did the General! Hence, there is no such thing as the General's policy
nor any other policy than the F[ederal] C[ouncil]'s."[38]

In the emergency situation of a war that threatened the country's existence,
"Army and Home" regarded its own activities as legitimate and as a matter of
course. According to Colonel Frey, though, there was yet another reason for the
army to organize presentations and classes. In reaction to the criticism that
civilian authorities, even the Head of the Military Department on behalf of the
Cabinet, were voicing, Frey composed an extensive memo that he submitted to
the adjutant general. In this statement he wrote: "The workers who actively
participate in these classes now would quit as soon as the political authorities
would organize the events. The Social Democratic Party, which is the workers'
party, opposes the Federal Council, on which it is not represented. If civilian
bodies organized the classes, that party would consider the presentations as government propaganda and would not want to have anything to do with them."[39]
Frey added that therefore only the army could carry out such propaganda
because it was the only body that was accepted as being "completely neutral."

This argument articulated by Frey was precisely the reason why Guisan
vehemently opposed cutting back the activities of "Army and Home," or putting them under the control of civilian authorities. At the end of 1941, he
replied to Federal Councilor Kobelt:

> You consider that economic and political issues should not be dealt
> with in the classes and presentations organized by 'Army and Home.'
> As I told you several times before, I agree that there should be no room
> for 'politics' per se in the army. However, that is no reason not to cul-
> tivate the civic sense and spirit; it plays an important role in a curricu-
> lum that is supposed to inform the dependable public about the diffi-
> cult duties of the present times. [In fact, the public] in all parts of the
> country and from all social ranks craves to be informed about the
> major issues that affect our existence as a nation.[40]

Hausamann provided the main argument for keeping the propaganda
activities under the control of the army, writing to the General at the end of
1941, "By now 'Home' is the army command's most important and most effective weapon on the domestic policy level. That is why the Federal Council
would like to wrest it from the commander-in-chief at all costs. However, that
must be prevented under all circumstances, otherwise the commander-in-chief
would not have any means left to address the people."[41]

In a lecture to the army staff on January 10, 1942, in Interlaken, Federal

Councilor Kobelt pointed out that "for the army to make politics in the civilian sector" carried with it "certain risks," and in his judgment "the activities of
the 'Army and Home' section should involve the 'Army' more than the
'Home'."[42] However, ultimately Guisan succeeded in securing the army's control over the section. During a conversation with Federal Councilor von Steiger
by the fireplace at the "Cranz Villa" in Interlaken in early 1942, he brought up
the subject of the propaganda service, of which Barbey, the head of the personal staff, wrote, "The General repeated that he would relinquish neither 'Army'
nor 'Home.' Mr. von Steiger can no longer have any doubts about that issue."
Barbey said that he admired "the patience and the warmth with which the
General pleads his case, the new arguments that he finds, and his well-chosen
words. The credit goes to him for anticipating and avoiding until today any
decline in the morale of the troops."[43]

In January 1942, following additional talks, Guisan and Federal President
Etter came to an agreement that satisfied both parties. "Army and Home"
would continue to report to the army but "the major guidelines of the curricu-
lum, the topics of the presentations, the names of the speakers, and the names
of the participants [would have to] be communicated to the Head of the
[Interior] Department on a regular basis via the office of the Adjutant
General."[44] Barbey was relieved, and noted in his diary: "The General was very
pleased when he came back from Bern. He met with Federal President Etter,
the Head of the Interior Department, and insisted on his position regarding
'Army and Home,' which has been, and will remain, a section of the army."[45]
Alfred Ernst considers the fact that Guisan was able to assert himself after several rounds of tough negotiations a "significant act" and one of the General's
major achievements, explaining, "If he had given in at that time, 'Army and
Home' would hardly have been capable of overcoming the widespread mistrust
among the civilians, nor of keeping up the determination to resist."[46]

Ultimately, the Federal government was pleased with the work accomplished by "Army and Home." At the beginning of 1943, the Federal Council
informed the General that it was "pleased to note that unlike in the earlier days,
the activities of the 'Army and Home' section have not given rise to any complaints since being governed by the new rules."[47] In early 1943, even Federal
Councilor Pilet-Golaz began praising the head of "Army and Home" by writing to him that he appreciated the objective reporting done by the military.
National Councilor Markus Feldmann commented to the General, "This is
quite interesting if one recalls how vehemently Pilet had criticized Colonel
Oskar Frey during 1940–41." At that time he had suspected that the Head of
the Department of Foreign Affairs was "looking for new bases in the press."[48]

"Army and Home" and the Interior Department cooperated well until the end of the war; however, in 1943 tension rose between the head of the section, Colonel Frey, and his direct superior, Adjutant General Dollfus. The dispute resulted in Frey's dismissal from his post. He was replaced by Major Roland Ziegler. Frey complained that he had not been confronted with straight language, "which is unfortunately often the case in the army and is extremely damaging."[49] When Frey refused to apologize to the adjutant general for this reproach, which both Dollfus and Guisan considered unjustified and offensive, he was sentenced to five days of detention by the commander-in-chief. The General explained his decision to Frey, writing, "Because you insist on your point of view and refuse to apologize, I must take disciplinary action against you. I regret that I have to do that because I respect you and appreciate the work you have accomplished. I sentence you to five days of detention and charge the infantry section with executing the sentence."[50] The dismissal and punishment must have hit Colonel Frey hard, taking a personal toll. It is uncontested that as one of the standard-bearers of the spirit of resistance, this officer, who had a strong sense of honesty, made a great contribution as a unit commander as well as by serving as head of "Army and Home."[51]

"Army and Home" received financial support not only from the military but from civilian organizations. In 1941, Dr. Näf, Secretary of "Pro Helvetia," told a contact in the military that his foundation contributed an annual 250,000 francs to the army's activities on behalf of psychologically preparing the Swiss to defend their country.[52]

In sum, one may say that the "Army and Home" section was a dynamic enterprise in spreading the spirit of resistance throughout the country. Not least among its achievements, it allowed the General to increase the army's political weight. After the war, the section, whose interesting history has not yet been fully written, was dissolved; after a transition period of several years, the "Information Service for the Troops" replaced it.[53]

Some time before "Army and Home" went into action, and one month before the formation of the Officers' Alliance, the "Gotthard Alliance" was founded. Some of the subsequent conspirators of the Officers' Alliance, such as Alfred Ernst, Walter Allgöwer, Gerhart Schürch, and others, played a leading role in the initial stages of this civilian organization. Denis de Rougemont has been credited with the idea of a civilian body that would propagate the spirit of absolute resistance, independent of political parties. On June 6, 1940, at a time when the defeat of France already loomed, he told his friend Professor Theophil Spoerri from Zürich, after a lecture, "One should start a movement in the whole country to promote resistance at all costs, with the Gotthard as a symbol and as a great military asset."[54] Spoerri agreed that this was "a good idea," so the two writers started contacting friends and acquaintances, and on June 22, the day France's capitulation was announced, the first meeting of the "Gotthard Alliance" was held in Bern. No one among the participants "believed in the final victory of the Axis Powers, but they thought for sure that the war would last five to six years."[55]

De Rougemont was unable to attend the founding meeting because the General had placed him under house arrest. However, he used his "imposed vacation" to draft the manifesto of the Alliance.[56] This manifesto was published in the form of a full-page advertisement containing the Gotthard Alliance's agenda in 74 newspapers at the end of June. Its first point read: "We demand that every Swiss never cease to be ready to put up unconditional resistance. Those who ask if there are any prospects of successfully putting up resistance are traitors."[57] Hence, it appears that this last catchy phrase, which was later used during the Officers' Conspiracy and by the "Action for National Resistance," was most likely coined by Denis de Rougemont. When General Guisan announced the establishment of the Réduit at the briefing at the Rütli, de Rougemont enthusiastically noted in his diary: "Our entire defense strategy [will be] focused around the Gotthard! Our dream has come true!"[58]

The founding members of the Gotthard Alliance included Swiss Germans and Swiss French, Protestants and Catholics, unionists and entrepreneurs.[59] Its public appeal was signed by personalities such as Gottlieb Duttweiler, Gonzague de Reynold, Friedrich Traugott Wahlen, Arnold Muggli, Paul Niggli, and others. The founders did not want to start a party but rather a federal "Alliance" which stood above the parties. A new group of men was to take the lead in the fight against defeatism and for defending the country at all costs. De Rougemont explained that a "new man" did not necessarily need to be a young man but someone who was "clear-headed" and was able to take over the "rhythm of the new times, [as] man and his work come before profit."[60]

There was some personal connection between the Gotthard Alliance and the Officers' Conspiracy. In his diary, de Rougemont said that he considered the Officers' Conspiracy a secret offshoot of the Gotthard Alliance inside the army, and that Corporal Lindt was the liaison between the two. He mentioned, "A house in Bern with two entrances allows us to maintain discreet contact with the representatives of the Alliance in the army."[61]

De Rougemont's interpretation does not seem to be misguided, because at the end of June 1940, Walter Allgöwer, acting in the name of all the founding members, made an attempt to recruit Colonel Däniker as a military expert for the Gotthard Alliance. He explained that the organization, which was about to be established, was "a large and solid national movement" which would strive, among other things, to get "incompetent Federal Councilors and top officials to resign." Allgöwer wrote to Däniker: "One of [the movement's] main goals is to completely overhaul the army and reorganize the Federal Military Department. You are expected to play a major role and take over a significant post in this process."[62]

Alfred Ernst, who initially considered the Gotthard Alliance a suitable organization to turn things around in order to save Switzerland's existence, donated 50,000 francs, practically all he had, to the cause of the new Alliance. On July 22, the day after the founding convention of the Officers' Alliance in Lucerne, he negotiated a written agreement with the Gotthard Alliance regarding his donation. This agreement stated that the donation was made by "an anonymous person" on condition that the leadership of the Alliance make a formal commitment "never, not even for strategic purposes, to cooperate with, nor contact, a movement of which one or several of the following individuals are members: Wille, Oehler, Wechlin, Hofmann, Thoenen, Buehler, Sartorius, Henne, Tobler, Haas, as well as persons who are listed on the manifesto of the National Revival Movement."[63] The list on that manifesto included the names of the known leaders of the Front movement and of other right-wing extremists. The fact that Corps Commander Ulrich Wille was the first one mentioned in the agreement indicates that at that time he was considered the main opponent of the resistance movement.

Corporal Lindt, on behalf of Captain Ernst, conducted the negotiations with the Gotthard Alliance. The leadership of the Gotthard Alliance made the following commitment:

a) To support the cause of unconditional resistance;
b) To reject once and for all the idea of a total State;
c) To recognize federalism, the freedom of conscience, and the freedom of religion as unalterable principles of Switzerland's existence;
d) To have no contact whatsoever with the National Revival Movement of the Front groups nor with other movements of which advocates of the Front movement, Colonel Wille, or Mr. Haas are members.[64]

During the investigation of the Officers' Conspiracy, Ernst explained that he donated the money in the "interest of the Gotthard Alliance's victory" and in order to give it "a chance." He added, "I am not asking anything from [the Gotthard Alliance] in return; I am sympathetic toward its activities, and I hope that it will soon be inspired by a different military spirit; if not, I will forget about it."[65]

Ernst's donation was used to finance the billboards, flyers, and large newspaper advertisements of the Gotthard Alliance. As an example, in Zürich

300,000 flyers were distributed carrying the title "Stop looking over the fence, stop being mercenaries." The text said that the "time of political mobilization" had come.[66] In addition, at the end of July 1940, a large number of copies of the brochure written by de Rougemont entitled "What Is the Gotthard Alliance?" were published.[67]

Acting on behalf of the Officers' Alliance, on several occasions Ernst personally held talks with de Rougemont about possible cooperation with the new organization. However, as Ernst later explained, "I was hoping that the Gotthard Alliance would indirectly support our activities, but it turned out that the impact created by the foundation of the Gotthard Alliance and its public statement did not meet my expectations, in spite of the goodwill of the founders."[68] Even before he was arrested, Ernst wrote to Lieutenant-Colonel Werder, "I am not pleased with the activities of the Gotthard Alliance so far. They seem to think that they can chat and discuss in the old-fashioned way. It would be very important if we could place people among the leadership of the Alliance who have the character of a soldier and whom we trust."[69] He suggested that Captain Paul Schäfer, the adjutant of Divisional Commander Bircher and a member of the leadership of the Gotthard Alliance, be entrusted with reinforcing the military element within the organization.

The leadership of the Gotthard Alliance was in the hands of people with good intentions, but to the conspirators they appeared too hesitant and indecisive. They had virtually no political experience, making them largely ineffective on the public relations level. Ernst later commented about his disappointment, "We overestimated the Gotthard Alliance because we lacked political experience. . . . There was little use in cooperating with somewhat unrealistic idealists."[70] The uncovering of the Officers' Conspiracy soon put an end to the relations with the Gotthard Alliance. In a letter to this author, August R. Lindt categorically denied that the Officers' Conspiracy was a secret offshoot of the Gotthard Alliance as stated by de Rougemont.[71]

The Gotthard Alliance did not receive support from workers tied to the Social Democratic Party, even though by that time they fully supported General Guisan. The Social Democrats immediately distanced themselves from the Alliance because of a sense of mistrust, as it included members known to tend toward the political right, such as Eibel, Gasser and de Reynold, and it had connections with the reactionary "Alliance of the People Without Subsidies," the "Swiss National Patriotic Federation," and the "League of Canton Vaud."[72] The management of Switzerland's Social Democratic Party considered the new organization a political threat. Party President Hans Oprecht and Werner Stocker, a future Federal judge, feared that by appealing to the unions, the Gotthard Alliance might split up the party; National Councilor Paul Meierhans called the new organization a "political Salvation Army."[73] Ultimately, the party declared that those who were members of the Gotthard Alliance could not at the same time be members of the Social Democratic Party. Nevertheless, several union leaders viewed the Alliance in a positive manner, thus causing substantial tensions within the party.

The Gotthard Alliance became involved in the campaign preceding the election of two new Federal Councilors in December 1940. In newspaper advertisements and at public meetings, it praised Professor Wahlen and Colonel Du Pasquier, who were not members of Parliament, as "new men."[74] However, the two candidates, whom the General also favored, were not elected by Parliament.[75] This incident demonstrated that the new organization had very limited power. Moreover, it ran into difficulties because there were doubts about its real intentions. A special report, which was probably written by Bureau "Ha," stated:

> In practice, the leadership of the Gotthard Alliance has so far applied the principle not to admit any Jews or Freemasons as members, even though the movement's agenda does not include any statement on this subject. A difficult situation has been created because the Freemasons have threatened to declare war on the Gotthard Alliance if it does not give up this policy. In Geneva, the Gotthard Alliance cooperates closely with the corporative movement, which in turn has connections with Fascists from Geneva.[76]

It is thus understandable that Hans Hausamann, who was himself a Freemason, belonging to the "Concordia" Lodge of St. Gallen, and his friends distanced themselves from the Gotthard Alliance. This in turn affected General Guisan's relationship with the organization.

In the winter of 1940–41, when it was headed by Theophil Spoerri, the Gotthard Alliance had about 8,000 members.[77] Its contribution to keeping the spirit of resistance alive must not be underestimated. However, as soon as the immediate threat of an invasion disappeared, it began to lose importance. It subsequently took an active part in promoting the government's emergency cultivation program, tried to mediate between capitalists and workers, and after the war fought for the establishment of Social Security. The Gotthard Alliance was formally dissolved in 1969.

Another organization founded by members of the failed Officers' Conspiracy was the "Swiss Federal Society." Its initiator, Gerhart Schürch, and his associates wanted to become active in public with the army command's approval. In the fall of 1940, Alfred Ernst told his superior, Colonel Masson, that he intended to join an "association of friends [which] supports the cause of unconditional resistance and the idea of the ancient Swiss Federal State without making party politics." He explained that this was a "perfectly legal association whose activities have absolutely nothing to do with the army," and added that it would carry out its activities in public and keep the General informed.[78] Masson did not object to Ernst's membership in this new organization.[79]

The Swiss Federal Society was officially founded on January 12, 1941. In its statutes it stipulated, "The Swiss Federal Society aims to gather the best people in the country in order to defend and apply once again on a political level Switzerland's federal principles."[80] Those who became members accepted to be "unconditionally ready to make sacrifices and endure hardship [as well as to] be glad to take on responsibility, which belongs to those who believe in the validity of Switzerland's federal principles and fight for their application even during emergency situations."[81]

One month later, the three former members of the Officers' Alliance—Schürch, Ernst, and Allgöwer—sent the General a copy of the statutes and informed him of the founding of their new association, explaining that they insisted on "telling [him] from the beginning about [their] activities" even though this was "a strictly civilian matter." They continued by stating, "We want to strengthen the determination to put up unconditional resistance against any attack and fight against defeatism everywhere. . . . Each one of us wants to be a full soldier in the army but also a full citizen in the State."[82]

The Society recruited a number of well-known personalities from northern and eastern Switzerland as members. The directory of the local chapter of Zürich had 23 names, including University Professors Hans Barth, Donald Brinkmann, Karl Schmid, and Richard Zürcher, as well as editors and writers such as Erwin Jaeckle, Max Rychner, and Viktor Jent (Winterthur).[83] Other members included Peter Dürrenmatt, Hans von Greyerz, Eric Mettler, and Mayr von Baldegg.[84] The group published hectographed booklets written by various members to promote its ideas.[85] However, the organization hardly made a substantial impact in the country. Karl Schmid, one of its members, commented that it resembled "something between a romantic castle and an arsenal."[86] It was formally dissolved in 1982.[87]

Unlike the Swiss Federal Society and the Gotthard Alliance, which conducted their activities in public to strengthen the spirit of resistance, the "Action for National Resistance" (ANR) operated as an underground organization. Ernst explained that there was no doubt that this body was founded as a result of the failed Officers' Conspiracy, adding, "In order to camouflage [this

fact], I did not become an official member of the 'ANR,' but we worked closely together."[88]

The idea to establish this secret civilian organization, which launched its
activities through local cells, was put forward by Hans Hausamann,[89] who
wrote to Federal Councilor Kobelt, "I had the opportunity to observe the game
between the different forces. I noticed that after Germany's victories influential
young and old conservative members of parliament suddenly discovered that
there was in fact no big gap between the conservative Catholic and the totalitarian fascist views of the state. This game behind the scenes was one of the reasons that prompted me to found the 'Action for National Resistance'."[90] In later
years, Hausamann continued to place great importance on the fact that he was
the founding father of the ANR, but not of the Officers' Conspiracy, and that
Feldmann and Gafner from Bern, Oprecht from Zürich, and Oeri from Basel
"acted as its godfathers."[91]

The minutes of an examination of Corporal Lindt conducted by the investigating judge a few days after the fact provide a detailed account of the circumstances surrounding the founding of the "Action for National Resistance."
According to Lindt's statement, the first meeting took place on September 1,
1940, at the restaurant of the Zürich train station. It was attended by eight
individuals, including Lindt, Captains Hausamann and Allgöwer, National
Councilors Dr. Oprecht from Zürich, Dr. Weber from Bern, and Bringolf from
Schaffhausen, Cantonal government member Nägeli from Zürich, and Dr.
Ernst von Schenck, a journalist from Basel. These people "agreed that it was
necessary to recruit individuals from all segments of the population and from
all parties who are willing to actively participate in strengthening the national
resistance."[92] They drafted an "oath" and decided to approach additional influential personalities with whom they planned to hold a second meeting one
week later.

On Saturday, September 7, about 25 individuals met in Zürich, including,
among others, Professors Karl Barth from Basel and André Oltramare from
Geneva, as well as a Ms. Staehelin from St. Gallen. Social Democratic National
Councilor Hans Oprecht opened the meeting. Hausamann spoke of
Switzerland's military and political situation and the need to fight with all
means against defeatism. At this meeting, the founding convention of the
ANR, a five-member action committee was appointed that included Oprecht,
Oltramare, von Schenck, Hausamann, and Lindt.[93]

Hausamann had given Colonel Werner Müller, Chief Security Officer of
the Armed Forces, confidential information about the upcoming meetings. He
explained:

I told Colonel Müller that I wanted to do things the right way and inform him about my plan. I also said that I would ask him to intervene on my behalf in due course in order for me to be able to personally inform the General. The General should be informed only once the 'Action' was ready to make an impact. Until then the General's time should not be wasted. I said that once we were ready, I would refer to the General's authorization of several weeks ago to address him personally and inform him about any subject matter.[94]

Chief of the General Staff Huber was also informed about Hausamann's new endeavor. At the end of September he reported to the General about it, writing that he had in no way influenced Hausamann nor approved the initiative. Huber stated that during an official meeting, Hausamann had approached him and "explained that he was in the process of convincing persons of different political backgrounds that it was crucial to unite the Swiss behind the cause of unconditional resistance. He said that the final goal was to make the General's difficult task easier and to make it possible for him to have the people united behind him during difficult times."[95] Huber added that he had authorized Hausamann to inform the General in writing about the group.

Hausamann provided information about the goal of the newly founded organization in a detailed report that the General undoubtedly saw, since his personal staff had a copy of it. He explained that the Action would undertake to rekindle and revive fighting spirit and the determination to resist to establish "the necessary favorable political and mental conditions for the army to do its job." "Therefore, the ANR," he added, "will become the most important instrument of our national defense, even though it is deliberately placed outside the army and is supported by Swiss citizens."[96] Hausamann said that unlike other organizations, the ANR would not present itself to the public with full-page advertisements. Instead, "The moving forces behind the Action [would] act and make publicity within their own spheres of influence, using all their efforts, until the front of resistance [was] once again completely closed." He continued:

That way the network will gradually spread all over Switzerland until the entire population has been reached. Within a short period of time, every single village shall have a resistance cell. Those who have committed themselves [to our cause] will not tire of intervening in discussions by defeatists, no matter where this may be, in parliament, in political meetings, at factories, in the family, at the restaurant. The driving forces shall not give up until their fellow citizens are convinced and join their cause. Through this kind of work the cells will grow.[97]

Hence, the General learned of the new resistance organization no later than three weeks after its founding. It was clear that it would have a connection with the army but that this connection had to remain as invisible as possible. Its initiator, Hausamann, resigned from the ANR but continued to keep a close eye on it. As he explained to the General, "I receded into the background as early as the late fall of 1940, once the Action's existence was secured, so no one would have any argument to attack it."[98] As the liaison, Lindt was formally discharged from the military. The chief security officer of the armed forces wrote to Guisan: "If the General agrees, I will discharge this man [Lindt] because he intends to continue his activities for the 'ANR,' which are not wanted in the military."[99]

After the founding of the ANR, only one additional meeting was held, which took place in Olten in the early fall of 1940. It had been suggested by Albert Oeri and was attended by about sixty individuals. No minutes were kept.[100] It appointed a working committee, which included Hans Oprecht, August R. Lindt, and Ernst von Schenck.[101] Afterward, these three men conducted the operations of the Action from the underground; no other meetings were held. Hausamann did not take part in the meeting in Olten, but others carried on the torch that he had lit. Schenck commented, "Within a short time, he taught us in his strict and unsparing manner that the projected union had to be accomplished right away."[102] Hausamann personally paid Lindt's salary as a secret functionary of the ANR; Lindt had to sign the receipts using a cover name.[103] It is likely that von Schenck was paid in a similar fashion.

The "Action for National Resistance" recruited new members according to the snowball system. Their party affiliation or religion was irrelevant; what mattered was their performance and the example they set. Even top magistrates or officers were admitted only if they had given proof, through their attitude and their public and private activities, that for them "to live as a Swiss or not live at all" was not just an empty phrase but the ultimate principle. Hausamann wrote: "For those who adhere to the 'ANR' the commitment toward the Swiss Confederation is above any other ties they have. As soon as they see that Switzerland's existence is threatened they do not show any further consideration for their family, party, or business."[104] Those who appeared to be trustworthy to join the cause were invited to sign an "oath" that was considered a declaration of membership. The oath, drafted in a common effort by Oprecht, Bringolf, Lindt, and von Schenck, read:

> The new Alliance of the Swiss fights for the liberty, honor, and independence of the Swiss Confederation, for individual freedom and the freedom of conscience, for the freedom of the federalist community,

for the rule of the people, for personal responsibility, for securing jobs and food for every Swiss, and against any defeatist, wherever he may be. I am determined and ready, and I vow, to sacrifice everything and everyone in order to fight for these objectives.[105]

Lindt kept the signed oaths for some time before forwarding them to Hausamann, who locked them up "in one of his safes as a symbol of the sense of unity."[106] Werner Rings reported that he saw "several hundred" of these oaths while Hausamann was still alive.[107] However, they are now missing, so they were probably destroyed. None were found at the Federal Archives in Bern nor at the Archives for Contemporary History in Zürich where Hausamann's unpublished papers are kept. Lindt kept a mailing list of the individuals who used to receive the ANR's weekly newsletter "Information der Woche." Since generally only those who had signed the oath received the information bulletin, the mailing list can be considered the equivalent of a list of members.[108]

Until the time the mailing list for the newsletter was discovered, the "Action for National Resistance" was believed to have had between 50 and 800 members.[109] Lindt's list includes 581 names from 20 cantons. This was probably the membership status toward the end of the war, as a note on the inside of the file folder containing the list said, "October 1, 1941: 368 [members]."[110] The largest contingent came from the cantons of Bern (162 members), Zürich (136), and the two semi-cantons of Basel (117). Eight percent (47 members) were women, most of whom were university graduates. A strikingly large number of members were clergymen, including several Catholic priests, as well as the pastors of the cathedrals of Zürich (Rev. Farner), Bern (Rev. Tenger), and Basel (Rev. Thurneisen). Other theologians included Prof. Karl Barth and, surprisingly, Leonhard Ragaz, a social theologian who was otherwise known to be a fervent pacifist. Moreover, the list included several conservative personalities, including National Councilors Albert Oeri, Markus Feldmann, and Max Gafner, historians Karl Meyer, Adolf Gasser, and Georg Thürer, editors Hermann Böschenstein, Reto Caratsch, and Max Ras, as well as virtually the entire leadership of the Social Democratic Party, including National Councilors Walther Bringolf, Hans Oprecht, Ernst Nobs, Emil Klöti, Willy Spühler, Max Weber, Arthur Schmid, Paul Meierhans, and Karl Dellberg. Four of the above-mentioned National Councilors, Feldmann, Nobs, Spühler, and Weber, were later elected as Federal Councilors. Author Jakob Bührer also signed on. A former anti-militarist, he stated that he was "happy to be able to join the local civil defense unit as a volunteer" after France's collapse.[111] One of the 17 Swiss French who became members of the ANR was Oscar L. Forel from Prangins.

Some outsiders considered it remarkable, if not incomprehensible, that left-wing politicians who had rejected the military and challenged the army at every available opportunity were now turning into staunch resistance fighters. Military Attorney General Trüssel wrote to the General:

> The leadership of the 'ANR' is in the hands of personalities who were among the most fervent anti-militarists before the war and who sabotaged the credit requests for the military. I would like to mention National Councilor Weber, who was sentenced by the court of the 3rd Division because he dodged his military service for political reasons, and Mayor Bringolf of Schaffhausen. . . . Before the war, many of these people held political views similar to that of Léon Blum in France. If their proposals had been successful, Switzerland would now have an army that would not be capable of putting up effective resistance.[112]

Others who were just as adamant proponents of the spirit of resistance, such as editors Willy Bretscher and Ernst Schürch, as well as Professors Edgar Bonjour and Jean Rudolf von Salis, were not included on the list of ANR members. Many thousands of other people who were ready to sacrifice their lives to fight for their country did not have the opportunity to sign an oath because through some circumstance they had not been contacted. It would be unfair to consider the members of the ANR as the only or the most fearless civilian freedom fighters, as some have assumed.

One of the few high-ranking officers of the general staff who became a member of the ANR was Colonel Oskar Frey from Schaffhausen, the head of the "Army and Home" section. Hausamann explained that "Army and Home" became "the willing instrument for the ANR to disseminate the information that it intended to spread."[113]

The ANR's activities brought positive results to the spirit of resistance and to public opinion regarding the General. In the winter of 1940–41, in a special report that dealt, among other things, with the ANR's activities and which was undoubtedly forwarded to Guisan, Hausamann wrote, "The General must notice that strong forces are at work which unite the people behind him. A large part of the credit for this activity goes to the 'Action.' The things that the ANR has accomplished so far in this respect alone justify its existence."[114]

The ANR also remained in "continuous contact" with the "Gotthard Alliance."[115] The fact that some individuals were members of two or all three organizations gave rise to a multi-layered network that had an unusual impact. In order to be able to establish contact in an emergency situation, Hausamann set up a radio network consisting of "20 cigar box-size stations generated by storage batteries and equipped with wire antennas; they were kept in the homes of trustworthy members who lived outside the Réduit."[116]

Ernst von Schenck from Basel edited the ANR's regularly published newsletter. It was typewritten, copied, and sent to all ANR members. The newsletter was the only link between them. It looked improvised but included top-secret, up-to-date information provided by Hausamann, which he received in part through his work as an intelligence officer. Lindt recounted that ANR members regularly met with members of Army Intelligence and of the "Press and Radio" section.[117]

Because the newsletter was sent out in closed envelopes, it was not considered a publication and hence was not subject to censorship.[118] It was not possible to subscribe to the newsletter; it was mailed to the members free of charge on the condition that they did not pass it on to anyone else. They were allowed to quote from it only verbally, not in writing. In one of his special reports, Hausamann wrote that the weekly bulletin was begun "to keep the moving forces of the 'Action for National Resistance' abreast of important events in Switzerland on which the press is not allowed to report for political reasons. The [newsletter] also provides information about the things written by the foreign press about Switzerland."[119]

The ANR newsletter was financed through private donations. It was said that Zürich's Mayor Dr. Emil Klöti provided financial assistance through the "Reptile Fund."[120] In the fall of 1940, Zürich's City Council approved its chairman's request to support the "Action for National Resistance" with 2,000 francs. One year later, it granted another 5,000 francs, and in 1942 once again 5,000 francs to the organization, bringing the total of its donation to 12,000 francs. According to the minutes, the City Council supported the ANR because it made "a useful contribution above the party level to mentally prepare the country to defend itself. Above all, its [newsletter] contains useful information that helps to mentally prepare the country's defense."[121] The newsletter was copied and mailed from the office of the Federation of Public Service Personnel, which was headed by Hans Oprecht.[122]

Information about some of the activities of the "Action for National Resistance" leaked to the outside, and it was suspected that the ANR might have some unofficial ties with the army. Some people were troubled by its existence. As early as December 1940, Corps Commander Labhart told the General of his reservations about the organization, which he felt was infiltrated by leftists, writing: "After reading the enclosed [ANR newsletter], the impression prevails that this newly created body follows tendencies that will not always be in line with our domestic and foreign policies; hence, the harmless declaration . . . appears to be nothing but a cover. Furthermore, I consider that the way in which they deal with the events abroad, particularly those in Germany, is dangerous and is not compatible with our neutrality policy." The Commander of the 4th Army Corps pointed out that the censorship authorities would probably not accept the ANR newsletter because this type of publication did not respect the rules applicable to the press. Moreover, he speculated that it was not improbable that "Capt. Hausamann intended to continue his former one-sided activities through this channel via National Councilor Dr. Oprecht."[123]

One month later, General Guisan replied to Labhart that he had investigated the matter and had come to the following conclusion:

> Men of all political camps, members of Parliament from all parties, representatives of both nationally recognized Churches have joined the 'Action for National Resistance.' It is therefore hardly appropriate to call it an undercover organization of the leftists. The information, which I have received from several sources, makes it possible to establish that at the present time there is no reason to forbid officers of the army to join this Action. It goes without saying, though, that no office of the army nor the intelligence service shall be allowed to cooperate with this Action.[124]

This passage indicates that once again not all the cards were placed upon the table. The General actually went so far as to reassure Labhart, "The criticism voiced by you against Capt. Hausamann has not been substantiated through the investigation. He is not on close terms with the [ANR newsletter]." He added that since it was established that "the army [could] in no way be associated with the 'ANR' nor with [its newsletter]," the army command had no possibility of intervening. It would be "the responsibility of the civilian authorities to have the law respected if those two institutions were not in line with the interests of the country."[125]

Hausamann managed to camouflage his ongoing contacts with the ANR and to deny his involvement in its newsletter. In truth, however, he personally wrote the draft of the report that his superior Masson submitted to Guisan in response to the General's internal investigation. In this draft, he (Hausamann) claimed, "Capt. Hausamann was ignorant of the existence of the [ANR newsletter] until he received a copy of it in the mail."[126] This sentence was used verbatim in the letter to the General signed by Masson.[127] To protect the people who were behind the newsletter as well as to create a false trail, it was said that the editor of the newsletter had been identified as Karl Keller, a journalist living at Marignanostrasse 22 in Basel, who was said to be a conservative driving force of the ANR.[128] Whenever it seemed necessary, one did not hesitate at all to use ploys.

A commitment to total defense was stressed by the ANR not only on the military level but on the psychological level to increase the chances of preserving Switzerland's political uniqueness. Alfred Ernst considered that the activities of the "Action for National Resistance" were "probably one of the decisive factors that influenced the destiny of our country. Without them, many things would have turned out differently."[129] Among the activities that contributed to making an impact was a brochure expressing the ANR's ideas. Written by Karl Barth, it was entitled "In the Name of Almighty God." History Professor Edgar Bonjour considered it "a real relief during the tensions of the year 1943"; however, it was banned from being distributed in public by the press monitoring office, of which Bonjour was himself a member.[130] This example indicates the extent to which some people were torn between their official duties and their personal inclinations during the complicated times of the Second World War.

Von Schenck made a strong statement about the facts of the matter, writing that it was "good to know that the resistance movement of 1940 did not in the first place grow out of the patriotism of the bourgeoisie, which had become insecure and was eager to become perverted to fascism in order to preserve its status. Instead, it was directed in a decisive manner by antifascists who were very eagerly discredited as hysterics once the battle was won in order to have a not very uplifting restoration generally accepted."[131]

The "Action for National Resistance" was the army's, and hence the General's, foremost discreet instrument, used effectively not only to consolidate the spirit of resistance but also in internal disputes against Pilet-Golaz, against Wille, and against Däniker. Hans Hausamann was the man who kept an overview of the many and diverse connections, pulling the strings extremely skillfully, and for the most part successfully in the background. His untiring efforts substantially helped shape the national spirit of resistance supported by General Guisan.[132]

Attempts to Arrange a Special Mission to Berlin

THE GENERAL'S PUBLIC EFFORTS IN 1940–41 to rekindle fighting spirit and to strengthen Switzerland's determination to put up resolute resistance contrasted somewhat puzzlingly with his simultaneous secret attempts to arrange a special mission to meet with Hitler in Berlin. In March 1939, Federal Councilor Hermann Obrecht had proudly declared, "The Swiss shall not go on pilgrimages to foreign countries." Nevertheless, in the summer of 1940, about three weeks after the briefing at the Rütli Meadow, Guisan recommended that the Federal government take a step toward appeasing the intimidating Third Reich in order to improve relations with it.

General Guisan initially submitted his proposal on August 14, 1940, in a detailed letter to Federal Councilor Minger, the Head of the Military Department. On November 9, he reiterated his suggestion in a letter to Federal President Pilet-Golaz. Bonjour first published the full texts of the two confidential documents in his book on the history of Swiss neutrality.[1] People in French-speaking Switzerland, especially in Guisan's home canton of Vaud, were shocked at the revelation of the General's totally unexpected faux pas, and were "distressed and repulsed" about its being made public.[2] Since then, historians Georg Kreis and Oscar Gauye have analyzed the two letters' origin as well as the political context of 1940 and 1941 in which they should be viewed.[3]

Guisan began his letter to Minger by outlining the new political situation, which had changed as a result of the victory of the Axis Powers in the West and by Germany's hegemony on the European continent. He argued that in this new situation "outdated [diplomatic] methods" should be abandoned in favor of new ones. The way the incidents between German and Swiss military aircraft were handled earlier in the year proved that Switzerland's envoy in Berlin was incapable of maintaining contacts with the leading officials of the Reich; instead, he only had access to secondary offices. Guisan claimed that this situation was "very troublesome" at the least, adding that in view of these facts, a special mission should be considered in order to initiate a broad exchange of opinions on political, cultural, social, and tourism issues.[4]

The General proposed Professor Carl J. Burckhardt as the "new man" who should be sent on a mission to Berlin on behalf of the Swiss government. He explained that the former High Commissioner of the League of Nations in Danzig was personally acquainted with Hitler as well as with Reichsmarshal Göring and Permanent Secretary von Weizsäcker. Hence, "Mr. Burckhardt would be perfectly qualified to try appeasing [Germany] and establish some cooperation [between the two countries]."[5] It is remarkable that in this letter General Guisan did not refrain from using terms such as "appeasement," "accommodation," and "cooperation." In order to cover up the mission, "at least in the beginning," he suggested camouflaging it as a Red Cross initiative, which would be easy to do because Burckhardt was a member of the International Committee of the Red Cross.

It is interesting to note that Corps Commander Wille also advocated sending a mission headed by Burckhardt to Berlin. The Federal Council had already discussed Wille's idea before the General submitted his letter of August 14 to Minger. In a letter to Federal President Pilet-Golaz dated August 12, 1940, Wille referred to two conversations held on July 29 and August 5 during which they had discussed the possibility of the Federal Council sending Prof. Burckhardt to ascertain Germany's plans. Wille wrote that Burckhardt would probably be "the most suitable personality to get in touch with Berlin." However, he argued:

> The most important thing is that the mission actually takes place; it should under no circumstances be delayed. I recommend that for the visits at Minister Funk's and at Mr. Schacht's he be accompanied by General Director Jöhr, who enjoys a high reputation in Berlin because of his impartiality and his expertise. Furthermore, I recommend sending a third person who can visit party leaders such as Minister Hess and Göring. From what I know about these gentlemen, the Chancellor listens to them. Perhaps Dr. Stegemann or Colonel Däniker could be that third person.[6]

Hence, Wille's idea was to send a mixed delegation to Berlin consisting of personalities with political, economic, and military backgrounds.

Around the same time, Colonel Däniker also strongly suggested sending a mixed delegation of "officers, economists, industrialists, journalists, etc." to Germany. He wrote to Wille, "I consider this matter to be of such extraordinary importance because I am convinced that something must be done. Everything you hear boils down to the same idea: it is about time to do something that indicates we are no longer inclined to fly around Europe as 'the odd one out'."[7]

Member of the Officers' Alliance found out that the Federal Council as well as the army staff were discussing the possibility of organizing a special mission to Berlin. On July 28, 1940, National Councilor Markus Feldmann was informed by Captain Hausamann that the latter had received reliable information that the Federal Council was examining whether "to send a delegation to Berlin whose mission would be to take note of Germany's wishes." Hausamann asked Feldmann "to verify this information and to tell Federal Councilor Minger that based on the current mood in the army this delegation will be shot before it can cross the border into Germany."[8]

On the same day, two other officers of the army staff, Colonel Plancherel, Head of the Press and Radio Section, and his subordinate, First Lieutenant Ernst, told Feldmann that efforts were being undertaken to enter into contact with the Germans by sending Prof. Burckhardt "on an official Red Cross mission to Berlin and at the same time giving him a political mission to clear up [Switzerland's] relations with Germany." Feldmann asked himself whether this mission was initiated by the army command or the Federal Council, or "if this was a mission like that of [former Czechoslovakian President] Hácha." The two officers "did not fail to indicate that they condemned this move; they said it completely misjudged the real situation." Ernst went so far as to state, "This move verged on high treason."[9]

A little later, in a letter to Chief of Intelligence Masson, Captain Waibel criticized the tendency to send "traveling salesmen" on political missions. Even German personalities who were well-disposed toward Switzerland were eyeing them with suspicion because they would make the country appear in a distorted light by making it look as though Switzerland was "willing to capitulate."[10]

There are no documents at the Federal Archives that indicate whether the political authorities reacted either in writing or verbally to the General's idea. It is possible that his letter was not forwarded to the Cabinet as a whole. In view of the close friendship between Guisan and Minger, it cannot be excluded that the suggestion was dealt with in a private conversation and that Minger succeeded in momentarily talking his friend out of pursuing the idea. Yet the General insisted, writing a letter to Pilet-Golaz, the Head of the Department of Foreign Affairs, on November 9 in which he recommended sending Burckhardt on a special mission to Berlin. Guisan referred to an alarming report by Ambassador Frölicher, who suggested sending former Federal Councilor Schulthess on a mission to intensify contacts with the Reich and ease tensions between the two countries. The General wrote that he would be pleased if Schulthess was entrusted with this mission, but that Burckhardt was another Swiss personality who would be able to take advantage of his connections with the German leadership. He added that he remembered that the Federal President also respected Burckhardt and therefore probably wanted to use his services during more critical times; but he wondered if these critical times had not arrived. Guisan suggested, "Among the various issues that could be dealt with by Mr. Burckhardt are exchanges in the areas of culture, art, and tourism. Moreover, would Mr. Burckhardt not be particularly qualified to try appeasing [Germany] and establish some cooperation in matters of the press, in which our two countries have been ceaselessly and often acrimoniously battling each other since the beginning of the war?"[11]

Pilet-Golaz, who on several occasions fended off critics claiming that his foreign policy was too accommodating toward Germany, ignored the General's suggestion. In the summer of 1943, during a conversation with National Councilor Feldmann, he insisted, "In the summer and fall of 1940, [he] had shrugged off repeated attempts by high-ranking Swiss personalities who urged him to send a delegation on a mission to Berlin, because he considered that if you gave the Germans an inch they would take a mile."[12] In the briefing he gave his successor, Federal Councilor Petitpierre, about the threats to which Switzerland was subject, Pilet-Golaz once again insisted that he had objected to any suggestion to "go on pilgrimages" to foreign countries. He added that he had rejected a proposal by the military to send an emissary to Mussolini, explaining, "During a 'crisis,' some did not hesitate to suggest sending a secret emissary to the Duce without the Federal Council's knowledge in order to 'plead our case' . . . I refused; this would have been like putting a finger between the jaws of the Axis, which would have snatched it and eaten us up."[13]

In contrast with these reassurances, M. L. Keller, a leader of the Front movement, reported Pilet-Golaz telling him during a meeting on September 10, 1940 "that he was fully aware of the need to get in touch with Germany and that he had someone very suitable in mind to accomplish this mission. However, certain incidents in connection with a speech prevented him from carrying out his plan. He said that Germany was ready to receive a special envoy."[14] Pilet-Golaz undoubtedly referred here to the General's speech at the Rütli.

Because the Federal Council failed to react to his suggestion, in early 1941 Guisan undertook a new attempt to have Burckhardt sent on a special mission.

He was prompted to do so by a letter from Adjutant General Dollfus, who informed the General about news he had received from his fellow partisan, National Councilor Heinrich Walther from Lucerne. Walther had written:

> In Berlin, the atmosphere toward Switzerland has virtually reached boiling-point. I recently received news directly from the government that makes me fear the worst. Hitler has for the first time talked bitterly about Switzerland, calling it a 'festering boil'. . . . Our Ambassador in Berlin, Dr. Frölicher, is liked well enough but he carries no 'weight,' nor is he able to create any weight for himself. The situation would change instantly if Dr. Burckhardt replaced Mr. Frölicher. This would be the best and most effective move one could make toward Germany. Dr. Burckhardt enjoys a very good reputation there and is trusted. Even Hitler would lend him an ear.[15]

The General sent a copy of this letter to Federal Councilor Kobelt, Minger's successor,[16] but the new Head of the Military Department did not react either.

In May 1941, the General made a last attempt to prompt a special mission to Berlin, going to see Federal President Wetter to speak to him in person about his suggestion. In the notes he prepared for the meeting on May 3, 1941, Guisan wrote that the moment had come to send Burckhardt to Berlin "to be able to hold discussions" because the time had come to ease tensions.[17] Shortly after, Guisan forwarded reports to the Federal President about aggressive language used by Reich Governor Sauckel while addressing Germans who lived in Switzerland. Hence, he suggested that Switzerland demand the same right in order to have Switzerland's voice heard in lectures in Germany. He asked, "Would Professor C. J. Burckhardt, whom I had recommended to the Federal Council on several occasions last year, not still be a suitable candidate?"[18] Wetter replied that in case a mission was to be arranged, Burckhardt would indeed be a suitable candidate, but he said that he did not think his role should consist of holding lectures, adding, "Such lectures would probably not be requested. However, Prof. Burckhardt might render great services to us in a different way through his connections."[19]

It is striking how persistently Guisan pursued the idea of sending a special mission to Berlin. In retrospect, one must say that it is fortunate this questionable undertaking was not carried out as it would have had damaging consequences, including to the General's reputation. One wonders what could have prompted the General—the embodiment of the spirit of resistance in the public eye—to suggest such a far-reaching step toward appeasement? Who might

have been behind this plan, influencing the commander-in-chief? Bonjour
speculated that the idea came "from an outside source, probably Colonel
Masson"; Kreis tended to agree with this opinion.[20] However, Gauye disagreed,
providing compelling evidence that Bernard Barbey, the chief of the General's
personal staff, played the leading role in this endeavor and drafted the relevant
correspondence.[21] Historian Daniel Bourgeois subsequently commented that
the plan contained "certain elements of Proto-Vichy France" and criticized
Bonjour for minimizing the significance of the letters, as they advocated going
on a "pilgrimage" to Hitler.[22]

The fact that the General repeatedly insisted on carrying out the plan can
be taken as proof that he considered it of great importance and fully identified
with it, even if someone else originally put it forward. It is unlikely that this was
a mere slip. The General made a carefully considered attempt to get on better
terms with the Third Reich in order to safeguard Switzerland's existence. Gauye
concluded that the mission aimed to open Switzerland up to the German
Reich.[23] However, the idea of a special mission can hardly be interpreted as a
manifestation of discouragement and defeatism on Guisan's part. On the contrary, he cunningly decided to take one step toward appeasement while continuing to be prepared to put up resistance.

This policy resembled that of Pilet-Golaz, the Federal President of 1940,
who was criticized on several occasions because of it. However, Guisan's idea
was to use foreign policy for dissuasive purposes. In his opinion, Switzerland's
foreign policy should be more active, dynamic, and aggressive than it had been.
Unlike Pilet-Golaz, Guisan wanted to actively use diplomatic channels to promote Switzerland's uniqueness and increase understanding of its neutrality during the war. For that purpose, he suggested that Federal President Wetter also
send special emissaries to London and Washington, which would have counterbalanced to a certain extent a special mission to Germany. In a report by the
personal staff, Barbey wrote, "In a personal and confidential letter dated June
27 [1941], the General presented to the Federal President suggestions that
would tend to increase the weight and profile of our representation in foreign
countries. Missions and conferences [could be organized] with renowned personalities who are well respected, such as Minister Sulzer in America and
Professor C. J. Burckhardt in Germany."[24] However, the General did not manage to convince Federal Councilors Wetter and Kobelt to initiate a more active
foreign policy. Wetter replied that Switzerland's ambassador in Washington,
Minister Bruggmann, who was married to one of the sisters of the Vice
President of the United States, would certainly not fail to inform the President
"about Switzerland's real situation."[25] Federal Councilor Kobelt, to whom the
General sent a copy of the letter, did not respond.

By suggesting strengthening relations with England and the United States as well, the General once again became involved in foreign policy issues. It is striking, though, that in this instance he did not address the proposal to Foreign Minister Pilet-Golaz but went behind his back to submit it to two of his colleagues in the Cabinet.

Guisan's suggestion to encourage closer ties with the leadership of Germany through a special mission must probably also be seen in an additional context. In the summer of 1940, following the successful campaign in France, Berlin refused to invite an official mission of Swiss officers to Germany. Switzerland's Military Attaché in Berlin wrote, "I was verbally informed that the matter was discussed directly with the Führer. He was against it, giving as reasons Switzerland's political position and attitude as well as General Guisan's speech, by which he meant the address at the Rütli."[26] Even though this reply was not an official rejection because no official request had been made, it unambiguously showed the bad light in which Switzerland's army was seen.

In contrast with this negative response, Germany welcomed a delegation of officers from Sweden, which was also a neutral country, for a visit to the battlefields in France. Sweden made more extensive concessions to the Third Reich than Switzerland during World War II, even though it was less exposed from a strategic point of view.[27]

In the late summer of 1940, the General considered the possibility of sending an air force mission to Germany. Colonels Isler, Magron, and Wuhrmann were to exchange experiences with Berlin regarding air combat, study the possibility of purchasing some "Fieseler Storch" aircraft, and raise the issue of accrediting an air force attaché in the German capital. On the General's orders, Colonel Logoz discussed the idea with Federal President Pilet-Golaz, arguing that following Germany's criticism that Switzerland was doing too little to prevent British aircraft from violating its air space, the mission would provide an opportunity "to show our willingness to improve our technical skills and to establish relations in view of future cooperation."[28] However, preliminary inquiries in Germany indicated that Swiss air force officers were not welcome there.

It seems that during the meeting with Logoz, Pilet-Golaz advocated using night fighters to stop English bombers from flying across Swiss territory. However, after consulting with Air Force Commander Bandi, the General strictly refused to carry out nighttime operations, considering them too difficult and risky. He stated, "I will take action only upon formal written orders by the Federal Council. . . . It is easy for these gentlemen to talk about this issue, sitting in their comfortable chairs." He said he would tell Divisional Commander Bandi to submit the relevant technical data, "which he completely ignores," to the Foreign Minister.[29]

As early as the beginning of August 1940, the General may have heard rumors that during their advance in France, the Germans had seized documents relating to possible Swiss military cooperation with France, the details of which would put a strain on Switzerland's stance as a neutral state.[30] Hence, he had to have an interest in improving relations with the German leadership so as not to have personal difficulties as commander-in-chief. In this difficult situation, Guisan did not hesitate to try to enter into contact, through private channels, with Counselor von Bibra, the official leader of the National Socialist German Workers' Party (NSDAP) in Switzerland. Hans Rufener, a lieutenant colonel in the Army who lived near the General's headquarters in Gümligen, had close relations with Guisan and was at the same time acquainted with Mr. and Mrs. von Bibra. According to research undertaken by Kreis, von Bibra wrote that in November 1940, Rufener had invited him to a "nice luncheon with General Guisan"; however, he declined the invitation, stating, "I asked Mr. Rufener not to invite me. I would have been happy to meet with General Guisan last winter, but at the present time I don't know what I could get out of a meeting with him."[31] For the commander-in-chief of the Swiss Army to be snubbed, albeit indirectly, by a National Socialist like Counselor von Bibra must have been worrisome.

In the fall of 1940, the commander-in-chief brought up the issue of a military mission to Germany once again, suggesting to the Head of the Military Department that it should include Divisional Commander Borel, Colonels Nager and Maurer, Major Steinrisser, and Captain Primault, who were all instructors.[32] Pilet-Golaz was consulted on the matter and expressed reservations about the mission, arguing that it would have a political aspect. He also reminded Guisan that the first attempt to organize a military mission had been blocked by Germany. Moreover, he explained that in meetings with Minister Köcher he had gained the impression that a formal request should be made only once there were signs that the tensions between Switzerland and Germany were easing. In addition, Pilet-Golaz said that a mission could only be successful if the selected Swiss officers were already known in Germany and could count on the goodwill of their friends in the German Army, which was hardly the case with the five officers the General proposed, regardless of their personal qualifications. He concluded that therefore it would be desirable to re-examine who should be sent on a mission to Germany, because "forcing another rejection would have negative consequences for German-Swiss relations as a whole. On the other hand, succeeding in having a mission with Swiss officers received by the German Army would contribute to creating a more friendly atmosphere between Germany and Switzerland, which would be strongly desirable."[33]

The General consequently suggested changing some members of the military delegation; he proposed to send Divisional Commander Bircher, Colonels H. Frick and Maurer, Majors Berli and Steinrisser, and Captain Primault, altogether a group which would be considered more pro-German.[34] Chief of the General Staff Huber agreed that Bircher's "excellent relations with several high-ranking German personalities should be used to advantage."[35]

Among the proposed military delegation, there was no mention of Corps Commander Wille, who would have undoubtedly liked to head a mission to Germany. The General would have preferred to send Wille to a more distant place, to the Balkans or the Far East. He offered the Chief Instructor the opportunity to travel to Greece or Japan, adding, "Should you intend to personally head the mission to Japan, I will leave it up to you to select the officers who will accompany you."[36]

Wille realized what was going on and had the impression that the army command intended to push him completely aside. He replied in an ironic fashion, writing, "I am as grateful to you to offer me some interesting distraction as I am displeased about the fact that you want to send me as far away as possible on an outlandish military mission." He said that Japan and Greece were out of the question, "but I will accept a mission to Germany or Italy. Concerning Colonel Däniker, I reiterate that he will be extremely useful for us on a military level during a mission to Germany."[37] However, the General did not consider Däniker for a mission either.

When the Third Reich reached the climax of its expansion of power, there was a tendency to want to make "pilgrimages" to Berlin. Based on the many various documents, one gains the impression that by making his own suggestions regarding a special mission to Berlin and by putting forward names of possible emissaries, Guisan also intended to take the wind out of the sails of other candidates who would not have been acceptable to him. In fact, Corps Commander Wille continued to insist unwaveringly on organizing a mission, long after the General, who was undoubtedly influenced in part by the resistance groups headed by Hausamann and Ernst, had dropped the idea. Wille finally went as far as to intimate that he would be a suitable head of a mission to Germany. In a top secret memorandum he submitted to Federal President Wetter four weeks after the beginning of Germany's Russian campaign, he explained that because of his position and the experience he had gained in his own country, as well as his "excellent knowledge of Germany and [his] acquaintance with German personalities of all ranks," he felt obligated to comment on the situation.[38] He argued that the "Axis' definition of power [was such] that their policies [would] not necessarily respect historical development nor Switzerland's legal situation and neutrality." The only positive aspect was that "according to my own, purely instinctive, feeling, Hitler and Mussolini [would]

prefer [to integrate] small Switzerland [into the new Europe] without using violence." He said that in that situation the question was unavoidable whether "a
Swiss in whom the Federal Council has full confidence should travel to Berlin
on an unofficial mission soon and meet with Hitler's influential entourage, and
if possible with Hitler himself, to find out about his inclinations and perhaps
exercise a favorable influence on him. [This special emissary] should at least
prevent rabble-rousers from exercising their influence."[39] Even if Wille did not
mention his own name in the memorandum, it is clear from the context that
he was thinking he should be the one to go on a special mission to Germany.
It is interesting to note that Wille did not follow official protocol in submitting
the memorandum, instead circumventing the General and handing it directly
to the Federal President. He explained that he did so because he did not believe
that the army authorities in charge—an expression by which he undoubtedly
meant Guisan—were "capable of making a carefully considered, objective,
impartial judgment."

Former Federal Councilor Musy was another person who considered himself a competent emissary for Switzerland to the Axis Powers, especially the
Third Reich. Following a trip to Germany in November–December 1942, he
informed the Foreign Minister about his excellent relations with German party
leaders and recommended himself for a special mission. He claimed that no one
in Switzerland knew Himmler better than he did, adding that Nazi ideologue
Alfred Rosenberg and his people were actually more dangerous for Switzerland
than Himmler.[40]

Luckily there were too many scruples to give in to the temptation of sending a special mission to Berlin. Even if it can be considered likely that in making his proposal all General Guisan intended to do was point out to Hitler
Switzerland's determination to put up resistance, one cannot overlook the dubi-
ousness of his plan. It is therefore not surprising that after the war Guisan
attempted to cover up, or at least play down, his part in trying to establish cultural relations with the Third Reich. When in 1953 Federal Councilor
Feldmann, who knew about the General's role, asked him a relevant question,
Guisan replied that "he would never have thought of making a proposal on this
matter, nor would he have gotten involved in such things."[41] Barbey also pretended to know nothing about the subject. When he heard, in 1969, that
Professor Bonjour had discovered the two revealing letters of August 14 and
November 9, 1940, addressed to Federal Councilors Minger and Pilet-Golaz,
and planned to publish them, he was reported as claiming that he "was completely stunned."[42]

Alfred Ernst rightly called the attempt to organize a special mission to
Berlin one of the "questionable aspects of the activities" of the commander-in-

chief, because Guisan was wrong to believe that Hitler would have been interested in accepting a solution that was acceptable for Switzerland. Ernst stated:

> Only one attitude was possible with regard to [Hitler]: absolutely reject any imposition and unambiguously express our determination to resist. You do not negotiate with the devil. If you stretch out your hand to him, you risk being eaten alive. The General should have thought about that. However, the fact that he did not must not be held against him in terms of his convictions. On the contrary, he made a wrong judgment, which is different from giving up one's convictions. In addition, one must take into consideration that Guisan was from French-speaking Switzerland; hence, it was more difficult for him to see the real nature of National Socialism than it was for Swiss Germans, who are closer to the neighbor to the North."[43]

The Files of La Charité

DURING THE CAMPAIGN IN FRANCE IN MID-JUNE 1940, several train cars full of confidential government and military files, which were to be transferred from Paris to Vichy, fell into the hands of German troops at La Charité-sur-Loire, 100 miles west of Dijon.[1] Some of the 1,800 boxes contained secret files of the French Army's Supreme Command, including the papers of Generalissimo Gamelin, who had already been dismissed by then. The documents were transported to Berlin, where a group of experts headed by Ambassador Hans A. von Moltke quickly realized that several documents referred to talks that the French and Swiss army commands had held regarding cooperation in the event of war. This discovery was first mentioned by Swiss historian Bonjour and was later analyzed in detail by Georg Kreis.[2] When the news became public after the war it contained fuel for domestic and foreign political controversy. During World War II, however, the German discovery weighed heavily upon General Guisan, and jeopardized his position as commander-in-chief.

One month following France's capitulation, Germany's Chief of the General Staff Franz Halder mentioned in his diary, "Written evidence of cooperation between France and Switzerland."[3] As early as the beginning of August 1940, the first news of the discovery reached Switzerland. The Swiss Embassy in Berlin telegraphed, "Mood is very bad against General because recent order to armed forces [at the Rütli] is considered to be directed against Germany. Supposedly documents found which incriminate Army Command."[4] If one assumes that General Guisan was informed of the discovery of the files as well, and was alarmed, it cannot be excluded that his letter of August 14 to Federal Councilor Minger in which he proposed sending Professor Burckhardt on a special mission to Berlin in order to improve relations with Germany's leadership was connected with the discovery of the files.[5]

German sources indicate that a first report on the documents discovered at La Charité was submitted to Hitler and others in early September 1940. After translating the documents, the Germans concluded:

The Swiss and French Armies have been in very close contact, for which there is written evidence from May 1939 to the end of March 1940. In order to formally remain neutral, they held unofficial talks rather than official meetings between their general staffs. On the French side, the liaison officer was a Colonel Garteiser of the staff of the French commander-in-chief at the northeastern front (General Georges). Based on his personal connections, Lt. Colonel Garteiser was in direct contact with the Swiss Army commander, General Guisan, and a small group of quite high-ranking Swiss officers. His task was to inform the concerned French general staffs about the results of his ongoing discussions. On the Swiss side, General Guisan and some higher-ranking Swiss officers participated in the discussions. The Swiss government was also informed about the talks. In a letter dated March 13, 1940, General Georges specifically stated that the Swiss government had asked to keep the matter strictly confidential in order to avoid repercussions in the country's domestic policy because the talks might appear as non-neutral conduct. The French strictly respected this wish by informing only a small number of general staff officers of the discussions. In spite of the unofficial nature of the talks, military documents were exchanged. The discussions focused on exchanging precise information about the organization and deployment of troops as well as the intentions of the army commands on both sides. In addition, they made far-reaching and detailed arrangements on coordinating the two armies in the event that the French Army was to 'intervene' in Switzerland. For instance, at one point it stated that French Lt. Colonel Garteiser and Swiss Colonel Gonnard [sic] would draft a plan for orders to certain Swiss units which would be submitted for review first to [Swiss][6] Army commander Guisan and then to French General Besson. There is no written evidence that France might have intended to march into Switzerland for offensive purposes. According to the wording in the documents, the French 'intervention' was planned in the event that German troops were to march into Switzerland first.[7]

This report, probably written by Ambassador von Moltke, gave a fairly accurate account of the collaboration between the Swiss and French army commands, except that the Federal Council was in fact not informed of the talks. In particular, the Germans realized that the French would intervene only after a German attack on Switzerland, not as a preventive step. This was definitely confirmed through additional secret files discovered at the Dampierre barracks in Dijon that belonged to the French 8th Army (Besson), which was designated for deployment to Switzerland. In a report, the representative of the Foreign Ministry at the Supreme Command of the Wehrmacht quoted document no. 14, which said, "It is assumed that the French troops will receive authorization to march into Switzerland three to four hours after Germany opens fire at its borders."[8] This report also stated that the files relating to cooperation with Switzerland included a total of 25 original documents.

In a second report, which was also submitted to Hitler and Foreign Minister von Ribbentrop, the issues were once again summarized. The report explained that even "recently discovered additional documents [did] not provide any evidence that France might have intended to march into Switzerland for offensive purposes. On the contrary, a fairly large number of documents indicate clearly that a French intervention was planned only in the event that German troops were to march into Switzerland first."[9]

The interesting report also pointed out that both the French and the Swiss had placed great importance on keeping the cooperation arrangements confidential, stating, "The documents show that the French set great store on camouflaging and keeping confidential their cooperation with Switzerland." The report quoted an order stating that no document was to include instructions "that could be interpreted as the result of prearranged agreements between the French and the Swiss general staffs." Moreover, an order dated March 29, 1940, stated, "Due to the obligation to keep everything confidential, which is easily understandable for diplomatic reasons, the phrase 'possible intervention in Switzerland' shall not be used any more in drafts, orders, etc. It shall be replaced by the term 'Maneuver H,' which stands for all relevant operations that have been planned."

The report explained that Switzerland also took adequate precautions. On November 26, 1939, according to one French document, "The Swiss were preparing very precise agreements but they do not want to present them to us until fighting starts." Also, the "Liaison Service" was reported to have received a less suspicious name. In addition, the report specified that only verbal arrangements had been made, explaining, "It appears that Colonel Garteiser meets only with a liaison person, and they proceed in a manner that allows officials to deny any cooperation at any time. However, it is too obvious that the Swiss general staff accommodates France's wishes, and vice versa, to leave any room for doubts concerning the collaboration. The documents provide perfect evidence on this matter."[10]

Initially, Germany did not seem to consider the files overly important. In the first half of September 1940, new information about the discovered files began leaking into Switzerland. In a letter intercepted and copied by Switzerland's censorship authorities, Swiss filmmaker Martin Rikli, who was a fervent advocate of National Socialism and worked for the Universum Film-AG (UFA) in Berlin, mentioned that documents had been discovered which did not discredit the Federal Council, "but it seems to me that the General's position is in jeopardy."[11] The Intelligence Bureau "Rigi" informed Army Intelligence about the intercepted letter.[12] Captain Max Waibel, speculating that the story of the documents had been made up to stage an intrigue against the commander-in-chief, wrote to the chief security officer, Colonel Müller, that he was personally handling the matter, explaining:

> I am most particularly pleased to have the opportunity to fight for a cause in which the General's personal prestige is at stake. I would very much like you to reassure the General; he has no reason to believe that the officers of the 'German' bureau do not have confidence in him. These officers will prove precisely in this matter that they stand up for the General with the same determination with which they would stand up for their own prestige.[13]

Waibel sent an "absolutely reliable person" to Berlin to look into the matter. The informant was unable to get in touch with Rikli, but he found out that Minister Frölicher had told some gentlemen "that being from French-speaking Switzerland (!), General Guisan was intolerable (!) for Germany and should be made to resign. Chief Instructor Wille should replace him. This solution would make a very good impression in Germany."[14] This information reinforced Waibel's opinion that the alleged discovery of secret files was part of a plot to cast doubts on Guisan's character and to have him replaced by the pro-German Wille. Waibel suspected that, considering the attitude of Switzerland's Ambassador to Germany, it would "not be surprising if no immediate nor determined action was taken against an intrigue which was being plotted in Berlin."[15]

The first written evidence that General Guisan had received information about an alleged discovery of files was dated September 23, 1940. In a hand-written note, he stated, "Files of 2nd Bureau found in Brest by Germans, including a letter [which says,] if German invasion, France will march i[n] t[o] Switzerland. Swiss maps are ready; they will find them in such and such place!! (L.F. Meyer, Miescher)."[16] Hence, National Councilor Ludwig F. Meyer from Lucerne, a friend of Guisan's, and Corps Commander Miescher must have received some vague information, which they communicated verbally to the General.

As late as mid-October 1940, the Swiss Intelligence Service was not sure what the alleged documents on "joint Swiss-French plans of operation" concerned. In another report to Colonel Müller, Waibel stated that he did not know if the rumor contained "a grain of truth," adding, "If such documents were actually found in Paris [sic], I would personally consider them as nothing but a matter-of-course precaution which the entire population would have expected to be taken and would have approved."[17] Waibel realized what intentions Germany could have by spreading a mere suspicion, and suggested being proactive about it. In his view, "If there is a possibility that such documents have fallen into the hands of the Germans, the Swiss should be informed in a careful and skillful manner about all the preparations that may be made to safeguard the country's neutrality. We have to pull the carpet from under the Germans' feet before they stage an artificial coup. We have to inform the people carefully so the German punch will miss the target." Waibel wrote that it was important to prevent the Germans from launching a joint political campaign with the pro-German revival movement in Switzerland that aimed "to replace the General by Wille or some other like-minded fellow." He said that allowing this to happen would be "the first step toward slavery" and considered that General Guisan was emerging more and more as a "cornerstone of our country's independence."[18]

Waibel's fears and premonitions were not unfounded; in fact, an intrigue aimed to get rid of General Guisan had already started in Bern. After speaking with Wille, probably on the afternoon of September 30 during a reception hosted by Germany's Military Attaché von Ilseman, Germany's Ambassador Köcher noted:

During an encounter with Colonel-Corps Commander Wille, we discussed the documents which had fallen into our hands during our advance. Colonel-Corps Commander Wille told me that I was a friend of Switzerland. After a long moment of silence, he continued and asked if it would not be better to bring the matter up officially, by which he meant General Guisan's arrangements with Gamelin, at the Federal Palace. I told him that this was out of the question because I had heard about the matter through purely private channels. He replied that he had too, but already on three occasions, and that he believed that the Federal Council would make efforts to get the General to resign if we brought up the matter. Wille considered that the best thing would be for the army to demobilize altogether; then the General could not remain in office, as he would automatically be left without any responsibilities. He said that the difficulty for the Federal Council was that it could not give any instructions to the General, who had to report only to Parliament but not to the Federal Council. He added that in fact it was not at all clear to whom the General had to report.[19]

Wille explained to Köcher that the arrangements with France had been made without the Federal Council's knowledge. When Köcher asked him if similar arrangements had not been made with the German Army, Wille replied that "he knew that this had not been the case."

Two days later, Köcher wrote a summary report to the German Foreign Ministry on his conversation with Wille. In it, he did not mention the idea of bringing up with the Swiss government the issue of the cooperation talks. However, he indicated that Wille had taken up "the subject of these documents" on his own accord.[20] In Berlin's response, the ambassador was instructed to say "that he knew nothing about the existence of these documents" if the matter was raised with him again.[21]

After the war, Wille stressed that Köcher had been the one who had first raised the subject of the "documents." Furthermore, he "very firmly" insisted to Federal President Max Petitpierre that he had "spoken with Mr. Köcher about political and military matters only when it was in the interest of our country, and especially when it was necessary to refute Köcher's and Ilsemann's comments about our commander-in-chief."[22]

It seems irrelevant who raised the subject first. What matters is what was said during the conversation. In this respect, there is hardly any doubt about the veracity of the German ambassador's testimony, for as a diplomat, Köcher had no interest in stating anything but the facts in the notes he took for his personal perusal shortly after the conversation had taken place. Nevertheless, Wille tried to deny these facts, claiming, in 1955, "At that time (summer–fall 1940), I did not know anything about the documents that had fallen into Germany's hands, and even today I do not know anything about General Guisan's possible agreements. I believe that they go back to the talks he had with Generals Pétain and Georges before the war."[23]

Based on the available written evidence, Wille's statements were clearly not true. In handwritten notes, Corps Commander Labhart wrote that on October 23, 1940, during the fall maneuvers of Border Brigade 7, Wille had personally informed him of the affair, about which he had already heard through Brigadier Rudolf von Erlach. A little later, Labhart asked Wille over the telephone whether he could use this information during a meeting with the General. Labhart wrote that "after giving it some thought," Wille recommended waiting for the time being and consulting with Dr. Wilhelm Frick, who was also informed. Labhart reported Wille as adding, "[If Dr. Frick's] indications were not sufficient, he would provide me with additional details."[24] In early December 1940, Labhart wrote in his diary that Wille had informed him "that the matter regarding the documents had gotten worse insofar as it was no longer the army but the party which was handling it. I told Colonel-Corps Commander Wille that I considered that the moment had come to inform the relevant authorities about the matter."[25]

Kreis provided an interesting overview of the channels through which the information and rumors about the documents of La Charité reached Switzerland.[26] According to his research, Brigadier Rudolf von Erlach, whose wife was a member of the Wille family, was one of the first Swiss to learn of the documents' discovery. Von Erlach reported that a former fellow student, Dr. Fritz Thoenen, had informed him as early as July 1940 about "letters that were very incriminating against our army command." An SS member had in turn informed Thoenen during a visit in Zweisimmen.[27]

In addition to the channels that Kreis reconstructed, in spite of missing written evidence, it is not unlikely that Corps Commander Wille also received discreet information early on through German Permanent Secretary Ernst von Weizsäcker. In the first half of September 1940, one of Wille's daughters, Gundalena von Weizsäcker, who was the Secretary's daughter-in-law, spent a few days in Switzerland. Wille wrote about this visit, "The Permanent Secretary told me through her that Hitler, who had generally viewed our country favorably, was becoming more and more angry with our press since the beginning of the war, to the point where it had become dangerous. He asked me to provide assistance to get Bern to halt this risky reporting as well as the rattling of sabers like at the Rütli on August 1 [sic]."[28] His statement seems to suggest that on this occasion Wille also received the first news about the discovery of the files.

During a reception in early October 1940, the host, German Counselor von Bibra, and Military Attaché von Ilsemann addressed Brigadier von Erlach to complain about Switzerland's army command, declaring impudently that Germany trusted neither the General nor his chief of staff. They asked "if it was not possible to nominate a new general and a new chief of the general staff. They said that a large part, maybe even a decisive part, of German-Swiss relations depended on that issue; indeed, they stated that this matter was even more important than the press."[29] Von Erlach told Labhart about the conversation, speculating that this information was a "well-meant warning and admonition." He added that this was "another reason not to hesitate any longer."[30]

A secret note, which was probably also submitted to the General in the late summer of 1940, stated about Labhart's attitude and his relationship to Wille:

Wille's entourage is extremely optimistic, as they expect Germany to make a number of demands toward Switzerland in the near future. They think that Germany will demand that the General resign. The only possible successor is Wille because Hitler wants him to be commander of the Swiss Army. Wille's entourage suspects that the position of the current chief of the general staff is also at stake, since Berlin views him as anti-German. They say that even though Wille and Labhart are not on good terms, the two corps commanders have practically joined forces to pursue common interests. Labhart views Wille's efforts to remove the General from office favorably, even if he does not know Wille's objectives. He is prompted by a strong resentment.[31]

Following a briefing at the commander-in-chief's headquarters on October 19, 1940, Labhart informed the General of the news he had received regarding the documents. Afterward, he wrote about the General's reaction, "He was visibly embarrassed when I told him, but then he said that he had been informed about the rumor for months (?). He added that L. F. Meyer had received similar information."[32] Labhart explained to the General that he was also concerned about the suspicion because the convention regarding possible cooperation with France had been drafted during the time when he was chief of the general staff. Therefore, Labhart suggested looking into the rumor because "it was possible that one of the gentlemen involved in working [on the agreement] had talked or wanted to play the role of 'fate'."[33]

At the General's request, Labhart confirmed the information in writing, and he formally requested an official investigation, stating:

> Even if it should be only a German attempt to spread unrest and mistrust in our country, I consider that the army command and the Federal Council must not be inactive regarding this information. In the interest of the country, an immediate investigation is necessary into the serious attacks against the army command. Being the chief of the general staff at the time when the convention was drafted, I was second in charge behind you, General, and was therefore responsible for the actions of the army command; hence, I request that an investigation be made.[34]

No more than two days later, the General informed Labhart that he had ordered internal inquiries to be made because the rumors were likely to be propaganda.[35] Labhart may have felt personally concerned by the alleged discovery of documents, but it did not take him long to suspect that these documents were more than just the preliminary drafts he had initiated when he was chief of the general staff. His suspicion was heightened when Lt. Colonel W. Frick told him that during a business trip to Germany he had been informed by an acquaintance who was an officer in the German Army's foreign service that the "incriminating documents" mentioned the name of, or were signed by, "a Lt. Colonel Gonard." Labhart informed the General about this latest news and requested that the Military Attorney General interrogate Gonard.[36]

Before acting on Labhart's suggestion, Guisan held a meeting behind closed doors on November 4 with his closest aides, Gonard and Barbey, and with Colonel Du Pasquier, who was well informed about the matter as commander of the ad hoc "Gempen Division." The law professor from Neuchâtel wrote in his diary that the General pulled a file out of the cabinet, and explained that he had been informed by Labhart that according to information received by Lt. Colonel Frick during a trip to Berlin, the Germans had discovered documents in France which proved that Switzerland had compromised its neutrality in favor of France. One of the documents was said to carry Lt. Colonel Gonard's signature. The General added that he had received the same information from National Councilor L. F. Meyer, who had connections in Germany. Du Pasquier recorded the General as saying, "Colonel Labhart suggests that the Military Attorney General carry out an investigation. What do you think about that?"[37]

Du Pasquier replied that in the current situation one had to avoid leaving the impression that one was trying to hide something. He suggested acting on the proposal, as it would have only advantages. He argued that it would allow Gonard, who denied putting anything in writing or signing any document, to justify himself and to defend himself against attacks in that matter. When the General asked him whether this procedure would not require the Military Attorney General to ask Germany for more precise information, Du Pasquier replied, "Certainly not. This concerns only the Swiss. Let us wash our linen among ourselves. The Military Attorney General will hear only Dr. Frick, L. F. Meyer, and Gonard. You will give him instructions beforehand to that effect."[38] Gonard agreed to the proposed solution without hesitation. Du Pasquier reported him to be "openly at war" with Labhart, suspecting that Labhart was staging an attack against him.

Du Pasquier further wrote about the conversation: "The General explained to me that there were two trends in the army: one group (Wille, Labhart, Däniker) considers that we have to immediately adjust ourselves to the German victory by changing our policies and institutions accordingly. The other group (including the General himself) rejects any such influence among our officers."

During that conversation, Du Pasquier and the General agreed that internal reforms were necessary "by reducing the power of the members of parliament," but these reforms should be carried out on Switzerland's own accord, without any pressure from outside nor any German money. On the way out of army headquarters, Barbey explained to Du Pasquier that the "pro-German clan" was challenging the commander-in-chief and that the attack on Gonard was actually aimed at the General. Du Pasquier was "quite distressed" when he went home, writing that the situation reminded him of the time when the Swiss border was occupied during the First World War and tensions rose among the army command because they did not sympathize with the same foreign country. He commented, "Here we go again!"[39]

The General followed Du Pasquier's advice, ordering the Military Attorney General to begin a preliminary investigation against Gonard. The following day, he informed Labhart about his decision, writing, "I am the first to wish for Lt. Col. Gonard that this investigation be carried out because the Head of the Federal Department of Military Affairs told me that you had accused [Gonard] of advocating the policy of the Western powers when you opposed his nomination as Head of Section on the general staff."[40]

Gonard made a handwritten declaration to the Military Attorney General, stating, "I have never written nor signed any letter nor any document that could have reached France, mentioning an activity of the army command that could have compromised it."[41] This reassurance was literally correct, but it did not tell the whole truth because it gave rise to the impression that Gonard had "absolutely nothing to do" with the preparations for cooperation with France.[42]

In his report to the General, Military Attorney General Trüssel concluded that according to Gonard's statement, he considered it to be "out of the question that any incriminating documents carrying his signature existed." He believed that someone had branded Lt. Colonel Gonard as a "quasi-Frenchman," thereby "making him appear suspicious in Germany." He added that it was probable that claims "which say that the General's 'entourage' [appeared] to have only one-sided information" were also directed against Gonard.[43]

Even though Trüssel believed it was unnecessary to continue the investigation, the General requested that it be extended to his informant, National Councilor Ludwig F. Meyer, and to Dr. Albert Riedweg, a lawyer from Lucerne, whose brother had forsaken his Swiss nationality to become an officer of the Waffen SS. Riedweg told the Military Attorney General that in Germany's opinion "the entire Federal Council" as well as the General were considered "absolutely unbearable," adding, "I am generally being told that the material discovered would be sufficient to justify a military intervention against Switzerland."[44]

In his final report, the Military Attorney General concluded:

> Dr. Riedweg's testimony provides the key to an explanation what kind of documents this might be about. Through his connections with his brother, who is a member of the German SS, this witness has apparently had the opportunity to speak with influential persons. They have told him two things:
>
> a) It is said that before the war, General Guisan, who was a corps commander at that time, held discussions with a higher-ranking French officer, of which the officer in question might have taken personal notes after the fact. It is possible that these notes were kept at an office of the French general staff. However, there are absolutely no indications in this respect. It is certainly excluded that there could be anything compromising about these discussions. It is of course also possible that if such discussions actually took place, the French officer in question took notes that went beyond what was actually said during the discussions. The General will be in the best position to judge the real value of this supposition, which appears highly implausible to begin with.
>
> b) Dr. Riedweg also discussed a visit to Paris, in April 1940, by a higher-ranking Swiss officer from the entourage of the commander-in-chief of the Swiss Army. In terms both of the date and of the officer involved, this information matches the military mission which was sent to France at that time and of which Lt. Colonel Gonard, the head of the General's Personal Staff at the time, was a member.[45]

After questioning all the members taking part in the mission of April 1940, the Military Attorney General concluded that during that time "nothing [had] occurred that would allow to cast any doubt on Switzerland's absolutely neutral conduct." Nevertheless, he argued that it was "not at all improbable" that the files of the French general staff included documents concerning that mission, but he considered it to be "absolutely excluded" that there might be any written evidence on the issue of cooperation between the two armies. He said that it should be noted "that the supposition that documents or deployment plans were exchanged [appeared] to be merely a fabrication."[46]

When considering what really happened during the preparations for possible cooperation, it is striking how harmless the Military Attorney General believed the matter to be; hence, his report appears to be well meaning. He made no mention of the far-reaching, detailed arrangements Barbey and Garteiser had made on the orders of their respective army commands. One major implication of Trüssel's report was that it provided both the General and Lt. Colonel Gonard with a clear exculpatory statement that afterward helped them to counter suppositions and suspicions.

During the first half of December 1940, Corps Commander Wille received a visit from his son-in-law, Carl Friedrich von Weizsäcker, who provided additional information on the discovered files on behalf of his father, the German Permanent Secretary. Wille initially considered directly informing the Federal Council about this new information. On December 14, he wrote a draft stating, among other things, "My sense of responsibility forces me to officially inform the Federal Council of the things about which I have received confidential information on December 7 from a German, C.F., whom I know to be highly reliable and benevolent toward Switzerland. It appears that he gave me the information with the intention to warn the Federal Authorities through this channel about an imminent threat to our country."[47] However, during a conversation with Däniker on December 16 at his home in Mariafeld, Wille decided to send the Colonel on this delicate mission. Däniker wrote in his agenda: "Meeting with W[ille] in Mariafeld re: procedure concerning the discovery in Paris."[48] The following day, Däniker wrote to the Federal President to request a meeting because he wanted to present to him in person "information from Germany which [was] of great significance and therefore urgent."[49]

In preparation for the meeting with Pilet-Golaz, which took place in the late afternoon of December 23, Däniker wrote some notes in which he stated, among other things, that his indications were based on a German informant "who tells nothing but the truth" and who was acting "out of affection for Switzerland, hence, in our interest." He added, "The informant personally saw a report by the desk officer at the Foreign Affairs Office in Berlin, which has undoubtedly been read by higher authorities, in which it was said the files that were discovered in Paris (files on military cooperation between Switzerland and France) should be kept secret for the time being in order to be able to use them whenever they were needed." As a result, Däniker suggested three "options to draw the consequences from this matter: Demobilizing most troops, making a commander-in-chief superfluous; The commander-in-chief should take a leave of absence at his own request, giving the heavy workload or his health as a reason (a leave which could later become permanent); Suspending [Guisan] as commander-in-chief (should be avoided if possible)."[50]

At the Federal President's request, Däniker put his statements in writing the following day and declared that he was prepared to repeat them in front of the whole Cabinet or the commander-in-chief.[51] Däniker clearly undertook his forceful initiative after consulting with Wille. He did not follow official channels, but instead planned to use the news about the files discovered at La

Charité to bring about the General's downfall. By intervening directly with the Federal Council, he tried to achieve what the German Ambassador had declined to do almost three months earlier. In view of the incriminating information, the Federal President transmitted Däniker's letter to the Military Attorney General and called the General to a meeting on the morning of December 31 to demand an explanation.

In this delicate situation, which risked jeopardizing his position, Guisan once again called on Du Pasquier for advice, summoning him to Gümligen. He explained to the law professor that he considered the whole matter a maneuver by the Germans to sack him as General, and the pro-German Wille, Däniker, and Labhart, who he said were his enemies, served as their front men. Moreover, he argued that Pilet-Golaz was jealous of him and was using the opportunity to get him into difficulties. Du Pasquier replied, "If the Germans fabricated this story, one has to limit oneself to denying it. However, if due to the stupidity of the French, the Germans obtained documents recording the meetings of Lt. Col. Garteiser, it would be better to make the first move and tell Pilet-Golaz that the French informed us of their intentions in the event of a German attack through Switzerland, but that we did not make any commitment toward them." Du Pasquier advised Guisan that the best strategy was "to keep as close to the truth as possible."[52]

Guisan followed Du Pasquier's advice. According to notes he wrote in preparation for the meeting with the Federal President, he explained that he had been kept up to date by the French Supreme Command about possible military precautions, but only during the time when France would have become Switzerland's likely ally in case of a German attack. He added that he had received this information without having to do anything in return; neither side had made any commitment nor done "anything that resembled a military convention." He argued that obtaining such "strictly personal and confidential" information was not only his right but in fact his duty as a soldier. Then he counterattacked, stating, "The Federal President has the right to receive an officer of the general staff without informing the General about it, even though this is not very trustful behavior. However, if he transmits to the Military Attorney General a deposition concerning the commander-in-chief without informing him, or without sending him a copy of the deposition, the President acts incorrectly toward the General, which the General will not tolerate any more in the future." Moreover, he said that it was known in Switzerland and abroad that Colonel Däniker opposed the General. It was important not to be lured by his suppositions that were based on German sources.[53]

That same day, the last of Pilet-Golaz' presidency, the General confirmed to the Federal President in writing that "[Referring] to this morning's meeting, I confirm that I have not concluded any military convention whatsoever with any foreign power. I have not had any communication on this subject."[54] This written declaration was a cunning, evasive response; it told only part of the truth, showing that Guisan did not trust Pilet. Under normal circumstances, this behavior by the commander-in-chief of the armed forces toward the President of the Swiss Confederation would be beyond what is considered dutiful loyalty. After the war, Pilet-Golaz told Federal Councilor Kobelt that he had not filed the General's letter among the official papers but kept it among his own papers after retiring from the government, because he wanted to respect its personal and confidential character.[55]

In the meantime, the rumors about the discovered files had also been discussed among members of Parliament. In December 1940, Gonard heard from several fellow officers, including Captains Robert Frick and Fred Kuenzi of the general staff, that Colonel Armin Meili, a National Councilor, had informed his fellow parliamentarians of the Radical Democratic Party about the documents and had mentioned his name in that connection. Gonard asked the General to look into the matter and to have Meili included in Trüssel's investigation, declaring that the accusations inflicted moral and material damages on him "in a careless and improper fashion."[56]

Colonel Meili told Military Attorney General Trüssel that in December he had provided to his fellow partisans confidential information which he had received as early as mid-July 1940 from von Bibra and which he had immediately relayed to Federal President Pilet-Golaz.[57] Trüssel considered it advisable to have the German diplomat testify to obtain more detailed information, arguing that von Bibra had either "committed an indiscretion about facts which had been reported to him by Berlin, or he carelessly made serious wrong accusations against a higher-ranking officer of the army." However, Trüssel concluded that it was up to the Department of Foreign Affairs to decide whether it was appropriate to hear von Bibra and to examine, if necessary, whether Switzerland's Ambassador should officially intervene in Berlin.[58]

Gonard, suspecting a new attack against him and the General initiated from Zürich, demanded that Colonel Meili be brought before a military court to have him convicted of slander and the spreading of rumors. As he wrote to the General, "The further the investigation progresses, the clearer it becomes that this affair originates in Switzerland and takes the shape of an intrigue and a plot which is ultimately aimed at you personally, as you had suggested to me earlier."[59] Guisan fully supported Gonard's request, stating, "I am determined to give Lt. Col. Gonard the opportunity to put things straight and to obtain full redress for the injustice that has been done to him."[60]

In January 1941, Colonel Eugster replaced Trüssel as Military Attorney General. Eugster had to pursue the case and informed the General that National Councilor Meili did not benefit from immunity because he had made his remarks during an internal meeting of his party, not during a session of the National Council; hence, Meili could "be held accountable as a citizen and as a soldier" for his action. He added, however, that according to international law it was not possible to take von Bibra to court, as he was accredited as a diplomat. The only step that could be taken was for the Federal Council to examine whether it should ask the German government to recall von Bibra from Switzerland.[61]

The Federal Council did not wish to take any action against von Bibra. The General was told that the Department of Foreign Affairs was highly interested in shedding light on the "unpleasant affair" but that the Foreign Minister opposed taking further steps in the matter, especially against von Bibra.[62] The minutes of the Cabinet meeting on January 31, 1941, read: "[Issue] of military convention with France. Pilet: Do we have any interest in asking Germany questions? No. Matter settled."[63]

Gonard's case against Meili dragged on until the spring of 1941. In the end, Federal Judge Eugen Hasler was called upon to arbitrate. In mid-March, based on the result of the investigation, which cleared him of any accusation, Gonard had declared, "I consider the sentence of a military court as the only act that can conclude this case."[64] However, four weeks later, he agreed to an out-of-court settlement by which Meili formally apologized to him, expressing his regrets about affecting in an unjustified manner his "honor and reputation as a soldier" by making statements about him in front of fellow partisans. Meili confirmed that "not even a suspicion [remained] against him." Gonard accepted the apology, granting that Meili had believed he was acting "exclusively out of concern for the well-being of the country and of the army [and] that the last thing that he wanted to do [was] to dig at Lt. Colonel Gonard."[65]

Meili promised to read the full text of his declaration to his fellow parliamentarians from the Radical Democratic Party at their next internal meeting. By this agreement, both parties were to consider the case settled in every respect. Nevertheless, Meili gained the impression that following the incident, he became persona non grata in the General's entourage. He was not called back to serve on the army staff but was suspended from duty in 1942.[66] It is probably not wrong to conclude that Meili was pushed aside because his critical remarks gave rise to the suspicion that he supported the group of officers that followed Wille and Däniker.

The commander-in-chief's entourage made efforts to cover up the tracks of their cooperation with the French Army, destroying their own file containing all relevant documents,[67] and making the watchful skeptics uncertain.

Nevertheless, there is no doubt that Wille's supporters continued plotting against the General in a systematic manner to have him replaced by someone who would be more submissive to the Germans.[68] In a report, Hausamann stated that certain officers were hoping that the expected offensive of the Axis Powers in the spring would result in the "conditions for Wille's and Däniker's efforts to carry away the victory." He added, "It is no secret that their goal consists of getting rid of the General."[69]

Hausamann was one of Guisan's most loyal supporters. In early March 1941, he wrote to the General:

> Some officers are clearly aiming to get you to resign in one way or another, General. . . . If the 'Däniker group'—let me call these officers by that name for lack of a better term—were allowed to proceed without meeting any opposition, there would be a serious risk of a critical situation in view of the good relations that the group entertains with the Head of the Department of Foreign Affairs. At that critical moment, Berlin would be made to produce the 'documents.' If on top of that one takes into account that by then a large number of Swiss, particularly the 'notables,' will be disheartened because they will be impressed once again by the expected initial military victories of the Axis, one comes to the conclusion that these gentlemen might have a good chance of being successful with their coup.[70]

The accuracy with which Hausamann predicted developments and perceived the imminent danger for the General at an early stage is surprising. During the summer of 1941, after Germany had staged its first impressive victories in its campaign against Russia, the efforts to have the commander-in-chief removed from office reached a new peak. Däniker's attempt at the end of 1940 having failed, it was Corps Commander Wille's turn, assisted by Däniker, to strike a new blow in connection with the documents of La Charité that were in German hands. In July 1941, he sent Federal President Wetter a detailed "Memorandum on the [current] situation."[71] According to Bonjour, the pieces of advice that Wille included in the memorandum all aimed to "further accommodate Hitler's Reich and, ultimately, to integrate [Switzerland] in the New Europe."[72]

In a letter to Däniker, Wille bluntly spoke about the "stupidity and incompetence" of the army command. In addition, during a meeting with the Head of the Military Department, he stated, "in strictly confidential terms," that it would be the Federal Council's duty "to remove an incompetent general from office." Kobelt wrote that he was amazed at Wille's choice of words. He added about the meeting, "[Wille] also argued repeatedly that there was in fact no longer any reason to keep the army on duty; instead, it should go back to pursuing its peacetime activities. Throughout the conversation, I kept feeling that this suggestion aimed to have the General dismissed."[73] On several occasions, Federal Councilor Kobelt indicated that in case Guisan was to leave office, the only possible successor as commander-in-chief would be Corps Commander Labhart, under whom he used to serve as chief of staff in the 4th Army Corps.[74]

Others speculated about Guisan's possible replacement as well. During a telephone conversation which was tapped by the Surveillance Service, Lt. Colonel Heinrich Frick, who was a friend of Kobelt's from university, explained to an unidentified person, "I told Kobelt that they should nominate Bircher as general and Däniker as chief of the general staff. I bet things would run more smoothly that way. He smiled; he is more inclined to choose Labhart."[75] It goes without saying that surveillance reports, including such tapped conversations, ended up on General Guisan's desk.

Based on the written evidence of the events surrounding the discovery of the files at La Charité, one comes to the surprising conclusion that the General's position was not at all secure in 1940–41; in fact, it was hanging by a single thread. Little more would have been needed to seal the commander-in-chief's fate. If Däniker's and Wille's advances had been combined with an official diplomatic move from Germany at the decisive moment, the General could hardly have held on to his position. After making repeated assertions that no arrangements had been made with France, his position would have become untenable for reasons of neutrality if the Germans had produced written evidence proving that the contrary was true. This author agrees with Georg Kreis, who wrote, "Even a diplomatic intervention resting on shaky foundations [could have] successfully demanded that Guisan be removed from office."[76] The General risked being convicted of lying in the eyes not only of the Federal Council but also of the whole country and the world. In that situation, Guisan's arrangements would have appeared as a flagrant violation of Switzerland's neutrality. This was bound to have had more disastrous consequences than the comparatively harmless "Colonels' Affair" or the case of Hoffmann/Grimm during the First World War. One can imagine what tensions this matter would have engendered not only in foreign policy but above all in the country itself, because most Swiss would probably have continued to support the General in view of his recent speech at the Rütli.

Considering the explosive tensions in the army command during 1940–41, only a spark was needed to topple the General. However, his opponents hesitated, which saved him. Their strategic move was engineered as a conspiracy and aimed to get the commander-in-chief to resign, yet it missed the decisive moment and subsequently began to fizzle out. In retrospect, it is difficult to decide whether Wille failed to recognize his chance at the time or if he put his personal ambitions behind the country's interests in order to spare it from a dangerous crisis, and possibly from unrest that could even have assumed the proportion of a civil war. Wille's descendants are convinced that the corps commander never intended to become general but only had the country's well-being in mind; they claim that he did not pursue the matter because of his patriotic feelings.[77] They think that in this instance imponderable factors once again worked in Guisan's favor.

The composure with which the commander-in-chief bore the pressure to which he was subject was admirable. It would be understandable if he had begun to have doubts about himself. However, there were no signs of that. At no moment during his public appearances did he give the impression that he was aware of the sword of Damocles hanging over him. Convinced that he had acted in line with his responsibilities, he appeared to be sure of himself, even when he communicated with the Military Attorney General and the Federal Council. Was he bluffing? In view of the facts known today, he certainly took a considerable risk. Guisan benefited from an unwavering attitude, however, as he was able to maintain his position and assert himself against his opponents. Subsequent events in connection with the files of La Charité proved him right.

Several authors have analyzed and evaluated Wille's attitude in connection with the intrigue that aimed to eliminate the commander-in-chief. Bonjour considers Wille's behavior "dangerously rebellious."[78] Kurz believes that his doings were "some of the darkest phenomena of a dark era."[79] Béguin called the intrigue "an act of high treason."[80] Based on historical research, Meienberg gave an impressive literary account of what he called the "Wille biotope," in which "plants such as the plot against Guisan were growing in the darkness of the night."[81] Kreis is more forbearing toward Wille, arguing that it would be unfair "to interpret [his actions] as a reckless move by an unscrupulous, ambitious individual who therefore also disregarded the country's interests"; instead, he thinks that Wille was driven only by the idea that the "compromising General [had] to be sacrificed to the appeasement strategy."[82]

In this author's opinion, research permits the interpretation that a conspiracy with many branches did indeed exist. Wille and his power base intended to fight systematically against the General, whom they did not consider a real "soldier." They intended to have him removed from office, take over his position, and realize their dream of a real soldierly life in a state at the side of the German Reich. It is obvious that in this endeavor Wille tried to stay in the background, pulling the strings without having to overly expose himself.

After Wille's death, alarmed by the publication of the German notes on him in 1961, the Federal Council once again looked into the corps commander's dubious machinations, but ended up deciding not to pursue the matter further. It conceded that it was "difficult to make an absolutely safe judgment on the issue" and was reluctant "to condemn someone who could no longer defend himself in respect to something that he denied while he was alive." At the same time, however, the government noted, "Though he disapproved of the General's decisions, Wille had no right to suggest an intervention by the German Ambassador to have the General removed from office. Even if one assumes that Wille believed he was acting in the interest of the country, his doings were culpable. If this had become known at the time, an investigation would have been justified."[83]

Through the warnings from Hausamann, Guisan was regularly kept informed of the intrigues against him and stayed on his guard. In 1941, he was reported as saying, "[Things] just don't work out with Wille. There is no room for a second general next to me."[84]

For some time, speculation continued about the extent and the exact nature of the documents discovered by the Germans at La Charité. As late as the summer of 1942, in connection with a detailed analysis of the military situation, Labhart suggested to the Head of the Military Department "in a strictly personal and non-committal manner" that the Federal Council "examine whether the troops should really continue to remain on duty." By making this suggestion, he undoubtedly aimed to have the General removed from office.[85] However, Kobelt replied that he did not want "to deal with this issue at this time."[86]

In addition, the German Embassy in Bern continually tried to make the General's removal from office an issue, even though the discovery of the files was not mentioned officially nor unofficially once the Foreign Affairs Office had issued instructions to deny having any knowledge about their existence. In 1942, Köcher wrote to Berlin, "In view of the existing evidence, [Germany could] no longer have confidence in Switzerland's army command." He declared, "If the General is not removed from office, it will not be possible to have trusting relations between Switzerland and us."[87] One year later, in fall 1943, he reiterated that Germany could "never acknowledge that Switzerland was really neutral as long as a man like the seriously handicapped General Guisan [was] in command of its army." Köcher rightly suspected that the Federal Council had not been "accurately informed" about the arrangements with the French army command, writing, "I do not believe that Guisan held his talks with the Federal Council's tacit approval. It is not in the mentality of the Swiss to make such shady moves. Moreover, being the solely responsible political authority, the Federal Council would have remedied this situation with rigor if it had discovered the truth." Only at this time, after a delay of three years, did Köcher try to take up Wille's suggestion of September 1940, writing to the German Foreign Affairs Office, "I consider that we can bring about a change among Switzerland's army command by making this an official complaint to the Federal Council. If necessary, we will threaten to publicize the material available. It will be possible to put aside the justified mistrust only once General Guisan and the guilty officers have been removed from the army command."[88]

By then, however, the military situation had begun to change on a worldwide level, and following Guisan's meeting with General Schellenberg of SS Intelligence in Biglen near Bern, the "incriminating documents" had virtually lost their meaning as a trump card.[89] The most opportune moment to use them against Switzerland was long gone and they were no longer anything but useless paper. Von Bibra realized this as early as the spring of 1943. Switzerland's Foreign Minister Pilet-Golaz wrote about Bibra's farewell audience in Bern before being sent to an outpost in Madrid:

He tells me that two years ago, he would very much have liked to show me and hand over to me the documents that have inspired Germany to mistrust us (Charité-sur-Loire). He often talked about them with Mr. Köcher. They both believed that if we could have been presented with the facts, the task would have become easier for everyone—the Federal Council, the Embassy, the German government. But he regrets that Berlin did not want to pursue the matter. He says that now [the documents] are nothing but sheets of paper.[90]

At that time, the file with the incriminating documents may no longer even have been in Berlin. After the war, several Germans took credit for dealing with them in a dilatory manner and finally destroying them out of goodwill toward Switzerland. In 1947, Hans Bernd Gisevius, a member of German Military Intelligence who was Vice Consul in Zürich for some time during the war, told the investigating military judge that he had never seen the documents but had been told by Admiral Canaris and General Oster "there was irrefutable proof of the fact that [the French and Swiss general staffs] had closely cooperated, and that the content of the documents was incompatible with Switzerland's neutrality." He explained that Switzerland could "not be thankful enough" to Canaris, the head of the German military intelligence service, for keeping the documents from being harmful to the country. He added, "Canaris deliberately chose to delay bringing the documents into the open, continually saying that the 'Switzerland file' was not yet ready to be presented."[91] Ambassador Frölicher also received information "that in this matter, Canaris and his desk had rendered outstanding services to Switzerland."[92]

In the German Foreign Affairs Office, Permanent Secretary von Weizsäcker, who worked with Canaris, reportedly held back the material because of his friendly feelings for Switzerland.[93] After being transferred to the Security Office of the Reich in mid-1942, the files were reportedly destroyed by SS General Schellenberg.[94] According to Colonel Werner Müller, Chief Security Officer of Switzerland's Armed Forces, it was Military Attaché von Ilsemann who "did everything" to save Switzerland from Germany's revenge after the documents were discovered at La Charité.[95] Probably several Germans played a part in preventing the documents being used as a means to put pressure on Switzerland. Unlike Kurz, this author considers it to be absolutely possible that Schellenberg himself destroyed the files in early 1943.[96]

After the war, when the discussion about the files of La Charité began, the Military Attorney General suggested asking General Guisan to write a detailed report on whether in 1939–40 "negotiations [with France] had actually taken place, who had taken the initiative, who had taken part in them, what their results were, and what conclusions the army command had drawn from them; also, whether someone had seen to it that the files discovered at La Charité were destroyed, and if so, who had done it when and with what means."[97] The Federal Council struggled with the question of whether it should take up the Military Attorney General's suggestion. Its members were not unanimous. Federal Councilor Petitpierre opposed putting any questions on that matter to Guisan, arguing that it was better to keep such negotiations a secret if they had really been held, adding, "It is better not to force the General to possibly lie about it."[98] Etter speculated that asking Guisan questions would not yield any results. The General was likely to reply that he did not know anything about such arrangements. Ultimately, though, Federal Councilor Kobelt was authorized to write Guisan to ask him for detailed information about the issue.[99]

Guisan annotated the letter from Kobelt by calling the affair of the files of La Charité "a farce."[100] He continued to refuse putting all his cards on the table, even for the benefit of the Federal Council, giving an evasive answer by claiming that he did not know the details of the "so-called affair of La Charité." He explained that he had heard about it only indirectly and considered the completely unfounded rumors about the papers as a means to put Switzerland under pressure, adding, "[That] is why I did not place any importance on them. Among the papers that were seized at the time by the Germans, were there really any that concerned Switzerland? I suppose, but I am not sure that the French general staff had to have undertaken some studies for the event that Germany attacked Switzerland, just as any other general staff would do." Further, he confirmed once again what he had told the Federal President in writing on December 31, 1940, that he had not concluded any military convention with any foreign army.[101]

Following the General's reply, which did not reveal anything new, the Federal Council was divided over the question whether to look further into this matter, because the information provided by the General did not match the credible information received through other sources. Oser, the Vice Chancellor of the Swiss Confederation, pointed out that in 1939, when he was staff secretary, he had been dictated a letter by Barbey which referred to military cooperation between France and Switzerland in case of a German attack.[102] Federal Councilors Celio, Kobelt, Nobs, and Stampfli were in favor of pursuing the matter further; Etter and Petitpierre wanted to leave things as they were, since they considered that any further steps would be the equivalent of an investigation against the General. Walther Stampfli insisted on the Federal Government's right to be informed about military secrets, stating, "We have to know whether the arrangements remained within the framework of our neutrality and within the army's authority." Etter asked what would be the consequences if suspicions about the arrangements were confirmed, and then gave the answer himself, stating, "The only possible outcome [is] a moral condemnation of the General if the facts are established. . . . Let's think about the General's situation!"[103]

Ultimately, the only further step was another round of questioning by a delegation of the Federal Council, for which Guisan was summoned to the Federal Palace on February 8, 1946.[104] Head of the Military Department Kobelt, who took part in the meeting together with Vice President Etter, reported that the General once again confirmed that he had never concluded, neither directly nor indirectly, any military convention with France, adding that the only purpose of the military mission of early 1940 was to make observations and to gather information. Moreover, he explained that Barbey had had contacts in Paris but only for informational purposes.[105] The Federal Council contented itself with these declarations and did not pursue the matter further.

In 1947, during a hearing before the National Council Committee dealing with the General's report on the army's wartime duty, Guisan did not diverge from his version of the facts. Bircher asked him the tricky question whether it was true that military arrangements had been made with France and whether the same right had been granted to Germany. Guisan replied in a concise manner, saying, "No convention whatsoever has been worked out, which is what I declared to the Federal Council at the time." Nevertheless, he admitted that officers who went on a mission in the spring of 1940 to visit the western front with the Federal Council's approval had received information about the formation of the French Army's right wing, which would have been useful for Switzerland in case of a German attack. He said that in addition, the command posts of the French troops that were stationed along Switzerland's border had readily provided information about their deployment plans.[106]

Ten years later, the Federal Council, consisting mostly of new members, took up the issue of the alleged documents on arrangements between the Swiss and French armies once again. At this writing, the official minutes of the Cabinet meeting have not yet been available to the public, but in a personal note, Foreign Minister Petitpierre, who was then Federal President, wrote, "It is being decided not to do anything. I draw my colleagues' attention to the most unpleasant aspect of this affair: the contradiction that exists between the documents and the statements made even in writing by the General and possibly by other concerned officers, according to which no negotiations had taken place between the Swiss and French Army Commands."[107] The government came to terms with the fact that there was a contradiction and did not go any further.

One may regret the commander-in-chief's lack of frankness in the matter of the arrangements with France, and one can argue that the concealment strategy went too far. The initiative, which was not sufficiently anchored on a political level, must be considered questionable, even if one does not put too much importance on the neutrality aspect of operational arrangements that appeared to be imperative from a military point of view. Military historian Alfred Ernst commented on this issue, "In retrospect, one has to say that the contacts with the French were understandable and even necessary considering the circumstances of that time. However, it turned out that contacts with a warring party entail political risks, even if they are initiated in a legally admissible manner."[108]

What is disturbing about the affair is that Guisan repeatedly and insistently denied that talks had been held and arrangements made with the French. Even if the General undoubtedly kept them secret in the interest of national defense, the fact that he denied the secret arrangements even to the Federal government, all the way to the end, must be considered questionable. His failure to admit the facts, which he should have done as a matter of course, at least after the war, is an indication that his mistrust of the Federal Council must have been serious and persistent. Yet surely some would have shown understanding for his actions and would undoubtedly have protected him. Wüst explained that even "some of his closest collaborators had difficulty in understanding that they had not been kept 'in the loop.' They asked themselves whether and why the General did not trust them."[109]

Telling the whole truth would above all have been appropriate on behalf of those individuals who had received information about the existence of the documents and informed the authorities, but who were subsequently accused of making malicious insinuations. This is one of the dark spots in General Guisan's career that make him appear in a somewhat dubious light. In a letter to his former comrade-in-arms, Divisional Commander Boissier, Corps Commander Georg Züblin expressed his disappointment about the ex-commander-in-chief's lack of fairness, writing, "I do not criticize the General for the measures he took; what upsets me is the lack of frankness toward the Federal Council and the general staff once the hostilities had broken out. And once the affair was uncovered, to me it did not seem very honorable to deny it and blame others as if everything had been malevolently made up."[110]

The Däniker Affair

THE CONTROVERSY RESULTING FROM THE DISCOVERY of the documents at La Charité-sur-Loire caused the General great difficulties. The attacks initiated by Däniker, Wille, and their followers as well as by German officials made it clear that in view of the general military and political situation, the commander-in-chief's position was in jeopardy. In this uncomfortable situation, the best thing for him to do was counterattack at the first possible opportunity. As early as the briefing at the Rütli, Guisan explained to the unit commanders that he was determined to dismiss any officer who failed to support him and who did not believe in unconditional resistance.[1] In particular, high-ranking officers whose negative influence could have devastating consequences had to be removed from office. Not everyone heeded this warning. Wille and Däniker failed to do so perhaps because they had a high sense of self-esteem and doubted Guisan's ability to assert himself, erroneously believing that he lacked leadership qualities. As late as July 1941, the General issued a clear warning intended for Colonel Däniker, telling Wille during a meeting, "I shall not tolerate his working against me behind my back."[2]

In the summer of 1941, the opportunity arose to part with Däniker after the latter had written a confidential official report following a trip to Germany and then agreed to its public distribution. Misjudging the situation, through this "Memorandum on Observations and Impressions During a Stay in Germany," Guisan's primary opponents in the army, Däniker and Wille, put a noose around their own necks.[3] The General's attack was initially directed against Däniker but took on the proportions of a purge affecting all pro-Germans and defeatists.

From April 30 to May 10, 1941, after the Axis Powers had attacked Yugoslavia and Greece, Colonel Däniker went on a private trip to Germany during which he undertook some studies and presented a series of lectures. Before leaving, he promised to Chief of Army Intelligence Masson to report on his impressions and experiences on returning home.[4] During his trip, Däniker, the commander of the Walenstadt training facility, had the opportunity to visit installations of the German Wehrmacht, such as the infantry and panzer training center for non-commissioned officers in Potsdam. Moreover, he met prominent political, military, and civilian people, of whom he wrote, "My observations are based on the contacts I had with personalities of the state, the party, and the Wehrmacht, as well as with industrialists, business leaders, journalists, and university professors. Some of these are German, some are Swiss who have been living in Germany for some time."[5] In Berlin, he was invited to dinner at the home of Franz Riedweg, who had just been promoted to the rank of Captain in the SS. Däniker gave an unusually favorable opinion of Riedweg, the head of the "Central Office for Germanic Affairs" and director of the infamous "Panorama Institute" in Stuttgart, where Swiss were recruited to serve in the SS. Däniker stated, "I would like to take this opportunity to point out that in my opinion Switzerland owes much to Dr. Franz Riedweg. In his position, he has connections with influential people, to whom he continually presents Switzerland's viewpoint. I am convinced that he has already been able to wipe out quite a few dark spots."[6]

Däniker's report dealt less with military issues than with what he called "the things that I had the opportunity to observe about political matters and in particular about German-Swiss relations." He wrote to ex-Federal Councilor Musy that the quintessence of his visit was the statement, "Stop being biased in favor of Germany's adversaries, stop continuously stirring up hatred against Germany, and mentally prepare for participating in a new Europe, which is also in Switzerland's interest."[7] In the memorandum he wrote, "If Switzerland really wants to have its special responsibility in Europe—hence, if it endeavors to be a really useful member of Europe—it must accordingly integrate into this Europe. The idea of this integration is not at all un-Swiss; in fact, in view of the way Switzerland was established and has existed, it is thoroughly Swiss. Participating in the new Europe does not at all contravene the concept of Switzerland but at the most a few archaic and outdated external forms. At the least, a good Swiss can just as well have his mind set on Europe and promote a new Europe as he can pay tribute to England or the United States."[8]

One of the key sentences of the memorandum stated, "What's more, curiously we are very proud to continue flying through the new Europe as a 'ricochet'." Däniker claimed that by remaining on the defensive, Switzerland would be all the more prone to be pulled into the war; in particular, "the publications and presentations by Colonel Oskar Frey have caused some damage lately."[9] He argued that the Third Reich was "preparing a decision concerning the problem of Switzerland," but it was not certain yet "which trend" would gain the upper hand.

One of Däniker's questionable conclusions was that it would be the fault of the Swiss themselves if they were to be attacked by Germany, for having failed to realize in time the real balance of power in a National Socialist-dominated Europe and refusing to draw the consequences from the new situation. Referring to the possible blood-guilt of the press, he stated, "I am convinced that things cannot continue in the same way, or else Switzerland is unfailingly heading for disaster. . . . No one will be able to clear his conscience and refuse to accept his share of responsibility after the fact by saying that he saw things coming if he cannot at the same time prove that he tried everything to steer the country off its bad course, even at the risk of causing damage to himself. Ultimately, everyone will be held accountable one day, even if it is just before his own conscience."[10]

If one replaces the term "new" with "National Socialist," which was undoubtedly what he meant to say, it becomes clear that Däniker advocated integrating Switzerland into the "continent sharing one common fate." However, one should note that Däniker believed "Switzerland [should] remain a nation of its own." "Therefore," he argued, "there can be no doubt that we want to be and will be ready to fight if demands are made that we must not and cannot accept, even if we know from the start that we have no prospects of winning this fight and are bound to perish."[11] Nevertheless, considering the contents of the entire memorandum, this qualifying statement does not blur the impression that, because of his admiration for Germany, Däniker fell victim to National Socialist propaganda and became the self-proclaimed advocate of a far-reaching policy of appeasement.

On May 15, 1941, Däniker submitted the original of his memorandum to Colonel Masson, attaching a "personal and secret" letter to it. Initially, it did not receive much attention among the army staff. Masson immediately confirmed receiving the document and approved of its contents, officially forwarding it to the chief of the general staff for the ultimate attention of Guisan. The Chief of Army Intelligence expressed his approval. "I thanked Colonel Däniker of the general staff for [the memorandum] and found it to be interesting, as some statements, particularly regarding the attitude of our press, correspond to my own view."[12]

Däniker initially produced nine numbered copies of his memorandum. He sent the second copy to Federal Councilor Pilet-Golaz; the third to his direct superior, Corps Commander Wille; the fourth to Divisional Commander Probst, the Chief Instructor of the infantry; and the fifth to Divisional

Commander Bircher in exchange for a report the latter had sent to him "which contained about the same statements." He submitted the sixth copy to his friend Lt. Colonel Heinrich Frick, the commander of Border Regiment 54. As Däniker explained, "I sent all these copies with an attached letter stating, 'personal and secret.' These words were not written on the memorandum itself."[13] Däniker kept the remaining three copies for himself but lent them to several close friends and officials, such as Councilor of State Mercier from Glarus and Corps Commander Labhart.

In the second half of May 1941, Labhart visited a unit at the Walenstadt training facility and afterward wrote in his diary, "I meet with Colonel Däniker, who informs me of his visit to Germany and presents me his report about the visit. He has also submitted this report to the army command and to Federal Councilor Pilet."[14] At the Foreign Minister's request, Däniker agreed to have the other members of the Federal Government read the memorandum as well. The Colonel insisted, however, that he had not given any copy to any member of the "National Movement of Switzerland," nor had he sent "a copy to Minister Frölicher, even though I suspected that he would be disappointed, thinking that I had not taken any action."[15] It follows that Däniker had agreed, during his visit to Berlin, to inform Frölicher about his observations there.

Unfortunately, there is no written evidence of the General's nor his chief of staff's first reactions to Däniker's report. Masson's comment indicates that the army staff shared Däniker's critical view of the Swiss media. However, it was not realized until much later that the report also contained some explosive material. Initially, the controversy erupted not over the contents of the memorandum but over the way in which a military document that was considered official and classified as "secret" was distributed to a large number of people. Five weeks after it had been submitted to Masson, Barbey informed Chief Security Officer Müller that the General had heard that Colonel Däniker had distributed to a number of officers the report of his impressions in Germany. He requested that Colonel Müller provide Guisan with a copy of the report.[16]

In fact, the half dozen copies that were distributed were not the only copies of the memorandum in circulation. With Däniker's approval, Lt. Colonel Frick made about one hundred extra copies of the report, which he considered "an important statesmanlike document,"[17] and mailed them or handed them out to friends and acquaintances. In most instances, he did not mark them as confidential, but commented that they should be used in the "interest of the country." In this way, within a few weeks, Däniker's memorandum had been widely distributed without his keeping track of the number of copies. Brunner and Bucheli, two members of the "Swiss Federal Movement," a Front organization, made 450 copies, which they sent to members and sympathizers of the group.

During the investigation, it was established that in the end close to 2,000 copies existed, not including surreptitious ones.[18]

The investigation report clearly indicates that the memorandum was distributed through three independent channels: first by Heinrich Frick, directly and via members of the "People's Alliance for Switzerland's Independence," to members of other pro-German "revival movements"; second, by National Councilor Paul Meierhans, the editor of the Social Democrat *Volksrecht* newspaper, who warned the resistance fighters about it; and third, by the German Consulate in Zürich, which made copies to use as propaganda material in Germany's favor. All three channels originally used one of the copies sent out by Lt. Colonel Frick; some of them received a copy indirectly. In Zürich, Däniker's memorandum was available for reading at a barber shop operated by a foreigner: "Upon request, clients could have a copy of it."[19] Hence, in a more or less deliberate manner, an official, "secret" document became a mass publication.

Däniker may not have intended to have his report so widely distributed, yet he allowed it to happen and actually made it possible. One gains the impression that he purposely allowed the breach of official confidentiality to take place. In the fall of 1941, in a letter to Federal Councilor Kobelt, Däniker claimed, "I regretted that the memorandum was widely distributed through an indiscretion, but I was totally unable to do anything against this, because I found out about the distribution only one month later through a coincidence."[20] However, he later admitted to the General that he was "not unhappy" about the report being disseminated without his personal involvement, as he hoped it would "have a good effect."[21] During the investigation, he explained, "I authorized my memorandum [to be copied] because I did not write it to have it filed in some desk drawer, but because I was deeply concerned about the future of our country and wanted to help improve the situation before it was too late."[22]

Däniker received widespread praise for the memorandum from his friends and acquaintances. According to a list which he personally compiled, among the persons who approved of his ideas were two corps commanders (Wille and Labhart), four divisional commanders (Bircher, Combe, Jordi, and Probst), two brigadiers (Gubler and von Erlach), and ten colonels.[23] Civilians, above all members of the "People's Alliance for Switzerland's Independence," also loudly applauded him. Hektor Ammann, the head of the archives of Canton Aargau, stated, "In general, the statements made by Colonel Däniker seem correct to me, even more so as they correspond to what Colonel-Divisional Commander Bircher reported. Overall, I agree with the opinions expressed in the document."[24]

National Councilor Roman Abt, a leader of the farming community, also supported the memorandum, stating to the investigating judge, Colonel Herzog, "The impressions I had received in Germany and which were confirmed by other good Swiss who had been there were the same as those of Colonel Däniker; I felt his memorandum to be a justified warning by a concerned patriot against the dangers that lurk for us." Abt added that even if he did "not fully agree" with some statements about the new Europe, he did not see "anything unpatriotic" about them. He said that he considered the "warning call absolutely justified and necessary," explaining that he had "used similar words [in the parliament's proxy committee] and kept pointing out that we must not provoke [Germany], because our destiny could easily be influenced through an accumulation of small provocations, even more so because ultimately our destiny depended on the decision of one single man."[25]

Two federal judges, Carl Jaeger and Eugen Hasler, also expressed their approval of Däniker's memorandum. Jaeger considered "Colonel Däniker's examination as a very commendable work." Hasler, who had been head of the Radio and Press Section of the army until the spring of 1940, wrote, "All I can say about this memorandum is that as far I know from my own previous experience and from other sources, it generally gives a correct reflection of the mood in Germany toward us, and that the way in which the press has been reporting and its attitude have in part contributed to this mood." Hasler did not want to comment on details but stated that Colonel Däniker could only have "written the memorandum in the army's and the country's best interest as he [saw] it, because there [was] no doubt about his good convictions as a Swiss."[26]

Samuel Haas, the director of the "Schweizer Mittelpresse" news agency, wrote to Däniker, "I consider the document to be an extremely commendable report; it corresponds mostly with my own information."[27] Even National Councilor Theodor Gut from the Radical Democratic Party agreed in large part with Däniker, writing to him, "Heinrich Frick sent me your memorandum. I read it with the utmost attention. It is precisely because I agree in large part with the therapy but not with all aspects of the diagnosis, about which it seems to me that we should come to an agreement, that I would prefer having a face-to-face conversation with you instead of corresponding with you in writing."[28]

Once Däniker's memorandum had been widely read and entered the hands of journalists and opponents of Wille and Däniker, it ceased to be just an internal army matter and turned into a political issue. Both the publicly recognized and undercover resistance movements that supported the General began to react. As early as the beginning of 1941, ten weeks before Däniker submitted his memorandum to Masson, Hans Hausamann had warned Guisan of the danger that Colonel Däniker—"the spokesman of a certain opposition among the officers' corps"—constituted not only for unity in the army but also for the General's authority. He wrote that it "was no longer admissible" for Däniker to continue "criticizing the army command." He recommended:

Colonel Däniker has to be faced with two alternatives: either he refrains from voicing any criticism against the army command toward a third party, or he draws the consequences as the type of soldier which he advocates would. There is no other option. If Colonel Däniker is not told clearly that the commander-in-chief shall no longer accept the constant derogatory criticism, we will come to see that considering the respect that Colonel Däniker enjoys among the officers' corps, more and more officers will begin to have doubts about the Supreme Command. This situation has already started developing and is spreading to the rank-and-file; hence, it has begun to manifest itself among the population.[29]

Hausamann explained to the General that Däniker was "fully convinced that our country is not subject to any threat from outside" and the Colonel could not be made to understand that this view was wrong. Hausamann continued:

Unlike him, based on our information, we consider that we will be erased from the map as an autonomous nation at the moment the Axis is convinced that it will not require many sacrifices [to conquer Switzerland], that it may in fact just require bringing the country into line with Germany. We will be ready for being brought into line from the moment our country is split in the fight for a democratic revival, which would inevitably cause a major breach of confidence. That is why we so adamantly advocate preventing serious conflicts on the domestic political level while the war lasts. . . . This is where I find fault with Colonel Däniker. Being the clear-thinking soldier that he wants to be, he should see things as they are.[30]

Hausamann's correspondence indicates that Guisan asked him to come up with a plan for winning Däniker over as a loyal collaborator, or casting him aside if necessary. As Hausamann wrote to the General, "The evil has to be eliminated without causing more damage than necessary. Pursuant to the request that has been put to me, please allow me to suggest the following procedure."[31] He suggested that the personal staff should be involved in taking action against Däniker. For that purpose, he drafted some letters and suggested that they be addressed to the colonel. He explained that regardless of how Däniker would react, "The commander-in-chief [had] to be able to take drastic measures if necessary." Hausamann indicated strongly that it was high time to take action against Däniker, not least in support of those officers who "fight among their comrades against Colonel Däniker's fateful activities." He said that he and his friends often heard comments such as "Our criticism of Colonel Däniker must be based on some mistake, otherwise the General would have disciplined him a long time ago."[32]

The task of secretly pulling the wires was very much to Hausamann's liking. In the 1930s, in connection with an attempt to build up Colonel Eugen Bircher as the possible future commander-in-chief, he had written to the popular troop commander, medical doctor, and military historian from Aargau, "You had better leave it up to us to eliminate vituperators. Consider us as your general staff members whose duty it is to relieve the commander of everything that could hinder him from carrying out his ideas."[33] In the case of Däniker, Hausamann, having the General's backing, must have felt in his element.

After submitting his proposal, Hausamann probably had a meeting on the subject with the General. Guisan took some handwritten notes, which read:

1. Däniker criticizes the Commander of the Army in classes and training sessions, and among officers. Lack of tact and correction.
2. He confuses my leniency toward him with weakness.
3. He uses inadmissible words (General not capable of commanding the army).
4. Received by Pilet just like Wille.
5. Press and radio should ask themselves above all if their press releases are good or bad for the army instead of considering only the point of view of the Department of Foreign Affairs.[34]

These notes indicate that the General was told that it was about time to take drastic action, and he hinted at a possible alliance between his opponents Pilet-Golaz, Wille, and Däniker.

In the case of the refractory colonel, General Guisan did not simply rely on the information he received from third parties. He wanted to make up his own mind about Däniker, summoning him to the command post in Interlaken to speak with him as an officer speaks with an officer. According to Kreis, Hausamann put the questionnaire and the outline for the meeting together at the General's behest.[35] Colonel Müller, the Chief Security Officer of the Army, had a microphone installed in the General's office to record on steel tape the conversation, which lasted more than two and a half hours.[36]

According to the tape recording, the General made a number of accusations against Däniker and told him that he would not tolerate colonels of the general staff "who should actually be locked up to get them to improve their behavior." He said he assumed that Colonel Däniker would draw the consequences on his own accord and resign from his position as a career officer if the meeting did not yield the results the General hoped for and expected.

One of the points the General held against Däniker was his "derogatory remarks about the speech at the Rütli," which he was said to have "qualified as 'provocative.'" Guisan continued:

> I am surprised that you, of all people, who correctly demands military thinking and a military attitude, failed very much to act like a soldier by criticizing my speech to third parties, and in a very disparaging manner. According to my view of a military attitude, you should have refrained from making critical remarks about your Supreme Commander to third parties; instead, if you really felt obliged to do so, you should have come to see me to present to me your point of view.[37]

Further, the General disapproved of Däniker's attitude regarding the documents of La Charité, stating, "The disseminated rumors are completely unfounded." He characterized the colonel's suspicions and his meeting with the Federal President as behavior that was "completely unlike that of a soldier." In addition, he rebuked Däniker because he had submitted the report about his trip to Germany—addressed to the Chief of Army Intelligence—to numerous other persons, "including the Head of the Department of Foreign Affairs, marking it as 'personal and confidential.' You apparently forgot to also send a copy to the General so that he could get to know your opinion as well as others. You failed to ask his permission to mail the report to the Foreign Minister." The General also criticized Däniker for allowing the memorandum to be distributed in large numbers, stating, "You undoubtedly know as well as I do that today hundreds of copies of your document continue to be circulated without you, the responsible author, doing anything to stop this from happening. I would like to draw your attention to the fact that you are responsible for all copies of this confidential document. The Federal Council will have to deal with the legal implications." In conclusion, the commander-in-chief asked the colonel, "Do you support the Federal government and the General without reservations or not?"

It was not difficult for Däniker to refute some of the accusations leveled against him. He denied ever describing the address at the Rütli as "provocative," as he was not present there and consequently did not know what was said. This statement permits the conclusion that Hausamann was mistaken in assuming Däniker had written a disparaging letter to the General following the briefing at the Rütli.[38] Regarding the documents of La Charité, Däniker explained that he considered it to be "a strictly political matter," not a military issue, and that was the reason why he had contacted Foreign Minister Pilet-Golaz, acting "as a Swiss citizen, not as a colonel of the general staff." With regards to the original of his memorandum, he said that by submitting it to Masson to the attention of the army command, he assumed that the report "would be on the General's desk within 24 hours."[39] However, he admitted being partly responsible for allowing the report to be distributed to so many people, as he had authorized Lt. Colonel Frick to copy it. Hence, he stated that he accepted "the full responsibility for this whole matter."[40]

Colonel Däniker explained that he did everything that he had done and continued to do "out of deep concern for our country, because we are heading toward a disaster." He conceded that he was deeply upset by this realization, so he could "state with a clear conscience that [his] actions [were] directed by this single principle. In this whole issue," he said, "my person does not matter in the least. I have been asking myself what has to be done to get out of our current situation. This is what the issue is all about for me, nothing else." He claimed that he often did not know what to do because he was so deeply concerned about the future of the country, since the situation was "extremely serious, both for the army and for the people."[41]

Strangely enough, Däniker criticized the lack of modern training instructions, which caused "the level of training in the army to deteriorate." Guisan, who had issued a number of training instructions since he had become commander-in-chief, was surprised at this criticism and replied that corps commanders and divisional commanders had told him the opposite. He said that he had recently asked Constam, the commander of the 6th Division, "'What do you think about the division's current training level? In what areas do improvements have to be made?' He clearly told me that he considered that much progress had been made with the new combat tactics."[42] The General added in handwriting to this passage of the minutes, "The Commanders of the 2nd and 4th Army Corps, and the commanders of Divisions 2, 5, 6, and 8 view the progress in training matters favorably. Only among some battalions belonging to the reserve troops, where the officers are not qualified enough, is there room for improvement."

Guisan did not consider the result of the official meeting to be very satisfactory. Concluding that "substantial facts of the matter needed to be looked into," he requested that the Head of the Department of Military Affairs order an administrative investigation against Däniker.[43] Barbey wrote about the atmosphere that reigned around the General following the meeting, "The General summoned him to a meeting in order to have him answer for [his memorandum]. Däniker believes that we have to adapt to the Axis on our own accord before we are forced to do so. He defends his viewpoint like a brilliant lawyer." Barbey stated that Däniker gave the "impression of a man with a delusion" and was a classical case of an "officer who [was] a brilliant, talented military scientist, [and had] a passion for political theories," a combination which was "quite rare" in Switzerland. However, Barbey thought there was a risk that Däniker could influence certain groups of people who might protect him; therefore it was "important to make sure that the damage remained limited and to prevent him from considering himself a victim who makes himself a martyr in his self-defense through his innate pathos."[44]

The General was determined to take resolute action against Däniker; however, he wanted to proceed in a subtle manner, and if possible without causing a great stir. According to Barbey, Federal Councilor von Steiger agreed, telling him that he was "surprised that this boil [had] not burst before and that [the command had] not been alarmed sooner nor intervened faster." The Federal Councilor argued that "after the quick victories during the German offensive against Yugoslavia, in the Balkans, and during the initial stage of its campaign in Russia, Däniker considered that he was home and dry and consequently showed his real face by publishing the memorandum. Von Steiger declared that, 'now Däniker has to be prevented from sitting on a high horse or making himself look like a martyr'."[45]

In August 1941, after a meeting dealing with deployment issues in the Réduit for the 2nd and 4th Army Corps, the General told the group of unit commanders that he had requested the Head of the Military Department to carry out an investigation against Colonel Däniker, an act which should be considered a warning, not as a mere administrative matter.[46] Barbey, who was also present, reported about the commanders' reaction that "Labhart defends [Däniker] with a few rather vague words. So does Bircher, but he says that he is not 'his friend,' as has been claimed by some. He explains that he has seen Däniker no more than two or three times during the last twelve months. Prisi favors a quick and resolute intervention."[47]

Barbey wrote that on their way back to the army headquarters in Interlaken, the mood was at a low point because of the "current differences among the top commanders." As he noted in his diary, "the Russian campaign abroad, the Däniker affair at home—the air is quite stale in the late summer. In addition, there is concern about the lack of agreement among the commanders; the crisis in the air force; the difficulty to find sufficient troops to relieve those that are on duty; and finally the fear that the determination to resist, which was confirmed one year ago at the Rütli, might not be kept up in the long run. Thought about that in the fog on the way back on the Brünig mountain pass, next to the General, who was more silent than usual."[48] One gains the impression of an increasing number of signs that the vigor required for an army to stick together and fulfill its obligation to the country was slackening.

On August 25, 1941, Colonel Däniker was ordered into another meeting with the General. In the course of the first meeting, he had told the commander-in-chief that he was willing to explain to him "openly and truthfully" his view about the current situation in Switzerland.[49] Guisan gladly accepted this offer. Their second conversation, an hour long, was also recorded on steel tape.[50] Däniker made a number of reproaches against the army command and against Guisan himself. He complained about the "decline in military thinking" in the army, claiming, "those who think like soldiers are ipso facto branded as Nazis." He criticized the "spying activities and suspicions" that had occurred in connection with the investigation of the Front movement, claiming that "not everyone [was] equal before the law at all . . . dissenters [were] being oppressed," and freedom of expression was not guaranteed, since pro-German newspapers such as the *Neue Basler Zeitung*, the *Front*, and the *Nationales Heft* had been banned. Däniker said, on the other hand, that the Army and Home section was using "itinerant political preachers" such as Colonel Oskar Frey and Captains Hausamann and Wartenweiler to influence public opinion. Moreover, he deemed that military training was not promoted and that "the young ones and the best ones did not have confidence" in the army.

Däniker compared himself with Adrian von Bubenberg, who had repeatedly warned others against provoking the Burgundian enemy in the second half of the 15th century and yet became the most dogged defender of his home country during the Battle of Murten. Däniker declared that he wished that everyone who was suspected of being unreliable be united in one regiment under his own command, stating, "If we were drawn into the war, this regiment would receive an honorable place in Swiss history books long after the other regiments are forgotten."[51]

Däniker criticized General Guisan personally for "being extremely interested" in matters dealing with the army's uniform and also interested in sports events, and he mentioned his "numerous visits with cantonal governments which included gala dinners."[52]

The colonel predicted that Switzerland was facing a worse fate than in 1798 when Napoleon conquered the country, as the state, which was "no longer healthy on the inside," was about to collapse. "In 1798," he continued, "Switzerland was kept together and it was able to rise again when the foreign rule was over. If the same thing should happen again now, Switzerland will not be kept together but will be split up."[53]

Exercising self-control, the General let Däniker talk for an hour, interrupting him only occasionally to raise some brief objections. At the end, he asked the colonel to put his "serious accusations" in writing. In an annotation to the minutes of the meeting, Guisan characterized Däniker as a "pathological man!"[54]

In the meantime, several of the General's supporters tried to incite him to take more resolute action against Däniker. In this connection, it is interesting to read notes by Paul Meyer-Schwertenbach, who was privately acquainted with the Guisan family. He was a captain in the army's security section, for which he accomplished several special missions. In this role, he was allowed to see the General and his wife at any time. When Mrs. Guisan asked him, during a visit after the General's first meeting with Däniker, if the colonel was the General's enemy, he replied that indeed he was and that there was a serious risk that the army might split into two camps, explaining, "This has not happened yet. The officers who support Däniker or who sympathize with him are not yet against the General, but they do not back him either. They admire the ability of the Germans and demand an energetic leader. [They] do not tolerate the General's kindness and indulgence. The people are also asking for a firm hand and would be grateful if the Federal Council and the Supreme Command showed more determination." Mrs. Guisan confided to her guest that one of the Federal Councilors had recently told her husband that "the General will not be General anymore after six days if Däniker seizes power." When Mrs. Guisan asked whether it was "still possible to fix the matter with Däniker," Meyer replied, "I don't know. In any case, the General will not be able to avoid the issue. One makes more mistakes by being kind than by being strict."[55]

The conversation with the General's wife about Däniker's intentions was a prelude to a meeting with the General. Mrs. Guisan told Meyer, "My husband would like to talk to you—here, in this informal atmosphere." The following day, the General called him to find out if they could meet at Mrs. Guisan's apartment in Bern. During their meeting, Meyer repeated his warning about the risk of the army splitting into two camps and encouraged the General to take more determined action against Däniker. According to his own notes, Meyer said, "Looking on is the same as standing by and being run over. The commander has to act with a firm hand because some of the best officers have gathered around Däniker. . . . Showing too much consideration for others is the most pernicious thing one can do during adverse times." He warned that Däniker's followers, who he said were "not traitors but revolutionaries," should not be allowed to go about their own business. Instead, one should become their leader or take resolute action against them in order "to put things straight."[56]

Shortly after the existence of Däniker's memorandum became known, Colonel Müller, the Army's Chief Security Officer, also pointed out to the General the risk that the army might be torn apart. He explained that Däniker's statements had generated political discussions in the army that resulted in the officers positioning themselves for or against Däniker and for or against the General. He considered the situation very serious, as it might bring about a rift among the officers' corps. He said that the first signs of "an underhand but fierce war" were already noticeable, and this would ultimately affect the Supreme Command's authority. Colonel Müller stated that it was not his job to pass judgment on Däniker's political opinions, but that he considered it his responsibility to tell the commander-in-chief that things could not go on like that. He considered it the General's duty to take action as long as there was still time, adding, "If such discussions continue to be tolerated, the moral unity of our officers' corps is bound to be destroyed."[57]

Corps Commander Prisi also believed it was his duty to inform the General about what he called Däniker's "subversive activities," writing to him, "There is an increasing sense of concern among the officers' corps. They are anxiously awaiting a reaction by the Supreme Command, demanding that something be done soon and Däniker be called to account. Most of all, they believe that they have the right to expect that this dangerous demagogue [sic] be put out of action so he will no longer be able to influence the mentality of his subordinates in a fateful manner through his position as commander of military training camps and courses."[58]

In the fall of 1941, Captain Paul Meyer had another confidential meeting with the General to report on the general mood in connection with the Däniker case. He noted about the meeting, "[Guisan] listens carefully. I stress that the case of D[äniker] has to be resolved once and for all, and quickly, to finally restore peace and quiet. The officers in Zürich in particular have become involved in this issue, and they are turning more and more into underground supporters of Däniker. The General replies that he is meeting with [Military Attorney General] Eugster the same day and will tell him once again that this matter has to be settled quickly. He says that he does not think that the matter should be brought before a military court. I agree with him. This leaves only two possibilities: sanctioning Däniker or dismissing him from the instructors' corps."[59]

In his function as an official security informant, Meyer told the General about additional subversive activities being undertaken against him. He reported, "Then I mention to him that certain gentlemen in the Federal Palace consider that the army and the General should be put off duty, as a military confrontation between Germany and Switzerland can be ruled out and the civilian authorities are in a better position to render relations with Germany tolerable. I tell him that Kobelt is ready to take things under control and that Labhart will be called back as chief of the general staff. The General says that he has been informed about this tendency by another source as well." It is difficult to determine whether this was factual information or if it was based on rumors spread as part of an intrigue or in an attempt to exercise some influence. In any case, it is interesting that Guisan did not hesitate to take note of the information with interest. When the informer left, explaining that he was sorry that he usually had to report "unpleasant matters," the General shook his visitor's hand and told him, "Meyer, please come back whenever you consider it to be necessary!"[60]

Corps Commander Labhart did not fail to notice the threat of imminent polarization in the army either; however, that was precisely why he tried to influence Kobelt not to treat Däniker too harshly. Following a meeting with Kobelt, he wrote in his diary: "Afterward, we discuss the case of Colonel Däniker; I admonish not to take too brusque action because there is a risk that all those who are not well-disposed toward the current army command will side with Däniker."[61]

On August 21, 1941, as requested by the General, the Federal Department of Military Affairs ordered an administrative investigation of Däniker on suspicion of his violating his duties as a Federal official. The investigation would look into how the "Memorandum" came to be distributed without proper authorization as well as how many copies had been distributed. One month later, on September 29, the General ordered that the process be continued by launching a preliminary military investigation, which was the equivalent of criminal proceedings.[62] Colonel Herzog from Lucerne, the Senior Judge of the 8th Division, was put in charge. He had to examine not only the origin and distribution of the memorandum, but also to what extent its content violated the Federal Council's decree banning subversive propaganda in the military.

During the investigation, which was extended to Lt. Colonel Heinrich Frick, Däniker was examined very extensively. During the first examination on October 9, which lasted eight hours, the colonel had to answer 80 questions. During a second round of questioning on October 20, he was asked another 23 questions. Däniker commented, "The whole interrogation was an extremely detailed exploration of my convictions."[63] Among other things, Däniker was asked about the rumor that he had promised to provide machine guns and ammunition from the Walenstadt training facility to the pro-German "revival movements" if they tried to stage a coup d'état. He categorically denied ever making such a promise, stating, "I considered it to be a mean thing to suspect me in this way, especially after being told that nobody had any doubt that my convictions were honest."[64]

When the preliminary investigation was initiated, the General informed Däniker in writing that he was suspended for the time being from his post as commander at Walenstadt. Because it did not take long for his suspension to become known in the military, it was inevitable that the colonel appeared to be publicly ostracized. Some officers were outraged about the steps taken against Däniker. At the same time, new rumors began spreading among the public about the controversial officer. One rumor held that some officers and soldiers planned to march on Bern. Däniker was said to be discouraging his supporters from carrying out this idea.[65]

While the investigation was under way, the Swiss Officers' Society submitted a petition to the Federal Council supporting Däniker, in which it pointed out considerable tensions among Zürich's officers' corps because of the investigation against their colleague and his suspension from office. Hence, the steps that had been taken against Däniker were questionable.[66] During a meeting with Federal Councilor Kobelt, National Councilor Hans Müller, a leader of the farming community, declared, "Punishing an officer simply because he has a pro-German attitude will have dreadful consequences. Däniker is concerned about our country and its future. The country is in great danger. Even the investigation itself is dangerous. The news of [Däniker's] suspension has spread through the country like wildfire and has caused great concern among officers who are as worried about Switzerland as he is."[67] National Councilor Roman Abt from Aargau went so far as to call Däniker's suspension and the military investigation "a national disaster, both on the domestic and foreign political level."[68]

Corps Commander Wille, who was Däniker's direct superior in his function as Chief Instructor of the Army, wrote to the commander-in-chief to beseechingly plead his subordinate's cause. He claimed that Däniker was "the victim of an intrigue" and emphasized the risk of a rift in the army and among the population, as many people's confidence had begun to waver. Wille wrote, "Comrades-in-arms and schoolchildren are discussing how they could manifest their support of and solidarity with the revered officer." Furthermore, he subtly admonished Guisan:

> I urge the General not to underestimate the extent of the concern nor the quality of the men in the military and among the population who offer Colonel Däniker their full support. Moreover, I consider that I am allowed to inform the General that my son-in-law, Weizsäcker . . .

has told me that the people who view us favorably [in Berlin] are very concerned about the investigation against Colonel Däniker, while those who are ill-disposed toward us have been making gloating comments.[69]

Before the investigation was concluded, Wille wrote to the General once again, telling him that he considered it his duty to inform him that a decision which did not result in the Colonel's rehabilitation "would outrage [his] sense of justice, and if [his] subordinate [was] unjustly disciplined, it would have to have serious consequences for [him] the superior."[70] He added that because the matter was significant not only from a military perspective but also on a political level, he had decided to inform the Federal Council about his initiative. The General was taken aback by Wille's failure to follow official procedure and he consequently reprimanded the corps commander.[71]

Regardless of the objections raised by members of the army as well as by civilians, the military authorities completed their investigation. Military Attorney General Eugster came to the conclusion that banned subversive propaganda had been disseminated by negligence. He argued that the pro-German "revival movements" considered Däniker's memorandum a suitable propaganda instrument and consequently distributed it in large numbers. In addition to the manner in which the memorandum was disseminated, the Military Attorney General considered as disparaging Däniker's analysis of tensions with Germany when he wrote, "I am not afraid of formally stating that we Swiss are in large part responsible for this crisis." He also viewed as derogatory Däniker's demand that Switzerland should integrate of its own accord into the European continent "sharing one common fate" and his statement, "If we choose not to contribute to rebuilding Europe, we will not be able to simply stand by, because the contribution will be forced upon us." In the end, "with most serious reservations and taking into account the subjective circumstances," Eugster decided not to bring the matter before a military court; instead, the commander-in-chief should settle it in the form of disciplinary action. Eugster wrote, "The file shall go back to the General for him to take disciplinary action and shall then be forwarded to the Federal Department of Military Affairs for examination in connection with Colonel Däniker's status as an official of the Federal Government."[72]

From a legal viewpoint, the Military Attorney General's decision to settle the matter through disciplinary action meant that the military proceedings had come to an end. Eugster explained to the Federal Police and Justice Department:

The procedure is settled by a single authority and the judge has the right to transfer this authority to another body recognized by the military code. There is no right of appeal against this decision; it is final and binding for both the suspect and the commanding authority that ordered the preliminary investigation. If the suspect is sentenced to disciplinary action, the commanding authority within the limits established by the law must define this disciplinary action.[73]

For Däniker, the commanding authority was Guisan, who as commander-in-chief had the right to pronounce sentences of up to 20 days of detention. The General sentenced Däniker and Frick to 15 days of detention in seclusion at the Gotthard fortress. In addition, both officers were suspended.[74] The sentence was final; the two officers had no right to appeal. In line with this disciplinary action, at the Military Department's request, the Federal Council decided not to renew Colonel Däniker's contract as a training officer; he was no longer a Federal official. A government press release was published in newspapers about the punishment of the two officers, stating, among other things:

According to the results of the investigation, Colonel Däniker distributed the memorandum, which he had termed secret to his superiors, among the population and in the army, and he had it distributed by others. Lieutenant-Colonel Frick played an important part in the distribution process. The Military Attorney General has decided to have the case settled through disciplinary action. The case records indicate that Colonel Däniker acted in an undisciplined manner by distributing his memorandum and also during the investigation, which is even more serious considering his high rank and his high position as a government official. As a consequence, the Army Command and the Federal Council no longer put their trust in him. The General has sentenced Colonel Gustav Däniker and Lieutenant-Colonel Heinrich Frick to several days of detention. The Federal Council felt compelled not to reelect Colonel Däniker as an official of the Swiss Confederation. In recognition of his many years of commendable service as a training officer, he is granted his entitlements to the pension fund. Colonel Däniker is suspended.[75]

Through this press release, which tried to calm public opinion, Däniker was publicly ostracized and cast from the military. However, the "Däniker affair" was far from over as the army command had hoped; instead, it had further repercussions, heightening tensions in domestic politics. The General forbade the press to publish anything on the matter, since it related to the military. However, the topic continued to generate heated conversations between Däniker's supporters and opponents. Both Däniker and Frick were board members of the "People's Alliance for Switzerland's Independence," had enjoyed a high reputation in the military, and had extensive personal connections. The matter remained in the news through private channels and in underground propaganda. Däniker, supported by Corps Commander Wille, wrote lengthy petitions to official bodies to contest the way the case had been settled.

First, Däniker opposed the Military Attorney General's decision to settle his case through disciplinary action. Claiming that "the accusations [were] false," he asked Guisan to bring him before a military court so that he would be able to defend himself.[76] In his reply, the General declined Däniker's request, calling the Military Attorney General's decision "final and binding for me."[77]

The possibility of bringing Däniker's case before a court martial had been considered earlier, but both the General's military and political advisors had rejected the idea. Hans Hausamann opposed a lawsuit from the very beginning. In the spring of 1942, he wrote to Kobelt that a trial would provide Däniker with an opportunity "to defend himself in front of a large audience," whereas for political reasons, the prosecution would have to use caution to publicly prove the colonel wrong. He added, "If Colonel Däniker and his public and secret supporters gain the upper hand, hordes of officers who are currently waiting to see how the whole matter is concluded will desert to his camp." Hausamann suggested carrying out a less spectacular but equally effective military investigation, arguing:

> If Colonel Däniker is dismissed unceremoniously, giving as a reason the government's lack of trust in him, the confidence of the population will receive a boost, most officers will say to themselves that something had not been quite right after all, and Colonel Däniker will lose his political platform. A small group of people will get very upset, but since they do not have any newspapers nor any supporters to stage large-scale gatherings, this will be a storm in a teacup.[78]

Hausamann's suggestion was followed, and it turned out to be feasible and successful. He wanted to avoid a show trial or create a public martyr. Politicians such as National Councilor Heinrich Walther from Lucerne also considered that a trial should be avoided partly because of the impression it might make in the Third Reich. Walther hoped that Däniker would be punished less harshly, writing to his fellow partisan in the parliament, Adjutant General Dollfus: "Let me repeat that I would consider as really fateful a sentence through which he would be stripped of his command, etc. Däniker is a very ambitious man. . . . His behavior was clumsy and not without danger, but I think that it would be even more dangerous to brand him a martyr. In Germany the case is being followed with great interest. Even Hitler has shown some interest in it."[79] In the end, the case was settled with relative discretion, and yet the controversial officer was destroyed as a military officer and ostracized within the country.

After serving his sentence, Däniker, who had studied law, submitted an extensive document to the General in his own defense which he had written during his detention in Andermatt. In this document, he once again brought up the issue of the memorandum, repeating that he had acted "as a responsible Swiss citizen [and] in the interest of the country and its future." He told the commander-in-chief that he "vehemently rejected" the Military Attorney General's decision, which he considered to be "challengeable in every aspect."[80] Däniker criticized the Military Attorney General for basing his accusations on "a one-sided and twisted interpretation of the records" and for "concealing all those essential facts that do not fit into his argument."[81] He protested against the accusation that he had made subversive propaganda and against being dismissed as an official of the Federal Government. He reiterated that he expected a military court to try his case.

The General replied in writing that the decision was final and irrevocable. His letter, drafted by Eugster, stated that the decision could "not be revoked under any circumstances; the matter is settled."[82] In an addendum, Däniker tried to defend himself once again, but at the same time took note of the fact that he had no right to appeal the decision.[83] Guisan forwarded the letter to the Military Attorney General, annotating it with the handwritten comment, "This man will not learn. Is it really necessary to respond? On the other hand, should he have the last word?" Eugster returned the letter to the General, suggesting not responding. He argued, "[His] writing style shows such a high degree of grumbling that it is useless to engage in further discussions with him."[84]

Däniker also protested to the Federal Council. He wrote Kobelt that he was aware that he could not appeal a decision by the Federal Council, but he added that he protested against "being dismissed as an official of the Swiss Confederation and against the way in which this dismissal has been carried out." He considered that history would be the ultimate judge in his case.[85]

Corps Commander Wille supported Däniker in his endeavors, writing a legal treatise entitled "Thoughts on the Military Attorney General's Decision Against Colonel Däniker," in which he challenged Eugster's arguments and demanded that Däniker be rehabilitated. Wille also included ill-concealed reproaches against the General and went so far as to claim that the Military Attorney General had made his decision not based on the facts but from a desire to do the Supreme Command and the Federal Council a favor. He said that Eugster deserved "to be pitied because to the best of his knowledge, with his evidence he probably wanted to render a service to the commander-in-chief and to the Head of the Military Department."[86] Guisan annotated this passage with the comment, "Three-fold insult! Federal Military Department, Military Attorney General, General!" Wille concluded his harsh attack with a formal request to recall Military Attorney General Eugster, who he thought had shown an "unforgivable lack of objectivity," and to have Däniker's case tried by a military court.

Wille informed the General that he had made 65 copies of his "Thoughts on the Military Attorney General's Decision Against Colonel Däniker," of which he was sending the commander-in-chief and the Head of the Military Department two copies each. He said that he reserved six copies for the other members of the Federal Council and would hold on to the remaining copies if he needed to provide further assistance to Däniker, or if he had to "defend [himself] against false accusations which somebody might pronounce against [him] because of [his] siding with Colonel Däniker or against [General Guisan] because his [Wille's] trustworthiness and his military discipline have been belittled."[87] In a handwritten annotation, Guisan understandably termed this announcement a "threat!" Several additional annotations indicate that the General carefully read Wille's "Thoughts," which he considered to be an "incorrect and impertinent" manifestation of the corps commander's opposition against him. Some of the comments Guisan made were "distortion of the truth! . . . untrue! [in four different places], personal attacks against the General! . . . well, well! A matter of discipline! . . . sophistry! . . . polemical! . . . outrageous!"[88]

On orders of the General, Captain Bracher forwarded Wille's document to the chief of the general staff, remarking that the General was "upset both about its content and its form" and would discuss with the Head of the Military Department in a few days about what steps to take, as he was "facing the question whether it [was] possible to continue working with Wille."[89] The General was so distressed about problems at work during those days at the end of May that he withdrew for an extended weekend to his home on the shores of Lake Geneva. During that time, he had Barbey inform him of new developments at army headquarters. The chief of his personal staff told him that Chief of the General Staff Huber also considered Wille's document "an unacceptable offense" against the General and believed that the moment had come to part with the Chief Instructor, adding, "Once this has happened, the officers who currently back W[ille] would in a way be disarmed and their opposition would break down."[90] Barbey reported Huber as thinking that Wille would be much less dangerous outside the army than in his present official functions. In addition, that would make it possible to have him put under permanent surveillance by the security section of the army. Barbey summed up Huber's statements by writing, "He considers that this matter has to be done with and that it is dangerous to put it off any longer."[91]

Corps Commander Prisi was also given the opportunity to read Wille's "Thoughts." He agreed that Wille's words were "an outrageous insult," both against the General and the Federal Council.[92] Prisi's and Huber's reactions reassured the General that he could dare to make a stand against Wille. On the same day, he signed a letter that Barbey had drafted as a response to Wille's document. In this letter, the commander-in-chief forbade the Chief Instructor to distribute additional copies of the "Thoughts," which he said contained incorrect and insulting statements against him and the Federal Council. He clearly stated, "I shall not tolerate this attitude," and formally reprimanded Wille, adding that he reserved the right to go into detail about the matter at a later date. The General then wrote, "I expect you to promise in writing, by this coming Saturday, June 6, 1942, that you renounce your direct or indirect opposition and criticism against the commander-in-chief. Otherwise I shall not hesitate to part with you."[93]

Wille took note of the reprimand and informed the General that he had in the meantime given three copies of his "Thoughts" to Colonel Däniker. He skirted the issue of making a declaration of loyalty but accepted the commander-in-chief's authority and left the impression that he was about to retreat. He wrote:

> I herewith make the declaration which you demanded from me. General, if I communicate to you my conviction as an officer in an official matter, I would not like you to consider this as personal opposition. In the case of Däniker, I would like you to consider my petition of May 18, 1942 which I addressed to you and the Federal Council as a step that I took to defend my former subordinate Colonel Däniker against the Military Attorney General and his disputable construction of the facts. I believe that this is a loyal attitude toward you and the Federal Council. Moreover, I consider that one is allowed to provide support to a comrade, even if he is a Colonel who has been suspended.[94]

Wille's declaration shows that he was not willing to acknowledge any wrongdoing. In an additional letter, Wille expressed his regret about the dispute, writing:

I regret if you feel that my different opinion is a violation of your authority. I did not nor do I intend to express criticism; I wanted to explain my own, different opinion about this very important issue in a matter-of-fact manner. . . . I honestly regret if my different opinion in the case of Däniker and my extensive explanation on how I reached this opinion met with the General's disapproval. I kindly ask you to judge the 'Thoughts on the Military Attorney General's Decision' as a whole, not according to individual passages, because I have never expressed my opinion in order to oppose the General as the commander-in-chief.[95]

Wille ended his letter by reassuring Guisan that it was "best to respect [the General's authority] by being a frank and honest soldier." Guisan had doubts about how honest Wille's assertions were, annotating the last sentence with a big question mark.

Kobelt also severely reprimanded Wille for his "Thoughts," writing on behalf of the Federal Council:

We have no reason to follow your request to have Colonel-Brigadier Eugster replaced as Military Attorney General. Nor shall we argue with you about the Federal Council's decision of March 31, 1942 to dismiss Colonel Däniker as a government official. This decision is final, and you have no right to contest it. Incidentally, the decision is based on valid reasons and clearly expresses the fact that Colonel Däniker no longer enjoys the Federal Council's confidence and that his contract could therefore not be renewed.[96]

Kobelt vehemently protested Wille's "impertinent imputation that the Head of the Military Department or the Federal Council ordered the investigation against Colonel Däniker because it had been pressured to do so by politicians and members of parliament." He added that it was clearly proven that Däniker had "made subversive propaganda in a negligent manner"; moreover, there were "serious indications that [allowed] the conclusion that [Däniker had] actually acted willfully."

Eugster for his part wrote an extensive treatise to explain further his decision against Däniker. In these "Observations about the Thoughts of Colonel-Corps Commander Wille," the Military Attorney General confirmed the results of his investigation, which had brought him to the conclusion that by distributing the "Memorandum," an act of subversive propaganda had been committed. He argued that Däniker's document, in which the colonel adopted

Germany's position that Switzerland was mainly responsible for the tense relations with the Third Reich and demanded that Switzerland integrate into the "New Europe," could have served as a pretext for hostilities. Eugster continued, "Offering a foreign state such an instrument is incompatible with the demands which he purported to make out of concern for the well-being of the country, most particularly if these demands conflict with the security measures taken by the state."[97] He said that one had to wonder whether Däniker was aware of the consequences of his statements and plans and was able to recognize the danger which they constituted for the existence of an independent state, adding, "It would be an insult to say that this officer, who studied history, military science, and law and has great experience in these fields, was not aware. Consequently, he must bear the consequences of his actions."[98]

Eugster used the opportunity to analyze Däniker's claim that he acted in the interest of and "for the well-being of his home country." He argued that this assertion was not at all acceptable as a means to exculpate oneself, since "all enemies of our Constitution declare the same thing and undoubtedly also believe in their assertions, even though they deliberately aim to destroy and harm our state in the form in which the majority of the people want it to remain." The Military Attorney General maintained that in spite of their declarations, the activities of these enemies were a threat to the state:

> These declarations are made even by supporters of political movements that want to completely give up our sovereignty as a state, that intend to do away with the state and the Constitution by using violence. Therefore, each case must be examined to see if their goals are compatible with the well-being of our state, that is, if the existence of the Constitution and our full independence continue to be guaranteed. Wherever this is not the case, the activities are a threat to the state.[99]

Eugster considered that the criticism and demands expressed by Däniker in his "Memorandum" were definitely a threat to the state.

The Military Attorney General's "Observations" were submitted only to the Federal Council and to Guisan. At Eugster's suggestion, Wille also received a copy; however, the General ordered him not to make use of it in any way.[100]

Major Georg Züblin was right when he wrote to Wille that the latter's attempt to support Däniker and have Eugster replaced would be unsuccessful, even though he agreed with Wille that the Military Attorney General had "not done his duty." As Züblin argued:

> Now that the Federal Council and the General have made their deci-

sions and issued their orders, I think that it is virtually out of the question that Colonel Eugster will not be protected. The matter is such that you cannot publicize it either and that only very few people really know about it. Hence, it follows that the country's top political authorities and the General will back Colonel Eugster because they want to save their reputations and because Eugster's view matches their own.[101]

Even though the case against Colonel Däniker was officially closed after over a year, the matter did not end. Supporters of the ostracized officer, who were mainly directed by the pro-German "People's Alliance for Switzerland's Independence," circulated a resolution in favor of Däniker and Frick. Rudolf von Erlach, who had just been promoted to divisional commander, informed the commander-in-chief about the upcoming resolution. He explained that the executive committee of the "People's Alliance," including his brother-in-law Andreas von Sprecher, intended to show their solidarity with Däniker and Frick, with whom they had worked. However, he said that the purpose of the resolution was not to criticize the government or the General, but simply to reassure them that the two sanctioned officers had "good patriotic intentions."[102]

The petition was signed by 575 persons and submitted to the Federal Council by its main proponent, Ed. Ramser. It stated that the two punished officers had been wronged, that "their actions were intended to serve solely the country's well-being," and that "they continue to deserve to be trusted."[103] It is interesting to note that the petitioners were mostly those who had signed the "Petition of the Two Hundred"; others who signed the appeal included young officers and NCOs.

The petition yielded no results. Military Attorney General Eugster remarked, "I know that the people from Zürich who signed are all members of the 'People's Alliance for Switzerland's Independence' or former members of the Front movement."[104] Waeger suggests that Federal Councilor von Steiger, who had been an influential member of the "People's Alliance" for two decades, once and for all turned his back on the organization after this affair.[105]

On May 7, 1942, at the Central Hotel in Zürich, Guisan met with Colonel Karl Brunner of the general staff, a training officer who had also tried to intervene in favor of his comrade-in-arms Däniker. Brunner had studied law and specialized in constitutional and administrative issues. He complained about "the materially and formally incorrect and unjust manner" in which the Däniker case had been settled. After the meeting, he recorded the conversation on paper. According to these notes, Brunner explained to the General that Däniker had "unfairly been denied" the right to defend himself appropriately, as stipulated in the law governing dismissals from an official government position.[106] Before the meeting, Brunner had consulted Däniker over the telephone. The ostracized officer asked him to tell Guisan that the General's assertion that the case had been handled correctly was "complete nonsense."[107]

After the fact, the General was verbally informed about the telephone conversation between Brunner and Däniker, which had been tapped by the Security Section of the army. Captain Paul Meyer took handwritten notes about this event, stating:

> I explain to [the General] that what I am about to tell him should be considered unofficial information. D[äniker's] telephone has been tapped since he was dismissed from his post. No one knows about this except M[asson] and M[üller]. I have just been given a report about a conversation between Colonels Brunner and Däniker that I have to inform [you] about even if the official meeting between [you] and B[runner] has already taken place.[108]

After carefully reading the report, the General declared that it was "impertinent of D[äniker] to say that the General had sentenced him in order to make a gesture toward England." Meyer then asked the commander-in-chief what to do with the recorded telephone conversation:

> I ask him if he wants to take note of this information officially, which would reveal that he knows about D[äniker's] telephone being tapped and will have to discuss the conversation with the Federal Council. In this case, I will have Colonel-Brigadier Masson submit the report on the tapped conversation to him. However, if he wants to take note of the conversation unofficially only, I will file the report with the other ones and inform him only when something develops against him or against the Federal Council which requires taking immediate action. The General thinks about it and decides to take note unofficially only for the time being. He says that he has a meeting with the Federal Council tomorrow and wants to hear what [it] will say about the D[äniker] case. . . . I tell him that the D case was far from being over. He agrees with me.[109]

In fact, the painful effects of the domestic political crisis dragged on for some time. However, the steps taken against Colonel Däniker eased tensions in the army and calmed public opinion. As Hausamann had predicted, only a small group of people continued showing their dissatisfaction, and their number decreased to the same extent as the German armies began to run into difficulties on the battlefields abroad. Däniker's prophecy that the German Wehrmacht would be insuperable and win every war thanks to its ideal military spirit turned out to be inaccurate.

The national resistance movements were able to focus their efforts on the fight against the appeasement policy advocated by Däniker. His controversial "Memorandum" provided "Army and Home," the "Gotthard Alliance," and the "Action for National Resistance" with a first opportunity to test their effectiveness. This author concludes that there is no doubt that the resistance movements successfully applied pressure and supported the campaign against Däniker with targeted activities.

After being disciplined and dismissed from the instructors' corps of the army, Däniker was offered a job as head of military technology and arms tests at Bührle & Co., a private machinery firm in Zürich-Oerlikon. In this civilian position, Däniker was able to put his reputation and expert knowledge into service for the company's armaments production, which went mostly to the Axis Powers.

At the beginning of 1943, the General and the Federal Council took note, with apparent uneasiness, of Däniker's request for a leave of absence in order to present a series of lectures in Germany to which he had been invited by the "German Society for Military Policy and Military Science." The Federal Council was asked by the army command to give its opinion and stated, "Legally there was no objection to this trip abroad; nevertheless, it should be recommended to Colonel Däniker to renounce going on the lecture tour."[110] It was considered desirable that Däniker drop his plan because there were fears that his trip to Germany could be viewed as a pilgrimage and that his case could be discussed again and give rise to polemics in the press. However, Däniker insisted on going, refusing to drop his request, which was eventually granted. In the end, though, the ostracized officer cancelled the trip of his own accord.[111]

The army did not make it easy for Däniker to come to terms with his fate. At the end of 1943, he was denied access to shooting demonstrations by the Armament Section in Thun, which presented a new set of weapons to top army officials. Chief of the General Staff Huber expressly declared that the suspended colonel, as a representative of the Bührle company, was not welcome. Däniker complained about this incident to one of his former comrades-in-arms, Divisional Commander Franz Nager, writing, "I cannot possibly commit suicide just so these people don't have to see me anymore."[112] He was under the impression that he had been "cunningly bumped off," and suffered even more from his isolation because he felt abandoned by former comrades who turned their backs on him. As he commented to Nager, "They pronounce big words such as justice, stalwartness, comradeship, etc., but they act the way they did in

Thun. And this was no exception at all."[113] In his reply, Nager appealed to Däniker's conscience, stating:

> You wrote that you were very distressed about the fact that those who condone your way of thinking or claim to be your friends 'just stand by without lifting a finger.' I think that your friends or close comrades do not question your loyalty to Switzerland, but they do not agree with your memorandum of 1941. . . . I do not see how these comrades or friends would be able to lift a finger on your behalf. I am not the only one who thinks like that; others who have been well-inclined toward you agree. In some personal matters, no one else can help his friend; everyone has to deal with these matters on his own.[114]

Nager wished Däniker "understanding and strength to find [his] way out of the fighting and polemics and to leave the responsibility to those who are responsible."[115]

Some of the soldiers who had trained under Däniker's direct command embarked on successful careers in the military. However, Däniker himself remained ostracized. It would have required a German attack on Switzerland or a victorious Third Reich to allow him to be rehabilitated.

During the dispute with Däniker, General Guisan's authority was challenged, but he emerged strengthened. Guisan's accurate instinct concerning the political situation contrasted sharply with Däniker's fateful misjudgments. The General received several letters congratulating him for taking drastic action against the Colonel. An anonymous letter stated, "[Your] decision in the matter of Colonel Däniker has triggered a wave of sympathy in your favor. Now everyone knows that the General makes absolutely fair judgments and expects and demands iron discipline and an unyielding attitude from his soldiers and his officers; in case of doubt, he acts with fairness and treats everyone the same way. The Swiss will never forget your excellent judgment."[116]

Influenced by foreign opinions and blinded by Germany's initial victories on the battlefield, Däniker continued to insist that he was justified all the way to the end of his life. He failed to realize that his conduct was incorrect and he viewed himself as a victim. By continuing to believe in ideas that conflicted with Switzerland's determination to remain independent, he completely marginalized himself. As with many of his contemporaries, he did not seem to see through the perniciousness of National Socialist tyranny. He considered "totally inexplicable" the development his case had taken because he was convinced that he had done "nothing, really nothing at all that is inadmissible in any way." He said that he could not understand why his "Memorandum" was considered subversive.[117] At the end of 1944, he stated that "the mental situation in parts of the army [was] very worrisome" and predicted that it would "take not just years but decades to eradicate the last root of the weeds that are being grown and cultivated today."[118] Even after the war, he complained that his case was "probably one of the saddest chapters of Switzerland's World War II history."[119]

Considering the way the war ended, Switzerland was without a doubt lucky that its military and political leadership did not follow the advice given by Däniker in his "Memorandum." In addition to the fateful disputes this would have triggered on the domestic front, one has to imagine what position Switzerland would have been in once the war took a different course, and even more so when the unconditional capitulation of Hitler's Germany became a reality. The result would have been a bloody reckoning in the country itself. Moreover, Switzerland's policy of neutrality would have appeared as even more dubious internationally than it indeed appeared after the Allied victory.

Legally speaking, Colonel Däniker and his supporters were certainly not traitors, but according to the large majority of public opinion they betrayed Switzerland's conception of itself at that time. During the years 1940–1942, they failed on the national level, even though they were convinced that the opposite was true. There was something tragic about their incorrect conduct. In 1947, in an obituary for the deceased Däniker, Georg Züblin, a career officer who was one of the colonel's most successful disciples, wrote, "Däniker was undoubtedly wrong. He believed in Germany's victory and assessed the military and political situation incorrectly at the time." However, Züblin argued that it was inadequate and unfair to conclude that Däniker had acted as a traitor.[120]

The way in which Däniker's most determined opponents viewed him indicates how difficult it was to make a judgment of his intentions. In the draft version of his account of the "Officers' Alliance" of 1940, Alfred Ernst wrote about Däniker, "I do not deny that he had good intentions. In addition, his goal was to keep Switzerland independent. He believed that the way to achieve this goal was by bringing Switzerland closer to Germany. This is where he was wrong. However, this mistake does not authorize us to consider him a traitor to Switzerland, even though his attitude turned out to be very dangerous for the country."[121] When Ernst edited the draft after consulting with former fellow members of the Officers' Alliance, he eliminated the passage quoted above, which Hausamann undoubtedly considered too lenient toward Däniker.[122]

In his report on the army's wartime duty, General Guisan did not mention the Däniker affair, which had once been of great concern to him as well as to the public. The Adjutant General's report was the only document in which the matter was mentioned, and there only in one sentence as "a case of banned propaganda," without even naming Colonel Däniker.[123]

22

Relations with the Federal Council

D<small>URING</small> <small>BOTH THE</small> F<small>RANCO</small>-P<small>RUSSIAN</small> W<small>AR OF</small> 1870–1871 and World War I of 1914–1918, relations between the Federal Council and Switzerland's Generals were strained. In view of the Swiss constitutional framework, frictions between the top political authorities and the supreme command of the armed forces were virtually bound to occur. During the mobilization of World War II, some crises and differences between the two bodies were caused by specific issues, while others were rooted in personal rivalries. Relations between the Federal Council and General Guisan, despite an unbroken show of unity in public, were extremely tense at several points.

In his postwar report, Guisan complained about a lack of communication with the Federal Council and openly noted some difficulties. Nevertheless, he gave a positive account of his relations with the government overall, stating, "Generally, the Federal President and the Federal Councilors were very receptive to every measure undertaken by the commander-in-chief. Most of them honored me with benevolence. With some I had a trusting relationship or even enjoyed friendship."[1]

The Federal Council was somewhat more reserved, albeit considerate, in its comments about relations with the General, writing in its report:

> One may say that during the period of wartime duty, relations between the Federal government and the commander-in-chief were for the most part quite good and were based on trust. During our cooperation we always kept our ultimate common objective in mind. Both parties repeatedly put personal opinions and requests last when the overall goal required them to do so. In many instances, to avoid conflicts, in

the country's interest the Federal Council granted requests by the General even though they went against what it considered to be the right thing to do; it did not want to jeopardize the whole endeavor because of a few individual issues. Both parties continually made serious attempts to find compromises in cases of conflicting opinions and divergent points of view.[2]

Several authors have since echoed the official versions, which were not so much incorrect as incomplete, and tended to paint an idealized picture of the relations between the two bodies from 1939 to 1945. This idealization is understandable because both parties managed to cover up tensions by displaying friendly attitudes during public appearances. Chapuisat concluded that the only differences between the Federal Council and the General occurred in connection with "issues where their respective authority had to be defined." He mentioned the problem of the Press and Radio Section and the tug-of-war regarding the "Army and Home" section.[3] De Reynold pointed out that Guisan tended to make his own policies; however, he quickly added that this did not cause any conflict with the government but only some differences of opinion.[4] On the other hand, historians such as Bonjour, Kurz, Gauye, Hofer, and Kreis have written about significant differences, some of which took on the proportion of conflict. In his memoirs, Hermann Böschenstein described how a careful observer could not fail to notice that there were "differences between the Federal Council and the General" and that Guisan's "personnel policy in connection with filling the top command positions [and] occasionally his style as a leader were contested."[5] Without dramatizing, one must note that at times the difficulties, which remained hidden from the public, formed a prolonged atmosphere of tension and a virtually ongoing series of disputes.

During the first phase of active duty, from 1939–40, when Federal Councilor Minger, a friend of Guisan's, was Head of the Federal Department of Military Affairs, there were no unresolvable differences. When Minger retired, very much to the General's regret, Guisan declared that not a single cloud had marred their good cooperation during the 16 months since the outbreak of the war. "On the contrary," he wrote to the former Minister, "on the Federal Council you showed understanding, offering the General and the Army valuable and energetic support in their task to defend our country by all means."[6] Minger for his part stated that their friendly relations had made it possible to constantly "stay in close contact," adding, "During the frequent meetings, we were always able to reach an agreement without having long debates about regulations. There was never a note of discord. I have very pleasant memories of serving our home country together with the General."[7]

According to the diary of the General's personal staff, during Minger's term of office Guisan was invited to at least seven Cabinet meetings, four of which were held during the critical time of Germany's western campaign when Switzerland called up all its troops for the second time.[8] In a conversation with Labhart, the Secretary of the Military Department, Colonel Burgunder, insinuated that Federal Councilor Minger was somewhat annoyed at some of the army's decisions and that it would be preferable for the General to discuss them with him.[9] However, such slight differences were easily smoothed out during personal meetings.

After his briefing at the Rütli Meadow, Guisan demanded that the government "be absolutely firm and determined, discouraging from the beginning even the slightest inclination toward disintegration in the country or toward pressure from outside."[10] During that time, he did not hold back his reservations about the Federal Council and even about Minger, as reported by Du Pasquier, who wrote in his diary following a conversation with Guisan: "The General also talked about the Federal Council, which he does not consider to be firm enough. He said to me, 'I don't have any confidence in Pilet-Golaz; Etter has less energy than it first appeared; Minger is the most solid of them all.'"[11]

Guisan knew that he owed his election as General to Minger, whom he viewed as "an understanding boss in every respect."[12] He was taken by surprise when his mentor announced his retirement from the government at the age of 60. Barbey noted in his diary, "The General, who has always admired Minger's down-to-earth and logical decisions, does not hide the fact that he is somewhat surprised; for a short moment he is puzzled. He knows what he is losing—most of all a friend."[13]

After Minger had made his announcement, some members of parliament considered Guisan his potential successor. National Councilor Gadient from the Grisons wrote to the General to ask him if he would consider running for the Federal Council, arguing that his election would infuse the population with new confidence in the government, since it had been shaken in previous months. Gadient added, "If you had a man among your top commanders who could more or less replace you, then I am convinced that at the present moment you would have to join the Federal Council as Head of the Military Department. The parliament will meet in ten days. I would appreciate your letting me know confidentially what you think about this proposal."[14] The General thanked Gadient for his "warm words" but declined without further deliberation, replying, "I do not think that your well-meant proposal is appropriate; first of all, because the Federal Council needs a younger man, not someone who is 65 years old. With the help of God and our people's confidence, I hope to be able to fulfill my task as commander-in-chief until the period of wartime duty is over."[15]

Minger was a politician of the people, which had a positive influence on the Cabinet's public image as a whole. Once he resigned, this image changed abruptly and deeply, and at the same time the government's relations with the army command began to deteriorate. Guisan would have liked his close friend Claude Du Pasquier to be elected to the Cabinet. As Barbey commented, "The General would consider this a very opportune solution."[16] However, on December 10, 1940, Parliament elected Karl Kobelt, a National Councilor and member of the cantonal government of St. Gallen, who was also a colonel and Labhart's chief of staff in the 4th Army Corps. Kobelt was not the official candidate of the Radical Democratic Party, of which he was a member, but of the National Alliance of Independents. He was elected with a rather slim majority in the fifth round of voting.[17]

Because Guisan had attempted to influence members of Parliament to vote against Kobelt, a fact which the latter did not fail to notice, relations between the commander-in-chief and the new Head of the Military Department were strained from the very beginning. During a reception organized by the staff of the 4th Army Corps for the newly elected Federal Councilor, Corps Commander Labhart discussed this matter with Kobelt. He later wrote in his diary, "During the reception, I addressed the issue of the machinations in connection with the election. Colonel Büchi had informed me that Adjutant General [Dollfus] had gone to see him before the election to influence him so he would vote for Du Pasquier rather than for Kobelt." He said that Dollfus had argued that in Labhart's 4th Army Corps, "there was a faction against the General," and it would therefore "not be good" to elect Kobelt. Colonel Alfred Büchi, a National Councilor from Zürich, informed Kobelt about Dollfus' intervention. Kobelt did not hesitate to immediately ask Dollfus for an explanation. Labhart wrote, "Something similar was reported to me by Councilor of State Löpfe during the reception in St. Gallen. He said that after the first or second round of voting, the General called up Councilor of State (Colonel) Chamorel to tell him that Colonel Kobelt was not acceptable to him."[18] Labhart wrote that Kobelt called these attempts "dirty tricks" but was aware that "they were part of an election process."

On December 18, 1940, the newly elected Federal Councilor, who was 17 years younger than the General, went to see the commander-in-chief at the army headquarters in Interlaken to officially report absent from his post as colonel on the general staff. On that occasion, Kobelt made the General understand that he knew about the attempts to block his election, and he protested against the claim that there was a faction against the General in the 4th Army

Corps.[19] Several differences that arose during the following years between the Military Department and the army command seemed to be rooted in mutual suspicion, which marred relations between the two very different personalities of Guisan and Kobelt from the start. Barbey did not mention anything about these early tensions in his diary. The only thing he noted about Kobelt's election was that, as expected, "the career politician" had won against the outsider. Following Kobelt's visit to army headquarters, he wrote, "The General says that he is very pleased about the first contact."[20]

Hans Hausamann later explained that during the preliminaries to the Federal Council election, National Councilor Holenstein from St. Gallen, a lieutenant colonel in the army, had also tried to prevent Kobelt from being elected. After Kobelt's victory, it was Holenstein, of all people, who was designated by his colleagues to congratulate Kobelt on behalf of the members of Parliament from St. Gallen. Hausamann claimed he told Holenstein over the telephone that he had known for a long time that "politics was prostitution" and he would therefore not be surprised at all about the "nice speech" Holenstein would have to make.[21]

From the moment Kobelt became Head of the Military Department, the commander-in-chief was no longer invited to attend regular Cabinet meetings, which Guisan took as an insult. In his postwar report, the General mentioned that "some misunderstandings could have been avoided and some deadlines could have been shortened" if the Federal Council had continued to invite him to plenary meetings or to delegations of the government after 1940. He said that in his opinion this should be "normal procedure," explaining, "As the senior authority and as a 'team,' it is up to the Federal Council to invite the General for a briefing when the situation seems to be tense, and even more so when differences of opinion or difficulties arise."[22] After the war, Guisan told a special parliamentary committee that he had expected "to be consulted, just as in 1939–40, whenever there were differences of opinion."[23] He said that unfortunately this was not the case.

During the first half-year of Kobelt's tenure, the General was asked to participate in a Federal Council meeting only once; however, this was not an official meeting but a conference at Federal President Wetter's apartment at which only Federal Councilors Wetter, Etter, Pilet-Golaz, and Kobelt were present for the government.[24] For this meeting on May 9, 1941, the General ordered Barbey to draft a situation report which Guisan intended to present. Barbey wrote, "[The General] gives me the files with which I need to draft a memorandum: an assessment of the situation, which looks bleak—yesterday Masson considered it to be 'bleaker than in May 1940'—and mentions the possibility of a surprise attack. Furthermore, the memorandum will have to outline the new basic concept based on Operations Order No. 13 and the duty schedules for the units. And last, it will emphasize the need to put the Press and Radio section under the Federal Council's supervision."[25]

Barbey later wrote that the General "was very pleased" about the outcome of the meeting. He said that regarding the Radio and Press section, the General had reminded Federal Councilor Pilet of a statement he had made to him earlier: "The army is your domain; it should not deal with politics. Politics is my domain."[26]

During Kobelt's tenure, General Guisan encountered difficulties similar to those faced by General Dufour almost one hundred years earlier. Dufour had complained that his efforts to keep in touch with the Federal Government "were very one-sided."[27] However, it would be incorrect to say that there was a lack of contact between the Federal Council and General Guisan. In addition to the liaison officers who maintained permanent contact between the army staff and the heads of the various departments, numerous meetings were held between the commander-in-chief and the Head of the Military Department or various other members of the Cabinet. Guisan was not invited to regular Federal Council meetings; yet, as he admitted, "I was allowed to see the Head of the Military Department, through whom I communicated in principle with the Federal Council whenever I wanted."[28] Based on a compilation of the meetings of one or several Cabinet members with the General, sixteen meetings were held in 1940, fifteen in 1941, eight in 1942, twelve in 1943, ten in 1944, and three in 1945.[29] Hence, there were a total of 64 meetings from 1940 to 1945, amounting to an average of one meeting per month.

After finishing his first year as Head of the Military Department, on January 10, 1942, Kobelt addressed the army staff in a secret speech in Interlaken, which was undoubtedly intended to improve relations between the civilian and military authorities. He explained that, based on his first experiences, he had "the feeling that the Federal Council's measures [were] not well understood by everyone." He gave his version of the definition of the government's responsibilities and advocated better mutual trust, adding that the Federal Council's "simple, clear, resolute, unchanging, and unalterable" objective was to safeguard the country's neutrality and independence. Kobelt also outlined his own role, stating:

> When he sent me his best wishes for the new year, the General wrote to me that as the Head of the Military Department I was the champion of the army on the Federal Council. This thought could be taken one step further by saying, in addition, that I am also the champion of the army in the Parliament and among the people. However, the Head

of the Military Department is also the champion of the Federal government in the army. Moreover, I am also a member of the Federal Council, and I feel that I bear a share of its responsibilities. The position of the Head of the Military Department cannot be precisely defined; it is an extremely difficult position. I want to serve the country.

Kobelt, who expressly declared that he did not want a discussion to follow his speech, finished by saying, "May the relationship between the army and the Federal Government be built on trust."[30]

Kobelt, who succeeded Minger following a successful career as a colonel on the general staff of the army, was "an expert rather than a statesman," as Kurz put it.[31] He seemed to have difficulties accepting that during wartime duty his authority was transferred in large part to the army command and that he was simply an executive. On several occasions, it turned out that Kobelt could not resist the temptation to deal with issues that were primarily the army command's responsibility. He did not hesitate to give Guisan unsolicited advice on how to draft plans of operation or conduct tactical training for the top commanders. There is evidence that on some occasions Kobelt consulted with his former superior in the army, Corps Commander Labhart, before making suggestions to the General.

It is obvious that Kobelt, and hence also Labhart, influenced Plan of Operations No. 14, which proposed measures in the event of an attack from the west.[32] Kobelt wrote to the General that he did not want to get involved in the commander-in-chief's decisions but "would like [him] to bear in mind that a second front called for measures that [were] different from those suggested in Operations Order No. 14." He argued that it was the Federal government's and the army command's ultimate responsibility:

to use [the army] as a last trump card against the Allies or the Axis powers. . . . [T]herefore, it seems advisable to me to plan for standby positions which will allow the army to be deployed to the north or west without abandoning the central area. It is up to the army command to decide which army units should be stationed in what sector of the standby positions in case the troops are called up. However, 'Case W 42,' which is the basis for Operations Order No. 14, runs way ahead of this scenario.[33]

It is hardly possible to interpret these critical remarks by the Head of the Military Department as anything other than an expression of doubt about the army command's capabilities on the operational level. Kobelt added that he hoped "to be able to count on [the General's] understanding that the Federal Council [could] not be indifferent as to whether the army [had] taken all the measures that [would] allow the responsible Federal authorities to make their decisions as independently as possible." This statement could be interpreted as a suggestion that the General might not be capable of taking all measures necessary to ensure that the political authorities maintained perfect freedom of action.

At the same time, Kobelt tried to influence the training activities for top commanders by suggesting that operational exercises be carried out in order to see if the plan of operations was suitable. The General expressed his surprise at Kobelt's proposal by annotating it with a big exclamation mark in red ink. Barbey laconically wrote underneath, "We know that."[34]

There is definitive evidence that Kobelt consulted with his former military commander Labhart before making suggestions to the General. The corps commander wrote in his diary that Kobelt had come to see him to ask his "opinion about Operations Order No. 14." Labhart continued: "I tell him that I do not think that this order is in line with our neutrality policy because it could be executed only once we have been attacked by the Allies at the western front. I consider that the best solution would be to move the mobile troops into the area north of the Napf mountain to Langenthal which would prevent [the Allies] marching through the lowlands toward the northeast or the west."[35] However, even in his own diary Labhart denied trying to influence the army command through an indirect channel. Following an extended meeting with Kobelt during a maneuver visit he wrote, "I had the opportunity to discuss several questions with Federal Councilor Kobelt. I was pleased to note that he agrees with me in practically all matters concerning the military. The army command is said to remark that Federal Councilor Kobelt usually consults with me on the issues, but that is not at all the case."[36] On a later occasion, Labhart complained to Kobelt that in its operations orders the army command asked to have tasks accomplished "but failed to make any means available."[37]

When there were no signs that the army command would heed his recommendations, at the beginning of the new year Kobelt reiterated his suggestion via the entire Cabinet by telling the General:

The Head of the Military Department had informed you about his serious reservations regarding Plan [of Operations] No. 14 as early as when the guidelines for the plan were published, and he recommended to you to carry out several operational exercises which were to deal with the various possible future operational options. As no operational exercises have been performed by the army since 1941, the top commanders of the army units have had very few opportunities to practice their skill at making quick operational decisions. Carrying out operational exercises is therefore highly recommended also in order to develop the skills of the commanders. Officers of the general staff also need to be offered more opportunities to deal with operational and tactical problems next to their mostly administrative activities.[38]

It is impossible not to note the criticism that these statements contained; they were an indication of the tensions that began to mount in relations between the Federal Council and the General. Barbey annotated the critical remarks with the comment, "This had already been planned by the General. The Cabinet should not write such things!"[39]

In the spring of 1943, Kobelt verbally submitted to the General a number of suggestions concerning the army. Guisan wrote about this:

Study several options, Case W[est] and S[outh], for example if Axis is thrown back toward our W[estern] fr[ont]. Uncertain cases. Plains could be useful to the Allies if we remain in the Réduit! This could incite the Germans to come and reinforce our def[ense] in the Jura, or inversely. Study these different possibilities in reduced op[erational] ex[ercises] (army unit commanders and chiefs of staff). Everybody at the same place and only in the form of a rough draft.[40]

The Head of the Military Department also made suggestions concerning mobilization and demolition procedures, about which the General wrote: "Assembly points for corps and arsenals to be moved further out, not just in the Réduit! Easier to assemble troops outside the Réduit and then bring them into the Réduit positions with their mat[eriel]. Do not blow up factories, dams, fuel depots, etc. too soon, certainly not before situation is clear! Danger!"[41]

Another issue that repeatedly caused friction between the Federal Council and the General was the question of how many troops should be called up, which units should be relieved by other units at what time, and who should be granted leave. For economic reasons, the Government often had an opinion that differed from the General's; consequently, it took long negotiations to come up with a compromise.[42] Georg Hafner undertook an interesting study on the "almost insolvable conflict" of how many soldiers should be kept on duty and how many should be made available for the war economy, a problem that caused continuous differences between the Army and the Department of Economics.[43] In the spring of 1940, Federal Councilor Hermann Obrecht declared that he was "extremely surprised" by the General's attempt to interfere in matters relating to the wartime economy. He explained that the commander-in-chief was expected to address the Department of Economics through the Military Department and "clearly and vehemently" opposed any attempt to change that procedure.[44]

Federal Councilor Stampfli, who replaced the seriously ill Obrecht on the Cabinet in the summer of 1940, became a model for the resistance movement in the field of the war economy. Hafner called Stampfli "the General's counterpart on the civilian level who counterbalanced him."[45] Stampfli was in command of the economic and supply aspect of the war, and he made a superb contribution to maintaining the spirit of resistance. Hafner correctly stated, "No General, no matter how popular he was, could have kept the troops' morale at a high level if the families at home had been starving."[46]

In the winter of 1942–43, the commander-in-chief demanded that the army's state of alert be heightened in view of the upcoming spring. He therefore requested to extend the time of service of the light troops and to call up eight infantry regiments and additional special troops. However, the government considered the military and political situation to be much less dramatic than did the General. At a meeting between a delegation of the Federal Council and the General, Stampfli stated:

> One may well say that Germany does not view Switzerland as an enemy; otherwise, we would not be the only country to receive coal, iron, and materials for our emergency cultivation program from them. On an economic level, we have no reason to complain about a hostile attitude. However, new negotiations will be held shortly on economic matters that will show if Germany's attitude toward Switzerland is still the same. Everything indicates that Germany wants to keep economic relations with us at the same level; there are even expectations that we will deliver more materials. Moreover, Germany has shown great interest in Switzerland's currency, which is the only currency that is still traded to a certain extent on the international level. All these factors indicate that there are currently no intentions to attack Switzerland.[47]

Foreign Minister Pilet-Golaz also did not believe that it was necessary to increase the number of troops on duty. He proclaimed that the military situation could "not be considered worse than at the time before Germany invaded France," adding that Germany had other concerns than to deal with Switzerland. In addition, he said that at the current time it was difficult to see any military threat "because by attacking us, Germany would lose everything and gain nothing."[48] The Cabinet delegation made the General understand that it would approve an extension of the time of service for the light troops but would not authorize eight additional regiments to be called up. In reaction to this meeting, Guisan reluctantly agreed to scale down his request for additional troops. The Federal Council ended up approving a call-up notice for four regiments, half the number of troops the General had originally requested.[49]

Federal Councilor Stampfli tacitly opposed the General until the end of the war but rarely showed his emotions during conversations. Nevertheless, Hermann Böschenstein reported Stampfli as openly telling him "on several occasions how displeased he was about the way in which the General appeared in public."[50] The Head of the Department of Economics was under the impression that the army command did not give the war economy sufficient credit for helping to guarantee Switzerland's independence. Hafner claimed that, contrary to the commonly held opinion, "Stampfli viewed the General's behavior as arrogant and believed that he did not care much about civilian matters."[51] Toward the end of the army's wartime duty, when Guisan protected an officer who had made derogatory remarks about the Federal Council, Stampfli wrote to him with indignation, "According to explicit orders by the commander-in-chief of Switzerland's armed forces, any officer is allowed to make derogatory, offensive remarks about members of the Federal Council without their complaint being heeded by the commander-in-chief of the Army. . . . This is characteristic of the degree of respect which the army command shows for the members of the top political authorities."[52]

From 1941 on, at the end of every year the General reported to the Federal Council on the army's activities, current problems, and projects for the upcoming twelve months. At the end of 1941 the General explained that because he had not been given any opportunity to meet with the Cabinet since May, he wanted to formulate in a memorandum the pending issues that needed to be resolved in the general interest.[53] The style and code number "8" indicate that these confidential reports were drafted by Barbey. In the first report, dated December 26, 1941, Guisan stressed the need to receive the authority to order measures necessary to call up troops and to quickly mobilize the entire army. He regretted that the Federal Council had not granted his earlier requests to keep more units on duty.[54] Kobelt noted that the first memorandum caused "some surprise and displeasure among the Federal Council, [adding,] what would happen if we also submitted a list to the army command with the things that were not accomplished or were not handled according to our wishes?"[55]

The "top secret" 1942 report caused a very unpleasant controversy between the Federal Council and the General. The report once again pointed out the unsolved issue of timely mobilizations of troops. Guisan wrote that what mattered for Switzerland's militia army to be ready to fulfill its duty in a war were not strategic studies and plans of operation, nor the level of training and armament, but "most of all—I have to insist on this point at the threshold of a year that is full of threats—the moment or the circumstances under which the army has all its forces mobilized and concentrated."[56]

The Federal Council did not agree with all of the General's declarations and considered it to be "necessary to state certain facts and views concerning this report that do not correspond with the General's statements."[57] In a detailed reply, the government told Guisan that it did not share his view of the military situation, arguing that the landing of British and American troops in North Africa and the occupation of Vichy France by the Axis Powers had actually decreased rather than increased the threat of a war for Switzerland. The analysis stated: "The military operations in North Africa and the Russian winter offensive in the East cause forces to be scattered, and the Axis powers are forced to adjust their military strength accordingly. . . . At the present time, there is hardly any strategic need to attack Switzerland. Moreover, there are no signs of an imminent threat to our country."[58] The Federal Council speculated that if Germany were to reconsider the "problem of Switzerland" and weigh the pros and cons of an attack on Switzerland, it would most likely decide to maintain the status quo. In addition, the Cabinet said that Switzerland's intelligence service would be able to recognize in time any serious threat to the country.[59]

In his reply, in which he was unable to conceal his anger, the General insisted on his view of the situation. Referring to a briefing with the corps commanders, who basically agreed with him that additional troops should be called up, Guisan wrote that he considered "as only partly correct" the statement that tensions eased for Switzerland due to the operations in North Africa and the Russian winter offensive. He was "really surprised" at the Federal Council's opinion that the intelligence service would be able to recognize in time any serious threat, arguing that even though it was "established that our intelligence service does work very well," in view of the characteristics of modern invasion strategies it was not always possible to see signs of an imminent attack. As the General explained:

> The attack will be staged in a way that the aggressor will get to his target before our troops are able to mobilize or reach their combat positions. The enemy will therefore focus most of its efforts on preventing us from properly mobilizing our troops and deploying them to the front. It will be impossible for us to overcome this handicap. For this reason, an attack will most likely be launched at the moment when our authorities' and our people's requests are granted to boost the economy

and to call troops off duty, hence, at the moment when the country's defense is neglected.[60]

In an ironic tone, the General added that he took "note of the feeling of safety" with which the Federal Council viewed the situation. He said that he did not come to the same conclusion, stating, "On the contrary, I consider that it will be precisely this feeling of safety and trust on which an enemy attack will be based. One of the most important conditions for successfully launching a surprise attack is to catch us off guard so we have an insufficient number of troops on duty." He argued that if the government felt truly as safe as it said it did, "it would be better to also call the remaining few troops off duty." However, he said that he believed that it would be "better to show our strength than to be forced to use it." The General concluded his letter by admonishing the Cabinet that if it did not agree with him on the necessity to reinforce the defense, it would have to bear the consequences, adding, "I would like to point out that [maintaining the current strength] might in the long run put a heavier burden on the soldiers than carrying out the measures stipulated in my request."[61]

The Federal Council was not willing to accept the commander-in-chief's reply. The following day, January 23, 1943, the Head of the Military Department addressed the issue in a meeting with the chief of the general staff. According to the minutes of the meeting, "Federal Councilor Kobelt [criticized] the incorrect, subjective, and impolite statements the General made in his reply to the Federal Council's letter. He [repudiated] the threat pronounced at the end of the letter."[62] Kobelt's oversensitive reaction continued in his subsequent written response to the General, in which he insisted on the Federal Council's viewpoint, refusing categorically to call up additional troops.[63]

Guisan was also annoyed because the government's reply of January 12 was not signed by the Federal President but only by the Chancellor of the Confederation, Georges Bovet, which seemed to be unusual. The General ordered Major Bracher, the liaison officer with the Federal Council, to inquire if this was standard procedure for the government. Bracher informed him that it appeared that this was done in certain cases. The General was puzzled by the procedure, noting, "This is not done with Cantonal Governments!"[64] Hence, he resented the fact that the commander-in-chief of the Swiss Army received less attention from the Federal Government than a cantonal government.

The annual report on the army's activities continued to be an integral part of Guisan's contacts with the Federal government until the end of the war. When Barbey asked him, in 1944, if he wanted to submit another annual report, Guisan replied, "Of course. As long as I don't get an audience with the entire Cabinet or with a delegation as in 1939–40, this report is necessary."[65]

At the end of 1942, relations between the Federal Council and Guisan were additionally strained by the issue of the General's son, who had been slated for promotion to colonel. The minutes of the Cabinet meeting of December 30, 1942, stated:

> At the meeting of December 29, the requests by the Military Department were granted, with the exception of Lt. Colonel Henry Guisan, whose promotion to colonel was postponed until some further issues have been clarified. Hence, he was temporarily transferred to the general staff without being promoted. Now that these issues have been clarified, based on a written report and a request by the Head of the Military Department, Lt. Colonel Henry Guisan is promoted to colonel on the general staff.[66]

Kobelt noted in his diary about Henry Guisan's promotion, "Federal Councilor Pilet raises concerns about promotion of Lt. Col. Guisan to colonel, makes allusions to Lt. Col. Guisan's relationship with a woman who is under surveillance on suspicion of espionage. Federal Councilor von Steiger shares these concerns, [says] that proceedings were pending re: expulsion of this woman."[67] Kobelt had been unaware of this matter and was willing to approve Guisan's promotion because there were no objections from a military viewpoint; nor were criminal proceedings pending. However, he wrote that the Cabinet decided to postpone the promotion and look further into the matter.

Immediately following the Cabinet meeting, a gala dinner was held with the General at the von Wattenwyl mansion outside Bern. At the time Guisan was informed about his son's promotion having been postponed, so as not to disturb the atmosphere at the event. The next morning, Kobelt looked into the matter, holding meetings with the Chief of Counter-Intelligence, Colonel Jaquillard, the attorney general's office, and the police section dealing with foreign nationals. Then he informed the General, writing, "I took on the unpleasant task of informing the General about the internal discussions at the Federal Council meeting."[68]

Kobelt's research yielded the following results: In the summer of 1942, counter-intelligence had been informed that Lt. Colonel Guisan had a relationship with Miss L., a German national who had a bad reputation in Lausanne because of her lifestyle. The cantonal authorities requested that she be expelled on suspicion of espionage. However, the surveillance cleared her from the suspicion, as "no incriminating evidence was found against her apart from her bad reputation." Once made aware of the special circumstances, the younger Guisan "was immediately willing to put an end to the relationship."[69]

The relationship, which had apparently triggered numerous rumors, was obviously no reason to undertake any other action, and Lt. Colonel Guisan's promotion was confirmed with a delay of one day. Federal President Etter informed his colleagues that there was no reason "that would justify further postponing the scheduled promotion."[70]

This incident, which was basically gossip, would not be worth mentioning if it had not had repercussions that annoyed the General to such an extent that at the end of 1942 he failed to send the Government his best wishes for the new year. The General suspected that his enemies were plotting against him, and wrote to Kobelt that to his knowledge this was the first time in the history of the Swiss Army that the Federal Council refused to promote an officer against requests by the Military Department, the commander-in-chief, and the corps commanders without first consulting with the officer's superiors. He considered this to be an expression of mistrust against the military command, whose authority was being questioned. Guisan demanded to be informed about the discussions, the investigation, and its results. He argued that he was entitled to this information both as commander-in-chief and as the father of the officer concerned.[71]

Guisan resented the fact that none of the Federal Councilors had told him about the matter, and he declared that if he had known about it he would not have attended the dinner at the von Wattenwyl mansion. Federal Councilor Kobelt tried to calm the General, explaining to him once again what had happened at the Cabinet meeting regarding his son's promotion and writing to him in an apologetic tone about the dinner: "I would have considered it as a piece of tactlessness to confront you with this unpleasant news at that event." Kobelt reassured Guisan that the Federal Council had made every effort to "proceed correctly in this embarrassing matter [and] to leave [the General] out of it as far as possible." He added that he was "very embarrassed that our first exchange of letters in the new year lacks the usual understanding."[72]

The General also addressed Federal Councilor von Steiger, the Head of the Justice and Police Department, to complain about the "Federal Council's very regretful decision" and to find out "what erroneous information" had caused the Federal Council to initially deny his son's promotion. He demanded that the injustice done to his son be made good and asked to see "the documents on which the Federal Council based its severe measure regarding Colonel Guisan." Von Steiger declined his request, replying, "Since we do not live in a military state, we are not authorized to hand out to the army files regarding proceedings undertaken by the police." However, he agreed to "verbally inform [the General] based on the case file" once all documents were available.[73]

At first, the General did not accept this option. As he was not satisfied with the government's responses, the exchange of letters continued throughout the month of January, now also involving the new Federal President, Enrico Celio, and Federal Councilor Pilet-Golaz. The General asked, "Who intervened how and why?" He appealed to Kobelt's sense of honor as a high-ranking officer and threatened to bring the case before Parliament "because this matter, which got off to a bad start, has repercussions on the position and the authority of the commander-in-chief of the armed forces."[74]

Kobelt annotated Guisan's letter with the remark, "I am not authorized to provide information on this matter." In his detailed reply, he explained:

> Contrary to what you assume, we would like to repeat that the promotion was postponed for objective reasons. The Federal Council could not decide otherwise if it wanted to fulfill its duty and assume the responsibility that it has regarding these issues. This was not at all a rash or hasty decision. . . . No injustice has been done to Colonel Guisan because his promotion was postponed. The delay was his own fault because he entertained a relationship with a suspicious person at a time when common Swiss citizens, let alone staff officers of the army, had to be very careful about dealing with foreigners."[75]

Thanks to Federal President Celio's mediation, on January 18 von Steiger and Guisan met and settled the dispute, at least superficially. The General wrote to the Head of the Military Department that the clarification he had received allowed him "to declare that this regrettable affair was over and done with."[76] Kobelt for his part assured the General that "this dispute [was] off the table" after receiving his letter.[77] When Guisan mentioned the matter once again a week later, still voicing reservations, Kobelt did not respond but wrote on the letter, "The General apparently has to have the last word, otherwise the tiresome exchange of letters will never come to an end."[78] The dispute was officially settled, but based on the available documents one gains the impression that both sides were left with a nasty taste in their mouths.

While he was looking into Lt. Colonel Guisan's past, Kobelt was also informed that the General's son was suspected of being involved in deliveries of barracks to the armed divisions of the German SS. He told the General about these suspicions, writing to him, "If this information is correct, I would like to recommend that you advise your son to stop doing such business with foreign countries in view of his father's position as Commander-in-Chief of the Swiss Army, even if from a legal point of view nothing could be held against him."[79]

The controversy surrounding Henry's promotion was not the only incident that gave the General headaches in connection with his son. Members of the personal staff witnessed on several occasions how the General indignantly reprimanded his son because of his loose tongue, his womanizing, and his way of handling money, even when he was a colonel.[80] Colonel Wyss, who was Henry's commander for an extended period, told Captain Paul Meyer that once he had to lock him up. Meyer reported that Wyss "said that [Henry's] mother and father went to beg him to release their son."[81]

Undoubtedly the most complicated relationship the commander-in-chief maintained with a Cabinet member was the one with Pilet-Golaz, like himself a native of Vaud. Pilet-Golaz allegedly called Guisan the "General of the chamois."[82] The differences between Guisan and the Head of the Department of Foreign Affairs were rooted not only in diverging opinions on foreign policy, especially relations with the Axis Powers, but also in personal animosities that may have been based on their different characters, talents, and inclinations and that are therefore difficult to ascertain. The two men who were supposed to work closely together in the interest of the country were on such bad terms that they ended up hardly speaking to each other. There is no doubt that the tensions between Guisan and Pilet-Golaz, aggravated by their contrasting personalities, were greater, and their tendency to plot against each other was stronger, than has been known to outsiders until now.

The difficulties surrounding the promotion of the General's son had just been overcome when the next, far more serious, incident arose. In February 1943, General Guisan transmitted to the Head of the Military Department a special report by Hans Hausamann's Bureau "Ha," according to which Pilet-Golaz had offered his assistance to bring about a separate peace agreement between the Third Reich and the Allies, because he considered that this would prevent the Russian armies from advancing further and thus save Europe from Bolshevism. Germany's envoy and military attaché in Bern were reported to have informed Switzerland's Foreign Minister that the German leadership was interested in concluding a peace accord with the Western powers because the situation of the Wehrmacht on the Eastern front and inside Germany was considered to be "very serious."[83]

The Bureau "Ha" report claimed that Federal Councilor Pilet had relayed the German diplomats' suggestion to the United States' envoy to Switzerland, Leland Harrison, with the remark that "the Anglo-Saxons should let the Russians fight this war on their own." It said that the American immediately cabled this information to Washington; however, President Roosevelt was reported to reply that the Allies would continue fighting until the Axis Powers capitulated unconditionally. The report indicated, "This is firsthand information. We do not say that we quoted the German envoy, the German Military

Attaché, and Federal Councilor Pilet-Golaz verbatim, yet we know that this was the way in which the American government was informed about the matter.[84]

Kobelt must have realized immediately that if this information was true and became public, Switzerland's Foreign Minister would be doomed to step down for non-neutral conduct. Kobelt questioned Pilet-Golaz about the matter the same day and wrote about it in his diary, "Mr. Pilet spontaneously declared that it was not true. Then I wrote to the General on that same day, February 9, 1943, that not one single word was true about the matter and that he should see to it that these rumors be stopped. Wrote the same letter to Hausamann and asked him to tell me who had provided him with this information and to see to it that the rumor would not spread nor do damage to the country."[85]

Hausamann, who had been promoted to major at the end of 1942, wrote a confidential letter to Chief of Intelligence Masson to confirm that his sources were perfectly reliable. He said that he could "declare as absolutely certain" what he had reported, even though he could not mention the names of his informants. He insisted, "Even if Mr. P[ilet]-G[olaz] denies it, it happened the way I reported it."[86] In a letter, Hausamann also assured Kobelt that he was convinced that the information about Pilet's initiative was correct, explaining, "I transmitted it only once I was absolutely sure that an error or a misunderstanding was excluded."[87] He said the only evidence that was missing to topple Pilet were the telegrams.

During a private meeting with Kobelt, Hausamann reiterated that he could not mention any names "because he had promised on his word of honor to keep the informant's name secret; he said that this informant had provided him with a lot of useful, accurate information before."[88] Kobelt speculated that this informant might be "a minister on the Allied side."

After receiving a copy of the Bureau "Ha" report directly from the General, Federal President Celio intervened as well. First he spoke with Kobelt "about differences between the General and Federal Councilor Pilet." Kobelt wrote about the conversation, "[Celio] says that he intends to consult with each member of the Cabinet on the matter of P[ilet], which causes him great concern. He tells me that the increasing attacks against the Foreign Minister cannot continue."[89] At the Cabinet meeting of February 16, Pilet-Golaz addressed the issue of his own accord after being shown the "Ha" report by the Federal President, "declaring in a convincing manner that not a single word about it was true."[90] In a written declaration, Pilet-Golaz stated that the accusations raised against him were false. He explained that he had last received Germany's envoy Köcher on February 16, 1943, that the military attaché was not with him on that occasion, and that no one had talked with him about an alleged initiative.

Moreover, he said that he had last seen the American envoy on January 11. He argued that if one used just a bit of common sense one would realize that the report was nonsense. He added, "The content of the report is absurd. It denotes a total lack of knowledge about the possibilities, the habits, and the most basic precautions [of diplomatic initiatives]."[91]

As both sides claimed to tell the truth, and Pilet-Golaz was determined not to let the matter rest, the Federal Council asked the General to order that "a preliminary hearing of evidence [be carried out] against persons unknown, and perhaps against Major Hausamann, the Intelligence Service, and the Security Service."[92] Moreover, in agreement with the Cabinet, Federal President Celio received the American envoy Harrison to inquire of him about the matter. Afterward Celio informed the General in writing that the statements in the Bureau "Ha" report were a deception from beginning to end, adding, "Minister Harrison, whom I personally invited into a meeting, formally denies having had any conversation of this kind with Federal Councilor Pilet-Golaz."[93]

The correspondence between Hausamann and the General in this controversial matter leaves the disturbing impression that the two men plotted against Pilet-Golaz to topple him as Federal Councilor. Guisan left it up to his trusted intelligence officer to handle the matter. Hausamann drafted the detailed reply to the Federal Council and wrote to the General in an attached letter:

> Please find attached the draft reply to Federal Councilor Kobelt's letter of February 9. The document is written in a way that you, General, will be implicated in this matter only indirectly from now on. Most of all, nobody, least of all Federal Councilor Pilet-Golaz, will be able to accuse you of having a personal interest in, or even of being personally involved in, having the case followed up. In view of the future, I consider this to be extremely important. The draft letter explains that you are interested in the incident only in the higher interest of the country. Because the information comes from a reliable source, which is also indicated in the letter, you really felt it to be your duty as commander-in-chief to inform the Federal authorities about it.[94]

Hausamann also gave Guisan advice on how to proceed with the matter, making himself indispensable to Guisan and offering to protect him. He wrote:

> General, please consider that Mr. Pilet-Golaz is virtually lying in wait to find a reason to attack you. Should it become necessary to mobilize members of parliament or take any other action in connection with the Pilet-Golaz matter, I would like to propose to you, General, that you

use my humble services. I know almost all these people and can easily contact them. If anything happens to me during that time, not much will be lost. However, if you have a mishap, General, the damage will be immense and cannot be foreseen.[95]

The letter to Kobelt stated that the author of the report had "the reputation of being reliable." He was said to be an officer who reported the news "because he considered that there was absolutely no doubt that it was true." The person who provided the officer with the information was identified as "a united nations [*sic*] diplomat who is accredited in Switzerland and is well-disposed toward our country; he wrote down for himself what Minister Harrison had told him about the matter at the American Legation. The informant personally saw the manuscript that was prepared during that meeting."[96] The letter further claimed that the informant was willing to try to obtain written evidence if desired, but in that event a large scandal would be inevitable. It added that the General did not want to pursue the matter but that he left it up to the Federal Council if it wanted to do so.

When Hausamann was told that the military authorities would hear the evidence in the matter, he reassured Kobelt that he would be able to provide the evidence but that this would take some time; nevertheless he claimed he would be able to prove that his information was not wrong. He considered that it was unusual to hear evidence regarding the origin and reliability of information received by the Intelligence Service, but he said that he welcomed this measure, explaining, "This case is about my professional honor as an intelligence officer, my reputation, reliability, and conscientiousness. Because I know what is at stake I am grateful that by announcing the proceedings by a military court I will be able to go ahead and produce the evidence."[97]

Hausamann gave a detailed explanation to Guisan why he thought that in the interest of the country Federal Councilor Pilet-Golaz should be made to resign as soon as possible, arguing:

The end of the war is in sight. Nowadays there is no doubt that the Allies will be victorious. Representatives of Switzerland will have to participate in the negotiations on how to reorganize the world. It will be decisive that the Swiss delegates, who are bound to be led by the Foreign Minister, enjoy the confidence and sympathy of the statesmen who will represent the Allied nations. However, Federal Councilor Pilet-Golaz can pride himself neither on the sympathy nor on the confidence of the Allies, nor does he enjoy the sympathy and confidence of his own people. . . . Knowing that several Federal Councilors have been holding meetings recently regarding Mr. Pilet, I could imagine that one is just waiting for the right opportunity to suggest to Mr. Pilet that he resign. Now this opportunity presents itself. . . . The first step in this direction has been taken, and I have reason to hope that the next, decisive step will follow soon. All the conditions have been set to make it happen.[98]

Hausamann explained that if he accomplished his goal, he would "render our country a service." He claimed that he did not have "any vile motives to take a stand against Mr. Pilet," which would make it easy for him to bear any grudge that would certainly be harbored against him in that connection. He said that after the Däniker affair and other similar cases he was used "to being considered a rabble-rouser and treated with hostility."[99]

Hausamann believed that success was close at hand; however, this was not so. The hearing of evidence, carried out by Colonel Achermann, the Senior Judge of the 8th Division, did not yield any conclusive results. As a witness, Hausamann declared that he had personally seen a "word-by-word translation of notes which a foreign diplomat [had] written at the American Legation in Bern in a foreign language based on information received from Minister Harrison." He added that he had had no personal contact with Minister Harrison himself but had received the information from an intermediary, a foreign diplomat who was not a staff member of the American Legation but who had access there. He said that "for the time being" he did not want to reveal that person's name.[100]

Based on the report by Colonel Achermann, Military Attorney General Eugster informed the General that Hausamann had "refused to reveal the source of his information." He explained that there was no legal means to force him to disclose the name of the informant because as an intelligence officer he was only a witness. He added that because the author of the accusations against Federal Councilor Pilet-Golaz was allegedly a member of the diplomatic corps, he fell under the principle of extraterritoriality; thus prosecuting the alleged source was out of the question. The Military Attorney General admitted that according to Article 93 of the Military Penal Code, Hausamann could be sentenced to a maximum of 90 days in prison and be fined up to 1,000 francs; however, he added that the intelligence officer had the right to refuse to make a statement if it was to his own disadvantage. In view of the complicated situation, Eugster recommended that the case be dropped and the case file be forwarded to the Federal Council for its information.[101]

After the investigation was concluded, in a meeting with the commander-in-chief, Military Attorney General Eugster, and Intelligence Chief Masson,

Hausamann insisted once again that his information was reliable. The General told Federal Councilor Kobelt about this meeting, "[Hausamann] claims he can prove, within three to four weeks, that his information is accurate. Until then he absolutely refuses to reveal the name of his informant. I have granted Major Hausamann a deadline of four weeks to produce the evidence which he says he can obtain and warned him that I would have to take action against him if he failed to do so."[102]

Shortly before the deadline was up, Hausamann had to admit that he had not been able to get the promised evidence, explaining that it was difficult to obtain it "because it [was] hardly possible anymore to carry any papers across several borders without taking great risks."[103] Consequently, he asked Guisan to extend the deadline by one month, until mid-June 1943. However, Guisan did not grant his request and informed the intelligence officer that he regretted that he had to relieve him of his duties on the army staff until further notice.[104] In a letter, the General also informed Chief of the General Staff Huber of his decision, which he said was made "with great regret."[105] After consulting with Huber, and undoubtedly with the General's accord, Masson decided to put Hausamann on leave but to let him continue to perform his intelligence job as a civilian. The Chief of Intelligence explained, "It is impossible for us to do away with the entire organization 'Ha' during this critical time for Switzerland. The chief of the general staff accepted my arguments and agreed to this solution."[106]

Hence, Hausamann was only formally dropped, even though the Federal Council had believed, and Pilet-Golaz had expected, that he would be suspended. With his Bureau "Ha," Hausamann proved to be indispensable to the army. During his "leave," his personal relationship with Guisan did not change significantly. He continued to have direct access to the General and continued to provide him with information on Pilet-Golaz' activities.

In the summer of 1943, Hausamann reported to Guisan that the Foreign Minister had told a third party that he had documents indicating that the General had proposed sending a mission to Berlin. If Guisan should continue to make critical remarks about the Federal Council's policy, according to this report, the Minister would not hesitate to make use of these documents. Hausamann wrote to the General, "It does not actually matter to me whether Mr. Pilet-Golaz really has any documents. However, in the interest of our country and our people I am very keen on preventing him from finding a pretext to use them. . . . Pilet-Golaz and others are of course very concerned about what history books will write about you, General, and about Mr. Pilet-Golaz' activities." He argued that the time was right to set the record straight if the Foreign Minister could be prevented from "letting the bomb explode." Hence, he argued that it was important not to tell Federal Councilor Pilet-Golaz that the General knew about his intentions, adding, "Instead, he should come to believe that for you, General, the Pilet-Golaz case no longer exists." Hausamann urged Guisan to be careful about what he said about the Foreign Minister, especially to very prominent politicians, because they would probably tell the Federal Councilor about his statements. Hausamann concluded his report by asking the General to continue to leave "working on the matter of Pilet-Golaz" up to him. He claimed that he made his request not because he wanted to push himself forward but because he had "nothing else in mind than to defend your interests and to relieve you of as many unpleasant things as possible."[107]

After working for the intelligence service as a civilian for eight months, at the beginning of 1944 Hausamann requested to be formally readmitted to the army staff or to be discharged altogether.[108] He made his request without being able to produce the promised evidence regarding Federal Councilor Pilet-Golaz' alleged attempt to mediate between Germany and the Western Allies. Because Masson could not do without the intelligence network Hausamann had set up, and because Hausamann declared that he was ready to apologize formally to Pilet-Golaz, the General resolved to again call officially on the intelligence officer's services.[109] Pilet was "terribly furious" because of Hausamann,[110] yet he was indulgent and agreed to this solution. He wrote to Kobelt that he was aware that the intelligence service had to use all possible means to come by certain information.[111] However, he demanded that Hausamann focus exclusively on gathering information on military matters and stay away from politics because he considered that his reports were often tendentious and biased. On March 1, 1944, Major Hausamann was officially readmitted to the intelligence service.[112]

The question of whether Federal Councilor Pilet-Golaz tried to intervene with the American envoy Harrison to bring about a separate peace agreement has remained unanswered to the present day. Bonjour tends to think that this was possible in view of the thoughtless manner in which Pilet "expressed his fear of Bolshevism taking over Europe" and of his "playing a risky game" as Foreign Minister of a permanently neutral state.[113] However, based on the documents available to researchers today, this author does not believe that Pilet-Golaz falsified the truth regarding the issue. National Councilor Albert Oeri certainly failed to be convinced by Hausamann's version when he accompanied the intelligence officer as a mediator to a meeting with former Czech Minister Kopecky, who was accredited as a diplomat at the League of Nations. Oeri wrote to the General about the one-hour meeting:

Following my conversations with Major H[ausamann], I expected [Mr. Kopecky] to inform me that U.S. Minister Harrison had told him that

Mr. P[ilet]-G[olaz] had made attempts to present the idea of a separate peace agreement to the Anglo-Saxon powers. This expectation did not materialize during the meeting. . . . [Kopecky] explained that he was under the impression Mr. Pilet-Golaz was influenced by German elements that would like to conclude a separate peace agreement with the Anglo-Saxons, and tried to intervene accordingly. But I would like to point out that [Kopecky] stated that this was his impression; he did not provide me with any more specific clues.

Oeri thought that if the above was all Hausamann had found out from the diplomat, and that if his report No. 225 was based on that information alone, one had to fear that he had been "rather amateurish during his excursion into the diplomatic realm." He concluded that even if there was no doubt Hausamann had meant well and acted out of patriotic concerns, he "would be served best if he could make a decent retreat and things were left as they were."[114]

When analyzing this shady affair, one has to keep in mind that the Americans would not have been particularly interested in protecting Switzerland's Foreign Minister, whose policy was viewed as pro-German. It would be difficult to understand why Harrison would deny Pilet's alleged initiative to Federal President Celio if Pilet had actually undertaken it, because the Allies would probably not have been uninterested in having Pilet-Golaz ousted from office. Moreover, the United States Legation would have reported any such initiative to Washington even if it had been denied to the Swiss authorities. However, among the U.S. State Department documents available to the public no relevant information has been found.[115]

Hausamann had strong analytical capabilities and powers of reasoning, but his vivid imagination sometimes seduced him into making exaggerated statements. In view of his unconditional willingness to risk his neck for the revered General, it is completely possible that he purposely misinformed others. It is unlikely that Guisan inspired the plot. However, considering the manifold connections, one receives the impression that he was not unhappy about the bold, if underhanded, move to bring about the downfall of Pilet-Golaz, his main opponent on the Federal Council. It is striking that in public opinion General Guisan managed to rise to the same level as the government or even higher. He appeared to be more powerful than the executive branch not only through his military command but also as a political authority. A train station manager once wrote to him, "[You] managed to do what no Swiss had managed to do since 1848: your word carried more weight than that of all seven Federal Councilors and of all party leaders combined."[116] This view was shared by many others in the country at the time.

Hans Hausamann was one of the people who tried to push Guisan to consolidate his position as commander-in-chief, asserting his independence from the executive branch of the government. In 1940, he wrote a seven-page memorandum on the constitutional relations between the Federal Council and the Army Command in which he stated that "according to the Constitution, [the General] reports exclusively to the Parliament [which elected him], not to the Federal Council."[117] He argued that therefore "the General [had] the natural authority" not only to hold the supreme command of the armed forces but also to decide on any measures that were necessary "to protect the Swiss Confederation from dangers coming from the outside or affecting the country's defense through outside influence if these measures [were] not decided by the Parliament itself." Hence, he wrote that the Army Command was "the absolute authority in all matters relating to calling up troops, training and arming troops, nominating officers, and requesting the financial means necessary for the national defense."[118] He pointed out to the General that there was an "urgent need for a determined, uniform organization of the national defense that covers the entire population and is free from anachronistic civilian inhibitions" and recommended that he "exercise his authority to the fullest."[119] Hence, there was no lack of effort by Hausamann to incite the General to assert himself and stand above the Federal Council.

The longer wartime duty lasted, and the more popular the General became, the more signs of envy and jealousy became apparent in the Federal Council. The General, who visibly enjoyed his popularity, overshadowed every member of the Federal government in all respects. This fact especially bothered Federal Councilors Pilet-Golaz and Kobelt, who would have liked to show themselves in public more often but did not have Guisan's charming manners nor the same opportunities he had to become the center of attention. Hans Rudolf Kurz, who worked closely with the Federal Council for many years, wrote, "It was not easy for [Kobelt] to bear the fate of having to stand in the shadow of those who were popular" and that he had "bitter feelings" about it at times.[120] Similarly, Hermann Böschenstein, a keen observer, stated that the Federal Council was "not always happy" about the publicity the General received. Kobelt in particular visibly suffered from "fading as Head of the Military Department next to the General on many occasions."[121] Barbey noted Liaison Officer Hans Bracher reporting that Federal Councilor Kobelt said soon after being elected, "Either him or me . . ."[122] Hence, it appears that Kobelt was prepared to risk a power struggle with the General. As mentioned earlier, personal prestige and human weaknesses played a part in the relations between the members of the Cabinet and the commander-in-chief.

From the available information, it would go too far to conclude that a continuous guerrilla war was going on between the Federal Council and the General, even though the frictions must not be overlooked. A public conflict never broke out. Officially, relations remained correct, and thus the difficulties were hardly apparent to outsiders. In 1962, former Federal Councilor Wetter asserted that "differences between the Federal Council and the General are pure imagination."[123] However, in view of the facts, this statement glossed over the true situation and may hardly be deemed valid. Hans Müller, who wrote a biography of Kobelt, also stated that relations between Kobelt and General Guisan were "better than some people had claimed."[124]

The tensions never caused spiteful personal remarks to be pronounced. It should be noted that, according to Marguth, during Kobelt's occasional visits to the General's quarters they quite liked playing cards together.[125] The private letters, exchanged at the turn of every year, except for 1942–43, expressed feelings of trust and kindness. At the end of his first year in office Kobelt noted, "Handwritten New Year's letter to the General. Pointed out that in areas which concern both the Federal Government and the Army, we had to deal with many difficult issues but were able [to solve] them to our satisfaction, staying on good terms and being inspired by the willingness to understand each other. In the new year, I will attempt to work together in the same way, in the interest of the country and the army. General expressed the same ideas in his reply."[126] In his New Year's letter of 1944, Kobelt wrote that it was due to the large responsibility both possessed that there were occasional differences of opinion, but he said that he was pleased to note that their "cooperation [was] becoming more and more understanding and trusting."[127]

On the occasion of the General's seventieth birthday, Kobelt congratulated him by acknowledging that the trust placed in him by the entire population could "not be appreciated enough," and said that it was thanks to this trust that the determination to defend the country and the readiness to serve in the army had been maintained in spite of the long duration of the state of mobilization. Kobelt ensured Guisan that he would "loyally continue to work with [him, adding] I believe that when it comes to the decisive issues, we have always been able to find a common ground. On this special day, I would like to thank you very much for making constant efforts to lend a hand in order to reach an understanding."[128] Guisan responded to the birthday letter with equal kindness, writing that it was normal that they could not always agree on everything but that it was essential that they were able to come to an agreement every time the most important issue, "the defense of our cherished and beautiful country," was at stake. The General also complimented Kobelt, stating, "I can imagine how delicate your task is; indeed, I am tempted to believe that it is even more delicate than mine."[129]

At the end of 1944, the two officials once again exchanged best wishes and complimented each other. Kobelt assured the General that he was happy to note that "during the past year, the problems that we had to deal with together could be solved once again in perfect harmony"; and he said that he would continue to "do everything to make it possible to work together in a pleasant manner."[130] The General made similar statements and went as far as declaring, "We did not have any trouble coming to agreements."[131]

When comparing the tensions between the army command and the Federal Council during World War I and World War II, one must note that they were not smaller between 1939 and 1945. General Guisan may never have threatened to resign, as his predecessor General Wille did on several occasions.[132] However, relations between General Guisan and the Federal Council were at times almost unbearably tense, even though an open conflict was avoided, at least until the end of the war, thanks to the goodwill of the parties involved.[133] Because censorship worked better than during the First World War, the public heard very little about the internal difficulties, but the army staff and Parliament were kept better informed.

It will always be delicate to define the powers of the military and of the political authorities at the Federal level during times of mobilization of the armed forces. As Corps Commander Hans Frick wrote to the Head of the Military Department after the war, "Politics and strategy cannot be strictly separated; they both have repercussions on each other."[134] In addition, in connection with certain differences of opinion during the war, one receives the impression that decision-making bodies competed with each other on a certain level of hostility to deal with their subconscious aggressions because there was no actual combat at hand. There is legitimate reason to believe that the rivalries would automatically have become secondary, rather than having fatal consequences, if Switzerland had become involved in the war.[135]

Cooperation with Chief of the General Staff Huber

DURING THE FIRST WORLD WAR, the chief of the general staff was at least as popular as the commander-in-chief. General Wille and his chief of staff, von Sprecher, were a team that presented itself to the outside world as a unified military command.

During World War II, the chief of the general staff did not enjoy nearly the same popularity as the commander-in-chief. Jakob Huber stood in the shadow of the popular and admired General Guisan, and his name was familiar neither to many soldiers nor to the public. Not many people knew what he looked like. Nevertheless, there is no doubt that Huber was one of Switzerland's most remarkable military leaders.[1] He and the General shared the bulk of responsibility for keeping the army fit and ready to fight.

It is normally part of a chief of staff's destiny to stand behind his more publicly recognized commander and quietly do his job, von Sprecher being an exception in this regard. Another reason for Huber's relative anonymity was that he was taciturn and introverted and did not like to be in the limelight. He represented the ideal soldier of the Roman Empire who preferred reality to appearances, though he had far more substance than could be appreciated at first glance. Max Häni, a future brigadier who was acquainted with both Guisan and Huber and knew life inside the army headquarters very well, wrote in his memoir, "Next to the dominant figure of the General, Huber was inconspicuous, but it would be wrong to claim that he had no personality. He knew about the General's need for recognition and let him enjoy all the public honors. He did his duty quietly but accomplished a great deal as a leader."[2] National Councilor Karl Steiner put it more bluntly, stating, "The General is the brand name, and his chief of staff represents the strength and the substance of the army."[3]

Guisan, the commander-in-chief, and Huber, the chief of the general staff who was nine years his junior, complemented each other in a way that in retrospect appears ideal. The army command needed an expert chief of staff who worked methodically behind the scenes as a balance to the lively and communicative personality of Guisan, who enjoyed public appearances. Even though Guisan, a Swiss French militia officer, and Huber, a Swiss German career officer, had completely different personalities, they had a number of common interests. They shared a concern for agricultural issues, began their military careers in the artillery, loved horseback riding, were pro-French, and both were practically bilingual. In the spring of 1940 Barbey wrote in his diary, "Guisan and Huber—a perfect match of dynamism and methodology."[4]

It repays study to look more closely at the relationship between the General and Huber, who, according to the army's doctrine, was the General's closest collaborator for more than five and a half years. When he considered the different options for his chief of staff after being elected commander-in-chief, Guisan listed Divisional Commander Huber as one of his top candidates. He noted about the Assistant Chief of Staff for the Rear, who was Chief of the General Staff Labhart's deputy at the time, "Quiet, upright, disciplined, has little imagination, reserved. Could be Chief Engineer, used to be a surveyor, knowledgeable."[5]

In December 1939, when he was looking for a suitable successor for Labhart, the General received an assessment of Huber's capabilities that contained some criticisms, but still concluded that Huber would be his best choice as chief of staff. The assessment said that Huber appeared "somewhat disillusioned" and lacked imagination, so he would not be "a first-rate driving intellectual force." It also stated that Huber had adopted bureaucratic habits over the years, which could make it difficult to get things done quickly. On the other hand, he was said to grant freedom of action to capable associates, which would balance his own passivity. The assessment came to the conclusion that "being above all disciplined, [Huber] will always be a loyal subordinate who carries out the General's ideas without trying to impose his own ideas here and there once a decision has been made. Overall, he is an acceptable solution."[6]

General Guisan repeatedly acknowledged Huber's performance and emphasized how well they worked together. In his postwar report he wrote:

> The Chief of the General Staff's realism sparked a general feeling of confidence, and I was fully aware how valuable this was. . . . One knows that I held Colonel-Corps Commander Huber in high esteem.

Some people wondered why we did not see each other every day and why we did not 'live under the same roof.' However, I consider that these people know little about the principles on which cooperation of this kind has to be based. The Chief of the General Staff came to see me, or I went to see him, whenever it was necessary, but I respected our mutual independence, the way it is supposed to be when everyone's preferences and work habits are taken into consideration.[7]

In an interview with Gafner, Guisan also mentioned his good relations with the chief of the general staff, describing them as "always excellent" in spite of occasional differences of opinion.[8] He called Huber a valuable collaborator and a perfectly loyal comrade, "and what's more, a loyal friend."[9] Walde, who wrote a biography of Huber, counted the General mentioning his chief of the general staff 38 times in his postwar report; on 15 occasions he quoted him extensively.[10] For instance, the four-page analysis of the tactical problems of a "mobile, aggressive defense" and of staying in staggered defensive positions during a potential combat in the Réduit, which Huber had given during a maneuver briefing in spring 1944, was quoted verbatim.[11]

In his diary, Barbey repeatedly praised Huber, who—in a telling indication of his personality—used to go to bed early at headquarters and get up just as early to go for a ride on his horse by himself. Barbey called him "a personification of common sense," adding, "He is taciturn, yet as different as we feel from him, or perhaps the more different we feel from him, the more we respect him. He is really a typical sterling 'old man,' as the British would say. He looks like one, too, with his brick-red face and his white hair, his bright eyes, and his good manners." Barbey referred to Huber's "legendary calm" which deserved to be better known, explaining, "One will never be able to appreciate enough the significance of the chief of the general staff's composure during times of real danger."[12] The Germans remarked about the chief of the general staff, "Reserved, correct, scholarly type. (Wife is French.)"[13]

In spite of the close cooperation between Guisan and Huber, their relationship was not always perfect. Reports highlighting the permanent harmony at work contrast with accounts that paint a less idealistic picture. There is startling evidence from some of the General's immediate subordinates and from Huber himself that clearly indicate relations between the two men at the top of Switzerland's armed forces were far from exemplary; in fact, at times they were "unsatisfactory." Statements describing flawless harmony must be disqualified in large part as too rosy. Tensions existed under which the chief of the general staff suffered, and he repeatedly said that he intended to resign. On two occasions he actually requested in writing to be relieved of his post, and the General had difficulty convincing him to stay on. Huber wrote about this to Federal Councilor Kobelt, "Both times the General refused to grant my request and reassured me that he had full confidence in me. Each time I believed him until he disproved his own words through new deeds. It was always easy to get back on good terms when we talked instead of writing to each other."[14]

Karl Walde was careful in his choice of words but did not fail to mention that Huber had "serious disputes" with the General.[15] The conflicts were rooted less in clashing operational or organizational views than in the fact that the commander-in-chief had set up a special staff that both Huber and his predecessor Labhart considered rivals of the army staff.[16] This additional body understandably weakened the chief of the general staff's position, and had particularly negative consequences when Huber was bypassed in discussions of certain issues or when he failed to be informed about a few important meetings. Huber was shocked above all when he found out that information had been kept from him that would normally have been communicated if the commander-in-chief had trusted him.

During wartime duty, Huber gave the impression that for the most part he patiently accepted everything that was imposed on him. After the war, however, he explained to Federal Councilor Kobelt that relations between him and the General had been far from "what you would expect them to be between a commander and his chief of staff." He said that he kept quiet as a soldier in order not to jeopardize the national defense, adding, "The General's good reputation was to the army's advantage. I promoted it as far as I could. I will continue to keep up appearances toward everyone the way I have until now, except with a few close friends."[17] Huber stated that he had been disgusted by the "constant bickering between the General and the Federal Council" and had advised the General to put an end to it. He wrote, "It is not my fault that the laws existing at the beginning of World War II allowed the General to rule as a dictator."[18] He concluded his 17-page letter to Federal Councilor Kobelt with the comment that the time of duty between 1939 and 1945, "which was not a time of perfect happiness," was now over.[19]

Hans Frick, who became Chief Instructor of the Armed Forces after the war, holding the rank of Corps Commander, wrote an extensive report to the Head of the Military Department in which he also addressed the issue of cooperation among the army command, stating, "There was a great lack of contact between the General and the chief of the general staff . . . not only during the tenure of Labhart but also of Huber." He argued that one of the major reasons for this shortcoming was the fact that the General had a special staff working for him:

During wartime duty, even strictly operational matters were handled by the General's personal staff without the chief of the general staff being consulted. He was simply informed in writing after the fact just like any other officer concerned. What was more, once the army headquarters had been moved from Spiez to Langnau, the distance to the General's headquarters was about 15 miles, so they had to drive 30 miles back and forth to see each other, which was rather time-consuming. . . . If the commander-in-chief is not willing or able to personally discuss the main issues with the chief of the general staff on a daily basis, there is either a lack of mutual trust, requiring a change of personnel, or worse, a lack of feeling superior to his staff. At any rate, the situation that existed during wartime duty must never occur again.[20]

The only possible interpretation of this passage is that Corps Commander Frick indirectly criticized the General's failure to project authority over the army staff, possibly because of a feeling of inferiority. Corps Commander Borel voiced similar criticism, saying that there had "never been enough personal contact" between Guisan and Huber.[21]

Huber had never commanded a division but had been commander of the Fortress of St-Maurice. During discussions among high-ranking officers, the chief of the general staff's operational capabilities as well as his communicative skills were not uncontested. At the end of 1939, Labhart wrote in his diary that he had received confidential information that "the heads of section for the rear were disappointed about Colonel-Divisional Commander Huber's way of doing his job."[22] Half a year later, he noted that two members of the army staff had reported "very strange things" about the work atmosphere there, saying about the troops, "They are sick and tired of serving in the army. They wish that a change would take place soon."[23] During strategic maneuvers in 1943 under Corps Commander Miescher, Huber was put in charge of the defending units. After a briefing, Divisional Commander Frick pulled the chief of the General's personal staff aside to explain to him "firmly" that he considered Huber's instructions to be "Meaningless and disastrous! That's what they are!"[24]

Huber was bound to be the target of plots aimed to oust him from his important position. As early as 1940, before the beginning of Germany's western campaign, Colonel von Werdt, Switzerland's Military Attaché in Berlin, probably acting on orders of the Swiss envoy Frölicher, went to Bern to stir up sentiments against Huber and to advocate having him replaced by Corps Commander Wille. The General received him and later noted about their conversation, "His mission was above all to propose Wille as Chief of the General Staff!"[25] In June 1940, Wille personally attacked Huber, complaining in writing to Guisan that Huber had "falsely claimed" that Wille was the "protégé" of Captain P. Mutterer, an instructor in the army who had been sentenced to six years in prison and had been stripped of his rank the previous month.[26] The General tried to calm Wille and recommended that he withdraw his complaint.[27] Even though the case was not resolved according to his liking, Wille declared that he would let the matter rest.[28]

In the summer of 1940, some pro-German officers who were close to Wille and Däniker made a concerted effort to have Huber replaced with Wille. At the end of July, Colonel Däniker informed the Chief Instructor that in the near future a delegation of officers would meet with the Federal Council and demand that Huber be removed from his post. As Däniker explained to Wille:

> Many soldiers and civilians demand that you be placed in an influential position with decision-making power. (There is even talk of replacing the commander-in-chief, but that does not seem feasible.) The current chief of the general staff is in large part responsible for the present impossible situation, even though this is in part because he has been passive and lets things take their course. He has become unacceptable in his position. In the current situation a person whom everyone trusts must replace him. You are that person. When the demands are presented to the Federal Council, though, the emphasis will be less on the negative performance of Divisional Commander Huber than on the urgent need to place you in the influential position of chief of the general staff, and that therefore Colonel-Divisional Commander Huber has to step aside. This is the domestic political and military aspect of the matter. The foreign political aspect is just as important. Naming you chief of the general staff is an act that will demonstrate, like no other, that Switzerland is making serious attempts to take the new situation into account and to participate in constructing a new Europe. Personally I believe that this is the only step that will give us some breathing space and make it possible to gain time to take additional steps, and many others agree with me.[29]

The statements made in that letter may well be an indication that replacing the chief of the general staff was considered by the group of officers around Colonel Däniker as a first step toward ultimately removing the General and having him replaced by Wille. When their demand did not yield any result, Frölicher admonished from Berlin, "Considering the animosity that exists here against the General, it would be useful if at least the proposed changes in the General's entourage were made."[30]

Some of the numerous responsibilities of the chief of the general staff included providing the commander-in-chief with documentation for assessing a situation, receiving the General's operational decisions, and then translating them into orders and instructions. He also monitored the orders' execution and secured the army's strength by organizing the supply of arms, equipment, food, and any other material. Setting up the new front in the center of the country required an enormous amount of work. Once the decision had been made in favor of the Réduit, Huber put his whole energy into implementing it. He felt very much at ease accomplishing this task. As an artilleryman he was convinced that defense was the decisive factor in war and that the artillery played a dominating role.[31] Deploying the troops into the Réduit positions and later bringing them back into a forward front required substantial logistical effort.

In view of its many and diverse tasks, it is not surprising that the army staff had an unusually high number of personnel. When Huber began his job on January 1, 1940, 1,381 persons were employed on the army staff. The number of staff reached a maximum four years later with some 2,800 individuals on the payroll, plus a battalion of about 900 men who stood on guard.[32] Huber tried to combat hypertrophy and red tape, but in the long run was not very successful because the workload was apparently gigantic and new tasks kept being added to the existing ones. For their part, even the Germans did not fail to notice how "staffs were bureaucratic and overly organized."[33] Even when taking into consideration that the complicated mechanisms of an army required an unusually high number of activities, it is surprising how many people the army staff included. It had apparently partly grown according to Parkinson's principle.[34]

In his postwar report, Guisan wrote, "I admit that there was a grain of truth in the criticism and the jokes made about the army staff having too many personnel and too many gold braids."[35] In the fall of 1941, the General and Huber made a joint effort to reduce the size of the army staff. At a briefing, Huber gave instructions to that effect, of which the minutes stated, "The Chief of the General Staff explains why it is necessary to reduce the army staff as ordered by the General and states the purpose of today's briefing. Based on the current organization, ways have to be found to cut back further the number of army staff immediately. In the areas where this is not possible, the reasons have to be identified to be able to inform the General and the Military Department."[36] Whenever possible, staff was put off duty for medical reasons. Huber referred to instructions by the General to the Surgeon General dated July 4, 1941, concerning the officers' fitness to go to war and demanded, "This order must be interpreted with caution. The physical efforts that an officer needs to make depend on the task that he has been entrusted with."[37] The efforts to cut costs resulted in a temporary reduction of the army staff to 1,400 in 1942, but two years later that number had doubled once again.[38]

The chief of the general staff was only occasionally invited to meetings between the commander-in-chief and the Federal Council. Walde was wrong to state that he participated in all meetings.[39] Most minutes of meetings did not mention Huber being present. Moreover, Huber rarely accompanied the General on inspection tours. On one occasion, in March 1941, he took the "Red Arrow" train to examine some booby-trapped objects along the Gotthard route. In the fall of the same year, he accompanied the General on the command train to Ticino, where they rode on a "cart" serving as a chairlift (often used to haul goods up mountains that are inaccessible by ground transport) to inspect positions of the 9th Division in the Bedretto valley.[40] Barbey asked himself if it was not his duty to keep the General from going on such an adventurous trip, "hanging in the air, with nothing to support his feet, and his arms crossed." However, he came to the conclusion that "even the smallest act that shows that the General is willing to take risks has an excellent effect on our troops that are not involved in combat."[41]

In many respects the commander-in-chief kept the chief of the general staff on a tight rein. When Divisional Commander Combe was assigned to the army staff in 1941, Huber was told by the General to "please submit to me the draft of the letter that you are going to write to him to give him his terms of reference."[42] In addition, Guisan ordered that unless it was marked "personal," all correspondence by the army units to the army command be submitted to the chief of the general staff before being forwarded to his own office. The General argued that this measure should substantially lower his workload so he would "have more time to visit troops."[43]

Huber was hard-working, and he expected everyone else to work effectively and strictly abide by the rules. Three months after taking on his post, he admonished the assistant chiefs of staff, "I insist once again that the tasks be completed more speedily."[44] Moreover, Huber demanded that he be able to contact at any time the heads of section who reported to him directly. On a Monday in the spring of 1941, when he was unable to reach the intelligence section for half an hour, he asked Masson for an explanation and ordered that he put in a request for the officer concerned to be punished. He made it clear to Masson that his office had to be permanently kept informed about the whereabouts of the responsible officers.[45]

During the second half of wartime duty, Barbey made critical remarks about the lack of contact between different sections of the army staff, such as the operational section and the intelligence service, writing:

To change that, the chief of the general staff should be the one who coordinates the activities of the two bureaus. But that is not the way he works; he seems to put more emphasis on the hierarchy than on an exchange of opinions and on information from third parties. That in turn results in the fact that many officers do not know each other and everyone works within his own soundproof walls unless subordinates in the different sections take the initiative to make contacts.[46]

In addition, the General was under the impression that the army staff was too slow in forwarding important information and reports to him, or failed to forward information altogether. In a meeting with Huber, he complained about failing to receive through official channels or in the "black folder" (which contained the most important intelligence information) a report on the German economic delegation with which Switzerland was negotiating.[47] During the same meeting, Guisan protested that six weeks after ordering to have a study done on how to defend the southern front he had not yet received a report on that issue.[48]

In the spring of 1944, the General once again urged Huber to make the army staff speed up its work. Regarding a meeting on preliminary work for a new plan of operations, No. 15, he noted, "How far have the studies and preparations come along? Have the army corps, the air force, and the anti-aircraft defense been informed? When will their draft orders be submitted to the General for approval? If they are not ready, why? It is important that this plan, which is most likely to be used under the current circumstances, be carried out as quickly as possible."[49]

On another occasion, a head of section inquired of the General's personal staff if it had received a report he had submitted one month earlier through the official channel. It had not. Huber considered the inquiry an act of "denunciation," but the General immediately rejected this interpretation, replying that the head of section had raised a legitimate question.[50] Huber was extremely touchy about such issues.

The first serious controversy between the General and Huber occurred in the summer of 1941. Huber complained about the arrogance of the General's personal staff and about the improper tone in which it communicated with him, writing, "Your letter No. 4265 was written in an unnecessarily offensive tone. If you are not satisfied with my performance, or if you do not have confidence in me, I request that I be dismissed. Spiteful letters do not contribute in the least to making my job enjoyable nor in boosting my job performance." Moreover, Huber considered that the issue that was raised in the letter could have been resolved during a five- to ten-minute conversation; instead, he was forced to "spend hours at [his] desk replying to the letter, thus wasting time" that he could have used for doing more useful work.[51]

Guisan responded that he was "surprised and saddened" by Huber's reaction, writing that he had believed that their mutual trust was unshakeable and that their harmonious working relationship could not be marred by anything. He explained that he had carefully pondered the letter, which he said he had for the most part written himself, before sending it off and could "see nothing spiteful nor offensive in it even after rereading it." He added that he could "not understand why [Huber] interpreted it in that way."[52] The dispute was settled the following day during a placating meeting, about which the General laconically noted, "Over and done with during meeting of July 3, 1941."[53] Huber gave in, but he later wrote about the confrontation, "Similar incidents and even more serious ones occurred several times later on."[54]

One year later, in early summer 1942, Corps Commander Huber offered to resign for the first time in a formal letter to the Head of the Military Department.[55] Without giving a reason, he asked to be dismissed as Chief of the General Staff of the Armed Forces and to retire as a Federal employee as of July 31, 1942, as he was still officially an Assistant to the Chief of the General Staff in the Military Department. In a personal letter to the General, he explained:

> During yesterday's inspection of class 1a of the general staff I found out that during my absence in the Grisons between June 10 and 13, 1942, you ordered Colonel Brigadier Corbat to a meeting in Interlaken about official matters that fall under my responsibility. Even though I came to see you for a briefing on June 15, 1942, during which probably the same issues were raised that you had discussed with Colonel Brigadier Corbat, you did not consider it necessary to inform me about the meeting. This is even more disturbing to me in view of the fact that I had told you a short time earlier how unpleasant it was for me to have matters that fall under my responsibility dealt with behind my back. Your acting this way brings me to the conclusion that you mistrust me, which is unacceptable to me. I am used to speaking openly with superiors and subordinates and I hate diplomacy in the military. I expect that my superiors and subordinates act the same way toward me. The army staff can work under normal conditions only if the Commander-in-Chief of the Armed Forces also abides by the service regulations that he has approved and by article 21 of the Military Service Regulations regarding the official channels that must be followed. On the other hand, I have no right to criticize your behavior toward me and the army staff. Therefore I regret that I see only one way to get out of this

situation, which is unacceptable for me. I am asking you to forward and support the enclosed letter of resignation.[56]

It is interesting to note that Huber, an upright soldier, felt that Guisan's inclination to use diplomacy and operate on several levels at the same time amounted to a disturbing sign of a lack of trust. One has to assume that an accumulation of minor incidents injured Huber and made him come to his decision to resign.

The General was astounded that Huber, who was usually composed and thoughtful, had expressed his feelings with such vehemence. He replied the same day, trying in a paternal and persuasive manner to calm him down, calling his reaction disproportionate, and refusing to forward his letter of resignation. He explained that he did not see anything inappropriate in the meeting with Corbat, which was held in connection with the latter being nominated commander of Class II of the general staff, arguing that as commander-in-chief he reserved the right to speak with any officer at any time. He added:

I do not consider this a lack of trust in you. Have you already forgotten how often I have told you that I have full confidence in you? . . . Let me tell you frankly that I am astounded at your letter; it is all the less understandable because your decision is out of proportion with the reason you put forward. In case that the decision is prompted by other reasons, I expect you to inform me of them. Moreover, I consider that a decision of this significance should have been preceded by a request for an official meeting. That is why I will not forward your letter to the Head of the Military Department.[57]

The General invited Huber to a meeting which took place two days later, at the end of which the chief of the general staff revoked his letter of resignation. However, the atmosphere continued to be tense, and it seems that Huber tried to avoid Guisan in the following months. Walde reported that during July and August 1942, he met with the commander-in-chief "less than once every fortnight."[58]

Huber also made a verbal offer to resign during a briefing by the General in the presence of the corps commanders in the late fall of 1944, when the idea of nominating younger officers for leading positions was discussed. Barbey reported:

Someone suggests that every army unit commander should offer to resign of his own accord after five years on his post. This offer would be accepted or denied depending on the requirements and the circumstances. This idea, which came as a bombshell and which had not been seriously considered by anyone before, triggers a rather confusing discussion. Huber, whom nobody had had in mind but who feels aimed at, albeit wrongly, blushes and declares, with a contorted face, 'In that case, I demand to be relieved of my post because at the end of the year I will have been Chief of the General Staff for exactly five years.' The General replied, 'You may submit your request, but I can already tell you now that it will not be approved!'[59]

In spite of such encouraging endorsements, Huber continued displaying hints that he was considering resignation. As early as during the third summer of the war, the chief of the personal staff had the impression that Huber showed "some signs of being tired, pessimistic, or fatalistic."[60] In early 1945, Huber noticed that Guisan once again went behind his back, writing, "New French Military Attaché, General Davet, negotiates directly with General Guisan, via Barbey. He may do as he likes, but this is not normal."[61]

Huber submitted another official letter of resignation to the attention of the Federal Council at the end of February 1945, giving his health, at the age of 62, as a reason. He explained that he no longer felt perfectly fit to go to war, that he felt that his time was up, and that he did not want to "have a reputation of someone who stays put in his position." He said that he had not offered to resign at the end of the previous year because he had thought the war would be over soon and that he would be able to hold out until the Swiss Army was demobilized. However, now he argued that because the Germans intended to withdraw into the Alps, the war could continue for several more years. He therefore requested to be dismissed as Chief of the General Staff of the Armed Forces as of the end of May in order to retire from public office.[62]

Walde refers to the constant tensions between the General and the chief of the general staff, suspecting that Huber's health was "not the real reason" but only a pretext to ask permission to resign.[63] The General once again refused to approve Huber's resignation and did not forward it to the Federal Council. He met with Huber the same night and talked him into staying on until the end of the war, which he said was in sight. The following day, the General told Huber in writing, "I confirm that it is my wish and my hope that you continue to pursue your task together with me until the time of wartime duty is over. Hence, as agreed yesterday evening, I am holding back your letter of February 28, 1945 to the attention of the Head of the Military Department."[64]

A certain degree of alienation between the two men continued to exist beyond the time when hostilities in Europe came to an end. Before the period of wartime duty was over, at the end of May 1945, there was a bitter exchange of letters between Guisan and Huber. Without the chief of the general staff's knowledge, the General had had a member of his personal staff write a memorandum on the "tasks and future structure of Army Intelligence" and submitted it to the Military Department. Huber was informed only when he received a copy of the memorandum. Huber bluntly criticized its content and once again found fault with the General's way of handling the matter. He wrote:

> The memorandum is full of commonplaces, untrue statements, and enigmas. I regret that this piece could not be submitted to the competent office of the army staff for examination before it was addressed to the Federal Council. If it were considered necessary to write a treatise on the future development of the intelligence service, it would have been better to have it done by an expert. It is better to have one's shoe soles replaced by a shoemaker than by a carpenter.[65]

At the end of his letter, Huber asked whether perhaps the future Chief of Intelligence had "already been designated and [was] perhaps even [identical with] the anonymous author of the memorandum."

The General responded in a rather aggrieved tone, stating that he did not accept either the content or the form of Huber's remarks, which he said surprised him. "This memorandum," he said, "can no longer be considered as 'anonymous' once it is addressed to you by the commander-in-chief. If I authorized you to make comments, it was not to let you discuss the content but only to express your opinion about the measures that result from it."[66]

The last time Huber complained to the General about his lack of frankness was shortly before the "salute to the flag," the official act that put an end to the time of World War II duty. In a four-page report, he commented on the Masson-Schellenberg affair, which was beginning to become known to the public, quoting the meeting in Biglen on March 3, 1943, as an example of "important issues in the army command that were kept secret from me."[67] Huber wrote to the Head of the Military Department, "The entire deal with Schellenberg happened behind my back. Attempts were made to keep it secret even after I happened to find out about it, even if the intelligence fell under my responsibility."[68]

On several occasions, the Head of the Military Department intervened to ease tensions between Guisan and Huber. In a private conversation with historian Jean Rodolph von Salis, Federal Councilor Kobelt basically characterized the relationship between Guisan and Huber as "awful," adding that he had to mediate several times when Huber intended to resign in order to convince him to stay on.[69]

The real state of the relationship between Guisan and Huber was also high-lighted by the way that Huber's report on wartime duty, which was very blunt and contained some military secrets, was published. Huber insisted on inform-ing Federal Councilor Kobelt of the circumstances, writing that he assumed the General would use his report as a basis for his own report rather than publish large parts of it as such. Moreover, he expected the report to be submitted only to the Federal Council and Parliament and that these two bodies would in turn decide whether it should be made available to the public. Huber explained that as chief of the general staff he had often been forced to tell delegations of Parliament top military secrets and show them top-secret fortifications. Hence, he did not think that it was improper to mention details about the military and that the report, if publicized, "might go too far in committing treason."[70]

On January 11, 1946, after receiving a draft version of the General's report on wartime duty for comment, Huber informed Guisan that he did not agree with the critical remarks about high-ranking officers. Huber was subsequently surprised to see that the commander-in-chief's version was published without taking his reservations into account. Huber stated, "I received the printed report by the General at about the same time as the Federal Council, Parliament, and the press. I was probably as upset about its content as the Federal Council and the officers and groups of officers that were being exposed to the public."[71] Huber admitted that he was baffled when he found out that his confidential report was distributed to the press and even to foreign embassies. If there had been a real relationship based on trust between Guisan and Huber, this mistake would not have happened, not even after wartime duty was over.[72]

One should note that regardless of a number of qualifying remarks that must be made regarding the alleged harmony in the relationship between Guisan and Huber, in view of the favorable results that their cooperation yield-ed the two officers complemented each other beneficially. On balance, the General made an extremely fortunate choice in deciding to nominate Jakob Huber as chief of the general staff. Huber played an essential role in elevating the commander-in-chief to his position of status, insofar as through his excep-tional energy, studied discretion, and great modesty, Huber did much to create the conditions that made it easier for General Guisan to become Switzerland's symbol of resistance during the Second World War.

Relations with
Subordinate Commanders

WHENEVER GENERAL GUISAN USED THE EXPRESSION "supreme command" of the armed forces, he meant "all officers ranked corps commander, divisional commander, and mountain brigade commander, as well as the chief instructors."[1] When Guisan became General in 1939, the supreme command of the army consisted of five corps commanders, whose average age was 61: Chief of the General Staff Labhart, 58; the three commanders of the army corps: Lardelli, 63, Miescher, 59, and Prisi, 64; and Chief Instructor Wille, 62. During the war these commanders were all replaced, except for the youngest, Labhart, who remained a corps commander past the war. In another significant change, when the army was mobilized in 1939, the General and the commanders of all three corps were militia officers; at the end of the war, the commanders of all four corps were career officers.

To outsiders, Guisan's relations with his subordinates appeared to be perfectly correct and he seemed to be on friendly terms with them. Beneath the surface, however, things frequently looked different. There were tensions and differences among the corps commanders as well as between them and the General. Barbey wrote on this subject: "Differences? Maybe. Or perhaps they reflect different fundamental beliefs and feelings between commanders with very different backgrounds and very different education that are intensified through the political, military, and mental situation we are in."[2] Each time a corps commander was made to retire against his own will, rumblings of discontent could be heard inside the army. Yet because secrecy was maintained and censorship was effective, the public did not find out about these behind-the-scenes events.

In his postwar report, the General used somewhat disguised language to describe the problems that existed, stating:

> Because wartime duty lasted for a relatively long period of time, some difficulties in the characters of our top commanders were bound to surface. Although I do not want to make excuses for flaws in anyone's character, I must be fair and admit that in most cases these flaws coincided with health problems. It was very obvious that some unit commanders [i.e., the corps commanders and divisional commanders] who belonged to the team when wartime duty began would have been incapable of surviving a campaign because an incurable illness was beginning to take its toll on them or because they were worn out and would hardly have been able to bear the efforts required to conduct a modern campaign.[3]

Even though none of his direct subordinates showed a lack of dutiful subordination toward the commander-in-chief, from the beginning Guisan considered the criticism voiced by a majority of the corps commanders (Wille, Labhart, and Miescher) as a concerted attack against his position.[4] On the other hand, during the first few years of the war, he knew that the two other corps commanders, Lardelli and Prisi, were loyal and supported him.

The General made efforts to be conciliatory and win over opponents by discussing issues with them. He was not someone who felt hostility toward those who did not share his point of view; instead, he skillfully tried to mediate and find compromises. Even when he decided to relieve someone of command, he tried to proceed with subtlety and caution so that only the person directly concerned and his entourage would be fully informed about the decision. Nevertheless, some breaches in relationships occurred, about which Chapuisat wrote, "[Guisan] was not spared disputes with those who seemed to have forgotten what great responsibility the General carried as commander of the Armed Forces. Measures were inevitable that hit a few officers very hard, but they also hit him because he did not like to hurt others."[5] When he made such decisions, Guisan sometimes felt misunderstood.

The General demanded that the army staff be courteous in their correspondence with the subordinate commanders. After receiving complaints from the corps commanders about letters written in an improper tone, he wrote to the chief of the general staff to insist that these officers should not have to deal with any red tape, adding, "It would be advisable to remind your subordinates that the commanders of the army units have had long careers during which they have been able to gain much experience that younger officers do not yet have."[6]

In another instance, the General demanded that von Erlach, the Head of the Operational Section, formally apologize to a corps commander during a meeting because he had used unacceptable language.[7]

After early 1940, Guisan began holding regular briefings with the corps commanders to maintain personal contact with them, especially before making important decisions. He informed them that because he could not visit them as frequently as would be useful, he intended to call them to meetings periodically, for it was essential to him:

a) To have my views about the requirements of the current wartime service understood all the way down to the units and that everyone act according to these views;

b) To continuously receive precise information about the state of affairs among the troops, their training, and their morale and about preparations in the different sectors of the front.[8]

Guisan believed it was crucial to contribute personally to setting uniform standards and to demand that established principles be followed throughout the armed forces. In his postwar report he remarked, "The meetings I organized with the commanders of the army corps every three to four months, or more frequently when necessary, did not have the purpose of carrying on the activities of the National Defense Committee, which stopped meeting when the wartime duty began. Instead, they served to discuss many diverse issues relating to training, armament, relieving troops, leaves, etc."[9] Toward the end of each year, the meetings also examined proposals for promotions and transfers. In addition, whenever the post of a unit commander became vacant, the General met with the corps commanders or consulted with them before submitting the name of his proposed candidate to the Head of the Military Department.

The first briefing with the corps commanders was held on April 29, 1940, in Bern.[10] The fifth, which took place on October 19, 1940, was preceded by a luncheon at the General's quarters in Gümligen.[11] Altogether, two dozen briefings, as evidenced in the form of confidential minutes taken by a member of the personal staff (usually Hans Bracher), took place with the corps commanders. When operational issues such as the deployment of the army to the Réduit positions were discussed, these briefings tended to turn into a council of war. Even though the Military Service Regulations of 1927 that were still in force stated, "Nothing good comes out of councils of war,"[12] Guisan continued a long tradition in Switzerland's military history. General Herzog and General Wille had held similar briefings during previous wars.

Seven to thirteen officers usually participated in the General's briefings with the corps commanders, including the chief of the general staff and a number of experts invited as consultants.[13] However, the General also held other meetings to which only a limited number of officers were invited, giving them the character of a "mini-council of war." On June 5, 1944, the day before the Allied landing in Normandy, Guisan met with five officers (the chief of the general staff, two assistant chiefs of staff [Ia and Ib], the chief of the personal staff, and the liaison officer with the Military Department) to decide what measures should be taken in reaction to alarming news that had reached Switzerland from Budapest.[14]

Before the General's briefings with the corps commanders, the chief of the personal staff typically prepared a list of items to be discussed. However, in spite of these preparations, the General did not feel very much at ease during these briefings. He was "uncomfortable," especially when the debates became fierce. Some officers were more eloquent than he was, and although Guisan appeared very self-confident during public appearances, he was rather insecure during these meetings.[15] In addition, the commander-in-chief was not very methodical while moderating discussions. Von Berchem participated in a briefing in the fall of 1944 dealing with possible additional measures to strengthen the western front in the Ajoie region. He reported that the General did not at all adhere to the traditional way of structuring a discussion, by first assessing the situation and then making decisions and issuing orders to subordinate commanders. Instead, he led a general discussion on instructions that might be taken into consideration.[16]

Labhart, the former chief of the general staff, made some critical remarks about Guisan's consulting with subordinate commanders through briefings. In early 1942, he wrote in his diary, "These briefings are in fact nonsense when you consider how much power the General has. I believe that the reason for holding them is to put the responsibility on other people's shoulders."[17] A year and a half later, Labhart noted about the manner in which a discussion was held: "When the question of the overall situation is raised, Corps Commander Prisi speaks first; he is skeptical and sees danger lurking on all sides. I for my part argue that we do not have much to fear from the Germans anymore, explaining that they are on the defensive everywhere and that shortening their front is crucial to them. If Germany wanted to seize our Alpine transit routes, it would have tried to do so a long time ago."[18] Regarding the influence he thought he was able to exercise on the supreme command, in part through the Head of the Military Department, Labhart speculated, "My meeting with Federal Councilor Kobelt seems to have yielded some results. All of a sudden the Army Command does not see any threat from the north anymore, even if in its letter of August 4, 1943 regarding the relieving of troops it had considered that threat to be still the same."[19]

In addition to the briefings, the General sought to keep in contact with his subordinates through personal visits. During face-to-face meetings, he explained the principles on which orders and instructions were based, cleared up misunderstandings, and provided additional details. He liked to visit the subordinate commanders as often as possible, stating, "One should avoid calling a commander away from his troops. Therefore I went to see them whenever this was possible rather than making them come to see me. For instance, when I noticed shortcomings during my inspections, I went to discuss them in private with the corps commander concerned or I called all four corps commanders to a meeting to solve a training issue in all four army corps."[20]

Five days after the briefing at the Rütli, the General went to see the commander of the 1st Army Corps, who did not seem to fully understand the maneuvers he was supposed to carry out in the advance positions outside the Réduit. Barbey described the visit with Lardelli, the only corps commander whom Guisan addressed using the informal German pronoun *du*, writing:

I accompany the General to Laupen, where he summoned Lardelli. From there we proceed to Murten, south of where tanks might make incursions through the fields. On the terrace of the Weisses Kreuz restaurant, the General, holding the map in his hand, discusses the corps' order, criticizing especially point 2. Lardelli's explanation: he does not understand the order that he signed because it is written in French, which he does not speak very well. The debate is quite lively between the two former comrades-in-arms, who succeeded each other as commander of the 1st Army Corps.[21]

In cases of doubt, Guisan did not hesitate to show his determination to have operations run his own way. He demanded that his orders be taken seriously and took resolute action when he noticed they were not being strictly followed. As he once wrote to the Commander of the 4th Army Corps, "I demand that my orders be read carefully and executed accordingly. In the future I shall take sanctions against the culprits."[22] When Corps Commander Labhart planned to carry out, with one of his regiments, an exercise that conflicted with the plan of operations, the General immediately intervened, stating firmly, "I see no reason to discuss once again the reasons that I had verbally explained to you. I insist that it is not up to you to use the troops under your command as you like after receiving very specific orders from me."[23]

The General reiterated his determination during a similar situation later. Referring to Huber, he remarked:

The Chief of the General Staff has informed me that the army staff's work is made very difficult because the army command's orders and instructions are not being read carefully. He explained that orders were frequently not executed correctly because the commander involved had a different view concerning that matter or considered as irksome the work that the staff had to do. I have to admit that I have repeatedly noticed the same thing as well; I consider that it should be possible for top-ranking commanders to execute the army command's orders according to the same principles the rank-and-file are asked to abide.[24]

It was important to the General that the troops be treated correctly by high-ranking commanders and that the latter set an example. In 1942, when he found out that in the 4th Army Corps the newly appointed Divisional Commander Rudolf von Erlach was often "stiff and short" with his subordinates, he asked Corps Commander Labhart whether this was true and demanded that this behavior cease.[25] He also opposed officers who believed they had special rights that went against the rules. For example, he confirmed a ruling by the Chief War Commissioner who had sentenced a colonel who was an affluent industrialist to a fine of 100 francs because he had eaten meat on a day when meat consumption was prohibited.[26] Similarly, the commander-in-chief wrote to the Adjutant General of the armed forces, Divisional Commander Dollfus, who regularly drove from his home at Kiesen Castle to the capital in a large official vehicle, "I regret to inform you that the numerous trips that you make between Kiesen and Bern in a large car, which obviously uses a lot of gas, have an unfortunate effect. I therefore kindly ask you to consider in what manner you could reduce gas consumption either by taking the train or by using a smaller vehicle."[27] Guisan undoubtedly had in mind his own adjutant, Captain von Ernst, who commuted by train from his home at Muri Castle to the General's command post in Gümligen every day to save on gasoline.[28]

As one would expect, the General vehemently rejected disrespectful criticism of his decisions. In February 1941, during a briefing in connection with operational exercises, he declared to the top commanders that he was not one of those people unable to accept criticism, so long as the criticism was correct and was addressed through official channels. However, he did not accept criticism that subordinates made at their offices or during training activities regarding principles and decisions by the army command, explaining, "That type of criticism undermines confidence in the supreme command. It shows a lack of loyalty and is dangerous and unacceptable at this critical period."[29]

Guisan advised those who had no confidence in the army command to resign of their own accord to show their loyalty or he would "make them understand" that they should do so. This concise statement was a clear warning addressed to the General's opponents inside the army, most particularly the group around Däniker.[30] However, it is not impossible that Guisan also had Corps Commanders Wille, Labhart, and Miescher in mind when he issued the warning.

The General was serious about this, as demonstrated by the sanctions enforced against Däniker, and Wille's dismissal.[31] Between 1941 and 1943, three additional corps commanders were relieved of their command in a rather unconventional manner. In connection with the establishment of a 5th Army Corps on December 3, 1940, an opportunity occurred to make changes at the corps level. The new army corps was dissolved again a short time later.[32] The Federal Council, which had to approve the new corps and the personnel changes, postponed its decision, asking for an explanation. The General, who accepted this request "without being annoyed or at least without showing any sign of being annoyed," ordered the chief of his personal staff to write a report to the government explaining why it was necessary to create a 5th Army Corps. Barbey stated, "Completed my job around midnight; of course the report mentions only military considerations." Five days later, the Federal Council approved the General's propositions.[33]

Operational considerations were the official reason for this new 5th Corps, yet it is perfectly obvious that personal reasons also played a role. This supposition is corroborated by a statement in the diary of Barbey, who wrote, "Of course there are reasons [for making the changes]; they are more or less valid and are based on personal or objective criteria." After mentioning strategic considerations, Barbey continued, "In addition, there is a more personal consideration. Why should the Federal Council deny this? Does it not know exactly that we cannot make anyone retire nor resign by any other means? Does it not think of the longest serving, loyal, dear comrades with whom it is difficult for a commander-in-chief to part because in our unfortunate system someone who retires looks as if he has fallen from grace or been ostracized?"[34]

Barbey's insinuations leave hardly any doubt that the changes at top command posts were made with the ulterior motive that it would be possible after a short while to replace, in a relatively careful manner, the oldest serving corps commanders or other officers, although no names were mentioned in the official documents. The decision in favor of a 5th Corps was of course tenable from a strategic point of view and could be explained with valid arguments, but it did not seem to be absolutely necessary; otherwise it would hardly have been desirable to cancel the decision as early as five months later.

In early spring 1941, the time had come to resolve personnel issues by restructuring the army once again. As Barbey explained, "After dinner, the

General comes to see me in my office and outlines the boundaries of the new sectors on a map. The 5th Army Corps is gone."[35] During a briefing the following day, the General explained to the corps commanders that the requirements of the new operations order, No. 13, which would go into effect on May 24, 1941, had made the changes necessary.[36] According to the minutes of this "confidential internal meeting," Prisi, who apparently saw through the game of hide-and-seek, voiced "considerable reservations, because of accusations that plans of operation [were] made based on personnel issues. Under the former plan, the sectors held by the army corps were just the right size. Under the new plan they [were] probably going to be a bit too large."[37]

It seems that the implicit intention of changing the structure once again was to make Lardelli, who had been transferred from the 1st Corps to the 5th Corps on December 3, 1940, redundant as corps commander. However, another solution happened to present itself. In early May, Miescher fainted at his command post, making it necessary for the commander of the 3rd Army Corps to stay in the hospital for an extended period of time, followed by sick leave. In this situation, Miescher resigned from his post. The General accepted his resignation, using the opportunity to dissolve the 3rd Corps. Its troops were assigned to another corps, the 5th Corps was renamed the 3rd Corps, and the staff of the dissolved corps were to remain available to the commander-in-chief as reserve commanders.[38]

It is understandable that this curious move considerably displeased the people concerned. When Miescher heard about these measures while convalescing on the shores of Lake Geneva, he wrote to the General:

In my letter dated May 6, 1941, I requested to be relieved of my command post. Today I can no longer make this request because I have already been relieved of it in the most thorough manner because the 3rd Army Corps has been integrated into the 2nd Army Corps and the 5th Army Corps has been renamed the 3rd Army Corps. Moreover, since I do not see how I could be used in another equivalent position, I would like to ask you to submit to the Federal Council my letter of resignation from the military.[39]

Even if the General tried to placate him by citing operational constraints, Miescher left the army a bitter man. He avoided further personal contact with his commander-in-chief, asking Guisan, "Please allow me to report absent from duty only in writing, without presenting myself in person."[40]

In a private conversation, Miescher later commented in a restrained but telling manner, "I am glad that I decided to resign of my own accord because it was not until afterward that I fully realized that this event and certain second-ary phenomena caused a rift in my life that could not be mended anymore."[41] As Labhart, who had been informed about the circumstances of Miescher's res-ignation by Colonel Iselin, the chief of staff of the 3rd Corps, noted in his diary, "It appears that the army command made some serious psychological errors. At least the General did not find it necessary to visit Colonel-Corps Commander Miescher during his illness; nor did he send the surgeon general to obtain infor-mation on his state of health."[42] The indignation among Miescher's former staff did not go unnoticed. The General's special service reported, "The officers of the dissolved 3rd Army Corps meet in Zürich every week, where they voice their utter resentment against the General's decision to dissolve their corps."[43] The German Military Attaché von Ilsemann reported to Berlin that Wille had told him the 3rd Army Corps had been dissolved because Corps Commander Miescher as well as his staff were considered "disagreeable subordinates." Miescher was said "to be the only corps commander who opposes the army command."[44]

In summer 1942, General Guisan suspected that a plot was directed against him in which Federal Councilor Kobelt and two acting corps commanders were involved. He asked himself what would be the best strategy to block these high-ranking opponents. After a meeting with Bracher, the liaison officer with the Federal Council, he noted:

K[obelt] wants to weaken Gen[eral]'s posit[ion] and increase K[obelt]'s authority. Labhart would like to eliminate the Gen[eral] by sending all troops off duty or putting the Gen[eral] on leave. If this is not possi-ble, the Head of the M[ilitary] D[epartment] should have a technical advisor available, a post for which L[abhart] recommended himself. He claims that art[icle] 208 of the S[ervice] R[egulations] is no longer valid and that it would be advisable to create a war cabinet that is placed above the Gen[eral]! As Chief of the G[eneral] S[taff] (it remains to be seen if he will hold this position again or if someone younger will!), he would be part of this cabinet in order to prep[are] the postwar army and as an advisor to the Head of the M[ilitary] D[epartment]. Critics include W[ille], Bir[cher], von Erlach. Answer: get closer to K[obelt], yield some authority to him. Destroy Lab[hart] through K[obelt]'s political friends. Closer relations with a[rmy] u[nit] commanders who are trustworthy. Hold individual meetings with Frick, Flückiger, Iselin, for ex[ample]. Drop Lab[hart] and Erlach. Invite assistant chiefs. Rejuvenate officers' corps.[45]

These revealing notes by the General prove what real or alleged machinations Guisan had to deal with while the war was in its fourth year. Federal Councilor Kobelt supposedly even had the intention to form a war cabinet. The countermeasures the General planned to take to block the "conspiracy" and maintain his own position clearly show his determination to counter his opposition.

Mutual trust among the men in the army's supreme command suffered heavily from such awkward circumstances. In 1944, Edmund Wehrli considered the fact that Guisan and Labhart sat down at two different tables at a restaurant in Schaffhausen as a clear sign of the lack of trust between them. It required his mediation as a major on the general staff to have the General, who was accompanied by Barbey and an aide, at least drink a cup of coffee with the corps commander after lunch.[46]

Among the corps commanders, General Guisan got along best with Lardelli, who had served in the same artillery unit as Guisan and continued to be a comrade during the war, and with Prisi. Following a staff exercise directed by the commander of the 2nd Army Corps, Prisi received special praise. As Barbey reported, "On our way from Olten to Lucerne, the General congratulates Prisi on the way in which he has planned and directed his exercise and keeps telling him how much he appreciates his 'loyalty' and that of others."[47] However, in spite of the good relations, the commander-in-chief decided to part with Corps Commanders Prisi and Lardelli at the end of 1943 in order to replace them with younger officers. In the fall of 1943 Barbey noted in his diary, "On his birthday, the General had to accomplish a painful task. He had to inform the commanders of the 2nd and 3rd Army Corps about his plans and to make them, as far as possible, submit the letter of resignation of their own accord. . . . After the two meetings, the General appeared to be relieved, the way one is relieved after doing one's duty, even though neither Prisi nor Lardelli have agreed to submit their letters of resignation."[48]

The General subsequently asked in writing for the two corps commanders to resign voluntarily. He wrote to Prisi that in view of the state of his health he was forced to ask him "very reluctantly," after eight years of successful service as corps commander, to resign from his post as of the end of the year in order to be replaced by someone younger. The General added, "It is with great emotion that I will part with you. Since the beginning of wartime duty, you have been a loyal subordinate to me and at the same time a good comrade who has offered me valuable support."[49] The General used similar terms in asking Lardelli to resign. However, both corps commanders refused to do so of their own accord. They both submitted as soldiers but were reluctant to quit their posts and believed that they were being pushed aside unjustly. Lardelli wrote the General that he felt absolutely capable of continuing to command his corps, arguing, "I am fit for service and I have neither rheumatism nor diabetes. Overcoming an illness thanks to being in good shape speaks in favor of the concerned person, not against him. General, please allow me to tell you frankly that the resignation which you have ordered is a heavy blow to me."[50]

Lardelli, who was 67, two years younger than the General, asked Federal Councilor Kobelt to find him a new job. He wrote that he had two sons who were still in school, which cost him a lot of money, and therefore asked the government to be "kind" and help him acquire a second income after retiring. He urged Kobelt, whom he knew well, "to [please] advance my cause if your position and honor allow you to do so!"[51] Moreover, Lardelli struggled with the thought that he was going to be replaced by Constam, with whom he did not get along. He requested from Kobelt, "If I have to resign, please do not appoint Constam as my successor. That would not work at all. He has no experience as a mountaineer and does not understand the people who live in the mountains. He represents a mentality that I cannot stand."[52]

During a briefing in Bern, the General explained that Lardelli's and Prisi's health was considered by doctors as being "at risk" and that it was "very difficult" for him to decide to relieve them of their posts because they were two loyal associates who were "capable of accomplishing their task." Potential successors included divisional commanders Constam from Zürich (a disciple of Wille), Flückiger from Bern, and Gübeli from Lucerne. In spite of Lardelli's reservations, the majority recommended Constam and Gübeli for the two vacant posts.[53] On January 10, 1944, the General organized a farewell dinner in honor of Prisi and Lardelli to which the other corps commanders were invited.[54]

In the fall of 1943, the General also decided to replace the commander of the air force and antiaircraft defense, Divisional Commander Hans Bandi, who was his direct subordinate. Barbey wrote about Bandi's reaction when he received the information, "The General received Bandi, who reacted vehemently as expected. Bandi grumbles about humanity, the institutions and traditions, about his subordinates and particularly about the General's personal staff. That is perfectly understandable to a certain extent."[55] The reasons for his dismissal had postwar repercussions, after publication of the General's report on wartime duty, causing heated public debate.[56]

Once the oldest serving top commanders had been replaced, Corps Commander Jules Borel from Neuchâtel turned out to be "the General's most critical and aggressive direct subordinate."[57] In January 1944, he and Guisan had a major dispute in connection with winter maneuvers, though their differences were temporarily smoothed over in an official meeting arranged by Huber.[58] But their relationship continued to be tense. The personal staff considered Borel "nervous and irritable." Guisan had Borel's handwriting analyzed by two different graphologists,[59] but it appears the results did not justify taking any sanctions against him. Nevertheless, as late as the spring of 1945, one month before the end of the war, the commander-in-chief criticized the commander of the 1st Army Corps as being passive, apathetic, and lacking initiative, arguing, "You do not suggest any solution, you do not make any propositions to me, nor do you ask my permission to hold training courses, exercises, etc. like the other corps commanders do. I remember your telling me jokingly one day, 'laziness is a virtue.' Perhaps that is true, but only if you make others work! . . . If your heart is not in it, you have to tell me."[60]

In an extensive letter to Federal Councilor Kobelt, Jules Borel confirmed that he had had "serious differences" with the General, explaining, "[They] could easily have been smoothed away if the General had not had a tendency to avoid resolving them directly with me in a face-to-face meeting. He preferred to have some of his close collaborators write to me in a crafty yet polite language, and then he obviously signed the letters. The result was an exchange of letters that turned into polemics and poisoned the atmosphere."[61]

Fortunately, the general public knew very little about the manifold tensions and difficulties the commander-in-chief had to face in his relations with his subordinate commanders, as censorship and secrecy prevented any information on this subject from leaking out. However, there is no doubt that the General's direct subordinates had to swallow some bitter pills. They tacitly succumbed, but the resentment that accumulated over time surfaced after the war.[62]

Casting Aside Chief Instructor Wille

RELATIONS BETWEEN GENERAL GUISAN and Corps Commander Ulrich Wille Jr. were complex and ambiguous. Guisan showed patience and intuition during the fierce conflict with Wille, the son of the commander-in-chief of Switzerland's armed forces during the First World War, until he succeeded, in his third year as general, in removing this dangerous opponent from the army staff. Even when the Däniker affair ended, a tense atmosphere continued among his supporters, many of whom were also close to Wille.[1] There is ample written evidence of a connection between Wille's "Thoughts" written in support of Däniker and his dismissal as Chief Instructor. However, the first minor difficulties in the relationship between Guisan and Wille arose as early as during the first mobilization.

Following a meeting with Corps Commander Wille on the afternoon of August 31, 1939, the day after his election, the General named the Chief Instructor of the Infantry as the Chief Instructor of the entire Armed Forces, effective September 3, 1939.[2] Wille, who had hoped to be put in command of the 1st Army Corps, initially protested. On the day the troops were mobilized, he wrote to the General that he wanted to thank him "for the matter-of-fact and friendly discussion" they had held but considered that the commander-in-chief's plan was unsuitable because the task that awaited him as Chief Instructor during wartime duty was insignificant. Training the mobilized units was the sole responsibility of their commanders, he argued, and in his note to Guisan he wrote: "The Chief Instructor's responsibilities during times of peace are transferred to the General during a war. The Chief Instructor does mostly administrative work. A former commander of the Central Training Facilities, of a division and a corps is hardly the right person to hold this position unless he is an old gentleman."[3] He explained that he did not want a job that required no effort, and made Guisan understand clearly that he considered the task assigned to him below his capabilities.

On September 2, the General discussed the issue with Labhart, who noted about the conversation, "Issue of assignment for Colonel-Corps Commander Wille, who wrote a letter to the General. I insist that Colonel-Corps Commander Wille has an important task as Chief Instructor of the initiation courses and training courses for non-commissioned officers and logistics teams."[4]

Even though Wille had the impression that he was being pushed into a secondary role, after a second meeting on September 4 he accepted the post. As he wrote in his diary, "General wants to make me his direct subordinate as 'Chief Instructor' and wants me to draft the order announcing my nomination."[5] Wille accepted after being reassured that as head of an independent main section on the army staff he would not report to the chief of the general staff but directly to the General. The following day, September 5, he accepted in writing and transmitted drafts of two orders to the General concerning training in the army. The first order announced his nomination and listed his terms of reference; the second order defined the goals of the training for mobilized troops.[6]

The General made some minor changes to the two orders written on his behalf, approved and signed them, and communicated them to the troops. The General's order to the Chief Instructor read:

1. I intend to standardize training in the entire armed forces.
2. According to the decree of January 4, 1938 regarding the structure of the army staff, the Head of Main Section III shall be responsible for training. I order Colonel-Corps Commander Wille to monitor the status and progress of training activities in the entire armed forces and to request the means necessary to standardize training.
3. Based on article 3 of the decree mentioned above, the Chief of the General Staff orders the Head of Main Section III to report directly to me. The terms of reference have been communicated to all troop commanders.[7]

On September 6 Wille noted, "At 14.00 hours, General calls to inform me that he has approved the drafts, except for the duration of training, which is reduced from six weeks to four weeks."[8] The order drafted by Wille, approved by the commander-in-chief, and addressed to all troops, read:

I herewith issue the following first instructions regarding the training of troops:

As long as the events beyond our borders do not pose any threat to the Swiss Confederation, all our energy must focus on improving the commanders' and troops' fitness to go to war. However, the men and horses must not be overstrained, as is usually the case during the short training courses during times of peace. The power of resistance will be enhanced only if the training is purposeful and is done in moderation; this requires four weeks of training at the very least.[9]

Two of the weeks were reserved for company commanders to carry out basic training activities with their individual units, and the remaining two were to serve for combat training among combined units up to the size of a regiment.

After this promising beginning, relations between Guisan and Wille appeared to develop satisfactorily. It seems that both sides initially showed some goodwill. The General sent the Chief Instructor a copy of the instructions with the handwritten comment, "Many heartfelt thanks. Kind regards." However, tensions built up surprisingly quickly and relations between the two officers worsened.

A first misunderstanding occurred as early as September 8, when Wille criticized the French version of his terms of reference, which had been translated by the General's office. He remarked that the French expression used for "monitor" in the phrase "monitor the status and progress of training activities" was "faire une enquête," which he said might be misinterpreted by the French-speaking troops of the 1st Army Corps as a one-time inquiry, which was not at all what he was expected to do.[10] The General replied immediately that he had clarified that issue with the commander of the 1st Army Corps right away.[11]

The first serious disagreement between the two men occurred as early as the first month of duty. Wille apparently was not able to refrain from making comments about the army command's operational and strategic measures, thereby overstepping his authority. In mid-September, Wille held talks on his own initiative with Chief of the General Staff Labhart and Colonels Frick and von Erlach to prepare instructions that would lower the degree of the army's defense alert. Wille noted about this action, which he considered to be necessary:

[To] abandon border protection wherever the current state of alert does not make any sense in view of the situation, e.g. from the mouth of the Aare river east to the Mont Blanc [sic]; call guards in the infantry and anti-aircraft defense, as well as light machine gun and machine gun operators, even the ones all the way in the interior of the country, off duty; deactivate part of the booby-trapped objects; prevent troops from being deployed to new sectors, do not let fortification projects get off the ground, cancel plans calling for winter quarters for 9th Division; allow time for urgently needed training!![12]

The same day, Wille verbally presented these surprising steps to the General in order to cut down on security measures along the front facing the Allies, arguing that the time was needed for carrying out training activities. He remarked, "The General approves of them and intends to discuss them with the chief of the general staff the same evening and have orders prepared accordingly."[13] However, there is no evidence of such orders being issued. If he really approved of the measures, Guisan must have changed his mind later on. Gonard, the General's operational advisor, undoubtedly began to exercise some influence on him.[14]

New frictions emerged only a few days later, when the commander-in-chief was forced to put Wille in his place and to reprimand him in a "friendly" but loud and clear way. Guisan wrote of being informed that during a visit with the 2nd Division, Wille had criticized operational and strategic arrangements made by the army command. He said that in the interest of a well-functioning army staff he felt obliged to remind the Head of Main Section III of his terms of reference, explaining that he was responsible exclusively for monitoring the quality of training among the troops and making suggestions to the commander-in-chief on how to improve training. He added, "In the future, will you therefore please abide by the terms of reference that I have given you in order to avoid frictions. Kind regards."[15] Wille apologized, saying that he had no intention of becoming involved in strategic matters. He explained that he had simply made some casual comments during lunch with a regiment commander about positions that were too far advanced.[16]

Almost at the same time, the Chief Instructor incited the General to rebuke him once again because he refused to execute instructions from the Military Department. Wille believed that there was a contradiction between the Military Department's instructions regarding financial compensation for Federal employees serving during mobilization and a decree by the Federal Council regarding operations among the army staff. He wrote to the General that he believed "these directives by the Military Department [did] not apply to Main Section III of the army staff, so he [would] not execute them."[17] Guisan transmitted the letter to the chief of the general staff to have the facts established and the implications examined by the Chief War Commissioner. At the same time, he wrote an unmistakable warning to Wille, stating, "I must protest against the tone you used in the last paragraph. I could not possibly submit the letter to the Head of the Federal Military Department in the current form because it is simply unacceptable."[18]

Eight weeks after the army had been mobilized, the General urged the Head of Main Section III to present the requested report on the status of training among the troops.[19] Wille was in no hurry at all and took another eleven days to submit his report. In it, he stated that the impressions he had gained during inspections were not very satisfactory, explaining, "In addition to the activities that serve to protect the border and the fortification projects, other factors have been disrupting the training schedule. Training activities virtually came to a standstill because some troops were ordered to go on leave soon after being mobilized and other troops were redeployed in order to carry out the fortification projects. Moreover, the weather was often unfavorable for productive combat training."[20] He added that combat training among individual units and among combined units had been neglected or completely forsaken. To a certain extent he criticized the commander-in-chief's measures by demanding that leave be limited in the future and that the time should not all be used to work on the fortifications; instead, "useful exercises" should be organized with the troops. Wille continued, "The troop commanders must have several weeks available to be able to train their units autonomously and responsibly, and to thoroughly plan and carry out exercises. The Supreme Command must not disturb the training schedules by redeploying troops or issuing any other orders unless there are compelling reasons to do so."[21]

In mid-December 1939, the "terms of reference for the Chief Instructor of the Armed Forces during wartime duty" that Wille had received when he was nominated were summarized in writing; Wille once again drafted them.[22] The General heeded the Chief Instructor's suggestions insofar as he ordered the troops to remain in their assigned sectors and quarters throughout the winter and that redeployments should be "avoided as much as possible," even within an army unit, in order not to jeopardize the execution of systematic training programs. Nevertheless, the fortification projects in the open terrain were to continue until "the positions [were] ready to be used by the defense and [resisted] any kind of weather over an extended period of time." Until March 1, 1940, for ten weeks, "at least twenty full days [had] to be used for training, at least twelve days of which [had to] be allocated for exercises among the units." No more than 35 percent of the troops were allowed on leave at the same time. Even when the number of troops on duty was low, exercises would be held to provide leadership training to unit commanders. If necessary, units could be combined to reach full combat strength.[23]

The General complained repeatedly to the Chief Instructor about the excessive formality during initial training courses but also realized that the instructors did not do much to change this habit. In the summer of 1940, the commander-in-chief suggested that the Chief Instructor convene a committee of training officers to examine possible amendments to the training regulations so that the infantry could integrate into their training the conclusions that had been drawn from the German campaigns in Poland and France.[24] In the spring of 1941, he ordered the chief of his personal staff to write a report to denounce and condemn what he called "'staccato' and other linguistic aberrations, drills, and excessive formalism."[25] Barbey called the existing formalities "offensive" and defined staccato as:

> The process whereby a man's natural flow of speech is interrupted when he starts his initial army training. Giving as a pretext that he must learn to speak clearly, he is forced to pronounce each syllable separately at the rhythm of a typewriter. He has to say certain words, such as 'Sir,' as if barking like a dog, and when he addresses an officer by his title, his voice has to resound like a drum. This forced way of speaking is not only unnatural but also distracting. If a man is a bit shy and nervous, he becomes tense, rolls his eyes, and replies by stammering his words with a thundering voice, concentrating on the staccato instead of listening to the question that he has been asked. As a consequence, you see young officers who have just completed their training ridicule themselves when they address troops for the first time because they do not know how to speak to them. One could consider this a ridiculously bad joke if it did not use up valuable time that should be spent on combat training.[26]

After the war, Guisan admitted that his admonitions were not sufficient "to get rid of these aberrations."[27] The personal staff's annual report for 1941–42 stated that the General tried to exercise some influence on initiation and officers' training courses by corresponding extensively with Chief Instructor Wille and the Chief Instructor of the Infantry, Divisional Commander Probst, addressing both training goals and work methods.[28]

Overall, Guisan was quite disappointed by Wille's performance. In his postwar report, he wrote that considering Wille's far-reaching authority, the Chief Instructor "lived up only in part to my expectations."[29] He stated that Main Section III had issued many technical regulations as well as rules concerning training with individual weapons, thereby fulfilling its technical mission. However, he argued that it had made "only a minor contribution" to drafting orders and instructions in which strategic principles were defined based on actual war experience. Moreover, it "did not exercise as much influence on the army's combat training as would have been desirable." Nevertheless, he admitted that these shortcomings resulted from several factors, "most of which had nothing to do with the character or the capabilities" of the person holding this position. Guisan explained that it was mostly "the army unit commanders who [were] sometimes overly sensitive and [had] trouble accepting the Chief Instructor's presence during maneuvers or exercises, unjustly considering it as having an adverse effect on their position and reducing their authority."[30]

After Germany's victory over France, Wille, who was increasingly dissatisfied with being given a secondary role, started fighting to improve his position. He was outraged because he had not received any information during the alert of May 1940 and had not been invited to the briefing at the Rütli.[31] Germany's victories on the battlefields, which appeared to confirm his own theories about the paramount importance of military spirit, undoubtedly reinforced his feelings of superiority toward the commander-in-chief. In the summer of 1940, Wille began expressing his intention to resign, probably in part because he felt that he had no influence but undoubtedly also to put pressure on the army command and improve his position. After the briefing at the Rütli, he first went to see Federal President Pilet-Golaz, who encouraged him to stay on. Wille confirmed the content of their conversation in a letter to the President in which he wrote, "When you asked me about it on July 29, I had to admit that I had not been invited to the briefing at the Rütli. At the same time, I informed you that because of that and because I was actually reduced to an insignificant position on the army command, I had to consider resigning. After you urged me to persevere in the interest of the country and to continue working with the initiation training and officers' training courses, I have given this idea some serious thought. However, I can no longer bear to make it look as if I share some responsibility on the army command. I am tired of being excluded from all matters concerning the service of the mobilized troops."[32] At the same time, Wille transmitted to the Federal President a draft of his letter of resignation but hoped that he would not need to officially hand it in, writing, "[By proceeding in this manner] I want to give the Federal Council the opportunity to do whatever it considers necessary to make my staying on useful for the army and bearable to me." He said that otherwise his love of his home country would force him to resign from the army command, whose leadership he said increasingly spoiled the spirit and training in the army. Hence, Wille counted on the Federal Council's assistance to improve his situation.

Pilet-Golaz avoided making any commitment and waited two weeks before he invited Wille to a personal meeting. Wille wrote, "On August 27, Federal President finally receives me after I wrote to him on August 12. He explains that I must not hand in my resignation because of the consequences this would have in the country and abroad. He asks me to hold out. I reply that I will think about whether I should submit my letter of resignation to the General, and if so, in what manner."[33] This explanation shows that during the uncertain, alarming situation in the summer of 1940, Wille had difficulties in making a personal decision. As indicated by the controversial move he made with Germany's envoy Köcher, he wanted to keep several options open.[34]

On August 30, the General held a meeting with the Chief Instructor which Wille mentioned in his notes: "Short meeting with General in Thun during which I announce that I am planning to resign. He promises to change my status."[35]

The following day, Wille put his concerns in writing and asked the General to improve his role. He began his letter by complaining about being put in "a secondary position" as Head of Main Section III and mentioned several incidents "by which the General made [his] situation, which was not to be envied to begin with, even more difficult." According to Wille, these incidents included his not being proposed as chief of the general staff as promised, the unsatisfactory handling of his complaint about Divisional Commander Huber, the surveillance activities that served to identify officers who were members of the Front movement, and his not being invited to the briefing at the Rütli. He continued in his letter, "My position in the army is all the more unbearable as I am called 'Chief Instructor' in the commander-in-chief's official letters, thereby making me appear to the outside world as the one who is mainly responsible for the state of training, even though I have absolutely no authority in training matters in the army." He claimed that because of this "pseudo title" he might be held partly responsible later on for shortcomings in training and that neither would he want to be "held responsible for the lack of discipline among many troops." Wille explained that the only way to correct this situation was "to show authority right where it [needed] to be shown," which required that "the General make unannounced visits to the troops or make [Wille] his legitimate deputy in training matters."[36] Since his "odd position [was] no longer bearable for [him] from an objective nor from a personal point of view," he demanded that the General name him as his deputy for the army's training matters and authorize him to give relevant verbal instructions directly to the unit commanders. Moreover, Wille demanded, "like the Chief of the General Staff, I should act as your personal advisor in issues relating to promotions and nominations of staff officers and unit commanders so that the observations that I make during inspections may be taken into account."[37]

The Chief Instructor backed up his requests, by which he demanded the right to inspect troops at his own will as the commander-in-chief's deputy, by enclosing the draft of an order by the General to the directly subordinate commanders. However, the General did not support this order, which read, "I herewith name Colonel-Corps Commander Wille, the Head of Main Section III, as my deputy in all matters concerning training in the armed forces and authorize him to issue training-related instructions to the army units in my name and to speak on my behalf after the highest-ranking unit commander present at exercise debriefings."[38]

Guisan handled Wille's presumptuous proposition in a dilatory manner by only replying one month later, submitting to him a counter-proposal in which he did not make him his deputy but simply authorized him "to make remarks and suggestions, before the debriefing, to the highest-ranking commander present regarding an exercise" in case the General could not attend the exercise.[39] The Head of Main Section III was to report to the General about the results of his inspections.

Guisan did not want to make any further concessions to Wille, even less so because the corps commanders decidedly opposed increasing the Chief Instructor's authority.[40] He was relieved to be able to inform his direct subordinates, "All [other] Corps Commanders have voiced their opposition to making Colonel-Corps Commander Wille the General's deputy."[41]

Since he was dissatisfied with Guisan's response and was not invited to another head-to-head meeting on the matter, in a letter dated October 10, 1940, Wille submitted his resignation to the Head of the Military Department, asking to be allowed to retire.[42] In an additional letter addressed to Federal President Pilet-Golaz, he explained that it was difficult for him to take this step after serving as an officer and instructor for nearly forty years, but that he did so because he was concerned about the "army command's badly thought-out measures, our army's blind attitude, and the public opinion being misled." He bluntly mentioned the real reason for his resignation, stating, "As long as the General listens to other advisors rather than me in issues relating to success in the war, even if as his direct subordinate I am close to him as well, my cooperation is insignificant. After waiting patiently for many months I have to draw the necessary conclusion and ask to be allowed to resign as a federal employee." He added that in the future he would put his "entire confidence in the Federal Council [and] continue to help safeguard the country's existence through the Cabinet during a time of great danger that many do not seem yet to see."[43]

It appears that in view of the country's delicate domestic and foreign political situation, in the fall of 1940 neither the Federal Council nor the General considered Wille's dismissal advantageous. One factor was that Wille had a sizeable number of supporters in the officers' corps. Negotiations were begun to convince him to withdraw his resignation, and after a four-week tug-of-war, a compromise was found. On November 12, 1940, he informed the Head of the Military Department that following several meetings and a written exchange of opinions with the commander-in-chief, "The relationship was based on the necessary trust once again" and that he had granted the General's request not to resign and to remain on his post as Head of Main Section III.[44]

It is obvious that Guisan's strategy was to keep Wille waiting. He would have preferred to cast him aside but the time was not right to do so. The General paved the way for the compromise by writing Wille that he was willing to discuss the status of his position. He explained that he had once again carefully deliberated the issue of Wille's authority but had unfortunately come to the conclusion that it was not possible to grant the Chief Instructor the right to inspect troops at any time because that would curtail the authority of the corps commanders, who were responsible for training their troops. He said that the best solution would be to grant the Chief Instructor the following powers:

1. As previously suggested, during exercises that the commander was unable to attend, before the debriefing he should be authorized to "make remarks and suggestions to the highest-ranking commander present regarding the exercise";
2. He should regularly report to the commander-in-chief on the observations and experience gained during visits at exercises and inspections of training courses.

Guisan explained that whenever it seemed useful to him, he would transmit the Chief Instructor's remarks to the directly subordinate commanders, thereby assuring that all training was done according to the same standard. As for promotions and nominations of officers, the General told Wille that he "gladly" agreed to consult with him and would therefore invite him to the relevant meetings in the future. He concluded his letter by stating that he expected Wille to agree to this solution and take back his resignation.[45]

Wille initially rejected the General's proposal, making him understand that he considered the concessions regarding his authority too insignificant. He wrote, "I do not want to bring about a change in my position toward the commanders of the army corps but toward you. You do not take advantage of my long-time professional activity when it comes to personnel issues or in training-related matters."[46]

Following this exchange of letters, Guisan held a meeting with Wille on November 2 at his command post in Gümligen to clarify the situation. After one hour, Wille agreed to the solution the General proposed. Guisan explained that he wanted to keep Wille as Chief Instructor but agreed to let him resign as

Chief Instructor of the Infantry, which continued to be Wille's official title as a federal employee, in order to move Colonel Probst into that position, promoting him to divisional commander.[47]

It did not seem to take the General long to see through Wille's deliberate attempt to push him aside. One can assume that Hausamann, whose intelligence service worked quite well in this respect, was able to inform him in time of the maneuver that Wille had initiated with the German envoy. Hausamann reported having repeatedly received information from Berlin that German circles were trying to oust Guisan to have him replaced by an officer who was more acceptable to the German leadership. He stated that the information was usually summarized and transmitted to the General.[48] One of the reports, which came "from a reliable source" but was qualified as a rumor, stated "that Wille was [Guisan's] only possible replacement because Hitler himself [wanted] him to be Commander-in-Chief of the Swiss Army." Therefore, Wille's entourage was reported to be "decidedly optimistic, thinking that Wille [wanted] Switzerland to be ruled by a military dictatorship . . . in agreement with Germany's intentions."[49]

According to a special report by Hausamann, in the fall of 1940 Wille told an informant, "The Swiss Army was an obstacle to improving relations with Germany because the most important positions on the army command were held by Swiss French or Swiss Germans who were known to side with Western Europe. He said that the Chief Executive Officer was missing, adding that the board of directors should resign during times like those and leave the management up to the Chief Executive Officer."[50] The General transmitted a copy of this report to Federal Councilor Minger in order to point out to him "Wille's dangerous dual role."[51]

Based on these and similar reports and his own observations, Guisan began to have increasing doubts about the Chief Instructor's true attitude. As early as the summer of 1940, one month before Federal President Pilet-Golaz received a delegation of the Front movement, Guisan annotated a report by the intelligence service which stated that Wille, Däniker, and others were mentioned in connection with the National Movement of Switzerland with the words, "Nazi group set up by Wille, Spoerri, Däniker, Brunner, Berli."[52] Following a meeting with Wille in the late fall of 1940, Guisan noted his impressions: "Stubborn opposition and mean criticism. Lack of truthfulness, not upright. Flaw of character, cannot be corrected. Says that he would have resigned but the F[ederal] C[ouncil] asked him to stay on!!"[53]

For the time being, Guisan felt obliged to keep Wille on his post and even praise him. In December 1940, he wrote to him, "I for my part would not like to miss this opportunity to express to you my high esteem for your many years of successfully working to improve our army's defensive potential as Chief Instructor of the Infantry. Since I am very well aware how valuable training is that prepares troops for a war, it is particularly important to me to know that you will continue to work with me as Head of Main Section III."[54] In reality, however, the General began studiously avoiding Wille, who seemed above him intellectually but whose need for recognition certainly displeased him. In addition, he began to have the chief of the general staff deal with more and more training issues in order to have problems relating to the ground troops handled by officers on the army staff rather than by Main Section III.[55]

Relations between Guisan and Wille, which were not very pleasant to begin with, worsened with the culmination of the Däniker affair. The situation turned critical when the Chief Instructor, in his "Thoughts About the Decision by the Military Attorney General," defended the author of the reprehensible "Memorandum" and attacked the General and the Federal Council.[56] At that time, the Military Attorney General recommended in a confidential letter that Guisan punish Wille not only by reprimanding him or by putting him on a temporary leave, as Guisan had suggested, but by parting with him once and for all. He argued that a temporary leave would only "cause new complications, [hence] dismissing him [was] the only solution."[57] With his letter, Eugster enclosed the draft of a notice of dismissal in which Wille was politely asked to resign from his post as Chief Instructor in the interest of "securing a unified spirit of training and leadership in our army."

The General would have liked to follow Eugster's recommendation, but first submitted a copy of the proposed notice to the Head of the Military Department in order to discuss the issue with him "if necessary."[58] As indicated by their correspondence, Kobelt subsequently held several meetings with the General to discuss Wille's dismissal. At Guisan's request, Kobelt summarized the results of their meetings, stating:

> You wanted me to inform the Federal Council of your intention in order for political concerns to be addressed first. In particular, you were afraid that the Head of the Department of Foreign Affairs might change his mind after the fact. Since you insisted, even though I repeatedly told you that this was an issue entirely up to the General to decide and not a political issue, of course I no longer hesitated to present the matter to the Federal Council. The Federal Council asked me to recommend to you to renounce dismissing Mr. Wille at the present time. Since you have already taken disciplinary measures against Mr. Wille by rebuking him, and since in his letter of June 5, 1942, Mr. Wille accepted the conditions that you had set on June 1, 1942 to be

able to continue cooperating with him, it does not seem to be acceptable to dismiss him after all.[59]

The day before receiving this written notice of the Federal Council's opinion, Guisan had already decided not to insist on dismissing Wille right away
but to part with him at the end of the year in connection with regular staff
changes in order to avoid causing a stir. He only wrote to the Chief Instructor
that he was not satisfied with his declaration after being rebuked because of the
"Thoughts," because he had failed to state an apology. He added that Wille's
attitude further diminished his confidence in him and consequently spoiled
relations between the army command and the Chief Instructor.[60]

Guisan hesitated for some time before deciding what would be most appropriate to do in this delicate case. In an internal note, the personal staff pointed
out to him that the commander-in-chief's authority might suffer among high-
ranking officers and political authorities if he did not dare to take resolute
action against Wille. According to the memo, "Getting Colonel-Corps
Commander W[ille] to cooperate loyally and actively seems to be out of the
question. Consequently, the whole issue would only be postponed, for which
the commander-in-chief would be held responsible."[61]

Politicians advocating unconditional resistance also encouraged Guisan not
to handle his opponent Wille with kid gloves. At the end of an 18-page paper,
Markus Feldmann, a conservative National Councilor and future Federal
Councilor, recommended to the General to "affirm resolute resistance against
activities by Wille, Däniker, Probst, Bircher, who agitate against the Federal
Council and the Army Command. If necessary, ruthlessly tell the public the
truth by means of a parliamentary interpellation during a joint session of the
National Council and Council of States. I consider that this move, undertaken
under the motto, 'against Wille,' could at once totally isolate Däniker and his
supporters in Swiss public opinion."[62] Guisan annotated this passage with the
comment, "Interesting, to be examined."

The General's cautious, careful strategy in dealing with Wille was exactly
what Barbey had advocated as early as the spring of 1942. When he examined
Wille's attitude, which he described with the words, "lack of mental discipline,"
the Chief of the Personal Staff considered that it was preferable to quietly discharge Wille than to sack him. He asked himself, "Does it make sense, in the
current situation, to make a big deal out of this issue and to cause a stir that
might be publicized both at home and abroad? I don't think so."[63] In the case
of Wille, a man with a famous name, it appeared all the more advisable to proceed with caution and to give the Chief Instructor the opportunity to save face
at the time of his retirement from the army.

At the end of the summer of 1942, the General's entourage still believed that Wille's supporters were very influential. After a conversation with Du Pasquier and Corbat, Barbey noted, "They are both afraid of the spirit of Main Section III and fear that Wille might create 'an army within the army'."[64] On the other hand, though, there were clear indications that following the sanctions taken against Colonel Däniker, numerous officers reconsidered their relationship with the army command and in the interest of their career tried to improve relations with Guisan and his loyalists. Moreover, it had become obvious that on the battlefields abroad, which had developed to Germany's disadvantage, Wille's predictions had failed to materialize, making many among his supporters question his supposed perceptiveness. Hence, Wille's reputation as a military leader was waning.

The tempestuous relationship between Guisan and Wille, which had never been really good, was beyond repair, leading to the final break in the fall of 1942. Wille's actual dismissal as Chief Instructor, which he tried to oppose, followed six weeks of an intensive exchange of correspondence between him and the General during which 18 letters were written, some of them several pages long. On October 20, 1942, during a meeting in Champvent, the General informed Wille of his intention to discharge him as Head of Main Section III as of the end of the year. He gave as a reason Wille's continued lack of trust, referring to his role in the Däniker affair. In a follow-up letter, he wrote, "As I told you on October 20, if all I did during the past summer following your attitude in the Däniker affair was rebuke you and issue a warning to you instead of stripping you of your post, it was because I wanted to spare you the unpleasant consequences of a measure that is taken outside the regular transfer period. However, I implicitly reserved the right to take this measure at a suitable time." In addition, Guisan considered it "normal" that after nine years of serving as a corps commander, it was time for Wille to make room for a younger officer. Hence, he said that he was obliged to ask him to resign as of December 31. He explained that he left it up to Wille to write the letter of resignation.[65] The General added, undoubtedly in order to make the dismissal more appealing to Wille, that "paying tribute to your education and experience in the military, I reserve the right to call on you for special tasks in the future, the same way I ask Corps Commander Miescher for assistance whenever it is needed."

Wille replied that he would not take the opportunity to submit his own resignation. He said that he was under the impression he was going to be punished after the fact for supporting Däniker, stating, "If you had discharged me in May to sanction me because of my petition [in Däniker's favor], I and everyone else would have known why. When I wrote my 'Thoughts About the Decision by the Military Attorney General Against Colonel Däniker' and submitted them to the Federal Council and you, I was aware that this might displease you. If the time to discharge me did not seem right to the Federal Council and to you, I do not see this as being considerate of me. . . . You cannot expect me not to fight with all means against sanctions, or what appear to be sanctions, at the end of my career as an officer and after serving in the military for so long."[66] The General tried to deny that the Chief Instructor's discharge was a sanction after the fact, explaining, "You must understand, as others have, that after serving as corps commander for nine and a half years you will be relieved of your position and discharged as of December 31, 1942, according to article 51 of the Military Service Regulations."[67]

On November 19, 1942, Guisan held one last meeting with Wille, at the office of the general staff at the Federal Palace in Bern. Wille noted, "The items on the agenda were:

1. The reason for my discharge is the petition of May 18, 1942 together with my 'seniority.'
2. Question if Prisi, Lardelli, Dollfus, who are older, will also be replaced. They will stay on!
3. Who will be my successor? My opinion about Labhart, Borel, Constam, Frick. Result: the General wants to think the issue over once again."[68]

A few days later, the General informed Wille that he had not altered his decision and restated that there was a lack of trust between them, which was detrimental to the army's overall interests. He added that "nobody is irreplaceable; it will be possible to find a successor for you and thereby make room for someone younger, as I wrote to you on October 26."[69]

In his written reply, Wille once again suggested that his being discharged would be seen mostly as a punishment after the fact for his support of Däniker, explaining, "Because the moment did not seem right to you back then, you refrained from taking sanctions against me and reserved the right to do so 'at a suitable time'." He claimed, though, that no one would fail to realize the real reason for his being discharged and why the General considered the time to be right. Wille concluded his letter with the ironic remark, "I unconditionally agree with you that 'nobody is irreplaceable'."[70]

The order by which the commander-in-chief officially informed the Chief Instructor of his discharge was dated December 8. The official announcement in the press was concise, stating that effective December 31, 1942, Colonel-Corps Commander Ulrich Wille would be "discharged as Head of Main Section III (Chief Instructor) and put at the disposal of the army command.

We would like to thank Colonel-Corps Commander Wille for the services rendered."[71] On December 19, 1942, the Chief Instructor participated for the last time in a briefing by the General with the corps commanders. The commander-in-chief expressed his appreciation for the work he had done and announced that he reserved the right to use Wille's services in the future and would possibly entrust him with special missions. According to the minutes, the discharged officer said nothing.[72]

Wille was not only disappointed but enraged at the way he was cast aside. When he realized that the rift between him and the General could no longer be mended, he wrote to his former subordinate Däniker, "This is the last act of revenge in the tragedy of which you are the victim."[73] One of his sons explained that Ulrich Wille considered his being discharged "the ultimate humiliation."[74]

At the end of December, Wille went to see the Federal Councilors to personally bid them farewell. He wrote that he "noticed that everyone was embarrassed, expressed their regrets, and ended by pronouncing words of thanks and appreciation," a scenario that was repeated seven times. Wille added, "The things that I weaved into the conversation served as a clue for each of the gentlemen to elicit to what extent, depending on their character, they disassociated from our commander-in-chief. All seven Federal Councilors attributed my conflict with the General to the fact that I judged him by my father's personality and adhered to my father's principles."[75] In addition, Wille wrote to Federal Councilor Kobelt to complain about the "lack of sincerity" during the proceedings undertaken against him.[76] The discharged corps commander, who had served in the army for 45 years, did not appear in person at the General's office to report absent from duty but did so only in writing.[77]

The way the announcement of the Chief Instructor's discharge was formulated and published, along with all the year-end transfers in the military, did not reflect the fact that Wille was discharged against his own will. The army and people were under the impression that this was a regular retirement, even more so because newspapers acknowledged the retired corps' commander's achievements. However, Wille himself would have preferred not to be obliged to save face. He addressed editors of several newspapers, including the *Bund*, to ask them to inform their readers that he did not retire of his own accord at all but had been forced to do so. Markus Feldmann, a future Federal Councilor, wrote to the General about this, "Because the concerned editors showed understanding and the censorship authorities intervened right away, this action was duly blocked."[78] Hence, Wille's "retirement" was not only quietly accepted by the public, but according to Feldmann it actually "made a good impression." He remarked that he did not hear any negative comments about this measure.[79]

Those among Wille's supporters who were informed, though, were shocked at the way the General had proceeded. Däniker, who still mistakenly believed that the situation would turn around, comforted Wille by writing to him, "This external separation from the system [also has advantages, because the opponent's victory is only temporary;] those who matter have a different view . . . and know exactly that when the time of desperation has come because of today's shortsightedness, salvation can only be obtained by personalities who have a deep affection for the country but not for persons who are to blame for its fall." Däniker considered that Wille's discharge was "part of the countless mistakes that will ruin not only our army but also our country and for which no one will want to be responsible later on."[80]

The blinded entourage of Wille and Däniker fell victim to the mistaken belief that one day the mood would turn in their favor and they would end up in positions of power. Däniker claimed that "many young people who will make a difference know exactly how things stand; [you] cannot pull the wool over their eyes. These young people will know where they stand and will keep their composure in any situation [because] they are real soldiers, not just some opportunists who stay in the army because they do not have a regular job." He sneered at Guisan, stating, "If today someone can do the exact opposite of what [the General] said the day before without even blushing, there is absolutely no hope that a soldierly attitude will be established."[81]

On December 8, 1942, Guisan met with the main candidate for the post of new chief instructor of the armed forces, Divisional Commander Marcuard, the chief instructor of the artillery.[82] On the same day, Barbey was ordered to draft new terms of reference for the chief instructor.[83] The order dated December 16, 1942, which was not to go into effect until March 1, 1943, stated:

> In accordance with the Commander-in-Chief's instructions, and in close cooperation with the Army Corps Commanders, the Chief Instructor shall ensure that the training during initiation courses and courses for future officers and the training for enlisted soldiers, officers, and combined units are based on one single standard. In case of differences of opinion between the Chief Instructor and the Commanders of the army corps, the General shall be the arbiter.[84]

When he nominated Marcuard, Guisan insisted on explaining to him in detail what he expected from the new chief instructor. He wrote to tell him that he wanted to see him "in person in order to give [him] a number of additional instructions concerning [his] new mission."[85] This request stresses how important personal contacts were to Guisan. No minutes were kept of the meeting that was subsequently held on January 6, 1943, at the command post in

Interlaken. However, according to notes that Barbey prepared for the General for that meeting, Guisan particularly addressed the issue of the main arm, the infantry, which he said was "in a severe crisis" mostly because its Chief Instructor, Divisional Commander Probst, was a formalist and showed little interest in combat training. He said that Probst liked the routine of the barracks and had a tendency to judge the instructors and troops only by their appearance, not by their fitness to go to war. "Moreover," he added, "Divisional Commander Probst has not issued any directives since becoming Chief Instructor in 1940; instead, all he has been doing is work according to the tentative directives that were issued by Colonel-Corps Commander Wille in May 1939, before wartime duty began!"[86] The General explained that it was only after receiving orders from him that Probst finally issued revised instructions on November 1, 1942.

These remarks make clear that the dispute with Wille was not only about the General's desire to assert himself but also to a large extent about the basic issue of the main focus of training in the army. However, it is quite common for such conflicts to involve a complex combination of objective military, political, and personal factors, as well as animosities and rivalries that prevent two dissimilar personalities from working well together. It is difficult for outsiders to perceive the subtle nuances of Guisan's and Wille's multifaceted relationship. The secret feud between the General and the Chief Instructor intensified following Germany's victories on the battlefields, turning into an open conflict and a serious power struggle. By neutralizing Wille, Guisan managed to inflict a decisive blow on the officers who had kindled internal opposition against him; and Däniker's supporters had lost their last significant stronghold. It was not until he had cast aside Colonel-Corps Commander Wille in the third year of his tenure that General Guisan became the uncontested leader of the entire armed forces.

Cases of Treason, Death Sentences, and Surveillance Activities

IN HIS POSTWAR REPORT, the Adjutant General stated that a total of 478 individuals, including 283 Swiss citizens, were sentenced because they had breached military secrets or carried out espionage.[1] However, statistics published by the Military Department listed 683 cases of treason between 1939 and 1945, 468 of which involved Swiss citizens.[2] Based on the divergent figures, one must conclude that a considerable number of cases went to trial only after the war.

Both sources agreed about the number of death sentences, all of which were pronounced between 1942 and 1944. Switzerland's divisional and territorial courts pronounced a total of 33 death sentences against 22 Swiss citizens and 11 foreign nationals. Fifteen of those were convicted in absentia.[3] Seventeen men, including 16 Swiss citizens and a citizen of Liechtenstein, were executed by firing squad. One French national was pardoned, his death sentence commuted by Parliament to life imprisonment. The death sentences and executions were approved by a large majority of the population. General Guisan also fervently advocated carrying out the sentences.

Switzerland's 1937 penal code, which went into effect on January 1, 1942, abolished capital punishment throughout the country. However, the 1927 penal code of the armed forces made provisions during times of war for the death penalty to be applied as the ultimate punishment in cases of treason and military espionage that could disrupt or threaten the army's activities. The penal code of the armed forces stipulated, "The provisions that apply during times of war are in force not only when Switzerland is at war but also at the

Federal Council's discretion when there is an imminent threat of war."[4] The Federal Council's decision had to be submitted to Parliament for approval.

In the spring of 1940, it appeared that the war might spill over into Switzerland. Spying activities were on the rise, attempts at sabotage were made, and there were fears that a pro-German "Fifth Column" could intervene. During that time, as early as May 3, Corps Commander Labhart suggested to Guisan that he should consider supporting the introduction of the death penalty. The General informed Labhart that he "completely" agreed with his proposition but that Federal Councilor Minger opposed putting the article regarding the death penalty during times of war into force.[5] However, when the entire army was mobilized for the second time, Guisan revisited the question with the Head of the Military Department, writing that he once again requested the Federal Council to introduce capital punishment as stipulated in article 5 of the military penal code. He argued that it was highly advisable, as a preventive matter, to pronounce very severe sentences in the interest of the country's security and the army's operational combat capability.[6]

Civilians also urged the Federal Council to put this article into force. In mid-May 1940, a group of young citizens from the city of Bern submitted a petition to the Head of the Justice and Police Department, Federal Councilor Baumann, to introduce the death penalty immediately. The petition stated, "In view of the alarming increase of espionage cases against Switzerland involving military secrets, and considering the increasing concern among our soldiers and civilians, it is absolutely necessary to threaten spies with the death penalty. In many espionage cases the death penalty is the only appropriate punishment. Its application will also deter those who are tempted to betray Switzerland in exchange for money or for some other reason."[7] During a meeting of the National Council's proxy committee, Gottlieb Duttweiler, the chairman of the National Alliance of Independents, requested that in severe cases of treason the death penalty should be applied, arguing, "It would be irresponsible to keep waiting."[8]

It is striking that during Germany's Western campaign the Federal Council chose not to put the provision for the military death penalty into force, which would have been very easy to do. The Military Attorney General explained that the government had reservations about applying the provision during that "time of an imminent threat of war" because it feared that this could make the population even more worried and lead to false interpretations by foreign countries during a time of extreme nervousness.[9] In consequence, on May 28, 1940, the Federal Council passed a special decree to amend the penal code of the armed forces, allowing the death penalty to be applied only for a number of offenses in connection with giving away military secrets and in cases of treason against the military.[10]

General Guisan called treason the "dark spot of wartime duty," explaining that espionage on behalf of foreign countries was spreading across the entire country like a "vast spider web."[11] People who sympathized with Germany and embraced National Socialism were particularly prone to betray their home country by revealing military or economic secrets. Most potential traitors belonged to groups of Swiss Nazis who advocated Switzerland's *Gleichschaltung* with Nazi Germany or who wanted to fully integrate Switzerland into the Third Reich. Others were weak characters or wayward individuals who were willing to betray their country for material reasons. Many convicts, whose motives could usually be determined during the trials, were members of spying organizations that had many different branches. Those who spied for ideological reasons were more dangerous, but those who did so for material reasons were more numerous. Peter Noll, a professor of penal law from Zürich, analyzed the lives of the 17 executed traitors based on their case files and gave an account of their trials.[12]

Attempts at espionage were initiated almost exclusively by Germany. In comparison, the spying activities by the Allies were insignificant. Moreover, only four minor cases involved Germany's Axis partner, Italy.[13] Germany's spying activities focused mainly on matters dealing with the army's organization and equipment, defenses at river crossings, barriers blocking access routes to valleys, and later the access routes to the Réduit. Gottlieb Trachsel, a colonel who was the deputy of the chief security officer of the armed forces for some time, described how during the search of one traitor's home, spying instructions that came from Germany were discovered. When two sheets of paper containing some irrelevant notes were chemically treated, instructions that had been written in invisible ink became legible. They read:

> *Troops:* unit number, color of lapels, insignia. What division or brigade do they belong to? Time and place of observation, where are they quartered, what is their assigned combat area? Where are the staffs of the 1st, 2nd, 3rd, and 4th Army Corps and of the divisions and border brigades stationed? Who is the commander? Which division and brigades belong to which army corps? Sectors assigned to the border brigades; where are the staffs stationed? Which battalions belong to which brigade, and where are they stationed? When, for how long, and where do units go on leave or are called up (based on the General's latest order)?
>
> *Armament:* number of infantry guns, trench-mortars, anti-tank guns, flame-throwers, submachine guns per battalion or regiment. Provide specifics about weapons if possible. Include three to four pro-

jectiles of anti-tank guns if possible. Exact description of flame-throwers: design, effect, how can you protect yourself against them?

Military infrastructure: secret plans regarding the Réduit, secret deployment plans, plans of operation for Gotthard, Sargans, Monte Ceneri, Samaden, Maloja, Ofen, and Simplon mountain passes, St-Maurice, Le Locle.

Reconnaissance: the areas of Urnerboden, Klausen mountain pass, Hilterfingen, Interlaken, between Lucerne and Bern, Entlebuch and valleys branching out south from there. Always indicate exact location, type of armament. Objects prepared for destruction: where is the trigger, how are the explosives attached? Same for minefields. Military transmitters: equipment, position, stationary or mobile, frequencies, call codes, times of transmission, secret code or key to military information. Logistics movements: where, what, and for whom?[14]

Requests for such detailed information had to be very alarming to the Swiss command. Military historian Hans Rudolf Fuhrer wrote a comprehensive study of these and many other details of the spying activities against Switzerland.[15]

The information about Switzerland's defense in which German intelligence was interested was typically part of the preparations for an invasion. Even after Germany's attack on Russia in the early summer of 1941, which diminished the immediate risk of Switzerland being drawn into the war, spying activities continued, giving rise to concerns that Switzerland might still be at risk after all. Some had the impression that in 1941 spying activities were actually being intensified.[16] In the spring of 1942, at a briefing with the army staff about current espionage cases, Chief of the General Staff Huber warned that spying activities against Switzerland were still being carried out in a systematic manner, adding, "Therefore one must conclude that Switzerland has not yet escaped the risk of being drawn into the war but that something is being plotted against us."[17] Colonel Jaquillard, the head of Counter-Intelligence, explained that Swiss citizens were being lured into working as intelligence agents by being promised that if caught they would "be released as soon as the Germans arrived in Switzerland and be rewarded for their services."[18]

Fuhrer states that the German army and party intelligence was "remarkably successful, which shows that Switzerland did not exactly excel in maintaining secrecy."[19] The German Army High Command summarized the results of their intelligence activities for internal use in an "Information Booklet on Switzerland." The information contained therein comes surprisingly close to Switzerland's actual military strength and the way in which the Swiss Army Command viewed it.[20] In the fall of 1940, the German Army High Command also took down some information in its war journal.[21] As contradictory as it may appear, it has been established that the information gathered by German intelligence was not altogether damaging for Switzerland but actually helped prevent the Germans from attacking because it had some dissuasive effect. The approximately 2,000 booby-trapped objects and roughly the same number of anti-tank obstacles about which German intelligence had been informed evidenced Switzerland's determination to defend itself and served as a deterrent.

Switzerland's military courts are formally independent of the army command and do not report to the commander-in-chief. Nevertheless, in some exceptional cases General Guisan, following General Wille's example during World War I, did not fail to assert his influence on the military's jurisdiction. In the winter of 1941–42, two Swiss were sentenced to 15 years in prison because they had given away military secrets. When a new espionage case went to trial, Guisan wrote to the Military Attorney General:

> I consider the death penalty appropriate, especially to serve as a deterrent. Those who receive heavy prison sentences might all hope that their pleas will be heard by their soul mates in and outside the country. Traitors must be completely cured of this hope. It is absolutely necessary to set an example to warn and deter them, even more so because potential invaders would not be lenient with us either. I would like to ask you to stay on top of this case and consult with the Senior Judge, but of course without interfering in the legal proceedings. I consider that this will help curb the widespread spying activities in Switzerland.[22]

This unambiguous statement shows that the General was determined to stop spying activities by employing the death penalty.

In the summer of 1942, when three low-ranking officers who were former members of the Front movement were indicted for treason, Guisan once again urged the Military Attorney General not to refrain from applying the death penalty, explaining:

> Even if I do not wish to interfere in the military's jurisdiction, I consider that the time has come to pronounce the death penalty against 1st Lt. Reimann, 2nd Lt. Kully, and 2nd Lt. Merkt. The army and the people urgently demand that traitors of this kind, who are officers on top of it all, receive a punishment that is appropriate for the crime they committed. Past experience has shown that only the death penalty can act as a deterrent in view of the increasing number of spying cases. It

can be dangerous to be lenient and take into consideration past practice; for once we must apply the penal law of the armed forces to the fullest extent.[23]

In view of the circumstances at the time, a large majority of the population undoubtedly welcomed capital punishment. However, once the first death sentences were pronounced, for numerous Swiss—especially for all those who had categorically opposed the death penalty—these cases became a matter of conscience. Even though not the General but Parliament had the authority to pardon death row prisoners, Guisan received numerous letters from both intellectuals and workers asking him to pardon the traitors in the name of humanity and Christianity.[24] Pacifist Max Daetwyler and author Walter Marti were among those who approached the commander-in-chief.[25] In addition, the mothers, wives, and children of the convicts wrote moving appeals for mercy to the General. Guisan had most of these letters answered by his personal staff, informing the petitioners that he fully understood the distress of the concerned families but that the issue did not fall within his authority. He later explained that he was glad not to have the right to pardon those who had been sentenced to death because it would have put too much strain on him to have to make a decision alone in this grave matter.[26] In 1942, the Military Attorney General sent the General a copy of a report in which he recommended to the Federal Council not to pardon the convicted traitors. Guisan commented in his handwriting, "Very interesting report which shows that its author is not only a legal professional but also a soldier!"[27]

National Councilor Karl Killer, the mayor of the town of Baden, chaired the special parliamentary committee that examined convicts' appeals for mercy. In the presence of Federal Councilors Kobelt and von Steiger and the Military Attorney General, the 13-member committee met for three entire days to discuss three cases of traitors who had been sentenced to death. Federal Councilor Kobelt explained that the second case, that of Quartermaster Sergeants W. Zürcher and J. Feer and Driver E. Schrämli, was an extremely serious espionage case. They had given away the locations of explosives depots and the degree of readiness of objects that had been prepared for destruction in an area covered by three divisions, as well as the addresses of the commanders in charge of carrying out the explosions in the event of an invasion. The case was particularly serious because a copy of the complete set of defensive measures undertaken by an army corps had been sold to the Germans. The Head of the Military Department added, "What is even worse, they also explained what safety measures had not been taken."[28] The pardon committee took note of 14 petitions against and 22 petitions in favor of pardoning the traitors. In a secret ballot, it rejected all three appeals for mercy.[29]

The members of the committee did not make the decision easy for themselves, though it was ultimately a deliberation of conscience. The decision placed a particularly great emotional strain on Chairman Killer, a Social Democrat who had vehemently opposed the death penalty for decades, speaking against it in public before the war. He brought himself to assume part of the responsibility for the executions; however, he also decided to resign from the committee. Some members of Parliament had maliciously begun calling the chairman of the pardon committee "the killer," which was said to have contributed to his resignation.[30] National Councilor Carl Miville, a Social Democrat from Basel, succeeded him.

During the difficult time of World War II, even men of God did not hesitate to advance arguments in favor of the death penalty. Emil Brunner, a theology professor from Zürich, considered that the state had not only the right but actually the obligation "to make use of [capital punishment] on behalf of God, for mercy's sake, in order to protect the people."[31] As late as the 1930s, Karl Barth wrote that the Gospel did "not support [the death penalty] in any way but actually rejected it"; yet when he felt the threat of National Socialism, he changed his mind and considered the death penalty justified against traitors, supporting his case with theological arguments. After the war, though, he stated, "I wish I had not written that!"[32] Historian Edgar Bonjour from Basel advocated a compromise, suggesting that traitors who were sentenced to death should not be executed until Switzerland was actually attacked. However, his idea was "supported only by a few."[33]

Once the first death sentences had been pronounced, General Guisan made no secret of his opinion that the convicts should be executed. According to newspaper reports, during a speech that he gave at the 1942 Autumn Fair in Fribourg, he stated that traitors should not receive any mercy and that "our first concern was security, which was more important than anything else. He said that humanitarian considerations played only a secondary role."[34] His speech was met with great applause. The *Neue Berner Zeitung* argued that the General had "expressed exactly what the overwhelming majority of the Swiss [were] thinking" because traitors deserved no mercy.[35] *Aufgebot*, a paper published in central Switzerland, also approved of the General's speech, writing that he did what everyone had expected from him. The paper commented:

> The General's words were welcomed in large parts of the country. . . .
> It was necessary for the top military commander to say these words to
> all incurable humanistic dreamers delving in sentimental humanitari-

anism who believe that the state does not even have the right to take the lives of its worst enemies. However, the Swiss who have common sense know that there are times when the life of a traitor has to be put to an end so as to prevent the country from being threatened, even if life is otherwise the greatest good that must be protected.[36]

During the time the pardon committee was meeting in Bern, Guisan personally voiced his opinion in the press, writing in the *Schweizer Illustrierte* magazine:

> Being loyal to one's country means serving one's country from beginning to end and making sacrifices! Those who do not do so for their own sake have a right to know that their sacrifices are not in vain. However, these sacrifices turn into an illusion through the disloyalty of traitors. It is the country's duty to its patriotic soldiers to put a halt to the activities of those who are not afraid to jeopardize the lives of thousands of soldiers and tens of thousands of civilians as well as the country's liberty and independence. The Swiss who serve in the army with their whole heart, making great economic sacrifices, must be protected from being shot in the back. Hence, traitors have to be eliminated from society in a way that will prevent them from committing similar offenses in the future. Respect for humanity is all very well, but let us apply it most of all in favor of the soldiers who protect our borders and their families. Mercy is due exclusively to our own and foreign victims of war. The most sacred interests and our country's future must be safeguarded. Our home country is more important than anything else. Therefore, the first tenet is, 'Be loyal to your country!'[37]

Not everyone appreciated the General influencing public opinion in such a dramatic manner. Samuel Haas, the director of the Schweizer Mittelpresse news agency, complained to the Head of the Military Department that "out of respect for existing traditions and for the dignity and authority of the pardon committee," the General should respect democratic procedures and abstain from personally interfering in the administration of justice. As he explained:

> I consider that it was inadmissible for him to demand publicly that the sinners pay for their sins with their blood, as he did in Fribourg and again recently in the *Schweizer Illustrierte*. By interfering in such a way, he discredits the procedure, which is supposed to be impartial. His interference might promote the rule of force or at least give the impres-

sion that law and order are not free from personal pressure and intervention. . . . His interventions are objectionable, to say the least. They certainly ill become a state that is founded on the rule of law.

Haas concluded his sharp protest by asking Federal Councilor Kobelt, "Don't you think that after these two incidents, in the name of our democracy and its laws, it is about time to put an end to this blurring of civilian and military power? Leaders of totalitarian states may subordinate jurisprudence to the political executive power and do away with the separation of powers, thereby shattering the confidence of those who believe that the legal system is impartial. However, this does not befit Switzerland."[38]

In fact, Kobelt also disapproved of Guisan's interventions. As an indication for his secretary who had to formulate a reply to Haas, Kobelt wrote on Haas' letter, "I basically share the view that the General should not have interfered. Shouldn't he be made aware of that?" The Secretary, Colonel Burgunder, who agreed that Guisan's interference was "awkward indeed," noted that the General was informed verbally, but Guisan explained that he had "acted with Federal Councilor von Steiger's approval."[39]

The first convict executed by a firing squad was army driver Ernst Schrämli in November 1942, even though he had been the second defendant to receive the death penalty.[40] The executions were carried out according to a special ordinance that the Federal Council had issued as early as the summer of 1940.[41] Based on this ordinance, the delinquent had to be shot by a group of twenty men from a distance of six paces, on orders of the commander of the prisoner's regiment. Apparently according to a long-standing tradition among Swiss mercenaries,[42] the execution squad, commanded by a low-ranking officer, consisted of comrades from the convict's company. The Senior Judge, the Military Attorney General and Clerk of the Military Court, the defense attorney, a chaplain, two medical officers, and if possible a representative of the government of the canton in which the execution took place had to be present. The place of execution had to be kept secret. If the convict did not belong to a unit bearing arms, the commander of his army unit had to put a regimental commander of his choice in charge of the execution. The commander of Infantry Regiment 26, Colonel Gossweiler, who was asked to perform the execution of a member of the auxiliary service in the spring of 1943, tendered his resignation after carrying out the task because he deemed that the role of executioner was incompatible with his position and personal honor.[43] Gossweiler's request was not granted. The General annotated the letter of resignation with the comment, "Why delegate a colonel? Too much honor for these traitors!"[44]

The highest-ranking officer who was sentenced to death and executed was Major Ernst Pfister, who was head of the Motor Vehicle Section on the army staff and had access to important secret files.[45] Pfister, who acted mainly out of political conviction, admitted that he had "given away practically all the information that he knew or was able to find out."[46] The court stated that the damage the defendant had done was "for the most part irreparable." As an additional punishment, he was demoted and executed as a simple private. After being tied to a post, the metal buttons on his uniform jacket were cut off.[47] One gains the impression that the executioners released their entire contempt for that staff officer during the execution.

When the number of death sentences began to rise, influential circles suggested to Guisan that the traitors be executed in civilian clothes instead of their uniforms. After more than a dozen executions had been carried out, Samuel Haas wrote to the General that the traitors did not deserve to die in the most honorable attire of their country and that it was a shame that the uniforms got riddled with bullets, adding, "Most people have objected from the beginning to the delinquents wearing their uniform during the execution and the shots being fired at the jacket of a Swiss Army uniform. This contradicts our traditional saying, 'uniform = suit of honor' and 'soldier = citizen in uniform'."[48] The General did not fail to notice this suggestion by the well-known director of the Schweizer Mittelpresse news agency and ordered the Military Attorney General to draft a reply. The Military Attorney General opposed changing the ordinance regarding the execution procedure, arguing that the convicts would be better made aware of the reprehensible nature of their crime if they wore the same uniform as their execution squad. He explained that spoiling the uniform was the price to pay with this procedure.[49]

The public reacted quite positively to the executions, even though many privately still opposed the death penalty. The people were pleased to note that the military courts did not hesitate to pronounce, in the interest of the state, the most severe punishment provided under the law. Many were indignant, though, that in spite of the executions that exclusively involved cases of espionage on behalf of the Third Reich, some high-ranking Swiss officers did not put an end to their private contacts with representatives of the German armed forces or the Nazi Party (NSDAP). National Councilor Markus Feldmann from Bern wrote to the General:

> When I think about the shocking details that had to be revealed, during the appeals for mercy, regarding Germany's organized spying activities against Switzerland and about the fact that the latest executed traitor, Reutlinger, a National Socialist, had been trained by the German

armed forces in Stuttgart to spy against Switzerland, I am enraged and incensed to see that under the present circumstances Swiss officers consider their friendly social contacts with the German Military Attaché compatible with Switzerland's dignity. It seems to me that a so-called 'international soldierly attitude,' as advocated by Wille and Däniker, could be rampant under which one's Swiss roots are not sufficiently emphasized.[50]

As early as during the first winter of wartime duty, the General forbade his officers to attend receptions by foreign diplomats without his prior approval.[51] In May 1941, he tightened this restriction by forbidding all soldiers to have "any contact" with representatives of foreign countries without his written approval.[52] However, this ban, which was difficult to monitor, was undoubtedly ignored by officers like Wille, Däniker, Bircher, and von Erlach, and even in the final stage of the war by Guisan himself.

The German Reich took due note of the execution of traitors in Switzerland. An agent reported that the executions had "a very good effect there, since Switzerland was not believed to have the courage to pronounce death sentences."[53] A report by Hans Hausamann's intelligence Bureau "Ha" stated that the executions were being "frequently discussed also among German party members." The report added that the fact that Switzerland dared to execute criminals who had been working for the Reich proved that it felt safer again. However, the death sentences were criticized as being an "arbitrary act that [had] nothing to do with the administration of justice."[54] Fuhrer suggests that from a German perspective the execution of traitors "put a serious strain on relations with Switzerland."[55]

As late as 1942, Divisional Commander Bircher erroneously believed that Germany's spying activities were not conducted by its armed forces but by "rather clumsy subordinate party offices." He personally tried to get the Reich to stop its espionage against Switzerland by intervening with his acquaintances in Germany. In addition, he asked a fellow medical doctor to plead with his friends to "put an end to the incidents" that strained relations with Germany and "whose consequences [could] not be predicted."[56]

In reality, three different German intelligence organizations were most active in Switzerland. They were independent of each other and occasionally competed. First, there was Admiral Wilhelm Canaris' "Foreign and Counterintelligence Office" of the German Armed Forces Intelligence (the Abwehr); second, the "Reich Security Central Office" of SS General Reinhard Heydrich, whose Office VI dealt with foreign intelligence under the direction of Walter Schellenberg; and third, the Secret State Police (Gestapo). Fuhrer estimates that more than 1,000 German and Swiss agents were simultaneously working in the country.[57]

In the fall of 1942, even before the first death sentences had been carried out, Foreign Minister Pilet-Golaz informed the German envoy that Germany's spying activities in Switzerland were unacceptable. Köcher reported to the German Ministry of Foreign Affairs, "The day before yesterday, Federal Councilor Pilet-Golaz pointed out to me in all seriousness that the continued military intelligence activities that we have been carrying out against Switzerland are bound to put a strain on the public."[58] It was probably in part due to this diplomatic move, but undoubtedly also as a consequence of the first death sentences, which acted as a deterrent, that the German Ministry of Foreign Affairs actually instructed the legation not to continue its intelligence activities in Switzerland. In early 1943, National Councilor Feldmann, who was well informed, reported to the General, "Around November 20, 1942, Permanent Secretary Weizsäcker sent a diplomatic courier to the [German] Legation in Bern giving specific instructions to stop actively supporting any intelligence activities against Switzerland."[59]

Nevertheless, espionage activities did not come to a halt following these instructions. In the spring of 1943, Admiral Canaris forbade his intelligence section, "War Organization Switzerland," to undertake any further activities against Switzerland. One staff member in Canaris' office noted, "A few days ago, Admiral Canaris informed me that he had decided to strictly forbid procuring any more intelligence information about Switzerland, since the information was not useful nor interesting to us and these activities were a political burden for us."[60] Hans Rudolf Fuhrer, who was the first historian to mention this ban on intelligence activities against Switzerland, found out that after the summer of 1943, no further espionage orders were issued concerning Switzerland.[61] The Masson-Schellenberg connection took credit for getting the Security Service of the SS to cease its activities at about the same time. This assumption does not seem to be far-fetched because it is striking that the situation improved following the General's meeting with SS Colonel Schellenberg in Biglen (see Chapter 29).[62]

Many espionage cases were successfully uncovered because of the extensive network of surveillance activities throughout the country set up by several organizations. These organizations, in large part independent of each other, included a special counter-intelligence service in the army whose establishment the Federal Council had approved on September 29, 1939. This service, commanded by Colonel Jaquillard, had actually started its activities at the end of August 1939, at the time the border troops were called up. It had to cooperate with the Federal Prosecutor's Office to take steps to prevent espionage, sabotage, "and any other equivalent activities directed against the army."[63] During the second month of the war, the counter-intelligence service received updated terms of reference from Chief of the General Staff Labhart.[64] In May 1940, at the time of Germany's Western campaign, the service had a staff of nine commissioners and 29 inspectors who usually did not wear uniforms while on duty.[65] During a conversation with Gafner, General Guisan quoted a German expert who said that Switzerland's counter-intelligence service "had been considered by far the most dangerous one and the number of agents who were uncovered was proportionately highest in Switzerland."[66]

In addition to the army's counter-intelligence service, the police of the territorial section, the army police, and the police of the Federal Prosecutor's Office handled security and surveillance measures. In the spring of 1940, Chief of the General Staff Huber ordered the heads of the different sections to meet once a month to promote cooperation among the different organizations. Additional meetings were scheduled as needed.[67] Moreover, the intelligence service carried out some surveillance activities on its own initiative. As Hausamann reported, "The fact that the intelligence service and the police cooperated obviously had consequences outside as well as inside the country. Whenever we received information that a Swiss citizen had taken out some insurance policy in the Reich, we contacted the police of that person's home town in order to have him put under surveillance." Vice versa, the police informed intelligence officers when they made observations that they thought might interest army intelligence. Thus, "by and by the various services and offices began working together and set up a network through which hardly anything major could slip anymore."[68]

Special security measures were taken to prevent espionage at army headquarters. Judging from annotations he made on a report by Jaquillard to Masson, the General showed a personal interest in the security measures. For example, he agreed to have telephone lines tapped at hotels where foreign travelers and diplomats often stayed.[69] As indicated by passages that he underlined, the commander-in-chief read several transcripts of tapped conversations, especially those that dealt with right-wing extremists and the combined entourage of Wille and Däniker, which was under constant surveillance. Within ten days, between February 16 and 25, 1942, he received 15 transcripts at his office.[70]

The fears concerning spying attempts at and around army headquarters were not ill-founded. In 1942, a porter working at the Jungfraublick Hotel stole a number of engineering plans to sell them to German agents. In Zweisimmen, another hotel porter broke into the office of a division staff as well as the private rooms of the divisional commander and other officers to search for documents in wastepaper baskets, among other places.[71]

The various and numerous surveillance activities occasionally ran into some hitches because they overlapped, and in some instances efforts were excessive to the point of becoming ludicrous. Because top authorities mistrusted their counterparts in other offices, they began snooping on each other. In the late fall of 1941, Captain Paul Meyer heard from Colonel Werner Müller, the chief of the Security Section, that Federal Councilor Pilet-Golaz, who as former head of the Communications and Railway Department was said to still have connections with relevant authorities, had the General's telephone calls monitored, and also kept fellow Federal Councilors under surveillance. Meyer was told that whenever the General was at his home in Pully, he used his neighbor's telephone to make calls, and that he had temporarily moved his personal quarters from Interlaken to the Beau Site Hotel in Bern.[72] Hausamann reported, "According to [his] informant's latest information, [Pilet's listening system was] located on the fourth floor at the Postal Service headquarters in Bern, where it was kept in a carefully locked office."[73]

Army security also began putting all officers on the general staff under surveillance, and even listened to the General's and the chief of the general staff's private telephone conversations. At the end of October 1942, the General summoned Captain Meyer, who was nominally in charge of evaluating tapped telephone conversations, into his office to find out whether "his and his son's telephone conversations [were] being monitored, [explaining that he was] under the impression that they were."[74] Meyer was able to reassure the General only in part, telling him that Jaquillard, the head of Army Counter-Intelligence, had the telephones of all officers in Interlaken tapped on his own initiative, with the knowledge of Chief Security Officer Müller. He explained, "I tell the General that neither Masson, nor the chief of the general staff, nor I as the one who is in charge of monitoring telephone calls knew about this. I say that if the public finds out, there will be a scandal because this is a violation of the telephone privacy act. . . . I tell him that this is becoming common knowledge and that people at the Federal Palace are informing even officers about it. I argue that the officers of the army staff are prisoners in Interlaken." Meyer described Jaquillard's illegal action as "identical to the methods used by the Gestapo." He reported about the General's reaction: "He is visibly incensed. He offers me a cigarette."[75]

At Meyer's recommendation, the General had his Chief of Personal Staff Barbey look into the matter and requested that the Military Attorney General inform him whether Jaquillard's action was permissible. Even before receiving a response, he ordered Masson to have all internal telephone monitoring activities at army headquarters stopped.[76] Regarding a meeting with Masson on the subject, Chief of the General Staff Huber noted:

A few weeks ago, you informed me about telephone conversations at army headquarters being tapped by the counter-intelligence service, a measure that had been ordered without your knowledge. I gave you orders to reprimand your subordinate, Colonel Müller on the general staff, and to order whatever was necessary to put an end to this mischief. After that I considered the matter to be closed. However, yesterday I received a letter from the General indicating that he has ordered an investigation and has solicited the opinion of the Military Attorney General on the matter. How did the General find out about this?[77]

In his report, Military Attorney General Eugster concluded that monitoring telephone calls "in a center with heavy travel activities like Interlaken [was] perfectly understandable, and nobody needed to feel offended because of it." He argued that "out of principle" it appeared to be advisable to inform the persons directly involved about the tapping activities, but that did not mean that officers on the army staff were automatically suspected of spying.[78] However, the General had an uncanny feeling about the scope of the monitoring activities, commenting about the Chief of Counter-Intelligence's influence, "Too powerful. Limit his range of action. Inquisition."[79]

At the end of November, Huber chaired a meeting with the army staff members who were responsible for tapping activities in order to resolve the issue. During the meeting he stated: "Monitoring telephone conversations of suspects is one of the regular tasks of the counter-intelligence service. It seems indispensable that the conversations of other people who use the same phone lines as the suspects are also monitored. At first I was a bit annoyed when I was informed that my private telephone conversations were being listened to; however, I accepted that fact as a military necessity."[80] It became clear through the meeting that both Chief of the General Staff Huber and Chief of Intelligence Masson had been informed a year and a half earlier that telephone conversations would be monitored in Interlaken and had approved that measure. Huber admitted, "It is justified to blame me for my bad memory because I had simply forgotten about the events of the spring of 1941. To be honest, though, the bigger portion of the blame has to be attributed to Colonel-Brigadier Masson because as the direct superior he is responsible for supervising the counter-intelligence service. He should be better informed about its activities than I am."[81]

The participants at the meeting were displeased that the tapping activities at army headquarters had been brought to the General's attention by a third party whose name was not revealed. Huber called the indiscretion an act of "denunciation by anonymous cowards" for whom it was apparently possible "to clandestinely bring their information to the General's attention and be taken seriously. . . . One has to wonder how many of these cowards exist on the army staff and what their names are. The fact that the informant has not been identified leaves a serious feeling of mistrust."

A meeting between the commander-in-chief and the chief of the general staff was necessary to resolve the issue. Based on his handwritten notes, the General told Huber, among other things:

> It is improper to speak about cowards! There has been no denunciation. Why did you not talk to me directly if you considered that there were some cowards involved instead of jumping to conclusions that are recorded in these inadmissible minutes? Obviously my task as commander-in-chief puts me in a position to gather a lot of information concerning the entire army. Gathering it does not mean adopting it! I must monitor these things. Masson [is] not well enough informed about what goes on.[82]

The General made Huber understand clearly that he wanted to be in direct contact with intelligence officers and that this fact should not result in any feeling of mistrust nor any disagreement. Around this time, apparently following the meeting by the army staff about the monitored telephone conversations, the General wrote on the back of an official letter:

> I take note of the fact that at the time [Masson] had approved of these surveillance activities. I also take note that the Head of the Intelligence Service was not well enough informed about the counter-intelligence service, which reports to him. In principle, I would like to state that it is the General's responsibility to closely examine, either directly or by going through the official channels, everything that happens in the army, hence also on the army staff, that could give rise to criticism. In particular, there is a very close connection between the position of the intelligence service and the decisions that must be made by the General, making it necessary for me personally to be continuously informed about its activities.[83]

The General reiterated that he did not accept that the army staff mistrusted him or was ill-humored because of his actions.

As a consequence of the affair concerning the tapping activities, Colonel Jaquillard, who felt that he had been unjustly attacked and had become the victim of a plot, asked to resign from his post as head of counter-intelligence.[84] Even though he made his request to the General as well, neither Guisan nor

Huber accepted his resignation.[85] As early as December 5, 1942, apparently to satisfy the requirements of the security section, Guisan authorized Huber to resume monitoring telephone calls of civilians in Interlaken but not of the officers at army headquarters.[86]

Overall, the extensive surveillance activities in Switzerland, which took on virtually totalitarian proportions, affecting simple citizens as well as the top army command, served their purpose in terms of state security. At a secret briefing in early May 1942, Chief of the General Staff Huber stated that there was "an enormous number of suspects" in the army, including "455 officers and 2,340 non-commissioned officers and soldiers; 400 cases [were] pending, 2,500 cases [were] closed for the time being. The suspects [had] to be kept under surveillance within the scope of the existing orders issued to intelligence officers and their organization."[87]

Nevertheless, in some instances the surveillance network did not appear to be dense enough. Noll mentions the case of a mysterious "Colonel X" who had financial difficulties, became involved in gunrunning, and was seriously incriminated in a trial of other traitors. One of the defendants testified that at the Germans' request he had paid "X" an amount of 5,000 francs in exchange for a large sealed envelope that he had to transmit to the German intelligence service. However, this ominous officer died before legal proceedings could be initiated against him.[88]

The traitors, who had various backgrounds and committed crimes of different severity, were all sentenced within the standards of the law. No innocent person was executed. However, Noll concludes that there were significant differences in the way the same crime was treated at different trials. "Sometimes," he wrote, "it depended on who else was in the same trial whether a criminal was sentenced to death or not. When other defendants committed more serious crimes, he could be lucky and get away with a prison sentence. When he was the most seriously incriminated of the entire group, he risked being sentenced to death."[89] Moreover, it is justified to ask whether those who received the heaviest sentences were actually those who were the guiltiest. There is no doubt that the leaders of the Front movement who advocated National Socialist ideas had led most convicts astray.

Like Switzerland, Sweden, another neutral state, was a playground for spies from warring nations, especially from Germany. In Sweden, 651 people were arrested because of espionage and treason, yet no death sentences were pronounced.[90] Switzerland considered that the penal law of the armed forces required capital punishment while the country was in danger. The executions, carried out with the approval of almost the entire population, appeared to be an act of self-defense by the state.

When analyzing Switzerland's history during World War II, it is paradoxical to note that to the outside world the country appeared to be perfectly united in its unyielding determination to fight any aggressor, but at the same time several hundred Swiss citizens were convicted of committing treason. By executing 17 traitors, Switzerland expressed its absolute determination to make any sacrifice to safeguard its independence. As the commander-in-chief of the armed forces, through his firmness, General Guisan helped shape the nation's position on this issue and helped carry the responsibility for the executions on his conscience.

The Schellenberg-Masson Connection

QUITE UNUSUALLY FOR A COMMANDER-IN-CHIEF of the armed forces, General Guisan became personally involved in the connection that Colonel Roger Masson, the head of Switzerland's Intelligence Service, maintained for an extended period of time with SS Colonel (later Brigadier General) Walter Schellenberg, Head of Foreign Intelligence at the Reich Central Security Office. Guisan's involvement in the connection culminated in a controversial meeting with Schellenberg in Biglen.[1] Since understandably no minutes were kept of the secret meetings between intelligence personnel and there is only sparse written evidence, research on this topic is necessarily limited to a number of individual pieces of information. Nevertheless, the material available at the Federal Archives in Bern, including unpublished private documents, is conclusive enough to gain a sufficiently clear picture of the undercover activities.

The secret connection between Masson and Schellenberg, which put an additional strain on relations between the army command and the Federal Council after it was uncovered, was clearly based on contacts that the German businessman and SS Captain Hans Wilhelm Eggen had established with Henry Guisan, the General's son. In 1941, the younger Guisan, who was a lieutenant-colonel at the time, met Eggen when the SS Captain (and Cavalry Captain of the German reserve) visited Switzerland to negotiate a 22 million franc contract for the purchase of "2,000 barracks for the front in the East" from the Lausanne-based Extroc company. Guisan was a member of Extroc's board of directors.[2]

For arranging the deal, the General's son received a commission of at least 13,000 francs.[3] He was not a trained businessman, as indicated in a report by one of his partners. He was on Extroc's board of directors above all because he had access to influential people, and his name could be used to establish contacts.[4] When the General found out about his son's dubious connections, which were not illegal but could have damaged the family's reputation and jeopardized the General's position as commander-in-chief, he made Henry explain himself and resign from the Extroc company, and he seems to have forbidden him to conduct any other similar activities.[5] It is unlikely that the negotiators and exporters involved were unaware what the wooden barracks delivered to the SS were used for, because by that time Switzerland knew about the existence of the concentration camps.

In 1941, the younger Guisan introduced Eggen to his friend, Captain Paul Meyer, who served in the Swiss Intelligence Service but was at the same time interested in business relations with Germany as a partner of the Zürich-based export firm Interkommerz AG.[6] In describing how he first came to meet Eggen, Meyer recalled, "Guisan told me that Eggen had connections to Himmler and would certainly be interesting for our intelligence service. I discussed the case with my superiors, Colonel Müller and Colonel Masson. I established contact with Eggen with their approval."[7]

Captain Meyer, alias Wolf Schwertenbach, described Eggen to his superior Masson as an interesting person who might be useful for army intelligence. For that purpose, he arranged a meeting between Eggen and Masson, which took place in November 1941 at the Schweizerhof Hotel in Bern. The Head of Army Intelligence pretended to be a journalist who had a general interest in the situation in Germany.[8] This first contact gradually developed into a trusting relationship. Masson explained, "I did not seek to establish this connection; it was the result of a coincidence, since Colonel Guisan had business ties with Eggen and was at the same time a friend of Captain Meyer."[9] He later declared that his prime motivation was not to procure intelligence but to use Eggen to dispel German doubts about Switzerland's determination to remain neutral and to stress Switzerland's readiness to defend itself against any aggressor.[10]

As early as December 1941, Masson informed the chief of the General's personal staff about the prospect of establishing an unexpected new connection to Germany. Barbey noted, "Masson tells me about the first contact he has established, through his staff member Capt. Meyer from Ermatingen, with a German from Himmler's entourage who supposedly has access to the Führer. . . . Himmler allegedly said that he wanted to meet Masson. Whatever happens, I advise him to keep the 'connection' a secret." Masson agreed with Barbey, adding that he had rejected the idea of establishing a direct telephone line between Ermatingen and Berlin.[11]

Meyer wrote notes for his personal use about the meetings with Eggen, a few of which were also attended by Masson. Some of the notes were found among Meyer's unpublished documents. About one meeting he had written:

> On April 10, 1942, we drive to Wolfsberg Castle with Eggen. During our conversation at the fireside, it becomes clear that Germany has made all the necessary arrangements in Switzerland to integrate the country into its economic area once it is victorious in the East. Eggen says that it looks as if Switzerland will be brought under the Nazi regime because above all the Swiss who have emigrated to Germany propagate the all-German idea and consider the democratic system to be rotten and outdated. He explains that Riedweg has been on a visit to Switzerland and the future leading figures are in the process of being named.[12]

Meyer replied that he doubted Germany would be successful with its plan, explaining that it would definitely face a "second case like Norway." He added, "The assertions that the Swiss make in Germany are wrong and dangerous, because everything will fall apart and nothing will be gained. I tell Eggen that the plan will result in Germany having to feed four million people, the transit routes to Italy being interrupted, and the exports by the industry coming to an end. Eggen says that Germany does not want that to happen under any circumstances."[13]

After being invited on several occasions to Meyer's home at Wolfsberg Castle, Eggen made efforts to arrange a meeting between Masson and his own superior, SS Colonel Schellenberg. In addition, as early as the spring of 1942, Eggen tried to get Meyer's support to arrange a meeting between the head of Switzerland's Security Section, Colonel Werner Müller, and SS Reichsführer Heinrich Himmler.[14] At Wolfsberg at the end of August 1942, Masson also introduced Eggen to Heinrich Rothmund, the head of the Swiss Federal Police Section, hoping that Eggen could arrange meetings for him in Berlin and get him a visa. However, Meyer wrote that Rothmund appeared to be insecure and cut "a poor figure." The following day, Eggen commented to Masson that Rothmund was "not a chief but an employee" and that it was useless to send him to Germany.[15]

Schellenberg initially intended to invite Switzerland's Chief of Intelligence to Berlin to meet him in person. Masson declined, however, and instead asked Schellenberg to see him in Switzerland. Because the SS Colonel was hesitant as well, on July 7, 1942, Paul Meyer flew to Berlin on Masson's orders to act as a mediator, disguising his mission as a "private trip." He was to get in touch with SS authorities and try "to put German-Swiss relations on a friendlier level" through a semi-official exchange of opinions. According to Meyer's notes, he did not go to Berlin to discuss intelligence matters but went on a political mission on behalf of the army command via a "secondary diplomatic channel." Meyer stated, "These meetings are expected to give both states the opportunity to present their requests and concerns through the most direct, unofficial channel."[16]

Meyer explained that in addition to improving overall relations between the two countries, his mission was to accomplish two goals. The first was to have German newspapers stop publishing defamatory articles about General Guisan written by the "International Press Agency" directed by Franz Burri, a Swiss living abroad. Switzerland's Department of Foreign Affairs had made little effort to protest the hostile articles through official diplomatic channels. Second, he would seek to have Lt. Ernst Mörgeli, who had been arrested in Stuttgart on suspicion of espionage, released from prison. Masson, who could undoubtedly count on the commander-in-chief's backing in this undertaking, deemed such contacts to be necessary, arguing that the leading personalities at the German Legation in Bern, Köcher and Ilsemann, were viewed as "people of a long-gone past." He explained, "It is a waste of effort to address the authorities who actually hold the power through this [official] channel," adding that Counselor von Bibra, the nominal German Nazi Party leader in Switzerland, was not the right person either, because he was despised in Bern after "overstepping his boundaries" and bringing Germany into discredit. Meyer stated that he advised the authorities in Berlin to recall von Bibra, "as proof of their honest efforts to improve the disturbed relations."[17]

Meyer's notes permit the conclusion that he acted with self-confidence during his meetings with leading National Socialist figures such as Schellenberg and Ernst Kaltenbrunner. He said, among other things:

> Even though we have cultural and economic ties with Germany and our well-being depends in large part on Germany, our hearts reach out to the oppressed. Germany is ill viewed in Switzerland because there is too much talk about Switzerland just waiting to be integrated into the Reich as a province. If our fears are allayed, the situation will undoubtedly change because we all admire Germany's energy, courage, organizational skills, and talent as a colonizer. . . . By curtailing the freedom of the press in Switzerland, Germany would knock down a pillar of democracy and put an end to our state system. During times like these, it is more difficult to lead a state according to democratic principles than according to totalitarian principles.[18]

Captain Meyer-Schwertenbach's candidness during his secret mission to Berlin indeed appeared to favor a softening of the hardened attitudes. On August 28, 1942, during another meeting at the Baur au Lac Hotel in Zürich, Meyer and Eggen managed to convince Masson that the time had come for a face-to-face meeting with Schellenberg. They argued that Masson had to confirm to the SS Colonel personally the information they had given him about the situation in Switzerland and the country's determination to defend itself, that General Guisan was not submissively dependent on England but was really neutral, that Masson was not working for British intelligence, and that the claims made by Swiss living in Germany were wrong. Eggen assured Masson that, by speaking with Schellenberg, "he would become a person in a position of trust," enabling him in the future to solve the problems between the two countries through the most direct channels, "since through the official channels that was not possible because the talks had come to a standstill." Eggen told Masson that "he had the chance to save Switzerland."[19]

Eggen suggested that Masson and Schellenberg should meet "somewhere along the Swiss border" in order to build a relationship of real trust between the two chiefs of intelligence. Masson agreed, having learned of the prospect of being viewed much more favorably by the Germans than before. When he left, at around 3 o'clock in the morning, he once again thanked Meyer very much for his efforts at mediating, adding that "now he had a clear picture of the situation and had to agree to the meeting."[20]

General Guisan authorized Masson to meet with Schellenberg.[21] In early September 1942, Masson informed the Chief of the General's Personal Staff Barbey that he intended to travel to the German border area in the near future "to meet a personality who has significant influence in Himmler's and even Hitler's entourage; a young, fine, very well educated General whose task he said made him the 'Masson of the SS'." He explained that this personality could advocate Switzerland's real message with the Nazi Party and SS officials who had a hostile attitude toward Switzerland and were gaining ground in Germany. Masson stated that he wanted "to show that we had been misjudged or misunderstood by our neighbor to the north, to confirm that we were absolutely determined to defend our country against any aggressor, and make Germany stop its current intensive intelligence activities in our country." Barbey, who immediately told Masson that he opposed the plan, understood that the Chief of Intelligence wanted to obtain the General's approval, stating, "A little bit later, he approaches the General, addresses him, and informs him of his plan. The General does not voice any objection."[22]

Barbey made some additional reflections about the proposal, agreeing that it was "perfectly normal for our Chief of Intelligence to risk an initiative of this kind if the information that he might gather [was] worth the effort; that is, if it [increased Switzerland's] chances of being alerted in time should the threat of hostilities become more acute." However, overall he did "not think much of Masson's role as an honest and perhaps sentimental advocate of Switzerland's goodwill and good cause, no matter how warmhearted and convincing he [was]." Barbey considered that "what could be of value [were] the exploratory talks he could hold."[23]

Captain Meyer arranged the details for Masson to cross the border to meet Schellenberg. For that purpose, he contacted Captain Peter Burckhardt on the general staff, an intelligence officer with the 5th Division:

> I summon Captain Burckhardt to Bern and discuss with him in my hotel room the upcoming meeting. Following Burckhardt's comments, we agree that Laufenburg should be the place to hold negotiations. The procedure will be as follows: Capt. Burckhardt will drive the two civilians [Masson and Meyer] to the meeting place. The border guards (Colonel Weiss) will be instructed by Masson himself that at such and such time Capt. B[urckhardt] will drive two civilians to the border. They shall be allowed to leave Switzerland for Germany without being checked. B. will wait in the car until we return.[24]

The car was to appear to be a civilian vehicle, for which the army police and counterintelligence were to provide the license plates.

Two days later, Meyer informed his superior about the plan. Masson agreed with it, with the reservation that he wanted to tell, either personally or through Chief of Security Müller, the commander of the border guards about the upcoming border crossing only after informing the General about the procedure.[25]

Masson gave Barbey an account of his meeting with Schellenberg, which took place on September 8, 1942, in Laufenburg-Waldshut. The chief of the General's personal staff noted in his diary: "[Masson] crosses the bridge and is received by Emissary Eggen, who drives him to a small restaurant near Waldshut. There he meets SS General Schellenberg, who is less than forty years old, has delicate features, clear eyes, an educated mind. . . . They leave the restaurant and take a walk in the forest above Waldshut. They sit down on a bench, from where they can see the blissful Swiss villages and the bunkers across the border."[26]

Captain Meyer-Schwertenbach, who accompanied Masson to Waldshut, described the circumstances of the meeting in more detail, writing:

[At] 16.00 hours I meet Ma[sson] and Capt. Burckhardt of the general staff in Basel. We drive to Laufenburg in Burckhardt's private car. Bu[rckhardt] walks up to the fence at the border, returning a few minutes later. He reports that everything is all right. At 17.00 hours sharp, Ma[sson] crosses the bridge with me. The [German] sergeant says, 'You have an appointment at 17.00 hours,' and asks us to sit down in his living-room. I give him a pack of cigarettes. He wants to send it to his son in Russia. Then E[ggen] arrives in his car. We get in and drive 10 km to Waldshut, where Sch[ellenberg] receives us. We have some brandy, and then the two gentlemen take a walk along a lonely path in the forest. They sit down on a bench. At 19.30 hours they return and declare that they have come to an understanding on every issue. Mörgeli. Rothmund should decide whether he wants to accept assistance by the SS or not. At 20.00 hours we have dinner (Mosel wine, champagne, cold cuts, etc.). At 21.00 hours back in Switzerland. We drive to Liestal, from there we take the train to Bern, Hotel Schweizerhof. Ma[sson] expresses his thanks.[27]

Masson later testified about the meeting with Schellenberg, who he said was "immediately on the same wavelength":

The discussion with Schellenberg was very cordial. It will remain engraved in my memory. The man facing me was very slender, educated, and talked about highly interesting things. . . . He also told me that Switzerland had friends in Germany on whom it could count, but that obviously overall (and particularly in Ribbentrop's entourage) people were very hostile toward us because of the attitude of part of our press and because of certain incidents. . . . We were all by ourselves during our discussion, outdoors, without any witnesses. I explained to him that I did not intend to address political or military issues, because I was not acting on official orders but on my own behalf. I told him that an honest discussion between two officers who are equally attached to their respective countries could result in a form of mutual trust that could be beneficial for the good relations that neutral Switzerland wished to entertain with all belligerent parties.[28]

Masson wrote that he left Schellenberg, whom he said made an "excellent impression," around 6:00 p.m. and that both parties had become convinced that their connection could contribute to easing tensions between Switzerland and Germany during that critical time. In addition, Masson "used the opportunity to assure Schellenberg that our government and our army was determined to defend our territory against anyone, no matter what happened." He stressed the fact that he and Schellenberg had never talked about exchanging intelligence information, adding, "Of course we talked about the general situation, the way in which it is done in Bern with the foreign military attachés."[29]

The day following his encounter with Schellenberg, Masson informed the chief of the General's personal staff that "everything had gone well" and that he was "very pleased." Barbey commented about the advantages and drawbacks of the connection, which he considered to be questionable from the very beginning:

> *Positive results:* we have the opportunity to 'speak' with someone from the Führer's entourage. Masson assured him of our determination to defend ourselves. After that statement has been repeated over and over again in speeches and orders of the day, it may have begun to sound like a lecture. Is in line with what we have been trying to prove to foreign countries since June 1940: the costs of an attack against Switzerland would be disproportionately high compared to its benefits. If Masson sees Schellenberg again, he can gain an impression—right or wrong—of Germany's arrangements against us; at least it will be an impression.
>
> *Negative results:* Schellenberg did not [meet Masson] without wanting anything in return. His not making any formal request so far does not mean anything for the future. No matter what affection he may have for Masson and Switzerland, Schellenberg is above all German and first of all a man of the Party. His educated mind does not make any difference. What does he expect from Masson, whether explicitly or not? What services does he want in exchange for his own? Whether he wants to or not, Masson is subject to a political 'temptation'; one can imagine the bridge that is being built for our Chief of Intelligence to divert him from exclusively procuring intelligence and lead him to the negotiating table.[30]

Barbey, who undoubtedly discussed the matter with the General, found it "difficult if not altogether impossible" to weigh the advantages and risks of the connection between Masson and Schellenberg. He was also concerned that if the Allies found out about the meeting, they might suspect that Switzerland was moving closer to Germany. Barbey was aware that this was just the beginning of the affair, stating, "The first act is drawing to a close. The real drama— if it is really a drama—will begin in the second or third act. . . . Perhaps

Waldshut was a stroke of genius; if not, it may have simply provided a useful contact."[31]

After the meeting in Germany, Masson met with the SS General, who he said did not look like a "ferocious Nazi" to him, on three other occasions. From October 16 to 18, 1942, Schellenberg and Eggen were invited by Dr. and Mrs. Paul Meyer to Wolfsberg Castle, where Masson went to see them. Half a year later, Masson was present when Schellenberg met General Guisan at the Bären restaurant in Biglen. In the fall of 1943, while Schellenberg was once again staying in Switzerland from October 16 to 18, Masson met with him again at Wolfsberg Castle.[32] Hence, the two chiefs of intelligence met on four occasions within one and a half years, a fact that Masson confirmed.[33]

The connection with the SS General did indeed yield some tangible results. After Meyer had spoken with Schellenberg in Berlin about the case of 2nd Lieutenant Mörgeli, assuring him that he had not been working as an agent for England, the SS officials produced the definite proof of their goodwill and influence. On Christmas Eve 1942, Mörgeli was released after spending nine months in prison and was personally accompanied to Dübendorf airfield by Eggen, where Captain Meyer received him. Meyer noted about the event, "moving moments at the hotel, tears. [Mörgeli] says that he does not know how to thank me. The fact that this Swiss officer has finally been released from prison is my most beautiful Christmas gift."[34] Masson was pleased to inform the General that Mörgeli had returned to Switzerland, explaining that his liberation had been made possible "thanks to certain relations that I have, without my having to do anything in return."[35]

Eggen spent Christmas Eve and Christmas Day 1942 as a guest at Wolfsberg. On that occasion, he informed his host that Schellenberg had plans to visit Switzerland for a few days in the early part of the new year and was hoping to meet General Guisan and see Masson again. According to Meyer's notes, Eggen also talked about the dismissal of Chief Instructor Wille, about which Permanent Secretary Weizsäcker had informed him. He called the matter "unpleasant" because Hitler and Himmler had "supported" Wille and efforts to ease tensions might suffer a setback. Meyer assured his German visitor that Wille's dismissal had been requested not only by the General but also by the Military Department.[36] Meyer called the personal staff in Interlaken on Christmas Eve to inform the General about the conversation. The following day, Captain Marguth, who had been able to reach the General, informed Meyer that Wille had "actually resigned," explaining that the General had intended to offer the outgoing Chief Instructor a special post, which Wille declined. Meyer added, "[The General] also expressed his well-deserved thanks to [Wille] during the meeting with the corps commanders. He said that this was not a dig at the North."[37]

On January 11, 1943, during two meetings that lasted a total of two hours, Captain Meyer reported to Guisan the results that had been obtained so far through the connection with Eggen and Schellenberg. Guisan considered the information important enough to take some personal notes about it, writing after the meeting with Meyer:

> [Has] had Moerglin [sic] freed after ten months of detention thanks to Cavalry Captain Eggen of the German Armed Forces, who personally brought Moerglin back [to Switzerland] by plane, without asking for anything in exchange. [He did it] simply out of prestige and in order to prove that he keeps his promises. Cavalry Captain Eggen is on Himmler's general staff and a direct subordinate of General Schellenberg, who establishes a direct link between Hitler and Himmler every week. Gen. Schellenberg is the Head of Foreign I[ntelligence]! Cavalry Captain views Switzerland very favorably, his mother is French. Gen. Schellenberg is the most influential person next to Hitler and Himmler. Through him Meyer succeeded in arranging for Rothmund to travel to Germany after Rothmund had unsuccessfully tried to obtain a visa through official channels for ten months! Eggen wants to see to it that the undercover intelligence against Switzerland comes to an end! Bibra has already been summoned to Germany because of that; they are not happy about his activities. It is not impossible that he will be recalled soon!

The General also noted a risqué statement that von Bibra had allegedly made to Federal Councilor von Steiger: "Stop building your shitty bunkers so you'll have cement for me!"[38]

Guisan took note of Meyer's conclusions, writing, "Currently we have no reason to fear the Germans, neither for political, nor economic, nor ideological reasons. However, Germany has to be sure that we will also defend our country against the Anglo-Saxons. They are glad if we defend our borders! Nowadays they no longer have the means to tackle us as well."[39] This conversation with Meyer, who had demonstrated the usefulness of the connection with Schellenberg, was probably the starting point for Guisan's decision, two months later, to meet the SS officer.

The following day, Meyer, who had also taken detailed notes about the content of the meeting, submitted to the commander-in-chief a list of the specific results that had been achieved by the connection with Eggen and Schellenberg. It stated:

1. [General Guisan] is now viewed by leading German authorities as a leading exponent of the Swiss people and the Swiss Army, and his correct and neutral position during wartime duty is no longer being questioned.

2. [The International Press Agency, which used to call the General] the prime enemy of the state, [has] completely ceased its hostilities against him.

3. [Colonel-Brigadier Masson] has been completely cleared of the suspicion [continually raised by Germany that he was collaborating with the British and United States Intelligence]; today he enjoys the trust of leading German authorities.

4. [It has become possible to obtain a visa for the Head of Switzerland's Federal Police dealing with foreign nationals, Dr. Rothmund, in order for him to be able to resolve] pressing police issues concerning the two states.

5. [Efforts have been successful to free Lt. Mörgeli, who had been imprisoned in Germany on suspicion of spying, and] to repatriate him to Switzerland without making any concessions in exchange.

Moreover, Meyer stated that the two chiefs of intelligence had held direct talks that were based on trust, and delegations of the Swiss Federal Department of Economic Affairs had received visas within a very short period of time in order to hold negotiations in Germany.[40]

These statements about the usefulness of the connection appeared to be markedly optimistic. Otto Püntner concluded differently that, contrary to other reports, Schellenberg and Eggen "did nothing or did not accomplish anything" with respect to a ban on the International Press Agency (IPA). He argued that the IPA depended on Reich Propaganda Minister Goebbels, who financed it.[41] Nevertheless, even if the IPA was not banned, the vehement attacks against General Guisan definitely came to an end.

When IPA director Franz Burri returned to Switzerland after the war, and was waiting at the regional prison in Zürich to be tried as a traitor before the Federal Penal Court, he wrote to General Guisan to "withdraw [his] accusations, express [his] regrets, [and to ask him] not to hold the embarrassing matter against [him]." He claimed that the IPA articles attacking the General had been written by "a third party" but had been published under his responsibility.[42] Guisan refused to accept the apology, writing to the Federal Prosecutor, "A man who called me "the first traitor" on several occasions should be well aware that it is rather late to come to his senses."[43]

Masson used his connection with SS officers Eggen and Schellenberg not only for purposes strictly related to intelligence. For example, he also rendered a personal service to his friend Gérard de Loriol, the owner of Allaman Castle on Lake Geneva. Through Masson's mediation, the two German officers managed to get de Loriol's yacht, which had been confiscated in southern France as enemy property by the Italians, back to its owner. On February 10, 1942, Masson drove Eggen to the shores of Lake Geneva to introduce him to de Loriol. Paul Meyer, who was also present, noted about the event, "Mr. and Mrs. de Loriol receive us. Drinking spree. Masson intervenes regarding the subject of de Loriol's yacht, which he says has been unlawfully seized by the Italians on the Côte d'Azur."[44] Meyer reported that Masson asked Eggen to get a German visa for de Loriol for him to travel to France and take care of his assets there. Masson later also successfully intervened in the same matter with Schellenberg. Meyer stated, "I know about this matter because I participated in some talks and received information from Eggen. Eggen and Schellenberg made their efforts purely as a favor, not as a service in exchange for another service. Subsequently de Loriol was able to travel to France with a German visa."[45]

The Masson-Schellenberg connection was questionable insofar as it became entwined with a number of private business ventures in which the intelligence officers who worked under him had an interest. In addition to Captain Paul Meyer, Captain Paul Holzach, the director of the Zürich-based Interkommerz Company, was sent to Berlin as a liaison and messenger. Both Meyer and Holzach played a double role in their relations with the SS authorities, also doing business with them. Hausamann commented that it was "appalling how [the two captains] mixed up official business and commercial matters."[46] Max Waibel, an officer on the general staff and future divisional commander, expressed his objection in somewhat less drastic albeit equally clear terms, stating, "They both got involved in lucrative business transactions, which were certainly even more profitable to the Gestapo and the SS than to Masson's intelligence officers, who also involved the General's son in the dubious deals. I had a meeting with General Guisan on that topic in order to open his eyes about his son's machinations and to warn him about General Schellenberg."[47]

Even though such business methods were viewed with scorn, they were not at all illegal. Nevertheless, there was a risk that mixing official military matters and business could harm the country's interests. The hearing of evidence and preliminary investigations that military courts carried out after the war, however, did not uncover any illegal actions. The investigators concluded, "During critical times that were completely different from the current ones, [the concerned persons] rendered great services to our country through their personal, selfless initiative." The investigating judge ended his report requesting that the proceedings be abandoned and that "the matter rest."[48]

During the hearings, Holzach testified about his role as a messenger for Masson, stating:

> Colonel-Brigadier Masson gave me the written information addressed to SS General Schellenberg in white, sealed, neutral envelopes. I did not know anything about the information that the envelopes contained; at the most, I made conjectures based on the short conversations that I had with Colonel-Brigadier Masson when I received them. The first letter, or rather the first conversation, was about a reply to General Schellenberg regarding information from Schellenberg to Masson that new rumors were spreading in Berlin about Switzerland displaying non-neutral conduct. During my first meeting with Schellenberg in Berlin, he had given me a sealed envelope addressed to Colonel-Brigadier Masson, which I carried with me to Switzerland. I do not know what the letter said.[49]

Meyer's private notes contain no direct indications about his business activities. However, there is no doubt that some of his trips to Berlin and some of Eggen's trips to Switzerland were primarily business trips. That was also the conclusion reached by Federal Judge Couchepin in his final report on the administrative investigation of Masson's case. He stated that as mediators and negotiators between Switzerland's Chief of Intelligence and SS General Schellenberg, both Meyer and Holzach made some trips to Berlin exclusively on orders of Army Intelligence, but also some trips for their own purposes. Often they combined the two issues during one trip. Couchepin said that it was certain that both men did business with Germany, either in their own names or on behalf of their firm, Interkommerz.[50]

The numerous documents at the Federal Archives about Meyer and Holzach permit the conclusion that it is not exaggerated to qualify the two men as capable intelligence officers who were willing to take great risks, but also as black marketers and war profiteers. There is absolutely no evidence, though, that Masson had any personal interest in these business transactions or had a share in them, even though he knew about them.

Masson immediately took to Schellenberg, who was 17 years his junior, and was convinced that his feelings did not deceive him. He believed that their mutual trust would remain unshaken even in the ruthless context of intelligence war. In conversations with those who knew about the connection, he almost affectionately nicknamed the SS officer "Schelli." The only thing that may appear nice about the Masson-Schellenberg connection was the feeling of idealistic friendship that the two officers shared beyond political and ideological boundaries. However, the irrational sense of trust and romantic military feeling that the Swiss officer displayed above all during a time of total war seemed to indicate not only carelessness but a remarkable degree of naivete. It will remain debatable whether the connection with Schellenberg was really useful in safeguarding Switzerland from being drawn into the war, as Masson firmly continued to believe. Miraculously, Masson's "naivete" did not affect Switzerland's interests negatively.

In his memoirs, Schellenberg unfortunately gave only a summary account of his relations with Switzerland's intelligence service. He explained that the efforts to establish personal contacts with Swiss intelligence were part of his attempts to "gain contact with important representatives of the Western Allies" through suitable people. Moreover, he stated that he tried to prevent "the plan [from being carried out] according to which Switzerland was to be occupied as a preventive measure, a plan that was considered on several occasions. . . . After getting in touch with Mason [sic] and Guisan, I managed to get Himmler to use his influence at the Reich Central Command against such military measures. . . . In these efforts to keep Switzerland out of the war, the assistance of Reich Minister of Economy Funk was useful; he was skillful at convincing the top leaders that Switzerland had to remain untouched as a hub for foreign currency transactions."[51] A report about the Nuremberg trial states that Schellenberg supposedly managed to destroy the files of his SS office before the end of the war.[52]

Not surprisingly, there are totally conflicting opinions about the character of the SS Intelligence Chief who claimed to be a special friend of Switzerland. Sweden's Count Bernadotte described how Schellenberg, who ardently defended the interests of the Red Cross in the final stage of the war, inspired him with a certain degree of confidence right away.[53] Arnold Kaech, Switzerland's military attaché in Sweden, also considered him "an unbelievably charming man" when he met him in April 1945.[54]

On the other hand, Schellenberg's rapid rise to the rank of brigadier general and to the position of head of the foreign branch of SS intelligence—he was said to be the youngest SS General at the time—appeared to be eerie. He was viewed as an "extreme schemer." A German diplomat characterized him as a "very dynamic man with an excellent mind and exceptional energy. But he was sick, incurably sick because he was conceited and over-ambitious."[55] The basic mistrust that Hausamann voiced about Schellenberg in a letter to Federal Councilor Kobelt was certainly not unfounded. He wrote, "It is surely no coincidence that SS General Schellenberg is Himmler's closest collaborator. There is undoubtedly nothing that he does without having his own interests in mind, nor does his subordinate Eggen."[56] In the spring of 1943, when Federal Councilor Pilet-Golaz asked an informant about Schellenberg following the Biglen affair, he was told, "The SS officer has a university education and is said to be very nice, but his real intentions are not clear. At any rate, it is advisable to be cautious."[57] After the war, Eugen Bircher told a National Council committee that one had to wonder whether Masson's connection with Schellenberg, "this wicked fellow," was acceptable, and he went on to say, regarding the next stage in that connection, "The General's contact with Schellenberg was definitely wrong and incomprehensible."[58]

28

The Meeting in Biglen

ON SEVERAL OCCASIONS AFTER THE WAR, General Guisan implied that his meeting with SS General Walter Schellenberg in Biglen was a rather unexpected one-time encounter. Three years after the war, in a speech given at a meeting of the Association of French-Speaking Swiss in Bern, he explained that one day in the spring of 1943, Colonel-Brigadier Masson called him up to tell him out of the blue that "a young German general is waiting at the border who absolutely wants to see you. I tell him that I do not like these guys very much. I won't receive him at headquarters, but why not somewhere else. So I agreed to receive Schellenberg."[1] In his postwar report, Guisan made a similar statement, writing:

> In early March 1943, Masson called to tell me that General Schellenberg, who was staying at our border for a short period of time, wanted to see me as soon as possible on an urgent matter. It was obvious that this meeting was important because I knew about the military preparations in southern Germany. Receiving the foreigner at my headquarters was out of the question. Hence, Masson chose a restaurant in the countryside, the Bären in Biglen.[2]

Military historian Hans Rudolf Kurz questioned these statements by the commander-in-chief that this was a unique, chance encounter, speaking in various publications about "several meetings between General Guisan and SS Major [sic] General Walter Schellenberg."[3] This contradiction, which seems to be far from trivial from a historical perspective, will be resolved in this chapter based on the existing written evidence.

According to handwritten notes by Captain Paul Meyer, alias Wolf Schwertenbach, the intelligence officer who was directly involved, the first preliminary talks in preparation for a meeting between General Guisan and Schellenberg were held as early as late January 1943 in the presence of Captain Eggen of the German Wehrmacht and Masson. Meyer informed General Guisan that "Schellenberg was willing, with the approval of his superiors Hi[mmler] and Hit[ler], to come to Switzerland to meet with him." He claimed that the Germans wanted to hear from the General in person that Switzerland was "firmly and unshakably determined to defend its [borders] against anyone," even if the Allies approached the country from Italy. He said that the leadership of the Third Reich would trust a binding promise by Switzerland's commander-in-chief and give up its intentions to occupy the country. General Guisan declared that he was "willing to make such a declaration to General Sch[ellenberg] if that was to any avail." Meyer summed up the meeting with General Guisan by writing, "I can continue the unofficial negotiations along that line."[4]

Following some additional preparations, two weeks later Masson gave Meyer official orders to start organizing, together with Eggen, a meeting between Guisan and Schellenberg in the near future.[5] Eggen flew to Berlin and then returned to Zürich a few days later to discuss further procedures with Captain Meyer and A. Wiesendanger, inspector of the Zürich city police, and to establish a tentative schedule for the visit. The discussion took place at Wiesendanger's office, followed by dinner at the Widder restaurant, during which Eggen reported on his negotiations in Berlin. Meyer noted, "He explained that Schelli had been to the Führer's headquarters to get permission to travel to Switzerland. . . . Hitler reportedly said that his trip was unnecessary, that the Swiss had lied to him and had cheated him for three years, and that he was not going to make any commitments with those people who continually take without giving anything in return. He said that since he knew their mentality, he knew what he would have to do with Switzerland if Italy was drawn into events. The Germans living in Switzerland, especially the Industry Committee, had told him everything about us. After consulting once again with the Reichsführer [Himmler] and then again with the Führer, [Hitler] allegedly [told Schellenberg], 'OK, go! You'll see that I was right, that you are being led by the nose.'"[6]

The following day, February 26, 1943, Meyer and Wiesendanger met with Masson from 3:00 to 5:15 p.m. to discuss the details of Schellenberg's upcoming visit and his meeting with Guisan. The first idea was to arrange for them to meet in Arosa, but Masson was against it because in that major winter sport resort there was a risk that other visitors would recognize the two officers, making it difficult to keep the meeting secret. The choice of venue was left up to General Guisan, who decided that Arosa was out of the question. However, he indicated that he had time "to meet Schelli Wednesday and Thursday [March 3 and 4, 1943] in Bern." Meyer and Wiesendanger promised to do everything they could to ensure a trusting environment. They said that they wanted to "allot enough time for the meeting and not be narrow-minded."[7]

Hence, it was agreed that Schellenberg should arrive in Switzerland in Eggen's company as an anonymous visitor on March 2, 1943, and stay there for a few days. Meyer offered to host the visitors during the first night at his castle. In anticipation of the border crossing at Konstanz, on March 1 Meyer asked Masson over the telephone:

1. Are the two gentlemen coming at Switzerland's invitation?
2. Will Wie[sendanger] be their official escort?
3. Do you agree to pick up the gentlemen in Zürich?
4. Have the border personnel at the main customs office in Kreuzlingen been notified that on 2 March after 1:00 p.m., the visitors' car should be allowed to cross the border there without being stopped?
5. How about gasoline, meal coupons, accommodations? I will take care of accommodations.
6. [Should] Wiesendanger [issue] security instructions and [organize] cars?[8]

Masson answered all questions affirmatively.

On March 2, 1943, Meyer and Wiesendanger picked up Schellenberg and Eggen at the border in Kreuzlingen as scheduled. Meyer commented, "Everything went smoothly." They brought their guests to Wolfsberg Castle, where the German license plates were replaced with Swiss ones in order to make the car less conspicuous. Then they took a walk with Schellenberg to discuss the topics of the meeting with General Guisan. They agreed that "[First] the General [should] make a declaration about Switzerland's absolute determination to defend itself and its intention to remain perfectly neutral; then there should be a declaration from the other side that [Germany] would respect [Switzerland's] sovereignty." Meyer once again explained to his visitor "Switzerland's cultural and political position and its international role" during times of both peace and war, adding that Switzerland was also capable of defending its borders toward the south, which would take some pressure off the German armed forces. Schellenberg told his host that at headquarters efforts had been made to dissuade him from traveling to Switzerland "because his life was considered to be in danger, as the English were going to catch him." He said that Kaltenbrunner had warned him as well. After dinner, the four men sat

The long-missing page from the guest book of the Bären restaurant in Biglen with the signatures of General Guisan, Walter Schellenberg, and other participants in the meeting on March 3, 1943. (Copy from the author's private archives) "by the fireplace and until 1.00 a.m [continued] discussing the upcoming events."

The following day, March 3, the party drove in two cars to Zürich, where they were met by Masson. In the afternoon, they continued their journey to the Bellevue Hotel in Bern. Masson, Schellenberg, Eggen, and Meyer were riding in the same car. Meyer noted, "We check in at the Bellevue without having to present any identification; Wiesendanger speaks with Director Schmid. Four suites."[9] He added, "Schelli's stomach is upset," which was probably due to the tension associated with his critical mission to a foreign country.

Masson had chosen the Bären restaurant in Biglen as the venue for General Guisan's meeting with Schellenberg. It was not very far from headquarters at Gümligen and renowned for its cuisine, even during the war. The Swiss government quite frequently hosted dinners for official foreign visitors there. In the winter of 1939–40, the guest book of the Bären included a delegation of Swiss and Russian negotiators, and on February 13, 1940, delegates who were holding economic talks between Switzerland and Germany.[10] Guisan knew the restaurant well, having previously eaten there on several occasions. At the beginning of wartime duty, when he went to have dinner there with officers on the army staff, he even wrote a poem into the guest book which read:

Im Bären z'Biglen im Quartier	At the Bären in Biglen, at his quarters,
Empfängt der General sein' Offizier.	The General receives his officers.
Gar herzlich ist Empfang und Gruss,	They are given a warm welcome,
Die Darbietung ein Hochgenuss.	The food's appealing and tastes delicious.
Der Wirt, die Küche und die Leute	The manager, the cook, and the staff
Bekunden ihre Liebe heute	Show their warm affection today
Gar herzlich und in eigener Art.	In their own very special way.
The Männerchor singt ganz appart.	The men's choir has a distinct style.
Den Kindern einen festen Kuss	A kiss to the children
Und Euch, Ihr Bigler, Gott zum Gruss![11]	And God bless you, people of Biglen!

On this evening, a small dining room was reserved for dinner with General Schellenberg. Meyer's account of the evening was concise, stating, "Joint dinner; six people, private room, table decorated in the colors of the country. Cheerful conversation about horses, purchasing horses, cavalrymen. Signing of the guest book. After eating—champagne—the lower house withdraws for two hours." Hence, Guisan and Schellenberg talked with each other for two hours without any witnesses being present. According to other coinciding testimonies and the guest book, the four other persons attending the dinner were Colonel-Brigadier Masson, SS Major Eggen, Captain Meyer, and Dr. Wiesendanger.[12] Meyer wrote about the rest of the evening: "Page cut out. Sat together until 12 at night, relaxed atmosphere. Then drove back to the hotel—General to his home—with headlights on!" The meeting lasted past the official closing time of the restaurant, so the manager asked permission from the police to keep the premises open late that night. Based on his accounts, he paid 5.50 francs for the extension permit.

The few phrases Meyer jotted down were the only authentic written evidence by one of the participants about the controversial meeting. Third parties who had been verbally informed about the meeting left additional accounts. Quite a few attempts were subsequently made to trivialize the episode, thereby causing unexpected controversy, which in turn led to inconsistencies and contradictory accounts about the event. It seems that, after the fact, Guisan was concerned about signing the guest book and made a telephone call to inquire about it. Meyer noted, "General calls about page!" In fact, that page from the guest book went missing. Masson claimed he had destroyed it. Bonjour speculated that the German guests might have taken it with them as a souvenir.[13]

The manager of the Bären complained to the General about the missing page and asked him to sign the guest book again, sending it to his headquarters in Interlaken. That was how Major Barbey, the chief of the personal staff, found out about the meeting, of which the General had not informed him.[14] In his personal diary, Barbey nevertheless indicated that he suspected the commander-in-chief was going to meet Schellenberg, writing, "I admit that this matter concerns and worries me because it is confidential and pressing and because I cannot find out more about it tonight, as I am busy with urgent matters at the command post."[15] He was outraged when he found out about the meeting afterward. Captain Sandoz, the General's 1st Adjutant, did not know about it either; he stated that the General had told him that he was going to meet with Masson.[16] On that day, the personal staff's diary recorded: "At 12.30 hours, the General leaves his command post. He drives to Bern and Biglen by himself. The General has meetings with Col-Brig. Masson and I[ntelligence] S[ervice]. The General spends the night at Beau-Site."[17]

Not only Masson but also Police Inspector Wiesendanger took credit for getting rid of the incriminating page in the guest book containing Guisan's and Schellenberg's signatures. After his death, his friend E. Walder related that Wiesendanger had told him that during a casual conversation at the fireside he had grabbed the guest book while everyone else was saying goodbye to General Guisan, tore the page out and then destroyed it.[18] As late as 1946, the owner of the Bären hotel wrote to General Guisan to tell him how much he regretted that this unique page was missing from his guest book.[19]

In fact, neither Wiesendanger nor Masson had told the truth. The page did indeed disappear but without being destroyed. Captain Meyer wrote in his notes that he carefully cut it out of the guest book to keep it for himself. He held on to the document until the 1960s, when he handed it over together with other papers to a reporter of the German news magazine *Stern*, who intended to publish the memoirs of Intelligence Officer Meyer-Schwertenbach.[20] However, since Meyer died unexpectedly in 1966, the project was dropped. The documents, some of which were photographed by the editors of *Stern*, remained in Hamburg, where they were forgotten and ended up lost, as Dr. Armin von Manikowski, a *Stern* editor, told this author. He kindly made some photographs that had been found again available for this book. The main document was the missing page from the guest book at the Bären.[21]

On March 4, 1943, the day after the meeting between Guisan and Schellenberg, Masson, Meyer, and Wiesendanger met the two Germans for lunch at the Schweizerhof in Bern, where Masson was staying. Before that, Meyer and Wiesendanger had drafted "a declaration written in pencil in which the General explained Switzerland's position. It [was] to be submitted to the Führer even though his name [was] not mentioned on the address."[22] They presented the draft to Masson, who had it written in ink in order to submit it to General Guisan for signature.

On the afternoon of March 4, Masson stayed in Bern, and Meyer and Wiesendanger accompanied the German guests to Zürich, where Wiesendanger took leave of them because he had to go back to work. The rest of the party was joined by Meyer's wife, Pat, on the train to Arosa that same evening, riding first class. They checked in at the Excelsior Hotel. Schellenberg signed in as "Dr. Bergh."[23]

During the weekend of March 6–7, General Guisan was scheduled to stay at the same hotel, to make an appearance at the Swiss Skiing Championships and to see Schellenberg again to hand him the written declaration which had been prepared. The SS General did not sleep well during the night, suffering from diarrhea and indigestion. A doctor was called, who prescribed opium drops as a painkiller. Pat Meyer took care of the patient. Toward the next evening, Schellenberg felt well enough again to go on a sleigh ride to Maran and Prätschli with the Meyers.

On Saturday morning, March 6, Guisan arrived at the Excelsior in the company of his aide, Captain Marguth. At noon, Schellenberg invited him for drinks in a separate hotel room. Captain Meyer accompanied him and wrote, "I picked up the General at his room and brought him to Schellenberg's room. There G[uisan] submitted the handwritten letter to Sch[ellenberg] in the presence of Wie[sendanger] and me. Cordial contact for 40 minutes."[24] Following that official exchange, Eggen and Mrs. Meyer, who had arranged a brunch with champagne, joined the group to welcome General Guisan, who was "very jovial." Some time later, Guisan's son "Gigi" [Henry Jr.], who was an official at the Skiing Championships, also showed up for the party, at which everyone spoke High German.

On that same Saturday afternoon, the Meyers and the two Germans took the train back to Zürich, where Masson was waiting for them. Then they all drove back to Wolfsberg in two cars. The following morning, they got up as early as 5 a.m. so the SS officers could get an early start on their way back to Germany. Mrs. Meyer gave Schellenberg, who still did not feel well, a blanket, a pillow, and a thermos full of rice meal for the trip. Eggen, too, was in poor spirits because he had just received word that his house in Germany had been destroyed by Allied bombers. Masson, Meyer, and Wiesendanger accompanied the Germans to the border. Meyer described the scene, writing, "Ma[sson] tells the head of customs that he takes responsibility for everything. Then the German car drives across the border without being checked. They intend to drive all the way to Berlin in one stretch. Eggen has tears in his eyes when they leave because he drives home without having a home. Sch[ellenberg] is also reluctant to leave."[25] After six days, the two SS officers' stay in Switzerland had come to an end; it remained to be seen what consequences the visit would have.

As had been agreed, the handwritten "letter" that Schellenberg received from Guisan in Arosa contained the General's declaration of Switzerland's absolute determination to defend itself. The document, dated March 3, 1943, stated:

> The balance in Europe requires Switzerland to be neutral toward all sides and in every respect. Its location and its historical mission have called it to be the custodian of the mountain passes across the Alps. The great statesman and Reich Chancellor Bismarck also recognized and declared that Switzerland always fulfilled this task with all its energy and means. Switzerland considers that accomplishing this task, which every Swiss acknowledges, is not only an honor but a matter of course. We are aware that our country's sovereignty depends on whether this conviction is abandoned or slackens. Therefore all Swiss and the entire army are completely willing to sacrifice everything to defend their independence and honor. Whoever invades our country is

our enemy. He will face a highly powerful, united army and a people imbued with one and the same determination. At that moment Switzerland will be steadfast and fight with one determination. The topography of our country enables us very well to defend our Alpine front, no matter what happens. This statement will remain unshakeable and unchangeable. There is no room for any doubt about that, neither today nor tomorrow.

The handwritten copy of the text, which is at the Federal Archives, includes an additional handwritten note by Guisan stating, "I summed up my conversation with Sch[ellenberg] on March 4 [sic], 1943 in Biglen by telling him that defending our neutrality is a commitment that we will honor without fail."[26] Jürg Fink was wrong, in his Ph.D. thesis, to call these clear and determined words by Switzerland's commander-in-chief a "somewhat questionable declaration."[27]

It is probable that Guisan's declaration reached Hitler, but there is no direct evidence to support that supposition. At the least, it is certain that von Ribbentrop was informed about the declaration and dealt with the text. The Reich Minister of Foreign Affairs transmitted the full text of Guisan's declaration to the German envoy in Bern and informed him about the content of Schellenberg's talks with the Swiss General in Biglen and Arosa. "Some time in the future," he added, "General Guisan should receive an affirmative verbal reply from Brigadier General Schellenberg, something that has not yet been done." Ribbentrop explained about the content of the talks:

> General Guisan declared that Switzerland would defend its southern fronts in the Alps against any attack, under any circumstances, to the last drop of blood. He said that he gave the Führer his officer's word of honor that Switzerland did not have [any contact] with the Allies that was in violation of its strict neutrality, but was firmly determined to defend the southern front against them to the end. General Guisan explained that if Switzerland had reason to hope that it would not be subject to a preventive attack from the German side, against which it would of course put up resistance, he even thought that it might be possible to demobilize some major forces of the Swiss Army to have them reintegrated into the economy, thereby making an indirect contribution to enhancing Germany's war potential while maintaining Switzerland's neutrality.[28]

In this author's opinion, there is no reason why there should be any doubt about the truthfulness of these statements. It is entirely possible that Guisan made such comments to Schellenberg during their discussions to keep him well disposed.

Ribbentrop also informed his envoy Köcher that during the meeting with Schellenberg, General Guisan "solemnly assured [the SS officer] that he had not made any arrangements with the French at the time, as had supposedly been claimed by us again and again, and that he had no contact at all with the Allies." However, he pointed out that this statement contradicted what was described in the documents found at La Charité, which he said indicated, "There were secret contacts between General Guisan and the French Supreme Command throughout the winter of 1939–40." Hence, Ribbentrop concluded, "The claim that General Guisan made to Mr. Schellenberg that he had not made any arrangements with the French is not true."[29] In addition, he commented that it was "clear that if General Guisan did hold such talks, he did so with the Federal Council's consent. The Federal Council could consequently deny the talks or agreements." The Germans were wrong about this last issue; research has shown that the Swiss government was not informed about General Guisan's dealings with the French Supreme Command.

As expected in view of the conditions in Switzerland, General Guisan's meeting with SS General Schellenberg could not be kept secret for long. The first person who heard rumors about it, just a few days after the fact, was Major H. Bracher of the general staff, who was in a delicate situation as the liaison officer between the Head of the Military Department and the commander-in-chief. He felt obligated to look into the matter. Bracher noted, "By chance [I heard] from a comrade in arms in Biglen (1st Lt. H. Voegeli, the owner of the mill in Biglen) that on Wednesday, March 3, 1943, General Guisan met a German general for dinner at the Bären in Biglen." First he inquired with Barbey and then with Masson, and finally he went to see General Guisan to ask him if the rumors were true so he could "refute them if necessary."[30]

The General did not deny that the meeting had taken place, and he told Bracher some details about the conversation. However, he claimed that he did "not know the name nor the rank of the German gentleman." Moreover, he denied that "there [was] any connection between the German SS General who [had] met Colonel-Brigadier Masson in the fall and his guest in Biglen."[31] Guisan also concealed from Bracher that he had given the German visitor a written declaration. Instead he maintained that "it was just a brief encounter." It is obvious that the General tried to cover up the event and downplay its significance.

Barbey received some details about the meeting from Masson on March 5; the General personally informed him only seven days later. Barbey wrote:

Yesterday the General came back after being away for a week. Early this morning, he calls me into his office, talks to me about Biglen, about the usefulness of his meeting with Schellenberg. He does not appear to have any interest at all in Schellenberg as a person. He does not indulge in any conjectures and does not draw any conclusions. It seems that what was important was not what he could hear during the discussion but what he told Schellenberg. It is what he would have told others as well, journalists and others: our absolute determination! . . . To be very honest, I would be totally relieved if I was certain that this path will not be further pursued and that nothing about this encounter will leak out that could be distorted or exploited inside the country and abroad. I have to admit, though, that if I had been with him at the moment when he made his decision and if he had honored me with the question what I thought about it, I would have advised him not to receive Schellenberg. That would have been my gut reaction and also my reaction after giving the matter some serious thought. A typical case of the boss taking a risk. It is the chief of staff's task to point out to him the risks associated with that risk, so to speak.[32]

Barbey, who was quick to realize that the meeting in Biglen could have highly unpleasant, incriminating consequences, made it clear that he did not feel at all comfortable about the matter.

On March 11, Major Bracher confidentially informed his direct superior, Federal Councilor Kobelt, about what he had been told by the commander-in-chief and by others regarding the encounter with the German general. However, he asked Kobelt not to tell Guisan who had given him the information because the "General [had] asked him to consider the information as highly confidential. But Bracher said that he considered it to be his duty to inform [his] superior [Kobelt]."[33]

The following day, Kobelt visited army headquarters in Interlaken and spoke with Guisan about the meeting in Biglen. The Head of the Military Department wrote in shorthand about his visit:

After discussing several other matters, the General explained that I might be interested to know that he had recently been to Biglen, where he met a German personality who gave him interesting information about the situation in Germany and Italy. . . . General Guisan told me that he was very glad to be able to explain to the German that Switzerland would always remain neutral and defend itself against any aggressor. He said that it was very important for the German official to spread that information abroad. When I asked him who had arranged that meeting and what the name of the German official was, whether the German had come to see him on an official mission and was acting on anyone's orders, the General told me that he had been brought together with the German by a trustworthy Swiss who was close to him but whose name he was not allowed to reveal to me. He said that he did not know the German's name; he was not on an official mission and had no orders. When I asked him if that person was a political, industrial, or military personality, the General explained that he was a private person, but that he was ranked general. He was not a general employed by the armed forces nor a suspended general, just someone ranked general. So I told him that I suspected that that person was a party general. The General replied that he did not think so. He argued that in any case it was very useful for the country that he was able to convince that person that we would remain neutral and defend ourselves against anyone. I replied that the Commander-in-Chief of the Armed Forces should take care not to enter into relations with foreigners to procure intelligence on his own, arguing that he had his organizations to do that. I pointed out to him how dangerous his undertaking was. I explained to him that if the German in question was a private person, such a discussion would not have the expected effect; if he was an official, it was none of the General's business to get mixed up with him. The General reiterated that he was very glad and that it was very useful for our country that he had been able to express himself. Then he got up and invited me for dinner.[34]

The extensive notes taken by Federal Councilor Kobelt indicate how important this member of the government considered the matter to be in terms of the country's policy. It is obvious that Guisan first tried to keep the meeting in Biglen, which had been prepared for well in advance, secret from the Head of the Military Department, and when he did not succeed in doing so, he tried to downplay it by providing imprecise information. Because there were significant differences between what the General had told him and what Bracher had told him, which did not bode well, the Head of the Military Department confidentially informed the Military Attorney General about the matter as a precaution.[35]

At the same time, Kobelt arranged with his liaison officer to inform the General that there were inconsistencies in the account of the meeting in Biglen. Bracher was to tell Guisan that if more people knew about the matter, the Federal Council would certainly be surprised to find out that it had been informed incorrectly by the commander-in-chief. He was to explain that he was in a moral conflict if he could not tell Federal Councilor Kobelt the truth, but that it was his duty to do so, adding that he wanted to give the General some advance notice so he could provide additional information to Kobelt on his own initiative if necessary.

On March 15, Major Bracher spoke with the General to explain his moral conflict and to ask his permission to openly inform Federal Councilor Kobelt. As Kobelt noted about his instructions to Bracher, "I asked Major Bracher to tell the General not to ask *him* to inform me, because his conscience would not allow him to hide the facts from his direct superior. Major Bracher undoubtedly had the right to say that because he had not been taken into the General's confidence but addressed the General first about the issue of his own accord based on information received from a third party."[36] This procedure was apparently designed to allow the General to save face by making an orderly retreat. However, Guisan used the opening only to a limited extent. Kobelt noted: "[The] General did *not* want Major Bracher to inform me, explaining that he was going to write me a letter later today." Guisan authorized Bracher only to tell Federal Councilor Kobelt that "the trustworthy person" who had organized the encounter was Colonel-Brigadier Masson. He claimed that "he did not know the German general, that he did not know his name, and that he considered it to be unlikely that he was Schellenberg."[37]

That same day, Guisan told Kobelt in a handwritten letter that there was no reason to put any particular importance on the matter. He glossed over the facts by saying, "I can assure you that there is no reason to be concerned. I was invited by Colonel Masson, who wanted to introduce me to a German person who had come to Switzerland for a few days for health reasons. It was a private invitation that I kindly ask you to consider as such. There is no need to attach any importance to it."[38]

As it turned out, Guisan was wrong to think that this letter would bring the "Biglen affair" to an end. Kobelt did not give up, asking to receive precise information about the events. He wrote to the General that he wished to speak personally with Chief of Intelligence Masson "in connection with the Biglen case."[39] Guisan forwarded Kobelt's letter to Masson, informing him that he did not object to his speaking with Kobelt. However, he also gave him instructions, stating:

> It is stupid how much importance is attached to this affair. I would like to ask you to make Kobelt understand that this is a *private* matter that concerns only you and me, as I told him in the letter of which you have a copy. If he talks to me about it, I will not give him any [information],

since I promised that person that I would keep his trip to Switzerland secret. I think that you will do likewise since it is a person from your I[ntelligence] S[ervice] who must remain unknown![40]

It seems that the chief of intelligence did not follow the commander-in-chief's instructions but his own conscience, telling Federal Councilor Kobelt the undistorted facts. After receiving Masson's explanations, which gave him a fairly clear picture of the events, Kobelt felt obliged to inform the Federal Council about the Biglen meeting. He wrote to the General that he assumed and "gladly [acknowledged] that both Colonel Brigadier Masson's actions and [the General's] willingness to meet [Schellenberg] in Biglen and Arosa were based on an effort to serve the country."[41] In its meeting of April 5, 1943, the surprised Federal government took note of the General's unusual foreign political move. The concise minutes of the meeting stated: "[The] Head of the Military Department reports on the General's meeting with a foreign high-ranking officer that had been arranged by Colonel Masson. He presents the draft of a letter by the Military Department to the General." The letter was approved after "a thorough discussion," about which the minutes did not give any details, even though they mentioned, "The Head of the Department of Foreign Affairs, Federal Councilor Pilet, did not participate in the discussion."[42]

The letter that Federal Councilor Kobelt addressed to the General on behalf of the government to express its point of view stated, among other things:

> Most of all, the Federal Council does not have the slightest doubt that your intentions were good and that you wanted to serve the country. Moreover, it acknowledges that the statements you made in the declaration you submitted [to the German official] probably matches the views that the Federal Council has repeatedly voiced in public. However, the Federal Council does not understand that the Commander-in-Chief of the Armed Forces enters into relations with high-ranking officials of a belligerent state and makes declarations without first informing the Federal Council about that intention nor giving it the opportunity to voice its opinion about the matter. The Federal Council also has serious concerns about the extraordinary circumstances of the talks in Biglen and Arosa as well as the unusual police escort, even more so because the meeting did not go unnoticed by the public. The fact alone that you met with high-ranking German officials can cause the Allies to become mistrustful if they find out about it. The Axis powers on the other hand may think that it is

absolutely possible that the Commander-in-Chief of the Armed Forces holds similar talks with Allied officials. They may even come to the false conclusion that it is the General, not the Federal Council, that decides Switzerland's stance in any war situation. And last of all, the people's confidence in the General might be shaken if the public at large finds out about the General's mysterious meeting with an SS Colonel.

The Federal Council considers that it is its duty to share its concerns with you and to stress the fact that the Federal Council alone is authorized to make *declarations regarding the country's policies* to official foreign persons and that based on the instructions to the army command the Federal Council alone decides about deploying the armed forces. Hence, the Federal Council asked me to urgently request you not to hold such discussions in the future until you have informed the Federal Council about them and received its authorization.[43]

The following day, the Head of the Military Department personally presented the letter to the commander-in-chief during a meeting. The statements in the letter left no doubt about the government's determination to assume the ultimate leadership role as defined in the constitution. The General annotated the letter, expressing his opinion that the Federal Council's reprimand was a pure act of jealousy. Moreover, he stated that he had informed Allen Dulles, the Special Representative of the President of the United States, about the encounter in Biglen. Also, he said that he did not think that the people's confidence in him would be damaged if the public knew about his contacts with a high-ranking SS officer. He concluded, "Jealousy! I can't believe it!"[44]

The Cabinet meeting of April 5, 1943, was also mentioned in some personal notes by Pilet-Golaz, who noted that Kobelt had informed the Federal Council about talks that the General "thought he had to hold" with high-ranking SS leaders at Masson's "instigation." He recorded:

The high-ranking leaders arrived in Zürich by car. They were escorted by two police officers. It appears that this precaution was taken at Hitler's request because he feared they might be ambushed. The General for his part went from Interlaken to Biglen. The discussion took place at the Bären hotel. A few days later, when the General attended the Skiing Championships in Davos (or Arosa?), one of the top German SS leaders once again stayed at the same hotel as he did. On that opportunity, the General allegedly gave him a written confirmation of the declarations that he had made in Biglen. . . . Needless to say that these meetings did not go unnoticed and that they are already being discussed in the country.[45]

In another letter to Kobelt, Guisan once again brought up the Biglen case, saying that he hoped this was the last time he would have to do so. He stated:

[The meeting] had only one goal, that of reestablishing confidence, and I dare to hope that this goal has been accomplished. The [statements that I made] can hardly be viewed as a 'declaration regarding the country's policies' because they only served to confirm what the Federal Council and the General have been saying over and over again: our determination to defend ourselves against anyone who infringes our neutrality, no matter where he comes from. This cannot be said often enough these days, and I acted according to the purpose of the mission with which I have been entrusted. This being said, I agree with you that this matter is closed, and I only regret that it has been given a meaning that it did not have.[46]

In his personal account of wartime duty, Guisan stated about the content of his conversation with the SS General in Biglen:

Schellenberg explained to me that he had come as a friend of Switzerland. He said that 'Case Switzerland' was becoming pressing for the German Armed Forces High Command, adding that some of Hitler's advisors favored attacking Switzerland whereas others, including himself, were against that plan. He stated that Germany knew that the Swiss were anti-German; therefore it was considered possible that Switzerland would give up its neutrality if the Allies put pressure on the government and the people to receive authorization to use Swiss territory for military purposes, which would in turn increase the risk for Germany. I replied that if he was not our guest I would consider as an insult the mere idea of Switzerland forsaking its neutrality. Then Schellenberg complained about the language that the Swiss press was using. I responded that the language that the German press was using against us was far stronger, which I argued was even worse because in Germany the press was the government's instrument, whereas in Switzerland there was no pre-publication censorship in place. I also used the opportunity to point out to him the wheeling and dealing of the 'Fifth Column' in Switzerland and the 'press correspondence' of Burri, a traitor who had called me the 'prime enemy of the state.' I believe I can say that my arguments did not fail to impress the young German General. He insisted, however, to have a personal declaration from me that our army would fight if our neutrality was infringed. It was not difficult for me to make this declaration, since I had done so on innumerable other occasions, verbally and in writing, and so had the Swiss Government, no matter where the attack originated.[47]

It is not impossible that one of the reasons Guisan favored meeting Schellenberg was the fact that his efforts to stabilize relations with Germany through a mission by Burckhardt or talks with von Bibra had failed.[48] The General definitely expressed in his own way Switzerland's determination to defend itself against anyone so that those who had to decide about "Case Switzerland" would know the dissuasive message. He later explained, "I do not know how much influence Schellenberg had on Hitler or Hitler's entourage. Some people say that my discussion was to no avail. In any event, it did not do any harm."[49]

Alfred Ernst, an initiator of the 1940 "Officers' Conspiracy" who became a corps commander after the war, called the Masson-Schellenberg connection, particularly the General's personal meeting with Schellenberg, an "unnecessary and dangerous . . . political mistake." He argued that this was not a dishonorable act but said, "It was beneath the dignity of Switzerland's commander-in-chief to shake hands with a member of the SS."[50] As with the prewar cooperation plans with France, General Guisan once again went as far as he was possibly allowed to go as military commander-in-chief of a strictly neutral country. The strange connection with Schellenberg looks even more ugly because some officers of Switzerland's intelligence service engaged in shady relations with high-ranking SS officials, conducting dubious private business. However, as odd as things were, one has to acknowledge that the arrangement worked, that it evidently brought advantages to Switzerland's intelligence service, and that Switzerland benefited from it more than it suffered damage.

Considering the case in retrospect, the General's behavior and attitude toward the Federal Council, the country's top executive body to which he reported, must be qualified as embarrassing. It was unacceptable behavior toward the government that Guisan was not willing to stand by the full truth from the beginning but tried to keep the meeting secret, then made attempts to talk his way out of it, and in the end attempted to get away with providing only part of the information. This lack of honesty appeared to be an expression of a clear lack of trust between the army command and the Federal Council. If Switzerland had not been threatened by the war, serious consequences would probably have been inevitable. In view of the General's popularity, however, and because it was in the country's interest to maintain the reputation of the commander-in-chief of the armed forces, the Federal Council could not risk causing a public scandal.

29

The 1943
"March Alarm" and
the Messerschmitt Deal

ONE REASON GENERAL GUISAN may have been convinced that meetings with Schellenberg yielded positive results was that the Masson-Schellenberg connection took credit for diverting the military threat that put Switzerland on alert in March 1943. The Swiss Intelligence Service's reliable "Viking" [Wiking] connection, which had ties all the way to the Führer's headquarters, had reported as early as the late fall of 1942 that Germany intended to attack Switzerland. In early 1943 new, more frequent warnings were received, culminating toward the end of March. On March 18, 1943, the Intelligence Procurement Office in Lucerne received a message from Viking which stated that "Case Switzerland" was once again being discussed in the German High Command and that it was not impossible that an attack on Switzerland would be decided before April 6.[1] The following day, another warning stated, "There is a serious threat. The Führer's headquarters is intensely discussing the urgent issue. No decision has yet been made, but the button may be pushed at any moment. Do not trust negotiations if there are any. An attack may be launched in the midst of negotiations; in fact, experience has shown that this is exactly when it will be launched."[2] According to another worrisome message, the Germans had created a special commando squad under the "agitator and driving force von Bibra" that had orders "to kill General Guisan shortly before the attack [was] carried out."[3]

In a small council of war, during which "the boss offered some 'Rössli' cigars," the General deliberated with Huber, Masson, Gonard, and Barbey.

The chief of intelligence gave a situation report. As Barbey later reported, "Masson explained that Viking had sounded the alarm bell. The German Army High Command was discussing 'Case Switzerland' at the current moment. The staff of General Dietl, the specialist for mountain warfare, was said to be at work in Munich."[4] In a calm atmosphere, Guisan agreed with Huber's and Gonard's suggestions to "put an end to the massive leaves on Sundays; a limited number of army unit staff members [were] to return to their war command posts; the planned operational exercise [was] postponed until later; a number of so-called 'mobilization exercises' [were to be held] by and for all border brigades; and finally the Federal Council [was] to receive a request to authorize taking the first preliminary steps toward quickly mobilizing all troops if necessary." Barbey wondered how it was possible that the participants at the meeting remained so calm and composed, reflecting, "What is the reason for this composure? Certainly not the confidence instilled by the Schellenberg connection (except for Masson perhaps), but the confidence in the 'Viking' connection. Rightly so or not."[5]

It is debatable whether Barbey's explanation was correct. It is absolutely possible that the commander-in-chief, as well as Masson, was confident because he believed that the relations with Schellenberg were effective. Be that as it may, on March 22 Viking was relieved to report, "The decision at the Führer's headquarters has been made. Switzerland will not be attacked for the time being. However, in early April—probably not before April 4, 1943—another country will be attacked, most likely Turkey. Due to special circumstances, the name of that country could not yet be determined, but we will know in a few days which country it is. In view of the [limited] German reserves, our informant considers a simultaneous action against Switzerland to be impossible as long as Switzerland's military is ready and makes an attack appear unlikely to be successful."[6] In the cover letter to that report, which he submitted to the General the following day, Masson wrote, "I am certain that our activities (which have been going on for more than a year) have played a crucial role in this matter."[7]

At approximately the same time, Masson received a similar message from his own direct connection with the SS. Barbey noted that this information put Masson in a wonderful mood, writing, "When I meet Masson, he is radiant; more than that, he is moved. He received a message from Eggen informing him that Schellenberg had said that we could be 'pleased with him.' According to his connection, the threat is gone, Switzerland is no longer 'a topic.' He says 'Viking' confirmed that 'Case Switzerland' had been 'called off.'"[8]

In spite of the positive news, the army command did not blindly trust this apparent easing of tension. On March 22, it informed the Military Department that the General had issued orders to mobilize an additional 130,000 troops to ensure that the army was ready, and it requested authorization to carry out mobilization exercises with the border protection units if necessary.[9] Three days later, in one of his special secret reports, Hausamann suggested taking precisely the same precautions, arguing that even though the alert had been called off, it appeared necessary to keep "an adequate number of troops on duty [because] the only language that [was] understood these days at German headquarters was that of weapons." Alluding to the Masson-Schellenberg connection, he added, "Meetings between prominent Swiss personalities and dubious German SS generals do not change anything about that fact."[10]

In his postwar report, the General explained that he did not want to make a judgment on how effective his declarations to Schellenberg had been; however, it is not difficult to see that he was convinced they were useful because he added, "By renouncing mobilization of the entire army [at that time], we took one of the greatest risks during the entire war."[11] On another occasion, Guisan repeated that he did not know to what extent his talks with Schellenberg had "contributed to the fortunate decision," but he believed that the SS general was capable of exercising "substantial influence on the decision," even though he did "not know for certain."[12] Gonard made no comment about that issue, but in 1943 he was convinced that the alert in March was "one of the most immediate threats that we faced during the war."[13]

At the time Viking sounded the alarm bell, Masson seemed to have so much trust in Schellenberg that he had the unfortunate idea to ask, through his SS connection, if there was indeed a real threat to Switzerland. He consequently sent Captain Meyer to Berlin in order to find out the facts from his German contacts. Upon returning from Germany, Meyer congratulated the head of the Intelligence Procurement Office in Lucerne on his "good intelligence service because the reports by 'Viking' had been correct, as he had been able to verify himself in Berlin."[14] Major Waibel remarked about this, "First I did not trust my ears; then I thought that Meyer's explanations about his mission to Berlin were a bad joke. When I realized what had happened, I addressed a serious written warning and complaint to the chief of intelligence."[15]

When the news reached them that "Case Switzerland [had been] called off," the intelligence officers working for the Masson-Schellenberg connection were absolutely convinced that by arranging the meeting between the SS General and Guisan, they had saved their country. After returning from Berlin together with Eggen on the evening of March 22, Meyer met with Masson and Wiesendanger in Zürich. Meyer noted: "We sit together until 12 at night, drinking a bottle of champagne. We are glad that we were spared that ordeal." Colonel Brigadier Masson wrote a thank-you letter to Schellenberg that Captain Meyer dictated, in which he said that he had to "thank [him] very much for everything [he] had done so far for [their] country and for the relations between the two states."[16]

Captain Meyer, who was persuaded that he had contributed to a significant historic act, sent the General a bouquet of spring flowers after returning home, writing to him:

> On this day, which will undoubtedly turn out to be a historic day in Switzerland's history on which God's providence has once again protected our dear country from danger and grief, the citizen and writer Wolf Schwertenbach [Capt. Meyer], who knows all about the events, would like to thank you for what you have done in a cerebral battle for the well-being of the country. Because I also know that psychological elements ended up turning the scale in our favor, I did not fail to notice how much weight your word and the word of Colonel-Brigadier Masson carried. That is why I also know that it was not only rational reasoning but to the same extent your heart that saved us, for what do words mean when they are not heartfelt; [your heart] provided the necessary feeling of trust when you pronounced that we would be merciless toward any intruder and fulfill our holy duty toward our home country in any situation. That was the only factor that decided our destiny this time. . . . Although I am aware that we are far from having escaped all dangers, this does not in the least diminish the success.[17]

Guisan, who was undoubtedly also convinced at that moment that his personal intervention had been successful, thanked Meyer for the flowers, replying that he was "pleased and touched" by his gesture. He also thanked Mrs. Meyer for "the lovely bag of sugar" that she had included for the horses. Moreover, as his top superior, he officially thanked Captain Meyer-Schwertenbach, writing, "I would like to take this opportunity to also express my heartfelt thanks to you for your cooperation in this difficult issue. I hope that our declaration created the necessary confidence."[18]

In his complaint mentioned above—which was not addressed directly to Masson (as erroneously stated by Waibel) but to his deputy, Chief of Security Colonel W. Müller—Major Waibel harshly protested against the connection with Eggen and Schellenberg, writing:

> I do not think that anyone still seriously believes that Eggen does not act with the full knowledge and approval of his superior, SS Reichsführer Himmler, even regarding those issues in which he apparently speaks in Switzerland's favor and against the Reich's interests.

Himmler of all people is not the primitive kind of person who would tolerate a traitor in his entourage whom he keeps on call for the Swiss, so to speak, in order to warn the Swiss against the Reich. . . . However, Himmler is probably capable of being personally in control of the connection to the Swiss Army Command so as to properly pull the wool over its eyes practically with his own hands, and unfortunately he has done so successfully.[19]

Waibel argued that if it was true that the information received by Viking had been checked through the Eggen connection, an "inexcusable mistake with far-reaching consequences" had been made because in that case Himmler had been "obediently told in person" that Switzerland was informed about talks in the immediate entourage of the Führer's headquarters. That in turn would make it possible for the SS to do whatever was necessary to eliminate the informants working for the Viking connection, thereby putting several people's lives at risk. He explained that the reliable alarm bell was lost due to Army Intelligence's own fault, adding that the Eggen connection was no equivalent replacement for the Viking connection but was in fact "a threat to our country." Waibel stated that he had trouble believing that Masson had said that it was thanks to his direct relations that Himmler made Hitler renounce taking any action against Switzerland; however, if this was actually true, it had to be considered a "fateful error." Waibel threatened to resign as Head of the Intelligence Procurement Office if the direct connection to the SS was not immediately interrupted.[20]

At first Hausamann suspected that the people who had tried to verify the Viking information in Berlin might be "innocent" politicians but certainly not an expert like his military superior Masson. In one of his reports following the alert in March 1943, Hausamann pointed out that similar incidents had happened at the time in Norway, Holland, and Belgium, writing, "One must not make the slightest demands on politicians who go and ask their prospective butcher whether he really intends to butcher them. What is worse, though, is that these politicians believe their German butchers more than their own intelligence service!!"[21] There is no doubt that when he made this comparison, Hausamann had events in Switzerland in mind. It had to be all the more disturbing that this time it was not politicians but the military that had blundered. Hausamann commented, "People who ask official or semi-official offices dumb questions jeopardize our best connections in the German camp or even bring them to an abrupt end."[22] It may not be wrong to suppose that Hausamann directed this attack against Masson and indirectly against the General. It is unlikely that at that point in time the intelligence specialist failed to notice who was involved in the connection.

Major Ernst, the head of the German desk, was also horrified when he found out about the query in Berlin, writing a beseeching letter of protest to Masson that stated:

> I am deeply concerned about your telling me that you checked with your German informants whether Switzerland was in danger. I am convinced that people like SS leader Schellenberg and Eggen have no honest intentions toward us but play a dangerous game with you which must have fateful consequences. I know that my warnings will not be heeded and that I risk your losing confidence in me. However, I consider it to be my duty to tell you openly that my confidence is shaken because of your relations with the SS and the query regarding the threats to which Switzerland might be subject. I am ready to resign if the SS leaders, who I think are capable of doing only bad things, continue to exercise any influence on Switzerland's intelligence service. I feel obligated to tell you frankly that I will do my utmost to fight against this influence that is fateful for our country, and I am ready to bear the consequences of my conviction. I have given very careful consideration to all of this. If I did not offer to resign earlier it was only because I [felt] obligated to stay at my post during these critical times.[23]

Ernst admitted that the chief of intelligence had acted with "good intentions" and that he would therefore continue to respect him personally; but he said that he was determined to resign from the Intelligence Service "if the SS's influence continued to exist." Otherwise his "work [did] not make sense anymore" because Masson allowed the "SS, our deadly enemy," to abuse him without his being aware of it.[24]

Masson's action caused a serious rift between key intelligence officers and their superior. Ernst and Waibel were not the only ones who reacted; Hausamann also threatened to resign and undertook efforts to have the chief of intelligence replaced, writing to the Head of the Military Department that it seemed to be "in Colonel-Brigadier Masson's and the country's best interest to [put] him in a different command post that [corresponded] to his rank." He explained that he and his comrades had come to the same conclusion, stating, "Because all the warnings that we have been addressing to our boss for nearly a year are to no avail, a change has to be made, or else we will have to go."[25] As Masson was not willing to abandon the SS connection, Ernst resigned from his post, arguing that his "basic views" differed from those of his superior. He asked to be transferred to the operational section.[26] Chief of the General Staff Huber granted his request, informing him that Chief of Operations Gonard "very much agreed with this solution."[27] However, Ernst was not transferred until fall 1943; he was to report to his new duty station on October 11. The two other intelligence officers remained at their posts.

Hausamann reported that upon returning to Germany, Schellenberg had made some "quite critical and disparaging" remarks to his superiors concerning his meeting with General Guisan.[28] There is no written evidence to support that opinion. On the contrary, Foreign Minister Ribbentrop signed a note that can be interpreted in a perfectly positive manner. It stated:

> In the matter of the meeting that was held in early March [1943] between Colonel Schellenberg of the Security Service and the General of the Swiss Army, Guisan, and in the course of which the Swiss General gave us assurances that Switzerland would resolutely defend the mountain passes across the Alps at its southern border against any enemy under any circumstances, no new contact has been made yet between Schellenberg and Guisan. According to my proposal which the Führer had approved the previous month, in April I authorized Mr. Schellenberg to verbally declare the following to General Guisan: Berlin has taken note of the General's information. One welcomes Switzerland's decision to defend its neutrality under any circumstances. However, one considers that the intention to defend the Swiss mountain passes across the Alps against any attack from the south is not a reality because the Axis Powers are determined to chase the English and Americans away from the Mediterranean as soon as possible.[29]

Since the view that it would be possible to throw the Allies out of the Mediterranean turned out to be too optimistic, shortly afterward Schellenberg requested modifying "the final phrase of the declaration that he was ordered to deliver." Ribbentrop consequently weakened that passage, "because the Axis Powers are determined to prevent the English and Americans from landing anywhere." In addition, the Reich Foreign Minister suggested to Hitler "that Schellenberg should enter into even closer contact with Guisan than had been planned so as to try to find out more about the intentions of Switzerland's military."[30]

According to the German Foreign Minister's note, in view of the favorable impression that Schellenberg had gained about Guisan, the leadership of the Reich planned to strengthen relations with Switzerland's commander-in-chief. However, it is striking that in its reciprocal declaration, Germany did not state that it had no intention of attacking Switzerland. The second meeting between Guisan and Schellenberg that was referred to in the note never took place. The

Germans contented themselves with maintaining contact with Masson. Based on Ribbentrop's note, however, it may be established as a fact that the leadership of the Reich took heed of Guisan's declaration.

The German Ministry of Foreign Affairs transmitted to the German embassy in Bern the declaration that General Guisan had presented to Schellenberg in Arosa. Minister Köcher commented, "The written declaration by the General to SS Brigadier General Schellenberg on March 6 does not include any phrase that contradicts Switzerland's official policy. I have reason to believe that by now the General, who is not well-inclined toward us, has learned his lesson."[31] Subsequently, the reliability of Switzerland's commander-in-chief was duly taken into account and his uprightness was valued as a guarantee for his sincerity. Köcher continued, "The Military Attaché has told me that even the Swiss officers who oppose General Guisan do not consider him capable of breaking a promise that he has made. This information by the Military Attaché is all the more significant as these officers obviously do not know that General Guisan gave SS Brigadier General Schellenberg not only his word of honor as an officer but also a written declaration." Schellenberg's meeting with Guisan undoubtedly strengthened the German leadership's trust in Switzerland's neutrality. As Köcher remarked, "In conclusion, I duly report that I believe the Swiss have the honest intention to and are determined to defend themselves against an attack by the English and Americans using all their available military strength."[32]

Germany's mistrust of General Guisan, which was rooted in particular in the documents that had been discovered at La Charité, was dispelled in large part only once he had met with Schellenberg. A few weeks after the meeting in Biglen, a report by an agent from Germany explained in what a surprising new light Switzerland's commander-in-chief was seen. The agent reported: "It is interesting that our informant stressed the fact that one did not have any doubt that the General was determined to defend himself against anyone, hence also against an attack by the Allies. However, one does not believe that the army and the people would march against the Allies at Germany's side and considers that the crisis which would develop as a consequence would provide an opportunity for the Allies."[33]

After the alert in March 1943, Chief of Intelligence Masson received an invitation to meet with Schellenberg in Berlin. Meyer-Schwertenbach noted that this meeting was to "further strengthen relations between us all for the well-being of the two states." On that occasion, Masson was supposed to meet SS Reichsführer Himmler as well.[34] General Guisan and Chief of the General Staff Huber approved of Masson's trip; however, the Federal Council refused to grant his request. When Masson asked for the Military Department's official authorization to accept the invitation, indicating that the army command had approved of the plan, Federal Councilor Kobelt told the General, "The Federal Council discussed the issue at today's meeting and asked me to inform you in regard to Colonel-Brigadier Masson that it could not authorize this trip. The Federal Council considers that it is not permissible for the Chief of Army Intelligence to travel abroad while the army is on wartime duty."[35] Moreover, Guisan was verbally reprimanded in connection with Masson's request. Von Steiger, the Head of the Justice and Police Department, reported to his colleague Stampfli that he had to tell the General what procedure he would have to follow in the future, stating, "I politely but firmly pointed out to the General that it was the General's responsibility to come to an agreement with the Federal Council before answering the concerned officer's request. The General realized that this view was correct."[36]

When Masson's request to travel to Berlin was denied, it appears that SS circles began to have new doubts about Switzerland's position. At the end of August, the month after the Allies had established themselves in Sicily and Mussolini had been ousted from Italy, Meyer-Schwertenbach received an urgent call from Eggen asking him to travel to Berlin immediately to confirm in person to Schellenberg that Switzerland would stay absolutely neutral toward the Allies and that the General's word was binding. Meyer noted, "On August 27, 1943, I drive to see Masson in Bern and tell him about it. I tell him that I am reluctant to go but will of course do so if it is in the country's interest. He asks me to go, because otherwise it will be seen as an unfriendly act as he cannot go himself. I go to see the General for lunch, and G[uisan] is of the same opinion; but he takes note of the matter only unofficially."[37]

On the morning of August 28, Meyer left by plane from Dübendorf for the capital of the German Reich. According to Meyer's notes, his visit was "camouflaged as a business trip"; it is likely that he actually had some business to take care of on the side. During dinner at Eggen's apartment in Berlin, to which the Schellenbergs were also invited, the SS General explained to the Swiss visitor, "I asked you to come because my opponents say that because Masson did not come, they are right about what should be done with Switzerland. They say that Ma[sson] did not play fair and that Switzerland has to be whipped instead of being courted." During his stay in Berlin, Meyer was scheduled to meet Kaltenbrunner, the Chief of the Central Security Office, but the meeting did not take place. However, the following day Schellenberg reported that he had "won against Ribbentrop's view," that he had gained new confidence and "believed that the connection still worked and Switzerland was keeping its word." He added regarding developments on the battlefields that Germany was fighting "an uphill battle" but that would change again because "the real combat [was] just starting." He argued that the reasons for the recent failures were the "lack of a unified command" and Ribbentrop's false judgments. He described Ribbentrop as "a camel who also made a false assessment of the English."[38]

Schellenberg for his part returned to Switzerland in the fall of 1943 to meet with Masson once again. From October 16 to 18, he stayed at Wolfsberg Castle in the company of Eggen and Wiesendanger.[39]

After the war, some insiders voiced doubts about whether the danger in March 1943 was real. Some German generals as well as Hans Bernd Gisevius, who had an important role in German Army Intelligence, suspected that the alert had been faked so that the SS officers could put themselves in the limelight among their Swiss friends. When he was heard by the Swiss investigating judge, Gisevius stated, "I could almost swear that in March 1943 no preventive action was planned against Switzerland; otherwise the Abwehr would certainly have known about it. This preventive action was certainly only a bluff by Schellenberg."[40] Fuhrer indicates that it is extremely difficult to decide whether the alert was based on a real threat or was simply a ploy. At this writing, neither of the two views can be firmly corroborated with written evidence.[41]

The last time the Masson-Schellenberg connection played a role was in connection with the inadvertent emergency landing at Dübendorf, on April 29, 1944, of a newly developed German nightfighter aircraft. The Messerschmitt 110 Cg+EN, which was equipped with top-secret instruments, had become crippled during an air battle over southern Germany.[42] When they realized they had landed on a Swiss airstrip, the three crew members immediately attempted to take off again, but the Swiss airfield security team prevented them from doing so.

It seems interesting that in this case the German government did not undertake any official steps through diplomatic channels to repossess the aircraft or have it destroyed; instead, the negotiations were held with Switzerland's intelligence service through Schellenberg and Eggen. Schellenberg wrote to General Guisan, referring to their personal acquaintance, "The aircraft is a product of top-notch technology. Both the engine and the equipment are based on the most recent findings of our highly developed air force technology. It would cause great damage to the Reich's war effort if details about the aircraft, or even parts of it, became known to Germany's opponents. I trust you as a person and your Federal Council that your country will remain strictly neutral; I would therefore like to meet with you as soon as possible in order to come to an agreement about the aircraft and its parts, which absolutely must remain secret."[43] In exchange, Schellenberg suggested that it might be possible to award patents or licenses to the Swiss Air Force.

Following the complications that the meeting in Biglen had caused, General Guisan was cautious enough not to see Schellenberg in person again. He thanked the SS Colonel "very much" for the trust that he placed in him but stated that he would order Switzerland's military attaché in Berlin to continue the negotiations.[44] The next day, Guisan flew to Dübendorf in Barbey's company to personally inspect the German aircraft, which was equipped, among other things, with two upward-firing 20mm guns.[45]

Subsequently, the negotiations were carried out between Masson and Eggen, with Burckhardt, the military attaché in Berlin, and Meyer acting as intermediaries. During a meeting with Federal Councilor von Steiger (Kobelt's substitute), Masson, Burckhardt, Rihner, and Barbey, Guisan was able to announce that in exchange for returning the special aircraft to them, the Germans were willing to sell Switzerland twelve Me-109 aircraft. Masson added that it was Eggen who had made the offer. With Hitler's approval, he had been authorized by Luftwaffe head Göring to conclude the deal. He said that Eggen knew that returning the aircraft was out of the question and would therefore agree to have it destroyed with all its secret equipment, as long as the German air force attaché and a German technician were allowed to participate in the operation.[46] At that point, speaking on behalf of the entire Federal Council, von Steiger protested against Masson negotiating with the Germans. According to the minutes of the meeting, he stated, "Colonel-Brigadier Masson is in charge of Army Intelligence, that is all. He is not authorized to do anything else."[47]

After the war, Eggen explained to a Swiss investigating judge that on Hitler's instructions the aircraft was slated to be destroyed in a German surprise attack. He said, "It was planned to identify the exact location of the aircraft and then destroy it in a bombing attack, or if it was not certain that the aircraft was totally destroyed, paratroopers were to intervene to blow it up."[48] Eggen was ordered by Berlin to go to Switzerland to find out where exactly the aircraft was located. Through Masson's mediation, Eggen was able to "visit the plane at a hangar in Dübendorf." However, upon returning to Berlin, he reported that the location was unsafe and that the Swiss intended to paint their national emblem on the airplane, which would make it difficult to identify. Eggen had not been interested in the staging of a surprise attack because that would have jeopardized his valuable relations with his Swiss informants. It appears that it was he who suggested the deal involving the twelve Messerschmitt fighters.

Eggen traveled to Switzerland in Military Attaché Burckhardt's company to negotiate with Masson. He obtained a promise that the aircraft in Dübendorf would be destroyed with German explosives in exchange for the delivery of the dozen Me-109s. As Eggen explained, "Once I had received final approval by the German authorities to blow up the machine and that the twelve Me-109s would be delivered, thanks to arrangements by the Swiss officers who were in charge, I was able to bring along the explosives on my flight back to Dübendorf. On Ascension Day, the aircraft and its ammunition were blown up and set on fire with gasoline." The destruction was carried out in the presence of the two Germans, Eggen and a Captain Brandt of the Luftwaffe, as well as, from the Swiss side, Colonel-Divisional Commander Rihner, Colonel-Brigadiers von Wattenwyl and Masson, and Captain Meyer.[49]

The Military Department reported to the Federal Council that Germany's request to have the special aircraft destroyed had been confirmed through official diplomatic channels, but that in the meantime the aircraft had actually been destroyed on May 18. It added, "In return, Germany has promised to deliver twelve Messerschmitt aircraft (Me-109G) under the condition that payment be made in a freely traded foreign currency. The Federal Department of Economy has agreed to this method of payment."[50] The agreed price was 500,000 Swiss francs per aircraft, which the technical authorities deemed as "adequate." In view of the fact that the war was in its fifth year, the deal was considered "a unique opportunity to acquire modern fighter aircraft that must not be missed." The six million francs were to be debited under the budget line "purchases of material during wartime duty."[51]

On May 20, just two days after the destruction of the special aircraft, the twelve German Messerschmitts were flown to Dübendorf. A banquet was held in Eggen's honor to thank him for his role as a mediator. Colonel Guisan, the General's son, who attended the event, considered that Eggen had "rendered immense services to our country." He reported to his father about the event, "On this occasion, Colonel-Divisional Commander Rihner, Colonel-Brigadier von Wattenwyl, and numerous other officers invited him to dinner, in the course of which he was not only thanked but also celebrated. He even made a speech."[52]

In connection with issuing visas for Eggen to travel to Switzerland, there were repeated disputes between Masson and Heinrich Rothmund, the Chief of the Police Section at the Justice and Police Department, which dealt with foreign nationals. Masson, who was able to count on the General's and the chief of the general staff's support, referred to Rothmund as a "saboteur of the interests of Army Intelligence."[53] Huber did "not understand that the Police Section made it difficult for the Chief of Intelligence to communicate with foreign agents."[54]

Rothmund had come to realize that the intelligence activities of the Eggen-Schellenberg connection were also tied to business transactions, and informed Federal Councilor von Steiger about the commercial aspect, explaining:

Mr. Masson is blind. He speaks of his 'Schelli' as if he was an intimate friend to whom he is much obliged. He says and writes that Mr. Eggen would like to move to Switzerland sometime in the future as if that was a matter of fact. In short, he allows Capt. Meyer to blindly lead him by the nose. At best, Messrs. Masson and Meyer no longer clearly see what is official business and what is private business, nor what is in Switzerland's general interest and what is in Messrs. Eggen's and Meyer's personal interest. . . . Messrs. Eggen and Schellenberg should be exorcised once and for all from Mr. Masson. In my opinion, the Chief of the German Intelligence Service and his collaborators have no business spending time in Switzerland during the war.[55]

During the last year of the war, increasing numbers of critics demanded that restraint be employed in relations with Eggen and Schellenberg. In the summer of 1944, when Masson told General Guisan that both Schellenberg and Eggen had been promoted in rank, Guisan reacted in a reserved manner, asking Masson only to instruct the military attaché in Berlin to verbally congratulate Schellenberg on his behalf.[56] That fall, Federal Councilor Kobelt reminded Guisan that he had always opposed the connection with the SS officers. Once again he warned him against these "inadmissible" relations, arguing, "It is unlikely that Eggen and Schellenberg, who are tied for good or ill to the regime in Germany, will supply us, of all countries, with important information about the rulers' intentions."[57] The Military Attorney General also wrote to Guisan that one had to "beware of getting into situations in which leading circles of the National Socialist regime could demand unachievable favors from us in return for merely imaginary services." He recommended that the General "agree to refuse giving entrance visas to Eggen in the future."[58]

General Guisan himself also began to show signs of mistrust. According to his handwritten notes, during a meeting with Masson in October 1944 he asked, "Do you have any personal interests in the 'wood syndicate,' or in any other business that Eggen does, either directly or through intermediaries?" Masson replied, "No, none. I was the one who asked E[ggen] to come to Switzerland. I need information for my service about Italy, among other things. I do not do this on my own behalf but for my country and under my responsibility."[59]

Masson did not let anyone deter him from maintaining his contact with the Eggen-Schellenberg connection, through Captains Meyer and Holzach, until the bitter end. In December 1944, Holzach brought a sealed letter from Schellenberg to Switzerland from Berlin. Masson explained to Commissioner Maurer of the Federal Prosecutor's office that the letter included "personal congratulations by General Schellenberg to General Guisan."[60]

After the war, Schellenberg turned himself in to the Swedish authorities in Stockholm and was extradited to the Allies in June 1945.[61] Eggen for his part managed to flee to Switzerland during the final days of the war, where he first hid at Wolfsberg Castle. On May 15, 1945, the General ordered a military investigation against him. On May 26 he was arrested but was set free again three months later. On September 11, 1945, the Military Attorney General decided to abandon the proceedings against Eggen because it was proven that he had rendered some services to Switzerland's Intelligence Service, especially in connection with the Messerschmitt deal. A short time later, at his own request, the SS Major was handed over to the American occupying forces at the border checkpoint in Chiasso.[62]

The Issue of Censorship

IN TERMS OF FREEDOM OF THE PRESS, the Second World War is a dark spot in Switzerland's history. Until 1939, press freedom had been accepted as a matter of course, unchallenged as a basic principle in the Swiss democracy. Before the war it was known that Guisan, anticipating army mobilizations, favored introducing a type of censorship under which printed media were to be controlled as a preventive measure before they went to press.[1] As early as the beginning of 1938, when the National Defense Committee discussed the possibility of introducing censorship in connection with media coverage of Austria's Anschluss to the German Reich, the future General recommended that "the press be more closely monitored by the Federal Government."[2] The other corps commanders and Federal Councilor Minger agreed with him. Minger stated, "Unfortunately the existing legal framework is insufficient to exercise a moderating influence on the media."[3]

The Federal Council had made provisions to introduce pre-publication censorship in case war broke out; however, when the army was mobilized in September 1939, it renounced putting these provisions into effect. One week after the troops were called to duty, however, the Cabinet issued a restrictive decree designed to protect the country in matters of intelligence. This decree in turn made it possible to set up a "Press and Radio Section" on the army staff which was ordered to monitor the media after publication. The terms of the decree introducing post-publication censorship read, among other things:

1. In order to safeguard the country both on the domestic and foreign levels and in order to maintain its neutrality, the Army Command shall monitor information and statements that are published or transmitted by mail, telegraph, telephone, news agencies, radio,

and through films and photographs; it shall take the necessary measures to carry out this monitoring activity. The Army Command shall designate the military and civilian bodies that are entrusted with this task.

2. The measures that are ordered must be appropriate for the situation at any given time. These measures shall include instructions, general or limited bans, the withdrawal of publication licenses, confiscations, censorship, the closing down of a publication, or similar steps.[4]

The first head of the Press and Radio Section, which was initially vested with very limited authority, was Colonel Eugen Hasler.[5]

General Guisan explained that the army had "never intended to monopolize" the press by censoring it.[6] On the contrary, the army soon considered the type of censorship that it had been ordered to exercise increasingly burdensome and asked to be relieved of this duty. In an appendix to his postwar report, Chief of the General Staff Huber gave a detailed account of the structure, activities, and problems of the Press and Radio Section of the army staff.[7] A report by Max Nef, written at the Federal Council's request for the attention of Parliament, gave a comprehensive overview of Switzerland's media policy between 1939 and 1945.[8] Historian Georg Kreis also wrote an authoritative account of all aspects of censorship.[9]

As the army command was in charge of monitoring both military and political information, ultimately the commander-in-chief was considered responsible for the decisions made and measures taken. The General consequently became caught in the line of fire. The press in his own country held him responsible whenever restrictions were imposed, and on the other hand foreign countries blamed him whenever Swiss newspapers attacked them because he had failed to prevent this from happening. Hence, at an early stage Colonel Masson advocated curtailing the freedom of the press by censoring the media before publication. As early as October 1939, during a briefing with Chief of the General Staff Labhart, Masson claimed that Germany's attitude toward Switzerland had been "very correct so far" but that Switzerland had to reproach itself for the attitude of its press toward Germany. As he explained, "One feels that the Swiss population, army, and press begin to display an attitude that can pose a serious threat to our neutrality. If a country wanted to intervene against us, the attitude and the remarks of our press and the mood among the population would provide it with enough reasons to go ahead and do it." He argued that the material collected in Germany could "turn into a very dangerous weapon against Switzerland."[10]

Labhart agreed with Masson's view, adding that there was indeed a "risk that one day Germany might lose its patience and send a sweeping thunderstorm across Switzerland." He expressed, though, "a feeling that we might get out of this war unharmed . . . under the condition that the army does its duty at the border and the people keep their composure and behave properly at the same time." However, because censorship matters were a political rather than a military issue, Labhart declared, "I do not want to be seen as a political figure in the army. It is ultimately up to the political authorities to decide this matter."[11]

In his postwar report, General Guisan wrote that he did not know why the general staff section had agreed before the war to take on the responsibility of censoring the press in every respect. He argued that the army should have had only one important task: "Maintaining military secrets and monitoring the information that could hamper the troops' morale and security." He stated:

It would have been sufficient to have this task carried out by military representation among the body in charge of censoring the press. The general staff section undoubtedly agreed to take on this task because the civilian authorities apparently showed no interest in the whole issue of the media and because military secrets had to be maintained at all costs. Under the critical circumstances at the beginning of the war, when I took over the command, I was not entitled to immediately oppose instructions that had been issued in response to an urgent requirement.[12]

During the winter of 1939–40, the army command continually received official and unofficial information concerning foreign publications and radio stations accusing Switzerland of non-neutral conduct. However, the army did not have the necessary means to evaluate and refute these attacks by the media that were part of psychological warfare. The General commented after the war, "The situation appeared to become more and more paradoxical when foreign media and diplomats blamed the army command for the reactions of our press which they disliked. They logically held, or at least they pretended to hold, the army command responsible for our news and opinions."[13]

Apparently, Guisan's first move to request a change in the unpleasant situation followed a meeting by the Committee for Media Policy on February 19, 1940, during which some editors criticized the Press and Radio Section, and through it the army command, because some restrictive measures prevented the press from fulfilling its mission of printing truthful information. Barbey, who went to see the head of the Section that day on Masson's orders, described the scene, writing, "Poor Colonel [Hasler] looks devastated from the attacks to which he has been subject. The Media Committee has been meeting since this morning, attacking the army command. . . . National Councilor Feldmann, the editor-in-chief of the *Neue Berner Zeitung*, and Meierhans of the *Volksfreund* newspaper gave a well-founded, insightful, and courageous account of the methods used by the Nazis to enslave the press in Austria, Czechoslovakia, and Poland." The editors concluded that the army command should no longer be in charge of monitoring the press on a political level because it was "not well enough informed" to be able to assess political opinions, "nor strong enough to take action" if needed.[14]

Unlike Barbey, Chief of Intelligence Masson opposed the army command giving up monitoring the press. When Masson heard Barbey's report about the meeting with the editors, he was "dismayed." Barbey explained, "He fears that I have betrayed him in this matter. But I actually never shared his opinion about the problems of our press, and I have repeatedly told him so."[15] Some party activists and members of Parliament had been seething for a long time because the army had evidently curtailed freedom of the press. Criticism was voiced in Parliament in both December 1939 and in early 1940. The army, however, had its defenders. During a debate, Federal Councilor Etter admonished in passing that the army should not be criticized because of the censorship issue, and Federal President Pilet-Golaz declared, "The General's position must not be jeopardized."[16]

At the end of February 1940, the delicate issue of censorship, which strongly affected him in several respects, caused Guisan to make his first attempt to have the situation revised. Based on a report that Barbey had submitted, he ordered his legal advisor, Colonel Logoz, to draft a letter requesting that the issue of censorship and the possibility of separating the Press and Radio Section from the army be discussed.[17] In this letter dated February 29, 1940, the General asked the Federal Council:

> Can the Press and Radio Section continue to report to the army command considering the responsibility that this entails? Or will the army have to ask that the Press and Radio Section report to the Federal Council in the future in view of the increasing number of civilian matters that it has to deal with? In the latter case, there will have to be a liaison between the army and this section in order to handle the issues that directly concern the army. I reserve the right to raise these delicate issues again if necessary.[18]

In opposition to Masson's opinion, the general staff had come to believe that it was necessary in the army's interest to move the section out of the army.

Chief of the General Staff Huber also considered that the army command should be relieved of the task of censoring the media, especially after Germany's military attaché had intervened with him to protest against a caricature that had been published in the *Weltwoche* newspaper.[19]

German officials in Berlin were indeed upset about Switzerland. Shortly before the beginning of the Western campaign, Reich Foreign Minister Ribbentrop wrote a memorandum in which he stated that the Führer was "incensed at the attitude of the Swiss press," arguing that Hitler had always wanted to be on good terms with Switzerland, so it would henceforth have to "do things differently."[20] During an audience with Swiss Envoy Frölicher, German Permanent Secretary von Weizsäcker complained that the Federal Council's measures to restrain the press were not very effective. He claimed that "one day Switzerland would have to pay for what its press was destroying."[21]

The Military Department's response to Guisan's proposal on the censorship issue was cool. The Head of the Department informed the General that a copy of the letter had been submitted to all members of the government and that it was "being considered to have a meeting between the Federal Council and the Army Command on this matter sometime in March."[22] On March 19, Guisan was invited to a Cabinet meeting. The minutes of the meeting state that the General first reported on the international military situation, "the way he sees it based on the reports and information that are available to him. . . . Then the question is examined whether the task of censoring the press should be taken away from the army and be transferred to the civilian authorities. The Council basically considers that the current situation should not be changed, and press and radio matters should remain the responsibility of the army."[23] The idea of a joint "Liaison Service for Press-Related Matters," consisting of seven army and civilian representatives, that would have to deal with common issues in the area of political censorship was, however, discussed.

In June 1940, during Germany's Western campaign, Colonel Perrier, who had replaced Hasler as Head of the Press and Radio Section earlier that year, complained to the General about his lack of authority, arguing that he did not have the means available to "discipline" the press. "As a consequence," he added, "I cannot personally, nor through the means that I have available, persuade the editorial boards that it is absolutely necessary to understand the situation, abide by the current contingencies, and be strict and disciplined." Hence, he suggested that the General ask the Federal Council to call upon the press to restrain itself.[24]

In a letter dated June 21, Guisan took up Perrier's suggestion and formally asked the Federal Council to resolve the matter either by giving him the authority to fully censor the press before it was published or by relieving the army from the task of monitoring the press. The General explained that practically all issues raised in connection with monitoring the press were political, particularly foreign policy issues. He added that under the current regulations, he was allowed to intervene only after the fact; that is, once an article had already been published. He concluded:

> Therefore I consider that the only way to prevent the pranks and excesses of the press, as well as the incidents that may result from them, from happening is by introducing pre-publication censorship. It is currently an indispensable weapon for the national defense both on the domestic and foreign levels. . . . Should the Federal Council fail to take this request into consideration, I would no longer be able to monitor the press with the current means. I would therefore ask the Federal Council to relieve me of this responsibility.[25]

The letter, which Barbey had drafted, was as clear as it could possibly be, but it did not meet with much response from the government. In a first reaction, Minger replied that the issue of censorship had been discussed on the Federal Council and that Federal Councilor Etter would contact the Press and Radio Section about it. Moreover, he explained that the commander-in-chief's request had been forwarded to the Justice and Police Department for examination.[26] The General responded that no matter who supervised the Press and Radio Section, the section itself had to be given additional authority immediately in order to place certain newspapers that followed a particular tendency under its "guardianship."[27]

One week later, after the armistice had been signed in France, the General received a detailed, negative response from the Federal Council. It had been drafted by the Justice and Police Department and stated:

> The Federal Council paid full attention to your letters of June 21 and 26 regarding the introduction of pre-publication censorship. It shares your view that at the present time, violations of neutrality by the press can have extremely serious consequences for the country. However, it considers that other means should be tried before introducing pre-publication censorship. Hence, it seems to us that ordering pre-publication censorship would go too far, even if it was applied only to articles dealing with foreign policy topics. In addition, for this measure to be effective, a large system of censorship officers would be required that is out of all proportion to the number of misdemeanors. . . . We doubt that Parliament would approve such a drastic measure at a time when troops are beginning to be demobilized.[28]

In his reply to Minger, the General insisted that it was "not normal" that censoring the press, either before or after it went to print, continued to be the army's responsibility. At the same time, he recommended urgently intervening with the Reich government through diplomatic channels because the campaign waged by the German press against Switzerland had become insulting since Germany's victory over France. He argued, "I consider that such a press campaign cannot and must not be accepted by a free country. We should ask for an explanation and defend ourselves. . . . We also have the right to protest and ask for explanations. The press campaign that Germany is carrying out against us is not only incompatible with safeguarding our honor, but it is also dangerous to accept without reacting."[29]

Guisan considered media policy a part of the national defense. There is no doubt that this is why he was determined in good faith to have censorship introduced. This was a serious request and he did not simply propose it as a means to put pressure on the Federal Council to relieve the army of the task of monitoring the press, as Bonjour suggests.[30] During those days, the General, along with Masson and Gonard, was a stout advocate of pre-publication censorship. Eibel, who served as Head of Office on the Personal Staff in the summer of 1940 and had the opportunity to discuss the issue of censorship with the General, established this view as a fact.[31] Guisan stood by his opinion, confirming to Federal Councilor Feldmann after the war, "In fact, the attitude of part of our press was dangerous to the extent that pre-publication censorship by the Press and Radio Section on the army staff was necessary. However, as the army command wanted to stay out of politics as a matter of principle, and in order to stay clear of potential conflicts, I repeatedly asked the Federal Council to relieve the army command of the task of censoring the press."[32]

The "Petition of the Two Hundred," which was submitted to the Federal Council on November 15, 1940, became a measuring stick for public opinion on the issue of media policy. The petition was launched by the "People's Alliance for Switzerland's Independence," a pro-German organization that had been demanding, since its inception in 1921, that Switzerland cancel its membership in the League of Nations. It was signed by 173 individuals and included eight points demanding that freedom of the press be further curtailed, certain printed media be "eradicated," certain influential editors be "cast aside . . . the persons whose political activities [had] had obvious negative consequences for the country be removed from public office," some cases be retried and some criminal investigations be re-examined by "impartial" authorities.[33] Had the petition been approved, it could have resulted in a far-reaching compromise with the German Reich on the intellectual level. By demanding that the editors of the most influential daily newspapers be removed from their jobs, the group reiterated the request that the German press attaché Dr. Trump had made in vain in July 1940, a few days after Germany's victory in France.[34]

The petitioners included 80 serving officers, including 32 staff officers (14 colonels, 11 lieutenant-colonels, and 7 majors), plus one retired colonel.[35] Several of them were said to have been influenced to sign the petition by their superiors in the military, without being fully aware that by doing so they had promoted a cunning attempt to bring Switzerland largely in line with Hitler's "New Europe." After the war, Hausamann, a declared opponent of the "Two Hundred," explained that he was "completely convinced that the large majority of the officers who signed the petition [would] not have done so if they had been civilians being their own masters. . . . Anyone who accuses these officers of failing to do their duty like any other soldier does them wrong."[36]

Possibly some of the signatories were naïve, believing that the petition was merely an attempt to clip the wings of the press. However, there is no doubt that even those petitioners who were guided by honorable patriotic intentions misjudged the situation and aspired to commit an act of political injustice. Their questionable understanding of democracy could have brought about the self-destruction of the country's political system. Above all, astute personalities like Hektor Ammann, Heinrich Frick, and Andreas von Sprecher, who were the first persons to sign the petition, had to be aware of the implications of censoring the press to accommodate Germany and of applying political pressure to have sentences that had been passed down by regular courts reconsidered.

Asked to examine the petition, the Federal Prosecutor suggested that the Federal Council publicly repudiate the "monstrous and incomprehensible demands" instead of replying to the petitioners in person.[37] However, the Federal Council unfortunately failed to follow his advice and classified the petition without reacting to it at all at that time.

In the spring of 1941, General Guisan received a copy of the petition for his information from one of its first signatories, Wilhelm Frick. He certainly did not sympathize with the political convictions of the Two Hundred. However, it is interesting that he thanked Frick for the mailing, telling him, "I noticed that your opinion about the attitude of the press matches mine." He also explained:

> However, not only the attitude of the press matters to the army command but to a much greater extent also the fact that the Press and Radio Section has to monitor the press on behalf of, and on orders of, the commander-in-chief, which causes nothing but trouble. Hence, I have already asked the Federal Council several times to relieve the army command of the task of censoring the press during wartime duty

because this censorship leads to nothing but unnecessary conflicts for the army during times of armed neutrality. Unfortunately, and much to my regret, the Federal Council did not make the changes that I had so urgently suggested. In case of war, the army will of course take all the measures [necessary] to make censorship efficient exclusively for its own purposes.[38]

After the war, when a quarrel flared up in connection with the Petition of the Two Hundred, causing a storm of indignation, in a letter to Federal President Kobelt, Guisan distanced himself from the demands of the petitioners. He claimed that he had not known about the petition or at least that he had not taken note of it, arguing that the letter to Wilhelm Frick dated April 4, 1941, did not refer to the controversial petition to the Federal Council but only to some personal statements by Frick and Frick's letter to the "Committee for Media Policy" which he said he had received at the same time.[39]

Even after the Federal Council had given him several negative replies in 1940, General Guisan remained focused on the issue of censorship and on the question of who should be responsible for it. When the "Liaison Office for Press-Related Matters," which reported to the Department of the Interior and was headed by editor Max Nef, began its activities on January 31, 1941, the commander-in-chief once again brought up the issue with the Federal Council. In his letter, which Barbey drafted based on notes by Colonel Logoz, the General asked Federal Councilor Kobelt to reexamine the question of who should oversee the Press and Radio Section. He apparently tried to gain the support of the new Head of the Military Department in this matter, asking him whether it would not be "the logical consequence of how things have evolved" to put the entire Press and Radio Section under the responsibility of the Department of the Interior. He argued, "It would not be difficult to find ways, with the help of the Press and Radio Section, that would satisfy both the Federal Council and the army."[40]

Kobelt took four weeks to reply to the General's letter, which indicates that he was not particularly interested in the issue. He simply informed him that the Federal Council was aware of the problem and had ordered the Justice and Police Department to reexamine the facts in coordination with the Military Department and the Department of Foreign Affairs.[41]

The General also attempted to win over the second newly elected member of the government, Eduard von Steiger, to advance a matter that seemed to have become more and more pressing in terms of the army's reputation. Barbey was sent to Bern to plead the army's cause. He reported about his visit:

The General sends me to see Federal Councilor von Steiger, the new Head of the Justice and Police Department, in order to talk to him about the issue of who should oversee the Press and Radio Section. I have with me copies of the letters through which the commander-in-chief has asked the Federal Council four times since February 1940 to take on the responsibility for this task. These letters remained unanswered. They explain why it seems to be abnormal for the army to be put in charge of such a task. The General has been so angry that some of this emotion undoubtedly transpires in my conversation with Mr. von Steiger. First he looks at me from the side; that is normal. Then he responds favorably, telling me that he has not dealt with this issue yet but will examine it very carefully, especially because he says that he perfectly understands the army command's reaction.[42]

Two days later, the General received von Steiger in Gümligen for a meeting, during which the issue of the press was undoubtedly addressed. Guisan reminded the Head of the Justice and Police Department about it after he had not heard from him for a month. The General showed his disappointment by writing that he could not believe that the government continued to have no interest in an issue of such significance and of which it had to be aware. He threatened to "monitor the press only regarding military aspects (secrecy of issues dealing with the national defense)" in the future if the Federal Council did not grant his request to change the existing situation.[43] In another letter, Guisan once again pointed out to the Head of the Military Department how important it was to him to put the Section under the Federal Council's responsibility. He argued that a change was "urgently required, as [he had] explained several times in letters regarding this issue."[44]

Because von Steiger was in principle interested in the issue, it was finally given some serious consideration on the Federal Council and a solution began to take shape. Nevertheless, it is surprising how slow the flow of communication moved and how patient Guisan remained. Kobelt ignored Guisan's letter, and von Steiger also waited one month before explaining to the General that there was much goodwill, but that in view of changing the reporting status of the section, some clarifications were taking time. He stated, "The army's urgent request to the Federal Council and in particular to the Justice and Police Department . . . to take on the full responsibility requires getting everything ready that is needed to take over the entire system."[45] However, the General's entourage suspected that the administration, in order to procrastinate, was making the transition look more difficult than it really was.[46]

On May 7, 1941, the General submitted to von Steiger a stack of reports and comments he had received from Switzerland's military attachés and from private individuals, mostly from individuals living in Germany. They were highly critical of the Swiss press and made accusations against the authorities, especially against the army command, declaring it responsible for the language that was used in "tendentious articles" directed against the Axis powers. In his cover letter, Guisan once again reminded von Steiger of the proposals he had made on earlier occasions and explained that he did not ignore the difficulties that transferring the Press and Radio Section to the civilian authorities entailed. He said that he also had an interest in avoiding "tensions or conflicts between the Federal Council and the army command," yet he reiterated, "Should the existing system continue to stay in place, I would be obliged to declare to the Federal Council that I will henceforth be able to take on with a clear conscience only the responsibility for censoring military information."[47]

In view of this warning cry, the Federal Council could no longer ignore the commander-in-chief's request and now responded more quickly. Two days later, the General was offered the opportunity to personally present the army's request during a meeting at Federal President Wetter's private apartment in Bern. According to a memorandum that he had Barbey draw up for the occasion, he pointed out that even though it was necessary in that difficult situation to show strength of mind and determination, one also had to keep quiet, search one's heart, and "call a halt to all protests or manifestations that [were] incompatible with the principle of neutrality." In addition, he said that he did not want to repeat what he had explained to the government some time ago, both verbally and in writing, but wanted to "make another urgent appeal" to the Federal Council to bring the Press and Radio Section under its authority.[48]

Guisan used a new argument during the talks, referring to the Scandinavian countries, Belgium, Holland, and the Balkans, where he said it was considered a matter of course that the civilian authorities censored the press. He said that it was difficult for him to see what important reasons could exist for this issue to be handled differently in Switzerland. He repeated, "Time is short, and you will certainly understand that the commander-in-chief can no longer accept to oversee an organization that receives instructions from various Federal Departments after being denied the right to use pre-publication censorship, which he had been asking from the Federal Council since the summer of 1940 as the only means to fulfill his mission." Guisan argued that the current "awkward situation" was potentially damaging to the interests of the state.[49]

During the entire first half of 1941, the two parties did not move much closer to reaching an agreement on the issue; however, thanks to Federal Councilor von Steiger's efforts, in the course of the summer a decisive step was made toward finding a solution. Barbey commented, "It is fitting to state that the military owes this to Mr. von Steiger, who was the most important, if not the only, supporter on the Federal Council of a change of status. His Department will be put in charge of a new task. Thanks are due also to Captain Gut, who has a clear picture of this confusing matter as well as the ability to make correct judgments and the patience and tact to bring the matter to a successful close."[50]

On August 29, 1941, the decisive meeting which put an end to the dilemma that had existed since early 1940 was held at Guisan's home in Pully. The only person who attended the meeting in addition to Federal Councilor von Steiger, the General, and the Chief of his Personal Staff Barbey was Theodor Gut, who had been working as liaison officer between the Federal Council and the Press and Radio Section. In line with the army command's request, it was decided that the task of censoring the press should be handled entirely by the Justice and Police Department. In an exchange of letters dated August 29 and September 5, 1941, the agreement was put into specific terms and confirmed in writing. On November 14, von Steiger submitted the proposal to the Cabinet, which unanimously approved it on December 30, 1941, and put it in force effective February 1, 1942.[51] During a reception on New Year's Eve of 1941 at Guisan's home, "Verte Rive," Federal Councilor von Steiger told the General, "I am offering you a beautiful Christmas present by taking over the Press and Radio Section."[52]

According to the agreement, the section, which included ten sub-sections, continued to be headed by officers, but they were detailed to the Department of Justice and Police. Colonel Perrier remained at its helm. A "Press Secretariat," headed by Captain Gut, served as liaison between the head of the department and the Press and Radio Section, which remained a military body. In fact, the basic change consisted of nominally putting the civilian authorities in charge of censoring the press. The emergency press legislation remained unchanged.

In contrast to this resolution of the Press and Radio Section issue, differences continued to exist until the end of the war regarding the "Army and Home" section, which the Federal Council would have liked to oversee or even close down.[53] As late as January 10, 1942, the Head of the Military Department made a speech to the army staff in which he advocated transferring that section to the Department of the Interior.[54] Another delicate issue was the Press Office at army headquarters, which the army command also wanted to keep under its auspices because it served as the army's own internal news agency and publishing house.[55] The General ultimately imposed his wishes in both contested matters.

The Press Office of the army staff, for which the General fought with determination and which continued to report to Masson's intelligence service, was the army's main public relations tool. It was in charge of informing the army and the population, through press releases and statements, about anything pertaining to the national defense as defined by the army command. The head of the Press Office, Captain Hans Rudolf Schmid,[56] a publicist, had a considerable number of reporters, correspondents, cameramen, and photographers available to accomplish the task. Between 1939 and 1945, a total of 63 soldiers, including one female soldier from the Women's Auxiliary Service, ranked anywhere from Member of the Auxiliary Service to Captain, took turns serving in the Press Office.[57] During that time, 1,347 articles, reports, accounts of maneuvers, interviews, and other features were published, two-thirds of which were written in German and the rest mostly in French. During the last five months of the war, from January to May 1945, the Press Office wrote 130 articles that were published in 250 different newspapers. Reports, news items, and photographs were censored internally. About 22 percent of photographs (5,600 out of 25,700) were declared secret and could therefore not be published.[58] The operating costs for the Press Office were not insignificant, amounting to 91,500 francs over a period of seven months. The office was mostly funded through the credit line that the General had available for his own headquarters.[59]

The new solution in terms of overseeing the Press and Radio Section turned out to be appropriate and remained in force until the end of the war. National Councilor Feldmann explained to the General that the new reporting structure proved to be "a political success," adding, "What a difference it makes when the Federal Council and head of department who is responsible for monitoring the press has to explain himself whenever Parliament voices any criticism. In the past, the Federal Council was able to hide behind the commander-in-chief of the armed forces."[60]

Controlling the newspapers after they were published was a relatively mild way of censoring the press. This method was maintained until the end of the war. Journalists from different political camps handled it not in a dictatorial manner but in a fairly democratic way. However, according to contemporary historian Jean Rudolf von Salis, this type of censorship was "a rather hypocritical exercise,"[61] meaning that its existence had to be kept as inconspicuous as possible to the public. Georg Kreis correctly qualifies the system as self-imposed censorship, explaining, "The instrument used by dictators and totalitarian rulers was enriched with some democratic ingredients, so to speak, in order to create a type of censorship that was appropriate for the democratic order of this small country."[62]

At the beginning of the war, Switzerland's press consisted of approximately 400 publications, daily and weekly newspapers. About half of their editors and journalists were of age to serve in the military: one third of them were officers, another third were non-commissioned officers, and a third belonged to the rank-and-file.[63] Many served in the Press and Radio Section. According to confidential instructions from the Section, the journalists' choice of topics was limited, and they had to write in a straightforward style. A decree made it forbidden to disseminate news and comments "that harm or jeopardize Switzerland's independence, security, or neutrality."[64] An inappropriate comment or style could entail "light" or "heavy" sanctions. Von Salis remarked, "Generally speaking, when committing the first offense, the culprit was reprimanded, warned, or his article was banned. I personally had the honor of being threatened with the heaviest type of sanction, imprisonment, right away because I had criticized the way in which military matters were censored."[65]

The staff of the official censorship bureaus included editors, university teachers, legal professionals, and publicists. For example, the censorship bureau in Basel was directed by Robert Haab, Professor of Civil Law; the staff also included historian Edgar Bonjour and Max Gerwig, the Senior Judge on the Civil Court.[66] Bonjour wrote about this "difficult and exciting" task, "In the morning, we very quickly checked whether any article violated the decree issued by the Press and Radio Section. . . . Using sharp language was of course permitted or often even desirable, especially when it came to refuting attacks by the German press." However, lecturing foreign countries was taboo and censored. Bonjour explained, "By being fortunate to be spared from the bloodbath, one does not gain the right to preach and moralize. . . . We had to pronounce quite a few warnings against our personal convictions simply because we had to respect the decree."[67]

It appears curious that Guisan repeatedly voiced concerns that the attitude of and articles written by the Swiss press might play a crucial part in influencing the German leadership's decision whether or not to attack Switzerland. He argued that the press had to be restrained so as not to irritate the German dictator through provocative language. A number of Germans claimed, especially in conversations with influential business and military people, that if Switzerland were attacked it would be because of its press. Schwarz commented that "unfortunately [this opinion] had more than just a few supporters."[68] Even the commander-in-chief, who was influenced by Masson in this respect, obviously tended to share this view. Gonzague de Reynold, who was in contact with Guisan, wrote in his diary that it would be "lamentable" if Switzerland were drawn into the war because of the carelessness of some irresponsible journalists, adding, "The entire Federal Council, and I may say also General Guisan, is preoccupied by this."[69]

Divisional Commander Bircher, who had the opportunity to meet with several prominent Germans while attending a surgeons' convention in Berlin in the spring of 1941, thought it necessary to send the General an "urgent report" through the Swiss Legation in which he pointed out that the mood toward Switzerland had "worsened and become less favorable." He added that several times the word "war" had been mentioned to him in connection with the attitude of the Swiss press. He told the General, "Germany is running out of patience because of the attacks by the Swiss press. . . . If our country suffers hardship and misery or is even drawn into a war, we will have to thank these ignorant, irresponsible press people for it."[70]

General Guisan, who must have studied Bircher's report carefully, took notes on what should be done:

1. Ease tensions immediately, send messenger to Berlin and Rome, launch counterattack.
2. Solve issue of the press in order to relieve Swiss command.
3. Government to take action among the population. We don't want to be beaten up by the press.[71]

It is possible that Guisan took these notes after Bircher had returned from Germany and he had met with him personally. At any rate, the notes indicate that the General's notion of the responsibility of the press for the possibility of an invasion had been reinforced, causing him to intensify his efforts to free the army command from the task of monitoring the press.

In some undated notes, the General gave a description of his concept of freedom of the press, stating, "The freedom of the press is sacred to me as long as it does not jeopardize Switzerland's integrity."[72] These words may have been part of a radio address to soldiers which is quoted in part by Chapuisat, in which General Guisan elaborated:

It would be undignified to put someone's personal opinion above public welfare by using the freedom of speech as a pretext. It would go against the country's interests to carry out ideological debates in public, especially during this time of upheaval. . . . Imagine there are some windbags in this besieged fortress. They are the abscesses that cause infections to spread. They are the same kind of traitors as defeatists and cowards. I call upon you to be disciplined and not to be part of those windbags.[73]

On the issue of press responsibility, Guisan's view was the same as that of Pilet-Golaz or that part of the army influenced by Wille and Däniker. In the summer of 1940, in an effort to pressure the government into further restraining the press, Wille told Federal Councilor Etter, "Nowadays the freedom of the press is nonsense. A government that lets the press do as it likes does not want to make policies that are different from those advocated by the press."[74] Däniker, who also made frequent reference to the responsibility of the press, repeatedly warned that the obstreperous language of the press posed a threat to the country. Councilor of State Löpfe, who struggled with Däniker to get him to change his mind, replied to the Colonel:

> You believe that the press carries the bulk of the blame for the tension. That is a primitive scapegoat theory that does not in the least look into the real causes of this attitude. Colonel, I am asking you, a high-ranking officer of the Swiss Army, 'Do you think that the press would have shown strength of character and Swiss uprightness if it had kept quiet about Austria, Czechoslovakia, Norway, Denmark, Holland, Belgium, Luxembourg, and Greece being raped?' By the way, all these countries were crushed without the press being to blame for it! Should Switzerland, a free country, be silent when it sees such a terrible amount of injustice, violence, and suppression?

Löpfe wrote that he did not think that by occasionally overstepping the boundaries, the press was creating any danger, adding that even Bismarck had explained to the Reichstag that "newspaper articles never cause a war."[75]

The idea that the press would be to blame if Switzerland were attacked was vociferously rejected for obvious reasons by intellectual and political leaders and by the group who had formed the Officers' Conspiracy, with backing for their views from a large majority of the population. Many realized that the idea was merely "part of the propaganda arsenal that Germany used in a systematic psychological war against Switzerland."[76] In July 1940, during a meeting of the editorial board of the *Neue Zürcher Zeitung,* Editor-in-Chief Willy Bretscher had to defend the newspaper's position, recalling that it was the Swiss press, in addition to other factors, that had "saved Switzerland during the past few years from being conquered without putting up a fight." He believed that the press had to continue its work along those same lines, arguing, "In the recent past, being nice and friendly did not keep any country from being attacked and occupied."[77]

In late 1940, after the Officers' Conspiracy had been uncovered, Alfred Ernst, who constantly undertook efforts to strengthen the spirit of resistance, wrote a long letter to Chief of Intelligence Masson in which he defended the attitude of the press, stating:

I am sure that further concessions by our press would not improve our position because the Germans basically do not care what we write. They would simply consider us as cowards and weaklings and would put even more pressure on us than in the past. The complaining about the supposed anti-German attitude of our press is just a pretext like any other they use. If they did not have this pretext anymore, they would come up with another one. Have you ever heard anyone say that the Romanian, the Belgian, or even the Dutch press had insulted or criticized Germany? And yet the Germans came up with more than enough reasons to invade these countries. . . . If we are no longer allowed to tell our people what is right and wrong and what is true and false, we weaken their sense of the idea on which our state is built. If we tacitly accept that it was 'politically necessary' or 'inevitable for strategic reasons' for the Germans to break their word, we pronounce our own death sentence.[78]

Federal Councilor Kobelt rejected the theory of press responsibility as well. According to Barbey, during the debriefing after an operational exercise by the army in February 1941, Kobelt addressed the issue of the Swiss press, among other things, "emphasizing that its attitude could be used only as a pretext, not as a reason to attack Switzerland, and if this was not the most suitable pretext, 'one' would simply find another one." Barbey commented that this was "perfectly clear" and that the statements by the Head of the Military Department had "made a good overall impression."[79]

As with their colleagues in the Social Democrat press, the editors-in-chief of the leading conservative newspapers in Switzerland, Ernst Schürch of the *Bund*, Willy Bretscher of the *Neue Zürcher Zeitung*, and Albert Oeri of the *Basler Nachrichten*, who were supposed to be "cast aside" and whose publications were targeted for "eradication" according to the Petition of the Two Hundred, complained about the freedom of the press being increasingly curtailed. According to the minutes of a meeting of the Joint Liaison Office for Press-Related Matters, National Councilor Oeri said, "Certain senior officials often tend to support the point of view of a foreign country rather than that of Switzerland." In addition, National Councilor Arthur Schmid of the *Freier Aargauer* criticized the fact that the existing censorship prevented the press from defending humanity by criticizing the cruelties committed by foreign countries. He added, "This would cause our populace to lose its intellectual autonomy, which in turn [would pose] a threat to the national defense."[80]

As early as during the Phony War, National Councilor Robert Grimm had used similar words in a speech at a plenary meeting of the Social Democratic

Party of Canton Bern, stating, "These days unfortunately there are officers who believe that if the freedom of the press was curtailed and the press was put in line with German interests by simply transmitting news, there would no longer be any cause for conflict between Germany and Switzerland. This naïve opinion by naïve military people must be countered with firmness."[81]

In 1943, National Councilor Markus Feldmann, an editor of the *Neue Berner Zeitung*, spoke with Pilet-Golaz about the issue of censorship, telling the Foreign Minister that Germany was not guided by the goodwill of any country's press in making its strategic decisions. If the Third Reich intended to attack Switzerland, it would do so "even if the entire Swiss press shouted, 'Heil Hitler'."[82] Feldmann, who told the General about this conversation most likely with an ulterior motive, recounted that Pilet-Golaz "fully agreed with my opinion that the press would not be the triggering factor if [Germany] had already made up its mind to attack Switzerland. However, he argued that Hitler might make an 'emotional decision' which could be triggered by statements made by the press, and this had to be prevented. He said that Hitler was unpredictable."[83] Hence, it appears that Pilet-Golaz and Guisan had similar views and shared the same concerns about the possibility that Switzerland's press might influence the Führer's decisions, even though they did not have much else in common.

History has shown beyond a doubt that the freedom of a responsible press, and of responsible media in general, is the most important tool for real democracy to exist in an independent state. A democratic society is unthinkable without the freedom of speech. Publicist Paul Schmid-Ammann commented in the *Nation* that freedom of the press was "the last trench in the fight for freedom."[84] Nevertheless, it was clear to everyone that in the middle of the war journalists had to restrain themselves and that representatives of the totalitarian regimes north and south of Switzerland should not be provoked unnecessarily through personal insults.

General Guisan's demand that pre-publication censorship should be introduced is questionable not only from today's perspective. Alfred Ernst wrote that one of the lessons of the period between 1939 and 1945 was the value of the freedom of the press, and that restraining it would bring "great risks and drawbacks." He added, "If out of consideration for foreign powers the press is no longer allowed to state the whole truth, over time the people's sense of what is right and wrong, and therefore its determination to put up resistance, will suffer. One does not believe the press when it is controlled."[85] Ernst bluntly called the General's attitude a "political mistake" but added in his favor, "When judging the General's political mistake, one has to take into consideration that his intervention in favor of pre-publication censorship, which was unjustified from an objective perspective, seemed to result from the unfortunate way in which responsibilities were assigned in press-related matters, which was later changed."[86]

Hermann Böschenstein agrees that in retrospect one has to admit that if pre-publication censorship had been introduced as the General advocated, "It would have put a fateful strain on the Federal Government in view of keeping up the spirit of resistance in the country."[87] In his personal account of the wartime period, Böschenstein echoed sensible political leaders in saying that he was "absolutely convinced that any blood-guilt theory [was] nonsense."[88] However, Böschenstein also gave Guisan some credit in connection with the censorship issue, stating, "How could he have realized the consequences of such a measure? He had never dealt with the problems that arise when the press is censored and so had to rely on his advisors."[89] This author tends to believe that the General's attitude can be explained through the political views that he had embraced in the 1930s.

In the course of the war, the traditional liberal forces and the mostly unified Social Democratic movement in Switzerland turned out to be strong enough to successfully withstand the pressure exercised by authoritarian right-wing groups to introduce pre-publication censorship. The Federal Council and the General wavered for too long before they hesitantly took the stand favored by the majority of the people.

On July 25, 1940, General Guisan summoned his unit commanders to the Rütli Meadow on Lake Lucerne where, according to legend, in 1291 three fearless Swiss Confederates made the oath of independence that led to the founding of Switzerland. Through this briefing the commander-in-chief managed to rally his officers, and subsequently the entire army and population, behind the idea of unconditional resistance. (Photo from Werner Rings, *Die Schweiz im Krieg*)

General Guisan talking with Colonel-Corps Commander Ulrich Wille (left) at the Allmend (commons) in Bern on August 31, 1940. (ArMa)

General Guisan leaving the central office for prisoners of war at the International Committee of the Red Cross (ICRC), followed by ICRC President Prof. Max Huber, in early 1941. (Photo from the ICRC archives)

Swiss Independence Day celebration, August 1, 1941. The General, Federal President Wetter, and the commander of the parading troops taking the salute at a review in front of the Federal Letter Archives in Schwyz. (BAr)

General Guisan talking to Federal Councilor Karl Kobelt, who became Head of the Federal Military Department in 1941. Kobelt was a former officer of the general staff, and occasionally got involved in matters that fell under the General's authority. (BAr)

General Guisan in discussion with Divisional Commander Eugen Bircher from Aargau during a review of the 5th Division in Root, on April 17, 1942. (Photo from the author's personal archives)

Colonel Gustav Däniker (right) during a shooting demonstration at the army's training facility in Walenstadt. (Photo from the archives of the *Weltwoche* newspaper)

A combat exercise of the 1st Grenadiers (33rd Regiment) was held before representatives of the Axis Powers at the Schwägalp, on July 15, 1942. General Guisan shakes hands with Captain Brunner, head of the exercise, as German officers (background) look on. (Photo by Hans Steiner)

A secret meeting at Wolfsberg Castle in 1943. Head of German SS Foreign Intelligence, General Walter Schellenberg, is flanked by SS Major Hans Wilhelm Eggen (left) and Albert Wiesendanger, commander of the Zürich city police. The castle had been put at their disposal by its owner, Swiss Captain Paul Meyer-Schwertenbach. (Still photo from an 8mm film by Patrizia Meyer-Schwertenbach)

The chief of Switzerland's Intelligence Service, Colonel-Brigadier Roger Masson, left, talking with Chief of the General Staff Jakob Huber. Masson's clandestine meetings with Walter Schellenberg would later become a source of controversy. (BAr)

1944 promotion ceremony for high-ranking officers in front of the monument at Les Rangiers, which commemorates wartime duty from 1914 to 1918. (BAr)

French General de Lattre de Tassigny introducing General Guisan to the commander of the troops holding a parade in Constance on June 13, 1945. (BAr)

The General in the company of Italian customs officers, released Allied POWs and armed partisans at the border at Chiasso on May 5, 1945. This photograph was originally censored from public view. (BAr)

The General insisted that a salute to the flag be held to commemorate the end of the war. Three Cabinet members represented the government at the event. In front of the Federal Palace on August 19, 1945 are, from left to right, Federal Councilors Enrico Celio and Karl Kobelt, Federal President Eduard von Steiger, and General Guisan. (Photo by Hans Steiner)

A bird's eye view of the salute to the flag in front of the Federal Palace.
(Photo by Hans Steiner)

General Guisan at his office at the barracks in Lausanne in 1945, working on his report on wartime duty. (BAr)

Reception for Britain's Field Marshal Bernard Montgomery at the Federal Palace in 1946. From left to right, General Guisan, an interpreter, Federal Councilor Petitpierre, Federal President Karl Kobelt, and Montgomery. (BAr)

After his retirement, General Guisan enjoyed walking and riding his horse "Nobs."
(BAr)

Soldiers carrying the General's coffin through the gates of the "Verte Rive" mansion. The coffin was wrapped with the Swiss flag. (BAr)

The Crisis of June 1944

DURING THE FIFTH YEAR OF THE WAR, relations between the civilian and military authorities underwent their most serious test when, in June 1944, General Guisan raised the question of whether part of the army should be mobilized once again in connection with the Allied landings in Normandy. Because of various frictions resulting from either policy differences or highhandedness, relations between the Federal Council and the General had by that time turned so sour that the two parties avoided each other as much as possible. It seems that tensions had become so great that one suspects that certain members of the government could hardly stand seeing the commander-in-chief.[1]

As early as the summer of 1942, when Plan of Operations No. 14 was prepared, the army command had discussed what measures would have to be taken if the Allies were to set up a second front in the West. Without being contradicted by anyone, Chief of the General Staff Huber had stated, "It would not make any sense to mobilize troops at the moment when the English land in France. It could take the Allies weeks or months to get near the Swiss border, which is when we would have to mobilize the army. Hence, no troops should be called up until our country is actually in danger."[2]

In May 1944, however, new and alarming information reached Switzerland through diplomatic channels. After the Germans had invaded Hungary, Minister Maximilian Jaeger, Switzerland's envoy in Budapest, reported confidential warnings from various people that the Germans were planning to take action in the near future against Switzerland as well. He explained that they were planning to do so less for strategic reasons than because they were concerned about having "a foreign body that [was] full of Allied spies" very close to the border of the Reich.[3] A few days later, at the end of May, Jaeger sent another warning to Bern, reporting claims that "Germany's military strategy against Switzerland [was] ready." The troops slated to carry out the surprise attack would allegedly be deployed to Alsace. This move would be "camouflaged as a precautionary step in case of an Allied invasion from the West."[4]

This pessimistic report caused the army command to examine what precautions it should take to meet the looming danger. The procedure that was followed provides an interesting example of how options were prepared at the top command level before the decision was made by the commander-in-chief. On June 1, Masson and his closest aides in the intelligence service met with Barbey to discuss the situation after receiving the worrisome information. They did not attach too much significance to the alert from Budapest, yet they noticed once again that there were relatively few troops on duty. They did not consider mobilizing the entire army, knowing that this measure "would neither be understood nor accepted," but they thought the warnings provided a good opportunity to bolster the defense by calling up additional troops. They aspired to have one or two divisions, or the entire border forces, called up and to increase the state of alert for the facilities that had been prepared for demolition in the event of invasion. However, they knew that Chief of the General Staff Huber would be very reluctant to approve these steps. In two meetings on May 31 and June 1, Masson had been unable to convince him that additional measures needed to be taken.[5]

At Barbey's suggestion, after thinking things over for a day, Masson decided to present a written assessment of the situation to Huber and to insist that "a minimal number of measures be taken, compatible with our economic situation." Huber forwarded Masson's proposal to the General, suggesting to him not to take any action for the time being. Instead, he proposed summoning the commanders of the army corps to a meeting on June 6 to find out what they thought about the situation.[6] Barbey informed the Head of the Operational Section, Gonard, about Huber's suggestion, telling him, "For now, the chief of the general staff does not think it is necessary to propose to the General to take any new measures, except for the following minor steps: increase the number of horses and motor vehicles for the reserve units of the 1st, 2nd, and 4th Army Corps up to the number stipulated in the regulations; and get the designated objects in the border area ready for demolition."[7]

In order to prepare for the briefing with the corps commanders, the General called Huber, Masson, Gonard, Barbey, and Bracher (the liaison officer with the Military Department), to a meeting at his command post. During that meeting, Huber reiterated his opinion that no additional troops should be called up, recommending that the army command should wait to receive additional information. He argued that the danger was not as great as it had been in 1940 because the Germans no longer had the same victorious armies available.

No decision was made at that meeting. The General decided only that the Federal Council should be contacted as soon as possible and that the results of the briefing with the corps commanders, which was scheduled for the following day, should be awaited.[8] It is striking that in this situation of uncertainty, there was no mention of the "Viking" connection, nor of the controversial "Schellenberg" connection, both of which apparently remained silent.

The briefing on June 6, 1944, which the General opened at 11:00 a.m. at the office of the general staff section at the Federal Palace, was dominated by the first news of the Allied landings in Normandy, which made the long-awaited second front in the West a reality. Barbey gave a detailed account in his diary of the struggle with the Federal Council regarding the issue of mobilizing additional troops. He described how Guisan was confident, stating, "The General speaks with his 'metallic' voice, which always sounds very clear and warm to me during critical moments. It is the same voice that I heard during the difficult times in 1940 and in March 1943, sometimes with a hint of cheerfulness. He explains to the corps commanders what he has been told by [Switzerland's envoy to] Hungary before the beginning of the invasion. Then he briefly reminds them of the significance of the Swiss sector on the European chessboard in connection with 'fortress Europe'."[9]

After Masson had given an assessment of the situation, Chief of the General Staff Huber developed his ideas. He suspected that the Germans might have intended to take care of "Case Switzerland" before the invasion began in the West, but that the landings on the southern coast of the English Channel had complicated things for them, thwarting their intentions for the time being. He warned, however, that Switzerland was not yet out of harm's way because the German Army still had two dozen divisions left with which they could attempt a coup against the country. Nevertheless, Huber considered that it was not necessary to call up the entire army, and that only precautions should be taken that would allow the troops to be mobilized if necessary. For that purpose, he suggested immediately calling up all border units, the demolition troops, and the air force and antiaircraft defense by means of public notices.[10]

All corps commanders and assistant chiefs of staff Gonard and Masson agreed with Huber that it was imperative to increase the number of troops, as only a third of the army was currently on duty. Barbey commented that he had "never seen before that everyone shared the same opinion at a briefing with the corps commanders."[11] The General agreed, concluding the briefing by stating, "All participants agree on the suggested reinforcement measures. These measures will be submitted to the Federal Council for approval."[12]

That afternoon, the General went with Barbey to see the Head of the Military Department at the Federal Palace to submit the request for calling up the designated troops. Kobelt agreed with the army command's proposal; in addition, he suggested also calling up the three light brigades except for the dragoon squadrons to replace the troops that were soon scheduled to go off duty. The General readily agreed with that suggestion.

While Kobelt went into a special Federal Council meeting, Guisan waited at Huber's office for the government's decision. During that time, the orders through which the additional troops were to be called up were being prepared for signature. It was not until 5:30 p.m., after Guisan had waited for three and a half hours, that the Head of the Military Department called the General into his office. Kobelt told the astonished Guisan that the government did not consider the situation following the start of the invasion to be very alarming and therefore rejected his request. He said that the Cabinet had only agreed to call up the air force and antiaircraft defense and the light brigades, but that it considered calling up the border units superfluous. A chronological account of the events, probably written by Barbey, stated, "The Head of the Military Department regrets that this decision was made against his proposal."[13] The Federal Council argued that the foreign political situation was no longer so threatening, and it feared that calling up too many troops could have adverse consequences for the country's economy and negative repercussions on the army's morale.

The General considered that by rejecting his request the government had interfered in his authority as commander-in-chief. He replied to Kobelt that he did not understand the decision and could not bear the responsibility of its consequences. Nevertheless, he said that in order to ease his conscience, he would order the general staff to examine the possibility of carrying out the "half-measure" that the Federal Council had decided.[14]

In a letter several pages long drafted by Barbey that same evening, the General explained to the Federal Council why he objected to their point of view. He once again argued why it was necessary to immediately call up all border units, formally reiterating his first request. The General expressed his indignation by stating that he took note of the Federal Council's decision not to grant his formal request, by which he said the government was questioning his right to call up troops as stipulated in articles 204, 208, and 210 of the service regulations. "It is therefore questionable," he said, "that effective measures could be taken within a useful period of time in order to guarantee the security of the country if the situation worsened." He clearly rejected the argument that calling up too many troops could lead to a negative atmosphere among the population, stating, "It is my honor to remind you that on May 11, 1940, the entire armed forces were mobilized while the end of the campaign in France was not yet in sight, and they all remained on duty until the end of June. The country understood why this was done. I do not think that it would not understand this today. On the contrary, I fear that it is wondering or will wonder why we seem to be reacting so slowly by taking half-measures."[15]

The following day, the General addressed a similar letter to Kobelt, emphasizing once again the importance of his request. He wrote:

> Even after giving it some more thought, I cannot agree with the Federal Council's proposal to call up only half of the border troops. Based on article 210 of the service regulations, I formally reiterate my request to call up all border troops by means of the existing public notices. I am willing to take economic interests into account by granting leaves and reorganizing the units depending on the situation. . . . Fortunately we have been spared from being drawn into the war until now. Can it not be justified to make an additional effort so shortly before the end in order to avoid being pulled into the whirl of events at the last moment? I believe that in view of all the sacrifices that have already been made for the national defense, it is worth taking these precautions, and I am convinced that the population will understand this procedure as well.[16]

The General used all his powers of persuasion, including operational, strategic, and psychological arguments, to encourage the Federal Council to change its mind, all of which led to a long bout of haggling over the number of additional troops to be called up.

Kobelt informed the Federal Council in writing about his conversation with the General on the evening of June 6. He wrote that he had essentially told the commander-in-chief that "Objectively speaking, the Federal Council's decision produces the same result as the [General's] request, but it proposes proceeding in a different way. In terms of reinforcing the troops that are already stationed in these sectors, it does not really matter whether all border troops are called up (by means of public notices) and then put on leave after all, or whether only part of the border troops are called up (by means of individual notices sent by mail). However, the solution proposed by the Federal Council will prevent the population from being concerned the way it might if it saw public notices. Moreover, it creates fewer disadvantages for the economy and cuts down on the considerable costs to the Confederation."[17]

Some corps commanders also began asking themselves why it was absolutely necessary to call up additional troops. As Labhart wrote in his diary, "I am not very sure why the Federal Council did not approve the General's requests that had been discussed during the meeting on June 6. Apparently there are some economic reasons. The fact that our situation has been eased through the Allied invasion in northern France on Monday may also have contributed to its decision."[18] Considering the trusting relationship between Kobelt and Labhart, it does not seem impossible that the two men discussed the situation afterward in private.[19]

For his part, General Guisan sought the support of former Federal Councilor Minger. He wrote to him that as his friend he set great store in informing him of the "regrettable incident" with the government. He expressed hope that based on his explanations, the Federal Council would reconsider its decision and give him the means necessary to "keep the country perfectly secure and to ensure that the troops be mobilized."[20] It appears that Minger did not deny his support to the General. The next day, on June 8, the two friends met twice in Bern for discussions.[21] During a briefing, Guisan provided Corps Commanders Borel and Labhart with the confidential information that he had "also asked Federal Councilor Minger's opinion" about the issue.[22]

In addition to diverging assessments of the military and political situation, economic reasons played an essential part in the Federal Council's negative response to Guisan. Federal President Stampfli, the Head of the Department of Economy, voiced "serious concerns" about calling up additional troops because the economy in the country urgently needed manpower.[23] It seems that industry put some pressure on the Federal Council in this respect. In the summer of 1944, Antoine Vodoz, the president of the executive branch of the government of Canton Vaud, wrote to the General:

> I also want to tell you that there is a certain lack of understanding on the part of the most important industrialists in German-speaking and French-speaking Switzerland about keeping on duty the troops that were mobilized last June. They thought that it would be good to put some pressure on the Federal Council. I cannot tell you more about this right now, but I really wanted to let you know about it in case you have not been informed about the current state of mind in certain circles.[24]

The discussion about the usefulness of calling up troops ended up taking the form of a trial of strength between Federal Councilor Kobelt and General Guisan. Based on the written evidence, one gains the impression that the Head of the Military Department wanted to make the General understand clearly that as the representative of the political authorities he was above the army command, and that as a colonel on the general staff he was also well-versed in military matters. On June 8, he asked the General to come see him at the

Federal Palace. The General showed up for the afternoon meeting in the company of the chief of the general staff and the chief of his personal staff. Brigadier Burgunder, the Secretary at the Military Department, accompanied the Federal Councilor. Kobelt once again explained the Federal Council's position. Guisan referred to article 210 of the service regulations and reiterated his requests, emphasizing with determination, "Therefore I demand that the border troops be immediately called up by means of public notices, and I regret that this measure was not taken right away."[25] Chief of the General Staff Huber said that he completely agreed with the commander-in-chief, that he regretted the delay, and that "calling up the border troops [seemed] to be the least that [had] to be done."[26]

After both Guisan and Kobelt had once again briefly presented their arguments, each side insisted on its own point of view. It did not help the General to stress that the corps commanders unanimously supported his request; nor did it help when Huber opined that it was better to do too much than not enough. The Head of the Military Department pointed out that he wanted to avoid a conflict between the General and the Federal Council; but to all appearances he seemed rather pleased to be wielding authority on behalf of the Federal Council, refusing to make any concessions. Kobelt closed the meeting after almost an hour by stating that he considered the topic of the discussion exhausted.[27] He explained that the Federal Council would once again examine the issue—which the General qualified as "haggling"—and would make a final decision at its regular meeting the following day, Friday, June 9.

It should be noted that even though there were serious differences of opinion on a matter of principle, the commander-in-chief was not invited to take part in the Federal Council's deliberations. Only Kobelt communicated his arguments to the Cabinet. After the meeting on Friday morning, Kobelt telephoned the General and asked him to go to Bern to reach a settlement with him at the Federal Council's request. Guisan, who was apparently not willing to make another appearance at Kobelt's office, pretended that he was not available due to other obligations. Hence, Kobelt decided to go see the General at his headquarters in Interlaken. During the meeting that evening, during the course of which Huber was asked to join them, a compromise was reached. Kobelt agreed to have the border troops called up, with the exception of the territorial troops; however, they were to receive personal notices in the mail instead of public notices being posted everywhere in the country, which could have alarmed the population.[28] Proceeding in that manner meant that another four days would go by until the troops reported for duty. Guisan reluctantly agreed to the proposal.

The government held a special meeting the following morning and approved the compromise. On June 10, 1944, Kobelt was able to inform Guisan, "The General is authorized to call up about 80,000 border troops, without using public call-up notices. [The Federal Council] considers that leaves should be granted as soon as possible to as many soldiers as possible and that the number of troops on duty should be reduced as soon as the situation permits."[29]

The troops called up by means of individual notices in the mail had to report to their duty stations on the morning of June 15. An official press release of only one sentence was sent to all media, stating, "Taking into consideration the overall situation, in agreement with the General, the Federal Council has increased the state of readiness of our army by calling up additional troops."[30]

On the 15th, the General issued an order of the day to the fresh troops to explain the purpose of their mobilization. Referring to the war situation he argued, "It is better to fill one post too many than to leave one post too many unfilled! [... I shall] see to it that the measures that have been taken are continuously adapted to the security situation in order to take into account the jobs that are vital to you and to the country."[31]

Guisan remained convinced that the measures he had proposed were necessary, and he declared that the population shared his opinion and had difficulties understanding why the troops were not immediately mobilized when the invasion began. However, several reports stated that a number of soldiers were reluctant to be called up; many reported late to their duty stations, and incidents occurred that came close to mutiny. At the Federal Council meeting on June 19, President Stampfli informed his colleagues that while he was driving through eastern Switzerland, he had noticed that many troops were very unhappy "because they were not convinced that their presence was indispensable."[32] At its following meeting, the Federal Council once again discussed the mood among the troops. Pilet-Golaz noted, "The troops are very dissatisfied; they actually came close to staging a mutiny, making a number of measures necessary."[33]

Labhart's diary shows that even high-ranking officers questioned the call-up of troops. On the day they reported to their duty stations, he noted:

> It is indeed difficult to understand why at the present time border troops are called up, especially at our northern border. There is no threat, and for the time being no refugees are expected to arrive either. Therefore I consider that the mobilization of the border troops in that sector should be cancelled altogether, or else some troops could be sent off duty. In addition, a large number of troops should be granted leave. The commander of the 6th Division shares this opinion.[34]

One must keep in mind that these sentences were written by a corps commander on the day that the troops reported to their duty stations.

The crisis of June 1944 left Guisan in a bad mood. He resented the fact that he had not been invited to attend any of the meetings during which the Federal Council had discussed his requests. Instead, he had had to negotiate exclusively with the Head of the Military Department, with whom he had a strained relationship. As he told Barbey, "It was up to the Federal Council to call me into a meeting, not up to me to ask to be heard. What would I have had to do if the Federal Council had not granted my request to be heard? I would simply have had to resign. However, I would not want to resign because I asked a wrong question."[35]

In a letter to Kobelt, the General complained that he had not been consulted during any of the four meetings the Federal Council held during that critical time. He considered that in view of the diverging opinions it would have been not only normal but advantageous and necessary to have him present his arguments in person, arguing, "The General is responsible for military measures that are decided." Guisan wrote that, like the Federal Council, he wished to avoid an overt crisis between the government and the army command; however, he said that it was important to him to set things straight in order to remove any ambiguities about what had happened during the previous week. "That way," he added, "considering the circumstances which might arise in a very short period of time as the war progresses, we will avoid having measures that may have to be carried out right away being delayed once again."[36]

In its response, which Kobelt was ordered to write, the Federal Council evidently tried to pour oil on troubled waters, stating:

> First of all, we think that it would be wrong to speak of a conflict or a crisis of confidence. Yes, there were some differences of opinion during the negotiations, but they could be eliminated by coming to an agreement in personal meetings between you and the Head of the Military Department. Moreover, we expressly declare that the Federal Council would not have categorically rejected a discussion with you on issues pertaining to the national defense in a plenary meeting or among a delegation, neither during the deliberations in question nor on any other occasion.

The letter not only said that the General had never expressed the wish to be heard directly by the Federal Council, but that his presence was unnecessary anyway because the Head of the Military Department had "defended the General's point of view to the Federal Council and explained all arguments supporting his point of view." The Federal Council said that it was convinced that rumors were unfounded that there were critical tensions with the army command, and that it knew "how to avoid conflicts" in the future as well, adding, "We believe that it is safe to assume that you share our opinion. After all, we both have the same objectives."[37]

In the meantime, the dispute on the issue of calling up troops had come to the attention of some members of Parliament. In his letter to the Federal Council, the General claimed that members of Parliament had addressed and questioned him about the existing discord. At its meeting on June 19, the Federal Council discussed that matter, and both Federal President Stampfli and Federal Councilor Etter rejected the General's version of the story, stating, "Contrary to what the General said, it was not members of Parliament who approached him about the differences of opinion between the Federal Council and the General . . . but it was the General himself [who approached them]."[38] The Federal President indicated that he knew at which restaurant the conversation had taken place and who the members were. The government was particularly displeased about Guisan's way of proceeding. The minutes of the meeting stated, "Mr. Etter pointed out that the General had not only weakened the Federal Council's position but also his own position, because through members of Parliament the public realized that the Federal Council was not as convinced as the General about the need to call up such a considerable number of troops right away."[39] During the discussion, Federal Councilors Celio and Nobs both said they were convinced that time would prove the government right.

It appears that Pilet-Golaz, who usually opposed Guisan, kept in the background during the discussions. Following another meeting during which the Federal Council criticized the army command, the Head of the Department of Foreign Affairs noted, "I did not say a word."[40]

The troops called up in June 1944 remained on duty for only a short period of time. As soon as a few days later, official discussions were held about calling them off duty again. During the last week of June, the Head of the Military Department intervened with the commander-in-chief to have the number of troops reduced. Kobelt wrote that the Federal Council wanted to be accommodating toward the agricultural sector, industry, and the business community. Before making any decision on that issue, the General insisted on consulting with his directly subordinate commanders and he called the corps commanders to a briefing in Bern on July 1.[41]

The meeting came to the conclusion that it was best to reestablish the deployment levels that had existed before June 15; that is, before the border troops had been called up. All corps commanders expressed that view, while the army command suggested releasing only about half of the newly mobilized troops from duty. Labhart noted his own contribution to the decision-making process: "Taking into consideration the current military and political situation (massive attacks by the Russians, bridgehead in Normandy), I request that the number of troops be reduced to the previous number." The three other corps commanders supported Labhart. He commented, "Consequently the army command had no choice but to make its decision along that line."[42] However, the troops that went off duty were only sent on leave, so that they could be called up again at any moment "without having to ask the Federal Council's approval."[43]

Since the two different interpretations of the right to call up troops as stipulated in articles 208 and 210 of the service regulations had ultimately triggered the crisis of 1944, the commander-in-chief asked the Federal Council to settle the matter once and for all. In an extensive missive, Guisan said that he regretted that the Federal Council had not addressed the fundamental matter in its letter of June 23 and that it had not responded to his earlier letter of February 8, in which he had raised the same issue.[44] The Federal Council considered that "this [was] not the time to exchange letters" on how to interpret articles of the service regulations and decided not to answer the General's note of June 27 "simply because [it did] not want to prolong the exchange of letters." Instead, it asked the Head of the Military Department to verbally inform Guisan about the government's view. During a meeting with the General on July 1, Kobelt declared, "The Federal Council would like to point out that it continues to advocate what it said in its letter of June 23, 1944. With due consideration for the responsibility that the Commander-in-Chief of the Armed Forces carries in terms of the national defense, the Federal Council considers that its appreciation of the situation was correct and that developments have shown that it was advisable not to attach too much importance to the reports by the Chief of Intelligence, Colonel Masson of the general staff. However, the Federal Council would like to avoid marring relations between the Commander-in-Chief of the Armed Forces and the Federal Council by continuing the exchange of letters; hence, it restricts itself to making these verbal statements."[45]

In spite of the Federal Council's clear message, Guisan initially did not want to let the matter rest. After receiving Kobelt's declaration, he persisted and wrote another letter addressing the issue, stating, "Please allow me to point out with regret, as I had the honor to tell you on earlier occasions, that neither in its reply of 23 June nor after receiving my note of the 27th, did the Federal Council want to raise the issue of how to apply article 210. Instead, it preferred to keep silent." In addition, the General recalled that his letter of February 28 [sic], 1944 to the Head of the Military Department, which addressed the same issue, had also remained unanswered, adding, "I had reason to consider this fact as an indication of [the Federal Council's] tacit agreement; however, the events of June 6 and the following days have shown me that it would be very desirable to make things clear on this topic."[46]

Since Kobelt had left for Valperra for rest and recreation, Kobelt's acting deputy, Federal Councilor von Steiger, answered the General's letter. In his immediate response, the Head of the Justice and Police Department managed to smooth over the differences. Von Steiger wrote that "at the present time it [could] not be decided" whether potential doubts about the Federal Council's way of interpreting the articles in question had to be removed by rewriting them or in any other manner, even less so as the Head of the Military Department was absent. He said, though, that the Federal Council was aware that there was a difference in the way the articles were interpreted. Regarding the procedure that should be followed in the future for calling up the border troops, von Steiger explained that the Federal Council had taken note of the General's suggestion that "when danger [was] looming once again, the troops should be mobilized by means of public notices right away, not by means of personal notices sent in the mail." He said that the Cabinet had not raised any objections to that suggestion, adding that "experience with the personal notices [had] clearly shown that this was not the right method to use, at least not from a psychological perspective."[47] Moreover, von Steiger assured Guisan that he would see to it that while he was acting as Head of the Military Department, the General would have the opportunity to personally defend his point of view before the Federal Council in case of differences. These explanations made it possible to provide Guisan with some satisfaction and to make it easier for him to make a dignified retreat.

The crisis of June 1944 was the most serious conflict between the Federal Council and the army command during World War II, escalating to a sort of trial of strength and ending in a compromise that was a defeat for the General. Guisan felt that the government's opposition to him in the matter of calling up troops was an affront. In this instance, moreover, the Federal Council had repudiated the entire army command because the chief of the general staff and all corps commanders had supported the commander-in-chief's request. Nevertheless, events showed that the Federal Council had indeed "assessed the situation correctly," as Pilet-Golaz remarked.[48] Even though the language used in the written and verbal communications during this lengthy and strenuous confrontation remained relatively polite, both sides were left with a bitter aftertaste that had further repercussions. The mutual uneasiness was later unequivocally expressed by the General in his report on wartime duty—and also by the Federal Council when it responded in its own report.[49]

Relations with the
Social Democrats

THE MISTRUST THAT CERTAIN UNIONS and Social Democrats had voiced against Guisan before he was elected General completely disappeared during the course of the war. It is surprising how quickly the reservations that still existed on both sides during the first months of wartime duty gave way to a genuinely trusting relationship.

As early as 1934, during a presentation, Corps Commander Guisan had stated, "An officer's first duty is to build and foster solidarity. . . . He can promote wonderful social actions if he is imbued with his mission, filled with love for those who are in need, and is aware of the responsibilities that all leaders carry with them."[1] The war provided the General with an opportunity to demonstrate, through his open-mindedness in socio-political matters, that his idea of "the social mission," of which military superiors had to be aware, was not merely lip service.

Following Germany's overwhelming victories in the West, which had led to a crisis in the spirit of resistance in Switzerland, the Psychological Service of the army stated in its weekly report that the Social Democratic workers were "skeptical" about the Federal Council and were "less convinced than other circles that the totalitarian powers [would] carry away the final victory." The report concluded that the workers "remain nationalist and continue to be reliable soldiers, but politically they remain cautious."[2] During the week of the briefing at the Rütli, at a management meeting of the Social Democratic Party of Switzerland (SPS), Party President Hans Oprecht claimed that the army command was beginning to realize that "the workers and farmers [were] the pillars of the national defense and of the spirit of resistance."[3] In the fall of 1940, the Social Democratic Party of Switzerland was the only major national party to recommend that Swiss voters approve the introduction of compulsory pre-military training.[4] At the SPS convention the following spring, Oprecht made it clear why demobilizing the army was out of the question in spite of the armistice in France, arguing, "Unionists must become the custodians of the foreign policy principle of absolute and integral neutrality, because the foreign political situation continues to be very unstable in spite of all the victories the Axis powers have won on the battlefields."[5] He called upon the delegates to "totally defend the country without the slightest reservation" and admonished them "to fight against any sign of defeatism."[6]

Even though social tensions existed, the workers had realized the importance of democratic institutions and they had an interest in defending Switzerland. Captain Hausamann reported that after a presentation he had given for the "General's Office for Public Outreach" at the Volkshaus in Bern, a worker stood up and shouted to the crowd, "Comrades, believe me, the Captain is right. I spent fifteen years abroad as a laborer, and that is where I discovered Switzerland."[7]

The more the Social Democratic workers became committed to resistance, the easier it was for the commander-in-chief to get closer to their leadership. Once the industrialists and the right-wing bourgeoisie had largely failed, focusing their attention on the Third Reich's "New Europe," General Guisan began using the Social Democrats for support in domestic political matters. He recognized that the working class was able to carry the state and he was eager to integrate them into national defense, strengthening determination to defend the country and at the same time boosting his own ability to assert himself. In the delicate domestic and foreign situation that surrounded the General for some time, he gladly accepted the support of the powerful class that had rejected national defense only a few years earlier. He must have been happy to have these new allies. Meanwhile, his primary critics, the entourages of Wille, Däniker, Bircher, and Pilet-Golaz, stubbornly continued to mistrust and oppose the Social Democrats.

Young officers in the General's own entourage, particularly Captains Hausamann, Ernst, and Frick, played a significant role as mediators in fostering the new relationship between Social Democratic workers and the army command. Hausamann, who had acted as unofficial liaison between the Military Department and the Social Democrats since 1938, and had earned their trust, made an especially substantial contribution to improving relations between the General and the Left.[8] In a letter to Federal Councilor Kobelt, the commander-in-chief was happy to relay Hausamann's report that during virtually every presentation, workers readily pointed out that times had changed, saying, "Who would have thought five years ago that one day an officer wearing a uniform would come to see us!"⁹ In the fall of 1941, after giving a presentation to 200 delegates of the Metalworkers' and Watchmakers' Union in Biel, Captain Robert Frick of the general staff told Guisan he was convinced that these unionists were totally reliable, stating, "There are certain people who are secretly staging a battle against you, but I think I can guarantee you that the unionists fully and sincerely support you."[10]

Hausamann's relations with the Social Democrats, above all with National Councilor Hans Oprecht, were so trusting that he was able to play a role in redefining the party's objectives. In 1942, when the SPS was drafting a new political program, Hausamann was offered the opportunity to write the introduction. Hausamann informed a comrade-in-arms about that fact, which had been unknown before the publication of this book, writing that the SPS committee had presented a draft of the new program to him. He explained:

> I considered that the program lacked a national context. . . . Moreover, there was no mention of the unconditional commitment to national defense. I bluntly wrote to the concerned gentlemen about that. They replied that the program dealt only with politics and the economy. However, I did not accept this as a final answer. The result was that I was allowed to write an introduction to the program. The gentlemen of the left-wing movement were grateful for that. They agreed with my arguments. They did not adopt my text verbatim; wherever I had put the word 'social,' they replaced it with the word 'socialist.' However, let us be glad that they went as far as they did.[11]

The key passage in Hausamann's introduction, which referred to commitment to the national defense, read:

> As long as there is no real community of free, democratic states, Switzerland's military preparations must not come to an end. Even after this war, Switzerland must maintain a well armed militia army in order to safeguard the country's independence. The better the state and the economy are organized and are able to guarantee every Swiss citizen a job and food by constantly increasing the country's productivity, the more robust this militia army will be. These are the principles on which the goal and purpose of every restructuring of the country are based.[12]

In the final version of the SPS program, dated December 1942 and published in February 1943, the introduction was one page long. The passage expressing the party's support of the national defense stated, "Even after the war, a strong militia army will be needed. The better the state and the economy see to it that every Swiss is guaranteed an existence, a job, and food by increasing the country's productivity and by awarding everyone a fair share of the goods, the more powerful this militia army will be."[13]

Hausamann informed his direct superior, Masson, as well as the General about his part in writing the introduction. In early 1943 he wrote to Guisan:

> Please allow me to send you the Socialist party program, the introduction of which yours truly initiated and which, at the request of the committee of the Socialist party, he also revised. . . . That way the Communists and supporters of Léon Nicole have once again been isolated. The leaders of Switzerland's labor movement have once again defined their position. On the other hand, the wind has been taken out of the sails of those who tried to cash in politically on the 'scare of Bolshevism' as propagated by Goebbels. The connection with the 'left' has once again turned out to be in the country's interest.[14]

The General thanked Hausamann for his information and efforts, replying, "It is good to hear that the party program includes an unambiguous declaration in favor of national defense."[15]

Hausamann's sideswipe at those who he said were using the "scare of Bolshevism" for political purposes was addressed at right-wing organizations such as the "Swiss National Patriotic Federation" (SNPF), the "International Anti-Communist Entente," and the "Anti-Revolutionary Action." These political structures had not overcome the trauma of the nationwide strike movement of 1918 and mistrusted the truce with the Social Democrats, even though the Social Democrats had taken on a new stance; hence they decided to continue fighting against anything that was "leftist." Out of fear that nationwide social unrest might flare up as during World War I, the SNPF, together with the "International Anti-Communist Entente" and the "Aubert League," made several attempts to discredit the Social Democratic leadership among the civilian and military authorities. For example, they tried to oust National Councilor Robert Grimm, a member of the Bernese cantonal government who had been at the helm of the strike movement of 1918, from his political offices and his key role in the economy. In 1940 and 1941, the SNPF intervened with the Federal Council in that matter but had to realize, "[Several] petitions addressed to the Federal Council on the same matter have not been answered or have not been taken into account."[16]

In fact, in the spring of 1941, Federal Councilor Stampfli responded to the

"Swiss National Patriotic Federation" that dismissing Grimm as Head of the Energy Section at the War Industry and Labor Office was out of the question, arguing:

> The main reasons for appointing Mr. Grimm to that position were his abilities as an organizer, his experience as an administrator, and the fact that the workers' insistent request to let them participate in the tasks of the war economy could not be ignored. The Head of the respective Department and the Federal Council were responsible for appointing Mr. Grimm as Head of the Energy Section and are in charge of keeping him in his position; therefore, as a matter of principle we must refuse to enter into discussions on that issue.[17]

SNPF Secretary Huber considered that his patriotic group should not "accept being treated like that" by the Federal Council. He wrote to SNPF President O. Heusser, "The last word [has not yet been said] in that matter. . . . Let the dance begin!"[18]

During a meeting with Kobelt in 1943, a SNPF delegation voiced fundamental objections to allowing Socialists to join armed vigilance groups. Notes taken during that meeting stated, "Serious reservations were voiced about supplying the vigilance groups with arms because unreliable elements could be dangerous (Socialists being encouraged to join the vigilance groups)."[19] However, the Head of the Military Department ignored such reservations, as did the commander-in-chief and the chief of the general staff.

In the summer of 1940, in a circular that was not supposed to be published, Théodore Aubert, the founder of an anti-Communist league that was named after him, exhorted his supporters that it was "a patriotic duty never to forget about November 1918 [because] as in 1918, the Left would not hesitate to use the first opportunity to stage a revolution."[20] On several occasions, Aubert tried to incite the General, with whom he was acquainted, and Barbey and Masson against the workers because they were allegedly unpatriotic and unreliable.[21] In December 1942, Aubert demanded to know from Guisan what the military had planned to ensure that the aluminum processing facility in Chippis, Canton Valais, could continue to operate smoothly in the event of difficulties with the employees there, which he considered likely.[22] Barbey ordered Masson to look into the matter. He reported that everything was calm at the industrial sites in Valais, and no special measures were required. He further argued that "organizing surveillance activities by the army at the present time would actually be a psychological mistake."[23]

In the fall of 1944, Aubert informed the General about his organization's fight against what he called "leftist subversion" and suggested setting up an internal newspaper in the army for the same purpose.[24] Guisan rejected the suggestion, writing on Aubert's letter, "This all pertains to the civilian authorities; the army will obviously feel the repercussions. Let us hope that it will remain morally strong enough to be a pillar of resistance in our country against subversive elements! The army command does everything it can to be just that."[25]

During the third year of the war, in 1942, the "Anti-Revolutionary Action" (ARA) was founded by Samuel Haas, the director of the Schweizerische Mittelpresse news agency who had also been a co-founder of the "Patriotic Alliance for the People" at the time when the Front movements were mushrooming. Industrialist Caspar Jenny was the ARA's president.[26] In Peter Dürrenmatt's opinion, Haas was a "difficult person" who had the "reputation of an ultraconservative agitator and propagandist."[27] When Haas founded the new organization, he tried to make it look as though he were acting in agreement with the army command; hence, Hausamann and his friends feared that their efforts to consolidate a truce with the Social Democrats could be set back. Hausamann commented that Haas was "misusing the army command" and "spoiling the broth." He argued that Haas' endeavor could only "germinate as long as he [was] able to keep the gap open between capital and labor."[28] He asked Federal Councilor Kobelt to recommend to Guisan that "in his own name and in the name of the gentlemen on the army command, he should refuse to be mentioned in connection with the ARA" because it was unacceptable that the commander-in-chief be made to appear to have relations with an extremely political organization that was "clearly directed against the workers."[29]

Hausamann and other resistance fighters thought that the agitation of the right-wing extremist members of the ARA could jeopardize their trusting relations with the Social Democratic leadership and call into question the content of the introduction to the new SPS program. Hausamann expressed his concern in a letter to a comrade-in-arms, writing, "If the gentlemen on the left heard that Haas and his emissaries continue referring to the army command in connection with their activities, without the army command protesting against it, we should not be surprised if the Socialist party leadership rejects the introduction, arguing that they will no longer be fooled. That is what would happen if it turned out that the General or Colonel-Brigadier Masson made a secret deal with Haas and his ARA in spite of all mutual assurances."[30] Hausamann saw through "Mr. Haas' dealings that [were] covered up with patriotic arguments." He unsparingly placed the faux patriots' cards on the table, writing that left-wing politicians were informed about the connections between the different right-wing groups: "They know that Huber of the Swiss National Patriotic

Federation (backed up by Bircher) and the famous Mr. Aubert from Geneva (with Musy in the background) have a say in Haas' new ARA, that the 'People's Alliance for Switzerland's Independence,' which is financed by the same people as Haas' ARA, have a hand in it, etc., etc."[31] Thanks to its intelligence information, Bureau "Ha," which feared for some time that even the General and Masson were "doing deals with Haas," was able to identify correctly the interconnections among the groups. Hausamann said that the commander-in-chief had been warned, through his initiative, about the possible consequences of being linked with the ARA, after which the General and the army's chief security officer, Colonel Werner Müller, "immediately distanced themselves" from that organization.[32]

Hausamann's suppositions about the General's involvement in Haas' organization were not unfounded. Captain Meyer-Schwertenbach's notes indicate that he received a top-secret mission from the General to take care of relations with Haas. On March 27, 1942, Guisan called "special Meyer" into his office to tell him:

I have a mission for you that requires utmost secrecy. I have not told anyone about it, neither the chief of the general staff, nor Masson, nor Müller. Here is what it is about. [The General pulled a document out of the drawer and continued.] Do you know anything about an Anti-Revolutionary Action? One of its initiators, Director Haas of the Mittelpresse, came to see me to tell me about it. High-ranking and top-ranking people are members of that Action. Let me give you the written presentation that Haas gave me. Read it! I want to be kept up to date on that Action and would like you to participate at its meetings in order to keep me informed. Contact Haas right away, he will fill you in about everything essential. I thought of you for this mission because you will attend the meetings in civilian clothes, not in your uniform. The army cannot be officially represented there at the present time. I do not want anyone to find out about your mission.[33]

Captain Meyer did not fully respect the General's order to keep his special mission secret, feeling obliged to inform his direct superior Colonel W. Müller, the Chief Security Officer of the Armed Forces. He told Müller that he had to take care of relations with Haas, who was considered "a controversial person among journalists." He added, "The General has ordered me to act as liaison person between him and the ARA. This is not an official military order because he would like to avoid the army being said to be connected in any way with the ARA. My mission is that of an unofficial observer."[34] Captain Meyer summarized the impression that he gained of the ARA's activities by stating that in view of the internal unity of the army it was "a superfluous organization."[35]

One could measure to what extent the working class was recognized as an entity supporting the state by the degree of readiness with which the conservatives allowed Social Democrats to help participate in the Federal Government. The Social Democrats' first attempts to get one of their representatives elected to the Federal Council were easily blocked by the conservative majority in 1929 and 1938. During the first wartime elections, in 1940, when Federal Councilors Motta, Obrecht, Minger, and Baumann had to be replaced, the Social Democratic candidates lost to the conservatives, in part due to foreign policy concerns. At a meeting of the SPS leadership in the summer of 1940, National Councilor Bringolf explained that Federal Councilor Pilet-Golaz had "declared that in consideration of foreign political problems it was not possible to accept a Socialist Federal Councilor in the government." He commented that this showed that domestic policy and foreign policy were intertwined and that "the country's top authorities [were] adapting to the course of the war."[36]

At an earlier meeting of the party leadership, National Councilor Willy Spühler, a future Federal Councilor, pointed out that more and more people believed that Germany would win the war and that "under these circumstances the conservative politicians [would] never be in favor of having the Social Democrats represented on the Federal Council."[37]

In December 1940, in a conversation with the German envoy, Federal Councilor Pilet-Golaz expressed his satisfaction at the fact that neither a Social Democrat, nor Markus Feldmann, who had a critical attitude, had been elected to the government. As Köcher reported to Berlin, "Switzerland's Foreign Minister told me that the two new Federal Councilors, von Steiger and Kobelt, were men of modern thinking from whom he expected to receive support for his policy of rapprochement with Germany and of tightening the reins in the country. The Federal Councilor took credit for blocking Mr. Feldmann's election."[38]

As an editor of the *Neue Berner Zeitung*, National Councilor Feldmann did not hide his negative opinion of the Third Reich. The pro-German entourage of Däniker opposed his candidacy also. During the run-up to the election, Colonel Däniker wrote to Hektor Ammann, the initiator of the "Petition of the Two Hundred," that "In Germany, Feldmann is considered one of the journalists who have contributed to a great extent to substantially disturbing the good relations between the two countries. Since we are working hard but not very successfully to normalize relations with Germany again, someone like Feldmann should be prevented from being elected to the Federal Council. If Feldmann were elected, the situation would substantially worsen in the near future."[39] Feldmann himself believed that through confidential channels, the German envoy Köcher had a hand in the election campaign. He later noted an informant who stated, "The German Legation made von Steiger Federal Councilor."[40]

As late as the fourth year of the war, right-wing parliamentarians had a deep aversion against accepting any Social Democrat on the Federal Council. For example, in the summer of 1943, National Councilor Heinrich Walther from Lucerne wrote to Federal Councilor Wetter, who considered resigning from the government, "The extremists [among the Socialists], above all the horrible Dr. Oprecht, whom I have always disliked very much in Parliament, and Dr. Meierhans, who used to be quite agreeable in Lucerne but keeps moving further to the left every day in Zürich [have the greatest say]."[41]

In contrast to such opinions, theologian Karl Barth had asked as early as 1941, "Why has it not been possible until now to see to it that the Social Democrats, who are the strongest political force among the workers and the largest political party, get a share of responsibility on the Federal Council?"[42] In fact, the situation at the Federal level seemed paradoxical insofar as the SPS was the strongest party in Switzerland with more than 28 percent of voters,[43] and in many cantons Social Democrats had long served in the government. In 1939–40, three cantons, including the two with the largest populations, had Social Democratic heads of government. Grimm in Bern and Nobs in Zürich were politicians who had been very well known since the nationwide strike movement of 1918; in Aargau, Social Democrat Rudolf Siegrist was the head of government. Political authorities in border cities such as Basel, Schaffhausen, and Geneva, as well as in Switzerland's largest city, Zürich, the capital, Bern, and in Biel, either had a "red" majority or had "red" members and a "red" mayor.[44]

There is no direct evidence of Guisan's opinion regarding Socialists joining the Federal Council; however, there was reason to believe that in agreement with the conviction of political advisors such as Hausamann, the General not only favored letting them participate in the Federal government but considered it a necessity to keep the people and the army united. Guisan was capable of learning; he realized that the Social Democratic leadership was becoming a reliable supporter of his own policies and he was determined to take this strong political force into account. He consciously opened up toward the Left to secure the workers' support for the national defense and their leaders' support for himself. The new support he gained by that move allowed him to dispense with former supporters who were taken aback by his strategy.

Once events on the battlefields had clearly begun to turn against Germany, and the Social Democrats had been able to extend their lead in Parliament by adding eleven seats during the 1943 National Council elections, their joining the Federal Council was overdue.[45] On December 15, 1943, Parliament elected Zürich mayor Ernst Nobs as the first Social Democrat to the Federal Council. He had no serious competition, receiving 122 out of 212 votes in the first round of balloting. Fifty-two members who still could not warm to a Social Democrat cast a blank vote, and Radical Democrat Theodor Gut from Zürich (who had declined to be an official candidate) received 38 votes.[46]

One organization that had supported increasing the number of parties in the government was the "Gotthard Alliance," which expressed its view in an "open letter" to the parties represented on the Federal Council before Nobs' election.[47] The new member of the Federal Government did not receive any premature praise but Gut wrote that he had "good prospects," adding, "Today this has to be considered as an experiment; however, in a short time this will be an experience, based on which a judgment will be made about the election."[48]

Nobs' election did not give the workers a share of power in the Federal Government proportionate to its strength in Parliament, yet it was a promising start.[49] In an essay, SPS President Oprecht unambiguously expressed what the Social Democrats meant by sharing responsibility, writing:

> Switzerland's workers are aware of the share of responsibility they have for the country's domestic and foreign policies. They do not want to shirk this responsibility, nor will they ever do so. Whether they like it or not, they are the first to bear the consequences of these policies; therefore they also want to have a direct say in them and participate in the decisions from influential positions, according to their strength. The workers did not waver in 1940; they will not change their attitude when the war draws to a close nor after the war is over. In the "New Switzerland" party program, particularly in its introduction, the political direction of Switzerland's labor organizations is clearly defined both toward the outside and the inside. That is it. Switzerland's workers will remain steadfast. However, Switzerland's workers also want to help shape the future.[50]

Guisan believed that reconciliation with the Social Democrats was necessary for the state and hence inevitable. He listened less and less to biased right-wing conservatives and over time virtually ignored them; their opinions caused more harm than benefit to the country.

To become better acquainted with the top labor leaders and to tighten relations with some of them, General Guisan invited a number of unionists and Social Democratic members of Parliament to his command post at Jegenstorf

Castle. As indicated in a letter by the General, Fritz Brechbühl, the head of government of Basel-Stadt, whom he had known since the beginning of the war, had brought up the idea for this meeting.[51] In view of the meeting, which was expected to be a general exchange of opinions, the commander-in-chief had Captain Bracher, the liaison officer with the Military Department, and Colonel Werner Müller, the Chief Security Officer of the Armed Forces, provide him with information about his guests and their roles within the Social Democratic Party. According to the list that Bracher put together for the General, the people who were invited to Jegenstorf on August 18, 1944 included: "Head of Government Brechbühl, Head of the Police Department, Basel; Government Member Gustav Wenk, Head of the Department of the Interior, Basel; National Councilor Ernst Herzog, Director of the Consumers' Association, Basel; National Councilor Robert Bratschi, Secretary General of the Swiss Railroad Workers' Federation, Bern; National Councilor Joh. Huber, Chairman of the National Council Proxy Committee, St. Gallen; National Councilor Hans Oprecht, SPS President, Secretary of the Public Service Personnel, Zürich; Dr. Lüchinger, Mayor of Zürich; National Councilor Dr. Meierhans, Editor-in-Chief of the *Volksrecht*, Zürich; National Councilor Walther Bringolf, Mayor of Schaffhausen."[52]

According to his notes, General Guisan called the meeting a "conf[erence] of Socialist Nat[ional] Counc[ilors] at my command post."[53] The following four topics were to serve as a basis for the discussion:

1. The workers' attitude in the army and their view on the army's existence after the war. Formal assurance by the Social Democratic Party that they will support the further existence of the army after the war.

2. View of the commanders of training facilities and instructors regarding advanced training courses for soldiers [and] non-commissioned officers who are members of the Social Democratic Party. These soldiers should no longer be discriminated against because of their political opinions and should no longer be mistrusted.

3. Formal declaration by the SP[S] that it will not tolerate any antimilitary propaganda inside and outside the army. This is particularly in reference to claims made by National Councilor Bircher and the [Swiss National] Patriotic Federation.

4. The question has been asked whether the Mot[orized] A[rmy] P[olice] Bat[talion] was formed especially as an intervention unit against workers, factories, and labor offices.[54]

The General summarized the results of the meeting in handwritten annotations, writing:

Re:1.   It was exemplary from 1939–1944. Is written in the party program due to Hausamann. Know their position, have to stick together and work together. Bolshevism = Bolsheviks [on a] national [level], National Socialism = nationalist Bolshevist, so no difference!

Re: 2.   That's the way it used to be because of negative attitude toward n[ational] d[efense]. But no longer the case according to 1.

[Re: 3.] Ask these gentlemen for more details, then [Colonel] Müller will prepare a letter to the Patriot[ic] Assoc[iation] for me.

Re: 4.   Never; is a unit that m[aintains] o[rder] like the entire army. Since Aug. 14, [1944], the Bat. has been on duty in Altdorf to train for its mission in the war.[55]

Both the General and the eight top Social Democratic politicians apparently were pleased with the results of the meeting, about which no minutes were kept and which surprisingly was not mentioned in Barbey's published diary. Guisan's confidence in the Social Democrats was strengthened, and the Social Democratic leaders for their part gave up their last suspicions that the army command might continue to cooperate secretly with right-wing organizations.

The General's eyes must have been opened in particular by the presentation that he had asked Chief of Security Müller to prepare for the meeting with the Socialists on the activities and significance of right-wing organizations. Werner Müller, a colonel on the general staff and Police Commissioner of the City of Bern, was a shrewd criminologist who did not let anyone fool him; he was able to write an unbiased report stating the facts. The political organizations he targeted included the "Swiss National Patriotic Federation" (SNPF), in which Guisan had played an active role in the 1930s. As the chief security officer informed the commander-in-chief, "I know for a fact that the SNPF made the mistake to send secretaries all around Switzerland to raise funds and solicit support from affluent people for a cell organization directed against the left. One of the SNPF secretaries claimed directly that the mood in the army was worse than in 1917. He said that numerous army units were no longer reliable because they had been 'infested' with leftist politics."[56] The organization was said to claim that Communist propaganda had infiltrated the army and therefore the SNPF was destined to organize the defense. Müller commented on this:

Everyone knows that such claims are absurd. Those who make such assumptions are moral criminals. I personally hope that the Swiss will not have to be informed about these and other incidents because this would obviously provoke a storm of indignation. The population, which includes hundreds of thousands of Swiss soldiers who are on their jobs, knows best how far-fetched the SNPF representative's claims are. Needless to say that unity in the army suffers heavily from such machinations.[57]

Among the organizations that had made "the fight against left-wing politicians their top priority," Müller also included the "National Revival Movement," the "Aubert League," and the "Society for the Promotion of Switzerland's Economy." He wrote: "The population considers that this fight is directed against the workers and rejects it. The most recent National Council elections and numerous recent cantonal ballots are a clear indication of that. Because the aforesaid organizations no longer dare to publicly stir up the population, they now try to carry out undercover activities. They all use the same argument, claiming to make preparations in order to be ready to brave coup attempts etc. by leftists. Public debates are replaced by the creation of local cells, secret defense organizations. Their establishment and maintenance obviously requires substantial financial means. In reality, though, the funds are all used for one and the same purpose: the secretaries of these organizations want to make a living for themselves."[58] He stated that the "Society for the Promotion of Switzerland's Economy," whose main goal seemed to consist of financing political activities, had provided funds to the Schweizer Mittelpresse news agency, the "National Revival Movement," the "Aubert League," and the "Swiss National Patriotic Federation."

Colonel Müller pointed out to the General that in view of the predominant opinion among the people, it would be unfavorable "for officers who [had] a lot of responsibility in the army" to be officially connected "with the leading figures of the aforesaid organizations." He said that when analyzing who called the tune in the various organizations, the same names occurred again and again, adding that some of them were the same people who were financing the pro-German "People's Alliance for Switzerland's Independence," of which Corps Commander Wille and Colonel Däniker were two of the most dedicated patrons.[59] After these interesting revelations by the knowledgeable Chief Security Officer of the Armed Forces, Guisan could hardly have any doubt with which side he should make an arrangement.

The trusting exchange of opinions at the General's command post soon yielded positive results. In their articles commemorating Guisan's 70th birthday on October 21, 1944, the Social Democratic newspapers were full of praise for the commander-in-chief's personality, attitude, and achievements. In the Zürich newspaper *Volksrecht*, the editor Meierhans, who had participated in the reception at Jegenstorf, stated that General Guisan had managed to transform the mistrust that the Left had initially shown toward him into "absolute trust," adding, "During more than five years of wartime duty, not once has the opposition voiced criticism against him in parliament, not even during the secret deliberations by the party. That alone shows that the General has fulfilled absolutely all the requirements that we had said were indispensable to successfully accomplish his difficult task as commander of the army." Meierhans concluded the article by writing that on his birthday, General Guisan "received feelings of gratitude from all classes of the population, not the least of which came from the working class."[60]

Before that time, the commander-in-chief had begun visiting industrial sites to express his recognition of the work that the employees were doing at their benches to support the national defense. Probably it was Hausamann who suggested that the General visit workers at their jobs. A confidential report submitted to him recommended that Guisan:

> Incessantly tell [the workers] what a privilege it is to be Swiss; let them know that one feels united with them for good or ill; show interest in their work; members of the government and high-ranking officers should visit factories that work for the army to show them how much importance they attach to their work. Do not forget the production facilities of the Swiss Federal Railways, visit a switch-tower for a change. It takes very little to get our workers enthusiastic, provided that [the contacts] are "heartfelt." It is completely up to us to prevent our workers from sliding off into a dangerous opposition, to wrest them from the hands of certain secretaries.[61]

The General marked those sentences with two long lines in red ink and added, "Visit factories and Swiss Federal Railways facilities."[62]

In his conversations with Gafner, General Guisan stated about his relations with the workers, "I drove to Geneva, to Sulzer in Winterthur, to Brown Boveri in Baden to see the workers, most of whom were my soldiers anyway, in their civilian lives. Sometimes I sent them a regiment band to give them a concert. These two large firms stopped working for half an hour or one full hour; the workers were of course paid for that time."[63] Visits to the factories apparently did not all go well and the General was not always pleased. Major Bracher, who accompanied him on some of the visits, wrote in a letter to the General that the commander-in-chief had been very pleased about the workers' attitude at the Thommen AG watchmaking facility in Waldenburg. At other places, where he was apparently ignored or snubbed, he was rather disappointed. Bracher wrote, "On our way back from Waldenburg, I permitted myself to ask you where you had observed these not very pleasant facts. You replied that you had not received a favorable impression about the mood and attitude of the workers at factories in Geneva (Hispano and Tavaro)."[64] The General believed that he had noticed a significant "difference in the workers' appearance and behavior" between German-speaking and French-speaking Switzerland. Bracher wrote to him, summarizing their experience: "On Wednesday, October 6, 1943, I was allowed to accompany you on your unannounced visit to Saurer in Arbon. Once again, the subsequent conversation focused on the workers' mood and attitude, which were excellent, unlike in Geneva. . . . On our way home, you talked about how you were struck by the difference in the workers' appearance and behavior."[65]

After the meeting in Jegenstorf, Guisan enjoyed a particularly trusting relationship with National Councilor Robert Bratschi, the Secretary General of the Railroad Workers' Federation and President of the Swiss Union Association.[66] In early 1945, in an order of the day, the General addressed the army to acknowledge the efforts of the employees of the civilian transport companies and to express the army command's appreciation to "all soldiers of the railroads and their superiors." The commander-in-chief emphasized the "relentless and loyal work by the railroad workers [who had] done so much to help accomplish the tasks" and had rendered the army great services. "Between September 1939 and the end of 1944," he stated, "our soldiers took more than one hundred million trips, including deployments, redeployments, and leaves. Moreover, 900,000 horses and mules as well as about six million tons of military goods were transported. When the situation suddenly made it necessary to move major units around in 1944, preparing 2,200 special trains for the military within one week and running them on time was a superb performance."[67] He said that unlike their colleagues in 1918, these "soldiers of the railroads" who were distinguished by receiving the commander-in-chief's thanks in one of his orders of the day would see no reason to participate in a nationwide strike.

Shortly before the war was over, in April 1945, the General invited ten media representatives, most of whom were officers, to a meeting at his command post in Jegenstorf to discuss what should be done to prevent a change in mood among the population at the end of the war. The media representatives included Colonel Holliger, President of the Swiss Officers' Society; Colonel Weber of the Schweizer Mittelpresse; Lieutenant-Colonel Uhlmann, editor at the *Schaffhauser Intelligenzblatt*; Major Schmid, member of the press office of the army staff; Major Wanner, Secretary General of the Swiss Federal Railways; Dr. Bridel, President of the Society of the Swiss Press; and Dr. Egger, Editor-in-Chief of the *Bund*. It is striking that no Social Democratic media representatives were invited. The General explained that he wanted to see them to explain the situation and ask them for their advice. He wanted to find "means and ways together with [them] to inform the population and the army about the order of the day," since it was to be expected that the real test was yet to come at the end of the war.[68]

The meeting considered the political situation in the country to be far better than in 1918; therefore, no major difficulties were to be anticipated in any respect. As the General explained, "During this war, the Social Democrats have shown that they are willing to stand up for the defense. We absolutely want to avoid having two camps as in 1918—those who support the army and those who are against it. Our soldiers have been loyal to the army until now and will continue to be so after the war."[69] The meeting decided to strengthen relations further between the army and the media; for that purpose, press conferences would be organized on a regional level during which military installations would be visited.[70]

SPS President Hans Oprecht qualified Guisan's impartial attitude toward the unions and the Social Democrats as "the result of a restructuring of society." During a discussion in the National Council after the war, he stated, "The General made a conscious effort to be in contact with the working class. Most of all, he insisted that the "Army and Home" section cultivate relations with the unions and cooperate with them because he knew how important workers were in the war and what role workers play for the army nowadays."[71] In the *Volksrecht* newspaper, Oprecht wrote, "It would have been hard to imagine General Wille receiving a delegation of the SPS and unionists at his headquarters. Guisan intentionally cultivated relations with the working class because he knew that workers play a completely different role in a motorized army than used to be the case."[72] This author leaves it open for discussion whether the commander-in-chief or the workers should be given the larger share of credit for bringing about the rapprochement, which was a major political achievement. Former Federal Councilor Spühler later stated bluntly that he was convinced that the workers had to be given "the major share of the credit for allowing Switzerland to get through the dangers of the time without being harmed socially; it was actually strengthened."[73]

Unlike his predecessor, General Wille, Guisan avoided making the strategic mistake of underestimating the political power of the working class. It was just as difficult for him as it was for the labor leaders to free himself within a few months from political preconceptions that had existed for decades; nevertheless he managed, in a democratic manner, to make the Swiss Federal state aware of the Social Democratic workers' new relationship with the national defense. Calling Guisan a friend of socialism would go too far, but the commander-in-chief turned out to be capable of recognizing the existing political forces and taking them into account. The Social Democrats thanked Guisan for his open-mindedness by clearly taking his side in the controversy surrounding his postwar report.[74]

The Troops' Morale, State of Training, and Armament

GUISAN PLACED GREAT IMPORTANCE ON FOSTERING the troops' morale and building a sense of community. As he explained in a presentation at the Federal Institute of Technology in Zürich before the war, "What matters most are human beings. The performance of equipment depends on those who manipulate it, on their abilities and reactions and their physical and moral endurance. Apart from good training and excellent discipline, morale is the key element that determines an army's worth."[1] The war of 1939–1945 provided the General an opportunity to put his ideas about the importance of soldiers' morale into practice with troops that were on duty for several years under constantly changing conditions.

Reconciling the bourgeoisie with the Social Democratic working class in the country was a major requirement for being able to meet the challenging task of defending the country both physically and psychologically.[2] The General and the entire army command were concerned that the mistakes made when the army was on duty between 1914 and 1918 could be repeated, and they frequently discussed how to avoid the problem. Barbey reported a dinner table conversation between Guisan's personal staff, the chief of the general staff, and some other guests:

> The situation in 1918 is recalled, which the older guests still vividly remember. Neither the General, nor the others [Huber, Masson, Corbat, Combe, Dubois] believe that there will be another nationwide

strike movement or unrest. They enumerate the precautions that can be taken to prevent this from happening again. Most of our top commanders are apparently well aware of what has been done during this war for the soldiers' social and economic well-being, and especially what was done to take away their worries at the moment when they were called to arms.[3]

General Guisan must be given the major share of credit for promoting, through his attitude and actions, a climate within the army—as well as between the army and civilians—that withstood the tensions and strains during the extended time the troops were on duty. During the first year of the war, labor leader Robert Grimm noted, "The Swiss were of one mind and united when the army was first mobilized. No serious dissent was apparent anywhere. The international situation weighed on everyone."[4] Yet this favorable mood had to be maintained for the six years during which the units were serving on a rotating basis. The General had a special interest in maintaining the spirit of unity, explaining:

Never before in military history had the troops' morale played such a great role; never before had it been fostered so consciously and systematically as during the last time the army was on duty. Modern human beings require attention to their thoughts when they wear soldiers' uniforms. They stay in touch with the rest of the world through newspapers and the radio and are exposed to the same risks as the civilians when enemy propaganda works relentlessly by using all admissible and inadmissible means.[5]

Some social measures the civilian authorities had taken were useful to Guisan in his efforts to keep up the troops' morale. The main measure consisted of paying all soldiers a daily stipend while they were on duty, an amount that could add up to several times a soldier's pay.[6] Also, the transport companies charged only half price to family members who visited their husbands, fathers, or sons at their duty station. For its part, the army gave the soldiers coupons allowing them to travel for free when they went on leave. Duty schedules, leaves, and dispensations were handled in a way that satisfied most affected people. A cleverly devised rationing system ensured that the low food supplies were distributed fairly. Soldiers had more to eat when they were on duty than at home. According to a list made during the fourth year of the war,[7] the daily food rations were as follows:

	For the Troops	For Civilians at Home
Bread	375–500 grams	225 grams
Meat	170 g	45 g
Cheese	80 g	13 g
Pasta	42 g	8 g
Nuts, corn	42 g	29 g
Rice	20 g	8 g
Oat, barley	21 g	8 g
Edible fat, oil	40 g	18 g
Sugar	40 g	16 g
Milk	3–4 dl	4 dl

Food rationing was thus far less drastic in the military than among civilians. General Guisan once commented that women wrote to him to complain that their husbands were "fed too well in the military so they were not happy about the food at home anymore when they got off duty."[8] Some soldiers, however, seemed to be insatiable. During a briefing with the corps commanders when discussing the units' quarterly reports, the commander-in-chief felt obliged to read a passage from the report from Light Brigade 1 which stated, "The troops are not satisfied with the three regular meals, but they 'devour' everything they find any time at daytime and nighttime." When the General dryly remarked, "I had always heard that there was enough food," all corps commanders readily agreed with him.[9]

The army command was aware that the defensive wall was only as strong as its weakest point and that an empty stomach could negatively affect the troops' endurance. Ernst Feisst, the head of the Swiss Federal War and Nutrition Office, commented that to a certain extent it was true that "not only the way to a man's heart is through his stomach but also the way to his heart for his home country."[10]

In spite of these circumspect measures, which yielded positive results, over the course of the six years, the troops' morale alternately declined and improved. Because the population and the military were closely connected, mood changes among one group affected the other. Bonjour wrote, "The public was irritable and nervous; it was cheerful at one moment and depressed the next. Whenever events in the war changed, they were hit hard."[11] In his postwar report, the General dedicated a whole chapter to the "Troops' Morale" in which he did not hide the fact that there were difficulties. He wrote, "From September 1939 to early 1940, overall the mood was very satisfactory,"[12] and then went into detail about the "causes for a temporary malaise that [affected] the troops' morale and the country's confidence" in the army's determination to put up resistance following France's defeat.[13]

The General repeatedly emphasized his concern about maintaining the troops' morale in order to keep up the power of resistance. As he explained to the Federal Council in the spring of 1941, "The soldiers' morale is closely linked to the morale of the entire population in Switzerland." He said that if one were determined to stand up to the existing signs of despair and demoralization, one should not hesitate to use all available means to do so, adding, "However, the measures that the military takes would not be sufficient if they were not accompanied by measures taken by the civilian authorities. The army cannot be indifferent to these measures as long as its mission is tied to them, whether we like it or not."[14]

One way to measure the health of the troops' morale might be to look at the number of suicides in the military. The data do not show a very favorable picture. During the first 21 months of wartime duty, 163 out of 1,376 deaths were caused by suicide.[15] When he was presented with these statistics, the General was moved to analyze the problem. As it turned out, eight suicides had occurred in September 1939, during the first month the troops were on duty; in May 1940 the number of suicides was twice that high. Research showed that about three out of four cases were due mostly to problems in the victims' civilian lives; a proportionately high number of suicides occurred during short leaves and on Mondays.[16] During the entire period of wartime duty, 323 soldiers committed suicide, while by comparison, only 60 soldiers did so during World War I. The Surgeon General commented, "In numerous cases, alcoholism played a crucial role, and at least one-third of the few cases that were caused by problems linked to the military could have been prevented at least in the short run if their superiors and comrades had been more observant or knew more about psychology."[17]

Around the same time, in 1941, Federal Councilor Kobelt addressed the issue of the troops' morale, explaining to Parliament's proxy committee:

> In addition to the training activities, great attention must be paid to the troops' morale. Unfortunately we noticed here and there that some soldiers were ill-humored because they were on duty for a long time; some older soldiers were ill-humored because they believed that they had to serve too long compared with the young ones; some tradesmen were ill-humored because they had to stay on duty whereas the farmers were allowed to go home, etc. I think that we have turned into weaklings. More drastic measures had been taken between 1914 and 1918, especially in the army. It is no use for officers to make nice presentations to the public on how to defend ourselves if the troops' morale is not boosted. The soldiers' morale can be boosted not only by

sport and leisure but also by demanding that they work hard so they feel they are needed in the military, so they trust the leadership, have confidence in the measures that have been taken, and above all gain confidence in themselves. The best way to fight defeatism is to have soldiers who are aware that everything is ready when they go off duty.[18]

It is not difficult to see that in these remarks, the Head of the Military Department felt criticism was due about the lack of tough combat training.

Guisan did not fail to exert a personal influence on the troops' mental readiness to fight. He did so not only through orders of the day and orders to the armed forces that were read aloud to the troops but also through verbal orders to subordinate commanders during briefings and through written instructions on training matters. At a briefing with the corps commanders in December 1941, he said:

A field army that is not involved in combat but prepares for a war is subject to a tough moral test. It is useless to perfect training and to bear enormous material sacrifices if the mental driving force does not remain kindled so that the troops may perform to their best ability at any moment. Fewer difficulties arise when the troops are under arms than when they are on call in the hinterland, where they are exposed to a more or less slackening morale. A large part of our population is slackening the reins and is becoming indifferent now that the focus of the war has shifted elsewhere. It believes that the threat is gone and the hostilities will end far away from our borders without affecting our country.

He argued that such wrong ideas could take a heavy toll on the army's power of resistance and therefore it was important to counter them at every opportunity. "Our commanding officers," he insisted, "must be able to answer any biased question by any ill-informed or malicious windbag and must show, through their whole attitude, that they know why they have to be ready."[19]

It was largely because of the General's admonitions and example that periods of emotional lows were overcome and the army's fighting spirit remained steady—or the "driving force remained kindled," to put it in his own words. He repeatedly pointed out the importance of military superiors of all ranks setting an example through their own attitude, exerting a positive effect on the troops' morale. He demanded that they should "make a great effort to show strict moral discipline in their actions." During the third year of the war, he told the corps commanders, "I have noticed that many officers have not yet understood that this is one of their basic duties."[20]

In his postwar report, the General did not overlook this problematic issue, mentioning "weariness and dissatisfaction" as well as "subversion by defeatists," adding, "I have to admit that in certain cases psychological mistakes were made by commanders, or they did not set a perfect example."[21]

Toward the end of the war, in some units there were increasing signs of soldiers growing tired of army service. According to quarterly reports by the troops, in the fall of 1944, "Some soldiers were shirking their responsibility and an increasing number of soldiers tried to avoid being called up by presenting a medical certificate." An "interesting phenomenon" was noticed among the troops at Sargans fortress, where "efforts to become unfit for service by extracting one's own teeth [demonstrated] a quite remarkable degree of someone being tired of serving."[22]

In spite of some difficulties, the spirit of comradeship and solidarity gained the upper hand because of the commander-in-chief's drive. Alfred Ernst, a member of the Officers' Conspiracy who made a fairly critical assessment of Guisan's merits, commented about the fundamental improvement of the atmosphere: "The General overcame major resistance in the army to assist a new spirit of freedom and comradeship to impose itself. He absolutely hated harassment, pedantry, and purposeless activities. He refused to accept artificial barriers between officers and the troops."[23] Schmid comments that the last thing the General had on his mind was anything that resembled radicalism in the military or "totally soldierly manners."[24] Officers who had been trained in the Prussian style had difficulty getting used to the General's style. Guisan had written as early as the 1930s, "A soldier must be able to trust his weapons, his leaders, his own strength, and his comrades. That is what moral cohesion is all about."[25]

One aspect of Guisan's character—his sociability and readiness to lend an ear to everyone—was extremely useful in promoting a feeling of trust among the population. He set great store by replying to every letter he received from all layers of society, including women and children. An aide on his personal staff had orders to answer every letter that was reasonable and included the sender's name and address.[26] Soldiers who did not follow official channels wrote many of the thousands of letters. They received a reply as well, occasionally combined with a slight reprimand. Guisan mentioned the case of a soldier who wrote that his roommate, who was acquainted with the General, was dying and that his last wish was to shake the General's hand. Guisan did not disappoint the dying man, recalling, "I drove to see him at the hospital and shook his hand. These are cases where one's duty as a human being comes first."[27]

Guisan's ability to socialize with anyone encouraged a feeling of trust among the soldiers. The General used inspections and visits to check not only on the troops' state of training but also on their morale. He explained that by "seeing them, speaking with them, and listening to them," he was able to feel "the pulse not only of the army but of all the Swiss . . . because soldiers do not primarily talk about what they do in the military but about their families, their worries, everyone and everything they had to leave at home."[28] That was why the General liked asking his men about their occupation and their family situation during his inspections, which he often carried out without prior announcement of his arrival. Even though he seemed paternal, he did not fail to notice shortcomings. Barbey reported that on an inspection of a battalion from Appenzell, "The General discovers spare shells, bottles of hard liquor in their pockets. Some company commanders are apparently not well informed."[29]

According to his own account, in February 1943, Guisan experienced an adventurous episode while he was inspecting troops guarding the Lötschberg railroad:

> At Goppenstein, a dragoon belonging to the reserve troops raised his carbine and shouted, 'Don't move, or I'll shoot!' I had a hard time telling the good man from the Ajoie region that I was the General; he said that anyone could tell him that! Without lowering his carbine, he slowly walked backward on a narrow path next to a ravine until he reached the bell at the watchman's house, which he rang to call the corporal. The soldier who pointed his gun at me did what he was supposed to do.[30]

On such occasions, the General showed his benevolence, even when he had to reprimand someone. The soldiers not only respected the General, but their hearts went out to him. They were convinced that he showed understanding for their service-related problems and their personal and job-related worries.

A detailed list exists of the visits and inspections the commander-in-chief carried out during the six years up to May 10, 1945. There were only a few units of the entire army, including the border and territorial battalions, that the General did not inspect or visit at least once during that time; to many of them he paid several visits. On average, he visited Swiss French troops somewhat more frequently than Swiss German troops. He went to see the 1st Regiment of Light Brigade 1 on twenty different occasions, Infantry Regiment 2 of the 1st Division on fourteen occasions, Light Regiment 5 on nine occasions, and Regiment 23 from Aargau on seven occasions. He showed the least interest in anti-aircraft defense, visiting only one out of ten detachments belonging to the 1st Army Corps; he never visited the antiaircraft units of the 2nd and 4th Corps.[31] A special list of his visits and inspections during one year, 1942–43, included 287 entries. On December 22 and 23, he attended seven Christmas parties for soldiers. Moreover, he made 105 "trips and appearances that did not serve strictly military purposes."[32]

For his visits throughout the country during the war, Guisan drove about 220,000 miles by car. He explained that he was on the road "by day and night, almost always with the windows open or the top down. That was healthy and the best way to air out my head after spending the day at the office."[33] The commander-in-chief had no aircraft assigned to him, but for urgent missions the command of the Air Force and Anti-Aircraft Defense let him use a Taifun or the army's only Fieseler Storch aircraft.[34] Denis van Berchem, a member of the personal staff, told this author during a private conversation, "The General had an urge to travel, see people, establish contacts, get his own impressions. That is when he felt in his element."[35] Part of the secret of Guisan's success lay in his ability to establish and maintain friendly contacts. Through direct encounters and conversations with soldiers, the General managed to inculcate a basic feeling of trust, which imbued the spirit of the entire armed forces.

Alfred Ernst summed up Switzerland's defensive potential during World War II in a nutshell by stating that the troops' morale was "good," the state of training was "inconsistent," and armament was "the weakest spot."[36] The state of training and issues related to training methods were the subject of a controversy among military experts at the very beginning of wartime duty. During the "Phony War," officers from the entourage of Wille and Däniker were among the first to argue that there was not enough time available for military training. During the third month of the war, Colonel Däniker complained to the Chief Instructor, "Apparently one believes that positions are what is most important for our army. I would prefer to fight with well trained troops in less well fortified positions than to fight in excellent positions with troops that are as insufficiently trained as they are now. If we are not allowed more time for training, building all these fortifications will be useless."[37] Däniker said that he expected Corps Commander Wille "to correct the false opinion that building fortifications was so urgent that training activities had to be completely neglected."

Criticism such as Däniker's was directed against Guisan, who was said to lack a grasp of the martial attitude that the German Wehrmacht had demonstrated during its victories. Däniker claimed that Guisan had "managed to let the army take several steps back in its development during the [first] eighteen months of wartime duty. . . . Military discipline has given way to a comedy. Influential positions are taken by dilettantes and people who have no character, or are overworked and have lost control as a result."[38] The Chief Instructor voiced similar complaints to the Head of the Military Department, albeit in a less virulent manner. Kobelt noted, "Wille expressed criticism about the way in which time was spent in the military. He said that too much time was spent on construction projects and standing on guard, and not enough time on systematic training, with a few exceptions. He explained that those troops who received training did so against the army command's orders."[39]

A few members of Parliament also criticized the lack of training. After the proxy committee had visited troops in the positions held during the first mobilization, National Councilor L. F. Meyer from Lucerne wrote to the commander-in-chief: "In order to relieve the army of duties that do not pertain to the military, the fortification work in the positions should be handed over entirely to construction companies. The army should dedicate its time to training activities. In some areas, training has been seriously neglected."[40] During a later proxy committee meeting, following a report presented by the Head of the Military Department, Councilor of State Keller from Aargau stated that he was shocked to hear that almost two years after being called up, the troops' state of training was still not adequate. He asked "whether one should not draw conclusions from this about the quality of the army command."[41] Federal Councilor Kobelt defended the army command, replying, "The troops have not yet been trained adequately because they had to be used to carry out the most urgent construction work. Moreover, the frequent rotations and leaves have made it impossible to conduct training as systematically as could have been done if the units had stayed on duty uninterrupted."[42]

The General had his own ideas about training methods that could help prepare the troops for combat. Unlike Chief Instructor Wille and instructors such as Däniker, Guisan rejected military formalism as well as drills and exercises at the barracks. He had declared at an earlier time:

> Less well-trained troops that you have under control are more valuable than well-trained troops that you do not have under control. It is the 'soldier's heart' that must be fostered and developed; therefore, an officer must love his men and gain their affection. In other words, the soldiers' mental and emotional attitude must be shaped. It is not sufficient to deal with their artillery, guns, and horses; most of all, one has to take care of the people who have to handle them.[43]

In addition to building fortifications, General Guisan placed great importance on modern training methods in the field. During a briefing at the end of 1941, he issued verbal directives on how to improve combat training. Among other things, he explained that initial training courses should not only deal with formal exercises. "For that purpose," he said, "the Chief Instructors must not only inspect what is done at the barracks but also make efforts to monitor the state of training in the field during combat exercises."[44] The General did not advocate a softening of the troops; on the contrary, through tough training during the times that a unit was on duty, he hoped to increase the spirit of resistance in the nation. As he commented, "Wartime duty provides a unique opportunity that must be seized. The same way in which we leave permanent fortifications to our successors that will show them our terrain's natural defensive strength, wartime duty must contribute, through the army, to building a stronger and tougher breed for the army in the future."[45]

Guisan repeatedly opposed meaningless drills at the barracks during initial training courses. Ernst has commented, "Thanks to his tireless efforts, [he managed] to gradually bring about a change in thinking and in action."[46] General Guisan had the correct impression that during training courses in the infantry, the army's main arm, essential skills were neglected in favor of less important drills and that experience from the war was not well taken into account. Going behind the Chief Instructor's back, he wrote directly to the Chief Instructor of the Infantry, demanding, "[I want] intensive combat training to be developed; it has to become the most important training activity in the infantry for officers, non-commissioned officers, and recruits. [I want] clumsy, ridiculous formalism to be completely eliminated as soon as possible; it is a waste of precious time."[47] He urgently recommended that Divisional Commander Probst carefully study the most recent combat strategies used in the war, to put the emphasis during his inspections on combat training. He added, "Leave your subordinates with the impression that they get their troops fit for the war instead of carrying out rituals at the barracks!"[48]

The General demanded that at the end of the initial training course, recruits had to be "complete soldiers who [were] capable of accomplishing their assigned task in a war."[49] Because many instructors were working according to a long-established routine, it was difficult to get them to train the recruits according to his ideas. In order to get closer to accomplishing that goal, temporary regiments were set up with recruits whose regular training period was extended by three months. This measure was based on an idea that Chief Instructor Wille had expressed during a meeting of the National Defense Committee before the war.[50] The General later considered that those regiments of recruits proved to be a failure because their "combat training was significantly inferior to that of the field units."[51]

It would be unfair to criticize General Guisan for not being concerned with training issues, as has been claimed by various people. He rejected formalism and demanded that new methods be used. A considerable number of instructions and rules and regulations were issued under his supreme command in an effort to improve training as a whole and combat training and maneuver exercises in particular. The Chief Instructor of the Armed Forces and the chief instructors of the different arms were responsible for supervising initiation courses and officers' training courses, and the corps commanders and divisional commanders were responsible for training the troops of the field army.[52] The commander-in-chief's written directives for training were drafted mostly by members of the personal staff based on his instructions. The "instructions on how to conduct a defensive battle" were drafted by Gonard, who was chief of the General's personal staff at the time. They were issued in November 1939, the third month of wartime duty, in adaptation of the 1927 "Field Service." The personal staff explained, "These instructions were the basis of the military doctrine that the Swiss Army adopted from the first months that it was on duty. They modified the concepts that had been adhered to until then in our army."[53]

As amendments to those instructions on combat strategies, during the first half of 1940, based on lessons that had been learned from the war until then, the General issued additional instructions that were to be taken into account during training activities. The "instructions on anti-aircraft defense" were issued in March 1940, the "directives on how to organize the defense against saboteurs, airborne troops, and tanks that break through the front" as well as the "instructions regarding demolitions and destructions" were issued in May 1940, and the "draft directives on anti-tank defense" were issued in June 1940. Moreover, some operations orders were amended by instructions on combat strategies. For example, in the fall of 1940, the operations order for the construction and manning of the Réduit had instructions attached with a total of 30 strategies on anti-aircraft and anti-tank defense, the use of reserve troops, demolitions, and general lessons for the defense.[54]

In the summer of 1941, instructions were issued "with the purpose of creating standard training methods" in the army. They included instructions on certain types of exercises to be carried out by army units during the six weeks they were on duty on a rotational basis, and on cooperation between the infantry and the artillery. Exercises during which two groups opposed each other were to be designed in a way that "the supposed enemy [had] more means available than the defending troops, the way it [was] in reality." Moreover, the commanders were told "not to hesitate to put troops that [were] called up into situations equivalent to the situations that they would encounter in a war."[55] It is interesting to note that those instructions were also initiated by the personal staff and went directly to the commanders of the army corps and divisions. Chief Instructor Wille and Chief of the General Staff Huber were informed only by sending them a copy of the instructions. Similarly, directives for maneuver and combat exercises were addressed directly to the army units.[56] In the summer of 1942, the Chief Instructor and the head of the Air Force and Anti-Aircraft Defense received supplementary instructions on the training goals that had to be accomplished with the infantry and the air force, respectively.[57]

At the beginning of 1941, the General had new regulations drafted for training the infantry, taking into account experiences in the war. For that purpose, a special committee chaired by Wille was set up, with the General and his personal staff supervising its work. In some notes that he prepared for a meeting with Huber, the commander-in-chief wrote: "Draft by committee of group III (Däniker) will not be accepted; the General will write to Col.-Corps Commander Wille about that."[58] Hence, the contribution by Däniker, who considered himself a specialist, was rejected. In a similar manner, another committee drafted new "regulations for the engineer troops."[59]

In his notes, Chief of the Personal Staff Barbey stated that he was the author of the "directives for training the infantry," which the General signed on July 14, Bastille Day, and which were addressed to Chief Instructor of the Armed Forces Wille and Chief Instructor of the Infantry Probst. Barbey commented, "[The directives make an assault] on a real Bastille, the ridiculous formalism that distracts the troops from what is important and wastes valuable time. The sharp style in which the text is written is meant to launch a crusade against the spirit created by the drills at the barracks."[60] Once they had found out that Barbey was the author of the directives, Corps Commanders Borel, Lardelli, and Prisi congratulated him and told him that they were pleased with them.[61]

The commander-in-chief paid special attention to training in the mountains, close combat training, and shock troop training. In order to coordinate training in the mountains, on November 18, 1941, the General ordered the creation of an "Alpine Central Office," which was directed by Major Ernst Uhlmann of the general staff and reported to the operational section instead of Main Section III.[62] Once Wille had been retired, the new Chief Instructor, Corps Commander Marcuard, was put in charge of the training courses in the mountains. The General wrote in a note for the file, "Certain reservations existed [before Marcuard's time] about the person [who should be in charge of training the mountain units]."[63]

Similarly, to improve close combat training for the infantry, Guisan ordered the creation of special grenadier companies, an idea that had been put forward by the army staff's "Section for Reforms in the Armed Forces." At a briefing chaired by the General on March 26, 1942, in Bern, Colonel Ernst Wagner informed the participants that it was planned to establish new units in the infantry called "Pioneer Companies," which would consist of a total of 100 shock troops, demolition troops, and troops operating flame-throwers. Chief

Instructor Wille tried to object to this endeavor, arguing that the need for such special units was "not urgent" and that not enough men were available. The General, who decided in favor of the new units specializing in close combat, asked the participants to come up with a more suitable name because the term "Pioneer" was already being used for engineering troops.[64] The first "Pioneer" training courses were to be held in the summer of 1942 on a trial basis.

The necessary preparations, particularly issues related to the number of troops and their equipment, were time-consuming. Barbey reported that Divisional Commander Constam from Zürich played a decisive role in putting the idea of the special units into practice. Montgomery's 1942 victory at the Second Battle of El Alamein showed the importance of specialized antitank troops taking on the enemy in close combat, and of close cooperation between sappers and the infantry. Barbey noted, "[The] General asked me to write a letter to Constam inviting him to analyze the issue. Among our high-ranking commanders, he is the one who shows the most understanding for cooperation between the arms."[65] Only in January 1943, after Wille was cast aside, was the final decision made to begin setting up and training the new units "as soon as possible, definitely in the course of the year."[66] On February 6, 1943, the General signed the order establishing the training for what Barbey called the "super infantrymen."[67]

At a briefing in the spring of 1943, the General informed the corps commanders that the new units to be integrated into the infantry regiments would be called "Grenadier Companies," adding, "That name should be the basis for the spirit among these elite troops and have a great impact on the attitude and morale among the corps."[68] The first grenadier companies went on duty in the summer of 1943. Barbey reported:

> For the first time, we saw one of the new organic grenadier companies, the one of Regiment 25, at work. It has been about six months since the General decided, after analyzing the lessons from the Battle of El Alamein, to create units in our army that are equivalent to the units that allowed the English to overcome the obstacle of an organized battlefield. . . . It was without doubt a good omen that from the very beginning the matter was put in the hands of a personality such as Constam instead of some office. That is why today we are witnessing an experience, which was made in the desert sand and which has been transferred and adapted to the situation in the heart of the Alps.[69]

In his report on the year 1943, General Guisan stated about the first experience with the new shock troops, "From the first months of 1943 on, the tentative creation of grenadier companies added highly appreciated support to our elite infantry regiments and opened up new ways of experimenting with anti-tank combat methods and with equipment. We noticed that this measure has already created positive emulation in our entire infantry."[70]

The example set by the grenadier companies encouraged the rest of the infantry to accomplish comparable performances. Other special units were established, such as infantry gun companies, intelligence companies, minelayer and demolition companies, and a motorized army police battalion, which was the first fully motorized unit in the army. The motorized army police battalion was slated to become a storm unit that was to defend the army command, resist paratroopers and saboteurs, and if necessary maintain order in the country.[71] Other novelties included the creation of a surveillance squadron consisting of professional fighter pilots, and as early as February 12, 1940, the creation of a women's auxiliary service that was based on the model of the Lotta in Finland.

Subject to availability, the entire army's equipment and weaponry were continually improved during wartime duty. Almost each time a unit went back on duty, the corps had received some new weapon or modern equipment with which it had to familiarize itself. In the infantry, such new weapons and tools as submachine guns, antitank rifles and missiles, rocket-launchers, flame-throwers, mines, hand grenades, explosives, and radio transmitters were intro-duced.[72] The antiaircraft defense received light and heavy antiaircraft guns. The artillery was reorganized and partly motorized. By the end of wartime duty, the antiaircraft defense and artillery had a total of 5,126 guns of a wide variety of calibers, of which 1,317 were field guns and howitzers, 696 were fortress guns, 166 were guns to be used in mountainous terrain, and 2,947 were anti-aircraft guns.[73] At the time the General retired, Gonard noted, "The main armament efforts focused on the antiaircraft and antitank defense."[74] During wartime duty between 1939 and 1945, a total of 2.5 billion francs were spent on armament and equipment, not including regular mobilization expenses.[75]

According to production statistics, in 1941 about 240 million pieces of ammunition were produced, in 1942 only 120 million pieces, and in 1943 as little as 60 million pieces. For the light infantry weapons, the spare shells were calculated to last for 11.2 days of fighting, and for the artillery and antiaircraft guns they were calculated to last 15 days.[76] During the briefing in connection with an operational exercise in 1944, Chief of the General Staff Huber stated, "[We now have so much ammunition stocked in the Réduit positions that] even if only one out of 1,000 shots is on target—assuming that fewer shots are on target would be a disgrace for a country with a long tradition of marksman-ship like Switzerland—we can kill one million enemies with our rifles and light and heavy machine guns."[77] Every soldier who went off duty was ordered to take 48 shells home with him for his carbine.[78] In the spring of 1941, the General approved a program by which ammunition supplies were to be increased. However, in spite of the seemingly impressive figures given above, and even though it was possible "to increase the supplies considerably," in his postwar report the chief of the general staff stated that the planned target had been only partly reached.[79]

Toward the end of the war, the soldiers on the whole were convinced that they had adequate equipment and had received adequate training. Even if they were aware that they had a lower number of heavy and mechanized guns, tanks, and aircraft available than a potential enemy, they were convinced that they would not make a useless sacrifice but would stand a real chance to defend the country. Hans Senn, a future chief of the general staff, argued that "apart from the lack of war experience," the state of training of Switzerland's militia army "matched that of any professional army. . . . The soldiers were physically well trained and were used to making great sacrifices. They mastered their guns so well under combat-like circumstances that the safety regulations could be relaxed without jeopardizing anybody's life."[80] For many years afterward, the officers and the rank-and-file who had served during World War II drew from the skills they had acquired on wartime duty and sustained among themselves the sense of community they had experienced during that time.[81]

The Final Phase of
Wartime Duty

THE ANGLO-AMERICAN INVASION OF THE CONTINENT at Normandy on June 6, 1944, offered Switzerland the prospect that its military and political situation would eventually improve. After the Allies next launched Operation Anvil, landing at the Gulf of Lyons on August 15, a large-scale pincer movement began to take shape against the German armies in France. If the Allies were successful, Switzerland would gradually be released from the grip of the Axis Powers. After landing in Provence, the troops of the French 1st Army commanded by General de Lattre de Tassigny methodically advanced up the Rhone Valley, supported by French resistance fighters of the Force Française Intérieure (FFI). They reached the Swiss border in as little as ten days.

The Federal Council approved General Guisan's request to call up individual divisions, light brigades, and border troops as necessary without any difficulty. On August 25, he signed a secret order instructing the corps commanders to cancel Operations Order No. 13, pull some troops out of the Réduit positions, and take the risk of facing a potential aggressor in the Jura Mountains and in the southwestern part of the Mittelland (midlands) if necessary. This strategy had first been studied under Gonard in the summer of 1942 as a possible variation of Operations Order No. 13, and again in more detail in early 1943.[1] The final order was drafted by Major Georg Züblin of the operational section on orders from the chief of the general staff. Barbey submitted the draft to Guisan for signature and reported, "[The General] is pleased with the personal instructions; he makes hardly any changes and signs it."[2]

On August 29, Light Brigade 2 was already stationed at the Ajoie near Porrentruy. By September 8, the border troops, consisting of five divisions, and three brigades had been stationed outside the Réduit positions on the western front.[3] The situation was identical to the campaign in 1940, except for the fact that the warring parties were moving in the opposite direction. In that situation, there was a certain risk involved in deploying Switzerland's troops, which were still neither very mobile nor powerful in terms of equipment and armament, at least beyond the fortified positions of the Réduit. As Alfred Ernst commented, "If we had been drawn into the war, we would have had to fight in improvised positions. The risk associated with this move was acceptable because as of the fall of 1944, it was unlikely that any large-scale attacks would be launched against us."[4] Barbey noted, "The General is aware of this risk and accepts it."[5]

The danger of Switzerland unexpectedly being drawn into the war was indeed only closely averted. Ten years later, it became known that during preliminary talks for the Yalta Conference, in the fall of 1944 in Moscow, the Soviet dictator Stalin had recommended that the Allies go through Switzerland to bypass Germany's western wall.[6]

That summer, the columns of the French 1st Army advanced northeast along Switzerland's western border from Pontarlier to Besançon before linking up, on September 12, with the armed forces of Operation Overlord that were advancing southeast from Normandy. In the course of the previous week, General Guisan had used the opportunity to speak with an injured French air force officer at the border checkpoint at Damvant. Barbey noted, "We take a look at his Citroën that is marked with a white star and is parked next to the customs building. It is the first vehicle of de Lattre's army that we have the privilege of seeing and touching. This is the army that was put together in Africa, landed in southern France, and is pulling us free from the grip [of the Axis Powers]." Guisan and Barbey admired the French officer's uniform. Barbey stated, "This is the first time we see the cap, the red neckerchief, the deep blue fatigues."[7]

In mid-September, General Guisan transferred his command post from Interlaken to the Mittelland.[8] The train that he used for that purpose was first stationed in Luterbach in Canton Solothurn for a few weeks and then in Delémont for some time.[9] On October 9, he moved to Jegenstorf Castle, which remained his command post until the end of the war. Like Gümligen Castle, the owners of Jegenstorf Castle were relatives of Major von Ernst, the General's 1st Adjutant. The castle had a sufficient number of rooms to fit the quarters of the General and his personal staff as well as their offices. Moreover, the arched basement could be used as a fallout shelter. Barbey wrote, "Under the guidance of Armand von Ernst, for whom this building has no secrets, we proceed from room to room to assign them to the staff. The General's room and office will be located in the southwestern wing on the second floor."[10]

"To be closer to the front," part of the army staff also moved from Interlaken to the lowlands.[11] At Gonard's suggestion, an "operational team" led by Chief of the General Staff Huber set up its quarters in Burgdorf. Barbey was surprised to learn that Masson and his intelligence service, whose input was relevant for operational tasks, had to remain in Interlaken.[12] The chief of the personal staff did not mention why this was so, but it is not impossible that this was an overt sign of a certain alienation between Huber and Masson, for which there were a number of clues.

In his report on wartime duty, the General wrote that "during the entire final stage of the war," he noticed "the staff and the troops had an urge [to serve in the sectors] which were close to the war events."[13] He took this urge into account by establishing a schedule that allowed as many units as possible to get a firsthand impression of the war. The General himself did not hesitate to repeatedly follow the action on the battlefields from a short distance near the border, mostly by looking through a collapsible telescope or by walking along the border. Barbey recounted an incident that happened while Guisan was visiting a border checkpoint at the village of Fahy in the Ajoie region: "When the General was speaking with a customs officer, we heard a noise that sounded as if some silk cloth was ripping, but we did not pay any attention to it. Several days later, we were told that an unexploded shell had landed a few yards from where the General had been standing."[14]

In October 1944, some troops of the 1st, 3rd, and 4th Army Corps were combined to form ad hoc Divisions 14 and 15. They were commanded by Colonels Samuel Gonard and Karl Brunner, respectively, and were stationed south of the Aare River as operational reserve troops.[15] Later that year, these troops of the two colonels, who were both instructors and whose training and performance had made them candidates for promotion to the rank of divisional commander, were aligned against each other during maneuvers. Gonard's 14th Division reportedly performed much better than Brunner's 15th Division.[16] As a consequence, Gonard was awarded the command of the 9th Division as of January 1, 1945, whereas Brunner had to content himself with the command of Mountain Brigade 11.

The fact that the two first-rate officers, equally ambitious and both born in 1896, were not awarded the same promotion caused an incident following the promotion ceremony, which the General conducted at the veterans' memorial at Les Rangiers on December 28, 1944. To the General's indignation, Colonel Karl Brunner, who was a disciple and supporter of Däniker, wrongly felt that he had been treated unfairly and protested by refusing to hand his dagger to Guisan to have it engraved in memory of the ceremony. Understandably, the General took this arrogant and undiplomatic act of protest badly. At a performance evaluation toward the end of wartime duty, Corps Commander Borel once again suggested Brunner for promotion to the rank of divisional commander;

however, the General objected, recalling the incident at Les Rangiers, which he qualified as "childish, a detail perhaps, but typical of his character."[17] Consequently, Brunner was not put in charge of a division until after the General had completed his tenure as commander-in-chief.

At the ceremony at Les Rangiers, the General promoted 44 officers, including two new corps commanders (Adjutant General Dollfus and Chief Instructor Frick), three divisional commanders, and three brigadiers. The remaining officers were promoted to border brigade commanders and regiment commanders. The numerous appointments at the end of 1944 brought younger blood into high-ranking positions. Dragoon Squadron 5 and the band of a cavalry regiment provided entertainment during the ceremony.[18] As with the previous year at the site of the battle of Sempach, the event was held without pomp but in a festive manner, as the General liked military events to be.[19] At noon, while the rumble of gunshots could be heard from across the border, the General addressed the promoted officers in front of the L'Eplatteniers monument. He reminded them of their challenging task as high commanders in the military, stating, among other things:

> Being a leader not only requires knowledge, determination, and faith, as I had stated last year. It also requires hope. A leader must believe in the victory that he prepares for and is determined to achieve. This war has provided an ever-increasing number of examples of troops that are in a seemingly hopeless situation, encircled and cut off from the rest of the army, but ending up playing a part in the whole picture all the way to the end provided that they do not lose hope. From the day of the Battle of Thermopylae until the present time, people have continually spoken about miracles that happen on battlefields. But are they really miracles? It is God's will, but certainly also the determination of every individual man, the determination of the commander. There can be a moment when his determination is decisive; it lasts longer than the iron rations and longer than the last shell. It lasts until all means have been exhausted.[20]

The General shared with the promoted officers his secret as a commander, explaining:

> Troops cannot be commanded from a distance. Paper, wires, and radio transmitters are no substitute for personal contact. The times when the commander was invisible and unapproachable are over. Today's military leaders, just like the great commanders of all times, go to the front

whenever and wherever it is necessary, not just anytime nor anywhere. They go to see their subordinates and talk to them, not to lecture them but to show them what they expect from them. They will do so especially during times of danger but also at the first sign of wavering.

The General reminded the officers more insistently than ever before of their duty to the whole country and of the need to respect soldiers as citizens, stating, "A leader must not forget that he commands human beings. I said so last year and am repeating it today: they are men who have a heart, a family, and a career as civilians. That is his way of being social."[21]

In view of the Germans' imminent defeat, Switzerland's neutrality became subject to a new test. It had become very unlikely that the retreating German armies would attempt to overrun "Switzerland the porcupine," as the Hitler Youth had boldly characterized the country in a song, on their way back to Germany. However, the political and military leadership faced the question of what should be done if the Allies infringed Swiss territory or tried to march through Switzerland. Ernst explained that to avoid being caught in an unwanted relationship of dependency on Germany in case the Allies infringed Switzerland's neutrality, "Only part of the available armed forces were to put up resistance against the invading Allies. The bulk of the army was to remain on standby in such a way that it could either intervene to fight the Allied forces attacking from the west or to counter a German attack."[22]

Senn put the two alternatives in that complicated situation in a nutshell, explaining, "In order to avoid entering the war on the wrong side, there were two options: either we could defend ourselves against both warring parties; or if the German Army gave us an ultimatum to accept their offer to support us and subsequently proceeded on their own authority, we could side with the Allies once they attacked."[23] Switzerland had to remain determined to defend itself and at the same time make every possible effort to avoid falling into the grotesque situation of being forced to become Germany's ally during the final stage of the war when the collapse of Hitler's Reich was imminent. In view of the circumstances, remaining completely neutral had become almost unbearable. Soldiers from Aargau who were debating what they should do if the Allies wanted to go through Swiss territory in one of the border areas concluded, "Shooting is out of the question; we would have to wave white handkerchiefs at them."[24]

In his postwar report, General Guisan wrote that soon after the landing of the French 1st Army, General de Lattre had given him "reassuring information" regarding his troops' advance along the Swiss border.[25] De Lattre expressed his views about respecting Switzerland's neutrality and avoiding incidents at the border in a conversation with 1st Lieutenant René-Henri Wüst from Geneva, who went to see him at his headquarters in Avignon on August 26, 1944, on orders of the intelligence service and with Guisan's agreement.[26] One month later, when the French troops had advanced as far as Switzerland's border area at Porrentruy, Corps Commander Borel informed General Guisan that General de Lattre would like to see him to discuss mutual steps to prevent incidents at the border. De Lattre suggested meeting General Guisan for a "military luncheon" at the Roches mountain pass.[27] Guisan would have liked to accept de Lattre's invitation, and through Major Bracher, his liaison officer with the Military Department, he requested Federal Councilor Kobelt's authorization to see the French general. However, Kobelt held the "opinion that a meeting between the two commanders-in-chief during the war [was] not appropriate." Hence, the meeting did not take place; instead, the local unit commanders were authorized to discuss border issues with the French Army.[28] In early 1945, after the French troops had crossed the Rhine and established a foothold in Lörrach, Germany, a few miles north of Basel, General de Lattre repeated his invitation to meet General Guisan at the border. Kobelt noted, "The invitation was once again declined for the same reasons."[29]

In his report, General Guisan gave a slightly different account of the facts, giving the impression that he was the one who declined the invitation. He wrote that he welcomed personalities who offered him "information from abroad" whenever he considered it to be appropriate. "However," he added, "I renounced receiving commanders of warring armies who were not allowed to enter Switzerland during the war because of its neutrality. In agreement with the Federal Council, one exception was made in the case of General Spaatz, the commander of the American Strategic Air Force, who in 1945 discussed with us ways to avoid repeating the tragic error that had led to the bombing of Schaffhausen in 1944."[30]

American Chief of the General Staff George Marshall had introduced General Carl Spaatz, the head of U.S. Army Air Force Operations in Europe, to Switzerland's authorities in a letter. He arrived in Bern on March 7, 1945, after the Americans had bombarded—again during clear weather conditions—the freight depot in Basel and suburbs of Zürich. Switzerland's commander-in-chief was present at the meeting chaired by Federal Councilor Kobelt. He considered Spaatz "very open and very fair by qualifying the bombings of Basel and Schaffhausen as 'stupid,' inexplicable, and inexcusable." Prior to the meeting, maps drawn at a scale of 1:250,000 had been transmitted to the American Military Attaché, Bernard Legge, on which the Rhine was marked in blue ink and the Swiss border in red ink. Using these maps they discussed with Divisional Commander Rihner, the commander of Switzerland's Air Force, technical measures that could help prevent misdirected bombings.[31]

Because the meeting between the commanders of the French and Swiss armies did not materialize, René Payot, a journalist and radio reporter from French-speaking Switzerland, with General Guisan's agreement, visited de Lattre's headquarters in Besançon where he spent three days. As an unofficial liaison person, he managed to obtain valuable firsthand information on the French Army. Upon returning from France, he reported his findings to the personal staff. Barbey summarized this information for the General, writing that de Lattre's army consisted of eight divisions with a total of about 160,000 troops, outfitted with top modern American equipment. No operations were planned near the Swiss border and Barbey added, "Switzerland has nothing to fear from the Allies." In addition, Payot reported that the French Army command was willing to detail a qualified liaison officer to the Swiss Army, and "General de Lattre would be happy to receive any officer or officers whom we would like to send to him."[32]

Following another mission to Besançon, Payot was invited for lunch at General Guisan's command post. He talked about Churchill having visited the French Army and the "high esteem in which the Prime Minister apparently held the Swiss Army and its commander." Barbey recorded the lively image that Payot drew of General de Lattre, writing, "[He has a] sense for operational matters which is very unusual in this war of materiel, [he has] ideas, enthusiasm, [he is] attentive and has one hundred [additional] captivating traits that are part of this already legendary figure."[33] In a conversation with Gafner, General Guisan also discussed Payot's activities as a liaison person, explaining that de Lattre had told Payot to let him know he was happy to have been assigned a sector by the Allies that bordered on Switzerland. Guisan quoted de Lattre as saying, "[The armies of the Axis Powers] put a chain around your country's neck. My army will try to free your borders from that chain and tenderly embrace your country instead." He was reported as saying that because he had great affection for Switzerland and its commander-in-chief, he was hoping "to be able render some services" to the country.[34]

In mid-November, the French operations to liberate Burgundy began. The Swiss Army command had been informed about the upcoming offensive several days in advance; General Béthouard, the commander of the French army corps that was stationed at the Swiss border, recommended that the Swiss mark their border with clearly visible signs and possibly evacuate the women and children out of a certain zone. Barbey noted, "[The French General says] that there is an inevitable risk of our receiving some 'scratches.' We will be informed in time about the moment when the offensive will be launched."[35] The information about the upcoming offensive reached Switzerland on November 15. Bracher noted:

As a sign of the good relations [between the two countries], in order to avoid incidents at the border, the commander of the French 1st Army Corps, which is stationed at the Swiss border, informs the commander of Switzerland's 2nd Army Corps, Corps Commander Gübeli, in a letter which is transmitted via special courier, that the decisive offensive on the opening of Belfort has just begun. Colonel-Corps Commander Gübeli informs General Guisan about it and is invited to thank the French commander for this information.[36]

Colonel Du Pasquier, the commander of the 2nd Division, received similar written information about the upcoming French offensive from the commander of the 9th Colonial Division, General Magnau. To Du Pasquier's surprise, the messenger wearing civilian clothes who transmitted the letter was French Lieutenant-Colonel Garteiser, who had been the liaison officer with the Swiss Army in 1939–1940.[37] Garteiser must have re-established contact with General Guisan's personal staff as early as October 1944. The General's papers included an unsigned note, which was probably written by Barbey, at the top of which Guisan noted, "Gart"[eiser]. The note stated that Switzerland was absolutely determined to defend itself against any infringement of its territory by the Allies and included a request that was apparently communicated to the French officer, stating, "It would be important for Switzerland's command to know that its territory will be respected by the Allies. A small sign, such as a simple 'moral reassurance,' would be worth something."[38]

General Guisan later told Gafner that de Lattre, whom he had met as early as 1938 in Strasbourg, was a real friend of Switzerland; during the entire campaign, the French General had made efforts "to remove all obstacles for us." Moreover, he was reported as recommending that the Swiss border be marked with the Swiss flag rather than the words, "Schweiz – Suisse – Svizzera" because his Colonial troops were illiterate. He had threatened them with the death penalty if they infringed Swiss territory.[39]

Toward the end of the war, neutrality restrictions were understandably no longer enforced very strictly toward the Allies. In early 1945, the French received the prototype of a 30mm gun produced by Hispano-Suiza, including ammunition, for test purposes. General Juin, the Chief of the General Staff of the French National Defense, thanked Switzerland's commander-in-chief "for approving this operation."[40] This gesture was undoubtedly a service rendered in exchange for the French 1st Army's generous consideration of Switzerland's interests during its drive along the Swiss border.

During the final stage of the French campaign against Germany, after the French had crossed the Rhine, Colonel Henry Guisan, the General's son, repeatedly visited the headquarters of the commander of the French 1st Army as an unofficial liaison officer. In two separate conversations, Colonel Guisan told this author that around Christmas 1944, while he was on duty with his regiment in Basel, he received the commander of the French troops, who was traveling incognito as a civilian accompanied by two adjutants, for lunch at the Casino Hotel. He reported that on that occasion, General de Lattre invited him to visit his headquarters, but he did not get an opportunity to do so until April 1945. Colonel Guisan explained to this author that he visited de Lattre in civilian clothes as a private citizen, but at "the General's personal official request." He added that he had spent a total of 10 to 14 days with de Lattre's staff, returning to Switzerland after every visit to verbally inform his father about it. He stated that he intentionally did not put anything in writing.[41]

Because the contacts between Guisan and de Lattre touched upon Switzerland's neutrality and were actually a matter that should have been handled by the Department of Foreign Affairs, the Swiss side tried to proceed with discretion and keep a low profile. When historian Jean Rodolph von Salis ran into the younger Guisan while visiting de Lattre's headquarters in Karlsruhe in the company of two journalists, the Colonel was "visibly uneasy" at being seen there.[42] Even Chief of the General Staff Huber was left in the dark about Colonel Guisan's visits with de Lattre. Huber later wrote to the Head of the Military Department, "I was not informed about a liaison officer being sent to the French Supreme Command before the end of the war. I found out about it through an incident during a reconnaissance mission along the northern border at the time the French were advancing there. The General certainly had valid reasons to hide this activity from me. He probably knew that I would not have agreed to it."[43]

After dinner on the evening of April 28 at the headquarters in Karlsruhe, de Lattre spoke with von Salis in private about Colonel Guisan's mission, saying that he was there on orders of Switzerland's commander-in-chief. Because von Salis considered that information confidential, he kept silent about it until, after the war, de Lattre spoke during a public speech in Colmar about a special envoy who had been sent to him by General Guisan. Von Salis subsequently wrote a detailed report about his conversation with the French General to inform General Guisan and Swiss Foreign Minister Petitpierre about it.[44]

Based on von Salis' report, Guisan asked his son to give a written account of the circumstances and purpose of his visits to the headquarters of the French 1st Army. Colonel Guisan explained that after getting to know Commander Georges, a liaison officer in the French 1st Army, during military sports events, he was invited to visit de Lattre's staff on several occasions. During these visits, he met a total of six times with the French commander-in-chief at his command post: once in Kandel, twice in Karlsruhe, and three times in Lindau. He said that he had made his visits at de Lattre's request, explaining that the French commander enjoyed discussing tactical and strategic issues with him in connection with his army's rapid advance, and that some of these issues addressed problems concerning Switzerland. He added, "I acted on my own behalf, pointing out at every opportunity that I had no mission whatsoever."[45]

The younger Guisan emphasized that it was only in connection with one of these personal exchanges of opinion that he pointed out to his host the importance of advancing along the Swiss border parallel to the Rhine all the way to Lake Constance so as to encircle the German troops in the Black Forest and prevent them from retreating through Switzerland. He also said that on a later occasion, he had voiced Switzerland's concern about the Russians advancing so rapidly through Austria that they might soon reach Switzerland's eastern border. Guisan maintained, however, that these discussions had a strictly private character, even though they were also intended to influence the French commander's decisions by making Switzerland's interests known to him. De Lattre was also given to understand that Colonel Guisan would be happy to be able to report to his father that France had taken Switzerland's status as a neutral country into account when making its plans. Nevertheless, he concluded, "It is my duty to point out that I never went on any mission to General de Lattre's; on the contrary, I was personally invited by him."[46]

The French gave a different version. In February 1946, during a prolonged conversation, General de Lattre told Switzerland's Military and Air Force Attaché in Paris, Pierre de Muralt, that while he was in Karlsruhe, after issuing orders to attack Ulm, a personal emissary from General Guisan urgently requested to see him. De Muralt continued:

Colonel G[uisan] explained to General de Lattre that he had been asked by his father to urge the French commander-in-chief not to focus exclusively on the operation against Ulm but to back it up with an operation at Switzerland's northern border between Basel and Constance in order to avoid having the German Army . . . forced to penetrate Swiss territory. The French commander-in-chief pointed out to the Swiss emissary the very serious inconveniences that modifying his plans would have for him, but declared that he was willing to think about his suggestion. After hesitating for an hour, which was extremely painful for him, he reluctantly decided to change his orders at the last minute and weaken the main push on Ulm by assigning one additional division and armored units as reinforcements to the right wing, which was originally supposed to stay behind to back up the main push on Ulm. The right wing received the new mission to clean up the region in the triangle between Basel, Lindau, and Ulm.[47]

De Lattre estimated that those rearrangements delayed the conquest of Ulm by three days and cost him additional losses during heavy fighting. He said that later on, Colonel Guisan returned to see him and thank him on behalf of Switzerland's commander-in-chief, but also to submit a new request: that French troops occupy the Austrian province of Vorarlberg, which borders Switzerland, to get there before the Russians did. De Lattre stated that he once again granted his Swiss colleague's request and changed his original plan, according to which he would have advanced on Innsbruck first with as many troops as he could.[48]

There are some obvious differences between de Lattre's account, as reported by de Muralt, and von Salis' and Colonel Guisan's report. General Guisan's explanations also differed considerably from what the French 1st Army's commander-in-chief told his Swiss visitors. After the war, General Guisan wrote to the Head of the Department of Foreign Affairs, "There is no need for me to confirm that I never sent Colonel Guisan on a mission to General de Lattre, but I authorized him to accept his invitations, knowing that the information he might obtain regarding the French 1st Army's movements would be valuable for us, especially at a time when I was concerned that the SS might destroy our factories along the Rhine."[49] He added that it was regretful that General de Lattre later let himself be carried away by "linguistic digressions" which did not correspond to the facts.

Guisan also reassured France's Military Attaché in Bern, General Gruss, that his son never visited de Lattre's headquarters on official orders, explaining:

Colonel Guisan . . . was fortunate to be invited by Commander Georges to visit the French 1st Army. General de Lattre was also very kind to invite him and receive him as a private person. These contacts resulted in an exchange of opinions about the problems that arose at our border due to the rapid advance by the French 1st Army in the Black Forest. However, the arguments that Colonel Guisan presented were always made in his own name.[50]

In the published account of the French 1st Army's operations, General de Lattre was a bit more cautious in his statements about contacts with the Swiss officer, but in principle he did not change his original version. "During the regular friendly visits that they made at my command post," he said, "officers of the Swiss Army insinuated that they would like our troops to arrive as quickly as possible at the Rhine between Basel and Schaffhausen, thereby ensuring that their border would not be infringed."[51] He stated that, so as not to disappoint the Swiss, he modified the plan of operations that had already been established, even though it was not imperative for his army to advance along the Rhine after taking Freiburg. He asked, "Was it not also our duty to take into account the permanent interests of the friendship between France and Switzerland, as Switzerland had always been loyal to France without ever failing to abide by the centuries-old rules of its neutrality?" He explained that after hesitating for a short time, he decided to take the risk of weakening the momentum of the main push, because, "At that moment, I decided in favor of the friendship between France and Switzerland."[52] That operation caused the Black Forest to be completely encircled and prevented approximately 65,000 German troops that were still stationed there, including some SS units, from reaching the Swiss border.

Based on the written evidence, one can hardly assume that the conversations Colonel Guisan held with General de Lattre were official talks—they were secret but were held on the Colonel's own account. However, based on the facts, it is also likely that General de Lattre was under the impression that the Swiss colonel was acting as an emissary for his father to transmit requests to him. This misunderstanding about the way in which the Colonel's moves should be interpreted caused serious differences between the two generals after the war.[53]

In addition to the controversial private "mission" by the General's son, during the last few weeks of the war representatives of the military went on two official missions to the French Army. In the second half of March 1945, Divisional Commander Corbat and Major Daniel visited French troops to obtain firsthand reports on the latest experiences in the war.[54] The second mission, originally scheduled to be headed by Chief of the General Staff Huber but eventually assigned to Divisional Commander Rihner, served primarily to study problems of cooperation between ground troops and the air force. The ten-member delegation included Barbey, the chief of the General's personal staff. During that mission from April 20 to 30, Barbey visited de Lattre's headquarters twice and witnessed the battles during the crossing of the Danube.[55] He wrote an extensive official report about his observations and activities during his visit with the French Army. It is striking that pages 60 and 61, on which a confidential conversation with General de Lattre must have been recorded, were carefully cut out of the report.[56]

As early as the last chaotic days of the war in Europe, the Head of the Military Department wrote a letter to Guisan requesting him to "think about closely examining and adjusting the measures that the military [had] taken to protect the country," indicating that the end of the war was in sight. He argued that the national debt had taken on alarming proportions due to spending for defense. Hence, it was the government's duty "to do everything they [could] and [were] allowed to do to decrease this debt on their own initiative instead of waiting to be put under pressure to do so by political and other democratic institutions." Kobelt wrote that he therefore considered it "necessary to prepare and, as far as possible, execute orders that [would] result in calling troops off duty and, as a consequence, contribute to cutting expenditures for defense." He explained that he believed that in the current situation it was "unlikely, if not altogether impossible" that Switzerland would be attacked. Guisan apparently did not agree with this view, annotating that passage in Kobelt's letter with the word, "Russians!"[57]

The General forwarded Kobelt's letter to Huber for comment and subsequently called him and the assistant chiefs of staff into a meeting. The reply, prepared by Huber and signed by the General, was evasive, stating that the suggestion would be examined but that no troops could be called off duty as long as the border remained closed, because "The troops that [were] currently on duty [were] all needed to guard the border."[58] The army command was extremely skeptical about demobilizing troops early. The General was concerned about how far the Soviets, who had shaken hands with American troops at Thorgau on the Elbe on April 26, could be trusted and how far west they would be able to advance in Austria.

As early as the beginning of 1945, when the war was approaching Switzerland from the east, the commander-in-chief ordered the general staff to undertake studies "to establish the principles for focusing the defense on the east."[59] In view of the Russians' rapid advance, he recommended that the chief of the general staff draft plans for "Case E[ast]" in order to "deal with this new type of danger, [adding] one must not forget about certain problems which the increasing victories by the Russians could cause inside our own country."[60] Chief of the General Staff Huber replied, "I consider that working out new plans of operation would not be advisable." Instead, he suggested making that issue the main focus of the next operational exercise.[61] Guisan agreed to that proposal.[62] Huber personally conducted the exercise that was held from April 6 to 14, 1945, in St. Gallen.[63]

Huber was not as concerned as the General about the potential danger emanating from the Russians. Shortly after the war, he declared, "When the German Reich was collapsing, and until very recently, omniscient people predicted that the Russians would definitely stage a war against Western Europe, that is, [against] the Anglo-Saxons, French, and ourselves. I never believed in that, considering these fears an unconscious suggestive effect of the German propaganda."[64]

For a short time, rumors about fanatic SS troops planning to retreat into a German "Réduit" in the Bavarian and Austrian Alps also gave rise to concern in Switzerland. It was feared that such an operation might prolong the war and cause new complications. However, the people who had planned the pullback for the Swiss Army into the heart of the country knew from experience about the problems that such an operation entailed. Hence, Gonard stated, "There was no reason to take this idea seriously."[65]

As early as April 13, 1945, the Federal Council decided as a precaution to completely close off Switzerland's borders to the north, east, and south—"as soon as, as far as, and as long as required"—to prevent the country from being flooded with refugees. Anyone trying to cross the border clandestinely was to be sent back; only Swiss citizens were allowed to cross.[66] The General enacted that decision on April 21, closing the border from Basel in the north to Altenrhein in the east.[67] Regarding the internment of German troops, it was ordered that only members of the regular German armed forces were allowed to seek refuge in Switzerland; members of the SS and party officials of the NSDAP were to be turned back at the border. The Grand Mufti of Jerusalem, a friend of the Nazis, who landed at Belpmoos near Bern on the afternoon of May 7 in a private airplane flown by a Luftwaffe captain, was sent out of the country the same night, shortly after midnight at St. Margarethen.[68]

According to the commander-in-chief's instructions, all requests for internment, which had to be examined by the Military Department, the Department of Foreign Affairs, and the Justice and Police Department, were to be decided in less than 30 minutes, regardless of the time of the day. However, supposedly it took up to five hours for certain decisions to be communicated to the troops at the border. The General demanded that the reason for the delays be looked into, suspecting that the territorial section, which was the link between the Federal departments and the army corps, was responsible.[69]

On May 2, 1945, German Army Group C, commanded by General von Vietinghoff, surrendered in Italy. Lieutenant-Colonel Waibel, the head of Intelligence Procurement Bureau 1, played a major part in the difficult, top-secret negotiations between Germany and the Allies, which had started in early March and were held in Zürich, Lucerne, and the canton of Ticino.[70] His direct superior Masson received only vague information about Waibel's role, and the commander-in-chief was not informed about it at all. After the war, when Waibel described, during public lectures, how he had contributed to bringing about the surrender of the German troops in Italy, Federal Councilor Kobelt asked the General whether he and Chief of Intelligence Masson knew about the intelligence officer's role as a mediator and whether they had approved it.[71] Guisan told Kobelt that he had been informed, through confidential reports by

Brigadier Masson, about the secret talks between SS General Karl Wolff and American intelligence chief Allan Dulles, but he had to admit, "None of these reports mentioned Lt. Col. Waibel's activity as a so-called mediator, so I did not know about his activities."[72]

Kobelt also asked Masson to explain himself on the matter. Masson replied that he had considered Waibel a "simple informant" and that his subordinate largely overstepped his authority.[73] When Waibel—who by acting as a mediator made a great contribution to shortening the war—made it known that he was about to publish his account of the events and had already found a publisher who was interested in his story, Chief of the General Staff Montmollin had the manuscript withdrawn and had the author renounce having it published.[74] Waibel's report was released for publication only twenty years after his death.[75]

On May 7, 1945, the armistice between Germany and the Western Allies was concluded in Reims, and on May 9 the armistice between Germany and the Soviet Union was concluded in Karlshorst-Berlin. Theodor Gut, editor of the *Zürichsee-Zeitung*, commented, "Never before in recorded history has Europe had to see so much fear and hatred, suffering and bloodshed, destruction and decay, horror and brutality as during the five years, eight months, and seven days of the war which has just ended on our continent." The war, which had brought untold misery, was "unreal and dark [like] a nightmare."[76]

On May 8, 1945, which the Allies declared Victory in Europe Day, General Guisan issued an order of the day to express his appreciation to the troops. He stated that the army had accomplished the duty with which it had been entrusted at the beginning of the war, and that through "divine providence" the country had remained unharmed. "Our army used to, and continues to, protect and shield us," he said. "It saved us from misery and suffering, from war, occupation, destruction, captivity, and deportation. . . . Honoring your oath of loyalty, you stayed put at your assigned positions. You proved to be worthy of your home country!"[77]

The Federal Council addressed the nation on the radio, expressing its satisfaction about the armistice. In its declaration, the government explained that the wartime restrictions, rationing, and other regulations dealing with the war economy could be lifted only gradually and that the peace entailed new tasks, especially social ones. It stated that the problems that had to be solved included social security, the protection of the family, prevention of unemployment, legislation in the agricultural sector, and the federal deficit. It added that the end of a war was a time "when expectations about the future [were] particularly great."[78]

When the armistice was announced, Switzerland's population was told that it no longer needed to black out its homes. At the same time, the army's measures to protect Switzerland's air space were cancelled. The General ordered:

1. As of May 8, 1945, foreign aircraft which infringe our territory will continue to be asked to land. However, these aircraft will only be fired at if they engage our fighter planes in combat activities.
2. The anti-aircraft defense shall cease fire until further notice.
3. In agreement with the Head of the Military Department, sirens shall no longer be used to alert the population.[79]

When the welcome news of the German Reich's capitulation became known, the chief of the General's personal staff, Barbey, was riding a train between Geneva and Bern. In the restaurant car, wine was "flowing by the gallons" and people were "laughing and singing" to express their joy.[80] Early the following morning, he met with the General to discuss when the troops should go off duty and how to officially celebrate the end of wartime duty in an appropriate manner. On the afternoon of "V-E Day," the General gathered his staff and personnel at Jegenstorf Castle to address a few words to them. Barbey reported, "He refrains from making eloquent statements and shows a certain concern about the near and distant future."[81] After dinner, Barbey made a speech, addressing the General: "Today is not Victory Day for us. Nevertheless, for you, for our army, for your officers who are gathered here around you, it is something no less beautiful: the day on which the task has been accomplished. . . . Today you told every soldier that he is worthy of his country. Please allow the Chief of your Personal Staff to tell you very simply, on behalf of his comrades, 'General, you are the first who is worthy of your country!'"[82]

Barbey suggested spending the rest of the evening in the nearby capital. While walking through the old town on the way to the Casino Hotel, the people in the streets recognized the General and followed him, giving him applause.[83] The *Berner Tagblatt* reported two days later, "When General Guisan walked on the arched sidewalks through the old town in the company of two personal aides, the public gave him long ovations. The crowd became so large that traffic on Market Street was temporarily blocked. The public kept cheering the General; the Commander-in-Chief of the Armed Forces reacted by thanking them."[84]

In the capital and in most other cities in the country, crowds gathered spontaneously that night, celebrating exuberantly. The *Berner Tagblatt* continued its report:

At nightfall, at first it looked as if the people of Bern were celebrating the Swiss National Holiday, but soon the scenery changed; street musicians showed up. People of more 'mature' age flocked to them, and soon after a few people started dancing on the square. Everybody started dancing through the streets arm in arm. New groups kept joining in, and in the end long lines of joyful people were shouting and singing through the city, cheering the Allies in a chorus, and screaming and laughing wildly. All of a sudden, one could hardly recognize Bern, a city that is usually calm and sober.[85]

The troops who were on duty celebrated the occasion in their own way. On the afternoon of V-E Day, the chief of the general staff put the relaxed duty schedule for Sunday in place for the army staff. The town authorities of Burgdorf invited the officers of the operational team to a snack at the Lueg.[86] On the evening of the same day, the soldiers on guard at the General's headquarters planted a peace tree in the middle of the town of Jegenstorf.[87]

Soon after the armistice, General Guisan invited the commander of the French 1st Army, General de Lattre de Tassigny, whom he had not been allowed to meet during the war for neutrality reasons, to a visit at Stein am Rhein on May 18, 1945 "to thank him for all the attention he had paid to our country."[88] Colonel Henry Guisan had already arranged the details of the meeting between the two commanders-in-chief in a meeting with the French general before the armistice was signed.[89]

On May 18, shortly after midday, General de Lattre, escorted by two motorized infantry regiments, arrived at the Swiss border at Ramsen, where Colonel Guisan welcomed him and accompanied him and his fellow visitors to their destination in Switzerland. De Lattre's companions included General Salan, who had forced the crossing of the Rhine at Speyer; General Valuy, who had been in charge of the drive along the Rhine to Lake Constance; General Béthouard, who had commanded the operations at Vorarlberg; Lieutenant de Lattre, the General's son; and the writer François Mauriac, whom Barbey had known since the time he lived in Paris. Mauriac, who was dressed in civilian clothes, asked Barbey, "Please tell me what I have to do; I am not used to such ceremonies at all and am afraid that I might do something wrong."[90]

General Guisan waited for his French visitors at the town of Stein am Rhein. He was accompanied by members of his personal staff, Corps Commander Labhart, the legendary Colonel von Tscharner, who had commanded the Moroccan 3rd Infantry Regiment before the war, and Divisional Commanders Corbat, Frey, and de Montmollin, three graduates of the Ecole Supérieure de Guerre in Paris. De Montmollin had been in the same class as de Lattre. A guard of honor made up of the 7th Division was standing on the main square of the town to receive the French visitors. Lunch was served at the Rheinfels Hotel and the aperitif was served on the terrace overlooking the Rhine. As Barbey reported about the meal, "Our guests raved about the boiled trout and the Fendant wine. . . . During dessert, the General addressed the chief of the French 1st Army, praised his strategy and his intuition to take aim at the Rhine. Then he offered him an alarm clock, playfully remarking that this instrument would perhaps not only help him get up in the morning but also go to bed at night." De Lattre's entourage reacted to that remark by laughing and shouting 'bravo' because they knew that their superior managed to do with very little sleep and expected the same from his staff.[91] According to the hand-written notes that he took for his speech, Guisan welcomed de Lattre as the first French general since Napoleon who had crossed the Rhine [into Switzerland] in a military operation.[92]

Barbey recorded that General de Lattre began his reply "in a low voice; his acknowledgement of our country and its army was so touching that we all gasped and my neighbor, General Davor, could not hold back his tears."[93] Chapuisat recounted that during his visit in Stein am Rhein, de Lattre also addressed press representatives, praising the Swiss Army and Guisan and recalling the saying by Jean Jaurès that "A national defense only exists if the nation puts its heart and its mind to it," and that this was very much the case in Switzerland.[94]

General Guisan informed the Federal Council about his intention to receive the commander of the French 1st Army only the day before the meeting, telling Kobelt that it would be an "intimate lunch among military people." Kobelt did not receive that message until after the meeting had started.[95] He was clearly aggrieved at being informed so late, writing to the General, "Your message reached me only on May 18, 1945, at a time when the talks were already in progress. However, I am glad to take note after the fact that from our side there were no further objections to that plan now that the hostilities have ended. . . . I would be interested to hear from you what common issues were discussed and what their results were."[96] The General was as irritated as Kobelt, telling the Federal Councilor, "I do not think any of the topics that General de Lattre and I discussed would be of interest to you, since the occupation zones have not yet been defined for good. Our meeting was just a simple get-togeth-er among military comrades."[97]

For Guisan's second meeting with de Lattre, the Federal Council was once again informed on very short notice. On June 12, the day before the meeting, Kobelt received a message from the General informing him that in return for the invitation of the previous month to Stein am Rhein, the commander of the French 1st Army had invited him "to lunch at a place that remained to be deter-mined on Lake Constance. . . . I consider it to be proper to accept the invita-tion. According to General de Lattre's information, the event will be a very sim-ple military affair. If I do not hear from you otherwise, I assume that you agree to this procedure."⁹⁸ The visit, which would take place as early as the following day, June 13, in Constance, was authorized by a decision of the Federal President.⁹⁹

General Guisan took ten officers with him to Constance, including Corps Commander Borel, Divisional Commanders Gonard and Du Pasquier, and Major Primault. It is interesting for several reasons that Chief of the General Staff Huber, who was supposed to be the top officer in the commander-in-chief's entourage, refused to accompany the General to Constance.¹⁰⁰ At the border checkpoint, General de Hesdin, commander of the Moroccan 4th Mountain Division, received the Swiss delegation. Barbey reported, "We drive to the Inselhof behind the cohort composed of Colonial cavalry troops, who ride on the asphalt streets of Constance that are decorated with flags, between two rows of French troops and German police. At the Inselhof, Generals de Lattre, Béthouard, Schlosser, etc. are expecting us, surrounded by their staffs and a large number of unit commanders of the 1st Army."¹⁰¹

The event was everything but "a very simple military affair," as Guisan had told the Federal Council. After lunch and the speeches, the two generals took the salute at a military show and watched the troops of General de Hesdin march past them. Barbey commented, "The parading units represent the French Army in its entire diversity, from the tanks of the 5th Armored Division and the bulldozers all the way to the romantic aspect, the colonial cavalry troops and the temporarily hired Moroccan troops on horseback." The French staff officers claimed that the preparations for the show and the parade had been more labor-intensive than some of the operations in the war. The Swiss felt less awkward about these efforts when they learned that other visitors were expected right after them, most of all General Devers, the commander of the American 6th Army Group to which the French 1st Army belonged.¹⁰² At the end of the glamorous day, de Lattre brought the Swiss visitors to Mainau Island, where French doctors and nurses were taking care of survivors of the concentration camps of Dachau, Buchenwald, and Mauthausen. Barbey reported, "We bend over groups of emaciated faces with protruding cheekbones, lying in rows of beds. If their eyes were not wide open, you would think that these deplorable victims were Chinese or miserable Orientals." De Lattre pulled General Guisan aside to tell him, "See, that is what I wanted to show you, so you can see for yourself."¹⁰³ The Swiss had to realize once again that destiny had spared their country from extreme misery and that it would take long for the wounds of the war to heal.

Two months later, on August 17, 1945, three days before wartime duty was officially over, Guisan met with de Lattre's successor as commander of the French 1st Army, General Koenig, in Switzerland. Shortly before the meeting,

General Guisan informed the Federal Council about his plan, writing to the Head of the Military Department that he was going to invite the French commander, who had expressed the wish to meet him at the border, for lunch "at Laufenburg, in a very intimate setting; no official reception is planned."[104] The two generals met in the middle of the bridge that crosses the Rhine, accompanied by five officers. One of the officers in Guisan's company was the new designated chief of the general staff, Corps Commander de Montmollin. The meeting did not include any military ceremonial; the group spent four hours together during lunch at the Solbad Hotel. The French officers accompanying General Koenig told Barbey that "the style, the energy, the youthfulness of [Switzerland's commander-in-chief] tremendously" appealed to them.[105]

Soon after the fighting ended in Europe, some members of Parliament rightfully requested that it was time to call the troops off duty and to lift the restrictions that had been imposed during the war, especially the emergency regulations concerning the press. However, the army responded in no uncertain terms that it wished to keep censorship in place at least as long as the General continued in office. At a meeting of the joint committee for media policy, National Councilors Bretscher and Feldmann, who were both editors of major newspapers, said they suspected that the army command's request to continue censoring the press "apparently aimed to thwart any criticism against the leading personalities in the army." Feldmann argued that the emergency regulations concerning the press had been introduced to protect the country, not the army commanders.[106] In a meeting with Federal President von Steiger, during which they discussed the suggestion made by the General early in the war to send a special mission to Berlin, Feldmann put his criticism into even plainer language, noting in his diary: "In this connection, I insisted that I was no longer willing to contribute to building a myth around the General which glorifies him as the one who saved the country from the Federal Council's weak hands. This myth downright falsifies history!"[107]

Guisan originally planned to end wartime duty and consequently step down as commander-in-chief on August 30, 1945. He informed the chief of the general staff, the adjutant general, and the two corps commanders, Huber and Dollfus, in writing that he intended to write to the Federal President and the Speaker of Parliament about his intention to resign exactly six years after being elected.[108] He first verbally informed Federal President von Steiger; however, von Steiger expressed his reservations right away, writing to the General, "I am sure that you will not hold any grudge against me if I tell you that I have noticed in the past few days that many citizens expect you to choose an earlier date."[109] He managed to convince Guisan that he might jeopardize or even spoil the sympathy, trust, and admiration he had gained among the population in the course of wartime duty if he delayed his resignation as commander-in-chief, arguing, "A people filled with chivalrous feelings would grant those three months to you and consider the date of August 30, 1945 as perfectly appropriate. However, unfortunately the Swiss listen more to cold reasoning. They would think that the date of August 30 is dictated by sentiment rather than necessity. . . . Would it not be regrettable if after such a wonderful performance, your resignation was associated with ungrateful criticism instead of genuine thankfulness?"[110] He explained that the Federal Council had wondered if it should do the General a favor by officially informing him of these considerations. However, von Steiger said that he decided to tell him personally, as the General was of course free to choose the date of his own resignation. However, he added that the Federal Council would like to avoid making this an issue for debate.

Von Steiger's flattering letter had the desired effect, and Guisan was sufficiently considerate to take the Federal President's concerns into account. In a letter sent by express mail, the General informed the Federal President that he considered the Swiss to trust him enough to understand that the troops had to remain on duty for a while; but he was willing to advance the date of his resignation to August 20, shortening the time of mobilization by ten days. He conceded that in fact the original date had been dictated by sentiment rather than necessity, even though much remained to be done for the army to wrap up their work.[111] Gonard's statement that the General picked the day of his resignation on his own is therefore not totally accurate.[112]

As early as the following day, General Guisan submitted his formal letter of resignation to the Speaker of Parliament. He wrote:

> Even if the armistice is not equivalent to peace, the ceasing of hostilities in Europe allows me to put an end to wartime duty soon and thereby also to alleviate the burden that this state of emergency entails for the country. Hence, I propose to the Federal Council to establish August 20 as the last day of wartime duty unless there are any unforeseeable circumstances. It is my honor to ask you to relieve me of my duties as Commander-in-Chief of the Armed Forces on the same day and to put me at the disposal of the Federal Council, according to article 51 of the Military Organization.[113]

The General wrote that the remaining time was needed to accomplish the various tasks connected with demobilizing the army. Moreover, he said that he would need additional time to write his report on wartime duty. Enclosed with the commander-in-chief's letter of resignation were letters of resignation by the

chief of the general staff and the adjutant general. It was up to the Federal
Council to decide whether to accept them.

The minutes of the Federal Council meeting dealing with the General's letter of resignation stated:

> The Commander-in-Chief of the Armed Forces, General Guisan, sub-
> mitted his letter of resignation to the Head of the Military
> Department, to the attention of the Speaker of Parliament. In this let-
> ter, he asks to be relieved of his command as of August 20, 1945. In a
> second letter, which is addressed to the Federal President, the General
> states that he has accomplished the task that the Federal Council
> defined for him on August 31, 1939 in his terms of reference. Based
> on the request by the Military Department, the Council decides the
> following: the General's letter of resignation will be forwarded to the
> Speaker of Parliament in order for Parliament to be able to decide on
> it in the course of the summer. The Federal Council recommends that
> Parliament accept the resignation. It expresses its thanks to the General
> for the services rendered.[114]

Hence, Guisan submitted his letter of resignation to Federal Councilor Kobelt
for presentation to the government. Barbey remarked that the General signed
the letter of resignation "without showing any sign of being moved."[115]

On the morning of June 20, 1945, Parliament received the General in the
presence of all seven Federal Councilors for a ceremony during which it accepted his resignation. The Speaker, National Councilor Pierre Aeby from Fribourg,
officially thanked Guisan on behalf of the nation. In his address, he stated,
among other things, "As a man who accomplishes his duty, you also showed
that you are a man with a noble sense of humanity and a good heart. The reverence with which you are received spontaneously each time you meet with our
good people is based on sincere affection. . . . General, the Swiss are proud of
you. They welcome you as a great soldier and a great fellow citizen and will be
grateful to you forever."[116] It is rare for someone to be applauded by Parliament
as long as General Guisan was on that day. He made a short reply, stating,
"Thank you, Mr. Speaker, for the kind words that you just addressed to me. I
only did what I had to do as a soldier: to watch over the country's safety during the six years that the World War lasted so that the country could live and
work in peace. The unity among the people and their confidence in me allowed
me to accomplish this task. My job is done. I am stepping down to join the
rank-and-file again and to be at my country's disposal."[117]

After a short ceremony, Speaker Aeby and Federal Councilor Kobelt escorted the retiring General out of Parliament. In front of the Federal Palace, a large crowd received him, singing the national anthem, accompanied by a cavalry band. They cheered him and crowded around him, making it difficult for him to get into his car.[118]

Thus, the General's official farewell at the Federal Palace was quite a show. However, behind the scenes some less respectful, whispering voices were heard. National Councilor Markus Feldmann, a future Federal Councilor, remarked in his diary, "During the more than heroic farewell to the General in Parliament, I had to try hard not to think about certain incidents, [otherwise I would have become] nauseous." He commented, "The truth had to be sacrificed to 'reasons of State' today."[119] As a result of relentless interventions, particularly on the part of National Councilor Feldmann, on August 7, 1945, the Federal Council decided to lift the restrictions to which the press had been subject during the major part of the war, thereby reestablishing freedom of the press in the area of foreign policy.[120]

The salute to the flag that the commander-in-chief planned to organize to step down from the command of the armed forces was at first not to the government's liking. From the discussions about whether or not such an official ceremony was appropriate, one gains the impression that the Federal Council feared it might turn into another tribute to Guisan instead of honoring the army and its accomplishments. Two days after the General had been given his farewell in Parliament, Barbey noted in his diary, "The sky is clouding up; Mr. Kobelt writes to the General that the Federal Council does not approve of the salute to the flag scheduled on August 19, the day before the troops go off duty. He writes that instead the Federal Council will invite him to a farewell brunch and will present him with a gift, about which they can come to an agreement at a later date."[121] It was thanks to former Federal Councilor Minger, who agreed "to defend the issue of the ceremony with the top authorities," that the government gave up its opposition and the General's plan was carried out.[122]

The General was not as successful in another endeavor he pursued during the final weeks of wartime duty: he would have liked to bring some new blood into the army command by placing some officers whom he trusted in influential positions. In early July, he submitted to Kobelt a list with suggestions for changes in top positions after his retirement. He proposed making Corps Commander Labhart resign, or at least reinstating him in the post of Chief of the General Staff Section, which was still his official title as a government employee. He suggested appointing Divisional Commander Gonard or Corbat as the new Chief of the General Staff, Corps Commander Frick as Inspector of the Armed Forces, and Divisional Commander de Montmollin as Chief Instructor. Among other proposed promotions for younger unit commanders, he recommended promoting his own son, Colonel Henry Guisan, to command of Mountain Brigade 10.[123]

Kobelt was not willing to follow the General's suggestions. After one month, he told him, "Taking into account all evaluations that have been communicated to us and all potential candidates, we have decided to propose to the Federal Council Colonel-Corps Commander Frick, the current holder of the post, as Chief Instructor. For the post of the Chief of the General Staff, we intend to propose to the Federal Council the current Chief Instructor of the Artillery, Colonel-Divisional Commander de Montmollin."[124] Kobelt did not say anything about Gonard or Colonel Guisan as candidates for promotion. Through that reply, the Head of the Military Department made the General understand clearly that he was no longer the decision maker in army personnel matters.

On the other hand, Guisan was so well respected and revered by the population that quite a few people would have liked him to stay on. Some young people from Lausanne publicly called upon the General to take back his resignation and remain at his post. In June, a student named L. Perrochon wrote an article entitled "The General Steps Down" in which he stated, "What if we did not accept his resignation? Tough luck for the Federal Council and Parliament. . . . OK, so we will not accept his resignation. The General will remain our General. His portrait is up, his example helps us, his courage gives us strength, his goodness makes us better, his confidence reassures us, his faith inspires us, so we tell him, 'Dear General, you can count on us, you can count on the young generation, they are following you!'"[125] The General was undoubtedly happy to read these words of devotion, responding to the student, "You say that you will not accept my resignation. However, that is what the law stipulates. On August 20, it will all be over. But the General remains your General, and I know that I can count on the young students as much as they can count on me."[126] On July 11, Guisan made a speech at the secondary school in Lausanne, from which he had graduated, during which he urged the students to keep their hearts open and to pass on the Swiss spirit of living peacefully together, reconciliation, loyalty, and fear of God during the upcoming rapprochement between the peoples on earth.[127]

One duty that the General set for himself before resigning was to bid farewell to the cantonal governments. Just as in September 1939, when he had traveled to the capitals of all cantons to introduce himself as commander-in-chief, he went on tour in August 1945 to report absent from duty. At several places, a ceremony was held in his honor, and at banquets at the end of the day, speakers paid tribute to him and he was presented with flowers. The trips took longer than expected, some of them taking place only after he had stepped down from office. On August 8, Guisan went to Frauenfeld and on August 15 to Chur and Appenzell, but he did not make it to Altdorf and Schwyz until September 7 and to Solothurn and Fribourg until September 19.[128] The first visits took place around the time of the dropping of the first atomic bombs on Hiroshima and Nagasaki, which inaugurated a new era not only in the history of war but also in the history of peace.[129]

The salute to the flag, which was the General's idea and for which Captains Mario Marguth and Beat Frey, two members of the personal staff, did a major share of the planning, turned into a distinctive ceremony that even impressed those who had originally opposed the idea. Guisan wanted it to be a symbolic act providing the population and the army with an opportunity to salute the standards "in a dignified manner. . . . The gathering should be neither a cele-bration nor a 'victory parade' but a simple event to express our gratitude."[130]

The commander of the 3rd Division, Walter Jahn, was responsible for organ-izing the August 19 ceremony, for which the standard-bearers of all regular and special units of the armed forces were summoned to the capital. Approximately 1,000 persons received an official invitation, including all incumbent and former Federal Councilors, the Speakers of both chambers of Parliament, the Presidents of all cantonal governments, the city authorities of Bern, top-ranking federal employees, all former corps commanders, divisional commanders, brigadiers, and regiment commanders who had served between 1939 and 1945, ten women rep-resentatives of the Welfare Office for Soldiers, and all serving commanders who were ranked battalion commander and higher.[131]

Former Federal Councilor Minger received a special personal invitation. The General wrote to him as early as three weeks before the event, "On 19 August, I am going to hold the salute to the flag which we have already dis-cussed together. It is my honor to invite you as a friend and a former Head of the Federal Military Department, and I will take the liberty to send you a detailed program ahead of time."[132] It appears interesting that Colonel Däniker, who had been disciplined, was not on the list of invitees, and the name of Lieutenant-Colonel Heinrich Frick was crossed out.[133] Among the few who did not accept the invitation were Divisional Commanders Bandi and Bircher, who had been made to resign. Bandi did not give a reason for declining the invita-tion; Bircher asked to be excused because he had to take care of his wife who had just undergone surgery.[134]

The day of the ceremony started at 10:30 a.m. with a public thanksgiving service for Protestants at the Cathedral and a thanksgiving mass for Catholics at Trinity Church. These were attended by the army command and representa-tives of the Federal authorities and cantonal governments. Barbey remarked about that part of the day, "Service at the Cathedral; it lacks solemnity and distinctive features. One would have preferred to have less time spent on the 'sermon' and more time on singing and organ playing, more solemnity."[135] After lunch, for which the General and his personal staff were invited to the Erlacherhof by the government of the city of Bern,[136] the persons who had received a personal invitation were asked to gather at the Bernerhof between 1:30 and 2:00 p.m., from where they marched to the grandstand that had been built in front of the Federal Palace. The General and the three Federal Councilors who attended the ceremony marched in front of everyone else. At 2:30 p.m. the march of approximately 400 standard-bearers began. When they arrived in Federal Square they formed a rectangle. A regimental band and a guard of honor consisting of a company of fusiliers, a company of recruits, and a detachment of dragoons who were on duty at that time provided the setting for the ceremony. The balcony on the second floor of the Federal Palace was reserved for the wives of the General, the Federal Councilors, and the unit commanders. Several thousand spectators surrounded the flag-bearers and crowded the access streets to Federal Square.

General Guisan and Federal President von Steiger made short speeches, addressing the standard-bearers representing the army and the people. The General briefly recalled the efforts that the population and the army had made to deal with the threat of the war, emphasizing the importance of national unity. He stated: "This sense of unity turned out to be crucial as the war was progressing. One single warring party surrounded us. We had to be prepared to fight on our own under extremely difficult circumstances. We decided to put up total resistance and to sacrifice ourselves. That is an experience that we want to remember forever. All Swiss stood closely united. It was no longer the army alone that was responsible for maintaining our freedom; workers, farmers, and civil servants all summoned up their strength to satisfy the country's vital needs." The audience was particularly pleased to hear that the General expressed his gratitude toward women, who "were bearing a large share of the material worries and, through their love, provided their husbands and children with immense strength." The General concluded his speech by saying, "May God protect you, banners! I am handing you back to the Federal Authorities unharmed. I expect those who supported me during the past six years to continue to serve you unwaveringly and to continue gathering new courage and new strength."[137] His words were met with great applause.

On behalf of the government, Federal President von Steiger expressed the country's thanks to the army and to the commander-in-chief, stating, "This morning, we paid reverence to God. Now the Federal Council and the Cantonal Authorities would like to thank you, General, all officers, non-com-

missioned officers, soldiers, and men and women who are members of an auxiliary service, for loyally safekeeping and guarding the country and tirelessly
doing your duty during those six years." The Federal President also paid tribute to women, explaining that they did their best during the time that the army
was mobilized "to keep the workshops, factories, and farms running." He said
he hoped that the people would successfully accomplish in harmony, justice,
loyalty, and peace the "tremendous tasks" that Switzerland's democracy now
faced, adding, "Therefore, today's salute to the flag is a day of exhortation. Let
it be a day of encouragement to increase our efforts."[138]

After the singing of the national anthem, the flag-bearers carried their banners past the saluting General into the Federal Palace. Before they were returned
to the various arsenals, the banners remained on view to the public for three
days in the foyer of the Federal Palace, in front of the statues of the three legendary Swiss Confederates swearing, on August 1, 1291, to free their land from
foreign tyranny.

Toward the evening of August 19, to conclude the memorable event, the
General summoned the staff officers, the serving regiment commanders and
commanders ranked above them to a last briefing at his command post at
Jegenstorf Castle. The Bernese cavalry band provided the setting for the briefing by playing military marches.[139] In the presence of the Head of the Military
Department and the Chief of the Main Section on the army staff, approximately 400 officers stood in a semicircle on the lawn in front of the castle, one army
corps next to another, similar to the briefing at the Rütli five years earlier. The
General made a long farewell speech, in which he talked about his "difficult and
multifarious" mission, adding, "Nevertheless, or precisely because of that, it was
also a very beautiful mission. I gladly acknowledge that. It is therefore all the
more difficult to say good-bye now." The officers felt grateful yet also pensive
when the General explained to them:

> The task that you are facing will not be easy. Let me tell you why.
> Gratitude is a short-lived feeling. Today public opinion acknowledges
> your merits in connection with keeping Switzerland a free country;
> however, this acknowledgment can soon fade. You will get only limit-
> ed moral credit for the time that you served in the course of the past
> six years, no matter how beautiful and valuable the memories are that
> you and all of us have kept of that time. That experience is yours alone
> and that of your comrades. Moreover, imagination is a rather rare gift.
> A large majority of our people prefers not to think about whether and
> in what ways our country could become subject to new threats in the
> future. Between 1920 and 1930, and even later, they did not deal with

that issue very much either. We will have to keep doing what we did at that time, especially from 1933 on, to shake them out of their apathy, stir up their conscience, and admonish them to be on their guard.[140]

The General also commented:

The times of 'playing soldiers' games' are over, never to return. During wartime duty, I fought against a certain tendency toward formalism and excesses, which I called 'the spirit of the barracks.' This common tendency is even more dangerous because we did not have to prove ourselves in the war. We can counteract this tendency if we think about the dignity of the men whom we have the honor to command and keep in mind that we may or must ask each one of them to sacrifice his life if necessary.

To be able to cope with the challenges of the future, Guisan suggested, "First we have to be Swiss and then soldiers; [we have to be able to continue] finding our own solutions for Switzerland [because] everything useful and durable that we have done so far has been based on solutions that were tailor-made for Switzerland. They were always the cleanest and best solutions." At the end, General Guisan assured his subordinates, "I will remain your older comrade in whom you can confide any matter and who will be happy to receive you whenever you need his advice."[141]

Federal Councilor Kobelt also addressed the officers in Jegenstorf, expressing his recognition to the commander-in-chief and his helpers, "particularly for the understanding cooperation with the Federal Government." He pointed out the tasks that would have to be accomplished by the Military Department after the war, explaining that because Switzerland was a democracy, the decision-making process would "naturally become more cumbersome and laborious" once again. Hence, he asked the officers to "take an active part in relentlessly informing the people, warning them against half-truths, refuting wrong ideas and opinions with good arguments, and fighting against secret and overt enemies of our national defense."[142]

General Guisan's statements at the final briefing in Jegenstorf, and his last order of the day, issued on August 20, 1945, were what could be called the military legacy of the Commander-in-Chief of the Swiss Army during the Second World War. The order of the day in which he bade farewell to the troops also contained some memorable phrases that have remained valid to the present. He wrote:

Serving in the army means doing one's best for the country. I would like all of you who served with dedication between 1939 and 1945 to develop more intensive and more human feelings. In this era where there are many different demands and disputes, these feelings will allow you to better grasp the value of life and health, which you vowed to sacrifice. If everyone who speaks and takes action nowadays appreciated these values, we would be able to look to the coming time of peace with more confidence.

General Guisan admonished the soldiers that the army had to "incessantly continue to develop, perfect itself, and gather new energy," or else it would become a heavy burden. Guisan concluded the order by assuring the soldiers he had commanded, "I will never forget you; it is very difficult for me to say good-bye to you." He added that he was stepping down but would always remain their comrade and their general.[143]

On the occasion of his retirement, General Guisan received numerous congratulatory letters and acknowledgments. Those congratulating him included foreign dignitaries such as the Apostolic Nuncio, Monsignor Bernardini, and the head of the French National Defense, General Juin. The Nuncio stressed Guisan's faith, stating, "Many people consider you, dear General, a great soldier embodying the perfect love of his country; I for my part think of you as a *believer*."[144] Juin acknowledged, "History will not fail to point out the role of the Swiss Army, which has turned into a formidable and dreaded instrument through the vigilance and determination of its commander. One may say that it was due to the army that your country was able to remain a safe haven and a haven of generosity in a Europe full of turmoil."[145]

Former Federal Councilor Minger once again told his friend that the honorable task of commanding Switzerland's armed forces could not have been bestowed on anyone more worthy than Guisan.[146] The General for his part confirmed to the former Head of the Military Department, "The day of the salute to the flag was also a special day for the one who assembled the tool with which the commander-in-chief was able to hold out at the border and in the Réduit positions during six years of wartime duty. Providence allowed me to take on the supreme command under your aegis. The cooperation between the Head of the Military Department and the General was based on mutual trust."[147]

On the evening of the day on which the troops went off duty, General Guisan, Chief of the General Staff Huber, and Adjutant General Dollfus were received by the government for a farewell dinner at the Lohn mansion in Kehrsatz outside Bern. On that occasion, Guisan was presented with the Federal Council's official gift, a grandfather clock from Neuchâtel. That gift was chosen after consulting with the General's wife; the two other gifts the government had considered offering him were a set of silverware and a sword of honor.[148]

The dinner ended on a note of discord which caused the General to complain to Federal Councilor Etter, writing, "Yesterday, following the dinner that the Federal Council generously offered to me, you expressed your surprise, or rather you criticized me for failing to express my thanks or pay tribute to the Federal Council during the salute to the flag." Etter suspected that the General had intentionally not mentioned the Federal Council in public. Guisan vehemently protested "against that insinuation," stating, "It is wrong and offensive; I cannot accept it." The General argued that during the salute to the flag, he had to thank all those who had been serving the country under his command, adding, "I have no authority to express thanks or pay tribute to anyone else. By the way, for what exactly should I have thanked the Federal Council? For the work it did in general during those six years? Of course you are the supreme authority in the country from which I received my terms of reference, but it was not up to me to thank you for that."[149] Federal Councilor Etter apologized to the General right away, sending him a handwritten letter in which he admitted that he went too far with his criticism. He explained, "I regretted after the fact that I made my remarks sound as if I was reproaching you. Let us remain what we have always been: real friends!"[150]

Although the troops officially went off duty on August 20, 1945, the General's personal staff remained on duty for a few extra days to file papers, hand some of them over to the Military Department, and to prepare the documents necessary to write the report to Parliament. On August 29, 1945, the flag at the commander-in-chief's command post in Jegenstorf was lowered for the last and final time.[151] The General's driver, non-commissioned Adjutant Eugène Burnens, and his secretary, non-commissioned Adjutant Konrad Huber, continued to serve as his personal aides for some time afterward. The General continued working at his office until August 29. On that day, Barbey knocked on his door to submit a few documents for signature. He described the mood, writing, "He shouts at me, 'Come on, come on', which was highly unusual for him. . . . A lump got into his throat. And into mine as well."[152]

That afternoon, Burnens drove General Guisan back to the shores of Lake Geneva, where he would continue his life as a civilian. Upon arriving in Canton Vaud, between Chexbres and Epesses his car was stopped by a group of young people who had blocked the road with a huge Swiss flag. They received Guisan with cheers and presented him with flowers. District authorities, the Mayor, and the Town Councilors of Puidoux as well as winegrowers from the region surrounded him, carrying a glass of wine in their hands to offer him a drink welcoming him to his home canton. The General was allowed to continue on his way home only after being symbolically kept as a prisoner for two hours.[153]

On the last day the army was demobilized, August 20, 1945, 33,202 troops remained on duty, almost half of whom were undergoing regular training courses. The remaining troops were serving at the frontier to assist the customs and border officials.[154] In the course of wartime duty between 1939 and 1945, a total of 900,000 men and women—20 percent of the country's total population—had been on duty. Approximately 500,000 of them were soldiers, 300,000 were serving in an auxiliary service or on antiaircraft units, and 100,000 were members of local civil defense units.[155] They were rightly proud to have contributed to safeguarding the country. After 2,180 days of wartime duty, the army was in perfect shape physically, psychologically, and in its training. After a six-year war, General Guisan relinquished the command of an army that was more experienced, rejuvenated, and mobile than he had found it.[156]

III

AFTER GUISAN'S SERVICE AS COMMANDER-IN-CHIEF (1945–1960)

Trouble with Masson

AT THE END OF THE WAR IN EUROPE, when the public began to hear bits and pieces about Chief of Intelligence Roger Masson's relations with the German SS leadership, Federal Councilor von Steiger wrote to the General, "There is no denying that members of Parliament and part of the people suspect that certain staff officers of the intelligence service and security service permitted themselves to do things incompatible with the ethics of a public servant." Von Steiger explained that he did not wish to pass judgment on anyone prematurely, but he felt obliged to inform the commander-in-chief that the government was continually receiving protests regarding this matter, with potential damage to the army's reputation. He stated that it appeared as if Colonel Masson "did not abide by the instructions he had received [and that his actions] blatantly violated the neutrality policy established by the Federal Council and infringed the penal code in several respects."[1]

The Federal President also asked the General to see to it "that similar encroachments by the intelligence service and security service come to an end once and for all." In view of that intervention, on May 14, 1945, in the week after the German surrender, the commander-in-chief ordered a preliminary evidentiary hearing.[2] During his examination by the investigating judge, Masson explained the importance of the army's intelligence ties with the German SS, though he openly admitted that some officers of the service, such as Colonel Werner Müller and Majors Hausamann, Ernst, and Waibel, had repeatedly protested against the connection with Schellenberg and Eggen. He added, "I did not share their concerns, considering the connection as valuable for our country. I am responsible for our country's intelligence service; hence, I am the one who decides which connections are maintained."[3]

In his report on the evidentiary hearing, the Military Attorney General did not refrain from criticizing Masson. He argued that the intelligence service could claim that special circumstances applied to its case and that "the right hand [was] not allowed to know what the left hand [was] doing." However, Military Attorney General Eugster explained that this should not apply to the chief of intelligence, stating:

> [Masson] blindly accepted everything that Schellenberg and Eggen told him as the truth. . . . Hence, the SS leadership was able to unscrupulously misuse his excessive trustfulness. It is no secret now and was no secret at the time of what things the SS leadership was capable. In the event of an attack on our country, the SS would certainly have taken advantage of this excessive trustfulness to pull the wool over our eyes at a critical moment. Because of his personal, albeit purely intellectual, relations, our Chief of Intelligence was bound to fail during such a critical situation.

Eugster also criticized Masson on the grounds that by establishing relations with the SS officers, Masson became personally involved in foreign political matters "without previously consulting with the Federal Government or obtaining its authorization."[4] Moreover, the Military Attorney General remarked that it appeared that Masson had been disobedient and abused his power, especially when he singlehandedly authorized the SS officers to travel to Switzerland without informing the civilian authorities. Nevertheless, in spite of substantial reservations, the Military Attorney General concluded that the country's neutrality policy had not been infringed, that no warring party had been favored, and that the intelligence service had not undertaken any illegal activity. Hence, he asked the commander-in-chief not to pursue the matter further but rather content himself with reprimanding the chief of intelligence.[5]

After the fact, the connection with the SS and the relations with Schellenberg also caused Guisan and Huber considerable trouble. Corps Commander Huber protected the chief of intelligence, writing to the General, "You and I both knew about the connection between Masson, Eggen, and Schellenberg, and we both tolerated it. If this connection were against Masson, our destiny would be closely tied to his."[6] It is impossible not to notice the critical undertone in the chief of the general staff's further remarks. He stated, "You knew about the connection even before I did. Masson informed me only after becoming persona non grata to you and remembering thereafter that he could take the official route and that taking the correct route could be more advantageous than taking the direct route." Huber explained that he had found out about the General's meeting with Schellenberg and Eggen only after the fact and "It was not until [I] saw some documents during the investigation that [I] received the first information about the circumstances of the meeting of March 3, 1943 in Biglen."[7]

Huber explained that he did not consider the connection with Schellenberg as inappropriate and therefore tolerated it, stating:

> The Third Reich was commanded by a lunatic who did not act rationally but according to spurs of the moment. If someone in his entourage could exercise some random influence in this kind of atmosphere, even if he was a lower-ranking person, it could be decisive. If a man in the Führer's entourage made it clear that Switzerland was not defenseless but was absolutely determined to use its weapons and other advantages, that it was not at all an easy prey like Denmark and Norway, that it was more useful to the Reich as a neutral country supplying materials than as a wasteland scattered with partisans, that the Swiss Army would be able to put up resistance for a long time in the fortified Réduit, that the Reich's communication channels across the Alps would be completely interrupted, etc., that kind of information could prevent [the Reich] from staging a war against us. The Masson-Schellenberg connection was an excellent means to get that message across to the Reich. I considered Masson to be willing and absolutely capable of exercising that kind of influence on Schellenberg.[8]

Huber probably made a realistic assessment of the SS informants' motivations, remarking:

> I never had any doubt that Schellenberg and Eggen did not act out of selflessness; their actions were certainly not governed by their affection for Masson. Their driving force could have been the Reich's interests or their own personal interests. I tended to favor the idea that Schellenberg and Eggen were looking out for their own interests; that was quite typical of Nazi leaders. I considered Eggen to be an upscale black marketer; my view of him improved somewhat when he negotiated the purchase of twelve Messerschmitt aircraft.

Huber also believed it was not impossible that the two SS officers had felt as early as 1943 that the Third Reich was doomed and thus tried to establish suitable relations in Switzerland "so they could take care of number one when the time came."[9] The chief of the general staff remorsefully admitted that he failed to realize that Masson's connection with Schellenberg might jeopardize Switzerland's "other antennas at the Führer's headquarters," by which he meant the Viking connection.

Masson, who was suspended from his post during the preliminary evidentiary hearing, wrote an account of the intelligence service's connection with the SS to the attention of the investigating judge in order to defend himself; however, he deliberately left out the fact that Guisan knew about the connection. He informed the General about the omission, writing:

> You will not fail to notice that neither your name nor the name of your son is mentioned in my report, even though I could have been tempted to cover myself behind your authority, at least regarding the principle of my contacts with Schellenberg, about which you were constantly kept up to date. In the report, the so-called 'Charité' affair is not mentioned either. I can tell you now that I was quite worried about that affair at the time and that it was the main focus of my initial activity with Schellenberg.[10]

Masson explained that it was not for him to make a judgment about the contacts with the French Army, which he said were without a doubt justified at the time, but that he had feared that documents existed which the Germans could have exploited against Switzerland. He added, "In the beginning, Schellenberg talked to me about them on several occasions and promised to me that he would make them disappear."[11]

The General undoubtedly recognized the significance of the insinuations that Masson made in his letter. He replied to him that he saw "no sufficient reasons" not to let him go back to his post and that he would receive him at his command post on August 10, 1945 at 15.00 hours to "inform [him] about the consequences of this matter."[12] Guisan left it up to Masson's direct superior, Chief of the General Staff Huber, to rebuke the chief of intelligence. Huber followed the Military Attorney General's recommendation, verbally reprimanding Masson because as late as 1944 he had defied the Federal Council's instructions and "the General's order of May 12, 1944" by letting German SS Major Eggen, a former cavalry captain, enter Switzerland without a visa.[13]

Masson's temporary suspension did not go unnoticed. Public sentiment escalated against the chief of intelligence, who was known to have favored a stricter censorship of the press. A flood of suspicions and rumors began spreading about Masson and attacks were launched against him. He was accused of non-neutral conduct, corruption, and even of giving away diplomatic and military secrets. Through his own clumsy behavior, he came under increasing pressure by those who started a polemic in the press after the war, wanting to purge the country of all Swiss who had been convicted or merely suspected of being willing to directly or indirectly accommodate the Third Reich when the threat of invasion was looming.

In the summer of 1945, Masson was careless enough to tell a foreign journalist about his intelligence service's connection with the SS officers, stating that their help had made it possible to avert an attack on Switzerland. On September 28, 1945, Swiss newspapers published an article by the Exchange news agency explaining that the London-based *Daily Telegraph* had printed an interview by American journalist Paul Ghali with Switzerland's Chief of Intelligence. The article read, "Masson told the correspondent that in March 1943, the Germans had intended to invade Switzerland and annex it after completing their campaign. He said that Hitler had personally ordered that all preparations be made for a military and a political campaign, and had thirty special divisions go into position near the border." The article explained that, surprisingly, the plan was dropped after Himmler's right hand, Walter Schellenberg, the head of the SS Secret Service, had managed to convince Hitler, thanks to Switzerland's Chief of Intelligence, that Switzerland was more useful as a neutral country than as an occupied country. The article continued by stating, "Schellenberg reportedly gave Hitler his word of honor that the Allies would face tough resistance if they tried to infringe Switzerland's neutrality and in that event the Swiss Army would undoubtedly fight the Allies. Hitler allegedly calmed down and was convinced by Schellenberg's arguments."[14]

This news from Britain came as a bombshell in Switzerland. The public was dismayed, and the entire press, from the conservative *Neue Zürcher Zeitung* to the communist paper *Vorwärts*, was outraged.[15] Except for the few officials who were informed, no one had known anything specific about the secret connection with the criminal SS. It appeared disturbing that Masson had been on close terms with an SS general who was one of Himmler's closest collaborators; at the same time he was blamed for awarding the sensational interview to a foreign journalist.[16]

During the 1945 fall session, National Councilors Eugen Dietschi (Radical Democrat, Basel), Urs Dietschi (Radical Democrat, Solothurn), and Walther Bringolf (Social Democrat, Schaffhausen) asked the Federal Council for an explanation of the matter. In reaction to these requests, Federal Councilor Kobelt stated:

> With all due respect for Colonel Masson's great merits in connection with expanding and heading Switzerland's intelligence service, I have to condemn the indiscretion that he committed in his interview with

a foreign press representative. He was not authorized to give out inside information. In addition, his statements were very subjective. If it had been possible to inform the press, Switzerland's press could have expected to be given priority."[17]

The Head of the Military Department explained that it was true that Masson had been in contact with SS General Schellenberg but that there was "nothing objectionable about that per se," because in his position, Masson had maintained relations with high-ranking officials of both warring sides. Moreover, the commander-in-chief had continually been kept up to date about the connection with Schellenberg and Eggen. He added, however:

> The information that was published in yesterday's *Journal de Genève*, according to which the Federal Council had approved of the Masson-Schellenberg connection, is inconsistent with the facts. On the contrary, the Federal Council warned against this connection on several occasions, and in particular the Head of the Federal Department of Justice and Police and myself pointed out on several occasions that the relations that Switzerland's Chief of Intelligence entertained with SS General Schellenberg were intolerable.

Kobelt informed Parliament that investigations had been undertaken against Masson on two previous occasions and that Masson had been "temporarily suspended from his job at his own request." The Federal Council would "of course ask [Masson] to explain himself."[18]

After his case had been publicly discussed in Parliament, the attacks against Masson intensified, even though he was said to have good personal qualities and to have acted out of good intentions, trying to serve the country. In his distress, Masson asked the General to make a public statement in his favor, writing, "General, with your great authority and immense popularity, you are the only one who can shield me from, and defend me against, all the slander! At the last briefing in Jegenstorf, you told us that you would stay with us and would not abandon us. At this grave moment in my own life and my family's life, may I ask you to make a gesture that I deserve, because you know the truth?"[19]

Masson added the draft of a "statement by General Guisan" to his imploring letter, which explained that the commander-in-chief had approved of the connection with SS officers Schellenberg and Eggen as being in the country's interest and had been fully informed about it at all times. The draft added that the Chief of Intelligence was an officer whose loyalty, conscientiousness, and love of country should not be questioned.[20]

Guisan could not bring himself to make such a public statement in favor of Masson. However, he wrote a letter to Federal Councilor Kobelt to support the cause of the former chief of intelligence along the lines indicated in Masson's draft statement.[21] Masson must have felt disappointed and abandoned by Guisan's evasive move. In another letter, in which he recalled the importance of the General's multifarious service, during which he commanded about 300,000 troops, including the intelligence service, security service, territorial service, and mobilization service, Masson wrote to the General, "Certain people were wondering why you did not defend me, because I was not a subordinate of the Federal Council nor of Mr. Kobelt. You did defend me, but your noble and worthy efforts were sabotaged by the two chambers of Parliament."[22]

Supreme Court Justice Louis Couchepin was entrusted with the task of carrying out the administrative investigation against Masson. In view of that investigation, as Hausamann wrote to Kobelt, "Now the truth must no longer be covered up, nor must the facts be withheld. . . . I still hope and believe that one can admit that Colonel-Brigadier Masson acted in good faith and had decent intentions. However, the people who used him and were covered up by him must be exposed without showing any mercy. One of these people is the General's son."[23] Hausamann's remarks made allusion to the not very transparent business relations that Captains Meyer-Schwertenbach and Holzach, who were in contact with Colonel Guisan, were able to combine with their activity for the intelligence service.[24]

Couchepin limited the scope of his investigation to the "Masson affair." He stated that it was undisputed that the Chief of Intelligence had acted in good faith and that his motivation had been irreproachable, but that he did make some mistakes. He explained that his granting an interview to a foreign journalist, which "bordered on naiveté," had been incompatible with his position as Chief of Intelligence, adding, "It was imprudent and inadmissible, especially with regard to the fact that the Federal Council has kept silent until now about the dangers Switzerland faced during the war, for Colonel Masson to publicly reveal that as chief of intelligence he personally entertained relations with the head of the Security Service of the SS."[25] The investigating judge concluded that Masson had breached the secrecy to which he had sworn as an official, but that it was not as serious as the press had initially made it appear. He stated that no military or diplomatic secrets had been given away. In view of all the circumstances, especially Masson's merits, this appeared to be a minor offense and therefore, a confirmation of the official reprimand that the Head of the Military Department had pronounced in Parliament should be the end of the matter. Hence, in early 1946, Kobelt once again formally rebuked Masson.[26]

Even if the disciplinary action taken by Kobelt concluded official involvement in the Masson affair, it did not come to an end. Rather, it began to show signs of a well-directed public campaign. Hans Rudolf Schmid, the army staff's former press officer, suspected that the attacks against Masson were indirectly aimed at the General as well. He claimed that the continuing attacks were staged by Hausamann, "who blandishes the Military Department and at the same time serves as an informant for leftist extremists."[27] After a telephone conversation with Schmid, Guisan noted, "The left will go as far as attacking the General because of his letter of Nov. 9, 1940 to the F[ederal] C[ouncil]. Grimm tries to decrease [the] General's prestige and demolish the F.C.!"[28]

In early 1946, the Zürich-based newspaper *Die Tat*, which supported Masson, launched a counterattack. Domestic affairs editor Kummer and H. R. Schmid claimed that Hausamann had plotted against the Chief of Intelligence "out of reprehensible motives, above all out of political and business interests. He incited National Councilors, politicians, and journalists against Colonel Masson [and] set up a devilish endeavor out of jealousy, mistrust, and ambition, and because he has an obsessive desire to pronounce suspicions." He was even said to have been involved in preparing a coup attempt.[29]

Hausamann, about whom Chief of the General Staff Huber commented, in a letter to the General, he was not surprised to see "after Masson, [had] also found a way to make it into the news,"[30] felt that the authors of the articles in *Die Tat* had unfairly attacked him. He started legal proceedings against them, accusing them of defamation and intentional libeling.

In connection with the new investigation, in which the military courts were involved, Federal Councilor Kobelt repudiated the claim that his actions had been influenced by Hausamann. He wrote to the Military Attorney General, "H[ausamann] never asked me to take any action against M[asson] nor to suspend him. M[asson's] case was 'staged' by M[asson] himself, not by H[ausamann]. I do not know who saw to it that Bringolf and Dietschi intervened in Parliament. H[ausamann] did not influence me when I answered their questions, nor did he try to do so."[31] Both former Federal Councilor Pilet-Golaz and General Guisan refused to serve as witnesses for the prosecution or the defense.[32] However, the Federal Council decided to authorize Masson to take the witness stand.[33]

The voluminous indictment against the authors of the *Tat* articles, written by Albert Züblin, a lawyer from Zürich, unsparingly uncovered the dubious machinations by some of Masson's subordinates and the minor involvement of the General's son.[34] It is a real treasure trove for those trying to find information about the secrets that Hausamann and his bureau knew. Hausamann, in order to justify himself, seemed determined not to spare any dirty laundry from the public.

Because of this, several people made efforts to prevent the case from going to court by trying to negotiate an out-of-court settlement. General Guisan personally went to see the editor-in-chief of *Die Tat*, Erwin Jaeckle, in Zürich in order to convince him, "in the higher interest of the country," to drop the dispute with Hausamann.[35] The General also tried to have Hausamann and his lawyer, who went to see him at Verte Rive in September 1947, drop their charges. Hausamann wrote to a lawyer friend that Guisan was willing to make a public statement saying that the aspersions cast on him were unfounded, but that the General asked him for a favor in exchange. Hausamann explained:

> What the General dared to ask from us during our visit was quite embarrassing for Dr. Züblin and me. We went to see him at Masson's request, who had told us that the General wanted to assess the situation with us. As you know, the General has been trying to get hold of a file containing documents that incriminate Federal Councilor Pilet, but I have consistently refused to give it to him. He made me understand that he could immediately make a written statement in my favor if I gave him these papers. Of course I refused to accept this shady horse-trading.[36]

Hausamann wrote further that he had clearly made the General understand that he set no store at all on a "declaration" that required him "to do something ugly" because both Guisan and Masson had "been playing rather nasty games" in that matter.[37] Hausamann later described the conversation with the General at Verte Rive in a similar manner to Captain Hans Seelhofer, a member of Kobelt's staff who wrote a note for the file about it.[38]

On the morning of September 22, 1947, the day that the trial was scheduled to begin, more than a dozen journalists showed up at the courtroom in Winterthur. Much to their surprise, they were told that the trial was canceled because it had been settled out of court. Defendants Kummer and Schmid had requested that an out-of-court settlement be negotiated. At the last moment, Hausamann decided to accept the defendants' request if they agreed to pay for all legal expenses and publish a declaration in the press that the accusations made in their articles against him were unfounded. The following day, the Military Attorney General was pleased to inform the Military Department that the case had been settled out of court, in part through the efforts of Senior Judge Egloff, the chairman of Zürich's jury-based court.[39]

From the files documenting the preliminaries of the trial that did not take place, one gains the impression that ultimately all parties involved were relieved that a major confrontation could be prevented, some because the state's interests were at stake and others because they had personal concerns. In letters to his comrade-in-arms, Max Waibel, and to Ernst Kaeser, a lawyer, Hausamann indicated that a trial would have revealed "how the General distorted history [as well as] quite a few not very positive things about Masson."[40]

Roger Masson took early retirement in 1947 and was therefore no longer an employee of the Federal Government. The last time he fell into disrepute was in connection with the Nuremberg trial, when Schellenberg's defense attorney asked to hear Switzerland's Chief of Intelligence as a witness. In the spring of 1948, the Military Attorney General informed Federal Councilor Kobelt that Masson told him that Schellenberg's German defense lawyer had come to see him and that Masson had written an account of his relations with the SS General for the defense. He added that General Guisan had agreed with this procedure and signed the report.[41] Since Masson had received an invitation to appear at Schellenberg's trial in person as a witness, he asked the Federal authorities' authorization to accept it. However, in a meeting with the Military Attorney General, Federal Councilors Kobelt and von Steiger concluded that Masson should not be allowed to appear at the Nuremberg trial, nor make any statement as a witness "in matters that resulted from [his] actions as an official." The following day, the entire Federal Council dealt with the issue, about which Kobelt noted, "The Federal Council has asked me to refuse to let Masson take the witness stand. It is surprised to note that Masson handed a written declaration to the defense without asking the Military Department's prior approval. The Federal Council would like to see that document after the fact and asks me to request it from Masson."[42]

The multi-page report was a well-intentioned account of the relations between the two intelligence chiefs. In exchange for the services that Schellenberg had rendered Switzerland, Masson wrote the report to spare the accused SS General from suffering the destiny of a war criminal.[43] General Guisan personally confirmed that "the declaration [was] correct, particularly concerning the services that were rendered to Switzerland by W. Schellenberg." He signed it, "General Guisan, former Commander-in-Chief of the Armed Forces from 1939 to 1945."[44]

After viewing the document, the Federal Council concluded that Switzerland's Chief of Intelligence should have asked the Military Department's authorization before writing the report. On behalf of the Federal Government, Federal Councilor Kobelt reprimanded Masson for providing assistance to Schellenberg, writing, "You were not authorized to issue a statement to a foreign court. For the time being, the Federal Council expresses its surprise and displeasure to you about the way in which you proceeded."[45]

Schellenberg was accused in Nuremberg of being an accessory to preparing wars of aggression, exterminating Jews, and killing Russian prisoners of war. He was found not guilty of the main charges against him but was sentenced to six years in prison because of "crimes against humanity and [his] membership in a criminal organization [the SS]."[46] Schellenberg's lawyer, Fritz Riediger, confirmed that his defendant owed his relatively mild sentence above all to the support he had received from Switzerland, part of which had been provided by former Federal Councilor Musy. In a letter of thanks to Masson, Riediger stated, "Schellenberg and I would like to express our heartfelt thanks to you. Please extend [our thanks] to General Guisan as well. It was only possible because of this selfless and very generous support to obtain such a favorable result."[47]

Afterward, General Guisan publicly acknowledged the achievements of the controversial Chief of Intelligence on several occasions, although he fell short of making the formal declaration that Masson would have liked. In his conversations with Gafner published in 1953, he praised Masson's "magnificent work," explaining, "It is my pleasure to use this opportunity to once again express my well-deserved recognition to him. He was a valuable staff member. . . . Colonel-Brigadier Masson constantly kept me current, thereby providing me with great satisfaction. The entire credit for this fact goes to the well-functioning intelligence service, which Masson had prepared and organized together with carefully selected agents."[48] On another occasion, the General remarked that Masson was "an example of a man with great merits whose downfall is brought about even though there is no obvious link between the accusations that are made against him in connection with his doing his duty and any actual wrongdoing. At this time, Colonel-Brigadier Masson, who is a sick man today, is owed a word of recognition."[49]

One would have liked Masson, whose merits were undisputed in several respects, to have been able to end his career in a more dignified manner. Pilet-Golaz, who knew the Chief of Intelligence well, described Masson as "a nice man, . . . yet also a man who on numerous occasions was credulous, imprudent, and naïve. In addition, he was easy to impress and tended towards extremes. I saw him tremble at my office and demand draconian measures to censor the press during some critical situations."[50] When analyzing the written evidence, one is left with the impression that Masson ended up bringing about his own downfall by rashly giving an interview to a foreigner. After that, he was blamed for being throughout the war a staunch supporter of censoring the press before it went to print. In councils he had repeatedly advocated introducing pre-publication censorship because he feared that the "excesses of [the Swiss] press" could provoke Hitler to attack Switzerland.[51] Moreover, his not being able to resist the urge to get involved in matters of national policy instead of focusing exclusively on his task as an intelligence officer turned to his disfavor. His emotional affection for Schellenberg, which could have had disastrous consequences for Switzerland, showed that he tended to have a romantic image of the military; however, that trait did not diminish his qualities as a human being.

Hans Hausamann, who provided ample evidence of his critical attitude toward certain activities by the Chief of Intelligence, summed up his final opinion about Masson by stating: "When you ask yourself what consequences the 'Masson case' had, the answer is, 'none.' The fact that he tolerated some spongers around him does not diminish his merits. What ultimately counts is that he was successful, which is proven."[52] What Hausamann said about Masson applies to an even greater extent to General Guisan.[53]

Report on Wartime Duty

ONCE WARTIME DUTY WAS OVER, General Guisan's main remaining task was to write the report he was required to submit to Parliament on his command of the army between 1939 and 1945. This report—which prompted serious disputes once it was published—was begun in summer 1945 and took about eight months to complete. Both the commander-in-chief and the chief of the general staff continued to receive their regular pay until they completed their reports. In addition, they received rations for two horses each and a monthly compensation for taking care of the horses, according to the regulations for instructors. The staff that remained at their disposal was compensated as any other soldier on duty.[1] The General, the chief of staff, and the adjutant general had no financing available after August 31, 1945. It appears that a request to extend the General's authority to spend funds until the end of the year was denied.[2]

The first order to establish files that would serve as a basis for writing the report on wartime duty was issued by the first chief of the general staff, Corps Commander Labhart, to the heads of Main Sections II and III as well as to the assistant chiefs of staff shortly after mobilization.[3] Shortly before the war ended in Europe, Guisan told Huber, "The report should be based on a systematic outline established by the chief of the general staff; each chapter should be written by a qualified officer. Please submit the outline to the General before giving any instructions to your subordinates."[4]

Guisan's own report, based on the files, was drafted by the chief of his personal staff, Bernard Barbey, who had been promoted to lieutenant colonel in 1944. At the end of May 1945, Barbey submitted a handwritten draft outline for the report to the General, stating that he wanted to start writing the report as soon as the outline was approved.[5]

Once the troops went off duty and the personal staff was dissolved, a small-scale team continued serving as the General's office staff. Until the end of September 1945, it remained at Jegenstorf Castle, and then relocated to offices on the third floor of the barracks in Lausanne, where Guisan had his office when he was commander of the 1st Army Corps.[6] This "office," which helped Barbey draft the report, consisted of Captain Marguth, non-commissioned Adjutant Konrad Huber, and Driver Burnens. The General wrote to his former first adjutant, Major Albert Mayer, "This is a major task that will keep me busy for six months, so I will stay on duty until the middle of next year with a scaled-down office."[7]

There is no doubt that Lt. Colonel Barbey drafted the major part of the General's report. Guisan himself indicated that Barbey wrote it.[8] Several other officers wrote individual chapters; for example, Major Charles Daniel of the general staff wrote the section about the various periods when Switzerland faced heightened threats of foreign invasion.[9] Other parts were written by Denis van Berchem, who was also involved in polishing the style of the final text.[10] The explanations regarding plans of operation were undoubtedly written by Gonard.

Chief of the General Staff Huber was not involved in drafting the commander-in-chief's report at all. When the General submitted the draft of the chapters on the "Assessment of the officers' corps" and on "The general staff of the armed forces" to him for examination and comment, he did not ask to make any changes or add anything, stating, "I never did and still do not agree on certain issues, but the report is supposed to reflect *your* views."[11] In comparison, Edgar Bonjour found out that Chief of Staff Frey-Herosé wrote General Dufour's report on the Civil War of 1847.[12]

Barbey had the draft of Guisan's report sent to him in Paris, where he was now serving as Counselor at the Swiss Embassy. After reviewing the document, he sent it on to van Berchem. Barbey wrote to the General, "As instructed by Adjutant Huber, I returned the second and final draft of your report directly to von Berchem by express mail. I corrected a number of details that will not require any major modifications."[13]

Barbey urged the General to publish the report as soon as possible. In early March 1946, he wrote to him from Paris that the more he thought about it, the more convinced he became that it was in the army command's interest to publish the report without delay because that was the only way to show its accomplishments in the right light and to take the sting out of increasing criticism from the press and other quarters. He wrote, "I do not think that Mr. K[obelt]'s arguments against first presenting only the French version are tenable. It seems to me that you alone can judge the—personal and general—interest that presenting the original French version entails under the current circumstances and in view of the criticism by the press."[14] He added that he allowed himself to "urgently and frankly" advise the General to do so in the same spirit that had guided him when he was serving on his staff.

In spite of Barbey's appeal, the General decided to wait until both his report and Huber's were available in the three official languages (German, French, and Italian). The General's report was translated from French into German by Captain Max Schneebeli, a lawyer in Zürich, and edited by Major Karl Schmid, a professor of literature at the Federal Institute of Technology in Zürich.[15] The reports by the chief of the general staff and the adjutant general were translated from German into French by Captain Bullet from Estavayer and 1st Lieutenant Verrey from Lausanne. Major Casanova from Magliaso translated the reports into Italian.[16] Eighty copies of the General's original report were initially printed on parchment as a bound gift edition and 3,000 copies were printed on regular paper as a paperback edition, of which 1,500 were in German, 1,000 in French, and 500 in Italian.[17] In addition, the Federal Chancellery printed several thousand copies as a popular edition that was put on the market in the summer of 1946.

The 273-page report was transmitted to the appropriate authorities during the session of June 1946.[18] On June 24, the General's aide Captain Marguth submitted it to the Speakers of the two chambers of Parliament and to the Federal Council. The General wrote an accompanying letter to the Speaker of the National Council in which he stated:

> Now that I have submitted my own report and the special reports by my direct subordinates that are meant to be appendices, I consider my task to be accomplished on the administrative level also. My report shows what the army accomplished during the six years of wartime duty that it was under my command, and it highlights, in a critical and constructive manner, the findings that one could not help making while the army was doing its duty. The occasional critical remarks were made with the perspective of using the experience of this past wartime duty for the future.[19]

The General's report was also accompanied by the original typewritten reports by the chief instructors, which were combined in one unpublished volume.

National Council Speaker Robert Grimm, the former driving force and leader of the nationwide strike movement of 1918, thanked the General that same day for the report and presented him his best wishes, adding, "Please accept my personal thanks for the services you rendered the country during the mobilization."[20] The following day, the General's report was distributed to the members of Parliament and to the press; later, it was even sent to the foreign embassies in Switzerland.

In a letter he wrote to the General after the report had been submitted to the authorities, Barbey clearly stated that it was no coincidence that some passages were provocative, explaining:

> In my opinion, the report will have accomplished its objectives if it
>   causes the following essential reforms to be sped up:
>   Establishing plans of operation during times of peace;
>   Making training less drill-oriented;
>   Putting more weight on the air force and admitting its commander
>   to the NDC;
>   Designating a first "officer in charge" (inspector) during times of
>   peace, according to the idea presented on the last pages of the
>   report.
>   I believe that if these objectives can be reached, [the report] is worth
>   a stir.[21]

Viktor Hofer, who analyzed the General's report and its consequences in a thorough and detailed study, points out that the way in which the report was submitted and published gave rise to some polemics. He remarks: "Some accused the General of trying to boost his popularity, others suspected him of attempting to inflict a hidden blow on the Federal Council, and a few even asked if Guisan was actually authorized to publish his report before Parliament had commented on it."[22]

In particular, the General's way of proceeding with the publication of the report incurred the Federal Government's displeasure. In 1919, General Wille faced a similar reaction when he submitted his printed report to the Speaker of Parliament, sent twelve additional copies to the Head of the Military Department to the Federal Council's attention, and asked permission to make the report available to bookstores for sale. Generals Dufour and Herzog had submitted the manuscripts of their reports to the Federal Council for approval before presenting them to Parliament. The Federal Council was indignant at Wille's acting on his own authority and denied his request, arguing that it was up to Parliament to decide whether his report could be published. Moreover, it stated, "Currently the situation in Parliament is as follows: on the National Council, Mr. de Dardel asked the Federal Council if it agreed with the report. The Head of the Military Department replied that he had not yet read it and reserved the Federal Council's right to analyze it and comment on it at a later

date. The National Council decided to forward the General's 'report' to the
Federal Council so the Government can present it to the two chambers together with its own report."[23] This passage and other statements in the minutes of
the Federal Council prove that at the end of the First World War similar difficulties occurred as in 1946 in connection with the commander-in-chief's report.

Hofer explains that General Guisan's report distinguished itself from the
reports of Switzerland's previous commanders-in-chief both in terms of its
length and its unusual frankness.[24] In their reports, Guisan's predecessors tended to gloss over or overlook tensions with the Federal government, leave subordinates whom they criticized unnamed, and name only people whom they
praised. Guisan, on the other hand, did not hesitate to reveal differences of
opinion, point the finger at failures and wrong moves, and mention shortcomings of, and errors made by, certain subordinates. Gafner correctly considers
that the talented writer Barbey revealed his authorship by employing a rather
indiscreet language to make points.[25] The report ruthlessly shed light on
Guisan's relations with the Federal Council, which had at times been problematic. In addition, Guisan harshly criticized the fact that no plans of operations
had been available when the war broke out.[26] Personal attacks against certain
subordinates, especially Divisional Commander Bandi, the sacked commander
of the air force and antiaircraft defense, were so unusual that they could be considered serious faux pas.[27]

Böschenstein calls the General's report "a mixture of convincing statements, extremely subjective arguments, obvious mistakes, and easily demon-
strable contradictions."[28] The critical remarks, some of which actually appear to
be designed to be provocative, caused not only the targeted parties to be
annoyed. Constam told Federal Councilor Kobelt that the report "would probably have been less polemical if officers such as the chief of the general staff had
been involved in drafting it; they would probably have argued more calmly
than a member of the personal staff."[29] Borel, the French-speaking corps commander, also criticized the General's report, writing to the Head of the Military
Department that the discrepancy between Guisan's and Huber's reports, the latter which he considered much "more objective and serene," was a sign of the
fact that there had "never been enough personal contact" between the two personalities. He added: "This is due to the existence of the General's personal
staff, with which he isolated himself during wartime duty and again to write his
report. If he had written it in cooperation with the chief of the general staff, one
can be sure that under the influence of that circumspect and level-headed officer, the General's report would have had more positive consequences."[30] Gafner
remarks that there "were about as many drawbacks as there were advantages to

the isolation to which the General subjected himself before publishing his report."[31]

The General's report described the main events and instructions to the army during the six years of wartime duty and included a number of critical and constructive statements, but it explicitly avoided making overall conclusions. Guisan explained that it was not his job "to draw the general conclusions [because] a new team [would] be responsible for tackling the urgent and difficult task of organizing the future army." He added that he intentionally retained differences of opinion that existed between his own report and some appendices written by others "in an effort to grant everyone freedom of expression."[32] Guisan was somewhat reserved yet confident in his assessment of Switzerland's chances of defending itself during World War II, stating, "I think that I may say with certainty that we would have been capable of taking logical and appropriate counter-measures in any situation, even in the event of a surprise attack, even though these counter-measures would not consistently have had the same effectiveness. We could have done so in any situation—with one exception."[33]

The report was divided into five chapters. In the first chapter, "The basic strategic decisions," which ran 67 pages, he described the process that led to the army's withdrawal to the Réduit and explained the Réduit's function as a deterrent, the course of the front with the three fortresses of Sargans, Gotthard, and St-Maurice as cornerstones, and the operational directives that he had issued to the four army corps. He did not refrain from mentioning the weaknesses of the Réduit. The next three chapters dealt with "the doctrine and the available forces" (82 pages), an "assessment of the officers' corps" (41 pages), and "the spirit of the armed forces" (40 pages). In the last chapter of 33 pages, "The General's terms of reference and the way he exercised the supreme command," Guisan made a critical assessment of his relations with the Federal Council in connection with the issue of which party should have the responsibility for calling up troops.

It is surprising how carefree the General, the chief of the general staff, and the authors of the appendices were about revealing details about the army command's operational considerations and about the national defense in general, such as numbers of available troops, equipment, and supplies. Bircher commented that the various reports were "the most valuable military and geography textbooks for anyone in foreign countries who [had] to deal with the issue of an attack on Switzerland."[34]

Federal Councilor Kobelt even requested an examination of how many instances occurred in the reports when the authors had ignored common secrecy regulations. Newly appointed Chief of the General Staff de Montmollin concluded that Guisan had done so in 18 instances, Huber in 47 instances, and the authors of the appendices in 30 instances.[35] Corps Commander Borel commented on the matter, "This imprudence is all the more surprising as during wartime duty, people who communicated a much smaller amount of information to foreign countries were severely punished."[36] All the other corps commanders agreed that the report on wartime duty went too far in revealing military secrets. Prisi remarked that Switzerland could "claim to be famous as the only country on the globe that [could] afford not to have any secrets from the rest of the world concerning its national defense."[37] Gübeli also regretted that "all the cards [had been] laid on the table" for foreign countries.[38]

Bircher was joined by other members of the National Council committee dealing with the General's report, such as National Councilor Clavadetscher from Lucerne, in voicing their "outrage" about the carelessness with which military secrets had been given away. National Councilor Holenstein from St. Gallen, a future Federal Councilor, stated that the commander-in-chief's report gave "rise to very serious concerns" in this respect.[39] It is justified to say that it would have been desirable to use more restraint in connection with the information that was provided about the Réduit, which is a permanent concept. Half a century later, however, there is no more need to make a secret of the arrangements that were made during the early 1940s, as the army's organization, equipment, and plans of operation in the positions in the heart of the country have since undergone several major changes.

The General's report was read with attention and considered sensational because of the frankness and bluntness with which it was written. A large part of the media and the population approved of it, but it was soon attacked from several quarters. Guisan undoubtedly expected that his report would not make everyone happy and would give rise to discussions, for he wrote in the preface, "I did not refrain from pointing out mistakes and shortcomings in my report. If some of my criticism is directed not only against institutions but also against individuals, it is not because I gave in to the currently widespread obsession with criticism. The only thing that matters and guided me was to prevent these mistakes or shortcomings from happening again and to examine the road that should be taken."[40] It may be pointless to ask whether Guisan had been able to foresee the unpleasant arguments that were triggered by the publication of his report. However, it is unlikely that he entirely expected to cause so many vehement reactions. Perhaps the most devastating opinion was expressed by publicist Hans Zopfi, who wrote to Colonel Däniker about the General's report, "That man caused damage to the army through his vanity and arrogance, and he may be considered as one of the destroyers of the army."[41]

Guisan received a disapproving letter from his former comrade-in-arms

Corps Commander Lardelli, who advised him, as a "loyal and good friend," to find the right words in the future in order to avoid the discussions turning into a feud. Lardelli wrote:

> What would distress me most is a cleavage between Swiss French and Swiss Germans. You were extremely good at getting the German-speaking officers and soldiers to support you. Do not forget that . . . the Military Department's position was not always easy; it may argue that it acted to the best of its knowledge and abilities. It does not need any malicious criticism but understanding, even if in retrospect that understanding may not have existed at the time, which I do not think is true. Such quarrels could end to your disadvantage, that is, they could undermine your popularity. That would be a crying shame.[42]

Guisan replied to Lardelli that he was convinced that the way he had proceeded was useful, arguing, "I believe that only frankness can pave the way for improvements."[43]

The General must have been particularly surprised about the harshness of attacks by some former subordinates who had always been rather compliant when he was commander-in-chief. The most vehement reactions came from two army unit commanders, Corps Commander Prisi and Divisional Commander Bandi, whereas the General's real enemies, Wille and Däniker, whose cases were not mentioned in his report, did not make any public statement. Prisi explained that his "Remarks on the General's Report" that he wrote in the fall of 1946 were originally meant to be a confidential document. He first submitted it to former Federal Councilor Minger and a few officers and members of Parliament with whom he was friends, and subsequently also to the Head of the Military Department, Federal Councilor Kobelt. When Guisan heard about the existence of the "Remarks," in a letter that he began with the salutation, "My dear Prisi," he asked his former subordinate for a copy of it.[44] Prisi granted his request, even though he claimed that the document had actually been addressed to the Military Department and that he was therefore allowed to assume that the addressee would inform the General about it. He added that he had "not in the least [intended] to do anything behind anyone's back" concerning the General's report.[45]

In the meantime, Prisi's "Remarks" had become public knowledge through an indiscretion. *Neue Politik*, a magazine initiated by members of the former "Two Hundred" and edited by Dr. Wilhelm Frick, was able to publish excerpts of the corps commander's statements without asking the author for his approval. Prisi tried to apologize to the General, telling him, "My remarks were not intended for publication by the press in the version that was printed [in the magazine]. The indiscretion that was committed is a serious abuse of my confidence."[46] Because some of his remarks had been communicated to the public and had subsequently been reprinted by several newspapers, Prisi decided to give *Bund* a copy of the entire document, which the Bern-based newspaper published in its entirety on November 20, 1946.[47]

Through Prisi's comments, which were a ruthless attack on Guisan in the form of an assessment, the controversy about the General's report climaxed before either the Federal Council or Parliament had actually discussed it. Prisi began his accusations by pointing out that the manner in which Guisan had published his report was debatable because he had acted rashly and high-handedly without duly informing the Federal Council. He said that it was even more disturbing that the statements made by the General had caused a fateful crisis of confidence in the army and among the population, explaining, "Many parts of the report are full of derogatory criticism. It does not include one word of acknowledgement to the subordinate commanders for their accomplishments in terms of organization, administration, training, and leadership. The commander-in-chief takes credit for the entire success, whereas the 'top commanders' are made liable and responsible for every shortcoming and failure." Prisi considered particularly offensive the fact that Guisan made a disparaging assessment of the abilities of certain army unit commanders who were serving at the outbreak of the war and whose training had not been worse than that of the commander of the 1st Army Corps who was elected General. He stated, "I consider the disparaging comments in the General's report about the top command of 1939 to be undeserved and not very fair from the point of view of comradeship. They are a defamation of the concerned officers before the public in this country and abroad," and he sardonically added that this was the expression of "the General's gratefulness."[48] Prisi argued that the chief of the general staff and the "top commanders" who were criticized had been continually at their posts, doing their jobs "unpretentiously and without much ado," and, unlike Guisan, "fortunately they did not have any time to accept the authorities' and the public's homage." Moreover, Prisi claimed, "There is absolutely no proof that the leadership of the army during wartime duty was infallible on the operational level."[49]

Prisi did not hesitate to make a number of sarcastic remarks. He pointed the finger at Guisan in connection with the replacement of the old guard in the army command by younger officers, which the General had advocated but never applied to his own case. He indicated that if the planned retirement age of 65 had been enforced equally on everyone, Guisan would not have been elected General in the first place, as he had turned 65 in 1939. Moreover, Prisi ridiculed Guisan's demand for the top commanders to be physically fit, stating, "The army unit commanders' famous physical fitness is not the answer to everything! As far as I know, the great Moltke won the wars of 1864, 1866, and 1870–71 without ever doing any gymnastics exercises in front of his staffs!"[50]

Prisi claimed that the General's report had created "serious moral damage" because it would not only serve "as ammunition to all anti-army elements" in their fight against the national defense and against the army as an institution, but it had also "made hundreds of thousands of conservative Swiss citizens waver in their confidence in the political leadership and the army command." The former commander of the 2nd Army Corps also criticized the lack of input by the General in training-related matters, stating:

> Curiously [he did] little to promote continued training for his subor-
> dinate commanders during the entire duration of wartime duty. . . . As
> far as I know, he did not personally direct one single operational exer-
> cise or maneuver but left those tasks to the chief of the general staff and
> the corps commanders. As far as I know, he never spoke at any brief-
> ing about the core of the matter but contented himself with making
> general, not very substantial, remarks, such as 'this is up to the com-
> manders,' 'I do not want to get involved in this matter,' 'so-and-so is
> responsible for that,' etc. when in fact the officers' corps of entire divi-
> sions and army corps were anxiously waiting to finally hear our top
> commander pronounce his views and theories on strategic and opera-
> tional issues! However, each time the officers were disappointed. There
> was indeed hardly any sense of his mentally leading the officers' corps![51]

Prisi remarked that Guisan could not be convinced "by any reasonable argument . . . not to boost the popularity for which he constantly strove by pre- senting himself to the public at large as the savior of the country who succeed- ed, through his great leadership qualities and hard work, in replacing a partly incapable corps of commanders by a better one that he selected and in making the insufficiently equipped troops fit to go to war!" Prisi considered that "in the interest of the truth," history would have to correct that image, explaining, "It is necessary to also play a different tune in public, if necessary through the press, not just in confidential reports."[52]

The two officers engaged in a serious quarrel, accusing each other of an unprofessional attitude and of damaging the army's image. As the General wrote to Prisi:

> One thing is certain now: You proved that you did not realize what

were the commander-in-chief's mission, his responsibility, and the circumstances that he was facing. He tried to do his job to the best of his knowledge and belief and, in spite of what you say in your 'Remarks' that are full of animosities, never allowed himself to be arrogant. You think that you are doing some damage to me with your document. However, you have done damage only to yourself and unfortunately particularly to the army! You will understand that I cannot approve of your unmilitary attitude, about which I am very disappointed.[53]

Prisi's attacks against his former superior appeared to be sensational at first, but the press in Switzerland did not pay much attention to them. In connection with the attacks, the General received countless letters from all parts of society telling him not to worry because the people would continue to be loyal and thankful to him.[54] Hans Rudolf Schmid, the former press officer for the army staff, wrote to the General that he was convinced that "Bern [was] taking its revenge," explaining:

The attitude of the Swiss German press in the matter of Prisi can be described as follows: the moderate, tactful conservative press (e.g. N[eue] Z[urcher] Z[eitung]) was reserved; the Social Democratic press made rather critical comments on Prisi's remarks; however, unfortunately it was above all the conservative press, which is strongly influenced by the correspondents who are based in Bern, that paid too much attention to the matter. It appears that Mr. Haas' Mittelpresse was also quite delighted to distribute Prisi's report.[55]

Schmid recommended that the General respond to Prisi's harsh attacks in an open letter to the press. However, Guisan refused to follow his advice, annotating that passage in the letter with a clear "No!"[56] Nevertheless, in another personal letter, the General reprimanded Prisi, telling him that he was playing "an unworthy game."[57] Barbey was also startled by Prisi's tough language, writing to the General from France, "I am indeed disheartened after reading this foolish and unjust paper, but I am not altogether surprised, as I know Col. Prisi's attitude since he was made to retire."[58]

Prisi could say in his favor that as a commander he had probably been one of the commander-in-chief's most loyal subordinates. However, while his provoking remarks set some things straight, the tone that he used and some statements that he made clearly went too far. His disappointment and sense of betrayal over the circumstances of his dismissal as corps commander evidently caused him to make a number of inaccurate statements. In addition, the fact that Prisi's comments were first published in the magazine of the "Two Hundred" made a bad impression on the public from the start; thus, unlike the General's report, they did not cause a major stir.

Prisi's criticism largely echoed the negative opinions of most high-ranking troop commanders. The two unit commanders from French-speaking Switzerland, Borel and Corbat, both agreed that the General's report was an attempt by Guisan to justify himself and at the same time issue a far-reaching indictment of others. As Divisional Commander Corbat argued, "[The report is a] plea in his own defense in which the General wants to justify his actions and moves in a rather detailed manner. The first-person pronoun is definitely not used with moderation in this historic document. The indictment is harsh. . . . In my opinion, the accusations that he makes are triggered above all by personal considerations and personal grudges."[59] Corps Commander Borel also considered that Guisan had "made a plea in his own defense," adding, "One cannot help thinking that the public would have received more objective information if the General had not left out from the report those errors, mistakes, and shortcomings for which he was partly responsible."[60] Even the new chief of the general staff, de Montmollin, commented that with his egocentric report, Guisan had "worked at his own glory."[61]

In a 29-page position paper on the General's report, Corps Commander Labhart admitted that it was understandable that Guisan "only [mentioned] facts that [spoke] in his favor." However, he wrote to the Head of the Military Department:

> The General will have to accept that those who had an insight into the circumstances will also voice criticism about measures that he took in the course of wartime duty but which are not mentioned or only alluded to in his report. . . . As expected, the report highlights the General as a person and his activities. It is striking how often it points out that everything that had been undertaken by the appropriate authorities before the troops were mobilized did not mean much and included shortcomings and careless mistakes, whereas the measures taken by the General, his requests to the Federal Council, etc. are supposed to stand up to any criticism. The General's criticism goes as far as making the common people who read his report believe that everything was rotten among the authorities who had been responsible for making preparations for the war and that the General was the savior in the country's hour of need.

Labhart also feared that the General's report might contribute to "undermining our army" among unbiased citizens and soldiers and that it would "take a lot of time and effort to regain their confidence."[62]

One gains the impression that the numerous serious retorts by high-ranking commanders resulted from feelings of resentment that had accumulated over the years, because they had not been able to voice reservations about the General during wartime duty. In a National Council meeting, Carl Miville from Basel explained that the criticism by these top officers "was not met with any understanding among the people." He went so far as to speak of a "Colonels' mutiny."[63]

The new top officers in the army, Chief of the General Staff de Montmollin and Chief Instructor Frick, expressed their disappointment about the fact that the General had not used the opportunity to present his ideas about a future reform of the army. Corps Commander Frick acknowledged that the General's report "definitely [included] some interesting and remarkable comments"; however, he added that it did "not, with a few exceptions, give any hints about the General's ideas on how the army and its training should be developed based on the experience from the war."[64]

Corps Commander Gübeli also said that he missed proposals on how "the urgent and difficult task of reorganizing the army" could be accomplished, adding, "It is too bad that that General is not able to make a commendable lasting contribution in this respect."[65] Borel for his part stated that it was "very regrettable" that the General did not reveal his personal ideas on how to solve the main forthcoming problems in national defense.[66]

Chief of the General Staff Huber truthfully denied having contributed to the General's personal report, and refused to be considered a "sleeping partner" in it. He told Kobelt in all frankness, "I regret that the General has damaged his own reputation along with that of the army."[67] The reprimands and reservations that these top-ranking officers expressed are impossible to miss.

In the chapter in which he assessed the officers' performance and addressed the issue of how to select officers in the future, the General expressed his view that among the dominant bourgeoisie there were fewer and fewer "people with a steadfast character," explaining, "[Today] new social forces dispute the bourgeoisie's right to supremacy. Leaders are emerging among the farming community and the workers who influence the country's destiny just as much as the class that has been in power until now. As a logical consequence of this development, the bourgeoisie, which is now involved only in part in leading the affairs of the state, feels less motivated to take on responsibility and has a lesser sense of obligation."[68] Therefore, Guisan emphasized the need to expand the pool of potential officers and to give above all those soldiers who had the necessary strength of character the opportunity to continue their training.

Viktor Hofer considers that these statements "to a certain extent supported the class struggle."[69] Corps Commander Borel suspected that these remarks
in Guisan's report were made in an attempt to curry favor with the political left,
stating that they apparently intended "to increase the General's popularity in
the social spheres where it was perhaps not yet that great."[70] Marius Corbat, a
future corps commander, objected that the General's remarks about the way in
which officers should be selected in the future were "a political and demagogic
flirt." He actually went as far as to imply that Guisan had moved close to
Communism when he stated, "The General has made himself the great ally of
Vorwärts and *Voix ouvrière*, etc. [two Communist publications in Switzerland];
he must be very surprised at this alliance!"[71]

The few magistrates who spoke favorably of the General's report as a whole
included former Federal Councilor Minger, Guisan's friend, who commented
extensively on it to Kobelt, his successor. Minger stated:

> Based on the lessons that the Second World War taught us, it was the
> General's duty to reveal unsparingly the mistakes and shortcomings of
> our national defense in order to prevent the same mistakes from being
> made again in the future. He fulfilled this duty with the perfect frank-
> ness of a soldier. Even if the tone and the words that he chose were
> sometimes quite sharp, for which he has been criticized here and there,
> they do not change anything about the fact that the General did not
> have the slightest ulterior motive, nor did he want to cause polemics.
> Being the straight soldier that he is, he did not reckon with intrigues
> and polemics; if some people try to exploit the report to cause
> polemics, the General will be the first to be outraged about it.[72]

Minger wrote that Guisan was not a man who considered himself self-
righteous or infallible. Instead, the report should be "viewed as a judgment by
a competent man [who would like] to give some useful advice on the future
development of our national defense." Hence, he argued that the General's
remarks should be "seen as instructions for the future rather than as criticism."[73]
It is interesting to note that some phrases in Minger's comments were taken verbatim from a long letter that Guisan had sent the former Head of the Military
Department one month earlier to defend his report.[74]

In his fundamental work on the conception of national defense, Alfred
Ernst mentions Guisan's ideas on the future development of Switzerland's security policy only in passing. He simply writes that, in his report, the General
"also gave some hints about our future combat strategies and the expansion of
the military," but that these hints were scattered throughout the text. Ernst con-

siders that the "main statement [was] an extensive quote from Colonel-Corps Commander Huber's final speech on the occasion of the operational exercise in 1944. Guisan quoted the chief of the general staff's remarks because he basically agreed with him."[75] In that passage, Guisan and Huber advocated building permanent structures in the Swiss plateau that would complement those in the Réduit and in the border areas in order to reinforce the terrain.[76]

The Federal Government, which considered several disapproving statements and reproaches to be unjustified, was displeased with Guisan's personal account of wartime duty. The Head of the Military Department was particularly dismayed at the sharpness of the General's reproaches. One week before the report was published, Federal Councilor Kobelt and his wife had been invited for lunch at Guisan's home. As Kobelt wrote to the editor-in-chief of the *Tribune de Genève*, "The personal attacks that were made a few days later in the printed report were all the more difficult to understand."[77]

Böschenstein points out that the Federal Council was in a difficult situation, stating, "It could not keep silent about the false statements in the [General's] report. However, it could even less accept the challenge that the report contained and begin a struggle against the former commander-in-chief."[78] The reputation both of the General, whose merits were uncontested, and of the army, which on the whole had passed a test with dignity, were at stake.

The Federal Council decided to publish a counter-report to set the record straight. This procedure was not unusual, as the Federal Council had also commented on General Wille's report after World War I. It gave a detailed explanation of why it did so again after the Second World War, stating:

> The General made ample use of the freedom of expression, a right that has always been very cherished among us, and presented his view without any inhibitions or any reservation. The Federal Council lays claim to the same right in its response. It is important to the Federal Government to comment on the issues about which it has been criticized in the General's report; however, it would like to state with at least the same insistence that rendering a different interpretation of certain facts is not the ultimate objective of its own report. Therefore, it will not comment on every detail, nor on matters that are of minor importance in the whole picture, even where it would be possible to refute them with facts. It would like to make a number of statements only because the General's report requires that the situation be made clear.[79]

The Federal Council, which characterized the General's attacks as exaggerated, did not want to add fuel to the fire but tried to stay clear of polemics in its response so as not to diminish Guisan's reputation, which had by then made him famous. It argued, "The Federal Council agrees with the General that criticism is not voiced for its own sake but in an effort to strengthen and consolidate the idea of our defense and to maintain the strength of our army. Both reports will accomplish that objective only if they jointly and freely strive toward it."[80]

Several contemporary authors who have written about the subject agree that it was thanks to Federal Councilor Kobelt that the government's reply did not take on the proportions of a counterattack; instead, it was objective, avoiding unnecessarily harsh statements.[81] Böschenstein calls the Federal Council's report "a remarkably honest and cautious document [in which] some of the General's major claims were soberly and objectively refuted with written evidence."[82]

The Military Department had the Federal Council's counter-report, which was more than 100 pages long, written by the talented writer Colonel Edgar Schumacher, the editor of a monthly magazine for officers of all arms. Schumacher, who was promoted to the rank of divisional commander the following year, wrote the first three, and most important, chapters, and Hans Bracher, Kurt Bührer, and (in part) Hans Rudolf Kurz wrote the remainder.[83] Schumacher was able to present the draft of the report as early as mid-December 1946. It was submitted to several civilian and military officials for examination and was discussed extensively by the government.

The "Report by the Federal Council on the General's Report on Wartime Duty," dated January 7, 1947, was thoroughly researched and carefully written. It stated the government's view on the contentious issues that Guisan had raised and contained "clear guidelines on the future organization of national defense."[84] The General had to accept that he was proven wrong regarding several issues, yet regarding other issues on which the government and the army command disagreed, it was one party's word against the other's.

Concerning the General's allegedly high-handed way of submitting his report to Parliament and publishing it, the Federal Council stated, "It would have been more useful if the General's report and the Federal Council's comments on it could have been presented to Parliament and the people simultaneously."[85]

Regarding the question of whether Guisan had abided by the obligation to maintain secrecy, the government came close to reprimanding him, stating:

One may ask oneself if it was appropriate and useful to publish things

that may be important for the Federal Council and the new army command to know and may be of use to Parliament but that are not
intended for a large audience and certainly not for foreign countries.
When wartime duty ended, the regulations with respect to maintaining secrecy that had been in force before the war were not repealed.
The army cannot possibly do without these regulations in the future.
If the Federal Council had had the opportunity to comment on the
reports before they were made available to the public, it would have
tried to prevent certain information about the current status of our
armaments from being published. However, it did not have that
opportunity because the General's report was submitted to the members of the Federal Council only one day before it was presented to the
members of Parliament, the press, and the Federal Department of
Foreign Affairs to the attention of the foreign news agencies, and only
ten days before it was sent to the foreign embassies.[86]

Concerning Guisan's complaint that after 1940 he had never been invited
to any government meeting to explain his point of view, it was easy for the
Federal Council to demonstrate that the General had been received by the
Head of the Military Department or a delegation of the Cabinet whenever he
desired, but that he had never expressed the wish to have more contact with the
government.[87] The Federal Council considered that it was difficult to say who
was ultimately responsible for determining how many troops should be called
up because the laws were not explicit and left room for different interpretations,
and thus they had to be improved. The government explained that because economic and political concerns were at stake in addition to military ones whenever the two parties assessed the situation differently, it would have to continue to reserve the right to make the final decision.[88] Moreover, the Federal
Council did not agree with the General concerning his criticism that no plans
of operations were available at the beginning of the war, and also his assessment
of the situation of the air force and anti-aircraft defense.[89]

The Federal Council's interesting explanations on "the issue of future combat strategies and the future development of our military" filled a gap that had
been left open in the General's report. They were written in reaction to a common wish that there should be an overall conception of the national defense.[90]
The statements made in that chapter pointed the way to the future of
Switzerland's defense in general and of tactics and combat strategies to be used
outside the Réduit in particular. Ernst explains, "The report established that the
army had to prevent a war merely by marking its presence. It suggested using a
purely strategic defense in the event of a war."[91] The idea advanced by some at

the time that the army should be split up into units of partisans was completely rejected; instead, it was envisaged to use guerrilla warfare and small-unit
strategies to support the operations of the field army.

The Federal Council concluded its report in an altogether conciliatory
manner, summarizing the great contribution that the Commander-in-Chief of
the Armed Forces had made from 1939 to 1945. It remarked, "The General
was able to promote a trusting relationship between the population and the
army during the entire time that the troops were on wartime duty. This helped
strengthen the unity of and the spirit of resistance among our people.
Moreover, the General was able to ensure that the relations between the officers, non-commissioned officers, and soldiers were good. We acknowledge his
merits and do not want to disparage them through our comments on his
report."[92] The Federal Council's factual and emphatic, but dispassionate, report
was "generally well received" by Switzerland's press and the public.[93]

The Federal Council's counter-report significantly complemented the
General's report regarding a number of issues and corrected it regarding some
others. Colonel A. von Erlach of the medical service wrote to his friend Bandi
that the Federal Council's statements would "make Guisan gasp in several
instances."[94] Gafner argues that Guisan had expected the Federal Council to
respond when he wrote his report and did "not take [its objections] badly."[95]
That statement is unlikely to be accurate. Guisan was rather annoyed by the
counter-report and examined what would be the best way to react to it. For that
purpose, on January 31, 1947, he invited a number of loyal officers to his home
by Lake Geneva to discuss the possibility of rebuking the Federal Council's reprimands and of organizing a campaign against the report.[96] Some "observations"
by Barbey about Prisi's remarks that the General had asked him to write and
that Barbey had submitted from Paris served as a basis for the meeting.[97] The
result of that meeting were Guisan's "Observations on the Federal Council's
report to Parliament regarding the General's report on wartime duty from 1939
to 1945." However, these observations were not submitted to the authorities
but were intended instead as a confidential document.[98]

The General wrote to Major Fritz Wanner of the general staff that at first
he sent his "Observations" only to one member each of the National Council
Proxy Committee and the Council of States Proxy Committee "to enlighten
them in view of possible debates," adding:

> As I would like to avoid any polemic in Parliament, I will send my
> observations to the Speaker only if the debate or the circumstances
> force me to do so. The same applies to the Federal Council. I am send-
> ing you my observations for your personal information so you can use

them as a basis for the articles that you are preparing in order to set things straight as well as to react against the unfavorable atmosphere that certain newspapers think they have to create around the General; one can guess by whom they are inspired (i.e. the *Schweizerische Mittelpresse*).[99]

In that letter, Guisan said that he considered the Federal Council's report "moderate and objective in its form [but] nevertheless fundamentally critical." He argued that Federal Councilor Kobelt used the counter-report to defend himself personally as Head of the Military Department, which "falsified" the perspectives of the General's report and, as it were, "eclipsed" its constructive parts.[100]

In his "Observations," the General wrote that in his opinion the Federal Council's report did not include anything that would be suitable to correct the statements made in his own report. Regarding the manner in which his report was submitted, he explained that he had followed his predecessor's example with the approval of the Speaker of Parliament and after consulting with the Federal Chancellor, who he assumed would also inform the Federal Council.[101]

The General protested vehemently against the accusation that he had failed to abide by the obligation to maintain secrecy, claiming that his own report and the chief of the general staff's report did not contain anything significant about the military that was not already general knowledge both in the country and abroad. He added that the fears the Federal Council had voiced over past situations were difficult to reconcile with the tendency of its own report to reveal certain principles of future defensive measures.[102] He also said that for the time being he had no intention of responding to, or commenting on, the "unfair and clumsy" pamphlets by Corps Commander Prisi and Air Force Commander Bandi, explaining that their attacks had basically been prompted by the measures taken against them during wartime duty.[103]

After both the General's official report and the Federal Council's counter-report had been published, special committees of the National Council and the Council of States examined the two texts closely in view of the forthcoming discussion on the floors of the two chambers of Parliament. Federal Councilor Kobelt and Chief of the General Staff de Montmollin participated in these committee meetings. The 26-member National Council committee, chaired by National Councilor Alfred Müller from Amriswil, included former Divisional Commander Eugen Bircher, Paul Chaudet, a future Federal Councilor, and the two Social Democrats Bringolf and Bratschi. Guisan was invited to one of the committee meetings in order to express his opinion about some unanswered questions and inconsistencies so that "all these issues [could] be clarified as much as possible," as the Chairman of the committee put it.[104]

During the meeting, the General remained self-confident and composed. He was assailed with so many questions that he refused to answer some of them. National Councilor Rudolf Reichling, a colonel, asked him if it had been useful, after Corps Commander Miescher's retirement, to dissolve the staff of the 3rd Army Corps, which had been working well together, to replace it with a new staff for the 5th Army Corps. He argued that he had noticed some "contradictions and inaccuracies" in that connection. Guisan explained that this was an internal matter of the army command, so he did not need to answer Reichling's question, adding that he regretted that he could not answer any other "question of that kind."[105]

When National Councilor H. Schnyder asked the General whether the army command's reports did not include information, such as operational arrangements, armaments, or ammunition that were considered secret, he reiterated that "the figures mentioned in the report were already known to foreign army staffs due to their intelligence activities. He said that neither his own report nor the reports of his subordinates included anything that was not already known."[106] Schnyder countered that common soldiers who had been brought to court did not understand "why they were severely punished for committing a minor offense in connection with the obligation to maintain secrecy, whereas [in these reports] much more important facts [were] openly presented." In addition, Schnyder argued that because of the details provided in the reports, foreign intelligence organizations could now check whether the information that they had procured was accurate. National Councilors Holenstein, a future Federal Councilor, and Colonel Jaquet from Basel voiced similar criticism. Moreover, Federal Councilor Kobelt intervened on several occasions, stating that he doubted that the German intelligence service knew all the details mentioned in the reports, adding, "It is regrettable that major military secrets have been revealed because now other foreign general staffs also have very valuable material available."[107]

Councilor of State Locher chaired the upper house committee consisting of 13 members. Similar to the National Council committee meetings, some questionable issues in the General's report gave rise to lively discussions. However, Guisan was not invited to attend any of its meetings. Councilor of State Fricker, a conservative from Aargau, regretted that the General, whose great merits during wartime duty, he said, were uncontestable, "frankly no longer found the right tone" in his report, adding, "He brought things up in public that he should have kept to himself or should have told only the Federal Council."[108] Lardelli from Grisons considered that the tone used in the Federal Council's report was "appropriate and authentic," whereas "the General's tone [did not seem] appropriate for the occasion. . . . That is not the way in which a General of Switzerland's Armed Forces is supposed to write to Parliament!"[109]

During a discussion about the relations between the Federal Council and the General, Federal Councilor Kobelt categorically denied that Guisan had been made to wait for hours before the Cabinet informed him of its decision regarding the number of troops that would be called up in June 1944. Kobelt argued, "I think the General makes a big deal out of the situation, particularly in this chapter. That is the only way I can interpret his statement that he was left waiting for many hours, because it is not true. Gentlemen, it is not true that the Federal Council was deliberating for four days without consulting with the General. During those four days, the General was consulted several times by the Head of the Military Department who acted as an intermediary between him and the Cabinet."[110] During the rest of the debate, Federal Councilor Kobelt tried to be conciliatory, emphasizing that considering the numerous major difficulties the war had entailed, the differences of opinion had been minor and should not be exaggerated after the fact.

After the two committees had discussed the General's report extensively, it did not cause a stir when the subject was placed on the agenda of the two full chambers of Parliament. While the Federal Council's report was commonly praised as a "masterpiece" and as "an example of a tactful and significant appreciation of the situation," some reservations were voiced about the General's report, even though his qualifications and performance as commander-in-chief were not questioned. National Councilor Armin Meili explained that gaining the army's and the people's confidence was the best reference a General could possibly have. He said that Guisan succeeded in an exemplary manner in accomplishing that "quintessence of a militia army."[111] On the other hand, National Councilor Schnyder voiced some reservations, stating:

> Not everything ran smoothly among the top command. One can tell that the General perhaps did not receive the kind of support that should have been expected from his top officers. But only one officer can become General; all others who were left out believe that they could have done a better job. That is the way it is. That is how a clique was formed which now occasionally manifests itself in a hidden or overt fashion during the discussion of the General's report.[112]

During the spring session of 1947, both the National Council and the Council of States "unanimously approved" the two reports. In the lower house, a total of 20 National Councilors voiced their opinion during the lively but worthy discussion. The upper house gave its approval tacitly.[113] In addition, both chambers approved a motion by the Council of States committee asking the Federal Council "to present to Parliament as soon as possible a draft revision of section 5 of the Military Organization of the Swiss Confederation dated April 12, 1907 by creating separate regulations for duty during times of emergency other than a war and actual wartime duty."[114] In other words, the government was asked to find a solution to avoid disputes in the future on the question of who had the authority to call up troops. That issue was resolved as early as 1949 when articles 211 and 212 of the Military Organization were revised.[115]

Hofer was able to demonstrate that in spite of the commonly held opinion that the General's report included few if any suggestions on the future development of Switzerland's defense, the report had a deep and lasting impact in terms of daily activities during training courses and the army's lifestyle. It is not difficult to trace back to General Guisan and his provocative report explicit demands such as eliminating monotonous drills, fighting the mentality that training should take place mostly at the barracks, motorizing the army, introducing modern means of communication, making the commander of the air force and anti-aircraft defense a member of the National Defense Committee, and clarifying the issue of who had the authority to call up troops.[116] Ernst comments that in some respects, Guisan advocated "surprisingly modern ideas."[117] It is completely logical for Switzerland's military to focus on the experience of victorious foreign armies and to be influenced by their ways of doing things because it has no modern war tradition of its own.

After the Second World War, Switzerland had the courage to wash the military's dirty linen in public, a spectacle that had not been common before. What happened in connection with the debate about the General's report may be considered a necessary self-cleansing process in a democracy that has responsible citizens. During the war, "censorship and self-inflicted censorship" had been in place, the army and its general had been beyond all criticism, and the opinion had been consistently maintained that all was well regarding the national defense. After the war, the General's report, which uncovered some shortcomings on its own, was discussed more fiercely than any other report by a Swiss commander-in-chief had ever been before. At the University of Basel's 1946 *dies academicus*, Dean Edgar Bonjour addressed the guest of honor, Guisan, by stating, "If we had not already bestowed an honorary doctorate on you on an earlier occasion, we would have to do so now for [your] performance as a writer of history." Much later, Bonjour expressed a certain degree of disillusionment when he recalled that event, remarking, "At that time, I did not know yet . . . that the General's report was in large part written by Bernard Barbey."[118]

In 1946–47, some people considered that the General failed to finish his career well because of the questionable way in which his report on wartime duty was written. The daily *Bund* commented, "After six years of being universally recognized, [Guisan] spoiled his own triumphant exit."[119] However, it is striking that even the most serious objections by top-ranking officers did not have a lasting effect.[120] Guisan's popularity turned out to be so vast and well established that not even justified criticism was able to diminish it. The damage was limited and the General's reputation hardly suffered at all. Three major contentious issues—the lack of plans of operation, the case of Air Force Commander Bandi, and the question of whether a General should be in office during times of peace—continued to be discussed in public for an extended period of time. It is therefore justified to consider them in more detail in the upcoming chapters.

The Controversy over Lack
of Plans of Operations

I<small>N HIS POSTWAR REPORT</small>, G<small>ENERAL</small> G<small>UISAN</small> complained that at the outbreak of the war no plans of operations had been available. That issue received a remarkable amount of attention, giving rise to concern and discussions among both military experts and the public. In his report, the General wrote, "What must be pointed out above all is the degree of preparation on the strategic level. As embarrassing as it may be, for the truth's sake I have to say that these preparations had a serious gap; we had no plans of operations available—none whatsoever."[1] Guisan continued, "At the end of September 1939, we may have encountered the largest threat on the strategic level during the entire war. We did not have several prepared plans or studies to choose from right away; therefore, we would not have been capable of putting a quick operational decision into practice swiftly and in an orderly manner."[2]

The General stated that he did not understand why plans of operations or studies by the general staff did not exist on the eve of the war. He characterized that shortcoming as "an act of carelessness [and] a sign of a lack of foresight and perhaps also of self-deception" that would have had fateful consequences in the event of an attack. He remarked, "I am convinced that the old military principle which says, 'Plan ahead but do not tie yourself down in advance,' still applies and will continue to apply, even in our special case. It is not enough to have *one* plan or *one* study ready; there must be five or ten of them in order to be forearmed against any possible threat and to be able to avoid needing to improvise when a threatening situation arises."[3]

The General's complaint made many people suspect that the experts in charge had seriously neglected their duty. His statement contained the accusation that preparations for war had not received enough attention, and the main culprit targeted by that accusation was Corps Commander Labhart, the chief of the general staff before the war. Corps Commander Borel told the Head of the Military Department it was regrettable that due to the way General Guisan wrote about the lack of plans of operations, public opinion was made to believe that someone had seriously neglected his duty and that this someone had to be Labhart. Borel added, "[Labhart] will obviously have no trouble justifying himself, but it will be difficult for him to do so without damaging the General's good reputation, which the General should be able to continue to enjoy if possible."[4] Borel argued that it was surprising that Guisan did not notice until the fall of 1939, after he was elected General, that there were no plans of operations available, since as a member of the National Defense Committee (NDC), he had been partly responsible for what he—unjustly—called a flaw.

The public soon asked whether the presumed culprits should be tried. Elements in the press, however, were quick to point out that plans of operations had fallen under the NDC's responsibility, but that as one of its members before the war, Guisan had apparently never complained that no plans were available.[5] So as not to further damage the army's or the General's reputation, Labhart renounced publicly defending himself, unlike Prisi and Bandi. However, he justified himself in a letter to the Head of the Military Department by denying that operational plans were required, questioning their usefulness. As Labhart argued, "Preparing scenarios for every possible case results in schematization, which is reserved for small-minded people. Perhaps the General is too fond of the former French doctrines, according to which orders and operational issues had to be planned in every little detail. I have been fighting my whole life against this small-mindedness, this schematization, which holds particularly great dangers for a militia army."[6]

The former chief of the general staff also refuted the claim that the commander-in-chief had reprimanded him in the fall of 1939 because no deployment plans existed. Labhart wrote that he set great store by the fact "that the General neither reprimanded nor reproached me in that matter," adding that both his memory and his diary entries would "prove the claim by the former Commander-in-Chief of the Armed Forces to be a lie."[7] In another letter to Federal Councilor Kobelt, Labhart reiterated, "I very firmly declare that the General never made any remark to me about the fact that plans of operations were not available at the outbreak of the war, neither at the time that I left my post as Chief of the General Staff nor later. As far as I know, no such remark was made either to my former subordinates, the Assistant Chief of Staff for the Front [Frick] and the Head of the Operational Section [von Erlach]."[8]

All other corps commanders except Lardelli agreed with Labhart that it would have been superfluous to prepare what the General called plans of operations. The most pungent public statement was made by Corps Commander Prisi. In his "Remarks," he explained that the fact that plans of operations had not existed was sensational for the public, or as he put it, "a nuclear bomb in the report, [but] for military experts it was more than strange." He remarked, "Only an aggressor can make plans of operations. . . . Nothing is more fateful than a defending party's cleverly devised 'plans of operations' that can never be matched against a future event in a war. If I have a choice between desk drawers and brains, I would very definitely prefer having empty drawers and resourceful, intelligent brains than having full drawers and empty brains." Prisi added that such long-term plans were "nonsense [for the defending party] from a military point of view, and the country would head straight into a disaster if a commander-in-chief wanted to abide by these outdated papers because of a lack of know-how."[9]

Prisi stated that Guisan's complaint showed a "surprising lack of knowledge of the limited possibilities of defending Switzerland and maintaining its neutrality in view of its military, geographic, and political situation." He explained that the two most important operations—mobilizing the troops and deploying them to the neutrality positions—had been prepared in detail and were successfully carried out during the first days of September 1939, allowing the General to take over the command of an army that had taken up its positions as planned. Prisi commented, "From there it was his job, the job of an inventive, resourceful leader who had to adapt to any given situation in the war by using his resources based on the information procured by the intelligence service and on his own quick decisions." Hence, he argued that it was not acceptable that those who had been in charge before the war were accused in retrospect by the commander-in-chief of neglecting their duty and defamed by him in public, adding, "According to Guisan's most recent statements, the fact that no plans of operations existed at the outbreak of the war would be a punishable offense for which the 'responsible' persons would have to be court-martialed."[10]

Karl Walde points out that the chief of the general staff's terms of reference of 1936 indeed made him responsible for preparing deployment plans and that this task was assigned to the Front group (not to be confused with the right-wing "Front" movement) two years later.[11] After the war, Corps Commander Hans Frick, who headed the Front group in 1939 as a colonel, explained:

> The various possibilities that existed for us were studied; however, as the Front group was very busy working on numerous other tasks, particularly on those associated with organizing the protection of the border and constructing the border fortifications, and as the Head of the Operational Section, Colonel von Erlach, was absent for extended

periods of time due to illness, it was not possible to put those studies into a final document. Moreover, at that time we considered that in our military and political situation, an army could not prepare any final deployment plans except for a so-called *deployment into neutral positions* because it was not clear who would be the enemy and how, when, and from what direction it would attack, and one could not know under what circumstances we would be targeted by an attack.[12]

In a letter to the Head of the Military Department, Frick "expressly" insisted that "the General's explanations were misleading if not altogether based on a foundation that [was] untenable from a military viewpoint" because the general staff was responsible for presenting studies and outlines for any possible situation but not actual "plans of operations." He added:

At the beginning of the war, General Guisan never spoke about any plans of operations either. The outline for deploying troops in the north was presented as soon as it had been requested. We would have been ready at any time to also present a report on all other possibilities that existed for 'Case North' or a combination 'North-South,' or for 'Case West,' but we were never asked to do so. That might have been due to the totally insufficient contact between the General and the Chief of the General Staff not only during Labhart's but also during Huber's tenure.[13]

Frick suspected that "the significance of the affection [for plans of operations] was suggested to [the General in retrospect] by someone who had an interest in discrediting the leading bodies of the general staff of that time."[14] That suspicion undoubtedly alluded to Gonard, the General's operational advisor, and Barbey, the chief of the personal staff.

During the 1938 operational exercises in which Guisan took part as corps commander, and during the 1939 exercises in which he even acted in the role of commander-in-chief, no one ever asked whether plans of operations had been prepared; instead, the plans for deploying the troops were established ad hoc by the general staff and presented within a few hours. As Frick explained, "At the debriefings of both exercises, which were attended by Federal Councilor Minger, neither the head of the 1938 exercise (Corps Commander Miescher) nor the head of the 1939 exercise (Corps Commander Prisi) nor anyone else considered it necessary to complain that no plans of operations were available."[15]

In internal comments on the General's report, other army unit commanders made practically the same statements, using arguments similar to Frick's. As members of the National Defense Committee, Corps Commanders Constam and Gübeli, who had both been promoted to that rank under General Guisan, explained that they attached no importance to plans of operations that were prepared in advance. Constam considered that such plans "could be fateful for a commander who [was] not very autonomous and rather insecure because they [did] not apply to special cases." Rather, he argued that more important than one or two dozen plans of operations was "a uniform terminology regarding the use of our resources for battle under the current circumstances and regarding the spirit in which the commanders and the troops [had] to be educated."[16] Gübeli took a dig at the militia officer Guisan, stating, "By virtue of his experience in the military and his having proven himself as a troop commander, as well as by virtue of his self-confidence, a General who makes his living serving in the army before being elected to that position will feel less need to be able to pull ready-made plans of operations out of a drawer."[17]

Former Divisional Commander Eugen Bircher, who spoke both on the National Council committee and in the lower house when the General's report was discussed, tried to shed some light on the term "plan of operations." He argued that Guisan's criticism about the lack of plans of operations was "justified neither from the point of view of military science nor history." He explained that the term "plan of operations" was used as a matter of principle in connection with offensive military plans, and that acting according to a plan of operations was "absolutely impossible for an army that [was] on the defensive." Bircher speculated that the misunderstanding had resulted from the fact that it was not clear how different terms were to be used.[18]

The new chief of the general staff, de Montmollin, also believed that "plans of operations [did] not need to be prepared in advance." He suspected that the argument was partly the result of personal differences, stating, "With his explanations concerning the issue of the plans of operations, the General sharply criticizes the preparations that were made by the general staff at the time. This can be attributed in part to the differences of opinion that existed between the General and Colonel-Corps Commander Labhart."[19]

Even Corps Commander Huber was rather skeptical about the usefulness of "plans of operations," although under his responsibility as chief of the general staff, about 20 of them had been drafted. His aversion to these plans became clear as early as 1942 during a lively discussion among the army staff, when Gonard and Masson disagreed on the way in which they should proceed with basic operational calculations. Barbey noted about this incident, "The chief of the general staff smiles, and in secret he is triumphant. He has always considered that these discussions were being led 'into the blue,' and in view of the much too uncertain situation, he softly repeats that these studies are inevitably theoretical. He says that what matters is to be ready to react quickly and spontaneously on the day of an invasion."[20]

On that occasion, the General made everyone understand that he considered those planning activities very significant. He recalled, "[It is important] to have our studies ready for any possibility; every possibility carries some implications not only on the military but also on the political level. We all must be able to reply at any moment, 'We are ready!' It is not enough to think of everything; everything has to be prepared."[21]

During the final phase of the war, the chief of the general staff flatly refused to prepare additional plans of operations. When the General suggested making new plans in view of the development that was taking shape in the East through the Russians' advance, Huber replied:

> I consider that it is not advisable to draw up new deployment plans as has been done so far. Deployment plans that were prepared on the basis of arbitrary assumptions were hardly ever realistic, as proven by past experience. If the development of the situation can be assessed and followed, it is better to renounce using plans that have been prepared in advance and to adapt to the development with a clear head and a flexible mind. In that case, there is a lesser risk of having to issue orders that cancel previous ones.[22]

It is striking that in that letter, Huber no longer used the term "plans of operations" but "deployment plans."

In his own report on wartime duty, Corps Commander Huber was cautious in his comments on the issue of plans of operations but made it clear that any such plan was "only the draft of an operation, so to speak," explaining, "It will in no case be possible to carry out a plan of operations without making sizeable changes to it because it is always based on assumptions that correspond only roughly to the subsequent specific situation. Hence, even if a plan of operations is useful insofar as it makes it possible to examine appropriate solutions, it will never be applicable as such in any particular case when the troops are actually mobilized."[23]

Huber wrote to the Head of the Military Department that he had never agreed with the General, who could "not ignore that [their] opinions diverged" on that matter, stating:

> None of the 22 operations orders that were prepared by the Operational Section in the course of wartime duty deserve to be called

that. They were exclusively 'deployment plans' or 'orders for moving into a defensive position,' some of which were complemented with directives on how to conduct battles. When I became chief of the general staff, three such orders had already been issued that carried that ostentatious title. I have always objected to that expression. However, we had more important things to do than discussing nomenclature. In the army, one knew what 'deployment' and 'operation' meant, even though the two terms were used indiscriminately. Unfortunately that confusion also exists in my report.[24]

For the future, Huber believed that in addition to the deployment plan for the unambiguous neutrality positions, only four deployment plans had to be available and had to be constantly adapted to the military and political circumstances: one plan each for cases "North-East," "West," and "South," plus one plan for manning the Réduit. He stated, "In my opinion, that is all that is needed!"[25]

In 1946, Federal Councilor Kobelt, the Head of the Military Department, was able to comment that all active corps commanders who were members of the National Defense Committee considered it unnecessary to have so-called plans of operations available, with the exception of plans for mobilizing the troops and for the first stand-by positions. He added, "Independent of each other, all members believe that the General goes too far with his demands regarding the plans of operations. The NDC unanimously agrees that we must not make any further commitment."[26]

In its counter-report to the General's report, the Federal Council adopted the National Defense Committee's unanimous opinion. It admitted that one could hold differing views regarding the need for ready-made plans of operations, but it considered that such plans were superfluous. However, it added that it was appropriate to have numerous operational studies available. The government insisted on stating that the lack of plans of operations was "due neither to a lack of foresight nor to self-deception but was the result of a conscious and deliberate choice," as it was important to allow the commander-in-chief to introduce his own ideas into deployment plans.[27] The Federal Council said that it wanted a General to be able to make his own decisions, but at the same time bear the responsibility for them. Ernst has written, "In agreement with Wille and his disciples, [the Federal Council] considered that plans of operations were dangerous because they could restrict the responsible commander's freedom of decision."[28]

The Federal Council did not fail to point out that General Guisan bore part of the blame for the fact that plans of operations did not exist. It recalled that before the war, as a member of the National Defense Committee, Guisan had the opportunity to demand that plans be worked out, but he never did.

After the fact, General Guisan did not at all deny that he was partly responsible for the shortcoming about which he had complained. On several occasions, he said that he was willing to accept part of the blame. As he wrote to his friend Minger:

> I have absolutely no intention of shirking the responsibility that I had as a former corps commander and member of the NDC, insofar as the NDC as a whole is made responsible to a certain extent for the fact that the plans of operations did not exist. However, the major share of the responsibility should have to be borne by the Chief of the General Staff Section. . . . If on September 4 or 5, 1939 it had been necessary to deploy the bulk of the armed forces for what was later called 'Case North,' the army staff (which was only roughly organized during those days and consequently did not yet operate smoothly; moreover, it was busy moving its quarters from Bern to Spiez) would certainly have been able to accomplish its tasks better and more successfully if it had been able to base itself on an existing plan of operations that included a list of the necessary means of transport.[29]

During a hearing on the National Council committee, the General explained that he wanted "to make it clear once again that his report [was] not intended as an indictment." Regarding the responsibility for the lack of plans of operations, he stated how "he had been a member of the NDC and should have dealt with the issue. He said that the purpose of his report was to draw posterity's attention to the mistakes that had been made to prevent them from happening again in the future."[30] During one of his conversations with Gafner, General Guisan confessed:

> As a former member of the NDC, I have to point the finger at myself first for not having dealt sufficiently with that issue. However, I still had in mind the time when I was an officer on the general staff from 1914 to 1918. At that time, those plans had been prepared in advance. And because such plans are part of the tasks of the general staff section, not the NDC, before 1939 I was completely permitted to assume that such studies were available. Yet I would like to say once again that I am primarily accusing myself for failing to draw the committee's attention to this issue, which seemed to be so fundamental to me.[31]

Contrary to what some claimed, Guisan did criticize his own role in connection with the lack of plans of operations; however, after the Federal

Council's counter-report was published, he continued to be convinced that plans of operations were necessary. In his "Observations," he remarked that it was "simply foolish" to claim that only an attacker could make plans of operations.[32] He explained to the National Council committee that the opinion expressed by the Federal Council was "a very bad conception. . . . One must not renounce such plans of operations. It has been said that such plans would tie the General's hands. However, if ten or more such plans exist, the General still has to decide which one he wants to carry out depending on the situation. There must be concentration plans with expected marching times, schedules, etc. It is not difficult to make minor changes here and there to those plans afterward."[33] It is interesting to note that in that document, Guisan for the first time used a new expression for what he demanded in connection with the different "cases," by speaking of "concentration plans," which had to include schedules and a list of the required means of transportation as well as an order of battle.

When analyzing the dispute about the lack of plans of operations, one cannot resist thinking that it was primarily a matter of terminology, as Huber had indicated. It turned out that even top-ranking staff officers did not agree among themselves what the expression "plan of operations" meant. What the General understood by that expression were not "plans of operations" in the traditional military sense, referring to offensives or maneuvers, but "deployment plans," because he expected to have plans available for deploying troops to defensive positions that were dictated by particular situations. As Huber explained to Kobelt, an "operation" is a movement of troops in a war to bring them closer to the enemy or to withdraw them from enemy contact during a combat.[34] It appears to be somewhat strange that the chief of the general staff did not remember that clear-cut distinction between a plan of operations and a deployment plan until after the war.

Corps Commander Hans Frick rejected the General's expression as "erroneous." He termed the movement of troops from the mobilization positions into all directions a "deployment into covering positions" (neutrality positions).[35]

During a meeting of the Council of States committee, Federal Councilor Kobelt unequivocally stated, "The mobilization positions had been prepared in every detail, including the requirements in terms of transportation. The troops took up these positions as planned. A second plan for the deployment of the troops to the neutrality positions had also been prepared in every detail and was carried out smoothly."[36]

Walde rightly points out that the controversy about the terminology may have been caused by the fact that in French, there was no equivalent expression available for "deployment plan," so the term "plan d'opération" was used.[37]

Hofer also attributes the arguments about that issue to the unclear way in which different terms were used, considering that it was "possible that the difference of opinion between the Federal Council and the General was not as great as it may have appeared."[38] A look at the way in which the expression "plan of operations" was used during the war makes it clear that General Guisan meant "deployment plans" when he said "plans of operations"; for example, "Operations Order No. 13" for manning the Réduit was actually a deployment plan.

In 1946–47, the issue of whether "plans of operations" in the sense of detailed deployment plans were useful and should therefore be worked out and periodically updated gave rise to heated debates among military leaders. Today, the general opinion prevails that they are an integral part of preparations for war. The type of operational studies that General Guisan said did not exist in 1939 and that he emphatically demanded in his report are a matter of fact today. The general staff of the Swiss Army continuously updates the arrangements for half a dozen possible scenarios.[39] Today's opinion about what the commander-in-chief of Switzerland's armed forces demanded in terms of "plans of operations" proves that General Guisan was right about this issue and the Federal Council was not.

Conflict with Air Force Commander Bandi

THE MOST SERIOUS PERSONAL CONFLICT caused by the General's report was the dispute that Divisional Commander Hans Bandi, who had been dismissed as commander of the Air Force and Anti-Aircraft Defense in 1943, carried out in public with the former commander-in-chief. In his report, the General not only complained about Switzerland's failure to have a "policy on airspace" before the war but also criticized conditions in the air force and antiaircraft defense, making its commander at the time personally responsible for many mistakes and naming him in several extended passages. The General argued that there had not only been shortcomings but "an actual crisis" in that arm.[1] He explained that he had consequently asked Corps Commander Miescher, who had resigned a short time earlier, to look into the situation and report to him. Guisan summarized the results of Miescher's analysis by stating, "The commander of the Air Force and Anti-Aircraft Defense and his chief of staff had an isolationist attitude. They seemed to prepare the air force for the time after the war rather than for the war that was threatening us every day. The staff's work was badly organized because the commander and the chief of staff jealously reserved dealing with the most diverse issues, both important and unimportant, for themselves. This attitude resulted in a widespread, almost complete lack of trust."[2] Guisan added that there was no doctrine on how to make use of the air force, nor any regulations on tactical matters, and that "there was a lack of understanding and willingness to cooperate with the ground forces."[3]

What caused a great stir in connection with the criticism was the fact that the General attached a separate report, which had originally been confidential, to his larger report to back up his statements against Bandi. This confidential report had been written by the new head of the air force and antiaircraft, Divisional Commander Fritz Rihner, at the General's request. In the attached report, Rihner listed the mistakes and shortcomings he had noticed when he took over the command of that branch. The General explained that he personally "made sure that the statements made therein were accurate and well-founded."[4] In his document Rihner claimed, among other things, that the "intelligence activities [had been] utterly neglected," the practical experience from the air combats in 1940 had "not been evaluated," expansion of the airfields in the Réduit was begun "only in mid-1942 after the commander-in-chief [had] applied some pressure" and even then was done "only hesitantly and reluctantly." He further stated that combat training for the air force and antiaircraft defense had been "severely neglected [and] even the General's instructions [had been] carried out reluctantly, cooperation with the ground troops [had not been] encouraged at all," and even "as of 1942, cooperation remained very limited, even though the General had expressly demanded" that it be intensified. Rihner also considered the radio equipment to be "totally insufficient" because only 43.5 percent of the fighter aircraft had been equipped, and the existing devices were neither reliable nor powerful enough.[5]

It was unusual for a dismissed army unit commander, whom the General accused of neglecting his duty, of lacking organizational and leadership qualities, and even of being disobedient, to be denounced so sharply with his name revealed. Prisi called this "the most outrageous occurrence that [had] ever happened; [it was the equivalent of] a posthumous execution in public."[6]

As hardly anyone publicly defended the former commander of the air force, who had been a rough and rather unfriendly superior, Bandi decided to speak up in his own defense.[7] In the spring of 1947, he addressed a 36-page document to parliament, the Federal Council, and the press. Its format, print, and design looked exactly like the General's report. Bandi stated that he vehemently rejected Guisan's accusations, not only because he wanted to justify himself but because he also wanted to provide his "former closest collaborators, who, with a few exceptions, accomplished their tasks in an exemplary manner, with the satisfaction they deserve."[8] He remarked that in the General's report "baseness [was] a criterion for writing a work of military history" and that he endeavored to "denounce the contradictions" that Rihner's report contained "and to clip some of the borrowed plumes with which [Rihner] strutted."[9] Bandi began every paragraph in which he set things straight by using the phrase, "In contradiction to the truth, Colonel-Divisional Commander Rihner claims ...," thereby accusing his successor of lying in several accounts. He concluded that "therefore [it was] proven that Colonel-Divisional Commander Rihner's document

[was] made up of misconceptions and distortions," so it was astonishing that General Guisan had declared that it was "accurate and well-founded."[10]

Bandi assured his readers that he did not claim to have made no mistakes, nor that the air force had been perfect under his command. Nevertheless, it was not difficult for him to prove that he was to be credited for building up the air force "from ground zero as of 1936" and for acquiring new planes, which had always been difficult for financial reasons.[11] Regarding the continual delays in the delivery of weapons, ammunition, and equipment, Bandi pointed out problematic relations with Colonel Fierz, the Director of the Armament Section, who he said was an "inventor, manufacturer, factory owner, monitoring authority, and buyer" all at the same time, and who would have liked to have been a tactical advisor for the air force as well. In addition, he said that Fierz always claimed "to be right."[12]

The beleaguered divisional commander also fought against Guisan's "hazy accusation" that he had displayed an isolationist attitude, qualifying it as "distorted criticism [that was] empty and at the same time laconic." He argued that because the General used to issue instructions for the air force and antiaircraft defense without consulting him, he had been "circumvented as an expert advisor and often forced to execute orders that showed a lack of expertise or consideration." As an example, Bandi remarked that Guisan had given orders to "fly American bombers," which he said would not have been possible "at the time out of foreign policy considerations."[13] Moreover, Bandi accused the General of having become involved in personnel matters of his staff and having ordered changes without his approval. He mentioned the example of the appointments of Colonels Rihner and Magron, who were not acceptable to him, as his deputies, adding, "The situation created by General Guisan was suitable to undermine any commander's position both upward and downward. I have been told that General Guisan went so far as ordering Colonel Magron into meetings [of Guisan's choosing] and instructing him not to reveal [to Bandi] the topic that was discussed there. Under such circumstances, no further comment is necessary about what one should think of the 'isolationist attitude' of which General Guisan accuses me."[14]

As indicated in Barbey's diary, Guisan's "Instructions for the Use of the Air Force" dated January 12, 1943, had indeed been drafted by members of the personal staff. Barbey noted, "I worked with van Berchem on the new instructions for the air force. We will be able to provide the General with the documents that he requested because of the almost unanimous opinions that we have polled from pilots of all ranks. There will be two texts: the instructions per se and a report on the training objectives and methods."[15] The draft instructions for the antiaircraft defense were developed in a similar fashion.[16] These directives for the air force and antiaircraft defense were drawn up in agreement with Gonard, the head of the Operational Section at the time.[17] Bandi did not know who had drafted these documents, but he found fault with the procedure, stating, "It does not bother me that things are criticized. What is incomprehensible, though, is that in matters relating to the air force, General Guisan was receptive to very amateurish objections."[18]

Bandi's remarks indicate that he suspected members of the personal staff, who had been in contact with some of his dissatisfied subordinates, of negatively influencing the General's attitude toward him. Historian Felix Müller wrote an interesting article that supports Bandi's suspicion.[19]

Bandi concluded his document by complaining that the injustice that had been done to him was an offense "against faith and honor," adding, "Therefore I am inalienably entitled to have my good name restored during my lifetime. In order to make that happen, I trust Parliament's incorruptible sense of responsibility, asking it not to approve Colonel-Divisional Commander Rihner's remarks, nor the conclusions that General Guisan has drawn from them [in his report]."[20]

It is easy to comprehend Bandi's vehement reaction; he considered that he had been unfairly attacked and denounced in public. The General's accusations contrasted sharply with the fact that at the end of 1941 he had been prepared to promote the commander of the air force and antiaircraft to the rank of colonel-corps commander in recognition of his merits. Chief of the General Staff Huber had brought the proposition for his promotion forward. The minutes of the General's meeting with the top unit commanders stated, "The General takes note of the fact that three army corps commanders (Labhart, Lardelli, Borel) reject the chief of the general staff's proposal to promote Divisional Commander Bandi to the rank of corps commander; one army corps commander (Wille) does not object to it but thinks that it would set a precedent; and one army corps commander supports it."[21] That close verdict may have caused the General not to promote Bandi at the time. Prisi explained, "The reason why [Bandi] was not promoted was because it was not indispensable for a chief instructor and air force and anti-aircraft commander to be promoted to corps commander. The majority of the corps commanders did not question his competence in military matters."[22]

When Bandi left his post at the end of 1943, former Federal Councilor Minger assured him, "You can resign with your head held high. You loyally managed your resources, and what you made out of our air force is a laudable chapter in the history of our national defense. You deserve the country's gratitude. It no longer falls under my authority to express any official thanks, but my personal thanks are all the more heartfelt."[23] In his comment on the

General's report, Minger's remarks on Bandi were also diametrically opposed to Guisan's, as he expressed his appreciation to Bandi and confirmed that he had done "a great job and brought the air force to a remarkable level under difficult circumstances."[24]

When dealing with the General's and the Federal Council's reports, the committees of the two chambers of Parliament also discussed Bandi's document. During one meeting of the Council of States committee, Emil Klöti from Zürich declared that he considered the case of Bandi "rather tragic. . . . That man worked with great enthusiasm, as I was able to see for myself. He was constantly busy fighting to get aircraft, fighting to get antiaircraft guns, and I must say that he was given a hard time in that respect." Klöti defended the General for having had the courage to uncover mistakes because the army was not allowed to keep such shortcomings secret from the people, to whom the army belonged. However, he argued, "In the case of Bandi, [the General] committed a faux pas."[25] Councilor of State Erich Ullmann went even further in criticizing the General, stating, "We have to be aware that the General made a great mistake by making Colonel-Divisional Commander Rihner's report available to the public in an appendix to his own report. He did the army a disservice by doing that. That was a faux pas. . . . What Bandi did in his document was not right either. I agree that Bandi had to defend himself if the General made a mistake, but the way he did it is not right either."[26] Federal Councilor Kobelt explained that Rihner had been "a staunch opponent of Bandi and Bandi a staunch opponent of Rihner" and stated that he understood why Bandi defended himself, adding, however, "The document that he wrote in his defense goes too far, both in its tone and in its contents."[27] The National Council committee had renewed doubts whether the General's entire report served to state the historic truth objectively. Bircher said that the accusations against Bandi had "shaken him both as a soldier and a human being."[28]

The Military Department submitted Bandi's document to the General for comments. Guisan replied, "There is not one word that I have to take out of my report; on the contrary, there is much that I could add to it!"[29]

In view of the reprimands and accusations that Guisan and Bandi made against each other, the Head of the Military Department, with the Federal Council's approval, ordered Divisional Commander Claude du Pasquier, a professor from Neuchâtel, to carry out an administrative investigation to shed light on the situation.[30] In a comprehensive 55-page report, Du Pasquier concluded that only some of Rihner's accusations on which the General's statements were based turned out to be tenable, explaining:

[The accusations are correct] especially concerning training and cooperation among the staff. On some other issues that Rihner's report raises (particularly the procurement of materiel), the criticism is unjustified. In some other respects, Rihner's statements are partly correct and
partly false. In addition, there are issues that in good faith may be
looked at from different perspectives and where opinions can be divided. Rihner's report also includes complaints that are factually correct
but are directed against the wrong person.

After a careful analysis, du Pasquier stated that Rihner's report (published,
after all, as an appendix to the General's report) was awkward insofar as it made
it look as if charges were being brought against Bandi, even though that was not
what it was supposed to do. He remarked, "The report lacked objectivity."[31]
Du Pasquier strove to settle the conflict amicably, concluding that the case
"should not be brought before a court nor entail any disciplinary sanctions."
The two concerned officers each received a copy of the investigative report in
order to "let Rihner know about the mistakes he had made" and to inform
Bandi about the corrections that were made. Du Pasquier recommended, "This
information should be considered personal; the report is not intended for publication, nor should it be passed on to a third party. However, a communiqué
should be published announcing that the matter has been settled."[32] With that
communiqué, the Bandi case was settled internally without bringing any details
to the public's attention.
From du Pasquier's report and from some other scattered information it
can be gathered that relations between Bandi and the General had begun to
turn sour as early as the second year of the war. The first time there was talk
about replacing Bandi was in connection with the examination of conditions in
the air force and antiaircraft defense that Corps Commander Miescher had
been asked to carry out in 1942. Bandi stated that Miescher's inquiries had
been made behind his back and that he never personally saw the results. He
explained that Miescher had held "discussions with numerous officers on the
back stairs" without his knowledge and that he had never been informed who
these officers were nor what they said, "so that [he] could confirm their statements, correct them, or prove them wrong." He argued that during these
inquiries, which he called "an insulting inquisition," he had been denied the
right to be heard.[33] However, Miescher's inquiries did not yield the expected
devastating results. Barbey remarked that Miescher's report was "something
between a study and an investigation"; consequently it could not be used "as the
decisive means . . . to get the boil to burst." Nevertheless, Barbey commented,
"All in all, [the report] is an essential piece of information without which it

would be impossible to take any action; it does not eliminate any difficulties, though."[34]

On December 21, 1942, when the General told the Head of the Military Department that it would be desirable to replace Bandi, Federal Councilor Kobelt clearly advised him not to do so for several reasons. He remarked to the General, "Bandi is a cross that we have to bear together."[35] During a meeting in early 1943 in Interlaken, the commander-in-chief reiterated his desire to dismiss Bandi. He considered making the current commander superfluous by restructuring the command of the air force and anti-aircraft defense. Kobelt wrote about that meeting in his diary:

> 12 March. Meeting with General in Interlaken regarding Bandi case. I oppose the proposed restructuring. I pointed out what the consequences would be if [Bandi] were relieved of his command. Bandi has a contract as a Federal employee until 1944 and would have to be kept on the payroll for two years even if he were not put in any other position. The General wanted to relieve Colonel-Divisional Commander Bandi of his command as of the end of the year. I recommended to the General not to go too far after Wille had been dismissed; I also reminded him of the cases of Labhart, Miescher, and Bircher. I recommended that the General continue to bear the cross. He agreed. . . . In his letters of 23 February and 7 March [1943], the General changed his mind again, wanting to remove Bandi from his post by restructuring the command. It is always dangerous to want to do some restructuring based on considerations that are linked to specific personnel rather than objective criteria.[36]

Kobelt consulted with Corps Commander Marcuard on that issue, who agreed that the General's planned restructuring should be rejected. Marcuard told Kobelt, "If B[andi] is not qualified, he should be asked to step down. However, in addition to some unpleasant traits of character, Bandi also has some qualities and undoubtedly also some great merits."[37]

Kobelt told the General that he should leave Bandi at his post until the end of 1943 so he could be replaced in connection with the regular replacements and transfers. Kobelt wrote in his diary, "I remarked that at the end of the year the question could be examined whether someone younger should replace [Bandi]. It seems that the General does not want to wait that long. He assured me that he would wait at least until the summer before replacing him."[38]

A few days after that meeting, during a private conversation with Federal Councilor Kobelt, German Minister Köcher surprisingly insinuated that he was informed about Divisional Commander Bandi's planned dismissal. Köcher said that Germany did not understand why "all higher-ranking officers who sympathized with Germany were removed," naming Labhart, Wille, Bircher, and also Bandi as examples. Kobelt commented, "It is interesting that Minister Köcher seems to be informed about the General's intention to dismiss Bandi. This proves that I was right to tell the General about that aspect of the problem."[39]

In the summer of 1943, General Guisan did not take any action on that delicate matter; however, that fall he took measures in time so he would be able to dismiss Bandi at the end of the year. In October, he informed the Military Department in writing about his determination to replace Bandi. Barbey noted that the General also informed Huber about his intention, stating, "The General summoned the chief of the general staff to show him the letter he wrote to the Military Department in which he asks to have Bandi replaced. This is an embarrassing and delicate matter because Huber and Bandi are friends. The General tells me that Huber did not 'resist' his move. However, [Huber] set great store on emphasizing the efforts that he considered Bandi had undertaken to follow the General's instructions."[40] Guisan also informed former Federal Councilor Minger about his decision, first verbally and then in writing, adding several documents to the letter in which he stated, "Col.-Div. Bandi should understand that it is in his interest to use health reasons as a pretext to step down from his command in an honorable fashion. Thank you for your efforts."[41] Minger apparently took over the task of speaking with Bandi to get him to agree to resign on amicable terms.

Bandi's long letter of November 13, 1943, to Federal Councilor Kobelt, in which he tried to prevent his dismissal from becoming reality, was to no avail. The decision had already been made against him. Following a medical examination by the Surgeon General, the official reason put forward for Bandi's retirement was a kidney stone that posed "a threat" to his health. The General noted, "There is a risk of B[andi] suffering from renal colic; during previous bouts, he became unbearable and was curt with his subordinates."[42] In the General's report, health-related considerations were not mentioned; the commander-in-chief emphasized that he had asked the Federal Council's approval for replacing Bandi because measures that he had ordered did "not entirely" meet his expectations.[43] On December 31, 1943, Bandi was relieved of his post and replaced by his rival Rihner. In connection with the dispute that arose after the war, Guisan confirmed to his friend Minger that "Bandi [had been] replaced for health reasons as well as for reasons linked to his character."[44]

The report that General Guisan asked Rihner to write about the situation in the air force and antiaircraft defense at the time Rihner took up his post on January 1, 1944 was probably written by his chief of staff, Major Primault.[45] It remains contested why and in what way that "personal and secret" report, which painted the situation in crude black-and-white terms and showed Rihner's predecessor in a bad light, was included as one of the reports on wartime duty. As Federal President, Kobelt asked Rihner for an explanation, and as Rihner was eventually attacked in the press, he turned to the General to ask him to make things clear in a public declaration. As Rihner wrote to the General, "This declaration could state that my report of early 1944 was written on your orders, that it was to list the shortcomings regarding the organization, equipment, and training in the air force and AD [antiaircraft defense], of which I was to make an inventory to confirm the findings that you had made on your own, and finally that you personally decided to publish this report after the end of wartime duty."[46] The General refused to make a public statement, annotating the letter with the words, "Intervene with my approval. If I dwelled on the air force in my report, it was because I had to intervene personally and because of that I also took on the responsibility."[47]

Rihner wrote to Kobelt that he had come to realize that the publication of his report "only caused damage" to the air force and to himself. He put great store on assuring Kobelt that the report had been written and published at the General's personal request, explaining:

After I had taken over the command during the first days of January 1944, the commander-in-chief informed me about the state of affairs in the air force and anti-aircraft defense. He asked me to write a 'status report' in which I was to write down every shortcoming that I noticed in the organization, operations, and equipment of the air force and anti-aircraft defense in order to define the starting position for the commander-in-chief and for myself, as it were. I submitted that report to the General as a personal and secret document. The last thing on my mind back then and now was to attack my predecessor personally and to cause damage to him in any way. I quite realized that various shortcomings I noticed had been considered as such also by my predecessor but that it often did not depend on him whether they could be corrected. . . . In any event, I pointed out to the General on several occasions that I did not think that my purely factual report of May 26, 1944 should be published because it was secret. I very much regretted that the General decided otherwise.[48]

In his investigative report, du Pasquier confirmed Rihner's version, explaining that it was the General who had insisted on publishing the air force and antiaircraft defense commander's report as an appendix to his own report, in spite of Rihner's objections. The General had declared that he would take "the responsibility for publishing it, but the contents [continued] to be the author's responsibility."[49]

During the hearings of the committee, National Councilor Odermatt asked Guisan what had prompted him to publish Rihner's report as an appendix, even though Rihner had submitted it as a "confidential" report and had considered that it was inappropriate to publish it. Guisan replied that he had set great store on publishing all reports "without cutting anything out of them."[50] National Councilor Oprecht subsequently asked him whether it was true that Rihner had recommended not publishing his report "and ended up leaving the decision up to the General after the General flatly refused to heed his recommendation." Guisan was evasive, replying that he could "not answer that question without consulting his files" but that he would "do so as soon as possible."[51]

In his written reply to National Councilor Alfred Müller, the chairman of the committee, the General did not deny that an exchange of opinions had taken place between Primault, the chief of staff of the air force, and Barbey in connection with the planned publication of Rihner's report. In addition, he mentioned that during a telephone conversation, Captain Zingg, an administrative aide in the air force and antiaircraft defense, had told Captain Marguth, the head of his office, about his concerns on that same subject. However, the General explained that these interventions came too late because by that time his report had already been printed.[52]

The following day, after the National Council committee had taken note of that written answer, Kobelt questioned the accuracy of the General's statement. According to the minutes of the meeting, Kobelt explained:

> The General's reply of March 3, 1947 to the chairman of this committee concerning the time of printing is not correct. When the exchange of opinions between Lt.-Col. Barbey and Lt.-Col. Primault took place in February 1946, the General's report was far from going to press. Only the drafts existed. The report went to press only in May. The General's claim that the concerns by the administrative aide of the air force and anti-aircraft defense at the end of March were voiced too late because his report had already been printed must be questioned.[53]

The committee let the matter rest even if it remained problematic.

Understandably the public did not find out about these differences, nor about the letters that several army unit commanders addressed to the Head of the Military Department to voice their concerns about the consequences of the public dispute between the General and Bandi. A few corps commanders, who were the commander-in-chief's former direct subordinates, did not hesitate to accuse the General of nothing less than showing an attitude unworthy of a soldier. Hans Frick, the Chief Instructor of the Armed Forces, wrote to Federal Councilor Kobelt, "It is hardly compatible with the military's ideals and the chivalry that becomes every officer to ask a newly appointed commander to criticize his predecessor in a report, and even less so to publish it. No matter with how much indulgence and consideration for his merits one views the General's report, this act is inexcusable."[54]

Corps Commander Labhart was equally adamant in his criticism, stating, "Making the successor to a command the prosecutor is unworthy of a soldier. Colonel-Divisional Commander Bandi did not deserve to be treated that way."[55] Corps Commander Constam also thought that Rihner's confidential report should not have been published under any circumstances. He argued that a commander was obliged to replace a subordinate commander if he did not seem to be in the right position, "however, [the commander] must not pillory [that subordinate commander] after the fact unless there is proof that he neglected his duty and at least some disciplinary action was taken against him. If that is the case, one should still consider whether one is doing a service to the army by [pillorying the subordinate commander]." He said that in most instances that was not the case, as exemplified in the Bandi affair.[56] Corps Commander Borel and Divisional Commanders Marius Corbat and Richard Frey voiced similar criticism.[57]

Chief of the General Staff Huber, who was informed about most details of the Bandi case, probably objected most vehemently to the commander-in-chief's way of handling the matter. He wrote to Federal Councilor Kobelt that as far as he could remember, it seemed to him that Bandi's document "reflected the facts" because his case was "one of the darkest chapters of wartime duty between 1939 and 1945." Huber explained that any other soldier had the right to appeal a decision but "the commanders immediately below the General [were] at a dictator's mercy without having any legal recourse." He argued that this situation explained why there was a public dispute, stating, "Having no legal recourse, Colonel-Divisional Commander Bandi ended up being driven so far that he forgot himself and became rude toward the General."[58]

The conflict with Bandi shows that General Guisan was not totally free of personal acrimony. By publishing Rihner's report against the author's will, he seems to have succumbed to a certain vindictiveness. Alluding to an expression that Prisi had used, Chief of the General Staff Huber commented on the matter, "By posthumously executing [Bandi] in public, injured vanity took its revenge in a less than noble manner."[59]

Issue of the
Peacetime General

ANOTHER ISSUE THAT WAS DISCUSSED WIDELY after being raised in General Guisan's postwar report was the structure of the army command during times of peace. The question of whether it was appropriate for Switzerland to institute the permanent post of an army inspector responsible for all aspects of the armed forces—a so-called "peacetime general"—had already been hotly debated before the war. Some were convinced that an army inspector, who had extended authority and to whom the corps commanders were to report, was necessary, while others believed that the National Defense Committee (NDC) should continue to be the leading armed forces authority in peacetime. Before the war, the Military Department had come up with a compromise between these two opinions that became law on June 22, 1939. The law stipulated that the NDC add two new members, a chief instructor and an army inspector, who were each to have the rank of corps commander. However, the army inspector, rather than possessing supreme authority, was to serve as a representative of the Head of the Military Department with the right to inspect any troops and to check if military doctrines and procedures were being uniformly followed. In 1939, Guisan had favored this compromise.[1] However, the law was not put into force at that time because the war broke out and the General was elected.

Based on his experience of the mobilization of 1939, at the end of his report the General proposed renaming the Military Department the "Swiss Federal Department of Defense," which would oversee the existing National Defense Committee and the armament section, and introduce an army inspector as a new function. As Guisan described it:

The "Army Inspector" would be ordered to command the entire armed forces in a war and prepare them for this task during times of peace. In other words, he would be responsible for overseeing their training and inspecting them. If a solution giving him maximum authority is chosen, this head will have full authority over the general staff, the commander of the air force, and the chief instructor; the two latter officers will have their own staffs to assist them. If a minimum solution is chosen, the Army Inspector will have the task of inspecting all ground forces and the air force and check the work that is done by the general staff. He will submit all requests for war material to the Head of the Military Department. Generally speaking, he will be the right-hand man and military advisor of the Head of the Military Department.[2]

Guisan suggested that Parliament elect the army inspector from among the army unit commanders. However, the rank of general was to be reserved for the commander-in-chief of the armed forces during a war and in other emergency situations when the army had to be called up. "That way," he argued, "the army would not only be administered but commanded during times of peace."

Guisan wrote that his proposal was only "a basis for further studies," yet he thought the overall direction of the new solution was "not open for discussion," explaining, "The important thing is to clearly establish the responsibilities and to bestow on the officer who would have the greatest responsibility during times of war the authority, and make available to him the means, that he needs to be able to prepare himself for that task in advance during times of peace."[3] Guisan's proposed solution aimed to automatically make the army inspector, who was responsible for making the troops fit for war, the general at the time of mobilization so that he could take over the command of the armed forces.

Guisan proposed this new way of electing the commander-in-chief on the grounds that the existing procedure, under which the general was elected only at the last minute before the beginning of hostilities, was "no longer adequate under the current circumstances and [would] certainly be even less adequate under future circumstances." He added, "Imagine the situation that we would have faced in the event of a sudden attack in late August and early September 1939, no matter if it had been preceded by an ultimatum or not."[4]

Guisan stated that being a member of the National Defense Committee, which was only a "committee," not a "council," did not sufficiently prepare the top commander for his task. "The future General's task," he said, "will become more and more difficult and varied. It is wrong to believe—or to pretend to believe—that he will always be able to take the reins by boldly improvising, and take control of all command matters under the best conditions and within a useful amount of time."[5]

After the end of the war in Europe but before the Swiss Army went off duty, on August 3, 1945, the Federal Council enacted the law regarding the expansion of the National Defense Committee that had been passed in 1939. However, with the approval of the proxy committees of the two chambers of Parliament, it did away with the paragraph that stipulated the establishment of the post of an army inspector with limited authority.[6]

In his report, General Guisan expressed his indignation at this development, stating, "I admit I was surprised that as the outgoing commander-in-chief, who got to know the personnel and had six years of firsthand experience, I was not consulted on that extremely important issue. If I had been consulted, I would have opposed eliminating that post."[7] In a letter to the Head of the Military Department, Guisan complained about not having been consulted. He told Kobelt, "Let me say once again that I consider the elimination of the post of army inspector a mistake, and as far as I know, the majority of the National Defense Committee and the Swiss Officers' Society share my view."[8] Indeed, four out of seven members of the NDC favored an army inspector, and a delegates' assembly of the Swiss Officers' Society had expressed its support for the proposed post with a two-thirds majority. However, while the media in French-speaking Switzerland supported Guisan's view, most newspapers in German-speaking Switzerland opposed it.[9]

The Federal Council did not share Guisan's opinion, rejecting the idea of a "peacetime general."[10] Moreover, the government was able to prove that it had asked the commander-in-chief's opinion on the matter before the end of wartime duty, and on that occasion, the General had commented that the 1939 law was "anachronistic."[11] In addition, before Guisan stepped down and before Parliament decided the issue, Kobelt had informed him, "While examining a decree by the Federal Council regarding the end of war-time duty, the proxy committees of both chambers unanimously considered that for the time being no army inspector should be appointed." He had told the General that the Federal Council intended to follow the committees' recommendation because it was convinced that the army's democratic structure, which he said the General had been emphasizing "in a very fortunate way" during the entire duration of wartime duty, should be maintained. Kobelt added, "It would go against that idea to bestow too much authority on one single high-ranking officer during times of peace."[12]

The General suspected that "personnel-related motives [could] have played a major role" in the Federal Council's and the proxy committees' decision not to establish the post of army inspector.[13] This supposition may not have been wrong, since Kobelt would have liked Labhart to become army inspector but some political officials and Guisan opposed him. In the spring of 1945, Labhart noted in his diary that Federal Councilor Kobelt had called him to a meeting to tell him:

> National Councilors Bringolf and Oprecht and another person came to see [me] to ask [me] whom [I] suggested putting in the top positions in the military [after the General's resignation]. They said that they had heard that [you] were going to be proposed as Army Inspector and Corbat as Chief of the General Staff. They said that they would oppose these nominations with all means, claiming that [you] were decidedly a militarist and pro-German and Corbat had been associated with the Front movement at the time. They argued that some younger officers should be placed in the leading positions. [I] clearly contradicted them. When [I] asked them whom they would consider as a suitable candidate for the post of the army inspector, they named Constam. [I] suspect that this move was initiated by the General, who is trying to get his people into the top positions. H. Frick is of the same opinion.[14]

These statements make clear what tactics were used to try to influence personnel-related decisions behind the scenes. When Labhart ran into National Councilor Grimm a short time later, he told him about his fellow partisans' initiative. Grimm, who was Deputy Speaker of the National Council at the time, "was very surprised at this action, calling it improper and declaring that he would put an end to it."[15]

A few days later, the Head of the Military Department told Corps Commander Labhart that Bringolf and Oprecht had come to see him once again. Labhart wrote, "Federal Councilor Kobelt explained that he had managed to convince the two National Councilors of my qualifications." They said that they would not oppose Labhart's taking on his original post as chief of the general staff; however, they were determined to prevent the law of June 1939 from being enacted by Parliament if it provided for the appointment of an army inspector."[16] As it turned out, the two National Councilors did not have to take any action in Parliament because the Federal Council decided to delete the paragraph concerning the army inspector from the law.

Military experts were divided over the question whether it was advisable to establish the post of peacetime general. Labhart called the army inspectorate not only desirable but also "inevitable and necessary," probably thinking that he was the one who would get the powerful post. However, he suggested that the army inspector be appointed by the Federal Council rather than be elected by

Parliament.[17] In a letter to Federal Councilor Kobelt, Corps Commander Huber, who also considered the change appropriate, called the way in which the General was usually elected "an anachronistic relic from the time when Switzerland was a confederacy."[18] Gonard, who rejected the existing procedure for the election of a commander-in-chief as "totally outdated," definitely supported the idea of a peacetime general, explaining, "Only a commander-in-chief who has already been designated during times of peace can order the strategic preparations that correspond to his personal ideas and for which he is solely responsible. He must be able to say in advance what he considers necessary, not only once the country is perhaps already affected by the first strategic bombings."[19]

Corps Commander Hans Frick also considered the last-minute election of a commander-in-chief as "an absolutely archaic procedure." Even though he did not "want to subscribe to all of [Guisan's] ideas," he agreed with the General that a strong army command was indispensable during times of peace, arguing, "A top officer, who stands above the Chief Instructor [is needed]. That top officer should be the Army Inspector, who would obviously have to have authority over the corps commanders, the general staff, and the Chief Instructor. The Army Inspector would of course be the designated commander-in-chief, but as long as Parliament elects the General, it would not be forced to appoint the Army Inspector to that position."[20] However, Frick also believed that the existing election procedure was outdated; he stated that in an effort to be ready in the event of a war, the "only objectively justifiable solution" was to have the commander-in-chief elected by the Federal Council in the future.[21]

It is striking that some officials who in 1939 had rejected the idea of an army inspector with significant authority had made an about-face by the end of the war, and the reverse was also true. Prisi, who was strictly against the institution of a peacetime general, reminded Guisan that he had repeatedly spoken out against introducing one when he was a member of the National Defense Committee. Alluding to Chief Instructor Wille, whom many had favored to become the proposed army inspector in 1939, Prisi commented that Colonel-Corps Commander Guisan had agreed with him on that issue when it appeared that "someone else was already dressed in his Sunday best."[22]

Corps Commander Constam believed that a peacetime general was superfluous, writing to Federal Councilor Kobelt, "What the army needs during times of peace is an expert body that is capable of monitoring the preparations for a war, initiating or proposing improvements, and commanding the military. Having a body with the same status as the Head of the Military Department is out of the question. Hence, General Guisan's proposal to establish a post for an army inspector, a.k.a. a peacetime general who is elected by Parliament, is unnecessary."[23]

Younger officers such as Hausamann and Ernst, who before the war had strongly advocated the idea of a peacetime general with extensive authority, changed their minds during the war and just as strongly rejected it afterward. Hausamann wrote to the Head of the Military Department, "Before the war, I fervently supported the idea. After studying events abroad during the war, I have become a staunch opponent. In our small country, a peacetime general can be particularly fateful." He stated that it would not be desirable "for everything to revolve around one person" in the army during times of peace. Progressive ideas, he thought, could only be introduced into the army if it was headed by a democratic body. "If there is a civilian top authority instead of a military one," he said, "everyone who has ideas has direct access to it. You can defend an idea even against the will of the civilian top authority without violating any rule on discipline. . . . An incompetent peacetime general can cause the army to stagnate or even to gradually die. An incompetent top civilian authority cannot do that."[24]

Alfred Ernst, who before the war had even considered launching a petition in favor of setting up the post of peacetime general, made a complete reversal.[25] As late as the fall of 1941, in an extensive report entitled, "Ideas on how to reform the armed forces," addressed to General Guisan, Ernst had argued that a commander-in-chief had to be in charge of the army during times of peace if Switzerland's defense was to be substantially improved.[26] However, in November 1946, he wrote in the *Volk und Armee* newspaper that a body consisting of several members was more suitable than a general to accomplish the tasks of Switzerland's militia army during times of peace. He stated that the National Defense Committee was an absolutely suitable body to oversee the army.[27] Based on his political experience during wartime duty, Ernst rejected any kind of authoritarian leadership, giving preference to a democratic institution that would formulate the army's demands and objectives during times of peace.

General Guisan deeply regretted the abolishment of the idea of an army inspector, and remained convinced that the Federal Council had made a wrong decision. During the hearing on the National Council committee dealing with his report, he once again emphasized the importance of having a peacetime general in office, stating that his proposal was "in accordance" with his report.[28] Several years after his resignation, during his conversations with Gafner, he repeated the idea that the Federal Council should appoint an army inspector as the supreme authority of the armed forces, especially in view of a possible attack by a foreign army. He explained that the decision should be left up to Parliament whether that army inspector should become general at the time the army was mobilized, adding, "If Parliament elects someone else, the army inspector could easily take over the elected officer's former post."[29]

When the Military Organization was amended on December 12, 1947, the National Defense Committee, which had been only an advisory body until then, received additional decision-making power on issues relating to the military. The advocates of a peacetime general viewed that solution as a poor alternative. Gonard considered that the question of the structure of the army command during times of peace was "the only strategic issue that [had] remained as significant as it was at the end of wartime duty."[30]

Some referred to the amended law of 1947, which stipulated that the commander-in-chief in charge of the army during emergency situations would henceforth have a more subordinate role to the Federal Council, as the "Lex Kobelt."[31] There has been no need in years since to test whether that solution has been useful, but four decades after the war new calls were raised for appointing a peacetime general. In an analysis of the leadership structure in the Military Department since 1848, former Chief of the General Staff Hans Senn came to the conclusion that a "supreme body" was an absolute requirement for a modern army command during times of peace, and that this necessity could not be argued away by pointing out the country's democratic traditions.[32] From a strictly technical viewpoint, this solution may appear necessary if the military is supposed to be in a permanent state of readiness. However, the issue of a peacetime general, as put forward by Guisan and others, contrasts with considerations of national policy that continue to carry more weight. As shown by General Guisan's example, electing a commander-in-chief in the event of a war is not only a military but also a highly political issue. If the Swiss Army intends to remain an army of the people based on the militia system, and which is deeply rooted in the nation, it will have to continue to bear the risk of not being commanded by a general during times of peace. One may easily argue that every corps commander, through his job, should acquire a comprehensive knowledge of all aspects of the army so that he would be capable of taking on the supreme command of the entire armed forces at any time.

Misunderstanding with de Lattre de Tassigny

GENERAL GUISAN'S RELATIONS with French General de Lattre de Tassigny took a turn for the worse after the war, as military historian Hans Rudolf Kurz was the first to describe.[1] The two generals disagreed on whether Switzerland's commander-in-chief had promised that his country would take care of a number of French soldiers who had been injured during the war in return for the strategic changes the commander of the French 1st Army had made in consideration of Switzerland's interests during his 1945 campaign along the Swiss border.

On February 2 and 3, 1946, celebrations were held in Colmar and in Guebwiller, France, to commemorate the first anniversary of the liberation of Alsace from German occupation. Guests from Switzerland included representatives of the government of Basel and radio reporters, including Jean R. von Salis, who was well known from his weekly reports and who held an extended private conversation with the French commander in Guebwiller. General de Lattre gave improvised speeches at both events. Much to his audience's surprise, he also spoke of the unusual military arrangements between the French and Swiss armies during the final stage of the campaign against Germany, revealing details that until then had been kept secret.[2]

During his first speech at the mayor's office in Colmar, de Lattre mentioned the visits that Colonel Henry Guisan, the son of Switzerland's commander-in-chief who was acting on his father's orders, had made to his headquarters in early 1945 to ask him to take the Swiss army command's requests into account in his plans of operations. Von Salis summarized de Lattre's statements in an eight-page confidential report that he submitted to General Guisan and Federal Councilor Petitpierre, Switzerland's Foreign Minister. As he wrote about the incident:

> I was stunned when General de Lattre committed an intentional indiscretion, explaining that during the first visit, on behalf of his father, Colonel Guisan had mentioned the government's and the army command's concerns about the 65,000 German troops that were stationed in the Black Forest. They might cross the Swiss border in case the French attack was launched in the north, forcing these units of the German armed forces to head toward the Rhine. So Colonel Guisan had gone to see the commander of the French 1st Army to ask him, on his father's behalf, to prevent the German troops from infringing Swiss territory. General de Lattre continued, "I could not disappoint the Swiss nor General Guisan; I canceled the orders, tore them up, changed my plans, issued new orders, and deployed one and a half divisions south along the Swiss border."[3]

Von Salis reported that Colonel Guisan had gone to see de Lattre once again at his father's behest to ask him to advance as quickly as possible along the Swiss border all the way to Liechtenstein. De Lattre addressed the Swiss who attended the ceremony, stating, "This time you were no longer afraid of the Germans, nor obviously of the Americans, but of someone else whom I prefer not to name. The French Army was happy to be able to do our Swiss friends a favor on these two occasions, and I would not hesitate one moment if I had to do it again."[4] The allusion to "someone else" undoubtedly referred to the Soviets, whose rapid advance had raised concerns among the Swiss army command, prompting it to study precautionary defensive measures.[5]

The following day, on February 3, 1946, before the official reception in Guebwiller, de Lattre approached von Salis, grabbed him by the shoulders, and after some initial small talk began "making very severe reproaches" against Switzerland and General Guisan. He once again mentioned Colonel Guisan's missions and repeated that he had changed his campaign plans twice in favor of Switzerland, stating, "I almost lost a battle because of that. I had to change my plans and detach troops to protect your border. I barely took in Ulm after losing three days. Lives were lost and people were injured just for Switzerland's sake." He added that when he had complied with the Swiss army command's request to occupy Vorarlberg, he did not lose any troops but was not able to conquer Innsbruck during his first assault.

De Lattre told von Salis that because of his repeated willingness to comply with the requests that Colonel Guisan had transmitted, he expected

Switzerland to do France a favor in return. He said that during their meeting at the Swiss border, he had talked to General Guisan about approximately 2,500 soldiers under his command who needed artificial limbs, which France could not afford. He explained to von Salis, "So I told General Guisan that I wanted Switzerland to provide these limbs to our mutilated soldiers free of charge." The disabled soldiers were expected to be admitted to Swiss hospitals to be fitted with the prostheses. De Lattre stated, "General Guisan promised to do that."[6]

De Lattre adamantly complained that Guisan did not keep his promise, saying that apparently nothing had been done at all. He had found out that Switzerland's Foreign Minister Petitpierre was not informed about the matter, commenting, "How is it possible that General Guisan, who had asked me a very great favor on behalf of his government, did not say anything about my request to M. Petitpierre?" He explained that this was not all. He had also found out that French soldiers who were staying in the Swiss resort of Leysin for rest and relaxation were not properly taken care of and were "starving to death" because France could afford to pay only nine francs a day for their accommodation and meals instead of the required twelve francs. He asked von Salis whether Switzerland could not pay the difference so that the French would receive the same meals as the Italians, Greek, and Yugoslavs, who could afford the twelve francs. De Lattre urged the Swiss radio reporter, "Will you please tell General Guisan and M. Petitpierre about this, Mr. von Salis?"[7]

De Lattre assured von Salis that he had intentionally discussed these matters in public the day before in Colmar and would continue to do so until Switzerland kept its promise. He said that his request was "a natural service in return" for what his army had done at General Guisan's request to protect Switzerland. Von Salis wrote that the French general gesticulated furiously while making his statements, which came as a total surprise to him. He had seen Colonel Guisan during a visit to Karlsruhe during the war but had never heard about any promise that the Swiss commander-in-chief had made to de Lattre. He promised the French commander that he would not fail to provide an exact account of what he had been told to General Guisan and the Federal Council. The conversation took place in the presence of Latour, the editor of the *Journal de Genève*, and General Gruss, the French Military Attaché in Bern.

After revealing high emotions in private, de Lattre was considerably more clement during his official speech in Guebwiller. He did not voice the slightest criticism but extolled his friendship with Switzerland and with General Guisan, flattering his Swiss audience by stating, "We will forever remain indebted to Switzerland because of everything that it did for us. Our gratitude has no limits. When you get back home, please tell General Guisan and your government that there is nothing but friendship, brotherhood, and love between France and

Switzerland, between the French Army and the Swiss Army, and between the commander of the French Army and the commander of the Swiss Army!"[8]

De Lattre's contradictory statements reflected the strange atmosphere at that meeting. The praise he expressed appeared to be as exaggerated as the reproaches he had made against Switzerland a short time earlier. Von Salis was not sure how serious de Lattre had been in both instances and whether he had made the accusations only in an effort to speed up the assistance to his mutilated and sick soldiers. He ended the extensive report that he submitted to General Guisan and Federal Councilor Petitpierre by commenting that the French victims of war undoubtedly considered themselves entitled to Switzerland's financial and medical assistance because they were convinced that they had spared Switzerland from making more serious sacrifices.[9]

General Guisan expressed his surprise at de Lattre's statements as transmitted to him by von Salis. He denied that the issue of the disabled soldiers had been raised during the meeting with the French General at the Swiss border. He annotated von Salis' report by stating, "The first time General de Lattre talked to me about it was on Sunday, November 4, [1945] in Montana [Canton Valais]."[10] In his short reply to von Salis, in which a sense of indignation was apparent, Guisan called de Lattre's remarks a linguistic faux pas. He speculated, "I can explain his digression only by his very fervent wish to assist his mutilated soldiers. He has set his heart so fully on that issue that he has made it *his* cause. If I am not mistaken, he does so without his government's knowledge. It seems to me that he let himself be carried away by his talent as a speaker; this has caused some confusion in him."[11]

Guisan also told the French Military Attaché, General Gruss, that de Lattre had expressed his request for assistance for the wounded men for the first time during his visit in November 1945 to Montana. He explained that because he was no longer commander-in-chief, he had invited the French general and Federal Councilor Petitpierre to his home in Pully so that de Lattre could personally make his request to the Swiss Foreign Minister. During that meeting at Verte Rive, Petitpierre was not able to make any commitment, but he promised to do all he could to get Schweizerspende/Don suisse, a humanitarian organization funded by both government and public sources, to take on this task. General Guisan enthusiastically supported that idea.

As Schweizerspende was an independently managed organization, complications arose that delayed assistance to the French war victims. Guisan asked the French Military Attaché to present his apologies to de Lattre for the delay, for which he said he was not liable, adding, "I hope that even after receiving this information he will not withdraw his friendship, which is so valuable to us."[12]

Federal Councilor Petitpierre informed von Salis that he had not been able to make any commitment to the French General, "I did not make the promise that General de Lattre claims I made to him," he said, "nor did General Guisan. I told him that I would try to get Don suisse interested in this idea. I could not do more than that, as Don suisse decides on its own how it uses the funds with which it is entrusted by Parliament and the generous public."[13]

In early 1946, René Payot, the director of the *Journal de Genève,* who had also attended the lunch at Verte Rive with de Lattre and Petitpierre, reminded General Guisan of the conversation with de Lattre about the wounded soldiers, stating, "In that connection, [de Lattre] recalled that at your request he had modified his strategy and renounced marching on Ulm and Munich with his entire forces in order to be able to eliminate the SS divisions that were stationed along our border that could have been tempted to infringe our territory. We all agreed that not only out of sympathy but out of gratitude we had to show some interest in these injured soldiers, who will not be able to be reintegrated into civilian life if they do not receive prostheses."[14] Payot considered that the Federal Council should take care of this matter, "because General de Lattre [had] rendered an immense service to our country that had been officially requested from him." Payot urged the General to use his entire authority in Bern to ensure assistance to the French victims of war without further delay.[15]

To express his regrets about the apparent misunderstanding with General de Lattre and to put matters right again, Guisan invited French Military Attaché Gruss and his wife to Verte Rive for lunch. Following that visit, General Guisan wrote to the attaché, "It was a great pleasure for me to be able to talk to you about the report that Professor von Salis had written at General de Lattre's request and to tell you how much that incident in Guebwiller/Colmar distressed me. It must be the result of a misunderstanding; I would be grateful if you could clear it up during your next visit to Paris." Guisan ended the letter with a postscript in which he stated, "According to the latest information I have received, it is likely that the management of Don suisse will approve the requested credit at its next meeting."[16]

The fact that François Jacques, an emissary from Paris, brought General Guisan a message from de Lattre shows how important the matter was to the French.[17] The visitor, who was invited to Verte Rive on the spur of the moment, undoubtedly received reassuring information, because afterward he wrote to Guisan, "I will personally tell General de Lattre how nice it was of you and your family to receive me."[18]

In the meantime, the issue of the French soldiers who had been disabled during the war had also been discussed between French and Swiss diplomats.

In early March 1946, Switzerland's ambassador to France, Minister Carl Burckhardt, informed Bern that his counselor, Barbey, had been summoned by General de Lattre to discuss the issue of the mutilated soldiers and to receive a message for General Guisan. De Lattre explained to Barbey how Switzerland could assist about 500 to 600 French wounded; he wanted 50 to 60 of them at a time to be admitted to Swiss facilities for three to four months to have them fitted with prostheses. De Lattre opposed the idea of Switzerland providing assistance by sending medical personnel and medical supplies to France. Burckhardt reported, "The General added that if [his] proposal could not be accepted by us, he preferred not to have any gesture, which he said would lose most of its value."[19]

Barbey for his part reported to General Guisan about the same conversation, telling him that he had been called to see de Lattre "to chat." He said that their conversation had been friendly, explaining, "He very much insisted on the fact that his friendship for you had not changed and that if he had to make another gesture toward Switzerland, he would not hesitate to do so. He warmheartedly asked me to personally inform you about that, several times repeating the same statement."[20] Concerning assistance to the disabled persons, Barbey's impression was that Switzerland should show some goodwill immediately or else not do anything at all and admit that it was not able to provide the requested assistance. He concluded, "In summary, it seems to me that the situation has much improved here and will be even better once we have made the gesture which is so important [to de Lattre]."[21]

In the meantime, Schweizerspende/Don suisse had agreed to cover the cost of 500 to 600 prostheses; however, initially no one agreed to cover the cost of the French soldiers' treatment and stay in Switzerland. Following a visit that he made in the company of Burckhardt, Barbey informed General Guisan that de Lattre continued to insist that the disabled persons be allowed to convalesce in Switzerland, adding, "He seems to have made commitments to his seriously injured soldiers last fall."[22]

Federal Councilor Petitpierre wrote to General Guisan that "for political reasons" Switzerland's ambassador was clearly in favor of granting de Lattre's request.[23] He argued that the requested assistance should be urgently provided, not only for humanitarian but for psychological reasons. Von Salis had voiced similar concerns in his report, stating that the people of France might rightly develop a hostile attitude toward Switzerland if the promised assistance to de Lattre's soldiers did not materialize and if the issue was discussed in public.[24]

In April 1946, Barbey told General Guisan that Minister Burckhardt had also discussed the issue of the disabled soldiers with French Foreign Minister Georges Bidault, asking him to "come to an understanding with General de

Lattre."[25] In order not to make the French wait any longer, Barbey suggested inviting at least 50 to 60 amputees to Switzerland for the time being to have them treated. The remaining disabled persons could be treated in France but Switzerland would pay for their prostheses. He argued that this was a partial concession to General de Lattre that would show Switzerland's goodwill. General Guisan transmitted Barbey's proposal to the Federal Council, commenting, "It seems to me that this solution could be accepted by the French government and by General de Lattre."[26]

By that time, details of de Lattre's speech in Colmar had made it into Swiss newspapers. The Basel-based Communist paper *Vorwärts* reported in detail about the French general's statements.[27] It asked whether Guisan's sending his son as a "special envoy" to the French Army's headquarters was compatible with Switzerland's neutrality policy. Other papers in the country took up the news. The Swiss French newspapers and *Die Tat* immediately sided with General Guisan, questioning the accuracy of the *Vorwärts* report.[28] Strikingly, the reactions of the conservative and Social Democratic newspapers, which could not have any political interest in supporting the Communists, were subdued. Hans Seelhofer, the head of the press service at the Military Department, was relieved to note that the matter did not cause a stir in public and was soon forgotten.[29]

During a Federal Council meeting in early May 1946, Petitpierre addressed the differences of opinion with General de Lattre concerning the disabled soldiers. The minutes of the meeting did not include any information on that subject, but Vice Chancellor Oser mentioned the Foreign Minister's statement in his handwritten notes, remarking, "The French General had asked Switzerland to take care of the mutilated soldiers of the 1st Army. We did not accept. Since he was displeased, during a convention [sic] in Colmar, de Lattre de Tassigny expressed his opinion, mentioning that he had taken into account Switzerland's—General Guisan's—requests during his campaign. It seems that the requests in question had been presented by Colonel Guisan."[30] Federal President Kobelt added that de Lattre was said to claim that, through his son who acted as a middleman, General Guisan had "negotiated" with him details of the campaign in Germany in order to defend Switzerland's interests.[31] It is presumed that at the meeting the Federal President, who was also the Head of the Military Department, was given carte blanche to find a solution that was satisfactory to both sides. Hans Rudolf Kurz, who was a member of Kobelt's staff at that time, reports that in the spring of 1946, "after some discussions [the Military Department] concluded the matter in a good way" in cooperation with Schweizerspende and the Red Cross.[32]

Based on a list that the French 1st Army had asked to be compiled, a total of 584 African and French officers, non-commissioned officers, and soldiers needed prostheses. Of these, 294 had lost a lower leg, 245 a leg, 15 both lower legs, 14 both legs, and 16 a lower leg and a leg.[33]

These disabled persons ended up receiving their prostheses, for which Schweizerspende/Don suisse had made 570,000 francs available, followed by a five-week stay in hotels in central Switzerland, for which the Swiss Red Cross had made 600,000 francs available.[34] A first group of 60 mutilated soldiers arrived in Switzerland on August 20, 1946, and was lodged at the Schweizerhof Hotel on the Brünig mountain pass; a second group of 65 disabled persons arrived on August 27, 1946, and was lodged at the Lützelau Hotel in Weggis.[35] Excursions, concerts, games, and other activities were organized for the convalescing patients. On September 21, General Guisan and his wife visited them at both places.

General de Lattre de Tassigny was very pleased about the manner in which the amputees of his army were taken care of. In the summer of 1946, General Guisan was able to inform the Chief Medical Officer of the Swiss Red Cross, Colonel Kistler, that "during his visit a week ago in Geneva, General de Lattre expressed his satisfaction about the fact that this project has been realized."[36]

General de Lattre de Tassigny apparently played two different tunes at the same time, and his behavior leaves an ambiguous impression. His speech in Colmar and his conversation with von Salis were not the only occasions on which he reprimanded General Guisan and expressed his anger at Switzerland. Kurz reports that he also expressed his disappointment at Switzerland's attitude "in a very sharp and bitter manner during several conversations with Switzerland's Military Attaché, Colonel von Muralt. He repeatedly and insistently told him that during the war, at the request of Colonel Guisan, who acted on his father's orders, he had had to make several dramatic decisions on a matter of conscience, changing his plans of operations in southern Germany exclusively in Switzerland's interest, which he said caused considerable drawbacks for him."[37] In his work on Switzerland's neutrality, Edgar Bonjour published the full text of a report that von Muralt had written on that subject.[38]

On another occasion, the French general tried to placate his Swiss counterpart, calling his critical remarks "a whim." After seeing de Lattre in Paris, Barbey was able to report to General Guisan, "During a conversation with General de L[attre], I referred to his speech in Colmar and to the delicate situation in which some of his statements had put you with respect to some political elements. General de L. ended up telling me that his speech in Colmar had been 'a mere whim.' I asked his permission to tell you about that. 'Of course,' he replied, 'I not only give you my permission, I would actually like to ask you to inform General Guisan about this and assure him of my loyal friendship.'"[39]

Guisan was relieved about this information and immediately told the Federal Council about the contents of Barbey's letter, adding that this should put an end to a matter about which too much ink had been wasted.[40]

In 1946, during a visit to the French World War II battlefields, a group of Swiss officers met with de Lattre. One of the participants reported that the French general used the opportunity to make very friendly comments about neutral Switzerland and its commander-in-chief, stating, "General de Lattre made a solemn and very official declaration of friendship for his 'great friend, General Guisan.' In response to our inquiries, General de Lattre also declared that Switzerland had never made any allusion to him about the Soviets. Furthermore, he explained to us that he had made 'a huge blunder' by joking-ly stating in Vorarlberg one day that he had kept the Soviet Army away from the Swiss border."[41]

The misunderstanding between Generals de Lattre and Guisan was closely tied to the different ways in which Colonel Henry Guisan's visits to the head-quarters of the French 1st Army were interpreted.[42] Kurz unambiguously demonstrated that, in this instance, "Switzerland's neutrality policy [did] not remain immaculate,"[43] an opinion with which one has to agree. It is unlikely that Switzerland's commander-in-chief is the only one who should be blamed for the differences of opinion that arose in connection with the care that dis-abled French soldiers were supposed to receive. These differences resulted from the various ways in which the services that de Lattre had rendered Switzerland were weighed. General Guisan undoubtedly told de Lattre that he would exam-ine and forward his request, while the French general, who was understandably impatient, interpreted this assurance as a binding promise. Switzerland, and especially the General, certainly did not lack goodwill, but the assistance was delayed for administrative reasons. Von Salis' report, which caused the Federal Council to become more actively involved in the matter, sped up the process, as de Lattre had hoped. However, the stinginess with which the Swiss initially tried to wiggle their way out of taking on a share of responsibility for taking care of victims of war—from which Switzerland had been spared through a spell of fortune—by haggling and negotiating does not leave the impression of a very accommodating country.

Honors and Postwar Travel

BOTH DURING WARTIME DUTY AND PARTICULARLY after his resignation as commander-in-chief, General Guisan was awarded many personal honors, such as honorary memberships in clubs (especially military associations), honorary citizenships of towns and villages, and honorary doctorates from universities.

The first of a total of seven honorary citizenships was bestowed on Guisan by the village of Mézières in Canton Vaud, where he was born. As early as the year the war broke out, the village council decided to name the commander-in-chief an honorary citizen.[1] On May 3, 1940, a few days before the beginning of Germany's turbulent Western campaign, Guisan and his wife were ceremoniously presented a document granting them honorary citizenship. In the speech he made to thank the village for the honor, he reminisced about his childhood, describing himself in the third person: "The doctor's son, as they used to call him, grew up in Mézières. Perhaps it was in those first years that he spent in the countryside among the villagers that he learned to understand people and above all their characters and ambitions. This understanding formed a solid basis for his career in the military, helping him to make correct assessments and decisions as well as to act as a mediator."[2]

On August 1, 1941, on the occasion of the 650th anniversary of the Swiss Confederation, the General and his wife were awarded an honorary citizenship of Pully, the town where the couple had been living for 35 years at the Verte Rive mansion. The town's executive had proposed to the municipal council "to bestow the honorary citizenship of the town of Pully to: 1. Henri Guisan, General, Commander-in-Chief of the Swiss Army; 2. Marie, the spouse of Henri Guisan, daughter of Christ-Charles Doelker and Marie, maiden name

Fricker."[3] At the public ceremony in Pully, Guisan made "a declaration of his conviction," stating:

> Only a people that is determined to defend itself will be respected. However, to defend itself, a people must be united. I believe in this unity, and I hope, or I should say I am convinced, that we will be able to leave Switzerland to you the way we want it to be, because as soldiers we know what we are preparing for. We know what is expected from us. We know that the sacrifice that everyone is making in our country may save us from having to make a much greater and more serious one. As soldiers we know that our home country's well-being has to take precedence over any personal wishes.[4]

After the end of the war, General Guisan was awarded honorary citizenships to Saignelégier (August 11, 1945), Interlaken (September 29, 1945), Thun (October 10, 1945), Lausanne (December 27, 1945), and the French border town Saint-Gingolph (August 18, 1948).[5] Interlaken, where the bulk of the army staff was stationed until the end of wartime duty, also awarded an honorary citizenship to Chief of the General Staff Huber. The proposal for making the two top commanders honorary citizens of Interlaken had been made by Max Häni, a former member of the Officers' Alliance who later rose to the rank of brigadier. It was "immediately unanimously approved."[6] Several publications mention that Guisan was also an honorary citizen of Avenches and of Canton Bern. However, these assumptions are based on misunderstandings. On May 30, 1946, one year after the end of the war in Europe, General Guisan was bestowed an honorary membership in the Citizens' Rifle Club of Avenches that was founded in 1611, but as the archive clerk of Avenches explained, "There is no mention of his being awarded an honorary citizenship."[7] In the case of Guisan's alleged honorary citizenship of Canton Bern, all the Bernese cantonal parliament did on September 10, 1945, was approve the decisions of the three Bernese municipalities of Saignelégier, Interlaken, and Thun. According to the minutes of the cantonal government meeting, on that occasion Guisan's name was entered in the registry of the citizens of Canton Bern "as a gift." No ceremony was held for that purpose.[8]

Two Swiss universities bestowed honorary doctorates on Guisan. During wartime duty, on August 26, 1944, the 500th anniversary of the Battle of St. Jakob an der Birs, the University of Basel awarded General Guisan an honorary Ph.D. at the request of the Arts Faculty. In a Latin eulogy that was probably written by Edgar Bonjour, the commander-in-chief was praised as the one:

who taught the Swiss the nature of modern warfare with illuminating explanations, made the army fit to go to war by taking into account the hereditary peculiarity of the Swiss, showed wisdom and insight in protecting the country from the current disastrous war that is devastating the world, and has contributed to keeping Switzerland out of harm's way with his unwavering courage and his excellent judgment. Hence, the entire country is obliged to him, and the city of Basel, which is devoted to fostering the works of peace at an outpost of the Swiss territory, owes him special thanks.[9]

In November 1945, the law faculty of the University of Lausanne, where he had studied for several semesters, awarded Guisan an honorary doctorate.[10] In his address, the General admonished the students to carry on the spirit of solidarity among the national community, stating, "You should become standard-bearers of humanity who pursue an ideal, leaders who are able to reconcile progress and traditions in all areas."[11]

A comprehensive overview of the General's personal papers reveals 75 certificates of honorary memberships to clubs and societies and 46 honorary diplomas and certificates of acknowledgment from additional associations and institutions.[12] Swiss and foreign musicians and painters showed their recognition by sending him works. Songs and pieces of music, especially military marches, were composed in his honor or were dedicated to him. Just weeks after the troops had gone on duty, Sergeant Stephan Jäggi, a well-known music director who conducted the band of Regiment 11 from Solothurn, composed the popular "General Guisan March."[13] Austrian composer Major Karl Hammerschmidt dedicated his march "Vivat Helvetia!" to the Swiss General.[14] For his 80th birthday, Guisan received the original score of a musical piece entitled "General Guisan, Military Parade with Drummers and Buglers" from the Frenchman Regis Duplessy.[15] Guisan asked his secretary Konrad Huber to thank the composer for his kindness, annotating Duplessy's letter by stating, "I do not know anything about music!"[16]

Guisan received a large number of portraits of himself and paintings by artists such as Traffelet, Hugentobler, Meylan, Hug, and others, most of which were dedicated to him. When painter Hermann Barrenschen offered him an oil-painted portrait, Guisan returned the favor by sending him a case of wine and a box of Havana cigars.[17]

As early as 1944, the neighborhood association of Pully de Port-Chamblandes suggested that the town authorities name one of the streets of the General's hometown after him.[18] Guisan would have liked to have the main road, "Avenue du 16 mai," renamed.[19] However, the town council did not grant his request; instead, after the war it decided to rename "Boulevard des Chamblandes," the road that went past Verte Rive, as "Avenue du Général Henri Guisan."[20]

Guisan did not particularly like traveling and did not see much of the world until he resigned from his post as commander-in-chief.[21] Before this, the only times he went abroad were for training at the agricultural schools in Lyons, France, and Hohenheim, Germany, and for occasional military missions to neighboring nations. After retiring and completing his report on wartime duty, though, he felt an urge to visit foreign countries, particularly northern Europe and the Mediterranean. The various trips he made as a private citizen from 1947 on included visits to Scandinavia and England.

His first destination was Sweden, where the Royal Academy of Military Science had appointed him a foreign member in early 1946. In view of that appointment, which was a rare honor, Major P. A. Welander, a military attaché and adjutant to Sweden's Crown Prince, contacted Guisan.[22] The Swiss General was only the third foreign national to be admitted to the Royal Academy as an honorary member, after Finnish Marshal Mannerheim (in 1925) and the Finnish artillery specialist Nenonen (in 1936). After receiving the certificate of his honorary membership from the Swedish envoy, Count Westrup, in Lausanne on May 24, 1946, Guisan wrote to the Head of the Academy, "Of course the honor that you have kindly bestowed on me goes to my country, to the Swiss Army, to its soldiers, as well as to my former collaborators. I am even more aware of the importance of your gesture, knowing how rarely it is made to foreign military leaders."[23]

Guisan and his wife left for Stockholm on June 7, 1947. Federal Councilor Enrico Celio, the Transport Minister, offered them return tickets on Swissair.[24] At the General's request, the Department of Foreign Affairs had a large map of Switzerland at a scale of 1:200,000, the size typically used in classrooms, sent to the Swiss Legation in Stockholm for his lecture at the Royal Academy.[25] Guisan wrote to Switzerland's envoy, who had informed him about the dress code, "All right, I will throw my tail coat in the suitcase in addition to my uniform, but I will not bring a tuxedo."[26] On 7 June, Mr. and Mrs. Guisan were received at Bromma Airport near Stockholm by Minister Valloton, who headed the Swiss delegation, and by General Count W.A. Douglas, the Head of the Swedish Army who was at the same time President of the Royal Military Academy. Guisan's escort in Sweden was the Swiss Military Attaché, Captain Arnold Kaech. The Swedish daily *Dagens Nyheter* reported about his arrival:

Saturday, a short 73-year-old man arrived at Bromma from Switzerland, a very young-looking trained farmer, the symbolic figure of Switzerland's liberty, the most popular citizen in his country, the creator of the unassailable fortress, the man who managed to shake up all Swiss men and women to put up resistance during a time of very difficult trials. Some of his fellow citizens were happy to make him the latest descendant in the line of William Tell, and others were not.[27]

On June 9, during a festive meeting, General Guisan was received at the Royal Military Academy. He presented a lecture in German on Switzerland's defenses during the Second World War which lasted 45 minutes and for which he did not use a manuscript. It was received with great applause. During his reply, Count Douglas, the head of the Academy, said that the personality of the Swiss general and his determination to fight to the utmost had "electrified Swedish hearts."[28] As Switzerland's envoy reported to Bern:

> From all sides, not only from the press but from the civilian and military authorities, we keep hearing the most flattering things about General Guisan. He made quite an impression in Sweden, and General Douglas assured me that the conference at the Academy had been one of the best since he had been there. There is no doubt that General Guisan's visit to Sweden was very valuable and useful for our country. Switzerland could not have found a better ambassador.[29]

General Guisan was also received by the elderly King of Sweden, Gustav V, for an audience, about which Valloton reported to the Swiss Foreign Minister: "The visit with the King was indispensable; the Swedish side would not have understood if, as the official guest at the Academy of Military Science, Switzerland's former Generalissimo had not made a short visit to His Majesty. According to Swedish protocol, I accompanied General Guisan and took part in the meeting, which lasted an exceptionally long sixteen minutes."[30]

Valloton wrote to the General upon the latter's return to Switzerland that his visit to Sweden had "literally [left a] dazzling impression" and that everyone "praised our General."[31] Even Sweden's left-wing extremist press made some flattering comments about Switzerland's commander-in-chief. The official publication of the Communist party had written on the occasion of Guisan's 70th birthday that the General was "politically rather conservative, [but] a comparison between him and the commanders-in-chief of certain other small states would definitely turn out in his favor." The paper added, "Guisan never considered becoming an ally of a potential enemy at any border; instead, he prepared himself for fighting at a time when others would have believed that fighting was no use. He knew that by doing so, he expressed the will of an overwhelming majority of the people. Many generals in other threatened countries were far from doing the same. Therefore, all we can do is express our respect for a General like Guisan."[32]

Guisan also made a presentation to the Swiss living in Sweden, this time in French, and had the opportunity to visit Swedish troops. Afterward, he wrote to the President of the Sweden-Switzerland Society, H. Hürlimann, that he had been received and honored in an "extremely friendly" manner by both civilian and military authorities. He said that the Swedes were "exquisitely polite," showing "every possible attentiveness" to him and his wife. He added:

> During my ten-day stay, I was very pleased to see that the efforts and customs of the Swedish people are comparable to ours. They also feel very attached to their country through their determination to remain independent and by keeping up their traditions. After having the great honor of visiting the field army, the air force, and the navy, I am convinced that their military education and training methods correspond to a great extent to ours.[33]

In early October 1947, Guisan traveled to Denmark at the invitation of the Swiss-Danish Society.[34] He gave presentations to the Swiss living in Copenhagen and at the Academy of Military Science and was received by King Frederik II for an audience. During the same year, he and his wife also visited England for the first time. At the West-Hartlpool shipyard near the Scottish border, a new freight ship owned by the Swiss-Atlantique shipping company named "General Guisan" was launched. The General's wife christened it.[35] In the spring of the following year, Guisan went to England again, this time at the invitation of the London group of the New Helvetian Society and nine other Swiss clubs, including the "Brotherhood of Canton Vaud," whose President, A. Renou, put together the program for the visit along with the President of the New Helvetian Society group, H.W. Egli.[36]

During a dinner in Guisan's honor on June 2, 1948, at the Dorchester Hotel in London, the Swiss living in England thanked the commander-in-chief for keeping the spirit of resistance alive on the European continent, just as Britain had remained intransigent after Dunkirk. The President of the Brotherhood addressed the guest of honor, stating, "Dear General, when people back home ask you, 'What did our compatriots in England do during the war?,' simply tell them, 'They humbly did their duty like the entire English people—and they were praying for us!'"[37] During his stay in Britain's capital, General Guisan was also invited to Winston Churchill's apartment.[38]

Later that same year, Guisan went to see Swiss communities in Besançon and Paris. The program for the visit in the French capital from October 28 to November 5, 1948 was organized mainly by the cultural attaché at the Swiss Legation, Bernard Barbey, the former chief of the General's personal staff, and by Military Attaché de Blonay.[39]

During the following years, Mr. and Mrs. Guisan traveled extensively: in 1949 to Italy and Sicily, in 1950 to Egypt, and in 1951 to the Mediterranean coast of France and to the North African states of Tunisia, Algeria, and Morocco. In all these countries, he was given a warm welcome by the Swiss living abroad. He made presentations to them and thanked them for their support and loyalty to their home country during the war.[40] When he traveled to Rome, he also visited the Swiss Guard at the Vatican and was received by Pope Pius XII. His wife (a strict Protestant) was reluctant to accompany him to that audience.[41]

General Guisan was mentioned on several occasions in connection with the governorship of the internationalized city of Trieste that was under United Nations administration after the war, and with the search for a neutral mediator in the conflict in Palestine. After Sweden's Count Bernadotte, the UN mediator in Palestine, had been murdered, the possibility of entrusting the former commander-in-chief of the Swiss Army with that difficult task was discussed in public. In early 1947, Federal Councilor Petitpierre informed the General that he had been mentioned in foreign newspapers, particularly the London-based *Daily Telegraph*, in connection with a possible mission to the Middle East, and that the French ambassador had made a preliminary inquiry into the same matter. However, he said that no official or unofficial request had been made.[42]

Even though in both instances no formal request was issued, Guisan received numerous letters from the population urging him not to accept any mission abroad. Minister Valloton wrote to the General from Stockholm to advise him not to bring "the hornets' nest" of Palestine down about his ears, explaining:

> I was not surprised to read that you are a possible candidate for replacing Count Bernadotte, but I am concerned. You will remember that on an earlier occasion, when your name had already been mentioned in that connection, I allowed myself to express to you my apprehension and my hope that you would decline. I am still of the same opinion, and unfortunately events have proven me right. Therefore I sincerely hope that you will not run away to Palestine! Life is too short, so why shorten it even more. Moreover, Switzerland needs you more than ever.[43]

Guisan replied to a major from Zürich who had written to him to voice similar concerns that he did not need to worry because "accepting this office [was] out of the question" for him.[44]

In the spring of 1948, Lt. Colonel Nakaschidse from Brussels wrote to General Guisan to gain his support for a worldwide humanitarian project. In view of future conflicts, the officer had the idea of setting aside neutral zones where civilians would be protected in order to ease the consequences of a total war. For that purpose, he suggested calling an international conference, similar to the conference that had resulted in the creation of the Red Cross organization. Nakaschidse reminded Guisan of General Dufour's role in the founding of the International Red Cross and asked him to follow in Dufour's footsteps with the new global project. "If I am not mistaken," he wrote, "Switzerland's commander at the time, General Dufour, was the first president of that institution. Perhaps it would be logical from a historic point of view that the current Swiss General take on a similar role."[45] Guisan replied that he was sympathetic to the idea but had to decline the offer, stating, "I do not feel capable, nor would I have the time that is required to accomplish that task. Even though I am retired and am 74 years old, I still have a lot of work to do and could not accept any new activity."[46]

Like General Dufour, who served two terms on the National Council after commanding the armed forces in the Civil War, and was elected to the Council of States at the age of 76,[47] after his resignation General Guisan had the opportunity to become a member of Parliament. Hermann Böschenstein states that Guisan would undoubtedly have been elected with a "brilliant" result if he had decided to run for National Councilor. Several political parties, even outside Vaud, would have been happy to make him one of their candidates.[48] Guisan, a conservative Protestant, however, had always been critical of the state being governed by parties and he had no desire to run for public office. He continued serving the state loyally but wanted to stay away from party politics, even more so after resigning as commander-in-chief.

Guisan's Retirement Years

AFTER SUBMITTING HIS REPORT ON WARTIME DUTY, the General asked the Federal Council to allow him to retire, either at the end of 1946 or after Parliament approved the report. Considering his numerous continuing obligations, that he said required extensive correspondence, he requested to have his office available to him until his retirement.[1]

It was not until six weeks later that the General received the Federal Council's reply. The government told him that because his report was completed, it did not see why he had to remain on duty; however, it was willing to establish December 31, 1946, as the date of his retirement, explaining, "The Federal Council would like to be as generous as possible toward the one who distinguished himself exercising the supreme command of the army during these difficult years, disregarding the considerations that speak in favor of an earlier retirement date."[2] Moreover, Guisan was informed that he would receive an annual 16,800 francs in pension payments, which was 60 percent of his last annual salary of 30,000 francs, plus a cost of living adjustment. At a meeting of the National Council committee dealing with the General's report, Federal Councilor Kobelt explained that the government did not want to be stingy and therefore "largely complied with the General's requests."[3]

Guisan's income and assets did not seem to make for a luxurious life, but for that time he could be considered to belong to the upper middle class. According to his personal bookkeeping records, in 1941 he had assets of 125,000 francs, at the end of the war 142,000 francs, and in 1955, when he was 81 years old, 160,000 francs.[4]

To keep down his mailing expenses, Guisan asked to be allowed to continue sending his mail post-free as if he were still serving in the army; however, the management of the Swiss Postal Service did not grant his request. On the other hand, he was offered a train pass that allowed him to travel free of charge anywhere on the network of the Swiss Federal Railways until the end of his life.[5] Other fringe benefits that the Federal Council granted him "until further notice" at his request included compensation for a stable lad and the maintenance costs for a riding horse.[6] In addition, he received a daily allowance of 300 francs whenever he represented the army at official events at the government's request.[7]

After his resignation, General Guisan maintained an active lifestyle and had numerous obligations. Even if he did not adopt another career for himself, he did not simply sit back contentedly at his mansion on Lake Geneva. In addition to giving presentations and representing the army at a wide range of events, which required some traveling, he continued dealing with military issues, fostered his many friendships, and spent more time with his family than he was able to do while serving in the military. The General remained in contact by mail with many former soldiers and their families. He received hundreds of letters of admiration and just as many letters from people who asked the former commander-in-chief for advice and assistance. He didn't hesitate to respond to all these letters in a conscientious and understanding manner, a task that was accomplished most of the time by his devoted staff members Mario Marguth and Konrad Huber. Furthermore, Guisan frequently lent an ear to imprisoned soldiers who had committed an offense during wartime duty and who asked him to support their request for pardon even though he was no longer in charge of the armed forces.[8] He annotated one of the many letters asking him for a recommendation and for assistance by stating, "This is one of many letters of good people who think that the General is Almighty God."[9]

A number of foreign commanders and statesmen received a gift copy of General Guisan's postwar report carrying a personal dedication. They included French generals Georges, Gamelin, Béthouard, de Lattre, and Juin, with all of whom Guisan was a friend or acquaintance, as well as de Gaulle, Mannerheim, and Churchill.[10] Most of them wrote a few kind words to thank him for the gift, and a few sent him their memoirs or the published account of their own military career in return. Upon reading Guisan's report, de Lattre noticed one common element in their military thinking: "[Guisan's] ideas about training matters, especially for the infantry."[11] Later de Lattre sent Guisan the history of the "Shock Battalion" of the French 1st Army, writing in the accompanying letter, "I think you will enjoy reading about the heroism of these young men. They had the same enthusiasm, fervor, and patriotism as the young men that I admired recently in Switzerland. Thank God yours did not have to pass the ultimate test of their worthiness, but I am more convinced than ever before that they would have done so magnificently if they had needed to."[12]

In the late summer of 1946, when Winston Churchill was vacationing in Bursinel near Rolle to paint, General Guisan, who was born the same year as the British Prime Minister, invited him to Verte Rive for lunch. In his letter thanking Guisan, Churchill called him "a great friend of world freedom."[13] The General for his part characterized the British statesman as an "incredibly fascinating person, a dynamic, communicative, convincing, striking, charming, and warm personality."[14] However, it appears that the host was somewhat disappointed that Churchill signed the volume of his memoirs that he offered him on that occasion without writing anything else.[15]

Unlike Corps Commander Ulrich Wille, who was said to have described the British Prime Minister as "a Don Quixote who [was] an adventurer during his entire life,"[16] Guisan had recognized at an early stage Churchill's importance and how his uncompromising attitude toward Germany was very inspiring for Switzerland. After the war, it became known that in December 1944, in view of upcoming negotiations with Stalin, Churchill had instructed his Foreign Minister Eden:

> Of all neutral states, Switzerland has the greatest claim to distinction. It is the only international factor that ties us with the horribly war-torn nations. What does it matter whether it has been able to grant us the trade privileges we desire, or whether it has granted too many to the Germans in an effort to stay alive? It has been a democratic state standing up for freedom among its mountains, and in thought, in spite of ethnicity, largely with us on matters of principle. I was surprised that U.J. [Uncle Joe, nickname for Stalin] was furious about Switzerland, but no matter how much I respect this great, good man, his attitude did not influence me in the least. He called the Swiss 'pigs,' and when he uses such words, he means them. It is my conviction that we must stand by Switzerland and explain to U.J. why we do so. The timing for delivering such a message has to be good.[17]

Finland's Marshal Mannerheim, who arrived in Switzerland in 1947 after resigning as state president, was received on several occasions at Verte Rive. General Guisan wrote about these visits, "I invited him twice or three times a year to my home, where he talked to me about his life in the military and about Finland."[18] Mannerheim had visited Switzerland as early as 1943. With the Federal Council's approval, he had entered the country using a false name and spent three weeks in Lugano to rest and relax. At that time, Guisan would have liked to have met with Finland's commander-in-chief, but the Federal Council denied his request for neutrality reasons.[19] Colonel Franz Nager, who had been detailed to the front in Karelia during the Finnish-Russian "Winter War," and who knew Finland's commander-in-chief in person, was not allowed to visit Mannerheim either.[20]

Guisan showed a theoretical interest in the discussion about army reforms that began after the war; however, as he told Gafner, "I did not want to interfere in matters that fell under the responsibility of those who are now at the helm."[21] Hence, he did not become involved in the dispute about the army's concept that had broken out between different groups of officers and which lasted until the mid-1960s.[22] It is striking that during those arguments, one group was led by former members of the Officers' Alliance, who had risen by then from the rank of captain to colonel. Ernst explains that this group was so coherent "because in addition to opposing the other group for objective reasons, comradeship and personal feelings of sympathy and antipathy came into play."[23]

In the spring of 1948, the former commander-in-chief complained to the Military Department that he had "never been informed" about planned measures for the future structure of the national defense, nor about the instructions for reorganizing the army and its combat strategies, even though he was interested in "being officially kept up to date about these issues."[24] Guisan may also have begun to feel concerned because instructors who had been close to Wille and Däniker were about to rise to the top ranks in the army.[25]

After the war, the army's activities were kept to a minimum for some time. In 1946, no refresher courses were held, and in 1947 they were shortened to two weeks. Nevertheless, unlike after 1918, majorities of the population and of Parliament were convinced that a powerful army was needed and that the national defense had to be further strengthened. Hofer considers that this favorable atmosphere for the army was not only due to the fact that tensions continued to exist during the Cold War, but also may be attributed indirectly to the former commander-in-chief's undiminished popularity.[26] Unlike his two predecessors, Generals Herzog and Wille, Guisan was almost totally spared from being subject to overt hostilities. Whenever he made a public appearance, young and old crowded around him, showing their enthusiasm and cheering him on. Mothers held their little children up as if they wanted him to bless them, and some people tried not only to shake his hand but also to kiss it in devotion. The Swiss identified him as a public figure who embodied the idea of a perfect union between the people and the army and as the person who had saved the country from the war. It is hardly an exaggeration to state that men and women revered him and paid tribute to him in a way that was atypical of Switzerland and that came close to the "cult of leadership" that was practiced in some foreign countries.

The veneration that Guisan enjoyed among the general public contrasted sharply with the reserve with which he was treated by political authorities. Hans Rudolf Kurz described an incident that may be considered typical of their attitude. On the day the army was honored at the 1954 Federal Shooting Contest in Lausanne, the guests of honor were invited to a banquet. The Federal Councilors, top-ranking army officers, and the members of the government of Vaud had already been sitting at the table for a while; the only one still missing was the General. Federal Councilor Kobelt remarked to Colonel Kurz, who sat next to him, "You will see, Guisan will be late so that everyone sees him and applauds only him." That was exactly what happened. The public gave the General a standing ovation to welcome him, whereas the other notables remained seated. During the meal, the atmosphere was frosty, and Federal Councilor Kobelt did not say a single word to the General.[27] It is impossible to miss the fact that Guisan enjoyed appearing in public. Corps Commander Züblin commented in a letter to a former comrade-in-arms, "The General always wanted to be a star, and so did Gonard."[28]

During the first years after the war, Switzerland's defense budget was relatively modest. An expert report written in view of the Confederation's 1948 mid-range financial planning recommended limiting the annual defense budget to 300 million francs because "more [was] not bearable for a small state."[29] Influenced by the Communist coup in Czechoslovakia, the continuing crisis surrounding Berlin, and particularly the outbreak of the Korean War in 1950, however, spending for defense was gradually increased by considerable amounts. General Guisan strongly welcomed this development. The armament program that Parliament approved on April 12, 1951 provided for an annual defense budget of 470 million francs, plus a special credit of 1.5 billion francs spread over five years.[30] These sums made it possible to modernize the army's weaponry and equipment based on the experience from wartime duty. The new equipment included aircraft and tanks, providing the army with new options in terms of mobile warfare.[31] This armament program was in line with the suggestions that the commander-in-chief and the chief of the general staff had made in their reports on wartime duty.

As part of the modernization program, the army did away with the cavalry, Guisan's efforts to prevent that measure from being carried out coming to no avail. Chief of the General Staff Huber, on the other hand, favored it. That difference of opinion had become apparent as early as wartime duty, when the usefulness of the cavalry was questioned among the army command. Divisional Commander Jordi, the Chief Instructor of the light troops, who was in charge of the cavalry, considered that this branch should be reduced in favor of motorized and mechanized troops. However, the General did not like the idea. At a meeting with the corps commanders during the war, he criticized Jordi, stating, "His aversion to the cavalry is dangerous." The chief of the general staff backed Jordi, explaining, "His attitude toward the cavalry is based on his opinion that this branch is outdated. We agree with that opinion. The role of the Cossacks is irrelevant in this respect. From a military point of view and in our specific case, the cavalry is no longer useful."[32] Guisan backed his own opinion with an argument that de Lattre de Tassigny had advanced in 1944 in a conversation with René Payot. The commander of the French 1st Army had asked Payot to tell Switzerland's commander-in-chief, "Please allow me to give you some good advice: do not entirely sacrifice your cavalry in favor of motorized troops. My horses and mules were of invaluable service to me in the Vosges Mountains."[33]

In the interest of boosting the army's power, reducing and then doing away with the formerly proud branch of the dragoons became indispensable. Guisan, who liked horses and whose report advocated maintaining the cavalry "for economic and social reasons," had difficulty accepting that fact.[34] At a meeting of the National Defense Committee in the spring of 1946, Chief Instructor H. Frick mentioned that at a recent convention for cavalrymen in Frauenfeld, the General had become "abusive toward the Chief Instructor of the light troops" and urged the participants "to fight for keeping their branch alive."[35] Federal Councilor Kobelt recommended to his fellow NDC members not to be deterred by this attitude, stating, "The National Defense Committee is not bound to heed the General's statements." A few months later, Corps Commander Constam told Kobelt, "I agree with the chief of the general staff regarding the reduction of the cavalry. One squadron of this picturesque branch per army unit is the maximum needed."[36]

Major Hans Hausamann also opposed doing away with the cavalry. In the daily St. Gallen *Tagblatt*, he wrote an essay on "The Military Situation and Our National Defense," in which he advocated maintaining the mounted branch. Guisan congratulated him on that article and told him that he completely agreed with his slogan, "Buy tanks but don't get rid of the cavalry."[37] When the cavalry was completely eliminated in 1972, the farming and horse-riding communities were shocked. Many dragoons and other Swiss from rural areas, including Vaud, never entirely got over that shock.[38]

Guisan was most particularly honored in private on his birthdays. On the occasion of his 70th birthday, during wartime duty, he was literally flooded with gifts, flowers, letters, and telegrams at his command post in Jegenstorf. Barbey noted, "The rooms on the first floor look like the backstage on the evening of a great premiere."[39] The public had received some discreet information about the upcoming event. The Press and Radio section had sent a press release to the newspapers ahead of time, stating, "General Guisan, who will celebrate his 70th birthday on October 21, would like to spend that day with his close family. He has expressed the desire for the press and the radio to keep their acknowledgments very simple if they plan to publish any. In addition, he is kindly asking the editorial boards and the radio studios that intend to commemorate the day not to do so before October 20."[40] The municipality of Lausanne sent the General 70 bottles of wine. A watchmaker where Adjutant Sandoz' wife held a leading position offered him a blank check for an amount up to 5,000 francs.[41] On October 19, the Federal government received Guisan for a festive meal at the von-Wattenwyl mansion; moreover, on the actual birthday, Federal Councilor Kobelt visited the General at Verte Rive in the company of his wife and daughter. Guisan expressed his sincere thanks for this gesture in writing.[42]

For the General's 80th birthday on October 21, 1954, the government of Vaud organized an official event. Federal President Rubattel expressed the Federal government's congratulations, and a bust of Guisan was dedicated at the Palais des Rumines. Following a military ceremony at the Place de la Riponne, the guests marched in a parade through the decorated city to the cathedral, where a public service was held.[43] The speakers at the banquet at Montbenon Casino included former Federal Councilor Minger, who expressed his gratitude for his friendship with Guisan. The former Head of the Military Department once again praised the smooth cooperation he had enjoyed with the commander-in-chief during the first year of the war, stating, "We did not need any regulations to work together; our mutual trust was the basis for our cooperation to develop very harmoniously. We got along so well that there was no room for differences of opinion to arise."[44]

Minger and Guisan remained friends beyond wartime duty. The year before his death, Minger sent the General a postcard from Vulpera, where he was on vacation, on which he wrote in verse:

Mein lieber General	My dear General
Das Alter hat auch seine Reize	Old age also has some attractions
Nicht die gleichen wie die Jugend	Not the same ones as when you are young
Man ruht sich aus in einer Beize	You get to relax in a pub
Macht aus dem 'Säuffeln' eine Tugend.	Having a drink or two becomes virtue.[45]

When his friend Minger died in 1955, the General spoke at the funeral in Schüpfen and on the radio, once again emphasizing how valuable their trusting cooperation had been for the country's security. He explained: "The National Defense Committee worked with him hand in hand, and we were amazed how well he understood the needs of the top command and of the army as a whole. His common sense manifested itself in all his decisions." Guisan added that after fulfilling his duty to the state, Minger, "a new Cincinnatus," went back to being a farmer.[46]

Guisan staunchly supported Switzerland's social security program, which was introduced in 1947. In addition, he was a member of the action committee chaired by Professor Carl Burckhardt that was fighting hard to obtain equal political rights for women.[47] The year before he died, he signed an appeal in favor of women's right to vote that was published during the campaign ahead of the plebiscite on that issue. The appeal stated:

> It is established that women render invaluable services to the community these days on the social and economic level. Moreover, one should not forget the extraordinary efforts that Swiss women made during the time the army was mobilized between 1939 and 1945, replacing their serving father, husband, and sons in the hinterland. . . . Don't they already play a significant role as citizens today in the family, educating their children, or on the job? So why should they continue to be denied the right to vote on federal issues? It would only be fair to make a step forward in that direction, and it would be extremely beneficial for the well-being of the community.[48]

Guisan did not live to see women's right to vote become a reality; on February 1, 1959, voters and a majority of the cantons clearly rejected the proposal.[49]

In the latter part of his life, Henri Guisan became a supporter of the "moral armament" that was advocated by the Oxford Movement, which had its headquarters in Caux above Montreux. He was in contact with its founder, Frank Buchmann, and wrote the preface to one of its brochures, "Ideology and Coexistence," which claimed that the policy of coexistence was a step toward the Third World War. In his preface, Guisan wrote, among other things, "Those who try to prevent our country from using the defensive weapons of the nuclear era, using religion or some higher ideals as a pretext, are playing the game of Communism."[50]

As he advanced in years, Guisan resigned from honorary positions, some of which he had held for a long time. He had stepped down from the International Olympic Committee (IOC) even before the beginning of the war. After the war he was asked to join the IOC again but declined, saying, "I stand by my principle that a management must regularly be replaced by younger members. One must not stay in a post forever—neither in the army nor on the International Olympic Committee."[51] In 1956, he resigned as chairman of the endowment council of the charity organization Schweizerspende, and in 1954, he resigned from the management council of the Swiss Red Cross, of which he had been a member since 1935.[52] When he was 78, he said that he intended to withdraw from public life and stop making presentations when he reached the age of 80.[53] However, he remained a member of the International Committee of the Red Cross in Geneva and President of the "General Guisan Foundation," which he had founded, until the time of his death. The Foundation was a postwar continuation of an assistance fund that the General had accumulated with contributions he received from private sources during wartime duty to provide immediate assistance to needy soldiers or their families in emergency situations.[54] Beginning in 1952, the General Guisan Foundation covered the educational expenses for children whose fathers had suffered an accident in the military. On average, it spent 100,000 francs annually for that purpose.[55]

During his retirement years, the General did not take note of the latest historical research providing new insight into the extent of the threat faced by Switzerland during World War II. For example, he remained convinced until his death that in 1940 a "Helvetia Army" and in 1943 a "Matterhorn Army" had been ready in the Black Forest to march into Switzerland.[56]

Most of the approximately 1,200 books that Guisan had at his home were bound in leather or linen, written in French, and concerned Swiss or European history or military subjects up to World War II. Twenty works dealt with Swiss serving in foreign armies, 64 with Napoleon's wars, six with the Civil War in Switzerland, 202 with the First World War, and 126 with the Second World War. He did not have Clausewitz' famous work "On War" but did have a biography of the Prussian General by Hubert Camus. The collected works of General Wille, edited by Edgar Schumacher, were also part of his personal library. Strikingly, he did not have any of the works of Eugen Bircher, the military historian, medical doctor, and divisional commander from the canton of Aargau. Guisan's collection included several works on the Battle of the Marne but not Bircher's publication.[57] He had very few literary books, which he probably received as gifts from the authors. He did not have much access to the arts, be it the theatre, music, or painting.[58] Major Sandoz, his adjutant, told this author that during wartime duty, the General regularly read the Bible and in the evening occasionally also a detective story.[59]

On October 29, 1957, Mr. and Mrs. Guisan celebrated their 60th wedding anniversary. Federal President Streuli congratulated them in a letter on behalf of the Federal government, and the cantonal government of Vaud did so as well on behalf of the people of Vaud.[60]

In the late summer of 1957, when the press reported that the General's favorite horse, Nobs, had to be killed following a heart attack at the age of 32,[61]

Guisan received dozens of letters of condolences and gifts from all over Switzerland. He had purchased the stallion, which he enjoyed riding during inspections and parades during wartime duty, in 1936 for 2,200 francs.[62] Barbey wrote from Paris that Nobs visibly enjoyed being ridden by the General and perfectly matched the personality of its master in every respect.[63] The exaggerated way in which not only officers but also men, women, and children whom he did not know expressed their condolences to him in writing took on Byzantine proportions, going beyond what is common in a democratic state. One admirer comforted the General with three verses of poetry entitled "I lost my horse."[64] When Monsignor Barras, the Catholic priest at Saint-Redempteur Church, went to see the stable during a visit at Verte Rive, he blessed Guisan's latest horse, Kursus, and the two white rabbits. His son recounted, "Mrs. Guisan was so touched by that gesture that afterward she insisted on seeing exclusively him; she preferred him even over the parish pastor!"[65] General Guisan continued to be fond of horses; an affection he said went back to his childhood, even after on his doctor's advice he stopped riding. He kept Kursus, one of the best dressage horses in Switzerland, which he had purchased after Nobs' death. In its old age, it marched in the General's funeral procession.[66]

The elderly General savored his memories and visibly enjoyed the affection and reverence shown to him by the entire country. One visitor remarked, "He did not in the least hide a certain vanity."[67] Chapuisat states that Guisan liked to please others but did not court anyone's favor. He apparently enjoyed the respect that he received, and that boosted his glamorous image because he considered it a recognition of his key position as commander-in-chief.[68] He was able to stand upright until his death. On the occasion of his 85th birthday in the fall of 1959, the former members of the General's personal staff organized a commemorative event at Jegenstorf Castle, in the same rooms where the commander-in-chief's command post had been located. This was the last time Guisan met with his former staff members.

During the night of April 7–8, 1960, after a short illness, General Guisan died at Verte Rive at the age of 85. When the news of his death was announced on the radio and in the press on April 8, the entire nation once again showed a spirit of solidarity, as it had during the war, mourning the General who had already been transformed into a legend. Böschenstein comments that the whole country in mourning "was something that was common for countries with a monarchist tradition but that probably happened for the first time in the history of the Swiss Federal State."[69] Here and there some people were astonished at someone being revered to such an extent as a hero in Switzerland. On the Swiss national radio, Karl Schmid, a professor of literature at the Federal Technical Institute in Zürich, acknowledged the commander-in-chief's significance on the national political level.[70] Across all party lines, the countless obit-uaries in the country's newspapers pointed out the immortal merits of the deceased General, "differing hardly at all" in their veneration for him.[71] In a let-ter to a friend, the editor Theodor Gut from Stäfa expressed what was felt by those who had been on duty during the war. He stated, "It has been a long time since I was shaken as much as by the General's death. Anyone who was as young as I was during the war is able to recognize only today what a great man he was, and hence also what a great loss this is."[72]

April 12, 1960, the day the funeral of General Guisan was held, was declared a national day of mourning. At 1:30 p.m., all churches in the country rang their bells to urge the Swiss to recall the hardships of the time of war and to remember the deceased General with respect and gratitude. At the same hour, the funeral procession began marching from Verte Rive to the Cathedral in Lausanne. The Federal Council had asked the commander of the 1st Army Corps, Samuel Gonard, to organize the funeral.[73] Gonard turned it into an impressive military show. Similar to the 1945 salute to the flag in Bern, the bearers of the army's more than 400 flags and a guard of honor the size of a combined regiment were called to Lausanne. The seven members of the National Defense Committee who were in the military—six corps command-ers and one divisional commander—marched next to the coffin, which rested on a gun-carriage pulled by six horses. They were followed by the General's last horse, which was saddled. The General's immediate family was followed by the incumbent and former Federal Councilors, the commanders of the army units, delegations of the two chambers of Parliament and of all cantonal governments, as well as by foreign diplomats and military attachés. The *Neue Zürcher Zeitung* reported that more than 3,000 persons attended the funeral "in an official or private function, representing the entire population."[74] Tens of thousands of people crowded the streets along which the funeral procession marched. When the procession entered the gothic cathedral, 24 Venom fighter aircraft flew over the huge crowd in two groups.

At the ceremony in the cathedral, Chaplain Edouard Mauris and Theology Professor Edmond Grin comforted the mourners, and in his funeral oration, Federal President Max Petitpierre acknowledged the unforgettable contribution made by the commander-in-chief to the country's well-being during a time of great difficulties. After the church ceremony, family members, as well as dele-gations of the army and the political authorities, went to the cemetery in Pully, where the burial was held. The flags of the battalions from Canton Vaud were lowered, and the troops made a last salute, firing three salvos. General Guisan's last resting place lies in the same cemetery where poet Charles Ferdinand Ramuz is buried beneath a simple wooden cross.

Posthumous Reputation

THE POPULATION OF A REPUBLICAN STATE does not generally display much gratitude toward its military commanders. It is said that they are indispensable when danger looms, but as soon as the threat is over hardly anyone takes note of them. If this is truly a rule, General Guisan was an exception. The high public esteem that the commander-in-chief gained during World War II, and which only increased during his retirement, definitely outlived him. The people who lived in and served Switzerland during wartime, with whom the General had made some sort of tacit oath of loyalty, remained emotionally tied to him, showing gratitude for the steadfastness he had demonstrated during the war.

After Guisan's death, during the session of June 1960, the Speaker of the National Council, Gaston Clottu, gave a speech in Parliament to commemorate the General's achievements. He praised him, stating, "Henri Guisan was not only a great soldier but a great citizen. Switzerland's authorities and population will never be able to thank General Guisan enough for what he did. For both the soldiers and the civilian population, the General became a major symbol of our determination to defend the country's independence and of the spiritual values that we share."[1] The members of Parliament rose to show their respect for the deceased General. Several cantonal parliaments held similar commemorative events.

On the first anniversary of the General's death, on April 7, 1961, his widow received letters from the Federal Council and the government of Vaud that recalled her husband's merits. The Federal Government's letter, signed by Federal President Wahlen, stated:

Many people in the entire country will once again silently pay tribute to the great citizen whom Parliament entrusted with the command of the army in August 1939 and who was able, during a time of danger, to earn the trust that had been placed in him by deeply influencing not only the soldiers that he commanded but also the population as a whole. I would also like to pay homage once again to his longtime faithful companion and express my sincere sympathy on this memorial day.[2]

Squares, streets, and promenades were named after Guisan in numerous towns and cities, both before and after his death.[3] In the spring of 1967, seven years after the General's death, a life-size monument representing Guisan on horseback was dedicated on the shore of Lake Geneva in Lausanne-Ouchy. The sculpture by Otto Charles Bänninger shows the commander-in-chief in a stylized uniform, unpretentiously sitting on the horse without holding any reins. In several other villages and towns, such as Chesalles-sur-Oron, Mézières, Avenches, and Interlaken, commemorative plaques recall General Guisan's achievements. Moreover, in May 1946, at the Cranz Villa in Interlaken, where the General's command post had been located between 1941 and 1944 and which now hosts the local administration, the meeting room was turned into a small museum containing paintings, arms, and a bust of Guisan.[4] Several hotels and restaurants in the country named rooms after Guisan. Museums in Avenches and at the castle of Morges have a few objects on exhibition that belonged to him.

There is no doubt that General Guisan was a father figure who symbolized an entire era. He appeared to embody the unity between the army and the people at a time when Switzerland was fortunate to be spared being drawn into the war. He reflected the circumstances and the atmosphere of a crucial time in history as well as a number of the country's traditional cultural aspects. Many Swiss not only glorified him but idolized and elevated him after his death. The common need for a heroic figure may have favored Guisan's being extolled as a perfect *dux helvetiorum.* In the spring of 1985, when some critical voices were raised in the media in connection with the 40th anniversary of the end of the war in Europe and the 25th anniversary of the General's death, emotions ran unusually high among the public.

In view of the extent to which the General was revered, it was inevitable that he was somewhat mythologized. A few of the achievements with which he is credited today were invented and thence carefully kept alive. Similarly, he is said to have had some peculiarities that were purely fictitious. One biographer stated about one of Guisan's alleged habits: "On Wednesdays he fasts, drinking only some lukewarm water. Nothing will make him give up that routine."[5] Members of his personal staff assured this author that this claim belonged in the realm of fantasy, as did some others.[6]

General Guisan not only became a national symbol; some actually raised him to the level of a cult figure. Intarsia, ashtrays, mugs, scarves, and other items carrying his portrait and sold at souvenir shops are an expression of his being venerated as a hero. This commercial exploitation often goes beyond what is considered good taste. In 1986, advertisements were run in which a couple of painted lead soldiers representing General Guisan on foot and on horseback were offered for sale at 245 francs; however, the press reported that the figurines did not sell very well.[7]

In 1971, Guisan's heirs sold the Verte Rive estate on Lake Geneva to the Swiss Confederation at a preferential price of four million francs. Private realtors would have offered considerably more for the house.[8] The Confederation promised not to change the building and to leave the living rooms, reception rooms, and the General's office as they were. In 1974, in agreement with the rest of the family, the General's son, who had the right to live there until his death, offered the General's personal memorabilia, office furniture, library, and gifts of honor to the Confederation.[9] In the meantime, Verte Rive has been turned into a museum, and an adjacent building became the home of the "General Guisan Research Pavilion," which was founded in 1975.[10]

In spite of the high reputation that General Guisan enjoys as a historic figure in Switzerland, younger generations do not know him very well. In a poll among recruits in western Switzerland in 1972, nine out of 324 young men, or 2.7 percent, claimed that they had never heard the name Guisan. On the other hand, one in five recruits had read a book on him.[11] Most of the young soldiers polled had a positive image of the General. However, the opinions ranged from one extreme to another, as he was described as a demagogue by some and as Switzerland's Julius Caesar by others. A draftsman called him a "con," whereas a drugstore employee termed him a "real man."[12]

Ives Delay exaggerated when he stated that General Guisan not only had an impact in Switzerland, but through his briefing at the Rütli in 1940 also became "one of the leading living symbols of freedom" in European history.[13] Churchill, Eisenhower, and de Gaulle did not mention Switzerland's commander-in-chief in their memoirs. He is not mentioned in Hitler's conversations nor in Ciano's diaries.[14] The average European did not know about General Guisan, either during the war or afterward, and that is unlikely to change in the future. The fact that Guisan's role is not well known abroad is also exemplified by a recent German research publication in which he is identified as "Chief of Switzerland's General Staff."[15] Even French General Koenig, who had been received by Guisan in Laufenburg after the war, addressed his thank-you letter to "General Guisan, Chief of the General Staff of the Swiss Army."[16]

In 1986, Myriam Decoppet-Guisan, the General's daughter, modestly concluded that her father had served as a figurehead during the war. She said that she did not dare to predict, and that it remained to be seen, what would remain of that image.[17] Past experience has shown that not only historic events but also historic personalities are subject to new interpretations with the passage of time. Contemporaries and subsequent generations often make different assessments of a major figure's achievements. In Henri Guisan's case, however, the assessment has remained quite the same. His historic significance for Switzerland has not been contested in the last few decades.

Afterword

IT IS NOT EASY TO REDUCE THE MULTI-LAYERED FACTS that are presented in this study to one common denominator. When analyzing the career and assessing the significance of the Commander-in-Chief of Switzerland's Armed Forces during World War II on a military and political level, one is presented with a unique personality who had strengths and weaknesses but whose record was exceptionally positive. Both the character and the achievements of Henri Guisan were far more complex than his legend describes.

General Guisan's main contribution consisted of successfully strengthening the discipline and the willingness of the troops to make sacrifices, and of creating close ties between the people and the army during the grueling years of wartime duty, thereby ensuring that the country remained determined to defend itself. It is hardly an exaggeration to say that between 1939 and 1945 the nation achieved a synthesis. The integrating force that the General embodied made Switzerland experience its strength as a nation at a time when it was under the impression that its existence was threatened; hence, the Swiss "Confederation" practically renewed its unity.

The commander-in-chief did not limit himself to commanding the army. During the summer of 1940—especially after his briefing at the Rütli, which had a decisive psychological effect—he increasingly turned into the *pater patriae*, the key public figure who largely, albeit indirectly, guided the country's political leadership. He was respected, and it would probably have been unthinkable to make any major decision in the country without being able to assume that he approved of it. As commander-in-chief, Guisan for his part did not fail to act as a stabilizing influence on the political level measures pertaining to the national defense that had the most far-reaching consequences.

He did not let subversive elements that tried to gain recognition for themselves disintegrate the nation, but successfully thwarted their efforts by giving optimistic speeches and issuing positive orders of the day that were addressed not only to the army but to the entire population. Moreover, he created the "Army and Home" organization as a specific tool to help him win over public opinion. He was able to act as a mediator through his legendary sociability, which allowed him to easily build up friendly relations with all layers of the population across all professional fields. The trusting relationship that Guisan had with the farming community, and was able to develop with the Social Democratic workers and their leaders in the course of wartime duty, was a major factor in creating a consensus in the country and strengthening the domestic front. The General's success was based less on extraordinary military capabilities than on his personal qualities.

Unlike the officers surrounding Wille and Däniker, Guisan realized that Switzerland was not only threatened by military powers but risked losing its spiritual and intellectual integrity because the totalitarianism that the Third Reich represented was a fatal danger for Switzerland's concept of freedom and democracy, and consequently for the state as a whole. It is largely due to the General's attitude that in spite of several hesitations, the small democratic state was able to pass the test in terms of morale and resolve, as he managed to take into account all political forces in the country. In view of the way the war ended, Switzerland would probably have emerged with a relatively unfortunate stance if Guisan had not become more open toward the left during a critical situation, even though he was initially tending in the opposite direction, and even though certain people tried to influence him to do otherwise. Guisan may serve as an example that the course of history is determined neither exclusively by basic economic forces nor solely by ideas, but that a person who carries large responsibility can also play an essential part during crucial moments.

The General's most impressive strategic decision was undoubtedly the withdrawal of the troops to the *Reduit* and the expansion of this mountain fortress. Even if the original idea for the defensive concept was not Guisan's, he took on the responsibility for putting it into practice; therefore, he has henceforth been inseparably associated with the Rütli and the *Reduit*. The setting up of defensive positions in the Alps, which became a symbol of the country's determination to put up resistance, is one of the enduring achievements of Switzerland's national defense establishment on the psychological, organizational, and military level. Guisan was not wrong when he wrote that the *Reduit* would remain important in the long term, as it would still be useful in the era of the atomic bomb due to its numerous underground installations in the mountains. He stated, "If I look at what was done from 1939 to 1945 in terms of fortifications and of preparing objects for demolition, I continue to be convinced that these works were necessary. I am sure that they will be useful and even indispensable as long as we will be forced to reckon with any maneuver by ground troops and an air force."[1]

The large number of orders and instructions that the General issued occasionally went beyond what the regulations stipulated. In accordance with the existing possibilities, he advanced the state of armament, equipment, and training, introduced new means of transport and communication, and modernized the artillery, anti-tank defense, air force, and anti-aircraft defense.

Just like the *Reduit*, creations such as the Personal Staff, "Army and Home," and even the briefing at the Rütli that are associated with Guisan were not initiated by the General but by others. Guisan was not someone who made hasty decisions; he liked having advisors, and the advice that he received from them was good. He was capable of accepting ideas from other people and making them his own. His basic skill as a leader consisted of selecting highly qualified and loyal officers to serve on his staff. He did not hesitate at all to take action, but it was in his nature to make careful deliberations before making decisions that had a far-reaching impact. He was not afraid of taking calculated risks. Once he had made up his mind, he adhered to his decisions and was able to motivate his entourage and the subordinate commanders to put all their energy into carrying them out. However, opponents who underestimated him interpreted his occasional tendency to calmly wait and see as a weakness.

Guisan's instinct not to view his role as commander-in-chief purely as a military one became apparent in his repeated attempts to exercise influence in the foreign political realm. The cooperation talks with France that he kept secret from the Federal Council, his meeting with SS General Schellenberg, and his efforts to have a special mission sent to Berlin were risky initiatives with which he went to the limit of what is considered a strictly neutral policy. He did not commit any "offense," but from a historic perspective one may be allowed to consider these actions as rather questionable. The lack of trust between the Federal Council and the army command was more serious at times than it appeared to outsiders, occasionally causing the General to play a double game that got him into embarrassing situations; and he subsequently tried to talk himself out of these situations by bending the truth. One must not overlook certain scratches in the country's image as a neutral state, even though they were inflicted with the objective of keeping Switzerland independent. Moreover, it is justified to voice reservations about Guisan's attitude regarding asylum matters and particularly about his demand that the press should be censored.

Was Guisan a strategist, a field marshal? Destiny did not challenge him to pass the test in a defensive war against a major power or to lead the army in a campaign. His strategic capabilities may be contested, and it is obvious that for operational questions he tended to follow the advice of others rather than coming up with his own ideas and theories. He was not a commander who made intellectual analyses, and behaving like an authoritarian martinet was the last thing on his mind. General Guisan did not perhaps qualify as a genius, but he was pragmatic and used common sense, instinctively making clear decisions at the right time and getting them accepted. He made a realistic, and hence correct, assessment of the powers that were at work in the military and political spheres and of the persons that exercised the power in the small state of Switzerland. Almost without exception, during his deliberations he realized what actions were expedient for specific situations, and he was able to intuitively make the right decisions. Guisan did not lack courage nor a good deal of cleverness; nor can it be denied that he had an understanding of issues pertaining to supplies and logistics and was able to resolve them. The "lives of others and the welfare of a great entity" were undoubtedly foremost on his mind, concerns which Clausewitz considered as major qualifications for a commander.[2]

It may be pointless to ask whether General Guisan would have passed the test if Switzerland had been drawn into the war, but the question has been asked many times, including by the soldiers who were on duty from 1939 to 1945. This author tends to believe that he would have remained an astute leader under the pressure of the war and would therefore have coped with his task as commander. Together with his staff which was determined to fight, he would have managed to use an aggressive defensive strategy, probably accomplishing more in this respect than some of his critics believed him capable.

It has been repeated several times that as the embodiment of the spirit of resistance, General Guisan turned into an integrating figure for the Swiss. The question is to what special qualities he owed his reputation, respect, and popularity. He was neither a magician nor an actor. He was not more intelligent, educated, or eloquent than many other people. What were the reasons for his success? He had a natural gift to instill confidence and create an emotional affinity; he was obliging and friendly, warmhearted, and paternal. These qualities made it easy for him to influence others. A secret to the General's success was his personal charm; even the toughest politicians succumbed to it. He was always in good shape, sharp, agile, and upright. His qualities made him an excellent role model. Personalities with psychological skills, especially his closest collaborators, contributed to projecting his image and boosting his charisma. His personal staff and the press office served to shape and reinforce the General's aura. They created an effective organization that resembled a public relations firm carrying out a marketing campaign.

Switzerland probably needed a hero in order to be able to seamlessly pass through the difficult years of World War II. Everything that seemed to help promote the image of the nation's representative was welcome in the sense that it strengthened the country's determination to remain independent. In this respect, Guisan, who was presented to the people as the embodiment of a true Swiss, fulfilled an additional historic role. By identifying themselves with him, it was easier for the Swiss to survive as a community. The General's style was fitting for the time, and his shining example was encouraging to others.

It would definitely be wrong to claim that the General, who was not indifferent to flattery, did not enjoy playing the role of an integrating force. He appreciated his great popularity and felt at ease when the public showed its affection for him. Guisan for his part was able to identify with the population. He gained a lot of public empathy through his public appearances in his gold-braided uniform, and as Chapuisat commented, "It was too easy to suspect him of fishing for popularity."[3] The characteristics that his rivals, such as Wille and Däniker, considered to be typical of a military featherweight were precisely what made both the soldiers and the population admire him. It must be said in the General's favor that even if he was not able to hide the fact that he liked portraying himself, he did not do so in an arrogant manner. When he appeared in public, he was aware that he was representing the army and was therefore expressing the nation's determination to put up resistance.

Switzerland was lucky that General Guisan played the role of an integrating force during the Second World War. As Ernst puts it, the country was privileged to have a personality as Commander-in-Chief of the Armed Forces who was able to maintain the national unity.[4] Guisan turned out to be the right man at the right time for the job of commander-in-chief. No other army unit commander would have been able to do justice to the task of maintaining peace and safeguarding the country's independence in an equally inimitable manner.

Some believe that Guisan was simply lucky and that favorable circumstances allowed him to play a leading role. He actually admitted, "Destiny has been smiling on me."[5] His balanced, well-tempered character allowed him to accomplish his difficult task with perseverance, intuition, and skillfulness. Guisan was lucky, but he earned his luck, and the country was lucky to have him. In the fall of 1940, following the General's visit with a mountain regiment from Wallis, its commander told his staff, "The fact that such a man is in command of our army is a sign of divine protection."[6] He did not disappoint his supporters but to a very large extent fulfilled the expectations that they placed in him at the time he was elected General. As commander-in-chief he did not suffer any major failures. His decisions, which have to be seen in the light of the circumstances of the time, remain undeniable achievements from a historic perspective.

It would be presumptuous to consider General Guisan as the only savior of Switzerland. He would probably not agree with Kimche, who qualifies him as the only hero among all statesmen and army commanders besides Churchill who was able to successfully fight Hitler with his own weapons and who successfully took a gamble with the Führer.[7] There were many different reasons why Switzerland was not drawn into the war. Its chances of surviving as a nation seemed to be dim for some time but remained intact because the country's political leadership managed to successfully overcome the complex social and economic problems that existed during the war. By rationing food items, farsightedly organizing the war economy, launching an emergency cultivation program, granting protection to tenants, establishing price caps, and most particularly by passing a law which entitled serving soldiers to a compensation for lost wages, the government made a major contribution to keeping the country united.

Research has shown that between 1939 and 1945, Switzerland was at no moment faced with an imminent military invasion. The staffs of both Axis Powers undertook studies for an attack on Switzerland, but at no point enacted their plans. Economic factors such as the production of war materials and the trading of gold with Germany, the fact that the country served as a hub for international intelligence activities, as well as the strategic fact that the Swiss Army protected a flank for both warring parties contributed in large part to keeping Switzerland out of the war. The course of the conflict, in which the Germans encountered unexpected and eventually overwhelming problems in Russia, was a key factor in Switzerland's being able to remain out of the crosshairs. Nevertheless, there can be no serious doubt that whenever the warring parties made an assessment of the situation, they took into account Switzerland's determination to put up resistance and safeguard its armed neutrality. It is established that the Swiss Army, whose defensive capability was believed to be effective, always played a significant part in Germany's strategic considerations. The Swiss Army acted as an effective deterrent. The decisive reason why Switzerland was spared by the Germans was probably their sober realization that Switzerland was more useful to them as an unharmed country that produced war materials for them than as an occupied but rebellious country, after strenuous conventional resistance, in which the industry was demolished and the access roads and railways were destroyed.

When looking at Switzerland's history during World War II, it is not difficult to see why its position has been seriously contested. Its policy resembled a risky balancing act. In retrospect, it appears as a stroke of fate that the country was spared from the war. No matter how hard one tries to identify the decisive factors that enabled the fortunate nation to come out of the dark years of the war sound and safe, there will always be some imponderable circumstances remaining. In view of the number of human errors, intrigues, miscalculations, and wrong conclusions that occurred, it is bordering on the miraculous that Switzerland was able to get through all perils unharmed and free. One cannot help thinking that ultimately it was coincidence or Providence that helped Switzerland remain free and independent.

Historians will doubtless have many details of Switzerland's political and military history between 1939 and 1945 left to assess. In his analysis, this author has come to the conclusion that the image that was created of General Guisan at the time does not need to undergo fundamental corrections. Even if the commander-in-chief's activities are assessed as relative, and even if Guisan was no superhuman being but made mistakes and had certain weaknesses, his accomplishments are not belittled. In fact, some of his obvious shortcomings make him all the more human and credible. A personality with the status of Henri Guisan does not need to be afraid of the truth. Whatever one may say against him, the final assessment will always be positive. The fact remains that the Swiss Army made a tremendous contribution to keeping Switzerland politically and intellectually independent during the Second World War, and the credit for that achievement goes to General Guisan.

Notes

Note: Abbreviations used in Notes are listed on pages 801–803.

Introduction

1. Benjamin Vallotton, *Coeur à Coeur, Le Peuple suisse et son Général.* Lausanne 1950, 134.
2. Pierre Béguin, "Die Schweiz und die Kriegswirtschaft," in *General Guisan und der Zweite Weltkrieg 1939–1945*, edited on the occasion of Guisan's 100th birthday. Lausanne 1974, 122–123.
3. Edgar Bonjour, *Erinnerungen.* Basel 1983, 12.
4. Edgar Bonjour, *Geschichte der schweizerischen Neutralität*, vols. IV–IX. Basel 1971–1976.
5. Carl Ludwig, *Die Flüchtlingspolitik der Schweiz in den Jahren 1933–1955, Bericht an den Bundesrat zuhanden der eidgenössischen Räte.* Bern 1957.
6. Hans Rudolf Kurz, *Die Schweiz im Zweiten Weltkrieg. Das grosse Erinnerungswerk an die Aktivdienstzeit 1939–1945.* Thun 1959. Hans Rudolf Kurz, *General Henri Guisan.* Zürich 1965. For his other publications, see the Bibliography.
7. Hermann Böschenstein, "General Henri Guisan, Zur zehnten Wiederkehr seines Todestages," in *Neue Zürcher Zeitung*, April 12, 1970, No. 166.
8. Viktor Hofer, *Die Bedeutung des Berichtes General Guisans über den Aktivdienst 1939–1945 für die Gestaltung des Schweizerischen Wehrwesens.* Ph.D. thesis, Basel 1970. Georg Kreis, *Auf den Spuren von "La Charité", Die schweizerische Armeeführung im Spannungsfeld des deutsch-französischen Gegensatzes 1936–1941.* Basel 1976. Daniel Bourgeois, "La Suisse et la Seconde Guerre mondiale, Guisan, Pilet-Golaz?" in *Alliance culturelle romande* November 23, 1977, 11–16. Oscar Gauye, "Le général Guisan et la diplomatie suisse, 1940–1941," in *Studien und Quellen* 4, Bern 1978, 5–68.
9. Oscar Gauye, "Au Rütli, 25 juillet 1940, Le discours du Général Guisan," in *Studien und Quellen* 10, Bern 1984, 5–56.
10. General Henri Guisan, *Bericht an die Bundesversammlung über den Aktivdienst 1939–1945* [n.p., Bern 1946]. *Bericht des Chefs des Generalstabes der Armee an den Oberbefehlshaber der Armee über den Aktivdienst 1939–1945* [n.p., n.d., Bern 1946]. *Bericht des Kommandanten der Flieger- und Fliegerabwehrtruppen, des Generaladjutanten der Armee, des Chefs der Ausbildung der Armee, des Chefs des Personellen der Armee an den Oberbefehlshaber der Armee über den Aktivdienst 1939–1945* [n.p., n.d., Bern 1946].
11. *Bericht des Bundesrates an die Bundesversammlung zum Bericht des Generals über den Aktivdienst 1939–1945, vom 7. Januar 1947.* Bern 1947.
12. Bernard Barbey, *Fünf Jahre auf dem Kommandoposten des Generals, Tagebuch des Chefs des Persönlichen Stabes General Guisans 1940–1945.* Bern 1948. Bernard Barbey, *Von Hauptquartier zu Hauptquartier, Mein Tagebuch als Verbindungsoffizier zur französischen Armee 1939–1940.* Frauenfeld 1967.
13. General Guisan, *Gespräche. Zwölf Sendungen von Radio Lausanne, geleitet von Major Raymond Gafner.* With a Foreword by ex-Federal Councilor Rudolf Minger. Bern 1953, p. 208.
14. Barbey 1967, 9.
15. Ibid., 8. Similar statement in Barbey 1948, 8–9.
16. When he died in an accident in France at age 70, in 1970, Bernard Barbey was a member of the Executive Council of UNESCO in Paris as a permanent representative of the Federal Council.

17. Reference works BAr 5795 and BAr J.I. 127, written by E. Tschabold and L. Andereggen, 1972 and 1973. See the Bibliography on pp. 776–803.
18. General to Maître Zumstein; Pully, 8/29/47, personal and confidential. Copy. ArVR.
19. Zumstein to Colonel H. Guisan; Lausanne, 3/14/66. ArVR.
20. Liliane Perrin, *L'Album privé du Général Guisan.* Lausanne 1986, 63 ff.
21. [Henri Guisan], *Grand Livre, Dépenses et Recettes, commencé par mon père en 1897 lors de mon établissement à Chésalles-sur-Oron.* [n.d., 1897–1955]. ArVR.
22. See the "Persons Interviewed" on pp. 800–801.
23. J[ean] R[udolf] von Salis, *Notizen eines Müssiggängers.* Zürich 1983, 85.

Chapter 1: Early Years
1. J.P. Zwicky, "Sammlung schweizerischer Ahnentafeln," in *Sonderheft, Schweizerische Heerführer.* Zürich 1940, 97ff.
2. Guisan 1953, 12f.
3. Perrin 1986, 59.
4. Ibid, 59.
5. Ibid., 54.
6. André Marcel, "Kindheit und Jugendjahre," in *General Guisan und der Zweite Weltkrieg 1939–1945.* Lausanne 1974, 12.
7. Perrin 1986, 25.
8. Answers the General gave students on a radio show, March 11, 1940. BAr 5795/175.
9. Guisan 1953, 13.
10. Marcel 1974, 20, 23.
11. Guisan 1953, 14.
12. Grade sheets, school year 1890/91, class A. BAr Nl Gui.
13. General to M. Pichler, Freudenstadt; Lausanne, April 26, 1947. Copy BAr Nl Gui.
14. Guisan 1953, 15.
15. It would be desirable from a biographer's viewpoint if a special study were done on Guisan's school years.

Chapter 2: University Studies and Vocational Training
1. Guisan 1953, 15.
2. Ibid., 16.
3. Marcel 1974, 19.
4. Guisan 1953, 16f.
5. Ibid., 17.
6. Ibid., 16.
7. Ives Delay, *La Grande Chance de la Suisse: Le général Guisan ou l'art de gagner la paix.* Echallens, [n.d., 1974], 28.
8. Guisan 1953, p. 17f.
9. Henry Guisan to the author on June 23, 1987 in Pully.
10. E.g. Edouard Chapuisat, General Guisan, Bern 1950, 50 and 70. Romansch is spoken primarily in the eastern canton of Graubunden (Grisons).
11. Valloton 1950, 217.
12. Böschenstein 1970.
13. Guisan 1953, 18.
14. Chapuisat 1950, 28.
15. Guisan 1953, 20.

Chapter 3: Guisan as a Farmer, Estate Owner, and Militia Officer
1. Guisan 1953, 18.
2. "Registre civique de Chesalles 1897." GAr Ch.

3. Guisan 1953, 18; "Federal census of December 1, 1900," in *Schweizerische Statistik*, Bern 1904, 170.
4. Guisan, *Grand Livre*, March 2,1897.
5. Ibid., "Récapitulation 1897." Cf. Perrin 1986, 65.
6. Ibid., March 29, 1897 and April 25, 1898.
7. Guisan 1953, 18.
8. Perrin 1986, 65.
9. Ibid., 49.
10. Myriam Decoppet-Guisan to the author, Zimmerwald, May 17, 1985. Guisan called his wife "Mery," and she called him "Chougnet." Perrin 1986, 51.
11. Guisan 1953, 19.
12. Guisan, *Grand Livre*.
13. Ibid., March 9, 1897. Quoted in Perrin 1986, 67.
14. "Procès verbaux du Conseil général de Chesalles," December 9, 1897. GAr Ch.
15. "Registre Bourse des Pauvres de Chesalles," March 25, 1898. GAr Ch.
16. "Procès verbaux des Assemblées électorales de Chesalles," November 6, 1898. GAr Ch.
17. Ibid., November 17, 1901.
18. "Procès verbaux de la Municipalité de Chesalles," December 31, 1901. GAr Ch.
19. Perrin 1986, 15.
20. Guisan 1953, 19.
21. Perrin 1986, 15.
22. "Catalogue des membres du Conseil communal de Pully," 1906/07. GAr Pu.
23. "Procès verbaux du Conseil communal de Pully, December 28, 1907," 80. GAr Pu.
24. "Catalogue des membres du Conseil communal de Pully," 1909, 1913.
25. "Procès verbaux du Conseil communal de Pully," 1908–1917.
26. Ibid., 1921. Also: "Registre des votations et élections 1921," 27ff. GAr Pu.
27. Guisan's political career would require another detailed study.
28. Perrin 1986, 17f. Unfortunately, the guest books are missing.
29. Marcel 1974, 22.
30. Henry Guisan to the author, Pully, September 25, 1984. Thousands of officers' job evaluations are at the Federal Archives, but those of Henri Guisan are missing.
31. Chapuisat 1950, 29f.
32. Guisan 1953, 31.
33. Ibid., 24.
34. Ibid., 27f.
35. *Diplomatische Dokumente der Schweiz*, vol. 6. Bern 1981, pp. 537ff. Details of the secret talks are mentioned in Hans Rapold, *Der schweizerische Generalstab*, vol. V. Basel/Frankfurt am Main 1988, pp. 282ff.
36. Cf. Chapter 9.
37. Guisan 1953, p. 31.
38. Ibid., pp. 28f.
39. "Lt. Colonels d'EMG de Goumoëns et Guisan, Rapport sur la visite des attachés militaires neutres aux 1ère et 2ème armées françaises, 19–25 août 1916." Confidential. BAr 27/12611.
40. Ibid., p. 9.
41. Ibid., pp. 11f.
42. Ibid., p. 8.
43. Ibid., pp. 20f.
44. Guisan 1953, p. 29.
45. "Lt.Col. Guisan, Visite des attachés militaires des pays neutres aux VIIe et VIIIe armées françaises, du 2–11 juillet 1917." Confidential. BAr 27/12618.
46. Ibid., p. 24.
47. Ibid., pp. 14f.
48. Ibid., pp. 7f. The United States declared war on Germany on April 2, 1917.
49. Ibid., p. 17.
50. Ibid., pp. 16f., 20.

51. Ibid., pp. 24f.
52. Guisan 1953, p. 29.
53. "Generalstabchef (von Sprecher) an EMD." Bern, 4/23/1919. BAr 21/11917.
54. "Verzeichnis der für den Ordnungsdienst nach Zürich aufgebotenen Truppen ab 4.9. 1918 bis Ende August 1919." BAr 27/12004.
55. Guisan, *Rapport sur le service d'ordre à Zurich du 13 mai au 13 juin 1919.* Colombier 6/18/1919. [15 pp.] BAr 21/11917. The following details are from this report, unless otherwise indicated.
56. "Kommando Ordnungstruppen Zürich (Sonderegger), Befehl für die Ablösung des Infanterieregiments 20." Zürich, 5/4/1919. BAr 21/11917.
57. Guisan to Cantonal Parliament member Ribeaud; Zürich, 6/6/1919. Copy BAr 21/11917.
58. Guisan, *Rapport sur le service d'ordre*, op. cit., pp. 3f.
59. Minutes of the Cantonal Executive Council of Zürich, 5/20/1919, No. 1442. StAr ZH.
60. Guisan, *Rapport sur le service d'ordre*, op. cit., p. 4.
61. Ibid., p. 15.
62. Report by the Cantonal Executive Council of Zürich to the Cantonal Parliament, 6/23/1919. StAr ZH.
63. Guisan 1953, p. 30.
64. Willi Gautschi, *Der Landesstreik von 1918.* Zürich/Köln 1968. Paul Schmid-Ammann, *Die Wahrheit über den Generalstreik von 1918.* Zürich 1968.
65. Guisan 1953, p. 30.
66. Ibid., p. 31.
67. Hans Rapold, *Der schweizerische Generalstab*, vol. V. Basel 1988, pp. 388, 394ff.
68. "Etudes opératives sur le cas de guerre avec la France (sans alliance), novembre/décembre 1921/février 1922." BAr 27/12790. "Memorial zum Aufmarsch an der Westfront im Krieg gegen Frankreich, Juli/Dezember 1925." BAr 27/12792. Quoted in Rapold 1988, pp. 399ff.
69. "Colonel Guisan, Aufmarsch West." 2/10/1926. BAr 27/12792.
70. Guisan, *Grand Livre*, 1909–1913.
71. Henry Guisan, born 1899, called "Riquet." Became a successful horse-jumping competitor, Colonel in the army, and President of the Swiss Ski Federation. Myriam Decoppet-Guisan, born 1901, called "Miry" or "Fifille" by the General. Married a physician, Dr. Gaston Decoppet, in 1934.
72. Perrin 1986, pp. 22ff.
73. Ibid., pp. 31f.
74. Ibid., p. 33.
75. Guisan, *Grand Livre*, "Cadeaux Noël 1928."
76. Perrin 1986, p. 66.
77. Ibid., p. 46. Raymond Gafner, "Passer le témoin," in *Général Guisan ... toujours vivant*, op. cit., p. 43.
78. Guisan, *Grand Livre*, 5/1/1928.
79. Bar Nl Gui

Chapter 4: Guisan as Divisional Commander and Corps Commander

1. Corps Commander Gübeli to Federal Councilor Kobelt; Lucerne, August 291946. BAr 5800/2.
2. Colonel H. Guisan to the Head of the Military Department (Scheurer); "Verte Rive," November 28, 1926. BAr 27/4923.
3. *Der Bund*, June 25, 1932, No. 291.
4. *Neue Zürcher Zeitung*, June 26, 1932, No. 1194.
5. Guisan 1953, 32.
6. Ulrich Wille, son of World War I General Wille, was promoted to the rank of Corps Commander and took over the command of the 2nd Army Corps.
7. Minutes of the NDC, October 9 to October 11, 1933, 12. Confidential. BAr 27/4059.
8. Ibid., February 3, 1936, and September 26, 1936, 1.
9. Ibid., November 28, 1933, 2.
10. Ibid., February 8, 1933, 11, and April 17–18, 1934, 12.

11. Ibid., October 9 to October 11, 1933, 7, and April 5, 1935, 2 f. The Federal Council's proposal to introduce a mandatory pre-military training was rejected in a national ballot on December 1, 1940 by 345,430 yea and 434,817 nay, with only 3-1/2 cantons accepting the proposal. Voter turnout was 63.6%. The opposition was strongest in rural areas where there was concern that farm boys might be overworked.
12. Ibid., February 3, 1936, 3. BAr 27/4060.
13. Ibid., April 17–18, 1935, 3.
14. Ibid., April 11, 1938, 5, and November 2, 1938, 18.
15. Minger to Guisan; Bern, August 14, 1934. BAr Nl Gui.
16. Guisan 1953, 32f.
17. [Henri] Guisan, En mission aux grandes Manoeuvres italiennes de l'Apennin Toscan-Emilien, Août 1934; October 15, 1934. BAr 127/42.
18. Ibid., 28.
19. Ibid., 29.
20. Ibid., 30.
21. Ibid., 31.
22. Ibid., 32.
23. Minutes of the NDC, July 12, 1937, 7f. BAr.
24. Walter Schaufelberger, "Dissuasion in der jüngsten Vergangenheit," in Die Zukunft der Milizarmee, Zürich 1985, 8f.
25. The public loan serving to finance armament investments of 235 million Swiss francs was tendered with 3% interest. Within three weeks, the loan was oversubscribed by 100 million francs.
26. Kreis 1976, 16ff.
27. Ibid., 15, 17.
28. Guisan 1953, 33.
29. Kreis 1976, 17.
30. Quoted in Kreis 1976, p. 17.
31. O. [Otto] F. [Frey], "Waadtländer Emotionen um General Guisan", in: Neue Zürcher Zeitung, 4/26/1985, No. 96; also by the same author: "Westschweizer und Franzosen als ungleiche Freunde," in: Neue Zürcher Zeitung, 8/9/1985, No. 182, and 8/14/1986, No. 186.
32. General Guisan to Marshal Pétain; AHQ, 4/24/1941. Carbon copy. BAr 5795/336.
33. Ibid., 3/29/1944. BAr 5795/338.
34. Kreis 1976, p. 46.
35. Henri Guisan, "Die Seele unserer Armee und die soziale Rolle des Offiziers", in: Neue Schweizer Rundschau, offprint, Zürich [n.d. 1934].
36. Ibid., p. 12.
37. Henri Guisan, "Les devoirs des universitaires à l'égard de la défense nationale", in: Schweizerische Hochschulzeitung, Zürich, 5/1/1937, p. 6.
38. Ibid., pp. 7, 9.
39. Henri Guisan, "Unser Volk und seine Armee," translated from French into German by Prof. Dr. Th. Flury, Zürich 1940, pp. 20, 27f.

Chapter 5: Politics in the 1930s

1. Guisan's cashbook mentions club-related expenses of 473 Swiss francs for 1927 and 686 francs for 1929. Guisan, Grand Livre, op. cit., 1927, 1929.
2. Guisan 1953, 81.
3. Guisan [1934], 27.
4. Henry Guisan Jr. to author; Pully, September 25, 1984.
5. SVV, Activity Report October 1931–October 1932. StAr AG. Depot AVV.
6. Willi Gautschi, Geschichte des Kantons Aargau, vol. 3. Baden 1978, 234 ff.
7. Minutes of the SVV committee meeting; Aarau, 12/18/1926. StAr AG. Depot AVV.
8. Katharina Bretscher-Spindler, "Konservativismus, Korporativismus und Faschismus: Zur Kontroverse um Guisans politische Ansichten," in Neue Zürcher Zeitung, April 19, 1985, No. 90.
9. Guisan [1934], 29.

10. Guisan to Head of Military Department (Minger); Lausanne May 3, 1934. Confidential. BAr 27/15085.
11. Ibid.
12. Beat Glaus, *Die Nationale Front: Eine schweizerische faschistische Bewegung 1930–1940.* Zürich/Einsiedeln/Köln 1969. Walter Wolf, *Faschismus in der Schweiz: Die Geschichte der Frontenbewegungen in der deutschen Schweiz 1930–1945.* Zürich 1969. Cf. also Werner Rings, *Schweiz im Krieg 1933–1945: Ein Bericht.* Zürich 1974.
13. Ernst Nobs, *Helvetische Erneuerung.* Zürich 1943, 32.
14. Minutes of the NDC, February 17, 1939, 2.
15. Ibid., May 21, 1938, 13.
16. See Chapters 11 and 26.
17. One piece of advice Stegemann gave Henne was to extend the Front's influence in the armed forces among both soldiers and officers. R. Henne, "Gespräch mit H. Stegemann," October 19, 1936, 11 ff. Handwritten. AfZ Hl He.
18. General to Minger; AHQ, May 4, 1940. Confidential. BAr 27/563.
19. Jules Sandoz to author; Biel, October 4, 1985.
20. Guisan [1934], 29.
21. Ibid., 18.
22. Lannurien, Maneuver Report, October 5, 1936. Quoted in Kreis 1976, 168.
23. Jann Etter, *Armee und die öffentliche Meinung in der Zwischenkriegszeit 1918–1939.* Ph.D. thesis, Zürich/Bern 1972, 125.
24. Ibid., 149.
25. Christoph Graf, "Vom Klassenkampf zur Konkordanz," in *Festschrift Ulrich Im Hof,* op. cit., 509.
26. Quoted from: Fred Luchsinger, *Die 'Neue Zürcher Zeitung' im Zeitalter des Zweiten Weltkrieges 1930–1955.* Zürich 1955, 170.
27. Minutes of the Social Democratic Party Committee, April 15, 1939, 9. SAr.
28. General to Minger; AHQ, May 4, 1940. Confidential. BAr E27/563.
29. Former Federal Councilor Pierre Graber to author; Ibiza, August 7, 1987.
30. Minutes of the NDC, April 24, 1939, 3.
31. Ibid., May 16, 1939, 3 f.
32. Ibid., 4.
33. Ibid., August 22, 1939, 1 f.
34. Ibid., 3.
35. Ulrich Wille, handwritten notes; August 22, 1939. ArMa.
36. Ibid.
37. Jakob Labhart, Diary, August 24, 1939. BAr Nl La.
38. Ibid.

Chapter 6: The General Is Elected

1. Max Waibel, "Bericht zum Buche von Jon Kimche 'Spying for Peace'." Bern February 26, 1963, 3. BAr Nl Lü.
2. Ibid., 7. Cf. also Bonjour, *Neutralität,* vol. IV, op. cit.,20.
3. Labhart, Diary, op. cit., August 25, 1939.
4. Ibid., August 26, 1939.
5. O.A. Germann, *Erinnerungen.* Bern [n.d., 1977]: privately published edition, 57.
6. Labhart, Diary, August 28, 1939.
7. Ibid.
8. Operational Section (von Erlach), "Assessment of the Situation." Bern, August 28, 1939, 10 a.m. BAr.
9. The full text is published in German in H.R. Kurz, *Dokumente des Aktivdienstes,* Frauenfeld 1965, 27f.
10. Head of Operational Section (von Erlach), "Assessment of the Situation," presented orally to the Chief of the General Staff on August 29. By the same author, "Assessment of the Situation," Bern August 30, 1939, 5 p.m. BAr 5795/328 and 348.

11. Labhart, Diary, October 29, 1939.
12. Kimche 1961, 6 footnote.
13. Military Organization of the Swiss Confederation of April 12, 1907, article 205.
14. Rudolf Minger, Foreword in *Guisan: Gespräche*, op. cit., 8.
15. [Representative] Hans Müller, "Erinnerungen an die Mobilisation 1939," in *Bulletin des Offiziersvereins Biel-Seeland*. Biel 1969, No. 7.
16. Stenographic minutes, House of Representatives, August 30, 1939, 525.
17. Guisan 1953, 45f. Quoted from tape recording of August 30, 1939.
18. Stenographic minutes, House of Representatives, August 30, 1939, 525. After quoting the short speech by the Chairman of the joint Senate and House session, the minutes state "(applause)."
19. Guisan 1953, 46.
20. Guisan to Labhart, AHQ, October 19, 1939. Nl La.
21. Mario Marguth, "Das Tagewerk und die Kommandoposten des Generals," in Kurz 1959, 35.
22. Guisan 1953, 47.
23. Labhart, Diary, Thursday, August 31, 1939.
24. Order to the Armed Forces; AHQ, August 31, 1939. BAr 5795.
25. The full text of the neutrality declaration is quoted in German in Bonjour, *Neutralität*, vol. VII, op. cit., 19f.
26. Fritz Hummler, "Tagebuch, 30.8.39," in *Bürger und Soldat*. Zürich 1944, 417.
27. Jacques Meurant, *La presse et l'opinion de la Suisse romande face à l'Europe en guerre 1939-1941*. Neuchâtel 1976, 182.
28. *Volksrecht*, August 31, 1939, No. 204.
29. Ulrich Wille to his wife, 8/30/1939. Quoted in Kreis 1976, 179.
30. Ibid., 180.
31. Däniker to Senator Löpfe; Walenstadt, October 2, 1940. Copy. AfZ Nl Dä.
32. Report by the French Ambassador, September 4, 1939. Quoted in Kreis 1976, 155.
33. Chauvin to the French Supreme Command, No. 285. Bern, March 29, 1941. Based on notes by Pilet-Golaz of December 8, 1943, who had a copy. BAr 2809/1, 5.
34. Report by attaché, May 28, 1936. Quoted in Kreis 1976, 157. Kreis indicates correctly that S. Gonard ended up assuming the role of Guisan's top advisor.
35. Oberkommando des Heeres, *Kleines Orientierungsheft Schweiz*. [n.p.] September 1, 1942, p. 95 (appendix 8). Confidential command matter. Copy. BAr 27/14348 A.
36. Labhart, Diary, Friday, September 1, 1939.
37. Hans Bracher, "Notizen." December 18, 1945, p. 3. BAr 5795/202. It appears that Captain Bracher, a member of the general staff, took notes for the General's report on the war. Cf. Chapter 36.
38. Ibid.
39. Federal Council to General, August 31, 1939. Draft. BAr 5800/1 and 27/14110. The edited version of the Federal Council is published in German in Guisan [1946], pp. 241f. and in Kurz 1965a, p. 36, and in French in Bonjour, *Neutralität*, vol. VII, op. cit., 31.
40. Note signed by Colonel von Erlach, August 30, 1939, 6:30 p.m. BAr 27/14110.
41. Labhart, Diary, Saturday, September 2, 1939.
42. Ibid., Monday, September 4, 1939.
43. Quoted in Bonjour, *Neutralität*, vol. VII, op. cit., 31.
44. General to Federal Council; Bern, October 11, 1939. BAr 5795.
45. Federal Council to General; Bern, November 3, 1939. BAr 5795.
46. Head of the Military Department (Minger) to General; Bern, November 9, 1939. Quoted in *Rapport de l'Etat-Major particulier du Général, 31.8.39- 31.12.39*, 4. Confidential. BAr 5795/200.

Chapter 7: The First Army Positions, 1939–1940

1. Huber [1946], tables 52 ff.
2. Chief of the General Staff (Labhart), "Bericht über Feststellungen am 2. Mobilmachungstag in den Armeekorps und Divisionen." AHQ, September 4, 1939. BAr 5795/348.

3. Huber [1946], 111.
4. Labhart, Diary, Friday, September 1, 1939.
5. Bonjour, *Neutralität IV*, op. cit., 25.
6. Guisan, "Rückblick auf meinen Aktivdienst, Aus meinen privaten Notizen." Offprint from No. 31 and No. 32 of the *Schweizer Illustrierte Zeitung*, [n.d., August 1, 1947], 5 f.
7. General Guisan to his direct subordinate commanders. Bern, September 2, 1939. ArMa.
8. Labhart, Diary, Saturday, September 2, 1939. Plan of Operations No. 1, September 2, 1939. BAr.
9. Operations Order No. 1, Bern, September 2, 1939, 18:45 hours. BAr 5795/282.
10. Huber [1946], 27.
11. Labhart, Diary, Tuesday, September 5, 1939.
12. Huber [1946], 27.
13. Guisan [1946], 13.
14. Guisan 1953, 93.
15. Frick to Federal President Kobelt; Bern, August 31, 1946. Carbon copy. Nl La.
16. Guisan [1946], 12.
17. Ibid., 20.
18. Alfred Ernst, *Die Konzeption der schweizerischen Landesverteidigung 1815–1966.* Frauenfeld/Stuttgart 1971, 67.
19. Kurz 1965 b, 23.
20. Guisan [1946], 19, 15.
21. On the controversy that this issue created, cf. Chapter 37, "The Controversy over Lack of Plans of Operation."
22. Ernst 1971, 101.
23. Oscar Adolf Germann, born 1889, died 1979, was Professor of Penal Law at the University of Basel as of 1930. When the war broke out, he was Colonel on the Operational Section of the General Staff; in December 1939, he was Assistant Chief of the Operational Section under von Erlach, and in early 1940 he was Chief of the Operational Section for several weeks. After Kobelt was elected Federal Councilor, he became Chief of Staff of the 4th Army Corps.
24. Germann to Assistant Chief of Staff for the Front; AHQ, Sept. 19, 1939, 13 f. BAr 5795/300.
25. Labhart to General; AHQ, September 20, 1939. BAr 5795/300.
26. Gonard to General; AHQ, September 22, 1939. BAr 5795/84.
27. Labhart to Federal President Kobelt; no date [summer 1946], 8. Nl La.
28. Ibid., 7. On the role of the General's personal staff, cf. Chapter 10 below.
29. *Rapport de l'Etat-Major particulier* [I], op. cit., 11.
30. Samuel Gonard, "Der Weg zum Reduit," in *Readers Digest, Der Zweite Weltkrieg.* Vol. I, Zürich 1971, 479 f.
31. General, "Beurteilung der Lage"; AHQ, July 10, 1940, 1. BAr 27/15067.
32. Ibid., 2.
33. Hans Senn, "Vom Versailler Vertrag bis heute," in *Krieg und Gebirge, Revue Internationale d'Histoire Militaire*, No. 85. Neuchâtel 1988, 244.
34. Operations Order No. 2; AHQ, October 4, 1939. BAr 5795/282. An informative map of the Limmat front under 'Case North' can be found in Hans Rudolf Kurz, *100 Jahre Schweizer Armee.* Thun 1978, 166.
35. Gonard 1971, 478.
36. Operations Order No. 2, op. cit.
37. General to Lardelli; AHQ, April 3, 1940. BAr 5795/303.
38. Oberbefehlshaber, "Instruktion für Verstärkungsarbeiten"; AHQ, September 23, 1939. ArMa.
39. Minutes of the briefing at the Chief of the General Staff's, November 9, 1939, 3. BAr 27/14151,1.
40. Ernst 1971, 152.
41. Werner Roesch, *Bedrohte Schweiz: Die deutschen Operationsplanungen gegen die Schweiz im Sommer/Herbst 1940 und die Abwehrbereitschaft der Armee im Oktober 1940.* Ph.D. thesis, Zürich 1986, 40.
42. Ernst 1971, 68, 103, 139 f. Kurz 1978, 165. Quoted in Franz Odermatt, *Zur Genese der Reduitstrategie.* Seminar paper, University of Bern 1983, 23 [unpublished].

43. Oberkommando des Heeres, *Kleines Orientierungsheft Schweiz*, op. cit., 33.
44. General to commanders of 1st to 3rd Army Corps; AHQ, November 17, 1939. ArMa.
45. General to command 2nd Army Corps; AHQ, September 27, 1939. ArMa.
46. Minutes of meeting between command of 3rd Army Corps and army command; Zürich, October 16, 1939. BAr 27/14151,1.
47. Minutes of the inspection and discussion of the Limmat front, January 4 to January 5, 1940. BAr 27/14151,1.
48. Edmund Wehrli, pro memoria; April 27, 1941. ArWe.
49. Labhart, Diary, September 28, 1939. Hans Hausamann, born 1897, died 1974, citizen of Basel and Unterstammheim ZH. Salesman in St. Gallen, lived in Teufen. As a militia captain, he created his own intelligence service, called 'Bureau Ha.' Was later promoted to major. He was an unusual, controversial officer who was the spokesman of the Swiss Officers' Society for many years. After Hitler seized power in Germany in 1933, Hausamann was willing to provide the Foreign Ministry of the Third Reich with advice on how to disseminate National Socialist propaganda in Switzerland; he wrote a letter to that effect to Consul General Crull dated 4/8/1933 (quoted in Humbel 1976, pp. 219 f.). However, Hausamann soon realized what Hitler's real intentions were and turned into a fervent patriot. He was instrumental in reconciling the Social Democrats with the conservative parties in the second half of the 1930's.
50. Labhart, Diary, October 25, 1939.
51. Guisan [1946], 22.
52. Labhart, Diary, October 25, 1939.
53. Barbey 1967, Sunday, November 12, 1939, 51.
54. Labhart, Diary, November 9, 1939 and November 14, 1939.
55. Ibid. Cf. Chapter 19 below.
56. William L. Shirer, *Der Zusammenbruch Frankreichs, Aufstieg und Fall der dritten Republik.* Munich/Zürich 1970, 567.
57. Mayor to Mrs. Guisan; Pully, October 1, 1939. GAr Pu A10.2.4.
58. Commander 3rd Army Corps (Miescher) to General; December 27, 1939. Confidential. BAr 5795/301.
59. Note on file re: meeting in Baden; February 13, 1940. BAr 27/14151,1.
60. Zürich Cantonal Executive Council (Nobs) to Federal Council; Zürich, June 3, 1940. BAr 2809/1,5.
61. Order of 4/20/1940, quoted in Kreis 1976, 99.
62. General, "Befehl betreffend Behebung der Eisgefahr auf armeewichtigen Gewässern"; AHQ, January 25, 1940. BAr 5795/142.
63. Labhart, Diary, November 15, 1939.
64. General to Labhart; AHQ, December 4, 1939. Confidential. Nl La.
65. Labhart, Diary, December 11, 1939.
66. Labhart to General; AHQ, December 28, 1939. Confidential. Nl La.
67. Ibid., 3.
68. Barbey 1967, Wednesday, January 31, 1940, 94.
69. Ernst 1971, 102.
70. General to Chief of General Staff (Labhart); AHQ, December 30, 1939. Confidential. Copy ArMa.
71. Huber [1946], 30. Operations Order No. 8, April 22, 1940. BAr 5795/289.
72. General to command of border brigade 5 (Renold); AHQ, March 27, 1940. Confidential. BAr 5795/287.
73. Barbey 1967, Wednesday, January 31, 1940, 94.
74. Roesch 1986, 40.
75. Minutes of the meeting concerning fortifications; September 29, 1939. BAr 27/14151,1.
76. Federal Military Department to Federal Council; Bern, July 25, 1941. Top secret. BAr 2809/1,5.
77. Guisan [1946], 174.
78. Minutes of the NDC, 2/3/1936, 5 f.
79. Ibid., March 11, 1936., 5, and 4/30/1936, 6.
80. Labhart to General; AHQ, December 5, 1939. BAr 5795/95.

81. Karl Kobelt, born 1891, died 1968, Ph.D. Federal Technical Institute Zürich. Member of the St. Gallen Cantonal Executive Council as of 1933. Commander of Infantry Regiment 31. Succeeded Minger as Federal Councilor and Head of the Military Department in 1941. Stayed on the Federal Council until 1954.
82. Order to the Armed Forces; AHQ, December 16, 1939. Confidential. BAr 5795/95.
83. Operations Order No. 4, January 22, 1940, 1. BAr 5795/285. A modified 2nd version of this order is dated May 14, 1940. Different in Bonjour, *Neutralität* IV, 65 f.
84. General to Huber; AHQ, March 26, 1940. Personal and confidential. BAr 5795/303.
85. Germann [1977], 66 ff.
86. Ibid., p. 67. Germann to Chief of the General Staff; May 17, 1940. Confidential. BAr 5795/303. Cf. Chapter 17 below.
87. Guisan [1946], 35. Bonjour, *Neutralität* V, op. cit., 36, believes that Switzerland's Armed Forces would have retreated to the West if they had cooperated with France and would have had "no other choice but to capitulate in the country's [southwestern] corner at Geneva or to continue fighting on French territory."
88. Ernst 1971, 68.
89. Order to the Armed Forces; AHQ, October 26, 1939, 00:45 hours. BAr. It is quoted in full in Kurz 1965 a, 48.
90. *Rapport de l'Etat-Major particulier* [I], op. cit., 15.
91. Guisan 1953, 81.
92. Guisan [1946], 267.
93. Ulrich Wille, "In Erwartung des Jahres 1940." Memorandum, January 20, 1940. ArMa.
94. Labhart to General; HQ, April 6, 1940, 1 f. Confidential. BAr 5795/142.
95. Ibid., 6.

Chapter 8: Replacing the Chief of the General Staff

1. Handwritten notes. No date [approx. 8/30/1939]. BAr 5795/449.
2. Barbey 1967, 19.
3. Robert Eibel to author; Zürich, March 13, 1985.
4. General to Labhart; AHQ, September 24, 1939. BAr 5795/449.
5. Minutes of briefing by Chief of the General Staff with Assistant Chiefs of Staff; September 22, 1939, 09:00 hours. BAr 5795/300 and 27/14151,1. Cf. Chapter 7 above.
6. General to Labhart; AHQ, October 13, 1939. Personal. BAr Nl La.
7. General to Labhart; AHQ, October 19, 1939. Carbon copy. BAr 5795/449.
8. General to Labhart; AHQ, October 4, 1939. BAr Nl La.
9. Labhart to General; AHQ, October 6, 1939. Personal. Carbon copy. BAr Nl La.
10. General to Labhart; AHQ,. October 19, 1939, 5. Carbon copy. BAr 5795/449.
11. Labhart to Minger; HQ, August 16, 1940. Personal. BAr Nl Mi.
12. Huber to Minger; Bern, May 25, 1938. BAr.
13. Huber to General; AHQ, November 8, 1939. Copy. BAr Nl La.
14. Karl J. Walde, *Generalstabschef Jakob Huber, 1883–1953.* Aarau/Frankfurt a.M./Salzburg 1983, 49.
15. General to Labhart; AHQ, December 13, 1939. BAr 5795/449.
16. Labhart, Note for file on meeting with the General, December 26, 1939, a.m. BAr Nl La.
17. Labhart to General; AHQ, December 19, 1939. BAr Nl La.
18. Ernst 1971, 458, footnote 13.
19. Order to the Armed Forces; AHQ, December 16, 1939. Confidential. BAr 5795/95.
20. Labhart to General; AHQ, December 23, 1939. BAr Nl La.
21. Häberlin to Labhart; Frauenfeld, December 25, 1939. Confidential. BAr Nl La.
22. Labhart to Häberlin; AHQ, December 28, 1939. Confidential. Carbon copy. BAr Nl La.
23. Handwritten notes. No date [fall 1939]. BAr 5795/449.
24. Robert Grimm, *Die Arbeiterschaft in der Kriegszeit: Rede vor dem Parteitag der bernischen Sozialdemokratie vom 18. Februar 1940.* Special reprint. Bern 1946, 23.
25. Labhart, Diary, December 27, 1939. One of the journalists was Hermann Böschenstein, who was reprimanded. Böschenstein 1978, 290 f.

26. Press office; AHQ, December 22, 1939. BAr Nl La.
27. Labhart, Note for file on meeting with the General, December 26, 1939, 3. BAr Nl La.
28. Official order; AHQ, December 18, 1939. BAr 5795/449.
29. General to Huber; AHQ, March 26, 1940. Personal. BAr 5795/449.
30. General to Labhart; AHQ, March 26, 1940. Personal. BAr Nl La. Labhart lost his official title, "Chief of the General Staff Section," only on August 20, 1945, at the request of the Federal Military Department. Minutes of the Federal Council meeting of August 14, 1945. Labhart retired as Commander of the 4th Army Corps at the end of June, 1947.
31. Note [unsigned], December 12, 1939. BAr 5795/449.
32. Ibid., points 4 to 6.
33. Labhart, Diary, December 22, 1939. BAr Nl La.
34. Ibid., 12/26/1939, and Note for file, December 26, 1939. BAr Nl La.
35. Labhart, Diary, December 30, 1939. BAr Nl La.
36. Ibid.
37. Ulrich Wille, Diary notes, December 26, 1939.
38. Ibid., December 4, 1939.
39. Probst to Wille; Bern, December 8, 1939. ArMa.
40. Kreis 1976, 194 f.
41. "Question du Haut Commandement, Etat le 9.12.39," 2. [Unsigned.] BAr 5795/422.
42. Study, December 6, 1939. [Unsigned.] BAr 5795/422.
43. Wille, Notes in his diary, December 11, 1939.
44. Wille to General; HQ, August 31, 1940. Personal. BAr 5795/465.
45. Ibid. Cf. also Chapter 25 below.
46. General to Wille; AHQ, October 4, 1940. Personal. ArMa.
47. Ibid., handwritten comment by Wille.
48. Minutes of the Special House Committee dealing with the General's Report, op. cit., 43.

Chapter 9: Cooperation with Foreign Powers
1. Guisan [1946], 25.
2. Cf. René-Henri Wüst, *Alerte en pays neutre*. Lausanne 1966, 70 f. Kreis 1976, 46 f. Kurz 1965, 17.
3. Kreis 1976, 47.
4. Ibid, 76. For information on the Colonel Affair, cf. Jürg Schoch, *Die Oberstenaffäre: Eine innenpolitische Krise (1915/1916)*. Ph.D. thesis, Zurich/Bern 1972.
5. Barbey 1967, 15.
6. Horst Zimmermann, *Die Schweiz und Grossdeutschland: Das Verhältnis zwischen der Eidgenossenschaft, Österreich und Deutschland 1933–1945*. Munich 1980, 400.
7. R.-H. Wüst, "L'histoire suisse d'hier," in *La Suisse* newspaper, June 8, 1965.
8. *Diplomatische Dokumente der Schweiz*, vol. 6, op. cit., No. 182,. 338 ff., No 298, 537 ff., and No. 400, 699 ff.
9. Barbey 1967, October 28, 1939, 36 f.
10. Kurz 1978, 161 f. Kreis 1976, 4, 26. Wüst 1966, 74.
11. Summary, July 31, 1939. BAr Nl Pp. The whole text is published in Kreis 1976, 211 f.
12. Senn 1988, 259.
13. Ibid., 244. Also by the same author, "Militärische Eventualabkommen der Schweiz mit Frankreich 1939/1940," in *Neue Zürcher Zeitung*, September 2, 1988, No. 204.
14. Kreis 1976, 173.
15. Quoted from Bonjour, *Neutralität* V, op. cit., 21, footnote 11.
16. Germann [1977], 60 f.
17. Labhart to General; AHQ, September 20, 1939, 14. BAr 5795/300.
18. Labhart, Diary, op. cit., October 4, 1939.
19. Ibid., October 5, 1939.
20. Ibid., October 7, 1939.
21. Ibid., October 26, 1939.

22. [Oscar Adolf] Germann, "Studie über die militärischen Grundlagen einer Kooperation mit den Westmächten im Falle Nord"; AHQ, October 24, 1939, 22. BAr 5795/300.

23. Labhart, Diary, November 2, 1939.

24. Peter A. Marti, "Die Studie Germann," in *SZG* February 1986, 236-256 reprinted the entire text, including Guisan's, Labhart's, and Gonard's annotations.

25. Germann, "Studie Fall Nord," op. cit., 20 f.

26. [Bernard] Barbey, "Rapport sur les travaux effectués à l'E.M.A. en vue d'une coopération éventuelle avec une armée alliée"; September 14, 1940. Confidential. BAr 5795/304.

27. Germann, "Studie Fall Nord," op. cit., 20 f.

28. Ernst 1971, 82 f.

29. Germann, "Studie Fall Nord," op. cit., 16 f. The plans for cooperation with the French Army in individual situations during World War I also stipulated an Allied Supreme Command. *Diplomatische Dokumente der Schweiz*, vol. 6, op. cit., No. 298, 538.

30. Annotation in Gonard's handwriting, "not absolutely decisive. Foch was supposed to 'convince' the Allies. We are under no obligation to accept missions that we consider to be impossible to accomplish."

31. Germann, "Studie Fall Nord," op. cit., 15.

32. Ibid., 19.

33. Ibid., 15.

34. Barbey 1967, Sunday, October 1, 1939, 25.

35. Ibid., 26 f.

36. Ibid.

37. Ibid., Monday, October 10, 1939, 28.

38. Ibid., Sunday, October 22, 1939, 31 f.

39. Kreis 1976, 169 f.

40. Barbey 1967, Saturday, October 28, 1939, 45.

41. Wüst 1966, 70, 71 f.

42. Cf. Chapter 20 below.

43. Barbey 1967, Sunday, October 28, 1939, 33 ff.

44. Ibid., 40.

45. Ibid., 44. The 20-page report by Barbey was undoubtedly among the files that were later destroyed.

46. Barbey 1967, Monday, November 20, 1939, 56.

47. Ibid., Friday, November 24, 1939, 59.

48. Ibid., Tuesday, December 5, 1939, 76 ff.

49. Lugand, *La Campagne de France mai-juin 1940*. Paris 1953, 30. Quoted in Edmund Wehrli, *Schweiz ohne Armee — eine Friedensinsel?*. Zürich 1985, 43.

50. Barbey 1967, Monday, December 12, 1939, 79.

51. Ibid., January 9, 1940, 86; March 4, 1940, 102 ff.; April 7, 1940, 121 f.

52. Ibid., Monday, December 12, 1939, 79.

53. Bonjour, *Neutralität* VII, op. cit., Documents, 238 ff.

54. Peter Andreas Marti, "Geheimabsprachen General Guisans mit Frankreich und Grossbritannien 1939/1940," in *Neue Zürcher Zeitung*, March 10–November 1984, No. 59.

55. "Air-Commander F.W.F. West to Kelly"; Bern, March 7, 1940 and March 27, 1940. Published in Bonjour, *Neutralität* VIII, op. cit., 238 f., 240 ff.

56. Jules Sandoz to author; Biel, September 11, 1986.

57. Claude Du Pasquier, *Journal*; February 12, 1940. BAr Nl DuPa.

58. Ibid., February 23, 1940.

59. Ibid., February 22, 1940.

60. Ibid., March 26, 1940.

61. Ibid., April 15, 1940.

62. Jules Sandoz to author; Biel, September 11, 1986.

63. Barbey 1967, Monday, March 4, 1940, 102.

64. Germann [1977], 64.

65. Barbey 1967, Friday, November 3, 1939, 48 f.

66. Ibid., Wednesday, November 1, 1939, 47.
67. Ibid., Monday, November 6, 1939, 50.
68. Ibid., Monday, February 5, 1940, 95.
69. Ibid., Monday, March 11, 1940.
70. Germann [1977], 62 f. Germann says that he found out about the direct contacts with the French Army only when Barbey's diary was published in 1967.
71. Barbey, "Rapport sur les travaux effectués," op. cit., 4.
72. Guisan [1946], 26.
73. Barbey 1967, Wednesday, January 31, 1940, 92 f.
74. Barbey, "Rapport sur les travaux effectués," op. cit., 4.
75. Labhart, Diary, op. cit., July 2, 1936.
76. Ibid., November 11, 1939.
77. Kreis 1976, 107. Cf. Chapter 12 below.
78. "Köcher an Auswärtiges Amt"; Bern, March 21, 1940. Copy of telegram. BAr EDI 1005/2.
79. "Attachébericht," April 8, 1940. Quoted in Kreis 1976, 113.
80. Kreis 1976, 113.
81. "Köcher an Auswärtiges Amt"; Bern, April 16, 1940. Photocopy of telegram. BAr EDI 1005/2.
82. Barbey 1967, Saturday, October 28, 1939, 34 f.
83. Ibid., Thursday, March 21, 1940, 112.
84. Germann [1977], 63.
85. On 'Case West A' and 'Case West B', cf. Chapter 7 above.
86. [Oscar Adolf] Germann, "Studie über die Grundlagen einer Kooperation mit der deutschen Wehrmacht im Fall W."; AHQ, April 9, 1940. [20 pages] The study was kept locked away at the Federal Archives and was made available for this study in 1986 at this author's special request.
87. Ibid., 5, 18.
88. Ibid., 16 f.
89. Hans Berli, born 1899, died 1952, Ph.D. in Law. Major on the general staff, training officer. Chief Instructor of the infantry from 1947 to 1951, ranked as a divisional commander.
90. Ernst 1971, 83.
91. Von Erlach to Germann; AHQ, February 5, 1940. BAr Nl Ge.
92. Barbey, "Rapport sur les travaux effectués," op. cit., 4.
93. Barbey 1967, Easter Monday, March 25, 1940, 112.
94. Ibid., 114. Followed further below by technical information on the use of 155-mm howitzers. Ibid., 125.
95. Ibid., 119, 125.
96. Ibid., 117.
97. Ibid., Tuesday, March 26, 1940, 116 f.
98. Head Federal Military Department (Minger), "Abkommandierung nach Frankreich"; Bern, April 9, 1940. BAr 5795/336.
99. De Blonay to Masson; Paris, April 11, 1940. BAr 27/12689.
100. "Ordre aux officiers de la mission militaire suisse en France"; AHQ, 4/22/1940. Confidential. BAr 27/12689. The General's backdated order was drafted by Gonard.
101. Colonel Schafroth, Note, March 11, 1960. BAr 27/12689.
102. Montfort to General; Bern, May 25, 1940. Personal and confidential. BAr 5795/336.
103. Barbey 1967, Friday, May 3, 1940, 135.
104. Ibid., Wednesday, December 20, 1939, 80.
105. Ibid., Thursday, March 14, 1940, 107 f.
106. Barbey, "Rapport sur les travaux effectués," op. cit., 5 f. Boissier's report, which mentions the files that were later destroyed, includes Captain de Brémond among the list of officers for whom a special order was prepared for their mission; hence, there may have been a total of twelve liaison officers. Cf. endnote 124 below.
107. Barbey 1967, Friday, May 10, 1940, 137.
108. Ibid., Tuesday, May 14, 1940, and Barbey, "Rapport sur les travaux effectués," op. cit., 7.
109. Barbey 1967, Tuesday, April 23, 1940, 128 f.

110. Ibid., Sunday, May 12, 1940, 138, and Wednesday, May 15, 1940, 142.
111. Ibid., Tuesday, May 21, 1940, 150 ff.
112. Ibid., Friday, May 24, 1940, 154 f. The Morvan is a hilly region west of Dijon with peaks as high as 900 meters above sea level.
113. Ibid., 155.
114. Ibid., Sunday, June 9, 1940, 164.
115. Ibid., 166.
116. Ibid.,168.
117. Ibid., 170. Cf. Chapter 10 below.
118. "Note sur l'appel éventuel à une coopération alliée"; AHQ, June 13, 1940 Confidential and strictly personal. BAr 5560 (B).
119. Cf. Chapter 17 below.
120. "Note sur l'appel éventuel," op. cit.
121. Barbey 1967, Tuesday, May 28, 1940, 157 ff.
122. Guisan [1946], 26.
123. Barbey, "Rapport sur les travaux effectués," op. cit., 7.
124. Boissier to Chief of the General Staff; AHQ, September 25, 1940. Confidential. BAr 5560 (B). The list of documents is published in Kreis 1976, 214 ff.
125. Huber, Note, September 30, 1940. BAr 5560 (B).
126. Barbey 1967, 128.
127. Barbey, "Rapport sur les travaux effectués," op. cit.
128. Wehrli 1985, 19. E. Bircher had made a written proposal to the Head of the Military Department, Federal Councilor Minger, in 1936 for precautionary military conventions to be concluded with the neighboring powers during a time of peace. Daniel Heller, "Das 'offene Loch': Eugen Bircher und die Verteidigung unserer Nordgrenze," in *ASMZ*, June 6, 1987, 370 f.
129. Edgar Bonjour, "Die Neutralitätspolitik der Schweiz während des Zweiten Weltkrieges," in *Brückenbauer*, May 1, 1985, No. 18.
130. Labhart, Note for file, November 3, 1939. BAr Nl La.
131. Huber to Kobelt, January 31, 1947, 9. BAr. Cf. also Klaus Urner, "Kompromittierende Neutralität 1940?" in *Neue Zürcher Zeitung*, August 24, 1970, No. 391.
132. Exposé by Head of Federal Military Department (Kobelt); Interlaken, January 10, 1942. Confidential. BAr 5795/146.
133. Karl Kobelt, Diary, June 26, 1946. Shorthand. BAr 5800/1.
134. "Weisungen betr. Handhabung der Neutralität durch die Truppe," October 10, 1939. BAr.
135. Lecture by Edgar Bonjour, UNESCO Seminar, Sigriswil, November 4, 1982. Also Bonjour 1981 c, 227 f.

Chapter 10: The General's Personal Staff

1. Bracher, *Notizen*. December 18, 1945. BAr 5795/202.
2. Labhart, Diary, op. cit., Saturday, September 2, 1939.
3. Presentation at the Archives for Contemporary History at ETHZ, October 24, 1984. Robert Eibel, born 1906, died 1986, from Zürich, grew up speaking German and French in Strasbourg. Ph.D. in Law. Later founded the Eibel public relations agency, which became known in Switzerland for its "Trumpf Buur" ads. Member of the National Council from 1963 to 1975 (Radical Democratic Party).
4. Guisan 1953, 49.
5. Guisan 1946, 254 f.
6. Huber to General; AHQ, June 28, 1941. Personal and confidential. BAr 4001 (C), 2.
7. *Rapport de l'Etat-Major Particulier*, Vol. I, op. cit., 9.
8. General to Labhart; AHQ, October 9, 1939. BAr 5795/449.
9. Huber to Kobelt; Brienz, January 31, 1947. BAr 4001 (C), 2.
10. Labhart to Commanders of Army Units; AHQ, October 11, 1939. BAr 27/14193,1. The diary's title was changed from "Journal du Bureau du Général" (Diary of the General's Office)

to "Journal de l'Etat-Major Particulier du Général" (Diary of the General's Personal Staff) only on February 16, 1942. BAr 5795/51-66.

11. Labhart to General; AHQ, October 14, 1939, 2 f. Personal. BAr 5795/449.

12. D. van Berchem, a member of the General's Personal Staff, explained to this author that Captain on the General Staff Rob. Frick had claimed that he was the one who came up with the idea of creating a special staff. Denis van Berchem to author; Vandoeuvres, September 9, 1986.

13. General to Labhart; AHQ, October 19, 1939, 3 f. Personal. BAr 5795/449.

14. Ibid., 7.

15. Armand von Ernst to author; Muri near Bern, August 7, 1985.

16. Labhart to Kobelt; n.d. [summer 1946]. BAr Nl La.

17. Marguth 1959, 32. The Personal Staff's diary mentioned the total number of officers, non-commissioned officers, and soldiers, which changed almost every day. BAr 5795/51 ff.

18. Roesch 1986, 58. Concerning the army staff, cf. Chapter 23.

19. Armin Meili, *Lorbeeren und harte Nüsse: Aus dem Werk- und Tagebuch eines Eidgenossen.* Zürich 1968, 168.

20. Chapuisat 1950, 99 ff.

21. Kreis 1976, 206.

22. Bracher 1945, 6.

23. Minutes of the Senate Committee dealing with the General's Report to the Federal Parliament on War-Time Duty 1939–1945 and the Federal Council's Report of January 7, 1947 on the General's Report. Rigi-Kaltbad, February 3–5, 1947, 25. Confidential. BAr.

24. [Bernard] Barbey, *Ordre réglant le service interne et les attributions des officiers de l'Etat-Major personnel du Général.* March 17, 1944. BAr 5795/89. Cf. Guisan, 1946, 256.

25. Jules Sandoz to author; Biel, September 11, 1986.

26. Jacques Boissier, Max Häni, Fritz Wanner to author; April 7, 1986, July 2, 1985, August 5, 1986.

27. Gonard to General; Lugano, September 12, 1940. Handwritten. BAr 5795/446.

28. Since Gonard was the 7th officer to join the General's Office, he often identified himself on letters which he drafted by writing, "7".

29. Barbey 1967, Saturday, October 28, 1939, 45.

30. Barbey 1948, 148.

31. General to Minger; AHQ, September 16, 1940. Personal. BAr 5795/446.

32. Barbey 1948, 281.

33. Armand von Ernst to author; Muri near Bern, August 7, 1985.

34. Barbey 1948, June 11, 1940, 13.

35. Cf. Chapter 12.

36. Barbey 1948, 76, 81.

37. Gonard to Barbey; July 11, 1940, 4. BAr 5795/85. Cf. Chapter 17.

38. Barbey 1948, November 10, 1944, 204.

39. Borel to Kobelt; Neuchâtel, August 14, 1946, 3. BAr.

40. General to Labhart; AHQ, December 9, 1939. BAr 27/14126.

41. Some of the examples of bad writing quoted by Barbey include, "Order re: horses that have volunteered to serve in the army"; and, "On the Alpine mountain crossings, the destruction of man-made constructions will remain in place as they are"; etc. Barbey 1948, October 23, 1941, 104.

42. Huber to Kobelt; January 31, 1947, 11. BAr.

43. On one occasion with Federal Councilor Kobelt, on three occasions with the corps commanders, and on five occasions with the Chief of the General Staff. BAr 5795. Cf. also Chapter 24.

44. General to Huber; AHQ, 5/29/1942. Strictly confidential. BAr 5795/87.

45. "A l'usage strictement personnel du Commandant en Chef"; June 11,1942. BAr 5795/87.

46. Notes, June 15, 1942, "Cas West à étudier". BAr 5795/87.

47. Huber to Kobelt; January 31, 1947, 9 f. BAr.

48. Barbey 1948, 50.

49. Ibid., Sunday, January 19, 1941, 67 f.

50. Ibid., December 8, 1943, 200.

51. *Rapport de l'Etat-Major Particulier,* op. cit., January 1, 1941-June 30, 1941, Vol. IV, 4.

52. Ibid., July 1, 1941-June 30, 1942, Vol. V, 2.

53. Denis van Berchem to author; Vandoeuvres, September 9, 1986.

54. Jules Sandoz, "In memoriam", in *Bulletin des Offiziersvereins Biel-Seeland* No. 7. Biel 1969, 9 ff.

55. Robert Eibel to author; Zürich, October 24, 1984.

56. Barbey 1948, 9, 76.

57. General to Huber; AHQ, December 9, 1940 and November 30, 1940. Personal and confidential. BAr 27/14190.

58. General to Huber; AHQ, December 9, 1940. Personal and confidential. BAr 27/14190.

59. Report by Intelligence Service, March 23, 1941. BAr 5795/451.

60. Order to relocate, March 26, 1941. Confidential. BAr 5795/250.

61. *Rapport de l'Etat-Major Particulier*, Vol. IV, op. cit., 26.

62. Barbey 1948, April 4, 1941, 78 f.

63. *Rapport de l'Etat-Major Particulier*, Vol. IV, p. 26. German industry owner Cranz, the father of a famous Alpine skiing champion, Christel Cranz, constructed the "Cranz Villa" in the 1920's. From 1935 to 1975 it was owned by a St.Gallen-based real estate company and was purchased by the municipality of Interlaken in 1975 to house the municipal administrative offices. Municipal Secretary Goetschi to author; Interlaken, July 3, 1989.

64. Barbey 1948, April 1, 1941, 79.

65. Guisan 1947, 23.

66. Jules Sandoz to author; Biel, October 4, 1985.

67. Marguth 1959, 33.

68. Jules Sandoz to author; Biel, October 4, 1985; and Denis van Berchem to author; Vandoeuvres, September 9, 1986.

69. Du Pasquier, Diary, op. cit., February 9, 1940. BAr Nl DuPa.

70. Jules Sandoz to author; Biel September 11, 1986.

71. Barbey 1948, October 25, 1941, 102.

72. Ibid., 102 f.

73. Ibid., early June, 1942, 125 f.

74. Jules Sandoz to author; Biel, September 1, 1986. The apartment was located at the "Beau Site," Schanzengraben 15 in Bern.

75. Notes of the Personal Staff [n.d., 1943]. BAr 5795/199. Marguth to Commander AHQ; January 21, 1944. Personal. BAr 5795/520.

76. Guisan [1946], 263. The General covered 350,000 km by car during the time of wartime duty; the car, a Buick, was driven by Adjutant Eugène Burnens. Delay [1974], 162.

77. General to Assistant Chief of Staff Ib; AHQ, October 24, 1940. Personal and confidential. BAr 27/14190.

78. *Rapport de l'Etat-Major Particulier* July 1,1940-December 31, 1940 [III], 24 ff. Cf. also Guisan 1953, 57.

79. General inspector of "Wagons-Lits" (sleeping car company) to General's Personal Staff; Basel, November 27, 1940. BAr 5795/252.

80. *Rapport de l'Etat-Major Particulier* [III], 27.

81. Denis van Berchem to author; Vandoeuvres, March 13, 1985.

82. Barbey 1948, July 22, 1944, 246, and October 15, 1941, 100.

83. Marguth to Group Id; AHQ, May 27, 1942. Confidential. BAr 5795/250.

84. Marguth 1959, 37 f.

85. Notes of the Personal Staff [n.d., 1942]. BAr 5795/199. Also Barbey 1948, February 22, 1942, 118.

86. Barbey 1948, May 11, 1944, 228 f.

87. Jules Sandoz to author; Biel, October 4, 1985.

88. Barbey 1948, May 10, 1941, 85 f.

89. Marguth 1959, 33.

90. Barbey to the General's Personal Staff; March 17, 1944. BAr 5795/89.

91. Gonard, "Allocution"; Lausanne, October 21, 1954. BAr Nl Go.

92. Böschenstein 1970. Felix Müller, "Der Einfluss von 'Maulwürfen' in Guisans Stab", in *Die Weltwoche*, September 11, 1986, No. 37, talks about a "French-speaking camarilla that surrounded the General."

93. Robert Eibel to author; Zürich, November 30, 1984.
94. Barbey to General; AHQ, December 13, 1940. BAr 5795/456.
95. Verkehrsverlag AG (Rimli) to General; Zürich, December 17, 1940. BAr 5795/456.
96. BAr 5795/456.
97. Barbey 1948, 10.
98. Cf. also Chapter 30 below.
99. Jules Sandoz to author; Biel, September 11, 1986.
100. General's Personal Staff; AHQ, August 27, 1944. BAr 5795/560.
101. Denis van Berchem to author; Vandoeuvres, March 13, 1985.
102. Cf. Chapter 15 below.
103. Cf. especially Chapter 22 below.
104. Böschenstein 1978, 283 f.
105. Jürg Wille to Däniker; December 3, 1940. AfZ Nl Dä 80.
106. Huber to General; AHQ, June 28, 1941. Personal and confidential. BAr 5795/86. Cf. Chapter 23 below.
107. General to Huber; AHQ, July 2, 1941. Personal and confidential. BAr 5795/86.
108. Guisan [1946], 257; Huber [1946], 430. Cf. also Chapter 36 below.
109. Guisan 1953, 51.
110. Ibid., 52.
111. Corbat to Labhart; Zürich, July 26, 1946. BAr Nl La.
112. Constam to Kobelt; Bern, August 31, 1946. BAr 5795/207.
113. Frick to Kobelt; Bern, August 31, 1946. Carbon copy. BAr Nl La.
114. Rudolph Iselin, *Erinnerungen und Erlebnisse*. Basel 1949, 123. Privately published book.
115. Minutes of the Senate Committee dealing with the General's Report, op. cit., 43. According to the regulations of 1961, a general staff officer will be assigned to the General's office in a future emergency. Group for General Staff Service (Froidevaux) to author; Bern, June 5, 1989.

Chapter 11: Investigation of the Front Movement

1. Minutes of the Briefing; Bern, April 29, 1940, 6. Confidential. BAr 27/14151,1.
2. Ibid, 5, and handwritten notes by Huber on the subject.
3. Minutes of the meeting on fighting anti-state propaganda in the armed forces; Bern, April 6, 1940. Confidential. PKAr AG.
4. Handwritten notes; no date [approx. April/May, 1940]. BAr 5795/85.
5. Order re: investigation of officers who are members of the so-called Front movement; AHQ, May 10, 1940. Confidential. BAr 5795/342.
6. Diary of the army staff, May 7, 1940. Confidential. BAr 27/14140. I personally saw the list of names on an earlier occasion at the Federal Archives, but by 1989 they were missing.
7. General to Minger; AHQ, May 21, 1940. BAr 5795/342.
8. Guisan [1946], 214.
9. Huber to General; AHQ, June 16, 1940. BAr 5795/468.
10. Overview, no date. BAr 5795/468.
11. Paul Schmid-Ammann, *Nation*, June 8, 1939, in *Mahnrufe in die Zeit*, op. cit., 88.
12. Decision by the Federal Council re: ban of anti-state propaganda in the armed forces, dated December 4, 1939. BAr.
13. Stämpfli to army staff (Logoz); Bern, November 16, 1939. BAr 27/11197.
14. General to Minger; AHQ, July 15, 1940. Confidential. Copy. AfZ Nl Dä 20,1.
15. Guisan [1946], 214 f.
16. Order re: the officers of the so-called Front Movement; AHQ, June 24, 1940. Confidential. BAr.
17. Guisan 1953, 135. No other indications were found regarding this incident.
18. Wille to General; HQ, May 31, 1940. Carbon copy. ArMa.
19. Bircher to army command; Div. HQ, July 25, 1940. BAr.
20. Däniker to General; Walenstadt, July 22, 1940. Personal and confidential. AfZ Nl Dä 20,1.
21. Däniker to General; Schuls, August 6, 1940. AfZ Nl Dä 20,1.

22. General to Däniker; AHQ, August 9, 1940. Personal and confidential. AfZ Nl Dä 20,1. Däniker wrote in an annotation to this letter, "someone's discipline is called upon when all other arguments have failed!"
23. Wehrli to his parents; May 19, 1940. ArWe.
24. Wille to General; HQ, August 31, 1940. Personal. Carbon copy. ArMa.
25. General to Wille; AHQ, October 4, 1940. Personal. ArMa.
26. Wille, annotations on the General's letter of October 4, 1940; HQ, October 8, 1940. ArMa.
27. Wille to Däniker; July 19, 1940. Handwritten. AfZ Nl Dä 80.
28. K[obelt], note for file; September 2, 1941. BAr 5800/2.
29. Files on the investigation of the Front Movement. BAr.
30. Files of the Federal Prosecutor's office. Cf. Chapter 26.
31. Minutes of the committee of the Council of States on the General's post-war report, op. cit., 39.
32. Minutes of the committee of the National Council on the General's post-war report, op. cit., 49.
33. Chief of the General Staff (Labhart), Directions re: combating anti-state propaganda in the armed forces; AHQ, December 9, 1939. BAr.
34. Huber to police section of the territorial service; AHQ, July 9, 1940. BAr.
35. General to Minger; AHQ, July 15, 1940. BAr.
36. Military Attorney General (Eugster) to General; Bern, April 25, 1944. BAr.
37. Alfred Ernst, "Der 'Offiziersbund' von 1940," in *CH: Ein Lesebuch*, ed. by the Swiss Federal Council, Bern 1975, 257.
38. Wille to Däniker; Mariafeld, June 30, 1940. AfZ Nl Dä 72,1.
39. Ernst to Chief Justice of the 8th division (Herzog); Worb, August 8, 1940, 4. BAr 27/5330.
40. Ibid., 6.
41. Hans Hausamann, *Rund um den Nachrichtendienst im zweiten Weltkrieg, von einem Nachrichtenoffizier gesehen.* Teufen, October 1947, 81 f. Unpublished manuscript. BAr 5800/1.
42. Ibid., 91 f.
43. Hans Hausamann, *Offiziersbewegung 1940.* Written 1946. Carbon copy, 4.
44. "Wochenberichte über die Stimmung im Volk [Ernst von Schenck], July 28, 1940 – August 4, 1940. BAr 4450/6105.
45. Minutes of the briefing of October 19, 1940 at the General's command post, 2 f. BAr 5795/145.
46. Guisan [1946], 215. Cf. Chapter 26.
47. Jean Rudolf von Salis, *Grenzüberschreitungen: Ein Lebensbericht,* part 2, 1939-1978. Zürich 1979,48.
48. E. Wehrli to his mother; June 30, 1940. ArWe.
49. Zimmermann 1980, 140 ff.
50. Hans-Ulrich Jost, "Bedrohung und Enge (1914-1945)," in *Geschichte der Schweiz und der Schweizer,* vol. 3, Basel/Frankfurt a.M. 1983, 175.

Chapter 12: Alert During Germany's 1940 Western Campaign

1. Etter to Federal Military Department, April 15, 1940. BAr 5795/85.
2. Minutes of Federal Council meeting, April 18, 1940. Excerpt. BAr 27/13001.
3. Directions concerning the behavior of reservists in the event of a surprise attack; AHQ, April 18, 1940. The full text is published in Kurz 1965 a, 56.
4. Jost Adam, *Die Haltung der Schweiz gegenüber dem nationalsozialistischen Deutschland im Jahre 1940.* Ph.D. thesis, Mainz 1972 [n.p., n.d., Bielefeld 1973], 31.
5. Bonjour, *Neutralität* IV, op. cit., 70 ff.
6. General to direct subordinate commanders; AHQ, April 18, 1940. BAr 27/13001.
7. General to Commander of Air Force and Anti-Aircraft Defense; AHQ, April 21, 1940. BAr 27/13001.
8. Guisan 1953, 103.
9. Barbey 1967, 123. "X" was probably Lieutenant-Colonel Schafroth, the deputy of Chief of Intelligence Masson.
10. [Charles] Daniel, Summary notes on the military risks (1939-1945); AHQ, 7/23/1945. BAr 5795/202.

11. R[oger] Masson, "Unser Nachrichtendienst im Zweiten Weltkrieg." In Kurz 1959, p. 74.
12. Minutes of the briefing of April 29, 1940, pp. 3 f. Confidential. BAr 27/14151,1.
13. Ibid., 6.
14. General to Head of Military Department (Minger); AHQ, May 4, 1940. Confidential. BAr 27/563.
15. Guisan 1953, 100. The Federal Council's decree on local civil defense units was dated September 16, 1940 and went into effect retroactively.
16. Instructions on organizing steps against saboteurs, airborne troops, and armored troops making incursions; AHQ, May 12, 1940. BAr 5795/342. The full text is published in Kurz 1965 a, 60 ff.
17. Diary of the General's Bureau [sic], May 9, 1940. According to the diary, Masson was with the General from 11:35 to 14:45, Huber from 17:00 to 17:55, and Dollfus from 17:40 to 18:45 hours.
18. Diary of the Army Staff, op. cit., May 10, 1940.
19. Guisan [1946], 26 ff.
20. Diary of the General's Bureau, May 10, 1940.
21. Barbey 1967, May 10, 1940, 137.
22. Guisan [1946], 202.
23. Huber [1946], 51 ff. Cf. Chapter 7 above.
24. Order of the day; AHQ, May 11, 1940. BAr 5795/170. The full text is published in Kurz 1965 a, 58.
25. Barbey 1967, Friday, May 10, 1940, 137.
26. Diary of the Army Staff, night of May 10-11, 1940.
27. Intelligence service of the army staff to Chief of General Staff; AHQ, May 10, 1940. Confidential. BAr.
28. Barbey 1967, Monday, May 13, 1940, 140.
29. Ibid., Tuesday, May 14, 1940, 141.
30. Paul Hausherr, *Feldgraue Tage: Erinnerungen aus den Jahren 1935–1945*. Baden 1975, 44 ff.
31. Masson 1959, 74.
32. [Marcel] Pilet-Golaz, "Aperçu destiné à M. le Conseiller fédéral Max Petitpierre, Chef du Département politique sur les dangers auxquels la Suisse fut exposée au cours de la guerre mondiale 1939–1945"; September 1945, 13 f. BAr 2809/1,4.
33. Max Iklé to author; Küsnacht (ZH), March 9, 1989.
34. Germann [1977], 67.
35. Hentsch to General; HQ, May 29, 1940. Copy. ArMa.
36. Wille to General; HQ, May 31, 1940. BAr 5795/85.
37. Kreis 1976, 201.
38. Diary of the Army Staff, night of May 14–15, 1940.
39. Cf. Chapter 18 below.
40. Robert Eibel to author; Zürich, November 30, 1984.
41. General to Huber; AHQ, May 12, 1940. BAr 5795.
42. Diary of the General's Bureau, May 14 and May 15, 1940. BAr 5795/51.
43. Army Staff, Intelligence Service (Masson); May 15, 1940, 09:15 hours. BAr 5795/328. Gonard annotated next to the last sentence, "they are available now."
44. Du Pasquier, Journal, op. cit., Thursday, May 16, 1940.
45. Minutes of Chief of General Staff's briefing, May 15, 1940, 10:40 to 12:40 hours. Confidential. BAr 27/14151,1.
46. Ibid.
47. Order to the Armed Forces; AHQ, May 15, 1940. "To be communicated to all combat troops right away." BAr 5795/170. Cf. illustration.
48. Order of the Day [no date, May/June 1940]. BAr 5795/170. Two documents were attached to the drafts: De Gaulle's 1940 Manifesto, and excerpts from a speech by General Gort, Commander of the British expeditionary corps in France.
49. Cf. illustration.
50. Daniel, Summary notes, op. cit., 5.

51. Guisan [1946], 27, 203.
52. Guisan 1953, 110; Guisan [1947], 10.
53. Perrin 1986, 31.
54. Köcher to Ministry of Foreign Affairs; Bern, May 22, 1940, telegram. Copy. BAr EDI 1005/2.
55. Pilet-Golaz 1945, 14.
56. Ibid., 15.
57. Ulrich von Hassel, *Vom anderen Deutschland.* Zürich/Freiburg i. Br. 1946, 151 ff. Von Hassel was one of the conspirators attempting to assassinate Hitler on July 20, 1944; he was executed thereafter.
58. Quoted by Heinz Bütler, *"Wach auf, Schweizervolk!": Die Schweiz zwischen Frontismus, Verrat und Selbstbehauptung, 1914–1940.* Bern 1980, 174 ff.
59. E. Wehrli to his parents; May 12, 1940, 18:30 hours. ArWe.
60. Ibid., May 19, 1940, 15:00 hours. ArWe.
61. General Management of Postal Service (Müri) to Pilet-Golaz; Bern, June 23, 1940. BAr 2809/1,5.
62. Guisan [1946], 28.
63. Ibid., 29.
64. Minutes of Chief of General Staff's briefing; May 10, 1940, 18:30 hours. Confidential. BAr 27/14151,1.
65. Handwritten notes [no date, approx. May/June 1940]. BAr 5795/85.
66. Operations Order No. 4; AHQ, May 15, 1940. Confidential. BAr 5795/291.
67. Samuel Gonard, "Die strategischen Probleme der Schweiz im Zweiten Weltkrieg," in Kurz 1959, 46.
68. E.g. Meurant 1976, 671.
69. E.g. Peter Dürrenmatt, *Kleine Geschichte der Schweiz während des Zweiten Weltkrieges,* Zürich 1949; by the same author, *Schweizer Geschichte,* Zürich 1963, 686; Sigmund Widmer, *Illustrierte Geschichte der Schweiz,* Zürich 1965, 432.
70. Guisan [1946], 27 ff.
71. Huber [1946], 15 ff.
72. Christian Vetsch, *Aufmarsch gegen die Schweiz: Der deutsche "Fall Gelb" — Irreführung der Schweizer Armee 1939/40.* Ph.D. thesis, Zürich 1973. Cf. Chapter 14 below.
73. Jules Sandoz to author; Biel, September 11, 1986.
74. Barbey 1948, 16.
75. Denis de Rougemont, *Journal d'une époque, 1926–1946,* [n.p., Paris] 1968, 424, 426 ff. *Gazette de Lausanne* June 17, 1940.
76. Gonard 1971, 479 ff.
77. Minutes of Chief of General Staff's briefing; AHQ, June 4, 1940, 1 f. Confidential. BAr 27/14151,1.
78. General, "Note sur l'appel éventuel à une coopération alliée;" AHQ, June 13, 1940. Confidential and strictly personal. BAr 5560 B.
79. Cf. Chapter 9 above.
80. General to Huber; AHQ, May 25, 1940. Personal, confidential. BAr 5560.
81. Minutes of Chief of General Staff's briefing; June 16, 1940. Confidential. BAr 27/14151,1.
82. Guisan 1953, 115.
83. Heinz Guderian, *Erinnerungen eines Soldaten.* Heidelberg 1951, 118. When Guderian reported his arrival at the Swiss border to the Führer's headquarters, his message was believed to be wrong. Guderian explained, "Hitler reacted by asking, 'your message is based on a mistake. You must be talking about Pontailler-sur-Saône.' However, I replied, 'no mistake. Have arrived at Swiss border at Pontarlier,' which reassured the supreme command of the *Wehrmacht.*"
84. Minutes of Chief of General Staff's briefing; June 16, 1940. Confidential. BAr 27/14151,1.
85. Ibid., June 20, 1940, 14:30 hours.
86. R[ené] Probst, "Flüchtlinge und Internierte in der Schweiz," in Kurz 1959, 223.
87. Guisan [1946], 31.
88. Köcher to Ministry of Foreign Affairs; Bern July 2, 1940. Published in Bonjour, *Neutralität VII,* op. cit., 98.
89. Guisan 1953, 73, 77.

90. Jules Sandoz to author; Biel, September 11, 1986.
91. Diary of the Army Staff, June 20, 1940.
92. Daniel, Summary notes, op. cit., 2.
93. Concerning the problem of returning internees, cf. Chapter 14 below.
94. Diary of the Army Staff, Saturday, June 22, 1940.
95. Report by the Personal Staff [III], op. cit., 4.
96. Johannes von Muralt (born 1877, died 1947), instructor in the artillery. Divisional commander after 1931. President of the Swiss Red Cross. On December 31, 1941, the Federal Commissioner's Office for Internment Matters became a section of the Adjutant's Office of the General; in the summer of 1944, it was placed under the Military Department.
97. Ludwig [1957], 185.
98. General to President Paderewski; AHQ, June 23, 1940. BAr 5795/336.
99. Diary of the Army Staff, June 22, 1940.
100. General to Pilet-Golaz; AHQ, June 16, 1940. Quoted in Ludwig [1957], 182.
101. Minutes of Chief of General Staff's briefing, June 16, 1940, 17:00 hours. Confidential. BAr 27/14151,1.
102. Quoted in Ludwig [1957], 184.
103. Pilet-Golaz 1945, 19.
104. Diary of the Army Staff, June 21, 1940. Report by Liaison Officer, First Lieutenant Vogel.
105. Minutes of army briefing; Bern, June 22, 1940. Confidential. BAr 27/14111.
106. General to Minger; AHQ, June 21, 1940. BAr 5800/2.
107. Ernst 1971, 68.
108. Huber to General; AHQ, June 20-21, 1940. Confidential. BAr 27/17396. Quoted in Roesch 1986, 42.
109. Guisan [1946], 33.
110. Ibid., 104 ff.
111. Diary of the Army Staff, June 4, 1940, 16:15 hours, message by front group. Lieutenant Rudolf Rickenbacher died during the incident because his parachute got caught. During later combats, four other pilots were killed: First Lieutenant Emilio Gürtler (June 8, 1940); Lieutenant Rudolf Meuli (June 8, 1940); Lieutenant Otto Link (June 20, 1941); and First Lieutenant Paul Treu (September 5, 1944). Report by the Commander of the Air Force and the Anti-Aircraft Defense, op. cit., 30 ff., 50, 131.
112. Walo Hörning, "Der Einsatz der Schweizerischen Luftwaffe im Neutralitätsdienst," in Kurz 1959, 177.
113. Tamaro to Foreign Ministry; Bern, June 5, 1940. Copy. BAr EDI 1005/2.
114. Hörning 1959, 175.
115. Report by the Federal Council to the Federal Parliament on anti-democratic activities conducted by Swiss and other nationals in connection with the war of 1939–1945 (based on a motion by Parliament Member Boerlin), part I, 12/28/1945, 119. Documents about this attempted sabotage are published in Bonjour, Neutralität VII, 99 f.
116. Minutes of Chief of General Staff's briefing; June 16, 1940. Confidential. BAr 27/14151,1.
117. Barbey 1948, 18.
118. Guisan [1946], 33.
119. Pilet-Golaz 1945, 19.
120. Köcher to Swiss Department of Foreign Affairs; Bern, June 5, 1940. Published in Bonjour, Neutralität VIII, op. cit., 83 ff.
121. Köcher to Swiss Department of Foreign Affairs; Bern, June 19, 1940. Published in Bonjour, Neutralität VIII, 92 ff.
122. Barbey 1948, 24.
123. Cf. Chapter 14 below. On the incidents in the air in May/June 1940 and their diplomatic consequences, cf. Ernst Wetter, Duell der Flieger und der Diplomaten. Frauenfeld 1987.
124. P. Schmidt, an interpreter, described the capitulation negotiations from his own perspective in his memoirs entitled, Statist auf diplomatischer Bühne 1923–1945. Bonn 1949, 484 ff.
125. Handwritten notes on the briefing with the corps commanders, June 22, 1940. BAr 5795/85. The details of the talks are described in Chapter 17 below.

126. Wille, Notes, June 22, 1940, 14:30 hours. Handwritten. ArMa.
127. Guisan [1946], 34.
128. Germann [1977], 68.
129. E. Wehrli to his parents; May 19, 1940. ArWe.

Chapter 13: Orders to the Armed Forces in June 1940
1. Cf. Chapter 12 above.
2. Order of the day; AHQ, June 3, 1940. BAr 27/14112.
3. Order to the Armed Forces; AHQ, June 3, 1940. BAr 5795/170.
4. General to the commanders of army units; AHQ, June 3, 1940. BAr 5795/170.
5. Nobs to Gut; Zürich, June 13, 1940. Carbon copy BAr Nl No.
6. BAr 5795/170. In a front-page editorial, Editor-in-Chief Willy Bretscher of the *Neue Zürcher Zeitung* (June 6, 1940) also thanked the General for "these right words at the right time." Published in Willy Bretscher, *Im Sturm von Krise und Krieg*. Zürich 1987, 253 ff.
7. Kurz 1965 a, 71 ff. published both orders verbatim; Bonjour, *Neutralität* VII, op. cit., 38 f. published the Order to the Armed Forces, and so did Chapuisat 1950, 77 ff.
8. Guisan [1946], 205 ff.
9. Guisan 1953, 112 ff.
10. Otto Weiss, *General Dufour als Heerführer*. Bern 1939, 50 ff., 66, 208 ff., 214 ff. Carl Helbling, *General Ulrich Wille*. Zürich 1957, 222 ff., 239 ff., 268 ff.
11. Edmond Grin, sermon delivered on April 12, 1960 BAr Nl Go. Professor E. Grin (born 1895, died 1977) was married to a first cousin of General Guisan. Mrs. M. Eglin-Grin to author; Basel, June 27, 1988.
12. Grin to his wife; May 28, 1940, 14:00 hours. Nl Gr.
13. Ibid., May 31, 1940, 21:30 hours.
14. Ibid.
15. Wille to General, personal memorandum; HQ, May 31, 1940, 1. BAr 5795/85.
16. Ibid., 6.
17. Huber to General; AHQ, June 3, 1940. Personal, confidential. BAr 5795/85.
18. Ibid. Gonard annotated, "this is just to make sure that destruction is executed on a broad scale."
19. Odermatt 1983, 45.
20. Confidential instructions to the commanders of the army units and troops; AHQ, June 5, 1940. BAr 27/14306.
21. Wille to General; Main Section III, May 22, 1940. Draft ArMa.
22. Wille, handwritten notes, May 23, 1940.
23. Wille, personal memorandum, op. cit., 7.
24. General to Wille; AHQ, June 5, 1940. ArMa.

Chapter 14: After France's Defeat
1. General to Commanders of 1st to 4th Army Corps and 9th Division; AHQ, June 23, 1940. Confidential. BAr 5795/303.
2. Minutes of briefing; Bern, June 22, 1940. Confidential. BAr 5795/145.
3. Minutes of briefing by Commander of 2nd Army Corps; Zofingen, June 24, 1940 Confidential. BAr 5795/145.
4. Order re: regrouping of the armed forces; AHQ, June 25, 1940 Confidential. BAr 27/14192,3.
5. Guisan [1946], 34. On the new strategic concept, cf. Chapter 17 below.
6. Ernst Schürch, *Als die Freiheit in Frage stand*. Bern 1946, 12.
7. The full text of the speech was published in Bonjour, *Neutralität* IV, op. cit., 117 f. in French, and in Kurz 1965 a, 74 ff in German.
8. Bonjour 1981 c, 225.
9. On the making of the radio address, cf. Bonjour, *Neutralität* IV, 115 ff.
10. Minutes of the Federal Council meeting, June 25, 1940. BAr.
11. Handwritten notes, June 23, 1940. BAr 2809/1,4.

12. E.g. A. Rütschi, Zürich, June 11, 1940; former National Councilor Duft, St. Gallen, June 14, 1940; Dr. Ed. Werdenberg, Davos, June 17, 1940. BAr 2809/1,5.
13. Wochenbericht, op. cit., June 25 – July 1, 1940.
14. Jules Sandoz to author; Biel, September 11, 1986.
15. Quoted in Markus Hohl, *Der Rütlirapport.* Seminar paper at the University of Bern [typed, no date], 9. BAr M 34.
16. De Rougemont 1968, June 26, 1940, 429 f.
17. Labhart, Diary, op. cit., June 25, 1940.
18. Minutes of army briefing; AHQ, October 19, 1940, 4. BAr 27/14126.
19. Alfred Ernst, *Zur Geschichte des "Offiziersbundes" von 1940.* January 1963 [1st version], 3. ArSchü. The quoted passage was crossed out in the draft and was omitted in the fair copy.
20. Ibid., 3 f.
21. Wartenweiler to army command; in the field, July 3, 1940. BAr 27/9076.
22. Hausamann 1947, 91.
23. *Wochenbericht,* op. cit., June 25–July 1, 1940, 3.
24. Feldmann to General; Bern, March 3, 1943, 3. Personal and confidential. BAr 5795/333.
25. Minutes of National Council Proxy Committee meeting, June 26–27, 1940, 6 ff., 18 f. BAr.
26. Grimm to Nobs; Bern, June 27, 1940. BAr Nl No.
27. Adam [1973], 315.
28. Minutes of closed Socialist Party meeting; Bern July 3, 1940, 7. SAr 1.110.30.
29. Ibid., 6.
30. Minutes of Socialist Party leadership meeting; June 29, 1940, 1 f. SAr.
31. Ibid., 3 f.
32. Du Pasquier, Diary, op. cit., June 25, [1940]. BAr.
33. Christian Gasser, *Der Gotthard-Bund: Eine schweizerische Widerstandsbewegung.* Bern 1984, 21.
34. Gautschi 1978, 375 f.
35. E. Wehrli to his mother; June 30, 1940. ArWe.
36. Grimm to Nobs; Bern, June 27, 1940. BAr Nl No.
37. Oeri to Federal Council; Basel, July 24, 1940, 4. Copy BAr Nl Wet. Federal Councilor Wetter annotated this passage of Oeri's letter with the phrase, "a bit much!"
38. Wille to Däniker; Mariafeld, June 30, 1940. AfZ Nl Dä 2.1.
39. *Wochenbericht,* op. cit., June 25–July 1, 1940.
40. Ernst Leonhardt, *Schweizervolk! Deine Schicksalsstunde ist gekommen! Was soll nun werden? Eine Abrechnung.* Edited by "Pressedienst der Schweizerischen Erneuerung," July 15, 1940, 30 f. BAr 5795/342.
41. Ibid., 31.
42. General to Head of Military Department, attn. Federal Council; AHQ, June 25, 1940. BAr 27/14111.
43. Bracher to Minger; AHQ, June 29, 1940. BAr 27/14111.
44. Federal Council to General; Bern, July 2, 1940 BAr 5795/151.
45. Barbey 1948, July 4, 1940, 26 f.
46. B[urgunder], regarding instructions to the General; Bern, June 29, 1940. Handwritten note. BAr 27/14111.
47. Cf. Chapter 17 below.
48. Order of the day; AHQ, June 28, 1940. BAr. Published in Kurz 1965 a, 79.
49. Barbey 1948, June 26, 1940, 24.
50. Guisan 1953, 116. Guisan [1946], 208.
51. Order to the armed forces; AHQ, July 2, 1940. BAr. Published in Kurz 1965 a, 79 f.
52. Order re: demobilizing part of the armed forces; AHQ, July 25, 1940. BAr 5795/303. Odermatt 1983, 60 f., and Kurz 1978, 181, mentioned the same numbers of troops. The discharged troops included the territorial reserves, territorial troops, and large parts of the artillery and special units.
53. Guisan 1953, 117.
54. Order re: demobilizing part of the armed forces, op. cit.
55. Roesch 1986, 62.

56. Hans Rudolf Kurz, *Operationsplanung Schweiz.* Thun 1974, 34.
57. Roesch 1986, 42.
58. Supreme Command of the [German] Armed Forces, Situation Report West; No. 406, July 30, 1940 and No. 413, August 28, 1940. Confidential. Photocopy. BAr 27/14348.
59. Hans Rudolf Fuhrer, "Von der Planstudie 'Tannenbaum' zum Märzalarm 1943," in *IPZ-Information* No. 3, Zürich 1980.
60. Daniel Bourgeois, *Le Troisième Reich et la Suisse 1933 - 1945* Neuchâtel 1974, 113 ff.; Vetsch 1973, 16 ff.
61. Ernst 1971, 68.
62. Quoted in Gisela Blau, ". . . aber nicht nur die Franzosen flohen vor den Nazis," in *Schweizer Illustrierte* No. 20, May 12, 1980, 37.
63. Hans Senn, "Die Haltung Italiens zum 'Fall Schweiz' im Jahre 1940," in *Neue Zürcher Zeitung,* May 14–15, 1988, No. 111.
64. Senn 1988 a, 251.
65. Guisan [1946], 163 f.; Huber [1946], 240; Hans Rudolf Kurz, *Nachrichtenzentrum Schweiz.* Frauenfeld/Stuttgart 1972, 107; Fuhrer 1980, 25.
66. Roesch 1986, 5 ff.
67. Supreme Command of the [German] Armed Forces, Notes for a presentation on an attack against Switzerland, June 25, 1940; draft of "Operation Tannenbaum," September 6, 1940. Copies. BAr 5800/1.
68. Cf. illustration.
69. Roesch 1986, 64.
70. Henry Picker, *Hitlers Tischgespräche im Führerhauptquartier.* 3rd, extended edition, Stuttgart 1976, 420.
71. Prisi to General; HQ, June 16, 1940. Personal and confidential. BAr 5795/328.
72. Hans Frölicher, Report to Federal Councilor Petitpierre on the tense moments in German-Swiss relations; Bern, July 10, 1945, 3 f. BAr 2809/1,4.
73. Cf. Chapter 12 above.
74. Minutes of the meeting of July 1, 1940, 3.15 p.m. at the Federal President's BAr 5795/160. The four pages of minutes were handwritten by B. Barbey. Published in Gauye 1978, 29-32.
75. The full text of the Federal Council's verbal note of July 1, 1940 was published in Bonjour, *Neutralität* VII, op. cit., 96.
76. Minutes of the meeting of July 1, 1940, op. cit., 3 f.
77. Bonjour, *Neutralität* IV, op. cit., 102.
78. Köcher to Foreign Affairs Office; Bern, July 2, 1940. Copy. BAr EDI 1005/2. Bonjour, *Neutralität* VII, op. cit., 97 f.
79. Frölicher, Report to Federal Councilor Petitpierre, op. cit., 3.
80. Bonjour, *Neutralität* IV, op. cit., 98. In the fall of 1940, Switzerland also returned the confiscated aircraft to Germany.
81. Hausamann 1947, 90.
82. Waibel to Masson; September 15, 1940. BAr 27/9943.
83. Frölicher, Report to Federal Councilor Petitpierre, op. cit., 3 f.
84. Hausamann 1947, 90.
85. Bonjour, *Neutralität* IV, op. cit., 109.
86. On economic pressure, cf. Bonjour, *Neutralität* VI, op. cit., 201 ff, 223 ff., and Robert U. Vogler, *Die Wirtschaftsverhandlungen zwischen der Schweiz und Deutschland 1940 und 1941.* Ph.D. thesis, Zürich 1983.
87. Hans Senn, "Schweizerische Dissuasionsstrategie im Zweiten Weltkrieg," in Bindschedler et al. 1985, 202.
88. Guisan [1946], 10.
89. General to Head of Military Department (Minger), attn. Federal Council; AHQ, July 4, 1940, 3. BAr 27/14274.
90. Odermatt 1983, 70, footnote 56. Cf. Chapter 19 below.
91. General to Head of Military Department (Minger), attn. Federal Council; AHQ, July 4, 1940. BAr 27/14274.

92. Ibid., July 18, 1940. Confidential BAr 27/14274.
93. Ibid.
94. Report, July 8, 1940, 21.00 hours, and July 18, 1940, 20.00 hours. AfZ Nl Ha.

Chapter 15: The Officers' Conspiracy

1. Guisan [1946], 215 ff.
2. Bonjour, *Neutralität* IV, op. cit., 181 ff.
3. Max Häni, *Lebenslauf.* Manuscript, Bern 1979, 32.
4. Waibel 1963, 9.
5. Gerhart Schürch to author; Bern, August 8, 1985.
6. Minutes of examination 1st Lt. Schürch; Bern, August 13, 1940. BAr E/5330.
7. Gerhart Schürch, "Notizen über meine Beiligung an der Offiziersverschwörung 1940." Bern, February 18, 1963, 6. ArSchü.
8. Alfred Ernst, "Der 'Offiziersbund' von 1940," in *Festschrift zum 75. Geburtstag von Hans Oprecht,* op. cit., 125 ff.
9. Ernst 1963 a, 13.
10. Hausamann [1946], 1, 10.
11. Fritz Wanner to author; Kilchberg, August 5, 1985.
12. Ernst to Lützelschwab; Schwenden, February 4, 1946. BAr Nl Lü. Lützelschwab did not get a chance to write the study.
13. Hausamann to Ernst; St. Gallen, February 7, 1963. Carbon copy ArSchü.
14. Gerhart Schürch to author; Bern, August 8, 1985.
15. Dr. Gerhart Schürch kindly made available to this author the only existing copy of the original draft, which is 18 pages long. It is herein referred to as "Ernst 1963 a."
16. August R[udolf] Lindt, "Aktiver Zeuge der Zeit," in *Ex Libris* No. 4, Zürich 1984, 16. Interview by A.A. Häsler.
17. August R. Lindt to author; Bern, May 17, 1985.
18. Gasser 1984, 23.
19. Minutes of examination Capt. Hausamann; August 4, 1940. BAr E/5330.
20. Ernst 1963 a, 8.
21. Waibel 1963, 9.
22. Hausamann [1946], 9 ff.
23. Ernst 1963 a, 4.
24. Cf. Chapter 22 below.
25. Ernst 1963 a, 7 ff.
26. Minutes of examination Capt. Ernst; August 3, 1940, BAr E/5330.
27. Gerhart Schürch to author; Bern, May 21, 1985.
28. Hausamann to Ernst Schürch; in the field, July 17, 1940. AfZ Nl Schü 3.1.
29. Ernst 1963 a, 7 ff.
30. Ibid., 8.
31. Ernst to Senior Judge of 8th division (Herzog); Worb, August 4, 1940. BAr E/5330.
32. Schürch 1963, 5.
33. Conversation General/Däniker; AHQ, August 25, 1941. Steel tape recording, 20. Confidential. BAr 27/4738.
34. Cf. Chapter 21 below.
35. Minutes of examination Lt.-Col. Werder; Aarau, August 6, 1940. BAr E/5330.
36. Fritz Wanner to author; Kilchberg, August 5, 1985.
37. Files BAr E/5330, 1982/1, vol. 9.
38. Minutes of examination Capt. Ernst, August 13, 1940. BAr E/5330.
39. Minutes of examination Capt. Uhlmann; Zürich, August 8, 1940. BAr E/5330.
40. Minutes of examination Capt. Heberlein; Schwyz, 8/7/1940. BAr E/5330.
41. Presentation, July 21, 1940. BAr E/5330.
42. "Zur heutigen Lage," n.d. [before July 21, 1940]. BAr E/5330.
43. Minutes of examination Capt. Uhlmann; Zürich, August 8, 1940. BAr E/5330.

44. Hausamann to Kobelt; Teufen, January 15, 1946, 4 ff. BAr 5800/2.
45. Gerhart Schürch, "Wächter - Denker - Mahner," in *Gedenkschrift zum 10. Todestag von Hans Hausamann.* St. Gallen 1984, 14 ff.
46. Minutes of examination Capt. Hausamann; Lucerne, September 5, 1940_*Gedenkschrift zum 10. Todestag von Hans Hausamann.* St. Gallen 1984, 14 ff. BAr E/5330.
47. Typed manuscript. An attached note reads, "the presentation was made on July 21, 1940 at the premises of the Schweizerhof in Lucerne." ArSchü.
48. Ibid., 5 ff.
49. Ernst to Senior Judge of 8th division (Herzog); Worb, August 4, 1940. BAr E/5330.
50. Minutes of examination Capt. Ernst; August 13, 1940. BAr E/5330.
51. Minutes of examination 1st Lt. Schürch; Bern, August 13, 1940. BAr E/5330.
52. Minutes of examination Capt. Häberli; Bern, August 14, 1940. BAr E/5330.
53. Minutes of examination Capt. Heberlein; August 3, 1940. BAr E/5330.
54. Gerhart Schürch to author; Bern, August 8, 1985.
55. Minutes of examination Capt. Burckhardt; Aarau, August 6, 1940. BAr E/5330.
56. Minutes of examination Capt. Wehrli; Bern, August 10, 1940. BAr E/5330.
57. Wehrli to Ernst; Zollikon, July 22, 1940. Confidential. BAr E/5330.
58. Ibid.
59. Wehrli to Däniker; Zollikon, August 18, 1940. AfZ Nl Dä 80.
60. Minutes of examination Capt. Ernst; August 13, 1940. BAr E/5330.
61. Häni 1979, 26.
62. Minutes of examination Capt. Waibel; Lucerne, August 4, 1940 and August 7, 1940. BAr E/5330.
63. Schürch to Ernst; Spiez, July 24, 1940. Confidential. BAr E/5330.
64. Schürch 1963, 6.
65. No. 1 [Ernst] to Lt.-Col. [Werder]; August 1, 1940. BAr E/5330.
66. Special Prosecutor (Hug) to General; Bern, August 17, 1940, 9. BAr E/5330.
67. To the members in charge at the army units; command post, July 29, 1940. Confidential, to be burnt immediately. BAr E/5330.
68. Special Prosecutor (Hug) to General; Bern, August 17, 1940, 8. BAr E/5330.
69. Minutes of examination Lt.-Col. Werder; Lucerne, September 5, 1940. BAr E/5330.
70. Ibid.
71. Minutes of examination Capt. Ernst; Lucerne, September 5, 1940. BAr E/5330.
72. Ernst to Senior Judge of 8th Division (Herzog); Worb, August 4, 1940, 6 ff. BAr E/5330.
73. Cf. Chapter 5 above.
74. Ernst to Senior Judge of 8th Division (Herzog); Worb, August 4, 1940, 7. BAr E/5330.
75. Ernst 1963 a, 2 ff.
76. Schürch 1984, 15.
77. No. 1 [Ernst] to Lt.-Col. [Werder]; August 1, 1940. BAr E/5330.
78. Ernst 1963 a, 12 ff.
79. Ernst to Senior Judge of 8th Division (Herzog); Worb, August 4, 1940. BAr E/5330.
80. Minutes of examination Lt.-Col. Werder; Aarau, August 6, 1940. Also, Special Prosecutor (Hug) to General; Bern, August 17, 1940, 9. BAr E/5330.
81. Ernst 1963 a, 14.
82. Ernst, personal notes, n.d. [before August 3, 1940]. BAr E/5330.
83. Ernst 1963 a, 13 ff.
84. Minutes of examination Capt. Heberlein; August 3, 1940. BAr E/5330.
85. Minutes of examination Capt. Hunziker; Zürich, August 8, 1940. BAr E/5330.
86. Hunziker to Intelligence Bureau 1; HQ, July 26, 1940. Confidential. BAr E/5330.
87. Minutes of examination Capt. Heberlein; August 3, 1940. BAr E/5330.
88. Minutes of examination Major Schönenberger; Walenstadt, August 8, 1940. BAr E/5330.
89. Ibid.
90. Labhart, diary, op. cit., Friday, August 2, 1940. BAr Nl La.
91. Ibid., Saturday, August 3, 1940.

92. Ernst 1963 a, 14.
93. Ibid.
94. Ernst to his wife; Worb, August 4, 1940. Copy. BAr E/5330.
95. Ernst to Senior Judge of 8th division (Herzog); Worb, August 4, 1940, 9. BAr E/5330. Hácha, the Czech President at the time, yielded to German pressure in March 1939 without putting up any resistance.
96. Ibid.
97. Minutes of examination Capt. Hausamann; August 4, 1940. BAr E/5330.
98. Ernst 1963 a, 14.
99. August R. Lindt to author; Bern, September 24, 1985. The following is based on what Lindt told me during an interview.
100. Ernst 1963 a, 14.
101. General, Order to carry out a preliminary investigation; AHQ, August 29, 1940. BAr E/5330.
102. Decision by the Military Attorney General (Trüssel); Bern, September 26, 1940. BAr E/5330.
103. Huber to General; AHQ, August 22, 1940. Personal, confidential. BAr 5795/442.
104. General, Decree on sentences; AHQ, October 3, 1940. Personal, confidential. BAr 5795/442 and BAr E/5330. Guisan's account on this matter in his postwar report is not very precise.
105. Huber to General; AHQ, October 3, 1940. BAr 5795/442.
106. Cf. Guisan [1946], 215 ff.
107. Ernst 1963 a, 15.
108. Häni 1979, 26.
109. Gerhart Schürch to author; Bern, May 24, 1985.
110. Hausamann 1947, 80 ff.
111. Waibel 1963, 10.
112. Ernst 1963 a, 15.
113. Ernst to Masson; Thun, October 16, 1940. Copy. ArWa.
114. Ernst to Wanner; Muzzano, October 3, 1940. ArWa.
115. Ernst to Gafner; on duty, July 30, 1945. Personal, confidential. Carbon copy. BAr Nl Er.
116. August R. Lindt to author; Bern, July 15, 1987.
117. Peter Burckhardt to author; Bern, February 10, 1986.
118. Minutes of examination Capt. Heberlein; August 3, 1940. BAr E/5330.
119. Military Attorney General (Trüssel) to General; Bern, September 9, 1940. Personal, confidential. BAr 5795/442.
120. General, Decree; AHQ, September 10, 1940. Personal, confidential. Military Attorney General to take action. BAr 5795/442.
121. Huber to General; AHQ, October 3, 1940. BAr 5795/442.
122. Huber to General; AHQ, January 1, 1941. Personal, confidential. Handwritten. BAr 5795/86.
123. Waibel 1963, 10, 14.
124. Hausamann [1946], 10.
125. Ernst 1963 a, 16.
126. Ernst 1969, 132.
127. Ibid., 133.
128. August R. Lindt to author; Bern, May 17, 1985.
129. Ernst 1963 a, 16.
130. Cf. Chapter 18 below.
131. Schürch 1984, 16.
132. Wille to Wetter; July 9, 1941. Carbon copy. ArMa.
133. Robert Eibel, Lecture at the Archives for Contemporary History; Zürich, November 24, 1984. Idem to author; Zürich, November 30, 1984.
134. Minutes of the National Council Committee dealing with the General's report, op. cit., 49.
135. Mario Andreotti, "Erneuerung eines Mythos," in Staatsbürger No. 3, May 22, 1985.
136. Walde 1983, 169.
137. Schürch 1963, 3.
138. Guisan [1946], 216.

139. It would be worth undertaking a more detailed scientific study on this complex "Officers' Conspiracy."
140. Swiss Association of Non-Commissioned Officers (Cuoni, Möckli), Resolution, July 21, 1940. BAr 5795/175.

Chapter 16: Briefing at the Rütli
1. Guisan [1946], 42.
2. Guisan 1953, 121.
3. Ernst 1963 a, 12.
4. H.R. Kurz, statement made at the AfZ; Zürich, October 24, 1984.
5. Barbey to Christine Gruner; Paris, May 14, 1967. Quoted in Christine Gruner, *Der "Rütlirapport" des Generals vom 25. Juli 1940*. Unpublished seminar paper, Basel 1967/68, appendix. BAr M34.
6. Gauye 1984, 7.
7. Barbey 1948, Tuesday, July 9, 1940, 29.
8. Armand von Ernst to author; Muri near Bern, August 7, 1985.
9. Ernst 1963 a, 12.
10. Guisan [1946], 211.
11. Hohl 1961, 14.
12. Ernst 1963 a, 12.
13. General to directly subordinate commanders; AHQ, July 18, 1940. Confidential. BAr 27/14124. Cf. illustration.
14. Alfred Schaefer, Interview in *Brückenbauer* No. 31, July 31, 1985.
15. Barbey 1948, 31; and Guisan [1946], 211.
16. Wilhelm Lützelschwab, "Notizen zur Geschichte des 'Offiziersbundes' von 1940"; March 1963. BAr Nl Lü.
17. *Die Woche* No. 30, 1960. Quoted in Hohl 1961, 15.
18. Barbey 1948, Thursday, July 25, 1940, 31.
19. Edmund Wehrli to author; Zürich, August 2, 1985; also Julius Stocker in *Die Woche*, 7/31/1960.
20. Walter Dieterle in *Die Woche*, July 31, 1960.
21. Lake Lucerne Navigation company (Ziegler, Buchmann) to author; Lucerne, January 8, 1988.
22. Ibid.
23. Hohl 1961, 37.
24. Du Pasquier, diary, op. cit., July 31, 1940.
25. Otto Kellerhals, diary notes; July 25, 1940. ArKh.
26. Jos. Ziegler-Zgraggen in *Die Woche*, July 31, 1960.
27. Guisan [1946], 210 f.
28. Barbey 1948, 31.
29. Ch. Gruner 1967/68, 10; and Hans Bracher in *Die Woche*, July 31, 1960. Bracher was also mistaken when he stated that it was Prisi, "the oldest serving corps commander in whose territory the Rütli was located," who reported the officers present.
30. Jules Sandoz to author; Biel, October 4, 1985. Also Edmund Wehrli to author; Zürich, August 2, 1985.
31. Kellerhals, diary notes, July 25, 1940.
32. Cf. photograph XXII.
33. Barbey 1948, Thursday, 7/25/1940, 31 f.
34. Guisan [1946], 211.
35. Diary of Mountain Infantry Regiment 15 (Lt. Col. Trachsel); July 25, 1940. BAr E 5970/130. Quoted in Gauye 1984, 11.
36. Du Pasquier, diary, op. cit., July 31, 1940.
37. Otto Kellerhals to author; Bern, August 28, 1985.
38. Edmund Wehrli, Interview with Gisela Blau, "... da fühlten sich viele Schweizer verraten," in *Schweizer Illustrierte*, May 19, 1980, No. 21, 70.

39. Edmund Wehrli, "Le rapport du Rütli vu par un témoin," in *24 heures*, April 11, 1985.
40. Edmund Wehrli to author; Zürich, August 2, 1985.
41. Hohl 1961, 21. Quoted in Gauye 1984, 12.
42. Jules Sandoz to author; Biel September 11, 1986.
43. Labhart, diary, op. cit., July 25, 1940.
44. Jules Sandoz to author; Biel, September 11, 1986.
45. Marguth to Huber; Bern, November 4, 1955. Handwritten. BAr 5795/173.
46. Note by Director of Federal Archives L. Haas, June 22, 1962 BAr. Cf. Bonjour, *Neutralität* IV, op. cit., 155.
47. Gauye 1984. The entire text of the manuscript is copied on 14-41.
48. Ibid., 50.
49. Rapport d'Armée au Rütli, July 25, 1940, 3 f. Personal, confidential. BAr 5795/173.
50. Ibid., 2. The sentence "this was also refused to me" was crossed out in the manuscript. Kellerhals noted in his diary, "the General also mentions the press and its escapades."
51. Cf. Chapter 14 above.
52. Grimm 1946, 6.
53. Rapport de l'Armée au Rütli, op. cit., 8k f.
54. General to Minger; AHQ, July 26, 1940. Personal. BAr 27/15067. Perrier worked as a lawyer in Vevey who was an associate of the contested M. Regamey, the leader of the "Ligue Vaudoise" and one of the people who signed the "Petition of the Two Hundred."
55. Rapport de l'Armée au Rütli, op. cit., 4, 10 ff.
56. Edmund Wehrli to author; Zürich, August 2, 1985. Also Major Wehrli, "pro memoria," February 27, 1941. ArWe.
57. Rapport de l'Armée au Rütli, op. cit., 14.
58. Ibid., 6 f.
59. General to Colonel E. Stalder, Zofingen; Pully, November 11, 1955. Carbon copy. BAr 5795/173.
60. Record, Grammoclub Ex Libris GC 707. BAr 5795/559. The General spoke in the past tense, quoting some passages from his speech.
61. Schaefer, Interview, op. cit.
62. Barbey 1948, 33.
63. Order to the Armed Forces; Rütli, July 25, 1940. BAr 5795/173, also 27/14124 The entire text was published in Kurz 1965 a, 90, and in Bonjour, *Neutralität* VII, op. cit., 184 f.
64. Kurz 1965 b, 55.
65. Guisan 1953, 60.
66. Alexander von Muralt to author; Arniberg, August 21, 1985.
67. Hans Bracher in *Die Woche*, July 31, 1960.
68. Schaefer, Interview, op. cit.
69. E.g. Edmund Wehrli to author; Zürich, August 2, 1985; and Jules Sandoz to author; Biel, September 11, 1986.
70. General, Radio address, August 1, 1940. BAr 5795/456.
71. Hohl 1961, 28.
72. Battle order, 5/1/1940. EMB.
73. Theo Frey to author; Weiningen, January 8, 1986.
74. Swiss Meteorology Center to author; Zürich, January 3, 1986.
75. Theo Frey in *Die Woche*, July 31, 1960.
76. "Ein 'Armee-Rapport' auf dem Rütli," in *Neue Zürcher Zeitung*, July 29, 1940, section 2.
77. *Basler Nachrichten*, July 31, 1940; *Tribune de Lausanne*, "Lettre du Rütli à un soldat," July 31, 1940.
78. Theo Frey to author; Weiningen, January 8, 1986.
79. *Neue Zürcher Zeitung*, August 3, 1940, No. 1111. It is possible that a soldier gave this response as a spontaneous reaction. However, it is more likely that this letter was also written by the Press Section of the army staff; its author could have been 1st Lt. Faesi again or Auxiliary Service Member Tobler, an editor at the national desk of the *Neue Zürcher Zeitung* who was also serving in the Press Section.

80. Köcher to Foreign Ministry; Bern, July 30, 1940, citissime, telegram Copy BAr 27/14124. Published in Bonjour, *Neutralität* VII, op. cit., 185 f.
81. Von Werdt to Intelligence Service; August 6, 1940.
82. Von Weizsäcker to Köcher; Berlin, August 5, 1940. Copy BAr EDI 1005/2.
83. Galeazzo Ciano, diaries 1939–1943, August 8, 1940; Bern 1947, 263. Apparently "General Guisan" was unknown to the Italian Foreign Minister, as he only talked about "some General."
84. Von Mackensen to Foreign Ministry; Rome, August 8, 1940, citissime. Copy. BAr 27/14124.
85. Ibid.; Rome, August 9, 1940. Copy. BAr 27/14124.
86. Hans Frölicher, *Meine Aufgabe in Berlin.* Bern 1962, 41 f.
87. Von Weizsäcker, Note; Berlin, August 8, 1940. Copy. BAr 27/14124.
88. German Legacy, Memorandum; Bern, August 10, 1940. BAr EPD 1943-45/3.
89. Federal Councilor Etter, Notes to the attention of the Department of Foreign Affairs; August 14, 1940, 1 f. BAr EPD 1943-45. A 14.48.4. Cf. illustration. The text of the notes was published in Bonjour, *Neutralität* VII, 190-193.
90. Ibid., 5.
91. Draft of a reply by Federal Council; August 19, 1940. BAr EPD 1943-45/3. This document was also published in Bonjour, *Neutralität* VII, 193 f.
92. Köcher to Foreign Ministry; Bern, August 26, 1940. Copy. BAr EDI 1005/2.
93. Department of Foreign Affairs to Minister Rüegger, Rome; Bern, August 29, 1940. BAr EPD 1943–45. A similar letter was sent to Frölicher in Berlin the same day.
94. Swiss Legacy (Thurnherr) to Department of Foreign Affairs; London, October 25, 1940. BAr EPD 1943–45.
95. Wille to Pilet-Golaz; Bern, August 12, 1940. Personal Carbon copy. BAr EDI 1005/1.
96. Wille, diary notes, op. cit., August 11–12, 1940.
97. Note, top secret, n.d. [before October 4, 1940]. Probably written by "Bureau Ha."
98. Order of the day, August 1, 1940. BAr 5795. The entire text was published in Kurz 1965 a, 91 f.
99. De Rougemont, diary, op. cit., July 10, 1940, 431.
100. Ibid., August 1, 1940, 433.
101. General, Radio address; August 1, 1940. Typewritten manuscript with handwritten corrections by Guisan. BAr 5795/175. The speech was recorded on vinyl on 26 July at the radio studio in Bern; on 1 August, the recorded speech was broadcast.
102. Pilet-Golaz, Speech on August 1, 1940. BAr 2809.
103. Ch. Gruner 1967/68, 14.
104. Weekly report on the mood among the population, July 23–July 29, 1940, 4. BAr 4450/6105.1.
105. Ibid., 5.
106. Ibid., July 28–August 4, 1940.
107. Report by 7th Division, May/June/July 1940; August 13, 1940. BAr 5795/124.
108. Report by 4th Army Corps; HQ, 8/7/1940. BAr 5795/124.
109. Hausamann to "Army and Home" service (Schüpbach); in the field, August 13, 1940. BAr 5795/124.
110. Adjutant General (Dollfus) to General; AHQ, August 22, 1940. BAr 5795/124.
111. Mountain Infantry Regiment 5 (Secretan) to Commander Mountain Brigade 10; command post, August 22, 1940. Personal, confidential. BAr 5795/124.
112. Henri Guisan, "Feierliche Höhepunkte des Aktivdienstes," in Kurz 1959, p. 25.
113. Minutes of the National Council committee dealing with the General's postwar report, op. cit., 49.
114. *Neue Zürcher Zeitung,* July 26–27, 1980, No. 172.

Chapter 17: The Réduit Strategy
1. Hans Rudolf Kurz, "Zur Geschichte des schweizerischen Réduit-Gedankens," in *Schweizerische Monatszeitschrift für Offiziere aller Waffen.* February 1947. Hans Rapold, *Strategische Probleme der schweizerischen Landesverteidigung im 19. Jahrhundert.* Ph.D. thesis, Zürich/Frauenfeld

1951, 67 ff., 143 ff. Ernst 1971, 98 f. Odermatt 1983. Walter Lüem, "100 Jahre Gotthardfestung," in *Neue Zürcher Zeitung*, January 31, 1986, No. 25, 35.

2. General Guisan, *Observations sur le rapport du Conseil fédéral à l'Assemblée fédérale concernant le rapport du Général sur le Service actif 1939–1945*. Lausanne, 2/9/1947, 5. ArWa.

3. Speech at the 125th anniversary celebration of the "Zofingerverein," quoted in Chapuisat 1950, 159.

4. Frick to Federal President Kobelt; Bern, August 31. 1946, 7. BAr Nl La.

5. Briefing with the Chief of the General Staff (Labhart); November 14, 1939. BAr 27/14151,1.

6. Ibid., 2.

7. Chief of the General Staff (Labhart) to General; AHQ, December 14, 1939. BAr 5795/301.

8. Odermatt 1983, 30.

9. General to Chief of the General Staff; AHQ, January 16, 1940. Personal, confidential. BAr 5795/302.

10. Cf. Chapter 7 above.

11. Germann [1977], 69.

12. General to Chief of the General Staff, May 17, 1940. Confidential BAr 5795/303. Quoted in Odermatt 1983, 32 f.

13. Huber to General; May 22, 1940. Confidential. BAr 5795/303.

14. Odermatt 1983, 35, 37.

15. General to Chief of the General Staff; AHQ, May 25, 1940. Personal, confidential. BAr 5795/303.

16. Ibid.

17. Odermatt 1983, 85.

18. Germann [1977], 71.

19. Barbey 1967, 155.

20. Barbey 1948, June 13, 1940, 16.

21. Frick to Commander of 4th Army Corps (Labhart); HQ, June 18, 1940. Personal, confidential. BAr 27/14268,2.

22. Ibid., 3.

23. Ibid., 5.

24. Labhart to General; no date [received by Personal Staff on June 21, 1940] Personal, confidential. BAr 5795/142.

25. Labhart to Kobelt; no date [summer 1946], carbon copy. BAr Nl La.

26. Gonard, "Appréciation de la situation, matin." June 22, 1940, 2 f. BAr 27/9911.

27. Ibid., 2, 5 f.

28. Germann to Chief of the General Staff; June 22, 1940. Confidential. BAr 27/14321. Quoted in Odermatt 1983, 52 f.

29. Minutes of the briefing; Bern, June 22, 1940, 1 ff. Confidential. BAr 5795/145.

30. Ibid., 2 f.

31. Ibid., 3.

32. Ibid., 7.

33. Ibid., 8 ff.

34. Ibid., 8.

35. Ibid., 5, 10.

36. Ibid., 10.

37. Ibid., 11 f.

38. Minutes of briefing with commanders of 2nd Army Corps; Zofingen, June 24, 1940. BAr 5795/145. Colonel P. Wacker, Chief of Staff of the 2nd Army Corps, kept the minutes.

39. Gautschi 1978, 385 f.

40. Huber to General; July 2, 1940. BAr 5795/304.

41. Barbey 1948, Monday, June 24, 1940, 23 f. The expression "small map" undoubtedly referred to the general map of Switzerland at a scale of 1:1,000,000.

42. Guisan [1946], 83.

43. Germann to Chief of the General Staff; AHQ, June 30, 1940. Confidential. BAr 5795/304.

44. Ibid., 3. Barbey annotated this passage, writing "very urgent if this project were adopted."

45. Guisan [1946], 35.
46. Gonard to Chief of the General Staff; July 1, 1940. BAr 5795/304.
47. Ibid., 6.
48. Cf. Guisan [1946], 36, and Barbey 1948, Saturday, July 6, 1940, 25. Roesch (1986, 69) had already pointed out this mistake by Guisan.
49. Strüby to Chief of the General Staff; AHQ, July 1, 1940. BAr 5795/304.
50. Ibid., 5.
51. Huber to General; AHQ, July 2, 1940. BAr 5795/304.
52. Barbey 1948, Thursday, July 4, 1940, 25 f.
53. Notes to the attention of the Commander-in-Chief of the Armed Forces; AHQ, July 5, 1940. BAr 5795/85.
54. Ibid.
55. Notes written in pencil by the General; July 6, 1940. BAr 5795/85. Cf. illustration.
56. Minutes of the briefing of July 6, 1940; Bern, July 7, 1940, 7 f. Confidential. BAr 5795/145. Captain H. Bracher of the general staff kept the minutes. The entire text of the minutes is published in Bonjour, *Neutralität* IX, op. cit., 379-392.
57. Ibid., 9.
58. Ibid., 10 a.
59. Ibid., 13.
60. Ibid., 20.
61. Labhart, diary, op. cit., July 6, 1940.
62. Prisi to General; HQ, July 8, 1940. Confidential. BAr 5795/304.
63. Barbey 1948, Tuesday, July 9, 1940, 27.
64. Gonard, Notes for an obituary of the General. No date [before March 15, 1959]. BAr Nl Go.
65. Barbey 1948, Tuesday, July 9, 1940, 27.
66. Directives for regrouping the army into a new defensive concept; AHQ, July 10, 1940. BAr 5795/304.
67. Operations Order No. 12, July 17, 1940. BAr 27/14298.
68. Gonard to Barbey; July 11, 1940. Handwritten. BAr 5795/85.
69. General to Huber; AHQ, July 10, 1940. Confidential. BAr 5795/304.
70. Walde 1983, 122 f.
71. Assessment of the situation; AHQ, July 10, 1940. BAr 5795/304.
72. Huber to General; AHQ, July 10, 1940. BAr 5795/304.
73. Barbey 1948, 28.
74. General to Federal Department of Military Affairs, attn. Federal Council; AHQ, July 12, 1940. Confidential. BAr 27/15067. The text is included in Guisan [1946], 37–42.
75. Cf. Chapter 7 above.
76. General to Federal Department of Military Affairs; July 12, 1940, op. cit., 6.
77. Cf. e.g. Bonjour 1981 c, 227; Kurz 1965 b, 49 f.; Roesch 1986, 49; Odermatt 1983, 74.
78. Cf. Chapter 14 above.
79. *Bericht des Bundesrates zum Bericht des Generals*, op. cit., 26.
80. Guisan 1947 a, 5.
81. Pilet-Golaz to Minger; Bern, July 16, 1940. Personal, confidential. BAr 27/15067.
82. Ibid.
83. Guisan [1946], 42.
84. Ibid., 43.
85. Operations Order No. 12, op. cit., subsection 4a.
86. Hans Rudolf Kurz, "General Guisan und die Kriegsparteien," in *General Guisan und der Zweite Weltkrieg*, op. cit., 83 f.
87. Huber to General; AHQ, November 26, 1940. Confidential BAr 5795/304.
88. Gonard 1971, 485.
89. Ibid., 482.
90. Roesch 1986, 48 ff.
91. Operations Order No. 13, May 24, 1941. BAr 27/14299.
92. Cf. above in this Chapter.

93. Alfred Ernst, "Die Armee im Aktivdienst," in Böschenstein 1963, 21. Karl Kobelt, "Vom Krieg zum Frieden," in Kurz 1959, 385. Kurz 1965 b, 49.
94. Huber to Kurz; Brienz, September 11, 1949, quoted in Odermatt 1983, 80.
95. Albert Züblin, "Über Ausbildung und Disziplin," in *Bürger und Soldat*, op. cit., 373 f.
96. Fritz Wanner, "Mit der Berner Division im Kriegsjahr 1940," in *Der Bund*, December 20, 1980, No. 299.
97. Guisan 1947, 13.
98. General to Huber; AHQ, June 6, 1941. BAr 5795/99.
99. Wilhelm Werder, "Die 5. Division," in *Festschrift Eugen Bircher*, op. cit., 328 f.
100. Barbey 1948, August 27–28, 1940, 38 f.
101. Ibid., November 5, 1940, 55.
102. Instructions on combat tactics in the defense, appendix to Operations Order No. 12, July 17, 1940. Confidential. BAr 27/14298.
103. Wille to General, August 31, 1940. Personal. BAr 5795/465. By the same author, complaint, November 2, 1940. BAr 27/14299,4.
104. Quoted in Guisan [1946], 137.
105. Constam to General; Küsnacht, January 8, 1941. BAr 5795/104.
106. Barbey 1948, January 19, 1941, 68 f.
107. Ibid., 86.
108. Instructions on combat tactics, appendix 1 to Operations Order No. 13; AHQ, May 25, 1941. Confidential. BAr 5795/171.
109. Ibid., 12.
110. General to Kobelt; AHQ, September 25, 1941. Confidential. BAr 5795/143.
111. Barbey 1948, Sunday, October 5, 1941, 96 f.
112. Guisan 1953, 131.
113. Directives concerning the fortification projects, July 24, 1940. Confidential. BAr 27/14321.
114. Ernst 1971, 152.
115. General to Labhart; AHQ, November 15, 1940. Personal, confidential. BAr Nl La.
116. Minutes of the conference, August 12, 1942. Confidential BAr 27/14126.
117. *Rapport de l'Etat-Major particulier* [III], op. cit., 16 f.
118. Military Department to Federal Council; Bern, July 25, 1941. Top secret. BAr 2809/1,5.
119. Huber [1946], 212.
120. Gonard 1959, 54.
121. Handwritten notes, no date [fall 1940?]. BAr 5560 (B).
122. Huber to General; AHQ, September 23, 1940, 2 f. BAr 5795/304.
123. Barbey 1948, Tuesday, September 9, 1941, 92 f.
124. Lardelli to General; HQ, October 15, 1942. Confidential BAr 5795/436.
125. Labhart to Kobelt; HQ, June 11, 1942. BAr 5800/1.
126. Bracher, Remarks on the critical summary report by Capt. Züblin of the general staff; November 3, 1942. Personal and confidential. BAr 5795/290.
127. Huber to General; AHQ, August 20, 1942. BAr 5795/436.
128. Pilet-Golaz 1945 20.
129. Daniel to General; AHQ, August 1, 1943. BAr 5795/337.
130. Stampfli to Walther, November 17, 1940. Quoted in Georg Hafner, *Bundesrat Walther Stampfli*. Ph.D. thesis, Zürich/Olten 1986, 224.
131. General to Labhart; AHQ, June 12, 1942. BAr 5795/146.
132. Notes taken during the conference of June 25, 1942. Confidential BAr 5795/146.
133. *Rapport de l'Etat-Major particulier* [V], op. cit., 4. Operations Order No. 14, September 1, 1942. Confidential. BAr 5795/87.
134. Handwritten notes by the General on "Case W[est] 1942." No date [July 1942]. BAr 5795/87.
135. Minutes of the conference, August 19. 1942. Confidential. BAr 27/14126.
136. Walde 1983, pp. 77 ff. Huber to General; AHQ, 11/27/1943. BAr 27/14301.
137. Barbey to General; AHQ, September 13. 1942. Personal, confidential. BAr 5795/87.
138. Ibid.
139. Cf. Chapter 31 below.

140. Order re: lifting of Operations Order No. 13; AHQ, July 9, 1945. Confidential. BAr 5795/338.
141. Guisan [1946], 90.
142. Ernst 1971, 352.
143. Quoted in Roesch 1986, p. 79.
144. Oberkommando des Heeres, *Kleines Orientierungsheft Schweiz*, op. cit., 33.
145. Quoted in Guisan 1953, 181.
146. Quoted in Chapuisat 1950, p. 209.
147. Guisan [1946], 264.
148. Kurz 1965 b, 50.
149. Gonard 1959, 41.

Chapter 18: The National Resistance Movement

1. Federal President (Etter) to General; Bern, September 2, 1939. BAr 5795/124.
2. General to Etter; AHQ, September 9, 1939. BAr 5795/124.
3. Samuel Haas, "Erste unverbindliche Ideenskizze für die Errichtung eines militärischen Aufklärungs- und Propaganda-Dienstes." N.d. [after September 1, 1939]. BAr 5795/124.
4. Order to the Armed Forces; AHQ, November 3, 1939. The entire text of the order is published, among others, in Kurz 1965a, 56.
5. Ibid.
6. Minutes of Federal Council meeting, March 19, 1940. Excerpt, p. 3. BAr 5795/546.
7. Hausamann to Labhart; Teufen, November 23, 1938 BAr 27/9860.
8. Hausamann to Schüpbach; in the field, August 13, 1940. BAr 5795/124.
9. Report by 'Ha', August 13, 1940, 20.00 hours, 5. ArSchü.
10. *Rapport de l'Etat-Major particulier* [III], op. cit., 10.
11. Schürch 1984, 17.
12. Guisan [1946], 217.
13. Hausamann to General; in the field, March 1, 1941, 13 f. BAr 5795/448,1.
14. Special Report by 'Ha', April 19, 1941. AfZ.
15. Guisan [1946], 218.
16. General to Etter; AHQ, February 13, 1941. Personal. BAr 5795/342. Excerpts were also published in Guisan [1946], 219.
17. *Rapport de l'Etat-Major particulier* [IV], op. cit., 22.
18. Barbey 1948, April 16 and 17, 1941, 83.
19. Schürch 1984, 17. Also Ernst 1963a, 13.
20. Order to the Armed Forces; AHQ, June 17, 1941. The entire text is published in Kurz 1965 a, 109.
21. *Bericht des Generaladjutanten der Armee an den Oberbefehlshaber der Armee über den Aktivdienst 1939-1945.* N.d., n.p. [Bern 1946], 274 f, 305.
22. Ibid.
23. Däniker to Schumacher; Walenstadt, May 28, 1941. AfZ, Nl Dä 80. He wrote letters to Ulrich Wille in which he expressed similar ideas.
24. Ulrich Wille, Memorandum on the situation in July 1941; Bern, July 9, 1941, 3. Strictly confidential. BAr 2809/1,5.
25. Labhart, Diary, op. cit., May 20, 1941.
26. Etter to General; Bern August 23, 1940. BAr 5795/85.
27. Minutes of the meeting, September 15, 1941, 16.00 hours. BAr 5795/86.
28. *Rapport de l'Etat-Major particulier* [V], op. cit., 18 f. includes a summary of the statements mentioned.
29. Ibid., 20.
30. Pilet-Golaz, Note; August 8, 1941. BAr 2809/1,5.
31. Gilliard to General; Lausanne, March 5, 1945. BAr 5795/90. Ambassador Dr. Lindt categorically denied that "Army and Home" was infiltrated by leftists. August R. Lindt to author; Bern, May 17, 1985.

32. Chief of the General Staff to Adjutant General; AHQ, October 24, 1941. BAr 5795/343.
33. To the Officers of the Armed Forces; AHQ, October 1, 1941. BAr 5795.
34. Memorandum "Beware of Political Movements"; AHQ, October 14, 1940. BAr 5795/342.
35. Handwritten notes. BAr Nl Mey. Capt. Paul Meyer, alias Wolf Schwertenbach, Ph.D. in law, born 1894, died 1966. Was the owner of "Wolfsberg" castle near Ermatingen on the shores of Lake Constance.
36. Ibid.
37. Special mission (Capt. Meyer) to General; AHQ, September 1, 1941. Personal and confidential. BAr 5795/460.
38. Handwritten note in a letter by H.R. Schmid; March 16, 1946. BAr 5795/342.
39. Frey to Dollfus; December 15. 1941, 14. BAr 57/9059.
40. General to Kobelt; AHQ, December 18, 1941. Quoted in Guisan [1946], 220 f.
41. Hausamann to General; in the field, December, 28, 1941. Carbon copy. BAr Nl Er.
42. Minutes of the lecture of 1/10/1941 in Spiez; AHQ, January 13, 1941, 7. Confidential. BAr 5795/146.
43. Barbey 1948, January 11, 1942, 112.
44. *Rapport de l'Etat-Major particulier* [V], op. cit., 20. Cf. Guisan [1946], 222.
45. Barbey 1948, 1/20/1942, 115.
46. Alfred Ernst, "General Guisan: Versuch einer Würdigung," in Böschenstein 1975, 33.
47. Federal Council to General; Bern, January 12, 1943. BAr 5795/88.
48. Feldmann to General; Bern, March 3, 1943, 10. BAr 5795/233.
49. Frey to Dollfus; April 9, 1943. BAr 5795/443.
50. General to Frey; AHQ, June 25, 1943. Personal. Copy. BAr 5795/443.
51. In Frey's biography written by Philipp Wanner (*Oberst Oskar Frey und der schweizerische Widerstandswille.* Münsingen 1974), the dispute with Dollfus and the sanctions imposed on Frey by the General are not mentioned. In his official post-war report, in the Chapter on "Army and Home" the Adjutant General did not mention Oskar Frey or his merits.
52. A. Forter, Report on my trip to Zürich on September 17, 1941; AHQ, September 17, 1941. BAr 27/9059.
53. On the activities of "Army and Home,"cf. Robert Vögeli, *Die gegenwärtige Organisation von Heer und Haus.* N.p. [Bern], December 1957. Typescript. Oskar Felix Fritschi, *Geistige Landesverteidigung während des Zweiten Weltkrieges: Der Beitrag der Schweizer Armee zur Aufrechterhaltung des Durchhaltewillens.* Ph.D. thesis, Dietikon/Zürich 1972.
54. De Rougemont 1968, 423.
55. Gasser 1984, 19.
56. De Rougemont 1968, 428 f. On the circumstances of de Rougemont's house arrest, cf. Chapter 12.
57. Quoted in Gasser 1984, 31.
58. De Rougemont 1968, 432 f.
59. René Leyvraz, Speech of 1940. Quoted in Gasser 1984, p. 29.
60. [Denis de Rougemont], *Qu'est-ce que la Ligue du Gothard?* Neuchâtel n.d. [1940], 6 ff.
61. De Rougemont 1968, 429 f.
62. Allgöwer to Däniker; Wangen an der Aare, June 26, 1940. BAr Nl Al.
63. Agreement with the Gotthard Alliance ; Bern, July 22, 1940. Carbon copy. BAr E 5330.
64. Lindt to Investigating Judge Hug; in the field, August 15, 1940. BAr E 5330.
65. Ernst to Senior Judge of 8th division (Herzog); Worb, August 4, 1940. BAr E 5330.
66. Gasser 1984, 53.
67. [De Rougemont 1940].
68. Ernst 1963a, 13.
69. No. 1 [Ernst] to Lt. Col. [Werder]; August 1, 1940. BAr E 5330.
70. Ernst 1963a, 13.
71. August R. Lindt to author; Bern, July 15, 1987.
72. Different in Bonjour, *Neutralität* IV, op. cit., 217.
73. Minutes of the management meetings of the Social Democratic party, July 20, 1940, 4, and July 27, 1940, 2 f.

74. Gasser 1984, 71 f.
75. Cf. Chapter 22 below.
76. Confidential; October 28, 1940. AfZ Nl Li 88.
77. Gasser 1984, 62.
78. Ernst to Masson; September 27, 1940. Carbon copy. BAr Nl Er.
79. Masson to Ernst; September 28, 1940. BAr Nl Er.
80. Statutes of the Swiss Federal Society; Bern, January 12, 1941. BAr 5795/343.
81. Ibid.
82. Swiss Federal Society (Schürch, Ernst, Allgöwer) to General; Bern, February 13, 1941. BAr 5795/343.
83. Mailing list of the Zürich chapter of the Swiss Federal Society, [n.d., approx. 1942]. ArJae.
84. Directory of the Swiss Federal Society, November 7, 1949. BAr Nl Al.
85. Swiss Federal Society, Booklets 1 to 5, August 1941–1942. ArJae.
86. Schmid to Allgöwer; Bassersdorf, January 11, 1947. BAr Nl Al.
87. Gerhart Schürch to author; Bern, May 21, 1985.
88. Ernst 1963a, 16.
89. Lindt 1984, p. 6. Also Schürch 1984, 17.
90. Hausamann to Kobelt; Teufen, March 1, 1943. AfZ Nl Ha.
91. Hausamann to Kobelt; Teufen, January 15, 1946, 5.
92. Minutes of examination; Luzern, September 20, 1940. BAr 5795/448.
93. Ibid.
94. Hausamann to special investigating judge (Achermann); in the field, September 20, 1940. BAr 5795/448.
95. Huber to General; AHQ, September 26, 1940. BAr 27/9850.
96. H[ans] Hausamann, *Die Schweiz im internationalen Spannungsfeld: (Was ist und was will die Aktion Nationaler Widerstand?).* N.d. [after September 7, 1940], 16 f. BAr 5795/448,1.
97. Ibid., 17 f.
98. Hausamann to General; Teufen, March 18, 1943. BAr 5795/448,1.
99. Müller to General; AHQ, September 26, 1940. BAr 5795/448.
100. August R. Lindt to author; Bern, February 10, 1986.
101. Von Schenck 1969, 107 f.
102. Ibid., 117.
103. August R. Lindt to author; Bern, February 1, 1988.
104. Hausamann [1940b], 16.
105. Oath; attachment to a letter by Huber to General; AHQ, September 26, 1940. BAr 27/9850.
106. August R. Lindt to author; Bern, May 17, 1985. Also von Schenck 1969, 118.
107. Werner Rings to author; Brissago, August 13, 1978.
108. This author expresses his gratitude to former Ambassador Dr. August R. Lindt for making available the mailing list for this publication.
109. Georg Thürer (*Die Geschichte des Kantons St. Gallen.* Vol. II, St. Gallen 1972, 524) mentioned "about 50 stalwarts." Thürer was a member himself. Walther Bringolf (Mein Leben. Bern 1965, 245) mentioned "250 members." A 1946 report by the government of the canton of Basel-Stadt (Basel 1946, p. 147) mentioned 800 members.
110. Fascicle, *"Bericht des Regierungsrates des Kantons Basel-Stadt über die Abwehr staatsfeindlicher Umtriebe in den Vorkriegs- und Kriegsjahren sowie die Säuberungsaktion nach Kriegsschluss. Aktion Nationaler Widerstand."* N.d. [after 10/1/1941]. ArLi.
111. Jakob Bührer, "Ein starker Zeuge," in *Festschrift Hans Oprecht,* op. cit., 199.
112. Military Attorney General (Trüssel) to General; Bern, September 23, 1940. BAr 5795/448,1.
113. Hausamann 1947, 94.
114. Special Report by 'Ha', 3. N.d. [approx. December 1940]. AfZ Nl Ha.
115. Gasser 1984, 22.
116. Schürch 1984, 17.
117. Lindt 1984, 17.
118. Based on a Decree by the Federal Council of September 8, 1939, no new newspapers or magazines were allowed to be established.

119. Special Report by 'Ha', n.d. [approx. December 1940]. AfZ Hl Ha.
120. Former Federal Councilor Willy Spühler to author; Zürich, June 12, 1987.
121. Excerpt from the minutes of the Zürich City Council meetings; November 8, 1940, October 25, 1941, and January 8, 1943. AfZ Nl Li. The donations were charged against budget item D 55, "Promotion of general culture."
122. August R. Lindt to author; Bern, February 10, 1986. Also von Schenck 1969, 110.
123. Labhart to General; HQ, December 11, 1940. Personal BAr 5795/342.
124. General to Labhart; AHQ, January 12, 1941. BAr 5795/342.
125. Ibid.
126. Hausamann, draft of letter, n.d. [before January 7, 1941]. AfZ Nl Ha.
127. Masson to General; AHQ, January 7, 1941. BAr 5795/342.
128. General to Labhart; AHQ, January 12, 1941.
129. Ernst 1963a, 16.
130. Karl Barth, *Im Namen Gottes des Allmächtigen 1291-1941*. St. Gallen 1941. Bonjour 1983, 101.
131. Von Schenck 1969, 123.
132. Regarding other resistance groups and movements, cf. Meyer 1965; the information in that book is still accurate.

Chapter 19: Attempts to Arrange a Special Mission to Berlin

1. Bonjour, *Neutralität* IV, op. cit., 226 ff., 236 f.
2. O[tto] F[rey], "Waadtländer Emotionen um General Guisan," in *Neue Zürcher Zeitung*, April 26, 1985, No. 96.
3. Georg Kreis, "General Guisan, Minister Frölicher und die Mission Burckhardt 1940," in *SZG* No. 1 and 2, Zürich 1977, 99–121. Gauye 1978, 5-68.
4. General to Minger; AHQ, August 14, 1940. Personal, confidential. BAr.
5. Ibid.
6. Wille to Pilet-Golaz; Bern, August 12, 1940. Personal. BAr EDI 1005/1.
7. Däniker to Wille; Walenstadt, September 10, 1940. ArMa. The following day, Wille used Däniker's exact words in a letter to the Federal President, except for leaving out the sentence about the "odd one out." Wille to Pilet-Golaz; September 11, 1940. Carbon copy. BAr.
8. Markus Feldmann, Diary, July 28, 1940, No. 872. BAr Nl Fm.
9. Feldmann to W. Stucki; Bern, February 4, 1946, 11. Copy. BAr 4001 (C). 1st Lt. Ernst Wilhelm, Ph.D. in law, Plancherel's assistant at the Press and Radio section, should not be confused with Captain Alfred Ernst of the general staff.
10. Waibel to Masson; September 15, 1940. BAr 27/9943.
11. General to Pilet-Golaz; AHQ, November 9, 940. Confidential, personal. Copy for personal information to Head of Military Department. BAr 5795/448,2.
12. Feldmann to General; Bern, July 15, 1943, 14 f. Personal, confidential. BAr 5795/333.
13. Pilet-Golaz 1945, 16.
14. M.L. Keller, shorthand notes, September 15, 1940. BAr 2809/1,4.
15. Dollfus to General; AHQ, March 6, 1941. BAr 27/9949. Quoted from Gauye 1978, 19 f.
16. Ibid., 20 f.
17. General's handwritten notes, May 3, 1941. BAr 5795/86. Cf. illustration.
18. General to Wetter; AHQ, May 21, 1941. Personal, confidential. BAr Nl Wet. Quoted from Gauye 1978, 23.
19. Wetter to General; Bern, May 26, 1941. BAr 5795/151.
20. Bonjour, *Neutralität* IV, op. cit., 231, 237. Kreis 1977a, 104 f.
21. Gauye 1978, 24 f.
22. Daniel Bourgeois, "Notes de Lecture," in *Relations Internationales* No. 30, Paris 1982, 243 f.
23. Gauye 1978, 65.
24. *Rapport de l'Etat-Major particulier* [IV], op. cit., 20.
25. Wetter to General; Bern, June 28, 1941. Carbon copy. BAr Nl Wet. 4/69. Quoted from Gauye 1978, 24.

26. Von Werdt to Intelligence Service; Berlin, August 19, 1940. BAr 27/12698.
27. Rudolf L. Bindschedler et al., *Schwedische und schweizerische Neutralität im Zweiten Weltkrieg.* Basel/Frankfurt a.M.1985.
28. Logoz, Report to General; September 5, 1940. Confidential. BAr 5795/85.
29. Ibid.
30. Cf. Chapter 20 below.
31. Notes by von Bibra; November 12, 1940. PAB. Quoted from Kreis 1976, 150 f.
32. General to Minger; AHQ, October 24, 1940. BAr 5795/336.
33. Pilet-Golaz to Minger; Bern, 11/1/1940. Copy. ArMa.
34. General to Minger; AHQ, November 14, 1940. Confidential. Copy. ArMa.
35. Huber to General; AHQ, October 19, 1940. BAr 5795/336.
36. General to Wille; AHQ, November 14, 1940. ArMa and BAr 5795/336.
37. Wille to General; AHQ, November 18, 1940. Personal. Carbon copy. ArMa.
38. Wille to Wetter; Bern, July 9, 1941. Strictly confidential. BAr 2809/1,5.
39. Memorandum on the situation in July 1941; July 9, 1941, 2, 5. Carbon copy. ArMa.
40. Pilet-Golaz, note; May 8, 1943 BAr 2809/1,5.
41. Gauye 1978, 38 f.
42. Ibid., 65 f.
43. Ernst 1975e, 28 f.

Chapter 20: The Files of La Charité

1. W. Mayer [Capt.], "Gefechtsbericht über den Vormarsch nach und die Einnahme von La Charité am 16. Juni 1940," in *Militär-Wochenblatt*, 126th year of publication, No. 6, August 8, 1941, 146 f. According to recent research by Hans Senn (1988c), it is probable that most documents relating to cooperation between France and Switzerland were found at the Dampierre barracks in Dijon, not at the train station of La-Charité-sur-Loire.
2. Bonjour, *Neutralität* IV, op. cit., 378 ff., 431 ff. Georg Kreis, *Auf den Spuren von "La Charité": Die schweizerische Armeeführung im Spannungsfeld des deutsch-französischen Gegensatzes 1936-1941.* Basel 1976.
3. [Franz] Halder, Diary, July 21, 1940. Quoted in [Peter] Burckhardt, Lt.-Col., *Bericht über meine Abkommandierung zur US-Army, EUCOM, Historical Division in Frankfurt, vom 14.10.48 bis 2.11.48.* Appendix II, 24 Confidential. BAr 5800/1.
4. Swiss Legacy to Department of Foreign Affairs; Berlin, August 3, 1940. Telegram. BAr EPD 1943-45/3.
5. Gauye 1978, 38.
6. The text erroneously stated, "French."
7. Note, September 3, 1940. Secret matter of the Reich. Was submitted to the Führer. Photocopy. BAr EDI 1005.
8. Representative of the Foreign Affairs Office at the Supreme Command of the Wehrmacht; Berlin, September 11, 1940. Confidential. Photocopy. BAr EDI 1005.
9. Note (Moltke); Berlin, November 7, 1940. Secret matter of the Reich. Was submitted to the Führer and to the Foreign Minister of the Reich. Photocopy. BAr EDI 1005.
10. Ibid. Apparently the French documents did not mention that the Swiss "liaison person" was Major Bernard Barbey. The texts of documents 7, 8, and 9 as well as other relevant documents are published in Bonjour, *Neutralität* VII, op. cit., 50 ff.
11. Martin Rikli to his parents; Berlin, September 8, 1940. Photocopy. BAr 27/9943.
12. Rigi (Waibel) to Intelligence Service; September 16, 1940, 17.25 hours. Telegram. BAr 27/9943.
13. Waibel to Müller; September 16, 1940. BAr 27/9943.
14. Waibel to Müller; September 25, 1940. Confidential. BAr 27/9943.
15. Ibid.
16. Handwritten note; September 23, 1940. BAr 5795/85.
17. Waibel to Müller; Thun, October 13, 1940. Quoted in Kreis 1976, 123.
18. Ibid.

19. Köcher, Note; Bern, October 1, 1940. Photocopy. BAr EDI 1005. The original is at the Political Archives in Bonn. Its full text is published in Bonjour, *Neutralität* VII, op. cit., 54 f.
20. Köcher to Foreign Affairs Office; Bern, October 3, 1940. Sealed, confidential. Published in Bonjour, *Neutralität* VII, op. cit., 55 f.
21. Foreign Affairs Office to German Legacy, Bern; Berlin, October 14, 1940. Secret matter of the Reich. Photocopy. BAr EDI 1005. Published in Bonjour, *Neutralität* VII, 56.
22. Wille to Petitpierre; Feldmeilen, July 28, 1955. Personal. BAr EDI 1005/1.
23. Ibid. The full text of the letter is published in Bonjour, *Neutralität* VII, op. cit., 61 ff.
24. Labhart, Handwritten note for the file; n.d. [before October 29, 1940]. BAr Nl La.
25. Labhart, Diary, op. cit., December 9, 1940.
26. Kreis 1976, 119 f.
27. von Erlach to Labhart; CP, October 15, 1940. Personal and confidential. Nl La.
28. Wille to Petitpierre; Feldmeilen, July 28, 1955. Personal. BAr EDI 1005/1.
29. von Erlach to Labhart; CP, October 15, 1940. Personal, confidential. BAr Nl La.
30. von Erlach to Labhart; October 18, 1940. By express mail. BAr Nl La.
31. Confidential; n.d. [summer of 1940]. AfZ Nl Li 88. The unsigned message probably came from Bureau "Ha."
32. Labhart, Note for the file; n.d. [after October 19, 1940]. Nl La.
33. Ibid.
34. Labhart to General; HQ, October 22, 1940. Personal, confidential. Carbon copy. Nl La.
35. General to Labhart; AHQ, October 24, 1940. Personal, confidential. Nl La.
36. Labhart to General; AHQ, November 1, 1940. Personal, confidential. Carbon copy. Nl La.
37. Du Pasquier, Diary, op. cit., Monday, November 11, 1940.
38. Ibid.
39. Ibid.
40. General to Labhart; AHQ, November 5, 1940. Personal, confidential. Nl La.
41. Gonard, Declaration; November 8, 1940. Handwritten. BAr 5795/447.
42. Kreis 1976, 145.
43. Trüssel to General; Bern, November 15, 1940. Personal, confidential. BAr 5795/446.
44. Minutes of statement; Bern, December 11, 1940. BAr 5330/1982,1,14.
45. Trüssel to General; Bern, December 17, 1940, 3 f. Personal, confidential. BAr 5795/447.
46. Ibid., 5.
47. Handwritten note, December 14, 1940. ArMa. The full text is published in Kreis 1976, 129 f.
48. Däniker's agenda; December 16, 1940. AfZ Nl Dä Quoted in Kreis 1976, 130.
49. Däniker to Pilet; December 17, 1940. Copy. AfZ Nl Dä.
50. Däniker, File for meeting with Federal President Pilet-Golaz, December 23, 1940. AfZ Nl Dä.
51. Däniker to Pilet-Golaz; Walenstadt, December 24, 1940. Copy. BAr 5795/440,1.
52. Du Pasquier, Diary, op. cit., December 30, 1940.
53. Note, December 31, 1940. BAr 5795/440,1. The full text of the note is published in Kreis 1976, 132.
54. General to Pilet-Golaz; AHQ, December 31, 1940. Personal, confidential. BAr 2809. Cf. illustration.
55. Pilet-Golaz to Kobelt; Lausanne, February 9, 1946. Confidential. BAr 27/10027.
56. Gonard to General; AHQ, December 19, 1940. Personal. Handwritten BAr 5795/447.
57. Minutes of statement; Zürich, January 7, 1941. BAr 5330/1982,1,4.
58. Trüssel to General; Bern, January 8, 1941. Personal, confidential. BAr 5795/447.
59. Gonard to General; AHQ, 1/19/1941. Personal, confidential BAr 5795/447.
60. General to Trüssel; AHQ, January 25, 1941. Personal, confidential. BAr 5795/447.
61. Eugster to General; Bern, January 28, 1941. Personal, confidential. BAr 5795/447.
62. Department of Foreign Affairs (Bonna) to General; Bern, February 3, 1941. Personal. BAr 5795/447.
63. Oser to Kobelt; January 16, 1946. Quoted in Kreis 1976, 132.
64. Gonard to General; Bière, March 15, 1941. Personal. BAr 5795/447.
65. Settlement; Bern, April 17, 1941. BAr 5795/447. It is signed by Meili, Gonard, and Hasler, the arbiter.

66. Kreis 1976, 135.
67. Regarding the destruction of the Swiss cooperation files, cf. Chapter 9 above.
68. Ernst 1975a, 257.
69. Hausamann, Report by a member of parliament; n.d. [approx. February 1941]. AfZ Nl Ha.
70. Hausamann to General; in the field, March 1, 1941, 11. BAr 5795/448,1.
71. Wille, Memorandum on the situation in July 1941, op. cit.
72. Bonjour, *Neutralität* IV, op. cit., 432.
73. K[obelt], Note for file; September 2, 1941. BAr 5800/2.
74. Report on tapped telephone conversation, August 5, 1941, 13.00 hours. BAr 5795/448,1.
75. Ibid.
76. Kreis 1976, 209.
77. Jürg Wille to author; Zürich, February 1, 1985. Fritz Wille to author; Gümligen, May 21, 1985.
78. Bonjour, *Neutralität* IV, op. cit., 432.
79. Kurz 1965b, 61.
80. Pierre Béguin speaking on Swiss national public television, French-speaking channel, January 3, 1978.
81. Niklaus Meienberg, *Die Welt als Wille und Wahn.* Zürich 1987, 139.
82. Kreis 1976, 197.
83. Declaration by Federal Council to the press, April 21, 1961. Confidential. BAr EDI 1005. Quoted in Bonjour, *Neutralität* IV, op. cit., 433.
84. Armin Meili, Remarks 1963. Quoted in Bonjour, *Neutralität* IV, 433.
85. Labhart to Kobelt; HQ, June 11, 1942. BAr 5800/1.
86. Kobelt to Labhart; Bern, June 16, 1942. BAr 5800/1.
87. Köcher to von Weizsäcker; Bern, September 28, 1942. Personal. Copy. BAr EDI 1005/2.
88. Köcher to Foreign Affairs Office; Bern, October 7, 1943. Secret matter of the Reich Copy. BAr EDI 1005/2.
89. Cf. Chapter 28 below.
90. Pilet-Golaz, Note, April 30, 1943. BAr 2809/1,5.
91. Minutes of statement; Geneva, May 14, 1947. Copy. BAr 5800/1.
92. Frölicher to Kobelt; Bern, February 10, 1950. Personal. BAr 5800/1.
93. Karl Heinz Abshagen, *Canaris, Patriot und Weltbürger.* Stuttgart 1949, 347 f.
94. Masson to General; August 3, 1945. Personal, confidential. BAr 5795/455.
95. Müller to Kobelt; Bern, December 18, 1945. Müller added, "what I am reporting here is probably the main reason why von Ilsemann later fell out of favor." BAr 5800/1.
96. Cf. Kurz 1972, 75. Cf. Chapter 27 below.
97. Eugster to Kobelt; Bern, January 4, 1946. Personal, confidential. BAr 27/10027.
98. Oser, Handwritten notes on the Federal Council meeting; January 15, 1946. BAr 5800/1.
99. Ibid., January 25, 1946.
100. From letter by Kobelt to General; Bern, January 28, 1946. Personal, confidential. BAr 5795/335.
101. General to Kobelt; Lausanne, January 30, 1946. Personal, confidential. BAr 5800/1.
102. Oser, Handwritten notes, February 5, 1946. BAr 5800/1.
103. Ibid.
104. Kobelt to General; Bern, February 5, 1946. BAr 5795/335.
105. Oser, Handwritten notes, February 15, 1946. BAr 5800/1.
106. *Protokoll der nationalrätlichen Kommission zur Behandlung des Berichtes des Generals.* Op. cit., 46.
107. M. P[etitpierre], Notes, March 16, 1956. BAr 2800/1.
108. Ernst 1971, 84.
109. Wüst 1965.
110. Züblin to Boissier; Küsnacht, February 10, 1977. ArBoi. Cf. Chapter 9 above.

Chapter 21: The Däniker Affair

1. Cf. Chapter 16.
2. Handwritten note by the General, July 22, 1941. BAr 5795/440.

3. Gustav Däniker, "Denkschrift über Feststellungen und Eindrücke anlässlich eines Aufenthaltes in Deutschland"; Walenstadt, May 15, 1941. BAr 5800. The full text of the memorandum is published in Bonjour, *Neutralität* VIII, op. cit., 261–272. The page numbers in the following notes are based on the text published in Bonjour. [Henceforth referred to as Däniker 1941a.]

4. Army Investigator (Eugster), "Entscheid in Sachen Däniker Gustav und Frick Heinrich"; Bern, March 26, 1942, 1 f. Signed carbon copy. BAr 5795/460.

5. Däniker 1941a, 261.

6. Minutes of examination; September 17, 1941. BAr 5330/1982,1,4. Concerning Riedweg's activities as a traitor, cf. *Bericht des Bundesrates über die antidemokratische Tätigkeit*, op. cit., part I, 93.

7. Däniker to Musy; Walenstadt, October 18, 1941. Carbon copy. AfZ Nl Dä 80.

8. Däniker 1941a, 270.

9. Ibid., 263 f.

10. Ibid., 271 f.

11. Ibid., 269 f.

12. Masson to Herzog; AHQ, October 8, 1941. Copy. ArMa.

13. Gustav Däniker, "Kurze Darstellung der 'Denkschrift'-Angelegenheit"; Walenstadt, November 21, 1941, 2 f. BAr 2809/1,5. [Henceforth referred to as Däniker 1941d.]

14. Labhart, Diary, op. cit., May 19, 1941.

15. Däniker 1941d, 3.

16. Barbey to Müller; AHQ, June 25, 1941. Personal, confidential. BAr 5795/343.

17. Frick to Däniker; May 21, 1941. AfZ Nl Dä.

18. [Jakob] Eugster, "Feststellungen des Armeeauditors"; Bern, July 1, 1942, 5 ff. Personal. BAr 5800/2.

19. Colonel W. Müller to Däniker; in the field, August 15, 1941. AfZ Nl Dä 20.4.

20. Däniker to Kobelt; Walenstadt, October 11, 1941. BAr 27/4783,1.

21. Däniker to General; July 14, 1942. BAr 27/4783.

22. Reply to question no. 35. Copy. ArMa.

23. Gustav Däniker, "Stellungnahme zu meiner Denkschrift"; Walenstadt, October 18, 1941. BAr 5330/1982,1,14.

24. H. Ammann, Written testimony; October 23, 1941. Copy. ArMa.

25. R. Abt, Written testimony; October 20, 1941. Copy. ArMa.

26. Jaeger to Herzog; November 3, 1941. Hasler to Herzog; Lausanne, October 16, 1941. Copies. ArMa.

27. Haas to Däniker; August 11, 1942. Copy. ArMa.

28. Gut to Däniker; July 18, 1941. Handwritten. AfZ Nl Dä 20.4.

29. Hausamann to General; in the field, March 1, 1941, 9 f. BAr 5795/448,1.

30. Ibid., 7 f.

31. Ibid., 10 f.

32. Ibid., 11.

33. Hausamann to Bircher; St. Gallen, December 16, 1934. Quoted in Gautschi 1978, 338.

34. Handwritten remarks; n.d. [approx. March 3, 1941]. BAr 5795/448,1.

35. Kreis 1976, 137.

36. P. Meyer, Several pieces of information. BAr Nl Mey.

37. Steel tape recording [I]; AHQ, August 12, 1941, 15.15 hours. BAr 27/4783,1. The typewritten version is 32 pages long.

38. Cf. Chapter 16.

39. Steel tape recording [I], 6 f.

40. Ibid., 8.

41. Ibid., 26 f.

42. Ibid., 27 f.

43. General to Kobelt; AHQ, August 15, 1941. BAr 5795/343.

44. Barbey 1948, 87 ff.

45. Ibid., 90 f.

46. Minutes of the conference of August 20, 1941; Rigi Kulm. Confidential. BAr 5795/440.

47. Barbey 1948, August 20, 1941, 88.
48. Ibid, 89.
49. Däniker 1941d, 6.
50. Steel tape recording [II]; AHQ, August 25, 1941, 15.27 hours to 16.27 hours. Confidential. BAr 27/4783. The typewritten version is 20 pages long.
51. Ibid., 10.
52. Ibid., 12. One common nickname for the General was "Henri the Banquet Master".
53. Steel tape recording [II], 19 f.
54. Ibid., 20.
55. P. Meyer, Diary notes, August 20, 1941. Handwritten. BAr Nl Mey.
56. Ibid.
57. Müller to General; AHQ, July 24, 1941. Personal and confidential. BAr 5795/460.
58. Prisi to General; HQ, August 16, 1941. Personal and confidential. BAr 5795/460.
59. P. Meyer, Handwritten notes; November 3, 1941. BAr Nl Mey.
60. Ibid.
61. Labhart, Diary, op. cit., August 30, 1941.
62. *Rapport de l'Etat-Major particulier* [V], op. cit., 29 ff.
63. Däniker 1941d, 12.
64. Ibid., 13.
65. P. Meyer, Handwritten notes; November 19–20, 1941. BAr Nl Mey.
66. Swiss Officers' Society to Federal Council; Lausanne, December 15, 1941. BAr 2809/1,5.
67. K[obelt], Note for file; October 8, 1941. BAr 5800/2.
68. R. Abt, Written statement; October 20, 1941. Copy. ArMa.
69. Wille to General; HQ, November 4, 1941, 14 f. Personal. BAr 5800/2.
70. Wille to General; HQ, March 4, 1942. Personal. BAr 27/4783 and 5795/460.
71. General to Wille; AHQ, March 11, 1942. Personal. Carbon copy. BAr 5795/460.
72. Army Investigator (Eugster), "Entscheid in Sachen 1. Däniker Gustav, 2. Frick Heinrich"; Bern, March 9, 1942. BAr 2809/1,5.
73. Eugster to Justice and Police Department; Zürich, March 18, 1942. BAr 2809/1,5.
74. General, Decree; AHQ, March 28, 1942. BAr 2809/1,5.
75. Press release; *Neue Zürcher Zeitung*, April 4, 1942, No. 538.
76. Däniker to General; Walenstadt, April 7, 1942. BAr 27/4782.
77. General to Däniker; AHQ, April 8, 1942. BAr 27/4782.
78. Hausamann to Kobelt; Teufen, Febru 9, 1942, 9 ff. BAr 27/4783.
79. Walther to Dollfus; November 21, 1941. Copy. BAr 5795/328.
80. Gustav Däniker, "Verteidigungsschrift gegen die vom Armeeauditor in seinem Entscheid vom 28. März 1942 gegen mich erhobenen Anschuldigungen"; Walenstadt, May 15, 1942. Copy No. 000001. Annotated by the General. BAr 5795/440,2. Däniker made a mistake regarding the date; the army investigator made his decision on March 26, 1942; March 28, 1942 was the day on which the General issued the decree establishing the sentences against Däniker and Frick.
81. Ibid., 25 f.
82. General to Däniker; AHQ, July 8, 1942. Confidential. BAr 5795/440,2.
83. Däniker to General; "Nachtrag zur Verteidigungsschrift vom 15. Mai 1942"; Walenstadt, July 14, 1942. Confidential. BAr 5795/440,2.
84. Remarks by Eugster, ibid.
85. Däniker to Kobelt; Walenstadt, June 18, 1942. BAr 2805/1,5.
86. Ulrich Wille, "Gedanken zum Entscheid des Armeeauditors gegen Oberst Däniker"; May 18, 1942, 32. Copy No. 001. Annotated by the General. BAr 27/4783. Just like in the files, where "Armeeauditor" and "Oberauditor" are used interchangeably, this publication uses "Army Investigator" and "Chief Investigator (of the Army)" to identify one and the same person.
87. Wille to General; Meilen, May 25, 1942. Personal. BAr 5795/440,2.
88. Wille 1942, 7 ff. Annotations by Guisan.
89. Bracher to Huber; AHQ, May 25, 1942. Personal and confidential. BAr 5795/440,2.
90. Barbey to General; AHQ, June 1, 1942. Personal and confidential, handwritten. BAr 5795/440,2.

91. Ibid.
92. Handwritten remarks by Prisi regarding copy No. 001 of Wille's "Thoughts"; May 29, 1942.
93. General to Wille; AHQ, June 1, 1942. Personal. Carbon copy. BAr 5795/440,2.
94. Wille to General; HQ, June 5, 1942. Personal. BAr 5795/440,2.
95. Wille to General; HQ, June 30, 1942. Personal, confidential. BAr 5795/440,2.
96. Kobelt to Wille; Bern, June 10, 1942. Carbon copy. BAr 5800/2 and 27/4783.
97. Eugster, "Feststellungen des Armeeauditors," op. cit., 12.
98. Ibid., 15.
99. Ibid., 14 f. Also Eugster to General; Bern, June 30, 1942. Personal. BAr 5795/440,2.
100. Eugster to General; Bern, July 3, 1942. Personal and confidential. Annotated by the General.
    BAr 5795/440,2.
101. Züblin to Wille; Bern, April 25, 1942. AfZ Nl Zü.
102. Von Erlach to General; July 2, 1942. Handwritten. BAr 5795/333.
103. Petition to the Federal Council; Zürich, July 17, 1942. BAr 27/4783.
104. Ibid.; annotated by the Military Attorney General.
105. Gerhart Waeger, Die Sündenböcke der Schweiz. Olten 1971, 184.
106. Brunner to General; Div. HQ, May 22, 1942. BAr 5795/440,2.
107. Report on tapped telephone conversation; May 4, 1942, 19.50 hours. BAr 5795/440,2.
108. P. Meyer, Handwritten notes; May 9, 1942. Nl Mey.
109. Ibid.
110. Minutes of Federal Council meeting, January 26, 1943. BAr.
111. Däniker to Kobelt; Kilchberg, February 13, 1943. BAr 27/4784.
112. Däniker to Nager; Kilchberg, February 8, 1944. Carbon copy. AfZ Nl Dä 80.
113. Däniker to Nager; Kilchberg, October 28, 1944. Carbon copy. AfZ Nl Dä 80.
114. Nager to Däniker; Div. HQ, November 7, 1944. AfZ Nl Dä 80.
115. Nager to Däniker; Div. HQ, November 16, 1944. AfZ Nl Dä 80.
116. Swiss soldier [anonymous] to General; May 1, 1942. BAr 5795/440.
117. Däniker 1941d, 9 f., 13 f.
118. Däniker to Wille; Kilchberg, December 29, 1944. Carbon copy. AfZ Nl Dä 80.
119. Gustav Däniker, "Im Dienste der Schweiz," in Schweizerische Politik, publication of the People's
    Alliance for Switzerland's Independence, issue no. 11, Zürich 1945, 27.
120. Die Tat, September 18, 1947.
121. Ernst 1963a, 11.
122. Cf. Chapter 15 above.
123. Bericht des Generaladjutanten, op. cit., 246. There is considerable material on Däniker's life and
    the Däniker affair at the Federal Archives in Bern and at the Archives for Contemporary
    History in Zürich which would make it worthwhile to undertake a special study on him.

Chapter 22: Relations with the Federal Council

1. Guisan [1946], 267.
2. "Bericht des Bundesrates zum Bericht des Generals," 21.
3. Chapuisat 1950, 112.
4. de Reynold 1963, 668.
5. Böschenstein 1978, 286.
6. Text of the farewell address, n.d. [1945]. Typewritten. BAr 5795/175.
7. Rudolf Minger, "Zum Geleit" in Guisan 1953, 10.
8. List of meetings, n.d. [1945]. BAr 5795/89.
9. Labhart, Diary, October 31, 1939.
10. Guisan, Notes for speech, end of 1940. BAr 5795/89.
11. Du Pasquier, Journal, November 4, 1940. Quoted in Kreis 1976, 126.
12. General to Minger's family; Pully, August 24, 1955. BAr Nl Mi.
13. Barbey 1948, November 11, 1940, 57.
14. Gadient to General; Chur, November 21, 1940. BAr 5795/77.
15. General to Gadient; AHQ, November 25, 1940. Personal. BAr 5795/77.

16. Barbey 1948, 57.
17. Menz 1976, 361 ff.
18. Labhart, Diary, December 17, 1940. Louis Chamorel, a farmer in Gryon, was a Councilor of State for the canton of Vaud.
19. Labhart, Diary, December19, 1940.
20. Barbey 1948, December 18, 1940, 60, 62.
21. Hausamann to Kobelt; Teufen, January 15, 1946. BAr 5800/2.
22. Guisan [1946], 267.
23. "Protokoll der nationalrätlichen Kommission zur Behandlung des Berichtes des Generals," 47.
24. "Rapport de l'Etat-major particulier du Général" [IV], 20.
25. Barbey 1948, May 8, 1941, 84 f.
26. Barbey 1948, May 10, 1941, 85. Cf. Chapter 30 below.
27. Weiss 1939, 176.
28. Guisan [1946], 266.
29. "Conférences du Général avec les Conseillers fédéraux dès le 10 mai 1940," n.d. [after July 17, 1945]. BAr 5795/207.
30. [Kobelt], "Referat des Chefs des EMD"; Interlaken, January 10, 1942, 8 f. Confidential. BAr 5795/146.
31. Kurz 1975, 99.
32. Cf. Chapter 17 above.
33. Kobelt to General; Bern, September 19, 1942. Personal and confidential. BAr 5795/87.
34. Kobelt to General; Bern, September 19, 1942.
35. Labhart, Diary, September 15, 1942.
36. Labhart, Diary, February 3, 1942.
37. Labhart, Diary, July 6, 1943.
38. Federal Council to General; Bern, January 12, 1943, 3. BAr 5795/88.
39. Federal Council to General; Bern, January 12, 1943, 3. Handwritten annotation by Barbey.
40. Handwritten notes, "Conf[érence] avec Kobelt du 29 mai 1943." BAr 5795/88.
41. Handwritten notes, "Conf[érence] avec Kobelt".
42. Cf. Chapter 31 below.
43. Hafner 1986, 222.
44. Obrecht to Head of Military Department (Minger); Bern, May 3, 1940. BAr 2809/1,5.
45. Quoted in Hafner 1986, 221.
46. Hafner 1986, 225.
47. Minutes of meeting on November 23, 1942, 4. Confidential. BAr 5795/87. The minutes were kept by Captain Hans Bracher of the general staff.
48. Minutes of meeting on November 23, 1942, 3.
49. Minutes of Federal Council meeting, November 27, 1942. BAr.
50. Böschenstein 1978, 283.
51. Hafner 1986, 225.
52. Stampfli to General; January 17, 1945. Quoted in Hafner 1986, 224.
53. General, "Aide-mémoire à l'intention du Conseil fédéral"; AHQ, December 26, 1941, 1. Confidential. BAr 5800/2.
54. General, "Aide-mémoire," 3.
55. Kobelt to General; draft, n.d. [early 1942]. BAr 5800/2.
56. General, "Exposé au Conseil fédéral sur l'activité de l'Armée en 1942"; AHQ, December 24, 1942, 13. Top secret. BAr 5795/199.
57. Minutes of Federal Council meeting; January 12, 1943. Excerpt. BAr 27/14820.
58. Federal Council to General; Bern, January 12, 1943, 1. BAr 27/14820.
59. Federal Council to General; Bern, January 12, 1943, 3.
60. General to Federal Council; AHQ, January 19, 1943. BAr 5795/88.
61. General to Federal Council, January 19, 1943, 2 f, 4.
62. Notes for minutes, January 20, 1943. Confidential. BAr 27/14820.
63. Federal Council to General; Bern, January 22, 1943. BAr 27/14820.
64. Annotations on copy of General's letter to Federal Council; AHQ, January 19, 1943. BAr 5795/88.

65. Barbey 1948, January 8, 1944, 203.
66. Minutes of Federal Council meeting; December 30, 1942. BAr Nl Ko.
67. Kobelt, Diary, December 29, 1942.
68. Kobelt, Diary, December 29, 1942.
69. Note for file (Bracher); Bern, December 30, 1942. BAr 27/14131. The General knew about his son's relationship with Miss L.; on November 18, 1942, he noted, "no job, lives off her friends' money." BAr J.I. 127.
70. Etter to members of Federal Council; Bern, December 30, 1942. BAr 27/14131.
71. General to Kobelt; AHQ, January 4, 1943. Personal. BAr 27/14131.
72. Kobelt to General; Bern, January 5, 1943. Personal and confidential. BAr 27/14131.
73. Exchange of letters General-von Steiger; January 7-8, 1943. Personal and confidential. BAr 27/14131.
74. General to Kobelt; AHQ, January 12, 1943. Personal and confidential. BAr 27/14131.
75. Kobelt to General; Bern, January 15, 1943. Personal. BAr 27/14131.
76. General to Kobelt; AHQ, January 21, 1943. BAr 27/14131.
77. Kobelt to General; Bern, January 25, 1943. BAr 27/14131.
78. General to Kobelt; AHQ, January 27, 1943. Annotation by Federal Councilor Kobelt, January 28, 1943. BAr 27/14131.
79. Kobelt to General; Bern, Jan. 5, 1943. Personal and confidential. BAr 27/14131. On the deal with the barracks, cf. Chapter 27 below.
80. Jules Sandoz to author; Biel, October 4, 1985.
81. P. Meyer, handwritten note; Interlaken, n.d. [approx. 1941]. BAr Nl Mey.
82. Sandoz 1969, 9 ff.
83. General to Kobelt; AHQ, February 8, 1943. Confidential. BAr 5800/1.
84. "Ha," Special report, February. 5, 1943, No. 225. Personal, confidential. BAr 5800/1.
85. Kobelt, Diary, February 9, 1943.
86. Hausamann to Masson; February 10, 1943. Confidential. BAr 5800/1.
87. Hausamann to Kobelt; Teufen, February 11, 1943. BAr 5800/1.
88. Kobelt, Diary, February 11, 1943.
89. Kobelt, Diary, February 12, 1943.
90. Kobelt, Diary, February 16, 1943.
91. Pilet-Golaz to Celio; Bern, February 16, 1943. Personal and confidential. Copy to Kobelt. BAr 5800/1.
92. General to Chief of General Staff (Huber); AHQ, February 17, 1943. Personal, confidential. BAr 5795/448,1.
93. Celio to General; Bern, Feb. 19, 1943. Personal, confidential. BAr 5800/1 and 5795/448,2.
94. Hausamann to General; in the field, February 16, 1943. BAr 5795/448,2.
95. Hausamann to General, February 16, 1943.
96. General to Kobelt; AHQ, February 16, 1943. Personal, confidential. BAr 5800/1.
97. Hausamann to Kobelt; Teufen, February 21, 1943. BAr 5800/1.
98. Hausamann to General; Teufen, February 25, 1943. BAr 5795/448,2.
99. Hausamann to General, February 25, 1943, 3 f.
100. Minutes of hearing; Lucerne, March 29, 1943. BAr 5795/448,2.
101. Military Attorney General (Eugster) to General; Bern, April 1, 1943. Personal and confidential. BAr 5795/448,2.
102. General to Kobelt; AHQ, April 13, 1943. Confidential. BAr 5800/1.
103. Hausamann to General; May 12, 1943. BAr 5795/448,2.
104. General to Hausamann; AHQ, May 16, 1943. Personal, confidential. BAr 5795/448,2.
105. General to Huber; AHQ, May 14, 1943. Personal, confidential. BAr 27/9844. Cf. illustration.
106. Note by Masson; May 19, 1943. BAr 27/9844.
107. Hausamann to General; Teufen, July 9, 1943. Carbon copy. AfZ Nl Ha.
108. Hausamann to General; Teufen, January 4, 1944. BAr 27/9844.
109. General to Kobelt; AHQ, January 8, 1944. Personal. BAr 27/9844.
110. Hausamann to Masson; October 10, 1943. BAr 27/9844.
111. Pilet-Golaz to Kobelt; Bern, January 19, 1944. BAr 27/9844.

112. Information by Group Id, March 1, 1944. BAr 27/9844.
113. Bonjour 1981 b, 317 ff.
114. Oeri to General; Bern, June 15, 1943. Handwritten. BAr 5795/448,2.
115. Erwin Bucher to author; Bern, August 21, 1986.
116. Hans Häfliger-Husi to General; Goldau, November 30, 1946. BAr 5795/207.
117. [Hans] Hausamann, "Politisch-militärpolitische Denkschrift zu Handen des Herrn Oberbefehlshabers der Armee"; October 9, 1940, 2 f. Carbon copy. ArSchü.
118. Hausamann, "Politisch-militärpolitische Denkschrift", 4 f.
119. Hausamann, "Politisch-militärpolitische Denkschrift", 6 f.
120. Kurz 1975, 100.
121. Böschenstein 1978, 283.
122. Handwritten note by Barbey on Federal Council's letter to General; Bern, June 23, 1944. BAr 5795/89.
123. Ernst Wetter, Notes on Kimche's book, *General Guisans Zweifrontenkrieg*, Zürich, August 8, 1962, 5. BAr Nl Wet.
124. Müller 1975, 82.
125. Marguth 1959, 36.
126. Kobelt, Diary, December 31, 1941.
127. Kobelt to General; January 3, 1944. BAr 5800/1.
128. Kobelt to General; October 21, 1944. BAr 5800/1.
129. General to Kobelt; AHQ, October 24, 1944. BAr 5800/1.
130. Kobelt to General; December 30, 1944. BAr 5800/1.
131. General to Kobelt; AHQ, January 4, 1945. Personal. BAr 5800/1.
132. Gautschi 1970.
133. Cf. Chapter 36 below.
134. Frick to Kobelt; Bern, August 31, 1946, 22. BAr Nl Ko.
135. Gafner 1974, 137.

Chapter 23: Cooperation with Chief of the General Staff Huber

1. Walde 1983.
2. Häni 1977–79, 41.
3. Steiner 1983.
4. Barbey 1967 (May 10, 1940), 136.
5. Handwritten notes, n.d. [after August 30, 1939]. BAr 5795/449.
6. "Question du Haut Commandement, Etat le 9.12.39" [unsigned, probably written by Gonard]. BAr 5795/422.
7. Guisan [1946], 155, 263.
8. Guisan 1953, 52.
9. Draft of Guisan's eulogy on the occasion of the funeral service for Chief of the General Staff Huber, March 16, 1953. BAr Nl Gui.
10. Walde 1983, 182.
11. Guisan [1946], 150–154.
12. Barbey 1948, 102, 151, 175.
13. Oberkommando des Heeres 1942, 95, enclosure 8. The statement that his wife was French is wrong; Chief of the General Staff Huber, who was born into a Catholic family, was married to Agatha Trepp, a Protestant from Splügen, canton of Grisons.
14. Huber to Kobelt; Brienz, January 31, 1947. BAr 5800/2.
15. Walde 1983, 66.
16. Cf. Chapter 10 above.
17. Huber to Kobelt; Brienz, Jan. 31, 1947, 4 f.
18. Huber to Kobelt, 11.
19. Huber to Kobelt, 17.
20. Frick to Kobelt; Bern, August 31, 1946, 7, 25. BAr 5800/2.
21. Borel to Kobelt; Neuchâtel, August 14, 1947, 7. BAr 5800/2.

22. Labhart, Diary, December 23, 1939.
23. Labhart, Diary, July 15, 1941.
24. Barbey 1948 (May 14, 1943), 178.
25. Annotation by the General in a report by Bureau "Ha", n.d. [approx. fall of 1940]. BAr 2809/1,4.
26. Wille to General; HQ, June 15, 1940. Personal. BAr 5795/465.
27. General to Wille; AHQ, July 1, 1940. Personal, confidential. BAr 5795/465.
28. Wille to General; August 31, 1940. Personal. BAr 5795/465.
29. Däniker to Wille; Walenstadt, July 30, 1940. Carbon copy. AfZ Nl Dä 80.
30. Frölicher to Bonna; Berlin, September 17, 1940. BAr. Quoted in Kreis 1976, 143.
31. It was typical for Huber to say as late as the 1930s that he did "not believe that tanks [would] be able to succeed in positional warfare." Walde 1983, 37 f.
32. Walde 1983, 124. Similar in Roesch 1986, 58.
33. Oberkommando des Heeres, 1942. Quoted in Schaufelberger 1985, 9.
34. Parkinson 1968.
35. Guisan [1946], 161 f.
36. Minutes of briefing by Chief of the General Staff; September 22, 1941, 1 f. BAr 27/14151,2.
37. Minutes of briefing, 1 f.
38. Jeker 1959, 239. Walde 1983, 124. By way of comparison, the headquarters of the Swiss Army that fought in the civil war of 1847 under General Dufour had a total of 153 staff, officers and soldiers combined. Weiss 1939, 49.
39. Walde 1983, 79.
40. Barbey 1948, 76 f., 100. Cf. photograph XXVI.
41. Barbey 1948, 100.
42. General to Huber; AHQ, January 6, 1941. BAr 5795/98.
43. General to Huber; AHQ, February 4, 1941. BAr 5795/98.
44. Minutes of briefing by Chief of the General Staff; April 16, 1940. BAr 27/14151,1.
45. Huber, Handwritten note; May 12, 1941. BAr 27/14139.
46. Barbey 1948 (January 8, 1944), 204.
47. Issues to be discussed with the Chief of the General Staff; June 15, 1943. BAr 5795/88.
48. Issues to be discussed.
49. Issues to be discussed with the Chief of the General Staff; February 18, 1944, 11.15 hours. BAr 5795/89.
50. Huber to General; AHQ, Jan. 27, 1945, and General to Huber; AHQ, January 31, 1945. BAr 5795/102.
51. Huber to General; AHQ, June 28, 1941. Personal and confidential. BAr 5795/86.
52. General to Huber; AHQ, July 2, 1941. Personal and confidential. BAr 5795/86.
53. Handwritten annotation by the General on the copy of his letter dated July 2, 1941. BAr 5795/86.
54. Huber to Kobelt; Brienz, Jan. 31, 1947. BAr 5800/2.
55. Huber to Kobelt; AHQ, June 27, 1942. BAr 5795/100.
56. Huber to General; AHQ, June 27, 1942. Personal. BAr 5795/100 and 5795/449.
57. General to Huber; AHQ, June 27, 1942. Personal, confidential. BAr 5795/100.
58. Walde 1983, 64.
59. Barbey 1948 (November 11, 1944), 268.
60. Barbey 1948, 135.
61. Huber, Handwritten note; January 23, 1945. BAr 27/14139.
62. Huber to Federal Council; AHQ, February 2, 1945. Submitted via the General's office. BAr 5795/449.
63. Walde 1983, 65 f.
64. General to Huber; AHQ, March 1, 1945. BAr 5795/449.
65. Huber to General; AHQ, May 29, 1945. BAr 5795/327.
66. General to Huber; AHQ, June 3, 1945. Personal, confidential. BAr 5795/327.
67. Huber to General; AHQ, July 26, 1945. Personal, confidential. BAr 5795/455.
68. Huber to Kobelt; Brienz, January 31, 1947. Cf. Chapter 28 below.

69. Jean R. von Salis to this author; Brunegg, June 21, 1984.
70. Huber to Kobelt; Brienz, January 31, 1947, 3.
71. Huber to Kobelt, 4.
72. Cf. Chapter 36 below.

Chapter 24: Relations with Subordinate Commanders
 1. Guisan [1946], 171.
 2. Barbey 1948, 88 f.
 3. Guisan [1946], 173.
 4. Cf. below in this Chapter.
 5. Chapuisat 1950, 132.
 6. General to Huber; AHQ, May 29, 1940. Personal. BAr 5795/449.
 7. General to Huber, May 29, 1940.
 8. General to directly subordinate commanders; AHQ, March 21, 1940. BAr 27/14126.
 9. Guisan [1946], 264.
10. Minutes of briefing; Bern, April 29, 1940. Confidential. BAr 27/14126. Regarding the items discussed during that briefing, cf. Chapter 11 above.
11. General to Commanders of army corps 1 to 4; AHQ, October 15, 1940. BAr 5795/85.
12. Military Service Regulations, Bern 1927, article 70 states, "The Commander makes his own decisions and is solely responsible for them. Nothing good comes out of councils of war."
13. For instance, the officers participating at the briefing on November 29, 1944 at the Federal Palace included the chief of the general staff, the four corps commanders, the chief instructor, two assistant chiefs of staff (Ia and Ib), the head of the Operational Section, the head of the Mobilization Section, the chief of the personal staff, and the liaison officer with the Military Department. Minutes of briefing; Bern, November 29, 1944. Confidential. BAr 27/14126.
14. Minutes of briefing; AHQ, June 5, 1944. Confidential. BAr 5795/89. Cf. Chapter 31 below.
15. Denis van Berchem; presentation at the Archives for Contemporary History; Zürich, March 13, 1985.
16. Denis van Berchem to this author; Vandoeuvres, September 9, 1986.
17. Labhart, Diary, January 20, 1942.
18. Labhart, Diary, August 13, 1943.
19. Labhart, Diary, August 13, 1943. Regarding Labhart's influence on Kobelt, cf. Chapter 22 above.
20. Guisan 1953, 62.
21. Barbey 1948 (July 30, 1940), 33.
22. General to Labhart; AHQ, March 19, 1940. BAr 5795/142.
23. General to Labhart; AHQ, June 6, 1940. BAr 5795/142.
24. General to Labhart; AHQ, October 10, 1941. Personal, confidential. BAr 5795/143.
25. Issues to be discussed with the Cdr. of 4th Army Corps; n.d. [after June 1, 1942]. BAr 5795/89.
26. General, Handwritten notes of a conversation with Military Attorney General Eugster; October 28, 1943. BAr 5795/455.
27. General to Dollfus; AHQ, September 10, 1940. Personal. BAr 5795/441.
28. Armand von Ernst to this author; Muri BE, August 7, 1985.
29. Notes for briefing on operational exercise; February 28, 1941. BAr 5795/86.
30. Barbey 1948, 75.
31. Cf. Chapter 25 below.
32. Cf. also Chapter 17 above.
33. Barbey 1948, 61 f.
34. Barbey 1948 (December 13, 1940), 61.
35. Barbey 1948 (May 7, 1941), 84.
36. Minutes of briefing; May 8, 1941. Confidential. BAr 27/14126.
37. Minutes of briefing; May 8, 1941. Addendum.
38. Minutes of briefing by Chief of General Staff; May 13, 1941. Confidential. BAr 27/14151,1. Also, General to addressees of Operations Order No. 13; AHQ, May 14, 1941. Confidential. BAr 5795/293.

39. Miescher to General; Glion-sur-Montreux, June 9, 1941. BAr 5795/459.
40. Miescher to General; Basel, November 21, 1941. BAr 5795/459.
41. Quoted in "Zur Erinnerung an Herrn Dr. Rudolf Miescher, Colonel-Corps Commander." Basel [author unknown], n.d. [1945], 11.
42. Labhart, Diary, May 22, 1941.
43. Special Service (Capt. P. Meyer) to General; AHQ, September 1, 1941. Personal, confidential. BAr 5795/460.
44. Report by Attaché; July 1, 1941. Quoted in Kreis 1976, 183.
45. General's notes on "Plot between Lab[hart], W[ille], and Kob[elt]; September 24, 1942, [information] by Bracher." BAr 5795/453. Cf. illustration.
46. Edmund Wehrli to this author; Zürich, August 2, 1985.
47. Barbey 1948 (February 19, 1942), 117.
48. Barbey 1948 (October 21, 1943), 193.
49. General to Prisi; AHQ, October 24, 1943. BAr 5800/1.
50. Lardelli to General; army corps HQ, October 30, 1943. BAr 5800/1.
51. Lardelli to Kobelt; army corps HQ, October 30, 1943. BAr 5800/1.
52. Lardelli to Kobelt.
53. Minutes of briefing; AHQ, November 4, 1943. Confidential. BAr 5800/1.
54. Labhart, Diary, January 10, 1944.
55. Barbey 1948 (October 27, 1943), 193.
56. Cf. Chapter 38 below.
57. Denis van Berchem to this author; Vandoeuvres, March 13, 1985.
58. Walde 1983, 67.
59. The analyses are at the Federal Archives at 5795/460.
60. General to Borel; AHQ, April 5, 1945. Personal. BAr 5795/460.
61. Borel to Kobelt; Neuchâtel, August 14, 1946, 3. BAr 5800/1.
62. Cf. Chapter 36 below.

Chapter 25: Casting Aside Chief Instructor Wille

1. Cf. Chapter 21 above.
2. General to Wille; AHQ, September 1, 1939. BAr 5795/465.
3. Wille to General; Bern, September 2, 1939. Carbon copy. ArMa.
4. Labhart, Diary, September 2, 1939.
5. Wille, diary notes, September 4, 1939. ArMa.
6. Wille to General; Bern, September 5, 1939. Carbon copy. ArMa.
7. Draft of order; September 4, 1939. Carbon copy. ArMa.
8. Wille, diary notes, September 6, 1939. ArMa.
9. General to directly subordinate commanders; AHQ, September 7, 1939. ArMa. Wille had suggested six instead of four weeks of training.
10. Wille to General; Bern, September 8, 1939. Carbon copy. ArMa.
11. General to Wille; AHQ, September 11, 1939. ArMa.
12. Wille, diary notes, September 15, 1939. ArMa.
13. Wille, diary notes, September 15, 1939.
14. Cf. Chapter 7 above.
15. General to Wille; AHQ, September 25, 1939. ArMa.
16. Wille to General; HQ, September 26, 1939. Personal. Carbon copy. ArMa.
17. Wille to General; HQ, September 25, 1939. Carbon copy. ArMa.
18. General to Wille; AHQ, October 3, 1939. ArMa.
19. General to Wille; AHQ, November 2, 1939. BAr 5795/85.
20. Wille to General; HQ, November 13, 1939. Carbon copy. ArMa.
21. Wille to General; November 13, 1939.
22. General, Terms of Reference for the Chief Instructor of the Armed Forces during the time of wartime duty; AHQ, December 16, 1939. Published in Guisan [1946], 190–192.
23. General, order regarding training; AHQ, December 17, 1939. BAr 5795/465. The draft written by Wille is at the archives in Mariafeld.

24. General to Wille; AHQ, September 7, 1940. BAr 5795/465.
25. Barbey 1948 (February 22, 1941), 77 f.
26. Barbey 1948 (June 28, 1942), 128 f.
27. Guisan [1946], 195.
28. *Rapport de l'Etat-major particulier* [V], 9.
29. Guisan [1946], 193.
30. Guisan [1946], 194.
31. Cf. Chapter 16 above.
32. Wille to Pilet-Golaz; Bern, August 12, 1940. Personal. BAr EDI 1005/1.
33. Handwritten note; August 27, 1940. ArMa.
34. Cf. Chapter 20 above.
35. Handwritten note; August 30, 1940. ArMa.
36. Wille to General; HQ, August 31, 1940, 2. Personal. BAr 5795/465.
37. Wille to General, August 31, 1940, 1.
38. Wille to General, August 31, 1940, 5.
39. Draft of a decree regarding exercises for the troops; AHQ, September 26, 1940. BAr 5795/465.
40. General to Wille; AHQ, October 4, 1940. ArMa.
41. General to Commanders of Army Corps; AHQ, October 15, 1940. BAr 5795/465.
42. Wille to Minger; October 10, 1940. Personal. Carbon copy. ArMa.
43. Wille to Pilet-Golaz; Bern, October 10, 1940. Carbon copy. ArMa.
44. Wille to Minger; HQ, November 12, 1940. Personal. Carbon copy. ArMa.
45. General to Wille; AHQ, October 23, 1940. Personal. ArMa.
46. Wille to General; HQ, October 25, 1940. Personal. BAr 5795/465.
47. General to Wille; AHQ, November 9, 1940. Personal. ArMa.
48. Hausamann 1947b, 89 f.
49. Anonymous report [by Bureau "Ha"?], October 4, 1940. BAr.
50. Report by Bureau "Ha", October 26, 1940, 2. Secret. BAr 5795/465.
51. General to Minger; AHQ, November 3, 1940. BAr 5795/465.
52. Handwritten note by the General on the "List of [pro-German] revival movements currently existing in Switzerland"; AHQ, August 6, 1940. BAr 5795/342.
53. Handwritten note, November 19, 1940, 9.45 hours. BAr.
54. General to Wille; AHQ, December 18, 1940. Personal, secret. ArMa.
55. Walde 1983, 121.
56. Cf. Chapter 21 above.
57. Eugster to General; Bern, June 16, 1942. Personal, secret. BAr 5795/440.2.
58. General to Kobelt; AHQ, June 18, 1942. Personal, secret. BAr 5795/440.2.
59. Kobelt to General; Bern, June 27, 1942. Personal, secret. BAr 27/4783. Cf. Chapter 21 above.
60. General to Wille; AHQ, June 26, 1942. Personal, secret. BAr 5795/440.2.
61. Anonymous note regarding case W[ille] – D[äniker], June 25, 1942. BAr 5795/440.2.
62. Feldmann to General; Bern, July 8, 1942,18. Personal, confidential. BAr 5795/333.
63. Barbey 1948 (May 13, 1942), 121.
64. Barbey 1948 (September 3, 1942), 140.
65. General to Wille; AHQ, October 26, 1942. Personal. ArMa.
66. Wille to General; HQ, November 7, 1942. Personal. Carbon copy. ArMa.
67. General to Wille; AHQ, November 9, 1942. Personal. ArMa.
68. Handwritten notes by Wille on General's letter of November 16, 1942 in which he set the date for their meeting. ArMa.
69. General to Wille; AHQ, November 28, 1942. Personal, confidential. ArMa.
70. Wille to General; HQ, December 2, 1942. Personal. Carbon copy. ArMa.
71. Decree; AHQ, December 8, 1942. ArMa.
72. Minutes of briefing on December 19, 1942. Secret. BAr 27/14126.
73. Wille to Däniker; Mariafeld, December 4, 1942. Nl Dä 80.
74. Jürg Wille to Däniker; barracks of Zürich, January 24, 1943. Nl Dä 80.
75. Wille to Däniker; Bern, December 28, 1942. Nl Dä 80.

76. Wille to Kobelt; Meilen, January 6, 1943. Personal. Carbon copy. ArMa.

77. Wille to General; Bern, December 29, 1942. Carbon copy. ArMa.

78. Feldmann to General; Bern, January 30, 1943, 34. Personal, confidential. BAr 5795/333.

79. Feldmann to General, January 30, 1943, 33.

80. Däniker to Wille; Kilchberg, December 31, 1942. Carbon copy. Nl Dä 80.

81. Däniker to Wille, December 31, 1942.

82. General, handwritten notes for a meeting with Marcuard, December 8, 1942. BAr 5795/87.

83. Barbey 1948 (December 8, 1942), 155.

84. General, Terms of reference for the Chief Instructor during wartime duty, effective March 1, 1943; AHQ, December 16, 1942. BAr 5795/454.

85. General to Marcuard; AHQ, December 30, 1942. Secret. BAr 5795/454.

86. Personal notes for Commander-in-Chief [n.d., before January 6, 1943]. BAr 5795/454.

Chapter 26: Cases of Treason, Death Sentences, and Surveillance Activities

1. Dollfus [1946], 258.

2. "Spione, Saboteure, Landesverräter: Übersicht über die bis Ende 1945 abgeschlossenen militärgerichtlichen Untersuchungen," March 1, 1946. Secret. BAr 27/10112.

3. Dollfus [1946], 259.

4. Penal code of the armed forces of June 13, 1927, article 5.

5. General's Personal Staff to Labhart; AHQ, May 15, 1940. BAr 5795/142.

6. General to Head of Federal Military Department; AHQ, May 14, 1940. BAr 5795/142.

7. Young citizens of the city of Bern (A. Bähler, lawyer; Dr. G. Roos; Dr. Hans Wirz) to Federal Council, May 15, 1940. BAr Nl Wi.

8. Minutes of meeting of National Council proxy committee, May 20–21, 1940. BAr.

9. Dollfus [1946], 247.

10. Ordinance of May 28, 1940 by the Federal Council amending the penal code of the armed forces. The ordinance was repealed at the time of the 1945 armistice; hence, the death sentences pronounced in the defendants' absence were not carried out when the convicts returned to Switzerland after the war.

11. Guisan 1953, 175, 179.

12. Noll 1980. Unfortunately the Military Attorney General obliged Noll to use false names in his book. In this author's opinion, there was no sufficient reason to hide the real names because at the time these names were repeatedly mentioned in the press and on the radio, making them common knowledge. Dollfus [1946], 262, also mentioned every single executed person by his real name.

13. Dollfus [1946], 257.

14. Quoted in Trachsel 1944, 131.

15. Fuhrer 1982.

16. Daniel 1945b, 7.

17. Minutes of meeting re: foreign intelligence activities, May 4, 1942. Secret. BAr.

18. Minutes of meeting re: foreign intelligence activities.

19. Fuhrer 1985, 423.

20. German Army High Command, *Kleines Orientierungsheft Schweiz*, 289 ff.

21. German Army High Command, War diary (October 2, 1940), vol. 1, 1982, 110.

22. General to Military Attorney General (Eugster); AHQ, February 7, 1942. Personal, secret. BAr 5795/343.

23. General to Military Attorney General (Eugster); AHQ, August 25, 1942. Secret. BAr 5795/48. Reimann and Kully were sentenced to death; Merkt to life imprisonment.

24. BAr 5795/481.

25. Daetwyler to General; Zumikon, January 18, 1943. Marti to General; Zürich, October 27, 1942. BAr 5795/481 and 5795/482.

26. Guisan 1953, 61.

27. Military Attorney General (Eugster) to Federal Council; Bern, October 23, 1942. Copy. BAr 5795/480.

28. Minutes of pardon committee meeting, November 2, 3, and 4, 1942, 6. Nl Ki.
29. Minutes of pardon committee meeting, 17. In every case, Parliament followed the committee's recommendation. For example, Schrämli's appeal for mercy was rejected by 176 nay and 36 yea. "Spione, Saboteure, Landesverräter," 53.
30. Gautschi 1978, 468.
31. Quoted in Noll 1980, 68.
32. Noll 1980, 69.
33. Bonjour 1983, 43.
34. *National-Zeitung*, October 2, 1942, No. 456; also, *Berner Tagwacht*, Oct. 2, 1942.
35. *Neue Berner Zeitung*, October 6, 1942.
36. "Das Wort des Generals," *Aufgebot*, October 15, 1942.
37. Guisan 1942.
38. Haas to Kobelt; Bern, November 6, 1942. Personal. BAr 27/14130.
39. Haas to Kobelt, handwritten annotations.
40. Cf. Meienberg 1974 and the 1977 movie by Richard Dindo on Schrämli's case, *Die Hinrichtung des Landesverräters Ernst S.*
41. Ordinance re: carrying out death sentences, July 9, 1940. BAr.
42. Noll 1980, 48.
43. Gossweiler to Command of 6th Division (Constam); Regiment quarters, April 20, 1943. BAr 5795/480.
44. Gossweiler to Command of 6th Division.
45. Dollfus [1946], 262.
46. Noll 1980, 139.
47. Noll 1980, 143.
48. Haas to General; Bern, April 3, 1944. Personal, secret. BAr 5795/481.
49. General to Haas; AHQ, April 4, 1944. Confidential. BAr 5795/481.
50. Feldmann to General; Bern, July 15, 1943, 33 f. Personal, confidential. BAr 5795/333. Feldmann must have written the letter knowing that the General had met with SS officers. Cf. Chapter 28 below.
51. Order by General; AHQ, December 14, 1939. BAr 27/4702.
52. Order by General; AHQ, May 17, 1941. BAr 27/13523. Cf. Kreis 1976, 78.
53. Report by agent [anonymous], December 23, 1942, 2. BAr 5795/333.
54. Report by Bureau "Ha," February 24, 1943. AfZ Nl Ha.
55. Fuhrer 1985, 415.
56. Bircher to Thoenen; Aarau, October 21, 1942. Copy. BAw.
57. Fuhrer 1985, 414 ff.
58. Köcher to von Weizsäcker; Bern, September 28, 1942. Personal. Copy. BAr EDI 1005/2.
59. Feldmann to General; Bern, January 30, 1943, 20. Personal, confidential. BAr 5795/333.
60. Intelligence Desk Switzerland (L. von Grote), remark; Berlin, April 10, 1943. Copy. BAr EDI 1005/2.
61. Fuhrer 1982, 35 ff.
62. Cf. Chapter 29 below.
63. Instructions regarding army counter-intelligence during wartime duty; AHQ, October 5, 1939. BAr 5795/342.
64. Chief of the General Staff (Labhart), army counter-intelligence; AHQ, October 27, 1939. Confidential. BAr 5795/342.
65. Diary of army staff, May 27, 1940.
66. Guisan 1953, 176.
67. Chief of the General Staff (Huber), Order re: cooperation between army counter-intelligence, police of territorial section, army police, and civilian police; AHQ, April 25, 1940. BAr 5795/342.
68. Hausamann [1946], 3.
69. Jaquillard to Masson; HQ, November 3, 1942. BAr 5795/451.
70. BAr 5795/436.
71. Minutes of meeting re: monitored telephone conversations in Interlaken, November 27, 1942, 5. BAr 5795/451.

72. P. Meyer, personal notes, [n.d.]. BAr Nl Mey.
73. Report by Bureau "Ha" to Colonel Müller, September 11, 1941. Personal. AfZ Nl Ha.
74. P. Meyer, handwritten notes, October 28, 1942. BAr Nl Mey.
75. P. Meyer, handwritten notes, October 28, 1942.
76. Barbey to Masson; AHQ, November 13, 1942. Personal, secret. BAr 5795/451.
77. Huber, notes, November 18, 1942. BAr 27/14139.
78. Eugster to General; Bern, November 16, 1942. Personal, secret. BAr 5795/451.
79. Handwritten note, November 18, 1942. BAr 5795/448,2.
80. Minutes of meeting re: monitored telephone conversations, 8.
81. Minutes of meeting re: monitored telephone conversations, 8.
82. Minutes of meeting re: monitored telephone conversations; handwritten remarks by General.
83. Handwritten notes by Guisan on back of letter to Masson dated December 1, 1942. BAr 5795/451.
84. Jaquillard to Chief of the General Staff; HQ, December 2, 1942. Personal, secret. BAr 5795/451.
85. Decisions by General and Chief of the General Staff; AHQ, December 10-11, 1942. BAr 5795/451.
86. General to Huber; AHQ, December 5, 1942. BAr 5795/451.
87. Minutes of briefing re: increasing foreign intelligence activities, May 4, 1942. Secret. BAr 27/10098,11.
88. Noll 1980, 181 ff.
89. Noll 1980, 47.
90. Wäsström 1985, 120 ff.

Chapter 27: The Schellenberg-Masson Connection

1. Cf. Chapter 28 below. SS Colonel Schellenberg was often given the title of brigadier general in the Swiss documents at that time, even though it seems that he was not promoted to that rank until the summer of 1944.
2. Basel-Stadt police department (Lützelschwab) to Kobelt; Basel, June 18, 1943. Personal. BAr 27/14131.
3. Basel-Stadt police department to Kobelt.
4. Shorthand minutes of conversation (Knecht); Bern, October 16, 1945. Copy. BAr 27/10027.
5. Kobelt, Diary, March 18, [1943]. Also Basel-Stadt police department to Kobelt.
6. Couchepin 1945, 6.
7. Minutes of examination Paul Meyer; Zürich, December 3, 1945. BAr 27/10027.
8. Paul Meyer, handwritten note, November 24, 1941. BAr Nl Mey.
9. Masson 1945, 2.
10. Masson 1945, 2, 5.
11. Barbey 1948 (Friday, December 12, 1941), 107.
12. Paul Meyer, note for personal file [n.d., after April 10, 1942]. BAr Nl Mey.
13. Meyer, note for personal file [after April 10, 1942].
14. Paul Meyer, handwritten notes, May 22, 1942. BAr Nl Mey.
15. Paul Meyer, handwritten notes, August 30, 1942.
16. Paul Meyer, note for personal file re: trip to Berlin, July 7–10, 1942. BAr Nl Mey.
17. Meyer, note for personal file re: trip to Berlin.
18. Meyer, note for personal file re: trip to Berlin.
19. Paul Meyer, handwritten notes, August 28, 1942. BAr Nl Mey.
20. Meyer, handwritten notes, August 28, 1942.
21. Couchepin 1945, 7.
22. Barbey 1948 (Thursday, September 3, 1942), 141.
23. Barbey 1948, 142.
24. Paul Meyer, handwritten notes, August 31, 1942. BAr Nl Mey.
25. Paul Meyer, handwritten notes, September 2, 1942.
26. Barbey 1948 (Tuesday, September 29, 1942), 143.
27. Paul Meyer, handwritten notes, September 9, 1942. BAr Nl Mey.

28. Masson 1945, 5 f.
29. Masson 1945, 6 f.
30. Barbey 1948 (September 9, 1942 and September 29, 1942), 143, 145 f.
31. Barbey 1948, 145, 146.
32. Couchepin 1945, 8.
33. Masson 1945, 7.
34. Paul Meyer, handwritten notes [n.d., after December 24, 1942]. BAr Nl Mey.
35. Masson to General; HQ, December 30, 1942. BAr 5795/327.
36. Paul Meyer, handwritten notes, [n.d., between December 24 and 26, 1942]. BAr Nl Mey.
37. Meyer, handwritten notes [between December 24 and 26, 1942]. Cf. Chapter 25 above.
38. General, handwritten notes, January 11, 1943. BAr 5795/333.
39. General, handwritten notes, January 11, 1943.
40. Meyer to General; AHQ, January 12, 1943. Personal, confidential. BAr 5795/455.
41. Püntner 1967, 136 ff.
42. Burri to General; Zürich, August 20, 1947. BAr Nl Gui.
43. General to Federal Prosecutor (Fürst); Pully, August 23, 1947. Carbon copy. BAr Nl Gui.
44. Paul Meyer, handwritten notes, February 10, [1943]. BAr Nl Mey.
45. Minutes of examination Paul Meyer; Bad Ragaz, August 7, 1945. BAr 5330/1982,1.
46. Hausamann 1947b, 20.
47. Waibel 1963, 13.
48. Capt. Wüest to Colonel Müller; Zürich, August 15, 1945. BAr 5330/1982,1.
49. Minutes of examination Holzach; Zürich, July 4, 1945. BAr 5330/1982,1.
50. Couchepin 1945, 64 ff.
51. Schellenberg 1979, 313 ff.
52. *Neue Zürcher Zeitung*, September 10, 1948, No. 1884.
53. Bernadotte 1945, 30 f.
54. Comment by A. Kaech during discussion at Archives for Contemporary History; Zürich, July 16, 1986.
55. Baron Heinz von Klimburg [n.d.]. File BAr.
56. Hausamann to Kobelt; Teufen, April 4, 1943. BAr 5800/1.
57. Information by "W", July 14, 1943. BAr 2809/1,4.
58. Minutes of meeting of National Council committee dealing with the General's postwar report, 27.

Chapter 28: The Meeting in Biglen

1. *Freies Volk* newspaper, Bern, February 20, 1948.
2. Guisan [1947], 16 f.
3. Kurz 1978, 192; also, Kurz 1974a, 89.
4. Paul Meyer, handwritten notes, January 27, 1943. BAr Nl Mey.
5. Meyer, notes, February 15, 1943.
6. Meyer, notes, February 25, 1943.
7. Meyer, notes, February 25, 1943.
8. Meyer, notes, n.d. [after March 7, 1943]. In the following passage, this author followed Meyer's account, unless otherwise stated. Meyer wrote the notes after the meeting in Biglen.
9. Schellenberg checked in at the hotel giving false information. He wrote that he was "Karl Schelkenberg, born 1904, manager of a factory, living in Frankfurt a.M." Bracher, notes, March 12, 1943. BAr 27/10022.
10. Guest book of the Bären restaurant, Biglen. Copy. BAr M 34/6.
11. Guest Book Bären, November 7, 1939.
12. Minutes of hearing Paul Meyer; Bern, May 28, 1945. BAr 5330/1982,1.
13. Bonjour, *Neutralität*, vol. V, 75.
14. Bracher, notes, March 12, 1943.
15. Barbey 1948 (March 3, 1943), 166 f.
16. Jules Sandoz to author; Biel, September 11, 1986. Also, Denis Berchem to author; Vandoeuvres, Sept. 9, 1986.

17. Diary of General's Personal Staff, March 3, 1943. BAr 5795/51,10.
18. Ernst Walder to Klaus Urner; Zürich, April 18, 1986. AfZ.
19. H. Berchtold-Schneider to General; Biglen, March 6, 1946. BAr 5795/455.
20. Patrizia V. Frey-Meyer to author; Petit-Vidy, February 13, 1987.
21. Arnim von Manikowsky to author; Hamburg, March 20, 1987. Cf. illustration.
22. Meyer, notes [after March 7, 1943].
23. Meyer, notes [after March 7, 1943].
24. Meyer, notes [after March 7, 1943]. Wiesendanger had joined them, arriving from Zürich.
25. Meyer, notes [after March 7, 1943]. While he was staying in Bern, Eggen received information by telegraph that his house had been destroyed in a bombing raid.
26. Declaration dated March 3, 1943. BAr 5795/334. On another copy of the document, the General wrote by hand, "text transmitted to Schellenberg in Arosa on March 6, 1943." BAr 27/10022.
27. Fink 1985, 90.
28. Ribbentrop to Köcher; Berlin, October 1, 1943. Personal. Copy. BAr EDI 1005/2.
29. Ribbentrop to Köcher. Concerning the documents in question, cf. Chapter 20 above.
30. Bracher, notes entitled, "General's Meeting with German Personalities," March 12, 1943. [3 pp.] BAr 27/10022.
31. Bracher, notes.
32. Barbey 1948 (March 10, 1943), 169.
33. Kobelt, diary, March 12, [1943].
34. Kobelt, diary, March 12, [1943].
35. Kobelt, diary, March 13, 1943.
36. Kobelt, diary, March 15, 1943.
37. Kobelt, diary, March 15, 1943.
38. General to Kobelt; AHQ, March 15, 1943. Personal, confidential. BAr 27/10022.
39. Kobelt to General; Bern, March 22, 1943. Personal, secret. BAr 27/10022.
40. Kobelt to General, March 22, 1943, General's handwritten annotations; AHQ, March 22, 1943, 18.00 hours. Personal, confidential.
41. Kobelt to General; Bern, March 29, 1943. Personal, secret. BAr 5795/334.
42. Minutes of Federal Council meeting, April 5, 1943. Excerpt. Secret. BAr 27/10022.
43. Kobelt to General; Bern, April 6, 1943. Personal, secret. BAr 5795/334. Published in Bonjour, Neutralität, vol. VII, 237 f.
44. Kobelt to General; April 6, 1943. General's handwritten annotations.
45. Pilet-Golaz, note, April 5, 1943. BAr 2809/1,4. The full text of his note is published in Bonjour, Neutralität VII, 237.
46. General to Kobelt; AHQ, April 7, 1943. Personal, secret. BAr 5795/334.
47. Guisan [1947], 17.
48. Cf. Chapter 19 above.
49. Guisan 1953, 18.
50. Ernst 1975e, 29 f.

Chapter 29: The 1943 "March Alarm" and the Messerschmitt Deal

1. Waibel to Masson; March 18, 1943, 18.15 hours, telephone call. BAr 27/14339.
2. Waibel to Masson; March 19, 1943, 17.25 hours, telephone call.
3. Information No. 3280, March 20, 1943, 08.30 hours. BAr 27/14339.
4. Barbey 1948 (March 20, 1943), 170.
5. Barbey 1948, 171.
6. Rigi (Waibel), Information No. 3285, March 22, 1943, 17.13 hours. Secret. BAr 27/14339.
7. Masson to General; March 23, 1943. BAr 5795/334.
8. Barbey 1948 (March 23, 1943), 172.
9. Measures by the Army Command in view of the current situation, March 22, 1943. BAr 27/14339.
10. Militärischer Rückblick, March 25, 1943, No. 514, 3. BAr 27/10022.

11. Guisan [1946], 53 f.
12. Guisan 1953, 150.
13. Gonard 1959, 47.
14. Statement by Waibel during a court hearing with a jury in Winterthur, September 15, 1947. BAr 27/9846. Quoted in Fuhrer 1980, 56.
15. Fuhrer 1980, 56.
16. Paul Meyer, handwritten notes, March 23, 1943. BAr Nl Mey.
17. Schwertenbach to General; Wolfsberg, March 25, 1943. BAr 5795/334.
18. General to Schwertenbach; AHQ, March 26, 1943. Carbon copy. BAr 5795/334.
19. Waibel to Müller; March 29, 1943. Personal, secret. BAr 27/9536.
20. Waibel to Müller.
21. Report by "Ha", March 24, 1943. AfZ Nl Ha.
22. It has not been established whether the alert in March 1943 was merely a bluff or whether anyone was actually arrested in Berlin after Masson had Viking's information verified there through the SS. Bucher 1988, 300 ff.
23. Ernst to Masson; March 27, 1943. Carbon copy. BAr Nl Er.
24. Ernst to Masson.
25. Hausamann to Kobelt; Teufen, April 4, 1943. BAr 5800/1.
26. Ernst to Chief of the General Staff (Huber); AHQ, June 25, 1943. BAr Nl Er.
27. Huber to Ernst; AHQ, July 18, 1943. BAr Nl Er.
28. Hausamann [1947a], 6. BAr 27/9846.
29. Ribbentrop, Note to the attention of the Führer; Fuschl, June 22, 1943. Copy. BAr EDI 1005/2.
30. Ribbentrop, Note to Führer.
31. Köcher to German Ministry of Foreign Affairs; Bern, October 7, 1943. Secret matter of the Reich. Copy. BAr EDI 1005/2.
32. Köcher to German Ministry of Foreign Affairs.
33. Rigi, Special report No. 51, April 20, 1943, informant Dietrich. AfZ Nl Ha.
34. Paul Meyer, handwritten notes, March 23, 1943. BAr Nl Mey.
35. Kobelt to General; Bern, June 25, 1943. Personal, secret. BAr Nl Mey.
36. Von Steiger to Stampfli; Bern, July 27, 1943. Personal, secret. BAr 2809/1,4.
37. Paul Meyer, handwritten notes, n.d. [after August 27, 1943]. BAr Nl Mey.
38. Meyer, handwritten notes, [after August 27, 1943].
39. Masson 1945, 7.
40. Minutes of hearing Gisevius, June 25, 1945. BAr 5330/1982,1.
41. Fuhrer 1982, 86.
42. Huber [1946], 21.
43. Schellenberg to General Guisan; Berlin, May 1, 1944. BAr 5795/433.
44. General Guisan to Schellenberg; Bern, May 4, 1944. Carbon copy. BAr 5795/433.
45. Barbey 1948 (May 3, 1944), 227. Also, Guisan 1953, 75.
46. Minutes of deliberations between Federal Councilor von Steiger, General, and Masson, May 12, 1944. Confidential. BAr 2809/1,4.
47. Minutes of deliberations.
48. Statement by Eggen; Zürich, August 10, 1945. Secret. BAr 27/10026.
49. Statement by Eggen, 5 f. (1953, 152) stated that the German Military Attaché attended the operation; in another passage (1953, 75), he said that the German Air Force Attaché was present. Based on Eggen's accurate testimony, both of these statements were wrong.
50. Federal Military Department to Federal Council; Bern, May 19, 1944. Urgent, secret. BAr 2809/1,4.
51. Military Department to Federal Council.
52. Guisan Junior to General; Regiment command post, November 15, 1944, 3 ff. Personal, confidential. BAr 5795/455. He began the letter with the salutation, "my dear daddy."
53. Masson to General; November 21, 1943. Personal, secret. BAr 5795/455.
54. Huber to General; AHQ, November 23, 1943. Personal, secret. BAr 5795/455.
55. Rothmund to von Steiger; Bern, May 5, 1944. BAr 2809/1,4.
56. Masson to General; June 29, 1944. Personal, secret. Also, General to Masson; AHQ, June 30,

1944. Secret. BAr 5795/433. It seems that it was only at that time that Schellenberg was promoted to Brigadier General.
57. Kobelt to General; Bern, October 20, 1944. Personal, secret. BAr 5795/455.
58. Eugster to General; Bern, October 28, 1944. Personal, secret. BAr 5795/455.
59. Handwritten notes by the General, n.d. [approx. Oct. 1944]. BAr 5795/455.
60. Report by the Federal Prosecutor's office (Mauser); Bern, April 5, 1945, 6. BAr 27/10026.
61. Schellenberg 1979, 419. Concerning Schellenberg's fate after the war, cf. Chapter 35 below.
62. Couchepin 1945, 22.

Chapter 30: The Issue of Censorship

1. Böschenstein 1978, 286 f.
2. Minutes of National Defense Committee meeting, March 16, 1938, 2. BAr 27/4059.
3. Minutes of NDC meeting.
4. Intelligence, dated September 8, 1939. Quoted in Guisan [1946], 222 f. The full text of the decree, which included seven articles, is published in Kreis 1973a, 429 f.
5. Eugen Hasler, born 1884, died 1965. Colonel in the infantry, Ph.D. in law, Supreme Court Justice from 1936 to 1950.
6. Guisan [1946], 222.
7. Huber [1946], 433 f.
8. Federal Council [1947a].
9. Kreis 1973a.
10. Minutes of meeting at the Chief of the General Staff's (Labhart's) office, October 10, 1939. BAr 27/14151,1.
11. Minutes of meeting at Labhart's office.
12. Guisan [1946], 223 f.
13. Guisan [1946], 124 f.
14. Barbey 1967 (Feb. 19, 1940), 96 f.
15. Barbey 1967, 97 f.
16. Kreis 1973a, 315.
17. Barbey 1967 (February 23, 1940), 100.
18. General to Minger; AHQ, February 29, 1940. BAr 5795/546. Quoted in Guisan [1946], 225.
19. Barbey 1967 (February 27, 1940), 101.
20. Ribbentrop, memorandum; Berlin, May 2, 1940. Copy. BAr EDI 1005/2.
21. Weizsäcker, memorandum; Berlin, May 14, 1940. Copy. BAr EDI 1005/2. The full text is published in Bonjour, *Neutralität* VIII, 32 f.
22. Minger to General; Bern, March 5, 1940. BAr 5800/2.
23. Minutes of Federal Council meeting, March 19, 1940. Excerpt. BAr 5795/546.
24. Perrier to General; June 5, 1940. BAr 2809/1,5.
25. General to Minger, attn. Federal Council; AHQ, June 21, 1940. BAr 5795/546.
26. Minger to General; Bern, June 24, 1940. BAr 5800/2.
27. General to Minger, attn. Federal Council; AHQ, June 26, 1940. BAr 5795/546.
28. Federal Council to General; Bern, July 2, 1940. BAr 5795/546.
29. General to Minger; AHQ, July 4, 1940.
30. Cf. Bonjour 1985. He expressed the same opinion on Swiss national television on April 8, 1985.
31. Robert Eibel during discussion at Archives for Contemporary History, Zürich, October 24, 1984.
32. General to Feldmann; Pully, November 4, 1953. BAr Nl Fm.
33. To the High Federal Council; Zürich, November 15, 1940. BAr. The full text is published in Bonjour, *Neutralität* IV, 368-371, and in Waeger 1971, 254–257.
34. Kreis 1973b.
35. Chief of Personal Matters in the Army; Bern, February 9/13, 1946. BAr 5800/2.
36. Hausamann 1947b, 82 f.
37. Stämpfli to Justice and Police Department; Bern, January 27, 1941. BAr 5800/2.

38. General to W. Frick; AHQ, April 4, 1941. Copy. BAr 5800/2.
39. The letter is published in Bonjour, *Neutralität* VIII, 252.
40. General to Kobelt; AHQ, February 1, 1941. BAr 5800/2.
41. Kobelt to General; Bern, February 28, 1941. BAr 5800/2.
42. Barbey 1948 (March 14, 1941), 77.
43. General to von Steiger; AHQ, April 14, 1941. Personal. BAr 5795/546.
44. General to Kobelt; AHQ, April 22, 1941. Secret. BAr 5795/546.
45. Von Steiger to General; Bern, May 12, 1941. BAr 5795/546.
46. Vodoz to Barbey; Vandoeuvres-Geneva, August 19, 1941. Personal. BAr 5795/546.
47. General to von Steiger; AHQ, May 7, 1941. BAr 5795/546. Quoted in Guisan [1946], 226.
48. Memorandum for presentation by the Commander-in-Chief of the Armed Forces to the members of the Federal Council present at the home of the President of the Swiss Confederation, on May 9, 1941; AHQ, May 9, 1941, 2 f. Secret. BAr 5800/2.
49. Memorandum for presentation, 3.
50. Barbey 1948 (August 22, 1941), 90.
51. Report by Personal Staff, vol. V, 17 f. Decree by Federal Council re: transferring the Press and Radio Section on the army staff to the Federal Council, dated December 30, 1941. BAr.
52. Barbey to Gut; AHQ, January 5, 1942. Personal. BAr 5795/546.
53. Barbey 1948 (October 8, 1941), 98.
54. Barbey 1948 (January 10, 1942), 111 f. On the issue of "Army and Home," cf. Chapter 18 above.
55. Barbey 1948, 90.
56. Hans Rudolf Schmid, born 1902, Ph.D., Press Officer of the 1939 National Fair.
57. List of reporters, n.d. (approx. May 1945]. BAr Nl Sd. The list included the names of some well-known artists, journalists, and photographers, such as Joseph Dahinden, Hugo Faesi, Theo Frey, Heiner Gautschy, Gottlieb Heinrich Heer, Charles Hug, Dölf Meier, Hans Staub, Otto Zinniker, and others.
58. Brief summary of the work done by the Press Office, September 1, 1939 to May 10, 1945. BAr Nl Sd.
59. Funds awarded to the Press Office, March 11, 1944 to Oct. 3, 1944. BAr Nl Sd.
60. Feldmann to General; Bern, July 8, 1942, 7. Personal, confidential. BAr 5795/333.
61. Von Salis 1979, 43.
62. Kreis 1973a, 335.
63. Schwarz 1944, 292, 310.
64. Huber [1946], 436.
65. Von Salis 1979, 43.
66. Bonjour 1983, 118.
67. Bonjour 1983, 119 f.
68. Schwarz 1944, 295.
69. De Reynold 1963, 650.
70. Bircher to General; Berlin, April 12, 1941. BAr 5795/546.
71. Bircher to General; handwritten notes by General.
72. Handwritten note, n.d. [after June 25, 1940]. BAr 5795/175.
73. Chapuisat 1950, 122 f.
74. Wille, handwritten notes, August 11-12, 1940. ArMa.
75. Löpfe to Däniker; Rorschach, September 1, 1941, 5 ff. AfZ Nl Dä 20.4.
76. Weber 1948, 169.
77. W[illy] Bretscher, verbal presentation by the Editor-in-Chief during the meeting of the board of administrators on the *NZZ*, July 1, 1940, 6. AfZ Nl Br 19.
78. Ernst to Masson; Thun, October 16, 1940. Copy. ArWa.
79. Barbey 1948 (February 22, 1941), 75.
80. Minutes of meeting of Liaison Office for Press-Related Matters, December 8, 1941. Confidential. BAr 5795/146.
81. Grimm 1946, 16.
82. Feldmann to General; Bern, July 15, 1943, 11. Personal, confidential. BAr 5795/333.

83. Feldmann to General, 12.
84. *Nation*, October 7, 1940. Quoted in Schmid-Ammann 1971, 112.
85. Ernst 1959, 136.
86. Ernst 1975e, 30.
87. Böschenstein 1970.
88. Böschenstein 1978, 289.
89. Böschenstein 1978, 286 f.

Chapter 31: The Crisis of June 1944

1. Cf. Chapter 22 above.
2. Minutes of meeting on August 19, 1942. Secret. BAr 5795/146.
3. Kobelt to General; Bern, May 20, 1944, 08.30 hours. BAr 5795/89.
4. Kobelt to General; Bern, May 31, 1944, 16.33 hours. BAr 5795/89.
5. Barbey to Bracher; AHQ, June 2, 1944. Secret. BAr 5795/89.
6. Masson, assessment of the situation on June 2, 1944. BAr 5795/89.
7. Barbey to Gonard; AHQ, June 3, 1944. Personal, secret. BAr 5795/89.
8. Minutes of meeting on June 5, 1944. Secret. BAr 5795/89.
9. Barbey 1948, 233.
10. Minutes of briefing; Bern, June 6, 1944, 11.00 hours. Secret. BAr 5795/89.
11. Barbey 1948, 234.
12. Minutes of briefing, June 6,1944.
13. Agenda, June 10, 1944. BAr 5795/89.
14. Agenda, June 10, 1944.
15. General to Kobelt, attn. Federal Council; AHQ, June 6, 1944. Secret. BAr 27/14245,69.
16. General to Kobelt; AHQ, June 7, 1944. Secret, personal. BAr 27/14245,69.
17. Head of Military Department to Federal Council; Bern, June 7, 1944. BAr 27/14245,69.
18. Labhart, diary, June 6, 1944.
19. Cf. Chapter 22 above.
20. General to Minger; AHQ, June 7, 1944. Carbon copy. BAr 5795/89.
21. Barbey 1948, 236, 239.
22. Labhart, diary, June 10, 1944.
23. Hafner 1986, 223. Hafner erroneously states that the General requested mobilizing the entire armed forces.
24. Vodoz to General; Lausanne, July 15, 1944. Personal. BAr 5795/89.
25. Barbey 1948, 238.
26. Minutes of meeting; Bern, June 8, 1944, 15.00 to 15.50 hours, 5. Secret. BAr 5795/147.
27. Minutes of meeting, June 8, 1944, 9.
28. Agenda, June 10, 1944. BAr 5795/89.
29. Kobelt to General; Bern, June 10, 1944, 10.20 hours. Secret. BAr 5795/89.
30. Press release, June 10, 1944. BAr 5795/89.
31. Order of the day; AHQ, June 15, 1944. BAr. The full text of the order is published in Kurz 1965a, 136.
32. Pilet-Golaz, notes, June 19, 1944. BAr 2809/1,4.
33. Pilet-Golaz, notes, June 23, 1944. BAr 2809/1,5.
34. Labhart, diary, June 15, 1944.
35. Barbey 1948, 240.
36. General to Kobelt; AHQ, June 14, 1944. Secret. BAr 27/14245,69.
37. Federal Council to General; Bern, June 23, 1944. Personal. BAr 5795/89.
38. Pilet-Golaz, notes, June 19, 1944. BAr 2809/1,4.
39. Pilet-Golaz, notes, June 19, 1944.
40. Pilet-Golaz, notes, May 23, 1944.
41. General, notes, July 1, 1944. BAr 5795/89.
42. Labhart, diary, July 1, 1944.
43. General to Huber; AHQ, July 4, 1944. Secret. BAr 5795/89.

44. General to Head of Military Department, attn. Federal Council; AHQ, June 27, 1944. Secret. BAr 27/14245,69.
45. Minutes of Federal Council meeting, July 5, 1944. Excerpt. BAr.
46. General to Head of Military Department; AHQ, July 5, 1944. Secret. BAr 27/14245,69.
47. Von Steiger to General; Bern, July 6, 1944. BAr 27/14245,69.
48. Pilet-Golaz 1945, 40.
49. Cf. Chapter 36 below.

Chapter 32: Relations with the Social Democrats

1. Guisan [1934], 22.
2. Weekly report, June 25–July 1, 1940.
3. Minutes of SPS management meeting, July 27, 1940, 2. SAr.
4. Gruber 1966, 119. On December 1, 1940, Swiss voters rejected the referendum by 434,817 nay and 345,430 yea (in five cantons there were more yeas than nays), even though the General had also voiced his support for the issue. 85.6 percent of eligible voters went to the polls.
5. Oprecht [1941], 11.
6. Gruber 1966, 119 f.
7. Hausamann, situation report to officers, October 15, 1943, 3. BAr 27/9853.
8. In the fall of 1940, Hausamann wrote to the General that he had declined to run for a position on the committee of the Radical Democratic Party, of which he was a member. Hausamann to General, September 26, 1940. BAr 5795/448.
9. General to Kobelt; AHQ, January 4, 1942. Personal. BAr 27/9862.
10. R. Frick to General; in the field, Oct. 2, 1941. BAr 5795/344.
11. Hausamann to XY [probably A. Ernst]; Bern, December 3, 1943. Carbon copy to Federal Councilor Kobelt. BAr 5800/1.
12. Introduction to SPS program, draft by H. Hausamann, December 3, 1942. BAr 5800/1.
13. "New Switzerland", SPS program; Zürich, February 1943, 1.
14. Hausamann to General; Teufen, February 18, 1943. BAr 5795/448,2.
15. General to Hausamann; AHQ, February 22, 1943. Strictly confidential. BAr 5795/448,2.
16. SNPF main secretariat (Huber) to Swiss Automobile Club; Zürich, May 10, 1941. BAr SVV 50.
17. Stampfli to SNPF; Bern, March 30, 1941. BAr SVV 50.
18. Huber to Heusser; Aarau, March 21, 1941. BAr SVV 50.
19. Notes on meeting of March 9, 1943 with Federal Councilor Kobelt in Bern. BAr SVV 25.
20. Th. Aubert, circular; Geneva, July 4, 1940. Not to be published. AfZ Nl Schü 1,1.
21. E.g. Aubert to General, Dec. 17, 1942, March 3, 1943, July 4, 1944, July 13, 1944, Sept. 20, 1944. BAr 5795/344.
22. Aubert to General; Geneva, December 17, 1942.
23. Masson to General; AHQ, February 23, 1943. Confidential. BAr 5795/344.
24. Aubert to General; Geneva, September 20, 1944.
25. Aubert to General, September 20, 1944, handwritten note. Also, General to Aubert; AHQ, September 26, 1944. Personal, confidential. BAr 5795/344.
26. Caspar Jenny, born 1890, died 1961, factory owner in Ziegelbrücke, one of the first signatories of the "Petition of the Two Hundred," member of the "People's Alliance for Switzerland's Independence" and board member of the "Aubert League." Moreover, he was a leading member of the "Patriotic Alliance for the People."
27. Dürrenmatt 1986, 63.
28. Hausamann to XY [probably A. Ernst], December 3, 1942.
29. Hausamann to Kobelt; Teufen, December 3, 1942. Confidential and personal. BAr 5800/1.
30. Hausamann to XY.
31. Hausamann to XY.
32. Hausamann to XY.
33. Paul Meyer, memorandum, n.d. [after March 27, 1942]. BAr Nl Mey.

34. Meyer to Müller; AHQ, July 24, 1942. BAr 5795/333.
35. Meyer to Müller.
36. Minutes of SPS management meeting, June 15, 1940, 5. SAr.
37. Minutes of SPS management meeting, May 22, 1940, 3.
38. Köcher to German Ministry of Foreign Affairs; Bern, December 14, 1940. Confidential. Copy. BAr EDI 1005/2. Feldmann was elected to the Federal Council in 1952, replacing von Steiger.
39. Däniker to Ammann; Walenstadt, November 25, 1940. AfZ VUS 133.
40. Feldmann, diary, June 8, 1945, No. 3436.
41. Walther to Werter; Kriens, August 5, 1943. BAr Nl Wet. Dr. Meierhans had been an editor of the Social Democratic newspaper *Luzerner Volksstimme* until 1935.
42. Barth 1941, 21.
43. Gruner 1969, 215.
44. Gruber 1966, 89 ff.
45. Gruber (1966, 231) calls the result of the 1943 elections "a remarkable slide to the left."
46. Shorthand bulletin of National Council meeting on December 15, 1943, 326. The first Catholic-Conservative candidate to be elected to the Federal Council was Joseph Zemp in 1891, 43 years after the civil war in Switzerland. The first Social Democrat was elected 25 years following the nationwide strike movement.
47. Gasser 1984, 124 f.
48. Gut 1954, 221.
49. The so-called "magic formula," under which two Radical Democrats, two Catholic-Conservatives (called Christian Democratic People's Party today), two Social Democrats, and one representative of the Farmers', Tradesmen's, and Citizens' Party (called Swiss People's Party today) share the power on the Federal Council, began only in 1959.
50. Oprecht 1944, 123.
51. General to Brechbühl; AHQ, August 12, 1944. Carbon copy. BAr 5795/343.
52. Bracher to General; Bern, August 12, 1944. BAr 5795/89. Herzog and Huber did not accept the invitation. On the other hand, National Councilor Reinhardt, City Council Member in Bern, attended the meeting, bringing the number of Socialist leaders who were present to eight.
53. Handwritten note, August 18, 1944. BAr 5795/89.
54. Meeting, August 18, 1944, 15.00 hours. BAr 5795/89.
55. Meeting, August 18, 1944. In his report on wartime duty, the General also addressed the issue of how officer candidates were selected. Cf. Chapter 36 below.
56. Note for file [Colonel Müller], August 15, 1944. Secret. BAr 5795/89. General Guisan annotated this passage with a question mark in red ink and asked, "who?" The unnamed SNPF Secretary must have been Dr. Arnold Huber.
57. Note for file, August 15, 1944.
58. Note for file, August 15, 1944.
59. Note for file, August 15, 1944.
60. Volksrecht, October 21, 1944, No. 248.
61. Information by anonymous, n.d. [probably by H. Hausamann, approx. 1942]. BAr 5795/85.
62. Information by anonymous, handwritten annotation by General.
63. Guisan 1953, 84.
64. Bracher to General; Bern, November 25, 1943. BAr 5795/88.
65. Bracher to General, November 25, 1943.
66. In a letter to Bratschi on the occasion of the latter's 60th birthday, Guisan wrote of their "trusting and friendly relations." General to Bratschi; Pully, February 5, 1951. Carbon copy. BAr 5795.
67. General, order of the day; AHQ, March 10, 1945. BAr 27/14112. The full text is published in Kurz 1965a.
68. Minutes of meeting on April 20, 1945 at Jegenstorf Castle. BAr 5795/550.
69. Minutes of meeting on April 20, 1945, 1 f.
70. Minutes of meeting on April 20, 1945, 7, 11.
71. Shorthand bulletin of National Council meeting on March 25, 1947, 125.

72. Volksrecht, March 26, 1947, No. 72.
73. Spühler 1985.
74. Cf. Chapter 36 below.

Chapter 33: The Troops' Morale, State of Training, and Armament
1. Guisan 1940, 27 f.
2. Cf. Chapter 32 above.
3. Barbey 1948 (November 2, 1943), 195.
4. Grimm 1946, 8 f.
5. Guisan [1947], 19 f.
6. The decree regulating the soldiers' compensation for wages and other income that they lost while they were on duty had been prepared by Federal Councilor Obrecht; it became the basis for Switzerland's social security system after the war.
7. Information by the Personal Staff, December 27, 1942. BAr 5795/250.
8. Guisan 1953, 153.
9. Minutes of meeting on June 23, 1943, 3. Secret. BAr 5795/147.
10. Feisst 1952, 79.
11. Bonjour 1983, 124.
12. Guisan [1946], 201 f.
13. Guisan [1946], 213 ff. Cf. Chapter 14 above.
14. Guisan, memorandum attn. Federal Council, May 9, 1941. BAr 5800/2.
15. Statistics on total number of deaths in the army, August 9, 1941. BAr 5795/85.
16. Strub 1941, 2.
17. Meuli 1959, 288. The total number of deaths (due to fatal illnesses and accidents) was 4,050. Meuli 1959, 287.
18. Minutes of Council of States meeting, June 26, 1941, 45 ff. BAr 2809/1,5.
19. Minutes of briefing, December 5–6, 1941, 14 f. Secret. BAr 27/14126.
20. Minutes of briefing, December 5–6, 1941, 15.
21. Guisan [1946], 230.
22. Remarks regarding the 1944 quarterly reports by the troops, 2.
23. Ernst 1975e, 33.
24. Schmid 1960, 9.
25. Guisan [1934], 19.
26. Cf. Chapter 10 above.
27. Guisan 1953, 87.
28. Guisan 1953, 73.
29. Barbey 1948, 59.
30. Guisan [1947], 15 f.
31. Visits and inspections until May 10, 1945. BAr 5795/378.
32. Inspections and visits serving military purposes, July 1, 1942 – June 30, 1943. BAr 5795/199.
33. Guisan 1953, 57. The General's driver during the entire time that the army was on duty was non-commissioned Adjutant Eugène Burnens from Morges. Guisan (1953, 57) described him as "a fabulous driver who was devoted to [him] like a friend."
34. Guisan 1953, 58.
35. Denis van Berchem to author; Vandoeuvres, September 9, 1986.
36. Ernst 1963c, 16.
37. Däniker to Wille; Mellingen, November 6, 1939. ArMa.
38. Däniker to Hausamann; Walenstadt, January 16, 1941. BAr 5795/448,1.
39. K[obelt], note for file, September 2, 1941. BAr 5800/2. Cf. also Chapter 25 above.
40. L[udwig] F[riedrich] Meyer, confidential remarks based on the visit by the Proxy Committee; Lucerne, end of April 1940, 7. BAr 27/14133.
41. Minutes of Council of States Proxy Committee meeting, June 26, 1941, 50. BAr 2809/1,5.
42. Minutes of Council of States Proxy Committee meeting, 50.
43. Guisan [1934], 22.

44. Minutes of briefing, December 5-6, 1941, 14.
45. Minutes of briefing, December 5-6, 1941, 17.
46. Ernst 1975e, 33.
47. General to Probst; AHQ, December 10, 1942. Personal. Carbon copy. BAr 5795/461.
48. General to Probst. The General was a staunch supporter of the Swiss Federal Institute for Physical Education and Sport in Magglingen, which he considered as a means to improve soldiers' fitness outside the army. Hirt 1969.
49. Minutes of briefing, December 5-6, 1941, 14.
50. Minutes of National Defense Committee meeting, April 24, 1939. BAr 27/4059.
51. Similar statement in Guisan [1946], 139 f. Minutes of briefing, December 5-6, 1941, 13.
52. Cf. Chapter 25 above.
53. *Rapport de l'Etat-Major particulier* [I], 10.
54. Amendment to the instructions for the defense; AHQ, October 21, 1940. Secret. BAr 5795/465.
55. Instructions on training; AHQ, September 16, 1941. Secret. BAr 5795/171.
56. Instructions re: topics for maneuvers and exercises; AHQ, March 1, 1941. Secret. BAr 5795/171.
57. Directives to the Chief Instructor of the Armed Forces on the training goals to be accomplished by the infantry, July 14, 1942. Directives to the Commander of the Air Force and Anti-Aircraft Defense on the training goals to be accomplished by the air force in the event of a war, August 19, 1942. BAr 5795/171.
58. Items to be discussed with Chief of General Staff, January 9, 1941. BAr 5795/86.
59. *Rapport de l'Etat-Major particulier* [III], 20.
60. Barbey 1948, 131 f. Instructions on training for the infantry; AHQ, July 14, 1942. BAr 5795/86.
61. Barbey 1948, 132, 137.
62. *Rapport de l'Etat-Major particulier* [V], 10.
63. Note for file on meeting with Chief of General Staff. September 7, 1943. BAr 5795/88.
64. Minutes of meeting on issues dealing with reforms in the army; Bern, March 26, 1942. BAr 5795.
65. Barbey 1948 (November 5, 1942), 150.
66. Minutes of briefing re: setting up of shock troops, January 8, 1943. BAr 5795/146.
67. Barbey 1948 (February 6, 1943), 164.
68. Minutes of briefing, April 6, 1943. BAr 5795/147.
69. Barbey 1948 (July 2, 1943), 182. The main instructor for grenadier training was Captain Matthias Brunner, born 1910, a specialist in close combat training. He later became the commander of the initiation courses for grenadiers in Losone and of the training facility in Walenstadt and was also a Military Attaché in Moscow and Sofia.
70. Guisan 1944, 8.
71. General's orders, January 15, 1943 and October 13, 1943. BAr 5795/89.
72. Huber [1946], 113 ff.
73. Valloton 1950, 100. Huber [1946], 89 ff.
74. Gonard 1945, 9.
75. Federal Council [1947a], 74, 96.
76. Statistics on production, by "Technical Service of the Army," n.d. [approx. end of 1944]. BAr 5795/89.
77. Quoted in Walde 1983, 148.
78. Guisan 1953, 91.
79. Huber [1946], 136.
80. 100 Jahre Füsilier Battalion 56, 36.
81. It would be worthwhile for a younger historian to write a special study on the different instructions issued for training during wartime duty under General Guisan.

Chapter 34: The Final Phase of Wartime Duty

1. The second front: study based on information procured by the Intelligence Service; AHQ, July 19, 1942. Secret. Studies of variations to Operations Order No. 13; AHQ, Jan. 20, 1943. Secret. BAr 27/14300,2. Cf. Senn 1988a, 253.
2. Barbey 1948 (August 25, 1944), 251.
3. Huber [1946], 42 f.
4. Ernst 1971, 140.
5. Barbey 1948 (September 10, 1944), 257.
6. Bonjour, *Neutralität* V, 408.
7. Barbey 1948 (September 7, 1944), 255.
8. Barbey 1948 (September 13 and 26, 1944), 258, 263.
9. Speech by Lt. Col. Barbey at the Beau-Rivage Hotel, Lausanne, August 28, 1954. BAr Nl Go.
10. Barbey 1948 (October 6, 1944), 264.
11. Guisan 1953, 166. Barbey 1948 (September 11, 1944), 257.
12. Barbey 1948 (September 11, 1944), 257.
13. Guisan [1946], 230 f.
14. Barbey 1948 (Nov. 16, 1944), 272.
15. Guisan 1953, 168.
16. Max Häni to author; Bern, August 15, 1985.
17. Minutes of meeting on February 2, 1945, 5. BAr 5795/259.
18. Instructions, December 15, 1944. BAr 5795/428.
19. Guisan [1947], 20.
20. Speech on December 28, 1944. The full text of the speech is published in Kurz 1965a, 145 f.
21. The speech is also published in Guisan 1959, 27.
22. Ernst 1963c, 21.
23. Senn 1988a, 254.
24. Major Schaefer to Army and Home section; Div. HQ, December 18, 1944. BAr. Quoted in Gautschi 1978, 485.
25. Guisan [1946], 64.
26. R.-H. Wüst in La Suisse, August 26, 1974. Quoted in Kreis 1976, 153.
27. Note for file (Bracher), June 18, 1945. BAr 27/14127. Bracher remarked that he put the notes together and Lt. Col. Barbey subsequently checked them.
28. Kobelt, shorthand notes, November 2, 1945. BAr 27/14127. Cf. Kurz 1987, 293.
29. Kobelt, shorthand notes, November 1, 1945. BAr 27/14127.
30. Guisan [1946], 268. The bombing of Schaffhausen on April 1, 1944 by three squadrons of Liberator bombers lasted 30 to 40 seconds, causing forty fatalities and seriously injuring another 33 persons. *Schaffhauser Magazin*, No. 1, 1984, 29.
31. Barbey 1948 (March 8, 1945), 290.
32. Barbey, conversation with Mr. René Payot, October 30, 1944. Secret. BAr 5795/330.
33. Barbey 1948 (November 23, 1944), 275.
34. Guisan 1953, 181 f.
35. Barbey 1948, (November 10, 1944), 268.
36. Note for file (Bracher), November 16, 1944. BAr 27/14127.
37. Du Pasquier, diary, November 17, 1944. BAr Nl DuPa. Cf. Chapter 9 above.
38. Notes for use by Commander-in-Chief, October 8, 1944. Secret. BAr 5795/331.
39. Guisan 1953, 82 f.
40. Juin to General; Paris, March 23, 1945. BAr 5795.
41. Henry Guisan to author; Pully, September 25, 1984 and June 23, 1987.
42. Von Salis 1979, 163. Also Jean Rudolf von Salis to author; Brunegg, June 21, 1984.
43. Huber to Kobelt; Brienz, January 31, 1947, 9. BAr 5800/2.
44. Von Salis to General and Petitpierre; Zürich, February 7, 1946, 2. Confidential. BAr 5795/533. Cf. Chapter 40 below.
45. Guisan to General; St. Sulpice, February 12, 1946. BAr 5795/533.
46. Guisan to General, 3. The full report is published in Bonjour, *Neutralität* VII, 336 ff. Kurz (1987, 297) mentions only three visits.

47. Report by Switzerland's Military and Air Force Attaché; Paris, February 23, 1946. BAr 5800. Bonjour, *Neutralität* VII, 339 ff.
48. Bonjour, *Neutralität* VII, 340.
49. General to Petitpierre; Lausanne, May 9, 1946. Personal. BAr 5795/533.
50. General to Gruss; Lausanne, February 20, 1946. Carbon copy. BAr 5795/533.
51. De Lattre de Tassigny 1946, 549 ff.
52. De Lattre de Tassigny 1946, 550.
53. Cf. above in this Chapter.
54. Barbey 1948, 292 f.
55. Barbey 1948, 296 f.
56. Barbey 1945. BAr 27/12692. Based on what he reported, Barbey must have returned to Switzerland early, on April 30, 1945. Barbey 1945, 63.
57. Kobelt to General; Bern, May 1, 1945. BAr 5795/379.
58. Huber to General; AHQ, May 5, 1945. BAr 5795/379.
59. Guisan [1946], 72.
60. General to Huber; AHQ, January 22, 1945. Secret. BAr 27/7311,1.
61. Huber to General; AHQ, January 26, 1945. BAr 27/7311,1.
62. General to Huber; AHQ, January 31, 1945. BAr 27/7311,1.
63. General service order; AHQ, March 17, 1945. Secret. BAr 27/7311,1.
64. Huber, report regarding calling troops off duty, August 16, 1945. BAr 4001/2.
65. Gonard 1971, 487.
66. Decree by Federal Council re: closing part of the border, April 13, 1945. Minutes of Federal Council meeting, April 13, 1945. BAr. The decree was not published.
67. General to Commanders of 2nd and 4th Army Corps; AHQ, April 20, 1945. Secret. BAr 5795/144. Huber ([1946], 48) stated that the border was closed on April 19, 1945.
68. Diary of army staff, May 7, 1945.
69. General to Huber; AHQ, April 24, 1945. BAr 5795/144.
70. Waibel 1959, 121 ff.
71. Kobelt to General; Bern, June 25, 1946. BAr 5795/327.
72. General to Kobelt; Lausanne, July 3, 1946. BAr 5795/327.
73. Masson to Kobelt; Mont-Pèlerin s/Vevey, July 5, 1946. BAr 5795/327.
74. Kobelt to General; Bern, June 25, 1946. BAr 5795/327.
75. Waibel 1981.
76. Zürichsee-Zeitung, May 8, 1945. Published in Gut 1954, 226.
77. Order of the day; AHQ, May 8, 1945. BAr 27/14112. The full text is published in Kurz 1965a, 152 f.
78. Kreis 1985.
79. Cancellation of measures to protect our airspace; AHQ, May 8, 1945. Urgent. BAr 5795/379.
80. Barbey 1948 (May 8, 1945), 297.
81. Barbey 1948, 298.
82. Barbey, speech addressed to the General in the evening of May 8, 1945, the day of the armistice in Europe. Handwritten, 2 pp. BAr 5795/195.
83. Barbey 1948, 298.
84. Berner Tagblatt, May 10, 1945.
85. Berner Tagblatt, May 10, 1945.
86. Diary of army staff, May 8, 1945.
87. Marguth (1959, 37) reported that the tree planted was a lime tree. However, it was in fact a copper beech and had grown into a sizeable tree by the time this book was written. Municipal Clerk A. Kurt to author; Jegenstorf, June 5, 1989.
88. Guisan 1953, 179.
89. Meeting on May 4, 1945. Confidential. Anonymous [probably H. Guisan Jr.]. BAr 5795/90.
90. Barbey 1948 (May 18, 1945) 299.
91. Barbey 1948, 300, and Guisan 1953, 180.
92. Handwritten notes, n.d. [prior to May 18, 1945]. BAr 5795/90.
93. Barbey 1948, 300.

94. Chapuisat 1950, 208.
95. Kobelt, shorthand notes, November 1, 1945. BAr 27/14127.
96. Kobelt to General; Bern, May 23, 1945. BAr 27/14127.
97. General to Kobelt; AHQ, May 30, 1945. BAr 27/14127.
98. General to Kobelt; AHQ, June 11, 1945. BAr 27/14127.
99. General to Kobelt; handwritten note, June 12, 1945. Kurz (1987, 295) states that the meeting in Constance took place on June 1, 1945.
100. Huber to Kobelt, January 31, 1947.
101. Barbey 1948 (June 13, 1945), 302.
102. Barbey 1948, 302 f.
103. Barbey 1948, 304.
104. General to Kobelt; AHQ, August 14, 1945. BAr 27/14127.
105. Barbey 1948 (August 17, 1945), 308 f. Also, Burgunder, note attn. Federal Councilor Kobelt; Aug. 20, 1945. BAr 27/14127.
106. Feldmann, diary, May 30, 1945, No. 3417.
107. Feldmann, diary, May 26, 1945, 4.20 p.m., No. 3412.
108. General to Huber, May 31, 1945. Confidential, personal. BAr 5795/102.
109. Von Steiger to General; Bern, June 2, 1945. BAr 5795/380.
110. Von Steiger to General.
111. General to von Steiger; Lausanne, June 3, 1945. Personal. By express mail. BAr 5795/380.
112. Gonard 1945, 16.
113. General to Speaker of Parliament (Aeby); AHQ, June 4, 1945. BAr 27/14115. Same letter to Federal President.
114. Minutes of Federal Council meeting, June 4, 1945. BAr.
115. Barbey 1948 (June 4, 1945), 301. Chapuisat (1950, 153) explained that the General was invited by the Federal Council to the meeting, at which he spoke. According to the minutes, that can hardly be true.
116. Shorthand bulletin of National Council meeting, June 20, 1945, 8.30 a.m., 252 ff. The full text of the speech is published in Kurz 1965a, 153 ff.
117. Kurz 1965a, 155.
118. Chapuisat 1950, 155.
119. Feldmann, diary, June 20, 1945, No. 3462.
120. Feldmann, diary, August 11, 1945, No. 3528.
121. Barbey 1948 (June 22, 1945), 305.
122. Barbey 1948, 305.
123. General to Kobelt; AHQ, July 3, 1945. Personal, confidential. BAr 5795/259.
124. Kobelt to General; Bern, August 2, 1945. BAr 5795/259.
125. *Le jeune gymnaste*, Lausanne, June 1945, 2.
126. General to Perrochon; AHQ, June 22, 1945. BAr 5795.
127. Chapuisat 1950, 162.
128. Entries in the diary of the Personal Staff, September 7, 1945 and September 19, 1945. BAr 5795/68. The diary was kept until December 31, 1946.
129. The bombings took place on August 6 and 9, 1945, causing at least 160,000 casualties.
130. Guisan 1959, 28.
131. List of invitees, n.d. [before August 19, 1945]. BAr 5795/381.
132. General to Minger; AHQ, July 27, 1945. Carbon copy. BAr 5795/381.
133. List of invitees.
134. Bircher to General; Lenzerheide, August 14, 1945. BAr 5795/381.
135. Barbey 1948 (August 20, 1945), 309.
136. City Council of Bern (Bärtschi) to General; Bern, July 30, 1945. BAr 5795/381.
137. The full text of the General's speech is published in Kurz 1965a, 158 f.
138. Kurz 1965a, 159 ff.
139. The details of the final briefing are described in Guisan [1946], 236 ff; Guisan 1959, 29 f.; Guisan 1953, 191 f.; Barbey 1948, 310; Marguth 1959, 37 f.; Chapuisat 1950, 213.

140. General, speech in Jegenstorf, August 19, 1945. Typescript. BAr 5795/380. The speech is published in Kurz 1965a, 162 ff.
141. Kurz 1965a, 164.
142. Kobelt, speech in Jegenstorf, August 19, 1945. Published in Kurz 1965a, 165 ff.
143. Order of the day, August 20, 1945. BAr 27/14112. Published in Kurz 1965a, 167.
144. Bernardini to General; Bern, Aug. 20, 1945. BAr 5795/195.
145. Juin to General; Paris, August 20, 1945. BAr 5795/195.
146. Minger to General; Schüpfen, August 17, 1945. BAr 5795/195.
147. General to Minger; AHQ, August 20, 1945. Carbon copy. BAr 5795/195.
148. Mrs. Guisan to von Steiger; Pully, July 20, 1945. BAr 27/14116.
149. General to Etter; AHQ, Aug. 22, 1945. Carbon copy. BAr Nl Gui.
150. Etter to General; Bern, August 23, 1945. BAr Nl Gui.
151. Guisan 1953, 196.
152. Barbey 1948, 311.
153. Chappuis 1983, 81 f.
154. Report from the front, August 20, 1945. BAr 5795/121.
155. Guisan [1947], 19.
156. Gonard 1945, 16.

Chapter 35: Trouble with Masson

1. Von Steiger to General; Bern, May 7, 1945. Personal. BAr 5330/1982,1.
2. General's order; AHQ, May 14, 1945. BAr 5330/1982,1.
3. Minutes of hearing, Bern, June 20, 1945. BAr 5330/1982,1.
4. Military Attorney General (Eugster) to General; Bern, July 16, 1945. Personal, secret. BAr 5795/455.
5. Military Attorney General to General.
6. Huber to General; AHQ, July 26, 1945. Personal, secret. BAr 5795/455.
7. Huber to General, 2.
8. Huber to General, 2 f.
9. Huber to General, 3.
10. Masson to General, August 3, 1945. Personal, confidential. BAr 5795/455.
11. Masson to General. Cf. Chapter 20 above.
12. General to Masson; AHQ, August 8, 1945. Personal. Carbon copy. BAr 5330/1982,1.
13. Huber, handwritten note, August 10, 1945. BAr 27/1413/9.
14. News item by Exchange news agency; September 28, 1945. BAr 27/10027.
15. Hofer 1970, 46.
16. Hausamann 1947b, 2.
17. Shorthand bulletin of National Council meeting, October 4, 1945, 646 f.
18. Shorthand bulletin, 647.
19. Masson to General, October 1, 1945. Personal, confidential. BAr 5795/455.
20. Masson to General.
21. General to Kobelt; Lausanne, October 2, 1945. BAr 5795/455.
22. Masson to General; Bern, Oct. 13, 1945. BAr 5795/455.
23. Hausamann to Kobelt, October 17, 1945. Handwritten. BAr 5800/2.
24. Cf. the account of the deal concerning the barracks in Chapter 27 above.
25. Couchepin 1945, 55 f.
26. Disciplinary order; Bern, February 28, 1946. BAr 27/10027.
27. Schmid to General; Thalwil, February 17, 1946. BAr 5795/455.
28. Handwritten note in Schmid's letter to the General; Thalwil, January 25, 1946. BAr 5795/455.
29. Die Tat, Jan. 27 1946 to March 25, 1946, No. 26 to No. 83. The incriminating passages that caused Hausamann to press charges were spread over 15 different issues of the newspaper.
30. Huber to General; Brienz, February 6, 1946. BAr 5795/207.
31. Kobelt to Eugster; Bern, February 20, 1947. BAr 27/9846.

32. Pilet to Kobelt; Lausanne, April 3, 1947; also General to Kobelt; Pully, April 5, 1947. BAr 27/9846.
33. Minutes of Federal Council meeting, April 16, 1947. BAr 27/9846.
34. Züblin 1947.
35. Statement by Erwin Jaeckle at Archives for Contemporary History; Zürich, March 21, 1984; also Erwin Jaeckle to author; Zürich, December 12, 1984.
36. Hausamann to Kaeser, attorney-at-law; St. Gallen, September 29, 1947. Carbon copy. BAr Nl Lü.
37. Hausamann to Kaeser.
38. Seelhofer, note for file, February 2, 1948. BAr 27/9846.
39. Eugster to Federal Military Department; Bern, September 23, 1947. BAr 27/9846.
40. Hausamann to Waibel; Teufen, September 26, 1947. Hausamann to Kaeser; St. Gallen, September 29, 1947. Photocopies. BAr Nl Lü.
41. Kobelt, diary, June 25, [1948].
42. Kobelt, diary, June 26, [1948].
43. Masson, statement in favor of "Walter Schellenberg"; Mont-Pèlerin s/Vevey, May 10, 1948. Carbon copy. BAr 5795/455.
44. Masson, statement "Schellenberg", 9.
45. Kobelt to Masson; Bern, July 31, 1948. Carbon copy. BAr 5795/455.
46. Report by Reuters news agency; Nuremberg, April 14, 1949. AfZ.
47. Riediger to Masson; Fürth/Bavaria, April 16, 1949. BAr 5795/455.
48. Guisan 1953, 74 f.
49. Guisan [1947], 18 f.
50. Pilet-Golaz 1945, 6.
51. Barbey 1948, 21, 30, 52. Cf. Chapter 30 above.
52. Hausamann 1947b, 98.
53. There was no biography of Masson at the time this book was published in German. A dissertation on his life and achievements on the army command would be worthwhile; there is a large amount of research material available.

Chapter 36: Report on Wartime Duty

1. Head of Military Department (Kobelt) to General; Bern, July 31, 1945. BAr 27/14122.
2. General's office (Marguth) to Military Department; Lausanne, November 16, 1945. BAr.
3. Chief of the General Staff (Labhart); AHQ, September 2, 1939. BAr 27/14193.
4. Meeting with the Chief of the General Staff on May 4, 1945, 2 f. BAr 5795/379.
5. Barbey to General; AHQ, May 24, 1945. BAr 5795/207.
6. General's instructions of August 23, 1945. BAr 5795.
7. General to Mayer; barracks of Lausanne, November 1, 1945. EMB Nl May.
8. Guisan 1953, 197.
9. [Daniel] 1945c.
10. Denis van Berchem to author; Vandoeuvres, September 9, 1986.
11. Huber to General; Brienz, January 11, 1946. BAr 5795/207.
12. Bonjour 1947, 15, 243.
13. Barbey to General; Paris, April 11, 1946. BAr 5795/533.
14. Barbey to General; Paris, March 6, 1946. Personal, confidential. BAr 5795/203.
15. Marguth to Schmid; barracks of Lausanne, February 6, 1946. Carbon copy. BAr 5795/203.
16. The translators received a compensation of six francs per page. Management of the Military Administration (Burgunder) to General's office; Bern, April 16, 1946. BAr 5795/203.
17. General to Federal Chancellor Leimgruber; Lausanne, March 25, 1946. BAr 5795/205.
18. Guisan [1946]. The two volumes of appendices included the reports by the Chief of the General Staff, by the commander of the air force and anti-aircraft defense, by the Adjutant General, and by the Chief Instructor, as well as the report by the Head of Personnel to the Commander-in-Chief.
19. General to Grimm; Lausanne, June 24, 1946. Carbon copy. BAr 5795/205.

20. Grimm to General; Bern, June 24, 1946. BAr 5795/207.
21. Barbey to General; Paris, July 16, 1947. BAr 5795/207.
22. Hofer 1970, 49.
23. Minutes of Federal Council meeting on September 29, 1919. Secret. Published in *Diplomatische Dokumente der Schweiz*, vol. 7/II, No. 95, Bern 1984, 226 f.
24. Hofer 1970, 53 ff.
25. Gafner 1974, 127.
26. Cf. Chapter 37 below.
27. Cf. Chapter 38 below.
28. Böschenstein 1975a, 114 f.
29. Constam to Kobelt; Zürich, August 19, 1946, 7. BAr 5795/207.
30. Borel to Kobelt; Neuchâtel, August 14, 1946, 7. BAr 5795/207.
31. Gafner 1974, 135.
32. Guisan [1946], 8.
33. Guisan [1946], 11. The "one exception" referred to the fact that no plans of operations were available at the outbreak of the war.
34. Minutes of the National Council committee meeting dealing with the General's report, 27.
35. Chief of the General Staff (de Montmollin) to Kobelt; Bern, January 25, 1947. BAr 5800.
36. Borel to Kobelt, August 14, 1946.
37. Prisi 1946.
38. Gübeli to Kobelt; Lucerne, August 29, 1946. BAr 5795/207.
39. Minutes of the National Council committee meeting dealing with the General's report, 25 f.
40. Guisan [1946], 7.
41. Zopfi to Däniker; Zürich, January 29, 1947. AfZ Nl Dä 80.
42. Lardelli to General; Chur, July 30, 1946. BAr 5795/207. The letter was annotated by Guisan; at the end he noted, "for Capt. Marguth to prepare a reply to Lardelli based on my annotations."
43. General to Lardelli; Lausanne, August 8, 1946. Confidential. BAr 5795/207.
44. General to Prisi; Lausanne, October 31, 1946. BAr 5795/207.
45. Prisi to General; Baden, November 2, 1946. BAr 5795/207.
46. Prisi to General; Bern, November 17, 1946. BAr 5795/207.
47. Prisi 1946.
48. Prisi 1946.
49. Prisi 1946.
50. Prisi 1946.
51. Prisi 1946.
52. Prisi 1946.
53. General to Prisi; Lausanne, November 22, 1946. BAr 5795/207.
54. The letters are filed at the Federal Archives at 5795/207.
55. Schmid to General; Thalwil, November 29, 1946. BAr 5795/207.
56. Schmid to General, November 29, 1946.
57. General to Prisi; Bern, November 26, 1946. BAr 5795/207.
58. Barbey to General; Chantilly (Oise, France), December 4, 1946. BAr 5795/207.
59. Corbat to Labhart; Zürich, July 26, 1946. BAr Nl La.
60. Borel to Kobelt, August 14, 1946, 6.
61. Quoted in Müller 1986.
62. Labhart to Kobelt, n.d. [summer of 1946]. Carbon copy. BAr Nl La.
63. Statement by Miville, shorthand bulletin of National Council meeting, March 25, 1947, 136.
64. Frick to Kobelt; Bern, August 31, 1946. Similar statement by de Montmollin to Kobelt, August 31, 1946. BAr 5795/207 and BAr Nl La.
65. Gübeli to Kobelt, August 29, 1946.
66. Borel to Kobelt, August 14, 1946. Similar statement by Corbat to Labhart, July 26, 1946.
67. Huber to Kobelt; Brienz, January 31, 1947. BAr 5800/02.
68. Guisan [1946], 187 f.
69. Hofer 1970, 179.

70. Borel to Kobelt, August 14, 1946.
71. Corbat to Labhart, July 26, 1946.
72. Minger 1946, 1 f.
73. Minger 1946, 10.
74. General to Minger; Lausanne, August 20, 1946. Personal. Carbon copy. BAr 5795/207.
75. Ernst 1971, 210 f.
76. Guisan [1946], 90, 150 ff.
77. Kobelt to E. Junod; Bern, August 8, 1946. Carbon copy. BAr 5800/2.
78. Böschenstein 1975a, 115.
79. Federal Council 1947b, 4 f.
80. Federal Council 1947b, 5.
81. Böschenstein 1975a, 115 f. Kurz 1975, 89. Müller 1975, 82.
82. Böschenstein 1975a, 115.
83. Hans Rudolf Kurz to author; Bern, August 13, 1985.
84. Hofer 1970, 66.
85. Federal Council 1947b, 6.
86. Federal Council 1947b, 40.
87. Federal Council 1947b, 25 f.
88. Federal Council 1947b, 26 f.
89. Cf. chapters 37 and 38 below.
90. Federal Council 1947a, 72 ff.
91. Ernst 1971, 218.
92. Federal Council 1947a, 109.
93. Hofer 1970, 69.
94. A. von Erlach to Bandi; Muri, January 24, 1947. BAr Nl Ba 16.
95. Gafner 1974, 128.
96. Fritz Wanner to author; Kilchberg, August 5, 1985.
97. Barbey to General; Chantilly, December 4, 1946. Handwritten [7 pp]. BAr 5795/207.
98. Guisan 1947a.
99. General to Wanner; Pully/Lausanne, February 22, 1947. Confidential. ArWa.
100. General to Wanner, February 22, 1947.
101. Guisan 1947a, 1 ff.
102. Guisan 1947a, 6.
103. Guisan 1947a, 1, 7. Also General to Wanner, February 22, 1947.
104. Minutes of National Council committee meeting dealing with the General's report, 39.
105. Minutes of National Council committee, 48.
106. Minutes of National Council committee, 48.
107. Minutes of National Council committee, 49.
108. Minutes of the Council of States committee meeting dealing with the General's report, 11.
109. Minutes of Council of States committee, 8.
110. Minutes of Council of States committee, 31. Cf. Chapter 31 above.
111. Shorthand bulletin of National Council meetings held in 1947, 141, 144.
112. Shorthand bulletin of National Council meetings held in 1947, 139.
113. Shorthand bulletin of National Council meetings held in 1947, 109 ff., 153. Shorthand bulletin of Council of States meetings held in 1947, 24 ff., 32.
114. Shorthand bulletin of Council of States meetings held in 1947, 32.
115. Federal decree of April 1, 1949 regarding amendments to the 1907 Military Organization. The revised article 211 stated, "When the country is in a state of *armed neutrality*, the Federal Council decides on calling up troops at the General's request. The General shall have the means available that the Federal Council assigns to him." The revised article 212 stated, "When the country is in a state of *war*, the General shall have all combat material and armed forces available that he needs to accomplish his task. He shall decide at his own discretion what means he needs."
116. Hofer 1970, 89 f., 132, 174 ff.
117. Ernst 1975e, 33.

118. Bonjour 1983, 147 f. Concerning the General receiving an honorary doctorate from the University of Basel, cf. Chapter 41 below.
119. *Der Bund*, March 16, 1947. Quoted in Hofer 1970, 74.
120. Ernst 1975e, 28.

Chapter 37: The Controversy over Lack of Plans of Operations

1. Guisan [1946], 15. Cf. Chapter 7 above.
2. Guisan [1946], 19 f.
3. Guisan [1946], 18.
4. Borel to Kobelt; Neuchâtel, August 14, 1946. Carbon copy. BAr Nl La.
5. *Nationalzeitung*, June 29, June 30, and July 4, 1946; *Vaterland*, July 4, 1946; *Volksrecht*, August 2, 1946. Quoted in Hofer 1970, 59.
6. Labhart to Kobelt, n.d. [summer 1946]. Carbon copy. BAr Nl La.
7. Labhart to Kobelt; Zürich, February 7, 1947. Carbon copy. BAr Nl La.
8. Labhart to Kobelt; Zürich, February 21, 1947. Carbon copy. BAr Nl La.
9. Prisi 1946.
10. Prisi 1946.
11. Walde 1983, 161 f.
12. Quoted in a letter by Chief of the General Staff Huber to General; Brienz, Aug. 30, 1945. BAr 5795/207.
13. H. Frick to Kobelt; Bern, August 31, 1946, 4, 6 ff. Carbon copy. BAr Nl La.
14. H. Frick to Kobelt, August 31, 1946, 7.
15. H. Frick to Kobelt, August 31, 1946, 6.
16. Constam to Kobelt; Zürich, Aug. 19, 1946, 2. BAr 5795/207.
17. Gübeli to Kobelt; August 27, 1946. BAr 5795/207.
18. Minutes of National Council committee meeting dealing with the General's report, 3 ff., 41.
19. Minutes of National Council committee meeting, 7, 42 ff.
20. Barbey 1948 (June 25, 1942), 127 f.
21. Barbey 1948, 128.
22. Huber to General; AHQ, January 26, 1945. Secret. BAr 4001/2.
23. Huber [1946], 186.
24. Huber to Kobelt; Brienz, January 31, 1947, 5 f. BAr 5800/2.
25. Huber to Kobelt, January 31, 1947, 7. Cf. also Huber [1946], 186.
26. Minutes of Council of States meeting dealing with the General's report, 25.
27. Federal Council 1947b, 12. Hofer 1970, 67.
28. Ernst 1971, 33 ff.
29. General to Minger; Lausanne, August 20, 1946. Personal. BAr 5795/207.
30. Minutes of National Council committee meeting, 45.
31. Guisan 1953, 95.
32. Guisan 1947a, 3.
33. Minutes of National Council committee meeting, 40.
34. Huber to Kobelt, January 31, 1947.
35. Frick to Kobelt, August 31, 1946, 3.
36. Minutes of Council of States committee meeting, 24.
37. Walde 1983, 162.
38. Hofer 1970, 113.
39. Ret. Chief of the General Staff Hans Senn to author; Bern, November 26, 1984. Also Divisional Commanders Hans Rapold and Gustav Däniker to author; Bern, March 23, 1984 and August 29, 1984.

Chapter 38: Conflict with Air Force Commander Bandi

1. Guisan [1946], 114, 109.
2. Guisan [1946], 107 f.

3. Guisan [1946], 109.
4. Guisan [1946], 115.
5. Rihner 1944, 178 f.
6. Prisi 1946.
7. Hofer 1970, 58 f.
8. Bandi 1947, 3.
9. Bandi 1947, 19.
10. Bandi 1947, 35.
11. Bandi 1947, 14.
12. Bandi 1947, 11 f.
13. Bandi 1947, 17 f.
14. Bandi 1947, 18 f.
15. Barbey 1948 (Sunday, January 10, 1943), 160.
16. Barbey 1948 (March 4, 1943), 167.
17. Denis van Berchem to author; Vandoeuvres, September 9, 1986.
18. Bandi 1947, 7, 8 f.
19. Müller 1986.
20. Bandi 1947, 36.
21. Minutes of meeting, n.d. [before December 5, 1941]. BAr 5795/86.
22. Prisi 1946.
23. Minger to Bandi; Schüpfen, December 31, 1943. BAr Nl Ba.
24. Minger 1946, 12.
25. Minutes of Council of States committee meeting dealing with the General's report, 35 f., 14.
26. Minutes of Council of States committee meeting, 36 f.
27. Minutes of Council of States committee meeting, 38.
28. Minutes of National Council committee meeting dealing with the General's report, 19.
29. General to Kobelt; Pully, January 30, 1947. Carbon copy. BAr Nl Gui.
30. Kobelt to Du Pasquier; Bern, February 19, 1947. BAr 27/15735.
31. Du Pasquier 1947, 51 f.
32. Du Pasquier 1947, 55.
33. Bandi 1947, 16.
34. Barbey 1948 (Wednesday, May 27, 1942), 124.
35. Guisan 1947a, 7.
36. Kobelt, diary, March 12, 1943.
37. Kobelt, diary, March 13, 1943.
38. Kobelt, diary, March 12, 1943.
39. Kobelt, diary, March 18, 1943.
40. Barbey 1948 (October 14, 1943), 190.
41. General to Minger; AHQ, November 2, 1943. Personal, secret. BAr Nl Mi.
42. Handwritten note by General, n.d. [after October 15, 1943]. BAr 5795/432.
43. Guisan [1946], 114.
44. General to Minger; Lausanne, August 20, 1946. Personal. BAr 5795/207.
45. Minutes of examination Bandi; Bern, February 28, 1947. BAr Nl Ba. Rihner 1944, 178 ff.
46. Rihner to General; Bern, July 19, 1946. Personal. BAr 5795/207.
47. Rihner to General, July 19, 1946, handwritten annotation.
48. Rihner to Kobelt; Bern, August 28, 1946. BAr 5795/207.
49. Du Pasquier 1947, 4.
50. Minutes of National Council committee meeting, 47.
51. Minutes of National Council committee meeting, 47.
52. General to A. Müller; Lausanne, March 3, 1947. BAr.
53. Minutes of National Council committee meeting, March 19, 1947, [II], 5.
54. Frick to Kobelt; Bern, August 31, 1946, 19. Carbon copy. BAr Nl La.
55. Labhart, notes, n.d. [summer 1946]. BAr 5795/207.
56. Constam to Kobelt; Zürich, August 19, 1946. BAr 5795/207.

57. Borel to Kobelt; Neuchâtel, August 14, 1946. Frey and Corbat to Labhart; Zürich, July 26, 1946. BAr Nl La.
58. Huber to Kobelt; Brienz, January 31, 1947, 12. BAr 5800/2.
59. Huber to Kobelt, January 31, 1947, 13.

Chapter 39: Issue of the Peacetime General

1. Hofer 1970, 82.
2. Guisan [1946], 272.
3. Guisan [1946], 273.
4. Guisan [1946], 268 f.
5. Guisan [1946], 270.
6. Hofer 1970, 82 f.
7. Guisan [1946], 270.
8. General to Kobelt; Lausanne, September 18, 1946. BAr 5795/259.
9. Hofer 1970, 86 ff.
10. Federal Council 1947b, 12.
11. General to Military Department; AHQ, June 8, 1945. Quoted in Hofer 1970, 82.
12. Kobelt to General; Bern, August 2, 1945. BAr 5795/259.
13. Guisan [1946], 270.
14. Labhart, note for file, n.d. [after June 16, 1945]. BAr Nl La.
15. Labhart, note for file, n.d.
16. Labhart, note for file, June 27, 1945.
17. Labhart to Kobelt, n.d. [summer 1946], 25 f. BAr Nl La.
18. Quoted in Walde 1983, 160.
19. Gonard 1971, 477.
20. Frick to Kobelt; Bern, August 31, 1946, 26. Carbon copy. BAr Nl La.
21. Frick to Kobelt, August 31, 1946, 24.
22. Prisi 1946.
23. Constam to Kobelt; Zürich, August 19, 1946, 6. BAr 5795/207.
24. Hausamann to Kobelt; Teufen, May 29, 1945. BAr 5800/2.
25. Senn 1986a, 38, 45.
26. Ernst 1941, 48.
27. Volk und Armee; Solothurn, November 1946. Quoted in Hofer 1970, 88.
28. Minutes of National Council committee meeting, 43.
29. Guisan 1953, 47 f., 55.
30. Gonard 1959, 43.
31. *Neue Zürcher Zeitung*, August 30, 1948. Quoted in Hofer 1970, 103.
32. Senn 1982, 180.

Chapter 40: Misunderstanding with de Lattre de Tassigny

1. Kurz 1987, 295 ff.
2. Cf. Chapter 34 above.
3. Von Salis to General and Petitpierre; Zürich, February 7, 1946, 1 f. Confidential. BAr 5795/533.
4. Von Salis to General and Petitpierre, 2.
5. Cf. Chapter 34 above.
6. Von Salis to General and Petitpierre, 3.
7. Von Salis to General and Petitpierre, 4.
8. Von Salis to General and Petitpierre, 6 f.
9. Von Salis to General and Petitpierre, 7.
10. Von Salis to General and Petitpierre, 2, handwritten annotation by Guisan.
11. General to von Salis; Lausanne, February 14, 1946. BAr 5795/533.

12. General to Gruss; Lausanne, February 20, 1946. Carbon copy. BAr 5795/533.
13. Petitpierre to von Salis; Bern, February 14, 1946. Carbon copy. BAr 5795/533.
14. Payot to General; Geneva, February 8, 1946. BAr 5795/533.
15. Payot to General.
16. General to Gruss, February 20, 1946.
17. Jacques to General; Zürich, February 23, 1946. BAr 5795/533.
18. Jacques to General; Zürich, February 27, 1946. BAr 5795/533.
19. Burckhardt to Petitpierre; Paris, March 5, 1946. BAr 5795/533.
20. Barbey to General; Paris, March 6, 1946. Personal and confidential. Handwritten. BAr 5795/533.
21. Barbey to General, March 6, 1946.
22. Barbey to General; Paris, March 26, 1946. Personal. BAr 5795/533.
23. Petitpierre to General; Bern, March 29, 1946. BAr 5795/533.
24. Von Salis to General and Petitpierre, 7.
25. Barbey to General; Paris, April 11, 1946. BAr 5795/533.
26. General to Petitpierre; Lausanne, April 15, 1946. BAr 5795/533.
27. Vorwärts; Basel, April 24, 1946.
28. Unsigned notes [by Hans Bracher?], February 1, 1947. BAr 27/14127.
29. Seelhofer to Barbey; Bern, June 25, 1946. Personal, secret. BAr 5795/533.
30. Oser, handwritten notes, May 3, 1946. BAr 5800/1.
31. Oser, handwritten notes, May 3, 1946.
32. Kurz 1987, 297 ff.
33. Prof. P. Decker to General; Lausanne, December 31, 1945. BAr 5795/533.
34. Swiss Red Cross (Luy) to Schweizerspende (Olgiati); Bern, August 9, 1946. BAr 5795/533.
35. Swiss Red Cross (Luy) to Schweizerspende (Oligiati); Bern, September 9, 1946. BAr 5795/533.
36. General to Kistler; Lausanne, July 17, 1946. BAr 5795/533.
37. Kurz 1987, 298.
38. Bonjour, *Neutralität* VII, 339 ff.
39. Barbey to General; Paris, May 24, 1946. BAr 5795/533.
40. General to Petitpierre; Lausanne, May 28, 1946. BAr 5795/533.
41. Seelhofer to Barbey; Bern, June 25, 1946. Personal, secret. BAr 5795/533.
42. Cf. Chapter 34 above.
43. Kurz 1987, 299.

Chapter 41: Honors and Postwar Travel

1. Minutes of village council meeting in Mézières, December 29, 1939. The text of Guisan's thank-you letter is published in Mézières 1987, 76.
2. Guisan 1953, 105 f.
3. Town Council to Municipal Council; Pully, July 9, 1941.
4. Guisan 1953, 136.
5. Bonnard and Belperrin 1973, 58.
6. Häni 1977–79, 41. Basel-Stadt Cantonal Archives (Zwicker) to author; Basel, March 3, 1989.
7. Town Archives (Gottraud) to author; Avenches, March 16, 1989.
8. Bern Cantonal Archives (Martig) to author; Bern, March 23, 1989. Official publication by the cantonal parliament of Bern, September 12, 1945, 585 f.
9. Basler Nachrichten, August 26–27, 1944, No. 364.
10. Program of the ceremony; Lausanne, November 8, 1945. BAr Nl Gui.
11. Tape recording of the speech on November 8, 1945. Text printed in Guisan 1953, 201 f.
12. Bonnard and Belperrin 1973, 59 ff., 64 ff.
13. Obituary for Stephan Jäggi, July 9, 1957. BAr Nl Gui.
14. Hammerschmidt to General; Vienna, November 16, 1954. BAr Nl Gui. Karl Hammerschmidt also composed military marches such as "Erzherzog Eugen" and "Erzherzog Friedrich."
15. Duplessy to General; Cormatin, France, June 14, 1955. BAr Nl Gui.
16. Duplessy to General, June 14, 1955.
17. Barrenschen to General; Basel, October 25, 1946. BAr Nl Gui.

18. Planning committee to Municipality; Pully, July 27, 1945. ArPu A.10.2.4.
19. General to Mayor Besson; Pully, July 27, 1945. ArPu A 10.2.4.
20. Minutes of Pully Municipal Council meeting, July 31, 1945. ArPu A 10.2.4.
21. Perrin 1986, 23.
22. Welander to General; Bern, March 21, 1946. BAr Nl Gui 48.
23. General to Douglas; Lausanne, May 31, 1946. BAr Nl Gui 48. Based on the available written evidence, it may be established that R-H. Wüst wrote the thank-you letter at the General's request.
24. Celio to General; Bern, May 23, 1947. Confidential. BAr Nl Gui 48.
25. Petitpierre to General; Bern, May 22, 1947. BAr Nl Gui 48.
26. General to Valloton; Lausanne, May 20, 1947. BAr Nl Gui 48.
27. Dagens Nyheter, quoted in Boéchat [1947], 2.
28. Boéchat [1947], 4, 8.
29. Valloton to Petitpierre; Stockholm, June 14, 1947. BAr Nl Gui 48.
30. Valloton to Petitpierre, June 14, 1947.
31. Valloton to General; Stockholm, June 17, 1947. BAr Nl Gui 48.
32. Ny Dag, October 26, 1944.
33. General to Hürlimann; Pully, October 31, 1947. BAr Nl Gui 38.
34. Guisan 1953, 200.
35. Guisan 1953, 200.
36. Egli to General; London, November 6, 1947. BAr Nl Gui 50.
37. A. Renou, speech; London, June 2, 1948. BAr Nl Gui 50.
38. Guisan 1953, 205.
39. BAr Nl Gui 52.
40. Guisan 1953, 201.
41. Perrin 1986, 51.
42. Petitpierre to General; Bern, January 20, 1947 and March 25, 1947. Personal. BAr Nl Gui 23.
43. Valloton to General; Stockholm, September 14, 1948 and September 25, 1948. BAr Nl Gui 48.
44. General to H. Mahler; Pully, September 28, 1948. BAr Nl Gui 48.
45. Nakaschidse to General; Brussels, n.d. [April 1948]. BAr Nl Gui.
46. General to Nakaschidse; Pully, April 28, 1948. BAr Nl Gui.
47. Gruner 1966, 943 f.
48. Böschenstein 1975a, 115.

Chapter 42: Guisan's Retirement Years

1. General to Military Department; Lausanne, August 5, 1946. BAr Nl Gui 4.
2. Federal Council to General; Bern, September 24, 1946. BAr Nl Gui 4.
3. Minutes of National Council committee meeting dealing with the General's report, 36. The General's pension was greater than the regular annual salary of a professor at the Federal Institute of Technology in Zürich, which amounted to 14,000 francs. Jean-R. von Salis to author; Brunegg, June 21, 1984.
4. Guisan, personal bookkeeping records 1940–41, 1954–55. Guisan made his last entries in 1955.
5. BAr Nl Gui 1,84.
6. General to Federal Council; Lausanne, December 9, 1947. Also, Federal Council (Etter) to General; Bern, December 19, 1947. ArVR.
7. Perrin 1986, 66.
8. The correspondence is located at BAr J.I. 127, vol. 1.
9. General to Primault; Pully, September 28, 1949. BAr Nl Gui 1.
10. Handwritten list of the copies that were dedicated to specific persons, n.d. [summer 1946]. BAr 5795/205.
11. De Lattre to General, August 10, 1946. BAr 5795/205.
12. De Lattre to General; Paris, September 20, 1947. BAr 5795/205.
13. Churchill to General; Bursinel, canton of Vaud, September 7, 1946. BAr 5795/205.
14. Guisan 1953, 204.

15. Perrin 1986, 23.
16. Report by "Ha", October 26, 1940. AfZ Nl Ha.
17. Churchill 1953, 437.
18. Guisan 1953, 203.
19. Kobelt to General; Bern, April 20, 1943. BAr 5795/337.
20. Kobelt to General, April 20, 1943.
21. Guisan 1953, 197.
22. For information on the conflict, cf. Ernst 1971, 175 ff.
23. Ernst 1971, 176.
24. General to Military Department; Pully, April 19, 1948 and May 7, 1948. Carbon copy. BAr Nl Gui.
25. The officers to whom Guisan alluded included Divisional Commanders Berli, Brunner, and Schumacher, and later Fritz Wille, the son of Ulrich Wille II who became Corps Commander.
26. Hofer 1970, 44.
27. Hans Rudolf Kurz to author; Bern, November 29, 1984.
28. Züblin to Boissier; Küsnacht, February 10, 1977. ArBoi.
29. Iklé [approx. 1980], 132, 190.
30. Kurz 1975, 94.
31. Ernst 1971, 232.
32. Minutes of meeting; AHQ, November 11, 1944. BAr 5795/147.
33. Guisan 1953, 181.
34. Guisan [1946], 97 f.
35. Minutes of NDC meeting, April 9, 1946. BAr 27/10027.
36. Constam to Kobelt; Zürich, August 19, 1946, 2. BAr 5795/207.
37. General to Hausamann; Pully, May 26, 1950. Carbon copy. BAr Nl Gui.
38. O[tto] F[rei] in Neue Zürcher Zeitung, January 28, 1985, No. 22. The cavalry was completely dissolved in a decree by the Federal Council dated December 19, 1972 that went into effect on January 1, 1974. Group for general staff services (Froidevaux) to author; Bern, June 5, 1989.
39. Barbey 1948 (October 21, 1944), 265.
40. Press and Radio section to editorial boards of Switzerland's newspapers, October 11, 1944. Confidential, not to be published. BAr 27/14113.
41. Bulowa Watch Co. Inc. to General. BAr Nl Gui 1/84.
42. General to Kobelt; AHQ, October 24, 1944. BAr 5800/1.
43. Cantonal Government of Vaud; Lausanne, September 22, 1954. Program. BAr Nl Go.
44. Quoted in Wahlen 1965, 203.
45. Minger to General; Vulpera, July 4, 1954. BAr 5795/561.
46. Quoted in Wahlen 1965, 207.
47. Schweizerisches Frauenblatt, No. 68, 1958.
48. Der Bund, January 14, 1959.
49. Women were not granted the right to vote on the federal level until a second vote was held on February 7, 1971. Woodtli 1975, 218 ff., 266 f.
50. Buchmann [1959], frontispiece.
51. General to A.R. Mayer; Lausanne, August 21, 1946. Carbon copy. BAr 5795/456.
52. Swiss Red Cross (Bucher) to author; Bern, March 16, 1989.
53. Guisan 1953, 205.
54. Guisan 1953, 198 f.
55. Decoppet 1986, 79 ff. After the General's death, the foundation was first chaired by Vaud government member Louis Guisan and as of 1982 by Maurice Decoppet, the General's grandson.
56. Hans Rudolf Kurz to author; Bern, May 24, 1984.
57. Bonnard and Belperrin 1973, 14 ff.
58. Perrin 1986, 46.
59. Jules Sandoz to author; Biel, September 11, 1986.
60. Federal Council (Streuli) to Mr. and Mrs. Guisan; Bern, October 28, 1957. Several files at BAr Nl Gui.

61. *Der Bund,* September 8, 1957.
62. Guisan, personal bookkeeping records, January 27, 1936. ArVR. The same document indicates that Guisan reduced the horse's actual value by 200 francs annually to account for amortization.
63. Barbey to General; Paris, September 14, 1957. BAr Nl Gui 25.
64. BAr Nl Gui 25.
65. Quoted in Perrin 1986, 52.
66. Kursus finished 6th in the dressage event at the 1952 Summer Olympics in Helsinki and 4th at the 1956 Summer Olympics in Stockholm (equestrian events were held in Stockholm although Melbourne hosted the other events of the Games that year).
67. Böschenstein 1978, 283.
68. Chapuisat 1950, 108, 215 f.
69. Böschenstein 1970.
70. Schmid 1960.
71. Schmid 1960, 11.
72. Gut to H.G. Wirz; Stäfa, April 16, 1960. BAr Nl Wi.
73. Gafner 1983, 45.
74. Report on the funeral, *Neue Zürcher Zeitung,* April 13, 1960, No. 1257. The other details in this Chapter concerning the funeral are taken from the same article.

Posthumous Reputation

1. Minutes of National Council meeting, June 7, 1960, 2 ff. The fact that the manuscript of the Speaker's speech is filed among Gonard's unpublished works gives rise to the supposition that Guisan's strategic advisor also had a hand in drafting the eulogy that was read in Parliament. BAr Nl Go.
2. Federal Council (Wahlen) to Mrs. Guisan; Bern, April 6, 1961. ArVR.
3. E.g. in Aarau, Basel, Geneva, Interlaken, Lausanne, Pully, St. Gallen, Winterthur, Zürich, and in other towns.
4. Municipal administration (Goetschi and Bieri) to author; Interlaken, July 3, 1989.
5. Marcel 1974, 22.
6. Jules Sandoz to author; Biel, September 11, 1986.
7. 24 heures, January 17–18, 1987. In Weinfelden in the summer of 1989 a restaurant served "pork roast à la General Guisan."
8. Perrin 1986, 71.
9. Henry Guisan to author; Pully, September 25, 1984.
10. The institution is now called "Center for Military History and Research."
11. Delay [1974], 185 ff.
12. Delay [1974], 190, 195, 208 f.
13. Delay [1974], 171.
14. Cf. Chapter 16 above.
15. Martin 1974.
16. Koenig to Guisan; Baden-Baden, August 31, 1945. BAr 5795/91.
17. Perrin 1986, 33.

Afterword

1. Guisan [1946], 89.
2. Clausewitz 1940, 234.
3. Chapuisat 1950, 216.
4. Ernst 1975e, 34.
5. Guisan 1953, 206.
6. Zermatten 1983, 37.
7. Kimche [1962], 28 f.

Bibliography

I. Primary Sources

Unpublished reference material (from public and private archives, private papers made available to the public, deposited documents)

Swiss Federal Archives (Schweizerisches Bundesarchiv), Bern (BAr):

Files of the General's Personal Staff	E 5795	
Files of the army staff	E 27	
Files of the Military Attorney General	E 5330 1982/1 Vol. 9	
Minutes of Federal Council meetings, 1939–1946		
Minutes of joint Council of States and National Council sessions, 1939–1946		
Minutes of Council of States meetings, 1939–1945		
Minutes of National Council meetings, 1939–1945		
Minutes of Council of States Proxy Committee meetings, 1939–1945		
Minutes of National Council Proxy Committee meetings, 1939–1945		
Files of Federal Councilor Kobelt, Karl (Nl Ko)	5800	
Files of Federal Councilor Petitpierre, Max	2800	
Files of Federal Councilor Pilet-Golaz, Marcel	2809	
Private papers of General Henri Guisan	Nl Gui	(J.I.127)
Private papers of Federal Councilor Baumann, Johannes	Nl Bm	(J.I.10)
Private papers of Federal Councilor Feldmann, Markus	Nl Fm	(J.I.3)
Private papers of Federal Councilor Minger, Rudolf	Nl Mi	(J.I.108)
Private papers of Federal Councilor Nobs, Ernst	Nl No	(J.I.4.1)
Private papers of Federal Councilor Wetter, Ernst	Nl Wet	(J.I.7)

Private papers of:	Allgöwer, Walter	Nl Al	(J.I.161)
	Bandi, Hans	Nl Ba	(J.I.159)
	Du Pasquier, Claude	Nl DuPa	(J.I.80)
	Ernst, Alfred	Nl Er	(J.I.140)
	Frick, Wilhelm	Nl Fr	(J.I.48)
	Germann, Oscar Adolf	Nl Ge	(J.I.142)
	Gonard, Samuel	Nl Go	(J.I.144)
	Hausamann, Hans	Nl Ha	(J.I.107)
	Labhart, Jakob	Nl La	(J.I.49)
	Lützelschwab, Wilhelm	Nl Lü	(J.I.137)
	Meyer-Schwertenbach, Paul	Nl Mey	(J.I.121)
	Petitpierre, Edouard	Nl Pp	(J.I.12)
	Schmid, Hans Rudolf	Nl Sd	(J.I.59)
	Schürch, Gerhart	Nl Schü	(J.I.52)
	Wirz, Hans Georg	Nl Wi	(J.I.122)

Deposited papers of the Swiss National Patriotic Federation (Schweizerischer Vaterländischer Verband)

Swiss Federal Military Library (Eidgenössische Militärbibliothek), Bern (EMB)
Private papers of Mayer, Albert R.   Fonds 1018–1020

Swiss Social Archives (Schweizerisches Sozialarchiv), Zurich (SAr)
File entitled "Die Schweiz im Umbruchsommer 1940"   Ar 1.124.8
Collection of letters   Ar 1.126.5
Minutes of meetings of the management and the executive of the Social Democratic Party of
    Switzerland, 1938–1945   Ar 1.110.28–33

Archives of Contemporary History, Swiss Federal Institute of Technology, Zurich (AfZ)
Private papers of: Bretscher, Willy   Nl Br
                   Däniker, Gustav   Nl D
                   Gisevius, Hans Bernd   Nl Gi
                   Hausamann, Hans   Nl Ha
                   Henne, Rolf   Nl He
                   Lindt, August R.   Nl Li
                   Schürch, Gerhart   Nl Schü
                   Züblin, Georg   Nl Zü
Various war-time tape recordings

Official archives of the canton of Zürich (Staatsarchiv des Kantons Zürich, StAr ZH)
Minutes of cantonal government meetings, 1 January–31 December 1919
Fascicle entitled "Unruhen in Zürich im Juni 1919"

Official archives of the canton of Aargau (Staatsarchiv des Kantons Aargau, StAr AG)
Deposited papers of the Patriotic Federation of the Canton of Aargau, 1919–1922

Municipal archives of Pully (GAr Pu), canton of Vaud
List of members of the Pully town council, 1885–1913
List of members of the town council, 1911–1977
Minutes of town council meetings, 1906–1929
Register of votes and elections, 1917–1962
File "Général Guisan" A.10.2.4

Municipal chancellery of Chésalles-sur-Oron (GAr Ch), canton of Vaud
Minutes of town parliament meetings, 1897–1904
Minutes of town council meetings, 1897–1904
Minutes of electoral assemblies, 1897–1904
Records of allowances offered to the poor in Chésalles, 1898
Register of births, marriages, and deaths in Chésalles, 1897

Archives of Henri Guisan, "Verte Rive," Pully (ArVR), canton of Vaud
Grand Livre, Dépenses et Recettes (Cashbook), begun by my father in March 1897 when I established
    myself in Chésalles-sur-Oron [no date, 1897–1955]. [Referred to as "Guisan, Grand Livre"]
Miscellaneous letters, notes, and other documents

Archives of Wille, "Mariafeld," Meilen (ArMa), canton of Zurich
Various files of Corps Commander Ulrich Wille, including:
files, 2 September to 31 December 1939;

miscellaneous files, 1940;
diary notes, 1939–1943;
correspondence with General Guisan;
files re: his dismissal as chief instructor of the army, 1940–1943

Military Archives of German Federal Archives (Militärarchiv des Bundesarchivs), Freiburg, Germany (MArF)

Reports by military attachés in Bern	RH 2/2923
Reports by German Armed Forces High Command, Foreign Countries I	RW 5/v.350
Foreign armies West, matters re: officers	RH 2/1515
Kleines Orientierungsheft Schweiz (Information booklet on Switzerland), status 1 September 1942	RHD 18/172
War diaries of the German Industry Commission in Bern	RW 45/42–45
Study by Major Zimmermann, 4 October 1940	RH 20–1/368
Pocket book on the Swiss Army, January 1940	RHD 18/173
Operation "Tannenbaum," 1940	RH 2/465

Service Historique de l'Armée de Terre (History department of the French ground forces, Vincennes (SHAT)

Conseil supérieur de la guerre (supreme martial council)

Note re: possible French intervention in Belgium and Switzerland, 7 April 1939. Top secret	1 N 47–1
Notes re: possible infringement of Swiss territory by German and Italian Armed Forces, 1930–1939	7 N 3086, EMA/2
Mobilization of outpost in Bern, 1939–1940	7 N 3093, EMA/2
Swiss Army personnel, 1939–1940	7 N 3089, EMA/2
Reports by military attaché, 1937–1940	7 N 3084/85, EMA/2
Various reports, 1939–1940	7 N 3086–3092, EMA/2
French-Swiss relations, 1939–1940	2 N 239–3

    Note re: our options for an intervention in Switzerland, 5 April 1939. Top secret; general instructions in case of intervention by our enemies in Switzerland, 22 May 1939. Top secret

Miscellaneous privately owned documents

Jacques Boissier, Bern (ArBoi): correspondence with Georg Züblin
Max Häni, Bern (ArHä): memoirs
Erwin Jaeckle, Zürich (ArJae): files of the Swiss Federal Society (Eidgenössische Gemeinschaft)
Otto Kellerhals, Bern (ArKh): diary notes, 1940
Karl Killer, Baden, canton of Aargau (Nl Ki): minutes of the pardon commission, 2, 3, and 4 November 1942 (owned by Mrs. Anna Killer-Friz, Baden)
August R. Lindt, Bern (ArLi): list of members of the "Action for National Resistance" (Aktion Nationaler Widerstand)
Gerhart Schürch, Bern (ArSchü): reports by Hans Hausamann, notes, draft reports
Fritz Wanner, Kilchberg, canton of Zürich (ArWa): miscellaneous correspondence, 1940–1947
Edmund Wehrli, Zollikon, canton of Zürich (ArWe): letters to his wife and parents, 1940–1941

Major single documents (in alphabetical order):

Allgöwer, W[alter], and G[erhart] Schürch, among others. Die Schweiz als Ziel, 2. Fassung eines ersten Texts vom Dezember 1936. ArSchü.
Armeestab Tagebuch, 1939–1945.
Barbey, [Bernard], Major. Rapport sur les travaux effectués à l'E.M.A. en vue d'une coopération éventuelle avec une armée alliée; 14.9.40, secret. [8 pp.] BAr 5795/304.
— Ordre réglant le service interne et les attributions des officiers de l'Etat-Major personnel du Général, 17.3.44. BAr 5795/89.

— Oberstlt., Rapport de la 2.mission suisse auprès de la 1. Armée française 20.4.–11.5.45, Carnet de route, AHQ, 18.5.45, confidentiel. [63 pp. und Anhänge] BAr 27/12692.

[Barbey], Observations sur les "Bemerkungen" du Col.Cdt. de Corps Prisi "zum Bericht des Generales" (15.8.46), unsigniert. [7 pp.] BAr 5795/207.

Bericht der Verbindungsstelle für das Pressewesen (Nef) zur Eingabe der "Aktion zur Wahrung der schweizerischen Neutralität"; Bern, 14.5.41. [18 pp.] BAr 5800/2.

Bircher, [Eugen]. Die Ursachen der Niederlage Frankreichs, Vortrag in der Allgemeinen Offiziersgesellschaft Zürich, 13.9.40. Typescript. [11 pp.] BAr 5795/436.

— Denkschrift an das Eidgenössische Militärdepartement, z.H. des Schweizerischen Bundesrates, 1.8.42. [34 pp.] BAr 5795/436.

Bracher, [Hans], Hptm. i. Gst. Militärpolitische Lage der Schweiz; AHQ, 24.6.40. [6 pp.] BAr 27/14111.

— "Zusammenkunft des Generals mit deutschen Persönlichkeiten," 12.3.43. [3 pp.] BAr 27/10022.

— Major. Bericht über die Abkommandierung zur 1. Französischen Armee, 30.4.–11.5.45. [23 pp.] BAr 27/12692.

— Notizen. 18.12.45. BAr 5795/202.

Bretscher, W[illy]. Mündliches Exposé der Chefredaktion, Sitzung des Verwaltungskomitees der "N.Z.Z.," 1.7.40. [12 pp.] AfZ N1 Br 19.

— Bemerkungen zur Unterredung General Guisan mit SS-General Schellenberg, 17.8.67. [3 pp.] AfZ N1 Br 19.

Burckhardt, [Peter], Oberstlt. Berichr über meine Abkommandierung zur US-Army, EUCOM, Historical Division in Frankfurt, vom 14.10.–2.11.48, geheim [13 pp.] BAr 5800/1.

Couchepin, [Louis], Colonel. Rapport d'Enquête concernant le Colonel-Brigadier Masson; Laussane, le 29 novembre 1945. [82 pp.] BAr 27/10027.

Daniel, [Charles]. Aufgaben und künftige Organisation unseres militärischen Nachrichtendienstes, 23.5.45, geheim. [11 pp.] BAr 5795/327.

— Major. Notes sommaires sur les dangers militaires (1939–1945); QGA, 23.7.45. BAr 5795/202.

[Daniel]. Die Gefährdung der Schweiz während des Krieges 1939–1945; AHQ, 8.8.45. [26 pp.] BAr 5795/327.

Däniker, [Gustav], Oberstlt. Zwischenbericht über den Aktivdienst 1939, 11.12,39. Durchschlag. [5 pp.] ArMa.

— Oberst. Denkschrift über Feststellungen und Eindrücke anlässlich eines Aufenthaltes in Deutschland; Walenstadt, 15.5.41. BAr 5800. [cited as: Däniker, Denkschrift]

— Folgerungen, Auszug aus der Bestätigung der 2. Unterredung [mit dem General] vom 25.8.[1941], geheim. BAr 5795/460.

— Stellungnahme zu meiner Denkschrift; Walenstadt, 18.10.41. BAr 5330/1982,1,14.

— Oberst. Kurze Darstellung der "Denkschrift"-Angelegenheit; Walenstadt, 21.11.41. [14 pp.] BAr 2809/1,5.

— Oberst. Verteidigungsschrift gegen die vom Armeeauditor in seinem Entscheid vom 28. März 1942 gegen mich erhobenen Anschuldigungen; Walenstadt, 15.5.42. Ex. No. 000001. Typescript. [26 pp.] Mit Randbemerkungen des Generals. BAr 5795/440,2. [cited as: Däniker, Verteidigungsschrift]

— Nachtrag zur Verteidigungsschrift vom 15.5.42; Walenstadt, 14.7.42, geheim. Bar 5795/440.2

Du Pasquier, Claude. Journal 1939–1946. BAr N1 DuPa.

— Divisionär, Bericht über die administrative Untersuchung in der Sache Oberstdivisionär Bandi gegen Oberstdivisionär Rihner; Neuenburg, 25.7.47. [55 pp.] BAr 27/15735.

Eggen, [Hans Wilhelm]. Zusammenfassung meiner Ausführungen vom 13./15.11.45. [21 pp.] BAr 27/10026.

Eidgenössische Gemeinschaft, Hefte 1–5, herausgegeben von der Gesamtleitung [n.p.], August 1941–1942. Typescript. ArJae.

Ernst, Alfred. Tätigkeitsbericht des Bureaus Deutschland der Nachrichtensektion; 15.10.40. streng vertraulich. Nur für den Chef der Sektion und dessen Stellvertreter bestimmt. Original. [15 pp.] BAr J.I.140/4,2.

— Hptm. i. Gst.. Gedanken zur Heeresreform; AHQ, 28.10.41. [48 pp.] BAr 5795/260.

— Zur Geschichte des "Offiziersbundes" von 1940, Januar 1963. [1. Fassung, 18 pp.] ArSchü. [cited as: Ernst, Zur Geschichte des "Offiziersbundes" (I)]

— Zur Geschichte des "Offiziersbundes" von 1940, Januar 1963. [2. Fassung, 14 pp.] AfZ N1 Li 57. Zwei Exemplare der Darstellung Ernsts "Zur Geschichte des 'Offiziersbundes' von 1940, Januar 1963" [2, Fassung, 14 pp.], befinden sich im BAr J.I.140/4,5, ebenso ein Exemplar im AfZ. N1 Li 57.

Etter, [Philipp], Bundesrat. Bemerkungen für das Politische Department, 14.8.40. Handschriftlich [5 pp.] BAr EP 1943–1945. A14.48.4.

[Eugster, Jakob], Armeeauditor. Entscheid in Sachen 1. Däniker Gustav, Oberst, 2. Frick Heinrich, Oberstlt., Bern, 9.3.42. [12 pp.], BAr 2809/1,5.

— Oberstbrigadier, Feststellungen des Armeeauditors zu den Gedanken des Oberstkorpskommandanten. Wille zum Verfahren gegen Oberst Däniker; Bern, 1.7.42, No. 3, persönlich. [15 pp.] BAr 5800/2. [cited as: Eugster, Feststellungen]

Feldmann, Markus. Tagebuch-Norizen 1939–1946, BAr N1 Fm.

— Politische Exposés an Oberbefehlshaber, persönlich und vettraulich. BAr 5795/335:
> Bern, 8.7.42 (I, 18 S.)
> Bern, 30.1.43 (II, 36 S.)
> Bern, 3.3.43 (III, 25 S.)
> Bern, 15.7.43 (IV. 37 S.)

— Erinnerungen. BAr N1 Fm.

Frick, Wilhelm. Bericht über meine Deutschlandsreise, Juni 1942, vertraulich. [18 pp.] BAr 5795/329.

Frölicher, Hans. Bericht für Herrn Bundesrat Petitpierre über die Gefahrenmomente in den deutsch-schweizerischen Beziehungen; Bern, 10.7.45, vertraulich, [7 pp.] mit handschriftlichen Notizen Guisans. BAr 5795/202. [cited as: Frölicher, Bericht für Bundesrat Petitpierre]

Gästebuch "Bären"-Biglen. Kopie. BAr M34/6.

Gästebuch "Schloss Wolfsberg". Kopie. BAr N1 Mey.

Germann, [Oscar Adolf, Oberst]. Studie über die militärischen Grundlagen einer Kooperation mit den Westmächten im Falle Nord; AHQ, 24.10.39 [22 pp.] BAr 5795/300. [cited as: Germann, Studie Fall Nord]

— Oberst. Studie über die Grundlagen einer Kooperation mit der deutschen Wehrmacht im Fall W., AHQ, 9.4.40, geheim. [20 pp.] BAr E 5560 (B).

Gisevius, Hans Bernd. Persönliche Aufzeichnungen über einige Erlebnisse, die ich im Zusammenhang mit der Person des Oberst-Divisionärs [sic!] Masson gehabt habe [undatiert, niche nach 1945]. AfZ N1 Gi I.4.6.3.

Gonard (Samuel), Manuskript der Trauerrede für General Guisan; Lausanne, 26.3.59, gesprochen am Radio, 8.4.60. BAr N1 Go.

Grin Edmond, Predigt; Lausanne, 12.4.60. BAr N1 Go.

de Goumoëns et Guisan, Lt. Colonels d'EMG. Rapport sur la visite des attachés militaires neutres aux 1 re et 2me armées française, 19–25 août 1916, secret. [23 pp.] BAr 27/12611.

[Guisan, Henri]. Grand Livre, Dépenses et Recettes. ArVR.

Guisan, Oberstlt. Visite des attachés militaires des pays neutres aux VIIe et VIIIe armées françaises, du 2–11 juillet 1917, confidentiel. [25 pp.] BAr 27/12618.

— Oberstlt. Rapport sur le service d'ordre à Zurich du 13 mai au 13 juin 1919; Colombier, le 18 juin 1919. [15 pp.] BAr 21/1912.

— Colonel. Etudes opératives sur le cas de guerre avec la France (sans alliance), novembre/décem bre 1921, février 1922. [53 pp.] BAr 27/12790.

— Oberst. Memorial zum Aufmarsch an der Westfront im Kriege gegen Frankreich, Juli/Dezember 1925 [14 pp.] BAr 27/12792.

— Oberst. Aufmarsch West, 10.2.26. [Studie zu einem Operationsbefehl] BAr 27/12792.

— [Korpskommandant]. En mission aux grandes Manoeuvres italiennes de l'Apennin Toscan-Emilien, Août 1934; Oktober 1934. [32 pp.] BAr 127/42.

— General. Beurteilung der Lage; AHQ, 10.7.40 [7 pp.] BAr 15067.

— General an Eidg. Militärdepartement. z.H. des Bundesrates; AHQ, 12.7.40, geheim.BAr 27/15067.

— Le Rapport du Rütli, 25.7.40. auf Schallplatte, Grammoclub Ex Libris GC 707. BAr 5795/559.

— Rapport d'Armée au Rütli, 25.7.40. Korrigiertes Typoskript. [26 pp.] BAr 5795/173.

— Aide-mémoire sommaire, Exposé fait par le Commandant en chef de l'Armée aux membres du Conseil Fédéral présents, le 9 mai 1941, au domicile du Président de la Confédération; AHQ, 9.5.41, secret. [9 pp.] BAr 5800/2.

— Unterredung Guisan/Däniker; AHQ, 12.8.41, 15.15–17.50 Uhr. Niederschrift der Stahlbandaufnahme. [32 pp.] BAr 27/4783,1.

— Besprechung Guisan/Däniker; 25.8.41, 15.27–16.27 Uhr, geheim. Niederschrift der Stahlbandaufnahme, [20 pp.] BAr 27/4783.

— Aide-mémoire à l'intention du Conseil fédéral , QGA, 26.12.41, secret. [8 pp.] Bar 5795/202.

— Exposé au Conseil fédéral sur l'activité de l'Armée en 1942; QGA, 24.12.42, très secret. [14 pp.] BAr 5795/199.

— Exposé au Conseil fédéral sur l'activité de l'Armée en 1943: QGA, 17.1.44, très secret. [15 pp.] BAr 5795/199.

— Exposé au Conseil fédéral sur l'activité de l'Armée en 1944; QGA, 10.1.45, très secret. [26 pp.] BAr 5795/199.

— Observation sur le rapport du Conseil fédéral à l'Assemblée fédéral concernant le rapport du Général sur le Service actif 1939–1945; Lausanne, 9 février 1947. [7 pp.] ArWa. [cited as: Guisan, Observations]

— Obervations sur "l'Eingabe" du Col.div. Bandi; Lausanne, 9 février 1947. [3 pp.] ArWa.

Haas, Samuel. Erste unverbindliche Ideenskizze für die Errichtung eines militärischen Aufklärungs-und Propaganda-Dienstes; [undated, nach 1.9.39] BAr 5795/124.

Häni, Max. Lebenslauf; Bern, 1977–1979. Typescript. ArHä.

Hausamann, [Hans]. Zusammenfassung meiner Darlegungen bei Anlass der ersten Besprechung mirt den Herren Nationalräten Bringolf, Oprecht, Dr. Spühler am 27.4.38, ab 20.00 Uhr im Hotel Savoy in Bern. Erinnerungsprotokoll. [undated, 6 pp.] ArSchü.

— Berichte 12.4.40–3.8.43. AfZ.

— Einleitendes Votum aus Anlass der ersten Zusammenkunft der Offiziere, welche in der Folge besprachen und beschlossen, bei Überfall den Kampf da auszulösen, wo sie gerade stehen, wenn der Befehl dazu aus irgendwelchen Gründen ausbleiben sollte. [Lucerne, 21.7.40. 6 pp.] ArSchü.

— Die Schweiz im internationalen Spannungsfeld (Was ist und was will die Aktion Nationaler Widerstand?); [undated, nach 7, 9, 40, 18 pp.] BAr 5795/448,1.

— Politisch-militärpolitische Denkschrift zu Handen des Herrn Oberbefehlshabers der Armee, 9.10.40. [7 pp.], ArSchü.

— Büro "Ha," Die derzeitige kriegspolitische Lage (Stand Mitte August 1941); [undated, 36 pp.] BAr 5800/1.

— Offiziersbewegung 1940; [verfasst 1946, Durchschlag, 10 pp.] ArSchü.

— Der Bericht Eggen; (undated, vor 12.9.47. 39 pp.) BAr 27/9846.

— Major, Rund um den Nachrichtendienst im zweiten Weltkrieg, von einem Nachrichtenoffizier gesehen, Teufen, Oktober 1947; [unpublished manuscript, 99 pp.] BAr 5800/1.

Huber, [Jakob], Generalstabschef. Erwiderung auf die Eingabe des Herrn Nationalrat Dr. Bircher an den Bundesrat; AHQ, 12.9.42. Verfasser: Hptm.i.Gst. P. Burckhardt. [20 pp.] BAr 5795/436.

— Korpskommandant an Bundesrat Kobelt; Brienz, 31.1.47. [17 pp. mit Beilagen. Kopie in Schreibmaschine] BAr 5800/2.

Journal du Bureau du Général 1939–1946; [seit 16.3.42: Journal de l'Etat-Major particulier du Général] BAr 5795/51.

Kellerhals, Otto. Tagebuchnotizen; 1940. ArKh.

Kobelt, [Karl]. Referat des Chefs des EMD, Interlaken, 10.1.42, geheim. Protokoll. [9 pp.] BAr 579/146.

— Bundesrat. Militärische Gefahren 1939–1945, Beantwortung der Interpellationen Dietschi-Basel und Bringolf vor dem Nationalrat. [4.10.45] BAr 27/10028.

— Bundesrat. Tagebuch EMD, Dezember 1941–[25.6.48], Stenographie. BAr 5800/1.

Labhart, [Jakob]. Tagebücher, 1936–1945. BAr N1 La.

Lützelschwab, W[ilhelm]. Notizen zur Geschichte des "Offiziersbundes" von 1940; März 1963 BAr N1 Lü.

Magron, Oberslt.. Berichr über meine Abkommandierung vom 20.9.–31.10.38 zur Aufklärungsgruppe 11 in Neuhausen bei Königsberg (Ostpreussen); Payerne, November 1938. [55 pp.] BAr 27/12056.

Masson, [Roger], Oberstbrigadier. La ligne Eggen-Schellenberg; Berne, le 14 juin 1945, secret. (14 pp.] BAr 5330/1982,1.

— Témoignage dans l'affaire Hausmann-Schmid/Kummer; Lausanne, 12.7.47. [17 pp.] BAr 27/1846.

— Attestation "Walter Schellenberg"; Mont Pèlerin s/Vevey, le 10 mai 1948. [10 pp.] Durchschlag. Mit handschriftlicher Erklärung von General Guisan. BAr 5795/455.

Meyer, L[udwig] F[riedrich]. Vertrauliche Bemerkungen als Ergebnis aus der Besichtigung der Vollmachtenkommission; Luzern, Ende April 1940, [8 pp.] BAr 27/14133.

Meyer, Paul. handschriftliche Notizen, 1940–1946. BAr N1 Mey.

Minger, Rudolf. Zum Generalsbericht; Bern, 28.9.46. (15 S.) BAr 5795/207.

Monatsberichte der Truppe, Januar 1940 bis September 1941. BAr 27/14822.

Nachrichtenbulletins der Armee. BAr 27/9984 und BAr 5795/342f.

Operationsbefehle Nos. 1–18, BAr 5795/281–299. [No. 13 ist in BAr 5795/294].

Pilet-Golaz, [Marcel]. Aperçu destiné à M.le Conseiller fédéral Max Petitpierre, Chef du Département politique sur les dangers auxquels la Suisse fur exposée au cours de la guerre mondiale 1939–1945, Septembre 1945. [44 pp.] BAr 2809/1,4.

Protokolle der Sitzungen der Landesverteidigungskommission 1932–1946. BAr 27/4059–4060. [cited as: Prot. der LVK]

Protokolle der Armeekonferenzen vom 29.4.40–29.11.44, geheim. BAr 27/14126. [einzelne Protokolle in andern Dossiers]

Protokolle der Dienstrapporte und Konferenzen des Generalstabschefs. Vol. 1: 1.9.39–31.12.40; Vol. 2: 1.1.41–20.8.45. BAr 27/14151.

Protokoll der Konferenz des Armeekommandos, Sektion für Polizeidienst; Bern, 9.12.39. [36 pp.] BAr 27/10098,12.

Protocole de la Conférence du 1.7.40, 15.15, chez le Président de la Confédération. [4 pp.] BAr 5795/160.

Protokoll der Konferenz betr. Bekämpfung der staatsgefährlichen Propaganda in der Armee; Bern, 6.4.40, geheim. PKAr AG.

Protokoll über die Begehung und Besprechung der Limmatstellung, 4./5.1.40. BAr 27/14151,1.

Protokoll Dienstrapport des Kommandanten 2.AK; Zofingen, 24.6.40, geheim. BAr 5795/145.

Protokoll der Vertrauensleutekonferenz der Sozialdemokratischen Partei der Schweiz; Bern, 3.7.40. SAr 1.110.30.

Protokoll der Konferenz betr. fremde Spionagetätigkeit, 4.5.42, geheim. BAr.

Protokoll der Konferenz betr. Telefonabhorchungen in Interlaken, 27.11.42. BAr 5795/451.

Protokoll über die Vorsprache der Herren Nationalräte Oprecht, Bratschi und Bringolf, sowie Parteisekretär Dr. Stocker, alle von der Sozialdemokratischen Partei der Schweiz, bei den Herren Bundesräten Pilet-Golaz, Kobelt und von Steiger, im Bundesratssaal am 8.11.44. [19 pp.] BAr 2809/1,5.

Protokoll der Sitzund der ständerätlichen Kommission zur Behandlung des Berichtes des Generals an die Bundesversammlung über den Aktivdiemst 1939–1945 und des Berichtes des Bundesrates vom 7. Januar 1947 zum Generalsbericht; Rigi-Kaltbad, 3.–5.2.47. vertraulich. [53 pp.] BAr. [cited as: Prot. der ständerätlichen Kommission zur Behandlung des Berichtes des Generals]

Protokoll der Sitzung der nationalrätlichen Kommission zur Behandlung des Berichtes des Generals an die Bundesversammlung über den Aktivdienst 1939–1945 und des Berichtes des Bundesrates vom 7. Januar 1947 zum Generalsbericht; Interlaken, 24.–26.2.47, vertraulich. [52 pp.] Sitzung vom 19.3.47 [II] BAr. [cited as: Prot. der nationalrätlichen Kommission zur Behandlung des Berichtes des Generals]

Quartalsberichte der Truppe 1941–1945. BAr 27/14822.

Rapport d'Armée au Rütli (General Guisan/Barbey), 25.7.40. [26 pp.] BAr 5795/173 (A47).

Rapports de l'Etat-Major particulier du Général, secret. BAr 5795/199f.:
31.8.39–31.12.39 [I]
1.1.40–30.6.40 [II]
1.7.40–31.12.40 [III]
1.1.41–30.6.41 [IV]
1.7.41–30.6.42 [V]

Renon, A. Allocution; London, 2.6.48. BAr N1 Gui 50.

Repertorium Nachlass General Guisan 1919–1939, 1945–1961, bearbeiter von E.Tschabold und L. Andereggen. 1972. BAr J.I.127.

Repertorium Persönlicher Stab des Generals 1939–1945, bearbeitet von E. Tschabold und L. Andereggen, 1973. BAr 5795.

[Rieser]. Militär- und Luftattaché in London, Bericht über Einsichtnahme in die von den alliierten Truppen in Deutschland erbeuteten Dokumente des Oberkommandos des Heeres, 21.9.51, vertraulich. [14 pp.] BAr 5800/1.

[Rihner]. Bericht der 2. schweizerischen Mission bei der 1. französischen Armee, 20.4.–11.5.45. [88 pp. und Anhänge] BAr 27/12692.

von Salis, J[ean] R[udolf]. an General Guisan und Bundesrat Petitpierre; Zürich, 7.2.46, vertraulich. [8 pp.] BAr 5795/533.

Schmid, Hans Rudolf. Etwas zum Bericht des Generals; Thalwil, 11.7.46. [4 pp] BAr 5795/207.

Schürch, Gerhart. Notizen über meine Beteiligung an der Offiziersverschwörung 1940; Bern, 18.2.63. ArSchü.

Spione, Saboteure. Landesverräter, Übersicht über die bis Ende 1945 abgeschlossenen militärgerichtlichen Untersuchungen, 1.3.46, geheim [87 pp.] BAr 27/10112.

Strub, Urs. Die Suizide in der Schweizerarmee von der Mobilisation 1939 bis und mit Dezember 1940; AHQ, 10.2.41. BAr 27/19809,1.

Tagebücher des Armeestabes 1940–1945. BAr 27/14140.

Tagebuch Geb.Inf.Rgt.15 1940. BAr 5795/130.

Waibel, Max. Bericht zum Buche von Jon Kimche "Spying for Peace"; Bern, 26.2.63. [Typescript, 15 pp.] BAr N1 Lü.

Wehrli, Edmund. Pro memoria, 27.2.42 und 27.4.41, ArWe.

Weisungen betr. Handhabung der Neutralität durch die Truppe, 10.10.39. BAr.

Weisungen betr. Bekämpfung der staatsgefährlichen Propaganda in der Armee (Generalstabschef Labhart); AHQ 9.12.39. BAr.

Weisungen betr. das Verhalten der nicht unter den Waffen stehenden Wehrmänner bei Überfall; AHQ, 18.4.40. BAr.

Weisungen für die Organization von Massnahmen gegen Saboteure, Luftlandetruppen und durchgebrochene Panzertruppen; AHQ, 12.5.40. BAr 5795/342.

Wetter, Ernst. Notizen über das Buch Kimches "General Guisans Zweifrontenkrieg"; Zürich, 8.8.62. [7 pp.] BAr N1 Wt.

Wille, Ulrich. Tagebuch-Notizen, 1939. ArMa.

— In Erwartung des Jahres 1940, Memorial; 20.1.40. [5 pp.] ArMa.

— Oberskorpskommandant an Oberbefehlshaber, Persönliches Memorial; HQ, 31.5.40. [7 pp.] BAr 5795/85.

— Memorial zur Lage Juli 1941; Bern 9.7.41, streng vertraulich. [5 pp.] BAr 2809/1,5.

— Gedanken zum Entscheid des Armeeauditors gegen Oberst Däniker, 18.5.42. Ex.No.001. [37 pp.] BAr 27/4783.

Wochenberichte über die Stimmung im Volk 1940 (Ernst von Schenck) BAr 4450/6105.

Züblin, A[lbert]. Klageschrift in Sachen Hans Hausamann gegen die Tageszeitung "Die Tat" betr. Ehrverletzung durch die Presse; Zürich, 7.7.47. [48 pp.] BAr 17/9846.

Published primary sources (published files, books, presentations, reports, memoirs, magazine and newspaper articles published during the war)

Akten zur Deutschen Auswärtigen Politik, Aus dem Archiv des Deutschen Auswärtigen Amtes, Baden-Baden 1956.

Amtliches stenographisches Bulletin der Bundesversammlung, Nationalrat und Ständerat 1939–1946.

45 ans plus tard: La seconde guerre mondiale en Suisse et ses conséquences vues par diverses générations, in: Alliance culturelle romande, Cahier No. 30. Yverdon, October 1984.

Armeebefehle des Generals 1939–1945. BAr 5795.

Armee-Einteilung 1.5.40, Ordre de bataille (OB). Nur für dienstlichen Gebrauch, Bern [n.d. 1940] BAr.

Arnet, Edwin. Das eidgenössische Wettspeil, Offizielles Festspiel der schweizerischen Landesausstellung 1939 Zürich, in: Das Büchlein vom eidgenössischen Wettspiel, Zürich 1939, pp. 89ff.

Auswärtiges, Amt. Weitere Dokumente zur Kriegsausweitungspolitik der Westmächte, Die Generalstabsbesprechungen Englands und Frankreichs mit Belgien und den Niederlanden, Berlin 1940. BAr 27/9932.

Bandi, [Hans], Oberstdivisionär. Eingabe zum Bericht von General Henri Guisan und zum Bericht des Kommandanten der Flieger- und Fliegerabwehrtruppen, Bern 1947. [cited as: Bandi, Eingabe]

Barbey, Bernard. Fünf Jahre auf dem Kommandoposten des Generals, Tagebuch des Chefs des Persönlichen Stabes General Guisans 1940–1945, Bern 1948 [cited as: Barbey, Fünf Jahre]. Original French title: "P.C. du Général. Journal du Chef de l'Etat-Major particulier du Général 1940–1945," Neuchâtel 1948.

— Von Hauptquartier zu Hauptquartier, Mein Tagebuch als Verbindungsoffizier zur französischen Armee, 1939–1940, Frauenfeld 1967 [cited as: Barbey, Hauptquartier]. Original French title: "Aller et retour, Mon journal pendant et après la (drôle de Guerre) 1939–1940," Neuchâtel 1967.

— Hommage au Général Guisan, Lausanne 1960.

Barth, Karl. Im Namen Gottes des Allmächtigen 1291–1941, St. Gallen 1941.

Béguier, Lieutenant-colonel. Les étapes d'un régiment Breton, le 71e R.I. et R.I.A., Paris 1953.

Bericht des Bundesrates an die Bundesversammlung über die antidemokratische Tätigkeit von Schweizern und Ausländern im Zusammenhang mit dem Kriegsgeschehen 1939-1945 (Motion Boerlin), I. Teil, 28.12.45; II. Teil, 17.5.46; III. Teil, 21.5.46. [cited as: Bericht des Bundesrates über antidemokratische Tätigkeit]

Bericht des Bundesrates an die Bundesversammlung über die schweizerische Pressepolitik im Zusammenhang mit dem Kriegsgeschehen 1939–1945, vom 17.12.46 [n.p., n.d., Bern 1947]. [cited as: Bericht Pressepolitik]

Bericht des Bundesrates an die Bundesversammlung zum Bericht des Generals über den Aktivdienst 1939–1945, vom 7.1.47, Bern 1947. [cited as: Bericht des Bundesrates zum Bericht des Generals]

Bericht des Regierungsrates über die Abwehr staatsfeindlicher Umtriebe in den Vorkriegs- und Kriegsjahren sowie die Säuberungsaktion nach Kriegsschluss, Dem Grossen Rat des Kantons Basel-Stadt vorgelegt am 4. Juli 1946, Basel 1946.

Bernadotte, [Graf Folke]. La Fin, Mes négociations humanitaires en Allemagne au printemps 1945 et leurs conséquences politiques, Lausanne 1945.

Boéchat, Jean F. Le Général Guisan en Suède, Lausanne [n.d., 1947].

Bonjour, Edgar. Erinnerungen, Basel 1983.

— Karl Barth und die Schweiz, in: Theologische Zeitschrift, Jahrgang 42, 1986, pp. 303–312.

Bonnard, Jacques, and Françoise Belperrin. Inventaire des Fonds et Collections du Général Guisan, Lausanne 1973.

Böschenstein, Hermann. Vor unsern Augen, Aufzeichnungen über das Jahrzehnt 1935–1945, Bern 1978.

Bretscher, Willy. Im Sturm von Krise und Krieg, Neue Zürcher Zeitung 1933–1944, Siebzig Leitartikel von Willy Bretscher, Zürich 1987.

Bringolf, Walther. Mein Leben, Bern 1965.

[Buchman, Frank]. Ideologie und Koexistenz, Genf [n.d., 1959].

Bührer, Jakob. Ein starker Zeuge, in: Festschrift Hans Oprecht, loc. cit., pp. 198–200.

Bundesblatt der schweizerischen Eidgenossenschaft, Bern 1939–1947.

Bürger und Soldat, Festschrift zum 70. Geburtstag von General Gulisan, Zürich 1944.

Chappuis, Albert-Louis. "L'arrestation" du Général Guisan, in: Général Guisan ... toujours vivant, loc. cit., pp. 81–85.

Chaudet, Paul. Verantwortung oder Verzicht, Bern [n.d., 1968].

Churchill, Winston. Der Zweite Weltkrieg, Memoiren, 6 Vols., Übertragung aus dem Englischen, Bern 1948–1954.

Ciano, Galeazzo. Tagebücher 1939–1943, Übertragung aus dem Italienischen, Bern 1947.

Couchepin, Louis, Oberst. Das Reduit. Wie unsere Armee die Schweiz verteidigt, Zürich 1943.

Däniker, Gustav. Werdendes Soldatentum, Bern 1940.

— Oberst. Zwei Jahre Deutscher Strategie, in: Schweizerische Monatsschrift für Offiziere aller Waffen, Oktober- und Novemberheft 1941, pp. 332 ff.

— Voraussertzungen für die Bewährung im Kampf, in: Allgemeine Schweizerische Militärzeitung No. 7, July 1942, pp. 337–443.

— Im Dienste der Schweiz, in: "Schweizerische Politik," Veröffentlichungen des Volksbundes für die Unabhängigkeit der Schweiz, Heft 11, Zürich 1945.

Der grosse Tag vor 20 Jahren, sieben Augenzeugen erzählen den Rütli-Rapport vom 25. Juli 1940, in: "Die Woche," 31.7.60, No. 31.

"Die neue Schweiz," Programm der Sozialdemokratischen Partei der Schweiz, Zürich, February 1943.

Die Schweizerishe Kriegswirtschaft 1939/1948, Bericht des Eidgenössischen Volkswirtschaft-departments. Bern 1950.

Dienstreglement 1933, Bern 1933.

Diplomatische Dokumente der Schweiz, Vol. 6 (1914–1918), Bern 1981.

— Vol. 7/11 (1919–1920), Bern 1984.

Dollfus [Roger]. Bericht des Generaladjutanten der Armee an den Oberbefehlshaber der Armee über den Aktivdienst 1939–1945 [n.p., n.d., Bern 1946]. [cited as: Bericht des Generaladjutanten]

Dürrenmatt, Peter. Zeitwende, Stationen eines Lebens, Lucerne 1986.

Eidgenössische Volkszählung vom 1.12.1900, in: Schweizerische Statistik, Bern 1904.

Ernst, Alfred. Erfahrungen aus dem Aktivdienst, in: Kurz, Die Schweiz im Zweiten Weltkrieg, loc. cit., pp. 134–144.

— Die Armee im Aktivdienst, in: Böschenstein, Bedrohte Heimat, loc. cit., pp. 16–24.

— Der "Offiziersbund" von 1940, in: Festschrift zum 75 Geburtstag von Hans Oprecht, loc. cit., pp. 125–134. [cited as: Ernst, Der "Offiziersbund")

— Der "Offiziersbund" von 1940, in: CH, ein Lesebuch, herausgegeben vom Schweizerischen
    Bundesrat, Bern 1975, pp. 257–264.

— Bürger, Christ, Soldat, Schriften, herausgegeben von Hermann Böschenstein, Frauenfeld 1975.

— Auf dem Rütli, Ansprache am Zofingertag, 7.7.69 (150 Jahre Zofingia), in: Böschenstein,
    Alfred Ernst, loc. cit., pp. 152–155.

— Vor dreissig Jahren – und heute? "Reformatio," Evangelische Zeutschrift für Kultur und Politik
    No. 8/1969. Wiedergegeben in: Böschenstein, Alfred Ernst, loc. cit., pp. 141–151.

Etter, Philipp. Die vaterländische Erneuerung und wir, Zug 1933.

Feisst, Ernst. Kriegswirtschaftliche vorbereitungen und Massnahmen, in: Festschrift Eugen Bircher, loc.
    cit., pp. 61–79.

Felddienst (FD), Bern 1927,

Feldmann, Markus. Nationale Bewegungen der Schweiz, Eine vorläufige Übersicht, Bern 1933.

Festschrift Eugen Bircher, Zum 70. Geburtstag, Gewidmet von der Aargauischen Vaterländischen
    Vereinigung, von Freunden, Kameraden und Mitarbeitern, Aarau 1952.

[Festschrift zum 70. Geburtstag von General Guisan], Bürger und Soldat, Zürich 1944.

Festschrift zum 75. Geburtstag von Hans Oprecht, Unterwegs zur sozialen Demokratie,
    Zürich/Wien/Frankfurt 1969.

Festschrift zum 70. Geburtstag von Hans Rudolf Schmid (n.p., n.d., Zürich 1972).

Foote, Alexander. Handbuch für Spione, Darmstadt 1954.

Frey, Oskar, Oberst. Die Lage der Schweiz 1941, Kultur- und staatswissenschaftliche Schriften der
    ETH 22, Zürich 1941. [Vortrag an der ETH am 24.1.41]

[Frick, Hans.] Bericht des Chefs der Ausbildung der Armee an den Oberbefehlshaber der Armee über
    den Aktivdienst 1939-1945 [n.p., n.d., Bern 1946). [cited as: Bericht des Chefs der Ausbildung]

Frick, Hans. Kriegslehren, in: Kurz, Die Schweiz im Zweiten Weltkrieg, loc. cit., pp.81–105.

Frölicher, Hans. Meine Aufgabe in Berlin, Bern 1962 [Privatdruck].

Gafner, Raymond. Passer le témoin, in: Général Guisan…Toujours vivant, loc. cit., pp. 41–47.

Gamelin [Maurice G.], Général. Servir, La Guerre (Septembre 1939–49 Mai 1940), Paris 1947.

Gasser, Adolf. Geheimdienstliches aus dem Zweiten Weltrieg, in: Ausgewählte historische Schriften
    1933–1983, Basel 1983, pp. 226–229.

Gasser, Christian. Der Gotthard-Bund, Eine schweizerische Widerstandsbewegung, Bern 1984.

Gerber, Urs. Ulrich Wille et sa conception de la neutralité, Son attitude face à l'Italie entre 1910 et
    1918. in: hyspo Cahier 5, Bern, April 1985, pp. 60–67.

Germann, O[scar] A[dolf]. Erinnerungen, Bern [n.d., 1977, Privatdruck].

Gisevius, Hans Bernd. Bis zum bitteren Ende, Hamburg/Berlin/Frankfurt 1947.

Gonard, [Samuel]. Hommage au Général Guisan, 30 août 1939–20 août 1945, Thun 1945.

— Die Strategischen Probleme der Schweiz im Zweiten Weltkrieg, in: Kurz, Die Schweiz im Zweiten
    Weltkrieg, loc. cit., pp. 39–57.

— Der Weg zum Reduit, in: Readers Digest, Der Zweite Weltkrieg, Vol. I, Zürich 1971, pp. 173–188.

— Hommage à Madame la Générale Guisan, in: Bulletin de la Section Vaudoise de la Société
    Suisse des officiers No. 5, Lausanne 1964.

Gos, Charles. Généraux Suisses, Préface du Colonel Commandant de Corps Guisan, Lausanne 1932.

Grieder, Fritz. Basel im Zweiten Weltkrieg, 135. Neujahrsblatt, Basel 1957.

Grimm, Robert. Der 12. Dezember des Bürgertums, Ein Nachwort zu den Bundesrats-Wahlen, Aarau
    1930.

— Die Arbeiterschaft in der Kriegszeit, Rede vor dem Parteitag der bernischen Sozialdemokratie
    vom 18. Februar 1940. Separatum, Neuauflage, Bern 1946.

Guderian, Heinz. Erinnerungen eines Soldaten, Heidelberg 1951.

[Gugger, Ivo.] Bericht des Chefs des Personellen der Armee an den Oberbefehlshaber der Armee über
    den Aktivdienst 1939–1945 [n.p., n.d., Bern 1946). [cited as: Bericht des Chefs des Personellen]

Guisan, Henri. Korpskommandant, Die Seele unserer Armee und die soziale Rolle des Offiziers, in:
    Neue Schweizer Rundschau, Sonderdruck; Zürich [n.d., 1934].

— Korpskommandant, Les devoirs des universitaires à l'égard de la défense nationale, in: Schweizerische Hochschulzeitung; Zürich, 1.5.37, pp. 6–9.

— General, Unser Volk und seine Armee, Zürich 1940.

— Treu zum Land, in: "Schweizer Illustrierte". 4/11/42.

— Nach einem Vierteljahrhundert, in: Gedenkbuch 25 Jahre Schweizerische Nationalspende für unsere Soldaten und ihre Familien 1918–1943, Bern 1945, pp. 30–34.

— General, Bericht an die Bundesversammlung über den Aktivdienst 1939–1945, [n.p., n.d., Bern 1946]. [cited as: Bericht des Generals)

— Feierliche Höhepunkte des Aktivdienstes, in: Kurz, Die Schweiz im zweiten Weltkrieg, loc. cit., pp. 15–30.

— Rückblick auf den Aktivdienst, Aus meinen privaten Notizen, Sonderdruck aus No. 31 und No. 32 der "Schweizer Illustrierten Zeitung" [n.d., 1.8.47. 23 pp.]. [cited as: Guisan, Rückblick)

— Gespräche, Zwölf Sendungen von Radio Lausanne, geleitert von Major Raymond Gafner, Mit einem Vorwort von alt Bundesrat Rudolf Minger, Bern 1953. [cited as: Guisan, Gespräche). Original French title: "Entretiens".

— Erklärung, in: [Buchmann Frank], Ideologie und Koexistenz, Genf [n.d. 1959], Frontispiz.

Gut, Theodor. Der politische Standort der Schweiz, Referat gehalten am 20. Oktober 1940 in der ordentlichen Delegierten-Versammlung der Freisinnig-Demokratischen Partei der Schweiz in Neuenburg, Stäfa [n.d., 1940].

— Reden und Schriften, Mit einer Einleitung von Willy Bretscher, Zürich 1954.

Halder, [Franz]. Kriegstagebuch, Vol. I, Vom Polenfeldzug bis zum Ende der Westoffensive, Stuttgart 1962.

von Hassell, Ulrich. Vom andern Deutschland, Zürich and Freiburg i.Br. 1946.

Hausamann, Hans. Das Schweizervolk hat sich nicht umzustelten, in: "der Schweizerische Beobachter," No. 14, Basel, 31.7.40.

— Wei es zu unserer Freundschaft kam, in: Festschrift Hans Oprecht, loc. cit., pp. 190–194.

— 1897–1974, Gedenkschrift zum 10. Todestag, St. Gallen 1984.

Hausherr, Paul. Feldgraue Tage, Erinnerungen aus den Jahren 1939–1945, Baden 1975.

Hillgruber, Andreas. Staatmänner und Diplomaten bei Hitler, Vertrauliche Aufzeichnungen über Unterredungen mit Vertretern des Auslandes 1939–1941, Frankfurt a.Main 1967.

Hirt, Ernst. General Guisan und die ETS Magglingen, in: Bulletin Offiziersverein Biel-Seeland No. 7, Biel 1969.

Hitler, Adolf. Monologe im Führer-Hauptquartier, Die Aufzeichnungen Heinrich Heims, Munich 1982.

Homberger, Heinrich. Schweizerische Handelspolitik um Zweiten Weltkrieg, Ein Überblick auf Grund persönlicher Erlebnisse, Erlenbach-Zürich/Stuttgart 1970.

— Schwerpunkte der schweizerischen Handelspolitik seit dem Zweiten Weltkrieg, in: Festschrift Petitpierre, loc. cit., pp. 55–67.

Hörning, Walo. Der Einsatz der Schwiezerischen Flugwaffe im Neutralitätsdienst, insbesondere ihr Kampfgeist im Juni 1940, Dem Andenken aller im Aktivdienst 1939–1945 abgestürzten Fliegerkameraden gewidmet, in: Kurz, Die Schweiz im Zweiten Weltkrieg, loc. cit., pp. 168–179.

Huber, Harald. Neue Aufgaben? Neuer Einsatz! in: Festschrift Hans Oprecht, loc. cit., pp. 185–190.

Huber, [Jakob]. Bericht des Chefs des Generalstabes der Armee an den Oberbefehlshaber der Armee über den Aktivdienst 1939–1945 [n.p., n.d., Bern 1946]. [cited as: Bericht des Generalstabschefs]

Hummler, Fritz. Der Grenzsoldat, Tagebuchblätter, in: Bürger und Soldat, loc. cit., pp. 411–437.

Iklé, Max. Aus dem Berufsleben, 2. Teil. Prifatdruck [n.p., n.d., Küsnacht-Zürich, ca. 1980].

Iselin, Rudolph. Erinnerungen und Erlebnisse, Basel 1949. Privatdruck.

Jaeckle, Erwin. Niemandsland der Dreissigerjahre, Meine Erinnerungen 1933–1942, Zürich 1979.

Jahrbücher der eidgenössischen Räte und Gerichte 1939–1946, Bern 1939–1946.

100 Jahre Füsilier-Bataillon 56, Geschichte, Erinnerungen, Veränderungen, Reinach 1975.

Jeker, Armin. Die Finanzprobleme der Kriegsjahre, in: Kurz, Die Schweiz im Zweiten Weltkrieg, loc. cit., pp. 234–241.

Kelly, David. The Ruling Few, London 1952.

Kobelt, Karl. Vom Krieg sum Frieden, in: Kurz, Die Schweiz im Zweiten Weltkrieg, loc. cit., pp. 376–388.

Kriegstagebuch des Oberkommandos der Wehrmacht, Vol. 1, München 1982.

Kurz, Hans Rudolf. Dokumente des Aktivdienstes, Frauenfeld 1965. [cited as: Kurz, Dokumente]

— Bundesrat Kobelt im Amt 1940–1954, in: Müller, Hans, Bundesrat Kobelt, loc. cit., pp. 85–100.

de Lattre de Tassigny [Jean-Joseph-Marie]. Histoire de la Première Armée francaise Rhin et Danube, Paris 1949.

Leonhardt, Ernst. Schweizervolk! Deine Schicksalsstunde ist gekommen! Was soll nun werden? Eine Abrechnung von Ernst Leonhardt, herausgegeben vom Pressedienst der Scweizerischen Erneuerung, 15.7.40. [31 pp.] BAr 5795/342.

Lindt, August R[udolf]. Aktiver Zeuge der Zeit, Interview (A.A. Häsler), in: "Ex Libris," No. 4, Zürich 1954.

Liss, Ulrich. Westfront 1939/40, Erinnerungen des Feindbearbeiters im OKH, Neckargemünd 1959.

— Noch einmal: La Charité 1940, in: Allgemeine Schweizerische Militärzeitschrift, 12/1967.

von Lossberg, Bernhard. Im Wehrmachtsführungsstab, Bericht eines Generalstabsoffiziers, Hamburg 1950.

Lugand, Lt.-Col. La Campagne de France mai-juin 1940, Paris 1953.

Mann, Golo. Mehr Scham als Freude, Interview (Klaus Lieber), in: "Brückenbauer," 1.5.85, No. 18.

Marguth, Mario. Das Tagewerk und die Kommandoposten des Generals, in: Kurz, Die Schweiz im Zweiten Weltkrieg, loc. cit., pp. 31–38.

Masson, R[oger]. Unser Nachrichtendienst im Zweiten Weltkrieg, in: Kurz, Die Schweiz im Zweiten Weltkrieg, loc. cit., pp. 69–80.

Mayer, W., Hptm. Gefechtsbericht über den Vormarsch nach und die Einnahme von La Charité am 16. Juni 1940, in: Militär-Wochenblatt, Jahrgang 126, No. 6, Berlin 8.8.41, pp. 146f.

Meili, Armin, Lorbeeren und harte Nüsse, Aus dem Werk- und Tagebuch eines Eidgenossen, Zürich 1968.

Meuli, H[ans]. Der Santätsdienst unserer Armee in den Jahren 1939–1945, in: Kurz, Die Schweiz im Zweiten Weltkrieg, loc. cit., pp. 276–292.

[Miescher, Rudolf.] Zur Erinnerug an Herrn Dr. Rudolf Miescher, Oberstkorpskommandant, Basel [anonym, n.d., 1945].

Mlitärorganisation der Schweizerischen Eidgenossenschaft, vom 12. April 1907. [cited as: MO 1907].

Minger, Rudolf. Zum Geleit, in: Guisan, Gespräche, loc. cit., pp. 7–10.

Montecuccoli [= Däniker], Das ABC zum Generalbericht, in: "Die Tat," 30.7., 2.8., 6.8. and 8.8.46, Nos.. 207, 210, 214, and 216.

Moralische Aufrüstung, Ideologie und Koexistenz, "Erklärung von General Guisan" [n.p., n.d., 1959].

Müller, H[ans]. Erinnerungen an die Mobilisation 1939, in: Bulletin des Offiziersvereins Biel-Seeland, Biel 1969, No. 7. [3 pp.]

Nobs, Ernst. Helvetische Erneuerung, Zürich 1943.

Oberkommando des Heeres. Kleines Orientierungsheft Schweiz; September 1942, geheime Kommandosache. Kopie. BAr27/14348 A. Publ. Von Schaufelberger, Walter, in: Allgemeine Schweizerische Militärzeitschrift, July/August 1977, pp. 289 ff. [cited as: Oberkommando des Heeres, Kleines Orientierungsheft Schweiz]

Oeri, Albert. O. Tagesberichte (Basler Nachrichten), Bern 1946.

Oltramare, Georges. Réglons nos comptes, Genf 1949.

Oprecht, Hans. Der zweite Weltkrieg und die schweizerische Arbeiterschaft, Separatdruck aus: Kultur und Arbeit, Schriften zur Wirtschafts-, Sozial- und Kulturpolitik [n.p., n.d., Zürich 1941].

— Pilet-Golaz' Fall und die politischen Konsequenzen, in: "Rote Revue," 4/1944, pp. 121–124.

Peer, Andri. Der Aktivdienst, Die Zeit nationaler Bewährung, Zofingen 1975.

Petitpierre, Max. Festschrift, Seize ans de neutralité active, Aspects de la politique étrangère de la Suisse (1945–1961), Neuchâtel 1980.

Picker, Henry. Hitlers Tischgespräche im Führerhauptquartier, 3. und erweiterte Ausgabe, Stuttgart 1976.

Prisi, [Fritz]. Oberstkorpskommandant, Bemerkungen zum Bericht des Generals, in: "Der Bund, 20.11.46, No. 541. [cited as: Prisi, Bemerkungen]

Probst, R[ené]. Flüchtlinge und Internierte in der Schweiz, in: Kurz, Die Schweiz im Zweiten Weltkrieg, loc. cit., pp. 222–233.

Pünter, Otto. Der Anschluss fand nicht statt, Geheimagent Pakbo erzählt; Erlebnisse, Tatsachen und Dokumente aus den Jahren 1930–1945, Bern 1967.

Raczek, F[ranciszek] K[sawery]. Oberstlt., Die Internierung der 2. polnischen Schützendivision in der Schweiz vor 25 Jahren (1940–1945), Stäfa 1965.

Reck, Oskar. Im Rekrutenregiment und spätter, Ein militärisches Experiment, in: Die Fünfte, loc. cit., pp. 128–130.

de Reynold, Gonzague. Mes mémoires, 3 romes, Genève 1960–1963, Vol. III: Les circles concentriques, jugements et prévisions, Genève 1963.

Rihner, [Fritz]. Bericht über die Verhältnisse bei den Flieger- und Flab.-Truppen am 1.1.44, in: Bericht des Kommandanten der Flieger- und Fliegerabwehrtruppen, loc. cit., pp. 178–188. [cited as: Bericht über die Verhältnisse bei den Flieger- und Flab.-Truppen am 1.1.44]

Rihner, [Fritz]. Bericht des Kommandanten der Flieger- und Fliegerabwehrtruppen an den Oberbefehlshaber der Armee über den Aktivdienst 1939–1945 [n.p., n.d., Bern 1946]. [cited as: Bericht des Kommandanten der Flieger- und Fliegerabwehrtruppen]

Robert, Olivier. Matériaux pour servir à l'histoire du doctorat h.c. décerné à Benito Mussolini en 1937, Lausanne 1937.

de Rougemont, Denis. Journal d'une époque, 1926–1946 [n.p., Paris], 1968.

[de Rougemont, Denis.] Qu'est-ce que la ligne du Gothard?, Neuchâtel [[n.d., 1940, 13 pp.]

von Salis, Jean Rudolf. Grenzüberschreitungen, Ein Lebensbericht, 2. Teil 1939–1978, Zürich 1979.

— Notizen eines Müssiggängers, Zürich 1983.

— Eine Chronik des Zweiten Weltkrieges, Radio-Kommentare 1939–1945, Zürich 1984.

Sandoz, Jules. In memoriam, in: Bulletin des Offiziersvereins Biel-Seeland No. 7, Biel 1969. [3 pp.]

Schaefer, Alfred. Interview, in: "Brückenbauer," No. 31, 31.7.85.

Schellenberg, Walter. Aufzeichnungen, Wiesbaden/Munich 1979.

von Schenck, Ernst. Aktion Nationaler Widerstand, in: Festschrift Hans Oprecht, loc. cit., pp. 107–123. [Schmid] Nachlass Prof. Dr. Karl Schmid 1907–1974, herausgegeben von Däniker Marie-Claire und Urner Klaus, Archiv für Zeitgeschichte ETHZ, Zürich 1983.

Schmid-Ammann, Paul. Mahnrufe in die Zeit, Vier bewegte Jahrzehnte schweizerischer Politik 1930–1970, Zürich 1971.

— Unterwegs von der politischen zur sozialen Demokratie, Lebenserinnerungen, Zürich 1978.

Schmidt, Paul. Statist auf diplomatischer Bühne 1923–1945, Bonn 1949.

Schneeberger, Ernst. Wirtschaftskrieg und "anderes," als Diplomat erlebt in Bern und Washington D.C. 1940–1948, Wädenswil 1984.

Schürch, Ernst. Als die Freiheit in Frage stand, Erinnerungen aus der Sturmzeit der Schweizer Presse, Bern 1946.

[Schürch, Gerhart.] Meinen Nächsten gewidmet zum 23. March 1970. [n.p., Bern]

Schürch, Gerhart. Wächter-Denker-Mahner, in: Gedenkschrift zum 10. Todestag von Hans Hausamann, St. Gallen 1984, pp. 9–23.

Schwarz, Urs. Schicksalstage in Berlin, Lenzburger Druck 1986.

— Die Presse als Glied der Landesverteidigung, in: Bürger and Soldat, loc. cit., pp. 289–311.

"Schweizerische Politik," Veröffentlichungen des Volksbundes für die Unabhängigkeit der Schweiz, Heft 11, Zürich 1945.

Die Sozialdemokratische Partei der Schweiz zur Armeereform, St. Gallen [n.d., 1947].

Spühler, Willy. Die Arbeiterschaft in Krise und Krieg, in: "Brückenbauer," 1.5.85, No. 18.

Stegemann, Hermann. Erinnerungen aus meinem Leben und aus meiner Zeit, Berlin/Leipzig 1930.

Steiner, Karl. Denker und Schaffer, hart wie Fels, in: "Wynentaler Blatt," 13.1.83.

Stucki, Walter. Von Pétain zur Vierten Republik, Bern 1947.

Thürer, Georg. Einige Erinnerungen an Hauptmann Hans Hausamann, in: Gedenkschrift zum 10. Todestag. Loc. cit., pp. 29–37.

Trachsel, Gottlieb. Fahneneid und Landesverrat, in: Bürger and Soldat, loc. cit., pp. 117–144.

Tschäni, Hans. Vor 40 Jahren: Ende des Aktivdienstes, in: Gegensteuer, Zürich 1987, pp. 85–93.

Valloton, Henry. La Suisse de demain, Lausanne 1940.

Vitali, Felice A., Zwischen den Grenzen, Lebensbericht eines Medienmachers, Locarno 1983.

Wahlen, F[riedrich] T[raugott]. Unser Boden heute und morgen; Etappen und Ziele des schweizerischen Anbauwerkes, Zürich 1943.

Waibel, Max. Die geheimen Verhandlungen über die Kapitulation der deutschen Wehrmacht in Italien, in: Kurz, Die Schweiz im Zweiten Weltkrieg, loc. cit., pp. 121–126.

— 1945 Kapitulation in Norditalien, Originalbericht des Vermittlers, Mit einem Kommentar von Hans Rudolf Kurz, Basel and Frankfurt a.M. 1981.

Wanner, Fritz. Mit der Berner Division im Kriegsjahr 1940, in: "Der Bund," 20.12.80, No. 299.

Warlimont, Walter. Im Hauptquartier der deutschen Wehrmacht 1939–1945, Frankfurt a.M. 1962.

Weber, Max. Die Schweiz nach dem ersten Kriegsjahr, in: Gewerkschaftliche Rundschau 9, September 1940.

— Der Kampf um die Kriseninitiative, in: Festschrift Hans Oprecht, loc. cit., pp. 39–55.

Wehrbriefe der Sektion "Heer und Haus," Nos. 1–34, AfZ Nl Li 17.

Wehrli, Edmund. Interview mit Gesela Blau, . . . da fühlten sich viele Schweizer verraten, in: "Schweizer Illustrierte," 19.5.80, No. 21, p. 70.

— Le rapport du Grütli vu par un témoin, in: "24 heures," 11.4.85.

Weitnauer, Albert. Rechenschaft, Vierzig Jahre im Dienst des schweizerischen Staates, Zürich 1981.

Von Weizsäcker, Ernst. Erinnerungen, Munich 1950.

Werder, Wilhelm. Die 5. Division, in: Festschrift Eugen Bircher, loc. cit., pp. 319–331.

Wüst, R[ené] H[enri]. Un nouveau chapitre inconnu de l'histoire contemporaine de la Suisse: L'accord secret de Lattre-Guisan, in: "La Suisse," 26.8.74.

Zermatten, Maurice. Esquisses d'un portrait-souvenir, in: Général Guisan . . . toujours vivant, loc. cit., pp. 27–37.

Ziegler, [Roland], Major. Histoire de la section "Armée et Foyer" 1939–1945, Bern 1945.

Zollinger, Albin. Geistige Landesverteidigung, in: "Die Zeit," Bern, June 1936. Wiedergegeben: Zollinger, Werke, Vol. 6, Zürich/Munich 1984, pp. 41–44.

Zopfi, Hans. Aus sturmerfüllter Zeit, Anekdoten und Erinnerungen, 2. Teil, Affoltern a.A. 1954.

Züblin, Albert. Über Ausbildung und Disziplin, in: Bürger and Soldat, loc. cit., pp. 373–389.

Zumstein, Jörg. Korpskommandant, In der Rolle des Oberbefehlshabers, in: Allgemeine Schweizerische Militärzeitschrift, 4.4.85.

II. Secondary Sources

Second-hand accounts, reference works

Abshagen, Karl Heinz. Canaris: Patriot und Weltbürger, Stuttgart 1949.

Accoce, Pierre, and Pierre Quet. Moskau wusste alles, Zürich 1966.

Adam, Jost. Die Haltung der Schweiz gegenüber dem nationalsozialistischen Deutschland im Jahre 1940, Diss. Mainz 1972 [n.p., n.d., Bielefeld 1973].

Andreotti, Mario. Erneurung eines Mythos, in "Staatsbürger," No. 3, 22.5.85.

Anet, Daniel. Pierre Ceresole: La Passion de la Paix, Neuchâtel 1969.

Arnold, Armin, and Rolf Rötlisberger. "Aus innen- und aussenpolitischen Gründen gestrählt," Cäsar von Arx, Philipp Etter und das "Bundesfeierspiel 1941," in "Neue Zürcher Zeitung," 30./31.7.83, No. 176.

Augsbourg, Géa. La vie en images du Général Guisan, Dessinée par le Caporal Géa Augsbourg, Lausanne 1939.

Beck, Marcel. Der Gotthard-Bund, in: "Badener Tagblatt," 20.10.84.

Beck, Roland. Dufour als militärischer Führer und Denker, in: "Neue Zürcher Zeitung," 12./13.9.87, No. 211.

Béguin, Pierre. Le balcon sur l'Europe, Petite histoire de la Suisse pendant la guerre 1939–1945, Neuchâtel 1951.

— Die Schweiz und die Kriegswirtschaft, in: General Guisan und der Zweite Weltkrieg, loc. cit., pp. 111–125.

Biaudet, Jean-Charles. Edmond Rossier et la censure pendant la seconde guerre mondiale 1939–1945, in: Etudes de letters, No. 2, Lausanne 1968, pp. 72–139.

Bindschedler, Rudolf L., and others. Schwedische und schweizerische Neutralität im Zweiten Weltkrieg, Basel/Frankfurt a.M. 1985.

Blaser, Fritz. Bibliographie der Schweizer Press, 2 Halbbände, Basel 1956 and 1958.

Blau, Gisela. Als die Nazis auf die Schweiz ein Auge warfen, in: "Schweizer Illustrierte," 5.5.80, No. 19.[I]

— . . . aber nicht nur die Franzosen flohen vor den Nazis, 12.5.80, No. 20. [II]

— . . . da fühlten sich viele Schweizer verraten, 19.5.80. No. 21. [III]

Bonjour, Edgar. Das Schicksal des Sonderbundes in eidgenössischer Darstellung, Aarau 1947.

— Geschichte der schweizerischen Neutralität, Vols. IV–IX, Basel 1971–1976. [cited as: Bonjour, Neutralität]

— Wirtschaftliche Beziehungen zwischen England und der Schweiz im Zweiten Weltkrieg, in: Schweizerische Zeitschrfit für Geschichte, 4/1972, pp. 591–620.

— Britisch-schweizerische Militärgespräche 1939/40, in: "Neue Zürcher Zeitung," 17.4.73.

— Wie lange glaubte Pilet-Golaz an den deutschen Endsieg? In: "Neue Zürcher Zeitung," 24./25.2.79, No. 46.

— Das Geschichtsbild von Pilet-Golaz, in: "Neue Zürcher Zeitung," 29.1.80, No. 23.

— Pilet-Golaz' Friedensbemühungen 1943, in: "Neue Zürcher Zeitung," 2.7.80, No. 151.

— England und der schweizerische Widerstandswille, in: Schweizerische Zeitschrift für Geschichte, 3/1981, pp. 332–335.

— Die Schweiz und Europa, Vol. 7, Basel/Frankfurt a.M. 1981.

— Henri Guisan, in: Die Schweiz und Europe, Vol. 7, loc. cit., pp. 223–228.

— Die Neutralitätspolitik der Schweiz während des Zweiten Weltkrieges, in: "Brückenbauer," 1.5.85, No. 18.

— General Guisan in heutiger Sicht, Vortrag an der 67. Stiftungsversammlung der Schweizerischen Nationalspende für unsere Soldaten und ihre Familien, gehalten im Rathaus Zürich, 30.8.86. Publ. in: "Tages-Anzeiger," 24.10.86.

Böschenstein Hermann, Bedrohte Heimat, Die Schweiz im Zweiten Weltkrieg, Bern 1963.

— General Henri Guisan, Zur zehnten Wiederkehr seines Todestages, in: "Neue Zürcher Zeitung," 12.4.70. No. 166. [cited as: Böschenstein, General Guisan]

— Alfred Ernst, Bürger, Christ, Soldat, Frauenfeld 1975.

— Bundesrat Kobelt und das Parlament, in: Hans Müller, Bundesrat Karl Kobelt, loc. cit., pp. 111–128.

Bourgeois, Daniel. Le Troisième Reich et la Suisse 1933–1945, Thèse Genève, Neuchâtel 1974.

— La Suisse et la Seconde Guerre mondiale, Guisan, Pilet-Golaz?, in: Alliance culturelle romande 23, November 1977, pp. 11–16.

— L'image allemande de Pilet-Golaz, 1940–1944, in: Studien und Quellen 4, Bern 1978, pp. 69–128.

— Notes de Lecture, Notice bibliographique sur les publications récentes concernant les relations internationals de la Suisse de 1848 à nos jours, in: Relations Internationales, No. 30, Paris 1982, pp. 231–248.

Les relations économiques germano-suisses pendant la seconde guerre mondiale; un bilan allemand de 1944, in: Schweizerische Zeitschrift für Geschichte, 4/1982, pp. 563 ff.

Brandell, Urs. Die Transitfrage in der schwedischen Aussenpolitik während des Zweiten Weltkrieges, in: Bindschedler u.a., Schwedische und schweizerische Neutralität im Zweiten Weltkrieg, loc. cit., pp. 82–96.

Braunschweig, Pierre-Th. Geheimer Draht nach Berlin: Die Nachrichtenlinie Masson-Schellenberg und der schweizerische Nachrichtendienst im Zweiten Weltkrieg. Diss. Bern, Zürich 1989.

(English translation: "Secret Channel to Berlin," Front Street Press, Rockville Centre, NY, 2003.

Brenzing, Klaus. Der Admiral, Leben und Wirken, Nördlingen 1973.

Bretscher-Spindler, Katharina. Konservativismus, Korporativismus und Faschismus, Zur Kontroverse um Guisans politische Ansichten, in: "Neue Zürcher Zeitung," 19.4.85, No. 90.

Bretscher, Willy. Das Verhältnis von Bundesversammlung und Bundesrat in der F?uuhrung der auswärtigen Politik, in: Festschrift Max Petitpierre, loc. cit., pp. 41–54.

Brügel, J.W. Nochmals: Der Fall Minister Frölicher, in: "Neue Zürcher Zeitung," 4.5.76, No. 103.

Brunner, Matthias. Die Ausbildung während des Aktivdienstes, in: Kurz, Die Schweiz im Zweiten Weltkrieg, loc. cit., pp. 187–194.

Bucher, Erwin. Die Schweiz im Sommer 1940, in: Schweizerische Zeitschrift für Geschichte, 2/1979, pp. 356–398.

— Pilet-Golaz im Urteil des englischen Gesandten, in: Schweizerische Zeitschrift für Geschichte, 4/1981, pp. 492–494.

— Zur Linie Masson-Schellenberg, in: Schweizerische Zeitschrift für Geschichte, 3/1988, pp. 176–302.

Burckhardt, Carl J. De Lattre de Tassigny, in: Begegnungen, Zürich 1958, pp. 237–251.

Bütler, Heinz. "Wach auf Schweizervolk!" Die Schweiz zwischen Frontismus, Verrat und Selbstbehauptung, 1914–1940, Bern 1980.

Cantini, Claude. Le colonel fasciste Suisse, Arthur Fonjallaz, Lausanne 1983.

Cartier, Raymond. Der Zweite Weltkrieg, 3 Vols., München 1967. Original French title: "La seconde guerre mondiales," Paris 1965.

Cattani, Alfred. Flüchtlingspolitik im Zweiten Weltkrieg und heute, in: "Neue Zürcher Zeitung," 15./16.3.86, No. 62.

Cerutti, Mauro. Mussolini bailleur de fonds des fascistes suisses, les relations entre le colonel Arthur Fonjallaz et le Duce à la lumière de noveaux documents italiens, in: Schweizerische Zeitschrift für Geschichte, 1/1985, pp. 21–46.

Chapuisat, Edouard. General Guisan, Bern 1950.

Chevallaz, Georges-André. Le role du Général Guisan Durant le service actif, in: Général Guisan . . . toujours vivant, loc. cit., pp. 9–19.

— Les plans italiens face à la Suisse en 1938–1943, Pully 1988.

Von Clausewitz, Karl. Vom Kriege, benützte Ausgabe: Insel-Verlag, Leipzig 1940.

Couchepin, Louis [Oberst]. Das Reduit, Wie unsere Armee die Schweiz verteidigt, Zürich 1943.

Dahinden, Martin. Das Schweizerbuch im Zeitalter von Nationalsozialismus und Geistiger Landesverteidigung, Diss. Zürich, Bern/Frankfurt a.M./New York/Paris 1987.

Däniker, Gustav [Jr.]. Dissuasion heute und morgen—ein persönlicher Exkurs, in: Die Zukunft der Milizarmee, Zürich 1985, pp. 27–30.

Das Deutsche Reich und der Zweite Weltkrieg, 3 Vols., Stuttgart 1979–1984.

— Vol. II: Die Errichtung der Hegemonie auf dem europäischen Kontinent, Stuttgart 1979.

— Vol. III: Der Mittelmeerraum und Südosteuropa, Stuttgart 1984.

Decoppet, Maurice. Fondation Général Henri Guisan, in: Perrin, loc. cit., pp. 79–81.

Delay, Ives. La Grande Chance de la Suisse, Le général Guisan ou l'art de gagner la paix, Echallens [[n.d., 1974].

Die Fünfte, 111 Jahre 5. Division, Aarau 1986.

Dragunow, G.P. Schweizer Geschichte und Gegenwart, Moskau 1978.

Dreifuss, Eric. Die Schweiz und das Dritte Reich, Vier deutschschweizerische Zeitungen im Zeitalter des Faschismus 1933–1939, Diss. Zürich, Frauenfeld 1971.

Dürrenmat, Friedrich. Interview zum 1. August, in: CH, Ein Lesebuch, herausgegeben vom Schweizerischen Bundesrat, Bern 1974.

Dürrenmatt, Peter. Schweizer Geschichte, Zürich 1963.

— Kleine Geschichte der Schweiz während des zweiten Weltkrieges, Zürich 1949.

Durrer, Marco. Die schweizerisch-americanischen Finanzbeziehungen im Zweiten Weltkrieg, Von der Blockierung der schweizerischen Guthaben in den USA über die "Safe Haven"—Politik zum Washingtoner Abkommen (1941–1946), Bankwirtschaftliche Forschungen Vol. 89, Bern 1984.

Emmenegger, Kurt. QN wusste Bescheid, Zürich 1965.

Ernst, Alfred. Die Ordnung des militärischen Oberbefehls im schweizerischen Bundesstaat, Basler Beiträge zur Geschichtswissenschaft 31, Basel 1948.

— General Henri Guisan, Versuch einer Würdigung, in: "Zofingia," Zentralblatt des Schweizerischen Zofingervereins, No. 7/8, St. Gallen 1971. Wiederabdruck in: Böschenstein, Alfred Ernst, Bürger, Christ, Soldat, loc. cit., pp. 28–34. [cited as: Ernst, General Guisan]

— Die Konzeption der schweizerischen Landesverteidigung 1815–1966, Frauenfeld and Stuttgart 1971. [cited as: Ernst, Konzeption]

— Der schweizerische Nachrichtendienst im Zweiten Weltkrieg, in Allgemeine Schweizerische Militärzeitschrift, Frauenfeld, 12/1972, pp. 567–662.

— Die Bereitschaft und Abwehrkraft Norwegens, Dänemarks und der Schweiz in deutscher Sicht, in: Neutrale Kleinstaaten im Zweiten Weltkrieg, Münsingen 1973, pp. 7–84.

Etter, Jann. Armee und öffentliche Meinung in der Zwischenkriegszeit 1918–1939, Diss. Zürich, Bern 1972.

Etter, Phillipp. Die Vaterländische Erneuerung und wir, Zug 1933.

Favez, Jean-Claude. Une mission impossible, le CICR, les déportations et les camps de concentrations nazis, Lausanne 1988.

Fink, Jürg. Die Schweiz aus der Sicht des Dritten Reiches 1933–1945, Einschätzung und Beurteilung der Schweiz durch die oberste deutsche Führung seit der Machtergreifung Hitlers, Diss. Zürich 1985.

[Frey, Otto], O.F., Waadtländer Emotionen um General Guisan, in: "Neue Zürcher Zeitung," 26.4.85, No. 96.

— Die Waadtländer zwischen Selbstgefühl und Selbstzweifel, in: "Neue Zürcher Zeitung," 3./4.8.85, No. 177.

— Westschweizer und Franzosen als ungleiche Freunde, in: "Neue Zürcher Zeitung," 9.8.85, No. 182, and 14.8.86, No. 186.

Frick, Gotthard. Die Reduitstrategie—aus der Sicht des möglichen Aggressors, in: Allgemeine Schweizerische Militärzeitschrift, 11/1987, pp. 746 f.

Frischknecht, Jürg, Peter Hafner, Ueli Haldimann, and Peter Niggli. Die unheimlichen Patrioten, Politische Reaktion in der Schweiz, Zürich 1979.

Fritschi, Oskar Felix. Geistige Landesverteidigung während des Zweiten Weltkrieges, Der Beirag der Schweizer Armee zur Aufrechterhaltung des Durchhaltewillens, Diss. Zürich, Dietikon-Zürich 1972.

Fuhrer, Hans Rudolf. Von der Planstudie "Tannenbaum" zum Märzalarm 1943, in: IPZ-Information No. 3, Zürich November 1980. [cited as: Fuhrer, Planstudie "Tannenbaum"]

— Spionage gegen die Schweiz, Die geheimen deutschen Nachrichtendienste gegen die Schweiz im Zweiten Weltkrieg 1939–1945, Diss. Zürich, Frauenfeld 1982.

— Die Schweiz im Nachrichtendienst, in: Bindschedler u.a., Schwedische und schweizerische Neutralität im Zweiten Weltkrieg, loc. cit., pp. 405–426.

Gafner, Raymond. Der Bericht des Generals, in: General Guisan und der Zweite Weltkrieg, loc. cit., pp. 126–145.

Gautschi, Willi. Der Landesstreik 1918, Zürich/Einsiedeln/Köln 1968.

— Die Verantwortlichkeit General Willes im November 1918, in: "Neue Zürcher Zeitung," zum 70. Geburtstag von Prof. Dr. phil. Leonhard von Muralt, 17.5.70, No. 223.

— Geschichte des Kantons Aargau 1885–1953, 3 Vols., Baden 1978.

— Guisan und Wille im gefährlichen Sommer 1940, in: "Neue Zürcher Zeitung," 20./21.8.88, No. 193.

— Der Kontakt General Guisans mit SS-Standartenführer Schellenberg, in: Scheizerische Zeitschrift für Geschichte, 2/1989, pp. 152–170.

Gauye Oscar, Le Général Guisan et la diplomatie Suisse, 1940–1941, in: Studien und Quellen 4, Bern 1978, pp. 5–68.

— Au Rütli, 25 juillet 1940, Le discours du Général Guisan: nouveaux aspects, in: Studien und Quellen 10, Bern 1984, pp. 5–56. [cited as: Gauye, Au Rütli]

General Henri Guisan und das eidgenössische Volk, Ein Buch der Erinnerung und des Dankes, Zusammengestellt von Mitarbeitern der Illustrierten "Die Woche," Olten 1960.

General Guisan und der Zweite Weltkrieg 1939–1945, herausgegeben zum hundertsten Geburtstag, Lausanne 1974.

Général Guisan . . . toujours vivant, Beiträge von Georges-André Chevallaz, Maurice Zermatten, Raymond Gafner, Albert-Louis Chappuis, Jacques Perrenoud, Max Petitpierre, Vulliens 1983.

Geschichte der Schweiz und der Schweizer, Vol. III, Basel/Frankfurt a.M. 1983.

Gilg, Peter. Die "Eidgenössiche Gemeinschaft" in: Festschrift Ulrich Im Hof, loc. cit., pp. 572–597.

Glaus, Beat. Die Nationale Front, Eine schweizerische faschistische Bewegung 1930–1940, Diss. Zürich, Einsiedeln/Köln 1969.

Graf, Christoph. Zensurakten as der Zeit des Zweiten Weltkrieges, Eine Analyse des Bestandes E 4450, Presse und Funkspruch 1939–1945, Schweizerisches Bundesarchiv, Inventare, Bern 1979.

— Vom Klassenkampf zur Konkordanz, Robert Grimm, Rudolf Minger und die schweizerische Demokratie, in: Festschrift Ulrich Im Hof, loc. cit., pp. 495–514.

— Die Schweiz in den 1930er Jahren, in: Studien und Quellen 9, Bern 1983, pp. 127–141.

Grieder, Fritz. Ein halbes Jahrhundert unter der Bundeskuppel, Über Herkunft und Tätigkeit von 71 Basler und Baselbieter Parlamentariern, 1920–1970, 163. Neujahrsblatt, Basel 1984.

Gruber, Christian. Die politischen Parteien in der Schweiz im Zweiten Weltkrieg, Vienna/Frankfurt/Zürich 1966.

Gruner, Christine. Der "Rütlirapport" des Generals vom 25.Juli 1940, Seminararbeit, Universität Basel, Wintersemester 1967/68 [ungedruckt], BAr.

Gruner, Erich. Die Parteien in der Schweiz, Bern 1969.

— Die schweizerische Bundesversammlung 1848–1920, Biographie, Bern 1966.

Guex, André (editor). General Guisan 1874–1960, Official Commemorative Work, Lausanne 1960.

Haener, Daniel. Der spanische Bürgerkrieg und die Schweiz, in: "Neue Zürcher Zeitung," 17.7.86, No. 163.

Hafner, Georg. Bundesrat Walther Stampfli (1884–1965), Diss. Zürich, Olten 1986.

Handbuch der schweizerischen Volkswirtschaft, 2 vols., Bern 1955.

Hart, Liddell. Die Verteidigung des Westens, Zürich 1951.

Helbling, Carl. General Ulrich Wille, Biographie, Zürich 1957.

Heller, Daniel. "Das offene Loch"—Eugen Bircher und die Verteidigung unserer Nordgrenze, in: Allgemeine Schweizerische Militärzeitschrift, 6/1987, pp. 365–372.

— Eugen Bircher, Arzt, Militär und Politiker, Zürich 1988.

Hillgruber, Andreas. Die Zweite Weltkrieg, Kreigsziele und Strategie der grossen Mächte, Stuttgart/Berlin/Köln/Mainz 1983.

Hirzel, Ernst. Der Ordnungsdienstauftrag der schweizerischen Armee, Diss. Basel 1974.

Hofer, Viktor. Die Bedeutung des Berichtes General Guisans über den Aktivdienst 1939–1945 für die Gestaltung des Schweizerischen Wehrwesens, Diss. Basel, Basler Beiträge zur Geschitswissenschaft 116, Basel 1970.

Hohl, Markus. Der Rütlirapport, Seminararbeit Universität Bern 1961 [ungedruckt], BAr.

ab Hohlenstein, Walther. General Guisan, Bildnis in Worten, Eich bei Sempach 1940. [Pages not numbered.]

Huber, Hans. Geistige Landesverteidigung, in: Kurz, Die Schweizer Armee von heute, Murten 1953, pp. 364–367.

Huber, Harald. Neue Aufgaben? Neuer Einsatz! in: Festschrift Hans Oprecht, loc. cit.

Humbel, Kurt. Nationalsozialistische Propaganda in der Schweiz, Diss. Zürich, Bern 1976.

Im Hof, Ulrich. Festschrift zum 65. Geburtstag, Gesellschaft und Gesellschafen, Bern 1982.

Isone, 10 Jahre Waffenplatz, 40 Jahre Grenadiere, Bern 1983.

Jaun, Rudolf. Das Schweizer Generalstabkorps 1875–1945, Eine kollektivbiographische Studie, Manuscript, Zürich 1987.

Joseph, Roger. L'Union nationale 1932–1939, Un fascisme en Suisse romande, Thèse Lausanne, Neuchâtel 1975.

Jost, Hans-Ulrich. Bedrohung und Enge (1914–1945), in: Geschichte der Schweiz und der Schweizer, loc. cit., pp. 101–190.

Keller, Paul. Marschall Pétains Reise durch die Schweiz im April 1945, in: "Neue Zürcher Zeitung," 24.4.85, No. 94.

Keller, W. Die Adjutantur im Wandel der Zeit, Herausgegeben vom EMD [n.p., Bern], 1978.

Kieser, Rolf. Erzwungene Symbiose, Thomas Mann, Robert Musil, Georg Kaiser und Bertold Brecht im Schweizer Exil, Bern 1984.

Kimche, Jon. General Guisans Zweifrontenkrieg, Die Schweiz zwischen 1939 und 1945, Zürich [[n.d., 1962]. Original English title: "Spying for Peace," London 1961.

Kopp, Otto. Der General und seine Rütli-Rede, in: "Vaterland," 20.7.85.

Kreis, Georg. Zensur und Selbstzensur, Die schweizerische Pressepolitik im Zweiten Weltkrieg, Frauenfeld and Stuttgart 1973.

— Juli 1940, Die Aktion Trump, Basel/Stuttgart 1973.

— Auf den Spuren von "La Charité," Die schweizerische Armeeführung im Spannungsfeld des deutsch-französischen Gegensatzes 1936–1941, Basel 1976. [cited as: Kreis, La Charité]

— General Guisan, Minister Frölicher und die Mission Burckhardt 1940, in: Schweizerische Zeitschrift für Geschichte Heft 1 und 2, 1977, pp. 99–121.

— Die schweiz und der Zweite Weltkrieg, Bilanz und bibliographischer Überblick nach 30 Jahren, in: La seconda Guerra mondiale nella prospettiva storica a trent anni dall'epilogo, Como 1977, pp. 219–241.

— Flüchtlingspolitik und Pressepolitik, in: "Neue Zürcher Zeitung," 4.5.79, No. 102.

— Der allmähliche Überang vom Krieg zum Frieden, in: "Neue Zürcher Zeitung," 8.5.85, No. 105.

Krieg und Gebirge, Revue Internationale d'Histoire Militaire, No. 85, Neuchâtel 1988.

Kurz, Hans Rudolf. Zur Geschichte des schweizerischen Reduit-Gedankens, in: Schweizerische Monatszeitschrift für Offiziere aller Waffen, Februar 1947, pp. 54 ff.

— Die Schweiz im Zweiten Weltkrieg, Das grosse Errinnergunswerk an die Aktivdienstzeit 1939–1945, Bearbeitet unter Mitwirkung der berufensten Persönlichkeiten, Thun 1959. [cited as: Kurz, Die Schweiz im Zweiten Weltkrieg]

— General Henri Guisan, Zürich 1965. [cited as: Kurz, Guisan]

— Nachrichtenzentrum Schweiz, Die Schweiz im Nachrichtendienst des zweiten Weltkriegs, Frauenfeld and Stuttgart 1972.

— Operationsplanung Schweiz, Die Rolle der Schweizer Armee in zwei Weltkriegen (with Introduction by Alfred Ernst), Thun 1974. [cited as: Kurz, Operationsplanung]

— General Guisan und die Kriegsparteien, in: General Guisan und der Zweite Weltkrieg, loc. cit., pp. 41–109.

— 100 Jahre Schweizer Armee, Thun 1978.

— Das grosse Glück der Schweiz, in: "Brückenbauer," 1.5.85, No. 18.

— Die Beziehungen des schweizerischen Armeekommandos zum französischen General de Lattre de Tassigny in den Jahren 1944 und 1945, in: "Der Fourier," No. 7, July 1987, pp. 292–300.

— Bundesrat Kobelt im Amt 1940–1954, in: Müller, Hans, Bundesrat Karl Kobelt, loc. cit., pp. 85–100.

Lachmann, Günter. Der Nationalsozialismus in der Schweiz 1931–1945, Ein Beitrag zur Geschichte der Auslandsorganisation der NSDAP, Diss. Berlin 1962.

Lasserre, André, La Suisse des annés sombres, Courants d'opinion pendant la deuxième guerre mondiale 1939–1945, Lausanne 1989.

Linsmayer, Charles. Die Krise der Demokratie als Krise ihrer Literatur, Die Literatur der deutschen Schweiz im Zeitalter der deistigen landesvertreidigung, in: Frühling der Gegenwart, Erzählungen III, Zürich 1983, pp. 436–493.

Longchamp, Claude. Das Umfeld der schweizerischen Ärztemission hinter die deutsch-sowjetische Front 1941–1945 (1967/68), Wirtschaftliche und politische Aspekte einer humanitären Mission im Zweiten Weltkrieg, Lizentiatsarbeit, Universität Bern 1983. [Typescript]

Luchsinger, Fred. Die Neue Zürcher Zeitung im Zeitalter des Zweiten Weltkrieges 1930–1955, Zürich 1955.

— Zum Bild der Schweiz im Krieg, in: "Neue Zürcher Zeitung," 13./14.7.85, No. 160.

Ludwig, Carl. Die Flüchtlingspolitik der Schweiz in den Jahren 1933–1955, Bericht an den Bundesrat zuhanden der eidgenössichen Räte [n.p., n.d., Bern 1957].

Lüem, Walter. Probleme der schweizerischen Landesbefestigung 1860 bis 1914, Diss. Zürich 1955.

— 100 Jahre Gotthardfestung, in: "Neue Zürcher Zeitung," 31.1.86, No. 25

Lüthy, Herbert. Die Disteln von 1940, in: Kreis, Juli 1940, Die Aktion Trump, loc. cit., pp. 85–110.

Maetzke, Ernst-Otto. Die deutsch-schweizerische Presse zu einigen Problemen des Zweiten Weltkrieges, in: Tübinger Studien zur Geschichte und Poltik 2, Tübingen 1955.

Marcel, André. Kindheit und Jugendjahre, in: General Guisan und der Zweite Weltkrieg, loc. cit., pp. 11–26.

Marti, Peter A[ndreas]. Geheimabsprachen General Guisans mit Frankreich und Grossbritannien 1939/40, in: "Neue Zürcher Zeitung," 10.11.3.84, No. 59.

— Beziehungen zwischen der Schweiz und Grossbritannien vom Ausbruch des Zweiten Weltkrieges bis zur Niederlage Frankreichs, Lizentiatsarbeit, History Seminar, University of Zürich, 1984. [Typescript]

— Die Studie Germann, in: Schweizerische Zeitschrift für Geschichte, 2/1986, pp. 236–256.

Martin, Bernd. Friedensinitiativen und Machtpolitik im Zweiten Weltkrieg 1939–1945, Düsseldorf 1974.

Matt, Alphons. Zwischen allen Fronten, Der Zweite Weltkrieg aus der Sicht des Büros "Ha," Frauenfeld/Stuttgart 1969.

Maurer, Peter. Anbauschlacht, Landwirtschaftspolitik, Plan Wahlen, Anbauwerk 1937–1945, Diss. Bern, Zürich 1985.

Maurer, Rudolf. Markus Feldmann (1897–1958), Werden und Aufstieg bis zum Ausbruch des Zweiten Weltkrieges, Diss. Bern 1965.

— Le Conseiller fédéral Marcel Pilet-Golaz, in: Alliance culturelle romande, Cahier No. 30, Yverdon 1984, pp. 29–33.

Maurois, André. Die Tragödie Frankreichs, Zürich 1941. Original French title:: "Tragédie en France."

Meienberg, Niklaus. Ernst S., Landesverräter (1919–1942), in: Reportagen aus der Schweiz, Darmstadt and Neuwied 1974.

— Die Welt als Wille und Wahn, Zürich 1987.

Menz, Peter. Der "Königsmacher" Heinrich Walther, Zur Wahl von vierzehn Bundesräten 1917–1940, Diss. Freiburg i.Ue. 1976.

Métraux, Peter. Die Karikatur als publizistische Ausdrucksform, untersucht am Kampf des "Nebelspalters" gegen den Nationalsozialismus, Diss. Berlin 1966.

Meurant, Jacques. La presse et l'opinion de la Suisse romande face à l'Europe en guerre 1939–1941, Neuchâtel 1976.

Meyer, Alice. Anpassung oder Widerstand, Die Schweiz zur Zeit des deutschen Nationalsozialismus, Frauenfeld 1965.

Mézières au fil du temps, Grandson 1987.

Möckli, Werner. Das schweizerische Selbstverständis beim Ausbruch des Zweiten Weltkrieges, Diss. Zürich 1973.

Müller, Felix. Was hat General Guisan nun wirklich gesagt?, in: "Die Weltwoche," No. 11, 14.3.85.

— Der Einfluss von "Maulwürfen" in Guisans Stab, in: "Die Weltwoche," No. 37, 11.9.86.

— Verbundene Augen—verbotene Bilder, in: "Weltwoche-Leader"; Zürich, July/August 1987, pp. 24–33.

Müller, Hans. Bundesrat Karl Kobelt 1891–1968, Eine Gedenkschrift, Bern 1975.

Nicolas, W[alter]. Der Terrtorialdienst seit 1887, in: 100 Jahre TerD, Frauenfeld 1988, pp. 9–13.

Noll, Peter. Die ethische Begründung der Strafe, in: Recht und Staat in Geschichte und Gegenwart 244, Tübingen 1962.

— Landesverräter, 17 Lebensläufe und Todesurteile 1942–1944, Frauenfeld/Stuttgart 1980.

Ochsner, Richard. Transit von Truppen, Einzelpersonen, Kriegsmaterial und zivilen Gebrauchsgütern zugunsten einer Kriegspartei durch das neutrale Land, in: Bindschedler u.a., Schwedische und schweizerische Neutralität im Zweiten Weltkrieg, loc. cit., pp. 216–235.

Odermatt, Franz. Zur Genese der Reduitstrategie, Die Reaktion der schweizerischen Armeeführung auf einen strategischen Sonderfall im Sommer 1940, Seminar, University of Bern 1983. [Typescript]

— Zwischen Realität und militärischem Mythos: Zur Entstehung der Reduitstrategie im Jahre 1940, in: Allgemeine Schweizerische Militärzeitschrift, 9/1987, pp. 549–552.

Padel, Gerd H[ellmut]. Die politische Presse der deutschen Schweiz und der Aufstieg des Dritten Reiches 1933–1939, Ein Beitrag zur geistigen Landesverteidigung, Diss. Zürich, Stäfa 1951.

Parkinson, C. Northcote. Parkinsons Gesetz und andere Untersuchungen über die Verwaltung, Düsseldorf/Vienna 1968.

Perrenoud, Marc. "La Sentinelle" sous surveillance, Un quotidian socialiste et la contrôle de la presse (1939–1945), in: Schweizerische Zeitschrift für Geschichte, 2/1987, pp. 137–168.

Perrin, Liliane. L'Album privé du Général Guisan, Lausanne 1986.

Piekalkiewicz, Janusz. Schweiz 39–45, Krieg in einem neutralen Land, Stuttgart 1978.

Rapold, Hans. Strategische Probleme der schweizerischen Landesverteidigung im 19.Jahrhundert, Diss. Zürich, Frauenfeld 1951.

— Der schweizerische Generalstab, Vol. V, Zeit der Bewährung? Die Epoche um den Ersten Weltkrieg 1907–1924, Basel/Frankfurt a.Main 1988.

Rentsch, Hans Ulrich. Neutraler Kleinstaat am Rande des Reiches, in: Europa und die Einheit Deutschlands, Herausgegeben von Walter Hofer, Köln 1951.

de Riedmatten, Chantal. General Henri Guisan, Autorité et Démocratie, ou la question de l'inspecteur et celle de la démocatisation dans l'armé 1939–1947, Lizentiatsarbeit, Fribourg 1982. [Typescript] BAr.

Riesen, René. Die schweizerische Bauernheimatbewegung (Jungbauern), Die Entwicklung von den Anfängen bis 1947, Diss. Bern 1972.

Rigonalli, Marzio. Le Tessin dans les relations entre la Suisse et l'Italie 1922–1940, Locarno 1983.

Rings, Werner. Schweiz Im Krieg 1933–1945, Ein Bericht, Zürich 1974.

Roesch, Werner. Bedrohte Schweiz, Die deutschen Operationsplanungen gegen die Schweiz im Sommer/Herbst 1940 und die Abwehrbereitschaft der Armee im Oktober 1940, Diss. Zürich 1986.

Rosen, Edgar R. Italien, Deutschland und die Schweiz im Sommer 1940, in: Schweizerische Zeitschrift für Geschichte, 3/1969, pp. 661–665.

Rosenberg, Martin. Was war Anpassung, wo war Widerstand?, Bern 1966.

Roth, Fritz. Die Schweizer Heimatwehr, Zur Frontenbewegung der Zwischenkriegszeit im Kanton Bern, Diss. Bern 1974.

Roulet, Louis-Edouard. La Suisse pendant la guerre, in: Revue d'histoire de la deuxième guerre mondiale, No. 121, Paris 1981.

von Salis, Jean Rudolf. Weltgeschichte der neuesten Zeit, Die grosse Krise und der Zweite Weltkrieg, Vol. III/2, Zürich 1980.

Schaufelberger, Walter. Das "Kleine Orientierungsheft Schweiz," in: Allgemeine Schweizerische Militärzeitschrift, July/August 1977, pp. 289 ff.

— Die Schweiz zwischen dem deutschen Reich und Frankreich 1914/1939, oder vom Nutzen der schweizerischen Armee, Zürich 1984.

— Overland—Die Landung der Alliierten, in: Allgemeine Schweizerische Militärzeitschrift 12/1984, pp. 638–645.

— Dissuasion in der jüngsten Vergangenheit, in: Die Zukunft der Milizarmee, Zürich 1985, pp. 7–10.

— Festschrift, Bumperlibum aberdran heiahan!, Aarau 1986.

Schmid, Hans Rudolf. Der General, Die Schweiz während des Krieges 1939–1945, Zofingen 1975.

Schmid, Karl. Über die Gestalt des Soldaten, in: Bürger und Soldat, loc. cit., pp. 79–97.

— Beim Tode von General Guisan, Olten 1960.

— Der General, in: Zeitspuren, Aufsätze und Reden, 2 Vols., Zürich 1967, pp. 42–50.

Schmid-Ammann, Paul. Emil Klöti, Stadtpräsident von Zürich, Ein schweizerischer Staatsmann, Zürich 1965.

— Die Wahrheit über den Generalstreik von 1918, Zürich 1968.

Schoch, Jürg. Die Oberstenaffäre, Eine innenpolitische Krise (1915/1916), Diss. Zürich, Bern 1972.

Schürch, Gerhart. Betrachtungen eines Bürgers zum Generalbericht, in: Schweizer Annalen, No. 3, 1946/47, pp. 138–147.

Schwarz, Urs. Die schweizerische Kriegsfinanzierung 1939–1945 und ihre Ausstrahlungen in der Nachkriegszeit, Diss. Zürich, Winterthur 1953.

— Die Presse als Glied der Landesverteidigung, in: Bürger und Soldat, loc. cit., pp. 289–311.

Schweizerischer Bundesrat (Herausgeber), CH, Ein Lesebuch, Bern 1975.

Semadeni, Erhard. Gebirgskrieg, in: Allgemeine Schweizerische Militärzeitschrift, 1/1986, pp. 5–9.

Senn, Hans. General Hans Herzog, Diss. Zürich, Aarau 1945.

— Die Entwicklung der Führungsstruktur im Eidgenössischen Militärdepartement, Frauenfeld 1982.

— Die öffentliche Auseinandersetzung um eine einheitliche und fachmännische Armeeleitung in den Jahren 1938/39, in: Festschrift Walter Schaufelberger, loc. cit., pp. 23–47.

— Schweizerische Dissuasionsstrategie im Zweiten Weltkrieg, in: Bindschedler u.a., Schwedische und schweizerische Neutralität im Zweiten Weltkrieg, loc. cit., pp. 197–215.

— Die Schweiz in der militärischen Planung ihrer Nachbarmächte zwischen den beiden Weltkriegen, in: "Neue Zürcher Zeitung," 1./2.286, No. 26.

— Vom Versailler Vertrag bis heute, in: Krieg und Gebirge, Revue Internationale d'Histoire Militaire, No. 85, Neuchâtel 1988, pp. 231–259.

— Die Haltung Italiens zum "Fall Schweiz" im Jahre 1940, in: "Neue Zürcher Zeitung," 14./15.5.88, No. 111.

— Militärische Eventualabkommen der Schweiz mit Frankreich 1939/40, in: "Neue Zürcher Zeitung," 2.9.88, No. 204.

Shirer, William L. Der Zusammenbruch Frankreichs, Aufstieg und Fall der Dritten Republik, Munich/Zürich 1970.

Siegenthaler, Paul. Der Oberbefehlshaber nach schweizerischem Staatsrecht, Diss. Bern, Zofingen 1946.

Simon, Christian. Monod-Waitz-Winkelried, Geschichtswissenschaft zwischen Patriotismus und Quellenkritik, in: Schweizerische Zeitschrift für Geschichte, 2/1987, pp. 443–454.

Späni-Schleidt. Die Interpretation der dauernden Neutralität duch das schweizerische und das österreichische Parlament, Diss. Zürich, Bern/Stuttgart 1983.

Spindler, Katharina. Die Schweiz und der italienische Faschismus (1922–1930), Der Verlauf der diplomatischen Beziehungen und de Beurteilung durch das Bürgertum, Diss. Basel 1976.

Stahlberger, Peter. Der Zürcher Verleger Emil Oprecht und die deutsche politische Emigration 1933–1945, Diss. Zürich 1970.

Strub, Urs. Die Suizide in der Schweizerarmee von der Mobilisation 1939 bis und mit Dezember 1940; AHQ, 10.2.41, BAr 27/19809,1. {Typescript]

Studer, Karl. Die Militärstrafgerichtsbarkeit im Bundesstaat, Diss. Bern, Aarau/Frankfurt a.m./Salzburg 1982.

Syfrig, Max et Defaye Christian. L'extrême-droite en Suisse, Lausanne [[n.d., nach 1968].

Thälstrup, Ake. Die schwedische Pressepolitik im Zweiten Weltkrieg, in: Bindschedler u.a., Schwedische und schweizerische Neutralität im Zweiten Weltkrieg, loc. cit., pp. 128–143.

Thürer, Georg. St. Galler Geschichte, Vol. II, St. Gallen 1972.

Todt, Manuel. Die politischen Beziehungen der Schweiz zu Deutschland 1934/35 im Urteil von zwei diplomatischen Berichten des deutschen Gesandten in Bern, Ernst von Weizsäcker, in: Schweizerische Zeitschrift für Geschichte, 1/1986, pp. 59–70.

Urner, Klaus. Kompromittierende Neutralität 1940?, in: "Neue Zürcher Zeitung," 24.8.70, No. 391.

— Neutralität und Wirtschaftskrieg: Zur schweizerischen Aussenhandelspolitik 1939–1945, in: Bindschedler u.a., Schwedische schweizerische Neutralität im Zweiten Weltkrieg, loc. cit., pp. 250–292.

— Emil Puhl und die Schweizerische Nationalbank, Zur Kontroverse um das deutsche Raubgold im Zweiten Weltkrieg, in: Schweizer Monatsheft 7/8, 1985, pp. 623–631.

Valloton, Benjamin. Coeur à Coeur, Le Peuple suisse et son Général, Lausanne 1950.

Vetsch, Christian. Aufmarsch gegen die Schweiz, der deutsche "Fall Gelb"—Irreführung der Schweizer Armee 1939/40, Diss. Zürich, Olten 1973.

Vögeli, Robert. Die gegenwärtige Organisation von Heer und Haus, Dezember 1957 [n.p., Bern], Typescript. [7 pp.]

Vogler, Robert Urs. Die Wirtschaftsverhandlungen zwischen der Schweiz und Deutschland 1940 und 1941, Diss. Zürich 1983.

Waeger, Gerhart. Die Sündenböcke der Schweiz, Die Zweihundert im Urteil der geschichtlichen Dokumente 1940–1946, Olten 1971.

Wahlen, Hermann. Bundesrat Rudolf Minger 1881–1955, Bauer und Staatsmann, Bern 1965.

Walde, Karl J. Generalstabschef Jakob Huber 1883–1953, Aarau/Frankfurt a.M./Salzburg 1983.

Wanner, Philipp. Oberst Oskar Frey und der schweizerische Widerstandswille, Münsingen 1974.

Wartenweiler, Fritz. General Guisan, in: Schweizerisches Jugendschriftenwerk No. 878, Zürich 1964.

Wäsström, Sven. Schweden als Arena der Nachrichtendienste, in: Bindschedler u.a., Schwedische und schweizerische Neutralität im Zweiten Weltkrieg, loc. cit., pp. 120–127.

Weber, Karl. Die Schweiz im Nervenkrieg, Aufgabe und Haltung der Schweizer Presse in der Krisen- und Kriegszeit 1933–1945, Bern 1948.

Wehrli, Edmund. Respekt vor wehrhafter Neutralität, Eine Episode aus dem Zweiten Weltkrieg, in "Neue Zürcher Zeitung," 7.9.83, No. 208.

— Schweiz ohne Armee—eine Friedensinsel? Schriftenreihe der Gesellschaft für militärhistorische Studienreisen (GMS), Heft 3, Zürich 1985.

— Vom zaghaften zum wehrhaften Reduit, Anmerkungen zu General Guisans operativen Über legungen, in: "Neue Zürcher Zeitung," 5. und 11.2.87, Nos. 29 and 34. [I and II]

Weingarten, Ralph. Juden in der Schweiz, in: Minderheiten in der Schweiz, Toleranz auf dem Prüfstand, Zürich 1984, pp. 75–94.

Weiss, Otto. General Dufour als Heerführer, Ein Beitrag zur Schweizer Geschichte des 19. Jahrhunderts, Bern 1939.

Wetter, Ernst, and Eduard von Orelli. Wer ist wer im Militär? Frauenfeld 1986.

Wetter, Ernst. Duell der Flieger und der Diplomaten, Die Fliegerzwischenfälle Deutschland-Schweiz im Mai/Juni 1940 und ihre diplomatischen Folgen, Frauenfeld 1987.

— Geheimer Nachtjäger in der Schweiz. Frauenfeld 1989. [Erst nach Drucklegung der vorliegen den Studie erschienen.]

Widmer, Sigmund. Illustrierte Geschichte der Schweiz, Zürich 1965.

Wistrich, Robert. Wer war wer im Dritten Reich? Ein biographisches Lexikon, Frankfurt a.M. 1987.

Wolf, Walter. Faschismus in der Schweiz, Die Geschichte der Frontenbewegung in der deutschen Schweiz 1930–1945, Diss. Zürich 1969.

Woodtli, Susanna. Gleichberechtigung, Der Kampf um die politischen Rechte der Frau in der Schweiz, Frauenfeld 1975.

Wüst, René-Henri. Alerte en pays neuter, La Suisse en 1940, Lausanne 1966.

— L'histoire Suisse d'hier, in: "La Suisse," May–July 1965.

Zehnder, Alfred. Die aussenpolitische Lage der Schweiz am Ende des Zweiten Weltkrieges, in: Festschrift Max Petitpierre, loc. cit., pp. 13–32.

Zimmermann, Horst. Die Schweiz und Grossdeutschland, Das Verhältnis zwischen der Eidgenossenschaft, Österreich und Deutschland 1933–1945, Munich 1980.

Zwicky, J.P. Sammlung schweizerischer Ahnentafeln, in: Sonderheft, Schweizerische Heerführer, Zürich 1940, pp. 97 ff.

— Schweizerisches Geschlechterbuch 1943, 7. Jahrgang, Zürich 1943.

Persons Interviewed

van Berchem, Denis, Prof. Dr. phil., Vandœuvres

Berlincourt, Alain, lic. jur., Bern

Boissier, Jacques, Divisionär a. D., Bern

Bonjour, Edgar, Prof. Dr. phil., Basel

Böschenstein, Hermann, Dr. h. c., Bern

Brawand, Samuel, alt Regierungsrat, Grindelwald

Bretscher, Willy, Dr. h. c., Zürich

Brunner, Marthias, Oberst a. D., Losone

Bucher, Erwin, Prof. Dr., Winterthur

Burckhardt, Peter, Divisionär a. D., Bern

Chevallaz, Georges-André, alt Bundesrat, Epalinges VD

Däniker, Gustav, Dr. phil., Divisionär, Zürich

Decoppet, Maurice, Lausanne

Decoppet-Guisan, Myriam, Zimmerwald

Eglin-Grin, Madeleine, Basel

Eibel, Robert (†), Dr. jur., Zürich

von Ernst, Armand (†), Muri bei Bern

Ernst, Hans-Ulrich, Brigadier, Bern

Frey-Meyer, Patrizia V., Petit-Vidy

Frey, Theo, Weiningen ZH

Freymond, Jacques, Prof. Dr. phil., Genf

Ganz, Anton Roy, Dr. Jur., alt Botschafter, Zürich

Gauye, Oscar. Dr. jur., Bern

Graber, Pierre, alt Bundesrat, Savigny VD

Guisan, Henry, Oberst a. D., Pully

Haab, Willy, Ittigen

Häni, Max, Brigadier a. D., Bern

Hirt, Ernst, Oberst a. D., Biel

Hunziker, Guido (†), Dr. ing., Baden

Iklé, Max, Dr. h. c., Küsnacht

Jaeckle, Erwin. Dr. phil., alt Nationalrat, Zürich

Jöhr, Eduard, Dr. Jur., alt Bundesrichter, Pully

Jollles, Paul, Dr. h. c., alt Staatssekretär, Bern
Kaech, Arnold, Brigadier a. D., Bern
Keckeis, Peter, Dr. jur., Zürich
Kellerhals, Otto, Dr. h. c., Bern
Kurz, Hans Rudolf, Dr. jur., Oberst a. D., Bern
Lamprecht, Franz, Dr. phil., Eglisau
Lindt, August Rudolf, Dr. jur., alt Botschafter, Bern
Maeder, Jean, Pully
von Manikowsky, Arnim, Hamburg
Mauris, Edouard, Prof. theol., Pully
Müller, Max (†), alt Stadtammann, Baden
von Muralt, Alexander, Prof. Dr. med., Bern
Perrin, Liliane, Lausanne
Rapold, Hans, Dr., phil., Divisionär z. D., Bern
Ritschard, Gustav, Unterseen
von Salis, Jean-Rudolf, Prof. Dr. phil., Brunegg
Sandoz, Jules, Biel
Schaefer, Alfred (†), Dr. jur., Oberst a. D., Zürich
Schaefer, Paul (†), Dr. phil., Wettingen
Schaufelberger, Walter, Prof. Dr. phil., Zürich
Schmid, Hans-Rudolf, Dr. phil., Zürich
Schmid-Ammann, Paul (†), Dr. h. c., Erlenbach
Schmutz, André, Pully
Schürch, Gerhart, Dr. jur., alt Nationalrat, Bern
Senn, Hans, Dr. phil., Korpskommandant a. D., Bern
Spühlr, Willy, Dr. oec., alt Bundesrat, Zürich
Stahel, Gertrud, Interlaken
Steinfels, Fritz, Zürich
Tschudi, Hans Peter, Dr. jur., alt Bundesrat, Basel
Vögeli, Robert, Dr. phil., Oberst z. D., Zürich
Wanner, Fritz (†), Dr. jur., Oberst a. D., Kilchberg
Wehrli, Bernhard, Dr. oec. publ., Zürich
Wehrli, Edmund, Dr. jur., Oberst a. D., Zürich
Weitnauer, Albert (†), alt Staatssekretär. Bern
Werder, Wilhelm (†), Dr. jur., Oberst a. D., Basel
Wille, Fritz, Dr. jur., Korpskommandant a. D., Gümligen
Wille, Jürg, Dr. jur., Zürich
Zwahlen, Margrit, Interlaken

List of Abbreviations

Archives, councils, organizations, unpublished documents

AfZ   Archiv für Zeitgeschichte (Archives of Contemporary History, Zurich)
AHQ   Army Headquarters
ANR   Action for National Resistance (in German: Aktion nationaler Widerstand, ANW)
APV   Association Patriotique Vaudoise (Patriotic Association of the Canton of Vaud)
ARA   Anti-Revolutionary Action (Antirevolutionäre Aktion)
ArBoi   Archives of Boissier, Jacques
ArHä   Archives of Häni, Max

ArJae	Archives of Jaeckle, Erwin
ArKh	Archives of Kellerhals, Otto
ArLi	Archives of Lindt, August R.
ArMa	Archives of Mariafeld
ArPu	Archives of Pully
ArSchü	Archives of Schürch, Gerhart
ArVR	Archives of Verte Rive
ArWa	Archives of Wanner, Fritz
ArWe	Archives of Wehrli, Edmund
ASMZ	Allgemeine Schweizerische Militärzeitschrift (military magazine)
AVV	Patriotic Association of the Canton of Aargau ("Aargauische Vaterländische Vereinigung")
BAr	Swiss Federal Archives (Schweizerisches Bundesarchiv), Bern
BBl	Bundesblatt der Schweizerischen Eidgenossenschaft (gazette of the Swiss Confederation)
BLS	Bern–Lötschberg–Simplon railroad
Div	Division
EMB	Eidgenössische Militärbibliothek (Swiss Federal Military Library)
FFI	Force Française Intérieure (resistance forces operating within France during World War II)
GAr Ch	Gemeinderarchiv (municipal archives of) Chesalles-sur-Oron
GAr Pu	Gemeindearchiv (municipal archives of) Pully
Gst	General Staff
HQ	Headquarters
IPA	International Press Agency (Internationale Presse-Agentur)
IPZ	Institut für politologische Zeitfragen (Institute for Contemporary Political Issues)
MarF	Militärarchiv des Bundesarchivs Freiburg i.Br. (Military archives of the German Federal Archives, Freiburg, Germany)
NDC	National Defense Committee (Landesverteidigungskommission)

Nl	*Unpublished documents of (Nachlass):*
Nl Al	Allgöwer, Walter
Nl Ba	Bandi, Hans
Nl Bm	Baumann, Johannes
Nl Br	Bretscher, Willy
Nl Dä	Däniker, Gustav
Nl DuPa	Du Pasquier, Claude
Nl Er	Ernst, Alfred
Nl Fm	Feldmann, Markus
Nl Fr	Frick, Wilhelm
Nl Ge	Germann, Oscar Adolf
Nl Gi	Gisevius, Hans Bernd
Nl Go	Gonard, Samuel
Nl Gr	Grin, Edmond
Nl Gui	Guisan, Henri
Nl Ha	Hausamann, Hans
Nl He	Henne, Rolf
Nl Ki	Killer, Karl
Nl Ko	Kobelt, Karl
Nl La	Labhart, Jakob
Nl Li	Lindt, August R.
Nl Lü	Lützelschwab, Wilhelm

Nl May	Mayer, Albert R.
Nl Mey	Meyer-Schwertenbach, Paul
Nl Mi	Minger, Rudolf
Nl No	Nobs, Ernst
Nl Pp	Petitpierre, Edouard
Nl Schü	Schürch, Gerhart
Nl Sd	Schmid, Hans Rudolf
Nl Wet	Wetter, Ernst
Nl Wi	Wirz, Hans Georg
Nl Zü	Züblin, Georg

NS	intelligence procurement office (Nachrichtensammelstelle)
NSDAP	National Socialist German Workers Party (Nationalsozialistische Deutsche Arbeiterpartei)
OKH	German Army High Command (Oberkommando des Heeres)
OKW	German Armed Forces High Command (Oberkommando der Wehrmacht)
PAB	Politisches Archiv (political archives) Bonn
PKAr AG	Polizeikommando-Archiv Aargau (archives of the police command of the canton of Aargau)
RAF	Royal Air Force (Britain)
R.A.M.	Reich Foreign Minister (Reichsaussenminister)
Sar	Schweizerisches Sozialarchiv (Swiss Social Archives), Zürich
SHAPE	Allied Supreme Headquarters, Europe
SHAT	Service Historique de l'Armée de Terre (History department of the French ground forces), Vincennes
SMP	Schweizer Mittelpresse (news agency)
SNPF	Swiss National Patriotic Federation (Schweizerischer Vaterländischer Verband, SVV)
SPS	Social Democratic Party of Switzerland (Sozialdemokratische Partei der Schweiz)
StAr AG	Staatsarchiv des Kantons Aargau (official archives of the canton of Aargau), Aarau
StAr ZH	Staatsarchiv des Kantons Zürich (official archives of the canton of Zurich), Zurich
SVV	Schweizerischer Vaterländischer Verband (Swiss National Patriotic Federation, SNPF)
SZG	Schweizerische Zeitschrift für Geschichte (Swiss history magazine)
UFA	Universum-Film AG

Miscellaneous

attn.	To the attention of
cf.	compare
e.g.	exempli gratia, for example
n.d.	no date
n.p.	no place
re:	regarding
[ ]	information added by this author
[...]	ellipsis in a quote

Index